Worldmark Encyclopedia of Cultures and Daily Life

Worldmark
Encyclopedia of
Cultures and
Daily Life

VOLUME 5 Europe
Second Edition

Editors

Timothy L. Gall and Jeneen Hobby

GALE
CENGAGE Learning

Detroit • New York • San Francisco • New Haven, Conn • Waterville, Maine • London

Worldmark Encyclopedia of Cultures and Daily Life, Second Edition

Editors: Timothy L. Gall and Jeneen Hobby

Product Management: Julia Furtaw and Carol Nagel

Manufacturing: Rita Wimberley

Gale
27500 Drake Rd.
Farmington Hills, MI 48331-3535

ISBN 978-1-4144-4882-4 (set)
ISBN 978-1-4144-4883-1 (vol. 1)
ISBN 978-1-4144-4890-9 (vol. 2)
ISBN 978-1-4144-4891-6 (vol. 3)
ISBN 978-1-4144-4892-3 (vol. 4)
ISBN 978-1-4144-6430-5 (vol. 5)

ISSN 0196-2809

© 2009 Gale, Cengage Learning

For product information and technology assistance, contact us at Gale Customer Support, 1-800-877-4253.
For permission to use material from this text or product, submit all requests online at www.cengage.com/permissions.
Further permissions questions can be emailed to permissionrequest@cengage.com

This publication is a creative work fully protected by all applicable copyright laws, as well as by misappropriation, trade secret, unfair competition, and other applicable laws. The authors and editors of this work have added value to the underlying factual material herein through one or more of the following: unique and original selection, coordination, expression, arrangement, and classification of the information.

While every effort has been made to ensure the reliability of the information presented in this publication, Gale, a part of Cengage Learning, does not guarantee the accuracy of the data contained herein. Gale accepts no payment for listing; and inclusion in the publication of any organization, agency, institution, publication, service, or individual does not imply endorsement of the editors or publisher. Errors brought to the attention of the publisher and verified to the satisfaction of the publisher will be corrected in future editions.

EDITORIAL DATA PRIVACY POLICY: Does this product contain information about you as an individual? If so, for more information about our editorial data privacy policies, please see our Privacy Statement at www.gale.cengage.com.

Library of Congress Cataloging-in-Publication Data

Worldmark encyclopedia of cultures and daily life / Timothy L. Gall, editor. -- 2nd ed.
    p. cm.
  Includes bibliographical references and index.
  ISBN 978-1-4144-4882-4 (set) -- ISBN 978-1-4144-4883-1 (vol. 1) -- ISBN 978-1-4144-4890-9 (vol. 2) -- ISBN 978-1-4144-4891-6 (vol. 3) -- ISBN 978-1-4144-4892-3 (vol. 4) -- ISBN 978-1-4144-6430-5 (vol. 5)
1. Ethnology--Encyclopedias, Juvenile. 2. Manners and customs--Encyclopedias, Juvenile. [1. Ethnology--Encyclopedias. 2. Manners and customs--Encyclopedias.] I. Gall, Timothy L. II. Title: Encyclopedia of cultures and daily life.
  GN333.W67 2009
  305.8003--dc22
                                                      2009004744

This title is also available as an e-book.
ISBN: 978-1-4144-4893-0
Contact your Gale sales representative for ordering information.

Printed in the United States of America
1 2 3 4 5 6 7 13 12 11 10 09

CONTENTS

JUSTIN CORFIELD. Department of History, Geelong Grammar School.

DIANNE K. DAEG DE MOTT. Researcher/Writer, Tucson, Arizona.

CATHARIN DALPINO. Department of Asian Studies, Georgetown University

MICHAEL DE JONGH. Professor, Department of Anthropology, University of South Africa.

GEORGI DERLUGUIAN. Senior Fellow, Ph.D., U. S. Institute of Peace.

CHRISTINE DRAKE. Department of Political Science and Geography, Old Dominion University.

ARTURO DUARTE. Guatemalan Mission to the OAS.

CALEB DUBE. Department of Anthropology, Northwestern University.

BRIAN DU TOIT. Professor, Department of Anthropology, University of Florida.

LEAH ERMARTH. Worldspace Foundation, Washington, DC.

NANCY J. FAIRLEY. Associate Professor of Anthropology, Department of Anthropology/Sociology, Davidson College.

GREGORY A. FINNEGAN, Ph.D. Tozzer Library, Harvard University.

ALLEN J. FRANK, Ph.D.

DAVID P. GAMBLE. Professor Emeritus, Department of Anthropology, San Francisco State University.

FREDERICK GAMST. Professor Emeritus, Department of Anthropology, University of Massachusetts, Harbor Campus.

PAULA GARB. Associate Director of Global Peace and Conflict Studies and Adjunct Professor of Social Ecology, University of California, Irvine.

HAROLD GASKI. Associate Professor of Sami Literature, School of Languages and Literature, University of Tromsø.

STEPHEN J. GENDZIER.

FLORENCE GERDEL.

ANTHONY P. GLASCOCK. Professor of Anthropology; Department of Anthropology, Psychology, and Sociology; Drexel University.

LUIS GONZALEZ. Researcher/Writer, River Edge, New Jersey.

JENNIFER GRAHAM. Researcher/Writer, Sydney, Australia.

MARIE-CÉCILE GROELSEMA. Doctoral candidate, Comparative Literature, Indiana University.

ROBERT GROELSEMA. MPIA and doctoral candidate, Political Science, Indiana University.

MARIA GROSZ-NGATÉ. Visiting Assistant Professor, Department of Anthropology, Northwestern University.

ELLEN GRUENBAUM. Professor, School of Social Sciences, California State University, Fresno.

N. THOMAS HAKANSSON. University of Kentucky.

ROBERT HALASZ. Researcher/Writer, New York, New York.

MARC HANREZ. Professor, Department of French and Italian, University of Wisconsin-Madison.

ANWAR UL HAQ. Central Asian Studies Department, Indiana University.

LIAM HARTE. Department of Philosophy, Loyola University, Chicago.

FR. VASILE HATEGAN. Author, Romanian Culture in America.

BRUCE HEILMAN. Doctoral candidate, Department of Political Science, Indiana University.

JIM HENRY. Researcher/Writer, Cleveland, Ohio.

BARRY HEWLETT. Department of Anthropology, Washington State University.

SUSAN F. HIRSCH. Department of Anthropology, Wesleyan University.

MARIDA HOLLOS. Department of Anthropology, Brown University.

HALYNA HOLUBEC. Researcher/Writer, Cleveland, Ohio.

YVONNE HOOSAVA. Legal Researcher and Cultural Preservation Officer, Hopi Tribal Council.

HUIQIN HUANG, Ph.D. Center for East Asia Studies, University of Montreal.

MARCEL IONESCU-HEROIU. Teaching Assistant, Cornell University

ASAFA JALATA. Assistant Professor of Sociology and African and African American Studies, Department of Sociology, The University of Tennessee, Knoxville.

STEPHEN F. JONES. Russian Department, Mount Holyoke College.

THOMAS JOVANOVSKI, PH.D. Lorain County Community College.

A. KEN JULES. Minister Plenipotentiary and Deputy Head of Mission, Embassy of St. Kitts and Nevis.

GENEROSA KAGARUKI-KAKOTI. Economist, Department of Urban and Rural Planning, College of Lands and Architectural Studies, Dar es Salaam, Tanzania.

EZEKIEL KALIPENI. Department of Geography, University of Illinois at Urbana-Champaign.

DON KAVANAUGH. Program Director, Lake of the Woods Ojibwa Cultural Centre.

SUSAN M. KENYON. Associate Professor of Anthropology, Department of History and Anthropology, Butler University.

ALLA GOLOVINA KHADKA. PhD Candidate, University of Pittsburgh

MARIA GROSZ-NGATÉ. Visiting Associate Director of the African Studies Program, Indiana University.

ADEL ISKANDAR. Center for Contemporary Arab Studies, Georgetown University

ASAFA JALATA. Professor of Sociology, The University of Tennessee, Knoxville.

THOMAS JOVANOVSKI, Ph.D. Lorain County Community College.

EZEKIEL KALIPENI. Associate Professor of Geography, University of Illinois at Urbana-Champaign.

SUSAN M. KENYON. Associate Professor of Anthropology, Butler University.

WELILE KHUZWAYO. Department of Anthropology, University of South Africa.

PHILIP L. KILBRIDE. Professor of Anthropology, Mary Hale Chase Chair in the Social Sciences, Department of Anthropology, Bryn Mawr College.

RICHARD O. KISIARA. Doctoral candidate, Department of Anthropology, Washington University in St. Louis.

SARAH KLUMP. Center for Eurasian, Russian and East European Studies, Edmund A. Walsh School of Foreign Service, Georgetown University .

KAREN KNOWLES. Permanent Mission of Antigua and Barbuda to the United Nations.

MELISSA KERR. Eurasian, Russian, and East European Studies, Georgetown University.

IGOR KRUPNIK. Research Anthropologist, Department of Anthropology, Smithsonian Institution.

LEELO LASS. Secretary, Embassy of Estonia.

ROBERT LAUNAY. Professor, Department of Anthropology, Northwestern University.

BENJAMIN LAZARUS. Eurasian, Russian, and East European Studies, Georgetown University.

CHARLES LEBLANC. Professor and Director, Center for East Asia Studies, University of Montreal.

RONALD LEE. Author, Goddam Gypsy, An Autobiographical Novel.

PHILIP E. LEIS. Professor and Chair, Department of Anthropology, Brown University.

MARIA JUKIC LESKUR. Croatian Consulate, Cleveland, Ohio.

RICHARD A. LOBBAN, JR. Professor of Anthropology and African Studies, Department of Anthropology, Rhode Island College.

DERYCK O. LODRICK. Visiting Scholar, Center for South Asian Studies, University of California, Berkeley.

NEIL LURSSEN. Intro Communications Inc.

GREGORIO C. MARTIN. Modern Language Department, Duquesne University.

HOWARD J. MARTIN. Independent scholar.

HEITOR MARTINS. Professor, Department of Spanish and Portuguese, Indiana University.

ADELINE MASQUELIER. Assistant Professor, Department of Anthropology, Tulane University.

DOLINA MILLAR.

EDITH MIRANTE. Project Maje.

ROBERT W. MONTGOMERY, Ph.D. Indiana University.

THOMAS D. MORIN. Associate Professor of Hispanic Studies, Department of Modern and Classical Literatures and Languages, University of Rhode Island.

CHARLES MORRILL. Doctoral candidate, Indiana University.

CAROL A. MORTLAND. Crate's Point.

FRANCIS A. MOYER. Director, North Carolina Japan Center, North Carolina State University.

MARIE C. MOYER.

NYAGA MWANIKI. Assistant Professor, Department of Anthropology and Sociology, Western Carolina University.

KENNETH NILSON. Celtic Studies Department, Harvard University.

MARTIN NJOROGE. PhD. SRF/UPenn Postdoctoral Fellow, Graduate School of Education, University of Pennsylvania.

JANE E. ORMROD. Graduate Student, History, University of Chicago.

JUANITA PAHDOPONY. Carl Perkins Program Director, Comanche Tribe of Oklahoma.

TINO PALOTTA. Syracuse University.

ROHAYATI PASENG.

PATRICIA PITCHON. Researcher/Writer, London, England.

STEPHANIE PLATZ. Program Officer, Program on Peace and International Cooperation, The John D. and Catherine T. MacArthur Foundation.

MIHAELA POIATA. Graduate Student, School of Journalism and Mass Communication, University of North Carolina at Chapel Hill.

MANSAH PRAH. Dean, Faculty of Social Sciences, University of Cape Coast, Ghana.

LEOPOLDINA PRUT-PREGELJ. Author, Historical Dictionary of Slovenia.

J. RACKAUSKAS. Director, Lithuanian Research and Studies Center, Chicago.

J. RAKOVICH. Byelorussian-American Cultural Center, Strongsville, Ohio.

HANTA V. RALAY. Promotions, Inc., Montgomery Village, Maryland.

SUSAN J. RASMUSSEN. Associate Professor, Department of Anthropology, University of Houston.

RONALD REMINICK. Associate Professor of Anthropology, Cleveland State University.

BRUCE D. ROBERTS. Associate Professor of Anthropology, Department of Anthropology & Earth Science, Minnesota State University, Moorhead.

LAUREL L. ROSE. Philosophy Department, Carnegie-Mellon University.

ROBERT ROTENBERG. Professor of Anthropology, International Studies Program, DePaul University.

CAROLINE SAHLEY, Ph.D. Researcher/Writer, Cleveland, Ohio.

VERONICA SALLES-REESE. Associate Professor, Department of Spanish and Portuguese, Georgetown University.

MAIRA SARYBAEVA. Kazakh-American Studies Center, University of Kentucky.

DEBRA L. SCHINDLER. Institute of Arctic Studies, Dartmouth College.

KYOKO SELDEN, Ph.D. Department of Asian Studies, Cornell University.

ELIZABETH SERLEMITSOS. Chief Advisor, National AIDS Council, Zambia.

ENAYATULLAH SHAHRANI. Central Asian Studies Department, Indiana University.

ROBERT SHANAFELT. Department of Sociology & Anthropology, Georgia Southern University.

TUULIKKI SINKS. Teaching Specialist for Finnish, Department of German, Scandinavian, and Dutch, University of Minnesota.

JAN SJÅVIK. Professor, Scandinavian Studies, University of Washington.

MAGDA SOBALVARRO. Press and Cultural Affairs Director, Embassy of Nicaragua.

PAMELA SODHY. History Department, Georgetown University

MICHAEL STAINTON. Researcher, Joint Center for Asia Pacific Studies, York University.

RIANA STEYN. Department of Anthropology, University of South Africa.

PAUL STOLLER. Professor, Department of Anthropology, West Chester University.

CRAIG STRASHOFER. Researcher/Writer, Cleveland, Ohio.

SANDRA B. STRAUBHAAR. Assistant Professor, Nordic Studies, Department of Germanic and Slavic Languages, Brigham Young University.

DAVID STRAUB. Masters Program in Central Eurasian Studies, Indiana University.

VUM SON SUANTAK. Author, Zo History.

MURAT TAISHIBAEV. Kazakh-American Studies Center, University of Kentucky.

CHRISTOPHER C. TAYLOR. Associate Professor, Anthropology Department, University of Alabama, Birmingham.

FATIMA TLISOVA. Kennedy School at Harvard.

EDDIE TSO. Office of Language and Culture, Navajo Division of Education.

DAVID TYSON. Foreign Broadcast Information Service, Washington, D.C.

NICOLAAS G. W. UNLANDT. Assistant Professor of French, Department of French and Italian, Brigham Young University.

GORDON URQUHART. Professor, Department of Economics and Business, Cornell College.

CHRISTOPHER J. VAN VUUREN. Associate Professor, Department of Anthropology, University of South Africa.

DALIA VENTURA-ALCALAY. Journalist, London, England.

CATHERINE VEREECKE. Assistant Director, Center for African Studies, University of Florida.

CAMILA VERGARA. Journalist, New York.

KORA BATTIG VON WITTLESBACH. Department of Romance Studies at Cornell.

GREGORY T. WALKER. Associate Director, Office of International Affairs, Duquesne University.

GERHARD WEISS. Department of German, Scandinavian, and Dutch, University of Minnesota.

PATSY WEST. Director, The Seminole/Miccosukee Photographic Archive.

WALTER WHIPPLE. Associate Professor of Polish, Germanic and Slavic Languages, Brigham Young University.

ROSALIE WIEDER. Researcher/Writer, Cleveland, Ohio.

JEFFREY WILLIAMS. Professor and Chair, Department of Sociology, Anthropology, & Social Work, Texas Tech University.

KOSTAS YIAVIS. Lecturer in Modern Greek, Cornell University.

GUANG-HONG YU. Associate Research Fellow, Institute of Ethnology, Academia Sinica.

RUSSELL ZANCA. Associate Professor of Anthropology, Northeastern Illinois University.

COUNTRY INDEX

PREFACE

The *Worldmark Encyclopedia of Cultures and Daily Life, Second Edition*, contains over 500 articles exploring the ways of life of peoples of the world. Arranged in five volumes by geographic regions—*Africa, Americas, Asia & Oceania* (two volumes), and *Europe*—the volumes of this encyclopedia parallel the organization of its sister set, the *Worldmark Encyclopedia of the Nations*. Whereas the primary purpose of *Nations* is to provide information on the world's nation states, this encyclopedia focuses on the traditions, living conditions, and personalities of many of the world's culture groups. Entries emphasize how people live today, rather than how they lived in the past.

Defining groups for inclusion was not an easy task. Cultural identity can be shaped by such factors as geography, nationality, ethnicity, race, language, and religion. Many people, in fact, legitimately belong in two or more classifications, each as valid as the other. For example, the citizens of the United States all share traits that make them distinctly American. However, few would deny the need for separate articles on Native Americans or African Americans. Even the category Native American denies the individuality of separate tribes like the Navajo and Paiute. Consequently, this encyclopedia contains an article on the Americans as well as separate articles on the Native Americans and the Navajo. Closely related articles such as these are cross-referenced to each other to help provide a more complete picture of the group being profiled. Included in this encyclopedia are articles on groups as large as the Han of China, with over one billion members, and as small as the Jews of Cochin, with only a few dozen members. Unfortunately, although the vast majority of the world's peoples are represented in this encyclopedia, time and space constraints prevented many important groups from being included in the first edition. Twenty-three new groups have been added to this second edition, and the editors look forward to including many more culture groups in future editions of this work.

New entries include in Americas: Sudanese Americans ("Lost Boys"); in Africa: Afar, Berbers, Ewe, Guineas of Guinea Bissau, Jola, Maldivians, San (Bushmen), Sao Tomeans, and Twa; in Asia and Oceania: Brunei, Coptic Christians, Kashmiris, Moro, Rajasthanis, and Timorese; and in Europe: Alsatians, Kosovars, Maltese, Montenegrins, Serbs, Tyrolese, and Vlachs.

Over 175 contributors and reviewers participated in the creation of this encyclopedia. Drawn from universities, consulates, and the press, their in-depth knowledge and first-hand experience of the profiled groups added significantly to the content of the articles. A complete listing of the contributors and reviewers together with their affiliations appears in the front of each volume.

ORGANIZATION

Each volume begins with an introduction that traces the cultural developments of the region from prehistoric times to the present. Following the introduction are articles devoted to the peoples of the region. Within each volume the articles are arranged alphabetically. A comprehensive table cross referencing the articles by country follows the table of contents to each volume.

The individual articles are of two types. The vast majority follow a standard 20-heading outline explained in more detail below. This structure allows for easy comparison of the articles and enhances the accessibility of the information. A smaller number do not follow the 20-heading format, but rather present simply an overview of the group. This structure is used when the primary purpose of an article is to supplement a fully rubriced article appearing elsewhere in the set.

Whenever appropriate, articles begin with the **pronunciation** of the group's name, a listing of **alternate names** by which the group is known, the group's **location** in the world, its **population,** the **languages** spoken, the **religions** practiced, and a listing of **related articles** in the five volumes of this encyclopedia. Most articles are illustrated with a map showing the primary location of the group and photographs of the people being profiled. The twenty standard headings by which most articles are organized are presented below.

INTRODUCTION: A description of the group's historical origins provides a useful background for understanding its contemporary affairs. Information relating to migration helps explain how the group arrived at its present location. Political conditions and governmental structure(s) that typically affect members of the profiled ethnic group are also discussed.

LOCATION AND HOMELAND: The population size of the group is listed. This information may include official census data from various countries and/or estimates. Information on the size of a group's population located outside the traditional homeland may also be included, especially for certain groups with large diaspora populations. A description of the homeland includes information on location, topography, and climate.

LANGUAGE: Each article lists the name(s) of the primary language(s) spoken by members. Descriptions of linguistic origins, grammar, and similarities to other languages may also be included. Examples of common words, phrases, and proverbs are listed for many of the profiled groups, and some include examples of common personal names and forms of address.

FOLKLORE: Common themes, settings, and characters in the profiled group's traditional oral and/or literary mythology are highlighted. Many entries include a short excerpt or synopsis of one of the group's most noteworthy myths, fables, or legends. Some entries describe the accomplishments of famous heroes and heroines or other prominent historical figures.

RELIGION: The origins of traditional religious beliefs are profiled. Contemporary religious beliefs, customs, and practices are also discussed. Some groups may be closely associated with one particular faith (especially if religious and ethnic identification are interlinked), while others may have members of diverse faiths.

MAJOR HOLIDAYS: Celebrations and commemorations typically recognized by the group's members are described. These holidays commonly fall into two categories: secular and religious. Secular holidays often include an independence day and/or other days of observance recognizing important dates in history that affected the group as a whole. Religious holidays are typically the same as those honored by other peoples of the same faith. Some secular and religious holidays are linked to the lunar cycle or to the change of seasons. Some articles describe unique customs practiced by members of the group on certain holidays.

RITES OF PASSAGE: Formal and informal episodic events that mark an individual's procession through the stages of life are profiled. These events typically involve rituals, ceremonies, observances, and procedures associated with birth, childhood, the coming of age, adulthood, and death. The impact of twenty-first century communications and global media on customs are addressed here.

INTERPERSONAL RELATIONS: Information on greetings, body language, gestures, visiting customs, and dating practices is included. The extent of formality to which members of a certain ethnic group treat others is also addressed, as some groups may adhere to customs governing interpersonal relationships more/less strictly than others.

LIVING CONDITIONS: General health conditions typical of the group's members are cited. Such information includes life expectancy, the prevalence of various diseases, and access to medical care. Information on urbanization, housing, and access to utilities is also included. Transportation methods typically utilized by the group's members are also discussed.

FAMILY LIFE: The size and composition of the family unit is profiled. Gender roles common to the group are also discussed, including the division of rights and responsibilities relegated to male and female group members. The roles that children, adults, and the elderly have within the group as a whole may also be addressed.

CLOTHING: Many entries include descriptive information (size, shape, color, fabric, etc.) regarding traditional clothing (or a national costume), and indicate the frequency of its use in contemporary life. A description of clothing typically worn in the present is also provided, especially if traditional clothing is no longer the usual form of dress. Distinctions between formal, informal, and work clothes are made in many articles, along with clothing differences between men, women, and children.

FOOD: Descriptions of items commonly consumed by members of the group are listed. The frequency and occasion for meals is also described, as are any unique customs regarding eating and drinking, special utensils and furniture, and the role of food and beverages in ritual ceremonies. Many entries include a sample recipe for a favorite dish.

EDUCATION: The structure of formal education in the country or countries of residence is discussed, including information on primary, secondary, and higher education. For some groups, the role of informal education is also highlighted. Some articles may include information regarding the relevance and importance of education among the group as a whole, along with parental expectations for children. In addition, literacy levels are described where appropriate.

CULTURAL HERITAGE: Since many groups express their sense of identity through art, music, literature, and dance, a description of prominent styles is included. Some articles also cite the contributions of famous individual artists, writers, and musicians.

WORK: The type of labor that typically engages members of the profiled group is discussed. For some groups, the formal wage economy is the primary source of earnings, but for other groups, informal agriculture or trade may be the usual way to earn a living. Working conditions are also highlighted.

SPORTS: Popular sports that children and adults play are listed, as are typical spectator sports. Some articles include a description and/or rules to a unique type of sport or game.

ENTERTAINMENT AND RECREATION: Listed activities that people enjoy in their spare time may include carrying out either structured pastimes (such as public musical and dance performances) or informal get-togethers (such as meeting for conversation). The role of popular culture, movies, theater, and television in everyday life is also discussed.

FOLK ARTS, CRAFTS, AND HOBBIES: Entries describe arts and crafts commonly fabricated according to traditional methods, materials, and style. Such objects may often have a functional utility for everyday tasks.

SOCIAL PROBLEMS: Internal and external issues that confront members of the profiled group are described. Such concerns often deal with fundamental problems like war, famine, disease, and poverty. A lack of human rights, civil rights, and political freedom may also adversely affect a group as a whole. Other problems may include crime, unemployment, substance abuse, and domestic violence.

GENDER ISSUES: New to this edition is a section focusing on women's issues including cultural attitudes, discrimination, status, health, sexual issues, education, and work and employment. Some discussion on the group's attitudes toward homosexuality may be included in this section, where relevant.

BIBLIOGRAPHY: References cited include works used to compile the article, as well as benchmark publications often recognized as authoritative by scholars. Citations for materials published in foreign languages are frequently listed when there are few existing sources available in English.

A glossary of terms and a comprehensive index appears at the end of each volume.

ACKNOWLEDGMENTS

The editors express appreciation to the members of the Cengage Gale staff who were involved in a number of ways at various stages of development of the *Worldmark Encyclopedia of Cultures and Daily Life, Second Edition:* Christine Nasso, Barbara Beach, and Leah Knight, who helped the initial concept of the work take form; and Larry Baker and Allison McNeill, who supported the editorial development of the profiles for the first edition. Carol Nagel and Ellen McGeagh were instrumental in the planning and scheduling of the second edition of this work. Anne Marie Hacht selected the photo illustrations and provided valuable review of the entries. Marybeth Trimper,

Evi Seoud, and Shanna Heilveil oversaw the printing and binding process.

In addition, the editors acknowledge with warm gratitude the contributions of the staff of Eastword Publications—Debby Baron, Dan Lucas, Brian Rajewski, Kira Silverbird, Maggie Lyall, Karen Seyboldt, Tajana G. Roehl, Janet Fenn, Cheryl Montagna, Jeneen Hobby, Dan Mehling, Karen Ellicott, Alexander Barnes, and Elizabeth Gall—who managed interactions with contributors; edited, organized, reviewed, and indexed the articles; and turned the manuscripts into the illustrated typeset pages of these five volumes.

SUGGESTIONS ARE WELCOME: Maintenance of a work the size and scope of *Worldmark Encyclopedia of Cultures and Daily Life, Second Edition, is a daunting undertaking; we appreciate any suggestions that* will enhance future editions. Please send comments to:

Editor
*Worldmark Encyclopedia
of Cultures and Daily Life*
Cengage Gale
27500 Drake Rd.
Farmington Hills, MI 48331-3535

INTRODUCTION

by
Roger Williams Wescott

Is Europe really a continent? Europe isn't nearly as sharply separated from Asia as the Americas are—or even as Africa is. Geographers often refer to large peninsulas, like India, as subcontinents. In many ways, Europe's relation to Asia is like that of India. It is at least as easy to go by land from the interior of Asia into Europe as it is to go from the interior of Asia into India.

Does this mean that we should call Europe a subcontinent rather than a continent? Maybe. But most Europeans prefer the continental designation. They point out that Europe has a uniquely long coastline, more extensive and more indented than that of any other land mass, including Asia itself. In addition to this strong geographic argument, Europeans also have a compelling historical argument. For most of the past few centuries, Europe has dominated the world in all areas of human endeavor. Finally, and perhaps most importantly, Europeans have a subjective reason for calling their region a continent. However limited it may be in area, Europe is their home as well as the center of what is generally called Western Civilization.

One might think that Americans, because they are an ocean away, would be less inclined than Europeans to recognize Europe as a continent. But Americans, from Argentina to Canada (including, of course, the United States) are predominantly European in ancestry. These European-Americans greatly outnumber both Native Americans and African-Americans, so they are inclined to take a rather European view of the geographic status of Europe.

While recognizing that there is cultural bias involved in calling Europe something more than a subcontinent, we shall here follow general practice in referring to Europe as one of our planet's major continental regions.

EUROPEAN TRAITS

There are two distinctive traits that seem to be characteristic of all the peoples of Europe. One of these traits is physical in nature and the other cultural. The physical trait is racial—all native Europeans are, in technical terms, Caucasoid or, in popular terms, white. In this respect, they resemble the peoples of northern Africa and western Asia but contrast with the peoples of Africa and the peoples of eastern Asia, termed Negroid and Mongoloid, respectively.

European Caucasoids are of three major varieties, or subraces. The most northerly of these is the Nordic subrace, whose members tend to be tall, blond, and blue-eyed. Of the nations of Europe, the one with the highest proportion of Nordics is Sweden. Although Nordics are now common in North America, their ancestors seem to have come exclusively from northern Europe. The most southerly of the subraces is the Mediterranean, whose members tend to be short, dark-complexioned, and brown-eyed. The European nation with the highest proportion of Mediterraneans is probably Greece. Between the Nordics and the Mediterraneans is a band of peoples of intermediate physical characteristics, known as Alpines. Those of Alpine subrace are typically of medium height, brown-haired, and gray-eyed. The Austrians are representative of Europe's Alpine population.

The cultural trait that characterizes all European peoples has to do with the structure of kinship, or family relations. All Europeans have what ethnologists term an Eskimo kinship system (so called because it is found in its simplest and most distinctive form among the Eskimos of arctic North America). Family life among people with this kinship system has the following characteristics:

Marriage is monogamous. Each married man has only one wife and each married woman only one husband. Kinship is bilateral. Each individual considers his father's relatives and his mother's relatives equally closely related to himself. (In other parts of the world, many peoples have unilateral systems, which trace kinship only through the father's line or the mother's line, but not both.)

The family is chiefly or exclusively nuclear. The core family consists of a pair of married parents and their children. If the family is extended, it is tri-generational, consisting of grand-parents, parents, and children—although such extended families are becoming rarer.

All of a person's relatives comprise a kindred, which consists of an equal number of mother's kinsmen and of father's kinsmen. (In this regard, a kindred contrasts with a clan, which consists of kinsmen from the mother's or father's side only. Clans were common in early Europe but are no longer found.)

Marriage is neo-local. This means that newlyweds preferentially set up a new and independent household of their own, rather than joining the household of the groom's family (which is known as patrilocal residence), or joining the household of the bride's family (which is known as matrilocal residence).

To compensate for the decreasing frequency of large extended families, many new-born children are assigned "back-up" parents, known as godparents. Ideally, these godparents serve as adoptive parents if neither the parents nor their kindred can care for the children. Godparenthood, however, is becoming both less common and less effective than it once was.

Besides race and kinship, there are other traits—linguistic and religious—that, though not universal in Europe, typify most European countries. The linguistic trait is one of language genealogy. Of the 36 independent countries of Europe, 33 have national languages that belong to the Indo-European family.

The Indo-European family also includes not only English and Spanish, but also such Asian languages as Persian and Hindi. Only three—Finland, Estonia, and Hungary—have national languages that belong to a different family, called Uralic.

There are certain Indo-European personal names that have spread sufficiently far beyond their area of origin as to be considered pan-European (referring to all of Europe). Examples of names of this kind, cited here in their English forms, are: from Germanic, *Frances,* meaning "of the Franks" (the conquering people for whom France was named); from Celtic, *Arthur,* meaning "like a bear"; from Romanic, *Patricia,* meaning "noblewoman"; and, from Hellenic, *Philip,* meaning "lover of horses."

The religious trait typifying Europe is Christianity. Christianity is the predominant and/or official religion of every European country except Albania and the European segment of Turkey. In both of these, Muslims outnumber Christians. Although Jews are found in every European country, Judaism is a minority religion throughout the continent. In the Americas, where Christianity is also predominant, it was clearly introduced there by European missionaries and colonists.

An archeological trait unique to Europe is the presence there of elaborate pre-urban structures composed of megaliths, or "big stones," which, unlike the stone blocks used in the ancient cities of Egypt or the Near East, were not cut at right angles or smoothly dressed. It is true that huge, rough-hewn stones of prehistoric age are found on most continents, but none of these constitute great circles like that at Stonehenge in England or mile-long avenues like those at Carnac in France.

Writing systems have developed on most of the world's continents. Only Europe, however, developed an alphabet of the type that regularly and consistently represents vowels as well as consonants. More specifically, it was the ancient Greeks who created this kind of alphabet by adding vowel signs to the early Phoenician syllabary of Lebanon, a script that contained signs for consonants only. This Greek alphabet was then modified in both western Europe to yield the Latin alphabet used in English and other languages, and in eastern Europe to yield the Cyrillic alphabet used in Russia.

Of all the arts, music has had the most distinctive development in Europe. European musicians were the only ones to create a musical notation that enables performers to read and recreate compositions with great precision. Only Europe has invented large and complex instruments, like the piano and the organ. And only Europe has constructed symphony orchestras involving over 100 instruments of diverse kinds. Probably the most uniquely European of all Western musical features, however, is counterpoint—the art of combining different melodic lines in a single composition. This form is evident in all so-called "classical" music—the Baroque compositions of Bach (1685–1750), the Rococo compositions of Mozart (1756–91), and the Romantic compositions of Beethoven (1770–1827).

If navigation may be called an art, Europeans, who had lagged behind the Phoenicians and even the Polynesians in long-distance sailing, eventually became its leading practitioners. As far as we know, no other people had ever sailed around the earth before the crew of the Portuguese/Spanish naval commander Ferdinand Magellan did so in the sixteenth century. And, by this circumnavigation, Magellan and his crew advanced science immeasurably by demonstrating that the earth must be shaped like a ball rather than flat or square-edged.

In the political realm, democracy is almost certainly a European invention. Outside of Europe, farm-villages were often democratically run, especially in India. But it was only in Europe that whole states, such as ancient Athens or modern France, were based, however tenuously, on such revolutionary ideological principles as freedom and equality. And, to the extent that democracy has become a global political ideal, that ideal stems primarily from the efforts and aspirations of Europeans and European-Americans.

In terms of its effect on the world outside of Europe, however, there was another European innovation that was probably even more transformative than was the democratic ideal. This innovation was the Industrial Revolution, beginning with the invention of a practical steam engine in eighteenth century England and culminating in the establishment of thermonuclear power stations. Although both the ancient Greeks and the medieval Chinese demonstrated the intellectual and mechanical skills necessary to launch this revolution, neither did. Perhaps they realized, or at least feared, that industrialization would destabilize their societies. If so, their apprehension has been justified by subsequent developments. After Europe industrialized itself and then industrialized the rest of the world, human technological and commercial power increased immensely. But warfare became more devastating, population increases outstripped agricultural resources, and pollution began to threaten public health nearly everywhere.

ENVIRONMENT

For a geography teacher who likes to draw free-hand maps of continents on the blackboard, Africa is a joy. A single broad stroke encloses all of it except the Indian Ocean island of Madagascar. Europe, on the other hand, is not so easy. It has a jig-sawed look, full of tiny twists, protrusions, and indentations. Even a professional wall map fails to show even half of the 80,000 kilometers (50,000 miles) of the intricately filigreed European coastline.

When these coastline complications are enlarged by archipelagos, islands, and peninsulas, the land/sea picture becomes even more elaborate. An archipelago (literally, "a ruler of the sea") is a collection of islands, like those of the Aegean Sea. A peninsula (literally, "nearly an island") is a projection of land, most but not all of which is coastal, like Iberia, a block of land politically divided between Portugal and Spain. A glance at these coasts makes it easy to see how the Greeks managed to colonize the Mediterranean region, founding cities like Naples in Italy and Marseilles in France, and how the Spanish succeeded in colonizing Latin America, most of which, before the revolutionary wars, was known as New Spain.

Topography

Away from the coasts, Europe consists mainly of highlands and plains. If we take the Ural mountains of Russia to be the boundary between Europe and Asia, then the only major European mountain system is the Alpine system. This system includes the Alps, the Iberian Pyrenees to the west and, to the east, the Carpathians of central Europe and the highlands of the Balkan peninsula. The system ends in the Caucasus range, generally taken to constitute a second mountainous boundary between southeastern Europe and southwestern Asia.

Geologists believed that the Alpine system was raised as the result of a collision or series of collisions between drifting continents—in this case, Europe to the north and Africa to the south. But because the Mediterranean Sea seems to separate these continents and serve as a presumptive buffer preventing collision, geologists have reformulated this collisional scenario in terms of plate tectonics. As they now picture the movements of the earth's surface, both continents and the oceans near them ride on crustal plates. And it is these plates rather than the continents themselves that collide, causing an uplift of land at the point or points of contact. When this uplift is sufficiently high, streams freeze and snow becomes compacted, producing glaciers, such as those in Switzerland. Among the other results of plate collision are earthquakes, of the kind frequently experienced in the Balkan hill country, and volcanic eruption. Among the northern Mediterranean volcanoes that have endangered towns are Mount Vesuvius in Italy and Mount Aetna in Sicily.

Complementary to the Alpine zone of southern and central Europe is the great plain of northern continental Europe, which stretches from the Ural mountains through Russia, Poland, Germany, and the Low Countries to France. This is the long, flat corridor through which wave after wave of migratory peoples have passed from the Eurasian steppes to the Atlantic seaboard during the period between the domestication of horses in Neolithic times and the eastward expansion of Russian peasant farmers in the sixteenth century. Among the many ethnic groups traversing this natural highway were the Indo-European ancestors of modern North Americans, the Uralians (ancestral to the modern Hungarians), the northern Turks (ancestral to the Chuvash of contemporary Russia), and the western Mongols (represented by the Kalmyks of contemporary Russia).

Climate

Overall, Europe is the least arid of all continents. The only part of the continent that can fairly be described as dry is the steppe country northwest of the Caspian Sea. As one moves north through eastern Europe, the land becomes progressively moister, until, in Finland, a fifth of the surface is covered by lakes.

The three major climatic zones of Europe are the Atlantic Maritime zone, typified by Britain; the Mediterranean Subtropical zone, typified by Italy; and the Inland Continental zone, typified by Russia. The Atlantic Maritime region is rainy and cool, with few extremes of temperature. The Mediterranean Subtropical region is rainy in the winter but dry in the summer. The Inland Continental region is both larger and more variable in climate than the other two, and must be divided into subregions, each with a distinctive climate. The five subregions, reading roughly from north to south, are (1) the subarctic subregion, represented by Finland; (2) the humid short-summer subregion, represented by Poland; (3) the humid long-summer subregion, represented by Hungary; (4) the elevated subregion, represented by Switzerland; and (5) the dry long-summer region, represented by Ukraine.

Soil, Water, and Forests

Until Europe was intensively farmed and urbanized, it had been heavily forested woodland. In the north, the forests consisted primarily of needle-leaf evergreens, such as pine, spruce, and fir. In the long central belt, they consisted chiefly of deciduous broad-leaf trees, such as oak, beech and ash. And, in the south, they consisted mainly of fruit-bearing trees, such as palm, olive, and orange. Agricultural and industrial deforestation, however, has turned the great forests of the past into scattered ornamental tree avenues. In more arid areas, such as southern Spain, trees have been largely replaced by scrub growth.

The life of any region depends largely on the quantity and quality of its soil and water. Most of Europe has fertile brown forest soil, now largely converted to agriculture. As one moves northward, the soil becomes increasingly acid, hospitable to needle-leaf trees but not to farming. Eventually, in Lapland (northern Scandinavia), even trees give way to low-growing lichens and mosses. Such tundra country provides good fodder for reindeer, but not for barnyard live-stock.

As one moves south, the soil becomes eroded and clay-like on the Mediterranean coast, where trees grow less tall than inland. The richest soil in Europe is probably the *chernozem*, or black earth, of Ukraine.

Europe has, in most places, a freshwater table that readily yields wells and fountains. Its sea water, by contrast, is saltier than most of the world's oceans. The Mediterranean is saltier than other oceans because evaporation from its surface, especially in the summer, exceeds the inflow of fresh waters from such rivers as the Rhone in France or the Tiber in Italy. And the reason why the northeast Atlantic Ocean is so salty is that it receives a salty surface outflow from the Mediterranean, through the Straits of Gibraltar between Spain and Morocco. The attractive blue color of the Mediterranean is due chiefly to the fact that its saltiness prevents the accumulation of green plankton, consisting of tiny floating plants, on its surface. The lack of edible plankton, in turn, prevents Mediterranean fish from becoming as large or as numerous as those in the Atlantic.

The relative mildness of the Atlantic coastal climate from Norway south to Spain is due to the transportation of warm, tropical American sea water from the Caribbean region by the so-called Gulf Stream. This stream—which may be regarded as a river in the ocean—moves slowly but steadily in a clockwise direction, assuring that Scandinavia is not nearly as icy as territories at a corresponding latitude, such as Greenland in North America.

The smaller seas of Europe have special characteristics. Both the Black Sea, between Ukraine and Turkey, and the Baltic Sea, between Finland and Denmark, have brackish water—water that is substantially less salty than that of the ocean. These seas receive more water from rivers than they lose through evaporation, and they are too far from the Atlantic Ocean to receive much salt water from it. The North Sea, between Britain and Denmark, would seem to have the potential to produce as much seafood as the Atlantic Ocean. However, because it is surrounded by six of the most active seafaring nations on earth, it is now virtually "fished out."

Agriculture

Most of Europe has a temperate climate, favoring growth of the kind of grass most nourishing to grazing animals. Southern Europe produces grapes of the type from which the world's most famous wines are made.

In Europe, as elsewhere, those plants that sustain the largest number of people are domesticated grains. All of Europe's grains, as it happens, originated elsewhere. Its wheat and rye were first cultivated in southwest Asia; its rice, in southeast

Asia; and its maize, in North America. Europe's other staple food crop, the potato, was first cultivated in South America.

Europe, like north Asia and north Africa, belongs to what is called the Palearctic (meaning "old northern") faunal zone. During the Ice Age, Europe was home to a number of large wild animals: the mastodon (an extinct elephant), the woolly rhinoceros, the giant cave-bear, and the Irish elk, whose antlers measured four meters (twelve feet) across. Even in early historic times, Europe still had lions and a type of buffalo called the aurschs.

Of the various animals basic to farming, only the pig was domesticated in Europe. Others now common in Europe—such as sheep, goats, cows, horses, chickens, ducks, and geese—were adopted from cultivators in Asia.

Fish and Birds

The fisheries of North Atlantic Europe produce an abundance of tuna, bluefish, mackerel, and sole. Those of the Mediterranean yield sardines, anchovy, bass, and flounder. Mediterranean divers harvest sponge and red coral, and southern European gourmets relish octopus and squid. Marine mammals, such as seals and dolphins, are found in both Atlantic and Mediterranean waters, although they are larger and more numerous in the Atlantic.

Such common European birds as sparrows, gulls, hawks, and owls are also wide-spread on other continents. A bird that can be considered distinctively European is the stork, because only in Europe does it nest on roofs and chimney-tops, coming to be regarded as a seasonal household lodger.

Of the many species of European insects, the only one that has a commercial importance comparable to that of the silkworm moth in China is the honeybee. European bee-keepers have long managed apiaries, in which they construct artificial beehives from which honey can be periodically withdrawn and consumed or sold.

In purely emotional terms, the most important animals in contemporary Europe are undoubtedly the cats and dogs that are kept as household pets. The love and care lavished on them is often second only to that lavished on children.

THE PREHISTORY OF EUROPE

Of all fossil human beings, the first to appear in Europe was one that scholars formerly referred to as *Pithecanthropus erectus* ("the upright ape-man"). To emphasize its close relationship to us, specialists have renamed this ancestor *Homo erectus* ("upright man").

Homo erectus

Remains of Homo erectus have been found in Spain, the French/Italian Riviera, and Hungary. He lived during the Lower Paleolithic Period, the earlier segment of the Old Stone Age. In geological terms, this was the middle of the Pleistocene Epoch or Ice Age. In chronological terms, Homo erectus lived between about 400,000 and 200,000 years ago. He stood about one and one-half meters (five feet) tall, and had a brain volume of around 57 cubic inches (950 cubic centimeters)—slightly smaller than that of most human beings today. His chief stone implement was a core tool of a type that archeologists call an Acheulean biface hand-ax. Besides this manual cutting tool, he may have made wooden spears (to the tip of which the ax could have been attached). It's also possible that he dug pits in the earth to serve either as traps for hunted animals or as shallow cellars for lean-tos or huts.

What is certain is that Homo erectus was carnivorous. In his habitations, excavators have found the remains of many fish, turtles, birds, and rodents. Surprisingly, perhaps, they have also found bones of some large animals—mammoths, woolly rhinoceroses, cave-bears, and even saber-toothed tigers. What is not clear is whether this early man killed such formidable beasts or merely scavenged their remains after they died or were killed by other animals. But he undoubtedly ate their meat and probably also used their bones as supplementary tools.

Men, women, and children of the species erectus constructed oval huts—about 10.5 meters (35 feet) long and 6 meters (20 feet) wide—from rocks, logs, and more perishable materials. These dwellings, which contained table-stones usable as either seats or foot-platforms, may have held a dozen or more inhabitants. A part of each hut contained abundant ashes and burnt bones, providing strong evidence that this primal human being used fire to warm his home, to cook food, and perhaps also to repel or stampede animals.

The skulls of Homo erectus are sometimes detached from the rest of the skeletons. Sometimes, too, the *Foramina magna*—holes at the bases of these skulls—are artificially enlarged by chopping. What these facts undeniably suggest is that this first European was a head-hunter, a cannibal, or both.

We may infer that Homo erectus was a relatively unimaginative creature, concerned primarily with survival. The prehistoric humanity that succeeded him, however, seems to have engaged in non-utilitarian activities of a type that we would call religious or artistic.

Neanderthalers

The earlier of these successors, Neanderthal Man, was known initially as Cyphanthropus ("bent-over man"), which derived from the fact that many Neanderthalers suffered from crippling arthritis; then as Homo neanderthalensis; and most recently, as Homo sapiens neanderthalensis ("the knowing man of the Neander Valley"). Neanderthal remains have been found in Spain, France, Germany, Italy, and the Balkan countries. Neandertalers lived in the Middle Paleolithic period of the Pleistocene Ice Age, between about 200,000 and 30,000 years ago. Like the erectus type, they were short, big-toothed, heavy-boned, and presumably muscular. But, unlike their Lower Paleolithic forebears, they had brains as big as ours. There was, however, a significant difference between their brains and ours—where our brains bulge in front, making us literal "high-brows," theirs bulged in back, in the occipital region believed to control large-muscle coordination. Neanderthalers were probably swift runners and powerful wrestlers, but less inclined than we to think and to plan for the future.

Archeologists refer to the main Neanderthal stone-working industry as Monsterian. Instead of focusing on core tools like hand-axes, it emphasized flake tools, such as awls and scrapers. Remains of bone and stone toggles suggest that Neanderthalers used them to fasten cloaks made from animal hides. Their motive in wearing clothes, we presume, had more to do with protection from ice-age chill that with modesty.

The most distinctive innovation in Neanderthal behavior was burial of the dead and construction of what look like shrines consisting of circles of animal skulls. The burial was clearly ceremonial, since, wherever graves contain more than one individual, all are arranged in the same ritual position, whether that position is flexed or extended. The skull circles may have been intended to propitiate the collective spirit of whatever animal the skulls came from (most often bears and goats). Pollen found in some graves suggests that flowers may have been placed with the deceased Neandertalers.

Neanderthal Man apparently hunted all the animals that were eaten by his Paleolithic predecessor, but the game that he most consistently killed and consumed was the deer.

Two mysteries remain with regard to the Neanderthalers. For communication, did they talk or employ a fully linguistic manual sign language? The complexity of their behavior suggests that they did. Yet, because they left no writing or pictorial representations, we cannot be sure. The other mystery is the cause of their disappearance. Did a natural disaster bring about their extinction? Did members of our subspecies, Homo sapiens sapiens, make use of superior weaponry to kill them off? Or were the Neandertalers, having a relatively small population, simply absorbed by the much larger population of our subspecies? As yet, there is no clear evidence favoring any one of these explanations.

Cro-Magnon

The period following the disappearance of the Neanderthalers is known, archeologically, as the Upper Paleolithic (recent Stone Age) and geologically, as the Upper Pleistocene (recent Ice Age). Since the beginning of that period, about 30,000 years ago, there has been only one human subspecies on earth, Homo sapiens sapiens, known to anthropologists as physically Modern Man. The kind of Modern Man that occupied Europe was Cro-Magnon, typified by fossil remains found in France and believed to resemble contemporary Europeans. Compared to Neanderthal Man, Cro-Magnon Man was tall and light-boned, with small teeth and a pronounced chin.

These Upper Paleolithic people followed the reindeer herds that then populated Europe. In addition to the stabbing and slashing weapons used by the Neanderthalers, they made new hunting tools: the spear-thrower, to bring down large mammals; the bow-and-arrow, to skewer birds; and the fish-hook, to catch underwater game.

To cultural anthropologists, the most interesting aspect of Upper Paleolithic European life is the art-work it produced. On the walls of Spanish and French caves, Cro-Magnon men painted strikingly life-like pictures of the many wild animals of their time. And they sculpted figurines, chiefly of buxom, pregnant-looking women. The wall-paintings are thought to reflect their concern for food and the figurines, their concern for reproduction.

Unlike their predecessors, Upper Paleolithic people were not confined to the Old World land-mass of Africa and Eurasia. They spread, presumably by raft, to Australia and the Americas. These and other accomplishments strongly suggest that they had language, even though they did not yet write it.

To the Paleolithic period described above, some archeologists add a Mesolithic, or Middle Stone Age, lasting from about 15,000 till about 10,000 years ago. The chief accomplishments of this period were the domestication of wolves, which became dogs, and the construction of sleds and boats for faster and more comfortable transportation over snow and open water.

The Pleistocene Ice Age ended around 10,000 years ago, giving way to the climatically milder Holocene Epoch in which we now live. The two chief differences between the Pleistocene and the Holocene were a pair of disappearances. The ice-sheet that covered northern Europe and much of North America vanished. So too did the Pleistocene megafauna—a collection of large mammals that we now know only from fossils or from Stone Age cave-paintings. Among these extinct animals are mammoths, woolly rhinoceroses, saber-toothed tigers, and giant cave-bears. Scholars still debate the causes of both the climatic shift and the extinctions. Some maintain that increasingly proficient Ice Age human hunters killed off these huge animals, although human populations were then so small as to make this explanation hard to believe.

Neolithic Age

By about 5,000 BC, Europe underwent a cultural transformation, initiating the Neolithic, or New Stone Age. This period gets its name from the fact that stone tools, most of which had been chipped, to yield a rough surface, began to be ground, to yield a smooth surface. But the most crucial development of the Neolithic Period was not its stone-working technique. It was, rather, the shift from food extraction to food production, constituting the so-called Agricultural Revolution. Where Europeans had previously hunted game and gathered wild plants, they now began to domesticate both. Sheep, goats, and pigs became livestock. Such grasses as wheat, barley, and rye became crops. The combination of herding and tillage produced the farm-village complex, involving irrigation, food storage, and a rapid increase in population. Farming, in turn, was accompanied by such cottage industries as pottery and weaving, all of which conspired to make a formerly nomadic population sedentary.

One of the most mysterious developments that grew out of the Agricultural Revolution was the megalithic complex, which involved the construction of huge, if crude, stone monuments along most of the Mediterranean and Atlantic coasts. Although the purpose of these monuments remains obscure, it is unquestionable that any society capable of erecting them without metal tools must have been well organized and highly motivated. Such motivation and organization may well have underlaid the transformative European expansion of historic times.

Indo-European Invasion

The last major occurrence in European prehistory was unquestionably the incursion of the Indo-Europeans from the east during the period from about 3,000 to 1,000 BC. The Indo-Europeans are so called because the speakers of their related languages are found from Europe through Iran to India to Bangladesh. The early Indo-Europeans were apparently an aggressive pastoral people who, though they could and did raise crops, more often migrated in search of better pasturage for their horses and cattle. Neither literate nor urban, they nonetheless smelted metals. From these they made weapons which, in combination with their mobility, enabled them to conquer or displace otherwise more culturally sophisticated peoples in southern and western Asia.

The major branches of the Indo-European family of languages are the following eight, each of which is represented here by a language spoken in Europe today. Of the languages that had been spoken in Europe before the Indo-Europeans arrived, the only one that survives today is Basque, the language of Pyrenean sheep-herders on the Bay of Biscay in France and Spain.

Language Family	Representative Language
Germanic	English
Celtic	Welsh
Italic	Spanish
Hellenic	Greek
Thraco-Illyrian	Albanian
Baltic	Lithuanian
Slavic	Russian
Iranian	Ossete

EUROPEAN HISTORY

Limitations of space prevent our giving Europe's recorded past the extensive attention that most historians would expect and demand. For brevity's sake we shall treat it as a sequence of cultural pulses.

Minoan Civilization

The earliest of these pulses is the advent of that blend of urbanism, literacy, and metallurgy that culture theorists call civilization. The first civilization of Europe, called Minoan, was centered on the island of Crete in the eastern Mediterranean, beginning about 1000 BC. Minoan maritime culture was spread throughout the Aegean region by Cretan naval and commercial crews. By around 1400 BC, Indo-Europeans from the Balkan area had entered the Aegean shores. We know them as Greeks and their civilization as Hellenic. About 900 BC, a third people from this area apparently migrated westward to Italy, founding the Etruscan city-states of the province now called Tuscany.

Macedonia and Rome

It is believed that these early southern European civil societies were mostly monarchial in their political organization. And monarchies, even more than other state organizations, tend to be expansionist. When one monarchy absorbs other monarchies or adjoining states, it becomes an empire. Two of the greatest empires of the ancient Mediterranean coasts were the Macedonian and the Roman. About 330 BC, the Macedonians from the northern shore of the Aegean Sea conquered the Greek city-states and then proceeded to absorb the Persian empire, which stretched from what is now Bulgaria eastward to what is now Pakistan. Meanwhile, the Romans were developing a powerful state adjacent to the Etruscans in Italy. By about 150 BC the Romans had annexed Carthage in North Africa, along with its colonies in Spain, Corsica, Sardinia, and Sicily. Soon thereafter it annexed Macedon and Greece. By about 125 AD the Roman Empire stretched from Scotland to Armenia and had no major military rivals in Europe, Africa, or Asia west of Iran.

Carthaginians, Arabs, and Others

Despite the fact that Indo-Europeans have dominated Europe for the past 3,000 years, there was never a time when other linguistic groups were without influence on the continent. In Pre-Roman times, the Iberian peninsula was controlled by Carthaginians from what is now Tunisia. And, in post-Roman times, the same peninsula was controlled by Islamic Arabs from Morocco, whose civilization was one of the world's most brilliant from about 900 to 1200 AD Linguistically, both the Carthaginians and the Arabs were Semites, speaking languages related to Hebrew. (The Jews, most of whom migrated to Europe after the fall of the Jerusalem Temple in 70 AD, maintained Hebrew only as a religious language. Their secular language came to be Yiddish, an Indo-European tongue closely related to German.)

Because the early Uralic-speaking peoples were preliterate, it is difficult to date their westward movement into Europe from the Ural mountains and valleys, but at least a dozen are known to have done so. Of these, the only conquering people were the Hungarians, who ruled a Balkan empire for centuries. The same dating problem pertains to the Altaic-speaking peoples, most of whom were Turkic, but a few were Mongolian. Of these, the only ones who are politically influential today are the Osmanli Turks of the Istanbul area who arrived there in the fourteenth century.

Most of these non-Indo-European peoples entering Europe seemed to the urban peoples already established there to be barbarians. It was, however, not so much their linguistic affinities as their nomadic habits that made the intruders seem barbarous. Around 350 AD, when the Roman Empire began to lose control of its northern frontiers, a host of Germanic migrants from the Rhineland and the North Sea and Baltic Sea coasts increasingly infiltrated southward. Chief among these tribal peoples were the Goths, who invaded Spain and Italy; the Franks, who conquered Gaul and changed its name to France; and the Vikings of Scandinavia, who raided the European coasts from the North Sea to the Black Sea. Rome had converted to Christianity in 313 AD, while the Germanic invaders remained pagan. The period of pagan incursions into southern Europe seemed to the people of the collapsing Roman Empire to be "Dark Ages." Between about 500 and 1000 AD, however, all the Germanic conquerors adopted Christianity and ceased pillaging urban churches and rural monasteries.

Medieval Period

The political system that replaced the central authority of imperial Rome is known as feudalism. The period that was feudally organized is known as the Medieval period or, alternatively, "the Middle Ages" (between ancient Rome and modern Europe). Medieval feudalism was characterized by a weakening of royal authority and an increase in the power of local lords—princes, dukes, and lesser noblemen. The duty of the feudal lords was to protect local peasant farmers from outlaws and invaders. The reciprocal duty of the peasants was to provide food and labor as well as occasional military service to the lords. This system held sway in most parts of Europe between about 700 and 1400 AD.

In 1054, Medieval Christendom underwent a schism, or split, between its eastern and western branches. The eastern branch, centered in Constantinople (modern Istanbul), capital of the Byzantine Empire, is known as Orthodox Christianity. The western branch, centered in Rome, the religious capital of the so-called Holy Roman Empire, is known as Catholic Christianity. Although the Orthodox Byzantine world was in decay, occasioned partly by military incursions of Persians and Turks, the Roman Catholic world was increasing in wealth and power.

Christianity had originated in what was known as The Holy Land (equivalent to contemporary Israel, Lebanon, and Syria).

Since about 630, however, its birthplace had been in the hands of Islamic conquerors from Arabia. Roman Catholic Europe now felt sufficiently strong—and more than sufficiently adventurous—to attempt to reclaim the cradle of Christianity from its current occupants. From about 1100 to 1300, the Normans and other western Europeans launched a series of Crusades, or holy wars, against the Moslem Levant. Although the Crusaders temporarily occupied the Bible's sacred sites, they were eventually expelled. But because Islamic civilization was, during this period, generally more elegant and more sophisticated than Christian civilization, Europe emerged from the Crusades more worldly and less provincial than it had been in Medieval times.

During the crusading period, western European kingdoms reversed the flow of power from royalty to feudal lords. Monarchs began to dominate their nobility, especially in England and France. Recovery of centralized royal power had become evident in Denmark to the north as early as about 1000, and in Portugal to the south by about 1400. By around 1500, most of the subjects of these kings began to think of themselves more as members of national communities than as members of provincial communities. In short, the sentiment that we now know as nationalism had effectively replaced localism along the Atlantic seaboard.

Exploration and Colonization

Until the fifteenth century, the world's greatest navigators had been Asian. In pre-Roman times, the Phoenicians of what is now Lebanon had sailed around Africa. About 1400, Chinese admirals crossed the Indian Ocean to trade with East African Muslim rulers. Soon, however, the Portuguese replaced the Chinese in the southern seas. And in 1492 the Spanish explorer Christopher Columbus crossed the Atlantic and made contact with native American Indians in the Caribbean islands.

Contact quickly turned to occupation. About 1500, the Portuguese claimed Brazil, and the Spanish began to colonize the rest of Latin America, enslaving or eliminating many of its indigenous peoples. In the sixteenth century, the French and English began competing for the conquest of North America. By the eighteenth century, English speakers had colonized the Atlantic coast, creating the populations that now constitute most of Canada and the United States. In the nineteenth century many western European nations extended their colonizing to Africa and Asia. Although most of the colonized nations regained their independence in the mid-twentieth century, many of them now employ English, French, or other European languages for official, academic, or commercial purposes.

Renaissance, Reformation, and Counter-Reformation

Meanwhile, a cultural transformation was occurring within Western Europe. Beginning around 1300 in Italy, the otherworldly religious focus of life in Medieval Christendom was giving way to a Renaissance, or rebirth, of classical Greek and Roman learning. This rebirth was not merely intellectual but artistic. Italian architecture began to rival that of the ancient Greco-Roman world; Italian sculpture equaled its prototype; and Italian painting surpassed it.

By the sixteenth century, the Renaissance had moved north of the Alps, producing the humanistic scholarship of Desiderius Erasmus (c.1466–1536) in the Netherlands and the poetic dramas of William Shakespeare (1564–1616) in England. The artistic flowering of Renaissance Europe led, without any cre-

ative interruption, to the development of the seventeenth and eighteenth century styles that are known as Baroque and Rococo. An example of Baroque visual art is the painting of Rembrandt van Rijn (1606–69) in the Netherlands; and, of Rococo auditory art, the music of Wolfgang Amadeus Mozart (1756–91) in Austria.

Parallel to the secular pulse of the Renaissance was the religious pulse known as the Reformation. What they perceived as spiritual laxity and ethical corruption in the Roman Church in the sixteenth century led two northern reformers to create the Protestant movement. About 1520, Martin Luther (1483–1546) in Germany broke with the papacy, abolished monasticism, and created a new church that is now denominationally prevalent in most of north-central Europe. About 1540, John Calvin (1509–1664) in Switzerland abolished the confessional and established a reformed church that is ecclesiastically ancestral to most of the non-Lutheran Protestant denominations of Europe and America.

The Roman Catholic response to Protestantism was to create a self-purifying movement known as the Counter-Reformation. In Spain, Ignatius Loyola (1491–1556) created the Jesuit Society to reinvigorate the Church spiritually and intellectually. And in Italy, the papacy convened a lengthy church council at Trent, to reformulate Catholic doctrine. While most of northwestern Europe became Protestant and most of southwestern Europe remained Catholic, some countries, such as Germany, were religiously divided. This division led to a Thirty Years' War—from 1618 to 1648—which devastated much of central Europe.

The dramatic rise of experimental science occurred at the same time as both the artistic Renaissance and the religious Reformation. Some salient events in this burst of scientific creativity include the demonstration in 1543 by Polish astronomer Nicolaus Copernicus (1473–1543) that the Earth circles the sun (rather than vice-versa, as "common sense" suggests). In 1609, the German astronomer Johannes Kepler (1571–1630) demonstrated that planets move elliptically around the sun, describing ovals (rather than perfect circles). In 1628, the English physician William Harvey (1578–1657) discovered the circulation of blood in the body. In 1638, the Italian physicist Galileo Galilei (1564–1642) conducted tests leading to his proposal of the law of acceleration of falling bodies. In 1662, the Royal Society of London was founded in England. Its best known president was Sir Isaac Newton (1642–1727), who invented calculus, proposed the corpuscular theory of light, and formulated the laws of gravity and motion, between 1669 and 1687.

Capitalism, Commonwealth, and Constitutions

During the feudal period of Medieval Europe, the economy was almost exclusively agricultural and barter was the chief means of exchange. When feudalism ended, capitalism made its appearance. Capitalism may be defined as a system in which the means of production are privately owned and prices are determined by free markets. It may be contrasted with state monopolies, in which the government controls both production and prices. During the sixteenth century, capitalism expanded rapidly, largely as a result of the rise of Calvinist Protestantism, which fostered industriousness and favored wealth—provided that wealth was invested frugally rather than expended luxuriously. In eighteenth century Britain, capitalism expanded further when its focus shifted from trade to productive industries like textile manufacture.

Until the seventeenth century, every major nation in Europe had a monarchical form of government, headed by a duke, prince, king, or emperor. In 1649, however, the Puritan rebels against the Stuart kings abolished the British monarchy and replaced it with a Commonwealth, which was in effect a republic. Although the monarchy was restored shortly afterward, it was made constitutional—that is, republic-like—in 1685. In eighteenth century France, republicanism became increasingly popular among writers and scholars until, in 1789, the Bourbon monarchy was replaced by a republic. Soon afterward, French nationalism intensified French republicanism to generate a patriotic fervor never previously seen in Europe. A young general named Napoleon Bonaparte (1769–1821) took advantage of this fervor to invade and occupy foreign countries from Spain to Russia. He then declared himself emperor. Until 1815 he ruled half of Europe. Although he was deposed and the old French monarchy restored, in 1870 France became a republic again and has remained so ever since. During the twentieth century, most former European monarchies became republics. Those that did not became constitutional monarchies, which may be described as de facto republics with royal figure-heads.

Romanticism

One of Europe's great artistic movements, which peaked in the early nineteenth century but remains strong, is Romanticism. Romanticism may be defined as an outlook that values feeling above thinking, love above duty, and the extraordinary above the ordinary. It was initiated by the Medieval troubadours of southern France, who wooed aristocratic ladies platonically by singing under their balcony windows. It did not become pan-European until the eighteenth century, when the newly prosperous middle class first defined an ideal marriage as one contracted between a man and a woman who had previously fallen in love. Decades later, Romanticism pervaded music, painting, and above all, literature. It is perhaps most fully exemplified by the lives of the English poets John Keats (1795–1821), Percy Bysshe Shelley (1792–1822), and Lord Byron (1788–1824). Besides being widely read, these three friends made enviable pilgrimages to glamorous Mediterranean shores and died dramatically premature deaths.

Democracy, Socialism, and Scientism

Modern European ideologies are, for the most part, products of the past few centuries. The political ideal is democracy, as manifest in the parliamentary government of republics and constitutional monarchies. This democracy is usually associated with the economic system known as capitalism. (In 1917, the Russian monarchy was overthrown by republicans whose goal was to empower the proletariat, or working class, not the middle class as in previous revolutions. Their ideology, which separated democracy from capitalism, was Marxism, the doctrine of Karl Marx (1818–83), a nineteenth century German scholar who lived in England. In place of capitalism, Marx advocated public ownership of the means of production. He referred to partial attainment of such ownership as socialism and to total attainment as communism. Though Russian communism was militarily successful and politically influential for seven decades, its national embodiment, the Soviet Union, collapsed in 1991. Since then, there have been no communist states in Europe. Most Europeans now doubt that democratic government can be effectively separated from a capitalistic economy.)

Outside the realm of politics and economics, the dominant European ideology is probably scientism, or the conviction that most contemporary problems can best be solved by applying to them the rigorously logical and experimental methods of science and mechanical technology. In a broad sense, this scientism can be equated with modernism, the belief that Medieval supernaturalism is impractical and irrelevant to material matters.

With regard to personal problems of an emotional nature, the most inventive response of the past century has probably been psychoanalysis, the therapeutic method devised by the Austrian physician Sigmund Freud (1856–1939) between 1882 and 1939. Freud saw most internal mental conflict as due to repression of unacceptable sexual urges into unconsciousness. For him, therapy meant bringing these unconscious inclinations increasingly into consciousness. Although many psychiatrists reject Freudianism as being no less cultist than Marxism, there is no question that psychoanalytic ideas have deeply influenced literature, psychological theory, and popular thought.

Between 1815 and 1914, scientism and modernism were accompanied by a profound and growing faith in human progress, it being implicitly understood that this progress was spear-headed by western Europe. But the two World Wars of 1914–18 and 1939–45, both of which centered on Europe, shook this faith. So too did the Holocaust, a non-military extermination of millions of Jews and Gypsies by Germany's National Socialist government toward the end of World War II.

Nineteenth century optimism was partially regained during the 1950s, when Europe recovered its prosperity and began to exploit atomic energy and to explore interplanetary space. Apprehension remained, however, over the danger that atomic energy would be used to produce bombs of the type that had devastated Japan and that rockets would be used to deliver those bombs more swiftly and irresistibly.

European Economic Community

To make the Space Age and the Atomic Age times of promise rather than of terror, Europe's statesmen began meeting soon after the German surrender of 1945. By 1949, they had established the Council of Europe, a continental proto-parliament, in Strasbourg: and, by 1957, the European Economic Community (better known as the Common Market) in Rome and Brussels. The purpose of these and other transnational bodies was ultimately to create a "United States of Europe" or its equivalent, preventing war between the constituent states of the continent. Events in eastern Europe, however, seem to have run against this unifying aspiration: the Soviet Union split into 15 independent nations and Yugoslavia into five. Furthermore, one of the formerly Yugoslavian states, Bosnia, erupted into civil war, which was stifled only by United Nations military intervention. To counter this persistent ethnic separatism and rekindle pan-Europeanism, the continent has little to offer beyond unconquerable hope and the equally persistent yearning for unity.

THE ECONOMY

Europeans have been farming, trading and engaging in small-scale manufacture since prehistoric times. Today Europe's farming is mechanized; its trade is accelerated by rapid transportation; and its manufacturing is done on a large scale. Europe is now one of the world's three economic power-houses (the other two being East Asia and North America).

Before the Industrial Revolution of the nineteenth century, Europe's wealth consisted largely of farm produce. Although her arable land was restricted in comparison with that of Asia or North America, her fields were intensively cultivated. And, although her forests were being converted into farmland, her timber yield in the northern and eastern parts of the continent exceeded that of more heavily forested continents like Africa and South America. Moreover, her extensive Atlantic and Mediterranean coasts were the scene of productive fishing enterprises.

After the Industrial Revolution, Europe benefitted greatly from the fact that it was rich in coal and iron. There was oil in the eastern parts of the continent and hydroelectric potential in its northern regions. The first steam trains and gasoline automobiles were of European manufacture. Today, rail lines and highways link all European nations and, along with steamships and airplanes, connect Europe speedily and profitably with other continents, both developed and developing.

About seven percent of the Western European population holds stock in major corporations like Unilever in Britain, Phillips in the Netherlands, Michelin in France, Fiat in Italy, or Volvo in Sweden. Such ownership is only about half as prevalent as stock-holding in North America, but it is twice that found in East Asia. As the cradle of Western Civilization, Europe has, for the past century, profited steadily from tourism. A majority of the cultural pilgrims to Europe come from Japan and the United States.

TECHNOLOGY AND POPULATION

Ten thousand years ago, all the world's peoples were hunters and gatherers. Their technology was limited to the wooden weapons used to hunt game animals and the woven baskets used to carry edible wild plants. It is unlikely that, with such survival techniques and simple tools, all of humanity could have numbered more than ten million individuals.

In Europe, population began to grow about 5000 BC, when small-scale vegetable gardening increasingly supplemented or replaced foraging. Those who planted crops had a far more reliable source of food than those who merely harvested what nature, unaided, provided. Around 2000 BC, large-scale plow agriculture replaced dooryard gardens, leading to a further jump in population. When farms no longer needed big families, a growing number of rural folk drifted toward temple complexes and market centers, turning them into real cities, with palaces and military garrisons.

Population, however, does not invariably swell. Adverse circumstances can make it decline. The first time such a demographic decline seems to have occurred in Europe was about 500 AD, when the centralized authority of Rome failed to maintain imperial order. Marauding bands of Germanic migrants then crossed the northern borders, disrupting the transportation of food and trade-goods and resulting in depopulation. Many cities, including Rome itself, shrank to village size. Many farms were abandoned, with the land reverting to uncultivated wilderness.

This depopulation was not halted till around 1000 AD, when the Dark Ages were supplanted by a new Medieval order. Medieval Europe grew around cathedral towns and royal capitals like London and Paris. Then in 1347, newly prosperous Europe was unexpectedly devastated by the Black Death, an epidemic of bubonic plague that had originated in East Asia and moved westward with lethal effect through Turkestan (a region of Asia that is now part of Turkmenistan, Uzbekistan, Tajikistan, Kyrgyzstan, Kazakstan, China, and Afghanistan) to the Black Sea coast. By 1400, this plague had wiped out a third of the European populace.

Since 1400, Europe's population has grown steadily. The first factor leading to population growth was the overseas colonization movement that exploited the resources of Africa and the Americas and brought wealth to all the Atlantic seaboard nations from Portugal to England. The second factor was the Industrial Revolution, which, soon after 1800, made Europe the manufacturing center of the world.

Since World War II, Europe's population growth has slowed despite continued growth in its industry, transportation, and communications. Among other reasons, this demographic slow-down may be due to European realization that small families are usually healthier and wealthier than large ones. Although Europe's total population is nearly a billion, it is now—alone among the continents—close to attaining zero population growth.

LAW

Although law can be scientific or religious in nature, we shall discuss it here only in its social, political, and economic applications. The earliest European law-giver of whom we have any appreciable knowledge is Solon, an Athenian statesman of the sixth century BC. His great legislative achievement was to abolish enslavement for debt and generally to equalize the rich and the poor in their relationship to public authority.

Roman and Common Law

The longest lasting of European juridical systems was Roman Law, which began in Etruscan Latium in the eighth century BC and lasted until the fall of the Byzantine empire in the fifteenth century AD. Initially, the Romans administered two kinds of justice—civil law for citizens of Rome and gentile law for conquered peoples. In the third century AD, however, this preferential system was abandoned in favor of a single standard of equal justice for all.

In England and its overseas colonies, Roman Law was largely superseded by Common Law. Common Law was a blend of Anglo-Saxon custom and Norman legislation. Before the Norman conquest of 1066 AD, wronged individuals and families had to seek redress for injustice from the parties who injured them. Thereafter, the courts of the British kings decided whether the law had been violated and how miscreants should pay for their misdeeds.

Napoleonic Code

In 1804, the French emperor Napoleon promulgated his own legal system, the Napoleonic Code. This code integrated various previous systems—local custom, ecclesiastical standards, royal edicts, and revolutionary justice—into a universalized system of law. The Napoleonic Code has remained prevalent in France and its colonies as well as influential in most of those European countries which the French, however briefly, conquered and controlled.

In the seventeenth century, Hugo Grotius (1583–1645) and other Dutch jurists began developing a code of international law to supplement the national codes of England, France, and other countries. Although international law is far harder to enforce than national law, it did exhibit coercive power in the Nuremberg trials after World War II, when Germany's National Socialist leaders were tried and, in some cases, executed for war crimes or crimes against humanity. It is the hope of ecumenically minded Europeans that such law will gain strength in the coming century and deter, if not wholly prevent, genocidal warfare.

GOVERNMENT

The earliest European governments of which we have written records were the limited monarchies of the Greek city-states, such as Athens and Sparta, beginning around 1200 BC. What limited these monarchies was the countervailing power of hereditary aristocracies and free yeoman farmers, who defended their communities in time of war. Like Athens, Rome was ruled by kings until about 500 BC.

Relatively democratic republican governments then replaced the monarchies in both Athens and Rome, with elections by popular assemblies. Within a few centuries, however, these classical democracies were replaced by expansive monarchies of an imperialistic cast. For centuries, much of ancient Europe was controlled by the Macedonian and Roman empires; Medieval Europe, by the so-called Holy Roman Empire and the Ottoman Turkish empire; and modern Europe by the Czarist Russian empire.

Intermittently, both monarchies and republics have become dictatorships, ruled despotically by men who were neither traditionally nor constitutionally authorized. During the sixth century BC, Athens was so ruled by Peisistratos (600–527 BC) and his sons, who were officially called tyrannoi (whence the English word "tyrant"). The most famous of Rome's dictators was, of course, Julius Caesar (100–44 BC), who was assassinated by the last Roman republicans in 44 BC. During the seventeenth century, England was ruled by Oliver Cromwell (1599–1658), who, though entitled the Lord Protector, exercised dictatorial power. In the twentieth century, Europe's two most powerful dictators were the Austrian Adolf Hitler (1889–1945), who held Germany and its conquered territories, and the Georgian Josef Stalin (1879–1943), who held the Soviet Union and most of eastern Europe from a power base in Russia.

City-states are extensions of single municipalities. Although they have sometimes controlled overseas holdings through naval power, they have rarely equaled nation-states or empires in area. In ancient Europe, the most influential city-state was undoubtedly Athens under General Pericles (c.490–429 BC). In Medieval Europe, it was probably Venice, which controlled much of the trade in the Mediterranean Sea. In modern Europe, city-states like Monaco (in France, but not part of it) and San Marino (in Italy, but not part of it) survive mostly as historical curiosities, having virtually no political weight among nations.

Associations among Nations

Associations of independent nations have not been common. During the fourth century BC, the twelve-state Achaean League of southern Greece tried valiantly but unsuccessfully to prevent the conquest of Greece by the expanding Macedonian Empire to its north. During the Middle Ages, the sea-faring cities of northern Germany created the Hanseatic League, to regulate and control trade in the North Sea and the Baltic Sea. In our century, two such associations have been created. The first of these was the League of Nations, headquartered in Geneva, which, after World War I, tried unsuccessfully to restrain Italy, Germany, and Japan from launching the military adventures that led to World War II. The second was the United Nations Organization, headquartered in New York but maintaining offices in Europe. The United Nations has many more members than the defunct League of Nations had. It also has the power to intervene militarily in interethnic conflicts in places like Cyprus and Bosnia. But whether it can exercise comparable control over the major nations remains to be seen.

Occasionally, leagues like these can themselves become nations. An example of such a development is Switzerland, which began as a confederation of Medieval Alpine cantons, or provinces, of the Holy Roman Empire in central Europe.

The type of territorial unit best known in contemporary Europe is, obviously, the nation-state. Nation-states are usually larger than city-states but smaller than empires. They are characterized by territorial continuity and by designation of a single vernacular as the official national language. During the Middle Ages, England and France were the first such nation-states to emerge from the ruins of the Roman Empire. In modern Europe, nearly every large ethnic territory from Spain to Russia has become a nation-state. In recent centuries, the political trend in most of these states has been to move from absolute monarchy through constitutional monarchy to democratically elective republican government.

Of all the states of twentieth century Europe, the most anomalous has been the Soviet Union. In some respects, it functioned as a nation, and in others as an association of nations. In terms of the wording of its constitution, it had the most democratic structure on earth. In practice, however, it was one of the most repressive of totalitarian countries. In the 1990s, it dissolved into a cluster of independent nations with complex relations to one another and to its core nation, Russia.

WARFARE

Among the positive traits technically cited as typical of civilization are urbanism, literacy, and metalworking. But civilization also has negative traits, foremost among which is war. All civilized societies have military institutions, even if, like Switzerland, some have not actually waged war for over a century.

Like the growth of population, the evolution of warfare depends largely on the development of technology. The earliest military invention to which we can assign even a rough date in European history is the war chariot. This Bronze Age innovation was a horse-drawn two-wheeled chariot that added a speed and mobility to battle that had been lacking in the clash of foot soldiers. About 1400 BC, aristocratic warriors from Mycenean Greece used chariots in their invasion and conquest of Minoan Crete, which, despite its strong navy, lacked swift and effective ground forces.

Around 1000 BC, iron replaced bronze (a copper alloy) as the metal of choice in southeastern Europe. Although iron swords and daggers are not always sharper than bronze weapons, iron is more widely available than copper and its alloys, such as brass and bronze. The result was a democratization of warfare.

Yeoman farmers who had been unable to afford bronze weaponry could now tip their spears and arrows with iron. Well-armed bodies of foot soldiers soon became much larger than in the Bronze Age.

The next Iron Age military innovation was the creation of the phalanx in Greece in the sixth century BC. A phalanx is a tight formation of foot soldiers with large shields and long spears that is virtually impenetrable to attacks by uncoordinated individual assailants. The city-state that made most effective use of the phalanx was Sparta, which defeated Athens in the Peloponnesian War of the late fifth century BC.

About the same time, the Scythians, a nomadic herding people from north of the Black Sea, began riding *on* horses rather than, as Mediterranean charioteers did, *behind* horses. Horsemen without chariots to pull can move even faster and maneuver more agilely than charioteers. By the third century BC, most of the herding peoples of the Eurasian steppes had put leather saddles and stirrups on their horses, making it easier than it had been in bare-back days for riders to hold their seats during raids and battles. This style of riding quickly spread throughout Europe, giving rise to what we know as cavalry.

In the second century BC, the conquering Romans began building stone roads, over which their legions could march easily and speedily from one military theater to another. To prevent erosion of their horses' hooves, they invented detachable horseshoes. The roads were built so well that, in Britain, they remain visible on the moors, and in rural Albania, people still travel on them. The only Roman engineering feat that remains more conspicuous than roads is the system of aqueducts, bringing water to cities and military garrisons all over southern and western Europe. Those in France remain prominent features of the landscape, and one in Segovia, Spain, is still used.

Because they included not only heavy infantry but also light infantry and cavalry, the Roman legions were more flexible and adaptable than Greek phalanxes. But, as Roman discipline began to falter in the fourth century AD, highly mobile horsemen from northern Eurasia were increasingly successful in raiding and looting the urban regions of Europe. From the Huns to the Mongols of the 13th century, steppe nomads put Christendom on the defensive. Heavily armored medieval knights could not move quickly enough to deal effectively with herding peoples who virtually lived on horseback.

Two fourteenth century inventions served to restore Europe's military advantage over the steppe peoples. The first of these was the archery long-bow, used by British yeomen to decimate French cavalry during the Hundred Years War. The second was gun powder, possibly a Chinese invention, that made it feasible to hurl projectiles from muskets and cannons. Thereafter, the only Asians who succeeded in conquering parts of Europe were those, like the Ottoman Turks of the seventeenth century, who adopted Western military technology.

The Industrial Revolution of the nineteenth century transformed European warfare by the introduction of large-scale steel manufacture. This permitted the making of long-range cannon and steel battle ships, as well as rapid transportation of troops by rail.

Twentieth century technology augmented this armament with battle tanks, machine guns, military aircraft, and long-range missiles. Since 1945, the specter of atomic warfare has haunted all continents, including Europe. The millions who died in World Wars I and II could become billions in an unrestricted thermonuclear exchange. The prevention of this prospect has become one of the primary goals of contemporary European diplomacy.

INTELLECTUAL LIFE

Europe's intellectual life unquestionably began in ancient Greece. Before the development of philosophy, Greek education consisted chiefly of memorizing passages from Homer's epic poetry and engaging in gymnastic exercise. The first Greek philosophers appeared in the fifth century BC. Known as Sophists, they were itinerant teachers, who, for a fee, would instruct their clients in the kinds of verbal skills needed to win a law case or an election. The Sophists were soon followed by the most famous ancient philosophers: Socrates (469–399 BC), who employed dialogue to arrive at insights; his pupil, Plato (c.428–c.348 BC) , who founded the first academy; and Plato's pupil, Aristotle (384–322 BC), who served as the tutor of Prince Alexander (356–323 BC) of Macedon.

In the fourth century, science began to emerge from philosophy. The earliest Greek physical scientist, in the modern sense of that phrase, was Democritus (c.460–c.370 BC), who originated atomic theory. The founder of medical ethics, as still taught, was the Greek physician Hippocrates (c.460–c.377 BC). The first mathematician was the geometrist Euclid (fl.300 BC).

During the Hellenistic Period that followed the Macedonian conquest, the Greeks developed, and the Romans continued, the liberal arts tradition, which balanced literary with scientific skills. Another intellectual link between Greece and Rome was the philosophy of Stoicism, which provided a pan-European ethic between the time of Plato and the advent of Christianity. Except in the areas of administration and engineering, the Romans were not intellectual innovators. They served rather to convey classical Greek educational standards to the rest of the continent.

During the Dark Ages, after the fall of Rome in 476, scholarship languished. What little remained was preserved in Christian monasteries and in Iberian centers of Islamic learning.

Birth of the University

The great academic achievement of the Middle Ages that followed was the creation of universities, whose professors were initially all priests. All of those universities remain major educational institutions today. The oldest universities are Bologna in Italy and Oxford in England; Paris in France and Cambridge in England; Prague in Bohemia and Heidelberg in the Palatinate (both at that time included in the Holy Roman Empire, or Medieval Germany).

In the sixteenth century, Europe underwent a Scientific Revolution, beginning with the heliocentric hypothesis of Polish astronomer Nicolaus Copernicus, who showed that the earth orbited the sun rather than the reverse. This revolution culminated in the work of Sir Isaac Newton, head of England's Royal Society, who formulated the Law of Gravity.

In the seventeenth century, the English philosopher John Locke (1632–1704) established the Social Contract theory, which served as the basis of liberal parliamentarianism in Britain, France, and America. In the eighteenth century, the English economist Adam Smith (1723–90) created the theoretical foundation of free-market capitalism. In the nineteenth century, for the first time, science became part of the standard curriculum of colleges and universities. And, in Germany, the Kindergarten movement led most European and other Western nations to adopt pre-school training as a means of preparing very young children for formal schooling.

Late in the nineteenth century, the English naturalist Charles Darwin (1809–82) made evolution part of the intellectual equipment of most scientifically oriented people. Just as Copernicus had removed our planet from the center of the astronomic stage, Darwin removed our species from the center of the biological stage. Both scholars made it harder for the thinking public to continue regarding terrestrial humanity as God's favorites or as lords of creation.

In the twentieth century, ancient Greek atomic theory bore fruit in atomic technology. This technology took two forms—one peaceful and the other military. The peaceful form was the use, in many parts of Europe, of atomic power as a means of generating electricity for domestic and industrial use. The military form was the construction of missile-borne thermonuclear weapons in England, France, Russia, and Ukraine.

The major institutional innovation of the twentieth century is probably the establishment of "think tanks," such as the Max Planck Institute for scientific research in Germany. Think tanks are designed to be on the cutting edge of intellectual exploration in every discipline, but especially those with medical, agricultural, and other practical applications.

The major technological innovation of the century is probably the computerization of communication, research, record-keeping, and storage of information, including in libraries. The chief purpose of computer use is to free human beings from such tedious tasks as computation and information retrieval and to permit them to devote their time and energy to more creative pursuits.

RELIGIOUS FAITHS AND PRACTICES

Religion is not easy to define. In its popular form, it cannot readily be distinguished from magic. In its theological form, on the other hand, it scarcely differs from philosophy.

The earliest European religious practices for which we have tangible evidence were the ritual burials and skull-shrine constructions of Neanderthal Man from the Middle Paleolithic Period. In the Upper Paleolithic Period that followed, Cro-Magnon Man painted his caves with animal shapes, which many archeologists interpret as expressions of hunting magic. During the subsequent Neolithic Period, preliterate farmers erected megaliths—huge stone arrangements that seem to have been correlated with the changing movements of stars or planets. Insofar as these celestial objects were regarded as divine beings, megalithic structures may have constituted religious architecture.

In historic times, the Greeks and Romans wrote explicitly about their pantheons of polytheistic deities, many of whom—such as Jupiter, king of Rome's gods—were associated with planets. Others—such as Aphrodite, the Greek goddess of love—were associated with human interests and activities. (From her name, we derive the word aphrodisiac, meaning something eaten or drunk to make one amorous.) Although all Europeans are now monotheistic, evidence of ancient polytheism is found in calendric names: Thursday was named for the old Germanic god of thunder, and the month of January was named for Janus, the Roman god of passages. Pagan temples, such as the Parthenon in Athens or the Pantheon in Rome, also survive to remind Europeans of their early religious beliefs.

When the power of the Roman Empire began to wane in the late second century AD, the authority of traditional Roman polytheism also waned. For spiritual consolation, Romans and their subject peoples turned increasingly to African and Asian creeds and liturgies. Among these were the worship of Isis, the Cult of the Unconquered Sun; Mithraism and Manicheisin; and Judaism and Christianity. It was not until the fourth century that Christianity emerged as the official religion of the Roman Empire.

During the Dark Ages and the Middle Ages, Christianity spread northward and westward. By the time of the Renaissance, all of Europe was predominantly Christian in affiliation. Like most successful ideological movements, however, Christianity experienced sectarian divisions. In the eleventh century, Catholic Christianity, centered in Rome, separated from Orthodox Christianity, centered in Constantinople (previously called Byzantium and now called Istanbul). Roman Catholics believed that Rome should be the acknowledged ecclesiastical capital of all Christendom, whereas Orthodox Christians held to the older doctrine that regional patriarchates in such places as Greece, Serbia, Bulgaria, and Russia should be granted ecclesiastical self-rule.

During the sixteenth century, Martin Luther in Germany and John Calvin in Switzerland initiated the Protestant Reformation, separating most of northwestern Europe from the Roman Communion. Protestants went even further than the Orthodox in asserting local ecclesiastical autonomy. The result was that, instead of a single Protestant Christian church, Protestantism produced a cluster of independent churches—Lutheran, Presbyterian, Baptist, and others.

For centuries in most parts of rural Europe there has existed a belief system distinct from (though not antagonistic to) the biblical faiths of Judaism and Christianity. This system, which is strongest in Ireland, is sometimes referred to as "the Fairy Faith." Its adherents believe in a host of spiritual beings, ranging from playful elves to ghosts of the dead but not equatable with scriptural angels and demons. Jewish and Christian authorities usually respond to this faith by ignoring it. When this proves impossible, they resort, with debatable success, to exorcising those spirits that seem to be possessing members of religious congregations.

Two other systems of thought that appear to have religious aspects are astrology and alchemy. Like the Fairy Faith, they probably antedate Christianity and stem from the ancient Near East. Astrology is the belief that the movements and conjunctions of heavenly bodies, when properly interpreted, foretell future developments in human affairs, both individual and collective. Alchemy is the belief that physical substances can be transmuted (without the use of "atom-smashers") and, in particular, that lead can be transformed into gold. Most modern opinion leaders—religious as well as scientific—now dismiss these beliefs as superstitions. But it is worth noting that even such a quintessentially authoritative scientist as Sir Isaac Newton not only took these systems seriously, but wrote extensively about them, not as a critic but as a contributor.

A nineteenth century system of thought that seems closer to the Fairy Faith than to biblical tradition is Spiritualism. Beginning in the United States, it quickly spread to England and then to mainland Europe. Spiritualism is the belief that, through mediumistic seances, one can contact the spirits of the dead and thereby alleviate the grief and loneliness of the bereaved.

In the twentieth century, Humanism has come to replace Judaism and Christianity among many rationalistically minded heirs of the biblical tradition. Although some Humanists consider themselves members of a new religious community while others do not, all agree in placing secular ethics before supernatural beliefs. Most Humanists regard themselves as advocates of the Greco-Roman tradition of "sweet reasonableness" in dealing with the most conflict-ridden issues in human life.

Some European rationalists eschew all of the aforegoing labels, on the grounds that religiosity is inevitably irrational. They point to religious differences as the chief cause of wars and atrocities in Northern Ireland, Bosnia, and the countries of the Caucasus. Many religious thinkers counter that religious faith, which usually counsels love and social harmony, cannot engender violent conflict. Instead, they say, unscrupulous political leaders use religious differences as a smoke screen to cover their personal or partisan lust for power over rival ethnic groups.

THE ARTS

Like religion, art overlaps extensively with other spheres of activity. In artifact design, it merges with craft; in architecture, with engineering; and in medicine, with science.

Among the visual arts, painting is preeminent. Although most ancient European painting has been lost, we still have murals from the ancient Aegean islands and vase paintings from mainland Greece. Many art historians hold that the pinnacle of European painting was reached in Renaissance Italy, the most striking example of which may be Michelangelo's religious works in the Vatican's Sistine Chapel in Rome. Other connoisseurs prefer the more secular Baroque portraits by Rembrandt in Amsterdam.

Music, when unrecorded (as most has been), is the most evanescent of the arts. Although Pythagoras (sixth century BC) and other ancient Greek scholars developed sophisticated mathematical descriptions of musical intervals, neither the Greeks nor the Romans have left us a written musical notation system adequate for the contemporary performance of ancient musical compositions. Written notation became adequate only in the Middle Ages. The Renaissance developed contrapuntal polyphony, combining diverse melodic lines. The following Baroque Period witnessed the expanded use of keyboard instruments—organ, harpsichord, and, finally, piano. Symphony orchestras reached maturity in the subsequent Rococo style. For many musicologists, the culmination of Western musical art was Classical, or pre-Romantic, composition, exemplified by the early nineteenth century concertos and symphonies of Ludwig van Beethoven (1770–1827) in Germany.

Verbal art can be either oral or written. When oral, it is often called oratory. Perhaps the most famous orator in European history was Demosthenes (d.413 BC) of Athens, celebrated for his Philippics—a series of speeches designed to arouse Greek opposition to the imperialistic ambitions of King Philip of Macedon, father of Alexander the Great.

When written, verbal art is known as literature. It takes at least three distinct forms—historiography, poetry, and fiction. Historiography is the recording of historical events. The writer generally regarded as having been Europe's first historian is Herodotus of Athens (c.485–425 BC), whose History was not only a chronological listing of past events, but also a cultural survey of non-Greek peoples, and a travel guide to foreign countries.

Most poetry takes the form of verse, involving regular sound repetition, such as meter or rhyme. One of the greatest European poems ever written is The Divine Comedy by Dante Alighieri (1265–1321) of Florence, Italy. Completed in 1314, it is a long religious narrative describing heaven, hell, and purgatory. In Italy, it defined Tuscan as the standard form of literary Italian. Outside Italy, it provided an authoritative picture of the soul's afterlife for most of Christendom.

Fiction is a vaguer literary form. Its most popular subform is undoubtedly the novel, which may be described as a prose epic. Many literary critics regard War and Peace by Count Leo Tolstoy (1828–1910) as the greatest European novel ever written. Published in 1869, it describes Napoleon's unsuccessful invasion of Russia in the early nineteenth century.

The only major kinesthetic art, involving expressive body-movement, is dance, which may be the world's oldest and most universal art. The most distinctively European dance form is ballet, which originated in fifteenth century Italy as dance theatre. Many dance historians believe that ballet reached its peak in St. Petersburg, Russia, under the tutelage of impresario Sergei Diaghilev in the early twentieth century.

Some arts are blends of sensory types. Sculpture, for example, blends visual with tactile art. Sculpture is widely regarded as having reached an early culmination during the Golden Age of Greece in the fifth century BC. By general consensus, the greatest ancient sculptor was Phidias of Athens, who created the 20-meter (60-foot) statue of Zeus at Olympia—considered at the time to be one of the Seven Wonders of the World. (The Italian sculptors of the European Renaissance emulated their Greek predecessors. Whether the Italians equaled or exceeded the Greeks cannot be determined, since the Greek statuary masterpieces survive only in small copies.)

Architecture blends visual art with engineering technology. As in the case of sculpture, critics disagree about the relative artistic merits of Classical Greco-Roman temples and Christian European cathedrals. And, even among those who favor cathedrals, admiration is almost equally divided between Gothic, Renaissance, and Baroque styles. Greco-Roman temples, however, strongly resembled those of Pharaonic Egypt and the ancient Near East. In terms, therefore, of a distinctively European (or non-Afro-Asian) style, the palm should probably be awarded to Gothic cathedrals, in view of the fact that the Gothic style was least derivative from Greco-Roman—and hence from non-European—models. The greatest of medieval gothic cathedrals were probably those of Amiens, Chartres, and Reims from thirteenth century France, all of which survive to this day.

Drama blends visual with both auditory and literary art. Literary historians have consistently rated verse drama above prose drama. Poetic drama throve in ancient Greece as well as in seventeenth century England, Spain, and France. Most critics now consider William Shakespeare the greatest of European dramatists and Hamlet the greatest of his tragedies. More traditionally minded classicists, however, continue to maintain the view that no subsequent writer has excelled the Athenian tragedian Sophocles (c.496–405 BC), and that no play has equaled his Oedipus trilogy.

Since the early nineteenth century, European art has become increasingly experimental and decreasingly inclined to emulate older models. Pessimists view this experimentalism as a sign of stylistic decay, while optimists view it as a promise of renewed creativity to come. But few observers deny that European art is in a state of ferment, the esthetic outcome of which remains to be seen.

FOLKLORE

Folklore is the tradition of the less sophisticated members of society. Until recently, most European folklore came from its peasant farmers. The folklore of Europe is distinct from that of other continents in several respects. Europe has a more homogeneous culture than do Asia and Africa. Unlike other continents, Europe has no professional storytellers to transmit its folklore orally from generation to generation. Because most continents still have preliterate peoples, they maintain a traditional ban on reciting inherited narratives during certain hours of the day or seasons of the year. In Europe, however, traditional tales may be told at any time when people have leisure to listen.

The best-known form of folklore is folk literature. Folk literature takes three major forms: myth, legend, and folktale. Myth deals mainly with supernatural beings, such as the pagan deities of early Europe. Pre-Christian stories about the amorous adventures of the Greek god Zeus are representative myths. Legend deals mainly with human beings for whom no firm historical records exist. Stories about Britain's King Arthur and the knights of his Round Table are legendary. Folktale typically concerns animals with the ability to talk and engage in behavior that can be morally evaluated. Fables such as that of *The Hare and the Tortoise* exemplify folktales.

In addition to these types of narratives, which are found world-wide, Europe has one that is more distinctive. This narrative is the fairy-tale, which combines natural with supernatural beings, humans with animals, and commoners with royalty. Typical of this type are the stories of Cinderella or Jack and the Beanstalk, in which humble youngsters attain regal status or fabulous wealth.

Not all folklore, however, is purely verbal in nature. Some is artistic, involving music, drama, or handicrafts. Examples are European ballad-singing, Maypole dancing, and the cottage manufacture of dolls, toys, or embroidered lace. Some celebrations, such as Christmas miracle-plays or pre-Lenten carnivals, merge several different folkloristic performances.

Some folklorists fear that folk traditions will soon disappear in Europe. Others believe that old rural traditions will be progressively transformed into stories and practices that represent the increasingly urban and mechanized life-style of modern Europe.

SPORTS

Explicit recognition of public athletic competition began with the Olympic Games of Greece, traditionally dated to the eighth century BC. The core event of the games was the pentathlon, which consisted of foot-racing, broad-jumping, throwing the discus and the javelin, and wrestling. Boxing and horse-racing were added to these events before the ancient games ended in Roman times. The Greeks themselves honored Olympic victors by writing odes and carving statues in their honor.

The imperial Romans had a more brutal taste in competitive sport. They forced slaves and war-captives to engage in physical combat with animals or with one another. The combatants, called gladiators, rarely survived many mortal contests in public arenas like the Colosseum. Medieval sport was more humane only in the sense that people were no longer killed for general entertainment. But bears were publicly baited—that is, prodded and stabbed till they died. This mode of amusement survives in the bull-rings of Spain and Portugal.

Modern Europe has a preference for ball-games—football (known as soccer in America), basketball, and volleyball as well as tennis and golf. But competitive fencing, bicycling, swimming, and rowing are also popular. So too are gymnastic events of various kinds.

Some games remain peculiar to a particular country. Examples are British cricket (similar to American baseball) and rugby (similar to American football).

In 1896 the Olympic Games were revived—first in Greece, later throughout Europe, and eventually on other continents. To the ancient events, archery, sailing, and track-and-field competitions were added. In 1924, Winter Olympics were inaugurated in the French Alps. These new events included skating, skiing, tobogganing, and ice-hockey.

Not all sports, of course, are competitive in nature. European children have long enjoyed swings and hobby-horses as well as playing pick-a-back. Today, increasingly affluent European adults enjoy beach vacations and tours of foreign countries. Those with limited budgets can still back-pack to less populous areas and find inexpensive hostels in which to stay.

ABKHAZIANS

LOCATION: Georgia (de jure within Georgia, de facto independent from Georgia)
POPULATION: Unknown but under 100,000 (2002)
LANGUAGE: Abkhazian
RELIGION: Islam; Christianity; pagan beliefs

¹ INTRODUCTION

Until the early 1990s, the Abkhazians were best known for their unusually long and active lives and a Black Sea coastal resort. In August 1992, soon after the dissolution of the Soviet Union, the Abkhazians made newspaper headlines as participants in a tragic armed conflict that erupted between them and the Georgians, a neighboring ethnic group (see separate entry). The dispute was over Abkhazia's post-Soviet status. The conflict led to the deaths of thousands of citizens, and it generated tens of thousands of refugees. Negotiations persisted in many formats over the years but never resulted in a peace treaty. In August 2008, war broke out again and the remaining Georgians in Kodori Gorge, Abkhazia, were expelled. After the war, which on the Abkhazian side was largely directed by the Russian army, Russia recognized the independence of Abkhazia. Only Nicaragua followed Russia's example. The international community still considers Abkhazia part of Georgia.

Abkhazians fear their extinction as a people, which has consolidated them as a group and shaped their collective cultural identity. In the 2003 census, which is disputed by the Georgians, there were fewer than 100,000 Abkhazians. The group's shared sense of vulnerability heavily influences their attitudes and behavior in interpersonal relations with each other and with non-Abkhazians, as well as their transmission of cultural values from generation to generation.

The Abkhazians are Caucasians. They typically have narrow faces, fair skin, and dark hair and eyes. Redheads are rare, and blondes even rarer. Gray hair appears quite late, and baldness is uncommon. They tend to be slender and have erect posture. Linguistically, culturally, and genetically, Abkhazians are related to the Abazins (or Abaza), Adyghey, Kabardians, and Circassians. These groups have always been neighbors of the Abkhazians in the Caucasus, but in the post-Soviet era have been separated from the Abkhazians because they live within the borders of Russia, in the North Caucasus. All of these peoples share many cultural traits, and in their large communities outside the former Soviet Union (in Turkey, the Middle East, Europe, and the United States for example), they have a fairly clear collective identity and are commonly known as Circassians.

² LOCATION AND HOMELAND

Abkhazia covers 8,500 sq km (3,300 sq mi) between the eastern shores of the Black Sea and the crestline of the main Caucasus range and from the rivers Psou (in the north) and Inguri (in the south). To the north, Abkhazia is bordered by Russia and to the south by the Georgian provinces of Svanetia and Mingrelia. Approximately 74% of the territory is mountains or mountain approaches. The coastal valleys are humid and subtropical. At higher altitudes the weather ranges from moderately cold to areas with temperatures so low that the snow never melts.

The relatively small distance between the coast and mountains gives Abkhazia a strikingly contrasting landscape.

Abkhazia has prime seacoast resorts that were always crowded with vacationers from all over the Soviet Union. Major cash crops are tea, tobacco, and citrus fruit. The two largest cities are Sukhumi, the capital, with a pre-1992 population of 100,000, but which now looks totally empty, and Tkvarcheli, an industrial center known for its coal. There are three urban resorts (Gagra, Gudauta, and Ochamchira), two rural spas (Pitsunda and Novy Afon), and 575 villages.

Abkhazians describe their country as harsh but beautiful. A legend says that when God was distributing land to all the peoples of the earth, the Abkhazians were entertaining guests. Because it would have been impolite for hosts to leave before their guests, the Abkhazians arrived late, and all that God had left were some stones. Out of these he created a land that was hard to cultivate but paradise-like in its beauty.

³ LANGUAGE

The Abkhazian language belongs to the northwest Caucasian family spoken by only the Abazins, Adyghey, Kabardians, and Circassians. There are very few words borrowed from other languages. Abkhazian is quite difficult to learn, although the large variety of consonants and vowels enables Abkhazians to pronounce foreign languages fairly precisely. The modified Russian Cyrillic alphabet currently in use does not fully represent the sounds of Abkhazian, which include a wavering trill, whistling noises, and a prolonged buzz. Much of the vocabulary preserves concrete images in the form of metaphor, for example, "helping leg" for staff and "mother's blood" for mother's brother. The language is rich in proverbs that guide everyday behavior and values.

The ability to make eloquent speeches is a highly prized and cultivated skill. It is the primary requirement for elders and community mediators, people held in the highest esteem in Abkhazian society. Ordinary people are also expected to make long and eloquent speeches and toasts at the family gatherings and public events that are a common feature of daily life. Many Abkhazians speak Russian as their first language.

Common girls' first names are *Amra*, *Asida*, *Gunda*, *Esma*, and *Naala*. Common boys' first names are *Adgur*, *Akhra*, *Daur*, *Alkhas*, and *Gudisa*. Prominent surnames are *Achba*, *Agrba*, *Avidzba*, *Kutsnia* (or *Kvitsinia*), and *Adleiba*, *Shamba*.

⁴ FOLKLORE

The oldest folk tales are about the Atzan midgets and the giant Narts. The Atzans were so small that they could walk on the stems of leaves, but they also displayed great physical power and courage. The downfall of the Atzans came when they rejected the existence of any authority, including God. They defiled their water sources and committed other sacrileges that compelled God to destroy them by fire. The Nart epics are shared by peoples throughout the North Caucasus. The Narts were warriors who fought, hunted, feasted, and engaged in martial games. They were the hundred giant sons of the same mother, Sataney-Guasha, who was known for her great beauty, perennial youth, and wisdom. Her husband became old and feeble and was not held in esteem. The brothers had one sister, named Gunda, whose beauty and gentleness drove her sisters-in-law to plot to kill her, and for this they were punished. The Nart tales depict Sataney-Guasha, the mother-in-law, as the

RUSSIA

Armavir

Nevinnomyssk

CAUCASUS MTS.

Gagra

ABKHAZIA
Gudauta

Sokhumi

Tkvarcheli

Ochamchira

Jvari

Mt. Shkhara
16,627 ft.
5068 m.

Enguri

Zugdidi

Rioni

Black
Sea

Senaki

Chiat'ura

Poti

K'ut'aisi

Samtredia

Zestafoni

Kobuleti

Ozurgeti

Borzhomi

Batumi

AJARIA

Akhaltsikhe

LESSER CAUCASUS MTS.

TURKEY

ABKHAZIANS

0   50   100 Miles

0   50   100 Kilometers

victim of her scheming daughters-in-law, in contrast to European tales, where mothers-in-law are the most likely villains.

5 RELIGION

Christianity was brought to Abkhazia from Byzantium in the 6th century, and the Sunni sect of Islam was introduced by the Turks in the 15th and 16th centuries. Neither of these religions, however, ever completely eroded pagan beliefs, which still remain very strong. Families may mark both Islamic and Christian holidays and also conduct pagan rituals. According to the ancient Abkhazian religion, Afy rules the thunder and the weather; Shasta is the protector spirit who rules blacksmiths and the arts; Azhvepshaa is the spirit of the forest, wild animals, and hunting; and Aitar is the protector of domestic animals. The supreme god is Antzva, the plural form of the word for mother. There are several sacred sites in Abkhazia where individuals and families pray to the spirits of the Abkhazian pantheon.

6 MAJOR HOLIDAYS

The most important secular holidays are the New Year (December 31 and January 1) and the Old New Year (January 13 and 14) according to the Julian Calendar (also known as the Old Style Calendar), which was followed until Soviet government was established. This is a time for family gatherings. Another popular holiday, celebrated after the fall harvest, is called the *lykhnashta* (Lykhny Meadow). This brings people from all over Abkhazia to the village of Lykhny, where spectators watch

breathtaking horse races and equestrian games and explore outdoor exhibits that boast produce and crafts from dozens of Abkhazian villages. Since 1993, September 30 has been celebrated as Liberation Day, which marks the routing of Georgian armed forces from Abkhazia. There is a parade of Abkhazian military forces and song and dance festivals.

7 RITES OF PASSAGE

It appears as though rites of passage were never part of Abkhazian culture. Until Soviet government was established in the 1920s, Abkhazians did not celebrate their birthdays or keep track of chronological ages. There are terms in the language that denote various stages of life. These stages are not defined by age; however, they refer to standards of behavior that fit a certain period in one's life.

8 INTERPERSONAL RELATIONS

All relationships are guided by an ancient code of honor known in the Abkhazian language as *apsuara*. This code is not merely a set of superficial manners, but rather a code of behavior dictated by a profound concept called Abkhazian *alamys*, or "Abkhazian behavior according to conscience." Such etiquette is typical of peoples who, like the Abkhazians, have survived through the millennia despite constant threats from formidable neighbors. In such cultures a high value is placed on honor befitting a true warrior. Thus, Abkhazian etiquette focuses on showing and expecting respect. This is reflected in the diverse forms of salutations, which vary considerably according to the age, social status, and gender of the parties. The most common greeting is "Good health to you." Other salutations are "Good day," "Glad to see you," and "Welcome." An older person must be the first to greet a younger one, and a person on horseback must be first to greet someone on foot. (It is necessary to raise oneself on one's stirrups, just as it is rude to stay sitting in a chair while saying hello.) Gestures are also important to the Abkhazians. When men meet, they make a hand-fist salute by raising the right hand. Handshakes, although not obligatory, are customary among younger people. It is also necessary to ask about the person's health, affairs, and relatives. Relatives greet each other with a gentle hug and a kiss on the left shoulder above the heart. It is customary to kiss children on the top of the head while placing a hand gently on the back of the neck. A common gesture of greeting for an elderly woman is to gently make a circle with her hand, which is intended as a blessing of safekeeping. Specific salutations are used depending on a person's trade and pursuits. To a blacksmith, one might say, "May your work bless you." To a hunter, the greeting would be, "May your game, good and killed, be waiting for you." The words of welcome spoken to a traveler back from a long journey translate as "Happy homecoming to you always." These words are also addressed to a soldier back from war.

The traditions of generous hospitality are sacred law and binding on every person. All guests must be given a heartfelt welcome, even if they are enemies, and never asked why they have come or for how long. Hosts offer guests their best food, which they reserve for just such occasions, and guests are provided the best sleeping accommodations. Abkhazians believe that guests bring wealth and good fortune, and they go to great lengths to please their company. A common saying is: "A guest brings seven pieces of good luck." Abkhazians maintain a space of at least a foot and a half between one another, and it is inappropriate to touch in most circumstances other than salutations. Shaking one's finger or similar gestures of displeasure and speaking in a loud voice are considered very rude behavior.

⁹ LIVING CONDITIONS

The majority of Abkhazians still live in rural areas in spacious stone or brick single-family homes with several bedrooms, a living room, a dining room, and a kitchen. The homestead is usually shared by three and four generations. Because land is plentiful, additional homes may be built on the same homestead to provide privacy for members of extended families. Traditionally, an Abkhazian kitchen was a separate structure. Now, however, kitchens are usually in the main house, and the old-fashioned kitchen has been replaced by a larger building where dozens of guests can be served at long tables. Abkhazian households are kept neat and clean, and there is usually ample space in the yard for lawns and for growing fruits and vegetables.

Increasingly, Abkhazians have settled in urban areas, where they live in the cramped, high-rise apartments typical of all the former Soviet republics. Apartments range from studios to three bedrooms and often accommodate extended families. In such housing it is difficult to maintain the traditional norms of Abkhazian etiquette, because the avoidance customs between certain family members require more space. The dilapidated water and sewage system inherited from the Soviet government causes the greatest inconvenience and considerable sanitation problems in urban areas. In city apartments, running water is available only a few hours a day, whereas homesteads in the countryside can provide their own water. Most Abkhazian city dwellers have close relatives still living in the countryside where they visit regularly, so they are not completely separated from their rural heritage and traditions.

¹⁰ FAMILY LIFE

The average number of children per family is two or three; more than five is rare. Perhaps small family size was an adaptation to conditions of frequent warfare, which made it important to be able to travel quickly and easily. Children are desired, and boys are important in the patrilineal system, but having children does not validate masculinity or femininity. An Abkhazian baby does not belong to its parents but to the family as a whole—to the aunts, grandmothers, grandfathers, brothers, and sisters. Family life, especially in rural areas, is distinguished by taboos that dictate everyday behavior in the home. For instance, couples do not show affection in public or in front of relatives, including their own children. No matter how old a man is, he must not smoke or shave in his father's presence. A daughter-in-law may not speak in her father-in-law's presence unless he has given her explicit permission, which may take many years and the event is marked by a feast. Although these customs are dying out, many are still practiced and their legacy clearly influences contemporary family relations.

In the public domain, women enjoy fairly equal opportunities with men. In the home, their duties are distinctly different. Men and male children do not cook or clean. Men slaughter animals and usually cook meat for feasts, however, it is common for boys to serve guests. Children and women do not usually join guests at the table, but remain standing throughout a feast, never conversing with the guests, and remaining ever vigilant that wine glasses and plates are kept full. Wedding ceremonies can involve hundreds of guests who are accommodated at long tables outside the house. The groom and his senior relatives and friends come to the bride's father's house to escort her to the wedding. There they have a feast with drinking and speech making that lasts a few hours. The bride then rides on horseback or travels by car to the groom's household, accompanied only by her bridesmaids and a male friend or relative of her own age to see to it that her rights are protected. No one from her family attends the wedding at the groom's home, where she and the groom remain concealed from all the guests in separate quarters throughout the big feast. When guests visit the bride, she must not smile or reveal any joy over her wedding. The groom may appear briefly, but he also must not exhibit any joy over the occasion. To do so would be considered immodest, especially with regard to the elders. To demonstrate how modest, self-disciplined, and traditional they are, a couple may wait a day or even longer before spending their first night together. For a long time after the wedding, the couple must go to bed later than everyone else in the household and wake up earlier so that no one sees them go into or emerge from their bedroom. Any manifestation of affection or sexual desire in the presence of others is scorned. The prevalent attitude toward sex is that it is good and pleasurable when it is strictly private.

¹¹ CLOTHING

Abkhazians wear predominantly Western clothing, but women maintain a few traditional restrictions in keeping with the high value placed on what they consider to be modest behavior and dress. For instance, women never wear slacks, shorts, or blouses with low necklines or straps. It is acceptable to wear swimming suits on the beach, but minimal body exposure is the norm everywhere else. Both men and women wear black clothing after the death of a close relative. Men wear black for a month or so, but women wear a black dress, scarf, stockings, and shoes for a year or even longer. Widows may remain in black the rest of their lives. The number of women in black is so great, especially since the 1992–93 war, that black attire may appear to a visitor to be the national costume. On holidays and during family feasts, the male elders wear the traditional *cherkesska*, a belted black garment with long sleeves, which falls to mid-calf, and has a row of cartridge pouches on the chest. This is worn over a plain long-sleeved shirt. The *cherkesska* is common to all Caucasian peoples.

The traditional headdress for men is a *bashlick*, made of soft brown or black cloth with two long ends hanging from either side of the head to well below the shoulders. In the cold, the cloth can be wrapped around the face, and in the summer the end pieces are tied together at the back of the head. Men also wear a long felt cape called a *burka* to protect them from heat and cold. When a shepherd or hunter sleeps in the open fields, he wraps himself in his *burka*. Pants are tucked into calfskin or kid boots that are so tight they must be soaked in water and grease before being worn the first time. Traditionally, women wore white pantaloons gathered at the ankles and a high-collared, long-sleeved coat of thick material, which flared out as it descended from the waist. From an early age until her wedding night, a girl wore a narrow corset made of soft animal skin or strong linen to shape a narrow waist, flatten the breasts, and

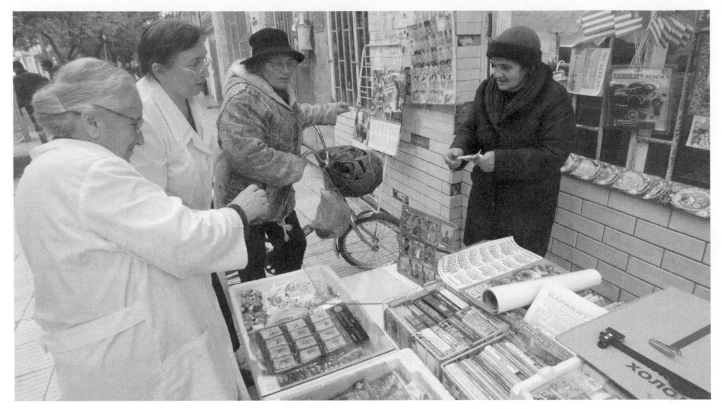

A street vendor selling small articles in the Abkhazian capital of Sokhumi. (Natalia Kolesnikova/AFP/Getty Images)

maintain an erect posture. Children and teenagers tend to wear stylish clothing much like their peers in any Western country.

12 FOOD

The everyday diet of all Abkhazians consists of homegrown and home-processed foods, including yogurt and cheese, abundant raw fruits and vegetables, moderate meat consumption, and even less fish. This diet is low in fat and calories. Instead of bread, they eat a bland cornmeal mush, and dip it and other foods into spicy sauces made with Abkhazian salt *(ajika)*, which is a tasty mixture of ground red peppers, up to a dozen herbs, and salt. Eating habits are formed in early childhood and persist consistently throughout a lifetime. The diet contains elements thought to be associated with low risk of heart disease and cancer. Meals are three times a day at regular times, with the biggest meal in the evening.

13 EDUCATION

Children begin school at the age of six and graduate at seventeen. All grades are taught in the same school facility, which is called a secondary school. Some schools are named after historical or literary figures, but most are distinguished only by a number. There are very few elective courses. Schooling in the cities continues to a higher level than in rural areas. Parents regularly supervise and help with homework throughout secondary school. Higher education is valued highly, so parents and teachers strongly encourage students to go on with their schooling. Abkhazia has one university and several colleges.

14 CULTURAL HERITAGE

Song, music, and dance are important to Abkhazian culture. There are wedding songs, ritual songs, cult songs, lullabies, healing songs, and work songs. There are special songs for the gathering of the lineage, for the ill, and songs celebrating the exploits of heroes. All of the arts are represented in Abkhazia. There are drama and dance companies, art museums, music schools, and theaters for the performing arts. Poetry and literature are also held in high regard.

15 WORK

Children learn how to work around the house and on the farm before they go to school, but it is like play for them. They are not required to do anything beyond their abilities. Throughout life, work is treated as an integral part of everyday living. An Abkhazian saying goes "Without rest, a man cannot work; without work, the rest is not beneficial." People continue working as long as they can.

16 SPORTS

The favorite spectator sports are soccer and equestrian contests. Every school has a soccer team. Most boys in rural areas learn how to ride horses and play fast-moving ball games on horseback. Traditionally, women also learned to ride, but this is no longer the case. Abkhazia has had two Olympic champions, one in javelin throwing and one in equestrian sports.

17 ENTERTAINMENT AND RECREATION

Most entertainment is informal, in small gatherings of family and friends at each other's homes. Whole evenings are spent in discussions and eating around a big table filled with a variety of tasty dishes, wine, vodka, and cognac. Both young and old participate. Dancing and singing are common at larger gatherings such as weddings, which are quite frequent in the fall. Throughout the year, going to the theater is also a common form of entertainment. People of all ages chat at length over coffee and snacks at outdoor cafes. Men play board games in courtyards until late at night

18 FOLK ART, CRAFTS, AND HOBBIES

Among the oldest crafts of the Abkhazians are basket weaving, pottery, woodworking, and metalworking. The designs are simple and utilitarian because most of the craft items were intended for use in the home. Contemporary craftsmen and artists produce a wide range of sophisticated works based on traditional motifs.

19 SOCIAL PROBLEMS

The economy has been practically at a standstill since the breakup of the Soviet Union and the armed conflict of 1992–93. This has created unemployment, theft, and drug use, which are the biggest social problems. Some people without jobs and money rob their neighbors, and some who have endured the trauma of war, turn to drugs to forget their pain. The legal system is unable to combat the problems of crime and drugs because the government has problems of a major proportion in rebuilding the country. In some areas of the capital city of Sukhumi there are blocks where two of every three homes and buildings are no more than crumbling walls, and hotels and public buildings have been demolished by the fighting. Nongovernmental organizations have emerged from the grassroots to deal with these problems but do not have significant resources. They focus on healing post-traumatic stress syndrome, promoting conflict resolution training, and the principles of civil society.

20 GENDER ISSUES

Women in Abkhazia significantly outnumber the men. The Soviet legacy has raised expectations of equality among Abkhazian women, but in reality they cannot compete equally for jobs with men and do most of the housework and child rearing. Gender roles in the home are quite rigid. A man would never be seen washing dishes, for example, although he may do them privately. Women are active in the NGO community but are poorly represented in the government and parliament. Many are widowed and families headed by females are among the poorest in the region.

21 BIBLIOGRAPHY

Benet, Sula. *Abkhasians: The Long-Living People of the Caucasus.* New York: Holt, Rinehart and Winston, 1974.

Garb, Paula. *Where the Old Are Young: Long Life in the Soviet Caucasus.* Palo Alto, CA: Ramparts Publishers, 1987.

Hewitt, George. *The Abkhazians: A Handbook (Peoples of the Caucasus Handbooks),* Basingstoke, UK: Palgrave Macmillan, 1999.

—revised by S. Jones

ADJARIANS

ALTERNATE NAMES: Adzharians; Ajarians, Acharans
LOCATION: Adjaria (within Georgia)
POPULATION: 376,016 (2002)
LANGUAGE: Gurian dialect in mountains, standard Georgian in cities
RELIGION: Mixed Sunni Muslim and Orthodox Christian

1 INTRODUCTION

The Adjarians (also called Adzharians or Acharans) are seldom mentioned outside of their native land. Adjarians are like Georgians in almost every respect except that a proportion of them are Muslim. By itself this situation does not cause tension and conflict, but it is important to realize that violent conflicts between communities (such as those in Bosnia-Herzegovina, or Northern Ireland) are rarely religious but almost always political.

In 1989–90, Georgia was among the first republics of the former Soviet Union where the local communist government effectively surrendered its power under the pressure of popular discontent. The political vacuum that followed was filled by a motley group that included self-serving opposition intellectuals, cunning black market entrepreneurs, and even self-professed honorable bandits. These new leaders had little in common except personal ambition and a strong belief in the cultural supremacy of the Georgian nation. They possessed no economic or state-building program at all. Instead, the new anti-communist leaders adopted nationalistic rhetoric and policies in an effort to gain popular support from common Georgians and to silence potential opponents. The aggressive nationalism of the new Georgian rulers soon led to rebellions in the peripheral parts of Georgia that had sizable non-Georgian ethnic minorities.

Adjaria was an autonomous province of Georgia where the sudden triumph of the new Georgian nationalists was met with grave suspicion. Although most Adjarians considered themselves Georgians, they also knew that many Georgians considered Adjarians "Turks" or at least second-class "Turkicized" Georgians because of their difference in religion. Georgians have been Christian since Byzantine times, at least since the 5th century. The ancestors of Adjarians were once Christian too, but in the 17th century the Turkish Ottoman Empire conquered Adjaria and many people converted to Islam, the religion of the new Turkish authorities. Adjaria remained under Turkish rule until 1878, when it was wrestled from the Turks by the Russian Empire. By that time Adjarians had been Muslim for some 10 to 15 generations and viewed themselves as a separate ethnic group with its own traditions derived from Islam.

After the Russian revolution of 1917, Lenin and the Bolsheviks created the Soviet Union, and Georgia became one of its 15 constituent union republics. In recognition of its religious and cultural uniqueness, Adjaria was granted limited autonomy within the Soviet republic of Georgia. Many Georgians who saw themselves as national patriots scoffed at Adjarian autonomy as a "foreign creation," arguing that Adjarians were Georgians just like everyone else. The Adjarians' Islamic heritage was deemed an unfortunate accident of history that had to

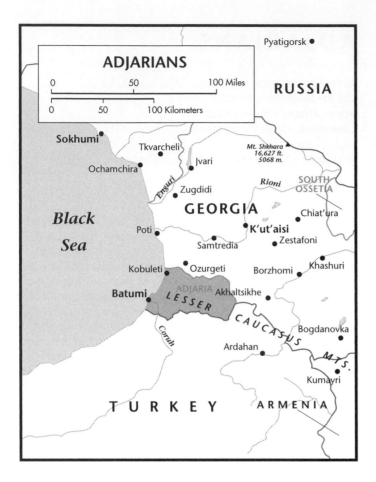

ADJARIANS

be redressed by making Adjarians once again Christian. While the Soviet Union existed, these Georgian nationalist projects were kept in check by the communist belief in internationalism, or what Soviet propaganda called "friendship among the nations." In 1990–91, however, abolishing Adjarian autonomy became one of the slogans proffered by the new post-communist government of Georgia. It appointed its own surrogate government in Adjaria, which was as disorderly as the one in Georgia proper. Virtually no one in the new government was a native Adjarian. This fact brought a huge crowd of worried and angry Adjarians into the main square of Batumi, the provincial capital. The demonstrators, both Muslim and Christian, were afraid that the new government would remove Adjarian autonomy.

The problems were not limited to religion, however. Adjarians today are a modern and quite secular people, many of whom consider themselves agnostic. As in any ethnic conflict, the crux of the problem was one of political power. The Adjarians wanted greater powers of self-determination than the new Georgian government would give them. Adjarians wanted to be treated with the same respect as other Georgians, including the right to retain their recognizably Muslim-Georgian names. The recognized organizer behind the Adjarian movement was Aslan Abashidze, who during the 1990s established a separate mini-state in Adjaria. Locally stationed Russian troops gave him support. At the same time, he proved an able diplomat, assuaging fears among some Georgians that Adjaria might secede. After 1990, Abashidze ruled his small country like a

virtual potentate, recognizing Georgia's authority over Adjaria only on paper. Adjarians credit him for two achievements: a well-armed peace amidst ethnic strife and civil war that engulfed most of the Caucasus in the 1990s and the cultivation of diversity and tolerance inside Adjaria. Compared with the tragic situations in Caucasia and in the former Yugoslavia, the outcome in Adjaria showed that ethnic conflict was not predetermined by religious and ethnic differences, but that political forces can both create and prevent ethnic conflicts. However, the peace was kept in part by Abashidze's own form of authoritarianism. Elections were rigged and the police suppressed all opposition. Abashidze's rule came to an end in May 2004, when he was overthrown by a domestic popular revolt inspired and supported by the new and youthful Georgian government that had came to power after the November 2003 Rose Revolution in Georgia

2 LOCATION AND HOMELAND

Aslan Abashidze was fond of saying that his land has no useful resources except its geography and the good humor of its people, but geography is strategically important. Adjaria is a tiny land (2,634 sq km/1,150 sq mi) of beautiful mountains and wooded valleys that descend to a thin coastal line of the Black Sea where the capital, Batumi, is situated. More than one-third of Adjaria's 400,000 people live in the capital. The climate along the sea front of Adjaria is one of the most humid in the world. A total of 160 cm (62 in) of precipitation is recorded annually, often destroying houses and crops. Before the 1930s, Batumi was one of the busiest oil-exporting ports in the world, serving as the main outlet for Baku oil from the landlocked Caspian Sea. In fact, at that time, the then-future Saudi Arabia received much of its kerosene from the Caucasus. The Caucasus is where the Swedish brothers Nobel (of the famous prize) developed a booming oil industry and laid one of the earliest pipelines to Batumi. Batumi, until the Russian invasion of Georgia in August 2008 was a growing oil and container port one again and a major trade hub on the road to Turkey. Adjaria's agriculture was best known for its tea and tangerines, but in recent years production has declined dramatically because export routes to Russia have been disrupted by wars and economic upheavals in post-communist countries.

It is impossible to know exactly how much of Adjaria's population consists of ethnic Adjarians, if by that we mean Muslim Georgians. Such a potentially divisive question has not been asked since the population census of 1926. It is no less difficult to tell how many Adjarians live in neighboring Turkey because Turkish statistics do not recognize ethnic minorities, but presumably there are many Georgian-speakers over the Turkish border. They, however, feel themselves to be both Turks and Adjarians.

3 LANGUAGE

Adjarians speak the Gurian dialect of the Georgian language (see entry on **Georgians**). This dialect is close to the language of medieval classical literature created in western parts of Georgia. Adjarians have no trouble understanding or speaking standard Georgian.

4 FOLKLORE

Adjarians share the same medieval folklore as other Georgians. They have, however, some local folk tales that display Turkish,

Armenian, and especially Laz influences (Lazes are a people of the Georgian language family who are also Muslim and live in North-East Turkey across the Georgian border).

The foremost hero of Adjaria's myths for a while was Aslan Abashidze, a former school principal and, curiously, grandson of the last Muslim ruler of Adjaria, Prince Memed Abashidze. With great admiration and passion, people told fabulous and incredible stories about their leader, whose courage, wit, and diplomatic skills were supposed to be proven by his exploits. His legendary showdown with Georgian nationalist leaders in April 1990 became the pinnacle of his personal legend, when after a meeting with the Georgian nationalists who were about to take over the government of Adjaria, Abashidze emerged from the government building with an AK-47 in hand saying that the meeting had suddenly flared up into a shootout, but that he and his bodyguards had proved better shots. These legends have been discredited after Abashidze fled to Moscow, escaping the wrath of his own people in 2004.

5 RELIGION

Although Adjarians have been Sunni Muslims for the past four centuries, today religion has lost much of its salience. After 70 years of Soviet-accelerated modernization, only a small number of elderly men can recite sacred Arabic verses from the Koran. Few people attend mosques even on Fridays, and virtually no women veil their faces. However, after the collapse of communism there was a Muslim revival that focused in most cases on the building of village mosques.

6 MAJOR HOLIDAYS

Muslim holidays are observed somewhat, especially the more pleasant ones. Like Lent and Easter in the Christian West, Ramadan is not observed with a month of fasting by many Adjarians, but almost everyone feasts after it is over. Because of Russian influence, which was strong during the Soviet period, Adjarians celebrate New Year's Eve. Many even put up Christmas trees, but nobody attaches any religious significance to this holiday. As in many former Soviet republics, February 23 is still celebrated as Men's Day, and women give small gifts to men. Few people seem to care that this date was meant to commemorate the first battle of the Soviet Red Army in 1918. Likewise, International Women's Day is celebrated on March 8 with flowers and chocolates offered to women, but it is no longer associated with the Socialist International movement. People have transformed these state and political holidays into celebrations of the seasons and gender. After independence, a number of Orthodox religious days have been introduced, such as St George's Day, Mariamoba (St Mary's Day), and others.

7 RITES OF PASSAGE

Muslim Adjarians follow Muslim traditions, although no longer very faithfully. For instance, male circumcision is still common. Like many other Muslims of Caucasia, Adjarians like to invite a special guest for the circumcision ceremonies. The *kirva*, who must be a Christian neighbor, would traditionally hold the baby boy on his lap during the operation. The special relationship between the Christian *kirva* and the child is akin to that of godparent and godchild in other cultures. Weddings are another major rite and are as lavish in Adjaria as elsewhere in Georgia and Caucasia.

8 INTERPERSONAL RELATIONS

Like all Caucasians, Adjarians are extremely etiquette conscious. They are infallibly polite and courteous under most circumstances, even when bargaining in the bazaar. Hospitality is supreme. A community values its members by their ability to live up to the norms of etiquette, including the availability of disposable income destined for conspicuous consumption. Like most Caucasians, Adjarians would starve if necessary to offer a feast to their friends and guests. In the 1960s and 1970s, when the Soviet Union's economy was booming, conspicuous consumption in Adjaria reached grotesque proportions. Corrupt local officials and wealthy peasants trading their citrus in the markets of Russian cities built themselves palatial houses, sometimes with ridiculously sumptuous decorations. In the 1970s, a group of Russian decorators who had previously worked in St. Petersburg in the restoration of the palaces of the tsars were lured to Adjaria with an offer of huge salaries. The mansions they helped to build rival Disneyland in both the purported impression and artistic taste.

Many Islamic norms, especially pertaining to relations between men and women, have been relaxed considerably in recent decades. Women in Adjaria dress and behave more like East European women than do women in many Arab countries or in Iran. Veiling is virtually non-existent.

9 LIVING CONDITIONS

Traditionally, most Adjarians lived in log cabins, which is the type of house most easily acquired, given the wooded mountainous environment. There were also houses made of stone and adobe found mostly near the seashore. In the 20th century, many Adjarians moved into towns, primarily Batumi. In the towns and modern villages, they prefer to live in private houses, sometimes very ostentatious two- and three-storied mansions. Such houses are endowed with all modern amenities, from hot water to air conditioning, and often have two toilets—one in a bathroom inside the house and another brick or wooden toilet in the backyard. As an old Adjarian man said resolutely: "no urban fashion will make me do my necessities inside the house where I live."

Many people who could not afford private homes were glad to receive virtually free apartments in the state-built high-rises. Because of centralized planning, these apartment houses look exactly the same in Adjaria as elsewhere in the former Soviet Union. Old village habits die hard, however, especially in an economy of chronic shortage. Many Adjarians keep chickens, turkeys, and sometimes cattle on the ground floor of their urban dwellings. Cows occasionally roam the streets of Batumi, including its beaches and the downtown area. Private homes are surrounded by fruit orchards of persimmons, figs, quince, tangerines, grapes, and kiwi, the latter of which was added several years ago. As part of the former Soviet Union, Adjaria experienced grave economic difficulties and disruptions after 1990 although since the ouster of Abashidze in 2004 the local economy has boomed as part of a new market-oriented Georgia. Georgia's GDP growth between 2004 and 2008 was in the range of 10–12% and tourism became a major industry in Adjaria. In 2006 the number of tourists in Adjaria increased by 27% compared to that in 2005. The number of new hotels, restaurants, cafes, and entertainment centers is increasing to accommodate the growing demand of tourism. The new international airport (5 km distance from Batumi port) was completed in 2007.

¹⁰ FAMILY LIFE

As elsewhere in the Caucasus, large extended families are no longer common in Adjaria. Nonetheless, the ties of kinship and neighborhood remain very strong. A modern family normally has two parents, one to three children, and grandparents if they are still living. Divorce is relatively rare, although not unknown. Many households are effectively run by women who also do most of the housework. There are no servants because the practice was considered extravagant in the socialist Soviet Union. Almost all private homes have pets—dogs, cats, and sometimes caged birds (canaries, or exotic parakeets). Wealthy people sometimes keep peacocks and pheasants to impress their guests and neighbors.

¹¹ CLOTHING

Traditionally, Adjarians dressed like Turks or other peoples of the Near East. This dress was completely replaced by modern European-style dress around the middle of the 20th century. Today, Adjarian men prefer Armani suits or tennis shirts and Levi's jeans (all of the brand names), and women try to follow French and Italian fashions in dress and makeup.

¹² FOOD

Adjarian cuisine is largely the same as Georgian. To this, Adjarian have added fish from the Black Sea—mackerel, flounder, and anchovies. Dolphins were hunted for meat in the past but mostly in times of hunger. In recent years, Muslim Adjarians began drinking wines and beer previously prohibited by Islamic law. Tea is the customary local drink.

¹³ EDUCATION

Governmental policies of the Soviet Union made high school education mandatory for all citizens including Adjarians. Education was conducted mostly in standard Georgian and in Russian. There are fewer classes in Russian language, as they have been replaced by English classes. At least formally, there are no illiterate Adjarians today. The older Islamic literacy in classical Arabic as well as in old Ottoman Turkish disappeared during the years of Soviet modernization. As in Georgia proper, the per capita number of college-educated people in Adjaria was among the highest in the former USSR. Almost as many women have higher degrees as men.

¹⁴ CULTURAL HERITAGE

Little can be described as specifically Adjarian cultural heritage. Most folk traditions (dances and music, for example) overlap with those of the Christian Georgians from the neighboring province of Guria. Islamic traditions are nearly forgotten due to rapid modernization during the Soviet years and hostility from the Georgian authorities. Today, Adjarians differ from other Georgians mostly by their Muslim first names. On several occasions in the past, especially in the 1950s and again in the early 1970s, Georgian officials have tried to change all Muslim names to Georgian Christian ones. For instance, all Memeds were mandated to become Michaels or Mamukas, and Gusseins to become Georges or Ghiorghis (Ghivi for short). A few Adjarians chose to resist, and some even went as

far as to protest at Moscow before the highest Soviet authorities. This kind of discrimination and similar attempts at forced "re-Georgianization" and Christianization of Adjarians fed the anxieties that in 1990 led to protests in the streets against the central government.

¹⁵ WORK

Adjarians are still mostly peasants with 55.7% of the population living in rural areas (2002). Because the Soviet Union was an isolated economy, it imported very few subtropical fruits from abroad, such as tangerines. Adjaria was one of very few places in the Soviet Union where the climate allowed the growth of tangerines, kiwis, and other tropical fruits. These crops brought monopolistic prices in the markets of Russian cities in the north and accrued never-before-seen wealth to many Adjarians. The reputed wealth of Adjaria was actually one major motivation behind the attempts of various Georgian paramilitary groups to invade what they called "Islamicized Georgia" in the 1990s. Thus, nationalist fervor was also a screen for the ordinary desire to plunder. After 1990, hardly anything was produced in Adjaria or grown for export. This changed after 2003 with some investments in tea and citrus fruits. Most inhabitants now derive their income from trading across the Turkish border, or from odd jobs.

¹⁶ SPORTS

Traditional sports include wrestling, archery, fencing, javelin throwing, horse riding, *tskhenburti* (a form of polo), and *leloburti* (a field game similar to rugby). In Adjaria, as in the rest of Georgia, soccer is quite popular. It is played in streets and yards as well as in stadiums.

¹⁷ ENTERTAINMENT AND RECREATION

Commercial recreation includes restaurants, cinemas, and pop music concerts. TV and video remain the cheap alternatives to modern mass entertainment, provided that electricity is uninterrupted in the evening. Many Adjarians now have access to cable. Otherwise, most Adjarians will enjoy themselves feasting in each other's homes.

¹⁸ FOLK ART, CRAFTS, AND HOBBIES

Adjarian folk art is similar to that of the Georgians. Pottery and rug making are still village crafts. Rugs are either woven in traditional patterns or made from compressed felt with abstract patterns. The colors most often used are deep red, brown, blue, and yellow. Metalworking, particularly with gold and silver, is an ancient skill that is still practiced. Metal chasing, which in Georgian is called *cheduroba*, is a treasured craft, as are enameling and jewelry making.

¹⁹ SOCIAL PROBLEMS

After the dissolution of the Soviet Union in 1991, Adjaria was effectively a separatist state ruled by a benevolent pasha. Its economy all but collapsed, unemployment was very high, and drug abuse soared. The crime rate was relatively low because, under Aslan Abashidze, one out of ten men served in the Adjarian police. This did not prevent massive corruption. Since 2003, employment has increased with the growth of tourism and foreign activity in the port, but most Adjarians still hover around the poverty line.

²⁰ GENDER ISSUES

Women in Adjaria face similar problems to those of their Christian Georgian neighbors. Despite formal equality in Soviet Georgia, women suffered wage and job discrimination and were expected to do the majority of the housework and childcare. In many ways, their position has worsened under new market conditions in Achara; female-headed households are more likely to be poor, women are concentrated in the semi-skilled positions and underrepresented in the senior jobs, and access to natal care has diminished while maternal mortality rates increased. Many Adjarian women support their families with cross border trade with Turkey, and a number have ended up as prostitutes in Turkish towns.

²¹ BIBLIOGRAPHY

Derlugian, G. "The Tale of Two Resorts: Abkhazia and Adjaria Before and Since the Soviet Collapse." Working Paper 6.2. Berkeley: University of California, March 1995.

Hale, William. "Turkey, the Black Sea and Transcaucasia," in *Transcaucasian Boundaries*, edited by J. Wright, S. Goldenberg, and R. Schofield, London, UCL Press, 1996.

Pelkmans, Mathijs. *Defending the Border: Identity, Religion and Modernity in the Republic of Georgia*. Ithaca: Cornell University Press, 2006.

—revised by S. Jones

ALBANIANS

ALTERNATE NAMES: Shqipëtarë
LOCATION: Albania; Macedonia; Greece; Kosovo
POPULATION: 3.6 million
LANGUAGE: Albanian
RELIGION: Evangelical Christian (Seventh-day Adventist, Jehovah's Witness, and others); Catholic, Muslim, and Orthodox

¹ INTRODUCTION

The Albanians are the direct descendants of the ancient Illyrians, whose territories in 1225 BC included all of former Yugoslavia—Dalmatia, Croatia, Bosnia, Herzegovina, Serbia, Montenegro, and portions of Macedonia and northern Greece. It is from one of the Illyrian tribes, the Albanoi located in central Albania, that the country derives its name. However, the Albanians call themselves *Shqipëtarë* and their country *Shqipëria*—generally accepted to mean "land of the eagles" because two of the Albanian words for eagle are *shqipë* and *shqiponjë*.

Now one of the largest cities in Albania, Shkodra, located in the northern part of the country, was also the capital of Illyria. The Romans conquered Illyria in 227 BC, a conquest for which they had to pay dearly by making frequent expeditions across the Adriatic Sea to quell chronic insurrections. During the civil war between Caesar and Pompeii, Albania served as the battleground in the contest for supremacy over Rome. The decisive battle between Octavius and Antony for the imperial throne of Rome was also fought on the Albanian seacoast. (In commemoration of his naval victory at Actium, the future Emperor Augustus built the new city of Nicopolos on the southernmost part of the Albanian seaboard. Its ruins may be seen in the modern-day city of Preveza, which was taken away from Albania and ceded to Greece by the Ambassadors' Conference of London in 1913.)

When the capital of the Roman Empire was transferred from Rome to Byzantium in AD 325, Albania, then known as the Thema of Illyricum, became a province of the eastern section of the empire. It remained part of the Byzantine Empire until the early Middle Ages, when certain feudal families managed to form independent principalities which eventually evolved into medieval Arberia (Albania), whose population was almost exclusively Albanian-speaking and also Albanian in terms of its history, laws, tradition, and culture. The Ottoman conquest of Europe began in 1354, when the Turks captured the Byzantine fortress at Gallipoli, located on a narrow peninsula where the Dardanelles opens into the Sea of Marmara. This military victory established the first Ottoman stronghold on European soil. The defeat of the Bulgarians at Maritsa in 1371, and also the defeat by the Turks of a Balkan coalition of Hungarians, Bulgarians, Romanians, Poles, Serbs, and Albanians on the plain of Kosovo in 1389, marked the eventual collapse of Serbia, Bulgaria, and Albania, which all then came under Turkish rule.

After conquering ethnic Albania, the Turks established a system of administration by dividing it into four provinces or "vilayets"— Shkodra, Kosovo, Manastir, and Janina. Ottoman domination of Europe lasted for more than 400 years before it went into decline, in large measure because of persistent un-

ALBANIANS

rest and nationalism in the conquered territories. After the defeat of the Turks by the Russians in 1877, the Great Powers evoked the Treaty of San Stefano the following year, signifying the break-up of the Ottoman Empire.

Ethnic Albania, still comprising four vilayets, was penalized by the Great Powers because it had been considered part of the Ottoman Empire for almost five centuries. The Albania of 1878 was divided and forced to cede the major portions of the vilayet of Shkodra to Montenegro, the vilayet of Kosovo to Serbia, the vilayet of Manastir to Macedonia, and the vilayet of Janina to Greece. What remained after the partitioning is, essentially, the nation of Albania as it exists today. Albania's neighbors continued to press for the total partitioning of Albania so that it would no longer exist as a separate political entity. The one person who prevented this from happening was President Woodrow Wilson of the United States, who declared, at the Paris Peace Conference in 1919, "I shall have but one voice at the Peace Conference, and I will use that voice in behalf of Albania." The conference eventually confirmed Albania's official boundaries.

Today, there are approximately 40,000 Albanians living in Montenegro, about two million in Kosovo, 100,000 in South Serbia, 600,000 in Macedonia, and at least 250,000 in northern Greece. In other words, there are as many Albanians living just outside of Albania's borders as there are within it, making Albania a country completely surrounded by itself. In February 2008, the Kosovo province declared independence from Ser-

bia. Despite protests from Serbia, the major European powers and the United States recognized independence.

² LOCATION AND HOMELAND

Present-day Albania is a small country located on the Adriatic Sea some 80 km (50 mi) from Italy. In a clockwise direction, beginning in the northwest, it is surrounded by Montenegro, Kosovo, the Former Yugoslav Republic of Macedonia, and, finally, Greece in the south. Albania is about 370 km (230 mi) long by about 144 km (90 mi) at its widest point, making it about the size of the state of Maryland. It has a population of approximately 3.6 million people, or about the same population as Greater Boston. Albania has an exceptionally beautiful seacoast, with white sandy beaches, that runs the entire length of the country, plus picturesque mountainous areas with significant winter sports (and ski resort) potential. The country has a typical Mediterranean climate along its southern part, where palm trees, oranges, and other citrus fruits grow in abundance. Some 36% of Albania is forested—mostly hills and mountains away from the fertile plains that hug the shoreline.

Albania has less land and air pollution than neighboring countries such as Romania, Slovakia, Hungary, and Poland. It is the world's third largest producer of chromium and has significant natural resources such as petroleum, copper, nickel, and coal. Thanks to the network of high-rise dams necessitated by its mountainous terrain, Albania has transmitted hydro-electric power all over the Balkans and as far west as Austria. Its forests are used essentially for five purposes: for firewood, as grazing land, as a source of forest plants, for recreation, and to supply the timber and paper industries. Although Albania had developed an internal railroad system, it was only in 1982 that it established a link into then-Yugoslavia, thereby gaining direct railway access to the rest of Europe for the first time in its history.

³ LANGUAGE

Albanian is not derived from any other language. It does not have a Slavic or Greek base, as is commonly believed, but is in fact one of the nine original Indo-European languages—the other eight being Armenian, Balto-Slavic, Germanic, Hellenic, Indian, Iranian, Latin, and Celtic. As such, Albanian is one of Europe's oldest languages. The Albanian alphabet is Latin-based and similar to that of English except that it is composed of 36 letters, including ë, ç, and the following nine digraphs, each of which is regarded as a single character: *dh, gj, ll, nj, sh, th, xh,* and *zh.* The Albanian alphabet does not have the letter *w.*

The Albanians are essentially a homogenous people but have been divided traditionally into two basic groups, the Ghegs in the north and the Tosks in the south, the dividing line being the Shkumbini River, which runs west-east almost across the center of the country. Both Ghegs and Tosks speak the same language but pronounce it with some differences. A typical example is the word *është,* which is the Albanian equivalent of the English word *is.* A Tosk would say EH-shtah, whereas a Gheg would pronounce it as AH-sht. The Tosk dialect is the official dialect of the entire country.

⁴ FOLKLORE

Fairies, snakes, and dragons are among the principal figures in Albanian mythology. Phenomena in Albanian folklore include the *kuçedër* (a snake or dragon with many heads), the *shtrigë* (a witch) and the *stuhi* (a flame-throwing winged being that guards treasures). To call someone a *kukudh* (goblin) is the ultimate insult, its full meaning being "a dwarf with seven tails who can't find rest in his grave." *Zana*, mythological female figures who help mountain folk in distress, are legendary, while the *ore* (fairy) also appears frequently in Albanian folklore, sometimes as an expression of fate—*I vdiq ora* (his luck ran out).

5 RELIGION

During Roman rule, in the 1st century AD, Christianity was adopted in the region of Albania, competing with Oriental cults (such as worshiping Mithra—the Persian god of light) and Illirian pagan cults. By the 16th century, almost all of Albania was Christian, the Orthodox religion being dominant in the south and the Roman Catholic in the north. In the 17th century, the Turks began a policy of Islamization by using, among other methods, economic incentives to convert the population. For example, some Albanians who adopted Islam received land and had their taxes lowered. By the 19th century, Islam became the predominant religion in Albania, claiming about 70% of the population while some 20% remained Orthodox and 10% Roman Catholic. These groupings remained stable until the Communist government outlawed religion in 1967, making Albania the world's only atheist state. Freedom of religion in Albania was restored only in 1989–90. However, the overwhelming majority of Albania's population was born under the Communist regime, which pursued an aggressively atheistic policy, and observations suggest that the historical 70-20-10 percentages are no longer valid. Following the collapse of the old Communist order, Albania has seen a religious revival of sorts, and some now believe that the religions with the most new adherents are evangelical Christian denominations, Seventh-day Adventists, Jehovah's Witnesses, and others. The current Albanian government includes Catholic, Muslim, and Orthodox members.

Different religious communities live together in harmony, and often religious holidays are celebrated together. For example, in Kosovo, on Aligjyni (Ali Day—August 2), both Muslims and Christians make a pilgrimage to Mount Pashtrik. Muslims do the pilgrimage in the morning, the Orthodox in the afternoon.

Although it is frequently referred to as a Muslim country, Albania has no state religion, and the Albanians are renowned for their religious tolerance. It is a little-known fact that Albania protected its own Jews during the Holocaust while also offering shelter to Jews who had escaped into Albania from Austria, Serbia, and Greece. The names of Muslim and Christian Albanian rescuers of Jews are commemorated at the Yad Vashem Memorial in Jerusalem and are inscribed on the famous Rescuers' Wall at the US Holocaust Memorial Museum in Washington, D.C. At the unveiling of the names of Albanian rescuers, the museum's director, Miles Lerman, gratefully stated, "Albania was the only country in Europe which had a larger Jewish population at the end of the war than before it!"

A joint Israeli-Albanian concert was held in Tirana on 4 November 1995 to commemorate the Albanians' protection of Jews from the country's Nazi occupiers during the Holocaust. Its participants included the Kibbutz Orchestra of Israel, the Opera Orchestra of Tirana, the National Choir of Tirana, and the Israel-Albania Society.

6 MAJOR HOLIDAYS

Albanian Christians celebrate traditional holidays such as Christmas and Easter, while Albanian Muslims observe Ramadan and the other religious holy days of Islam. Whereas other peoples in the Balkans refer to themselves as Christians or Muslims, an Albanian invariably says, "I am an Albanian" rather than a Christian or Muslim. *Dita e Verës* (Spring Day), derived from an ancient pagan holiday, is still celebrated in mid-March in Elbasan. All Albanians, wherever they are located in the world, joyously commemorate November 28 as Albanian Independence Day (*Dita e Flamurit*), for it was on that day in 1912 in the Albanian seacoast town of Vlora, that the venerable Albanian patriot, Ismail Qemali, first raised the Albanian red-and-black, double-headed eagle flag and proclaimed Albanian independence from the Ottoman Turks after almost 500 years.

Other public holidays include May 1 (Labor Day), October 19 (Mother Teresa Day), and November 29 (Liberation Day). If a public holiday happens to fall on a Saturday, then the previous Friday is taken as a non-working day. If a public holiday falls on a Sunday, then the following Monday is taken as a non-working day.

On St. Nicholas's Day (December 6), Christians and Muslims roast a pig or lamb and light candles for dead souls.

7 RITES OF PASSAGE

Most Albanians mark the major life events, including birth, marriage, and death, within either the Christian or Muslim religious tradition.

With the absence of funeral parlors, wakes for the deceased are generally held at home for a period of two or three days before burial.

8 INTERPERSONAL RELATIONS

Albanians are taught early on to respect their elders. To this day in some villages and in the smaller cities of Albania, youngsters kiss the hand of an elder male visitor when first greeting him. An eldest son, almost from the date of his birth, is groomed to become the eventual head of family upon the death of his father. It is the general custom in Albania for men to embrace each other upon meeting and kiss each other on the cheeks, and for them to walk along together with their arms linked.

There is an elaborate protocol of greeting exchanges when entering the home of an Albanian family. For example, after first being served the *qerasje* (treat), consisting of *liko* (a jam-like sweet) along with a drink or Turkish coffee by the hostess or other female member of the family, the visitor will inquire about the health of each member of the hostess's family in a careful and deliberate manner, and then the hostess will, in turn, inquire about the health of each member of the visitor's family. Only after this procedure is completed, will people relax and begin normal conversation.

The Albanians are very expressive people, using their eyes (rolling them upwards), hands (gesticulating), and bodies (shoulder shrugging) to reinforce their statements. They are great mimics and have a good sense of humor. Before World War II, dating was unheard of; later, dating one's betrothed became acceptable, but the couple was almost always chaper-

Albanians keep dogs mainly for keeping guard or herding sheep and other livestock. Lamb, rather than beef or pork, is the most common meat in the Albanian diet. (Cory Langley)

oned. Sacrosanct to all Albanians from olden days to more recent times is the concept of the *besa* or pledged word. More respected than a written contract was the verbal *besa-besën* agreement sealed by a handshake or embrace, and woe to the person who violated it! The greatest insult in Albania is to call a man *i-pabëse,* someone who has broken his word or who is disloyal or without honor.

9 LIVING CONDITIONS

Under the rule of President, and later King, Zog (1925–1939), the first rudimentary attempts were made to establish a system of health care in Albania. The post–World War II government of Albania undertook the construction of hospitals and clinics and expanded preventive health care by draining malarial swamps and instituting the inoculation of children against diseases such as measles and polio. Under rigid Communist rule from 1946 to 1991, many Albanians were forced to live in large, poorly constructed apartment buildings that provided only a couple of rooms to accommodate a family of four or more people. Many dwellings still lack central heating, and there is a shortage of water and frequent electric power outages in the larger cities. With the advent of democracy in 1992, new construction is already under way to rectify these problems.

The standard of living has also improved with the recent availability of household conveniences such as washing machines, dishwashers, and microwave ovens—items many Albanians did without until 1992. Throughout the 1990s and into the new century, living conditions have improved considerably, mirroring the economic expansion of the country. However, people living in the countryside still suffer from poor health care, an under-developed infrastructure, and lack of services.

10 FAMILY LIFE

Women were previously relegated to a secondary role in Albania, especially in relation to the eldest son of the family. By the age of 10, they were preparing their dowries—a tradition that was largely abandoned by 1950, although still practiced occasionally. During World War II, women came into their own, serving courageously in the partisan forces against the Italian and German invaders. After liberation, they were encouraged to enter the professions. Albanian families tend to be small, with the average being two children. The Albanian husband is not generally a helpmate to his wife, believing that the household is the province of the female. Arranged marriages were once the norm in Albania, but a prospective bride or groom almost always had the option of refusing to accept the proffered candidate and could hold out until a more suitable one was found. Elderly parents still reside with their children, where they are treated with honor and respect. Cats are quite common in single-family homes in larger cities, but dogs are used mainly for keeping guard or herding sheep and other livestock. There is no word for "pet" in the Albanian language.

11 CLOTHING

At one time Albanians could identify each other by the way they dressed. Each region had its own characteristic style of clothing, which was influenced by ethnic tradition and religion and differentiated by region, clan (fis), sex, and age. Historically, Albanians tended to spend a remarkably high proportion of their income on dress. In 1805 the English poet Lord Byron, visiting southern Albania (where he wrote a good portion of *Childe Harold's Pilgrimage*), called Albanian dress "the most wonderful in the world." Nowadays, their distinctive traditional clothing may be seen chiefly at theatrical or folk dance performances.

Until 1991, Albanian clothing styles, like those in other former Communist countries, tended to be unfashionable. Albania, in particular, had been isolated from other countries in Europe for almost 50 years. The media were heavily monitored, keeping Albanians unfamiliar with clothing and hair styles popular in the West. Today, Albanian men and women have easy access to the latest worldwide fashion trends through magazines and television, and this can be readily seen in their appearance.

12 FOOD

As a result of almost 500 years of Turkish subjugation, Albanian cuisine has been thoroughly influenced by those occupiers (although Italian influences prevail along the coast). Per capita bread consumption is sizable, looming unusually large in the Albanian diet. In fact, the word *bukë* (bread) is the normal word for "meal."

The main meal of the Albanians, as is the case throughout the Balkans, is lunch, which is usually accompanied by salad or fresh vegetables. Typical Albanian dishes include *lakror* (a mixture of eggs, vegetables, or meat, and butter encased in thin, multilayered pastry sheets) and *fërgesë* (a dish frequently made with minced meat, eggs, and ricotta cheese). Lamb, rather than beef or pork, is the most common meat. An unusual (and very tasty) pinkish trout *(Koran)* is found in Lake Ohri at Pogradec. Albania is also blessed with abundant seasonal fruits, such as grapes, cherries, figs, watermelon, peaches, quince, and oranges along with almonds, walnuts, hazelnuts, and olive trees. Albania manufactures beer and both red and white wines, although the national drink is *raki*, a clear, colorless brandy produced from grapes. Albania also produces an award-winning, three-star cognac called *Skanderbeg* (after its legendary folk hero) that is prized throughout Europe.

13 EDUCATION

Education in Albania has been stimulated and nurtured by nationalism. Under the Ottoman yoke, the teaching of the Albanian language was strictly forbidden, and Albanians of the Greek Orthodox faith were required to attend Greek schools, while Catholics were taught Italian, and Muslims, Turkish. The opening of the first school (*Mësonjtorja*) in which the Albanian language was taught (in Kore in 1887) was a milestone. The first Albanian-language elementary school for girls was opened, also in Kore, in 1892. Higher education in Albania really began with the American Vocational School (Shkolla Teknike) established by the American Red Cross in 1921, which eventually became part of the University of Tirana, when the latter was founded in 1957. Other institutes of higher education were located in Shkodra, Gjirokaster, and Elbasan. Since the overthrow of Communist power in 1992, new universities have been founded in Kore and Vlora. The literacy rate in 2003 was estimated at 87%.

14 CULTURAL HERITAGE

The Albanian flag is a deep red color with a black, double-headed eagle at its center. It is derived from the personal standard of Albania's great 15th-century folk hero, Gjergj Kastrioti, surnamed Skanderbeg which, translated into English, means Lord Alexander, after Alexander the Great. Skanderbeg, the leader of the Kastrioti clan, united all of the fiercely independent Albanian clans to fight the Ottoman Turks for some 25 years, until his death in 1468. He prevented the Turks from overrunning all of Europe and postponed the inevitable Ottoman conquest of the entire Balkan peninsula. Such was Skanderbeg's fame throughout Europe that the renowned Italian composer Vivaldi and the French composer Francoeur both composed operas about him, and Voltaire believed that the Byzantine Empire would have survived had it possessed a leader of Skanderbeg's stature.

Albanian folk music shows some Turkish and Persian influences. It sounds typically Balkan but is mainly polyphonic in the south and homophonic in north and central Albania. Music is played on folk instruments such as the *çifteli* (a long-necked two-stringed mandolin) and the *gërnetë* (a type of clarinet used for popular music). Other instruments are the *gajda* and *bishnica* (wind instruments) and the *sharkia* and *lahuta* (stringed ones). Before World War II, the Albanian government could not afford to provide education in the field of music. However, Albania eventually saw the establishment of seven symphony orchestras.

Albania has also produced writers of international renown such as Ismail Kadare, Albania's most influential and important writer, whom many believe worthy of a Nobel Prize. Kadare is the author of *The General of the Dead Army*, a novel describing how an Italian general, accompanied by a Catholic priest, returned to Albania after World War II to collect the remains of Italian soldiers who had fallen in battle. In 1982 Kadare's book was made into an Italian film starring Marcello Mastroianni as the general. Other important Albanian writers are novelists Dritero Agolli, Fatos Arapi, Rexhep Qosja, and Xhevair Spahiu, short story writer Naum Prifti, and humorist Qamil Buxheli.

15 WORK

During the Communist era, Albanians (especially youth brigades) were often conscripted to provide "volunteer" labor, such as building roads and railway beds, and preparation of new ground for agriculture. Students were required to donate one month of free labor during their summer vacations to terrace the hills, for example, and to plant citrus and olive trees. Although Albania is ideally suited for agriculture and tourism, the Communist government undertook a program of heavy industry that employed many people.

Because there was no real incentive to work, some western observers believe that Communism destroyed the Albanian work ethic. After 1992, however, a new spirit of entrepreneurship surfaced, and Albanians quickly developed a surprising number of private enterprises. Also, in 1992, Albanians finally experienced the five-day work week, a welcome relief from the previous six-day work week under Communism.

In recent years, labor force participation and employment levels have lagged beyond population growth. In 2005 only 57.8% of working-age people were gainfully employed, with men having a considerably higher participation rate (68.5%) than women.

¹⁶ SPORTS

Without question, Albania's favorite sport is football (the common European term for the game known as soccer in the US). Championship matches in Albania date from 1930, and an Albanian Football Federation was founded in 1932 and became a member of the International Football Federation (FIFA). Albanian teams have taken part in both Balkan and European championship games. For example, in 1965, one Albanian team eliminated Northern Ireland, while another eliminated the Federal German team (by draws in both cases). Today, Albanians fervently follow the fortunes of British, German, and Italian football teams. Second only to football is volleyball, in which both men's and women's teams have become Balkan champions. Basketball is becoming increasingly popular, and many Albanian cities have fielded teams of both sexes, who enter their respective national and international competitions. Chess continues to gain favor, especially with youngsters, and tennis, having long been labeled by the Communists as a "capitalist sport," is steadily winning enthusiasts.

¹⁷ RECREATION

Albanians are inveterate storytellers, and in coffee shops throughout the country, men are often found regaling each other with humorous stories (especially about the former Communist regime) or listening with reverence to the deeds of Albanian folk heroes. Until 1991, the Albanian film studio, (Shqipëria e Re /New Albania) used to produce between 10 and 20 movies each year. Currently, it turns out only documentaries and other short subjects, so television is exceptionally popular.

Albania presents several extensive folk dance/song festivals that attract international visitors, and its citizens are faithful attendees of classical music performances. With the advent of democracy in 1992, Albanians are now more exposed to dramatic and musical performances from other countries in Europe, the Middle East, and elsewhere, which they attend in growing numbers. Albanians are great socializers, and after taking a late afternoon nap, they enjoy a leisurely promenade along their wide streets during the evening on the way to meet friends and relatives before partaking of a late dinner. Discos are extremely popular with the younger set.

¹⁸ FOLK ART, CRAFTS, AND HOBBIES

Albanian women and even girls as young as eight have always been praised for the intricate embroidery (qëndisje) which they create to decorate their dwellings. In the course of preparing their dowries, several young women will get together to make beautiful doilies (çentro) to place on furniture. Using a small loom (vegël), they create colorful rugs for floors, and with other hand tools they produce sweaters, socks, gloves, and other items, using wool, cotton, acrylics, and fur. Ounë me grep (lace making) is a traditional folk art that has been passed down from generation to generation.

Men usually work with metals such as copper, brass, and aluminum to craft decorative plates, wall hangings, and utensils. Portraits of Skanderbeg abound, as well as pastoral scenes featuring the beautiful mountains and lakes of Albania. The capital, Tirana, is becoming well known for its delicate pen-and-ink drawings as well as for its acrylic, watercolor, and oil paintings. An outstanding ceramist, Mira Kuçuku, has a fashionable gallery on Rruga Zhon Dark in downtown Tirana—her beautiful pottery has already been exhibited in several countries in Europe. Hobbies including stamp collecting, birdwatching, gardening, butterfly collecting, and storytelling, are favorite pastimes all over Albania.

¹⁹ SOCIAL PROBLEMS

Having only emerged in 1992 from almost 50 years under the most repressive and isolated Communist government in Europe, Albanians are learning the ways of democracy. Significant progress has been made in the new century, with Albania openly stating its intent to join the European Union (EU). In June 2007, George Bush was the first US president to ever visit Albania, and noted its position as a close ally of Washington. In April 2008, Albania was invited to join the North Atlantic Treaty Organization (NATO), at the Bucharest (Romania) summit.

For a long time, the main broadcaster of radio and TV was the public station RTSh. Nowadays, the public station is facing fierce competition from private TV and radio stations that have mushroomed in the larger urban centers. Many people own satellite dishes, and Italian and Greek TV can be picked up via terrestrial reception. Sensationalism often defines the articles of the print media. Dependence on outside revenues, as well as ownership that is politically biased, limits the objectivity of these papers.

²⁰ GENDER ISSUES

Throughout Eastern Europe in the 1950s (and Albania was no exception), the newly laid socialist foundations created a desire for more independence for women. The new consumer culture that communism started to define (centered around privatized leisure—like the purchase of a radio or TV, and domesticity—goods designed to assist with housework) reinforced, to some extent, traditional sex roles, but it also challenged them by articulating female aspirations for greater social recognition and independence. The Albanian communist regime emphasized the role of women as an integral part of socialist labor. Throughout the 1960s and 1970s, employment levels among women continued to rise, although in predominantly "feminine" sectors. In 1961, women accounted for 73.7% of workers in textiles, 69.7% in the health services, 60% in food processing, and 50% in retail.

In 2004, the Assembly of Albania passed a law that called for the promotion of equal opportunities among men and women. The direct purpose of the law was to eliminate direct and indirect discrimination on the grounds of gender in the country's public life. Homosexuality continues to be a contentious issue.

²¹ BIBLIOGRAPHY

Elsie, Robert. *A Dictionary of Albanian Religion, Mythology and Folk Culture.* London: C. Hurst and Co., 2001.

Feffer, John. *Shock Waves: Eastern Europe after the Revolutions.* Boston: South End Press, 1992.

Hupchick, Dennis P. *The Balkans: From Constantinople to Communism.* New York: Palgrave Macmillan, 2002.

Hutchins, Raymond. *Historical Dictionary of Albania*. Lanham, Md.: The Scarecrow Press, Inc., 1996.

Jacques, Edwin E. *The Albanians: An Ethnic History from Prehistoric Times to the Present*. Jefferson, N.C.: McFarland & Company, 1994.

Konitza, Faik. *Albania: The Rock Garden of Southeastern Europe*. Boston: VATRA, 1957.

Logoreci, Anton. *The Albanians: Europe's Forgotten Survivors*. London: Victor Gollancz, 1977.

Pettifer, James and Miranda Vickers. *The Albanian Question: Reshaping the Balkans*. London: I.B. Tauris, 2006

Pittaway, Mark. *Brief Histories: Eastern Europe 1939–2000*. London: Arnold, 2004.

Skendi, Stavro. *The Albanian National Awakening: 1878–1912*. Princeton: Princeton University Press, 1967.

Sula, Abdul B. *Albania's Struggle for Independence*. New York: Privately published by the family of Abdul B. Sula, 1967.

Vickers, Miranda. *The Albanians: A Modern History*. London: I.B. Tauris, 2001.

—revised by Marcel Ionescu-Heroiu

ALSATIANS

LOCATION: Alsace, France
POPULATION: 1,817,000
LANGUAGE: French; Alsatian and Frankish dialects
RELIGION: Roman Catholicism; Lutheranism; Calvinism; Judaism

¹ INTRODUCTION

Located between Germany and France and in proximity of other European nations, the region known as Alsace has attracted travelers as well as invaders through history. Alsatians survived five centuries of rule by the Roman Empire and Teutonic invaders. Unification of Europe by Charlemagne brought peace to Alsace. However, Charlemagne's grandsons divided Europe again. In 870 the Franco-German border was established on the Moselle River, marking the beginning of the French-German dispute over the region. Alsace was added to France by the Treaty of Rijswijck in 1697. Alsatians saw their region annexed by Germany from 1870 to 1918. In 1918 Alsace was returned to France, but was again annexed by the Germans during the period of World War II from 1940 to 1944. When the war ended, Alsace was again returned to France in 1945.

As a result of the periods of German control and influence, Alsatian architecture, cuisine, dress, and dialect have been influenced by Germany. However, despite the constant presence of foreign powers, Alsatians developed a strong sense of identity. People there see themselves first and foremost as Alsatians, which is reflected in the use of their regional language.

Alsace is one of the regions of France. Politically it is one of the most conservative regions of France, where the conservative right won the 2004 regional elections. Alsatian regional government is an equivalent of state government in the United States. Since 2004 the conservative party has controlled the Alsace regional council. Not surprisingly, the French president Nicolas Sarkozy, nominated by the conservatives in the 2007 presidential elections, amassed the greatest support in Alsace. Alsatian politicians are known for supporting national identity issues. This region is also very supportive of European integration.

One of the most pro-EU regions in France, Alsace is home to numerous European institutions and organizations. The Center for Information on the European Institutions (CIIE) is based in the capital of Alsace, Strasburg. The CIIE is the official information network of the European Union. Its major task is to inform the general public on the operations of the institutions and to provide news on European policies. Moreover, Strasburg is one of the three official locations of the European Parliament. This legislative body of the European Union is the only institution to be directly elected by European citizens. The European Parliament in Strasbourg is the official place where the members of the European Parliament come together on a monthly basis to adopt community texts.

Other European Union organizations situated in Alsace include the European Court of Human Rights, the European Pharmacopoeia Commission, the headquarters of EUROCORPS, the European Science Foundation, the Assembly of European Regions, and others. Additionally, the Alsace Office in Brussels is the representational tool used by Alsatian territorial associations and local consular bodies to represent their concerns to the European Union. Being the hub of the EU administration, Alsace is situated at the heart of European politics. This strategic position has been extremely good for Alsatian economy and allows the region to keep its distance from the centralized French national government.

² LOCATION AND HOMELAND

Alsace is the smallest French region. It is located at the eastern border of France between the Vosges mountains to the west and the Rhine river to the east. It also shares borders with Germany and Switzerland. Stretching along the Rhine, Alsace is 193 km (120 mi) long and 48.2 km (30 mi) wide. Currently, it is divided into two departments: the Lower Rhine and the Upper Rhine.

The climate in most of Alsace is similar to the towns of southern France. The temperature is fairly mild, averaging to 18°C (64°F) in the summer and 2°C (35.6°F) in winter. Colmar is the second driest town of France. An abundance of sunshine and mild winters allow the fertile lands along the Rhine river to produce lavish crops of grains, hops, tobacco and cabbage. Other crops grown in the region include wheat, corn, potatoes, asparagus, and root vegetables, such as beets. The area surrounding the eastern foothills of the Vosges has a warm and sunny microclimate with little rainfall. It is perfect for growing slow-ripening wine grapes.

The small but beautiful region of Alsace is known for its verdant forests, rounded hills, splendid vineyards, serene lakes, and picturesque panoramas. The Vosges mountain range at the west of Alsace is made of old mountains. Its summits are called balloons due to their unique rounded shape. The Grand Balloon peaks, including *Ballon de Guebwiller,* are the highest in Alsace, reaching 1,737 m (5,700 ft). Located at the very south of the region is the Jura mountain range.

Alsace has quite a few lakes. The most famous lake is White Lake located at the high altitude of 1,055 m (3,461 ft). At 955 m (3,133 ft) sits Lake Noir (Black Lake) known for its hydroelectric powerhouse. Lac des Truites, also called Forlen Lake, is the highest lake of the Vosges mountains. It can be found at an altitude of 1,061 m (3,481 ft). Alsace's two longest rivers are the Rhine and Ill. Between those rivers lies the area called the *Ried,* or reed country. This reed country is marked with marshland and wet grassland.

Its close proximity to the capitals of France, Germany, and Switzerland places Alsace at the heart of Europe. The capital of the region is Strasbourg. With more than 263,941 inhabitants, Strasbourg is an important economic and administrative center of Europe. Many people in this city are employed in the banking sector or other businesses. Strasbourg has excellent high speed highways and express trains connecting it with Paris, France; Frankfurt, Germany; and Basel and Zurich, Switzerland. Other large cities of Alsace include Sélestat, which is particularly famous for its city library, its festivals, and its market; Wissembourg, with more than 70 houses built in the18th century; and Hunawihr, known for its burgeoning vineyards and flocks of storks. Colmar is a spawning industrial town with multi-colored, half-timbered, crooked houses and charming alleyways at the center of the city. Historical buildings are extremely well-preserved here. A fortress town of Neuf-Brisach is acknowledged for its military architecture.

Although the majority of Alsatians live in cities, a portion of the population resides in the countryside. Alsatian quaint villages, sparkling with half-timbered houses, sit peacefully among the vineyards. It is customary for traditional country houses to be adorned with elaborate wood carvings. People also decorate their dwellings with flower window boxes, overflowing with geraniums and other colorful perennials.

³ LANGUAGE

Since 1945, standard French has established itself as the prominent language of the region. Originally, the name Alsace comes from Alemannic expression "Ell-sass," which means "Seated of the Ill." One of the biggest rivers of Alsace is Ill. After 1996 the German Elsass was prominently replaced with French-sounding Alsace.

Although Alsace is considered a French-speaking area, the traditional language of the region is Alsatian. The Alsatian language is the Alemannic dialect of Upper German and is fairly similar to Swiss German. Frankish dialects of Western Middle German are heard in the north of Alsace. However, neither Alsatian nor Frankish dialects are official languages of Alsace. About 25% of the local population is fluent in the Alsatian dialect. Also, the Alsatian and the Frankish dialects are now recognized as languages of France and are taught in French high schools. Furthermore, the local dialects are seen on shop signs and menus. The desire to safeguard national identity encourages Alsatians to preserve the traditional Alsatian language. The overwhelming presence of French media makes the survival of Alsatian among younger generations rather challenging, but since it is an important part of the local identity, people hope that it will survive.

⁴ FOLKLORE

Traditional music, folk dances, songs, games, anecdotes, and legends are among the most popular forms of folklore that can be seen in the region. Many aspects of Alsatian folklore are inspired by or rooted in German folklore and traditions. Thus, Alsatian folk music shares many common features with German folk music. High-spirited melodies played with trumpets, flutes, accordions, and drums prompt the listeners to get up and dance. Most villages and towns have their own folk ensembles with members of all ages.

Alsatians have many beliefs, stories, and superstitions related to storks. A stork (*la cigogne* in French) is the national bird of Alsace. Enjoying their special status, these stately birds like to make their nests atop the roofs of tall buildings. They prefer to build their nests high so that young storks can swoop off the roofs as they learn to fly. A stork is considered to be a symbol of good luck, happiness, and fidelity throughout Alsace. In French folklore babies are delivered by a rabbit in a cabbage patch; in Alsatian folklore (like in German folklore) babies are brought by a stork. Therefore, when an Alsatian child wants a younger brother or sister, he or she needs to place a piece of sugar on the windowsill to attract the stork, hoping that the bird would grant a precious package in exchange for a sweet treat.

From Strasbourg to Colmar, from the Vosges mountains to the Rhine, Alsace is saturated with history and legends. One of the well known Alsatian legends is about King Dagobert. Falling in love with a Kuttolsheim beauty, he built a pipeline to bring white wine from her village to Strasbourg. It was such a commercial success, as well as a demonstration of his love, that Strasburg built another pipeline for red wine.

In addition many castles, churches, or other places of local importance have fascinating and at times mystical legends about people who lived in them or events that happened there. For example, the village of Andlau has a legend about the foundations of its Abbey of Ste. Richarde in 880. According to the legend, the site for the abbey was chosen by a she-bear, who scratched her paw on the ground designating where the monastery must be built. The abbey's 12 centuries old crypt has a small wooden door above the very ground scratched by the bear. As legend has it, if a person puts his or her sore limb into the niche in the crypt's floor and touches the ground, that person will be cured of these sores. One can also see a stone bear near the door. According to one local belief, any woman who sits by that stone bear shall be assured of many children.

The District of Wintzenheim is another place steeped with legends. Centuries-old lore continues to pervade the Five Castles and Brand wine region. As the legend has it, the Brand hillside was fertilized by a dragon's blood. People also say that the Pflixbourg castle, located near the three castles of Eguisheim, is a home for the ghost of a White Lady imprisoned by a wicked fairy.

Fascinating local traditions and superstitions include a custom called Andresle practiced in Illzach. For this ritual, on Saint Andrew's Eve a girl must take an apple form a widow without saying thank you for it. She then must cut it in two and eat one half of it before midnight. The other half must be eaten after midnight. Then, in sleep, the girl will see her husband to be.

5 RELIGION

For five centuries (from the 9th century until 1648) Alsace was a part of the Holy Roman Empire, which established Catholicism as the official religion of the region. However, after 1948 Alsace was divided into numerous virtually sovereign landlordships, forcing the people to adopt the religion of their prince. As a result, most of the Alsatian population is Roman Catholic, but there is also a considerable number of Protestants.

Additionally, unlike the rest of France, the Alsace and Moselle are the only regions that continue to follow the Napoleonic Concordat of 1801, under which public subsidies are granted to Roman Catholic, Lutheran, and Calvinist churches, and to Jewish synagogues. Following the concordat also implies that public education in each of those faiths is offered and supported. Since in France religion and state are separate, the religious policies in Alsace and Mocelle are the subject of constant disagreement between the two regions and the rest of France.

Alsace is known for its large Jewish community. The set of laws that provide religious equality and ensure that representatives of the deferent religions are treated as civil servants made Alsace a favorable destination of the Jewish people. However, this set of laws was adopted only in the early 19th century, while the Jewish community uninterruptedly existed in this area for over 800 years. The continued presence of Alsatian Jews reflects itself in the numerous ancient synagogues and cemeteries spread across the region, as well as in other aspects of the Jewish heritage.

6 MAJOR HOLIDAYS

Alsatians are merry people and love to celebrate. Whether it is a religious holiday, a local festivity, or a two-day parade, people here take their time to get together and celebrate. Many religious holidays, such as Christmas, are not distinct to Alsace. Yet, they acquire unique characteristics of the region and feel very Alsatian.

Similarly to most Europeans, Alsatians celebrate a number of Christian holidays, such as Christmas, Epiphany, and Easter. The Christmas season traditionally begins with the feast of Saint Nicolas, marked with special songs, legends, and gingerbread. At the wake of Christmas Eve, the streets throughout the region are lit with Christmas lights, the Christmas markets are set up, and the delicious aroma of cinnamon and biscuits fills the streets and homes. Alsatian Easter is particularly loved by children. It is the time of year when children hunt around the gardens in search of jolly-colored Easter eggs, carefully hidden by their parents. To celebrate the Epiphany, Alsatian children dress up as the three kings. A special dish made at Epiphany is the delicious *galette des rois* pastries.

Alsatians greatly enjoy festivals and carnivals. The midwinter Candlemas carnival marks the beginning of the festival season. The size and grandeur of the costumed procession depends on the village or town. For example, in Mulhouse the festive procession marches through the streets of the city for two days. The *corsos fleuris,* or flower floats festival, is another important event in Alsatian holiday culture. During this festival held in September, flower floats are assembled. Decorated with thousands of dahlias, the floats pass through the towns and villages. The most famous *corsos fleuris* parade is held in Sélestat. The first flower parade was organized in Sélestat by the Association of the Outdoor Gardeners of Alsace in 1927. The goal of the event was to attract young people to the gardening profession. This beautiful festival is enjoyed throughout the region, bringing joy and happiness to the hearts of the people.

Additionally, Alsace can boast its culinary and wine-related festivals. Each year multiple celebrations are put together to acknowledge Alsatian culinary, winemaking, and brewing traditions. From spring to autumn, villages and towns celebrate beer making, successful cherry crops, harvesting season, fried carp, or whatever else Mother Nature may grant.

Although there are some festivals celebrated by the whole region, many celebrations are local. Thus, the city of Ribeauvillé marks the end of summer with the Fête des Ménétriers (Musicians Festival). Bringing together artists and performers and offering theatrical and musical entertainment rooted in medieval times, this festival celebrates art and is a spectacle not to miss. In the same manner, each year a major folk festival (the Ami Fritz festival) is held in Marlenheim. Based on an Emile Erckmann and Alexandre Chatrian novel (1864), this festival brings to life traditional wedding rituals captured in the novel. During two days, visitors observe the nuptial parade, all sorts of folk entertainment, and a magnificent firework display.

There are a number of festivals celebrated by a given town or village to honor a local saint. They are called *Kilbe* in Upper Alsace and *Messti* in Lower Alsace. In medieval times, these lively events would end with a grandiose mass, followed by funfairs and a country market. Among such local holidays, the *Feux de Saint-Jean,* or the Saint John Fires Day, stands out. This summer celebration takes place in the valleys of Vosges mountains. People come together to make and light the fires dedicated to St. John. In the past, people lit the St. John fires to celebrate the sun before it begins its annual decline. Honoring St. John and celebrating the bliss of the sun was believed to guarantee a better harvest.

7 RITES OF PASSAGE

Traditional rites of passage in the villages and towns of Alsace include carnivals, calendar and votive festivals, and other types of folk rites. Varying from village to village, these festive events carry villagers into a new season or signify successful harvest. Also, each religious community in Alsace has its own rites of passages. For example, baptism plays an important role in the Christian community, while *brit milah* (the covenant of male circumcision) and naming ceremonies mark a passage through life in Judaism.

Other rites of passage in Alsace are related to the significant stages of human life, including birth, marriage, and death. Those could be religious or secular ceremonies, depending on a family. Religious or secular, each of these events is surrounded with rich ceremonial culture. Some observers note that Alsatians developed a particularly interesting and complex ritual that help them to cope with death.

8 INTERPERSONAL RELATIONS

In general, Alsatians are a very outgoing and community-oriented people. There is nothing that Alsatians enjoy more than their *fêtes*: the annual village fairs and festivals. Multiple festival and holiday occasions provide Alsatians with plenty of opportunities to set out tables and benches on the street and bring food, wine, and the accordion to relax. If one should name a sole major feature of Alsatian people, it has to be their conviviality.

Turbulent historic events, both happy and tragic, have shaped the character of the Alsatian people. Thus, on one hand Alsatians are very open and tolerant towards each other and towards the foreigners. On the other hand they are proud of their local identity, so that little things like usage of the Alsatian dialect, telling of a local joke, joining in the singing of an old tune or inviting people for a traditional Alsatian meal really warms people's hearts. In sum, despite their recent tumultuous history, or possibly because of it, one senses a delicate joie de vivre prevailing throughout the region.

9 LIVING CONDITIONS

As of 2008 Alsace has a population of 1,817,000 people and it is the third most densely populated region in metropolitan France. By 2030 it is estimated to increase by 12% to reach 2 million. Strasbourg, the capital of Alsace and a major port on Rhine, and other big cities, such as Mulhouse and Colmar, are busy industrial and administrative centers placing Alsace at the center of international trade.

An industrial and banking region at the heart of Europe, Alsace is not immune to the vicissitudes of the global economy. However, the dynamism of its businesses, convenient geographic location, appropriate regional legislature, and the ability of Alsatian businesses to establish themselves as the *sine qua non* of their corporate partners brings the region economic development, stability, and growth.

The thriving economy provides people with employment opportunities so that Alsatians have a relatively high standard of living. The regional government supports an open economy and creates good conditions for international employers. At the same time it provides its citizens with a strong social base, such as free public education and affordable medical care services.

There are approximately 130,000 foreigners residing in a region. Foreigners amount to 7.4% of the total population of Alsace and 4% of the total population of foreigners in France. Germans account for 16,000 residents. Furthermore, Alsace hosts 8.4 million tourists per year, 2.7 million of which are French tourists. The next in numbers stand visitors from Germany, Belgium, Switzerland, Italy, and Britain. Tourist accommodations range from luxurious hotels and holiday homes to inexpensive camping sites. Tourist industry annually brings Alsace over 2.5 billion euros.

10 FAMILY LIFE

The structure of the typical Alsatian family is similar to that in the other parts of France. Families usually have one or two children. Unfortunately, over the past decades a significant percent of couples ended in divorce. Especially it is a problem in bigger cities. However, people value their families and turn to close and extended family members for emotional and financial support. Despite the divorces, parents take their role as guardians and providers very seriously.

Both in the countryside and, to a lesser extent in bigger cities, people enjoy spending time with family and friends. Adult children visit their parents and grandparents on regular bases. Such visits usually involve a prolonged meal and a hearty conversation in the family circle.

Over the centuries Alsatians demonstrated different attitudes regarding intermarriages. At times communities, including Alsatian Jews, were somewhat secluded and intermarriages were difficult, if not condemned. At the same time located at the crossroads of France and Germany, Alsace has a long history of mixed German-French unions. At present, Alsatians do try to maintain their traditions, language, and identity, but it does not preclude them from entering mixed marriages.

Alsatians are fairly laid back and hospitable people, and they welcome visitors and foreigners. Yet, it is only with their close friends and family that they are free to completely be themselves. In addition to forming strong bonds with family members, Alsatians give their heart and soul to close friends. Friends are expected to be available when needed and it is common for friends to see each other almost every day

11 CLOTHING

Contemporary dress code in Alsace is fairly similar to that in the rest of France. However, Alsatians are proud of their traditional costumes. These outfits went out of fashion a long time ago, but they are readily worn at festivals and celebrations. For example, folk costumes are the highlight of the 14 July parade. The history of Alsatians costume is presented to the viewer in museums throughout Alsace.

Until the 19th century dress was an important symbol of social status in Alsace. Thus, types of the local outfit were roughly divided into a set of clothes worn by poor peasants, outfits of wealthy city-dwellers, and attire of the nobility. The French Revolution changed that. After 1820 people began to acquire a new sense of identity that reflected itself in one's style of dress. If before the revolution outfit symbolized social sta-

A boy wearing an Alsatian costume in Alsace, France. (© Steven Vidler/Eurasia Press/Corbis)

tus, after the revolution it turned into a reflection of political inclinations, religious beliefs, age, and feelings.

Over time, outfits of nobility and bourgeoisie disappeared giving place to modern fashion. However, the attire of Alsatian peasants continues to live on in a new capacity of national Alsatian costume. Interestingly, the various elements of the Alsatian peasant costume were inspired by the style of the French nobility and bourgeoisie and adapted to local needs with variations from one area to another.

Alsace is a big province, and it is hard to pin down a sole traditional costume. Different folk communities such as people from the Munster valley have their distinct dress. However, in general, traditional female costume consists of white shifts with ruffled cuffs and collars and long skirts, symbolizing modest and hard-working peasants. The skirt's length, color, and decoration carry a religious meaning. For the Protestants, the skirt is knee-length. It is adorned with a velvet ribbon and the typical colors are green, purple, brown, blue, and sometimes red. The Catholic woman's skirt is long and the hem of the skirt is decorated with black velvet. It does not have any ribbons on it. As for the color, girls tend to wear bright red-colored skirts and older women prefer other deep colors, but never green.

Another important element of women's traditional costume is an apron. In the Middle Ages it was made of linen and it was always plain white. Since the 1820s women have been making aprons of silk and satin. The apron is tied around the waist with two ribbons that are crossed on the back and tied into a big bow in front. Initially, aprons of young girls looking for a groom were tied with a big cord with numerous knots showing the amount of land included in the dowry. Stockings and silk shawls are also part of the female costume. Originally, stockings were knitted over the evening gatherings and demonstrated variety of patterns and elaborate stitches. Today, however, the stockings are mostly machine made.

Traditional male costumes include black trousers and white shorts with long pleated sleeves. Shorts are typically made of linen or cotton. A principal item of the male costume is a waistcoat. Originated during a bloody peasant war in the 16th century, Alsatian vest is often red, although older men prefer darker colors. A final cloth article is a black hat made of felt. It could be easily recognized for its narrow brims and a flat crown.

In the past, Alsatian women put considerable effort and skill into costume making. Certain articles worn during celebrations were made to last the whole life and were handed over from generation to generation. Now, of course, most of the traditional costumes are machine made. Yet, there are few people who continue hand-knit stockings and do embroidery.

12 FOOD

The Alsatian dishes could be described as a unique blend of German and French cuisine with distinct Alsatian flavor. Alsatian charcuteries offer a great variety of delicious hams and sausages such as *cervelat* (smoked pork), or *Montbéliard* (lightly smoked pork). Arguably, the best-known Alsatian dish is *choucroute*–a dish made of cooked sauerkraut garnished with sausages, smoked meats, and potatoes. Other local variations of *choucroute* are sauerkraut with goose or duck or more modern recipes, such as *choucroute de la mer,* where fish and seafood replace the meats. Another famous Alsatian food is *baekeoffe.* Originally, this casserole made of three different marinated meats and potatoes was a traditional Monday lunch. Women would drop off all the necessary ingredients at the baker's in the morning where it would cook in the oven for at least three hours. Then, they would pick it up on their way home for lunch.

Alsace is also well known for its traditional *flammekueche,* or Alsatian onion tart, made of cream, onions, and lardoons topped with a thin layer of bread dough and cooked in a wood-fired oven. Another favorite, *tarte flambée* could be roughly described as Alsatian pizza. One might go to the restaurant, place the order, and have the waiter start bringing the small tarts one after another, with a side salad and, of course, wine. When one is full, he or she has to notify the waiter that it is enough. The waiter would mark it down and bring the bill. Another regional specialty, *matelote du Rhin,* is a scrumptious fish stew made of freshwater fish marinated in white wine. The list goes on.

Furthermore, Alsace stands out for its breads and pastries. Alsatian bakers offer their customers different kinds of *bretzels* (Alsatian version of pretzels), *brioches* (light slightly sweet bread made with a rich yeast dough), *bredele* (Christmas biscuits), gingerbread, and *springerle* (anise-flavored cookies) Ethnic deserts include *kougelhoff,* the famous yeast cake baked in a special mold, *tarte au fromage blanc* (Alsatian cheesecake), *bierwecke* (Alsatian fruit cake), and *glace au miel de sapin aux fruits des bois* (honey ice cream with berries). As the variety and quality of Alsatian food demonstrates, Alsace is believed to produce some of the greatest chefs in the world.
In addition to numerous dishes enjoyed throughout Alsace, different parts of the region carry on their unique food traditions. Thus, a concentration of small ponds in southern Alsace allowed this area to develop its own version of fish and chips (*carpes frites*). Dusted in soft wheat semolina carps or parts of a carp are pan-fried or deep fried. Perfect in their delicious crunchy crust *carpes* are served with French fries or a green salad.

It is true that many Alsatian dishes have their equivalent in France and Germany. Yet, Alsace bestows French or German recipes with their distinct characteristics. For example, French *pot au feu* gets a special twist in Alsace, where this dish of boiled beef is served with distinctly Alsatian array of greens, radishes, tomatoes, cucumbers, carrots, beets, and horseradish sauce.

Without a doubt Alsatians are proud of their wine. There are about 65 miles of vineyards in Alsace, where perhaps the most diverse selection of grapes in France are grown. Preferred white wines are *Riesling, Tokay-Pinot Gris, Gewurztraminer, Muscat d'Alsace, Sylvaner, Pinot Blanc, Klevener, Edelzwicker,* and *Crémant d'Alsace.* Main red wines produced in the region are *Pinot Noir Rouge d'Ottrott* and *Rouge du Stephansberg.* Alsace is also one of the major beer-producing regions of France. Famous breweries in the proximity of Strasbourg produce superb *Kronenbourg Beer, Fischer Beer, Heineken Beer, Météor Beer, Kanterbräu Beer, Schutzenberger Beer,* and other beer varieties. Other traditional alcoholic drinks include a range of

eau-de-vie (fruit brandy). Made of local fruits and berries, such as plums, pears, and raspberries, it is sold in tall, slim bottles decorated with labels that look like parchment.

Gourmets in food in wine, Alsatians developed a wonderful tradition of pairing regional wines with ethnic dishes. Thus, *Winstubs,* the down-to-earth restaurant-bars offer their customers a perfect combination of a late-harvest *Gewürtztraminer* with *foie gras* (delicacies made of duck or goose liver) or a *Sylvaner* with escargots. Another favorite combination is a *Pinot Blanc* with onion tart or a *Riesling* with *choucroute.*

¹³ EDUCATION

Education in Alsace is similar to that in the other provinces in France. It is compulsory for children aged six to sixteen. Public education is free. However, in comparison to France, in Alsace there is no separation of church and state. Following the set of laws established by the Napoleonic Concordat of 1801, regional government provides subsidies to the Catholic, Lutheran, Calvinist, and Jewish public schools. There are of course secular schools so that parents are to able send their children to secular public school if they choose to. Additionally, there are some fee-based private schools that include religious schools and international schools. The absence of separation of church and state causes on-going debates between France and Alsace. Some people criticize Alsatian regional government for providing special privileges only to the designated religions. Others argue that since Islam is the second largest religion in France it should thus enjoy comparable status with the four official religions.

At present there are 103 secondary schools and 31 Apprenticeship Training Centers in Alsace. Moreover, Alsace has several strong universities, including the University of Strasburg. The University of Strasburg is known for its courses in theology and is particularly famous for its courses on Protestant theology. In addition to offering classic curricula, institutions of higher education are offering new courses in information and communication technologies.

Furthermore, these institutions provide excellent programs in business and business administration. Increasing number of universities form partnerships with local and international businesses. Such partnerships ensure that over the course of his or her studies student acquires relevant skills. It also allows universities provide recent graduates with placement immediately after graduation. Moreover, regional government encourages exchange programs and supports international mobility of the local students. Over the few past years the region allocated a significant amount of financial aid for international exchange programs.

¹⁴ CULTURAL HERITAGE

As it was mentioned numerous times throughout this article, Alsatian culture is greatly influenced by France, Germany, and other surrounding countries. As many other aspects of Alsatian culture, architecture of the region is a blend of various influences. Hence, it is not unusual to see a fine gothic cathedral in Strasburg and an excellent example of a Romanesque church, such as the Saint Foy de Sélestat in Sélestat. The houses of the little France district in Strasbourg and the little Venice in Colmar add to Alsatian architecture a touch of Renaissance. At the same time, the traditional half-timbered houses are still preserved in most of the Alsatian villages. The village of Riquewihr, referred to as the pearl of Alsace, is particularly known for this type of structure. Impressively, over 90% of the houses in this village date to the 16th century. Other types of the region's rural buildings reflect the many faces of Alsace's varied geographical and cultural identity. Perhaps it is the elegance with which Alsatians are able to blend these influences and mix them with their local traditions that makes this place unique.

Having been a disputed territory in the past, the region experienced lots of grief, but it also marked Alsace with a rich cultural heritage. The birthplace of numerous leading Alsatian celebrities, it is a land of art and culture. Internationally renowned artists from the region include Tomi (Jean-Tomas) Ungerer and Frédéric Auguste Bartholdi. Tomi Ungerer, born in 1931 in Strasburg, is best known for his erotic and political illustrations as well as illustrations for children's books. In 1998 he was awarded the Hans Christian Andersen Award for illustration. In 2007 his hometown dedicated a museum to him: the *Musée Tomi Ungerer*. Frédéric Auguste Bartholdi (1834-1904) is a legendary sculptor and architect from Colmar. His most famous work is the Statue of Liberty presented in 1886 to the United States.

Alsace has 250 museums. Mulhouse is a home for the largest rail museum of Europe called the Cité du Train, and its Museum of Automobiles presents its visitors with the largest automobile collection. *Musée du Jouet* in Colmar exhibits more than 2,000 toys. There are also several museums dedicated to various aspects of Alsatian traditional lifestyle, history, and its admirable gastronomy.

Moreover, Alsace boasts Europe's highest concentration of feudal castles that also bear witness to its turbulent history and display richness and diversity of architectural styles. The legendary Haut Koenigsbourg castle is one of France's most frequently visited monuments. Additionally, Alsace has more than 400 ruined castles. Other prominent cultural sites in Alsace include the 142 meters tall cathedral of Notre-Dame in Strasbourg (the second highest cathedral in France) and le Mont Sainte-Odile monastery ruins (a very popular place dedicated to the patron saint of Alsace) in the Vosges Mountains.

15 WORK

Alsace is primarily an urban area rated among the top three of the most urbanized regions in France. 93% of all Alsace inhabitants live in cities and only 7% of the population remains in the countryside. Major cities include the regional capital of Strasbourg with more than 263,941 residents, industrial city of Mulhouse with over 110,000 inhabitants and Colmar being home for over 65,000 people. Main rural areas are Fessenheim with a population slightly over 2,000 and Rhinau with a population of 2,300.

According to statistics, Alsace has a relatively young population. Approximately 69,000 are students. In 2007 8.6% (73,725 people) of the working population were unemployed. Yet, the standard of living is comparatively high with an average salary of 17,457 Euro per year. The greatest source of jobs in Alsace is the service sector with key branches of Commerce, Health, Administration, and Education. Employing more than 303,210 people, the service sector is now the principal driving force of the Alsace's economy. The industrial sector provides jobs for 151,243 people, or a third of the working population. Major industrial branches specialize in mechanical equipment,

textiles, electronics, and plastics. Companies specializing in biotechnology are blossoming. Among the leaders in biotechnology is the Peugeot PSA industrial site in Sausheim, producing over 400,000 vehicles per year. The construction sector employs more than 25,000 people. Nearly 63,100 Alsatians living in border areas commute for their work to Switzerland and Germany.

Only 7,187 people are employed in agriculture. At the same time Alsatian rural lands covers 40% of the territory. Furthermore, Agriculture is a sector essential to the regional economy. Consequently, people employed in the agriculture enjoy favorable conditions and subsidies.

16 SPORTS

In Alsace, sports bring together tens of thousands of people. Soccer and handball are among the most favorite sports. Professional and semi-professional sports in Alsace include basketball, handball, football, ice hockey, volleyball, and badminton teams. Also, people in Alsace enjoy a great variety of outdoor sports. For example the region is known for its ski resorts. Among the best resorts are the Lac Blanc (white lake), Gérardmer, Markstein, le Bresse and Schnepfenried, Champ du Feu and Grand Ballon located at an altitude of 1424 meters. In the summer many local families, as well as tourists, enjoy hiking. Popular water sports include canoeing, kayaking, and rafting.

Multiple sports clubs are supported by the local government. In fact the number of sports and health clubs is growing, thus contributing to the diversity of athletic activities. To encourage a high level of local sportsmanship, the government provides hundreds of the most talented athletes with generous grants. This support has bought Alsace quite a few champions.

Among such champions is Thierry Omeyer. A handball player, Thierry Omeyer was crowned in the European Championship of 2006 as the best goalkeeper of the tournament. He also won three Men's World Handball Championships (two in 2003 and one in 2007). Other famous Alsatian athletes are Sébastien Loeb, four-time World Rally Champion, and Mehdi Baala, a middle-distance athlete competing mainly at 1500 meters. Baala won two European Championships (2002, 2006), a World Championship (2003), and a European Cup (2008). Paul-Henri Mathieu from Strasbourg is a renowned tennis player and a member of French national tennis team. Arsène Wenger, the most successful manager in the history of French Arsenal Football Club in terms of trophies, is also a native of Alsace. Among Alsatian champion swimmers are Nicolas Rostoucher, Amaury Leveaux, and Aurore Mongel.

17 ENTERTAINMENT AND RECREATION

In addition to museums, castles, great food and wine, teahouses, pottery workshops, and numerous festivals and parades, Alsace is known for its *rue de vin,* or wine rout. This wine trail has existed in Alsace for centuries, producing one of the most sophisticated Rieslings, Sylvaners and Pinot Auxerrois. Towns and villages along the wine rout are surrounded with picturesque gardens full of flowers. Many villages compete with one another in flower contests for best flower display. Welcoming signs to those places often designate whether a given village is one of the eight most beautiful villages in Alsace. The signs also show villages' flower rating (with four stars indicating a top rating).

18 FOLK ART, CRAFTS, AND HOBBIES

Traditional art pottery and artistic furniture have been produced in Alsace for centuries. This crafts-making was originally influenced by France and Germany, but over the time Alsatian craftsmen developed their unique styles and techniques. The tradition of pottery making in Alsace goes back as far as the Middle Ages. It blossomed until in the middle of the 19th century it was trammeled by the onset of industrialization. However, traditional pottery-making never disappeared completely, remaining a cherished aspect of the Alsatian culture.

At present, Soufflenheim and Betschdorf are two acclaimed centers for pottery making. Soufflenheim earthenware could be easily recognized for its colorful designs in the shades of yellow, blue, green, and brown. It is often adorned with illustrations depicting Alsatian folk dressed in traditional clothing, elegant birds and delicate flowers. Betschdorf pottery is of a more simple design. Manufactured from grey clay, it is decorated with cobalt blue. It is particularly known for its grey and blue tones. In fact, Betschdorf's pottery is designed more for storage while Soufflenheim's are especially suited for cooking. Although today traditional pottery is made primarily for the tourists, craftsmen did preserve their skills and techniques and styles. Very little in traditional pottery-making process has changed since 1717. Many potters' workshops are open for visitors, so that people can observe how the pottery is made. Both Betschdorf and Soufflenheim hold special pottery festivals in September to celebrate the wonderful craftsmanship of the area.

Alsace also has a rich tradition of painted furniture making. While this tradition does not originate from Alsace, it has become an integral part of the local crafts production since the Middle Ages. Alsatian craftsman-made furniture includes chairs, closets, four-poster beds, cabinets, and other articles. The furniture either painted in one color, usually a deep red or a color imitating wood or is decorated with various patterns. The decorative schemes range from elaborate floral designs common in the Kochersberg to geometric motifs prominent in Alsace Bossue to stylized roses, animals, and figures used in the south of Strasbourg. Original pieces of Alsatian painted furniture are highly sought after and considered to be invaluable items for collectors of artistic furniture.

Additionally, there is a longstanding tradition of illustrated folklore. Modern artists such as Pat Thiebaut produce various illustrations of Alsace continuing the tradition. Folkloristic images often depict bucolic scenes of rosy-cheeked children in their colorful folk costumes. Other patterns include portrayals of the Alsatian way of life. These folkloric illustrations depict men and women, boys and girls dressed in Alsatian costumes dancing in the village square, picking fruit, herding geese or strolling in the verdant countryside with an Alsatian village of half-timbered houses in the background.

19 SOCIAL PROBLEMS

Alsace is one of the most stable and prosperous regions if France. It has relatively low unemployment and a low crime rate. The population growth is an impressive 6.8% per year. The regional government provides a reasonable safety net of benefits to Alsatian citizens and offers favorable conditions and employment opportunities to foreigners. In sum, it seems on the surface that people in Alsace do not really have glaring social problems.

In reality, however, there are several serious social issues within the region. For one, Alsatians are engaged in a constant struggle to create their unique political and cultural niche in the realm of a centralized French state. Having preserved their unique identity through centuries of violence, it is very important to the Alsatian community to stay true to the essence of their culture. Two major aspects of Alsatian identity include the local language and the regional set of laws concerning hunting, social insurance, public holidays, the church, and the retirement system. There is considerable discrepancy between regional and national laws and Alsace is constantly asked to re-think their regional legislature. This naturally triggers negative feelings and anxiety on the part of Alsatians. Dissemination of French media and its impact on regional language is another issue that challenges the Alsatian social scene. The Alsatian language is being displaced in the public sphere by the dominance of the French language. To deal with these problems, the Alsatian regional government is attempting to welcome international business and to become closely engaged with the supranational institutions of the European Union. Whether this approach will help Alsatians to preserve their identity and their language and establish their place of power in the French political and cultural arena remains to be seen.

20 GENDER ISSUES

In modern Alsatian society, men and women have almost equal opportunities. Women are distancing themselves from the traditional gender roles by pursuing higher education and careers. It has become normal for a woman to combine motherhood with work. Consequently, approximately 80% of the Alsatian women in their thirties are employed and many of them are raising young children. To support women in their educational and professional pursuits, the French national government provides French mothers with generous benefits. In fact, France has one of the most generous childcare systems in Europe. This is one of the factors contributing to the impressive growth rate of the Alsatian population.

Furthermore, in comparison to men a higher percentage of women have degrees from institutions of higher education. Many women are employed in businesses and a significant number of women hold powerful positions in the local government. One of the initial forces that brought women into politics was the Women of Alsace movement in the 1960s. It was during this time that the first two women were elected mayors in Alsace.

In addition to striving for gender equality, Alsatian society is open-minded about gender minority issues. A number of recourses are available for members of the gay, lesbian, bisexual, and transgender community (GLBT or LGBT).

The open-minded and progressive Alsatian society has not eradicated gender inequality completely. Women occupy important leadership positions, but there is still a gender-based wage differential. According to the National Statistics Institute report, the average annual net salary of men in 2006 amounted to €20,195 while average annual net salary of women was only €14,320. Alsatian women's gross average hourly wage is also significantly lower than that of men's. The wage issue along increasingly dominates local and national political agenda. In light of the debates, the French national government passed proactive legislation to combat gender-based discrimination.

21 BIBLIOGRAPHY

Byrnes, Joseph F. *The Relationship of Religious Practice to Linguistic Culture: Language, Religion, and Education in Alsace and the Roussillon, 1860-1890*. Church History, Vol. 68. 1999.

Comité Régional du Tourisme d'Alsace. http://www.tourisme-alsace.com/en/culture-heritage-alsace/ (June 5, 2008).

Ferrari, Gustave. *Ten Folk-Songs of Alsace, Lorraine and Champagne Harmonized by Gustave Ferrari*. English translations by Deems Taylor. New York: G. Schirmer, 1919.

Kahn, Bonnie M. My *Father Spoke French: Nationalism and Legitimacy in Alsace, 1871-1914*. New York : Garland Publishers. 1990.

Koch, Susan. *Toward a Europe of Regions: Transnational Political Activities in Alsace*. Publius, Vol. 4, No. 3 (Summer 1974). New York: Oxford University Press. pp. 25-41.

Morgan, Heather. "Vins d'Alsace." *NationalGeographic.com*. http://www.nationalgeographic.com/traveler/archive/2000-07-4-0.html (June 27, 2008).

Région Alsace. http://www.region-alsace.eu/dn_education-and-training/education-and-training-05042007-142208.html (June 1, 2008).

Ungerer, Tomi. *Tomi: a Childhood under the Nazis*. Publishers Group West, 1998.

—by A. Golovina Khadka

ALTAYS

LOCATION: Altai Republic in Russia (the Altay Mountains of South Siberia)
POPULATION: 68,000 (2002)
LANGUAGE: Turkic Dialects; Russian
RELIGION: Russian Orthodox Christianity, Native Altay religion

1 INTRODUCTION

Altay (also spelled Altai) is a term used to refer to a number of Turkic ethnic groups in the Russian Federation inhabiting the Altay district (*krai*) located in South Siberia. The Altays are in fact divided into two major divisions, the Northern Altays, comprising the Tubalars, Chelkans, and Kumandins, and the Southern Altays, comprising the Altay proper, or Altay-Kizhi, the Telengits, Telesy, and Teleuts. The Northern and Southern Altays differ considerably in language, history, and material culture. Historically, the Southern Altays were frequently misnamed White Kalmyks, Biy Kalmyks, or Mountain Kalmyks, and the Northern Altays were called "Tatars." Many ethnographers and historians consider the Altays' South Siberian homeland to have been the original homeland of the Turkic peoples in general. Furthermore, the Altays are of special interest to historians, ethnographers, and linguists because of their preservation of very archaic cultural traits.

The Altays are descendants of numerous Turkic as well as Samoyedic and Ketic peoples who lived in the Altay Mountains. The Turkicization of these communities was an ongoing ethnic process completed by the end of the 18th century. The ancestors of the Altays were varyingly subjects and constituent elements in the powerful Inner Asian states that emerged in the Altay and Sayan Mountain regions of South Siberia and came to dominate the steppes of eastern Inner Asia. This area came under Mongol control in the early 13th century, and the Altay region appears to have been a borderland between the lands of the Ulus of Jochi and the Ulus of Tului. As a result, the lands of the Southern Altays became the easternmost territory of the Blue Horde, centered on the lower Syr Darya River in Central Asia, and the lands of the Northern Altays became the northwestern border of the Mongol successor states in Mongolia. In the 15th century, the Altays came under the control of the Junghars, a powerful Western Mongolian confederation, and remained under their control until the annihilation of the Junghars by the Manchus in 1756. It was in that year that the Northern and Southern Altay tribal leaders petitioned to the Russian authorities to put themselves under Russian rule, and since 1756 the Altays have been subjects of Russia.

2 LOCATION AND HOMELAND

Numbering only around 68,000, the Altays are a small ethnic minority in Russia; however, by Siberian standards they constitute a relatively large group. The homeland of the Altays is the Altay Mountains of South Siberia in Russia. Most of the Altay population is located within the Altay Republic, which contains within it the so-called Altay Highland Autonomous District (*Gorno-Altaiskii avtonomnyi krai*). Although Altays constitute less than 2% of the population of the Altay District (Russians make up the vast majority of the district's popula-

ALTAYS

0 500 1000 Miles

0 500 1000 Kilometers

are closely related to Kazakh and Kyrgyz. The Northern Altays, on the other hand, speak dialects of the Northeast branch, which are related to Khakass, Tuvan, and more distantly, Yakut. Among both Northern and Southern Altays, Russian is also widely spoken, and substantial numbers of Altays have been linguistically assimilated by the Russians.

Altays typically have a first name, a patronymic (taken from the father's first name), and a surname. To a large degree Altays have preserved old Turkic names such as the men's names *Karga* and *Malchi,* and the women's names *Aylu* and *Sarï*. Since the Christianization of numerous Altay communities in the 19th century, Russian names have become more widespread, although it is common for Russian names to be "Altayized": *Temekey* (from *Timofei*) and *Banush* (from *Vaniusha*).

⁴ FOLKLORE

The Altays have rich folklore traditions, consisting of various songs, stories, and fairy tales. The Altays are especially well known for their composition and performance of oral epic poetry. The best known of these epics is entitled *Maaday-Kara*. Epics are typically performed at night, with a bard singing the verses in a style of throat-singing and accompanied by a horse-hair-stringed instrument called a *topshur*. The epic tradition of the Altays (and South Siberian Turks in general) is one of the richest in the world, and Altay epics continue to be collected by folklorists today.

The Northern and Southern Altays possess distinct epic traditions shaped by the peculiarities of each group's historical development. The Southern Altays, who were under the rule of the Golden Horde, retained epics such as *Alïp Manash* and *Idegey*, which depicted 15th century political events on the Central Asian steppes and in the Volga Valley. The Northern Altays, on the other hand, retained an epic tradition more similar to that of their South Siberian neighbors, the Khakass, Tuvans, and Yakuts.

⁵ RELIGION

Despite the conversion of numerous Altay communities by Russian missionaries in the 19th century, the Altays, both Christians and non-Christians, have remained firm adherents to their native religious traditions, which persisted even during the Soviet period, when manifestations of religious life were discouraged or suppressed. The resistance of the Altays to adopting Christianity, Islam, and Buddhism (all three of which are represented in Southern and Western Siberia) has resulted in the retention of very archaic religious traditions since abandoned by most other Turkic peoples. In the traditional Altay world view, the Universe was divided into three levels (the Upper World, the Middle World, and the Underworld) linked by the World Tree *(Bay Terek)*. Altays considered themselves inhabitants of the Middle World, and the community's link to the Upper and Lower Worlds was the shaman *(qam)*. Shamans functioned as healers and played other roles in Altay religious ritual. They also functioned as heroic figures, with shamanic journeys serving as the plots for epic poetry and other forms of folklore. In their performances, during which their souls would travel to the spirit worlds, shamans would typically wear a specific costume and accompany their performance with a drum. In the early 20th century a millenarian religious movement emerged among the Altays and other Turkic peoples of the region known as Burkhanism, which existed into the 1930's.

tion) they constitute a much larger proportion of the population of the Altay Highland District. The Altay District shares borders with Kazakhstan to the southwest and Mongolia to the south. Overall Altays constitute about a third of the population of the Altay Republic.

The Highland District has an area of 96,600 sq km (37,300 sq mi), and the district's mountains can reach over 13,000 ft (3,900 m). The mean temperature in January is between –30°C (–22°F) and –15°C (2°F), and in July the mean temperature is 15°C (62°F). Roughly 25% of the territory of the Highland District is covered by evergreen forests.

The traditional economy of the Altays was nomadic stock breeding, supplemented by limited cereal agriculture. A steady loss of pasture land to Russian colonization beginning in the early 19th century has resulted in a gradual increase in the role of agriculture in the Altays' economic life. Nevertheless, stock breeding has always held a very important position in Altay life, especially among the Southern Altays.

The Altay Mountains are very rich in wildlife, especially deer and squirrel, and the Altays have traditionally exploited the area's extensive forests. The hunting and gathering of forest products, especially furs, continues to be an important supplementary activity in Altay economic life.

³ LANGUAGE

The Altays speak a number of Turkic dialects that are to varying degrees mutually intelligible. The Southern Altays speak dialects of the Kipchak (or Northwest) branch of Turkic, which

⁶ MAJOR HOLIDAYS

The various communities forming the Altays and their constituent clans had a series of festivals that featured sacrifices and libations to the spirits of the Upper World and the Underworld, as well as to ancestral spirits and tutelary spirits. Such festivals were held at specific times according to the seasonal calendar and often involved the sacrifice of horses to *Erlik*, the spirit of the Underworld, and to *Ülgen*, the supreme deity of the Upper World. Modern-day Altays also celebrate the major Soviet and Russian holidays, including Victory Day (May 9) and New Year's Day (January 1).

⁷ RITES OF PASSAGE

Traditionally, when an Altay woman was giving birth, all men had to leave the *yurt* (tent) and stand outside. During childbirth, men were expected to frighten away evil spirits by making noises and running around the yurt. After the child was born, the head of the family would name the child after the first thing he laid his eyes on.

Young Altay men usually chose their own brides, and a young man's father or a formal matchmaker would go to the bride's father to arrange the match. Once the bride's dowry (*kalïm*) was agreed on, a wedding date would be fixed then both parties would sit around the fire and begin to feast.

Altays were commonly buried with grave goods, and it was common for wealthy Altays to be buried with one of their horses. The dead were buried in varying ways, commonly on the third day after death. The Telengits commonly placed the body on the ground and built a wooden structure over it in the shape of a small house. Other Altay groups placed the dead on platforms that were suspended in trees. In more recent times, especially during the Soviet era, the dead were simply placed in graves. A series of memorial feasts was usually held after the death of a family member. The first memorial feast was held on the day of the death, and a sheep or goat was slaughtered. Other memorial feasts were held on the sixth, seventh, or ninth days.

⁸ INTERPERSONAL RELATIONS

The traditional greeting ceremony among the Southern Altays was as follows. When a guest arrived at the yurt of an Altay, it was customary for him to come in and, without saying a word to the yurt's owner, take out his pipe, fill it, and light it from the hearth fire. The host would then do the same, and the two would exchange pipes saying "*nä tabïsh bar?*" ("What news is there?"). They would then answer "*Tabïsh yok*" or "*Tabïsh yoghïla*" ("There is no news"). They would then inquire about each other's health. If there was more than one visitor, the host would greet each one in the same way, in order of rank. Such exchanges generally took place only between men; women usually stayed home or remained silent during the ceremony. Altays are generally reported to have been quiet, polite, and reserved with one another, and observers of traditional Altay society have identified respect for elders as a feature that distinguishes them from their neighbors. Despite the rigid divisions between the sexes, men and women would freely interact with one another, and it was common for young people to arrange their own marriages.

⁹ LIVING CONDITIONS

Observers of the traditional life of the Altays have frequently commented on the general state of poverty of this group. The decimation of herds as the result of pestilence or sudden changes in weather frequently led to famine and the impoverishment of whole communities. The integration of the Altays into the Soviet economy probably did not completely liberate them from the economic risks of stock breeding in this remote area.

The traditional housing of the Altays is the yurt, the round felt tent common to most Inner Asian pastoral nomads. Among the Northern Altays, cone-shaped summer dwellings made from felt and tree branches were also common. More sedentarized Altays also constructed log houses similar to those of the Russian peasants who had migrated to the Altay Mountains. During the years of Soviet rule, the Altays were encouraged to move into Russian-style dwellings on collective farms. However, traditional dwellings continue to be used, especially when the Altay herders lead their herds to summer pastures.

While the relative isolation of the Altays has certainly preserved the archaic features of their culture, it has at the same time resulted in a relatively low standard of living.

¹⁰ FAMILY LIFE

In traditional Altay society, sex roles were very clearly distinguished. Men were primarily engaged in stock breeding and hunting, while women performed agricultural work, including haying, as well as domestic chores. Child-rearing was also the responsibility of women. Most accounts of traditional Altay society describe respectful and almost formal relations between spouses, especially in the presence of a third party. An Altay man was responsible for the welfare not only of his wife and children, but also for any unmarried female relatives. When a man's father died, the man would not only receive his father's property, but also any unmarried female relatives living in his father's house. Married daughters were considered to have left the family and were not eligible to inherit property from their kinsmen.

Marriage among the Altays was generally monogamous, and marriages could be arranged either between the parents or between bride and groom. A bride would typically bring a dowry (*qalïm*) provided by her parents.

The various groups making up the Northern and Southern Altays were themselves divided into clans (*seok*). Clans were not merely collections of related groups. The economic life of Altay society, especially among the Northern Altays, was closely structured along clan lines. Hunting grounds and pastures were divided up along clan lines, and members of one clan were banned from the lands of another.

¹¹ CLOTHING

Traditional Altay clothing, generally the same for men and women, consisted of pants and a long shirt that went down below the knee. Over this they wore a long belted robe with wide sleeves. This clothing was often made of Chinese materials. Overcoats were typically made of sheepskin and hats of lambskin with a wide upturned brim of fox or sable fur. Married women also wore a special sort of sleeveless overcoat. Altays wore soft-soled leather boots, into which they tucked their pants. Some northern Altay groups also wove fabric for shirts and pants from hemp.

Ivan Kobzorenko carries his last surviving hen in Gonukhovo village in the Altai region of the Russian Federation. The bird flu had been confirmed in 36 populated areas in Russia in 2005. (© Andrey Kasprishn/epa/Corbis)

Over the course of the 20th century, Russian clothing became more common among the Altays. Throughout the Soviet period, however, traditional clothing, which was quite practical for the harsh climatic conditions and the demands of stock breeding, was still frequently worn.

12 FOOD

The mainstay of the Altay diet was traditionally the products of their herds—meat and dairy products. Altays prepared various products from milk, including a yogurt-like drink called *ayran*. They also distilled a mildly alcoholic drink of fermented mare's milk called *chegän*. In addition, various sorts of hard cheeses were prepared. The main animals eaten for meat by the Altays were horses, followed by sheep and goats.

The Southern Altays supplemented this diet of meat and dairy products with some cereal crops, primarily barley, which was grown in lowland areas. In areas where Altays practiced agriculture and came into contact with Russian peasants, they also engaged in the growing of vegetables and the baking of bread. The Northern Altays supplemented their diets with a variety of forest products, such as berries and roots, as well

as fish. All Altay groups consumed substantial amounts of tea and tobacco as well.

13 EDUCATION

No formal educational apparatus existed for the Altays until the establishment of an Altay Christian Mission in 1868, when efforts were made to create an Altay alphabet and teach Altay converts literacy in translated Altay biblical texts and in Russian. The children of Altay converts could also be sent to Russian Orthodox monasteries. However, the vast majority of Altays had no access to formal education in any language.

With the establishment of Soviet power in the Altay lands, attempts were made to create an Altay literary language, as well as a Soviet-style intelligentsia. The Soviets created mixed Russian-Altay schools, and the current educational system in the Altay region is essentially an adaptation of the system created during the Soviet period. There are a number of higher educational institutions in the Altay region, and a few Altays also study in larger institutions in Moscow, St. Petersburg, and elsewhere.

14 CULTURAL HERITAGE

One of the most treasured aspects of the Altay cultural heritage is the recording and publication of the Altay oral epics, which are of tremendous value not only for our understanding of the Altays, but of Turkic and Inner Asian peoples in general.

The preservation of Altay cultural heritage is closely linked to the preservation of Altay religious traditions. Despite their partial conversion to Christianity in the 19th century, there is currently a renewal of interest among the Altays in their shamanic traditions, which they have been free to express since the collapse of the Soviet Union.

The Altay musical tradition is similarly rich and also linked to the epic and shamanic traditions. In addition to epics performed in the style of throat-singing, Altay musical folklore includes genres of a religious nature such as libation and shamanic songs. Despite the prominence of Altay vocal music, especially throat-singing, Altays also had several popular musical instruments. These include horse-hair fiddles, stringed lute-like instruments, and a sort of a metallic Jew's-harp called a *kobïs*.

15 WORK

Much of Altay life consisted of tending and milking the herds, making felt, and doing agricultural work such as planting and harvesting barley and mowing and gathering hay. Observers of traditional Altay life often comment on the tediousness and monotony of all the agricultural work and chores such as the milking of livestock and the making of dairy products such as cheese, yogurt, and butter.

Altays have continued to work in collective farms created during the Soviet era. The prosperity of collective farms varies considerably from farm to farm, depending on the resources allotted to the collective as well as the efficiency and organization of the collective farm's president and workers.

16 SPORTS

Like other Turkic peoples, the Altays enjoy horse racing, archery, and wrestling. The wrestling is a type influenced by the Mongol style in which two competitors square off standing, grab each other by the shoulders, and try to force one another to the ground.

[17] ENTERTAINMENT AND RECREATION

The performance of oral epics, which typically took place during winter nights and were accompanied by music, not only entertained but instructed the Altays in the values, history, and mythology of their community. Religious ceremonies, with their feasting and songs, likewise had a recreational element to them. Summers were the time of most abundant leisure for the Altays, especially Altay men, whose main recreational activities were drinking fermented mare's milk and hunting.

[18] FOLK ART, CRAFTS, AND HOBBIES

The Altays were known as especially skilled blacksmiths. Altays believed blacksmiths to be vested with religious power. Another important medium of Altay folk art is wood, and many objects intended for everyday use were often carved with elaborate designs. Religious images of ancestral and other spirits were often made of wood, cloth, and animal hair, or combinations thereof. The most elaborate creations of Altay folk art were shamans' drums and other elements of the shamanic costume.

[19] SOCIAL PROBLEMS

As with many other small, formerly nomadic groups in Siberia, the Altays have experienced numerous social problems as a result of their marginalization in Soviet, and now Russian, society. The Altays have always been plagued by poverty, which, despite Soviet claims, was not only not successfully alleviated, but may actually have been exacerbated during the Soviet era. The assaults of tsarist missionaries and Soviets on the most fundamental pillars of Altay society—particularly shamanism, religious rituals, and the clan-based social structure by which scarce resources were allocated—severely undermined Altay society. Furthermore, the introduction of cheap grain alcohol such as vodka further exacerbated Altay social problems.

[20] GENDER ISSUES

In traditional Altay society the nomadic economy and dispersion of Altays into small social units limited social segregation of the sexes. At the same time a clear division of labor was evident in nomadic Altay society, with women focusing on childrearing, food preparation, and textile production.

During the Soviet era, particularly during and after World War II, Altay women began to gain access to Soviet education, and began to enter to some degree the industrial, and to a much more limited degree, the professional workforce.

[21] BIBLIOGRAPHY

Alekseev, N. A. *Shamanizm Tiurkoiazychnykh Narodov Sibiri.* Novosibirsk, Russia: 1984.

Butanaev, V. Ia. *Burkhanizm tiurkov Saiano-Altaia.* Gorno-Altaisk, 1994.

Diószegi, Vilmos. "Libation Songs of the Altaic Turks." *Acta Etnographica Academiae Scientiarum Hungaricae* 19 (1970): 95–106.

Forsyth, James. *A History of the Peoples of Siberia: Russia's North Asian Colony, 1581–1990.* Cambridge: Cambridge University Press, 1994.

Ivanov, S. V. *Skul'ptura Altaitsev, Khakasov, i Sibirskikh Tatar.* Leningrad, 1978.

Krader, Lawrence. "A Nativistic Movement in Western Siberia." *American Anthropologist* (N.S.) 58 (1956): 282–291.

Potapov, L. P. "The Origins of the Altayans." *Studies in Siberian Ethnogenesis.* Toronto: 1962.

———. "The Altays." *The Peoples of Siberia.* Chicago: University of Chicago Press, 1964.

Radlov, V. V. *Iz Sibiri.* Moscow, 1989. (Translation of *Aus Sibirien I-II.* Leipzig, 1893).

Toshchakova, M. *Traditsionnye Cherty Narodnoi Kul'tury Altaitsev (XIX - nachalo XX v.).* Novosibirsk, Russia: 1978.

—by A. J. Frank

ANDALUSIANS

LOCATION: Spain
POPULATION: 8.059.431 (2007)
LANGUAGE: Castilian Spanish
RELIGION: Roman Catholic

1 INTRODUCTION

Andalusia, located in southern Spain, has a distinctive culture influenced by its Mediterranean climate and its historical tolerance of diverse ethnic groups. Tartessos, home of the once powerful Tartessian civilization, was founded in Andalusia. Its coastal area was colonized by the Phoenicians during the latter part of the 2nd millennium BC. With the fall of the Phoenicians, Carthage became the dominant sea power of the western Mediterranean. The Romans conquered Andalusia and renamed it Baetica. In the 5th century AD, it was invaded by the Vandals and then by the Visigoths.

The Moors (Muslims who invaded from North Africa and seized control of the region in the 8th century AD) ruled all of Spain for three centuries and Andalusia until 1492. This period was a time of both cultural and economic wealth for the region, which reaped the benefits of Islamic advances in philosophy, medicine, the arts, and other fields, as well as the religious tolerance practiced under Islamic rule. Córdoba had a prestigious university and became the largest and richest city in Western Europe, and one of the largest in the world. In addition, the Moors brought to the region sophisticated irrigation and cultivation techniques, building aqueducts and waterwheels throughout Andalusia and neighboring Valencia and making the land bloom. The word "Andalusia" is derived from the Arabic name for Spain: Al-Andalus.

When Christian forces based in Castile finally drove the Moors out of Granada in 1492, their religion (as well as that of the Jews) was suppressed, and the rich cultural life that had flourished in Andalusia was largely destroyed. Much of the region's wealth was confiscated, and a long period of economic decline began. The conquering Castilians—warriors rather than farmers—let the extensive irrigation systems of the Moors deteriorate, turning the fertile farms into pastureland. The *latifundio,* or large landed estates, became a way of life; large portions of land were placed under the control of absentee landlords, leaving Andalusia one of Spain's poorest regions. However, since Spain's entry into the European Community in 1986, Andalusia has seen economic progress. Since 1985, Andalusia is an autonomous community administered through the Junta de Andalusia, it has a local parliament and president. It is one of the four historic regions of Spain.

2 LOCATION AND HOMELAND

Andalusia is located in the southernmost part of the Iberian Peninsula between the Sierra Morena Mountains and the Mediterranean Sea. It is bound by Portugal to the west, the Spanish provinces of Extremadura, Castile-La-Mancha, and Murcia to the north, the Mediterranean to the southeast, and the Gulf of Cádiz to the southwest. The largest region in Spain, Andalusia includes the provinces of Huelva, Seville, Cádiz, Córdoba, Málaga, Jaén, Granada, and Almería. It is a land of contrasts, containing Spain's highest mountains (the Sierra Nevada chain that rises to heights of over 3,350 m (11,000 ft), its hottest lowlands (the Andalusian Plains), the white beaches of the Costa del Sol, and the Las Marismas marshes, home of the Coto de Doñana National Park. Andalusia is crossed by the Guadalquivir River, known as the "father" of old civilizations. Seville, located 64 km (40 mi) inland on the river, is Spain's most important western port.

Andalusia is the Spanish autonomous community with the greatest number of inhabitants and the second-largest in surface. Among its cities, Seville is the third largest in Spain, with a population of approximately 1,813,908 inhabitants.

3 LANGUAGE

According to the 1978 constitution, Castilian Spanish, the language of the central and southern parts of the country, is the national language. It is spoken by a majority of Spaniards and used in the schools and courts.

4 FOLKLORE

Flamenco is a Spanish style of music and dance that originated in Andalusia by the end of the 18th century. It was developed mainly by the gypsies, although it has several elements that reveal possible Roman, Arabic, Jewish, African, and American substrata. It is expressed by song (*cante*), guitar music, clapping of the hands (*palmas*), and dancing. The greatest performers are said to be distinguished by a type of inspiration that goes beyond artistic technique called *duende,* a mysterious and charming power that cannot be defined.

The name *cante jondo* expresses its deep feeling, and the 20th century Spanish composer, Manuel de Falla, considered it to be the old traditional song, while the *cante flamenco* embodied modern tendencies. Flamenco singing is divided into *cante grande* (with mainly gypsy influence) and *cante chico* (with folkloric and popular roots).

Flamenco music offers a great diversity of songs, with more than 60 different kinds of palos, or traditional varieties of *cante flamenco.* Among the best known are the soleá, seguiriya, peteneras, fandango, tango, and tanguillo. The most popular performers include Lola Flores, Manolo Caracol, Camarón de la Isla, and guitar player Paco de Lucia.

5 RELIGION

Like people in the other regions of Spain, the Andalusians are overwhelmingly Catholic. The Catholicism of Andalusia has a strong element of belief in the miraculous, and some scholars believe it is possible to trace the region's devotion to the Virgin Mary to the mother goddesses of pre-Christian religions. They are particularly known for the colorful Holy Week (*Semana Santa*) celebrations held in their cities and towns.

6 MAJOR HOLIDAYS

Andalusians celebrate the major holidays of the Christian calendar and Spain's other national holidays, including New Year's Day, Epiphany, St. Joseph's Day (March 19), the Day of St. Peter and St. Paul (June 29), St. James's Day (July 25), and Andalusia Day, on February 28, to commemorate the date of the successful referendum vote on autonomy. The most famous celebration is Seville's *Semana Santa,* or Holy Week, celebration, which begins on Palm Sunday and ends on Easter Saturday. Although each Andalusian city and town has its own religious processions, the most beautiful and spectacular take place in Seville. Each day up to 11 processions of *pasos* (floats)—some lasting as long as 12 hours—pass through the town, organized by members of religious brotherhoods called *cofradías*. The night-time processions by candlelight, accompanied by special march music, are especially beautiful.

Andalusia is noted for festivals and celebrations of many kinds that take place in the region throughout the year. Carnival celebrations are especially famous in Cádiz, with street parades, fancy dress, and satirical music competitions. Seville is noted for its famous *feria,* held at the end of April. It is held on fairgrounds containing booths called *casetas.* Seville's feria lasts an entire week, during which the town is on holiday and almost all normal business shuts down. Other festivities are Jerez's Horse Fair in May; Huelva's Romería del Rocío, when horse drawn carriages and processions converge from all the south on el Rocío; Saint John's night and its bonfires; Corpus Christi; the Virgen del Carmen processions in the coastal cities and fishing villages; and many other festivities and celebrations.

7 RITES OF PASSAGE

Baptism, first Communion, and marriage could be considered rites of passage for Andalusians, like most Roman Catholic Spaniards. These events are the occasion, in most cases, for big and expensive social gatherings in which the family shows its generosity and economic status. At times, families dig into their savings or borrow money in order to pay for such displays.

8 INTERPERSONAL RELATIONS

In the cities, office hours begin at 9:00 AM and traditionally include an extended afternoon lunch break beginning at 2:00 PM. Workers then return to their offices from 4:00 to 7:00 PM. The day typically ends with a walk with friends or family or visits to neighborhood bars for a few drinks, *tapas* (appetizers), and conversation. Dinner is often eaten as late as 10:30 PM. It is customary to shake hands, and in a social setting women usually kiss their friends on both cheeks. Young groups are formed by co-workers, fellow students, or people from the same town to go together to discos, organize parties and excursions, and date among themselves. It is not unusual to have lifelong friends known since kindergarten.

9 LIVING CONDITIONS

Reflecting the Andalusians' Moorish heritage, houses in the region have traditionally been built of stucco with thick walls and few windows to protect residents from the heat of the sun, although Andalusia's older houses may also be built of stone. Windows overlook patios filled with potted plants, and the house is often built around a shady central courtyard, sometimes including a fountain, in which the family can relax and cool off. Houses in Seville often have intricately carved wrought iron gates over their doors and windows.

Spain enjoys an excellent system of National Health Insurance, and the Andalusians have access to the same level of modern medical care as their neighbors elsewhere in a country with an average life expectancy of 78 years. Rail service connects the region's major cities to each other and to Madrid, including the AVE, Spain's newest rapid train, which was created for the World's Fair in Seville in 1992. Elsewhere in the area,

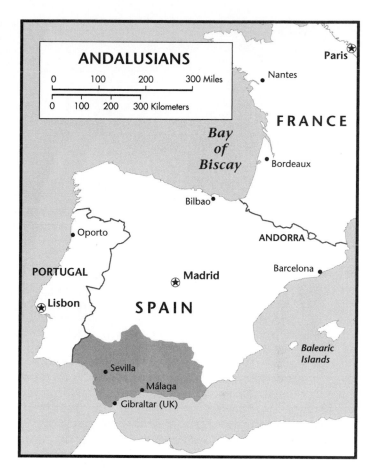

buses are the most efficient means of transport, with links between most Andalusian villages and towns and the rest of the country. Several airports connect Andalusia with other parts of the world.

10 FAMILY LIFE

Most Andalusian households consist of nuclear families (parents and children only), although they do sometimes include one or more grandparents. Male participation in the domestic sphere is limited, and women have almost exclusive responsibility for childrearing, with the father maintaining a more distant and formal role. Because of unemployment and other causes, it is customary for many young adults between the ages of 20 and 30 to continue living with their parents.

11 CLOTHING

For everyday activities, both casual and formal, Andalusians wear modern Western-style clothing similar to that worn elsewhere in Western Europe and in the United States, Boutiques and ready-to-wear shops can be found all over. Although young people wear sports clothes and blue jeans, the average Andalusian pays more attention to personal appearance. Businessmen wear a suit and tie, businesswomen dress fashionably in suits or dresses and high heels. However, traditional costumes can be seen at the region's many festivals and in flamenco dance performances. Women's attire consists of solid-colored or polka-dot dresses with tightly fitted bodices and flounced skirts and sleeves worn with mantilla shawls, long earrings, and hair

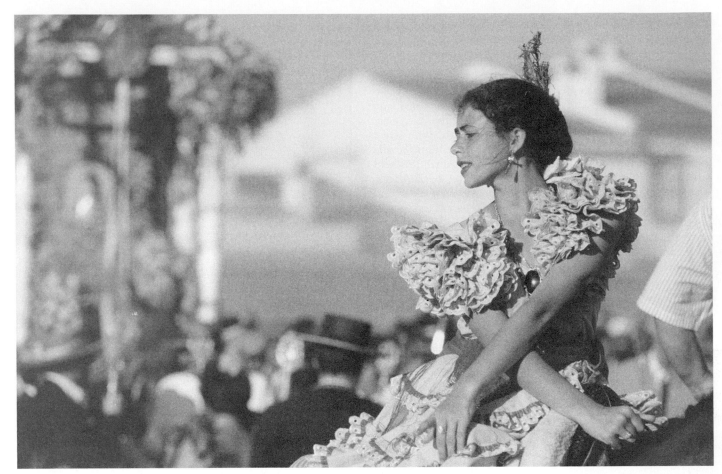

A young woman in traditional Andalusian dress during Pentecost Festival, El Rocio, Spain. (© Pawel Wysocki/Hemis/Corbis)

ornaments, such as combs or flowers. Male flamenco dancers wear white shirts with black suits and broad-brimmed black hats.

¹² FOOD

Typical Andalusian dishes include gazpacho, pescaíto frito (fried fish), several kinds of shellfish, jamón (cured ham), and prepared olives. Gazpacho is a cold soup made with tomatoes, peppers, cucumbers, and olive oil that has become common fare in Spain. While today gazpacho is usually prepared using a blender, the ingredients were traditionally pounded by hand in a special bowl called a *dornillo*. *Pescaíto frito* fried in batter is available throughout the region at special shops called *freidurías*. Some of the types of fish used for frying include sole, whiting, red mullet, and anchovies. A salad of lettuce and tomatoes is served with most dishes, but these are usually the only vegetables that accompany a meal. Andalusia's most popular drinks are white wines, different kinds of *manzanilla* and sherry, and ice-cold beer.

There is a rich variety of Andalusian deserts, heavily influenced by medieval Andalusian cuisine, like pestiños (deep-fried pastry bathed in honey), polvorones (almond cookies), amarguillos (almond macaroons) and alfajores. Tapas, said to have originated in Andalusia, are popular in all of Spain and include shrimp-fried squid, cured ham, chorizo (spicy Spanish sausage), and potato omelets (called tortillas).

The wines of Jerez are famous the world over. Other standouts are the *manzanilla* of Sanlúcar, the white wines of Cádiz, and the Moriles, Montilla, and Málaga wines, among others. The liquors of the region are also popular, included the Rute and Cazalla *anis*, and the rums from Motril.

¹³ EDUCATION

Andalusian children, like other Spanish children, receive free, compulsory schooling from the ages of 6 to 14, when many students begin the three-year *bachillerato* course of study, after which they may opt for either one year of college preparatory study or vocational training. Today, each Andalusian provincial capital has its own university; the one in Seville being highly regarded throughout Spain.

¹⁴ CULTURAL HERITAGE

Andalusia has an ancient cultural heritage dating from prehistoric times. It features beautiful examples of Roman architecture, such as the ruins of the city of Itálica, near Seville, and Moorish buildings, such as the Alhambra in Granada, the Mezquita in Córdoba, and the Giralda and Torre del Oro in Seville.

Andalusia is the birthplace of many illustrious people. Philosophers and writers include Séneca the Younger, San Isidoro de Sevilla, Averroes, Maimónides, Luis de Góngora, Gustavo Adolfo Bécquer, Juan Ramón Jiménez, Antonio Machado, Federico Garcia Lorca and Rafael Alberti. Famous statesmen include the Roman emperors Hadrian and Trajan, and former president Felipe González. Manuel de Falla is a famous Andalusian guitarist. Diego Velázquez and Pablo Picasso are the regions well-known artists.

Andalusia hosts numerous cultural events. The International Exposition was held in Seville in 1992. At the end of June, there is an International Festival of Classical Music and Flamenco dancing in Granada. There is also an International Festival in Córdoba in July, and Flamenco contests in September in Ronda.

15 WORK

Andalusia is primarily an agricultural region but the service sector, particularly tourism, retail sales, construction, and transportation have grown very quickly. According to the Spanish Institute of Statistics, the GDP per capita of Andalusia, 17401 euros in 2006, is still the second-lowest in Spain. At the same time, the economic growth rate for the 2005–2006 period was 3.72 % one of the highest in the country.

16 SPORTS

The Andalusians share their countrymen's passion for soccer (called *fútbol*), especially in Seville, where there is an old rivalry between the Betis and the Sevilla, the two home soccer clubs. Andalusia's other sports include tennis, swimming, hunting, and horseback riding.

Bullfighting is known as the "*fiesta nacional,*" the national sport. The sport originated in Andalusia, where Spain's oldest bullrings are located (in Seville and Ronda). At the beginning of the bullfight, or *corrida,* the *torero* (bullfighter) sizes up the bull while performing certain ritualized motions with his cape. Next the *picadores,* mounted on horseback, gore the bull with lances to weaken him, and the *banderilleros* stick colored banners into his neck. Finally, the torero confronts the bull alone in the ring. Exceptionally good performances are rewarded by giving the torero one or both of the bull's ears.

17 ENTERTAINMENT AND RECREATION

In a region affected by extremely hot weather much of the year, Andalusian life moves at a leisurely and casual pace. Much social life centers around the neighborhood bars where one can relax with a cold drink and a plate of tapas. However, people also enjoy staying home and watching television, which is found even in the smallest village.

18 FOLK ART, CRAFTS, AND HOBBIES

In addition to leather crafts (the word "cordovan" comes from Córdoba), the Andalusians are known for their ceramics, which are distinguished by the geometric designs that originated with the Moors (based on the Islamic prohibition against representing living things in art). The art of Andalusian builders and stone carvers has survived in such famous buildings as the Alhambra Palace in Granada, the Giralda Tower in Seville, and the mosque in the city of Córdoba.

19 SOCIAL PROBLEMS

Andalusia is a poor region with high rates of unemployment and much of the land concentrated in large holdings (latifundios). Andalusians tend to emigrate to other regions, mainly to Cataluña, and from the countryside to the cities. Unemployment and poverty are linked to delinquency, alcoholism, and drug dependency, problems that the Andalusian cities, mainly Sevilla, Cádiz, and Málaga, share with other developed countries.

20 GENDER ISSUES

Married women in Andalusia maintain close ties to their mothers. Common-law marriages are not unusual. Only church marriages were formally recognized in Spain until 1968, when civil ceremonies were first allowed by law. Divorce has been legal since the 1980s, although a man is much more likely to divorce his wife than vice versa. While the tradition of *machismo*, the public assertion of masculinity, is seen by many as belittling women, Andalusian women actually have an ever-increasing role in society and a high degree of economic independence, competing favorably with men for the region's jobs. Many women are found holding municipal and government posts and managing businesses. A large percentage of women attend university. Evidence of the secular nature of contemporary Spain can be seen in the widespread support for the legalization of same-sex marriage in Spain. In June 2005 a bill was passed to allow gay marriage, making Spain the third country in the European Union to allow same-sex couples to marry.

21 BIBLIOGRAPHY

"All Criss-Cross in a Great Big Square." *The Economist* (March 7, 1987): 53.

"Andalusians." *Encyclopedia of World Cultures (Europe).* Boston: G. K. Hall, 1992.

Caba Landa, Pedro and Carlos Caba Landa, *Andalucía, su comunismo y su cante jondo.* Madrid: Renacimiento, 2008

Carr, Raymond. "The Invisible Fist." *The New York Review of Books* (May 28, 1987): 41.

Cross, Esther, and Wilbur Cross. *Spain. Enchantment of the World Series.* Chicago: Children's' Press, 1994.

Crow, John A. *Spain: The Root and the Flower.* Berkeley: Univ. of California Press, 1985.

Fabricant, Florence. "Andalusia: Spain and Moor." *Harper's Bazaar* (February 1986): 32.

Grande, Félix. *Memoria del flamenco.* Madrid: Punto de lectura, 2007

Hooper, John. *The New Spaniards.* Suffolk, England: Penguin, 1995.

Hubbard, Monica, and Beverly Baer. *Cities of the World.* Detroit: Gale Research, 1993.

Jacobs, Michael. *A Guide to Andalusia.* London: Viking, 1990.

Lye, Keith. *Passport to Spain.* New York: Franklin Watts, 1994.

Madariaga, Salvador. *Spain: A Modern History.* New York: Frederick Praeger, 1958.

Moss, Joyce, and George Wilson. *Peoples of the World.* Detroit: Gale Research, 1993.

Schubert, Adrian. *The Land and People of Spain.* New York: HarperCollins, 1992.

Tremlett, Giles. *Ghosts of Spain.* New York: Walker and Company, 2008

—revised by S. García Castañeda

ANDORRANS

LOCATION: Andorra (Principality of Andorra) (between France and Spain)
POPULATION: 81,222
LANGUAGE: Catalan, French, Spanish, some English
RELIGION: Roman Catholic; some Protestants, Muslims, Hindu and Jews

¹ INTRODUCTION

The autonomous principality of Andorra is a tiny, mountainous nation in Western Europe. This isolated rustic region was virtually unknown to the outside world until the mid-20th century. Since that time, improved transportation and communications have strengthened its ties to neighboring countries, and it has grown to be a popular tourist destination for vacationers from Spain, France, and other countries throughout Europe.

At one time, the land that is now Andorra formed part of the Roman Empire. The Romans were succeeded by Germanic tribes and, in the 9th century AD, Moorish invaders who entered present-day Europe from North Africa. Charlemagne, the Frankish ruler who challenged the Moors and established the Holy Roman Empire, is credited with freeing Andorra from Moorish rule and is generally considered the country's first national hero. Charlemagne's grandson, Charles II, granted control of Andorra to a Spanish noble, the Count of Urgel. In the 12th and 13th centuries, authority over the region was disputed by the bishops of Urgel and the French Count of Foix, who signed agreements in 1278 and 1288 establishing a system of joint rule over the area. The Count's claim on Andorra eventually passed to France's head of state. Except for a brief period following the French revolution, France's leaders (including all its presidents since 1870) have had the title of Prince of Andorra, sharing official control of the region with the bishops of Urgel. Andorra paid a nominal sum—under $10 in present-day U.S. currency—to each ruler every other year until the adoption of its present constitution in 1993. (The bishop of Urgel traditionally received part of his payment in produce and livestock, including 12 hens.)

Andorran farmers began raising tobacco in the 19th century, but their country remained isolated and relatively impoverished until the establishment of improved transportation and communication systems in the 1930s, thus laying the foundation for development of the nation's tourist industry following World War II. In the wake of a constitutional crisis in the 1930s, Andorra's General Council ruled that all male citizens aged 25 and over could vote, whereas the vote had previously been restricted to heads of families. In 1970 the voting age was lowered to 21 and women were given the right to vote. Andorra became a parliamentary democracy in 1993 when it adopted its first constitution, which retained the nation's relationship to its French and Spanish princes but limited their powers. Under the constitution, political parties and trade unions were legalized for the first time. Andorra became a member of the United Nations in July 1993.

² LOCATION AND HOMELAND

Andorra is located on the southern slopes of the Pyrenees mountains between France and Spain. With a total area of 468 sq km (175 sq mi), it is one of the world's smallest nations—about half the size of New York City. Much of its terrain has elevations of 2,500 m (8,200 ft) or more above sea level, and its highest peak reaches 2,946 m (9,668 ft). The land also includes picturesque meadows, fields, and lakes, and the Valira River, which flows into Spain. Only about 4% of Andorra's territory is cultivable. The Madriu-Perafita-Claror Valley, in Andorra, was also designated a UNESCO world heritage site in 2004.

About two-thirds of Andorra's 81,222 people live in urban areas, mainly the capital city of Andorra la Vella and the second largest city Escaldes-Engordany. Andorra has one of the highest population densities in Europe: 173 per sq km (449.5 persons per sq mi). Native born Andorrans make up only about 36% of the population. The greatest number of foreign-born residents are Spaniards, who account for over half the population. Other sizable groups include the Portuguese (10%) and French (over 6%). The diverse ethnic mix of people attracted to present-day Andorra also includes Belgians, Germans, Poles, North and South Americans, British, Australians, Filipinos, Moroccans, Indians, and others.

³ LANGUAGE

Andorra's official language is Catalan, a Romance language similar to the Provençal spoken in the south of France. Catalan is also the official language of Catalonia, an autonomous region of Spain located in the northeast corner of that country, and is spoken in the Spanish region of Valencia, the Balearic Islands, and the French department (or province) of Pyrenees Orientales. Besides Catalan, most Andorrans also speak French and Spanish, and many speak even more languages, such as English, if they are engaged in tourism or commerce. Official government documents are printed in Catalan.

⁴ FOLKLORE

Andorra's most famous religious shrine, the church at Meritxell, is the subject of a popular legend. It houses a statue—the Virgin of Meritxell—that is said to have been found on a snowy hillside surrounded by blooming plants hundreds of years ago. Travelers who found the statue tried repeatedly to move it to a covered area in town, but each time it disappeared only to be found once again on the hillside surrounded by flowers. Finally, it was decided that the statue was destined to remain in that spot, so a church was built to house it. The statue became Andorra's most important religious emblem and a popular destination for pilgrimages.

The lake of Engolasters is the subject of two more religious legends. One claims that the lake was created by flooding when Jesus Christ, disguised as a poor traveler, was turned away by a woman he had approached and caused a flood to show her the evil of her ways. According to another legend, the stars fall from the sky in order to stay in the beautiful lake permanently.

A famous character from secular lore is Andorra's "White Lady," who is part of all major festivals. According to tradition, she was a princess abused by a wicked stepmother. After surviving her stepmother's attempt to have her killed, she married a man who headed a rebellion against her father and stepmother, and the two became Andorra's most illustrious couple.

5 RELIGION

More than 90% of Andorrans are Roman Catholics, and Catholicism influences many aspects of Andorran society. Even today the government of Andorra has a special relationship with the Catholic Church. The importance of Catholicism is reinforced by the fact that one of the principality's two princes is a Spanish bishop. In addition, the church's traditional parish system forms the basis of the country's administrative structure. All public records are kept by the church, and only Catholic marriages are officially recognized in Andorra. The country also has small populations of Protestants (including New Apostolic Church, Mormons, Anglicans, Reunification, and Jehovah's Witnesses), about 100 Jews, and about 2,000 Muslims and Hindus.

6 MAJOR HOLIDAYS

Andorra's holidays include New Year's Day (January 1), Good Friday, Easter Monday, the Andorran National Day (September 8), and Christmas (December 25), as well as other holy days of the Christian calendar. The National Day is observed by making a pilgrimage to the shrine of the Virgin of Meritxell, Andorra's most important religious site. In addition to these national holidays, Andorra's seven parishes all have their own local festivals.

7 RITES OF PASSAGE

Baptism, first Communion, and marriage are considered rites of passage for Andorrans, as they are mostly Roman Catholic.

8 INTERPERSONAL RELATIONS

Life centers around the family for most Andorrans, and fathers traditionally exert tight control over their wives and children. The Roman Catholic Church also plays a central role in the social life of Andorrans. For example, only Catholics are permitted to get married in Andorra.

9 LIVING CONDITIONS

Many Andorrans still live in traditional slate-roofed stone farm houses, often built against mountainsides to leave stretches of level land free for planting. Most of these rural houses have livestock areas or tool sheds on the ground floor, a kitchen and family area on the second floor, and bedrooms on the third. The country's rapid development in recent decades has led to a boom in both residential and commercial construction. However, due to Andorra's scarcity of flat land, it is difficult to find space for the new buildings. Modern multi-story apartment blocks and rustic village houses crowd in on each other with only narrow lanes in between. While this aspect of Andorra's economic development has drawn criticism, many of its people have regarded it as a necessary price that must be paid for the advantages brought by increased prosperity and closer ties with the outside world.

Before the 1930s, when the first roads to France and Spain were built, Andorra had no vehicles whatsoever—not even horse-drawn carriages. All transport was by pack animals. Over the past half-century, the tiny nation has rapidly joined the modern world; by the 1980s, it had one motor vehicle for every four inhabitants. Although Andorra has no railways, excellent roads provide passenger and freight transport routes to both France and Spain. There are also several cable cars in

operation. With no commercial airports of its own, Andorra must rely on international airports in Barcelona, Spain and Toulouse, France for air connections.

Average life expectancy in Andorra is 76 years. Catholic priests and lay personnel play an active role in the administration of the country's hospitals.

10 FAMILY LIFE

Family allegiance and cohesion are central to life in Andorra, although the absolute control traditionally exercised by fathers has diminished over the past half-century due to the social changes brought about by the opening of Andorra to tourism and commerce. A desire for change was already evident in the constitutional crisis of the 1930s that resulted in the granting of suffrage to all men over 25. Previously, the principality's political structure had reinforced its patriarchal tradition by limiting the vote to male heads of households. Women were granted the right to vote in 1970.

11 CLOTHING

Andorrans wear modern Western-style clothing like that common throughout Western Europe and in other developed nations. Traditional costumes—still worn for folk dancing and on special occasions—reflect the influence of Catalonia. Women wear full, flowered skirts over white petticoats; blouses (sometimes covered by flowered shawls); long, black, fingerless net gloves; and black espadrilles with white stockings. Men wear white shirts, dark knee-length pants, white stockings,

People look over a lake and hills in the Pyrenees mountains of Andorra. (© Morton Beebe/Corbis)

and black shoes. They may also wear broad red sashes ties at the waist.

¹² FOOD

During its centuries of isolation, Andorra evolved its own cuisine, distinct from that of its neighbors, France and Spain. Favorite dishes are often based on farm produce and freshly caught game. One popular type of dish is a stew made from hare, wild boar, or chamois (mountain goat), in which the animal is simmered in its own blood (the hare stew is called *civet).* Other favorite meats include lamb chops (often grilled on hot stones), sausages, and ham (which may be fried in honey and vinegar to create the dish *rostes amb mel).* Common entrees also include *trinxat* (boiled potatoes and cabbage), grilled trout (often caught in a nearby stream and seasoned with garlic and black pepper), and omelettes made with wild mushrooms. Andorra also has distinctive regional desserts, most notably *coques,* flat cakes made with grape syrup, brandy, and other flavorings. The village of Canillo is known for a special dessert called *coca de canel,* consisting of dried fruit simmered in wine and sugar.

¹³ EDUCATION

Andorra has a literacy rate of virtually 100%. Schooling is compulsory from age 6 to 16. About 35% of Andorra's primary schools are French; 35% are Spanish and 29% are Catalan but follow a Spanish curriculum as well. Andorrans who attend college usually do so in France or Spain. However in 1997 the University of Andorra was established. Because the number of students makes it impossible for the University of Andorra to develop a full academic program, it serves primarily as a center for virtual studies, connected to Spanish and French universities.

¹⁴ CULTURAL HERITAGE

Andorra has an old and rich folk heritage which is perpetuated in its folk dances. One of the most popular dances is the *sardana,* which is also the national dance of Catalonia in northeastern Spain. The dancers—young and old, male and female—form a circle or a long line, holding their clasped hands high in the air to perform this slow, graceful dance. Short, sedate steps alternate with longer, bouncy ones, and the dancers must pay close attention to the music to know when it is time for each type of step. While the sardana only attained its present form in the 19th century, it is based on an older dance that was formerly held in the open air after certain church services.

In addition to the sardana, which is popular throughout Andorra, various regions have their own dances, including the *marratxa* of Sant Julia de Loria, the *contrapas* of Andorra la Vella, and the *Bal de Santa Ana* of Les Escaldes, all of which are performed only on special occasions. Folk singing is also a popular pastime, and traditional pantomimes are still performed as well.

15 WORK

Until the 1930s most Andorrans were farmers and shepherds. They traditionally followed the Catalan pattern of leaving most or all of their land to one child (usually the eldest son) to prevent it from being split up into smaller holdings. This practice left the other children without a livelihood, forcing many to emigrate—today there are more ethnic Andorrans in France and Spain than in Andorra itself. With the growth of tourism since the 1950s, however, improved employment opportunities have kept more Andorrans at home, as well as attracting immigrants from Spain, France, Portugal, and other countries. Under Andorra's constitution, approved in 1993, the formation of trade unions was allowed for the first time in the country's history. Adoption of the constitution is also expected to create jobs in the newly expanded public sector. Trade has become especially prominent in Andorra because of the lower tax rates for manufacturing and Andorra's Tax free Status. Also, the tourist industry has blossomed because of the number of products that can be purchased duty free, in addition to Andorra's attractive recreational opportunities. Tourism now accounts for more than 80% of Andorra's gross domestic product (GDP).

16 SPORTS

Located high in the Pyrenees, Andorra has the perfect climate to make it a prime ski area. It is snow-covered for six months of the year, but its skies are usually clear and sunny, providing a picturesque view of its beautiful scenery as well as safe skiing conditions. Its resorts attract visitors from France, Spain, and other countries throughout Europe. Each resort offers ski lessons through the Andorran National Ski School. Once the ski season is over, Andorra's mountains are still frequented by hikers, mountaineers, and rock climbers. Hunting, fishing, cycling, and horseback riding are other popular outdoor activities. Competitive sports include rugby, soccer, tennis, golf, and auto racing.

17 ENTERTAINMENT AND RECREATION

Andorrans receive both television and radio broadcasts from neighboring countries. In addition, Andorra has two powerful radio stations of its own, with the highest transmitter in Europe. Andorrans who spend their leisure time in outdoor pursuits have an unusual resource located in the scenic mountains of their country—a series of 21 uninhabited cabins that are open to the public for use as overnight shelters.

18 FOLK ART, CRAFTS, AND HOBBIES

Traditional Andorran crafts include elaborately carved pine-wood furniture, pottery, and ironwork. A regional specialty is a class of products known as *musicatures*, which are decorated in a distinctive style with a knife point. These designs are found on many types of items, including wooden, leather, and even metal handicrafts, as well as furniture.

19 SOCIAL PROBLEMS

While tourism has brought new economic opportunities to Andorra since the 1950s, it has also marred the country's pristine landscape. In mountainous areas, high-rise residential accommodations for skiers have crowded out older wooden buildings. Towns have been overrun with tourist shops and restaurants and there has been a major increase in heavy automobile traffic. Real estate speculation has driven up property prices, making it difficult for young couples to afford their own homes.

20 GENDER ISSUES

Women in Andorra gained the right to vote in 1973. Today women have the legal capacity to act on equal terms with men. While there remain gender inequalities in the areas of employment and child care, the Andorran government has attempted to close these gaps. Women's rights are protected in the Andorran Constitution as well as the European Convention on Human Rights. However, culturally, those in the 45–65 age range still harbor sexist attitudes. Andorra has very strong laws against prostitution, which can result in imprisonment. Abortion is illegal except in order to save the woman's life.

Homosexuality is legal in Andorra and same sex partnerships were legalized in Andorra in 2005.

21 BIBLIOGRAPHY

"Andorra." *Convention on the Elimination of All Forms of Discrimination Against Women.* http://www.un.org/womenwatch/daw/cedaw/reports.htm (April 2008).

"Andorra." In *International Religious Freedom Report 2007.* U.S. Department of State, http://www.state.gov/g/drl/rls/irf/2007/90161.htm (April 2008).

"Andorra." UNESCO World Heritage. http://whc.unesco.org/en/statesparties/ad (April 2008).

"Background Note: Andorra." U.S. Department of State. http://www.state.gov/r/pa/ei/bgn/3164.htm (April 2008).

Carrick, Noel. *Andorra.* New York: Chelsea House, 1988.

"Concept of Same-Sex Marriage Has a Long History." *The Irish Times*, 13 December 2006. p. 18.

Deane, Shirley. *The Road to Andorra.* New York: Morrow, 1961.

Gall, Timothy, and Susan Gall, ed. *Worldmark Encyclopedia of the Nations.* Detroit: Gale Research, 1995.

Ministry of Tourism of the Government of Andorra. *Portal Turístic d'Andorra.* http://www.andorra.ad/en-US/Pages/default.aspx (April 2008).

Paris, Sheldon. "Andorra Consists of a Cluster of Mountainous Valleys." *Stamps* (April 1, 1995): 3.

Sasseen, Jane, et al. "Europe's Pocket Fortresses." *International Management* (March 1993): 28.

Taylor, Carry. *Andorra.* Santa Barbara, Calif.: Clio Press, 1993.

Valls-Russell, Janice. "Andorra Loses Its Innocence: Popping out of the Pyrenees." *The New Leader* (April 5, 1993): 9.

—revised by C. Corrigan

ARMENIANS

ALTERNATE NAMES: Hay
LOCATION: Armenia (in the southwest of the former Soviet Union)
POPULATION: 8–10 million
LANGUAGE: Armenian
RELIGIONS: Armenian Apostolic Church; some American Christian sects

¹ INTRODUCTION

The precise origins of the Armenian people, who call themselves *Hay*, are controversial and the subject of debate by historians and archeologists. Regardless of whether Armenians are indigenous to the region they inhabit—appearing there as early as the 28th century BC according to some—or whether they migrated there later, their presence in the Anatolian Highlands and the Ararat valley was documented by the 5th century BC in the writings of King Darius I of Iran (521–485 BC), Herodotus (b.484 BC), and Xenophon (401–400 BC).

Between the 1st and 5th centuries AD, Armenian kingdoms fell alternately under the political and cultural influence of the Roman and Iranian empires, between which they were situated. Between the 7th and 9th centuries AD, Armenia was buffeted by waves of Byzantine influence from the west and Arab invasions from the south. By the 11th century, Armenians who had prospered within the Byzantine Empire and who had settled in the Cilician plain on the Mediterranean coast of Asia Minor established their own independent state (AD 1080–1375). Because of its strategic location, Cilician Armenia fell within the sphere of European affairs until it was weakened and then destroyed by Mamluk invasions in the 13th and 14th centuries.

From the 16th to the 20th century, much of Western Armenia fell within the boundaries of the Ottoman Empire, while Eastern Armenia (Transcaucasian Armenia) fell within the Russian Empire. Centers of Armenian culture and learning formed in Constantinople in the West and Tiflis in the East. In the 19th century, Armenian nationalism emerged in both locales. Armenian political parties formed just before pan-Islamic policies in the Ottoman Empire grew to threaten the role of non-Muslim minorities, including Armenians. Massacres of Armenians took place in the 1890s, and Armenians, largely through the medium of political parties, began to organize themselves in resistance.

When Turkey joined the Central Powers against Russia in World War I (1914), Armenians became suspect due to their ties to Armenians in the Russian Transcaucasus, who had supported their political organization. In 1915 Armenians in Anatolia were disarmed and imprisoned and then deported to concentration camps in the Syrian Desert. As many as 1.5 million are thought to have perished, and hundreds of thousands fled to the Russian Transcaucasus, the Middle East, Europe, and the United States. Since 1948, these events have been referred to as the Armenian genocide. The genocide has occupied a central role in the cultural and political life of Armenians around the world.

Following the formation and dissolution of a Transcaucasian Federation (1918) and an independent Armenian Republic (1918–1920), Armenia succumbed to the Red Army, was absorbed into the Transcaucasian Soviet Federated Socialist Republic (1922), and became a union republic of the Soviet Union (The Armenian Soviet Socialist Republic) in 1936. After the emergence of a powerful national movement in Armenia (1988–1990), Armenians voted in favor of independence from the Soviet Union in 1991, just months before its collapse in December. Armenia adopted its national constitution on 5 July 1995 and has held democratic elections for president and parliamentary positions since that time, though the elections have been continually marred by accusations of electoral fraud.

² LOCATION AND HOMELAND

The newly independent Republic of Armenia is located in the southwestern part of the former Soviet Union and shares borders with Iran to the south, Turkey to the west, Georgia to the north, and Azerbaijan to the east. The country is landlocked and largely arid, encompassing the plain of the Ararat valley and cross-cut by small mountain chains. Despite one significant lake, Lake Sevan, Armenia possesses few natural or energy resources. Although the territory of the Republic of Armenia is only 30,100 sq km (11,620 sq mi), Armenians have historically occupied a much larger territory between the Black Sea and the Caspian Sea, spreading across eastern Anatolia (in modern Turkey) and into contemporary Iran and Azerbaijan.

The Armenian Plateau in eastern Anatolia was included in what is known as Greater Armenia, east of the Euphrates river, while a smaller region, to the west of the river, is known as Lesser Armenia. In the 1st century BC, under the rule of Tigran the Great, Armenian influence extended from the Caucasus mountain range to Cilicia, as far east as the Caspian Sea and as far south as Egypt. For two millennia, Armenian polities and communities have formed and dissolved within this larger area.

As of 2008, estimates of the world-wide Armenian population range between 8 and 10 million, 3 million of whom reside in the Republic of Armenia. Significant diaspora communities exist in the United States, France, former Ottoman territories (Jerusalem, Syria, and Lebanon), formerly communist countries (Georgia, Russia, Bulgaria, and Romania), and Iran. Some diaspora communities are very old, such as the ones in Madras, India and in San Lazzaro, Italy, but many date to the Armenian genocide and the subsequent dispersion of Armenians from their Anatolian homeland.

The Republic of Armenia itself is more ethnically homogeneous than other republics of the former Soviet Union, with Armenians constituting more than 95% of the total population. Large communities of Azerbaijani Turks and Kurds resided in Armenia until 1988, when they began to migrate out as conflict grew between Armenians and Azeris in the neighboring republic of Azerbaijan. Other minority populations in Armenia include Russians, Greeks, Yezidis, and Jews.

³ LANGUAGE

The Armenian language occupies an independent branch of the Indo-European family tree and has been spoken since antiquity. The Armenian language was written for the first time in the early 5th century (AD 406), when its alphabet was invented by the scribe, Mesrop Mashtots, so that the Christian liturgy and scriptures could be translated and written for an Armenian audience. The alphabet has 36 characters, some of which were modeled after Greek and Syriac cognates.

The Armenian language has numerous dialects, some of which are mutually unintelligible. However, two standard printed dialects exist: Western and Eastern. Western Armenian was the dialect of Armenians in the Ottoman Empire and was standardized as the literary language of Armenians in Constantinople. Armenian diaspora communities throughout the Middle East, Europe, and North America, which descend from Armenians who fled the Ottoman Empire, use the Western dialect. Eastern Armenian was the dialect of Armenians in the Russian Empire and Iran. It was standardized as the literary language of Armenians in Tiflis in the 19th century and was reformed in the Soviet era. Eastern Armenian is the official language of the Republic of Armenia and is also used by communities in the former Soviet states and in Iran. Western and Eastern dialects of Armenian use the same alphabet and are grammatically similar, although there are some consistent differences between them. Grabar, the classical Armenian language, is the language of the church liturgy but is no longer spoken conversationally.

Armenians everywhere consider the ability to speak the language an important part of being Armenian. For example, a survey of Armenian Americans showed that 81% thought Armenians should speak Armenian. Even though Eastern Armenian, along with Russian, had already been an official language of the Armenian Soviet Socialist Republic, and most Soviet Armenians were bilingual, the growth of a national movement in 1988 intensified sentiment about the language. With independence, Armenian began to replace the Russian language in many official contexts, such as government documents and street names, and the Armenian people began to replace Russian words in their speech with Armenian equivalents.

4 FOLKLORE

Armenian folklore is deeply historical, drawing upon centuries of national heroes. Mesrop Mashtots, for example, has often been depicted in works of art and educational and historical publications. A large statue in his image adorns the Armenian Manuscript Library (Matenaderan) in the capital city, Yerevan. Other folk heroes include the mythical ancient King Ara; the 5th-century warrior Vartan Mamikonian, who was martyred defending Armenians against the Persians; and modern guerrilla fighters (called *fidayi*). Folklore pertains both to ancient and medieval Armenian kingdoms and to daily village life before the genocide.

Another body of Armenian folklore is biblical or Christian in nature. For example, many people believe that Noah's Ark landed on Mount Ararat—a once-volcanic mountain that sits on the Turkish side of Armenia's contemporary western border. Gregory the Illuminator (Grigor Lusavorich') is the saint and popular national hero credited with bringing Christianity to Armenia by converting its King Trdat III in AD 301, making him the first ruler to adopt Christianity as a state religion. Tradition holds that Gregory the Illuminator saw visions of fire in which Christ himself showed him the site where the first Armenian church should be built. Erected on the site of an ancient pagan fire temple, that church became the cathedral of Etchmiadzin and has remained as the center of the Armenian Church.

5 RELIGION

According to some, Christianity was introduced in Armenia by the apostles Thaddeus and Bartholomew and is therefore apostolic. But, it was not until King Trdat III's conversion that Armenia was Christianized, shortly before the official Christianization of the Roman Empire. The Armenian Apostolic Church, to which the vast majority of Armenians belong, broke with the Council of Chalcedon in the late 5th century AD and has maintained a monophysitic doctrine since then, attesting to the single, divine nature of Christ. The Armenian liturgy has changed little from its classical form, canonized in the Middle Ages.

Not all Armenians are members of the Armenian Apostolic Church, partly due to the pressures of communism in Soviet Armenia and the attraction of other Christian faiths in the diaspora. Nevertheless, the Armenian Church has played an important role in the preservation of Armenian history and culture. Armenian church architecture dating as far back as the 7th century and medieval illuminated manuscripts produced in Armenian monasteries are national monuments and treasures.

6 MAJOR HOLIDAYS

Armenians celebrate major Christian holidays, such as Easter and Christmas (which they observe on the Orthodox date of January 6). As elsewhere in the Orthodox world, Christmas is considered to be primarily a religious holiday rather than an occasion for elaborate gift-giving. Like other people of Europe and North America, Armenians celebrate the New Year on January 1, when it is popular to go from house to house visiting friends and relatives. Birthdays are celebrated with parties for friends and extended family members. In addition, it is customary for the person whose birthday it is to treat classmates or co-workers to a special treat, such as chocolate or brandy.

Other occasions are traditionally marked with celebration in Armenia as well. For example, if someone enjoys very good luck, such as high grades on an exam or a new job or new home, it is customary to treat friends and co-workers to a celebration (*magharich*). On Vardavar, a pre-Christian spring holiday, young boys and teenage men splash water on passersby in the street, a practice which can be viewed as either a playful celebration or an inconvenience.

In the Soviet era, Armenians celebrated state holidays, such as May Day and International Women's Day.. Armenians now celebrate the anniversary of their nation's independence from the Soviet Union (declared on 23 August 1990). Around the world, Armenians sadly commemorate the Armenian genocide on April 24. On December 7, the anniversary of an earthquake that devastated northern Armenia in 1988, many Armenians visit cemeteries in mourning.

7 RITES OF PASSAGE

Major rites of passage in Armenian society include birth, marriage, and death. Birth is celebrated by family and friends, as is a baby's first tooth, which is an occasion for gift-giving and a playful ritual in which a baby is presented with a number of items from which to choose, such as a pencil and a pair of scissors. The baby's choice is thought to foreshadow its future choice of a career, so that choosing the pencil might mean that a baby will become a writer or a teacher.

Traditionally, Armenians celebrated engagement as well as marriage, as a symbolic union of two families. A marriage is commonly performed in church as well as in a state registry office and is celebrated with a big party at the home of the groom's parents. When the bride and groom enter the home for the first time as a married couple, Armenian flat bread (*lavash*) is placed over their shoulders and together they break a small plate on the threshold with their feet for good luck. In traditional families, a new bride's parents might visit her in her new home on the fortieth day after marriage, at which time her trousseau (*ozhit*) will be ceremoniously presented to her.

Funerals generally take place on the third day after death, when friends and family gather sorrowfully at the home of the deceased. The funeral procession is often accompanied by sad, traditional music. The seventh and fortieth days after death are commemorated at the cemetery and with a ritual toasting and a meal. After that, death is remembered with visits to the cemetery at each anniversary as well as at the new year.

8 INTERPERSONAL RELATIONS

Relations among kin and friends are very close in Armenia. Friends and family visit one another frequently and without invitation. Unlike the United States, where it is considered impolite to visit someone's home unannounced, in Armenia it is impolite to fail to visit spontaneously. When a guest arrives, it is common to serve food and drink. A meal consisting of hot and cold dishes is appropriate at any time of day, while in the afternoon or late evening, pastries, chocolates, fruit, and coffee are likely to be served. Most social gatherings are accompanied

by toasting with alcoholic drinks. Like other peoples of the Caucasus, Armenians toast one another's families, health, and fortune as a sign of affection and respect. Friends and co-workers also give each other small gifts of food, jewelry, or flowers as gestures of affection.

Armenians greet one another with handshakes or with kisses on the cheek. Women and men alike are physically affectionate with friends of the same sex, and it is as common to see two men walking down the street arm-in-arm as it is to see two women doing so. Teenage boys and girls date one another, but conservatively. Families are concerned about protecting the honor of their daughters before marriage; therefore, dates usually consist of visits to the movies or conversations in cafes. Because Armenians move infrequently, most adults retain their childhood friends and acquaintances.

9 LIVING CONDITIONS

In the Soviet era, Armenians enjoyed one of the highest standards of living among Soviet republics. Armenia was heavily industrialized and urbanized, with a developed capital city, an international airport, and a subway system. More than one-third of the population lives in Yerevan. Another third lives in other industrial and urban centers, such as Gumri (or Gyumri), Vanadzor, Vagharshapat, Hrazdan, and Abovyan. The remaining third lives in villages of varying sizes across the country.

Like other Soviet peoples, Armenians suffered periodic shortages of goods, such as butter, meat, and toilet paper. However, delicious fruits and vegetables are grown locally, including apricots, pears, apples, plums, grapes, peppers, tomatoes, eggplants, and more. Compared to other republics of the former Soviet Union, Armenians enjoyed a wide variety of goods, services, and urban amenities such as public transportation, telephone communications, indoor running water, and electricity.

In urban Armenia, most families live in apartment buildings that range in height from 4 to 15 stories. By American standards, apartments are small, with a kitchen, living room, separate toilet and washroom, one or two bedrooms, and possibly a balcony. Because of these space constraints, children and grandparents rarely have their own bedrooms, but instead sleep together on beds or sofas in the living room or balcony. Parents sleep together in the bedroom, sometimes with one or more children.

In villages, many Armenians have private houses, ranging in size from two rooms with a kitchen to very large houses and, in recent years, mansions of many rooms. Village homes may be attached to small farming plots and small barns where animals, such as cows, pigs, chickens, goats, and sheep, are kept.

10 FAMILY LIFE

In cities, towns, and villages alike, adults live with their parents even after marriage, when a new bride will move into her husband's parents' home. Children care for their parents in old age, and grandparents play a large role in the upbringing of their grandchildren. Siblings and cousins play together as children and usually remain close throughout adulthood. Traditionally, Armenian kinship has been patriarchal, meaning that the eldest man is the head of the extended family household and has authority over the affairs of the entire family.

Armenians carry flowers to pay their respects at a memorial for victims killed under the Ottoman Empire in the Armenian capital of Yerevan, Armenia. Armenians consider their deaths as genocide, yet this is a flashpoint in relations between Turkey and the West. (Hakob Berberyan/AFP/Getty Images)

In villages and towns, marriages are sometimes arranged by older relatives and friends. Divorce is far less common in Armenia than in the United States, but it does occur, as does remarriage. Armenians prefer to have large families, although the birthrate has declined somewhat in the first years of independence. Participation in the extended family is a central part of daily life.

11 CLOTHING

For more than 100 years, urban Armenians have dressed like other urban peoples of Europe. Men wear suits, sweaters, slacks, and leather jackets. Women prefer to wear dresses, jewelry, cosmetics, and high heels. Jeans are popular with young men and young women alike. As elsewhere in the world, Armenians follow Western fashion trends through magazines, television, and movies.

Traditional costumes are worn for dramatic performances and for dance, as well as for occasions of cultural importance. For both men and women, traditional dress includes baggy pants below long shifts or overcoats. Distinctive regional adornments include sheepskin hats, engraved metal belts, and jewelry, sometimes made of coins. Women wear their hair in two long braids.

12 FOOD

Armenians eat many foods common to other former Soviet peoples, including beet soup *(borscht)*, roasted meat *(khorovadz,* or *shashlik)*, potatoes, and stews. Other Armenian delicacies are fresh trout from Lake Sevan *(ishkhan)*, grapevine leaves stuffed with rice, ground meat, and herbs *(dolma)*, flat bread *(lavash)*, chicken porridge *(harissa)*, and yogurt *(madzun)*. In the diaspora, Armenians also eat many other foods that are popular throughout the Middle East, such as hummus, tabbouleh, baba ghanouj, and shish kebab.

13 EDUCATION

Armenia has its own state education system. School begins with kindergarten and lasts through the equivalent of American high school, with a total of 13 grades. In the past, both Russian-language and Armenian-language schools existed. The majority of schools have Armenian-language curricula, although there are also specialty schools offering other languages, such as English, French, Greek, and Persian. Even in villages children attend school. The literacy rate is nearly 100%.

After graduating from school, many young adults choose to go to the Yerevan State University, to the State Engineering University, or to one of numerous other state and private institutions of higher learning. Students choose familiar concentrations, such as computer science and physics, and the university offers programs in language, philosophy, history, and literature. Armenia has a large number of technical and vocational training schools and an American University with English-language graduate programs in business, engineering, political science, and health.

14 CULTURAL HERITAGE

Armenia has rich traditions of church music and folk music alike. Choral arrangements by the Armenian composer Komitas (1869–1935) were inspired by both folk songs and liturgical music and continue to be extremely popular. Folk music performed on traditional instruments and contemporary Armenian pop music (called *Rabiz*) and rock and roll are also popular. Since the language was first written in the 4th century, a vast body of Armenian language literature has emerged, including religious texts, histories, epics, poetry, drama, political writings, and modern novels. In addition, Armenia has established traditions of opera, ballet, folk dance, and cinema. Armenians of all ages take great interest in their musical, literary, and artistic traditions, and these traditions influence popular culture significantly.

Armenians have contributed to international cultural traditions in literature, painting, architecture, music, politics, and science. Novelist William Saroyan, painter Martiros Sariyan, physicist Victor Hambartsumian, and composer Aram Khachaturian are a few examples of Armenians who have made significant cultural contributions.

15 WORK

Work in Armenia is much like work in other industrialized and post-socialist economies. Garment and shoe production and computer technology are prominent among Armenia's light industries, while chemical industries include the production of neoprene rubber. Women constitute a large proportion of the work force and are represented among teachers, doctors, musicians, physicists, researchers, factory workers, and governmental and non-governmental administrators, as well as in the service sector. Men predominate in certain professions, such as management, government, transportation, and restaurant service. In addition to wages received for formal employment, many Armenians supplement their salaries through involvement in small-scale trade and investment.

In rural Armenia, farmers work the land and care for livestock, while women are more likely to engage in domestic work. After independence, Armenia shifted away from the large-scale agribusinesses of the Soviet era back to smaller-scale family farms. Men and women alike bring fresh produce to cities and towns for sale in central markets. Even the smallest towns and villages have schools, regional administrative representation, shops, and other kinds of non-agricultural employment.

Despite steady economic growth since independence, unemployment in Armenia remains high and one-quarter of the population continues to live below the poverty level.

16 SPORTS

In recent years, Armenians have particularly excelled in wrestling, weight-lifting, and boxing, for which they have received numerous Olympic medals. Skiing and tennis are also popular sports, but soccer is perhaps the most popular. In the 1970s and 1980s, the Armenian soccer team, Ararat, drew huge crowds and in 1973 became the champion of the Soviet Union.

17 ENTERTAINMENT AND RECREATION

Popular forms of recreation include movies, music, and traditional and modern dance. The Armenian symphony in Yerevan gives weekly performances at the Opera House that draw large crowds of all ages. Also performed there are national operas and ballets. Armenian men like to play backgammon and chess at home and in city parks when the weather is nice, and Armenians of all ages enjoy walks and visits to outdoor cafes. In the summer, the most popular forms of relaxation are trips to the beach at Lake Sevan, where it is possible to sun and swim, and picnics in the countryside, where meat and vegetables are roasted over open fires.

18 FOLK ART, CRAFTS, AND HOBBIES

Popular Armenian folk arts include woodworking, stone-carving, metalworking and jewelry, painting, embroidery, and rug-weaving. Each of these arts incorporates and embellishes traditional and even ancient motifs, such as the modern production of small salt dishes *(aghamanner)*, which may be made of elaborately carved wood or pottery in the form of ancient fertility symbols. In addition to several museums that feature folk arts and crafts, an art fair known as Vernissage is held near the Republic Square in Yerevan every weekend. Vernissage appeals not only to tourists, but also to local artists and the general public, who come to appreciate one another's work.

19 SOCIAL PROBLEMS

In February 1988, a national movement emerged in Armenia in support of the national self-determination of Armenians living in the autonomous region *(oblast)* of Nagorno-Karabakh in neighboring Azerbaijan. An ethnic conflict between Armenians in Nagorno-Karabakh and Azerbaijani Turks erupted into a full-scale war for independence. Despite an enduring cease-fire, the conflict does not appear to have a quick or simple conclusion.

In response to territorial conquests of Armenian forces in Nagorno-Karabakh, the Azerbaijani government imposed a total energy blockade on Armenia by disrupting the flow of oil and natural gas to the republic from pipelines passing through its territory. The blockade resulted in an energy crisis of catastrophic proportions between 1991 and 1996, when Armenia restarted its nuclear power plant. During the five-year crisis period, only 30% of Armenia's industry functioned, the gross national product underwent a five- to six-fold decline and citizens received as little as two hours of electricity daily. The impact of this dramatic decrease in the standard of living was reflected in health and marriage statistics. Between 1993 and 1994, the marriage rate decreased by 20% and between 1992 and 1993 the birth rate decreased by approximately 25%.

The social and economic impact of the energy crisis was exacerbated by the after-effects of an earthquake measuring 6.9 on the Richter scale that devastated three major industrial centers in northern Armenia on 7 December 1988. The earthquake killed 25,000 people, injured 31,000, left more than half a million homeless, and caused approximately $20 billion worth of damage. The combined effects of the earthquake, the war in neighboring Azerbaijan, and the collapse of the Soviet economy severely reduced the standard of living in Armenia in its first five years of independence, which were also characterized by an increase in crime, disease, and mortality.

Fortunately, the quality of life in Armenia has been improving steadily since then with the growth of a new middle class. In the past decade poverty and inflation rates have decreased dramatically, and the value of Armenian currency has stabilized. The conflict over Nagorno-Karabakh and its political and economic effects remains a serious problem, however.

20 GENDER ISSUES

Armenian culture retains its traditional patriarchal values, resulting in oppressive conditions for both women and homosexuals. Although women are guaranteed equal rights in the Armenian constitution and do, in fact, make up over half the student population in institutes of higher education, Armenia still has the lowest representation of women in its government in the region and women continue to earn less than men in the workplace. Also, there are no laws against domestic violence, although rape and sexual assault are prohibited, and no known shelters exist for victims of domestic violence. Because of the high rate of emigration by Armenian men since independence, Armenian women are left with no one to marry and support them, leaving young Armenian women vulnerable to sexual trafficking. The Armenian government approved a plan for prevention of trafficking in 2004 and continues to work at its implementation.

Although Armenia officially decriminalized homosexual activity in 2003, a strong stigma is still attached to homosexuality. The Armenian Apostolic Church views homosexuality as an illness and homosexual activity as a sin, disallowing practicing gays from receiving communion. Gay clubs remain underground, and the majority of Armenians still view homosexuality with contempt. A recent survey revealed that over 86% of young Armenians would refuse to live near or work with a known homosexual, indicating that societal attitudes towards homosexuality will take some time to change.

21 BIBLIOGRAPHY

Armenia Information. http://www.armeniainfo.am (4 August 2008).

Armenian House. http://armenianhouse.org (4 August 2008).

Bakalian, Anny. *Armenian-Americans: From Being to Feeling Armenian.* New Brunswick, NJ: Transaction Books, 1993.

Bournoutian, George. *A History of the Armenian People.* Vol. I. Costa Mesa, CA: Mazda Publishers, 1993.

———. *A History of the Armenian People.* Vol. II. Costa Mesa, CA: Mazda Publishers, 1994.

Discover Armenia. http://www.armeniaemb.org/DiscoverArmenia/index.htm (4 August 2008).

Harutyunyan, Shushan. "Armenia's Animosity Towards Gays." *The Rainbow Report.* http://therainbowreport.blogspot.com/2007/08/armenias-animosity-towards-gays.html (4 August 2008).

Hoogasian-Villa, Susie. *Armenian Village Life Before 1914.* Detroit: Wayne State University Press, 1982.

Lang, David Marshall. *The Armenians.* London: Unwin Paperbacks, 1988.

Walker, Christopher. *Armenia.* New York: St. Martin's Press, 1990.

—revised by Dianne De Mott

AUSTRIANS

LOCATION: Austria
POPULATION: 8.4 million (2007)
LANGUAGE: German; Italian, Slovene, Croatian, Hungarian, and Czech in the border provinces; English
RELIGION: Roman Catholic; Protestant

1 INTRODUCTION

From the defense of Vienna against the Turkish Empire in 1683 to the Krushchev-Kennedy summit meeting in 1961, Austria has historically been a place where East meets West. The great 19th-century diplomat Prince Metternich said "Asia begins at the Landstrasse" (the Viennese street that leads eastward from the city's center). A neutral nation since it regained its sovereignty after World War II, Austria is the third home of the United Nations (after the United States and Switzerland) and the seat of the Organization of Petroleum Exporting Countries (OPEC).

Located at the center of Europe, the landlocked nation of Austria wielded great military and commercial power for much of its history. The Celts who settled there in the middle of the first millennium BC called the area *Ostarrichi*—the empire in the East. (This name was later Germanized to become Österreich.) The Celts were followed by Romans in 14 BC, Germanic and Slavic tribes beginning in the 5th century AD, and, in the 10th century AD, the Babenburger dynasty, which helped establish Christianity throughout the area. In 1278 Austria's most illustrious historical period began with the accession of the Habsburg monarchy. With its capital city at Vienna, the Habsburgs' Austro-Hungarian Empire was to rule over much of Europe for over 600 years, expanding through war and marriage. At various times the empire included Burgundy (part of present-day France), Bohemia, the Netherlands, Spain, northern Italy, Hungary, Slovakia, Poland, and parts of the former Yugoslavia. With good reason, the Habsburgs had the letters *AEIOU*, which stood for *Austria est imperare orbi universo*—all the earth is subject to Austria—inscribed on their tombstones.

After a century of decline, the Habsburgs were defeated in World War I and their empire was dismantled. The newly created Republic of Austria retained only six German-speaking provinces of the former empire plus Burgenland and Vienna—the empire of over 50 million had become a state of 6.5 million. Once occupying an area as large as Texas, it had shrunk to approximately the size of Maine. Although the Allied powers had forbidden a union, or *Anschluss,* between Austria and Germany, it was forcibly achieved in 1938 with the invasion by Nazi Germany under Adolf Hitler. Following Germany's defeat in World War II, Austria was governed by the Allied powers until 1955, when it returned to independence. In 1995 Austria became a member of the European Union. Permanent neutrality is a part of Austria's constitution, although this stance is becoming increasingly controversial.

2 LOCATION AND HOMELAND

Three-fourths of Austria is mountainous, but valleys and Alpine passes allow for domestic travel and also make the country an important crossroads between different parts of Europe. The Alps, divided into three ranges, are located mostly in west-

AUSTRIANS

0 100 200 300 Miles

0 100 200 300 Kilometers

ern and central Austria; their highest peak is Grossglockner, at 3,797 m (12,457 ft). To the east lie the Carpathian foothills and the lowlands. The fertile Danube Valley lies beyond the Northern Alps and broadens into the Hungarian Plain near Vienna. Still further north is the Bohemian plateau, with elevations of between 351 m and 899 m (1,150 and 2,950 ft).

Austria's population was about 8.4 million in 2007. Unlike the ethnically diverse peoples of the former empire, the Austrians of today are a relatively homogeneous population, with the vast majority of Austrians (91%). There are six ethnic groups officially recognized in Austria: Burgenlandic Croatians, Roma, Slovaks, Slovenians, Czechs and Hungarians. These are concentrated in the east and south of the country. Among the population changes wrought by World War II—in addition to the deaths of 280,000 men drafted into the army—was the decimation of Austria's Jewish population, which had numbered nearly 200,000 in a 1934 census count but was, in ethnic terms, far larger.

Cities and towns with populations over 10,000 are home to about half the population—one-fifth of Austrians live in Vienna alone. The main population trends in modern times have been the shift from rural to urban areas and an east-to-west migration pattern.

³ LANGUAGE

Nearly 98% of Austrians speak German, although at least four different dialects are in use. The most common dialect is known as the Southern dialect. It sounds similar to the way people speak in Bavaria. One can also hear Italian, Slovene, Croatian, Hungarian, and Czech spoken in the border provinces, and many people in large cities and resort areas speak English. Croatian and Slovene are official languages in Burgenland. Certain Austrian words—especially culinary terms—differ from those used in Germany, reflecting Austria's diverse ethnic past. These include *Zwetschken* (plums) from the Bohemian *svestka*, *Palatschinken* (pancakes) from the Hungarian *palacsinta*, and *kafetier*, from the French term for a coffeehouse owner.

⁴ FOLKLORE

The great German epic, *Das Niebelungenlied*, was written in Austria around 1250 AD. It combined the warrior gods and goddesses of Teutonic myth with the realities of court life in the Middle Ages. Vienna's Museum für Volkskunde houses exhibits on Austrian folklore.

⁵ RELIGION

The religious legacy of the Habsburg empire—whose capital, Vienna, was the seat of the Holy Roman Empire—can be seen in the continuing predominance of Roman Catholicism in present-day Austria. In spite of the official separation of church and state, some 74% of Austrians were Roman Catholic in 2007 and numerous churches, shrines, monasteries, and cathedrals can be seen throughout the country. Other commonly seen signs of religious faith include roofed crosses called *Wiesenkreuz,* which are found in the Tyrol, and, further south, *Bildstöcke,* covered posts decorated with religious scenes. In the country, religious festivals, processions, and pageants take place throughout the year. In urban areas, religious observance is often more casual and typically limited to holidays and major events such as births, weddings, and funerals. About 4.7% of the population was Protestant in 2007, with the Evangelical Lutheran Church and the Presbyterian Church having the greatest number of members. About 4.2% of the population was Muslim. Less than 1% was Jewish.

⁶ MAJOR HOLIDAYS

Many Roman Catholic holidays are public holidays in Austria. In rural areas, the eve of Epiphany (January 6) is celebrated by children regaling neighborhood farms with a traditional carol in honor of the Three Kings to bless them for the coming year. Epiphany also marks the beginning of the carnival, or *Fasching,* season, which is celebrated until Ash Wednesday, the beginning of Lent. Vienna, in particular, is renowned for its two months of festive balls. Other religious holidays include Easter, Easter Monday, the Feast of the Ascension, Whitmonday, Corpus Christi, the Feast of the Assumption *(Maria Himmelfahrt)* on August 15, All Saints' Day *(Allerheiligen)* on November 1, the Feast of the Immaculate Conception on December 8, Christmas, and Boxing Day (Saint Stephen's Day) on December 26.

In some cities the evening of December 5 is a night of mischief in the name of Krampus, a devilish figure who, according to some legends, comes to call on naughty children. On this night, youth (particularly teenage boys) will dress in Krampus masks and costumes and run through the streets rattling chains and bells to frighten their friends and neighbors. In some areas, a parade of costumed Krampus characters is held. According to legend, the arrival of St. Nicholas on December 6 sends Krampus away as the saint forgives all the naughty children and distributes presents. Christmas parties and celebrations often begin with St. Nicholas's Day. Many houses and churches display wooden cribs at this time of year. Labor Day is celebrated on May 1 and there is also a national holiday on October 26 to celebrate the 1955 Declaration of Neutrality.

A number of traditional observances, both religious and secular, are carried out in rural areas. The feast of St. Leonard (the patron saint of livestock) is observed in November by festive horse-and-cart processions to mass and many villages still burn the "demon" of winter during Lent; in Vorarlberg, the explosive-filled figure of a witch is blown up at the top of a water tower and it is said that the weather for the coming year will come from the direction in which the head flies. In the Tyrol, *Schemenlaufen* (procession of ghosts) is celebrated every four years by a parade of men in masks ringing out the winter with bells. The feast of St. Martin on November 11 is celebrated as children go door to door with paper lanterns and candles to sing for their friends and neighbors. They are generally rewarded with a small treat.

7 RITES OF PASSAGE

Because of the strength of Roman Catholic practice in Austria, almost all newborns are baptized. The ceremony provides the parents with the opportunity to extend the bonds of godparenthood to close friends. Godparents are expected to visit on the child's birthday, provide presents on important occasions, and to take responsibility for the care of the child in the event of the parents' death. The godparents hold the child at the baptismal font while the priest sprinkles the baby with water. First Communion is practiced only in those families who are themselves church-goers, a much smaller number than the number of baptisms.

Childhood is filled with a number of firsts, from the first tooth to the first school holiday spent entirely with friends and away from parents. There are no special rites to mark puberty, but graduation from the teenagers' last school is marked with a party and gift-giving. Weddings are gala affairs involving fancy clothes and feasting among family and friends. Church weddings are common but are not required socially.

The experience by adults of the death of a parent is a significant moment. Most relations between parents and adult children are close, as both generations play an active role in raising children. This is marked by adult children calling their parents by the same nickname that the grandchildren call them. When these grandparents die, the loss is deeply felt and friends and family rally to support the mourners. Death is marked by the sending of a formal printed notice by mail to all of the deceased's acquaintances and distant family. In the countryside, the funeral is held in the church, followed by interment in a grave. In the cities, and especially in Vienna, it is held in memorial chapels in the cemeteries themselves. Here, grave interment is available, but cremation is more common.

8 INTERPERSONAL RELATIONS

In public Austrians are both courteous and formal, a legacy from the days of empire when many defined themselves by aristocratic position or by their place in an elaborate civil service hierarchy. A doctor or other professional is generally addressed as *Herr Doktor, Magister,* or *Professor.* Civil servants have honorifics consisting of various prefixes and the suffix *rat*

(councilor), such as *Hofrat* (Privy Councilor), *Gehiemrat* (town councilor), and a variety of others. Women are commonly addressed as *gnadige Frau* (madam). The greeting *Grüss Gott* (God bless you) is often used instead of *Guten Tag* (good day). People shake hands when they meet and part, doors are commonly opened for women, and a woman may have her hand kissed upon being formally introduced.

9 LIVING CONDITIONS

In the late 19th and early 20th centuries, Austria—and Vienna in particular—was known as a center for innovations in medicine. It was here that Sigmund Freud invented psychoanalysis (his former home at No. 19 Berggasse is now a museum). Austrians continue to enjoy a high standard of health care with the help of the comprehensive national health insurance program. Life expectancy was estimated at 79 years in 2008, with 76 years for men and 82 years for women.

The state controls Austria's modern, efficient transportation system, which includes 6,500 km (4,040 mi) of railroad and 11,102 km (6,900 mi) of highway and expressway *(Autobahns).* The Danube River is a means of transporting both people and goods. With Austria's well developed road and rail networks, its people rely little on domestic air travel to traverse their small country. However, when it comes to international travel, Austrian Airlines, the national airline, maintains Austria's tradition as a major connecting point between Eastern and Western Europe. During the Cold War, many foreign airlines used Vienna as a transfer point between East and West.

Because of a population shift from the country to larger towns and cities after World War I, housing in rural areas remains plentiful and cheap. Most city dwellers now live in one- or two-room flats with a separate kitchen; less than one-fourth occupy homes with four or more rooms.

10 FAMILY LIFE

While the number of marriages has declined and the number of divorces has increased, the most important Austrian family unit is still the nuclear family *(Familie),* which often establishes its own household near one partner's (usually the wife's) family soon after marriage and may eventually be joined by a widowed grandparent or unmarried aunt or uncle. Regular visits are exchanged with the extended family *(Grossfamilie),* consisting of grandparents, aunts, uncles, and first cousins, while a wider network of relations *(Verwandschaft)* comes together for major events such as weddings. Children who go through baptism may have a godparent, with whom he or she maintains a special relationship until adulthood.

11 CLOTHING

Modern Austrian dress generally resembles that of the northeastern United States. The traditional peasant costumes are largely reserved for holidays and festivals, when one can still see women in embroidered blouses, lace aprons, and full dirndl skirts and men in *lederhosen* (knee-length leather pants) with wide suspenders, short jackets without collars or lapels, and green-brimmed hats decorated with feathers or other regional adornments. A traditional costume worn on more formal occasions is the *Stierer Anzug,* consisting of gray or brown breeches embroidered in green, a colorful cummerbund, bright vest, long flared coat with ornamental buttons, and high top hat.

Traditionally dressed dairy farmer Sepp Hinterseer leads his cattle from the summer pastures in a procession to the city of Lofer, Austria. Austrian farmers decorate their cattle with ribbons, tree branches, and headdresses to celebrate a summer of good fortune and health. (AP Images/Kerstin Joensson)

12 FOOD

The Austrian love of good food and drink dates back at least as far as the Turkish siege of Vienna in 1683, when sacks of coffee beans left behind by the retreating Turks were used to open Vienna's first coffee-house and introduce the Austrians to the then-exotic brew (after slow initial sales, *mélange*—a local steamed-milk variant still consumed today—was introduced, and the rest is history).

Perhaps the most characteristic Austrian dish is the *Wienerschnitzel*, a breaded and golden-fried veal or pork cutlet. Traditionally, it is eaten with a few drops of fresh lemon juice and a vinegared potato salad. Also popular are Hungarian *goulasch;* a variety of soups with special ingredients; stews, typically served with dumplings; and hot sausages, which are often served with beer as snacks. The justly revered Austrian pastry chefs are the creators of such delicacies as apple strudel (*apfelstrudel), milchrahmstrudel* (a cheese crepe swimming in vanilla custard sauce), *Sachertorte* (a rich chocolate cake with a layer of apricot jam under its thick, smooth icing and plenty of whipped cream, or *Schlag*), and *Dobostorte* (alternating layers of sponge cake and chocolate butter cream glazed with caramel). In the 19th century, it became common to eat dinner late in the evening. To assuage their hunger, many city-dwellers would take a break between 4:00 and 5:00 PM for a special meal called *Jause* that consisted just of pastry and coffee. Many still eat this meal today.

Wine is a very important Austrian food. The area around Vienna and the Burgenland produce wonderful dry white wines. In nice weather, Austrians love to visit vineyards to drink the wine right out of the barrels. The vintners provide pleasant gardens with picnic tables and a buffet where people can buy roast meats, raw vegetables, vinegared salads, fresh cheeses, breads, rolls, and sweets to go with the wine. These are called *Heurigen,* which means "this year's vintage." The atmosphere of these gardens, the wines, and the foods that are eaten with them are distinctively Austrian.

13 EDUCATION

Children attend primary school from the ages of 6 through 10, when they are tested and tracked into either a continuing elementary school, a basic high school (*Hauptschule*), or a college preparatory school (*Gymnasium*). Formal secondary education continues through age 14. Some form of secondary training is required through age 15. A majority of students continue with some type of post-secondary schooling, including apprentice training, technical schools, vocational colleges, and universities. After some 200 years of free and compulsory education, Austria has a nearly 100% literacy rate.

14 CULTURAL HERITAGE

Vienna's famed reputation as a center for the arts—particularly music—began and flourished during the Habsburg empire. Maximilian I founded the renowned Vienna Boys' Choir in 1498. The six-year-old Mozart first played for the Empress Maria Theresa in 1762. The musical capital of Europe for much of the 19th century, Vienna was the birthplace or adopted home of many of the greatest classical and romantic composers from Haydn, Beethoven, and Schubert to Brahms and Mahler (and continuing on to the 20th-century atonal school of Schöenberg). It was also the home of the waltz, which reached the height of its popularity with such works as *Tales from the Vi-enna Woods* by Johann Strauss, Jr. Today, Austria's two great centers for classical music are Vienna—with its world-famous Boys' Choir, Philharmonic, and State Opera—and Salzburg, the birthplace of Mozart and site of an annual festival that draws thousands from around the world every summer.

For much of Austria's history, the works of its authors were considered part of German literature. However, a uniquely Austrian identity was already present in early-19th-century drama, flowering at the beginning of the 20th century with the influential group of writers and poets, including Arthur Schnitzler, Hugo von Hofmansthal, and Stefan Zweig, who were known as *Jung Wien* (Young Vienna). The Austro-Hungarian empire also claimed two of the greatest contemporary writers in German, Rainer Maria Rilke and Franz Kafka, both from Prague.

Spending time at coffeehouse is a cultural tradition that remains strong throughout the country. In the 19th and 20th centuries, the coffeehouses of Vienna were notable as the gathering places for some of the most prominent scholars, philosophers, writers, musicians, and artists in the country. Rather than simply ordering a cup to go, it is not uncommon for patrons to spend a few hours at a coffeehouse, reading, relaxing, or engaging in conversation with friends and colleagues.

15 WORK

Each of the three major economic groups—labor, management, and farmers—is represented by its own organization: trade unions, a management association, and the farmers' federation. In 2005 about 70% of the labor force was employed in some type of service related industry. Industry and manufacturing accounted for about 27% of the work force while only about 3% was employed in agriculture. People generally work from the ages of 15 to 60. Retirees enjoy generous pensions and high social status. Social legislation in Austria is very generous to working people. Even the youngest and most inexperienced workers are guaranteed five weeks of paid vacation per year. This number increases with seniority to eight weeks per year. Workers receive an extra month's salary before Christmas season begins and before the vacation season begins. This means that workers are paid for 14 rather than 12 months every year. Austrians receive free medical care.

16 SPORTS

Skiing is Austria's leading winter sport, but the natural beauty and variety of the country's scenery are conducive to outdoor activities of all kinds. Other winter activities include ice skating and tobogganing, while popular summer sports include bicycling, mountain climbing, sailing, hiking, canoeing, and swimming. Many Austrians, like their fellow Europeans, are avid fans and players of soccer (which is called *football*).

17 ENTERTAINMENT AND RECREATION

Austrians—most notably the Viennese—are legendary for their gaiety of spirit and enjoyment of life. According to a famous saying, "In Berlin, the situation is serious but not hopeless; in Vienna, the situation is hopeless, but not serious." Austrians are enthusiastic supporters of the arts and participants in all kinds of outdoor activities. Their love of fine food, conversation, and leisure coalesces around the coffeehouses and *Konditoreien* (pastry shops) where many hours are spent reading, socializing, or just relaxing and sipping a *brauner* (coffee with milk), a *konsul* (black coffee with cream), or one of the more elaborate coffee drinks, such as the *kaisermelange* (black coffee with an egg yolk and brandy).

[18] FOLK ART, CRAFTS, AND HOBBIES

Crafts produced by Austrian folk artists include wood carvings, ceramics, jewelry, glassware, wax figures, leather products, and embroidery, as well as items made of wrought iron and pewter. A *Heimatwerk* (local crafts organization) in each province runs shops that sell the products of area craftspeople.

[19] SOCIAL PROBLEMS

Austria has a relatively low rate of violent crime for an industrialized nation. However, it has a higher incidence of white-collar and property crime. Alcoholism, suicide, and absenteeism from work are also serious problems. The scale of domestic abuse is emerging as a problem as well. In 2007 the Women's Ministry estimated that about 10% of all adult women had suffered from some type of violence while in a relationship. People from Greece, Yugoslavia, Turkey, the Middle East, and Africa who settle in Austria are subject to employment and housing discrimination and overt racial hostility, expressed verbally and through graffiti. Anti-Semitic and anti-Roma sentiments are still a point of concern. Austria has a small illegal underground right-wing extremist movement which recruits young people (skinheads) who agitate against foreigners and commit acts of random violence.

[20] GENDER ISSUES

Male and female roles in the family are not equal, in spite of the increased responsibilities women assumed in Austrian society during the two world wars and the continuing wages that working women bring to the household. For much of the 20th century, Austria had one of the highest proportions of women in the labor force; however, in 2007 it was estimated that women's salaries were about 17% lower than those for men in equal employment. Generally, more women than men were unemployed and women were more likely to have temporary or part-time positions. Women have been underrepresented in the civil service despite labor laws that require the government to hire women of equivalent qualifications ahead of men in areas in which fewer than 40% of the employees are women. Women are eligible for two years of paid maternity leave after the birth of a child. In many families, the woman's early return to work is made possible by grandparents who are willing to care for the child during the day. Women also are eligible to retire five years earlier with full benefits.

Social legislation alone cannot alter centuries of practices that promoted the role of men as fathers and breadwinners within the family. Austrian men continue to be raised, for the most part, in families that do not encourage them to take an equal share of household responsibilities with their sisters. As adults, Austrian men continue to look at the household and child-rearing as inherently female activities, regardless of the wage contribution of their wives. Women have their first child after their own careers are established. This age can vary from 19 to 30, depending on the woman's education.

[21] BIBLIOGRAPHY

Area Handbook for Austria. Washington, DC: U.S. Government Printing Office, 1976.

Evans, R. J. W. *Austria, Hungary, and the Habsburgs: Essays on Central Europe, c.1683-1867.* Oxford: Oxford University Press, 2006.

Gall, Timothy, and Susan Gall, ed. *Junior Worldmark Encyclopedia of the Nations.* Detroit: UXL, 1996.

Haywood, Anthony, and Kerry Walker. *Austria Travel Guide.* Footscray: Lonely Planet Publications, 2008.

Hubbard, Monica M., and Beverly Baer, ed. *Cities of the World: Europe and the Middle East.* Detroit: Gale Research, 1993.

Illustrated Encyclopedia of Mankind. London: Marshall Cavendish, 1978.

Lichtenberger, Elisabeth. *Austria: Society and Regions.* Vienna: Austrian Academy of Sciences, 2000.

MacHardy, Karin Jutta. *War, Religion and Court Patronage in Habsburg Austria: The Social and Cultural Dimensions of Political Interaction, 1521-1622.* New York: Palgrave, 2002.

Moss, Joyce, and George Wilson. *Peoples of the World: Western Europeans.* Detroit: Gale Research, 1993.

Rotenberg, Robert. "Austrians." In *Encyclopedia of World Cultures (Europe),* ed. Linda A. Bennett. Boston: G. K. Hall, 1992.

—revised by K. Ellicott

BASHKIRS

LOCATION: Bashkortostan Republic, in Russia (in the Southern Ural mountains)
POPULATION: 1.8 million (2002)
LANGUAGE: Bashkir; Russian
RELIGION: Islam

1 INTRODUCTION

The Bashkirs are a Turkic Muslim people living within the Russian Federation. Bashkirs first appear in historical sources in the 10th century AD, as the inhabitants of the southern Ural mountains, the area which they still occupy today. The origins of the Bashkirs are obscure. Although today the Bashkirs speak a Turkic language, some historians consider them to have originally been Hungarian speakers who remained in the Ural mountains when the ancestors of modern Hungarians began the migration that eventually led them to settle in Central Europe. Whether or not this is the case, there can be little doubt that there was always a strong Turkic ethnic element among the Bashkirs and that this element became dominant before the end of the Middle Ages. Traditionally, the Bashkirs were a pastoral nomadic people, leading their herds of sheep, cattle, horses, and camels along fixed migration routes, but under Russian rule the Bashkirs increasingly practiced agriculture.

Politically, the Bashkirs have always been subjects of more powerful neighbors. The earliest sources identify them as subjects of the Volga Bulgarian state, centered in the middle Volga region. Before their subjection to Russia in the 16th century, the Bashkirs found themselves subjects of various steppe polities. These include the Mongol World Empire, the Golden Horde, the Noghay Horde, and the Kazan Khanate. Following the Russian conquest of the Kazan Khanate in 1552, the Bashkir leaders likewise became subjects of Russia. Until the late 17th century, subjection to Russia was a largely formal affair, but Russian influence gradually increased in Bashkir lands as a result of Russian peasant and military colonization and increased taxation. Despite a series of violent Bashkir rebellions, over the course of the 18th century, the Bashkirs and their lands became increasingly integrated into the Russian state.

With the advent of the Russian Revolution of 1917, the Bashkirs found themselves divided among various political forces and embroiled in the Russian Civil War. Although no actual Bashkir independence movement emerged at that time (the Bashkirs were the only Turkic people to voluntarily join the Soviet Union), the Bashkirs were eventually granted by the Soviet authorities in Moscow an "autonomous" territory within the Russian Republic. This territory eventually became known as the Bashkir Autonomous Soviet Socialist Republic (ASSR), and it has become known simply as the Republic Bashkortostan since the break-up of the Soviet Union in 1991.

2 LOCATION AND HOMELAND

Bashkir territory has traditionally encompassed the southern Ural Mountains as well as adjoining steppe regions to the south and in Western Siberia, that is, straddling the imaginary line separating Europe and Asia. Most Bashkirs live in the Russian republic, where 1.2 million Bashkirs constitute just under 30% of the republic's population. The remaining Bashkirs mainly reside in provinces and republics in neighboring Bashkortostan. Except for the rugged terrain of the central southern Urals, Bashkir territory is characterized by a mixture of evergreen and birch forest with steppe, or prairie. Roughly 40% of the republic's territory is forest. The northern parts of Bashkir territory are the most wooded and receive the most rainfall, while the southern regions frequently suffer from insufficient rainfall and have much sparser tree cover. The central southern Ural Mountains are largely forested, and the highest point in Bashkortostan is Yamantaw, which has an elevation of 1,638 m (4,900 ft). Much of Bashkir territory is uncultivated and is home to a rich variety of wildlife, especially in the Ural Mountains region, where there are large populations of bears, wolves, deer, and smaller mammals and birds.

The climate of Bashkortostan is markedly continental, characterized by long, harsh winters and cool, dry summers. The mean temperatures for January are –16°C to –14.5°C (0°F to 4°F), and for July 18.5°C to 20°C (69°F to 72°F).

The territory of the Republic of Bashkortostan encompasses 144,000 sq km (56,000 sq mi), an area slightly smaller than the state of Iowa. According to the 1979 Soviet census, the Bashkirs numbered 1,371,000, but made up less than 25% of the population of Bashkortostan, occupying third place in the republic's ethnic composition after Russians and Tatars. It is believed that the 1.8 million Bashkirs now account for less than 20% of the republic's population.

3 LANGUAGE

The Bashkirs speak Bashkir, which is a Turkic language of the Kipchak, or Northwestern, branch of the Turkic language family. Bashkir is most closely related to, and mutually intelligible with, Tatar, a Turkic language spoken widely by the Tatar population of Bashkortostan as well as in neighboring regions. Bashkir is also closely related to Kazakh. Bilingualism is typical among rural Bashkirs, but Russian is the dominant language in urban areas. In northern and western Bashkortostan, where there is a large Tatar population, the linguistic division between Bashkir and Tatar has essentially evaporated.

The Bashkir literary language is based on dialects spoken in the far southeastern reaches of the republic, dialects that are the most linguistically distant from Tatar and closest to Kazakh. Nevertheless, it is widely used, along with Russian, by the Bashkirs for everyday communication. There are newspapers and books published in Bashkir, as well as radio and, to a lesser extent, television broadcasts.

Because the Bashkirs are Muslims, Bashkir names are commonly adapted from Arabic names, as well as from some Turkic ones. Some common men's names are *Äkhmät, Mökhämet, Ildus,* and *Bulat.* Some common women's names are *Gulnara, Gölfiya,* and *Zukhra.* However, Russian and Western given names are increasingly common among the Bashkirs as well.

4 FOLKLORE

Like the other traditionally pastoral nomadic peoples of Inner Asia, the Bashkirs have a rich repertoire of folklore which includes songs, poetry and tales. The most remarkable genre in Bashkir folklore, however, is the heroic epic. While Bashkir folklore (particularly the epic tradition) has its roots in the Bashkirs' Inner Asian nomadic past, the conversion of the Bashkirs to Islam in the 14th century resulted in the insertion of Islamic themes and interpretations into Bashkir folklore.

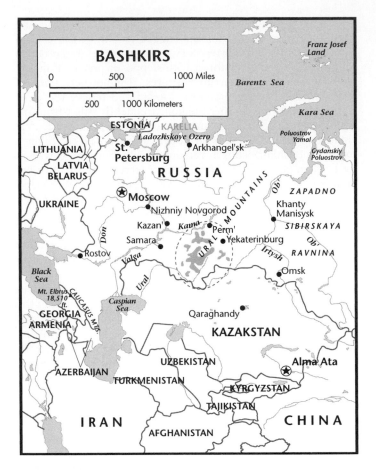

BASHKIRS

Some of the more famous epics include *Ural Batïr*, an ancient epic about the formation of the Bashkir people, and *Idheügey menän Moradhïm*, which describes historical events in the Golden Horde in the 15th century.

Bashkir heroes traditionally corresponded to the heroes of the epics; therefore it is not surprising that historical figures deemed to be heroic became the subjects of heroic epic poetry. The most prominent among these figures was Salavat Yulayev, a Bashkir commander during the Pugachev Rebellion of the 1770s. Yulayev, himself an accomplished poet in the Bashkir language, became the subject of a large cycle of Bashkir folklore. He was canonized in Soviet times as the Bashkirs' national hero and remains so today. A massive Soviet-era bronze statue in the Bashkiria capital of Ufa is very much a Bashkir national landmark.

Bashkir folklore retains a rich cycle of myth. In addition to myths recounting the creation of the world, the various Bashkir tribes and clans have retained myths of their own groups' formation. The category of myth can also include Islamic legends, particularly those concerning the Prophets and famous Sufi Shaykhs.

⁵ RELIGION

Historically the Bashkirs have been an overwhelmingly Muslim people. The conversion of the Bashkirs to Islam appears to have begun on a large scale in the 14th century, with the conversion of the Golden Horde to Islam. However, Bashkir Islamization legends are quite numerous and vary widely, including

accounts of their conversion at the hands of the Prophet Muhammad himself, Volga Bulgarian missionaries, or to Central Asian Sufis such as Ahmad Yasavi. Since the collapse of the Soviet Union and the lifting of Soviet anti-religious policies, there has been a resurgence of interest in Islam and a sharp increase in mosque construction in Bashkir villages. Seventy years of Soviet repression of religions, including Islam, resulted in the marginalization of Islamic knowledge and ritual in Bashkir society. The vestiges of traditional Bashkir religious life are most evident in rural Bashkir communities, especially among the older generation. These Islamic practices include reading from the Koran, ritual fasting, and pilgrimages to nearby Muslim saints' tombs.

Traditional, specifically Bashkir beliefs are equally deep-rooted, especially in rural communities. These include beliefs in various spirits thought to inhabit different buildings and natural features, as well as tutelary spirits of livestock, and amulets. Such beliefs are often artificially distinguished from Islamic beliefs, however, since tutelary spirits are often Muslim saints and amulets contain verses from the Koran, and the Bashkirs themselves understand their beliefs to be part of a unified Muslim belief system.

⁶ MAJOR HOLIDAYS

Historically, Bashkirs have observed major and minor Muslim holidays, the most prominent of which among the Bashkirs is *Qorban Bayramï* (the commemoration of the trial of Abraham and his willingness to sacrifice his son), which typically takes place in early June. This festival historically involved the sacrifice of animals and large communal feasts. Today, *Qorban Bayramï* is an official holiday and people get the day off from work to relax. Various festivals not of a strictly Islamic character but rather corresponding to the agricultural calendar are also observed. One such festival is *Sabantuy* (also called *Habantuy*), or "the plow festival," which is held after spring planting. *Sabantuy* festivities today involve playing picnic-style games. Another traditional festival is the clan and tribal gathering, called *Yïyïn*, usually held in early summer. In the past, these gatherings involved sacrifices of animals, but now there are only feasts and various games and dances. The Muslim season of Ramadan is not strictly observed by most Bashkirs.

While such festivals are still common in rural areas and seen by Bashkirs as being thoroughly "Bashkir," holidays officially promoted during the Soviet era are also widely observed, especially in urban areas, where Bashkirs are integrated into larger, primarily Russian environments. While specifically Soviet holidays such as May Day and the Anniversary of the October Revolution are generally ignored, less political Soviet holidays such as New Year's Day (January 1) and Victory Day (May 9) are widely celebrated.

⁷ RITES OF PASSAGE

Traditionally the Bashkirs observed numerous and complex rituals to mark the primary life cycle rituals of birth, marriage, and death. Bashkirs believed that a newborn was especially vulnerable to the "evil eye" (*qatï küdh*) during the first 40 days after its birth, and a number of amulets were hung around its crib. Another ritual involved the pretended sale of the child to the midwife, as protection against evil spirits who might seek to harm the actual parents. After 40 days, a name was given to the child, traditionally by a mullah. To what extent these rituals are practiced today is unclear. Home births are still common in rural areas, but name-giving is usually carried out by the parents of the child.

Puberty rites *per se* are not well documented among the Bashkirs, but the conscription of young Bashkir men into the army, usually at age 18, has generally functioned as a *de facto* and *de jure* puberty right. Induction into the armed forces also had its rituals meant to protect the life of the young soldier.

Bashkir weddings, especially in rural areas, were traditionally quite complex, involving countless rituals and large-scale feasting. In the past, brides would have been around age 15 and grooms around age 18. Today, the ages of the bride and groom are typically between the ages of 18 and 20. Weddings in rural areas continue to retain older rituals, but urban weddings are usually performed by civil authorities and correspond to the wedding traditions of Russian society.

Death and funerary rituals among the Bashkirs have tended to be the most impervious to the changes brought about by Soviet and Russian society. Today, as throughout the Soviet period, the dead are buried in Muslim cemeteries. The deceased is typically wrapped in a shroud and buried with a headstone with an Arabic or Bashkir inscription. On the third, seventh, and fortieth days and the first anniversary after a death, memorial feasts are held. Remembrance feasts for the dead in general are held during *Qorban Bayramï,* when families go to cemeteries and have a meal at the graveside of relatives or have prayers read.

8 INTERPERSONAL RELATIONS

Superficially, the interpersonal relations of Bashkirs differ little from those of Russian society as a whole, and this is especially true in urban settings. However, especially in rural areas, traditions of Bashkir hospitality are still observed. In traditional Bashkir society, guests were treated with considerable respect, and it is still common in rural areas for elaborate feasts to be held in honor of guests.

9 LIVING CONDITIONS

In urban areas, Bashkirs generally have access to hospitals, although the quality of care in these hospitals is generally poor. In rural areas, clinics and doctors can be very distant from Bashkir settlements, and it is common for Bashkirs, both urban and rural, to depend to a large extent on traditional forms of medicine, particularly herbal medicine.

Most urban Bashkirs live in large apartment blocks. For urban Bashkirs, as for urban citizens of Russia in general, vacant apartments are hard to find as apartments rarely change hands. Urban apartments rarely have more than two bedrooms, and in many cases consist of only one room with a communal bathroom and kitchen. Apartments often go without gas or hot water for weeks at a time. In Bashkortostan, telephone numbers are assigned to individuals rather than to residences. In order to get telephone service, an individual must register, which usually involves waiting in lines and completing forms for bureaucratic approval. It is then up to an individual to find someone who can install a telephone line to his or her house or apartment.

In rural areas, Bashkirs tend to live in wooden houses. In Bashkir villages, there is typically electricity, but no running water or private telephones. Water is usually obtained from wells. The quintessential traditional Bashkir dwelling is the felt yurt *(tirmä),* which was the traditional dwelling of Inner Asian steppe nomads. This was a round tent with a conical roof, constructed of lattice-work surrounding long wooden tent poles over which thick felt was draped. Although such tents are no longer used by Bashkirs today, they retain a powerful symbolic significance for Bashkirs.

Very few Bashkirs own private automobiles, and as a result most Bashkirs depend on public transportation. In rural areas bus service is often irregular, and many Bashkirs rely on animals, primarily horses, for transportation.

Generally, however, living standards among Bashkirs have broadly improved since the late 1990's, as the Russian economy has expanded.

10 FAMILY LIFE

In traditional Bashkir society, most men had only one wife, although wealthy Bashkirs could have as many as four wives. Polygamy, especially with more than two wives, was very rare however, and became illegal after 1917. Bashkir women have traditionally worked, either performing agricultural work, or in urban areas holding paid jobs. Before 1917 Bashkir families were typically very large, with a woman commonly bearing 15 or 16 children in a lifetime. Because of high child mortality rates, however, perhaps only four or five children might survive into adulthood. During the late Soviet era, family size among the Bashkirs was generally similar to that of ethnic Russians in general, less than two children per family, which is far lower than the fertility rates for most Muslim groups in the former Soviet Union.

The Bashkirs have retained a large and extended kinship network and a deep-rooted system of clan and tribal identities. Some of the major Bashkir tribal groupings were the Usergan, Ming, Qïpsaq, and Burjan. Tribes are divided into clans and sub-clans, and awareness of one's affiliation with clans and tribes remains high, even though the distinctions between these tribes were blurred during the Soviet years. Since the collapse of the Soviet Union, several tribal-based political movements have emerged among the Bashkirs.

11 CLOTHING

Traditional Bashkir clothing was strongly influenced by the region's harsh climate, as well as by Bashkir conceptions of Islamic precepts. Traditional Bashkir winter clothing consisted of long, thick hats, usually made from the fur of animals such as wild cats or fox. Coats and jackets were also made of wild animal fur, as well as reversed sheepskin. High boots made from soft leather were also common.

Islamic headgear, especially the skull-cap, was once commonly worn by Bashkirs. Women generally covered their heads with scarves, and before 1917 some Bashkir women wore veils as well. Islamic headgear is still occasionally worn by Bashkir men and women, especially the older generation.

Today the everyday clothing of Bashkirs is thoroughly Westernized and differs in no way from that worn by Russians.

12 FOOD

Bashkir staple foods today consist of dark bread, potatoes, meat, and various vegetables, especially cabbage, onions, and beets. Traditional foods include horse-meat sausage, honey, mutton, and fermented mare's milk *(kumys).* Large-scale feasts are an important element in Bashkir dietary custom, both on religious occasions and to welcome guests. Specific dishes are served for specific religious occasions such as memorial feasts and animal sacrifices.

Bashkirs often eat a *vak-belyash*, a round pastry filled with meat and potatoes, for a quick meal. Tatars in Bashkortostan may eat a *uch-pochmak*, which is like the *vak-belyash* except that the pastry is triangular. The Bashkirs are famous for their *kulama*, a type of soup where each person puts in what they like. Each ingredient is prepared separately in its own dish. Typical *kulama* ingredients include horse meat, onions, *lapsha* (square noodles), and carrots. Each individual puts what he or she wants into a bowl and then pours some broth over the top. The broth, traditionally made with horse meat, is now usually made from beef.

13 EDUCATION

Before 1917, most Bashkirs had some sort of access to Islamic education. Nearly every village mosque had attached to it an Islamic primary school *(mäktäp)* and secondary school *(mädräthä)*. Although access to instruction depended to a large degree on material conditions of the village and the energy of the village's *imam* (leader of the congregation), children and older students would be taught basic literacy in Arabic and Bashkir. Several large and prestigious *mädräthäs* were also located in Bashkir territory (in Sterlibashevo and Sterlitamak), and it was common for Bashkir students to study in major centers of Islamic learning both in Russia (Kazan and Orenburg) and in Central Asia (Bukhara and Samarqand).

After 1929, Islamic education was for all intents and purposes outlawed, and Bashkir education was taken over by the state. In Soviet times, education became compulsory, and higher education was entirely in the Russian language. Bashkirs typically receive eleven years of schooling, although some opt for higher education in universities in the capital, Ufa, or in other institutions in Russia. Bashkortostan has a controversial affirmative action educational program that encourages rural Bashkirs to seek a university education in Ufa. The program involves a quota system, in which one-third of the students must be from urban areas (such as Ufa), one-third from villages, and one-third from rural areas. There is much competition for acceptance to the university among urban residents (mostly ethnic Russians) because there are so many vying for the limited number of spaces. In villages and rural areas, however, the university must actively recruit just to meet its quotas. As a result, the competition to get in is not as tough for those in the villages and rural areas (who are more likely to be Bashkirs). In order to maintain this program, the university has set up separate remedial education classes. Most Bashkirs who do finish their university studies stay in Ufa to look for a job rather than return home.

Bashkortostan is home to some large educational institutions, including Bashkir State University in Ufa, and a number of technical and pedagogical institutes in Ufa and in the republic's smaller cities. Many Bashkirs also study in larger Russian cities, especially Moscow and St. Petersburg, as well as abroad, particularly in Turkey and Western Europe.

14 CULTURAL HERITAGE

The Bashkirs have retained a rich cultural heritage, and Bashkir music is especially fascinating because of its retention of archaic Inner Asian traditions. Most interesting is the musical tradition of throat-singing *(ödhläü)*, which exists nowhere else in western Inner Asia, but is well known in Mongolia and South Siberia. In *ödhläü*, the singer is able to produce two notes at once in his or her throat. Another characteristic of Bashkir singing is that it is based for the most part on a pentatonic scale (one with five tones per octave). A particularly characteristic Bashkir musical instrument is *quray*, which is a kind of reed flute held vertically. Traditional Bashkir dance is similarly archaic, and is commonly performed at gatherings and religious occasions.

Although the Bashkirs are well known for their oral literature, especially their oral epic poetry, Bashkir written literature, based on the Arabic script, was well developed before 1917. This literature includes tribal genealogies *(shäzhärä)* containing historical narratives, as well as historical chronicles. Bashkir Islamic literature was also well developed before 1917 and remains virtually unstudied. This literature was written in Arabic as well as in Turkic; in fact, a substantial body of literature produced by Bashkirs was written in Arabic.

Beginning in 1917, the Soviet authorities encouraged the creation of a formal Bashkir culture which includes European-style literature, classical music, classical dance, and so forth. The economic crises of the 1990's and the reduction of state subsidies for cultural institutions severely impacted Bashkir cultural life, from which it is currently recovering.

15 WORK

The Bashkir economy was historically based on semi-nomadic stockbreeding, cereal and mixed agriculture, and the hunting and gathering of forest products. Today, stock breeding, agriculture (including beekeeping) together with industrial manufacturing, oil and petrochemical production, and service industries form the basis of the Bashkir economy.

16 SPORTS

One of the most popular sports among Bashkirs, as among many other Turkic peoples, is wrestling. In addition, horse racing is quite popular as entertainment during Bashkir festivals. The most popular spectator sports are hockey and soccer.

17 ENTERTAINMENT AND RECREATION

Contests associated with the *Sabantuy* festivities are a favorite activity among the Bashkirs. One such traditional game is a pillow fight between two contestants who stand on top of short pillars and try to topple each other. There are also potato sack races and a log pole climb (with a prize on the top for the winner). A popular amusement is *nardoy*, a Turkic game similar to checkers that is played on a large board. Traditionally a common feature of public celebrations was competitions of improvised verse, known as aytïs.

18 FOLK ART, CRAFTS, AND HOBBIES

The Bashkirs are especially skilled at weaving, particularly woolen carpets. Bashkir carpets are generally flat-woven and feature simple geometric designs. Handicrafts in general are still widely engaged in, partly for supplemental income, but especially because of the lack of retail establishments in rural areas.

¹⁹ SOCIAL PROBLEMS

Bashkirs share many of the social problems being experienced in Russia and the rest of the former Soviet Union. This includes increasing rates of alcoholism, crime, unemployment, and poverty. In certain areas of the Republic of Bashkortostan rural poverty among Bashkirs is especially severe. Despite the ethnic diversity of Bashkortostan, no single ethnic group constitutes a majority, and ethnic tensions have not exploded into violence. The Bashkir movement for full political independence receives limited support among Bashkirs as a whole.

The most severe social problem facing Bashkirs is without a doubt their republic's environmental degradation. Bashkortostan's position as a moderate oil producer and especially the presence of petrochemical installations in the cities of Ufa and Neftekamsk have caused catastrophic pollution to the region's air and water. Most serious are high levels of toxins such as dioxin in urban areas, especially Ufa.

²⁰ GENDER ISSUES

In traditional Bashkir society there were sharp and clear-cut gender divisions in terms of division of labor and social interaction. Before 1917 both Bashkir customary law and Islamic law regulated the rights and obligations of men and women, and Islamic law became increasingly prominent until the Bolshevik Revolution of 1917. Russian law allowed Bashkirs to use Islamic law, or sharighat, to regulate family law and inheritance law. In particular it regulated divorce, the division of household property, and child custody. Similarly, Islamic law allowed for the division of property, both male and female, among heirs. Before 1917 many Bashkir women had access to Islamic education. Small boys and girls were educated together, but older girls and young women were educated separately by women, usually the wives of the village imam. As in much of the Islamic word, women were especially prominent as Quran reciters. Women also participated extensively in specific religious rituals, especially pilgrimage to local shrines.

Child-rearing, traditionally, in Soviet times and since 1991, has generally been relegated to women, as are specific domestic duties. Although women always contributed substantially to farming and stock-breeding, during the Soviet era, during and after World War II Bashkir women entered the service and industrial workforce in large numbers, and obtained greater access to Soviet education.

²¹ BIBLIOGRAPHY

Bikbulatov, N. V., and F. F. Fatykhova. *Semeinyi byt bashkir, XIX–XX.* Moscow: 1991.

Donnelly, Alton. *The Russian Conquest of Bashkiria.* New Haven: Yale University Press, 1968.

Frank, Allen J. *Islamic Historiography and 'Bulghar' Identity among the Tatars and Bashkirs of Russia.* Leiden-Boston: Brill Academic Publishers, 1998.

Rudenko, S. *Bashkiry.* Moscow-Leningrad: 1955.

Torma, Jozsef. "Magic and Name-giving among the Bashkir," *Altaic Religious Beliefs and Practices.* Budapest, 1992, 361-369.

Usmanov, Kh. F. (ed.) *Istoriia Bashkortostana s drevneishikh vremen do 60-kh godov XIX v.* Ufa, 1997.

—revised by A. J. Frank with acknowledgment to M. Tabatchnik

BASQUES

LOCATION: Northwest Spain and southwest France
POPULATION: almost 3 million
LANGUAGE: Euskera (Basque language); Spanish; French
RELIGION: Roman Catholic

¹ INTRODUCTION

The Basques are a single people who live in two countries: northwest Spain and southwest France, where the Pyrenees meet the coast of the Bay of Biscay. The Basques may be the oldest ethnic group in Europe. They are thought to have inhabited the southwestern corner of the continent since before the migration of Indo-European peoples to the area approximately 5,000 years ago. Surviving invasions by the Romans, Visigoths, Arabs, French, and Spanish, they resisted domination by outsiders until the Middle Ages when much of their territory was usurped by Spaniards, Gascons, and Catalans. In 1516 the Basques on the Spanish side of the Pyrenees agreed to Castilian rule but won the right to retain a degree of self-government. By 1876 all Basque lands were divided between France and Spain; however, nationalist sentiments ran high among the Basques—especially on the Spanish side—throughout the 19th century.

In the 1930s the Basques supported the Republican side in the Spanish Civil War in exchange for promises of autonomy, but their hopes were dashed with the victory of Generalissimo Francisco Franco. During the years of the Franco regime (1939–1975) the Basque language and culture in the Spanish provinces were ruthlessly suppressed, and their local government went into exile in Paris. By the 1950s, resistance groups had formed, most notably the ETA (Euskadi Ta Askatasuna, or Basque Homeland and Liberty), which continued its terrorist acts throughout the 1970s and 1980s, even after Spanish rule over the Basques was liberalized following Franco's death in 1975. Vizcaya, Guipúzcoa, and Alava, which make up three of the four Basque provinces, were unified in 1980 as the Basque Autonomous Community, and its inhabitants were granted limited autonomy, recognition of their language and culture, and control over their schools and police force. Today, it is one of the most decentralized regions in the world, with more autonomy than just about any other similar region in Europe. The seats of the Basque parliament and government are in Vitoria-Gastei. The parliament elects the *lehendakari* (president), who forms a government following regular parliamentary procedures.

ETA is an illegal armed Basque organization. It was founded in 1959, demanding Basque independence and self-determination from a Marxist-Leninist interpretation. According to official figures and ETA communiqués, since 1969 it has killed over 800 people, maimed hundreds more, and committed dozens of kidnappings. The group is proscribed as a terrorist organization by both the Spanish and French government, as well as the European Union.

² LOCATION AND HOMELAND

Basque country consists of three regions on the Spanish side of the Pyrenees (Vizcaya, Guipúzcoa, and Alava) and three on the French side (Labourd, Basse-Navarre, and Soule). These

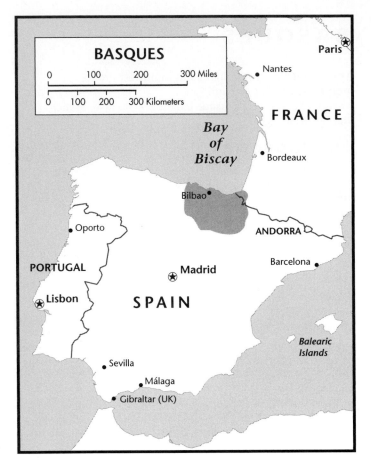

BASQUES

| 0 | 100 | 200 | 300 Miles |
| 0 | 100 | 200 | 300 Kilometers |

Nantes

Paris

FRANCE

Bay of Biscay

Bordeaux

Bilbao

ANDORRA

Oporto

Barcelona

PORTUGAL

Madrid

SPAIN

Lisbon

Sevilla

Balearic Islands

Málaga

Gibraltar (UK)

Romance language and belongs to no other known language family. Some scholars have suggested that it may have originated in the Caucasus region of Russia or in North Africa, and others have found similarities to Finnish and Berber. It was the universal language of rural Basques until the end of the 19th century, although it had no written literary tradition and was spoken less frequently by town dwellers. The Franco regime's suppression of all Spanish regionalism in the mid-20th century caused the number of Basque speakers in Spain to decline sharply (as opposed to France, where the figures are higher). In recent years, Basques in both France and Spain have promoted, with some success, the use of their traditional language, mainly by means of the *ikastolas*, or Basque language and culture schools, and it has become more common in literature and the media since Franco's death in 1975. Every province and town in Spain's Basque country has a Spanish and a Basque official name, both of which appear on all road signs.

The Basque language is notoriously difficult (regional folklore has it that the devil tried to learn Basque for seven years and gave up). There are many different grammatical tenses and a variety of possible forms for each word, depending on gender and other factors. In addition, there are a number of different dialects, although a person who speaks one dialect can generally understand the others. Basque is also rather exotic when contrasted with other Western tongues. For example, intensity may be expressed by repeating a word twice ("very hot" is *bero-bero*), a feature unknown among European languages but common among Polynesian ones. The language also lacks generic terms for "tree" and "animal": there are names for specific trees (oak, maple, etc.) but not for trees in general.

SAMPLE WORDS AND PHRASES

welcome	ongi-etorri
beach	hondartza
yes	bai
no	ez
see you later	gero arte
hello, how are you?	kaixo, zer moduz?

"Happiness is the only thing we can give without having" (proverb): *Izan gabe eman dezakegun gauza bakarra da zoriona.*

4 FOLKLORE

Through centuries of storytelling, the Basques have evolved a rich and colorful mythology. In ancient times their land was supposed to have been peopled by a race of giants called *jentillak,* who lived side by side with its human inhabitants until the coming of Christ, when they disappeared, leaving behind only one of their number named Olentzero. Olentzero is a folk character that appears in country festivals and celebrations, and is represented in the form of dolls and straw figures. According to legends, the lamiak were female spirits who looked like beautiful women with long golden hair; they had chicken feet, lived in caverns, and could wield either a helpful or a harmful influence. Besides legends and tales, the Basques have a rich and ancient folklore that encompasses various rituals and dances. The Katcha-Ranka is a dance performed in fishing villages. A person representing St. Peter is carried in a coffin through the village and to the waterfront by dancers who then proceed to symbolically beat him as a threat to ensure a good

territories, collectively, are called Euskal-Herria (Land of the Basques) or Euskadi. It has been nearly a thousand years since these regions were unified politically. The area is geographically varied, containing the ridges and foothills of the Pyrenees and a short coastal plain along the Bay of Biscay, as well as steep, narrow valleys and mountain streams. Although Basque nationalists claim Navarre as part of their territory, Navarre is a different autonomous community.

With 2.141.860 million inhabitants (2007), the land of the Basques, with an extension of 7,234 sq km (2,793 sq mi), is a densely populated area (293.73 per sq km). The people are unevenly distributed, with most living in Vizcaya and Guipúzcoa provinces. Fewer than 10% live in the region's largest province, Alava, which encompasses about 40% of the land area. About half the people who live in Basque country are Basques. More than 1 million have other ethnic backgrounds.

The port city of Bilbao is its largest city with a population of 354,145, followed by San Sebastián with 183,308. Blood types and other genetic information about the Basques suggest that they are an ancient people (possibly even descended from Cro-Magnon man) who inhabited the region long before the arrival of other European groups. According to a Basque saying, "Before God was God and boulders were boulders, the Basques were already Basques."

3 LANGUAGE

The Basque language, also known as Euskera, is Europe's oldest living language. It is unrelated to Spanish, French, or any other catch when they go out fishing. Cultural expressions, such as dancing and singing, often are tied to religious occasions.

5 RELIGION

Almost all Basques are Roman Catholics. Traditionally an unusually high percentage chose to become priests or nuns, although this number, together with church attendance generally, has fallen since the Second Vatican Council. Two of the church's most renowned theologians, St. Francis Xavier and St. Ignatius Loyola, who was the founder of the Jesuit order, were of Basque origin. Basque Catholicism, like that in many other areas of Spain, is characterized by a strong devotion to the Virgin Mary.

6 MAJOR HOLIDAYS

As elsewhere in Spain, most Basque holidays are those found in the Christian calendar. Special holidays include celebrations for Saint John, the Virgen de Begoña, the Virgen del Carmen (patroness of sailors and fishermen), and the Virgen Blanca. The celebration for the Virgen Blanca takes place on and around August 16, including weeklong celebrations of the Semana Grande Donostierra in San Sebastián and Bilbao. In addition, villages celebrate their own festivals with performances by folk musicians, dancers, and *bertsolariak,* traditional singer/storytellers who can improvise and sing rhymes on any topic.

7 RITES OF PASSAGE

Besides baptism, first Communion and marriage could be considered a rite of passage for Basques as with most Spaniards. These events are the occasion, in most cases, for big and expensive social gatherings in which the family shows its generosity and economic status.

8 INTERPERSONAL RELATIONS

In rural communities where families often lived on individual farms in relative isolation, a special relationship developed with one's neighbors, especially the nearest neighbor, called the *lehen auzo,* or "first neighbor." The role that first neighbors play sometimes even surpasses that of blood relatives. The best man and chief bridesmaid at weddings are chosen from the household of the lehen auzo, and its members are informed of a serious illness or impending death before the family's closest relatives. In an emergency, the lehen auzo temporarily takes over the running of his neighbor's farm. When there is a death in the family, custom traditionally requires that the lehen auzo be informed before the village bell tolls. The wider neighborhood, or *auzoa,* is also an important source of social support.

9 LIVING CONDITIONS

People in the rural regions of Basque country live in large stone farmhouses called *caseríos, or baserriak* (the plural of *baserria*). They are often as high as three stories, with animals kept on the ground floor, the family living space on the second floor, and hay and other crops stored on the third. They may either be built at a distance from one another or located in clusters of about 10 or 12. As a result of economical prosperity, cities and towns are much more extensive than a quarter of a century ago, and there are new areas developed with modern apartment buildings.

The Basques have access to the same level of modern medical care as their neighbors in Spain or France, countries with average life expectancies of 78 and 77 years, respectively. However, some Basques, particularly members of the older generation, still believe in the effectiveness of certain types of folk remedies, especially those involving various herbs.

Basque cities and towns are connected by bus and trains. Bilbao, the industrial center of the Basque region, is also Spain's busiest port. Located on the Bay of Biscay, it can accommodate tankers weighing up to 500,000 tons. Bilbao, Vitoria, and San Sebastian have airports. Bilbao's Sondika Airport, a beautiful building, is the busiest in northwest Spain, and the city is connected by rail with the rest of Spain and with France.

10 FAMILY LIFE

In rural areas, Basque households generally include the maternal or paternal grandparents, as well as unmarried aunts or uncles. It is not uncommon for cousins, even first cousins, to marry. The most important concern for rural dwellers is the perpetuation of the family farm, or *baseria*. In every family, one son or daughter is designated from childhood as heir to the farm. When he or she gets married, ownership of the farm is transferred to the new couple as part of the wedding arrangements. All adults in the household participate in child rearing. The whole family helps with the farm work, including children and grandparents, who assist with easier tasks. In urban areas, the nuclear family is the norm, sometimes joined by an elderly grandparent or unmarried aunt. Well-off families may have a live-in nanny or servant. In urban areas, family life is like in other parts of Spain.

11 CLOTHING

The Basques wear modern Western-style clothing for both casual and formal occasions. The single most distinctive item of traditional Basque clothing, which is still worn throughout the country, is the flat wide black beret (*boina*) worn by Basque men.

12 FOOD

The Basques are known for their excellent cuisine, much of which involves seafood. The Basque version of bouillabaisse, or fish stew, is called *ttoro* and includes mussels, crayfish, congers, and the head of a codfish, as well as three other kinds of fish. Cod itself (called *bacalao*) is also extremely popular; a book entitled *264 Recipes for Cod* is sold in Bilbao. Other specialties include fresh tuna with tomatoes, garlic, and spices; *txangurro* (spider crab); and hake *(merluza) kokotchas,* made with garlic and parsley. Red peppers are a dietary staple and find their way into seafood sauces, chicken recipes, and omelettes. "Gateau Basque" (Basque cake) is made from eggs, flour, sugar, and rum. A favorite national beverage is *txakoli,* a fruity white wine produced in coastal areas, often in small family cellars.

13 EDUCATION

School for the Basques, as for other Spanish children, is free and compulsory from the ages of 6 to 14, when many students begin the three-year *bachillerato* course of study, after which they may opt for either one year of college preparatory study or vocational training. About one-third of Spain's children are

Traditional Basque dancers hold torches in Bilbao's San Mames soccer stadium during a celebration of the official Basque language, Euskera. (AP Images/EFE, Txema Fernandez)

educated at private schools, many of them run by the Catholic Church.

Advanced studies are offered through the University of the Basque Country, founded in 1968, and the universities of San Sebastián and of Vitoria; the private University of Deusto, run by the Jesuits, is the oldest and most prestigious university in the Basque country.

¹⁴ CULTURAL HERITAGE

Besides, ancient stories and songs of a folklore, which were transmitted orally, there is not a sizeable literary heritage written in Euskera (the Basque language). Yet, there are well-known Basque authors who wrote in Spanish, such as Antonio de Trueba, Arturo Campion, Francisco Navarro Villoslada, writer and philosopher Miguel de Unamuno, and novelist Ignacio Aldecoa. In the 20th century, along with an upsurge of nationalism, a flourishing cultural, literary, and artistic movement began. Now, a great amount of Euskera-language books are published each year. Outstanding musicians are Juan Crisóstomo Arriaga, called "the Spanish Mozart," and composer Maurice Ravel. Artists include painter Ignacio Zuloaga and sculptor Eduardo Chillida.

Since 1997, when the Guggenheim Museum was opened, Bilbao has become a center of attraction for tourists and art lovers. The building is the work of the Canadian/American architect Frank Ghery. Built with reflective titanium panels, it is considered to be one of the world's most spectacular buildings

in the style of deconstructivism. Other museums are the Museum of Fine Arts in Bilbao and the San Telmo Museum in San Sebastián.

¹⁵ WORK

Fishing and agriculture have long been important occupations for the Basque. The traditional farm holding, or *basseria*, is a family enterprise in which each household raises its own crops (corn, wheat, and vegetables) and livestock (chickens, pigs, cows, and sheep), and certain resources including pasture lands and fuel wood are held in common by each village. The past 50 years have seen an increase in commercialization and mechanization, dictated by the demands of urban markets. However, Basque herders still follow the seasonal patterns of their ancestors, moving herds of sheep, cows, and goats up to mountain pasture lands from June to October while their wives take charge of the family farm.

The Basque country was the first part of Spain to become industrialized, and it has long been known as a center of Spanish industry, especially the city of Bilbao. The region's history as Spain's iron and steel capital led to the development of automobile and machine tool manufacturing, as well as shipbuilding. Although the iron industry and shipbuilding have declined, they still are a source of economy in the Basque country.

Other important sectors of the economy include the manufacture of railway cars, automobiles, and iron construction materials; a sizeable commercial fishing fleet that ventures as far away as the coasts of Ireland and western Africa; retail businesses; and tourism. Bilbao has traditionally been an important financial center. The Banco de Bilbao-Vizcaya (BBV) bank ranks among the one hundred largest banks in the world. Today, the Basque Autonomous Community is one of the wealthiest in Spain.

The Basque Technological Park in Zamudio is the home of many companies in high-tech industries, including telecommunications, biotechnology, and robotics.

16 SPORTS

The Basques have a rich tradition of sports in which skill and physical strength are the main components. Among these are competitions like *aizkolariak* (featuring teams of woodcutters racing to chop a tree trunk in two in the shortest time), dragging or lifting of heavy stones, foot races, and bowling. *Regatas de traineras* are rowing competitions among long narrow boats with a 13-member team. Every fishing town in the northern coast of Spain has its own team and *trainera* to compete at the annual rowing championship in San Sebastián.

The region is known internationally for the game called *frontón, pelota vasca,* or *jai-alai,* a handball- or squash-like ball game played at very high speeds. There are several forms of pelota, including some in which the ball travels at up to 241 km/hr (150 mi/hr). The game has been played for centuries in an outdoor court called a *frontón,* which often shares a wall with the village church. Today, it is also played in indoor courts as well. The fastest form of pelote, called *cesta punta,* is played on an outdoor court with a second wall called a *jai-alai.*

Basques are very fond of soccer and Bilbao has its own team, the Atlético de Bilbao, that has consistently been one of the best teams in the country.

17 ENTERTAINMENT AND RECREATION

Like other people throughout Spain, the Basques spend many leisure hours socializing with friends at tapas bars, which serve light food and drinks. They also enjoy each other's company at the more than 1,500 gourmet societies, or *txokos,* in their region. These are private dining clubs that were formerly all-male haunts but now welcome women (although men still tend to do the cooking). Television is a popular form of relaxation, and Spain has a private television station (TV Vasca) that broadcasts in the Basque language. *El mus is* a popular card game.

18 FOLK ART, CRAFTS, AND HOBBIES

The traditional Basque decorative arts consist primarily of wood carving and engraving on stone, both practiced mainly on door-lintels and tombstones. The Basques have a well-developed tradition of oral storytelling, which was one of their main forms of entertainment before urbanization (and television); Basques would often invite their neighbors over for an evening of tale-spinning. Basque folk music is sung and played on traditional instruments including the *txistu,* a three-holed flute, and the bagpipe-like *dultzaina.* Dozens of folk dances have been preserved, and many villages have folk-dance groups that perform regularly. Two especially spirited dances are the *Bolant Dantza* (flying dance) and *La Espata Dantza* (sword dance).

19 SOCIAL PROBLEMS

The iron, steel, chemical, and paper industries of the Basque region have created a serious pollution problem in its cities, and motor vehicle emissions have aggravated the situation. There is considerable river pollution as well. Bilbao's metals industries must deal with an outmoded infrastructure and increased competition from the new European Union.

The most pressing problems are ETA activities. Although the group represents the views of only a small minority, it continues to fight for full independence, and has killed over 800 people since 1968.

Other problems include alcoholism and drug dependency, mainly in the big cities.

20 GENDER ISSUES

Women have an ever-increasing role in society and a high degree of economic independence, competing favorably with men for jobs. Many women hold municipal and government posts, such as councilwomen, mayors, or university professors, and many are employed in or manage business. A large percentage of women attend universities.

21 BIBLIOGRAPHY

Abercrombie, Thomas J. "The Basques." *National Geographic* (November 1995): 74–96.

Collins, Roger. *Basques.* London: Basil Blackwell, 1990.

Douglass, William A. "Basques." In *Encyclopedia of World Cultures (Europe).* Boston: G. K. Hall, 1992.

Facaros, Dana, and Michael Pauls. *Northern Spain.* London: Cadogan Books, 1996.

Gaines, Lisa. "Spain's Basque Country Still Maintains Its Independent Spirit." *Travel Weekly* 52, no.66 (August. 23, 1993): 48.

Gallop, Rodney. *A Book of the Basques.* Reno, NV: University of Nevada Press, 1970.

Lee, Denny, "Bilbao, 10 years later". The New York Times, September 23, 2007

Moss, Joyce, and George Wilson. *Peoples of the World.* Detroit: Gale Research, 1993.

Westwood, Webster. *Basque Legends.* New York: AMS Press, 1977.

—revised by S. G. Castaneda

BELARUSANS

PRONUNCIATION: Byeh-lah-ROOS-ans
ALTERNATE NAMES: Byelorussians; "White Russians"
LOCATION: Belarus
POPULATION: 9.7 million
LANGUAGE: Belarusan
RELIGION: Christian (Russian Orthodox, Roman Catholic, Pentecostal, Baptist, other sects); minority of Muslim, Jewish, and other faiths

¹ INTRODUCTION

The history of the name *Belaya Rus* (variously translated as "White Russia," "White Ruthenia," "Byelorussia," "Byelorussiya," or "Belarus") is quite different from the history of the East Slavic Belarusan people. The name originated in the 12th century and initially designated various parts of northwestern Russia or Ukraine. Since the 14th century it has also been applied to eastern territories of present-day Belarus.

The meaning of "white" in White Russia, as applied to present-day Belarus (pronounced byeh-lah-roos«), is something of a puzzle. Historians have proposed various explanations for the term. "White" could refer to the beauty of the land, for instance, or to the abundance of snow, to the white complexion of the people, or to freedom and independence. The word "white" in those distant times signified "free," or "independent." Over the course of many centuries, the Belarusans have stubbornly struggled to defend their independence, language, culture, and national way of life. Another explanation of the color white has a religious context. The term *beloruski* was used for the first time by Prince Andrei Bogolubski who, having sacked Kiev in 1169, assumed the title "Prince Beloruski" to underscore true Orthodox faith.

The name *Belarus,* which in its contemporary meaning signifies either the modern Belarusan state or the entire ethnographic area settled by the Belarusans, dates back only to the last decade of the 19th century, when the Belarusan political movement began to develop. Its earlier variant was *Belaya Rus.*

Rus—distortedly translated by many as "Russia"—was a patch of land in the triangle formed by three cities: Kiev, Chernigov, and Perayaslavl in present-day Ukraine. But, as a result of the expansion of the Kievan Rus state, which spread during the 10th century over the vast territories of Novgorod, Pskov, Polacak, Muscovy, and other regions, *Rus* acquired a new meaning, and its scope was substantially changed. When the center of power in that empire moved by the mid-14th century to Muscovy, the quintessential Rus went with it.

The ancestors of the Belarusans have been known throughout history under various names. The earliest embodiment of statehood on Belarusan territories were the principalities of Polacak, Turau, and Navahradak (Novohorodak), named after their respective main cities. Ruled toward the end of the 10th century from Kiev, they asserted themselves early on as independent or semi-independent dominions. The Polacak principality, occupying more than half of present-day Belarus, was settled by a tribe of Kryvicans, one of the largest groups of East Slavs who moved into the area in the 6th century AD. The territory occupied by the Kryvicans stretched beyond the confines

of the Polacakan princes. In the 13th century, the territories of Polacak, Navahradak, and other Belarusan cities merged to defend their territories from the German religious order of the Teutonic Knights. This merge established the new duchy, further known as the Grand Duchy of Litva, Lithuania, Rus, and Samogitia (GDL), or simply as Lithuania. At the time of the political union between the GDL and the kingdom of Poland in 1569, when Ukraine was transferred from the GDL to the Polish kingdom, Belarus remained in the duchy. During this period, some Lithuanian princes embraced Eastern-rite Christianity, and Belarusan was the official language of the ducal chancellery and courts. In 1562, during the war with Muscovy, the gentry of the Grand Duchy formed a so-called confederation (i.e., a temporary military-political agreement), exploiting the thrust of the moment, and demanded closer ties with Poland. In 1569 a real federation concluded in the Polish city of Lublin established the new relationship between the two states. When the Polish kingdom fell apart in the last half of the 18th century, Russia took over the Belarusans' homeland.

The first attempt at independence from Russia began in 1863, when about 75,000 Belarusan farmers and some of the local nobility led a violent rebellion against the Russians. Although the revolt failed, it helped to solidify the national spirit and helped the movement for independence grow during the late 1800s. In 1918, an independent Belarusan Democratic Republic was declared out of the collapse of the imperial Russian government, despite the German occupation of World War I. The new Bolshevik government in Moscow refused to recognize the legitimacy of the new republic and arranged the overthrow of the new Belarusan government. In 1919, the Communists formed the Belarussian Soviet Socialist Republic (BSSR). In 1920, the Poles occupied much of the new country, but they later withdrew from all but the westernmost parts. The BSSR formally joined the Soviet Union in 1922. For its subservience to the regime, the Soviet Union rewarded the BSSR by focusing on its industrial development. The BSSR was also awarded a large amount of territory in the west that had been part of Poland but was ceded to the Soviet Union in the famous 1939 deal between Hitler and Stalin, the Nazi-Soviet Nonaggression Pact. Much of this "new" part of western Belarus in 1939 was actually the same territory that Belarus had given up to Poland after World War I.

The Soviet plan of restoration and industrialization after World War II initially helped the Belarusans during the 1960s and 1970s. Many factories produced weapons-related equipment and heavy machinery. However, by the 1980s, a lack of consumer goods, poor quality of life, and environmental problems (like contamination and deforestation) caused the Belarusans to distrust the Soviet government. During the 1986 Chernobyl nuclear power disaster in nearby Ukraine, the Soviet government delayed telling the people about the situation for several days. By that time, however, hundreds of thousands of people had been exposed to the radioactivity, and about 20% of the farmland was contaminated.

Labor strikes by factory and transportation workers in April 1991 helped further the cause of independence. After the failed coup in August 1991, Belarus became the sixth republic to secede from the Soviet Union. In December 1991, the capital of Belarus, Minsk, became the capital for the new Commonwealth of Independent States (CIS). (The CIS is a loose confederation of some of the former Soviet republics that addresses military and economic issues.

The first constitution of the newly independent Belarus was ratified in March 1994, and Alexander Lukashenko was elected president in July of that year. Since then, Lukashenko has wrested increasing control over the government of Belarus to establish an authoritarian regime. In 1996, Lukashenko manipulated a national referendum to reform the constitution, giving him increased powers over the government and removing term limits on the presidency. He declared himself the winner of presidential elections in 2001 and 2006, both of which were deemed fraudulent by international observers, as were other local and parliamentary elections that solidified Lukashenko's influence. Belarusan opposition leaders and protesters have been harassed, beaten, jailed, or made to "disappear," and the media is controlled by the government. Freedom House, an organization that grades countries on civil and political freedoms, recently gave Belarus the lowest scores possible.

The political situation in Belarus has prohibited the development of international relations, isolating Belarus and inhibiting its economic development. The transition from Soviet republic to independent nation continues to prove difficult for Belarus.

² LOCATION AND HOMELAND

Belarus is situated in the eastern part of the European continent. It borders Russia in the north and east, the Ukraine in the southeast, Poland in the west, and Latvia and Lithuania in the northwest. The Belarusan homeland is a landlocked nation that occupies 207,600 sq km (83,040 sq mi), which makes it about as large as the U.S. state of Minnesota, or about three times as large as Belgium and the Netherlands combined.

The major cities of Belarus are the capital Minsk (also spelled Miensk), with a population of over 1,800,000 people in 1992; Homel (Gomel), 506,000; Mahilou (Mogilev), 363,000; Viciebsk (Vitebsk), 356,000; Brest, 269,000; and Hrodna (Grodno), 255,000. Other large cities include Pinsk, Sluck, Baranavichy, Orsha, Hlybokaje, and Salihorsk.

The terrain of Belarus is predominantly flat, with hilly areas occupying only 8% of its territory. The Belaruskaya Hrada is a range of elevated terrain that runs from the southwest to the northeast part of Belarus. The highest point is 346 m (1,135 ft) above sea level. The climate of Belarus is temperate continental with a mild and humid winter, a warm summer, and a wet autumn. Annual precipitation ranges from 55 cm to 70 cm (21–28 in). The mean temperature in January is –6°C (20°F) and 18°C (64°F) in July, with high humidity. The climate of Belarus is favorable for agriculture. The territory of Belarus includes 3,000 streams and 4,000 lakes that are used for transportation and power generation. The largest lake is Naroch, which covers 80 sq km (31 sq mi) and has a maximum depth of about 25 m (82 ft). The principal rivers of Belarus are the Dneper, the Pripyat, the Berezina, the Western Dvina, and the Neman. The average density of river networks is 43.6 km for every 100 sq km of land (or about 70.1 mi of rivers per 100 sq mi of land). There are also sources of mineral water.

The inalienable part of the Belarusan landscape is bogs and swamps, which are of large climatic and hydrological significance. Their total number is about 7,000, and they occupy about 13.4% of Belarus's territory. Much of the swampland is in the south and is sparsely populated. The forests of

Belarus constitute over 33% of its territory, with a total area of 8,055,000 hectares (19,900,000 acres). The territory of the Republic of Belarus includes deposits of oil, oil shale, coal and lignite, iron ores, nonferrous metal ores, dolomites, potassium and rock salts, and phosphates. There are huge deposits of peat, fire and refractory clay, molding sand and sand for glass production, and different construction materials. The industry of Belarus has developed a number of deposits, making it possible not only to meet the requirements of the republic, but also to export natural resources.

About 25% of the population of Belarus was killed during World War II. Combined with the numbers killed in the Soviet purges, the population of Belarus in 1945 was only 67% as large as it was in the early 1930s. The population did not return to prewar levels until the mid-1970s. As of 2008, Belarus had 9.7 million inhabitants, of which 81% were ethnic Belarusans. The ratio of ethnic Belarusans to non-Belarusans has increased due to the emigration of ethnic Russians to Russia since independence. A law passed in 1992 made every inhabitant of Belarus a citizen, including all the ethnic Russians who had moved there over the years. Many of the Russians, however, declined to accept Belarusan citizenship but still live in Belarus.

There are also many ethnic Belarusans in Poland and in other parts of the former Soviet Union (such as Russia, Ukraine, Kazakhstan, Latvia, Lithuania, and Estonia), as well as large numbers living in the West (primarily in Great Britain, Germany, France, Belgium, the United States, Canada, and Argentina). The total population of Belarus has declined since independence due to emigration in search of better economic opportunities.

³ LANGUAGE

The development of the Belarusan language was stifled by Polish and Russian dominion for centuries. For example, during the time of the Russian tsars, the public use of the Belarusan language was strongly discouraged. Baltic influences also have helped shape the Belarusan language. The Belarusan language of the 1500s was the same as that used throughout the Grand Duchy of Lithuania. These influences caused the language to remain in a somewhat dormant state throughout those centuries. Modern Belarusan, therefore, is still very close to the old Eastern Slavic language, with some words borrowed from modern Polish and Russian. There are three primary Belarusan dialects: southwestern, northeastern, and central. Written Belarusan is based on the central (Minsk) dialect. A person who knows the Belarusan language can understand Russian and Ukrainian very well and will also comprehend Polish, Czech, Slovak, Bulgarian, and Slovenian.

During the Soviet era, the Belarusan language suffered because of the dominating influence of Russian, which is similar. Belarusans came to know the Russian language through exposure, and the Soviet government tried to change the Belarusan language by making the words and grammar sound more like Russian. Many Belarusan children were taught their own tongue as a second or even a third language in school. By the early 1940s, there were no Belarusan-language schools operating. It was estimated that only 11% of the population in the early 1990s was fluent in Belarusan. The constitution of Belarus proclaimed Belarusan as the official language in 1991, but a new constitution was adopted in March 1994. The Russian language has become so much a part of everyday life for Belarusans that it was voted an official language in May 1995 by leaders sympathetic with Russia.

Since independence, Belarusan has become the primary language of instruction. Belarusan and Russian are both official state languages in Belarus, though the government plans to phase out the use of Russian gradually. However, pro-Russian officials in Belarus have recently slowed down or stalled the implementation of this policy. The population of Minsk is almost entirely composed of Russian-speakers. Metro and street signs are now posted in both Russian and Belarusan, more courses at the university are now being taught in Belarusan, and most local radio stations now broadcast in Belarusan.

Everyday terms in the Belarusan language include *dobraga zdarovya* (hello), *tak* (yes), *nye* (no), *kali laska* (please), *dzyakooi* (thank you) and *da pabachenya* (good-bye).

⁴ FOLKLORE

The image of the tragic Rahnieda has sunk deep into the memory of the Belarusan people. There are numerous tales of the heartbroken princess who wanders across her native land consoling those in grief, healing the wounds of injured soldiers, and helping the unfortunate. The story of Princess Rahnieda begins with Prince St. Vladimir.

In his younger pre-Christian days, the future Christianizer of Rus, Kievan Prince St. Vladimir, ruled Novgorod, which was given to him by his father Svyatoslav (d. 972), the warrior-builder of the Kievan empire. To Vladimir's dismay, his father gave the prestigious Kievan seat to another son, Yaropolk.

Knowing he would have to fight for Kiev, Vladimir decided to secure himself an ally by marrying Rahnieda, the daughter of the Belarusan prince Rahvalod from the city of Polacak. Rahnieda, however, preferred Yaropolk. Rahnieda not only pricked Vladimir's pride by her refusal but also injured his ego by calling him *rabynic* (born of a servant). Rumor had it that Vladimir's mother was a servant in the household of the grand prince Svyatoslav. This was sufficient pretext for Vladimir and his cunning uncle, Dobrinya, to descend on Polacak, kill Rahnieda's parents and two of her brothers, and force the princess to become his wife. Soon afterward, Vladimir gained the Kievan seat by killing his brother Yaropolk.

Rahnieda gave birth to a boy, whom she named Iziaslau. She continued to hate her husband. Rahnieda decided to kill Vladimir in his sleep, but the scheme did not work: Vladimir awoke in time and thwarted his wife's revenge. He wanted to punish Rahnieda by death, but, as the chronicler states, their young son, Iziaslau, made him change his mind. Iziaslau stood up for his mother. With a sword in his hand, he said, "Don't think that you are all by yourself here!" Impressed by the courage of his first-born, Vladimir decided merely to banish both Iziaslau and Rahnieda to their native Polacak and even ordered a city built for the two of them, appropriately named Iziaslau (today known as Zaslauje, located near Minsk). According to legend, Rahnieda became a nun, taking the name of Anastasia, and spent the rest of her life in a monastery near the newly built city of Iziaslau, where she died around the year 1000.

⁵ RELIGION

Christianity came to Belarus soon after Rahnieda's husband, Kievan grand prince Vladimir, baptized his subjects in 988. The Byzantine variant of Christianity became the state religion and was spread throughout the realm by force of decree. Some historians believe that Polacak's first bishopric emerged as early as 992, and that Turau's came in 1005. One of the most famous religious leaders was St. Euphrosyne of Polacak (c. 1120–1173). Christened Pradslava, the young princess chose to become a nun. She transcribed books, initiated the building of churches and monasteries, and founded schools, libraries, and orphanages. St. Euphrosyne is remarkable not only for her works, but also for her courage and devotion to Christian ideals. During the Second Crusade she visited the Holy Land on a pilgrimage to Jerusalem, where she died in 1173 and soon afterward was canonized.

Revered today by Orthodox and Catholics as the patron saint of Belarus, St. Euphrosyne symbolizes the civilizing power of Christianity. Her name was immortalized by (among other things) a splendid gem-studded cross created at Euphrosyne's behest by a Belarusan master, Lazar Bohsa. Of exquisite beauty, the relic survived centuries of turbulence until World War II, when it mysteriously disappeared.

The Belarusan people, Christianized originally in the Byzantine rite, became multiconfessional as a result of the advantages Catholicism enjoyed in the Grand Duchy, followed by the Reformation, Counter-Reformation, and Polish as well as Russian counterpressures. Over the centuries, however, the peoples of the Grand Duchy of Lithuania, Rus, and Samogitia were able to work out a peaceful compromise marked by religious tolerance and interethnic cooperation between Orthodox and Catholic, Jew and Tatar. In 1622 King Sigismund III prohibited any public controversy against Catholics. A wave of takeovers of Orthodox Church buildings and monasteries swept Belarus. Just as Protestants a century earlier had taken over Catholic churches, now the Uniates, instigated and supported by state authorities and the Vatican, did the same to Orthodox shrines. Catholicism, having lost much ground to the Reformation in Western Europe, found a small counterweight in the East.

When the Polish element began to dominate the political life of the Belarusan territory, the religious union inadvisably became a tool to make the Belarusan people more Polish. Many Belarusans, dissatisfied with social conditions and opposing the growing pressure to join the Uniate Church, fled south into the Ukrainian steppes to join the Cossack group. In 1696, by decision of the General Confederation in Warsaw, the Belarusan language in the Grand Duchy lost its official status and was replaced by Polish. Moreover, Catholicism became increasingly identified as the "Polish creed," thus deepening and complicating the Russo-Polish antagonism.

In their geopolitical striving toward Western Europe, the tsars used the convenient pretext of "liberating" their co-religionists of the "Russian faith" from Polish Catholic domination. In 1839 the Uniate Church in Belarus, to which about 75% of the population adhered, was forcibly converted to Russian Orthodox. The name Belarus was officially banned, replaced either by the name of individual governorships or by the term West Russia, (with such variants as Northwest Russia and Northwestern Province).

Before 1917, Belarus had 2,466 religious congregations, including 1,650 Orthodox, 127 Roman Catholic, 657 Jewish, 32 Protestant, and several Muslim communities. Many congregations were destroyed during the early Soviet years, and religious leaders were typically exiled or executed. Congregations that were allowed to exist were often controlled by the government in order to advance a nationalist agenda. During the 1980s, the relaxation of controls against religious institutions (coupled with the celebration of the millennial anniversary of Christianity in Russia) initiated a small religious revival in Belarus.

The new constitution of Belarus guarantees religious freedoms; however, a 2002 law and 2003 concordat with the Belarus Orthodox Church (BOC) give the BOC a privileged status and effectively repress the practice of other religions. In 2008, about 80% of Belarusans identified themselves as Orthodox, 14% as Catholic, 2% as Protestant, and the remaining 4% as Jewish, Muslim, or other faiths. Those who are not members of the BOC, particularly Protestants and Jews, suffer harassment and discrimination.

6 MAJOR HOLIDAYS

Kolady (Christmas) is one of the most prominent traditional holidays in Belarus. The holiday season starts with a solemn, elaborate supper on *Kootia* (Christmas Eve). Twelve or more dishes are prepared and served. The pot containing a dish called Kootia is placed on a stand in the corner under the icons. The head of the home starts by saying grace. The dishes are served in a specific order, with a portion of each put aside for the ancestors. Kootia is the last course of the supper.

The tradition of Christmas caroling dates back to the Middle Ages. Young people would travel from house to house. They carried a giant lighted star, representing the Star of Bethlehem, and sang carols called *Kaladki;* some would dress in animal and bird costumes. The goat was always the favorite—a re-

versed sheepskin coat and a goat's head, complete with beard and horns, were used. They sang and entertained with humorous presentations and games. Along with the merrymaking, the carolers would praise the host and his family. In return, they received goodies, money, and small presents.

Another beautiful Christmas tradition was the Batlejka Show. This was a puppet show of the Nativity, performed with wooden puppets. This tradition has become popular again. Christmas tree decorating and the Christmas tree show are also very popular in Belarus. Young people usually decorate the tree with handmade toys. They also prepare grab bags for the Christmas Tree Show. The show is an elaborate presentation of singing and dramatic readings. After the show, Dzied Maroz (Father Frost) or Sviaty Mikola (St. Nicholas) distributes the presents.

Easter is one of the most joyous holidays in Belarus. The Easter festivities usually begin with Palm Sunday, which is called *Verbnica* in Belarusan (from the word *viarba*, "willows"). Each girl brings a bouquet of pussy willows, decorated with artificial flowers and evergreen twigs, to church. After the service, there is a contest to select the girl with the prettiest bouquet. After Mass and the blessing of eggs on Easter morning, a common brunch called a *razhaveny* is held in the church hall; *babkas* (Easter bread), *kaubasy* (sausage), and other traditional foods are served. The people then go home to take a brief nap because the Easter Mass lasts the entire night.

Easter Sunday is a day of enjoyment. People play games, crack eggs, and have contests to select the best painted eggs. It is also traditional to visit friends, relatives, and neighbors on Easter Sunday. The Easter celebrations in Belarus last for two or three days. This tradition is especially popular with young people.

7 RITES OF PASSAGE

Completion of high school and university are important moments that mark the passage into adulthood. Entrance into military service is also revered in the same way.

8 INTERPERSONAL RELATIONS

Belarusans typically shake hands upon greeting each other, but family members and close friends will often greet each other with a hug. Unlike Russians, the Belarusans do not use patronymics when addressing each other. Family ties among Belarusans are strong, and a traditional sense of kinship among families is still apparent in modern society. There is a custom among Belarusans that "no one should walk the street hungry," and this tradition has led to an informal system where individuals respond to others in need. Belarusans do not have the custom of avoiding eye contact with those who appear destitute.

9 LIVING CONDITIONS

The health care system for Belarusans in the homeland today is in bad shape, as is common throughout the former Soviet Union. There is a lack of both trained personnel and adequate technology. The burden of the 1986 Chernobyl fiasco completely overwhelmed the health care system, and it has yet to fully recover. Various forms of cancer brought about by radioactive contamination have affected many adults and children, and birth defects and infant mortality rapidly increased after the accident. The most common causes of death are cardiovas-

Farmers in the village of Postrash, Belarus, load sugar beets into a cart. While Belarus once had to curtail food exports, food imports from Russia and Moldova have grown dramatically. (AP Images/Sergei Grits)

cular disease, cancer, accidents, and respiratory disease. There is mandatory HIV testing of all hospital inpatients.

About 75% of all the housing in cities and in many of the villages was destroyed during World War II. Many people lived in makeshift shacks after the war while massive urban housing projects were being constructed. Now, many of these same housing projects are in disrepair. A shortage of urban housing was common throughout much of the former Soviet Union, but the problem was made much worse in Belarus because of the 1986 Chernobyl disaster, which required the resettlement of thousands of people from the contaminated area. About three-fourths of the population lives in urban centers today. Most urban Belarusans have small apartments in multistory, prefabricated buildings. The process of privatizing housing has been slowly progressing.

Because of the flat terrain, an extensive railroad system has developed into the major method of transportation across Belarus. Minsk is an important railroad junction for lines that connect the Baltic states with Ukraine and for the line that links Moscow with Warsaw. The railroads have historically had an important role in the development of industry, as well as strategic military importance. Since there is such a reliance on railroads, cars are a secondary form of transportation for many Belarusans. As a result, many of the roads outside of urban areas are unpaved, making it hard to transport agricultural products to the cities. A vast system of canals and navigable rivers is also widely used to transport both freight and passengers within Belarus.

10 FAMILY LIFE

Marriage and family are very important to Belarusans. One traditional Belarusan wedding gift is a *rushnik*—a handcrafted towel. Wedding guests are traditionally greeted with round rye bread and salt on a rushnik.

11 CLOTHING

The male Belarusan folk costume consists of a long, embroidered white linen shirt, girdled with a wide embroidered belt (sash), white linen trousers, and black leather boots or bast sandals. Wide-brimmed straw hats are worn in summer and jerkins and sheepskin coats are worn in winter.

The typical female folk costume is a loose white dress. Occasionally, a blouse with embroidered shoulders was worn over a flounced skirt. An embroidered apron and kerchief completed the outfit.

National costumes are still worn in Belarus, especially in the southern areas. There are regional variations. Many modern clothes are now decorated with traditional embroidery.

12 FOOD

Belarusan cuisine includes dishes made with potatoes, beets, peas, plums, pears, and, particularly, apples. The dishes are relatively simple and healthy and vary with the seasons. The inclusion of a large variety of grains and mushrooms reflects the land and soil characteristics.

Potatoes are the most abundant and popular food. Belarusans boast of being able to prepare potatoes in over 100 different ways. Carrots and cabbage are also popular. Veal, pork, fowl, and venison are the most common meats. *Kaubasy* (sausages), pork chops, and other meats are often smoked. Belarusans also love freshwater fish. A small river lobster, *ugry*, is considered a Belarusan delicacy.

Many Belarusan dishes are similar to those of Slavic groups. Some typical Belarusan specialties are potato pancakes with bacon, *vireshchaka* (pork ribs with gravy and pancakes), *varley kuccia* (hot barley cereal with bacon and fried onion), birch and honey *kvass* (a fermented drink), and *holodnik* (cold beet soup with cucumbers, dill, hard-boiled eggs, radishes, and sour cream). Belarusan cooks honor their guests with traditional greetings such as, "Guest into the house—God into the house."

13 EDUCATION

Required public education lasts about nine years, after which students may attend two or three more years of secondary education. Many of the secondary schools are trade and professional schools. Most Belarusans who want to go to college in the homeland attend the University of Minsk or the Academy of Sciences. Several theological schools have also opened in recent years.

14 CULTURAL HERITAGE

The Belarusan culture was originally developed in the old principalities of the Belarusan cities of Polacak, Smolensk, Turau, etc. Belarusan culture reached its highest stage of development as part of the Grand Duchy of Lithuania, where Belarusan was the official language. Francishak Skaryna, Vasil Tsiapinski, Symon Budny, Symon Polacki, Sciapan Zizani, and other scholars contributed to the development of Belarusan and other Slavic cultures. Cultural ties with the West were also maintained through the universities in Prague, Germany, Italy, and Krakow.

Dr. Francishak Skaryna printed the first book in Belarusan—the Bible—in 1517. The Belarusan Bible was the second Slavic Bible to be translated into a native language. Skaryna's Bible also established the first printing press on Belarusan soil, and Belarusan printing owes its beginning to him. He published 23 books of the Bible between 1517 and 1519. After moving from Prague to Vilna (Vilnius), then the center of Belarusan political and cultural activities, Skaryna published several more books of the Bible, beginning in 1522. All his books have lengthy introductions and epilogues in Belarusan explaining the book's content, meaning, and relation to everyday life. He also included comments on literature, history, geography, philosophy, and the sciences.

As stated in the draft of the new Constitution of the Republic of Belarus, modern Belarusans pride themselves on having a "centuries-long history of the development of Belarusan statehood," as reflected in "the Statutes of the Grand Duchy of Lithuania." The Statutes of the Grand Duchy of Lithuania (which, as codes of law, were promulgated in 1529, 1566, and 1588) stand as a monument to the role played by Belarusan culture in the early period of the Grand Duchy. Written in Belarusan, the official language of the ducal chancellery, these statutes contain local-custom laws as well as decisions of the administration and courts. The 15th and 16th centuries left behind a wealth of documents, including historical chronicles, original literary works, translations of the classics, religious treatises, and biblical studies that attest to the fruitful development of Belarusan culture in the Grand Duchy of Lithuania.

Belarusan literature developed most strongly in the 19th and 20th centuries. The most famous Belarusan writers are Maksim Bagdanovich (1891–1917), Janka Kupala (1882–1942), Jakub Kolas (1882–1956), Alojza Pashkevich (Ciotka) (1876–1916), Ryhor Baradulin (b.1935), Janka Bryl (b.1917), and Vasil Bykau (b.1924).

Folk dancing, which originated centuries ago, expresses the feelings, work habits, and lifestyle of the Belarusan people. Dances, such as *Bulba, Lanok,* and *Ruchniki,* reflect work processes; the *Miacelica* and *Charot* demonstrate humanity's relationship to nature; and the *Liavonicha, Mikita,* and *Yurachka* express human feelings and folk tales. Belarusan folk dances are characterized by richness of composition, uncomplicated movements, and a small number of rapid steps. The dances can be adapted for varied groups and solos. Ethnographers have identified over 100 Belarusan folk dances. Belarusan dances are unique in that they are often accompanied by singing.

15 WORK

Underemployment was a problem during the Soviet years and is still present today, which accounts for the low official unemployment rates. Rather than just lay off workers, factories and businesses often will shorten the number of work hours, reduce wages, or force employees to take unpaid leave. In 2004 the government instituted a policy of short-term contracts for state employees (about 80% of Belarusan workers), effectively allowing them to fire workers by not renewing their contracts. Contracts may last up to five years, but most are only one year.

16 SPORTS

Soccer and hockey are popular team spectator sports that Belarusans also enjoy playing. Sports societies and organizations were prominent in the Soviet years, and the government liberally advocated public participation in a wide variety of sports. Many of the former "sports palaces" built by the Soviet government have been converted to health clubs. International competitions, such as the Olympics, have become very important national rallying events for Belarusan athletes. Belarusans have become internationally prominent in gymnastics and acrobatic activities.

17 ENTERTAINMENT AND RECREATION

Until the 19th century, during the spring and summer it was common for Belarusan boys and girls to gather together outdoors in groups at twilight for singing. People would also traditionally gather around the fireplace in the winter for singing. Fishing in the rivers and streams of Belarus was formerly a popular activity, but irrigation projects and pollution of waterways during the Soviet era have greatly diminished sport fishing.

18 FOLK ART, CRAFTS, AND HOBBIES

Ceramics and pottery are traditional Belarusan crafts. The most famous type of Belarusan ceramics is probably *charnazadymlenaya*—a type of black, smoked pottery developed centuries ago. Other famous styles of ceramics are named after the

Belarusan place of origin, such as *Garadnianskaya* (from Garadnaia village, in the Stolin region) and *Ivianetskaya* (from Ivianets, in the Valozhyn region).

Weaving and textiles are also popular traditional crafts. Different types and colors of straw are woven together to make contoured pictures for hanging on walls. Traditional Slavic color motifs make frequent use of red (which signifies goodness and joy) and white (which represents purity). Red and white are also the national colors of Belarus and are used in patriotic designs. Flowers and trees are often the objects depicted in Belarusan handicrafts. Textiles from the upper Dzvina River region often show a Baltic influence because of the historical connection between Baltic and Belarusan cultures.

¹⁹ SOCIAL PROBLEMS

Belarus has long been caught in the middle of Central European history, which has made it necessary for the Belarusans to get along with their neighbors. Ethnic tensions in Belarus are less substantial than elsewhere in the former Soviet Union, and relations with Russians remain generally good. This situation must be maintained because, as a people in a landlocked nation, the Belarusans cannot economically afford to be unfriendly to their neighbors. The transition toward a market economy has been greatly slowed, however, by President Lukashenko's authoritarian policies.

Increased crime, particularly organized crime activities, such as drug and human trafficking, plagues Belarus given its geographic position as a transfer point between Eastern and Western Europe. The failure of Lukashenko's government to provide civil liberties has resulted in the isolation of Belarus from the international community, and Russia is beginning to exert pressure on Belarus to repay its debts, placing Belarus in a tight position politically and economically. These realities have caused a rise in conflicts between those who identify themselves as pro-Western versus those who are pro-Eastern, or European versus Slavic.

Belarusans also continue to suffer the economic and social costs of the 1986 Chernobyl nuclear power accident in Ukraine. About 70% of the radiation from that accident blew across Belarus, affecting over 2 million people, including about 600,000 children. The costs of this accident decades later include an increase in various forms of disease (such as leukemia and other cancers) and birth defects, which have risen by 40% since the accident. Much of the cropland was ruined with radiation, and contaminated water, livestock, produce, and soil are still widespread. Some marshlands in the south still retain high levels of radiation. In 2004, the government nevertheless introduced plans to reopen some of the contaminated land to agriculture.

²⁰ GENDER ISSUES

Belarusan culture holds fast to its traditional patriarchal values, resulting in oppressive conditions for both women and homosexuals. Although women are guaranteed equal rights in the Belarusan constitution, they still struggle for equal representation in government and the workplace. Motherhood is considered more important than individual women's rights, making it difficult to institute reforms providing better treatment of women in the workplace. Women represent the highest percentage of the unemployed in Belarus, and about 12% have suffered sexual harassment at work. Many women work in unsanitary or unsafe conditions.

Life at home is no better. Nearly one in three women have experienced domestic violence, and rates of poverty among women continue to increase. All this leaves Belarusan women vulnerable to sexual trafficking. Promises of jobs or marriage in foreign countries lure disadvantaged women to place themselves in the hands of traffickers, who sell them into prostitution. The Belarusan government has been in the forefront of the eastern European efforts to combat human trafficking, establishing shelters and hotlines for women at risk.

Although homosexual activity is not illegal in Belarus, a strong stigma is still attached to homosexuality. The Belarusan Orthodox Church, to which the vast majority of Belarusans belong, views homosexuality as a sin. Most homosexuals remain closeted and keep their social life underground. Discrimination is widespread and there are no laws specifically against homophobic crimes.

²¹ BIBLIOGRAPHY

Bely, Anatol. *Uladary staraszsytnay Belarusy.* Skryzaly Spadzhny 1996, #2.

Fedor, Helen, ed. *Belarus and Moldova: Country Studies.* Lanham, MD: Federal Research Division, Library of Congress, 1995.

Immigration and Refugee Board of Canada. "Responses to Information Requests: BLR100656.E," http://www.irb-cisr.gc.ca/en/research/rir/?action=record.viewrec&gotorec=449808 (11 August 2008).

Kipel, Vitaut. *Byelorussian Americans and their Communities of Cleveland.* Cleveland, OH: Cleveland State University, 1982.

Korosteleva, Elena A., Colin W. Lawson, and Rosalind J. Marsh, eds. *Contemporary Belarus: Between Democracy and Dictatorship.* New York: Routledge Courzon, 2003.

Stop Violence Against Women. "Freedom House Report Labels Belarus, Russia (Chechnya), Turkmenistan and Uzbekistan as Among the World's Most Repressive Societies," http://www.stopvaw.org/2May20059.html (11 August 2008).

UN Committee on Elimination of Discrimination Against Women. "Campaign Needed to Raise Awareness of Women's Human Rights in Belarus," http://www.un.org/News/Press/docs/2004/wom1430.doc.htm (11 August 2008).

US Department of State. "Background Note: Belarus," http://www.state.gov/r/pa/ei/bgn/5371.htm (7 August 2008).

Virtual Guide to Belarus, http://belarusguide.com (7 August 2008).

Zaprudnik, Ian. *Belarus: At a Crossroads in History.* Boulder, CO: Westview Press, 1993.

—revised by Dianne de Mott

BELGIANS

LOCATION: Belgium
POPULATION: About 10.4 million
LANGUAGE: Dutch (called Flemish in its regional spoken version); French; German
RELIGION: Roman Catholic; smaller numbers of Muslims and Jews

1 INTRODUCTION

Centuries of foreign invasion and occupation—by the Romans, French, Burgundians, Spanish, Austrian, and Germans—have made the people of Belgium resilient and enterprising. When Rome invaded in 58 BC, Julius Caesar called the region's Belgae tribes the toughest opponents he had faced. Some of history's major battles have been fought in this small country, including the Battle of Waterloo that signified the downfall of Napoleon Bonaparte and the Battle of the Bulge in World War II. Although it was recognized as a distinct region, Belgium did not become a nation until 1831. Today some of the world's most important international organizations, including the European Union (EU) and the North Atlantic Treaty Organization (NATO), are headquartered in Brussels. But tensions between the Dutch-speaking Flemings of the north and the French-speaking Walloons of the south have led in recent years to constitutional amendments granting these regions formal recognition and autonomy. Belgium was locked in a political stalemate beginning in June 2007 when elections failed to produce a new government. The question arose as to whether or not Belgium should cease to exist as a country, and that the territory would be split into two—the mainly Dutch-speaking Flanders and French-speaking Wallonia regions. The crisis was temporarily resolved in March 2008 when a new government was formed, and major reforms of state were planned.

2 LOCATION AND HOMELAND

Located in northwestern Europe, Belgium is one of the "low countries," so called because much of its land is at or below sea level. This small country, about as large as the state of Maryland, often serves as a crossroads between its larger neighbors. Belgium is often the point of departure or arrival for those crossing the English Channel, and it only takes about three hours or less to drive from its capital, Brussels, to the neighboring cities—Paris, Bonn, and The Hague. Belgium's major geographic divisions are the coastal lowlands, the central plain, and the high plateau of the Ardennes. Its principal rivers are the Scheldt and the Meuse.

Belgium is one of the world's most densely populated countries, but it is run so efficiently that overcrowding is not a problem. Belgian society is overwhelmingly urban: over 90% of the people live in one of 135 major cities. The Flemish and Walloon populations coexist but maintain sharply separate ethnic and linguistic identities. Traditionally, the Walloons were considered the dominant group because their region led the nation in industrial development and also because of the perceived superiority of their French cultural roots. However, since World War II, a shift in economic development from heavy industry toward commerce—much of it reliant on the port city of Antwerp—has favored the northern, Flemish region (also known

as Flanders). The Flemish have surpassed the Walloons in numbers as well.

3 LANGUAGE

Belgium has three official languages: Dutch (also called Flemish in its regional spoken version), French, and German. Approximately 60% of Belgians speak Flemish, 40% French, and less than 1% German. Flemish is the language of the northern provinces and French of the southern ones, while most German speakers live in eastern Liège along the German border. There have been longstanding conflicts between the Flemish and the French-speaking Walloons over language use in schools, courts, business, and government. Many visitors to Belgium will be surprised by the fact that signs on highways will indicate cities' names in two languages (e.g., Brussels/Bruxelles, Luik/Liège, Bergen/Mons). The 1970 constitution specifies four autonomous linguistic areas, one for each of the three languages plus Brussels, which is bilingual. (Most people in Brussels actually speak French, although the city itself is surrounded by a Flemish-speaking region.)

NUMBERS	FLEMISH
one	een
two	twee
three	drie
four	vier
five	vijf
six	zes
seven	zeven
eight	acht
nine	negen
ten	tien

DAYS OF THE WEEK	DUTCH
Sunday	zondag
Monday	maandag
Tuesday	dinsdag
Wednesday	woensdag
Thursday	donderdag
Friday	vrijdag
Saturday	zaterdag

4 FOLKLORE

Many of Belgium's colorful festivals are based on local myths, including the famous Cat Festival of Ypres. According to legend, cats were brought into medieval Ypres when the city was overrun by rats, but the cats multiplied so fast that they became a problem themselves and people took to throwing them off the tops of buildings (an act that is ritually repeated during the festival with toy cats). Other festivals with mythic origins include the pageant of the Golden Tree in Bruges and the Ommegang in Brussels. Folklore also surrounds Belgium's traditional puppet theater, whose marionettes are based on characters from the lore of their particular cities. These include Woltje in Brussels, Schele in Antwerp, Pierke in Ghent, and Tchantchès in Liège.

Another important festival in Bruges is the Procession of the Sacred Heart, held in summer. Originally a Catholic holiday, the celebration attracts many people both from Belgium and surrounding countries.

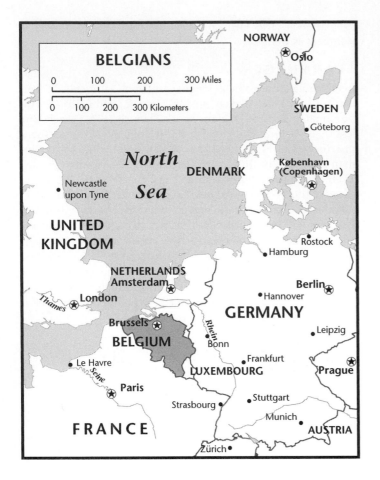

dance thought either to symbolize or to have been learned during the 15th-century Spanish conquest of the Incas in Peru. Men dressed in bizarre padded and brightly colored costumes and white hats adorned with enormous ostrich plumes dance down the street in formation throwing oranges (symbolizing pieces of gold) at the spectators, who are also pelted with water-filled sheeps' bladders. The occasional foreigner who throws oranges back at the men will risk being beaten up by other inhabitants of Binche. The Binche festival is so popular that the Belgian railways have extra trains run on that day.

Other festivals include Brussels' Ommegang, in which thousands of people parade in colorful costumes; the Cat Festival of Ypres (commemorating feline rat control during the Middle Ages); the Parade of the Giants in Ath; and the Nivelles carnival, graced by ritualized fights between people on stilts.

7 RITES OF PASSAGE

Rites of passage include major Catholic ceremonies such as baptisms, first Communions, marriages and funerals. Although most Belgians do not really practice Catholicism, the important events in a person's life tend to be occasions of major family reunions stressing their religious heritage. Special gifts and wishes will be given for baptisms, first Communions, and marriages. Many young people do not get married, but live together; however, compared to the Netherlands where this is a common practice, Belgium seems to be a bit more conservative.

8 INTERPERSONAL RELATIONS

Belgian manners are generally formal and polite, and conversations are marked by frequent exchanges of compliments and repeated handshaking. Relatives shake hands, hug, or kiss each other on the cheek, while friends usually hug. Men and women or two female friends—but never two men—might exchange kisses on the cheek, and women can sometimes be seen walking down the street arm-in-arm. American-style "high fives" have become popular among Belgian youth.

Both official Dutch and official French have a polite form to be used when addressing another person, but both Flemish and Walloons tend to use the informal *jÿ* (Dutch) and *tu* (French) more often than the Dutch in Holland or the French in France.

9 LIVING CONDITIONS

Belgium has no significant housing shortage and few slums. Traditionally, many Flemings lived in walled cities, although villages and other types of settlements were common as well. Brick and limestone are the most popular materials for Belgian houses and public buildings—wooden structures are relatively rare due to the nation's scarce timber resources. The distinctive "stepped-gable" style seen in 17th- and 18th-century houses has influenced modern architectural styles. In a number of Belgian homes, a portion of the first floor is used for business activities: common terms for a dwelling that is used this way include *winkelhuis* ("shop house") and *handelshuis* (business residence). Many houses have large kitchens in which closely knit Belgian families can gather.

Belgians receive modern medical, psychological, and geriatric care in state-run hospitals and clinics, as well as from private doctors. Fully 99% of the people are covered by the na-

5 RELIGION

Belgium is a predominantly Catholic country; about 75% of the population identifies itself as Roman Catholic. Muslims, mostly migratory workers from Turkey and North Africa, are the second-largest religious group, numbering 364,000 in 2005. Muslims outnumber Belgium's Protestants and Greek and Russian Orthodox. Belgium has a Jewish population of some 42,000, the fourth largest Jewish community in Europe in 2005. While Belgian Catholics are commonly baptized and receive a religious education, many do not otherwise actively practice their religion. Some are even outright nonbelievers who avoid leaving the church because of its link with many social services, at the parish and other levels. Beauraing and Banneaux in Wallonia are popular destinations for pilgrimages, as is Lourdes in France.

6 MAJOR HOLIDAYS

Belgium's legal holidays are New Year's Day, Easter Monday, Labor Day (May 1), Independence Day (July 21), All Saints' Day (November 1), and Christmas. Another important day is the Anniversary of the Battle of the Golden Spurs on July 11. However, in addition to these official holidays, the people of Belgium find many other occasions to celebrate. Belgians have a well-known fondness for festivals of all kinds, both sacred and secular.

One of the most famous is the Shrove Tuesday Carnival at Binche, from which the English word "binge" is thought to derive. It is known for the "March of the Gilles," a ritualized

People cruising on a canal. Belgium is one of the so-called "low countries" of Europe because much of its land is at or below sea level.
(Cory Langley)

tional health plan. In every Belgian city or town, a committee administers health and hospital services.

Belgium has an excellent waterway system—many of its cities are linked by a network of rivers and canals whose center is the port of Antwerp, which also handles the majority of foreign trade. The rail system, with its hub at Brussels, is also well developed. Helicopter service is available between Brussels and several other cities on the European continent.

10 FAMILY LIFE

The Belgian family is traditionally an economic unit. Many couples work side by side in either business or farming, and traits considered desirable in a marriage partner often include those that will lead to a compatible working relationship. Instead of divorcing, couples who are in business together may remain legally married in order to protect the business, maintaining separate households with new partners. Among extended families involved in the same business or trade, several nuclear families may live in neighboring houses near their business. Men and women tend to marry young—in their teens and twenties—and begin their families early. Most families have between two and four children, and children generally live with their parents until they marry. The elderly are commonly cared for in homes run by religious orders, social or political organizations, or other types of groups. Women account for roughly 40% of the work force (but 90% of the part-time workforce), although salaried women earn about 15% less than men.

11 CLOTHING

The traditional costumes of the Flemings and Walloons are a thing of the past—Belgians, especially in the city, wear modern Western-style clothes, with men expected to wear jackets to white-collar jobs (although it is often acceptable for women to wear slacks). The traditional dark-colored garb can still be seen on some farms, with women in aprons and men wearing caps.

12 FOOD

Belgium is known for its rich, tasty food—the Belgians' daily consumption of calories is among the world's highest. They are great meat eaters and spend up to one-third of their food budget on various types of meat including pork (the most popular), beef, chicken, rabbit, and veal, which are all popular. Two of the best-known dishes are *carbonades* of beef (stewed in beer) and a chicken or fish chowder called *waterzooi*. Belgian cooking uses many rich sauces made with butter and cream, and mayonnaise is widely used as well. It is often eaten as a dip with the popular Belgian chips whose distinctive taste comes being cooked in two different kinds of fat, one of which is used only when the chips are nearly done. The plentiful North Sea and Atlantic Ocean catch includes many varieties of fish as well as eels, cockles, and mussels, all of which are considered delicacies. Other Belgian specialties include waffles, over 300 varieties of beer, and chocolate.

Locals and tourists linger at tables in Groenplaats (Green) Square in Belgium. (Paul Kenward/Getty Images)

13 EDUCATION

Education is compulsory from the ages of 6 through 15, and nearly all children start earlier with nursery school and kindergarten. Belgium has an unusually high literacy rate—adult illiteracy is virtually nonexistent. Depending on the region, classes may be taught in either French, Dutch, or German. Both the public, or "official," schools and the private "free" schools (largely Catholic) are financed by the government, and historically there have been conflicts between secular and religious schools. Belgium has eight major universities, including institutions in Brussels, Ghent, Liège, and Antwerp.

14 CULTURAL HERITAGE

Belgium has played a prominent role in European culture since the 15th century. Among the most famous elements of Belgium's cultural heritage are the paintings of Pieter Breugel the Elder, Jan van Eyck, and Peter Paul Rubens and the compositions of Orlando di Lasso and César Franck. Belgium has literary traditions in both French and Flemish dating back to the Middle Ages, although French has been used by Flemish authors at various times since the 16th century. Modern Bel-

gians writing in French include the Nobel Prize-winning dramatist Maurice Maeterlinck and the popular detective novelist Georges Simenon, who was born in Liège. Prominent modern painters include expressionist James Ensor and surrealist René Magritte.

15 WORK

The Belgians—who are largely Catholic—demonstrate what Americans call the "Protestant work ethic." Traditionally considering work something of a moral duty, they put in long hours: a businessman who arrives at the office at 9:00 is considered lazy. Small, family-run businesses were long the norm in Flanders, while industry was primarily the domain of the Walloons, especially in the Liège area. In recent years the north has undergone increased industrialization, and the service and tourist sectors have expanded rapidly. However, farmers still grow vegetables, fruit, and grains, and commercial fishing and fish processing dominate the North Sea cities.

16 SPORTS

The most popular participatory sport in Belgium is bicycling. Belgians use their bicycles to commute to work, take recreational cycling trips to the countryside, and participate in races. In the winter, some racers practice on indoor tracks, while others can be seen braving the elements on their cycles even in snowstorms. Belgians also participate in soccer in addition to watching it, and there are many regional teams. Other common sports popular in Belgium include tennis, horseback riding, hiking, and skiing.

One Belgian sport specific to western Europe is sand sailing, which is done on a sort of mini-car with sails called a "sand yacht" that is driven along the coast and powered by the wind. Also popular, especially in Wallonia, is pigeon racing. As many as 100,000 pigeons may be entered in a single race, with owners competing from other countries including France and Spain.

17 ENTERTAINMENT AND RECREATION

Like many other Europeans, Belgians are avid soccer fans. There are 18 teams in the national league, although many of the players, unlike professional athletes in America, hold other jobs in addition to playing soccer. Concerts and theater are popular evening pastimes in the cities, and Brussels also has opera, ballet, and café cabarets. Traditional puppet theaters featuring wooden marionettes have enjoyed a resurgence in popularity following a period of decline after World War II.

18 FOLK ART, CRAFTS, AND HOBBIES

Traditional Belgian crafts include lacemaking (for which Brussels is especially famous), tapestry, glass, and pottery. Other folk arts include folk opera, street singing, as well as both marionettes and hand puppetry. Antwerp has a particularly lively puppetry tradition that at times has been used as a vehicle for social and political dissent. Popular hobbies include stamp collecting, model trains, and gardening.

19 SOCIAL PROBLEMS

Traditionally, ethnic differences between Belgium's Flemings and Walloons have been sources of social conflict, and even threatened to divide the country in 2007 and 2008. There are also religious divisions within the country. In particular, the degree of separation between church and state has been a divisive issue both between Catholics and non-Catholics and within the Catholic community itself. Schools, hospitals, trade unions, and numerous other institutions can be divided into those that are "secular" and those with strong church involvement. Strong differences of opinion still exist about the government's arrangement for the subsidization of Catholic-run schools. Another divisive issue—one which cuts across religious, class, and ethnic differences—is abortion. Social problems include unemployment, high rates of immigration, gradually increasing crime, and the high taxes needed to support Belgium's wide-ranging system of social benefits.

[20] GENDER ISSUES

Women won the right to vote in Belgium in 1919, and restrictions on the suffrage were dropped in 1948. Abortion was only legalized in Belgium in 1990. As of 2000, women made up 24% of the lower house of parliament, and 28.8% of the upper house. Approximately 55.7% of Belgian women hold a secondary degree, 53.1% hold a bachelor's degree, and 7.6% are in senior management. The government made a concerted effort in the 1990s in involve women in politics.

Belgium decriminalized homosexuality in 1843 and legalized same-sex marriages in 2003—it was only the second country to do so worldwide. Gay and lesbian couples have the same rights as heterosexual ones, including inheritance and adoption. In 2006 the country's first gay church was inaugurated in Ghent.

[21] BIBLIOGRAPHY

Flood, Merielle K. "Flemish." In *Encyclopedia of World Cultures* (*Europe*). Boston: G. K. Hall, 1992.

Fodor's Belgium. New York: Fodors Travel Publications, 2004.

Gall, Timothy, and Susan Gall, ed. *Junior Worldmark Encyclopedia of the Nations*. Detroit: UXL, 1996.

Gross, Joan. "Walloons." In *Encyclopedia of World Cultures* (*Europe*). Boston: G. K. Hall, 1992.

Hargrove, Jim. *Belgium. Enchantment of the World Series*. Chicago: Children's Press, 1988.

Hubbard, Monica M., and Beverly Baer, ed. *Cities of the World: Europe and the Middle East*. Detroit: Gale Research, 1993.

Illustrated Encyclopedia of Mankind. London: Marshall Cavendish, 1978.

Moss, Joyce, and George Wilson. *Peoples of the World: Western Europeans*. Detroit: Gale Research, 1993.

Pateman, Robert. *Belgium*. 2nd ed. New York: Marshall Cavendish Benchmark, 2006.

Stallaerts, Robert. *Historical Dictionary of Belgium*. 2nd ed. Lanham, MD : Scarecrow Press, 2007.

Wickman, Stephen B. *Belgium: A Country Study*. Washington, DC: U.S. Government Printing Office, 1984.

—revised by J. Hobby

BOSNIANS

LOCATION: Bosnia and Herzegovina
POPULATION: 3.9 million (2005)
LANGUAGE: Serbo-Croatian (Bosnian)
RELIGION: Islam; Eastern Orthodox Christianity; Roman Catholic Christianity

[1] INTRODUCTION

Bosnia is the only republic of the former Yugoslavia that was established on a geographic/historical basis rather than on an ethnic one. "Bosnian" refers to someone who lives in the nation of Bosnia and Herzegovina (usually referred to as Bosnia, for short), not to a particular religious or ethnic group. Throughout its history, Bosnia (and its companion, Herzegovina) has found itself on the frontier between empires. As part of the Balkans in AD 100, Bosnia was a territory of the Roman Empire. When the empire split into two halves, Bosnia, Slovenia, and Croatia were ruled by the western Roman Catholic empire, and Serbia by the eastern Orthodox Byzantines. During the 5th century AD, Slavic peoples from Central Europe occupied the region. It is from these peoples that modern-day Bosnians are descended.

The 12th century brought domination by Hungary and Austria, which would later join forces as the Hapsburg Empire. Parts of the region remained under Austro-Hungarian rule until the 20th century. From 1328 to 1878, Bosnia was occupied by the Ottoman Turks. During this time, many Bosnians converted to Islam, the religion of the Ottoman rulers. The Austro-Hungarian Empire once again took over Bosnia in 1878. Serbia had become independent in 1815, and Croatia had gained semi-independence in 1867. Most Bosnians wanted to unite with Serbia. By 1900, all Bosnians wanted to rid themselves of foreign rule, and tensions were mounting. In June 1914, Archduke Franz Ferdinand, heir to the throne of the Austro-Hungarian Empire, was assassinated by a Bosnian Serb nationalist named Gavrilo Princip in Sarajevo. The Austro-Hungarians accused the Serbians of engineering the assassination; Serbia denied it and turned to Russia, and later France and Great Britain, for support. The Austro-Hungarians drew Germany to their side and declared war on Serbia and its allies—soon the world was involved in the worst war it had ever seen, World War I.

Following the defeat of the Austro-Hungarian Empire and Germany in World War I, Serbia's allies supported its bid for independence. The Kingdom of the Serbs, Croats, and Slovenes, to be ruled by the royal family of Serbia, was established in December 1918. In 1929, King Alexander dissolved the Parliament and declared himself ruler of the kingdom, which he renamed Yugoslavia. Alexander was assassinated in 1934 by a Croatian nationalist. His successor granted Croatia limited self-rule in 1939, but conflicts continued within the kingdom. Then, the Axis powers (Germany and Italy) invaded in 1941, and Yugoslavia entered World War II. During this war, a leader named Josip Broz, known as Marshal Tito, took power.

The second Yugoslavia—Tito's Yugoslavia—was declared in Bosnia (at a conference held in Jajce) in 1943. When the Axis powers were finally defeated in 1945, Tito took full command and created a communist state that attempted to find a mid-

BOSNIANS

0   100   200   300 Miles

0   100   200   300 Kilometers

dle ground between East and West. Following Tito's dramatic break with Russian dictator Joseph Stalin in 1948, Yugoslavia's "self-management" model and the partial restoration of property rights led to rapid growth and relative prosperity from the mid-1950s to the late 1970s. Until its breakup, Yugoslavia and its brand of communism were relatively progressive. As the country began to unravel after Tito's death in 1980, the Communist Party, especially in Serbia, became much more repressive, and the Serbians once again began to dominate. Slovenia and then Croatia seceded from Yugoslavia in 1991. Wars were waged by all parties, justified on nationalistic and religious grounds. As these wars spread from small sections of Slovenia (though its secession was peaceful) to Croatia, it became apparent that Bosnia would soon declare independence as well, and this would likely cause great anger in Serbia. The Republic of Bosnia and Herzegovina declared independence in 1992, with its capital at Sarajevo.

Another war began in 1992 as Serbia embarked on a campaign of "ethnic cleansing"—a form of genocide aimed at eradicating non-Serbs from large sections of Bosnia in order to achieve eventual political union with a greater Serbia. Conflicts with newly independent Croatia ensued as radical members of that state sought to create, from the multinational Bosnia and Herzegovina, a Croatian state called Herzeg-Bosna, with its capital at Mostar. By 1994–95, the international community finally began pressuring the warring sides to enter into serious negotiations. The Bosnians and the Croatians were the first of the three combatants to sign a cease-fire, but they continued fighting the irregular Serbs, who remained determined to create a greater Serbia in the majority Serb sections of Croatia and Bosnia. The North Atlantic Treaty Organization (NATO), at the insistence of France and the United States, finally threw its considerable military resources behind ending the bloodiest war Europe had seen since World War II. A peace accord was negotiated at a military base in Dayton, Ohio, in November 1995 and was formally signed by the combatants—Alijia Izetbegovic of Bosnia, Franjo Tudjman of Croatia, and Slobodan Milosevic of Serbia—in Paris on 14 December 1995.

2 LOCATION AND HOMELAND

Before the war began in 1992, Bosnia's population was 4.5 million—approximately 44% Muslim, 31% Serbian, and 17% Croatian, along with small numbers of Gypsies, Albanians, Ukrainians, Poles, and Italians. Bosnian Muslims have historically been more urban than their Christian counterparts. Bosnia's major cities are Sarajevo (the capital), Banja Luka, Zenica, Tuzla, and Mostar.

Bosnia is located in the west-central region of the former nation of Yugoslavia on the Balkan Peninsula. It is bounded by Croatia to the north, Serbia to the east, and Montenegro to the south. There is a very short coastline to the west on the Adriatic Sea. Bosnia comprises four distinct regions. Northern Bosnia contains more than 70% of the cultivated land in the former republic and is characterized by low-lying plains, changing to rolling hills and isolated mountains to the south. Central Bosnia, where Sarajevo is located, is a mountainous region with a number of peaks over 2,000 m (6,560 ft). The mountains are part of the Dinaric Alps range. There is low population density outside the cities. Western Bosnia and upland Herzegovina form a region of bare limestone ridges and barely fertile valleys. Lowland Herzegovina, cut through by the Nertva River, is home to the regional capital of Mostar. Bosnia's short stretch of coast on the Adriatic Sea lies along the rocky beaches of Neum.

The climate in Bosnia and Herzegovina ranges from humid summers and harsh winters in the north and central regions to a Mediterranean climate in lower Herzegovina. Strong winds are common, almost constant in some areas. The *jugo* wind brings rain; the *maestral* (or mistral) brings cooler air during the summer heat; and the *bura* brings bitter cold from the northeast during the winter. Earthquakes occur frequently. There is a wide variety of plant and animal life in Bosnia. Many wild animals, such as bears, wolves, lynx, and wild boars, still live in the mountains and forests.

3 LANGUAGE

The official language of Bosnia is Serbo-Croatian, although many Bosnians refer to the dialect they speak as "Bosniac." Romany dialects (Gypsy), Albanian, and Ukrainian are spoken by substantial minority groups, and most students are exposed to some English or German in school. Conflicts among the ethnic groups in Bosnia extend even to the alphabets they use. Though all speak Serbo-Croatian, the Croats and Muslims use the Roman alphabet, whereas the Serbs use the Cyrillic alphabet. The common form of the word "hello" is written *zdravo* by Croats and Muslims; for the same word, Serbs write çäðàâî.

Serbo-Croatian belongs to the Slavic branch of the Indo-European language family—more specifically, to the group of South Slavic languages that includes Bulgarian, Macedonian, and Slovenian. Serbo-Croatian is a language that is rich in loan words from other European languages, as well as from Turkish, Arabic, Persian, and, more recently, English. In the 19th century, folklorists and linguists standardized Serbo-Croatian to regularize spelling and phonetic correspondence between spelling and pronunciation. "Write as you speak and speak as you write" was the slogan of this movement. Thus, Serbo-Croatian has no silent letters (such as the *k* in "knife") or diphthongs (such as the *oa* in boat), as English does.

"Please" is *molim* (pronounced MOU-leem) in Serbo-Croatian, and "thank you" is *hvala* (pronounced FA-la). "Yes" and "no" are *Da* (or *Jeste*) and *Ne*. The numbers 1 to 10 in Serbo-Croatian are *jedan (jedna, jedno), dva* (or *dvije* for feminine nouns), *tri, Thetiri, pet, šest, sedam, osam, devet,* and *deset*.

Women's first names tend to end in *-a* and *-ica* (pronounced EET-sa). Almost all Bosnian family names end in *-ic* (which means "child of," like John-son). Family names often indicate ethnicity. *Sulemanagic,* for example, is a Muslim name derived from the name of the Muslim hero Suleiman. Family names are passed down the male line from father to children.

⁴ FOLKLORE

Given the ethnic diversity in Bosnia and Herzegovina, there is no particular folklore that can be said to be specifically Bosnian.

⁵ RELIGION

Bosnia, like many isolated areas, developed a mixture of religious beliefs and practices that diverged from the mainstream. In the medieval era, Bosnian Christians embraced Bogomilism (an anticlerical, dualistic sect), which was considered heretical by the Roman Catholic Church. In the Ottoman era, many Christians found reason to convert to Islam. Their motives for conversion ranged from a simple preference for Islam, to escaping Catholic persecution of the native Bogomil Christian sect, to retaining rank in the local nobility, to escaping taxes placed on the Christian peasantry. About 44% of Bosnians today are Muslim. Sufism (mystical Islam) also became established in Bosnia. Islam in modern Bosnia has evolved into a tolerant form, with some practices diverging sharply from what is considered orthodox in other Islamic countries. Many Bosnians treat their religion as many Americans do theirs—something that is observed only on holy days and on major religious holidays. Fundamentalism was discouraged both by the Yugoslavian government and by the religious community.

Serbians (31% of the population) are mostly Eastern Orthodox, and Croatians (17%) are mostly Roman Catholic. The Eastern Orthodox Church broke from the Roman Catholic Church in AD 1054. Although the two faiths remain quite similar today, the chief difference is that the Eastern Orthodox Church has no pope. Questions of faith are instead decided by a consensus of all the bishops of the church. Other decisions, such as the placement of individual priests in parishes, are also made less hierarchically and more democratically in the Eastern Orthodox Church, in which congregations elect their priests. In the Roman Catholic Church, priests are appointed by bishops. Eastern Orthodoxy does not believe in purgatory, indulgences, the immaculate conception, or the assumption of Mary—it considers them all "innovations" made by the Roman Catholic Church. Mysticism also finds a more welcome home in the Eastern Orthodox Church than it does in the Roman Catholic Church.

⁶ MAJOR HOLIDAYS

Bosnians celebrate a number of religious, secular, and family holidays. Especially in the cities, where intermarriage is common, families might celebrate the state New Year holiday, both Orthodox and Catholic Christmases, and the traditional New Year's Day, along with the secular holidays of Marshal Tito's birthday on May 25 and the Day of the Republic on January 9. Eastern Orthodox Christian families also celebrate the *slava,* or saint's name day of the family.

Muslim festivities center on *Ramadan,* the month of ritual fasting. Exchanging household visits and small gifts is a particular feature of the three days at the end of Ramadan, called *Bajram* (known as *Eid Al-Fitr* elsewhere). During this period, the minarets of all the mosques are illuminated with strings of electric lights.

The Bosanska Korrida festival, during which bulls are encouraged to fight one another, attracted large numbers of country folk before it was disrupted by war in the 1990s.

⁷ RITES OF PASSAGE

Weddings are a major time of celebration, is army induction day, when young men leave for their compulsory national service. Other major life transitions are marked by ceremonies that are appropriate to each Bosnian's religious tradition.

⁸ INTERPERSONAL RELATIONS

During the worst of the war years of the 1990s, the social fabric of Bosnian society, once a unique and successful example of multiculturalism, was very nearly destroyed, and it is still in the process of healing. There are still Serbian Orthodox churches in Sarajevo (though many of the mosques in the Serb-controlled Republika Srpska have been demolished), and more and more, young people are looking beyond the ethnic hatred. Though the bitterness has not disappeared entirely and the city of Sarajevo is filled with NATO peacekeepers, normalcy is nonetheless returning.

⁹ LIVING CONDITIONS

Much of the infrastructure of modern Bosnia—especially Sarajevo, the capital—was developed during the Austrian occupation (1878–1914). The first railroads, museums, public transport systems, and waterways for commercial transport were built then. Craft guilds were organized, and new systems of agriculture were developed. In the villages, most people were farmers and lived in small houses built of stone or wood. Some modernized farms existed, but the majority relied on traditional methods, using plows pulled by oxen and horse carts for transportation. Before the regional wars (1992–95), about three-fourths of village homes had electricity, and nearly all had running water. Since the war, nearly three-fourths of the population (more than 3 million people) have lost their homes; 150,000 Bosnians are dead or missing; and more than 2 million are refugees. There are more than 500,000 refugees in Croatia, 400,000 in Serbia, another 400,000 in Germany, and 350,000 in other European countries.

As the 20th century progressed, more and more people left their villages to find work in the cities. As a result of the fighting, many villages have been destroyed and their residents forced to leave. Cities have also been hard hit. In Sarajevo, many people have no electricity or running water and little

Two Bosnian refugee girls play at a refugee camp near Tuzla north of Sarajevo. (AP Images/Amel Emric)

food. For years, they lived in fear of being killed or wounded by the Serb paramilitaries that laid siege to the city. Before the war, life in the big cities had been modernized—people lived in apartments with televisions and modern appliances, they drove cars, and so on. The war left large parts of the city in rubble, though major internationally funded rebuilding plans were instituted beginning in the late 1990s, and Sarajevo is retaining its prewar Hapsburg feel. There are elegant pedestrian walkways, classically Central European sidewalk cafés filled with young, fairly affluent people, an internationally recognized film festival, and museums with quite modern collections, similar to those one might see in other mid-sized European cities.

10 FAMILY LIFE

Much of the social structure of Bosnia reflects European custom, with some Mediterranean cultural aspects. Emphasis is on the nuclear family, although there is still some evidence of the Slavic extended family social pattern of co-dwelling, called *zadruga*. Although women have been guaranteed full equality and entry into the workforce, this has come to mean that they often hold down two jobs—one at the office or factory and one at home. Men rarely do housework. The Muslim custom of polygamy was seen only in one isolated region of the country. Most marriages follow the modern custom of love matches. Arranged marriages have mostly disappeared. Family size has decreased as education and prosperity have increased.

11 CLOTHING

Although only a generation ago, Bosnia was well known for its wide variety of folk costumes, little of this variety can be seen today, except in isolated mountain villages and in the stage costumes of amateur folklore ensembles. Most urban Bosnians dress in the Western style now; blue jeans are extremely popular. In large cities such as Sarajevo, older men can occasionally be seen wearing the urban Muslim costume of breeches, cummerbund, striped shirt, vest, and fez. The baggy trousers traditionally worn by women (called *dimija*) were adopted by all three ethnic groups as a folk costume. They are rarely seen on the streets of cities nowadays, but they are still common in rural districts. (Folk costume researchers say that one can tell the altitude of a woman's village by how high on the ankles she ties her dimija to keep her hems out of the snow.) Even the most devout Muslim women in Bosnia do not wear the *chador* (or *chadri*, as it is known elsewhere), a one-piece garment worn over the head that reaches to the ground, with a mesh insert over the eyes and nose. Headscarves and raincoats are more frequently worn instead, especially on religious holidays.

12 FOOD

The cuisine of Bosnia shows influences from Central Europe, the Balkans, and the Middle East. Dishes based on a mixture of lamb, pork, and beef, especially in the form of sausages (called *ćevapčići*) or hamburger-like patties (called *pleskavica*), are grilled along with onions and served hot on fresh *somun* (a thick pita bread). Bosnian hotpot stew (*Bosnanki lonac*), a slow-roasted mixture of layers of meat and vegetables, is the most typical regional specialty. It is usually served directly at the table in a distinctive vase-like ceramic pot. Turkish dishes, such as *kebabs* (marinated pieces of meat cooked on a skewer), *burek* (meat- or vegetable-filled pastry), and *baklava* (a sweet, layered dessert pastry) are common. Pizza is readily available, often served with a cooked egg in the middle. It is generally eaten with a fork rather than with the hands. Homemade plum brandy, called *rakija* in Bosnia and imported to the United States as *slivovitz*, is a popular drink for men; women tend to prefer fruit juices. Turkish coffee and a thin yogurt drink are also popular.

¹³ EDUCATION

Most Bosnians (96%) are literate. Since the country was restructured following the Dayton Accords, education systems have changed. A nine-year system of compulsory education for children ages 6–15 was implemented in 2003–04. Secondary schools offering various curricula exist throughout the nation, leading some students to vocational training and others to university. The Republika Srpska, the Serb-controlled section of Bosnia, maintains its own system of schooling, its own curricula, and an independent ministry of education. In 2003–04, it was reported that roughly 375,000 students were enrolled in 1,871 primary schools, and 160,000 students attended 304 secondary educational institutions in all of Bosnia. There were 72 institutions of higher education in Bosnia (excluding the Republika Srpska).

¹⁴ CULTURAL HERITAGE

The arts are highly developed in Bosnia and Herzegovina. With three major ethnicities to draw on (Serbian, Croatian, and Muslim), a great wealth of song, dance, literature, and poetry is available. The Ottoman and Austrian occupations also left rich architectural legacies. Sculpture in Bosnia dates to the pre-Islamic era, evidenced by many carved figures of humans and animals. This tradition carried over into the Islamic period, although the usual Muslim prohibition against representing the human form did not take hold. Still, Islamic arts such as calligraphy and fine metalworking became features of Bosnian art. Before the war, much energy was devoted to religious and domestic architecture. Houses featured walled compounds with their distinctive gates, carved wooden ceilings and screens, and built-in seating covered with fine weavings. *Kilims* (handwoven carpets) and knotted rugs were common. The custom of giving a personally woven dowry rug, with the couple's initials and date of marriage, has only recently disappeared. Other textile arts, such as silk embroidery, were also common domestic arts.

Music and dance especially reflect Bosnia's great diversity. Bosnian music can be divided into rural and urban traditions. The rural tradition is characterized by such musical styles as *ravne pesme* (flat song) of limited scale; *ganga,* an almost shouted polyphonic style; and other types of songs that may be accompanied by the *šargija* (a simple long-necked lute), wooden flute, or the *diple* (a droneless bagpipe). The urban tradition shows a much heavier Turkish influence, with its melismatic singing (more than one note per syllable) and accompaniment on the *saz,* a larger and more elaborate version of the šargija. Epic poems, an ancient tradition, are still sung to the sound of the *gusle,* a single-string bowed fiddle. However, this rich heritage of folk music is disappearing under the influence of Western pop music and new native pop music in a folk style played on the accordion. *Sevdalinka* songs (derived from the Turkish word *sevda,* "love") were traditionally the most widespread form of music in Bosnia and Herzegovina. These deeply emotional songs speak metaphorically and symbolically of love won and lost. They came to symbolize Bosnia to natives and foreigners alike.

Bosnian folk dance is probably the richest and yet least known of all the regional folk dances of the former Yugoslavia. Dances range from the silent *kolo* (accompanied only by the sound of stamping feet and the clash of silver coins on the women's aprons), to line dances in which the sexes are segregated, to Croatian and Serbian dances like those performed across the border in their native countries. Like music, however, these folk dances are rapidly being replaced by Western social dances and rock and roll.

¹⁵ WORK

Before the war, about 40% of Bosnians worked in industry. Major industries included textiles, food processing, coal and iron mining, automobile-related industries, and the manufacture of steel. Agriculture contributed 11.5% of gross domestic product (GDP) in 2005; the major crops are now tobacco and fruit. The industrial sector contributed 27.8% of GDP in 2005. Before the communist era, almost all Bosnians were farmers. The communists changed Bosnia from a farming nation to an industrial nation during the 1960s to the 1980s. Bosnia still retains a substantial rural population, however, especially in the northern region of Bosanska Posavina, just south of the Sava River. This population lives in small towns and villages throughout the region, engaging in agriculture and its supporting or related industries. They are not poor peasants—their homes generally have electricity and indoor plumbing, and they may own a small tractor, an automobile, a television, and a DVD player and may have an Internet connection. Most have completed their primary education through the eighth grade. Some, especially those outside the primarily agricultural zones, are miners or factory workers. City dwellers have the same sorts of jobs as those in the Western world, such as teachers, bankers, engineers, truck drivers, merchants, and librarians.

¹⁶ SPORTS

Soccer is the favorite sport of Bosnians. Official matches draw spectators from all over the country, and informal games spring up constantly in parks, on playgrounds, and in the streets. If actual goals are not available, makeshift ones are created from old netting, clothes, rags, and even plastic bags. Outdoor sports such as hiking, skiing, swimming, and fishing are also very popular in Bosnia,. The 1984 Winter Olympic Games were hosted by Bosnia in Sarajevo. In 2002–03, the first soccer league in the country, featuring teams with players from all the main ethnic groups, began regular play. The national soccer team is currently ranked fifty-ninth by FIFA (International Federation of Association Football).

¹⁷ ENTERTAINMENT AND RECREATION

Bosnians enjoy the same sorts of entertainment and recreation as Americans—they watch television, listen to pop music, read comics, go to movies, and play games. Outdoor activities such as hiking, hunting, mountain climbing, skiing, swimming, and fishing are also popular. A traditional form of recreation is *korzo*—walking along the main street of the village, town, or city in the evening and stopping to chat with friends or have a cup of coffee in the *kafana,* or coffeehouse. (Kafanas are often restricted to men only.)

Folklore festivals and competitions between amateur performing groups were a major feature of contemporary Bosnian life before the war. Bosnian amateur folklore groups, called Cultural Art Societies, were found throughout the republic. They were required to perform the dances, music, and songs of the three major ethnicities in Bosnia, as well as the folklore of the other republics of Yugoslavia. Successful performances at local festivities could earn such a society the privilege of performing abroad.

18 FOLK ART, CRAFTS, AND HOBBIES

The main folk art in Bosnia is carpet weaving. The cities of Mostar and Sarajevo are famous for their rugs, which are made from brightly colored wools in a variety of intricate designs.

19 SOCIAL PROBLEMS

The worst social problem for Bosnians is, of course, the effects of the war from 1992 to 1995. It is estimated that 150,000 Bosnians were killed (or remain missing) as a result of the war. In Sarajevo, more than 60% of the homes were destroyed. The environment suffered heavy damage from bombings, fires, and acid rain resulting from gases released into the air. Historic buildings and structures, including the 16th-century Stari Most (Old Bridge) in Mostar, were destroyed, although some have since been rebuilt.

Thirteen years after the signing of the Dayton Accords, normalcy has returned to much of Bosnia, but this does not mean there are no social problems. There is a significant marginalized population of Roma (Bosnia's largest ethnic minority) living on the outskirts of major cities in squalid conditions. There is also a continuing low-level hostility between the Bosnian-Croat entity and the Serb enclave living in Republika Srpska.

In recent years, Bosnia years become a transit point for both drug and human trafficking. Corruption is a significant problem.

20 GENDER ISSUES

As a traditionally liberal, nearly secular, and partially modernized nation, Bosnia's gender issues mirror those of the former Warsaw Pact nations of Eastern Europe. Bosnia's founding documents and constitution define gender equality in slightly different ways. According to the United Nations Development Programme, the country has committed itself to achieving full gender equality in all legislative authorities of the state. It reported in 2006 that the country was making progress toward bringing its laws regarding gender equality in line with developed-world standards.

In terms of female health standards and reproductive rights, abortion is widely used as a form birth control; sex education is insufficient, and gynecological services are badly lacking.

Bosnia offers no legal recognition for unmarried couples, both heterosexual and homosexual. The traditional family forms the core of much of rural society, though this has fragmented a bit in the cities, where homosexuality and cohabitation are tolerated.

21 BIBLIOGRAPHY

"Bosnia and Herzegovina Making Progress Towards Gender Equality." United Nations General Assembly, Committee on the Elimination of Discrimination Against Women. http://www.un.org/News/ Press/docs//2006/wom1557.doc.htm (March 8, 2008).

The Bosnians: An Introduction to Their History and Culture. CAL Refugee Fact Sheet Series No. 8. Washington, D.C.: Refugee Service Center, Center for Applied Linguistics, June 1994.

Cohen, Lenard J. "The Disintegration of Yugoslavia." *Current History: A World Affairs Journal,* vol. 91, no. 568 (November 1992): 369–75.

Donia, Robert J. "Bosnia: A Short History." *Slavic Review,* vol. 54, no. 2. (Summer 1995): 505–6.

Erlanger, Steven. "The Dayton Accords: A Status Report." *New York Times,* March 8, 2008.

Flint, David. *Bosnia: Can There Ever Be Peace?* Austin, TX: Raintree Steck-Vaughn, 1996.

Ganeri, Anita. *Why We Left: I Remember Bosnia.* Austin, TX: Raintree Steck-Vaughn, 1995.

Smith, Huston. *The Religions of Man.* New York: Harper & Row, 1958.

—revised by J. Henry

BRETONS

LOCATION: Brittany region of northwestern France
POPULATION: 2.9 million
LANGUAGE: French; Breton
RELIGION: Roman Catholic

¹ INTRODUCTION

Located in the northwestern corner of France, Brittany is often compared to Wales because of the Celtic origins of its people, as well as their ruggedness and independence. The two regions—both located at the western edges of their respective countries—are about the same size, and the Bretons, like the Welsh, have historically shown a determination to preserve their cultural and linguistic traditions despite political control by a much larger ruling power. The Bretons have also been compared to the Irish because of their strong emphasis and love for tradition, their large and catholic families, and their history of poverty in comparison to their ruling powers. Although the past two centuries have brought about a dramatic decline in Brittany's isolation from the rest of France, its people still retain their identity as a distinct cultural and ethnic group.

The Bretons arrived in their current homeland in the 5th and 6th centuries AD, fleeing the Anglo-Saxons invading the British Isles. The coastal part of Brittany had long been called Armorica ("land by the sea") and the interior Argoat ("land of forest"). The arriving Celts, however, simply called the entire region Petite Bretagne ("little Britain"), sometimes shortened to Bretagne. The area was an independent duchy from the 9th century until 1532 when it was formally annexed to France. Until the French Revolution in the 18th century, however, it retained its own parliament and autonomous administration. After the Revolution (in which the Bretons had sided with the royalists), Brittany was split into separate administrative divisions called *départements* and ceased to exist as a political entity. (Since 1964, it has consisted of four départements: Finistère, Côtes-d'Armor, Ille-et-Vilaine, and Morbihan. The Loire-Atlantique département, which had traditionally belonged to Brittany, was transferred to another region, a move which angered many Bretons.)

The linguistic and cultural isolation that had been fostered by Brittany's political autonomy began to decline during the 19th century thanks to a number of developments, including the inauguration of a military draft, the beginnings of mandatory public education, improved transportation, and the development of industry. World War I further contributed to the Bretons' assimilation into the French mainstream, resulting in a strong (but ultimately unsuccessful) movement for the return of political autonomy to Brittany. The Front de Liberation de la Bretagne was much like a small scale Irish Republican Army (IRA) with their use of sporadic attacks in pursuit of a free Brittany. The group has largely disappeared today. The region suffered great losses in both world wars (Brittany lost 12% of its population in World War I, although the Bretons accounted for only 6.5% of France's total population). In the postwar period, Brittany has prospered. Agriculture has been modernized, and the growth of industry has decreased the region's traditional dependence on fishing (although fishing remains an important source of income and employment). In recent years, Breton regionalism has focused on cultural and linguistic preservation and economic, rather than political, autonomy.

² LOCATION AND HOMELAND

Located at the westernmost edge of continental Europe, Brittany is virtually a peninsula, surrounded by water on three sides: to the west and south, the Atlantic Ocean and to the north, the English Channel. Slightly larger than Wales, it is 215 km (134 mi) long with 1,200 km (746 mi) of coastline. The coast is extremely jagged, with many islands, reefs, islets, and estuaries. Much of the interior is laid out in a checkerboard pattern of fields and pastures separated by stone walls and hedges called *bocages*. A traditional east-west division into Upper and Lower Brittany (Haute and Basse Bretagne) delineates cultural differences between the western half of the region, where both French and Breton are spoken and some of the old customs are still followed, and the east, which has more thoroughly assimilated the culture and language of the rest of France.

Most of Brittany's towns and cities are found along the coast. The area has a population density of 53.5 per sq. km. The largest include Vannes, Quimper, Concarneau, Brest, Morlaix, and St. Malo. Rennes is the only important city in the interior. Formerly the capital of Brittany, today it is home to one of two universities in the region and is an important industrial center. In the past 25 years, increasing numbers of Bretons have emigrated from rural areas, mostly to Paris and other French cities and, in lesser numbers, to other countries.

³ LANGUAGE

Breton is a Celtic language related to Welsh and Cornish. It was brought to the French coast in the 5th and 6th centuries AD by British Celts; flourished in the 9th century, when the duchy of Brittany was at the peak of its power historically; and declined after France's annexation of the region in the 15th century. Today, there are only a small number of people who speak Breton as their first language, while greater numbers speak both French and Breton. The modern nationalist movement has worked to revive the Breton language, as seen by the existence of the Union for the Defense of the Breton Language (UDB). Nevertheless, the use of Breton as a first language has declined rapidly, and there are few Bretons who do not also speak French. The Breton language has been effectively excluded from primary and secondary schools. By the beginning of the 21st century, the number of Breton speakers in Brittany was estimated at fewer than 600,000. Estimates of those who can read the language are far smaller (under 10,000).

There are four Breton dialects: Trégorrois, Léonard, Cornouaillais, and Vannetais. Many Breton surnames are derived from the word "ker" (which means house) plus another syllable based on a Christian name. Examples include Kerjean ("house of John"), Kerbol ("house of Paul"), and Kerber ("house of Peter"). Syllables commonly found in Breton place names include "plou," or "parish" (Ploudaniel); "lann," or "church" (Lannion); "ker," or "house" (Kermaria); and "gui," or "town" (Guimiliau). Other common words found in Breton place names are *bihan* (small), *braz* (large), *men* (stone), and *mor* (sea).

⁴ FOLKLORE

A Celtic aura of magic and mystery pervades Brittany, a land of legends and superstition. Many folk customs and legends center on death, symbolized by a character named Ankou, who figures in a multitude of tales depicted as a skeleton carrying a scythe and often riding on a wooden cart. It is said that deaths are foreshadowed by the creaking of his cart. When a person dies, the doors and windows of the family house are traditionally left open so that the spirit of the deceased (commonly pictured as an insect) can easily fly out, and mirrors are turned to face the walls.

The medieval legends of King Arthur and the Knights of the Round Table are popular in Brittany, as is the tale of Tristan and Isolde. The town of Quimper is said to have been founded by King Gradlon after his former capital, the city of Is, was destroyed when his daughter, bewitched by the Devil, let in the floodwaters of the sea. Escaping with her on horseback, the king received an order from Heaven to throw her into the sea, where she turned into the mermaid Marie-Morgane. It is said that if mass is ever celebrated in one of the drowned city's churches on Good Friday, the city will be restored and the mermaid will become human again.

5 RELIGION

The Bretons—an overwhelmingly Catholic people—are known for the strength of their religious beliefs, especially their devotion to their hundreds of local saints whose painted wooden statues decorate the region's multitude of churches. Every town has its patron saint, and special saints are prayed to for specific ailments (for centuries, such prayers were the Bretons' most trusted form of medical intervention). Although religious observance, even among this devout group, suffered a decline during the 20th century, Catholicism has remained stronger in Brittany than in many other parts of Western Europe, and most Bretons are still baptized, married, and buried within the Catholic tradition. Bretons are also noted for their religious monuments (including nine cathedrals), pilgrimages, and the traditional festivals known as *pardons*. According to tradition, every Breton is supposed to make a pilgrimage to all nine cathedrals in the course of his or her lifetime to avoid having to make this pilgrimage after death.

6 MAJOR HOLIDAYS

Bretons celebrate France's religious, historical, and patriotic holidays throughout the year. These include New Year's Day (January 1); Epiphany (January 6); Labor Day (May 1); Bastille Day (July 14), which is France's national holiday and the equivalent of Independence Day in the United States; the Feast of the Assumption (August 15); All Saints' Day (November 1); World War II Armistice Day (November 11); and Christmas (December 25). The French observe Christmas by attending a midnight mass.

The most famous and important of Brittany's regional holidays are the *pardons*, local religious festivals usually centering on a particular saint or legend. Pilgrims attend them to make or fulfill vows, seek miraculous cures, and, above all, to seek forgiveness for their sins. The main event of every pardon is a procession, usually in the afternoon. Men and women wearing traditional costumes carry multicolored banners, candles, and religious relics to a final destination, usually a church or chapel. Although the pardons are directed by priests, and sometimes even bishops, once the procession is over they assume the character of a secular fair or festival, with refreshments, dancing, and games. Pardons mostly take place between March and the end of October. The most famous is Le Folgoët's *Grand Pardon*, which begins at 4:00 PM and lasts until the following day. However, the traditional Breton customs and clothing are most prominent in the western half of the region.

7 RITES OF PASSAGE

The Bretons live in a modern, industrialized, Christian country. Hence, many of the rites of passage that young people undergo are Roman Catholic rituals, such as baptism, first Communion, confirmation, and marriage. In addition, a student's progress through the education system is marked by many families with graduation parties.

8 INTERPERSONAL RELATIONS

In most ways, life for 21st-century Bretons differs little from life in the rest of France. Because the influence of the Catholic Church is so strong, church festivals are important social events for many Bretons.

9 LIVING CONDITIONS

Many of the houses found today in Brittany are built with the traditional pink, grey, and black stones of the area and have thatched or slate roofs. In older dwellings, the family's living area is composed of only one or two rooms, with additional structures, such as barns, attached to the house itself. Modern houses often retain the look of the older homes but are much more spacious inside, with an exterior of whitewashed cement.

Three young Breton women wear traditional lace headdresses during the Fete des Brodeuses (festival of lacemakers) in Brittany, France. The festival celebrates Breton culture. (Travel Ink/Getty Images)

The Bretons receive high-quality modern health care through France's comprehensive national health care system, which covers both private care and state-operated facilities. The average French life expectancy is 81 years. Traditional Breton folk medicine included homemade herbal remedies and the services of a healer called a *diskonter,* who practiced spells transmitted from one to generation to the next.

France's modern, efficient transportation system is centered on the city of Paris, which can make direct travel between provincial locations difficult. However, rural Bretons enjoy the advantage of quiet and relatively uncrowded roads, especially compared with the congested traffic that has become the norm in Paris and other parts of France. The state-owned railways are punctual, with clean, modern trains. Brittany has 600 km (373 mi) of navigable rivers and canals.

10 FAMILY LIFE

Most couples in Brittany have both civil and church weddings, although the civil wedding alone is legally acceptable. In spite of their strong Catholic religious tradition, many Bretons practice birth control, limiting the size of their families to two or three children in contrast to the larger families that were formerly the norm. Also, couples tend to have their children while they are young. Divorce, while legal, still carries a stigma for many Bretons. Most women in Brittany are part of the paid labor force at some time in their lives, and many have found employment in technical and professional fields.

11 CLOTHING

For everyday casual, business, or formal wear, Bretons wear modern Western-style clothing like that of people elsewhere in France and Western Europe. However, their distinctive traditional costumes are still seen at *pardons* and other festivals, and may also be worn on special occasions such as baptisms and weddings. The men's costumes include broad-brimmed hats with ribbons, embroidered waistcoats, short jackets, and, in some areas, baggy homespun breeches called *bragoubras.* Women wear black or colored dresses, often with elaborate embroidered, brocaded, or lace-trimmed aprons of satin or velvet. The most distinctive feature of the women's costume is the elaborate lace headgear, which varies from region to region but is generally called a *coiffe.* The best-known coiffes are stiff white lace bonnets ranging from a modest-sized cap to the coiffe worn by the women of Bigoudènes, a stiff cylinder over a foot high with streamers in back. Younger women often modernize their costumes by wearing skirts that are shorter than ankle-length and fashionable footwear instead of the traditional black buckled shoes.

12 FOOD

Much of the cuisine in Brittany is similar to that elsewhere in France, although the region is known for its excellent seafood, especially lobster, crawfish, cod, tunny, and sardines. Regional specialties include a fish soup known as *cotriade* (similar to the bouillabaisse eaten in other parts of France), a lobster dish know as lobster à l'armoricaine, a beef-and-vegetable dish called *potée bretonne,* and wheat or buckwheat crèpes, with a range of fillings that include ham, cheese, eggs, jam, fresh fruit, and honey. Cider is the most popular local beverage in Brittany, which is not one of France's wine-producing regions.

13 EDUCATION

As elsewhere in France, education in Brittany is free and compulsory between the ages of 6 and 16. Children attend school on Saturday mornings and have Wednesdays off. Secondary education begins with four years at a middle school called a *collège,* followed by three years spent either at a general *lycée* for those planning to go on to college or at a vocational *lycée.* After receiving their *baccalauréat* degrees, students may go on to a university or to a *grand école,* which offers preparation for careers in business or government service. In Lower Brittany, the Breton language is taught as an optional subject in secondary school and at teacher training schools.

14 CULTURAL HERITAGE

Brittany has over 250 Celtic Clubs whose mission is the revival and preservation of Breton folk music and dance and other traditional customs. The traditional performance arts are also kept alive through regular gatherings such as the *Abadenn Veur* held every July in Quimper. The most popular Breton folk instruments are the *biniou* (a small bagpipe) and the *bombarde,* which is similar to an oboe. The accordion and the Celtic harp are also widely used for traditional music. Special folk dances traditionally performed at the religious festivals called *pardons* include the Ribbon Gavotte, the Tobacco and Handkerchief Gavotte, and the *Dérobée,* where a man "steals" a young woman from her escort. The folk art of Brittany is found in churches and on statues as well as in paintings and tapestries.

Famous Breton authors include the medieval poet and philosopher Peter Abelard; Alain-René Lesage, author of *Gil Blas;* the science-fiction writer Jules Verne; and the experimental novelist Alain Robbe-Grillet, who wrote the script for French director Alain Resnais's famous 1961 film *Last Year in Marienbad.* There has been a revival of writing in the Breton language since the 1920s, before which point Breton was suppressed by the French authorities.

15 WORK

Although many small farms have been abandoned with the rise in mechanization since World War II, Brittany is France's foremost agricultural producer. The region is responsible for about 30% of France's fishing industry. The major principal crops are artichokes and cauliflower. Other major employers are light industry and the service sector. Forty percent of France's telecommunications research and development is based in Brittany. The ferry industry is also significant, with 2.7 million annual passengers, mostly from the United Kingdom, and huge amounts of shipping. However, the ferry business has suffered with the increased usage of train travel and especially the Channel Tunnel to the UK. Brittany's unemployment rate is still low compared to the rest of France.

16 SPORTS

The Bretons, like people throughout France, love soccer ("football"). On the coast, popular water sports include sailing, windsurfing, skin-diving, and deep-sea fishing. Other favorite pastimes include fishing on the river banks of inland areas, and hiking or cycling through Brittany's countryside.

17 ENTERTAINMENT AND RECREATION

The Breton *pardons,* while primarily religious festivals, are also a popular source of entertainment. In some areas, the secular portion of the festival even includes performances by jazz and rock groups. Bretons, like the other people of France, have more leisure time over the weekend than they did before the 1960s, when factories were open on Saturday mornings. Domestic activities such as gardening, home improvement, and cooking have become popular leisure-time pursuits: about one-third of the French people spend some of their time gardening. Approximately 95% of the French people own television sets, and the average viewing time is three hours per day. Bretons, like people in other parts of France, like to use their long summer holidays to take vacation trips, either to the beach or to other destinations.

18 FOLK ART, CRAFTS, AND HOBBIES

Traditionally the Bretons have been skilled woodworkers, known for their chests, sideboards, dressers, wardrobes, and clock cases. A unique regional feature is the old-fashioned box bed, which was something like a bunk bed with sliding doors on the sides. It provided both protection against the winter cold and privacy in the small, traditional houses of rural Brittany. Large chests for linen or grain and two-door wardrobes are other important pieces of traditional Breton furniture. Pottery is another important Breton craft.

19 SOCIAL PROBLEMS

There is concern among Bretons about the decline of their language and traditional way of life. The use of Breton as a first language is confined mostly to the elderly, and few children are learning it as they grow up. The teaching of Breton is limited to secondary and teacher training schools, and is only found in Basse Bretagne (Lower Brittany).

The creation of a single European economic market in 1992 provided new economic opportunities but also created challenges for the Breton economy. Traditional fishing practices, for example, have had to be modified to conform to the quotas and restrictions of the European Union and its member states. The transformation to larger farms has created pollution problems for the area.

Alcoholism is a significant social problem in Brittany. Alcoholism in France is less of a problem in the wine-growing regions than in the northern area of the country, and especially Brittany.

Brittany has a history of high levels of emigration. Most Bretons emigrate to Paris and other European regions.

20 GENDER ISSUES

With Brittany's large Catholic population the issues of abortion and gay rights are somewhat contentious. The women's movement in Brittany was not as significant as those in other Western European countries and in other regions of France.

21 BIBLIOGRAPHY

Ardagh, John, ed. *The Penguin Guide to France.* New York: Viking Penguin, 1985.

———. *France in the New Century: Portrait of a Changing Society*. London: Penguin Books, 2000.

Badone, Ellen. *The Appointed Hour: Death, Worldview, and Social Change in Brittany*. Berkeley: University of California Press, 1989.

Bell, Brian, ed. *Brittany. Insight Guides*. Boston: Houghton Mifflin, 1994.

Brittany. Michelin Guides. Harrow: Michelin Tyre, 1991.

Gall, Timothy, and Susan Gall, ed. *Worldmark Encyclopedia of the Nations*. Detroit: Gale Research, 1995.

Howarth, David and Georgios Varouxakis. *Contemporary France: An Introduction to French Politics and Society*. London: Arnold, 2003.

"Regions of France, Brittany (Bretagne)." Internet French Property. http://www.french-property.com/regions/bretagne/about.htm (April 2008).

Timm, Lenora A. "Bretons." In *Encyclopedia of World Cultures*. Boston: G. K. Hall, 1992.

—revised by C. Corrigan

BULGARIANS

LOCATION: Bulgaria
POPULATION: 7.7 million
LANGUAGE: Bulgarian
RELIGION: Bulgarian Orthodox Christian; Muslim; Protestant and Catholic minorities

¹ INTRODUCTION

Like the republics of the former nation of Yugoslavia, Bulgaria has undergone a difficult period of political and economic change since the collapse of communism in 1989. However, this ethnically unified people has escaped the violence that has ravaged its Slavic neighbors to the west, even as it has faced the challenges of this latest chapter in a turbulent history that includes centuries of foreign domination.

In the 7th century AD, the Bulgars, an Asiatic people, migrated to the area that is now Bulgaria, mingling with Slavic tribes already living in the region. The Bulgarian state, formed in 681 and recognized by the Byzantine Empire, officially adopted the Christian religion in 865. After several centuries of autonomy under three different dynasties, interrupted by a period of Byzantine rule in the 11th century, the Bulgarians were conquered by the Ottoman Turks in 1396 and remained under Ottoman rule for nearly 500 years. In 1878, the northern part of Bulgaria achieved independence from the Turks, with the rest of the area following in 1886.

The Bulgarians sided with Germany in both world wars. In 1944, Soviet troops entered the country, and the newly established communist government was consolidated. Unlike some of its neighbors, Bulgaria, headed by a single leader—Todor Zhivkov—remained steadfastly loyal to the Soviet government throughout the communist era. In 1989, Zhivkov was forced from office. Two years later, a new constitution was approved, and Bulgaria elected its first noncommunist, multiparty government, choosing philosophy professor and former dissident Zhelyu Zhelev as president. The parliamentary democracy elected the first monarch in postcommunist Eastern Europe (King Simeon Saxe-Coburg-Gotha) to the position of prime minister in 2001. In 2004, Bulgaria joined the North Atlantic Treaty Organization (NATO), and in 2007, the nation became a member of the European Union (EU).

² LOCATION AND HOMELAND

Bulgaria is located on the Balkan Peninsula of southeastern Europe, covering an area of 110,910 sq km (42,823 sq mi). The country's geographic areas and climatic zones are defined by the Balkan Mountains, which cut across its center from east to west and serve as its principal topographical feature. North of the Balkans is the Danubian Plain; to the south lie mountains and the Thracian Plain. The Black Sea coast to the east constitutes a third distinct geographic area.

Approximately 85% of Bulgaria's 7.7 million people are ethnic Bulgarians. Turks, who account for slightly less than 10% of the population, are the largest ethnic minority, followed by Roma (Gypsies), who make up about 5%. Other minority groups include Armenians, Macedonians, Tatars, and Circassians. As a result of the country's low birth rate (growth rate of –0.51%), Bulgaria's population has fallen since 1991.

³ LANGUAGE

Bulgarian is a Slavic language that is written using the Cyrillic alphabet. There are many regional dialects throughout the country, and the grammar and vocabulary of Bulgarian have been influenced by non-Slavic Balkan languages, notably Turkish. Bulgarian is the official language of Bulgaria; it is widely spoken by its residents, even among those who speak other languages as their primary tongue, such as Turkish, Armenian, Greek, or Romanian. Nearly 85% of the people in Bulgaria speak Bulgarian; the remaining 15% speak other languages.

These are some common Bulgarian words (transliterated into the Roman alphabet here):

hello	*zdraveyte*
good-bye	*dovizhdane* (informally, *ciao*)
yes	*da*
no	*ne*
right	*dyasno*
left	*lyavo*
today	*sot*
tomorrow	*nesër*

The days of the week in Bulgarian are as follows:

Monday	*e hënë*
Tuesday	*e martë*
Wednesday	*e mërkurë*
Thursday	*e enjte*
Friday	*e premte*
Saturday	*e shtunë*
Sunday	*e diel*

⁴ FOLKLORE

A favorite character of Bulgarian folktales for hundreds of years has been Sly Peter, with his many ways of outwitting others. Other popular folk figures are the freedom fighters known as *hajduks,* who resemble the English folk hero Robin Hood, and Marko Krabjevic, who rides a magic horse and carries an invincible sword. A more recent addition is Bai Ganyu, a character created at the turn of the 20th century by author Aleko Konstantinov. During the communist era, this blundering figure, originally conceived of as a peasant, metamorphosed into an engineer in stories mocking the government's emphasis on achievements in science and technology.

The tough-minded, pragmatic Bulgarian character is revealed in the following proverbs:

> If evil does not come, worse may arrive.
> The dog barks to guard itself, not the village.
> When there's no work to be found, join the army.
> Work left for later is finished by the Devil.

⁵ RELIGION

The Bulgarians are not a strongly religious people. The major organized religion in Bulgaria is Bulgarian Orthodox Christianity, which approximately 83% of Bulgarians identify as their religion, although many have a limited familiarity with its teachings. Bulgarians' religious observance is mostly a matter of tradition rather than deeply held personal beliefs. Approximately 12% of Bulgarians are Muslim, and there are small Protestant and Catholic minorities (less than 1% each).

⁶ MAJOR HOLIDAYS

Official holidays include the New Year (January 1 and 2); Liberation Day (March 3), which commemorates Bulgarian independence from the Ottoman Empire in 1878; Easter Monday (in March or April); Labor Day (May 1); the Day of Letters (May 24), which honors the Cyrillic alphabet and Bulgarian education and culture; and Christmas (December 25 and 26). Many Bulgarians also observe the holy days of the Eastern Orthodox calendar, including a number of saints' days. Until the collapse of communism in Bulgaria in 1989, the country's national patriotic holiday was observed on September 9, the day on which Soviet troops arrived in the capital city of Sofia in 1944. After the fall of Bulgaria's communist regime, this Soviet-style celebration (together with its date) was replaced by one that was judged more meaningful to Bulgaria's history and national aspirations.

⁷ RITES OF PASSAGE

Religious ceremonies marking important life events include christenings, weddings, the blessing of a new house, and funerals. Rural villagers still observe the tradition of refraining from any kind of singing, dancing, or music making for at least six months after the death of a relative or close friend.

⁸ INTERPERSONAL RELATIONS

Bulgarians greet each other by shaking hands; close female friends may exchange kisses on the cheek. The most common formal greetings are *Kak ste?* (How are you?) and *Zdraveite* (hello). More informal versions, used among friends, relatives, and coworkers, are *Kak si?* and *Zdrasti* or *Zdrave*. In formal situations, last names are used with the titles *Gospodin* (Mr.),

Gospozha (Mrs.), or *Gospozhitsa* (Miss) or with professional titles. It is common to say hello to strangers in rural but not in urban areas. Bulgarians observe a much smaller zone of personal privacy than in most Western European nations and the United States: People tend to stand or sit close together when conversing, speak in louder voices, and make physical contact more frequently.

The Bulgarian gestures for "yes" and "no" often confuse people from the West. "Yes" is indicated by shaking one's head from side to side, while "no" is signaled by one or two nods up and down (often accompanied by clicking of the tongue). Pointing with one's index finger and (for men) crossing an ankle over the opposite knee in public are considered rude.

9 LIVING CONDITIONS

Housing in Bulgaria is mostly privately owned. Two-story brick houses with a plaster finish resembling stucco have largely replaced the traditional single-story rural houses made of wood, mud bricks, or stone and plaster. Houses in most villages are built close together and surround a central village square. As protection against the cold winters on the Danubian Plains, some houses in that region are built virtually underground, with only the roof showing above ground level. Although brick and stucco houses are also found in urban areas, much residential construction since the 1950s has consisted of multistory concrete apartment complexes, and most urban dwellers live in apartments rather than houses. Urban families often retain ownership of houses in the country, maintaining gardens on the property, using them as vacation cottages in the summer, or moving their elderly parents into them.

Bulgaria has a national health system that provides free medical assistance of all types, including an extensive network of pediatric facilities and special facilities for patients with tuberculosis. However, in some cases, public health care facilities are underequipped, and better care can be obtained at private facilities by those who can afford to pay for it. Life expectancy averages 68 to 76 years, and the infant mortality rate is 19.85 deaths per 1,000 live births.

Having long served as a connecting point between Europe, Asia, and Africa, Bulgaria has a well-developed, reliable transportation system. Both national and international express trains cross the country, and more than half the nation's rail system is electrified. In the cities, transportation is available by bus, streetcar, trolley, taxi, and private automobile. Almost all families own cars, but many do not drive them on a regular basis because of the high price of gasoline, preferring to use public transportation instead. Bulgaria has three international airports and two major waterways, the Danube River and the Black Sea.

10 FAMILY LIFE

Family life is very important in Bulgaria. The three-generation extended family is common in rural areas, whereas the nuclear family predominates in cities. Single adults are generally expected to live with their parents until they marry, and children often care for their elderly parents. In addition, it is not unusual for young married couples to live with one set of parents until they can afford to own a home. In line with Bulgaria's low birth rate, families tend to be small. In the cities, families usually have no more than two children; in the country, families are somewhat larger. Children are very close to their grandparents, who often care for them while their parents are working. The role of grandmothers is considered so special that there is a holiday dedicated to them—Grandmother's Day on January 21.

Bulgarian women have traditionally enjoyed a relatively high degree of freedom and responsibility. Under socialism, the quality of their education improved, and they joined the workforce in greater numbers, partly because restrictions on men's incomes made it necessary for many families to have two breadwinners. Today, women account for almost half the Bulgarian labor force and hold many of the same jobs as men. In urban areas, many women are employed in banking, finance, and insurance.

11 CLOTHING

Bulgarians wear modern Western-style clothing. On the whole, they are very careful about their appearance, dressing up even for casual occasions and carefully ironing the natural fabrics they favor, such as cotton, wool, and silk. However, fashionable Western clothing is expensive, and many women take care of their families' cold-weather needs by knitting sweaters themselves. Special care is lavished on the dressing of children, who often can be seen wearing imported clothing and lovingly hand-knit items.

The traditional colorful, richly ornamented Bulgarian costumes once worn are seen today only at festivals or dance performances. Styles vary from one region to another, but embroidered white shirts or blouses are common, worn with elaborately embroidered vests. Women may wear colorful aprons or jumpers over their skirts, and men often wear wide waistbands over their pants and shirts. Red is seen in almost all costumes, either as a background color or in the embroidery, and many costumes also feature some black.

12 FOOD

Many Bulgarian dishes feature meat, especially pork and lamb. Favorites include *kufteta,* a fried patty made with meat and breadcrumbs; *moussaka,* a casserole of pork or lamb with potatoes, tomatoes, and yogurt; and *sarmi,* pepper or cabbage stuffed with pork and rice. Fresh fruits and vegetables are an important part of the Bulgarian diet, especially in the summertime. A popular vegetable dish is *shopska,* a salad made with cucumbers, tomatoes, and a Bulgarian cheese called *cerene. Tarator* is a cold soup made from cucumbers, yogurt, garlic, dill, and walnuts.

Yogurt—eaten by Bulgarians starting at the age of three months—is a dietary staple that is served at virtually every meal. Another important staple is bread, usually bought fresh every day. A popular snack is a slice of warm bread topped with feta cheese and tomato slices. Favorite desserts include *baklava* (layers of thin, flaky pastry dough filled with nuts and saturated with a sweet syrup) and *banitsa* (a layered pastry filled with cheese or pumpkin). Bulgarians enjoy espresso and Turkish coffee. A favorite wintertime drink is an aperitif called *greyana rakiya,* which is made from plum or grape brandy heated with honey.

13 EDUCATION

Education is highly valued in Bulgarian society. The literacy rate is nearly 100%. Schooling is free and compulsory from the ages of 6 to 16, and it remains free at higher levels. A large ma-

A Bulgarian Muslim bride looks at her make-up during her two-day wedding ceremony in the village of Ribnovo, Bulgaria. The people of this mountain village are famous for performing their unique wedding ceremonies in winter time only. (AP Images/Petar Petrov)

jority of students complete high school. After the seventh or eighth grade, students decide which type of specialized high school they want to attend (there are as many as five types in urban areas), and they must take a qualifying examination to get into the school of their choice. Bulgaria has some 20 universities, as well as many three-year training facilities. University admission has traditionally been highly competitive, although in the past, students who were admitted did not have to pay tuition. Recent years have seen the introduction of private colleges that charge tuition, as well as the establishment of tuition charges for some students at public universities.

¹⁴ CULTURAL HERITAGE

Bulgarian culture underwent a resurgence when Ottoman rule ended. Leading literary figures included poets Hristo Botev, Dimcho Debelyanov, and Geo Milev, all of whom died violent deaths at a young age, either in battle or at the hands of the police. Ivan Vazov, a major Bulgarian literary figure, was a novelist, playwright, poet, and travel writer. Another 20th-century Bulgarian novelist was Dimitar Talev, author of *The Iron Candlestick (1952)*. The visual arts were revived in Bulgaria during the 19th century, especially the tradition of realistic painting, which became evident in the works of such 20th-century painters as Vladimir Dimitrov, Zlatyo Boyadjiev, and Ilya Petrov.

Bulgaria's lively, rhythmically complex folk music is popular with international folk dancers the world over. Although different regions have their own characteristic sounds, there is an underlying unity to the music, with songs grouping themselves into two main categories. The first group consists of songs with a long line and free meter, such as harvest songs and ballads. The second group has strict meters and includes dance songs and Christmas carols. Bulgarian folk music is played on instruments such as the *gaida* (bagpipes), *kaval* (seven-hole reed pipe), *gadulka* (pear-shaped fiddle), *tambura* (fretted lute), and *tupan* (cylindrical drum). A relatively new offshoot of Bulgaria's folk music tradition is the extremely popular genre known as "wedding music," dating back to the 1960s and 1970s, which is an adaptation of folk tunes for an amplified band consisting of clarinet, saxophone, accordion or synthesizer, guitar, electric bass, drums, and vocalist.

The best-known Bulgarian folk dance is the *horo*, a fast, swirling circle dance. Another favorite is the *ruchenitza*, often featured in dance competitions.

¹⁵ WORK

A significant problem confronting the country's labor force is the "brain drain" that has occurred since the 1990s as a result of immigration to the West in response to deteriorating economic conditions. More than 450,000 Bulgarians have left for

Germany, France, Canada, the United States, and other countries, many of them well-educated professionals, and most are not expected to return. Although the skills of these lost workers are sorely needed, Bulgaria cannot provide jobs for many of those who are still in the country, and unemployment during the mid-1990s rose above 10%, though it declined to about 8% in 2007. The workforce in 2007 was about 3.44 million, with 8.5% employed in agriculture, 33.6% in industry, and 57.9% in services. There are two major agricultural areas: The Danubian Plain specializes in the cultivation of roses, wheat, sunflowers, sugar beets, and potatoes, while in the Maritsa River Valley, rice, cotton, grapes, watermelon, and tobacco are grown. Bulgaria is known for its wines, and in 2002 it was the 13th largest wine producer in the world. Bulgaria's major industries are electricity, gas, and water; food, beverages, and tobacco; machinery and equipment; base metals; chemical products; coke; refined petroleum; and nuclear fuel.

16 SPORTS

The mountains of Bulgaria provide an excellent setting for its many ski enthusiasts, hikers, and tobogganers. Vacationers often head to Bulgaria's coastline to swim, fish, or boat. Soccer and basketball are also popular. There were countrywide celebrations when the Bulgarian soccer team defeated the Germans in the World Cup quarterfinals in 1994. As in other European countries, professional soccer players are celebrities, and almost all boys learn to play soccer at a young age. Basketball is more popular among young people in the cities than among those in rural areas. Volleyball, track, rowing, wrestling, and weightlifting are other favorite sports.

17 ENTERTAINMENT AND RECREATION

The Bulgarians are an industrious people who like to spend their leisure time in productive pursuits, even just catching up on household chores. Women often sew or knit while they socialize. There is an old village tradition, called the *sedenka,* of gathering for an evening of sewing, embroidering, or knitting, and there are even special sedenka songs that form part of the country's folk music tradition. Wine making is a favorite leisure time pursuit among Bulgarian men, and gardening is another very popular hobby. Even sedentary time is more likely to be spent reading or socializing in a coffeehouse than watching television.

18 FOLK ART, CRAFTS, AND HOBBIES

The skills of many fine but anonymous Bulgarian artisans can be seen in icons and other church art, which reached a high point in the 18th and 19th centuries. Prominent among contemporary crafts is the weaving of intricately patterned cloth and carpeting.

19 SOCIAL PROBLEMS

There are some interethnic tensions between the Bulgarians and the minority Turks and Roma. The plight of the Roma has been a cause for concern, as they tend to live in substandard housing on the outskirts of cities and have very high unemployment rates and a relatively short life expectancy.

In the 1990s, the Bulgarians struggled, both politically and economically, to adapt to the realities of the postcommunist era. Living standards for all except the wealthiest segment of the population declined, and political instability slowed the pace of economic reform. Since then, the Bulgarian government has focused on reversing the "brain drain" caused by the collapse of the Soviet Union.

The accession of Bulgaria to the European Union prompted new regulations on industry and agriculture, and the country and government continue to focus greatly on Euro-Atlantic relations.

With the collapse of the Soviet Union and the reduction of regulation, crime has been on the rise in Bulgaria. It is second only to Columbia in the production of counterfeit currency, and the country has a significant problem with the illegal sale of weapons to other governments.

20 GENDER ISSUES

The regulation of women's concerns has been and continues to be insufficient in Bulgaria. There are no laws against gender discrimination, and the workforce is replete with discriminatory hiring practices and sexual harassment. After the fall of communism, 65% of women were unemployed. One in every five women in Bulgaria has been the victim of spousal abuse, illegal trafficking, or enforced prostitution. However, many women's groups are forming, such as the Women's Alliance for Development. There are now far more women in politics. In 2008, 26% of the members of parliament were women; many high positions in business have been filled by women, and more and more women role models are emerging.

As a member of the European Union, Bulgaria has outlawed discrimination based on sexual orientation, and homosexual acts were decriminalized in 2001. However, Bulgaria does not allow same-sex marriage and gives few rights, such as domestic partnership arrangements, for homosexual or heterosexual couples. The European Union has dictated that member states, including Bulgaria, take action to reduce violence based on discrimination; however, Bulgaria has been slow to prosecute cases in which homosexuals are the victims. Bulgaria has yet to remedy inequality in the age of consent for homosexuals. The age of consent remains higher for homosexual couples, whereas most European countries have changed this statute. Although Bulgaria lags the rest of Europe in its views on homosexuality, pressure and influence from the European Union is beginning to change the situation.

21 BIBLIOGRAPHY

Bokov, Georgi, ed. *Modern Bulgaria: History, Policy, Economy, Culture.* Sofia, Bulgaria: Sofia Press, 1981.

Bulgarian Helsinki Committee. "Bulgarian Legislation about Homosexuals." http://www.bghelsinki.org/special/en/2001homosexual.html (6 May 2008).

Crampton, R. J. *A Short History of Modern Bulgaria.* Cambridge, UK: Cambridge University Press, 1987.

Creed, Gerald W. "Bulgarians." In *Encyclopedia of World Cultures (Europe),* edited by Linda A. Bennett. Boston: G. K. Hall, 1992.

McIntyre, Robert J. *Bulgaria: Politics, Economics, and Society.* London: Pinter, 1988.

Otfinoski, Steven. *Bulgaria. 2nd ed.* New York: Facts on File, 2004.

Population Reference Bureau. "Data Comparisons by Geography: Bulgaria: Summary." http://www.prb.org/pdf07/07WPDS_Eng.pdf (6 May 2008).

Stavreva, Kirilka, and Lynnette Quek. *Bulgaria. 2nd ed.* New York: Marshall Cavendish, 2007.

US Department of State, Bureau of European and Eurasian Affairs. "Background Note: Bulgaria." http://www.state.gov/r/pa/ei/bgn/3236.htm (6 May 2008).

—revised by C. Corrigan

BURIATS

ALTERNATE NAMES: Buryats; Buriaad
LOCATION: Russia (mountains of Southeast Siberia)
POPULATION: 515,175 (445,175 in Russia, 2002), (70,000 in Mongolia)
LANGUAGE: Buriat, Russian
RELIGION: Tibetan Buddhism; native religious practices, Eastern Orthodox Christianity

¹ INTRODUCTION

The Buriats (sometimes spelled Buryats) are an Asiatic people who inhabit the steppes and mountains surrounding the southern half of Lake Baikal in Southeast Siberia and speak a language belonging to the Mongol branch of the Altaic language family. The Buriats' name for themselves is Buriaad (or, less commonly, Buriaad-Mongol). The origins of the Buriats and the exact time at which they arose are unclear, but anthropological, linguistic, and archaeological evidence suggests that the ancestors of the modern Buriats may have been formed sometime during the Bronze Age (between 2500 and 1300 BC) along the shores of Lake Baikal and the Selenga River from Mongol tribes who mixed with native Siberian groups who spoke Turkic, Tungus, and perhaps Samoyedic languages. Russian soldiers and explorers first encountered the Buriats in the late 1620s and conquered them over the course of the 17th century. Most Buriats fought fiercely against the Russian invaders, and uprisings and attacks on Russian forts continued for decades, although some groups submitted voluntarily to the Russians in order to stop paying tribute to the Mongol khans and to escape the wars that were occurring in Mongolia at that time between Mongols and Manchus and between rival Mongolian leaders.

² LOCATION AND HOMELAND

The Buriats in Russia numbered around 445,175 as of 2002. The main area of Buriat settlement is the Republic of Buriatia, which contains 249,500 Buriats and is part of the Russian Federation. Buriatia covers about 351,300 square kilometers (135,600 square miles) along Lake Baikal, making it 1.5 times larger than Great Britain. About 49,300 Buriats also live in the Ust'-Ordynsk Buriat Autonomous District to the west of Lake Baikal, and 42,400 more live in the Aga Buriat Autonomous District to the east. Altogether, 445,175 Buriats live inside the boundaries of the Russian Federation. Outside Russia, 70,000 Buriats live in Mongolia, and a few thousand live in northern China. Most of Buriat territory is mountainous taiga. Rolling steppes are to be found east and southeast of Lake Baikal, and in some places steppe valleys extend deep into the taiga. The highest parts of the Buriat Republic lie in the Eastern Sayan mountain range to the southwest of Lake Baikal. Buriatia's climate is harsh and continental. Because Buriatia is far from the moderating influence of the sea and high above sea level, temperatures are extreme and precipitation is sparse. Winters are long, dry, and very cold (the average January temperature ranges from –23°C to –27°C [–9°F to –17°F]). Summers are short, hot (the average July temperature is 20°C [68°F]), and relatively rainy. Most of the region's 300 mm (12 inches) of annual precipitation falls during the summer.

Wild animals found in forested areas of Buriatia include deer, reindeer, elk, boar, squirrel, bear, lynx, and wolverine. Hamsters and marmots also live in the steppe areas. There are numerous species of birds, including ducks, and fish in the Buriat lands. Freshwater seals can be found on the many islands that dot the shoreline of Lake Baikal. Lake Baikal is the deepest continental body of water in the world, reaching a depth of 5,700 feet (1,737 meters). The lake contains about 20% of the world's freshwater reserves.

³ LANGUAGE

The Buriat language belongs to the Mongolian family and is divided into numerous dialects and subdialects. The Buriats did not have a written language until the early 17th century, when they began to write in Classical Mongolian, a literary language traditionally employed by most of the Mongol peoples. In this flowing vertical script, words are written from top to bottom in columns of text that read from left to right. After 1929, Buriat was written in the Latin alphabet, which was in turn replaced by the Russian (Cyrillic) alphabet in 1938. The Buriat literary language used today is based on the Khori dialect of the eastern Buriats and is written in the Cyrillic alphabet with extra letters for Buriat sounds that do not exist in Russian. Some common Buriat male names are *Baatar* ("hero") and *Mergen* ("wise"); common female names include *Gerelmaa* ("light") and *Erzhena* ("mother-of-pearl"). Because many Buriats practice the Tibetan form of Buddhism, names of Tibetan origin, such as *Sodnom* ("virtue"; male) and *Geleg* ("luck"; male) are also widely used. Some Buriats use Russian names such as *Mikhail* (male) and *Tania* (female).

⁴ FOLKLORE

The Buriats have a rich heritage of folklore that has accumulated over hundreds, perhaps thousands, of years. The most remarkable genre of Buriat folklore is the *uliger*, or epic poem, which has been compared to the *Iliad* and *Odyssey* epics of the ancient Greeks. The Buriat epic poems all describe the struggles of mythical heroes such as Geser, Alamzhi-Mergen ("Alamzhi the Wise"), and Shono-Bator against various enemies and monsters. (The Buriats' favorite hero, Geser, is actually of Tibetan origin.) All Buriat *uligers* are very long, ranging from 2,000–3,000 to 25,000 lines in length. Some have developed several versions in different regions of Buriatia. The *uligers* have been most faithfully preserved in western Buriatia, perhaps because Buddhism is much less widespread there than among the Buriats east of Baikal, so the *uligers* have not had to compete with Buddhist tales. Because most Buriats were illiterate until the 20th century, the *uligers* were passed down orally from generation to generation, memorized and publicly recited by *uligershens* (bards). The Soviet persecution of Buriat national culture almost destroyed the *uligershens*. The Geser epic was banned for several years after World War II because Russian Communists misinterpreted several lines as anti-Russian, and new *uligershens* were no longer trained to replace the older ones who were dying out. In the past decade, Buriat cultural institutions have begun the slow, difficult work of preparing new *uligershens*.

⁵ RELIGION

The traditional religion of the Buriats was shamanism. Mountains, rivers, forests, and the sky were all considered to have

their own spirits or gods that had to be respected. Animals, too, had their own spirits that had to be respected. For instance, it was forbidden to refer to certain animals directly by their usual Buriat names during the hunt lest they take offense at this impertinence. Thus, a *shono* (wolf) was called *tengeriin nokhoi* (heavenly dog). The Buriats also held fire to be sacred and sacrificed meat, milk, fat, liquor, and butter to it. A tribal priest, or shaman, was responsible for communicating with the gods. Like the Native American "medicine man," the shaman performed rituals at births, marriages, and burials and officiated at sacrifices, the most important of which was the horse sacrifice to the sky god Tengri. The shaman also prayed for and gave medicine to the sick and divined the future. There were both male shamans and female shamans, and the profession of shaman was hereditary.

Buriats east of Baikal adopted the Tibetan form of Buddhism in the 1600s. Most western Buriats remained shamanists, but some adopted Buddhism or Russian Orthodox Christianity. The Buddhism practiced by the Buriats has incorporated many shamanist beliefs and rituals. Buddhist *datsans* (monasteries) filled cultural and educational as well as religious needs, since they contained schools, libraries, and printing facilities. The Soviet government destroyed the monasteries and imprisoned or killed almost all of the Buriat lamas (Buddhist monks or priests) and shamans in the 1930s as part of its war against religion. Buriat religious practices had to go underground until the 1980s, when Soviet leader Mikhail Gorbachev abandoned the government's anti-religious policies. Now some of the previously destroyed *datsans* are being rebuilt, entirely new ones are being opened, *datsan* schools are again training lamas, and shamans can practice openly without fear of persecution.

6 MAJOR HOLIDAYS

The *Tsagaalgan* (New Year's Festival) is the most popular Buriat holiday and is celebrated by feasting and drinking that, in theory at least, can last through the entire first month of the year (the *sagaan hara* or "white month"). Since the Buriats formerly used the lunar calendar, the Buriat New Year falls on a different day each year in the Gregorian calendar. Buriats also celebrate the Western New Year's Eve and New Year's Day (31 December and 1 January). Buddhist Buriats also attended *tsams*, festivals held at the *datsans* that featured dramatic dances by lamas in elaborate masks and costumes depicting gods and demons. Shamanist Buriats also celebrated holidays called *tailgans* that began with animal sacrifices to local deities and ended with feasts, horse races, wrestling matches, and archery contests. There were three major *tailgans*—spring, summer, and fall—every year as well as many minor ones. Christian Buriats and those who lived in areas with large Russian populations also observed Christian holidays such as Easter and Christmas. Because all these holidays had religious aspects, they were banned by the Soviet regime, but in recent years Buriats have begun to observe them openly again. Of the Soviet-era secular holidays celebrated throughout Russia, the most popular among the Buriats are International Women's Day (8 March) and the anniversary of the Soviet victory over Nazi Germany (9 May).

7 RITES OF PASSAGE

Buriats have traditionally called upon shamans or lamas to bless the birth of a child. Because childlessness is considered a great misfortune by the Buriats, and infant mortality rates were high before the spread of Western medicine, superstitious parents temporarily gave newborns unappealing names or names inappropriate to their sex in order to make them less attractive to evil spirits that might otherwise harm them. For this reason, it is still common to refer to infants in uncomplimentary terms. A mother, for example, might say that her baby is *muukhai* ("ugly") even though she considers him beautiful.

The Buriats have no special rites of passage for childhood, puberty, or adulthood. Buddhist Buriats consider children to be without sin until they are about eight years old, but attaining this age is not marked by any special ritual. Buriats traditionally disposed of their dead by exposing them in the open air on the ground or on a raised platform. Weapons, saddles, and other everyday items were sometimes buried with their owners, and the deceased's horse was sometimes killed. Shamans were cremated and their ashes placed in tree trunks; groves that contained these trees were considered sacred, and it was forbidden to take wood from them. Cremation was also common in traditional Buriat society, especially among Buddhist Buriats. Buriats now bury their dead in cemeteries or cremate them.

8 INTERPERSONAL RELATIONS

Upon receiving a guest in one's home for the first time, it is customary to present him or her with a *khadag,* a strip of silk approximately one yard long and a little less than one foot wide. The host places the *khadag* across his or her outstretched arms and transfers it to the arms of the guest. This practice, along with the word *khadag,* is of Tibetan origin. It is considered poor manners to hand someone an item with one's left hand when in polite company.

9 LIVING CONDITIONS

The nomadic eastern Buriats' traditional form of housing was the yurt, or *ger*, which was covered with felt cloth and held in place by a wooden frame. The doorway of the *ger* always faced south. The *ger* could be quickly taken apart and reassembled when the family moved from pasture to pasture. Because most western Buriats lived in mountainous areas unsuitable for nomadism, they used eight-sided permanent wooden "yurts." As a result of Russian influence, some also adopted log cabins and houses. At the present time, rural Buriats live in wooden houses in collective farms and villages, and urban Buriats live in Soviet-type apartment buildings or private wooden houses. Because of the persistent shortage of desirable housing during the Soviet period, it was not uncommon for Buriats in Ulan-Ude and other Buriat cities to live for years or even decades in crowded apartments with relatives or in dilapidated wooden houses that lacked indoor plumbing while waiting for suitable apartments of their own.

Like all Mongol peoples, Buriats have traditionally been excellent horsemen, and horses are still widely used for transportation in the countryside. Buriats living in cities, on the other hand, use public trolleys and buses and, to a much lesser extent, private automobiles.

Before the Soviet period, Western medicine was virtually unknown among the Buriats; instead, they were treated by shamans who knew herbal folk medicine and lamas trained in Tibetan medical practices at Buddhist monasteries. Western medicine has become widespread since the October Revolution of 1917 and is provided by the government at low cost. Many Buriats combine Western medical treatment with traditional methods of healing. Buriatia contains numerous mineral springs that are used for medicinal purposes, the most famous of which are located at Arshaan, southwest of Lake Baikal and are used by people from all over Buriatia, and indeed, from all parts of the former Soviet Union.

10 FAMILY LIFE

Traditional Buriat society was made up of *esege zon* (large tribes) organized on a territorial basis and *otog* (clans) that were based on kinship rather than territory. Wealthy clan members were obligated to help poorer clan members and widows and orphans who belonged to their clan. Clans, in turn, were divided into families. There were two types of traditional Buriat families: small nuclear families consisting of the male head of a household, his wife, several children, and sometimes his parents; and extended patriarchal families that combined the households of several brothers into a single settlement under the leadership of their father or the eldest brother. The nuclear family has always been the more common type, and the large patriarchal families have now faded into the past. Nevertheless, ties between members of related nuclear families are still strong, and it is not uncommon for parents, grandparents, and unmarried adult grandchildren to live under the same roof. Buriat couples usually have two or three children, and families tend to be larger in the countryside, where housing is in greater supply than in the cities.

A Buriat man and his Russian wife with their three daughters in Maloye Goloustnoye, Siberia. (© Dean Conger/Corbis)

Traditionally, most marriages were arranged by the parents of the prospective pair. The groom's family was required to pay a "bride-price" to the family of his prospective wife; if they could not afford to pay the bride-price in money, livestock, or other property, the groom was required to work it off at the home of his future in-laws before the marriage could take place. The difficulties caused by this practice sometimes led a prospective groom or his family to kidnap a bride from another clan rather than pay for her. Families who wished to gain financially by a marriage sometimes arranged it long before their children were old enough to marry. The minimum age of marriage was 15 or 16, but in practice women usually married between the ages of 17 and 21, and men between 18 and 25. (Men married later since they had to provide the bride-price.) Marriage between clan members who shared an ancestor within the preceding nine generations was forbidden. Polygamy was permitted, but only wealthy men could afford to have more than one wife. During a traditional wedding ceremony, the bride was brought on horseback to the groom's home, where she bowed to the gods of the groom's clan and sacrificed food and drink to them. Among Buddhist Buriats, lamas performed additional rituals to ensure the marriage's success. Buriats are now married in civil ceremonies. During the 20th century, marriages for love have replaced arranged marriages, although some parents still use unofficial "matchmakers" to help their children find suitable mates.

¹¹ CLOTHING

The traditional Buriat garment for both men and women is the *degel*, an ankle-length robe of felt, fur, or cloth that is fastened on one side with buttons or hooks. A lighter version of the *degel* worn in summer was called a *terlig*. Men also wore hats of cloth or fur and belts to which were attached knives in sheaths and elaborately decorated pouches for tobacco, snuff, and firemaking flints. Women wore trousers and shirts under their *degels* and sometimes an embroidered vest on the outside. Both sexes wore boots, or *gutal*, with thick soles and toes that curled slightly upward. (Men carried their pipes in the tops of their boots). Women, especially wealthy ones, wore elaborate silver earrings, rings, headdresses, and trinkets. Today almost all Buriats wear Western clothing (suits, dresses, etc.). Few Buriats even own traditional clothing, which cannot be purchased in stores, and those who do wear it only on holidays or other special occasions. The Buriats in the Aga Buriat Autonomous District represent a major exception to this tendency, however. Almost all Buriats their own and wear traditional clothing.

¹² FOOD

Because Buriats have traditionally been a livestock-breeding people, it is not surprising that most of their national dishes feature meat and dairy products. A particularly esteemed delicacy is sheep's tail, which consists of very fatty meat; it is given to the most honored guest as a sign of esteem. Customary foods include boiled mutton, *süsegei* (a type of sour cream), *eezgei* (a dish similar to cottage cheese), blood sausages, butter, *buuza* (steamed dumplings filled with ground mutton or beef), and various types of yogurt. A recipe for *buuza* follows.

Buuza
(Buriat meat dumplings)

Filling
850 grams (1¾ pounds) lean mutton (Beef, pork, or horsemeat may be substituted)
220 grams (8 ounces) pork or mutton fat
3 onions
130 milliliters (4½ ounces) water
9 grams (1 tablespoon) flour
3 grams (1 teaspoon) salt

Dough
350 grams (2½ cups) flour
2 eggs
60 grams (2 ounces) water
dash of salt (optional)

Grind the meat in a meat grinder. Finely chop the fat and onions and mix them thoroughly with the meat, water, flour, and salt. Set aside.

Mix the dough ingredients together in a bowl. Roll the dough by hand into a tube about 2 centimeters (¾ inch) wide, then cut the tube into pieces (about 2 to 4 centimeters ¾ to 1½ inches) long. Use a rolling pin to shape the pieces into thin circles.

Place 50 grams (slightly less than ¼ cup) of the filling onto each of the dough circles. Pinch the edges of the circles together in tiny folds at the top of the meat, leaving a small hole in the center to let steam escape. Steam the dumplings over boiling water until the juice from inside is clear, 18 to 20 minutes. Serves 4 to 5.

(Translated and adapted from G. Tsydenzhapov and E. Badueva, Buriatskaia kukhnia (Buriat Cuisine), Ulan-Ude: Buriatskoe knizhnoe izdatel'stvo, 1991, 50–51.)

Buriats are fond of tea, which they sometimes drink in the Tibetan style with milk, salt, and barley. The Russian influence on Soviet food production has made cabbage, potatoes, and other vegetables, as well as bread, sugar, and canned goods staples of the Buriat diet. The wooden and leather containers and utensils formerly used to prepare, store, and consume food have been replaced with metal, glass, and enamel ones purchased in stores. Food and drink are preferably given to guests or respected persons with both hands, or, if this would be impossible or awkward, with the right hand (preferably supported symbolically at the elbow by the left). When vodka or *darasun* (a liqueur made from fermented milk) is drunk, the first drops from a bottle are spilled into the fire (or, as is more common today, onto the electric or gas stove).

¹³ EDUCATION

Prior to the October Revolution, most Buriats were illiterate. Some Buriats attended local Russian elementary, and much more rarely, secondary schools. Most schools in the Buriat lands taught in Russian, not Buriat, because there were few Buriat teachers. Very few Russian teachers knew Buriat, and the Russian government opposed the use of Buriat and other non-Russian languages in the classroom. Russian Orthodox missionaries also established religiously oriented elementary schools, but these institutions were unpopular among the Buriats, who associated them with forced assimilation. Some Buddhist Buriats attended schools at the datsans, and there they learned Tibetan (the ritual language of Buriat Buddhism), Classical Mongolian, Buddhist theology and philosophy, and sometimes Tibetan medicine. Pre-revolutionary Buriats who did not attend school occasionally learned to read and write from relatives or tutors in Russian or Classical Mongolian.

The Soviet government made school attendance mandatory and universal. As a result, illiteracy has been practically eliminated among the Buriats. Most Buriats graduate from secondary school, and a sizeable proportion go on to attend colleges or trade schools. These advances have not come without a price, however. The Soviet regime attempted to use schooling as a tool of Russification (that is, replacing native cultures and languages with Russian), especially during the 1960s and 1970s. Teaching in the Buriat language was intentionally reduced, leading to a sharp decline in the number of young Buriats who knew their own language. Even those who spoke Buriat fluently could not read or write well in it. Since Gorbachev abandoned the policy of Russification in the 1990s, Buriat educators have increased the Buriat language's role in the classroom as both subject of study and means of instruction.

¹⁴ CULTURAL HERITAGE

Many aspects of the Buriat cultural heritage were represented in the Buddhist monasteries *(datsans)*. *Datsans* contained libraries of religious and secular literature in Classical Mongolian and Tibetan and even printed books in these languages. Artist-monks painted icons and carved statues of Buddhist deities and copied scriptures onto lacquered wooden pages using inks made of precious stones. The lavishly decorated monasteries were in themselves unique architectural monuments.

In addition to epic poems and other forms of oral folk literature, the Buriats possess historical chronicles written in Classical Mongol in the 18th and 19th centuries. During the 20th century, Buriat writers have adopted Western literary modes such as the novel, short story, and play. The most famous modern Buriat author is Khotsa Namsaraev (1889–1959), whose works attack the real and alleged shortcomings of traditional Buriat ways of life and speak in glowing terms of the new Communist society. Although most Buriats find these propagandistic themes crude and distasteful, they still respect Namsaraev for his excellent literary style.

¹⁵ WORK

The Buriat economy traditionally centered around the breeding of cattle, sheep, horses, and goats. Some Buriats to the south and southwest of Lake Baikal also raised yaks. The Buriats in the steppe lands to the east and southeast of Baikal were nomads, moving their flocks to new pastures after they had exhausted an area's grass and water. Most nomadic Buriats moved twice a year, but rich Buriats who owned large herds changed residences up to a dozen times a year. Buriats west of Baikal also raised livestock, but because they usually lived in rugged mountain areas where movement was difficult, they were more sedentary. Western Buriats traditionally raised barley, wheat, and other grains. Buriats on both sides of Baikal engaged in hunting, particularly squirrels, sables, bears, elk, and deer, and those who lived near lakes or rivers also fished. When the Soviet government collectivized agriculture and animal husbandry in the 1930s, the Buriats lost their herds and were forced to settle in collective farms. Because the issue of private land ownership has not yet been settled in the former Soviet Union, most Buriats still live and work in the collective farms.

[16] SPORTS

The most widespread sports among Buriats of all ages have traditionally been archery, horse riding, and wrestling, sports that are common among other Mongol-speaking peoples as well. *Surkharbaan* (archery festivals) are held every year at the town, district, and all-Buriat level, and include horse races and wrestling matches in addition to the archery contests. Buriats also enjoy Western spectator sports common throughout the former USSR such as soccer, basketball, and volleyball.

[17] ENTERTAINMENT AND RECREATION

The traditional forms of Buriat entertainment—watching horse races and archery contests and listening to bards recite epic poetry—have been supplemented by modern ones. In addition to the Russian-language news and entertainment programming of the national stations in Moscow that broadcast by satellite to the entire Russian Federation, there are several hours each day of Buriat-language radio and television programs from stations in the Buriat capital, Ulan-Ude. Since the early 1990s, Buriat-language television broadcasts have been videotaped and sent to television stations in the city of Irkutsk west of Baikal to be rebroadcast to Buriats who live outside their republic. Buriats enjoy watching Russian and Western films; young Buriats especially like American action-adventure films and East Asian martial-arts movies. A Buriat-language theater in Ulan-Ude stages plays by Buriat authors and translations of works by Russians and other non-Buriats. There is also an opera house in Ulan-Ude that performs Buriat, Russian, and Western compositions.

[18] FOLK ART, CRAFTS, AND HOBBIES

Because many Buriats were traditionally nomads, Buriat craftsmen have tended to focus on portable and relatively small items of everyday use such as saddles, tools, chests, clothing, storage trunks, and religious statues (shamanist *ongons*, or representations of deities, and Buddhist figures). The techniques they employ include carving, embroidery, stamping, and embossing. Although Buriats have long worked in leather, wood, bone, felt, iron, and stone, they are especially talented at crafting silver and even today produce very detailed and beautiful silver knives, pipes, buckles, buttons, rings, earrings, bracelets, and other jewelry.

[19] SOCIAL PROBLEMS

Modern Buriats face many of the same social problems that confront people in other parts of the former Soviet Union. A collapsing economy, rampant crime and corruption, alcoholism, and environmental degradation are foremost among these. In addition, they must confront threats to their cultural integrity that stem from specific historical circumstances. Although the Bolsheviks initially encouraged the formation of a multicultural state in which all cultures and languages would enjoy equal rights, Stalin and his successors considered Russian language and culture superior to those of the USSR's other peoples and pursued a policy of Russification aimed at wiping out non-Russian cultures and languages with a mixture of persecution and neglect. The Buriat language was almost entirely removed from schools, and Buriat book and newspaper publishing declined in quality and quantity. Even worse, propaganda subtly but unceasingly fed Buriats (especially young ones) the message that "Buriat-ness" was equal to "backwardness" and that there was nothing in their cultural heritage of which they could be proud. Only in the last decade has the end of censorship and official Russification allowed Buriats to criticize these policies and to begin to slowly repair, primarily through education and the press, the damage done.

[20] GENDER ISSUES

The social position of women was somewhat inferior to that of men in traditional Buriat society. For example, a woman had to observe many taboos in dealing with her husband's family: she was forbidden to address her mother- and father-in-law by their names, to sleep in the same dwelling with them, to walk in front of them, or to appear before them without covering her head with a cap. Buriat women now have legal rights equal to those of men, but sexist attitudes are still common. Although most Buriat women are employed outside the home, many husbands refuse to help them with household tasks. Historically, collectivization and the Second World War brought profound changes to traditional Buriat gender roles. The integration of the Buriats into the Soviet economic system, and into Soviet society shifted gender roles to some degree, but also provided Buriat women with increased educational opportunities.

[21] BIBLIOGRAPHY

Czaplicka, M. A. *Aboriginal Siberia: A Study in Social Anthropology.* Oxford: Oxford University Press, 1914 (reprinted 1969).

Forsyth, James. *A History of the Peoples of Siberia: Russia's North Asian Colony, 1581-1990.* Cambridge: Cambridge University Press, 1992.

Galdanova, G. R. *Dolamaistkie verovaniia buriat,* (*The Pre-Buddhist Beliefs of the Buriats*). Novosibirsk: Nauka, 1987.

Humphrey, Caroline. *Karl Marx Collective: Economy, Society and Religion in a Siberian Collective Farm.* Cambridge: Cambridge University Press, 1983.

Mikhailov, T. M. *Buriatskii shamanism.* (*Buriat Shamanism*), Novosibirsk: Nauka, 1987.

———. "Buriaty" (The Buriats). In *Narody Rossii: Entsiklopediia* (The Peoples of Russia: An Encyclopedia). In Russian. Ed. V. A. Tishkov. Moscow: Bol'shaia Rossiiskaia Entsiklopediia, 1994.

Montgomery, Robert W. *Late Tsarist and Early Soviet Nationality and Cultural Policy: The Buryats and their Language.* Lewiston, New York: Edwin Mellen Press, 2005.

Vyatkina, K. V. "The Buryats." In *The Peoples of Siberia.* Ed. M. G. Levin and L. P. Potapov. Trans. Stephen Dunn. Chicago: University of Chicago Press, 1964.

Zhukovskaya, Natalia. "The Buriats." In *Encyclopedia of World Cultures. Vol. 6, Russia and Eurasia/China.* Ed. Paul Friedrich and Norma Diamond. Boston: G. K. Hall, 1994.

—revised by A. Frank

CASTILIANS

LOCATION: Central Spain
POPULATION: Approximately 11 million
LANGUAGE: Castilian Spanish
RELIGION: Roman Catholic

¹ INTRODUCTION

Castilians, who inhabit Spain's central tableland, have dominated Spain politically since the 16th century. The area traditionally referred to as "Castile" (meaning land of castles) comprises two present-day regions: Castile and León and Castile-La Mancha. Its original inhabitants were Iberians and Celts who were conquered by the Romans and the Moors. The *Reconquista*—the centuries-long crusade to drive the Moors from Spain that began in the 8th century—was centered in Castile, a region known for its religious devotion and fierce warriors, epitomized by the regional hero El Cid, who became the subject of epic poetry.

By 1492, when the Reconquista was finally completed with the expulsion of the Moors from Granada, Castile had became a center of political as well as military power, a result of the 1469 marriage of Isabella of Castile to Ferdinand of Aragon. The pair united the two territories 10 years later when Ferdinand succeeded to the throne of his kingdom. Ferdinand and Isabella made important governmental reforms, notably, reducing the influence of the nobles and crusading orders and consolidating power in the hands of a central authority with a regional seat in Castile. (Castile also became the center of authority for the Spanish Inquisition, beginning in 1478.) In the following centuries, the fortunes of Castile, located at the center of power, rose and fell with those of the Spanish Empire. The golden age of the 16th century was followed by wars that eroded Spain's power, and the Bourbon dynasty was installed at the close of the Wars of the Spanish Succession (1701–14).

Castile was caught up in the 19th- and 20th-century struggles between supporters of the monarchy and those who desired the formation of a republic. In the 20th century, Spain remained officially neutral in both world wars. Coming to power at the end of the Spanish Civil War (1936–39), the regime of Francisco Franco aided the Axis powers during World War II, with the result that Spain was left out of the Marshall Plan that aided in the postwar reconstruction of Europe. The nation did, however, become a member of the United Nations in 1955. Predominantly rural areas such as Castile—where the postwar period was referred to as the "years of hunger"—experienced large-scale emigration. Following Franco's death in 1975 and the installation of a democratic regime in 1978, Castile experienced greater opportunities for economic development. Spain became a member of the North Atlantic Treaty Organization (NATO) in 1982 and joined the European Union (EU) in 1986.

² LOCATION AND HOMELAND

Castile is located within Spain's central tableland, or *meseta.* It is a region of hot, dry, windswept plains broken in places by chains of low mountains, with elevations varying from 600 m to 900 m (2,000–3,000 ft) above sea level. There are few trees, and much of the terrain is covered by *encinas,* which are similar to dwarf oaks, or by scrub. The main bodies of water are the Duero and Tagus rivers. The seasons are quite extreme, switching from very cold to very hot almost immediately, with little spring or fall. Castilians traditionally describe their climate with the following proverb: *Nueve meses de invierno y tres mese de infierno,* or "Nine months of winter and three months of hell."

The Castile region represents one-third of the territory of Spain and about one-quarter of the population of approximately 45 million, mostly concentrated in major urban areas such as Madrid, Toledo, and Valladolid. The rural areas, by contrast, are much less densely populated, and their population continues to fall as residents relocate to the cities or immigrate abroad. Madrid has a population of 5.5 million.

³ LANGUAGE

Though several distinct languages are spoken throughout Spain, Castilian *(Castellano)* is the country's national language, a status it garnered as a result of Castile's long-standing political dominance. Used in government, education, and the media, Castilian is the language that people in other countries identify as "Spanish." Two of the main regional languages—Catalan and Gallego—are Romance languages that bear some degree of similarity to Castilian. Euskera, a language spoken in the Basque Country, is very different not only from Spanish but from any other European language. Other Spanish dialects include Andalusian, Aragonese, Asturian, Leonese, and Valencian. Spain's linguistic differences have been a source of political tension, and today, Catalan, Gallego, and Euskera (Basque) are also designated—together with Castilian—as official languages in their respective regions. They are taught in the schools and appear alongside Castilian on all street signs.

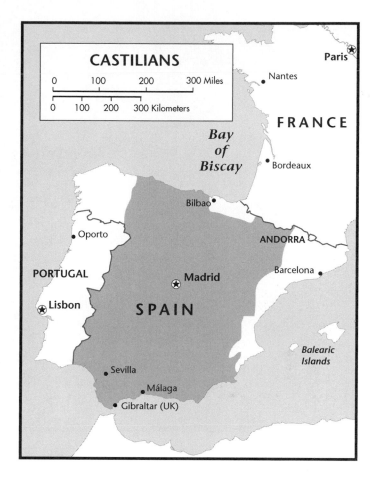

NUMBERS

one	un, uno
two	dos
three	tres
four	quatro
five	cinco
six	seis
seven	siete
eight	ocho
nine	nueve
ten	diez

DAYS OF THE WEEK

Sunday	domingo
Monday	lunes
Tuesday	martes
Wednesday	miércoles
Thursday	jueves
Friday	viernes
Saturday	sábado

⁴ FOLKLORE

The Castilians' great cultural hero is El Cid Campeador, an actual historical figure (Rodrigo Díaz de Vivar) of the 11th century whose life passed into legend with the composition of the Spanish national epic based on his life, *Cantar del Mio Cid (The Poem of the Cid).* This warrior of the *Reconquista* (the Christian reconquest of Spain from the Moors) is celebrated for qualities that still resonate with Castilians: a strong sense of honor, devout Catholicism, pragmatism, devotion to family, and integrity.

⁵ RELIGION

The Castilians, like the Spanish population in general, are overwhelmingly Roman Catholic. They are known for their adherence to church doctrine and high degree of religious observance. Many attend church every Sunday, and a number of women go to services every day. However, the traditionally strong influence of village priests over their parishioners' lives has declined in recent years.

⁶ MAJOR HOLIDAYS

Besides New Year's Day and the major holidays of the Christian calendar, Castilians celebrate the national holidays of Spain: Saint Joseph's Day (March 19), the Day of Saint Peter and Saint Paul (June 29), Saint James's Day (July 25), and National Day (October 12). The most important religious holidays in Castile are Easter and Christmas. In addition, every village observes the feast day of its patron saint with a gala celebration that includes many distinctly secular events, such as bullfights, soccer matches, and fireworks. Residents parade through the streets carrying huge papier-mâché figures called *gigants* (giants) and *cabezudos* (big heads or fat heads). The gigants are effigies of King Ferdinand and Queen Isabella, while the cabezudos portray a variety of figures from history, legend, and fantasy. Madrid's Festival of San Isidro comprises three weeks of parties, processions, and bullfights.

Locals and tourists sit at a café in Segovia, Castilla y Leon, Spain, with the ruins of a Roman aqueduct in the background.
(© Alan Copson/JAI/Corbis)

⁷ RITES OF PASSAGE

The sacraments of baptism, first communion, and marriage are occasions for large and expensive social gatherings at which families show their generosity and economic status. Military service is also considered a rite of passage for Castilians, as it is for most Spaniards. *Quintos,* young men from the same town or village who go into military service in the same year, form a closely knit group that collects money from neighbors to organize parties and serenade girls. The period of compulsory military service has been greatly reduced since the 1990s, and the government plans to replace compulsory military service with a voluntary army.

⁸ INTERPERSONAL RELATIONS

Tempered by the harsh, barren landscape of their homeland, Castilians are known for their toughness, frugality, and endurance. Isolated by Castile's vast expanses of arid land, rural inhabitants rely closely on their immediate neighbors, living in small clusters of houses. They tend to be suspicious of outsiders and new ideas.

⁹ LIVING CONDITIONS

Although Castile is home to large cities such as Madrid and Toledo, it remains a primarily rural region, and much of its population is dependent on agriculture. In rural villages, the traditional house combines the family's living quarters with a stable and barn that have a separate entrance. The kitchen is arranged around an open-hearth fireplace (*chimenea*). The most

common building material is stucco, although stone houses are common among wealthier inhabitants.

Castilians have access to the same level of modern medical care as their neighbors elsewhere in Spain, where the average life expectancy is 78 years. Despite their reliance on modern medicine, it is not unusual for Castilians to invoke the healing powers of a patron saint when a loved one is ill, and traditional folk medicine, including herbal remedies, is still practiced in some remote rural areas.

Castile is the hub of Spain's transportation network. All of the nation's highways, rail lines, and air routes pass through Madrid because of its central location. The city also has a modern subway system. In the country, dirt and gravel roads are common, and burros are still used for transportation in some small villages.

¹⁰ FAMILY LIFE

Castilians tend to delay marriage until the age of about 25, when the man has completed his military service and the couple has achieved a degree of financial independence. Courtships are carefully monitored, as scandal reflects not only on the couple themselves but also on the reputations of their respective families. During the marriage ceremony, members of the wedding party hold a white veil over the bride and groom to symbolize the future submissiveness of the wife to her husband. Newlyweds are expected to set up their own household, although it is common for the bride's parents to help the couple buy or build a house, which is often located in the parents' own neighborhood. Only church marriages were recognized in Spain until 1968, when civil ceremonies were first allowed by law. Divorce has been legal since the 1980s. A man is much more likely to divorce his wife than vice versa. Because of the intensity of the divorce process and the strong Catholic influence in the country, Spain has the third lowest divorce rate on the European continent.

11 CLOTHING

For everyday activities, both casual and formal, Castilians wear modern Western-style clothing, similar to that worn elsewhere in Western Europe and in the United States. Traditionally black clothing was worn to church, and the elderly in rural villages still observe this custom.

12 FOOD

Pork and other pig products—ham, bacon, and sausages—are staples of the Castilian diet. The region's most famous dish is *cochinillo asado,* roast suckling pig, for which the city of Segovia is especially well known. The city of El Bierzo is known for another popular dish, *botillo,* composed of minced pork and sausages. Castile has a traditional soup—*sopa castillana,* containing pork, eggs, bread, garlic, and fat—but it is no longer widely eaten. Beans of all kinds are a regional staple, including red beans, white beans, chickpeas, and lentils. Tapas, the popular snacks eaten throughout Spain, are also popular in Castile. Tojunto, beef or rabbit with tomatoes, is a typical dish of the area. Bizcochos borrachos are sponge cakes soaked in brandy. Serrano ham and olla podrida (rotten stew) are well known in León. Saffron is often used in cooking, and it is highly prized in the area. Like people in other parts of Spain, Castilians take an extended lunch break at midday, called a siesta. This tradition has waned as people have become busier; only about 25% of Spaniards still take a siesta. Castilians typically eat dinner late, between 9:00 pm and midnight.

13 EDUCATION

For young Castilians, like other Spanish children, schooling is free and compulsory from the ages of 6 to 14, when many students begin the three-year *bachillerato* course of study. Subsequently, they may opt for one year of college preparatory study or vocational training. Castile is home to Spain's oldest university—the Pontifical University of Salamanca, founded in 1254—as well as the University of Madrid, which has the highest enrollment in the country.

14 CULTURAL HERITAGE

Castile's literary tradition dates back to the 12th-century epic poem *Cantar del Mio Cid* (Poem of the Cid), which celebrates the life and exploits of Rodrigo Díaz de Vivar, a Castilian warrior who gained fame during the *Reconquista.* The fictional El Cid, embodying the ideal Castilian, has captured the popular imagination for generations, serving as the subject of a play by the French playwright Corneille and a Hollywood movie starring Charlton Heston. The most famous Castilian writer is Miguel de Cervantes, author of the 17th-century classic *Don Quixote,* a masterpiece of world literature and a milestone in the development of the modern novel. At the turn of the 20th century, the poet Antonio Machado, a member of a group of writers and artists called the "Generation of 1898," wrote of Castile's decline from its onetime position of power:

Castilla miserable, ayer cominadora,
envuelta en sus andrajos, desprecia cuanto ignora.

Miserable Castile, yesterday lording it over everybody, now wrapped in her rags scorns all she does not know.

15 WORK

Castilian agriculture consists of small family farms that raise barley, wheat, grapes, sugar beets, cork, tobacco, olives, and other crops. Many farms also raise poultry and livestock, and almost all farm families have at least one or two pigs. Income from the family farm is usually supplemented by a small business or by salaried jobs—often in government—held by one or more family members. Tourism is a major employer in the city of Burgos, and Valladolid is an industrial center and grain market. Food processing plants employ many workers in Salamanca.

16 SPORTS

The most popular sports in Castile are soccer (called *futból*) and bullfighting. Bullfighting events are often conducted during fiestas. Spaniards have a love for sports and events that involve big crowds and loud cheering. Other favorite sports include cycling, fishing, hunting, golf, tennis, and horseback riding. Horse racing takes place in Madrid at Zarzuela Hippodrome.

17 ENTERTAINMENT AND RECREATION

Spaniards spend more time and money on collective celebrations than any other country in the world. Castile's warm climate fosters an active nightlife in its cities, much of it outdoors in streets, plazas, taverns, and restaurants. These are known as fiestas, and they are a strong part of the culture. After work, Castilians often go for a stroll (*paseo*), stopping to chat with neighbors along the way or meet friends at a local café. A dinner date in Madrid may take place as late as 10:00 or 11:00 pm, followed by a trip to a local club. Sunday afternoon is another traditional time for a stroll. Castilians, like people throughout Spain, also enjoy relaxing at home with their favorite television programs. The dance of Jota is known in Castile, and the bolero is a dance that has been performed in La Mancha since the 16th century.

18 FOLK ART, CRAFTS, AND HOBBIES

Castilian pottery is typically decorated with brightly colored pictures of birds and other animals. Fine swords have been made of Toledo steel—famous for its strength and flexibility—since the Middle Ages. Craftspeople continue this tradition to the present day, inlaying the steel with gold and silver and crafting intricate designs on swords, jewelry, and other objects. The Spanish government has taken steps to ensure that traditional crafts, or *artenia,* survive against competition from mechanized industry.

19 SOCIAL PROBLEMS

As in other rural areas of Spain, Castile has suffered from a high rate of emigration since World War II. Between 1960 and 1975, the population of Castile and León declined from 2.85 million to 2.55 million; that of Castile-La Mancha dropped from 1.38 to 1.04 million. The Castilian provinces of Avila,

Palencia, Segovia, Soria, and Zamora had smaller populations in 1975 than in 1900.

Because of its long coastline, Spain has had many problems with foreign parties in North Africa, Latin America, and Europe, trafficking drugs along the border. The country also has problems with alcohol, tobacco, and drugs, as do other modern nations.

20 GENDER ISSUES

Spain has historically been a male-dominated society, and women have stood in the background for much longer than in other Western European countries. The women's movement began in 1976 with marches in Madrid. Spain's 1978 constitution included an equality clause for all Spaniards, thereby creating a legal basis for women's equality. The most offensive restrictions on women's rights took place during the Franco era. During the 1980s, women gained more rights to ownership and property. Laws allowing women to seek sanctuary from abuse were created at this time. Divorce laws were enacted in 1977.

Homosexuals were highly repressed under the Franco regime—more so than any where in modern Europe, with the exception of the Salazar regime in Portugal. The 1978 constitution, however, gave homosexuals equal rights. The 1960s and 1970s brought far more tourism to Spain, exposing urban areas to gay culture. In all, 80% of homosexuals in Spain live as couples, a reflection of the country's strong sense of family and the importance of relationships. As of 2008 Spain was one of five countries in the world that had legalized same-sex marriage.

21 BIBLIOGRAPHY

Cross, Esther, and Wilbur Cross. *Spain*. Chicago: Children's Press, 1985.

Crow, John A. *Spain: The Root and the Flower*. Berkeley: University of California Press, 1985.

Facaros, Dana, and Michael Pauls. *Northern Spain*. London: Cadogan Books, 1996.

Gratton, Nancy. "Castilians." In *Encyclopedia of World Cultures (Europe)*, edited by Linda A. Bennett. Boston: G. K. Hall, 1992.

Hubbard, Monica M., and Beverly Baer, eds. *Cities of the World: Europe and the Middle East*. Detroit: Gale Research, 1993.

Kenny, Michael. *A Spanish Tapestry: Town and Country in Castile*. London: Cohen & West, 1961.

Lye, Keith. *Passport to Spain. 2nd ed.* New York: F. Watts, 1994.

Madariaga, Salvador de. *Spain: A Modern History*. New York: Praeger, 1958.

Ortiz-Griffin, Julia L., and William D. Griffin. *Spain and Portugal Today*. New York: Peter Lang, 2003.

Schubert, Adrian. *The Land and People of Spain*. New York: HarperCollins, 1992. Stanton, Edward F. *Culture and Customs of Spain*. Westport, CT: Greenwood Press, 2002.

US Department of State, *Bureau of European and Eurasian Affairs*. "Background Note: Spain." http://www.state.gov/r/pa/ei/bgn/2878.htm (7 May 2008).

—revised by C. Corrigan

CATALANS

LOCATION: Spain (Catalonia region in the northeast)
POPULATION: About 7 million
LANGUAGE: Catalan
RELIGION: Roman Catholic

1 INTRODUCTION

The Catalan people live in an area of northeast Spain—Catalonia—that was officially declared an autonomous region in 1979. Historically, Catalonia also included Andorra, the Balearic Islands, and the French department (or province) called Pyrenees Orientales—areas where speakers of the Catalan language can still be found. Following centuries of foreign rule by the Romans, Visigoths, and Moors, Catalonia became an independent political entity in AD 988 and united with the kingdom of Aragon in 1137. Together, the two regions established an empire that eventually extended to Sardinia, Naples, Sicily, and Greece. After the marriage of King Ferdinand and Queen Isabella in the 15th century united the kingdoms of Aragon and Catalonia with those of Castile and León, the Catalans struggled for centuries to preserve their political and cultural identity. In the mid-17th century, part of their territory—called Roselló—was incorporated into France, and a bid for Catalan independence in the following century failed.

However, by the 19th century Catalonia had become a major economic power in Spain due to the growth of trade and the coming of industrialization, an area in which it was a pioneer. It has remained one of Spain's wealthiest and most developed regions, attracting large numbers of immigrants from the south throughout the 20th century. During the years of Francisco Franco's dictatorship (1939–1975), Catalan regionalism was suppressed and the local language outlawed. Following Franco's death and the installation of a democratic national government, Catalonia attained the status of an autonomous region—the Generalitat de Catalunya—with its capital at Barcelona.

In 1992 it gained the international spotlight as host to the summer Olympic games. The same year marked an economic milestone for the region, together with the rest of Spain, as the country was fully integrated into the European Community. Autonomous Catalan government has a Statut d'Autonomia; on August 2006 a reformed version of the Statut was approved.

2 LOCATION AND HOMELAND

Covering an area of roughly 32,000 sq km (1,236 sq mi)—about the size of Maryland—Catalonia is located in Spain's northeastern corner. It is bound to the north by the Pyrenees mountains, to the east and south by the Mediterranean Sea, to the southwest by Valencia, and to the west by Aragon. The region is dominated by the Pyrenees; its highest point is Pico de Aneto at 3,404 m (11,176 ft). Its coastline includes the cliffs and coves of the Costa Brava, and the Ebro river, flowing to the Mediterranean, marks its border with Valencia. Catalonia is divided into four administrative provinces: Lleida, Girona, Barcelona, and Tarragona. The Catalan-speaking co-principality of Andorra, in the Pyrenees, is an independent country.

As of 2006 Catalonia had a population of 7,134,697 million people, roughly 15% of Spain's total population. Much of the region's population growth—up from barely 2 million in 1900—is due to immigration, as the Catalan people themselves have a relatively low birth rate. Over one-fourth of the region's inhabitants live in Barcelona, whose population numbers over 1.5 million.

³ LANGUAGE

Catalan, a Romance language like French, Italian, and Castilian Spanish, is the official language of Catalonia and is also spoken, with regional varieties, in Andorra, the Balearic Islands, and the French department (or province) of Pyrenees Orientales. Road signs in Catalonia are printed in both Catalan and the national language, Castilian. Catalan is similar to the Provençal language spoken in the south of France. From the1930s to the mid-1970s, Catalan, like other regional languages in Spain, was suppressed by the Franco regime. Now that the language can be heard on television and radio and is taught in the schools, the number of Catalan speakers is rising by about 20,000 each year, although Catalan is still spoken by only half the population. However, most residents of Catalonia claim they can understand it even if they are not proficient speakers. The Institut d'Estudis Catalans deals with all elements of Catalan culture, and works on standardizing the Catalan language.

The most common Catalan names are Jordi (the equivalent of George) for men and Montserrat for women. Núria is also a popular woman's name. Catalan was the official host language for the 1992 Olympics in Barcelona.

EXAMPLES

beach	platja
good day	bon dia
please	si us plau
welcome	benvinguts
common sense	seny

⁴ FOLKLORE

Catalan folkloric tradition is distinctive and very rich. A few examples are the *sardana*, a purely Catalan dance, and the *habaneras*, choral songs characteristic of the marine localities of the Costa Brava. Many of the religious festivities, like the Patron Saint Day (Festa Major) have a folkloric component, and it is customary to have civic processions in which *gegants* and *capgrossos* are paraded (Section 6, *Major Holidays*), or to have competitions of *colles* (teams) of *castellers*. A castell is a human tower built during festivities in many places in Catalonia, and its members usually come from the town of Valls, in the southern part of the country.

Fire has a predominant role in many festivals, and *correfocs* are amongst the most striking of them. The name comes from groups of men dressed as devils that dance in the streets and throw firecrackers and small rockets. The Feast of La Merced that takes place in Barcelona in September features an enormous correfoc that include fire-breathing dragons. Perhaps the most spectacular of the Catalan fire festivals is the nocturnal Patum of Berga in June, which incorporates dances featuring angels, demons, and mythic characters and animals.

Traditional male Catalan garb includes the distinctive *barretina*, a sock-shaped red woolen hat that can be seen at festivals, often worn with a white shirt and black slacks and vest.

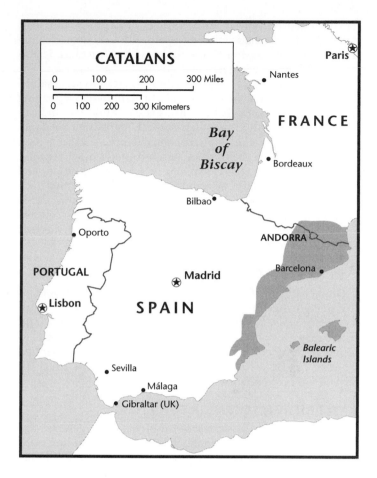

Women's traditional festive costumes include much elaborate lacework in both black and white.

⁵ RELIGION

The majority of Catalans, like most other people in Spain, are Roman Catholics. However, the industrialization and modernization of Catalonia, as well as outside cultural influences, have decreased the role of religion in the lives of many people in the region. While most Catalans mark major events such as baptism and marriage with the appropriate religious ritual, many are not regular churchgoers. A 1967 law guarantees freedom of religion in Spain. The recent waves of immigration, especially during the 1990s, have lead to an increasing number of Muslims, who have about a million members in Spain. Islam is today the second largest religion in the country, after Roman Catholicism. Other religious minorities include Protestants, evangelical Christians, and Jews. Due to its flourishing industry, Catalonia attracts a steady influx of immigrants, both from the south of Spain and from abroad.

⁶ MAJOR HOLIDAYS

In addition to the standard holidays of the Christian calendar, other religious dates celebrated in Catalonia include Epiphany (*Reis*) on January 6; Pentecost; the Feast of St. George (*Sant Jordi*), Catalonia's patron saint, on April 23; and several summer festivals marked by fires and fireworks, including the feasts of St. Anthony on June 13 (in Balears), St. John, on June 24, and St. Peter on June 29. The Day of the Dead (*Dia dels Difunts*) is celebrated on November 2. Instead of Maundy Thursday, which is observed elsewhere in Spain, the Catalans celebrate Easter Monday. Boxing Day, one day after Christmas, is also observed. The Catalan national holiday is *La Diada* on September 11. Towns and villages celebrate their individual saints' days every year in a "main festival," or *festa major*, climaxing in an all-night dance that begins as late as 11:00 PM and can last until dawn. All Catalan festivals are marked by the dancing of the *sardana*, the Catalan national dance. Another typical feature is the presence of ritual figures called giants *(gegants)*, enormous papier-mâché forms up to 4.5 m (15 ft) high, and bigheads *(capgrossos)*, big painted cardboard heads that men wear over their own. They go through the streets and dance accompanied by a group of musicians *(donzainers)*. Each town has its own gegants and capgrosos, and they enter gatherings *(aplecs)* and competitions.

7 RITES OF PASSAGE

Besides baptism, first Communion and marriage could be considered rites of passage for Catalans, as with most Spaniards. These events are the occasion, in most cases, for large and expensive social gatherings in which the family shows its generosity and economic status. Compulsory military service, another rite of passage, was abolished in Spain in 2001. The armed forces are now all volunteer.

8 INTERPERSONAL RELATIONS

The Catalans have a strong sense of national, cultural and linguistic identity, and generally have a reputation for being hard-working, ambitious, and conservative. Since the 1960s, there has been a steady improvement in the Spanish economy mainly due to industrial development and tourism, as well as an evolution in customs. The Catalans frequently travel abroad and have adopted customs from other cultures in the last 25 years or so. The economic prosperity has allowed many people to also have a vacation home in the country or an apartment at the beach.

In the cities, office hours begin at 9:00 AM and traditionally include an extended afternoon lunch break beginning at 2:00 PM. Workers then return to their offices from 4:00 to 7:00 PM. The day typically ends with a walk *(paseo)* with friends or family and/or visits to neighborhood bars for a few drinks, appetizers *(tapas)* and conversation. Dinner is often eaten as late as 10:30 PM. In some places, such as Barcelona, however, the traditional afternoon siesta is no longer the rule. Both blue and white collar workers have a paid month vacation which they usually spend by the sea, in the mountains, or travelling abroad. Travel to faraway or exotic places has become quite popular due to the affordable travel packages offered by travel agencies. Like other Spaniards, the Catalans are considered to be friendly and outgoing. It is customary to shake hands and in a social setting women usually kiss their friends on both cheeks. Young groups are formed by co-workers, fellow students or people from the same town that go together to discotheques, organize parties and excursions, and date among themselves. The average citizen spends a great deal of time out of the house. There is an active street life; many people live downtown, frequent bars and restaurants, and go to bed late. Spaniards move from place to place less frequently than Americans and, once they get a job, many aspire to return to their birthplace and settle there. Regional loyalties are usual-ly strong and the new autonomous status of the old provinces has strengthened this feeling. It is not unusual to have lifelong friends known since kindergarten.

9 LIVING CONDITIONS

Catalonia today is a consumer society that relies on credit cards, loves to go shopping, and is interested in cars, gadgets, and entertainment. Cars are commonplace and have become a problem in big cities (parking, pollution, congested traffic, car theft). The public transportation system is excellent and thus many people who work in cities have moved to towns in the periphery that are now part of suburbia. Catalonia has an excellent system of highways and bus services, and RENFE, Spain's national rail network, connects all major cities and is developing a service of ultrarrapid trains, called AVE. The first of this kind was the Madrid-Sevilla line started for the 1992 World Expo, and it was followed by the Madrid-Barcelona line. There is also a Catalan railway company that services Catalonia. It has bus links with most large European cities, and Barcelona has a clean, well-lighted, modern subway system. Major ports include Barcelona and Tarragona, on the Mediterranean. The region has three international airports; the principal airline serving Barcelona is *Iberia*, the major Spanish air carrier. In the years preceding the 1992 summer Olympics, a large-scale urban redevelopment program was undertaken in Barcelona. It included a new marina for pleasure cruisers housing Olympic visitors, as well as new highways and a new airport. In addition, 2,000 new apartments were created.

10 FAMILY LIFE

Economic interests have traditionally played an important role in rural, and even some urban, marriages. According to custom, the older son *(l'hereu)* inherited all the family property, which resulted in the creation of many wealthy estates but also in a high rate of emigration. In cities the nuclear family makes up the household, while in the country a family may include grandparents as well as aunts and uncles. The last three decades have seen a weakening of family ties among many Catalans. Today's Spanish families are much smaller than in the past and usually have two children, and the mother has most of the responsibility for rearing them. In general, when children reach adolescence, their relationship with their families diverges based on gender. A teenage male, while continuing to revere his mother, begins spending much of his time with other young men, while teenage daughters and their mothers grow closer than ever. Even after a daughter is grown and married, her mother continues to play a prominent role in her life. Yet these traditional patterns are also changing and young men and women are as independent as their economy allows it. Today people live longer lives, have fewer children than before—actually the birth-rate is one of the lowest in Europe—and fewer people live in their homes with extended family members. Spanish people usually marry within their own social class. Only church marriages were recognized in Spain until 1968, when civil ceremonies were first allowed by law. Divorce has been legal since the 1980s.

11 CLOTHING

Like in the rest of Spain, both in town and in the country, Catalans conform to the average European fashion standards, and boutiques and ready-to-wear shops can be found all over the country. Although many young people wear sports clothes and blue jeans, the average Catalan pays more attention to personal appearance than his or her American counterpart. Businessmen wear a suit and tie, businesswomen dress fashionably in suits or dresses and high heels. The Catalan fashion industry has greatly developed, and it is an important source of income; it produces over 90% of Spain's textiles.

12 FOOD

Catalonia has a rich culinary tradition. The earliest Spanish cookbook in existence—the *Llibre de Sent Sovi*—was written in the Catalan language in the 14th century. Typically Mediterranean flavors predominate in Catalan cuisine: olive oil, garlic, onions, tomatoes, nuts, and dried fruits. A favorite Catalan dish is *escudella i carn d'olla,* a boiled meal-in-a-pot comparable to the French *pot-au-feu.* Meats and sausages are simmered with vegetables; the broth is then served with pasta as a first course, with the rest served as an entrée. Catalonia is known for its fish casseroles and for cured and smoked meats, such as *butifarra,* a type of sausage. Popular seafood includes squid, crab, shrimp, fresh sardines and tuna, salmon, trout, and dried and salted codfish.

A Catalan staple, eaten as a snack or a meal accompaniment, is *pa amb tomáquet,* bread smeared with tomato and sprinkled with oil and salt. *Coca* is the name given to a type of bread that can either be served with a meal in a style that resembles the *pa amb tomáquet* (with tomato or garlic, oil, salt, and other toppings such as anchovies) or as a dessert, topped with pine nuts and sugar or crystallized fruit. Other popular desserts include *crema catalana,* a custard dish topped with caramel; pine nut tarts over *cabell d'angel,* caramelized spaghetti squash; and *postre de músic,* or "musician's dessert," the mixture of dried fruit and nuts traditionally given to traveling musicians. Catalan wine and champagne *(cava),* are excellent and are exported both to Europe and the Americas. Catalans are especially fond of mushrooms, of which about six dozen edible varieties grow in their homeland, and mushrooms often appear sautéed as an hors d'oeuvre *(tapas)* or as an ingredient in soups, sauces, and stews.

Today's Catalan avant-garde cuisine is well known all over the world: famous chefs are Carme Ruscallada and Ferrán Adriá, who with his El Bulli Restaurant in the Costa Brava tops the *European Restaurant Ranking.*

13. EDUCATION

Catalan children, like other Spanish children, receive free, compulsory schooling from the ages of 6 to 16, when many students begin the three-year *bachillerato* course of study, after which they may opt for either one year of college preparatory study or vocational training. Schooling is both public and private. Today the study of the Catalan language is required in the region's schools. University education is general. Spain has 31 state-run universities and an increasing number of private ones. Students receive a diploma after three years of general study and a *Licenciatura* upon completing a program of specialized study lasting two or more years. Barcelona has three excellent universities; Universidad Central, Universidad Autónoma, and the most recent, Universitat Pompeu Fabra, a creation of the Catalan Government; there are several other universities, both public and private, in the rest of Cataluña.

A record-setting ten-story human pyramid in Tarassa, a Catalan town, Spain. Creating human pyramids, also known as "Castells," is a tradition based in the Catalan region. (AP Images/EFE/Ignes)

The Biblioteca Nacional de Cataluña was one of the first libraries in Spain.

14 CULTURAL HERITAGE

Catalonia has an impressive cultural heritage. Catalan art and architecture is especially prominent in connection with two widely separated periods in the history of art and architecture, Romanesque and modernist. The region contains some 2,000 buildings erected during the Romanesque period, which flourished from around AD 1000 to 1250 (as well as half a dozen impressive Gothic cathedrals). At the turn of the 19th century, the Modernist style was championed by architects like Antoni Gaudí, the builder of the Sagrada Familia church (The Sacred Family), a Catalan shrine, Casa Milá and La Pedrera. Modernist painters are Ramón Casas and Santiago Rusiñol. Among the moderns, the great Catalan names are those of Joan Miró, Salvador Dalí, and Antoni Tàpies. Pablo Picasso, perhaps the single most powerful influence on 20th-century art, was not Catalan but spent his formative years in Barcelona. Each one of these artists has a museum in the city devoted to their work. Barcelona has a new Museum of Contemporary Art.

In the middle of the 19th century Cataluña enjoyed a literary revival, called the *Renaixença,* spearheaded by the poet and priest Jacint Verdaguer. Modernism followed, and then *Noucentisme.* Well-known 20th-century writers include Salvador Espriu, Mercé Rodoreda, Manuel de Pedrolo, and Llorenç

Villalonga. Cataluña is also well represented in the world of music by cellist Pablo Casals and opera singers Montserrat Caballé and Josep Carreras.

Catalan culture was a Guest of Honor at the 2007 Frankfurt Fair.

15 WORK

Catalonia—one of the top five industrialized regions of Europe—has been called "the factory of Spain." Catalan industrialization began with textile production in the 19th century. Other important industries include chemicals, leather, construction materials, automobiles, and appliances. The region also has the greatest number of small high-tech companies in Spain. *La Caixa* savings bank is the most powerful of its kind in Europe. The *Fira* de Barcelona (the Industrial and Commercial Fair of Barcelona) organizes conventions and exhibits of international character in various sectors of the economy.

Since the early 1970s Spain has developed a prosperous tourism industry. Since the 1970s Spain has been the second most visited country in the world after France. In 2007 almost 60 million foreign visitors arrived in Spain. Among the preferred destinations are the Costa Brava beaches and the city of Barcelona. Parallel to summer tourism Catalonia offers cultural tours, international conventions and sports meetings, as well as cruises. There is ample hotel accommodation as well as bed-and breakfast *Turismo rural* (Country tourism) places and a network of beautiful deluxe Spanish-government-sponsored hotels (*Paradores*) located in historical buildings.

About 10% of economically active Catalans are engaged in agriculture, horticulture and animal husbandry, 45% in industry, and 45% in the service sector. Seeking higher living standards, many people migrate from the countryside to the cities and to industrialized areas, like Barcelona and other parts of Cataluña. Spain's economic prosperity attracts a growing work force (some it enters the country illegally) coming from economically or politically unstable areas. It mainly comes from North- and Sub-Saharan Africa, Spanish America and the East of Europe. The majority work in agriculture and in construction.

16 SPORTS

The most popular sport is soccer (called *fútbol*). League matches are played on Saturday and Sunday afternoons from September through May, with tournaments in the summer. Madrid has two teams in the top division, and Barcelona's team, known as *Barsa*, is world-famous. It forms the basis of a sporting club, with over 100,000 members, one of the oldest such clubs in Europe. Membership passes from father to son, and some 80,000 members, called *culés*, have permanent seats for matches in the Camp Nou stadium, the largest in Europe and the second largest in the world. The Futbol Club Barcelona is a Catalan institution, as they say, *Més que un club* ("More than a club"). The 1992 Olympics were hosted in Barcelona. Basketball and tennis are also gaining popularity as spectator sports.

17 ENTERTAINMENT AND RECREATION

Catalans generally vacation in their own region, although they also enjoy traveling abroad to other countries. Participant sports include *fútbol*, cycling, squash, hunting and fishing, sailing, tennis, golf, and horseback riding, hiking or climbing in the Pyrenees. Winter sports include Nordic and cross-country skiing, ice skating, and ice hockey. There are many excellent beaches in the Costa Brava and the Costa Daurada, and ski resorts in the Pyrenees.

Many, especially the young, prefer to go to the beach in summer and to the countryside and the mountains for hikes and picnics. In the evenings, they go dancing or have a drink with friends. The mild climate has fostered an active night life, much of it outdoors in the streets, plazas, taverns, and restaurants. A dinner date may take place as late as 10:00 or 11:00 pm and be followed by a trip to a local club.

The fine arts have played an important role in the Catalonian heritage, and according to their cultural level, Catalans enjoy frequenting the opera houses, theaters, and museums in Barcelona and other cities. Like other people in Spain, the Catalans enjoy go to concerts, to the theater, and to movies, and watching television; most TV stations in the region broadcast in the Catalan language.

18 FOLK ART, CRAFTS, AND HOBBIES

The Catalan national dance is the *sardana,* a circle dance universally performed at festivals and other special occasions throughout the country. The dancers form a circle, holding their clasped hands high in the air. Short, sedate steps alternate with longer, bouncy ones, and dancers must pay close attention to the music to know when it is time for each type of step. While the sardana only attained its present form in the 19th century, it is based on an older dance that was formerly held in the open air after certain church services. The bands that play music for the sardana are called *coblas* and consist of the *flabiol,* a three-holed flute that is played with one hand while the player beats a small elbow drum called a *tabal;* woodwind instruments called *tenoras* and *tibles;* the brass *trompeta, fiscorn,* and *trombó;* and the *contrabaix,* or double bass. A regular sardana session, or *audació,* consists of half a dozen dances, each lasting about 10 minutes. Marathon sessions called *aplecs,* however, include 24 dances played by three or four different *coblas* and last all day. Group singing is very popular among Catalans, and many belong to traditional Catalan choirs.

19 SOCIAL PROBLEMS

As Spain's most prosperous region, Catalonia has been spared many social problems, and Catalan efforts to maintain cultural identity and independence—unlike those of the Basques—have remained peaceful, centering largely on the Catalan language, whose use was forbidden during the Franco era and previously as well. The traditional Catalan family structure has been weakened in the postwar decades, and immigration to the region has resulted in social and cultural discrimination and sometimes violent conflict. With the rest of the developed countries of the world Spain shares a drug problem and crime in the big cities.

20 GENDER ISSUES

Like in the rest of Spain, Catalan women have an increasingly prominent role in society. Approximately 15% of Spain's armed forces are women and the Defense Secretary in 2008 was a woman. Many women hold municipal and government posts as councilwoman, mayor, university professor, or director general, and several have been, and are, ministers of the crown, employed or manage businesses, and a large percentage go to the university. Evidence of the secular nature of contemporary

Spain can be seen in the widespread support for the legalization of same-sex marriage in Spain; in June 2005 a bill was passed to allow gay marriage, making Spain the third country in the world to allow same-sex couples to marry.

21 BIBLIOGRAPHY

Andrews, Coleman. *Catalan Cuisine: Europe's Last Great Culinary Secret*. New York: Collier Books, 1992.

Carreras, Carles, and Gary W. McDonogh. "Catalans." In *Encyclopedia of World Cultures (Europe)*. Boston: G. K. Hall, 1992.

"Catalonia." *Nation's Business* (May 1988): 66.

Conversi, Daniele. *The Basques, the Catalans, and Spain*. Reno: University of Nevada Press, 1997.

Crow, John A. *Spain: The Root and the Flower*. Berkeley: University of California Press, 1985.

Eames, Andrew. *Barcelona. Insight Guides*. Boston: Houghton Mifflin, 1995.

Finnegan, William. "Our Far-Flung Correspondents: Catalonia." *New Yorker* (28 September 1992): 66.

Hooper, John. *The New Spaniards*. Suffolk, England: Penguin, 1995.

Hunt, Carla. "Catalonia to Showcase Art, Culture." *Travel Weekly* (8 October 1990): E3.

Lye, Keith. *Passport to Spain*. New York: Franklin Watts, 1994.

Moss, Joyce, and George Wilson. *Peoples of the World*. Detroit: Gale Research, 1993.

Riquer, Martí de. *Historia de la literatura catalane*. 6 vols. Barcelona: Aruedl, 1980.

Schubert, Adrian. *The Land and People of Spain*. New York: HarperCollins, 1992.

Terry, Arthur. *A Companion to Catalan Literature*. Woodbridge: Tamesis, 2003.

Thomas, Benjamin. "Catalonia: The Factory of Spain." *Forbes* (11 June 1990): A1.

Tremlett, Giles. *Ghosts of Spain*. New York: Walker and Company, 2008.

Vallverdu, Francesc. "A Thousand Years of Catalan History." *UNESCO Courier* (May 1989): 26–28.

Williams, Roger. *Catalonia*. Insight Guides. Singapore: APA Publications, 1991.

—revised by S. Garcia Castaneda

CHECHENS

LOCATION: Chechnya territory between Russia and Georgia
POPULATION: Unknown
LANGUAGE: Chechen, Russian
RELIGION: Islam

1 INTRODUCTION

The Chechens (Nokhchii, singular Nokhchuo) inhabit a small territory in the Caucasus Mountains between the Russian and Georgian republics. Throughout their long history in the Caucasus Mountains, their strong sense of national pride has kept them prepared to fight to retain their homeland. The mountainous territory has protected them not only from enemies but from outside influences in general. Thus, the Chechens have retained many traditional customs and practices.

Throughout the 19th and 20th centuries, the Chechen people and their territory have been threatened. In particular, the Chechens have struggled against Russian interference. During the 19th century, the Chechens joined other peoples of the North Caucasus to defend their territories from Russian attack. These struggles, known as the Caucasian Wars, lasted over 70 years. The Chechens gained a reputation for being the most determined, skillful, and aggressive fighters among the North Caucasian peoples. Ultimately, the Russian forces, which substantially outnumbered the North Caucasian fighters, were victorious. The Chechens and others who were involved in the wars were brutally repressed, and many were killed as the Russians attempted to consolidate their power in the territory. Large numbers of Chechens were forced to flee, with many emigrating to Turkey.

When the Russian monarchy collapsed in 1917 and Soviet power replaced the Tsarist regime, the Chechens experienced a brief period of relative freedom as part of the short-lived Republic of Mountain Peoples. In the 1920s, the early years after the imposition of Soviet government, the state granted the Chechens considerable opportunity to express and develop their national culture. The state even assisted the Chechens, providing linguists and other expert scholars to help the Chechens develop a standard national alphabet. This alphabet, based on Latin rather than Cyrillic characters (like English rather than Russian letters) bore some resemblance to modern Turkish.

This period of relaxation ended by the late 1920s, as Iosif Stalin (himself of Caucasian origin) emerged as the new Soviet leader. Chechen schools were forced to expand their Russian language curriculum, the publication of Chechen-language books and newspapers was curtailed, and the public practice of Chechen cultural and religious customs was restricted. This repression heightened throughout the 1930s. Many political and cultural leaders among the Chechens were arrested, exiled, or executed. This situation culminated in the late 1930s with the arrest of many local cultural leaders, whose activity was seen by the Soviet government as dangerous and subversive. In response, many Chechens participated in armed resistance. The Soviet government had difficulty containing the Chechens, as the Soviet Union was preparing to fight Nazi Germany in World War II.

RUSSIA

Terek

Terek

Terek

Nal'chik

Vladikavkaz

Malhachlala

SOUTH
OSSETIA
Tskhinvali

GEORGIA

T'ianet'l

Gori   Kura

Alazani

Lagodekhi

T'elavi

T'bilisi ✪

Iori

Tsnori

Bolnisi

Shaumyani

ARMENIA

Kirovakan

CHECHENS

0   50   100 Miles

0   50   100 Kilometers

AZERBAIJAN

Despite the difficult relations between the Chechens and the Soviet regime, however, the Chechens supported the struggle against Nazi Germany and contributed to the Soviet victory. Nevertheless, the Soviets continued to view the Chechens as a threat. Soviet suspicion of the Chechens led to the brutal deportation of the entire Chechen population in the winter of 1944. In the course of a few days, the people of Chechnya were rounded up by the Soviet army and secret police, loaded into boxcars, and transported to remote regions of Kazakhstan, Central Asia. Many died on the way, and many more died in their harsh, new living conditions. Those who survived were denounced as traitors and suffered severe discrimination. During this period, Chechens were often denied employment opportunities or entrance to schools and universities. They were not permitted to assemble in groups or to engage in their traditional cultural practices. Despite these brutal conditions, some Chechens were still able to publish and circulate a secret Chechen newspaper during the years of exile.

After Stalin's death in 1953, Nikita Khrushchev rose to power. Under this new leadership, the Soviet government began to reconsider the Stalinist decision to deport the Chechen people. In 1956, the Chechens were permitted to return to their homeland. Although they had spent over a decade in exile, the Chechens returned in massive numbers to their native territory. Conflicts arose when the returning Chechens discovered that, in their absence, new settlers—many of whom were ethnic Russians—had taken over their territories. Clashes and animosity between Chechens and Russians living within Chechen

territories have persisted down to the present. The difficult relations between the two groups heightened the long-standing Chechen resentment of Russia.

The Chechen people have, in general, adhered strongly to their cultural practices and customs, resisting active attempts by the Soviet government to stifle Chechen cultural self-expression. Soviet policies of Russification (Russianization) in Chechnya were not effective, and Chechen intellectuals attempted to strengthen Chechen culture from the 1960s to the early 1980s.

By the mid- to late 1980s, under Soviet leader Mikhail Gorbachev, the state's policies toward freedom of expression grew more permissive. Thus, Chechens began to work energetically on their cultural development. However, this relatively free political climate provided the Chechens with opportunities to discuss the possibility of splitting from the Soviet Union and forming an independent, sovereign Chechen state. By August 1991, with the collapse of the Soviet system and rise of Russian president Boris Yeltsin, ideas of national independence gained widespread support in Chechnya.

In November 1991, the Chechens formed a government under leader Dzhokhar Dudaev and declared Chechnya an independent state. Boris Yeltsin immediately contested the declaration and refused to negotiate with Dudaev. Tensions between Russia and Chechnya continued to escalate and, in December 1994, Russia launched an air attack on Chechnya, precipitating a brutal war. Although severely outnumbered, the Chechens managed to prevent Russia from gaining control in Chechnya. The war lasted for nearly two years, with massive casualties on both the Chechen and Russian sides. Much of Chechnya was destroyed.

Fighting came to an end in 1996 when General Alexander Lebed successfully negotiated a cease-fire treaty between the two sides. However, the treaty did not resolve the issue of Chechnya's independence. Instead, the treaty postponed the issue until the year 2000, when a referendum of Chechen citizens was to be held on the question of independence from Russia. Chechnya continued to consider itself an independent state, and Russia continued to treat Chechnya as part of the Russian federation. Dissension, desperate economic conditions, and armed bands created a violent and chaotic period between August 1996, when a cease fire was signed, and October 1999, when Russia once again invaded Chechnya. During the interval between wars Chechnya grew to be dangerous, with numerous kidnappings and murders. In August 1999 the warlord, Shamil Basaev, invaded the Andi highlands of Daghestan. Russia was suddenly confronted with the prospect of losing Daghestan. Although Basaev retreated, Yeltsin's successor, Vladimir Putin, launched a second war in October 1999. Major fighting began to die down in 2006, after the death of Basaev, but sporadic fighting persists and the future of Chechnya remains an open question.

² LOCATION AND HOMELAND

The Chechen territory is located between Russia and Georgia in the Caucasus Mountains, between the Black and Caspian seas. The mountainous terrain has been strategically important for Chechnya. Chechen fighters have been able to withdraw into their familiar, mountainous territory, hiding and launching attacks from well-concealed bases. Thus, they have fought successfully against opponents of greater strength and numbers.

The mountains also support sheep-farming, the traditional Chechen occupation. The flatter territories of Chechnya accommodate other industries. Until the destruction of Chechnya in the recent wars with Russia, Chechnya had a major oil-refining industry, as well as an important pipeline that transported oil to Russia.

From 1934 to 1992 Chechnya shared official boundaries with the neighboring Ingush people, in a republic called Checheno-Ingushetia. The 1989 Soviet census reflected conditions in the former Checheno-Ingushetian Republic. In 1989, 957,000 Chechens lived in Checheno-Ingushetia, comprising 57.8% of the population. Ingush and ethnic Russians accounted for 13% and 23%, respectively. Because the Chechens maintained a majority in the republic, they had greater opportunity than other groups to develop their cultural and political identity.

The breakup of Checheno-Ingushetia was precipitated by the Chechen decision to form an independent state and the Ingush decision to remain a part of the Russian Federation. The two nations had been long-standing allies, with similar languages and cultures. The split was remarkably peaceful and free of contention. Local ethnic Russians living in Checheno-Ingushetia did not play a prominent role in this process. Many Russians left the territory in the late 1980s and early 1990s, concerned about rising anti-Russian sentiment among Chechens and Ingush.   Because of the devastating war with Russia, and the large number of Chechen casualties, it is difficult to know how many Chechens live in Chechnya. The 2002 census lists 1.1 million Chechens and 361,000 Ingush. During the wars many Chechens fled as refugees to other areas of the Caucasus, especially Ingushetia, which welcomed them. The capital city, Grozny, has been reduced to rubble by repeated shelling and air raids. During the present time of relative peace and stability, rebuilding is underway under the appointed governor, Ramazan Kadyrov, who has conscripted many former Chechen fighters into his security apparatus.

³ LANGUAGE

The Chechen language is unique to the Caucasus region and not related to any languages outside of this region. Within the Caucasus, only the Ingush language (the language of the neighboring Ingushetians) and Batsby or Kisti of northern Georgia are closely related to Chechen. These three languages form a distinct branch of the Northeast Caucasian family, which includes the Dagestani languages.

Until 1991, Chechnya had two official languages, Chechen and Russian. Russian was taught in all schools, and many radio and television broadcasts were in Russian. A working knowledge of Russian was required for any prestigious or important job; consequently, most Chechens had a fluent command of Russian. One effect of the wars has been an interruption in education. Consequently, many young Chechens no longer have a command of Russian.   After 1991, Chechen national identity and rising anti-Russian sentiment resulted in movements to purify the Chechen language and increase its use. Thus, a Chechen thesaurus prepared in the early 1990s replaced many words derived from Russian with new, Chechen equivalents. A new school curriculum to increase Chechen language teaching was developed, and Chechens tried to increase the number of publications and media broadcasting in the native language.

With the new president the situation with Russian language turned to the old times again and currently there is a bilingual system in Chechnya.

⁴ FOLKLORE

Because the Chechens did not develop a widely-used written language until the early 20th century, folklore was passed on orally from generation to generation. The traditional epic folk tale, which can be found in various forms throughout the Caucasus, was a traditional folkloric form. Such tales feature stories of heroism, hardship, and sacrifice, reinforcing values of bravery and personal or family honor. The Chechens used these folk tales to present historical events. Thus, events of the Caucasian Wars, the deportations, and the hardships suffered during the Soviet period are expressed in traditional form, passing stories of national survival to the next generation. The Chechens (and Ingush) also had a distinctive tradition of Nart lore, ancient and garbled tales about a race of heroes.

⁵ RELIGION

Islam is the traditional Chechen religion. Despite efforts of the atheistic Soviet regime to eradicate the practice of Islam, the Chechens continued to adhere strongly to their religion throughout the years of Soviet power. However, because the practice of Islam was not permitted during these years, many conventions of Islam, particularly public prayers, were not maintained. Instead, a sect of Islam called Sufism gained strength in Chechnya. Because Sufism emphasized secrecy and mysticism, it was well-suited to the need to observe religion in secrecy during the Soviet period.

Islam remained a strong force among Chechens. The weakening of Soviet repression during the late 1980s intensified the public expression of religion. The daily prayers (*namaz*) were heard again, religious publications became more widely available, and people began to make the traditional pilgrimage to Mecca. Traditional dress, featuring head-covering for both men and women, became more widespread. The public celebration of major Islamic festivals, such as Ramadan and Eid al-Fitr, also increased. However, like most cultural practices in Chechnya, the development and revival of organized, publicly-observed religion was disrupted by the wars with Russia.

As the second war has wound down, some Chechens have returned to Groznyj. Now, large groups of men are allowed to gather to perform the circle dance, the *zikr* (Arabic *dhikr*), a form of mystic prayer. The Chechen *zikr* is unique in the Muslim world. It is so intense that the chanting and rhythmic movement of the men can be heard blocks away.

⁶ MAJOR HOLIDAYS

During the years of Soviet power, the celebration of religious or national Chechen holidays was discouraged. In particular, traditional celebrations were curtailed during the deportations in the 1940s, when the Chechen people were dispersed throughout various regions and harshly repressed. Even after their repatriation and return to their homeland, the Chechens were still restricted by Soviet authorities from celebrating their religious holidays.

The Soviet holiday of the Day of the Revolution (October 7) has been turned into the National Pride day of Russia and is celebrated in Chechnya, too. The Day of International Socialism (May 1) is still an official holiday. People are not required to attend work on these days, and the holidays are often marked by state-sponsored fireworks and cultural displays. New Year's Day, another holiday acceptable to Soviet power, was widely celebrated.

After the collapse of Soviet power and the Chechen declaration of independence in 1991, the Chechen government tried to create new holidays. In particular, November 9 was declared a national holiday in celebration of Chechen independence. The Chechens also celebrate Deportation Day on February 23. Religious holidays have regained popularity. The 1994–96 war with Russia, however, interfered with the replacement of Soviet holidays by the new Chechen holidays. The social fabric now remains damaged, and holidays seem not to be particularly important.

⁷ RITES OF PASSAGE

When a baby is born, he or she is registered with the local authorities, giving the birth date and name. Even in contemporary Chechen society, the birth of a boy is viewed as an especially important occasion. Family and friends hold celebrations welcoming the new son. Boys are usually circumcised in a traditional ceremony, in adherence to Islamic requirements. The festivities surrounding the birth of a daughter are much more modest.

In contemporary society, a child's first day of school, which begins in the first grade at the age of seven, is viewed as an important transition toward greater maturity. For males, this process is completed when they leave school and choose careers.

Traditionally, Chechens married young. Men usually married by the time they were 16 or 17, and many girls married before they were 14. Marriage marked the end of childhood and the initiation into the responsibilities of adult life. Young Chechens did not have a distinct teenage period in which they could enjoy greater independence without yet assuming adult roles. In contemporary Chechen society, most young people spend some time in high school, and many go on to university, enabling them to enjoy some years of relative freedom before assuming adult roles. However, by North American standards, the teenage period for Chechens is brief. Even today, many young men are married by age 20, and many girls marry at age 17 or 18. Most young couples have children soon after marriage. Once their children marry, parents gain prestige and authority in the household.

Rituals surrounding death are generally religious, although deaths are always registered with local authorities. Even during the Soviet period, death was marked by a religious ceremony. In addition, the family of the deceased generally holds a large feast for mourners.

⁸ INTERPERSONAL RELATIONS

Chechen men, as do those in Western countries, greet one another with handshakes. In most other respects, however, interpersonal behavior follows Chechen tradition. Women are expected to behave modestly and deferentially in the company of men, keeping their eyes lowered. When a man enters the room, women stand in respect. At most social gatherings, men and women interact separately, with men congregated in one room (usually the living room), and women in another (usually the kitchen). Children remain with the women most of the time. Segregation by gender is not strictly observed in the workplace, although there is a tendency for men and women to spend most of their time in the company of their own gender.

Chechens place great importance on displays of hospitality toward guests. In a Chechen home, guests can expect to receive the best food and the most pleasant accommodations that the hosts can afford. If a guest is not shown proper hospitality, this is regarded as shameful for the entire extended host family. This can cause some intergenerational friction, as the younger generation today tends to have a much more casual and relaxed attitude toward the treatment of guests. Visiting is an important part of Chechen social life, and guests are expected to return invitations and extend hospitality to those who have entertained them in the past.

Chechen clans, *teips,* serve, among other things, as exogamous social units. Dating is not usually part of Chechen social life. Premarital sexual relations among teenagers are strongly discouraged, and such relations between young men and women can even start feuds between their families. Marriages are sometimes arranged by families, as each family is seeking to marry into another family of at least equal, if not superior, wealth and social standing. Many young people choose whom they will marry, although they may ask for parental approval. Young men and women generally become acquainted in public settings and have little privacy during their courtships. Chechen parents exert considerable pressure on their children to marry other Chechens. This is particularly true for women, as married women are considered to belong to the culture of their husbands.

Chechens are among the few peoples of the Caucasus who continue to observe avoidance customs in everyday life. Avoidance customs limit the contact that an individual may have with his or her in-laws. For example, according to Chechen avoidance customs, a son-in-law is not allowed to speak to, or even see, his mother-in-law. Similarly, relations between daughters-in-law and fathers-in-law are limited by avoidance customs. Because the daughter-in-law often lives with her husband's parents, avoidance between daughter-in-law and father-in-law cannot be strictly observed. However, they will often limit their contact and may speak to one another only indirectly through a third party. Even if these customs are not practiced, young Chechen women are expected to show great deference and respect to their fathers-in-law.

⁹ LIVING CONDITIONS

Traditionally, most Chechens lived in isolated mountain villages. Because extended families and clan groups lived in close proximity, traditional dwellings featured several large buildings in a courtyard enclosed by a wall. The buildings of the courtyard also housed farm animals, such as cows, chickens, and horses.

The rural population of Chechnya has remained large, but many Chechens, particularly the younger ones, have chosen to move to towns and cities. Most urban residents live in apartments. However, in contrast to many other cities in the former Soviet Union, most Chechen towns and cities also have a large number of small houses, set behind walls with their own small courtyards. Even in cities, people may keep some small livestock, such as chickens.

Living conditions in Chechnya deteriorated sharply after the first war with Russia in 1994–96. Many towns, cities, and rural areas were destroyed, and thousands of people were

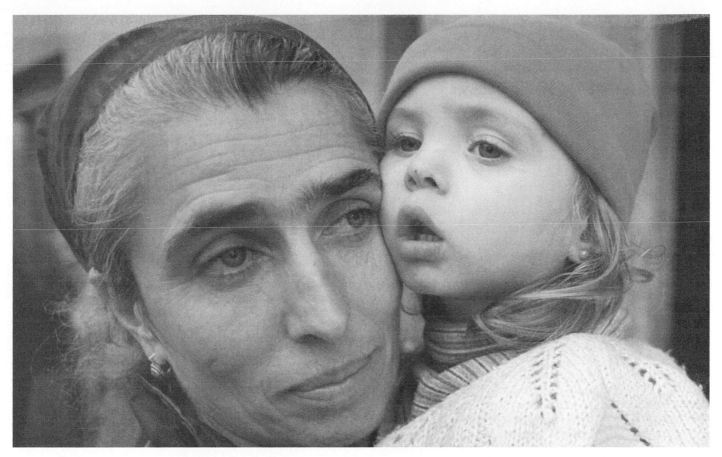

Chechen refugee Zula Uzuyeva looks on while holding her granddaughter Mata in the Duisi village, a remote region of Georgia near the border with Chechnya. The area was home to about 7,000 refugees from the war in Chechnya. (AP Images/Shakh Aivazov)

forced to flee their homes. The supply of water and electricity became unreliable. Service has been partly restored as the second war tapers off.

Maintaining an adequate food supply has always been difficult in the former Soviet Union and, in Chechnya, food selection and variety were often poor. This problem has been particularly acute for urban dwellers, whereas rural people have been able to produce and store food more easily. Since the war, the food situation has deteriorated even more. Russia stopped importing food and Chechen farmland and reserves of food were destroyed. Other basic essentials, such as medical supplies, have become difficult to obtain since the war.

10 FAMILY LIFE

Traditionally, Chechens lived in large, extended family units. Parents lived with their sons and the sons' wives and children in several buildings in a single large courtyard. Many rural families still live in these large family units, as the additional labor provided by family members helps to bolster the economic welfare of the whole family.

In urban areas, few families live in the traditional, extended family groups. Sons are still encouraged to start their own families in their parents' house, moving out only after several years of marriage or after the birth of the first child. One son, usually the youngest, is expected to stay and raise his family in his parents' home. Sons and their families are expected to show great respect and deference toward the son's parents,

particularly to his father. Married couples rarely live with the wife's family. Chechen men consider living in the home of their wife's father to be dishonorable.

After marriage, when a young couple moves in with the husband's parents, a bride may have a difficult adjustment period learning to adhere to the practices and instructions of other household members. The youngest wife in the household is considered the lowest person in the family hierarchy. Therefore, she usually does the bulk of the work and unpleasant tasks. However, young wives can look forward to a time when their own sons will marry and bring a new wife into the household. Although young married people almost always spend a period of time living with the groom's parents, a couple who has married without the consent of their parents may choose to live in a different town or city for a few years, until the parents accept the marriage.

Traditionally, Chechen marriages were arranged by the families of the bride and groom. The bride and groom could not be related, even distantly. They had to come from separate *teips* (clans). Young women were expected to provide a dowry of household objects, linens, livestock, and, sometimes, money to the groom's family. In turn, the groom's family paid a bride-price to the woman's household. According to Islamic law, the woman was allowed to keep her dowry, or its cash value, in the event of divorce from or death of the husband. Dowries and bride-prices were declared illegal under Soviet law, but many families, especially those in more isolated rural regions, continue to use them to negotiate the marriage of their children.

Occasionally, if a man could not obtain the consent of the woman's family, he would arrange a "kidnapping marriage." The woman was kidnapped by the groom and some of his friends and then taken immediately to be married. Sometimes, these marriages would be prearranged between the bride and groom. However, a man may choose to kidnap and marry a woman who may have refused to give consent. Although declared illegal under Soviet law, kidnapping marriages persist to the present day. If a woman is kidnapped and objects strenuously to the marriage, her family may try to have the marriage dissolved. If the man's family is of lower social standing than the woman's, the kidnapping marriage could result in a feud between his and her relatives.

Polygamy was traditionally practiced among Chechens according to the Quranic restrictions that a man could have no more than four wives and that he must provide each with a lifestyle of equal quality. During the years of Soviet power, polygamy was outlawed and the practice ceased. However, since the fall of Soviet power and the rise in Islamic consciousness, interest in such traditional institutions as polygamous marriage has grown. Although polygamy is not widely practiced, some Chechen men take a second wife. These are often men whose first wives have either been unable to produce children or who have not given birth to sons. Such men are generally older and must also have considerable financial means, as the second wife must be provided with the same lifestyle as the first. Typically, the man will obtain a second apartment or house for the new wife. Thus, a second marriage is not only a means of bringing more children into the family, but also of displaying prestige and wealth. Most women, especially first wives, object strongly to the practice of polygamy. However, for some women, becoming a second wife is one way to gain many of the social advantages of married life and yet retain some measure of independence.

11 CLOTHING

The traditional Chechen national costumes were elaborate and very similar to the costumes worn by other Caucasian peoples. Women wore long, flowing dresses with fitted bodices. Women wore long scarves over their heads but did not cover their faces. Men's clothing was more practical, with tall leather boots and loose-fitting trousers convenient for horseback riding. Men's pride in their fighting skill and bravery in battle was expressed in their clothing, wearing tightly-belted jackets decorated with loops into which bullets (originally, silver tubes with pre-measured musket charges) were inserted. The number of bullets increased with a man's age and battle experience. Men also covered their heads, wearing tall lamb's wool hats, usually in black or grey.

In modern times, men and women wear Western-style clothing, although some men, particularly those in rural regions, continue to wear boots and loose-fitting trousers. Women always wear skirts or dresses that fall below the knee. Especially in the cities, women wear jewelry and use cosmetics. Unlike their North American or European counterparts, Chechens of both genders continue to wear head coverings. Older women often wear wool head-scarves, usually in grey or black. The head-covering of younger women is often purely symbolic, usually consisting of a silk scarf, folded and wrapped around the head to resemble a thick headband. According to the new State law established by president Ramzan Kadyrov women must cover their heads, especially the TV broadcasters and University students. Even the female manikins must have their heads covered in the stores. Men, especially middle-aged or elderly men, still wear traditional lamb's wool hats.

Recently, as Chechen nationalism has become a widespread and powerful force, more men have adopted the traditional head covering. Sometimes, a colored band of cloth is sewn around the hats, most commonly green, the Chechen national color. White cloth bands indicate men who have completed the pilgrimage to Mecca. With increasing awareness of their Islamic identity, some Chechens, especially young people, have adopted very conservative Islamic dress. Some Chechen women have chosen to wear a full head covering, although the practice is not traditionally Chechen. Efforts to impose Muslim norms of dress in the cities are meeting with resistance from Chechen women.

12 FOOD

Lamb and mutton are staples of the Chechen diet. These meats are served in a variety of ways—roasted, stewed, or ground and shaped into patties. The internal organs of the sheep are ground together and made into a sausage-like dish. Like all Muslims, Chechens do not eat pork or pork products. Thus, pigs are not raised in Chechen agriculture.

Tomatoes, red or green peppers, or eggplants are often stuffed with a ground lamb mixture and baked. Milk products, such as butter and cheese, are also an important part of the diet. Fruits, fresh in summer and dried in winter, are the most common dessert.

Traditionally, Chechen men and women dined separately. The men ate together in the dining room as the women cooked and served the food. Then the women and children ate in the kitchen. Larger, more traditional families, where many generations are dining together, often observe this segregation today. However, younger, more-modern families tend to eat together rather than in segregation. North American visitors to traditional households will usually be invited to eat in the living room with the men, even if the visitors are women.

13 EDUCATION

In the 19th and early 20th centuries, before the rise of Soviet power, formal education was not a traditional part of Chechen life. The exception was for boys who were interested in a clerical career. These boys went to special Muslim academies where they were taught to read and write Arabic. Those few who were interested in administrative careers had to leave Chechen territory to learn Russian. Until the 1920s, the Chechens did not have a written language.

The Soviet government took steps to ensure that all children, both boys and girls, would receive an education. In the 1920s a written Chechen language was created and a school curriculum in both official languages (Russian and Chechen) was instituted. Education until the tenth grade was mandatory for both boys and girls. At first, parents were reluctant to send their children to school but, by the 1930s, most children were receiving at least an elementary education. A university was opened in the capital city, Groznyj.

In contemporary times, children continue to attend school until tenth grade. Universities and trade institutes offer further career training to high school graduates. Many high school graduates, particularly boys from cities and towns, choose to continue their education. Girls sometimes do not take advantage of higher education opportunities, choosing instead to marry and raise a family. People in rural areas often remain at home and work in the family farming business.

Unfortunately, the wars with Russia have interfered with formal education. Most schools were not able to remain open during 1994–96 and have only recently (2006) begun to function again. Many educational buildings and supplies were destroyed. Primary school children in the late 1990s and early 2000s often did not have the opportunity to learn the basic skills of mathematics and literacy.

14 CULTURAL HERITAGE

During the years of Soviet power, the central government exercised strict control over the publication of literature and the writing of national histories. Thus, Chechen authors and historians were forced to write according to the Soviet government's version of events. Many historical events, particularly the Caucasian Wars and the 1944 deportations, were distorted. However, after the relaxation of central authority in the late 1980s, Chechens began to publish works that presented more authentically Chechen versions.

Chechens express great pride in their culture and began in the late 1990s to publish collections of Chechen memoirs and folklore. Traditional music is very percussive and energetic, with drums and accordion as the main instruments. Although European and North American classical and rock music is available in Chechnya, Chechen music is still very popular, even among young people.

As in many areas of life, artistic and cultural activity has diminished as a consequence of the wars with Russia. These severely interrupted the development of cultural renewal by many talented and innovative Chechens.

15 WORK

Traditionally, Chechens were sheep farmers, with men living a seminomadic life accompanying the herds through mountain pastures. In the 20th century, opportunities for education and urban employment have grown, and many people chose to leave farming, obtain higher education, and work in the towns or cities. Oil refining has been an important part of the Chechen economy, drawing many workers. The process of urbanization was interrupted during the Soviet period by the deportations; in addition, many Chechens became unwilling to remain in agriculture.

After the collapse of Soviet power, many jobs that had formerly been funded by the government were no longer supported. The transition from a state-driven to a market-based economy was difficult for some, who were unable to find new areas of employment. For others, the transition opened up new fields of work, such as the import/export area. Because many Chechens have links with other countries, particularly Muslim countries such as Turkey, with its large (50,000) Chechen diaspora, import/export is a popular career choice. For the most part, Chechens have made a smooth transition to new economic conditions. Extended families are often involved in a single family business.

However, as the Chechen economy was beginning to develop, war with Russia broke out. Much of the infrastructure,

including oil refineries and pipelines, was destroyed. Because of closed borders, the import/export business became difficult. Furthermore, the local market deteriorated greatly, as many Chechens were forced into hiding. However, the current reconstruction of the country is underway, with great likelihood of economic recovery.

16 SPORTS

A popular traditional Chechen sport is horseback-riding. Riding has always been part of the job of sheepherding, but is also enjoyed as a recreational sport. Many young boys from rural areas learn to ride as they help with the herding, and become more skilled as they grow older. Recreational riding features daring tricks on horseback, and is common among young people in the countryside.

Wrestling is another popular sport. Boys start to wrestle at a young age and, as they get older, are often encouraged to pursue the sport seriously. During the Soviet years, many coaches and wrestlers on the Soviet national team were from Chechnya. Recently Chechnya has a strong soccer team Terek, which with the financial support of the Chechen president Kadyrov became one of the most famous teams in Russia

17 ENTERTAINMENT AND RECREATION

In Chechnya, entertainment centers are around the family and the home. There are few cafés, restaurants, or theaters. Thus, most people entertain at home. Home entertainment is quite lavish and guests are treated to elaborate and lengthy meals. Visits are reciprocated, as guests are expected to entertain their hosts in their own homes at a later date.

Some socializing also takes place at work or school. Often, people will invite the families of friends and coworkers to their homes. Young people, who may wish to get out of the family environment from time to time, may get together in groups and go for walks, especially in the early evenings.

Most Chechen homes have televisions, radios, and stereos, and watching television and listening to music are popular pastimes. Predictably, the wars with Russia have interrupted the leisure time of Chechens.

18 FOLK ART, CRAFTS, AND HOBBIES

Weaving and knitting are traditional folk arts among Chechens. Even in the 1990s and 2000s, rural Chechen women continue to weave and knit, producing fine garments. Children may have opportunities to learn music and visual arts in school.

19 SOCIAL PROBLEMS

The most urgent social problems in Chechnya today are the consequences of war with Russia. Many people spent almost two years as refugees in neighboring territories, returning to disrupted lives and destroyed homes in their native region, only to flee a second time in 1999. Chechens have experienced massive destruction. Education was disrupted and opportunities for a normal social life and secure living environment have been delayed for young people of the late 1990s and 2000s. Furthermore, many youths were exposed to, and even involved as fighters in, great violence. Many were orphaned and some were badly injured. With all these deaths, those who were fighters or who lost loved ones must come to terms with the Chechen obligation of vengeance. The future consequences of these events are cause for concern.

20 GENDER ISSUES

In general, the status of Chechen women was lower than the status of women in Soviet society. However, the Soviet norms of equal education for girls and boys and equal access to health care and social security had made a positive impact on their lives. A set of cultural prejudices against women's public roles has been maintained and was reinforced by the recent militarization of society. The social infrastructure, health care, and insurance systems were practically ruined by the Chechnya authorities under the connivance of the federal government, and resources were allocated to the armed groups. Women became primarily responsible for the survival of their families. Girls in Chechnya nearly lost the possibility of going to school. It is almost impossible to get information about rapes and violence against women in armed conflicts in Chechnya because, in accordance with some traditions, a raped woman is expected to commit suicide or be murdered by her relatives.

The Chechen woman, like all women in the Caucasus, has always been defined by her humility, which is expressed through respect and deference towards members of the "stronger" sex. However, despite living in a patriarchal society, women have a genuine role in it; they do indeed have some rights and are far from being oppressed. Western culture has strongly influenced Chechnya within recent years. Chechen women have to work to help support their families. Because of the lack of jobs for men, the unsettled conditions in which they live, and the difficulties entailed in traveling within the republic, women are often compelled to be the sole breadwinners in the family.

21 BIBLIOGRAPHY

Babchenko, Arkady. *One Soldier's War.* Nick Allen, translator. New York: Grove Press, 2006.

Bennigsen, A., and S. E. Wimbush. *Muslims of the Soviet Empire.* Bloomington: Indiana University Press, 1986.

Benningsen-Broxup, Marie, ed. *The North Caucasus Barrier.* London: Hurst and Co., 1992.

Colarusso, John, "Chechnya: the War without Winners." *Current History* 94 (October 1995): 329–36.

Gammer, Moshe. *The Lone Wolf and the Bear.* London: Hurst & Co., 2006.

Henze, Paul B. *Chechnya, a Report.* London: International Alert, 1992.

Isaev, Ruslan. "The Chechen woman and her role in the 'new' society," *Prague Watchdog,* 2004.

King, Charles. *The Ghost of Freedom, a History of the Caucasus.* Oxford: Oxford University Press, 2008.

Kozlov, V. *The Peoples of the Soviet Union.* Trans. by P. M. Tiffen. Bloomington: Indiana University Press, 1988.

Nekrich, Aleksandr M. *The Punished Peoples.* New York: W. W. Norton, 1978.

Shah-Kazemi, Reza. *Crisis in Chechnya.* London: Islamic World Report, 1995.

Tolstoy, Leo, *The Raid.* Virginia: Orchises Press, 1996.

Wixman, Ron. *Language Aspects of Ethnic Patterns and Processes in the North Caucasus.* Chicago: University of Chicago Press, 1980.

—by J. Ormrod, J. Colarusso, and F. Tlisova

CHUKCHI

ALTERNATE NAMES: Lygoraveltlat; Chukchee
LOCATION: Russia (Chukchi peninsula in northeastern Siberia)
POPULATION: 15,767 (2002)
LANGUAGE: Chukchi, Russian
RELIGION: Native form of Shamanism; Eastern Orthodox Christianity

1 INTRODUCTION

The Chukchi are an Arctic people who chiefly inhabit the Chukchi peninsula, or Chukotka, in the extreme northeastern section of Siberia that faces North America across the Bering Strait. Archeological and linguistic evidence suggests that their original homeland probably lay further to the south along the shores of the Sea of Okhotsk, from which they migrated to their present area about six thousand years ago. The Chukchi who live in the interior of the Chukchi peninsula have traditionally been herdsman and hunters of reindeer; those who live along the coasts of the Arctic Ocean, the Chukchi Sea, and the Bering Sea have customarily hunted sea mammals such as seals, whales, walruses, and sea lions. The Chukchi call themselves the *Lygoravetlat* (singular: *Lygoravetlan*), which means "genuine people." The word "Chukchi"—sometimes spelled "Chukchee"—is itself a plural form of the Russian word *Chukcha* (feminine: *Chukchanka*), which is their word for an individual *Lygoravetlan.* The reindeer Chukchi also call themselves *Chavchu* ("rich in reindeer"), whereas the coastal Chukchi call themselves the *Ankalit* ("sea people"). Interestingly, the reindeer breeders among the neighboring Koriak people have also been known to call themselves "Chavchu."

The Chukchi were one of the last Siberian peoples to fall under Russian rule. Russian Cossacks and adventurers in Siberia first learned of the Chukchi from the neighboring Yukagirs and Koriaks in the 1640s, but no serious attempt was made to conquer them at first. Russia was at that time occupied with subduing Siberia's other indigenous peoples, and in any event the harsh tundra lands inhabited by the Chukchi were relatively poor in sable and other valuable fur-bearing animals sought by the Russians. But Chukchi raids on nearby Cossack settlers, combined with a need to find new sources of furs after stocks in other parts of Siberia had been depleted, led Russia to launch a series of vigorous military campaigns against the Chukchi in 1729. The Chukchi put up a ferocious resistance and, when surrounded, they frequently committed mass suicide rather than surrender. By the 1760s, the Russian government decided that the cost of vanquishing the Chukchi was too high in terms of money and troops and ended the war on the condition that the Chukchi cease attacking Russian settlers and pay the *yasak* (the yearly tax that native Siberians paid in furs). Since Chukchi territory was quite isolated from the rest of the Russian empire and its cold, harsh climate was unattractive to outsiders, the Chukchi suffered much less than most other Siberian peoples from Russian colonization and exploitation and government interference into their way of life under the Czarist regime and the early Soviet period. Most Chukchi contact with the Russians came through trade, in which the Chukchi received knives, kettles, and other cooking utensils, vodka, tea, tobacco, and sugar in exchange for their fox furs and ivory. American whaling ships also participated in this kind of barter with the Chukchi in the late 1800s. This relatively independent existence came to an end in the 1930s, however, when herdsmen and sea-mammal hunters were forced into state-supervised economic collectives. Chukotka became a region of mines and gulags (concentration camps) as Stalin's campaign to rapidly develop Soviet industry increased demands for the tin and gold that lay under Chukchi soil. Furthermore, the arrest of millions of Soviet citizens during that decade's waves of mass political repression created a need for isolated areas in which to build prison camps. Later in the Soviet era, the Chukchi were culturally afflicted as the frequent subjects of ethnic stereotype jokes told by Russians.

2 LOCATION AND HOMELAND

The Chukchi presently number slightly over 15,000, all of whom live in the Russian Federation. About 11,900 Chukchi live in the Chukchi Autonomous *Okrug* (Russian for "district") within the Magadan *Oblast* (Russian for "region," but similar in structure to a province). Almost all of the remainder dwell in the northernmost reaches of the Koriak Autonomous District (1,500) and in the Nizhnekolymskii *Raion* (a Russian divisional term for "district") of the Sakha (also known as Yakut) Republic (1,300). Most of the territory inhabited by the Chukchi is tundra, with some taiga areas in the south. The climate is harsh, with winter temperatures sometimes dropping as low as −54°C (−65°F). The cool summers average around 10°C (50°F). Coastal regions, especially along the coast of the Arctic Ocean, are damp and foggy; the climate is drier the further inland one goes. In the forested regions, larch, poplar, and birch trees are the most typical form of plant life; lichens and short, scrubby alders and cedar are common in the tundra. Reindeer, foxes, squirrels, and brown bears inhabit the inland regions, while walruses, white whales, killer whales, seals, and polar bears are found in coastal areas. Cod and fresh- and salt-water salmon are the most common fish.

3 LANGUAGE

The Chukchi language belongs to the Paleoasiatic language family's Chukotka-Kamchatka (or Chukotic) group, which includes other languages spoken in far northeastern Siberia such as Itelmen (Kamchadal) and Koriak. The speech of women differs phonetically from that of men: for example, the sound "r" in male pronunciation becomes "ts" in female pronunciation. Thus, the word for "no" is pronounced *krym* by men and *ktsym* by women. Children of both sexes initially learn only the female forms of words from their mothers. There are several dialects and subdialects of Chukchi, but they differ only slightly from each other; the most widely spoken ones are the coastal Uelen dialect and the inland Pevek dialect. Although non-Chukchi linguists (the most famous of which was the Russian Vladimir Bogoraz, 1865–1936) used Latin and Cyrillic (Russian) letters and linguistic symbols to record Chukchi during their research, in the 19th and early 20th centuries, a few native Chukchi speakers made isolated attempts to develop a sort of hieroglyphic writing. Consequently, the Chukchi did not have a written language until 1931, when they adopted the Latin alphabet. Since 1937, Chukchi has been written in a special form of the Cyrillic alphabet that includes extra letters for Chukchi sounds that do not exist in Russian. The Chukchi written language is based on the Uelen dialect. Around 75% of

the Chukchi claim to have a fluent command of their people's language, although the real percentage may actually be lower than this.

Until well into the 20th century, most Chukchi had only one given name. The practice of using a surname came only after an increased Russian presence led to pressure to adopt a family name (based on the father's given name) to facilitate school registration and other bureaucratic paperwork. Some Chukchi personal names reflect natural occurrences at the time of the person's birth—for example, *Tynga-gyrgyn* ("sunrise"; male) and *Gyrongav* ("Spring"; female). Other names, such as *Umqy* ("polar bear"; male) *Galgan-nga* ("duck"; female) are the names of animals native to Chukotka. Parents sometimes give their children names that reflect a quality that they hope the child will come to possess—for instance, *Omryn* ("robust fellow"; male) or *Gitingev* ("beautiful woman"; female). Some Chukchi use Russian first names such as *Yuri* (male) and *Nina* (female).

4 FOLKLORE

Chukchi folklore includes myths about the creation of the earth, moon, sun, and stars; tales about animals; anecdotes and jokes about foolish people; stories about evil spirits called *kelet*, which traditional Chukchi beliefs hold responsible for disease and other misfortunes; and stories about shamans with supernatural powers. Many Chukchi myths and stories have close equivalents among the neighboring Koriaks, Eskimos, Itelmen (Kamchadal), and even some Native American peoples. The Chukchi also possess numerous historical legends about ancient battles between the Chukchi and the Koriaks and Eskimos.

In one Chukchi folktale, several shamans (tribal priests) and the storyteller are traveling on the ocean when their boat develops a leak. One shaman succeeds in stopping the leak with the aid of seaweed-spirits. When they approach land, he tells the seaweed-spirits to depart; the leak reappears, and he challenges the other shamans to stop it. Their powers are weaker than his, they are unsuccessful, and they drown. The shaman who was able to master the seaweed-spirits swims to safety together with the teller of the tale.

5 RELIGION

Chukchi religious beliefs and practices are often described as a form of shamanism. Animals, plants, heavenly bodies, rivers, forests, and other natural phenomena are considered to have their own spirits. Fire created by friction (instead of matches or lighters) and the tools used to make it are considered sacred.

Although both men and women can become shamans (tribal priests similar to Native American "medicine men") if chosen by the spirits, male shamans are considered more powerful since they do not have to undergo the exhaustion and stress of pregnancy and childbirth. Formerly, some shamans were homosexual men and women who assumed the clothing, speech, and mannerisms of the opposite sex and took "wives" or "husbands" of their own gender. Such shamans were very rare and considered the most powerful of all. Most shamans claim to have been trained in their profession by the spirits themselves, although some learn from older shamans. During their rituals, Chukchi shamans fall into trances (sometimes with the aid of hallucinogenic mushrooms), communicate with the spirits and allow them to speak through them, predict the future, and cast spells of various kinds. Not all religious activities require the aid of a shaman. Most are performed privately within the family and take the form of drumming and chanting, which along with the magic charms and amulets carried by some Chukchi, are intended to heal the sick, punish enemies, ensure good luck in herding and hunting, and obtain wealth and love. Chukchi shamanism (and shamanism in general) may be considered to have suffered less than other religions from the Soviet government's anti-religious policies. Since most shamanist activity took place in the home, there was no stable religious hierarchy to attack, and so it was relatively easy for shamanism to survive underground.

During the late 19th century Russian state-supported missionaries succeeded in spreading Orthodox Christianity among the Chukchi, and before 1917 the Chukchi formally were Russian Orthodox. During the Soviet era anti-religious policies and initiatives were directed against both the Russian Orthodox Church and Chukchi shamans. Both of these religious traditions have reemerged since 1991, although the Chukchis have also been exposed to increased missionary activity since 1991, this time primarily from Protestant missionaries.

6 MAJOR HOLIDAYS

The most important traditional Chukchi holidays were festivals in which sacrifices were made to the spirits the Chukchi depended upon for success in their livelihoods. Among the reindeer Chukchi, these sacrifices took place in autumn. After shouting and firing guns to frighten away *kelet* (evil spirits), participants slaughtered some reindeer and used their blood

to anoint themselves and their sleds. This ritual was followed by feasting (the sacrificial reindeer were eaten) and drumming. Similarly, coastal Chukchi households presented sacrifices to the sea-spirit. At some point during the summer or fall, the best hunter in the family walked down to the seashore, showed his harpoon and other weapons to the sea, and asked its spirit for success and safety in hunting during the coming year. One of the family's women gave a sacrifice of blood soup and reindeer-stomach sausage (considered a delicacy since it was not an ordinary part of the coastal Chukchi diet). Occasionally, a dog was killed and given to the sea in this ritual.

7 RITES OF PASSAGE

The birth of a Chukchi child has traditionally been surrounded by many rituals and rules, although the degree to which these are observed has probably lessened as a result of modernization. After a woman has discovered that she is pregnant, she must go outside every day as soon as she awakens, look at the rising sun, and circle her dwelling in the direction of the sun's movement. When the time comes for her to give birth, no men can enter the sleeping chamber where she is giving birth, as it is thought that bad luck may accompany them. The reindeer Chukchi anoint infants with reindeer blood several days after birth. Both the inland and coastal groups build a small tent for the afterbirth and place it in the tundra.

Death, too, has customarily been accompanied by a series of precise ceremonies. The deceased is placed naked, save for coverings over his or her face and genitals, in the sleeping chamber and is watched over for a day or so in case he or she comes back to life. At this time, it is forbidden to beat drums or make other loud noises. After the watch is completed, the corpse is washed, dressed in new clothing, given gifts of tobacco and a bow and arrow or spear (for men) or sewing and skin-dressing tools (for women). The corpse is then taken into the tundra for disposal either by cremation or exposure. (In the latter case, the body is dismembered to allow evil spirits to leave and is left to be devoured by wild animals. It is considered a bad sign if animals refuse to eat the corpse.) The inland Chukchi sacrifice reindeer in honor of the dead or present the dead with especially fine reindeer antlers; the coastal Chukchi sacrifice dogs.

8 INTERPERSONAL RELATIONS

Because of the harsh climate and difficulty of life in the tundra, hospitality and generosity are highly prized among the Chukchi. It is forbidden to refuse anyone, even a stranger, shelter and food. The community is expected to provide for orphans, widows, and the poor. In general, stinginess is considered the worst character defect a person can have. For example, it is unthinkable for a Chukchi to refuse to share his tobacco if asked. There is an anecdote about a man who was killed for this very reason.

The Chukchi have great respect for their elders. During the summer, when the frozen soil melts and travel by sleds becomes impossible, elderly people who cannot walk are carried by young men on their shoulders. In earlier times, when old people asked to be killed if they became sick or feeble, this request could not be refused. (Euthanasia was usually performed by stabbing through the heart or shooting, as these methods were the quickest and hence most merciful forms of death.)

⁹ LIVING CONDITIONS

Reindeer-herding Chukchi were nomadic and lived in settlements of two or three families. The traditional Chukchi form of housing was the *yaranga*, a conical or rounded reindeer-hide tent with a box-shaped inner sleeping chamber made of fur that was large enough for several people. Maritime Chukchi originally lived in semi-underground houses made of earth or sod with whalebone frames, but in the 19th century they too adopted the *yaranga*, which they considered more comfortable. *Yarangas* were lit by lamps that burned reindeer or sea-mammal fat. Some Chukchi still live in *yarangas*, but the one-story wooden houses common in the former Soviet Union's collective farms and the prefabricated concrete apartment buildings typical in its towns are now encountered far more frequently.

The coastal Chukchi traditionally used dogsleds and skin boats for transportation, while inland Chukchi rode in sleds pulled by reindeer. Both groups used snowshoes. These traditional methods of transportation still survive, but are increasingly supplemented by air travel, motorboats, and snowmobiles.

With the exception of shamanist chants and prayers, medical care was unknown among the Chukchi prior to Russian contact, most likely due to the lack of medicinal plants and minerals in the Chukchi lands. Not surprisingly, disease was widespread. Smallpox and influenza, brought by infected Russians or those who had been in contact with them, were especially deadly because the Chukchi had no immunity to them. Blindness and eye infections were common, particularly snow-blindness and inflammation from sweat, dirt, and exhaustion (most common among herdsmen who had to stand watch over their reindeer for long periods). Western medicine became much more widespread in the Soviet period. Treatment was provided either free of cost or for modest fees; nevertheless, its availability and quality were, and still are, insufficient to meet Chukchi needs. As a result, diseases such as tuberculosis and alcoholism are major problems in Chukchi communities.

One peculiar malady that is common among the Chukchi and other Arctic peoples is "Arctic hysteria." A person affected by Arctic hysteria is seized by sudden fits of rage, depression, or violence and often harms others or himself. Murder and suicide are sometimes committed in this state.

¹⁰ FAMILY LIFE

Traditionally, Chukchi lived in encampments of several nuclear families who were usually related to each other and who shared reindeer herds or sea-mammal-hunting equipment. Polygamy was widespread, especially among wealthy Chukchi, until it was banned by the Bolshevik government. The nuclear family with one or two children living in its own dwelling is now typical of the Chukchi. Sexual attitudes have customarily been fairly tolerant (although incest, rape, and intercourse with girls who have not reached puberty are prohibited). Sexual activity usually begins before marriage, although there is little stigma attached to unwed motherhood.

One practice formerly common among the Chukchi was the "group marriage" in which two or more male friends had the right to occasionally sleep with each other's wives. Sometimes this privilege was granted to esteemed visitors as well. The children of women whose husbands formed part of a group marriage were considered relatives and were forbidden to marry each other.

In a traditional Chukchi wedding, a reindeer was sacrificed and the couple anointed with its blood. Red ocher was substituted for reindeer blood among the maritime Chukchi. If the bride was to become part of the groom's household, she traveled to his family's home for the ceremony. On the other hand, if the groom had agreed to join his father-in-law's family, the ceremony took place at the latter's home. The marriage partner who was joining the spouse's family gave up all of his or her property to it. Weddings of this type have now been largely replaced by civil ceremonies.

¹¹ CLOTHING

Chukchi women traditionally wore a *kerker*, a knee-length coverall made from reindeer or seal hide and trimmed with fox, wolverine, wolf, or dog fur. In addition to the *kerker*, women also wore robe-like dresses of fawn skins beautifully decorated with beads, embroidery, and fur trimmings. Men wore loose shirts and trousers made of the same materials. Both sexes wore high boots and leather undergarments. Children's clothing consisted of a one-piece fur coverall with a flap between the legs to allow the moss that served as a diaper to be easily changed. Present-day Chukchi wear Western clothing (cloth dresses, shirts, trousers, and underclothes) except on holidays and other special occasions.

¹² FOOD

The staple foods of the inland Chukchi diet are products of reindeer breeding: boiled venison, reindeer-blood soup, and reindeer brains and marrow. One dish, *rilkeil*, is made from semi-digested moss from a slaughtered reindeer's stomach mixed with blood, fat, and pieces of boiled reindeer intestine. Maritime Chukchi cuisine is based on boiled walrus, seal and whale meat and fat, as well as seaweed. Both groups eat frozen fish and edible leaves and roots. The Chukchi are very fond of tea, which they have drunk since they began trading with Russians in the 18th century. Traditional Chukchi cuisine is now augmented with canned vegetables and meats, bread, and other prepared foods purchased in stores. The Chukchi formerly boiled their food in wooden, bark, or metal kettles and ate with spoons or their hands from cups, bowls, and plates made of wood, bone, and ivory. Metal and ceramic vessels and knives, forks, and spoons are used today.

¹³ EDUCATION

Prior to the Soviet period, all Chukchi were illiterate, with the exception of a handful who had learned Russian from Russian settlers or at one of the few schools run by Russian Orthodox missionaries. Education only began to take root among the Chukchi in the 1920s and 1930s, when the Soviet government launched a campaign for universal education and literacy throughout the country. In 1926, the Institute of the North (now the Pedagogical Institute of the Peoples of the North) was established in Leningrad (St. Petersburg) to train native teachers for the Chukchi and other Siberian and Arctic peoples. Most Chukchi children study in primary and secondary boarding schools, because their settlements are too small and far apart to allow a school to be built in each one. Literacy in Russian is now virtually universal, but due to the Soviet government's policy of forced assimilation, this cannot be said of literacy in Chukchi.

[14] CULTURAL HERITAGE

In addition to their rich oral folklore tradition, the Chukchi have developed their own body of literature in the 20th century. Since the 1950s, the most famous Chukchi writer has been Yuri Rytkheu, whose poems, novels, and short stories are written in both Chukchi and Russian. Publishing in both languages has allowed Rytkheu to make a significant contribution to the development of the modern Chukchi literary language, while at the same time making his works on themes common to all of Russia's Arctic peoples accessible to them. Since the growth of freedom of speech and the press in the former USSR in the 1980s, Rytkheu has become a visible and outspoken critic of policies harmful to Russia's Arctic and Siberian peoples.

[15] WORK

Although both sexes share responsibility for running the household, they have different tasks. Chukchi men drive their reindeer in search of vegetation and travel to the edge of the taiga to gather firewood, fish, and hunt sea mammals. Women's work in the household includes cleaning and repairing the *yaranga*, cooking food, sewing and repairing clothing, and preparing reindeer or walrus hides. It is considered unseemly for a man to perform work usually done by women.

[16] SPORTS

Traditional Chukchi sports are reindeer- and dog-sled races, wrestling, and foot races. Competitions of these types are often performed following the reindeer sacrifices of the inland Chukchi and the sea-spirit sacrifices of the coastal Chukchi. The coastal Chukchi, like the neighboring Eskimo, enjoy tossing each other high into the air on walrus-skin blankets.

[17] ENTERTAINMENT AND RECREATION

Among children, foot races and playing with dolls (girls) and lassos (boys) are the most typical pastimes. Chukchi of all ages have traditionally enjoyed listening to folk tales, reciting tongue-twisters, singing, and dancing. Ventriloquism, besides being a staple of the shaman's repertoire, is a common amusement.

[18] FOLK ART, CRAFTS, AND HOBBIES

Sculpture and carving on bone and walrus tusk are the most highly developed forms of folk art among the Chukchi. Common traditional themes are landscapes and scenes from everyday life: hunting parties, reindeer herding, and animals native to Chukotka. Under the Soviet regime, Chukchi artists were "encouraged" to carve portraits of Lenin and representations of patriotic themes such as the May 9 holiday commemorating the Soviet victory over Nazi Germany. In traditional Chukchi society, only men engaged in these arts, but there are now female sculptors and carvers as well. Chukchi women are also skilled at sewing and embroidering.

[19] SOCIAL PROBLEMS

Pollution caused by Soviet-era mining and industry, poverty, poor diet and medical care, and widespread alcoholism have led to high rates of tuberculosis and other diseases among the modern Chukchi. Chukchi alcoholics, like those in other parts of the Soviet Union, sometimes die from drinking industrial fluids that contain alcohol. Moreover, pollution, weapons testing, strip mining, and overuse of industrial and mining equipment and vehicles have greatly damaged Chukotka's environment and endangered its ability to support traditional Chukchi economic activities.

Although many of the early Bolsheviks advocated equal rights for the USSR's peoples and supported the preservation and development of their cultures and languages, Stalin and his successors adopted a policy of Russification intended to destroy non-Russian cultures through persecution and neglect (while, of course, denying this officially). For the Chukchi, like the other native Siberian peoples, the 1960s and 1970s were the most destructive period in this regard. The government abolished many native settlements, dispersed their former inhabitants, and made Russian the language of instruction in Chukchi schools. When the Soviet leader Mikhail Gorbachev relaxed the USSR's policies towards censorship and the nationalities during the 1980s, writers, teachers, and other concerned Chukchi began to criticize these policies and to participate in native-rights organizations such as the Association of the Small Peoples of the North. They have also begun to expand Chukchi-language teaching and publishing.

[20] GENDER ISSUES

Women's status in traditional Chukchi society was clearly inferior to that of men. Women could not eat until the men in the household had been served, and females received the less desirable cuts of meat. Wife-beating was also common. Nevertheless, they could own property (such as reindeer herds) and were permitted to divorce abusive husbands. The status of Chukchi women has improved markedly in the 20th century as a result of Soviet policies of sexual equality, and women now serve as administrators, teachers, and doctors.

The severe economic collapse in the Russian north strongly affected Chukchi women, who faced additional burdens in the face of chronic unemployment and economic difficulties.

[21] BIBLIOGRAPHY

Antropova, V. V., and V. G. Kuznetsova. "The Chukchi." In *The Peoples of Siberia*. Ed. M. G. Levin and L. Potapov. Trans. Stephen Dunn. Chicago: University of Chicago Press, 1964.

Bartels, Dennis A., and Alice L. Bartels. *When the North was Red: Aboriginal Education in Soviet Siberia*. Montreal: McGill-Queen's University Press, 1995.

Bogoras, Waldemar (sic—Vladimir Bogoraz). *The Chukchee*. Vol. 7 of The Jesup North Pacific Expedition. Ed. Franz Boaz. New York: AMS Press, 1975. (Reprint. Originally published: Leiden: E. J. Brill; New York: G. E. Stechert, 1904-1909 sic.)

Crossroads of Continents: Cultures of Siberia and Alaska. Ed. W. Fitzhugh and A. Crowell. Washington, DC: Smithsonian Institution Press, 1988.

Czaplicka, M. A. *Aboriginal Siberia: A Study in Social Anthropology*. Oxford: Oxford University Press, 1914.

Dunn, Michael, "Chukchi Women's Language: A Historical-Comparative Perspective." *Anthropological Linguistics* 42(3): 305-328.

Fondahl, Gail. "Siberia: Native Peoples and Newcomers in Collision." In *Nations and Politics in the Soviet Successor States*. Ed. Ian Bremmer and Ray Taras. Cambridge: Cambridge University Press, 1993.

Forsyth, James. *A History of the Peoples of Siberia: Russia's North Asian Colony, 1581-1990.* Cambridge: Cambridge University Press, 1992.

Kerttula, Anna M. *Antler on the Sea: the Yup'ik and Chukchi of the Russian Far East.* Ithaca, NY: Cornell University Press, 2000.

Slezkine, Yuri. *Arctic Mirrors: Russia and the Small Peoples of the North.* Ithaca, NY: Cornell University Press, 1994.

Spravochnik lichnykh imen narodov RSFSR (Handbook of personal names of the peoples of the RSFSR). Ed. A. V. Superanskaia and I.M. Guseva. Moscow: Russkii iazyk, 1989.

Sverdrup, Harald U. *Among the Tundra People.* Trans. Molly Sverdrup. San Diego: University of California Press, 1978.

Zharnitskaia, Maria. "The Chukchee." In *Encyclopedia of World Cultures. Vol. 6, Russia and Eurasia/China.* Ed. Paul Friedrich and Norma Diamond. Boston: G. K. Hall, 1994.

Zharnitskaia, Maria and V. A. Turaev. "Chukchi." In *Narody Rossii: Entsiklopediia* (The Peoples of Russia: An Encyclopedia). Ed. V. A. Tishkov. Moscow: Bol'shaia Rossiiskaia Entsiklopediia, 1994.

Ziker, John P. *Peoples of the Tundra: Northern Siberians in the Post-Communist Transition.* Prospect Heights, IL: Waveland Press, 2002.

—revised by A. Frank

CHUVASH

LOCATION: Russia (Chuvash Republic in Middle Volga River region)
POPULATION: approximately 1.8 million
LANGUAGE: Chuvash
RELIGION: Christianity; some pagan rituals survive

¹ INTRODUCTION

The Chuvash are Turkic-speaking people who have lived in the Middle Volga region of the Russian Federation for centuries. They are considered to be descendants of the ancient Bulgars, who maintained a state in the Middle Volga River valley from the 10th to 13th centuries. As an ethnic group, the Chuvash were formed chiefly on the basis of the Turkic-speaking Bulgars who came in large masses in the 7th century from the Caucasus region. The Bulgars and the subdued and partially assimilated indigenous Finno-Ugric tribes settled down on both sides of the Middle Volga and formed the Bulgar state. Great Bulgaria occupied a sizeable territory, in which the Samara and Ulyanovsk oblasts (regions), the Tatarstan, Chuvash, Mari, and Udmurt republics, as well as western regions of Bashkortostan are now situated. In the first half of the 13th century, further development of the Bulgar civilization through the ethnic integration of Turkic-speaking and Finnish-Ugric tribes was interrupted by the defeat of the Bulgar state in 1236 by hordes of the Mongol Tatars. The Bulgar state became an *ulus* (region) of the Golden Horde. The disintegration of the Golden Horde and the formation of the Kazan khanate gave rise to the formation of Chuvash, Tatar, and Bashkir groups.

There is no common opinion about the origin of the name *Chuvash*. This term is not found in written documents until early in the 16th century. It is believed that the names Savir, Suvar, and Suvaz, used by some classical and medieval writers, actually refer to Chuvash ancestors. These names belonged to tribes that were a part of the Bulgar tribal confederation during the latter part of the first millennium AD. It was the Suvars who moved along the left bank of the Volga and then crossed the river in the 13th century when fleeing the Mongol-Tatar invasion. Later, the Suvars mixed with indigenous inhabitants of the region, resulting in the formation of one of the Chuvash subgroups, the Anatri. The Chuvash had been under the sway of the Kazan khanate between 1445 and 1551. In the Kazan khanate, the term *Chuvash* meant mainly villagers (*yasak*) professing paganism. However, the urban Muslim population, chiefly people in service *(sluzhilye lyudi)* were called "Tatars" in official documents. Beginning in the 16th century, a small proportion of them—those living east of the Volga—were Islamized, adopted the Tatar language, and became integrated into the Tatar culture. Beginning in the 15th and 16th centuries, the Chuvash people came under the growing influence of the Russian people and their culture. In 1551 the majority of the Chuvash were subjugated by the Russian state. Chuvash villages were built in secluded places and away from roads to make it difficult for the czar's tax collectors to find them.

The Chuvash consist of three main ethnic subgroups: the Upper Chuvash, or *Viryal*, in north and northwestern Chuvashia; the Lower Chuvash, or *Anatri*, in south and southeastern Chuvashia; and an intermediate group, the *Anat Enchi*.

Up until 1920 (before the formation of the Chuvash Autonomous Region), the basic area of inhabitance of the Chuvash people was not officially localized. The pre-revolutionary period, the territory that makes up present-day Chuvashia, was divided among two or three provinces.

The Chuvash Republic established during the Soviet period contains 18,300 square kilometers (7,066 square miles). The territory consists of three vegetation zones: a forest zone in the north and forest-steppe and steppe zones in the south. Forests occupy 30% of the territory with pine, oak, fir, and birch, predominant. The republic is crossed by the Volga, Sura and Tsivil rivers and contains 400 lakes. Bears, wolves, foxes, lynxes, elks, muskrats, squirrels, and martens are widely distributed. The climate is temperate to continental with cold winters and warm summers. The average temperature in January is –13°C (9° F) and in July is 19°C (67°F). The Chuvash rank fourth among the peoples of the Russian Federation (after Russians, Ukrainians, and Tatars). According to the 1989 census, the Chuvash population in Russia was 1,773,645, including 906,992 people (49.2%) in the Chuvash Republic. In 1989, more than 50% of the Chuvash lived elsewhere in the Soviet Union. The largest pockets of settlement were in Kazakhstan, Ukraine, and certain regions in Siberia. In Russia, there are large groups of Chuvash in Tatarstan, Bashkortostan, Samara Oblast, Ulyanovsk Oblast, Moscow Oblast, Tyumen Oblast, Krasnoyarsk Oblast, Kemerovo Oblast and Orenburg Oblast. Until quite recently, the population of the republic was mostly rural and agricultural. In 1926, 1.6% of the Chuvash lived in urban areas; in 1989, the percentage of urban Chuvash increased to 46.5%. According to the 1989 census the population of Chuvashia was 1,338,023 people, including: Chuvash, 906,922 (67.78%); Russian, 357,120 (26.7%); Tatar, 35,689 (2.7%); Mordvin, 18,686 (1.4%); Ukrainian, 7,300 (0.5%); Mari, 3,800 (0.3%); Belarusian, 2,200 (0.2%); and 0.4% other. Thus, 98.6% of the population of the Chuvash Republic consists of people representing four nationalities: Chuvash, Russian, Tatar, and Mordvin. They comprise to a certain extent the indigenous population of the Chuvash region.

The towns of Chuvashia are among the oldest in the Middle Volga region. The most ancient is Cheboksary, the capital of the republic, the first written record of which dates to 1469.

³ LANGUAGE

The Chuvash speak Chuvash, one of the ancient languages of the Altai branch of the Turkic family. It has two dialects: upper (*viryal*) and lower (*anatri*). The Chuvash literary language has been formed on the basis of the lower dialect. The Chuvash language by virtue of a number of peculiarities differs more widely than others from the Turkic languages. There are many Chuvash words in Mari, Udmurt, Russian, and other languages. Likewise, the Chuvash language has borrowings from Arabic, Persian, Kypchak-Tatar, Finnish-Ugric, and Russian. In the early 20th century, the language of the tombstone epitaphs written by the ancient Bulgars was determined to be quite close to the Chuvash language, which was the most archaic in appearance among the Turkic languages. The epitaphs are evidence of an Old Chuvash writing system formed on the Arabic basis. In ancient times, the ancestors of the Chuvash used a runic written language. Elements in Chuvash embroidery and tribal signs that graphically correspond to the runes testify to this fact. Later, in the 11th through 13th centuries in

The Lower Chuvash preserved the ethnic features of the Bulgar Chuvash; in the culture of the Upper Chuvash, Mari elements are recognizable. The Chuvash have a number of stable ethnographic and linguistic parallels with Turkic peoples of the Altay and southern Siberia. This becomes apparent in common characteristics of their dwellings, utensils, food, clothing, ornaments, embroidery, as well as pagan religious beliefs, mythology, folklore, and the pentatonic basis of folk music. The physical appearance of the Chuvash indicates the complexity of their ethnogeny: 10.3% of the Chuvash have Mongol features, 21.1% have European features, and 68.6% have mixed Mongol-European features.

After the revolution of 1917, the Chuvash asserted a right to political autonomy, and in 1920 they were rewarded with the establishment of a Chuvash Autonomous Region, which was transformed into an Autonomous Soviet Socialist Republic in 1925. The Chuvash ASSR became the Chuvash Soviet Socialist Republic at the end of the Soviet era in 1990 and was renamed the Chuvash Republic in 1992. Chuvashia is a presidential republic. It has its own constitution, national anthem, emblem, and flag.

² LOCATION AND HOMELAND

The territory occupied by the Chuvash people was first named "Chuvashia" in the first quarter of the 16th century by a traveler named S. Gerberstein. The Chuvash inhabit mainly the right bank of the Volga and areas along some of its tributaries including the Sviyaga and Tsivil Rivers.

Great Bulgaria, Arabic script was established officially. Relics of the Chuvash language proper (the Old Chuvash written language) include books and manuscripts from the 18th and 19th centuries: dictionaries, grammar books, translations from Russian, and original texts. In these books, Chuvash words are written in Latin or Russian letters, without any additional signs for designation of specific Chuvash sounds. The "new" Chuvash written language in use today originated in 1871. The first Chuvash alphabet considering the basic peculiarities of the language was created by the Chuvash enlightener I. Y. Yakovlev on the basis of the Russian alphabet. Some changes in the Chuvash alphabet were made in 1872, 1973, 1933, and 1938. The modern Chuvash alphabet consists of 37 letters. All 33 letters of the Russian alphabet plus four additional letters with diacritical marks that designate specific sounds of the Chuvash language: à, è, ç, and ÿ. The letters with superlinear diacritical marks convey vowels, and the letter ç with its underlinear diacritical sign conveys a consonant.

Among the Chuvash living in the republic, 15% don't speak their mother tongue, and old Chuvash names such as *Elembi, Atner, Narspi,* and *Setner* are no longer popular. However, there is an effort in recent years to revitalize the Chuvash language. It is being introduced into school curriculum in an effort to promote Chuvash culture.

4 FOLKLORE

A great variety of genres and richness of content are characteristic features of the Chuvash oral tradition, which includes historical songs, fairy tales, myths, legends, charms, proverbs, sayings, and riddles. The most developed genres are songs, fairy tales, and calendar poetry. The Chuvash have a rich and original mythology about the beginning and structure of the universe. The Chuvash mythological system of the universe has three main stages: (1) the self-generation of the cosmos from chaos; (2) the activity of creators in the form of animals; and (3) the activity of anthropomorphous creators. Chaos in the Chuvash mythology is usually manifested in the form of water elements—the primeval ocean *talai*—or in the form of a fight between fire elements and water elements. In one popular version, chaos is described as non-existence, absolute zero.

Anthropomorphous characters appear in later Chuvash myths: Tura, who in earlier myths personified heaven, was considered Supreme God, and Shuittan the embodiment of evil, was later considered a master of the lower world. Tura is a creator, and Shuittan performs the duties of his opponent, clumsily imitating the actions of Tura. Earth and Heaven are interpreted as feminine and masculine components of a sacred matrimonial couple in the beginning of cosmogonical process. God created a man and all the most sophisticated elements of the universe: the earth, cosmic supports, the world mountain (*Amatu*), the world tree (*Ama yivashch*), inland waters, useful plants, and domestic and wild animals, used for food. Shuittan created spirits, who were hostile to man: water-sprites (*shyvri*), wood-goblins (*arshchuri*), fiery dragons (*vutli shchelen*), spooks (*vere shchelen*), werewolves, and so on.

In Chuvash folk tales, three characters often unite and act as a single whole—a main hero and his helpmates, for example. Basic actions are repeated thrice, heroes fight with three-headed or three-eyed creatures, and so on. To Chuvash ancestors, certain numbers had symbolic meanings, connected with a mythical view of the universe. Numbers with symbolic or sacred meanings are 1, 2, 3, 4, 5, 7, 9, and 12.

5 RELIGION

The majority of the Chuvash were forcibly Christianized in the middle of the 18th century, thus becoming the only large Christian Turkic population in Russia and later the Soviet Union. Because the Chuvash were converted to Russian Orthodoxy early in their history, they do not feel closely related to the Muslim Turks. Islamization took place mostly among the urban populations—aristocrats, traders, and craftsmen—while the rural inhabitants maintained their animistic practices. Animistic mortuary rites were practiced by the great majority of Bulgars as late as 1400 AD, and the Chuvash continued to observe these rites until they were Christianized. The Chuvash believe themselves to be the victims of oppression by the Tatars; they are even proud of the participation of their ancestors in the subjugation of the Kazan khanate by the Russians. Because of the adoption of Christianity, they became highly Russified.

The majority of Chuvash profess Christianity, but some remnants of paganism survive in their religious idea of the universe. Wedding and funeral rites, worship of *kiremet* (a sacred tree, an offering place), and agricultural festivals such as *surkhuri* (solstice), *shchavarni* (Shrovetide), *shchumar chuk* (praying for rain), and *man chuk* (great offering) are all indicative of the vitality of paganism.

6 MAJOR HOLIDAYS

During the last millennium, the Bulgars and later the Chuvash maintained close contact, economic cooperation, and cultural relations with many peoples who profoundly influenced the Chuvash calendar, festivals, and rites. Among these influences were Arab, Iranian, Mari, and Tatar. For more than four hundred years, the Chuvash have been governed by Russia, and this has affected the rites of the Chuvash. They adopted a number of Russian folk calendar holidays such as Shrovetide, *shchavarni, semik shchemik,* and others, although these holidays were enriched by traditional Chuvash rites and at times assumed quite a different form. After the conversion of the Chuvash to Christianity their ritual repertoire was considerably widened with such holidays as Christmas (*rashtav*), Palm Sunday (*verpanni, kachaka prashchnike*), Whitsuntide (*truiski*), and other Christian holidays. Chuvash traditional new year is called Surhuri. Previously celebrated around the fall and spring equinox, it is now celebrated on January 13, due to Russian influence as this is Orthodox new year. Surkhuri means sheep leg, as in the past on this day the legs and head of the sheep were offered. Today, it is celebrated in a fashion similar to Halloween, with children going from house to house to request nuts or pastry.

One of the most highly regarded holidays of the Chuvash calendar is *akatui* (*aka* means "plough," and *tui* means "holiday" or "wedding"), a spring festival dedicated to agriculture. Although this holiday combines a number of rites and ceremonial rituals it is much more a secular holiday than a religious one. For the rituals of the *akatui*, beer is brewed, food is prepared, and eggs are colored. The celebration of *akatui* on different days in different homes begins and lasts a week. On a certain day a person who is prepared to celebrate, invites his relatives and neighbors, and a rich table is laid. At the head of the table, an *altar* (a keg) of beer is placed, and in the middle of the table on a special embroidered towel, a dish with a round loaf of bread and cheese is placed. To complete the ritual part of the festival, all village people go out into the field, taking with them a round loaf of wheat bread, cheese, eggs, pies, beer, and a traditional dish called *sharttan*. Here songs, dances, and revelry begin. On the day of the *akatui*, a village becomes boisterous and busy. In the meadow on the outskirts of a village, various competitions take place: horse-races, running races, jumping, wrestling, archery, and so on. The most popular event is a type of wrestling in which a towel is used as a waistband. Each wrestler holds a towel in his hands and wraps it around the waist of his opponent. The undefeated wrestler is called *pattar*, the title given for the strongest hero, and he is usually rewarded with a ram. Another central event of the *akatui* contests is horse-racing. The winners are presented with embroidered towels, with the prizes usually tied to the horses' necks. Various amusing events, such as potato-sack races and three-legged races round out the festival. Strength and adroitness are demonstrated in such contests as weightlifting, fights with stuffed sacks on a balance beam (played like a pillow fight), and tug-of-war.

⁷ RITES OF PASSAGE

Active atheistic propaganda and the closing of churches in the Soviet period promoted the estrangement of the Chuvash population from religion, but the new civil rites (initiation as workers or growers, first salary day, full-age day, etc.) did not become popular. Traditional rites and rituals are most stable among rural families. In the country, one can see traditional wedding rites such as the bride on the day after the wedding going to the well to draw water. Funeral rites also combine elements of pagan, Orthodox, and modern civil rites.

⁸ INTERPERSONAL RELATIONS

Interpersonal relations of the Chuvash are shaped by traditions of hospitality and mutual aid. *Nime* (pronounced "ni´-me") is a type of collective assistance arranged by countrymen to carry out labor-intensive or troublesome tasks. This tradition has its roots in ancient times, when *nime* saved and guarded peoples. The life of a peasant included many moments that required collective efforts for the timely fulfillment of work. This custom is usually practiced when a villager wants to build a house or to gather in the harvest. The host invites one of the community's most respected individuals and appoints him *nime pushche*—the head of the team. The next morning, the *nime pushche* calls upon the villagers to volunteer to help their countryman. After the day's work, the host invites all participants of *nime* to share a meal. Before leaving, the guests seat the host at the head of the table, treat him to beer, sing a thanksgiving song, and go home saying "*tavssi*," which means "thank you for the meal."

⁹ LIVING CONDITIONS

Almost half of the Chuvash population lives in towns. Working at big factories or in service, the city mode of life affects the well-being, behavior, and spiritual interests of former villagers. Living in town dwellings with modern conveniences, wearing city clothes, consuming Russian food, and using manufactured utensils, urban Chuvash gradually deviate from Chuvash material culture. The majority of families can't afford a car, so they usually use public transportation, mainly buses and trolley buses. However, this is slowly changing, and

the numbers who own cars are much higher than in 2000. Although the well-being of Chuvash villagers is improving, cultural and welfare facilities in the countryside are not as readily available as in town. Many villages experience difficulties on account of bad roads.

The primary type of Chuvash settlement is a village called a *yal*. The most common Chuvash dwelling is a complex type of cottage with a passage and a storeroom. Nearby is the outhouse, a barn, a bathhouse called a *muncha*, and a cattle-shed or a sheep-cot called a *vite*. A shed called a *sarai* or *karta* serves as a storage place for tools and firewood, a summer cookhouse, and a cellar. The houses are built from wood or bricks, and house fronts are decorated with a style of carving that was known as far back as Volga Bulgaria. Ancient ornamental motifs have survived in the Chuvash art tradition to the present. Chuvash engravers borrowed and remade many elements of Russian and Tatar art tradition. In the interior of the house, a very significant place is occupied by a Russian-style stove. Beds are covered with embroidered sheets and laces or colored bedspreads.

Industry in Chuvashia is well developed and includes engineering, production of heavy machinery, and chemical industries. Lumber and forestry are also important industries. Agriculture also plays an important role, and important crops include hops and potatoes. The banking and communication systems in the republic are well developed.

¹⁰ FAMILY LIFE

As a rule, Chuvash families are not large. In town, couples usually have one or two children, whereas in villages couples might have three or four. Men and women usually marry between the ages of 18 and 24. Very often newlyweds have to share an apartment or house with their parents as there is a shortage of affordable housing. Women as a rule work full-time and in addition have many household chores. It is not customary in Chuvash families for men to help their wives about the house. The divorce rate is much higher in towns than that in the countryside, but divorce rates have been declining. Favorite pets are cats and dogs.

¹¹ CLOTHING

Nowadays traditional Chuvash clothes are worn mainly by women in the country. Such clothing (a woman's shirt in particular) can be subdivided in accordance with ethnographic groups—*turi*, *anat enchi*, and *anatri*. Although the clothing is basically the same from group to group, there are a number of local peculiarities in cut, ornamentation, composition, manufacturing methods, color combination, and ways of wearing. The ornamentation of the traditional costume also varies depending on sex, age, and season. Each piece of clothing has its own tracery of a distinct composition form and color combination. The Chuvash woman's costume and its ornamentation have much in common with the clothes of the peoples in the Caucasus and Central Asia. Some similarities can also be drawn with the clothing of the Finnish-Ugric peoples. Chuvash national clothing is closely connected with the agricultural tenor of life. The primary article of the traditional Chuvash costume is a shirt called a *kepe*, which is shaped like a tunic and belted with a girdle. A dress is worn with an apron or a pinafore called a *chershchitti* or a *sappun*, which is remarkable for its bright colors and abundance of ornament (embroidery and laces). Women also wear a head band (*surpan*), a forehead decoration (*masmak*), a head dress (*khushpu*), a cap decorated with coins and beads, or a turban. Until recently, the Chuvash wore stitched shoes. Now they usually wear high leather boots or shoes.

12 FOOD

Vegetables are prevalent in the Chuvash diet. Bread grains include rye, barley, spelt, oat, millet, buckwheat, and wheat. Barley is used for brewing. Pulse products such as peas and lentils are also of great importance in the Chuvash diet. The major baked food is a rye bread, called *khura shchukar,* which women in the countryside sometimes still bake at home. Pies are common, and fillings include cabbage, carrots, beets, rutabagas, meat, potatoes, peas, cottage cheese, eggs, spring onions, berries, and apples. The most delicious, dainty, and festive dish is *khuplu,* a large round pie made of unleavened dough. The filling of *khuplu* is complex. The first layer is made of half-cooked porridge and finely chopped potatoes; the second layer is made of finely minced meat; and the third layer is made of a thin layer of fatty meat and fat.

Everyday soup is called *yashka. Shurpe,* a soup made from either meat or fish, is cooked mainly on high days and holidays. A particular soup gets its name from the seasoning used, such as *veltren yashki* (soup with stinging nettle) or *shchamakh yashki* (soup with a kind of dumplings). Other soup ingredients include flour, groats, fresh cabbage or sauerkraut, carrots, onions, and occasionally beets and wild herbs. Meat soups are cooked from mutton, beef, and pork. Of great importance in the Chuvash diet are different types of porridge: millet porridge, buckwheat porridge, and less often rice porridge.

Potatoes appeared in Chuvash cuisine in the 19th century, and the Chuvash prefer potatoes boiled in their jackets. These are served with vegetable oil and a relish of sauerkraut, pickled cucumbers, spring onions, garlic, turnip, cabbage, carrot, cucumbers, or pumpkins. Black radish and horseradish are used as appetizers and for medicinal purposes. Apples, currants (red, white, and black), raspberries, cherries, ashberries, and bird-cherries are widely used. Wild strawberries, bilberries, raspberries, and different kinds of mushrooms are also gathered in the forest and preserved for the winter and used as filling in pies.

National meat dishes are of ancient origin, as meat played an important role in Chuvash rituals. Meat was traditionally eaten during offerings in honor of pagan gods and spirits during ceremonial rites. Sacrificed animals (horses, bulls, or rams) were slaughtered in observance of special rituals. Pork became a part of the Chuvash diet only in the 19th century. Poultry (hens, geese, and ducks) are widely used. Hens' eggs are used for preparing various dishes, including *shchamarta ashalani* (scrambled eggs), *shchamarta khapartni* (a milk omelet), and *meserle shchamarta* (eggs that are first hard-boiled and then cut in half and fried).

The most famous national meat dishes are *sharttan, tultarmash, sukta, shchurme, yun,* and *shurpe.* The most prestigious dish is *sharttan,* which is prepared in both summer and winter after slaughtering a ram. The stomach of the slaughtered animal is thoroughly washed out and stuffed with boneless mutton. To avoid spoiling, the meat stuffing is salted down. The stuffed stomach is sewn up with a thick thread so that it resembles a round loaf of bread, then put on a frying pan and cooked

in the oven for three or four days. The cooked *sharttan* is kept cool. *Tultarmash* is prepared from the insides of a slaughtered animal. The animals' guts are stuffed with fat or small pieces of fat meat and groats, the ends of the guts are tied up with thick threads, then the *Tultarmash* is boiled in a copper cauldron and broiled in the oven. *Tultarmash* is eaten hot, often with *shurpe. Yun tultarmash* is prepared just like *tultarmash;* its ingredients are fresh blood, fat, and groats.

Shurpe, a popular meat dish of the Chuvash, is prepared from the heads, legs, and internal organs of cattle. On St. Peter's Day it is customary to slaughter a ram and invite relatives and neighbors to taste *shurpe.* From sheep's, cow's, and pig's heads and legs, meat jelly with onions and garlic is prepared. Fish is mainly used for the soup called *pula shurpe.*

Milk dishes are very diverse. *Turakh uirane* (sour milk diluted with water) is used in the summer as a wonderful thirst-quenching drink, and many dishes are prepared from cottage cheese. A highly popular folk drink is a type of beer called *sara.* Strong beer is not made for everyday use, but for holidays it is thick and heady. Grain alcohol was introduced to the Chuvash at the end of the 19th century. The beer produced in Chuvashia today is known throughout Russia for its excellence, and visitors make sure to try it. Cheboksary is home to a beer museum, illustrating the importance of this beverage in the republic.

The Chuvash diet resembles the diet of peoples living in different geographical zones. One group of Chuvash dishes (including *shchamakh, ash-kakai, shurpe, sharttan,* and *tultarmash*) has similarities to diet traditions of Turkic and Iranian-speaking peoples. Other dishes—starchy foods and porridges, pickled provisions, smoked foods, for example are the result of ethnocultural contacts with Finnish-Ugric peoples and Russians.

13 EDUCATION

Chuvashia is a republic of total literacy. All citizens of the Chuvash Republic have equal opportunities for education, which is provided free of charge. Educational ties with foreign schools have become popular, and include a Turkish boarding school, several German schools and a French school. The learning of English is also considered important. In Cheboksary, there are four very competitive higher educational institutions, with some 20,000 students: a University (where foreign students study as well), a Pedagogical Institute, an Agricultural Institute, and a Cooperative Institute. There is also an Academy of Sciences. The university also has exchanges and connections with 20 foreign institutions. Education in Chuvash families is considered to be very prestigious, and parents try to provide a good education for their children. Since 1993, the numbers of those who chose to study higher education increased from 134 per 10,000 of the population to 186 per 10,000 of the population by 2008.

14 CULTURAL HERITAGE

"My nation has preserved one hundred thousand words, one hundred thousand songs, one hundred thousand designs," said the enlightener of the Chuvash people, I. Y. Yakovlev, at the end of the 19th century. Chuvash folklore includes epic tales, everyday songs, fairy tales, and legends. The highest achievement of Chuvash poetry is the epic poem *Narspi* by Konstantin Ivanov, which is considered a masterpiece of world literature. Chuvashia is often called "Land of A Hundred Thousand

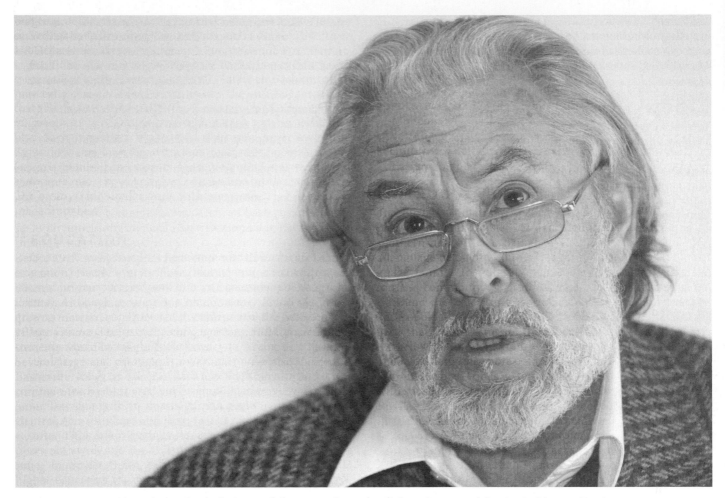

Chuvash poet Gennady Aigi reads his poetry during his 70th anniversary celebration in Moscow, Russia.
(Denis Sinyakov/AFP/Getty Images)

Songs." The Chuvash folk song is one-voiced and there are several different genres: everyday songs (lullabies, lyrical, comic), ritual songs, labor songs, and historical songs. Chuvash music is pentatonic (played on a five-note scale) and played on various folk musical instruments: *shakhlich* (a pipe), *shapar* (bagpipes made from a bull's stomach), *sarnai* (bagpipes made of goatskin), *kesle* (a psaltery), and *parappan* (a drum). The cultural life of the Chuvash people now centers around professional literature, theater, cinema, and fine arts.

¹⁵ WORK

The Chuvash are a very hard-working agricultural people, and they consider those who cannot till the land lazy. Even though about 50% of the population lives in towns, they go down to the country to work in their vegetable gardens or in the fields almost every weekend. They grow vegetables (particularly potatoes) and fruits and berries to store for the winter. A relatively high percentage of people, about 22%, engage in agriculture full time to make a living. The level of unemployment, at 2.2% in 2008, while lower than 10 years prior, remains higher than the Russian average of 1.6%.

¹⁶ SPORTS

Chuvashia is home to 3,500 sports facilities, including stadiums, pools, sports halls, running tracks, ice skating facilities, and other winter sports facilities. Chuvash athletes have become Olympic champions in boxing, track and field events, cycling, weightlifting, wrestling, and fencing. However, most of the population is not involved in organized sports. The government of the republic, to remedy this, has since 2004 instituted programs to encourage sports and increased the numbers of hours spent on physical activities in schools. Both children and adults participate in soccer, volleyball, basketball, tennis, ice hockey, and field hockey. Swimming, track and field events, skiing, cycling, boxing, wrestling, weight lifting, and karate are among the most popular sports among youth, especially in big cities. Popular spectator games are soccer in the summer and ice hockey in the winter.

¹⁷ ENTERTAINMENT AND RECREATION

In towns, people are very fond of going to the movies or concert halls, and Cheboksary in particular offers opportunities for entertainment and recreation. People there can attend plays at the Chuvash Drama Theater (which is also very popular among villagers) or go to the National Opera and Ballet Theater to enjoy ballets, opera, and concerts. In the countryside where there are not as many facilities and opportunities for recreation, people usually watch television or take part in amateur concerts. On winter evenings, farm people might get together, drink beer, dance, and sing Chuvash folk songs. Women sit by the fire spinning or knitting warm socks and sweaters, embroidering towels, shirts, napkins, etc.

¹⁸ FOLK ART, CRAFTS, AND HOBBIES

Chuvash folk art is rich and various. Its main branches are embroidery, tracery weaving, sewing with beads and silver, woodcarving, ceramics, and wickerwork. The old Chuvash folk art has its own particular features, its specific national form. Its main characteristic distinction was unusual development of the geometric ornament and the absence of topical motifs. In such branches of folk art as woodcarving, ceramics, and wickerwork there are no marked distinctions between the different Chuvash ethnographic groups, although there are striking differences in embroidery. Viryal embroidery, with its miniature elements is sewn with black, red, green, yellow, and blue threads, frequently on a colored ground; Anatri embroidery is large and decorative. The tracery of the Anat Yenchi is close to that of the Anatri. Embroidery has always been the most developed branch of Chuvash art. In the past, Chuvash clothing as well as the interiors of houses were decorated with embroidery that contained complex images presenting certain ideas and notions about the universe. The technical devices of making traceries vary, and embroiderers use more than thirty kinds of stitches. The decorative works of the factory Pakha Tere (Fine Embroidery) are widely known over the whole world. The masters borrow from the rich store of ancient folk art and apply it in creating modern works. There isn't a single settlement in the Republic that does not boast its own embroiderers. They embroider towels, curtains, bags, napkins, runners for tables and TV sets, bookmarks, and so on.

In the past, woodcarving reached a high level, and almost every Chuvash village had its own potters. The toy horses, whistles, and crockery they produced were well known for their delicate forms and lines. Wickerwork was also common and master weavers used with great skill the natural color of the birch bark, rod, and bass. Rod was used for the wickerwork of small baskets; bass for baskets, boxes, footwear, and toys; and birch bark for bags, plates, and dishes. In the modern period, crockery and wicker furniture are of particular interest. Cots, chairs, and rocking chairs are fine specimens of wickerwork. Souvenirs (pencilholders, powdercases, dolls, figures of people, animals, etc.) are displayed at exhibitions around the world. Jugs, plates, tureens, milkpots, and beermugs are known for the refinement of their forms. All of these items are closely connected with the folk traditions, characteristics with crockery of the past century.

¹⁹ SOCIAL PROBLEMS

Social problems in Chuvashia are similar to those in other republics and regions of the Volga basin and Russia in general. The rural areas of the republic, which are populated mostly by Chuvash, have the highest population density among the rural regions of Central Russia—more than 50 persons per square kilometer (130 persons per square mile). This concentration of population in the countryside has lead to unemployment, and youth are forced to leave their villages and migrate to towns or other parts of Russia. Ecological problems threaten the plant, animal, and human populations of the republic. Children are especially vulnerable. Emissions from the Novocheboksarsk chemical plant, which is currently engaged in destroying chemical weapons, threaten all forms of life in the region. The Novocheboksarsk plant causes respiratory diseases that are far more prevalent in Chuvashia than elsewhere in the Russian Federation, as well as high infant mortality. Cultural and welfare facilities are much worse in the countryside than in town. The general commercialization and urbanization of life for the Chuvash have eroded many traditional values, such as diligence, hospitality, open-heartedness, chastity of women, strength of marriage bonds, and readiness to come to the aid of others. Crime, alcoholism (among both men and women), and drug abuse are on the rise. Domestic violence can be a problem. Families in which there is only one parent are particularly vulnerable to social problems.

²⁰ GENDER ISSUES

Today, the situation of Chuvash women is similar to that of most other women in Russia. Chuvash women, as women of most ethnicities under the Soviet Union, were actively encouraged to join the workforce. Chuvash women are known to hold important positions within their community, obtaining success both in business and civil careers. Domestic violence is a social problem suffered by Chuvash women. Generally, women are responsible for household life with little assistance from men.

²¹ BIBLIOGRAPHY

Bromley, Y. V. *Glavnyi redaktor. Narody mira. Istoriko-etnograficheskii spravochnik.* Moscow: Sovetskaya Entsiklopedia, 1988.

Chuvashskoe narodnoe iskusstvo. Albom. Cheboksary: 1981.

Degtyarev, G. A. *Chuvashskii yazyk dlya nachinayushchikh.* Cheboksary: 1991.

Ivanov, V. P., G. B. Matveev, and N. I. Egorov. I d./sost. Skvortsov. *Kultura Chuvashskogo kraya.* Cheboksary: Chuvashskoe knizhnoe izdatelstvo, 1995.

NUPI Center for Russian Studies. "Ethnic Groups: Chuvash." http://www.nupino/cgi-win/Russland/etnisk_b.exe?Chuvashian (June 2008).

Official Site of the Government Organs of the Chuvash Republic. "Speech made by President Nikolai Fyodorv, 2004." http://gov.cap.ru/hierarhy_cap.asp?page=./103/8407/8413 (June 2008).

Russian American Chamber of Commerce. "The Chuvash Republic: Regional Profile." http://www.russianamerican-chamber.org/regions/chuvash_republic.html (June 2008).

Sergeev T. S., and Y. N. Zaitsev. *Istoriia i kultura Chuvashii. Vazhneishie sobytiya, daty.* Cheboksary: Izdatelstvo "Chuvashia," 1995.

Shnirelman, Victor A. "Who Gets the Past?" *Competition for Ancestors among Non-Russian Intellectuals in Russia.* Washington: The Woodrow Wilson Center Press, 1996.

—revised by M. Kerr

CIRCASSIANS

ALTERNATE NAMES: Adyges, Cherkess
LOCATION: Russia; Turkey; Syria, Jordan, Israel, USA
POPULATION: 5.5 million (approx.)
LANGUAGES: Adyghe (Circassian, Kabardian; Russian, Turkish, Arabic, Hebrew, English)
RELIGION: Historically Muslim

¹ INTRODUCTION

Adyghe (a-DEE-gay) is the self-designation for a group of Caucasian peoples who are commonly called "Circassians" by others. Today, three branches of Adyghes live in the Russian Federation: the Kabardins, the Cherkess, and the Adygheians. Few surviving ethnic groups are more ancient then the Adyghes. Their ancestors lived in roughly the same area of the Northwestern Caucasus for the past 6,000 or 7,000 years, since the earliest agriculture and the beginning of metal tool-making.

During much of their history, the Circassians existed independently. They had neither formal states nor towns. The main political units were clans and territorial communities similar to the ancient Greeks and Romans or the Iroquois confederation. Adyghe societies were elaborately subdivided into the ranks of princes, four degrees of nobles called *warqs,* the free commoners (*tfoquat'l, tkhwaquat'l*), and up to five different slave and serf statuses reserved for captives, aliens and conquered populations, and debtors. All Circassian communities were once ruled by princes, but in the 17th through 19th centuries the Shapsugh and Natukhay tribes along the Black Sea shore rebelled against their princes and expelled all aristocrats in a series of dramatic revolutions. These democratic Circassians were henceforth ruled by regular meetings of all citizens that usually took place in sacred groves. The meetings determined communal affairs and elected various magistrates. In wartime, Circassians elected temporary warlords and formed highly disciplined detachments of young men. All free commoners were expected to purchase arms and perfect their use. Defense of ancestral land and community was a sacred duty to Circassians, surpassed only by the obligation of the blood feud.

In the 1780s, the Russian empire expanded into the Black Sea basin, previously controlled by the Turkish Ottoman Empire. Neither the Turks nor the Russians had much interest in the poor and inaccessible mountains inhabited by fiercely independent highlanders, but the supply routes of Russian armies into the newly acquired provinces in Georgia and Armenia wound through the ridges of the Caucasus. This logistic fact made the mountain passes strategically important. The arrogance of Russian colonial governors and Cossack settlers soon provoked anti-Russian rebellions, which eventually led to a prolonged war. The outcome was the devastating Caucasian war, the longest war in Russian history that raged for more than 100 years and ended in 1864 with the defeat and ethnic cleansing of most Circassians from their homeland. The Circassian democratic societies (the Shapsighs, Natukhais, Abadzekh, and Ubykh) fought particularly fiercely. As a consequence the Ubykh, who had a distinct language, are now extinct as an ethnic group. Those who remained became Russian subjects and later Soviet citizens. Most Circassians were resettled in the Ottoman Empire, with the majority of their descendants living today in Turkey. Only 3% of the Circassian population lives in their homeland, with 97% living in exile. Contemporary researchers studying the history of the Circassians regard it as an example of genocide.

² LOCATION AND HOMELAND

The Circassians and their kin, the Ubykhs and Abkhazians (Abazas), dwelt in a triangle running along the east coast of the Black Sea northwards to the Sea of Azov, then eastward along the south shore of the Kuban River to the center of the North Caucasus, and then southwards, over the Caucasus massif, back to the homeland of the Abkhazians. The region consists of temperate steppes and rolling foothills, leading up into the snow-capped Caucasus. The region south of the mountains is semi-tropical.

The stratified and militaristic society of the Circassians prevented them from being conquered for thousands of years. In the west, the lands of Circassians were washed by the extremely treacherous waters of the Black Sea, where sailing ships could navigate only for several months during the year. The coast had few good harbors and many malarial swamps. Only the ancient Greeks were interested in founding colonies or fortresses on such a coast. The mountains rising immediately from the seacoast and extending to the east almost until the Caspian Sea provided impregnable refuge against nomadic invasions from the Eurasian steppe, from the ancient Scythians to the Mongols of Chinggis Khan.

Only modern technology changed the situation, first bringing the Russian regular armies and navy, then European settlers of primarily Slavic origin. After ethnic cleansing the Circassians were reduced to a small native minority. The formerly inhospitable sea coast, not unlike Florida, became the prized vacation spot in Russia. Many mountain slopes became ski resorts. There is still considerable wilderness in the mountains, partly incorporated in the Caucasian Nature Preserve.

Today the Circassians have autonomy within three separated small republics (Kabardino-Balkaria, Karachai-Cherkessia, and Adygheia) of the Russian Federation. The Kabardins number about 500,000, the Cherkess around 49,600, and the Adygheians about 116,000. Descendants of Circassians still live in Turkey (roughly 4.5 million, with estimates varying significantly) and Syria (35,000). Smaller groups are found in Jordan, Israel, and the United States (8,000 in and around Paterson, New Jersey).

³ LANGUAGE

The Circassian dialects (East and West) form, together with Abkhaz, Abaza, and the nearly extinct Ubykh, a separate language family, usually called North West Caucasian. These languages are unusual for their high degree of complexity. The most elaborate forms of Circassian—the Bzhedukh and Shapsigh varieties—have nearly 70 consonants and only three vowels. All forms of Circassian show a contrast between /k/ sounds and ones made farther back against the edge of the soft palate, usually represented /q/. Four kinds of s-like or sh-like sounds are made. These, as is the case with the /k/ and /q/ sounds, are further modified by rounding the lips. Sounds are made that are aspirated, much as with English /p/, /t/, /k/; voiceless unaspirated, as with Italian /p/, /t/, /k/; voiced, as with English

/b/, /d/, /g/; and with the vocal cords closed, written /p'/, /t'/, /k'/. These contrasts also occur among the /s/ and /sh/ sounds. There are many fricatives made in the back of the mouth, where /k/ and /q/ are made. Clusters of up to three consonants can occur. The vowel systems are the simplest known: a neutral vowel, such as the 'a' in sofa, a slightly open vowel, close to the /e/ in English bet, and for most languages, an /a/.

Nouns are made up from a basic set of about 200 roots through elaborate processes of compounding, so that even words such as "face" consist of a compound, /na-pa/, which means eye-nose. The verb can apply to every noun in a sentence as well as adding various sorts of geometric information and expressing the speaker's attitude toward the object of the sentence. The syntax of the sentence is elaborate. The verb is always at the end. The syntax expresses whether or not an action has been accomplished. If the action is accomplished, then the object is marked by an "absolute case" in Adyghean, which is /-r/. If it is not accomplished, then the subject carries this case but the object is marked with an "oblique case," which is /-m/. Such a system is called "ergative."

The North West Caucasian languages may be distantly related to Hattic, an ancient language of Anatolia (modern Turkey). Hattic is found only in religious rituals within Hittite documents. In the early 21st century, recent research suggested an even more distant link with the Indo-European language family.

In the 1600s an Ottoman scholar, Evliya Çelebi, was sent by the Sultan to record the languages of the Caucasus. Some of his report has survived, along with a folktale about his return. When Çelebi entered the presence of the Sultan after his long and arduous journey, the Sultan asked him what the Cherkess (Circassian) language sounded like. Çelebi took out a sack of pebbles from the sleeve of his caftan and rattled it at the Sultan. "This, O Sultan, is how Cherkess sounds."

4 FOLKLORE

The pride of the Circassians is the epic of the Narts, also called Nart sagas, which is an immense poetic narrative about the emergence, upbringing, and exploits of a warring band of mythical heroes called the Narts. The major Narts were Sosruquo, She Bardinuquo, Pataraz, and Warzameg. The chief heroine was Satanay, whose name means "mother of one hundred." She was the eternally youthful and all-knowing wife of Warzameg and mother to the mythical heroes. The Nart tradition also contains dance songs, humorous couplets, and even lullabies.

The Nart is found in varying forms among other North Caucasian peoples, some of whom, like the Ossetians, are totally unrelated to the Circassians. The more archaic Nart songs help scholars "read" pictures they find on artifacts from the excavations of Scythian and Sarmatian graves. The epic's many layers have been created over thousands of years. On the one hand, the Nart epic overlaps with Greek myths, with episodes such as the story of Prometheus. On the other hand, it includes sagas about the lives and deaths of the Circassian historical personalities known to have lived as recently as 400 years ago (such as the warrior Aidamyrkan). Several peoples have preserved and enriched the original epic in their languages, thereby making it part of their cultural heritage. As the epic has passed through different languages and epochs, unique transformations have

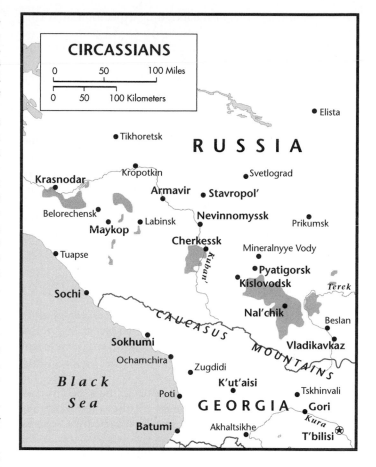

occurred to the ancient songs. The Circassian form is particularly archaic and mixed with local lore.

The Circassians also have fables reminiscent of those of Aesop. Circassian lore generally shows strong ties with that of ancient Greece, the steppe Iranians (Scythians and Sarmatians), and the Eastern Slavs (Russians, Ukrainians, and Byelorussians).

5 RELIGION

The majority of Circassians today consider themselves Muslim, although few practice any religion in daily life. Their recent ancestors were Christians. Earlier ancestors were pagans who worshipped a varied pantheon of gods, including Tlepsh, the god of the forge (akin to the Greek Hephaestus or Roman Vulcan), as well as the spirits of sacred mountains, groves, and streams. Distant ancestors several thousand years ago used to build impressive stone megalith structures, similar to those found in Celtic Europe. In the Northwestern Caucasus, the megaliths usually had the shape of houses with enormous stone tops closing the round entrance. Scholars suspect that these "houses of giants," or dolmens, were designed to hold spirits. Later, Byzantine Greeks spread Christianity among the Circassians, but the conversion was very superficial. Circassians began gradually converting to Islam after Byzantium fell to the Muslim Turks in the 15th century. Islam took root in the North Western Caucasus when it became the religion of those seeking democracy and resisting the Russian advance. As late as 1824, engravings of a Flemish trading expedition show Circassians making offerings to a cross in a sacred grove.

Religion fell into disuse during the Soviet period, but recently there has been some resurgence in reaction to the traumatic experiences of the post-Communist transition. In addition, Jama'ats (Islamic societies) have formed.

6 MAJOR HOLIDAYS

Since the fall of the Soviet Union in 1991, Circassians have begun commemorating 21 May—the day in 1864 when the last highlander warriors were defeated by the Russian troops and driven to the Black Sea. Despite being nominally Muslim, Circassians celebrate New Year's Eve (like the rest of the former Soviet peoples) with Christmas trees, gifts, and fireworks. The concept of a "World Tree," depicted as a woman, is still alive in the Nart sagas, so the Christmas tree has a natural interpretation in Circassian lore.

7 RITES OF PASSAGE

In the past, little boys and sometimes girls were often given to foster families for upbringing. This custom was called *atalyk* (a Turkic word) or /p"wer zeshtara/ (one taken as a student or fosterling) and was used to strengthen the bonds of kinship among the highlander clans and social levels, since the princes and nobles fostered their children to their servants and workers. Children were not to be returned to their biological parents until they were fully educated young adults, usually around eighteen. The moment of return was an occasion for great celebration. Most Circassians would thus have two sets of parents and brothers and sisters. Insult or murder of any relative, either biological or the foster atalyk, would be avenged by all men of both clans. Sometimes Circassians chose people of another language or even Christians, Armenians, or Russian or Ukrainian Cossacks to be their atalyks, which served to prevent conflicts. Sometimes a fosterling would continue to live with his foster parents. This was a great honor for the foster family and such a child was called a *qana* (one who stayed).

Historically, marriage was by abduction. In most cases, this abduction was a pre-arranged drama. The bride wore a leather corset with 48 knots. The corset with all its leather thongs intact had to be presented after the first nuptial night to show the groom's self-restraint and respect for his bride. Such weddings were the occasion for prolonged feasting. When a true abduction (one that had not been pre-arranged) took place, the brothers and male cousins of the abducted woman would launch a prolonged pursuit. Sometimes these ended tragically; sometimes they ended by the abducted bride's family becoming reconciled to their new son-in-law.

When a person was seriously or terminally ill, close friends or relatives would post a metal plate to the doorframe of the sick room and conduct *tschapsh*. They would come to the door, strike the metal plate loudly to frighten away any evil spirits and then enter in high spirits, making jokes, both as a sign of contempt for the same spirits and to lighten the mood of the ill person. They would then sing to the bedridden one. After death, close friends and relatives would speak to the corpse and reminisce about their lives together and how they would be reunited in the afterlife of beautiful meadows and hills.

8 INTERPERSONAL RELATIONS

Like other warrior peoples, ancestors of Circassians developed highly elaborate etiquette and a rigorous set of rules of behavior called Adyghe *khabze*, which can be translated as "the Adyghe way." The rules of khabze demanded very proud and noble conduct in every respect, from the very upright way one walks or rides a horse to civic attitudes toward community affairs. Respect of elders was paramount. For example, there is a story of a young man who lived with his foster *atalyk* parents and never saw his real father. Gravely wounded in battle, he asked to see his biological father once before he died. When the father came, the dying young Circassian stood to greet him according to the rules of khabze. The father embraced his son, making an effort not to cry, and left immediately, saying: "My son grew up truly a good Adyghe who must stand up when an elder person comes, but I cannot see him stand on his feet bleeding." Once the father left, the son dropped on the floor dead.

A husband's relations towards his wife were highly formalized in public, as was a father's signs of affection for his children. In contrast a woman's relations with her brother, or an uncle's to his nieces and nephews, were spontaneous and overtly affectionate. This peculiar pattern, which did not govern private feelings, is called the *Cherkess–Omaha* kinship system.

Formerly a young woman had her own room in which to receive suitors. The behavior of these suitors was overseen by the woman's brothers, who were responsible for maintaining her honor. Women nevertheless had wide latitude in matters of love and sex and even to this day retain considerable autonomy in these aspects of their lives.

These customs were observed in all social levels of their society.

Adyghe khabze is no longer fully observed in modern society but the rules of hospitality, protection of strangers, and respect to the elders are still very strong.

9 LIVING CONDITIONS

Traditionally, Circassians were proud but poor. They lived in long adobe houses covered with reeds or straw that could be easily expanded if one of the sons married. The main house and its satellites were enclosed within a compound. All transportation was by foot, on horseback, or oxen-driven carts with huge wheels because the roads were no more than mountain paths. The people grew corn, millet, and fruit trees, and bred sheep and horses. Their houses had chairs and cots reminiscent of those seen on Greek urns, with carpets on the floor and sometimes on the walls. The poorer people are reported to have eaten without plates, putting thick corn meal with pieces of smoked cheese or meat straight onto the low tables. Native words for dish, pot, and drinking horn indicate that such utensils were known.

This way of life changed during the 20th century. Today, Circassians live in large brick houses or in city apartments. From the 1950s to the 1970s, when the Soviet economy was rapidly growing, many Circassians seized the opportunity to get a higher education, train for a skilled job, or make a small fortune by producing cash crops and selling them in Russia. During this period, many built spacious homes and bought cars or motorcycles. Young people became interested in Western jeans, sneakers, electronics, and DVDs. With the near-collapse of Soviet economy, after 1991 most Circassians experienced severe hardship like the rest of post-Soviet society.

¹⁰ FAMILY LIFE

Traditional Adyghe domestic life was characterized by an extended family, itself embedded within larger clan and blood lineage patterns. The eldest man was the arbiter in disputes and represented the family to the public. The eldest woman ran the household with the help of her daughters and daughters-in-law.

In the past, families that were extremely poor could even exchange their children for horses or sell them into slavery. Women were especially prized in the Turkish and Arab harems of the Middle East, and more than one Turkish sultan and powerful courtier was born to an Adyghe concubine mother. Adyghe men came to dominate the Janissary army of the Ottoman sultan and, for two centuries, ruled Egypt as the Circassian Mamlukes.

Today, in Russia the bulk of domestic work in the household still is done by women. Urbanization somewhat changed the traditional gender roles.

In the diaspora Adyghe household dynamics tend to retain certain traits that set them apart from the communities among which they live. Respect for elders and freedom of women are still apparent.

¹¹ CLOTHING

Traditionally, the most prized possessions of a man were his ornamented dagger; his *fascha* (Circassian suit) or *cherkesska* (from Turkish Cherkes), a robe-like jacket with bandoleers of cartridge-like measured musket charges sewn on the breasts; and his fur hat. Men wore a sort of peaked head-cloth that wrapped around the neck. Men also wore a sort of leather sock as a riding boot. Women wore long dresses with embroidered ornaments and (at least on festive occasions) silver or gold belts and necklaces. Women had no overcoats and in cold weather rarely ventured outside their homes. Noblewomen wore elevated platform shoes. Veiling of women, however, was never a part of Adyghe tradition. Men wore felt capes called burkas in winter and sharp-domed hoods called *bashlyk*.

Modern Circassians dress like Europeans except that old men in villages occasionally wear traditional hats made of karakul (dense, curly lamb's wool), which are expensive and thus are objects of ethnic pride. Women, especially in towns, use European-style makeup and perfume. They are often very stylish.

¹² FOOD

Traditional food was very simple—corn meal, sheep's cheese, ground walnuts, fresh fruit, and dried or smoked meat. As life improved in the latter half of the 20th century, the Adyghe diet became much more varied due to numerous Russian and fellow Caucasian borrowings. The typically Adyghe dish is *shipsera pastera* (literally, gravy and pasta), in which wheat flour is slowly heated in a pan until it browns slightly; it is then added to chicken or turkey broth until it becomes dense like sour cream. Sometimes herbs (cilantro or parsley) and chopped leeks or onions are added to the broth just before the fried flour. Cooked chicken is chopped and served with this dish. This can be found in some cookbooks as "Circassian Chicken." Some Circassians use a lot of red pepper with shipsera pastera. All tend to use garlic extensively in their main dishes.

¹³ EDUCATION

Most Circassians are literate today, primarily in Russian or the language of their host nation (Turkish, Arabic, Hebrew, or English). Their native language has no traditional alphabet and is written with Russian letters plus special sign combinations for the numerous sounds not found in Russian or any other Indo-European language.

Traditionally, young men and women were taught dance. Young men were also taught horseback riding. The nobles had a special form of martial arts training. Various handicrafts were also taught, such as weapon-making, metal-working, leather-tooling, rug-making, cloth-making, and sewing.

¹⁴ CULTURAL HERITAGE

Adigha kafa (Circassians dances) are similar to the dances of all other North Caucasian peoples. The rhythm is provided by drums and wooden clackers, and the melody, once produced by national violin (*shichapshyna*) and flute (*c'amyl*), in recent times produced by either the Caucasian fiddle (*pshina*) or, more commonly, the accordion. There are both slow and incredibly fast dances, some resembling acrobatic tricks. For example, men sometimes dance with several daggers in their teeth, throwing one after another into the ground. Men dance in extremely upright postures, on their toes, with arms extended up and to the sides, facing their partners. There is also a dance where the men whirl about on their knees. Women make graceful circles with their arms, shyly looking down. In olden times a traditional round dance was conducted on horseback as a show of horsemanship.

Written literature and theater in the Circassian languages were created after 1917 as part of he Soviet policies of promoting and modernizing ethnic cultures. There is a great deal of poetry written and even some novels of high quality.

¹⁵ WORK

Until recently, with the exception of a few princes, all Circassians tilled the soil. Today, very few still farm or raise horses, but a sizable number work as high government authorities, managers, teachers, doctors, and technicians. There are also Adyghe businessmen, bankers, and traders—a previously unthinkable development because Adyghe *khabze*, the traditional code, deemed such occupations treacherous and unworthy of real men.

¹⁶ SPORTS

Equestrianism has always been very prestigious. In addition, Circassians are particularly fond of wrestling and martial arts, which is not surprising given their traditional values. Many Circassian men and women are extremely strong and athletic.

¹⁷ ENTERTAINMENT AND RECREATION

Television and movies have been very popular since they appeared several decades ago. Today, however, video is replacing them. Young men frequently visit dancing clubs and discos that exist in every village. Young women are free to attend, assuming they follow the norms of modesty. Violent confrontations between young men over female partners are commonplace and are often considered a form of entertainment in itself. Many older Adyghes are concerned, and the press and cultural figures regularly express sorrow over the loss of ancient values.

[18] FOLK ART, CRAFTS, AND HOBBIES

Folk dance groups and circles of traditional musicians and craftsmen exist with state support wherever Circassians live in large enough numbers. Promotion of folk traditions is considered a healthy remedy to the social problems of modernity and is seen as important for the survival of the culture itself.

[19] SOCIAL PROBLEMS

The sense of social and political dissatisfaction is one of the main problems of the Circassian society. Circassians are forced to live in conditions of discrimination at all levels. They fear that policies pursued by Russia will soon lead to the loss of Circassian language and assimilation. Fictitious autonomy in the three forcibly separated republics cannot compensate Circassian desire for political autonomy. Circassians are denied the right to elect leaders of their republics, who are appointed by the Russian government. Russia prevents the repatriation of descendants of Circassian exiles seeking to return to ancestral land. Even obtaining a tourist visa to visit Circassia in most cases meets a refusal. Repeated deportation of immigrants is not uncommon. Acute social dissatisfaction often forms protests and has even resulted in armed rebellion against Russia. The last uprising occurred in 2005. The situation is seriously aggravated by unemployment and underemployment and by the proximity of war zones in Chechnya and especially in Abkhazia, where many Circassian volunteers fought and then brought home their arms.

[20] GENDER ISSUES

According to statistics, the Circassian population is centered in the regions of Russia with the lowest rate of gender differences in income levels. Circassian women receive equal career opportunities and equal payment. However, in politics and in the corporate world, the percentage of the women in leadership positions is still relatively low, both in Russia and in the countries of the diaspora.

The historical and cultural traditions of Circassians held that women had a free and honorable position in society. In modern society, young women are free to choose a husband, and marriage follows the customs of modern European nations. Divorce and low birth rates are growing problems of Circassian society. For a modern Circassian woman there are no prohibited professions. Circassian women have followed many career paths, including performing arts, law, science, politics, business, and the fine arts.

[21] BIBLIOGRAPHY

Abdurakhmanov, A. M. "Totemistic Elements in Rituals and Legends about Animals." *Caucasian Perspectives* (1992): 392-405.

Arutiunov, S. A. "Yazyki narodov Kavkaza" and "Glottogenez i etnogenez na Kavkaze." In: *Narody Kavkaze: antropoligiia, linguisitika, khoziastvo,ed.* Abusheshvili M. G., S. A. Arutinunov, and B. A. Kaloev. Moscow: Institut etnologii i antropoligii, 1994.

Baddeley, John F. *The Rugged Flanks of the Caucasus.* 2 vols. Ayer, NH: 1973.

Benningsen-Broxup, Marie, ed. *The North Caucasus Barrier.* London: Hurst and Co., 1992.

Colarusso, John. Kabardian (East Circassian). Munich: LINCOM-Europa, 2006.

———. *Nart Sagas from the Caucasus, Myths and Legends from the Circassians, Abazas, Abkhaz, and Ubykhs.* Princeton: Princeton University Press, 2002.

———. "Abkhazia." *Central Asian Survey* (1995): 75–96.

———. "Chechnya: the War without Winners." *Current History* 94 (October 1995): 329–36.

———. "The Woman of the Myths: the Satanaya Cycle." *The Annual of the Society for the Study of Caucasia* 2 (1989): 3–11.

Comrie, Bernard. *The Languages of the Soviet Union.* Cambridge University Press, 1981.

Edwards, Mike. "The Fractured Caucasus." *National Geographic* 189, (February 1996): 126–31.

Goldenberg, Suzanne. *Pride of Small Nations.* London: Zed Books, 1994.

Grant, Bruce and Lale Yalçin Heckmann, ed. *Caucasus Paradigms. Halle Studies in the Anthropology of Eurasia,* vol. 13. Berlin: Lit Verlag Dr. W. Hopf, 2007.

Henze, Paul B. *The North Caucasus: Russia's Long Struggle to Subdue the Circassians.* Santa Monica, CA: Rand Corporation, 1990.

Hewitt, B. George, ed. *The Northwestern Caucasian Languages.* Delmar, NY: Caravan Books, 1989.

Iskander, Fazil. *Sandro of Chegem.* New York: Random House, 1983.

———. *The Gospel According to Chegem.* New York: Random House, 1984.

King, Charles. *The Ghost of Freedom, a History of the Caucasus.* Oxford: Oxford University Press, 2008.

Kumakhov, M. A. ed. *Adygskaja (Cherkesskaja) Énciklopedija.* Moscow: The Akbashev Foundation, 2006.

Maier, Frith. *Trekking in Russia and Central Asia.* Seattle, WA: The Mountaineers, 1994.

Wixman, Ronald. *Language Aspects of Ethnic Patterns and Processes in the North Caucasus.* Chicago: Department of Geography, University of Chicago, 1980.

———. *The Peoples of the USSR.* Armonk, NY: M. E. Sharpe, 1984.

Yagan, Murat. *I Come from Behind Kaf Mountain.* Putney, VT: Threshold Books, 1984.

—revised by J. Colarusso and F. Tlisova

CROATS

LOCATION: Croatia
POPULATION: 4,492,000 (est. 2008)
LANGUAGE: Croatian
RELIGION: Roman Catholic vast majority; Eastern Orthodox, Muslim

¹ INTRODUCTION

The Croats are a people with a long and rich history who today live in their own independent, newly democratic country—Croatia, a land whose historical experience was heavily determined by its geographic location. Croatia has been the borderland between the Western Roman Empire and the Byzantine Empire, the Roman Catholic and Eastern Orthodox spheres of influence, the Ottoman Empire and Western Europe, and the Communist bloc countries and free Europe. Croatia is culturally and geographically in Central Europe but has bridged the Eastern and Western worlds throughout its history. This position as a borderland has had significant effects on Croatia's history and development.

In the 7th century AD, the Croats settled the regions of Dalmatia (a former Roman province on the coast of the Adriatic Sea), Pannonia (northern and northeastern Croatia), and Istria, as well as parts of today's Bosnia and Herzegovina, Montenegro, and southern Hungary. Local Croat lords began to emerge in the 9th century to lay the foundations for the medieval state. The first Croat king, Tomislav, assumed the title in AD 925. The Croats were Christianized in the early Middle Ages, entering the Roman Catholic community and the Western European cultural sphere from the beginning of their history.

The Croatian crown was incorporated into the Hungarian dynasty in 1102, thereby increasing Hungarian influence in the northern Croat provinces. In the early 1400s, the Dalmatian cities became part of Venice, a rising city-state and sea power with whom the Croat kings had long clashed. The rest of Croatia was governed under the feudal system, the standard in Western Europe at the time, by joint Croat-Hungarian kings and various powerful lords.

Following a century of invasions into southeastern Europe by the Ottoman Turks, the Croat nobles and knights fought an epic battle at Sisak in 1493. The "flower of Croat chivalry" fell on the battlefield, and a long period of Turkish ascendancy in this part of the world began. Croatia, unlike Serbia or Bosnia, was never entirely conquered.

In 1527, following another great Turkish military victory over the Hungarians the previous year, the Croat noblemen elected Ferdinand Habsburg of Austria as their new king. In the 16th century, Croatia was progressively reduced in size by Ottoman expansion. Croatia's political center was shifted to Zagreb, in the north, from the old Croat heartland in coastal Dalmatia. The visible symbols of Croatia's continued autonomy lay in the assembly of nobles—the Sabor—and the office of the Ban (the royal governor). From this time onward, foreign imperial powers had a decisive influence on Croat affairs.

The famous Croatian Military Border (Krajina) was established by Austria to hold the line against the Turks in the 16th and 17th centuries. Various Croat frontier regions, devastated by constant wars, were repopulated with Eastern Orthodox settlers from the Balkans who served as colonists. This was the origin of the Serb community in Croatia. As the Ottoman Empire began to recede in the late 19th century, these areas reunited with the rest of Croatia.

Croatia became known as the "remnants of the remnants of the once-great kingdom" and as a "bulwark of Christendom" for preventing further advances by the Muslim Turks into Christian Europe.

During the 17th century, the present-day borders of Croatia were largely carved out in battles with the Turks. But, the power of the Croat aristocracy declined steadily in the face of Austrian military control over the border. As a result of this situation, together with Venetian dominance in Dalmatia and Hungarian demands on the rest of the country, Croatia's independence was reduced in the 18th century. A final imperial interlude came during the era of Napoleon. Dalmatia, Istria, and parts of northern Croatia and Slovenia entered the French empire from 1809 to 1813 as the Illyrian Provinces (finally reverting to Austrian rule in 1815).

The 19th century saw the development of modern Croatian nationalism in the various attempts by the Croats to reassert control over their own destiny. In the 1830s and 1840s, a Croat movement arose in opposition to rising Hungarian and German nationalism. The adherents of the Croat National Revival sought to unify the diverse Croat lands both culturally (through a standardized written language) and politically (by joining the divided provinces into one kingdom). The Illyrian Movement sounded the main themes of 19th-century Croatian history: linguistic unity with the Serbs and political unity with all South Slavs.

Croatia remained split into several distinct regions, even within the reformed Austro-Hungarian monarchy after 1867. As a result, many politicians desired Croat independence from Vienna and Budapest and agitated for an independent Croatia, rejecting ideas of South Slavic community or "Yugoslavism." Friction between Croat individuality and South Slavic unity has been another key feature of modern political history in Croatia.

Dissatisfaction with the situation in Austria-Hungary increased steadily in the three decades before 1914. The emerging idea of Yugoslav unity outside the Habsburg empire was gaining momentum, and some hoped to unite the South Slavs in one state and defend their territory from stronger, non-Slavic foreign powers like Austria, Hungary, and Italy.

At the end of World War I in 1918, as the Austro-Hungarian monarchy finally collapsed, the Croatian provinces proclaimed unity and independence and (along with Slovenia, Bosnia-Herzegovina, and Vojvodina) joined the new Kingdom of Serbs, Croats, and Slovenes. Ironically, while all the Croat lands were finally united, the new South Slavic union ruled by the Serbian Karađorđević dynasty was never democratically approved or validated by the Croatian people.

In fact, the Croat political parties, soon dominated by Stjepan Radić's Croat Peasant Party, rejected the new order and remained opposed to the unfair and centralizing policies of the Serbian-dominated government. The constitution of 1921—the centralist foundation of the new royal regime—was adopted over the objections of the Croats and others. In 1928, Radić was killed on the floor of parliament in Belgrade by a Montenegrin deputy of the ruling party. Using this event as a pretext, King Aleksandar instituted a harsh dictatorship in 1929. He tried to

CROATS

0   100   200   300 Miles

0   100   200   300 Kilometers

At the end of World War II in 1945, the partisans, with Allied and Soviet support, emerged victorious. Their overall leader was Josip Broz Tito, who also became the postwar dictator of Yugoslavia (until his death in 1980). Croatia became a republic in a new, federated Yugoslavia. All power was in Communist hands and dissent was not tolerated. The Yugoslav political and economic power structure was at first centralized in Belgrade. The ruling Communist regime was particularly harsh on Croat opponents who desired more freedom for the people of Croatia. In 1971, Tito purged or imprisoned much of the liberal Croat Communist Party leadership and its supporters due to their excessive national (i.e. non-Yugoslav) loyalty. A new constitution in 1974 brought decentralization and inefficiency.

Like the first, monarchist Yugoslavia (1918–1941), the second, Communist Yugoslavia (1945–1991) was also founded on force and kept alive by threats of force. Neither state had genuine democratic legitimacy or achieved widespread popular support in Croatia. Many Croatians believed that Communist Yugoslavia was exploiting Croatia's economic and natural wealth while reducing the Croats to second-class citizens in their own country. It came as little surprise, then, that when Croatia's first free elections in some 50 years were held in 1990, the Communists lost. When a referendum on independence was held in 1991, the vast majority of Croats (97%) voted for independence from Yugoslavia.

After centuries of foreign domination and unrepresentative rule, the Croats were finally given a historic opportunity to decide their fate for themselves. Croatia's independence (declared in June 1991) was recognized by the world beginning in January 1992.

Unfortunately, Croatia's transition to democracy and independence from Communist Yugoslavia was not accomplished peacefully. The Yugoslav central Communist government in Belgrade and the Yugoslav People's Army (JNA), both overwhelmingly controlled by the Serbs, were adamantly opposed to the secession of Croatia (and Slovenia) from Yugoslavia. This contributed to the outbreak of hostilities in 1990–91, as the Serb minority in certain parts of Croatia, supported by the Yugoslav government and the JNA, launched a rebellion against the democratically elected government of Croatia. By the time United Nations peacekeepers became involved in 1992, almost 30% of Croatia had been conquered and occupied by the Serb forces, with dozens of Croatian cities and towns damaged or destroyed, 20,000 people killed, and 250,000 people forced from their homes. Fighting continued off and on until August 1995, when the Croatian army and government regained control over most of the rebel Serb occupied territory.

Reintegration of the country and privatization went swiftly, beginning under the Catholic-dominated nationalist government of Dr. Franjo Tuđman. Since his death in 1999 power has shifted from right to left to right again in a multiparty system of changing coalitions. The country appears united in the drive to meet the requirements to become part of the European Union. Croatia applied for EU membership in 2003 and is likely to become a full member in 2010.

² LOCATION AND HOMELAND

Croatia had an estimated population of 4,492,000 in 2008 living in the country, comparable to the population of Alabama. They included 89.6% ethnic Croats, 4.5% Serbs, and a mix of small groups, such as Hungarians, Italians, Slovenes, Bosniaks,

erase long-standing national differences by force and changed the official name of the state to Yugoslavia. There was stubborn resistance to this policy in Croatia, where integral Yugoslavism was seen as a mere cover for the old policy of Serbian expansion. In short, Serbia was considered a threatening foreign power trying to subordinate and assimilate Croatia.

By 1939, the government of the Yugoslav prince and the new Croat leader, Vladko Maček, agreed on a formula for Croatia's autonomy within Yugoslavia. However, this Croat–Serb Agreement was a flawed and short-lived solution. The new Banate of Croatia was opposed by the Communists, by right-wingers, and by influential circles in Serbia.

When Germany and Italy invaded Yugoslavia in April 1941, the country quickly fell apart. An Independent State of Croatia was proclaimed by anti-Yugoslav nationalists (Ustasha) in Zagreb in collusion with German agents. Maček went into seclusion and his party—the most popular and powerful in Croatia—was banned. Most Croats were not sorry to see the end of the repressive royal Yugoslavia, but when Croatia's wartime rulers committed many crimes of their own, a vigorous resistance movement against the fascist order arose. During World War II, the pro-Axis government in Croatia was opposed by pro-Allied insurgent forces called partisans, who were directed by the Communist Party of Yugoslavia. The Communist Partisans achieved significant support from Croats in Dalmatia, much of which was annexed by Italy in 1941, and from Croatian Serbs.

and Roma. Nearly as many ethnic Croatians may live outside the country as in it.

Croatia has experienced extensive demographic changes since 1991. After Croatia declared independence from Yugoslavia in June of 1991, armed local Serb rebels, supported by the Yugoslav Army, forcibly expelled hundreds of thousands of Croats and other non-Serb minorities from their homes and set up two Serb-run regions within Croatia's boundaries. In 1995, as Croatia reclaimed most of the territory occupied by Serb forces, tens of thousands of Serbs left Croatia to trek to Serbia, instigated by their own defeated leadership and fearing retaliation.

All citizens of Croatia are guaranteed extensive personal and civil rights under the constitution of 1990, which was amended in 2001. Minorities in Croatia have also been granted extensive rights to cultural and linguistic autonomy, in addition to all rights of every Croatian citizen.

Croatia is located in southeastern Europe, across the Adriatic Sea from Italy. It is shaped like a boomerang, bordered on the north by Hungary and Slovenia, on the south by Bosnia and Herzegovina with the southern tip touching Montenegro, on the east by the Vojvodina province of Serbia, and on the west by the Adriatic Sea.

Croatia has an area of 56,538 sq km (21,829 sq mi), which is about the size of West Virginia. Croatia's Adriatic coastline is 1,778 km (1,100 mi) long and dotted with over 1,000 islands, which add another 4,058 km (2,522 mi) of coast.

Croatia's capital is Zagreb, located in northern Croatia, with a metropolitan area population of over one million. Other major cities are Split (metropolitan area over 200,000) in Dalmatia; Rijeka (ca. 150,000), a major port at the very north end of the Adriatic Sea; and Osijek (over 100,000) in Slavonia.

Croatia's natural landscape varies widely from region to region. Rolling hills and fertile plains characterize the Pannonian region in north/northeastern Croatia. Rugged mountains stretch straight into the Adriatic Sea in the Croatian coastal region, with a mountainous hinterland whose land is rocky and less fertile. The Dinaric Alps region, in northwestern Croatia, is mountainous and heavily wooded.

Croatia's climate is Mediterranean and very mild along the coast and more continental and harsh in the interior. Along the Adriatic Coast, summers are sunny, dry and warm, and winters are mild and similar to those of southern California. In the interior, there are hot summers, cold winters, and four very distinct seasons, as in the U.S. Middle Atlantic.

The homeland of the Croats has in some historical periods also included areas of today's Bosnia and Herzegovina. Approximately 750,000 Croats lived in Bosnia and Herzegovina before the recent war there. Estimates of the number of Croats living outside Croatia range from 2.5 to 4 million. Most emigration occurred in the last 150 years, although Croats have been leaving their ancestral lands since the Turkish invasions (1400–1800), for both political and economic reasons. Countries with large numbers of Croats include the United States, Germany, Australia, Canada, and Argentina. The Burgenland Croats, a particularly tenacious community of Croats, have lived in eastern Austria for 500 years and still preserve their language. Interestingly, more people are now immigrating into Croatia than are leaving.

³ LANGUAGE

The Croats speak Croatian, a South Slavic language of the Indo-European family. Croatian is written in the Latin alphabet. It has 30 letters, each of which is pronounced and has an independent sound. There are several regional dialects. Many words in the Croatian language reflect the foreign cultural influences on Croatia through the centuries. The Croatian language has German (*šrafciger,* "screwdriver"), Hungarian (*čizme,* "boots"), Italian (*pršut,* "prosciutto;" *lancun,* "bedsheet") and Turkish (*šećer,* "sugar;" *jastuk,* "pillow") words, but language traditionalists seek to eliminate as many foreign words as possible.

Common Croatian words include *dobar dan* (good day), *kako ste?* (how are you?), *dobro* (well), and *hvala* (thank you).

⁴ FOLKLORE

Croatia's traditional folk culture is enormously wealthy and diverse because of the many different cultural influences to which the different regions of Croatia were exposed at various points in history. The cultures that influenced Croatian folk culture through the centuries are Hungarian, Austrian, Venetian, Balkan, ancient Croatian, ancient Mediterranean, and Turkish. The Croats borrowed elements from these cultural influences and incorporated them into their own uniquely Croatian folk traditions. Croatian traditional folk culture is as varied as that of any other region of the same size in Europe.

Traditional Croatian folk culture is manifested in dances, songs, holiday traditions, folk tales, and other forms.

⁵ RELIGION

The dominant religious tradition of the Croats has been Roman Catholicism since the early 7th century, when the Croats converted to Christianity. The Croats have steadfastly maintained their religion for 13 centuries, and Catholic tradition and values remain one of the defining factors of Croatian national and cultural identity.

Minority religions among the Croats include Eastern Orthodoxy. A smaller percentage of people in Croatia practice Islam. Some claim no religion.

Religion in Croatia during the Communist period (1945–1991) was relegated to the private sphere. Since the establishment of democracy in Croatia, religious freedom is guaranteed under the Croatian constitution, but the Catholic church is often able to dominate.

⁶ MAJOR HOLIDAYS

Croatia today has a number of official national holidays. Many of these are associated with Catholic holy days and traditions. These include Epiphany (January 6), Easter Monday, Corpus Christi on a Thursday typically in May, the Feast of the Assumption of Mary (August 15), All Saints' Day (November 1), and Christmas (December 25-26).

Other non-working holidays are New Year's Day, International Labor Day on May 1, Anti-Fascist Struggle Day on June 22, Croatian National Day on May 25, Victory and Thanksgiving Day on August 5, and Independence Day on October 8. In addition, Jews are excused from work or school to celebrate Yom Kippur and Rosh Hashanah, Muslims to celebrate Ramadan Bairam and Kurban Bairam, and Orthodox Christians to celebrate Christmas on January 7.

Most of the notable holiday customs are associated with the church holidays. The day before the start of Lent (known as fat Tuesday or Mardi Gras to some) is celebrated by dressing in costumes and making special doughnuts. Easter is celebrated by coloring and sharing eggs, preparing and blessing food baskets, and attending church services. On All Saints' Day (November 1), people visit cemeteries, light candles and place chrysanthemums on the graves in remembrance of their deceased loved ones. On the eve of St. Nicholas Day, December 6, children leave their shoes out for St. Nicholas to leave them gifts. The family gets together on Christmas Eve to decorate the Christmas tree and attend midnight Mass. Christmas day is celebrated with family by exchanging presents and holiday greetings.

7 RITES OF PASSAGE

Traditional rites of passage have declined in modern times and are not distinctive in Croatian society today. Three main rites of passage still observed are baptism, marriage, and death.

The birth of a child is observed, among Christians, through the rite of baptism, where a child is welcomed into the church through the pouring of water and symbolic acceptance of the faith through the godparents. Newborns generally receive gifts of gold jewelry on this occasion.

Marriage is conducted in city hall and/or in church, usually followed by a reception. Weddings in small towns and rural areas can be large affairs with the whole village attending, while urban weddings tend to be smaller. A wedding is often an all-day family affair. Wedding guests ride through the streets in a procession of decorated cars, honking horns and waving.

Like birth, death is usually marked with Roman Catholic rituals, including a funeral mass, graveside service, the laying of flowers, and the marking of grave sites with headstones. The wake takes place just hours before the burial in a facility on the cemetery grounds, and the people walk in procession behind the casket to the grave. After the funeral, family and friends attend a lunch called *karmine*. Death notices appear in newspapers but are also posted on trees and poles around the neighborhood.

High school graduation is a major milestone. The *maturalni ples* (senior prom) is a major event. There is also the graduation trip, which is a group trip, often abroad.

8 INTERPERSONAL RELATIONS

The Croats are traditionally a warm, friendly, open, and sociable people who value family and friendships and like to make outsiders feel welcome. Croats greet one another openly and, in familiar circumstances, affectionately. Common greetings include saying good day, shaking hands, and hugging and kissing each other once on each cheek. Displays of affection, such as holding hands and modest kissing, are very acceptable in public.

The Croatian lifestyle lends itself to a great deal of social interaction. People generally walk or use public transportation, work in their gardens, sit on their balconies, shop daily in neighborhood stores, and frequent cafes. Croats get to know their neighbors well and have many friends and acquaintances.

Croats pride themselves on their hospitality, and food and drink are immediately offered when one enters a Croatian home. It is considered impolite and can offend the hosts if the offer of food or drink is declined.

A major facet of interpersonal relations is the linguistic distinction between the formal *vi* and familiar *ti*, meaning you. Elders, professional peers, and professors are examples of groups one would address using the formal terms. Peers, friends, and family are usually addressed in the familiar.

Dating in Croatia today is similar to dating in the U.S., usually beginning informally in high school. Young men and women choose whom to date and whom to marry.

9 LIVING CONDITIONS

The Croatian health care system is relatively well developed. Health care is provided by the government, and all citizens are entitled to it. Because of the quality and accessibility of health care, people in Croatia have a high life expectancy: 79.3 years for women and 72.5 years for men.

Croatian consumers have access to and purchase a wide variety of goods and services from small retailers, specialty stores and boutiques, department stores, and open-air markets. Although consumer prices are high in relation to salaries, the selection is large. Just about anything that is available in the United States can be purchased in Croatia.

Croats live in permanent dwellings including single-family homes, multi-family homes, and apartments. The interior layout of an average Croatian home includes separate rooms for a kitchen (usually with eating area), a bathroom or shower, a toilet, a living room, and bedrooms. In most Croatian homes, regardless of location and the economic status of the owners, one will find most of the amenities considered basic by an average American family. This includes television sets, refrigerators, stoves, telephones, washing machines, stereo systems, VCRs, and DVD players. In many homes one can find personal computers, satellite dishes, and video game systems. Cell phones are ubiquitous.

Many Croatian families own cars, but mass transportation is the most popular and efficient mode of travel in Croatia. Electric trams and extensive bus networks transport people within cities. Railroads and buses also transport people throughout the country and into other European destinations. Air transportation is also available. The driving age in Croatia is 18, and cars generally have manual transmission.

10 FAMILY LIFE

Croats are very family oriented. The basic Croatian family unit is the nuclear family of parents and children living in one home. It is not uncommon for extended families of parents, children, and grandparents to share a dwelling. Aunts, uncles, and cousins, godparents, a couple's best man and maid of honor, and longtime family friends are also considered as family and interact with each other often for family events, holidays, and informal visiting.

Family activities are very important. Weekends are considered family time, when families have a special dinner together, take strolls in town, go out for coffee, and visit friends and family. Families often vacation together on the Adriatic Coast during the summer, often in their own summer home, which may be the ancestral home.

Women have a very important role in Croatian society and generally have the same opportunities as men. It is common for women to work, but they are also the pillars of the home.

Croatians at Ban Jelacic square in Zagreb, Croatia. Weekends are considered family time, when families have a special lunch together, take strolls in town, go for coffee, and visit friends and family. (Embassy of the Republic of Croatia)

Croatian social policy recognizes the importance of this dual role of women. For example, women who work receive at least half a year paid maternity leave and six more months at partial pay, with a guaranteed job when they return.

The Croatian birth rate mirrors the general trend in developed countries: it has been declining in recent decades. It is common to have one to two children, and families with three or more children are considered large today. Marriage is the overwhelming lifestyle choice in Croatian society, and a mutually exclusive, monogamous relationship is the standard.

The Croatian family structure is still rather patriarchal. The man is considered head of the household, although the woman tends to have more household responsibility.

11 CLOTHING

Croats today wear the same types of clothing found everywhere in the developed world. The styles and norms, especially for the younger generations, are very contemporary and parallel those in Croatia's trendsetting neighbor, Italy. U.S. urban styles are also popular, especially Levi's jeans and Nike tennis shoes. Young people are very particular about their appearance and dress stylishly. This is true for all income levels in both rural and urban settings and in all regions.

One would be hard pressed today to find evidence of the rich traditional folk dress of Croatia's recent past. Remaining fragments of traditional dress can be found mostly among the older population as manifested by women wearing a headscarf or traditional hairstyle.

12 FOOD

Croatian food and cooking are as diverse as Croatia's landscape and differ according to region. Regional cooking is shaped by the available food in each region, as well as by tradition and outside influences.

Adriatic cuisine is light and incorporates the bounties of the sea and sun, such as fish, squid, pasta, and fresh fruit and vegetables. The kitchen of the northeastern regions (Danubian) is hearty and spicy, characterized by pork dishes, smoked meats, stews and pickled vegetables, and rich desserts. The Alpine region boasts food that is rich and mild, such as fried veal, poultry, potatoes, and green vegetables. Grilling is very common, and a favorite is *ćevapčići*, small spicy sausages made from ground meat.

Some traditional Croatian dishes are *sarma* (stuffed cabbage), *bakalar* (cod), *purica i mlinci* (turkey and special pasta), *pašticada* (a marinated beef dish), and *Zagrebački odrezak* (stuffed veal schnitzel). Soup is very common and is eaten with almost every main meal and throughout the year. Special traditional breads are made for celebrations, such as Easter. Fancy, rich pastries and cakes are also important to the Croatian kitchen.

Croation childen attend class in the central Bosnian village of Gornji. Walls separate Croats and Muslims at the school.
(AFP/Getty Images)

Croats eat three to four meals a day. Breakfast is very important and may include bread, spreads, and yogurt. It is also common to eat *marenda or gablec,* a light snack at mid-morning, commonly fruit or baked goods. Dinner, usually between 2:00 pm and 4:00 pm, is the main meal of the day and can include soup, salad, and an entree. Supper is eaten in the late evening and is small and light.

Sunday dinner is the most important meal of the week. It is usually earlier, between noon and 1:00 pm, and more elaborate than weekday dinner. It is the big family meal, and guests are often invited.

¹³ EDUCATION

Croatia possesses an excellent system of education that provides universal public education for all its children. The quality of education is generally uniform throughout the country, so that students in smaller urban and rural communities receive the same quality of instruction as their urban counterparts. This excellence in education has produced an adult literacy rate of 98.7% among the Croatian population.

The curriculum and courses are rigorous, and students must study hard to pass. Students in elementary (and secondary) school typically take more than twelve classes, including chemistry, history, math, physics, a foreign language, and Croatian language and literature. Essentially, Croatian students must choose their general career path in eighth grade, when they choose a high school. The high school system is organized into two categories: trade schools and college preparatory *(gimnazija).* Trade schools prepare students for careers ranging from nursing to machining to construction to tourism, while the college preparatory program prepares students for university study.

In addition to polytechnic schools, Croatia has universities in Zagreb (established in 1669), Split, Rijeka, and Osijek, Zadar, Dubrovnik, and Pula.

Legally, only elementary school is compulsory, but most Croats today finish secondary school.

Croatia is in the process of changing its education to conform to the Bologna Process, so that standards will be compatible with those of the rest of Europe.

14 CULTURAL HERITAGE

The Croats have a deep and rich cultural heritage that reflects Croatia's Western and Central European traditions as well as the diverse history of its regions. The Croatian cultural heritage is revealed in art, music, theater, sciences, architecture, literature, and the academic tradition. Remnants of ancient Rome found in Croatia include Emperor Diocletian's Palace in Split, the ruins of Salona near Split, and the Roman amphitheater in Pula. Churches in Dalmatia reflect beautiful and unique Gothic and Romanesque architecture and design, beautifully represented in Poreč, Trogir, Zadar, and Šibenik. Dubrovnik, a remarkably preserved medieval walled city, has been called the Jewel of the Adriatic. Dubrovnik served as the intellectual and cultural center for the Croats for centuries.

15 WORK

Both men and women in Croatia work and contribute to the support of their families. Croatia has about 1.8 million people in its work force. In 2008, the average monthly take-home salary in Croatia was about US$1,050. The kuna is the Croatian currency (approximately 4.9 kuna per US$1 as of 2008).

Social policy and tradition in Croatia are quite generous to the average worker. Croatian workers receive at least four weeks of vacation per year, in addition to national holidays. Employee benefits include universal health insurance, generous sick leave, accumulating seniority and pension benefits regardless of change of employers, maternity, paternity and family leaves, and bonuses for dependents. It is also common for employers to provide subsidized meals, transportation, and vacation packages for employees.

Students sometimes work, but the jobs are often seasonal and temporary. Typical jobs for young people are waiting tables in cafes or working in tourism during the summer. The types of jobs traditionally held by young people in America, such as retail, restaurant, and clerical work, are usually held by people with families to support.

Retirement age varies and is based on age and length of employment. Most Croatians can retire by 64. The pension system recently was changed to one partly based on fixed contributions to mandatory private funds.

16 SPORTS

Sports are extremely popular in Croatia. Team sports like soccer, basketball, volleyball, handball, and water polo are very popular, as are tennis, bocce, swimming, hiking, running, and aerobics. The hands-down winner for most popular sport is soccer, called *nogomet*.

Soccer is also the most popular spectator sport in Croatia, with professional and amateur teams throughout the country. The sport has a long tradition that has resulted in the formation of intense team loyalties and the erection of numerous stadiums. Watching soccer matches is a sport in itself, but fan violence is a problem. Basketball is continually gaining popularity as well.

In proportion to its population, Croatia has produced an extraordinary number of world-class athletes across a wide range of sports. Today, some of the most famous Croatian sports stars are Goran Ivanišević and Iva Majoli in tennis, Toni Kukoč of the Chicago Bulls, Dino Rađa of the Boston Celtics, and the late Dražen Petrović of the New Jersey Nets in basketball.

17 ENTERTAINMENT AND RECREATION

Most Croats, especially young people, relax and socialize in the cafes that line the main streets of large cities and small towns alike. Even residential neighborhoods have numerous cafes. In the summer, outdoor tables are filled, and the streets are filled with people and activity.

Croats also like to go to the movies. The most popular movies are the major American productions that appear in theaters in Croatia quite soon after their release in the United States. Croatian theaters also regularly offer domestic and international films as well. Movies are in their original languages with subtitles in Croatian, occasionally dubbed.

Theater, including musicals, dramas, and comedies, is also very popular in Croatia; most cities boast their own theater. Also popular are classical music concerts, ballets, and modern dance performances.

Every Croatian household, from the largest urban center to the remotest village, possesses a television. Croatia has national state-sponsored channels, private networks, and local stations. Croatian television offers domestic programming for the whole family, such as children's educational shows, comedy series, documentaries, and specialty shows. Croatian television also regularly broadcasts American and other foreign shows and movies, including Desperate Housewives and Grey's Anatomy.

In addition, many homes have satellite dishes that can receive CNN, MTV, the Cartoon Channel, ESPN, British Sky Movies, and just about anything else available to the international satellite network.

American popular culture influences countries throughout the world through music, movies, television, and MTV, and Croatia is no exception. Croatian popular culture resembles American pop culture, with a bit of a European twist. Young Croats today are hip. Fashions are a sophisticated, cosmopolitan mix. Techno, rap, and international and domestic pop music are popular.

Croatia has a strong popular music tradition of its own and has dozens of music festivals in all the larger cities including Split, Vinkovci, Zagreb, and Pula. Croatia also has a number of magazines devoted to pop culture, and television programs featuring music videos and fashion.

Young Croats spend a great deal of their free time going out. Streets are very safe, even after dark. The most popular hangouts are cafes, but discos (nightclubs) are also very popular and often stay open all night on the weekends.

18 FOLK ART, CRAFTS, AND HOBBIES

Traditional Croatian crafts include folk dress and footwear, woven household textiles, musical instruments, lace, jewelry, and other ornaments. There is also a strong tradition of Croatian folk song and dance. Regions are highly differentiated. The inland plains are in the cultural sphere of neighboring Hungary, while the mountains of the northwest are more like Slovenia. The coast has been influenced by Italy across the Adriatic, while the rugged Dinaric Mountains that rise up from the coast preserve archaic Balkan features. One distinctively Croatian art form is filigree jewelry. Earrings are found in medieval graves that are very similar in design to ones that craftspeople make today.

[19] SOCIAL PROBLEMS

The most significant social problems in Croatia today are still related to the 1991 warfare between the Croats and the Serbs, who were joined by an insurgent Serbian minority in Croatia. The war left 16,000 Croats dead, over 5,000 still unaccounted for, 25,000 permanently disabled, and approximately 200,000 displaced from their homes. Exacerbating this situation is the fact that Croatia is in the process of transforming itself from a Communist country to a democracy and establishing a free-market economy.

Croatia's social safety net is stretched very thin in providing care and services to all the war victims and their families. In addition, the war caused over $15 billion in material damage. Reconstruction is ongoing.

In addition to the extensive costs of reconstruction, Croatia is also denationalizing government-owned factories and businesses and restructuring the economy. An initially high unemployment rate has in 2008 come down to 12.4%. The cost of living is high, while the average salary is approximately $12,700 per year, net, and people are dissatisfied and often pessimistic.

Croatia is currently experiencing increased drug use and abuse among its young people. Areas that are most vulnerable are those on the Adriatic coast, because of the ease with which drugs can be brought in by sea, and larger urban areas.

[20] GENDER ISSUES

Patriarchy, under communism up to 1991, persisted but was not officially encouraged. With the transition to capitalism and a multiparty system, patriarchy reasserted itself as an ideology, attempting to curtail women's reproductive rights and push women back into the home. A smaller proportion of women are employed now than 20 years ago. Their salaries are not on par with those of men. Women suffer discrimination in employment and are disproportionately represented among the unemployed. A newly vociferous Catholic Church played a big role in this. Female members of parliament declined from 17% to 4.8%. Beginning in 1995, the government began to put principles of gender equality back on paper. In 2004 the Office of Ombudsperson for Sex Equality and the Government Office for Sex Equality became operational. However, it is still women who do the housework and caregiving. Schools that are still dominated by conservative and clerical voices are a major part of the problem. Nevertheless, women are reasserting their rights through nongovernmental organizations. The Center for Women's Studies has been operating in Zagreb since 1995. Domestic violence has been recognized as an issue, although there is but one inadequate shelter, and police have yet to learn to take it seriously.

Annual gay pride events have taken place in Zagreb since 2002.

[21] BIBLIOGRAPHY

Cuvalo, Ante. *The Croatian National Movement, 1966–1972.* New York: Columbia University Press, 1990.

Gazi, Stephen. *A History of Croatia.* New York: Philosophical Library, 1973.

Glenny, Michael. *The Fall of Yugoslavia: The Third Balkan War.* New York: Penguin, 1992.

Guldescu, Stanko. *The Croatian-Slavonian Kingdom, 1526–1792.* The Hague: Mouton, 1970.

Omrcanin, Ivo. *Diplomatic and Political History of Croatia.* Philadelphia: Dorrance, 1972.

Republic of Croatia. Central Bureau of Statistics. *Statistical Information 2008.* Zagreb: Central Bureau of Statistics of the Republic of Croatia, 2008.

Silber, Laura, and Allan Little. *Yugoslavia: Death of a Nation.* New York: TV Books, 1996.

Stellaerts, Robert, and Jeannine Laurens. *Historical Dictionary of the Republic of Croatia.* Metuchen, NJ: Scarecrow Press, 1997.

Tanner, Marcus. *Croatia: A Nation Forged in War.* New Haven: Yale University Press, 1997.

United Nations. Commission on the Status of Women. Statement submitted by Sanja Sarnavka to 49th session, 28 February–11 March 200, http://www.un.org/womenwatch/daw/Review/documents/panel-1/sarnavka_formatted.pdf.

—revised by T. Alt and W. Browne

CZECHS

LOCATION: Czech Republic
POPULATION: 10.2 million
LANGUAGE: Czech
RELIGION: Christianity (Roman Catholic and Protestant)

¹ INTRODUCTION

The Czech Republic (formerly known as Czechoslovakia) is a young nation: On 1 January 1993, it ended its union with Slovakia after more than three-quarters of a century of relatively calm coexistence.

The area now known as the Czech Republic has been inhabited since the earliest settlement of Europe. The first known settlers of the region were the Boii, a Celtic people from whom the name Bohemia is derived; they were followed by the Germanic Marcomanni tribe at the beginning of the Christian era. In the 5th to 7th centuries, Slavs began to settle in the region, and in the 9th century, Christianity was embraced by its inhabitants. During this period, the kingdom of Bohemia was founded. It reached its political and cultural height during the 14th century under King Charles I. The capital of the kingdom was Prague, where Charles constructed many buildings, including the Hradcany Castle, and, in 1348, founded Charles University, the first university in Central Europe.

During Charles's reign, the religious reformer Jan Hus (1369–1415) attacked the authority of the Roman Catholic Church and the privileged position of the Germans in Bohemia, who had been immigrating to the country since the 11th century. Hus was eventually excommunicated for his views. Conditions in the region worsened when the Roman Catholic Habsburg dynasty of Austria ascended to the Bohemian throne in 1526. The Czechs rebelled against the Habsburgs but were defeated in 1620. Over the next three centuries, Bohemia was reduced to a mere province of the Habsburg Empire.

The Slovaks had no independent state of their own before 1918, having been absorbed by the Hungarians as early as the 10th century. During World War I, Czech and Slovak representatives abroad, including Tomas Masaryk, Eduard Benes, and Milan Stefanik, won support from the Allied powers for the creation of a Czech-Slovak republic. Thus, Czechoslovakia was established in Prague immediately after the war, uniting Bohemia, Moravia, and Slovakia as one nation. The Czech National Council seized power in Prague, the Habsburgs were deposed, and Masaryk was elected president. A Western-style democratic republic was established, enjoying stable government during the interwar period, only to be torn apart as Adolf Hitler exploited the Allies' appeasement policy in the infamous 1938 Munich agreement, under which the Czech territory was ceded to Germany. The following year, Hitler brutally annexed Bohemia and Moravia as a protectorate and turned Slovakia into an independent fascist state.

In 1945, the communists, with Soviet backing, gained political power. In February 1948, a communist overthrow brought the country under Soviet domination. After Stalin's death in 1953, there was a general loosening of political strictures in Eastern Europe, including Czechoslovakia, and a mild liberalization of conditions was permitted. However, it did not last long, and the traditional Stalinist system was reemployed.

The year 1968 is remembered as the "Prague Spring," when a new regime under President Ludvik Svoboda, a World War II hero, began to liberalize and democratize Czechoslovak life and loosen the country's association with the Soviet Union. This move was met with hostility by the Soviet Union and other socialist countries in Eastern Europe. The Soviet Union and its Warsaw Pact allies put an end this wave of democratization, as some 650,000 Soviet, East German, Polish, Hungarian, and Bulgarian troops invaded and occupied the country. Though the intervention was condemned worldwide, Soviet troops remained in the country. President Alexander Dubcek was replaced by another Slovak, Gustav Husak, in 1975, and the reforms of the Prague Spring were almost entirely scrapped. There were repressions and arrests, and by 1982, the opposition had been successfully neutralized.

After the fall of the communism in Hungary and Poland, the so-called Velvet Revolution came to Czechoslovakia. The communist government resigned, and Vaclav Havel, a former dissident playwright, became the president of a free and democratic Czechoslovakia in 1990. He attempted to preserve the Czech-Slovak union, but three years of debate and popular votes resulted in the separation of the two nations on 1 January 1993.

The Czech Republic became a member of the North Atlantic Treaty Organization (NATO) in 1999. The nation, along with many other Eastern European countries, joined the European Union (EU) in 2004. It was set to host the EU presidency during the first half of 2009.

² LOCATION AND HOMELAND

The Czech Republic is bordered by its former federal partner, Slovakia, to the east; by Austria to the south; by Germany to the southwest and northwest; and by Poland to the north. The Czech Republic comprises the historic lands of Bohemia and Moravia (commonly called the Czech lands) and the southwestern portion of Silesia.

The country covers an area of 78,865 sq km (30,450 sq mi), approximately the size of South Carolina. Its landscape is made up mostly of wooded hills, valleys, and small, heavily farmed plateaus. The capital city is Prague, which has a population of 1.6 million.

The Czech Republic has a population of about 10.2 million, the majority of whom (90%) are Czech. Other minorities include Moravians (380,000), Slovaks (193,000), Poles (52,000), Roma/Gypsies (171,000), Germans (39,000), Silesians (11,000), Ukrainians (22,000), and Vietnamese (18,000).

³ LANGUAGE

Czech is the official language of the republic. It belongs to a group of Slavic languages that use the Roman rather than the Cyrillic alphabet. The Czech language comprises two forms: formal, written Czech (*spisovna cestina*) and everyday conversational Czech (*hovorova*). Many regional dialects exist.

Russian is understood by many in the Czech Republic, but it is rarely used. English, French, and German are used in business dealings, but they are not spoken by the general population.

Common phrases in the Czech language are *dobry den* (hello or good day), *kde je?* (where is . . . ?), and *kolik to stoji?* (how much does it cost?).

4 FOLKLORE

A major folklore festival is held each year in Stráznice, in eastern Moravia. During the communist era, the government encouraged the country's folkloric traditions but used them as an instrument of control within a larger framework of political activities, thus alienating a number of Czechs, especially young ones, from their heritage. Some artists, however, managed to express dissent in the form of folk songs and fairy tales.

5 RELIGION

According to the country's 2001 census, 26.8% of Czechs are Roman Catholics and 2.1% are Protestant. Surprisingly, 59% of the people are not affiliated with any organized religion. The majority of those who claim a religion are Christian. Many Czechs turned to Protestantism following Jan Hus's campaign to reform the Roman Catholic Church in the 15th century. The communist regime used various methods to eliminate religion from the lives of the Czechs, but the Catholic Church maintained an underground presence. After the demonstrations and uprisings of 1989, those who had been forced to say mass in hideouts were able to pray openly. In April 1990, Pope John Paul II celebrated mass in Prague before a crowd of more than a half million Czechs.

6 MAJOR HOLIDAYS

In addition to religious holidays, the Czechs celebrate several important national holidays. The end of World War II is commemorated on May 8. On July 5, Czechs celebrate the arrival

of Saints Cyril and Methodius, two Byzantine priests who introduced Christianity to the Slavs. July 6 is Jan Hus Memorial Day, the anniversary of the day when the religious leader was burned at the stake in 1415. October 28 marks Czechoslovak Independence Day. The Velvet Revolution is commemorated on November 17, but people do not take the day off work.

On the eve of December 5, Czech children wait for the arrival of Saint Nicholas. Usually a person dressed as Saint Nick and two people dressed as an angel and a devil walk the streets. Live carp is sold on the street for Christmas Eve dinner, and Christmas trees are set up in town squares. A fruit bread called *vanocka* is eaten during Lent and in the days before Christmas. On New Year's Day, people give each other small marzipan candies for good luck.

7 RITES OF PASSAGE

Most Czechs observe major life events, such as births, weddings, and deaths, within the Catholic or Protestant religious tradition.

8 INTERPERSONAL RELATIONS

A stranger who is meeting someone for the first time or a young person who is greeting an elder gives a firm handshake; both people say their last names, then they give a standard salutation, such as *teši mne* (pleased to meet you) or *dobrý den* (good day). When a man and woman meet, the man usually waits for the woman to extend her hand first. People address each other by their last names unless they are well acquainted. *Dobrou chut*, which means "bon appetit," is generally countered with *dekuji* (thank you). Failure to do so can be construed as a sign of ignorance or vulgarity. The terms for good-bye are *na chledanou* or the more informal *ciao*. When conversing, Czechs often gesture with their hands for emphasis.

At the beginning of a business meeting, it is customary to offer some sort of beverage to the attendees. Czechs do not do much entertaining at home, and they refrain from making unannounced visits to each other's houses. Inviting guests to dinner generally means taking them out to eat.

Using a person's title (which often corresponds to his or her educational level) is also customary among Czechs.

9 LIVING CONDITIONS

The health care system in the former Czechoslovakia was under strict state control. All people associated with the medical field were state employees. Health care standards were never high, and medical equipment was often outdated in clinics and hospitals throughout the country. The 1990s brought privatization in several sectors, including medicine. Private medical insurance companies have been established and health standards have improved. Life expectancy ranges from 72.3 to 78.5 years of age, and the death rate is relatively low (10.69 deaths per 1,000 live births). The infant mortality rate is 3.38 deaths per 1,000 live births. However, the birthrate is falling rapidly, thereby stunting the country's population growth.

Though many people have second homes in the country (called *chaty*), the Czech Republic has a serious housing shortage. Many city dwellers live in large apartment complexes. Young couples rarely begin married life in a home of their own and usually live with one set of parents for several years.

New railroads, highways, and airports were built after World War II. Today, the Czechs have a well-developed system of highways and public transportation, and increasing numbers of people own cars, especially the domestically produced Skoda. The government is constantly upgrading transport technology, and tourism in the Czech Republic is booming.

10 FAMILY LIFE

Families in rural areas tend to be larger than urban families, which usually have no more than two children (childless urban couples are not uncommon). Although most mothers work outside the home, they still have primary domestic and child-rearing responsibilities. Grandparents often help with child care. Parents and adult children commonly maintain strong ties, often sharing a country house or a car, and adults routinely assume responsibility for aging parents. The incidence of divorce has risen sharply over time, reaching nearly 40% by the late 1980s and 67% by 2003. Czechs are opting to marry later and have fewer children than before.

11 CLOTHING

Traditional Czech dress, characterized by white lace and embroidered materials, is worn on special occasions. For men, a holiday costume might consist of a white shirt with wide sleeves gathered at the wrists and white trousers. Both shirt and pants are frequently decorated with embroidery. A brightly colored vest decorated with embroidery and buttons is worn over the shirt. Women wear gathered skirts and blouses made of simple materials such as linen and cotton. These clothes are embroidered, however, to give them a rich appearance. To complete this costume, an apron, again heavily embroidered, may be worn. Both men and women complete their festive costumes with boots. In rural parts of southern Bohemia and southeastern Moravia, folk costumes are still worn. Otherwise, Czechs dress in modern, Western-style attire.

12 FOOD

Czechs borrow many of their cooking traditions and dishes from neighboring countries. Goulash, a hearty Hungarian stew, is a staple dish in the Czech Republic. Lunch is the main meal for most Czechs, while breakfast and dinner are lighter meals. Czechs enjoy eating hearty dishes such as roasted meats, wild game, vegetables, dumplings, and pastries. One of the most popular Czech dishes, *vepro-knedlo-zelo,* includes roast pork, sauerkraut, and *knedliky* (dumplings), which are made by boiling or steaming a mixture of flour, eggs, milk, and dried bread crumbs. Often, dumplings are filled with fruit. Popular snack foods include ham on bread and sausages in buns, both widely available from sidewalk vendors. Czechs also enjoy smoked meats, herring, sardines, goose, duck, hare, and venison. In today's increasingly health-conscious climate, many Czechs have begun to favor lighter foods over the traditional fare, which is high in fat, laden with heavy sauces, and time-consuming to prepare. The current trend is toward leaner meats and more vegetables.

Czechs enjoy drinking beer with their meals. The best Czech beer comes from a town called Plzeň, where the first brewery was established in 1295. This is where the Pilsner was created, and it is also the home of Pilsner Urquell. The Czech Republic is the sixth largest beer-producing country in the world. Red wines from the many wineries of Moravia are also quite popular. Slivovitz, a plum brandy made in the region, is sometimes consumed after dinner.

13 EDUCATION

The Czech Republic has had a near 100% literacy level since the early 1990s.

Czech education has historically been influenced by politics. The Habsburgs, for example, forced students, teachers, and writers to use the German language. The communists' main requirement was that children master the principles of socialism, and under communist rule, religious and private schools were banned. (Under the new government of the Czech Republic, they have been reinstated.)

In 1994, the structure of the Czech educational system was reformed. Children now attend grade school for five years (from age 6 to 11) and then receive eight years of secondary schooling. Students may choose an academic or technical track, and there is a third track for aspiring teachers. School is mandatory for children between the ages of 6 and 15. The Czech Republic has 23 universities or university-level facilities. The oldest is Charles University, which was founded in 1348. Czech students pay one-fourth of their university expenses.

14 CULTURAL HERITAGE

Prague is the center of Czech culture. Its many ancient churches and buildings withstood the fighting of World War II.

The Czechs have made great contributions to music and literature. Perhaps the most famous Czech writer was Franz Kafka. Kafka, a German who lived in Prague, influenced subsequent Czech authors such as Milan Kundera, Josef Skorecky, and Ivan Klima.

Vaclav Havel, a famous playwright whose sarcastic criticism of communism landed him in prison, became president of Czechoslovakia in 1989 and served as president of the Czech Republic from 1993–2003.

Czechs enjoy the writings of both modern and classical playwrights in hundreds of theaters throughout the country. Young children (and adults) find joy in watching puppet theaters and mimes.

Czech folk music has become world famous through its incorporation into the compositions of prominent Czech composers, notably Antonin Dvorak.

In the 1980s, rock music was closely tied to political opposition and an up-and-coming underground club scene. Czechs enjoy rock, jazz, and classical music, and they host one of Europe's biggest music events, the Prague Spring Music Festival.

15 WORK

The Czech Republic is one of the most industrialized countries in the world. Rich, fertile soil allows for a major farming industry, and coal and other minerals have been mined for centuries.

During the communist era, workers earned fixed wages and had little desire to increase their productivity. Food shortages and lack of housing, fuel, and electricity became the norm.

In 1989, the Czech Republic shifted to a free-market economy, accompanied by higher wages and a better standard of living for workers. Although salaries remain low, the vast majority of the Czech population is employed. Private enterprise has created many new jobs for those laid off from the declining industrial sector. Jobs in tourism and other areas of the service sector are growing. As of 2007, unemployment stood at 6.6%.

The Czech workforce numbers 5.17 million. Industry, construction, and commerce make up 40% of the workforce, gov-

Frantiska Polackova (l) and her granddaughter decorate Easter eggs in downtown Prague, Czech Republic. The eggs are a Czech Easter tra-
dition that survived communism and today provides an authentic souvenir for tourists. (Michal Cizek/AFP/Getty Images)

ernment and other services make up 56%, and agriculture makes up 4%. The country's natural resources include coal, coke, timber, lignite, uranium, and magnesite. The main agricultural goods are wheat, rye, oats, barley, hops, potatoes, sugar beets, hogs, cattle, and horses.

16 SPORTS

Czechs are no strangers to outdoor recreation. The mountainous landscape provides an excellent setting for skiing, rock climbing, and hiking. Water sports are enjoyed in the lakes of southern Bohemia.

Perhaps the most popular sport played by young Czechs is tennis, made famous by international Czech greats Martina Navratilova, Ivan Lendl, and Jana Novotna. Soccer is the most popular team sport. Hockey, volleyball, and basketball are also popular. The sport with the longest tradition in the Czech Republic, however, is gymnastics.

17 ENTERTAINMENT AND RECREATION

Czechs spend much of their leisure time enjoying their native mountains, fields, and woodlands. Urban dwellers frequently spend weekends and vacations in their country homes, where many enjoy gardening, planting and tending to fruit trees, and working on home improvement projects. Camping is also a popular activity; numerous campgrounds can be found throughout the countryside. Other outdoor activities include hiking, swimming, and gathering berries and mushrooms.

There are a number of mineral springs and health spas in the Czech Republic, where for a fee visitors can soak their ailments away in mineral water, mud, or peat. Other leisure activities include movie- and concertgoing, watching television, and dancing (a traditionally popular dance is the polka, a lively folk dance). Gathering in bars or pubs is a traditional after-hours activity for men, while women enjoy visiting close friends at home. Czechs enjoy traveling by both car and bus, especially with the lifting of travel restrictions since the demise of communism in Eastern Europe.

18 FOLK ART, CRAFTS, AND HOBBIES

Glass works and other decorative wares are among the folk arts of the Czech Republic. Bohemia in particular is known for its unusual crystal objects and deep red garnet stones.

19 SOCIAL PROBLEMS

Although the Czech Republic has significantly improved its economy and has established a democracy, social problems remain. Prices for energy and everyday items have increased significantly. As a result of rapid industrialization during the communist era, high levels of air, water, and soil pollution remain. Two distinct economic classes are now emerging from the single class formed by communism: a rich capitalist class and a lower class that is struggling with the new system.

Crime also became a major problem after the fall of communism. Organized crime in drug trafficking, money laundering, and prostitution is significant. Hate crimes, especially against Gypsies (Roma), are a big problem in the country as well.

The health care system was left in shambles after the fall of communism and continues to struggle today.

20 GENDER ISSUES

Discrimination and sexual harassment remain important issues for women in the workplace in the Czech Republic. While the communist government made work compulsory for both men and women, today women performing the same jobs as men are often paid half the salary. However, Czech women do not seem to be in favor of American-style feminism, believing that it drives a wedge between men and women. Some women's groups have formed since 1992, but they have been slow to gather steam. As of the first decade of the 21st century, there were high female employment rates in both full- and part-time work, but women tended to have fewer support structures to combine a balance of work and life.

Abortion was legalized in 1957, but until 1986, a woman wanting an abortion had to appear before a committee that would decide whether she was eligible.

Czechs' attitudes toward homosexuality are mixed. More than half of Czech citizens claim they have never met a homosexual, and about one-third believe that homosexuality is a disease. From 1948 to 1961, homosexual behavior was illegal. However, in March 2006, the Czech Republic adopted a same-sex partnership law. Lesbian and gay families are now legally recognized.

21 BIBLIOGRAPHY

Cravens, Craig. *Culture and Customs of the Czech Republic and Slovakia*. Westport, CT: Greenwood Press, 2006.

Holy, Ladislov. *The Little Czech and the Great Czech Nation: National Identity and the Post-Communist Transformation of Society*. New York: Cambridge University Press, 1996.

Ivory, Michael. *Essential Czech Republic*. Lincolnwood, IL: Passport Books, 1994.

Otfinoski, Steven. *The Czech Republic. 2nd ed*. New York: Facts on File, 2004.

Skalnik, Carol. *The Czech Republic and the Slovak Republic: Nation versus State*. Boulder, CO: Westview Press, 1997.

US Department of State, *Bureau of European and Eurasian Affairs*. "Background Note: Czech Republic." http://www.state.gov/r/pa/ei/bgn/3237.htm (7 May 2008).

—revised by C. Corrigan

DANES

LOCATION: Denmark
POPULATION: 5.4 million (2008)
LANGUAGE: Danish; English; German
RELIGION: Evangelical Lutheran Church of Denmark; small numbers of Roman Catholics, Muslims, Jews and others

1 INTRODUCTION

Denmark is the smallest Scandinavian country after Iceland. It has one of the world's highest standards of living, with an advanced system of government-supported social benefits supported by heavy taxes on its citizens. The country's principal port, the capital city of Copenhagen, is a leading center of international trade. The Danes were sailors and merchants by the era of the Vikings (AD 800–1050). The nation expanded its territory between the 14th and 18th centuries but had lost much of it, including Norway, to the Swedes by 1814. Denmark is a constitutional monarchy, ruled since 1972 by Queen Margrethe II.

2 LOCATION AND HOMELAND

Situated between the North Sea and the Baltic Sea, Denmark consists of the peninsula of Jutland and over 400 nearby islands, of which about 100 are inhabited. The Kingdom of Denmark also exercises sovereignty over Greenland and the Faroe Islands. Denmark's capital city, Copenhagen, is located on the nation's largest island, Zealand (Sjaelland). The Danish landscape is characterized by gently rolling hills and flat plains. The lowest points in the country, on the western coast, are below sea level, and dikes reclaim the land for agricultural use. The longest river is the Guden and many small lakes dot the land.

Denmark is a highly urbanized nation. About 85% of its 5.4 million people live in cities, with over one-third in the four largest cities of Copenhagen, Aalborg, Odense, and Arhus. Descended from northern Germanic tribes, the Danes are among the most ethnically homogeneous people in Europe. One out of every 13 Danes has the last name of Jensen. A small German minority lives in southern Jutland.

3 LANGUAGE

Danish, a Germanic language, is the official language of Denmark and is universally spoken in Denmark proper. The people of Greenland and the Faroe Islands speak their own languages. (Greenlandic [Inuit] is a non-European language, related to certain indigenous Canadian languages; Faroese is a distant relative of Danish.) English and German are widely spoken.

NUMBERS	
one	en/et
two	to
three	tre
four	fire
five	fem
six	seks
seven	syv
eight	otte
nine	ni
ten	ti

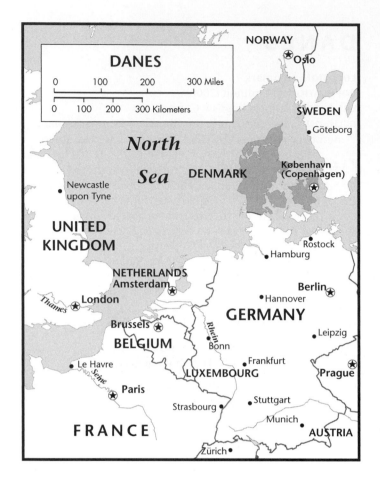

DAYS OF THE WEEK

Sunday	søndag
Monday	mandag
Tuesday	tirsdag
Wednesday	onsdag
Thursday	torsdag
Friday	fredag
Saturday	lørdag

⁴ FOLKLORE

In pre-Christian Scandinavian legend, the god Thor was said to cause thunder by wielding a hammer in the heavens; Viking warriors wore miniature hammers around their necks in his honor. Beautiful maidens called Valkyries were thought to transport Vikings killed in battle and transport them to the court of Odin—the leader of the gods—at Valhalla. (Much Viking mythology was later re-popularized in the operas of the 19th-century German composer Richard Wagner.)

Denmark was the first Nordic country to adopt Christianity as its official religion under King Harald Bluetooth in the 10th century.

During a later period of Danish history, the red and white national flag, the Dannebrog, was said to have descended from heaven on 15 June 1219, turning the tide in the Danes' battle against Estonia at Lindanaes.

According to legend, witches are thought to fly over Denmark on Midsummer's Eve, and on Midsummer's Day (June 24) firecrackers are traditionally set off all over the country to scare them off. The Danes traditionally believe that storks

bring good fortune and the beech tree is something of a national emblem.

⁵ RELIGION

About 83% of the population belongs to the Evangelical Lutheran Church in Denmark, the established religion of the country. It is headed by the Queen (who by law must be a member of the church) and supported by the state through subsidies and a tax levied on members. The Danish parliament is the legislative authority for the church. There is also a minister for church affairs in the prime minister's cabinet. While only about 3% of all church members attend services on a regular basis, nearly all members are baptized, confirmed, and married in the church. This is, in part, due to the fact that the church is the primary agency responsible for registering births, marriages, and deaths. Women make up a substantial percentage of the nation's ordained Lutheran ministers. Danish churches are known for the ship models that often hang from ceilings or archways.

The Danish constitution has guaranteed freedom of religion since 1849 and there are small numbers of Roman Catholics, Jews, and members of other faiths living in Denmark.

⁶ MAJOR HOLIDAYS

Besides the general Christian holidays of Christmas, Easter, and Pentecost, the Danes celebrate several other religious days as national holidays, including Holy Thursday, Good Friday, Easter Monday, *Store Bededag* (Common Prayer Day) on the fourth Friday after Easter, Ascension Thursday (the fortieth day after Easter), Whitmonday (Pentecost Monday), Christmas Eve, and Boxing Day. Queen Margrethe's birthday on April 16 is a school holiday, on which many children watch the parade of the royal guard at Amalienborg Square in Copenhagen. Another holiday for children—comparable to Halloween in the United States—is the Monday before Shrove Tuesday, when they dress up in traditional costumes and visit their neighbors asking for money to buy candy. Danes celebrate Liberation Day (May 5) and Constitution Day (June 5) as well.

The Danes also celebrate American Independence Day (July 4) in honor of Americans of Danish descent, who are invited to homecoming festivities including concerts, rallies, and lectures. Thousands attend this event every year.

⁷ RITES OF PASSAGE

Denmark, like most of its European neighbors, is a modern, industrialized country. Hence, many of the rites of passage that young people undergo are connected with their progress through the education system. Additionally, religious rituals such as baptism, confirmation, and marriage are important to those who observe them. The Danes place special emphasis on the birthdays that mark each decade of a person's life. One's sixtieth birthday in particular is considered an important occasion, to be celebrated by a gathering of relatives.

⁸ INTERPERSONAL RELATIONS

Danish manners are more formal than those in the United States. There is a great deal of polite handshaking and men raise their hats as a gesture of respect. The word *tak* ("thank you") is used often and can also mean "please" or "I beg your pardon." When drinking the national liqueur, aquavit, the

Queen Margrethe II of Denmark waves to the crowd in Amalienborg Castle square. Queen Margrethe was in the city to thank Copenhagen for the thousands of tulips presented to her for her 60th birthday. (Francis Dean/Getty Images)

Danes habitually offer up a courteous toast of *"Skol."* Professional titles such as "Doctor" or "Master" are commonly used in addressing people, as well as titles that indicate one's rank in business or government. Danes tend to be organized and punctual and can appear to be cool toward those they don't know well.

⁹ LIVING CONDITIONS

With its extensive system of social services, Denmark has one of the world's highest standards of living. In spite of a shortage of housing, most Danes own their own houses or apartments. Danish homes are made of brick and wood or of stucco. Although they are usually small, they appear more spacious than they are due to the well-known Danish talent for domestic design. Homes typically have light furniture and few wall hangings. The spare, graceful Danish furniture popular throughout the world is made of beautifully finished wood and characterized by its gently curving lines. Denmark has virtually no slums and elderly Danes often live in retirement communities affiliated with a nearby hospital.

Denmark has an excellent health care system. Complete medical care is provided free of charge to all Danish citizens and each person has his or her own private physician; however, this system is supported by high taxes. There are several private health care facilities as well as those sponsored primarily through the government. Life expectancy as of 2008 was about 78 years, with 76 years for men and 81 years for women. The major causes of death are heart disease and cancer.

Denmark's network of roads, airports, railroads, and ports is modern and efficient. Its many islands are connected by tunnels, bridges, and ferry boats that can accommodate up to 2,000 passengers and 400 cars. The major cities are served by extensive public transportation networks. About one Dane in four owns a car and more than half the population uses bicycles for short trips. Danish railway ridership is increasing after years of decline.

¹⁰ FAMILY LIFE

The Danes' social lives tend to focus largely on the nuclear family, although to a somewhat lesser degree than those of their Scandinavian neighbors. It is generally considered permissible for couples to live together before marriage and most couples do so. In addition, many Danish marriages are "paperless" common-law unions with no formal ceremony. Children are shown a great deal of care and respect in families and by society as well. Working parents generally have no problems in taking time off from their jobs in order to care for children and most parents are allowed flexible work schedules that allow them extra time to pick up their children from school or attend school meetings and functions.

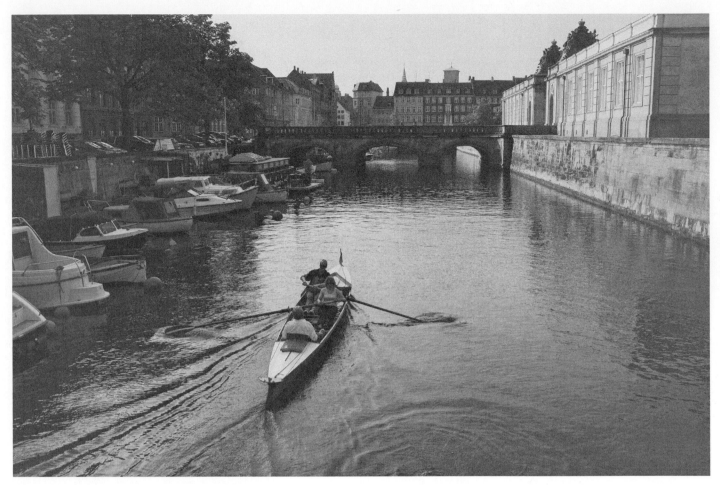

Danes row a boat down the Fredriksborg Canal in Copenhagen, Denmark. (© Hans Strand/Corbis)

At least half of all Danish marriages end in divorce and single-parent families are common. Since 1988 same-sex couples in a monogamous, long-term relationship have been entitled to the same rights as married heterosexual couples.

11 CLOTHING

The Danes wear modern Western-style clothing, dressing carefully for business and casually for less formal activities. Among young people, casual dress typically includes leather jackets, T-shirts, and jeans. Traditional folk costumes, which may still be seen at festivals, are worn by folk dancers. Women wear blouses and jackets, layered petticoats, scarves, and bonnets, and their costumes are decorated with gold and silver stitching. Men's costumes consist of sweaters, jackets, and knickers (pants that come to just below the knee) worn with high, white woolen socks.

12 FOOD

Danish food includes a wide variety of fish, meat, bread, cheese, and crispbreads. The Danes usually eat three meals a day. Breakfast usually includes cereal, bread with cheese, or yogurt. Lunches often include open-faced sandwiches called *smørrebrød,* consisting of thin slices of bread (especially rye) with such toppings as smoked salmon or eel, tongue, ham, shrimp, caviar, eggs, or cheese. Dinner typically includes some type of meat with potatoes, rice, or pasta. One traditional Danish dish is roast duckling stuffed with apples or prunes and served with red cabbage and boiled potatoes. Popular pastries include almond cakes made with generous amounts of butter and coffee cakes called *kringler.* The average Danish annual beer consumption of 40 gallons per person is the highest in Scandinavia and aquavit (snaps), a spiced liqueur made flavored with caraway seeds, is a popular after-dinner drink. The Danish place great emphasis on arranging their food so it is visually attractive as well as tasty. The popular smørrebrød may be garnished with twists of cucumber, tomato, dill weed, beets, citrus fruit, or onion rings.

13 EDUCATION

Virtually all Danish adults are literate. Free primary, secondary, and—in most cases—postsecondary education is funded by high taxes. Elementary education lasts nine years, followed by three years of schooling at either a technical or business school, or, for those preparing to enter a university, secondary school (called gymnasium). Students graduating from a gymnasium must pass an exam before going on to the university level. There are numerous afterschool programs and youth clubs offering educational opportunities for children and young adults. The oldest university in Denmark is the University of Copenhagen, founded in 1479. Most cities in Denmark have a wide variety of schools and institutions offering extra educational opportunities for both children and adults. For instance, lecture series for adults are popular at many institutions, including libraries, museums, and churches. There is also a system of Folk High Schools that offer short- and long-term courses on special topics, such as music, art, religion, athletics, politics, and more.

14 CULTURAL HERITAGE

Denmark has a distinguished ballet tradition; the Royal Danish Ballet was founded in 1829. The compositions of Carl Nielsen, Denmark's most renowned composer, are performed throughout the world. Dieterich Buxtehude is another classical musician and composer from Denmark. The pianist-comedian Victor Borge (d. 2000) delighted generations of international audiences. The state subsidizes the Royal Theater in Copenhagen, which presents dramas, ballet, opera, and modern dance. Amateur theater and musical groups are very popular.

Perhaps the most famous Dane connected with the arts is the prince whose story was dramatized by William Shakespeare. *Hamlet* is performed every year in the courtyard of Kronborg Castle, located in Helsingør, where the Hamlet of legend is said to have lived. Among Danish writers, the most famous is Hans Christian Andersen, the author of such beloved fairy tales as "The Ugly Duckling," "The Emperor's New Clothes," and "The Red Shoes." In the 20th century, Karen Blixen, who wrote under the pen name of Isak Dinesen, has gained renown for her memoirs, *Out of Africa,* which were popularized by the release in the 1980s of the American movie based on them. Denmark has a successful film industry of its own.

The 19th century philosopher Søren Kierkegaard is studied around the world. Niels Bohr won the Nobel Prize in Physics in 1922 for his work toward understanding atomic structures and quantum mechanics. His son Aage Niels Bohr won the Nobel Prize in Physics in 1975 for his own studies in quantum mechanics.

15 WORK

Danes have the same variety of employment options that can be found in most other European nations. While work is important to the Danes, there is a somewhat better balance between work and personal life than might be found in countries such as the United States. The average workweek is about 37 hours. Most workers are given five weeks of paid vacation each year and are typically allowed to take up the three weeks consecutively during the summer months. Employers respect the importance of family life and are generally flexible when it comes to scheduling options so that their employees have the time they need to care for family members. There are generous options for maternity and paternity leave in relation to childbirth and adoption.

Most Danes work in businesses with fewer than 100 employees. Altogether, about 76% of the labor force is employed in the service sector, 21% in industry, and only 3% in agriculture, forestry, and fishing. Unemployment is generally low. About 80% of all wage earners belong to a union.

16 SPORTS

In addition to its popularity as a spectator sport, soccer (*fodball*) is also a participant sport for players of all ages: it is estimated that as many as 300,000 Danes play. Children play it at school, after school, and on weekends and holidays. Volunteer-run clubs throughout the country are dedicated to turning young players into pros. At least one out of every four Danes belongs to a sports club of some kind. The proximity of the sea has bred an interest in water sports including sailing, rowing, and swimming. Other popular activities include rugby, tennis, handball, archery, fencing, cycling, skiing, and rifle shooting. Every year, Athletics Awards (*Idraetsmaerket*) sponsored by Queen Margrethe are presented to men and women who have passed qualifying tests based on age.

17 ENTERTAINMENT AND RECREATION

The Danish people enjoy spending leisure time with their families, whether to attend a sporting event or to observe a holiday. The most popular spectator sport is soccer (called *fodball*), with the main national rival being Sweden. Danes often enjoy athletic activities such as jogging, cycling, or long-distance running purely for exercise rather than competition. Bridge and chess are also popular leisure-time pursuits. Large numbers of bridge fans attend national tournaments featuring the top players.

18 FOLK ART, CRAFTS, AND HOBBIES

Folk dancing is popular in Denmark; some 15,000 men and women participate in this activity on a regular basis. The Danish Country Dancing Society, one of the best-known folk dance troupes, has been in existence since 1901. Crafts include work in silver, glass, porcelain, and pewter, as well as textiles. Modern Danish furniture was pioneered in the 1930s. Denmark has an outstanding system of folk museums, including parks that contain relocated, renovated rural and urban buildings that are centuries old.

19 SOCIAL PROBLEMS

In the early 2000s discrimination against ethnic and religious minorities, especially Muslims, was a problem. Such discrimination may be attributed both to stereotypes of Muslims as terrorists and to anti-immigration sentiments. There have also been reports of anti-Semitism. As more immigrants have arrived, particularly from Africa and the Middle East, there has been an increase in anti-immigrant sentiment, primarily based on the perception that immigrants are unwilling to integrate and that the increase in immigration might cause an increase in crime. The government does have antiracism and antidiscrimination laws in place and most cases of discrimination have been investigated and brought to trial.

However, an international uproar occurred in 2005 and 2006 with the publication in the Danish newspaper Jyllands-Posten of twelve editorial cartoons, most of which depicted the Muslim prophet Muhammad. The newspaper announced that it wished to contribute to the debate regarding criticism of Islam and self-censorship. Further examples of the cartoons were reprinted in newspapers in more than 50 other countries. This led to protests across the Muslim world, some of which escalated into violence, resulting in more than 100 deaths. While a number of Muslim leaders called for protesters to remain peaceful, other Muslim leaders issued death threats. Danish Prime Minister Anders Fogh Rasmussen described the controversy as Denmark's worst international crisis since World War II.

Some religious minorities, particularly Catholics, have claimed discrimination based on the preferential treatment allowed for the Evangelical Lutheran Church of Denmark (ELCD). While the constitution provides for religious freedom, religious equality is not guaranteed. The ELCD enjoys privileges and government financial support that are not offered to other religious organizations.

20 GENDER ISSUES

About 75% of all women and 82% of all men are active in the workforce. In most families both the husband and wife work outside of the home. Although men and women have equal rights under the law, women's pay is not yet equal to that of men. In 2007 it was estimated that women in the private sector earned approximately 21% less than men. The Danish Women Citizen's Society, created in 1871, works to further women's rights on such issues as working outside the home. Housewives have their own association, Husmoderforeningen, whose activities parallel those of professional groups. Many of the rights currently enjoyed by women were won by the modern feminist movement that began in the 1970s. In Denmark it was spearheaded by a group of women calling themselves the Redstockings, who launched protests in cities throughout the nation wearing bright red hose.

While prostitution is legal in Denmark, trafficking in persons is not. There have been reports that the country is being used as both a destination and a transit point for the illegal trafficking of both women and children. Women who are forced into prostitution are generally foreigners lured to Denmark from their homes in Russia, Eastern Europe, Southeast Asia, and West Africa with the promise of higher wages and a better life. There is a national task force in place to investigate and dismantle illegal trafficking operations. Several groups have formed to identify and assist trafficking victims.

21 BIBLIOGRAPHY

Bennett, A. Linda, ed. *Encyclopedia of World Cultures (Europe)*. Boston: G. K. Hall, 1992.

Bondeson, Ulla V. *Nordic Moral Climates: Value Continuities and Discontinuities in Denmark, Finland, Norway, and Sweden*. New Brunswick, NJ: Transaction Publishers, 2003.

Denmark in Pictures. Minneapolis: Lerner Publications, 1991.

Gall, Timothy, and Susan Gall, ed. *Junior Worldmark Encyclopedia of the Nations*. Detroit: UXL, 1996.

Hintz, Martin. *Denmark. Enchantment of the World Series*. Chicago: Children's Press, 1994.

Hubbard, Monica M., and Beverly Baer, ed. *Cities of the World: Europe and the Middle East*. Detroit: Gale Research, 1993.

Illustrated Encyclopedia of Mankind. London: Marshall Cavendish, 1978.

Ministry of Science Technology and Innovation, Denmark. "Work in Denmark." http://www.workindenmark.dk (23 April 2008).

Moss, Joyce, and George Wilson. *Peoples of the World: Western Europeans*. Detroit: Gale Research, 1993.

Salmon, Mark. Denmark: *A Quick Guide to Customs and Etiquette*. London: Kuperard, 2006.

Taylor-Wilkie, Doreen. *Denmark*. Insight Guides. Singapore: APA Press, 1992.

—revised by K. Ellicott

DOLGANY

ALTERNATE NAMES: Dulgaan
LOCATION: Russia (Taimyr peninsula and along the Yenisei River)
POPULATION: 7,261 (2002 census)
LANGUAGE: Dolgan; Russian
RELIGION: Orthodox Christianity; native form of shamanism

1 INTRODUCTION

The Dolgans are one of approximately thirty "Numerically Small Peoples of the North" in Russia. The Numerically Small Peoples are indigenous groups who have lived in the Far North for thousands of years, relying on the land and its natural resources to provide food, clothing, and shelter. Their spiritual life is also rooted in the land and the animals with which they share the tundra and taiga. Although their lives have changed rapidly as industrialization has spread throughout the world over the course of the past one hundred years, the land and its resources continue to provide a livelihood and spiritual anchor for the Dolgans. The contemporary Dolgan people are officially recognized as an amalgam of Sakha, Evenki, Entsy, Russian, and Nganasany peoples. The name "Dolgan" is derived from one of the Tungus clans from whom the contemporary Dolgans originated. The ethnonym, or ethnic self-designation of the Dolgans is "Dulgaan," but this is a very recent (19th century) name. Prior to that, groups used names originating from their past ethnic identities or the territories in which they lived.

Indigenous peoples in both Czarist Russia and the Soviet Union were considered "primitive" because they lived in the harsh arctic environment and made their living off the land. In the Soviet Union, the government implemented policies designed to "modernize" indigenous peoples and thus bring them into the fold of socialist society, whether they wanted to be modernized or not. Collectivization, universal education, and assimilation were three primary focal points of government policy. Collectivization entailed confiscating people's property, including their reindeer herds, and organizing economic activities on the basis of collective (*kolkhozy*) and state farms (*sovkhozy*). Education is generally acknowledged as a positive development except when students are denied the right to learn in their Native languages, and their cultures are disparaged by teachers and administrators. This is a problem which is only today being addressed. The Dolgans were expected to assimilate into the dominant Soviet society—to stop thinking of themselves as Dulgaan and start thinking of themselves as Soviet. Their lives as nomadic reindeer herds and hunters would end as they adopted modern industrial occupations and lifestyles. Their distinctive way of life, culture and beliefs would merge and eventually disappear into the larger "Soviet people."

The 2002 Russian census recorded 7,261 Dolgans in the whole Russian Federation. The Dolgan people today are one of the most politically powerful groups in their territory, and many senior officials of the Taimyr Autonomous *Okrug* are Dolgans. Political activism is especially important for native peoples as they begin to address the social and economic problems which have resulted from discriminatory government policies.

2 LOCATION AND HOMELAND

The Dolgan people live on the Taimyr peninsula and along the lower portions of the Yenisei River in the Taimyr (Dolgano-Nenets) Autonomous *Okrug* in Russia. The Taimyr Autonomous *Okrug* is an administrative unit within Krasnoiarsk *krai*, and has its administrative center in the port city of Dudinka. The total population of the *okrug* recorded in the 1989 Soviet census was 55,803. Of this total, 8,751 were members of indigenous groups (Dolgans, Nentsy, Evenki, Nganasans, and Entsy), and the Dolgans numbered 4,939. Although the Dolgans (along with the Nentsy) are the titular nation of this *okrug*, they are a numerical minority, the majority of the population is Russian. Some Russians have lived for generations in the region, but most are relatively recent immigrants who moved to the *okrug* to work in the large industrial centers, the shipping industry, and the mining complexes. The *okrug* occupies 862,100 square kilometers (332,900 square miles, or about twice the size of Sweden), and competition for land is a serious problem. The traditional economic activities of the Dolgans, Nenets, and other Native peoples require large tracts of land that are relatively free of human disruption. The industrial economy of the *okrug* is intensive, focused in large cities and settlements along the arctic coast and inland waterways. As industrial activities such as mining and processing minerals increase, they encompass land from surrounding rural areas, leaving fewer resources for native peoples.

The Taimyr Autonomous *Okrug* is located entirely north of the Arctic Circle. Winters are long and cold, with a mean January temperature in Dudinka of –30°C (–22°F). Summers are short and cool, with an average July temperature of 2°C to 13°C (36°F to 55°F). Humidity is relatively high, and strong winds blow throughout the year. Precipitation totals 110 mm to 350 mm (4.3 in to 13.8 in) per year. Permafrost is widespread.

Arctic, tundra, and forest-tundra ecological zones are all represented in the Taimyr Autonomous *Okrug*. The arctic zone has almost no shrubs or lichen and only sparse mosses and liverworts. The tundra has willow and arctic birch trees, mosses, lichens, liverworts, and grasses. The forest-tundra zone has large expanses of lichen where reindeer graze, and the entire Khatanga River Valley north of 68° latitude is covered with forests of larch, spruce, and birch. The wildlife that inhabits this diverse environment includes seals, walrus, and beluga whales along the arctic coast; fish on the coast and inland waterways; and wild reindeer, bighorn sheep, arctic fox, lemmings, ermine, hares, and wolves throughout the *okrug*. Bird species are also varied, especially during summer migrations when ducks, geese, and wading birds join local residents such as the ptarmigan and willow ptarmigan. Polar bears live on the ice floes along the northern coast and arctic islands.

3 LANGUAGE

The Dolgan language today is classified as a distinct language, although as late as the 1950s it was considered to be a dialect of Yakut, which is spoken by the Sakha. It is classified as a member of the Turkic language group, which is itself part of the Altaic language family. Most Dolgans speak both the Russian language and Dolgan. There was no written Dolgan language until quite recently. In 1973, the first Dolgan language book

was published using the Yakut alphabet. A Dolgan primer has been prepared to help teach the language in school. In 1991, the Dolgan language began to be taught in the lower grades.

4 FOLKLORE

Dolgan folklore is rich and varied. Historic legends tell of travel to faraway places. Epic tales are sung and describe ways of life totally foreign to the Dolgans in which heroes struggle against persons in league with the evil spirits. Most popular are short stories which tell of the everyday life of nomadic people, explain the origins of animals, and describe the metamorphosis of animals into people. Storytellers were considered to be chosen by the good spirits, and especially gifted storytellers might create their own schools and have young apprentices. Storytellers often worked with shamans to cure illnesses. The Dolgans believed that the images evoked by a storyteller could be made visible. A storyteller would be called to the bedside of the sick person and begin to tell an epic tale. As soon as the evil spirit making the person ill appeared to help defeat the story's hero, the shaman would cast a spell to remove the evil spirit from the sick person's body and thus effect a cure. The power of storytelling was believed to be so strong that stories were not told before a hunt in case the images brought forth might scare the game away.

5 RELIGION

Traditional Dolgan religion can be said to be Eastern Orthodox Christianity, since their adherence to Christianity was a factor in their formation as a people from the 16th to the 19th century, and which distinguished them for their unbaptized neighbors, such as the Nganasan. At the same time Dolgan religious practice incorporated many aspects of Siberian shamanism. It is based on a respect for the land and animals which embody spirits that guide hunting, herding, birth, death, and the behavior of individuals and society. Their animistic beliefs divide spirits and gods into three categories: *ichchi, ayyy,* and *abaasy. Ichchi* are invisible spirits which can bring to life anything they enter. *Ayyy* are spirits which help humans in their daily lives, such as in the hunt and in domestic matters. *Abaasy* spirits are evil, causing sickness and death. Shamans serve as mediators between humans and the spirits. Storytellers often help shamans in identifying the cause of illness or misfortune. The Dolgans believe that after death they will live in another world with their kinfolk.

By the beginning of the 20th century, the Dolgan people were said to have all been converted to Orthodox Christianity. Traditional beliefs never completely disappeared, however, but instead were practiced secretly or incorporated into Christian ritual and practice. Although religious practices were discouraged in the Soviet Union, Orthodoxy is still strong and the role of shamanism in traditional culture is being revived in some areas.

⁶ MAJOR HOLIDAYS

In addition to the Soviet secular holidays celebrated by all peoples in the former Soviet Union, the Dolgans celebrate Russian Orthodox holidays such as Easter and Christmas.

⁷ RITES OF PASSAGE

Traditional Dolgan beliefs held that death was caused by evil spirits who stole souls and carried them off to the underworld and then invaded a person's body and ate it. Some groups of Dolgans built log structures over their graves, while others felled a tree, which would be carved with various designs, over the gravesite.

⁸ INTERPERSONAL RELATIONS

Marriages were traditionally arranged by parents who used a matchmaker to negotiate the payment of "bridewealth" and assure that a sufficient dowry would be provided. Bridewealth, paid by the husband to his bride's family might include furs and reindeer. A bride's dowry would include household goods and clothing. The wedding would be held at the parents' home, and the newlyweds would live with the groom's family until they were able to establish their own home. Marriages today are arranged by individuals themselves (sometimes in consultation with elders), but they are still accompanied by celebrations with families and friends. Young married couples still often live with parents until a separate apartment can be found and furnished.

Social rules governing the activities of men and women and their behavior towards one another were stringently followed in traditional Dolgan society to ensure such things as successful hunting, and healthy births, and to ward off the attention of evil spirits. The world of men was outside the *chum* or tent, among the reindeer and in the forests. Women dominated the household and were responsible for its maintenance and internal harmony. Although the tasks of men and women might sometimes overlap (for example, men would help build a tent

or sled tent), each was primarily responsible for their own part of the Dolgan world. Within Dolgan society, there continue to be strong traditions of sharing among kinfolk and care of the elderly. In times of need, an individual's relatives can be counted upon to help. The elderly, regardless of whether or not they are one's immediate relatives, are always provided with assistance in the form of food, shelter, or whatever else might be needed.

⁹ LIVING CONDITIONS

Dolgans who live in the tundra, herding and hunting, tend to live in traditional types of dwellings—tents made of reindeer skins (or occasionally today canvas or tarpaulin) or small huts built of wooden frames covered with skins or fabric on sled runners. These sled tents can be pulled by reindeer and were adopted from Russian merchants. The families of herders and hunters might also have apartments in villages where they spend part of the year. Today many Dolgans live in small settlements (300–600 people) of wooden apartment buildings heated with coal. Plumbing is generally absent in these homes. Villages often have a medical clinic, a general store, and an elementary and/or middle school. Dolgans who live in large cities live in modern apartment buildings with plumbing and central heating. They shop in stores, attend school, and work in stores, hospitals, schools, factories, and so on.

Transportation in the tundra is often by reindeer-pulled sleds, although helicopters, airplanes, snowmobiles, and all-terrain vehicles are used as well. Canoes purchased from the Sakha or from Russian merchants are used for river transport and fishing.

¹⁰ FAMILY LIFE

The nomadic life of Dolgans herders and hunters is rigorous and demanding. As families move their reindeer from pasture to pasture, they must also move their homes and possessions with them. Among the nomadic reindeer breeders, men are generally responsible for the animals, hunting, and fishing. Women in traditional households are responsible for making fur clothing; preparing food; maintaining the tent; sled tent, or house; and child care. Some herding families have both mobile sled tents and apartments in a small village associated with a *sovkhoz,* or state farm. Each family today has its own tent. In the past, extended families predominated, whereas today the nuclear family is more common. Orphans and children from poor families are often taken into families of relatives to be raised, a practice that was common in the past and continues to be important today. In towns and cities where Dolgans have nontraditional jobs, women are still primarily responsible for the home and child care in addition to working outside the home. Young married couples and single people often live with their parents because housing is generally in short supply.

¹¹ CLOTHING

Traditional and manufactured clothing are often combined by the Dolgans, depending on their jobs and where they live. People in towns and cities tend to wear modern clothes made of manufactured cloth and perhaps fur coats and hats in winter. In rural villages and in the tundra, there are also manufactured clothes, but traditional types more suitable for hunting and herding activities are often seen. Russian-manufactured clothing was in use by the Dolgans by the early 20th century, and household garments of this type were worn by many people. A cloth coat called a *sontap* was worn by men and women in both summer and winter. In the winter, a second coat of fox or rabbit fur was worn beneath the cloth coat. Sometimes in winter instead of a cloth coat a short deerskin parka was worn. Belts embroidered with beads were sewn onto the outside of both men's and women's garments. Men's shirts and women's aprons were almost always decorated with embroidery. Hats (*bergese*) shaped like hoods were also ornamented with embroidery and beadwork.

12 FOOD

Traditional foods include reindeer meat, fish, fowl, and other game animals. Meat and fish were traditionally eaten boiled, dried, or raw (frozen or fresh). Fish were also sometimes fermented in pits in the ground. Reindeer milk was used by the Dolgans. Plant foods such as tea and sugar were introduced into the Dolgan diet long ago and have become integral parts of every meal.

13 EDUCATION

Educating the children of reindeer herders, who spend most of the year away from any village, has always been a difficult task. When universal education was first introduced by the Soviets, it was proposed that traveling teachers would move with the herding groups until they could be settled in permanent villages. This solution to the problem was short-lived, however, and the decision was made to send the children of nomadic herders to boarding schools, often far from their parents and other relatives. This resulted in children who knew the Russian language but not their own Dolgan language. Children were also taught that traditional ways of living and working should be abandoned in favor of life in a modern industrial society; thus, they learned little about their own cultural traditions and the land on which their families depended. Settling families in permanent homes in villages was another means of educating children and today most villages have schools that include the eighth class and sometimes the tenth class. After this point, students must leave their village to receive a higher education, and such a journey for 15- and 16-year-olds can be daunting. Today attempts are being made to change the educational system to include studies of Dolgan traditions, the Dolgan language, reindeer herding, and land management in addition to reading, writing, and arithmetic. Traveling teachers have again been proposed as one possible solution to the problem of combining education and a nomadic lifestyle, but even this system would have limitations, especially as children grow older and require more specialized instruction. Educational opportunities at all levels are available to the Dolgans Taimyr, other regional centers, and Moscow.

14 CULTURAL HERITAGE

Archaeological evidence shows that Samoyedic peoples had settled the Taimyr area by the first millennium AD, and these people were ancestors of the present-day Dolgans, Nentsy, and other indigenous peoples. They too were nomadic hunters and reindeer herders (although on a smaller scale than today). In the mid-16th century, Russian traders, trappers, and government representatives began moving into the Taimyr region; thus, the Native peoples have a long history of contact with Europeans. Beginning in the 17th century, travelers journeyed along the "Great Russian Road" across the Taimyr Peninsula from Lake Piasino east toward the Khatanga and on to the Anabar River and Sakha. Travelers on reindeer and dog sleds plied this route from one camp or settlement to the next. Peoples of diverse origins, languages, and cultures lived along this road, and it was along this route that the intermixing of peoples began which eventually lead to the formation of the contemporary Dolgan people.

In the 1926/27 Soviet census, the Dolgans were said to be composed of people descended from several ethnographic groups: Dolgans proper, Sakha, Evenki, Russia old peasants, and some Nentsy and Entsy. The Dolgans proper consisted of four Tungusic clans, one of which was named "Dolgan" or "Dulgaan." Only in the 19th century was this name used by the government to refer to people who called themselves by other names. Today this ethnic designation is recognized by the government and by the people themselves as an ethnic self-designation or ethnonym. Dolgan culture is also an amalgam of elements taken from each of the original ethnic groups: riding reindeer from the Evenki, herd dogs from the Nentsy, women's fur coats from the Sakha, and so on.

15 WORK

Work is often difficult to separate from other aspects of life among indigenous peoples. Although the Dolgans were traditionally hunters of wild reindeer, today there are many laborers, doctors, teachers, and other professionals among this group, and some people combine traditional occupations with nontraditional work on a seasonal basis.

The traditional Dolgan economy was focused on hunting wild reindeer in the north and elk and mountain sheep in the south. Ptarmigan, ducks, geese, and small game animals such as rabbits as well as fish were also important in the diet. Trapping polar fox was a significant commercial activity which allowed the Dolgans to trade for manufactured foods and goods. Reindeer breeding was oriented toward transportation: reindeer were ridden and used as pack animals during parts of the summer, and in winter they pulled sleds. Reindeer breeding requires a nomadic lifestyle as reindeer must frequently be moved to new pastures. The Dolgans had regular seasonal routes of migration not only to take advantage of pasturage, but of hunting and fishing opportunities as well. All of these activities continue to be important today, although they are more formally organized and sometimes conducted in nontraditional ways.

During the Soviet period, the traditional economic activities were reorganized by the government within the system of state farms, or *sovkhozes*. Work brigades moved the reindeer along traditional migration routes, going north in the summer and south in the winter, and changing routes on a regular schedule to maximize the use of available pasturage for the reindeer. Additional activities such as fur farming (raising foxes in cages), dairy farming, and vegetable growing were added, and fishing has become an important commercial activity. The Dolgans worked as laborers on the state farms and in the fishing industry. Today these state farms are being reorganized again in official attempts to encourage privatization and stimulate production. Educational and employment opportunities have also lead to substantial Dolgan participation in local government and nontraditional occupations in education, health care, construction, business, and so on.

[16] SPORTS

There is little information available on sports among the Dolgans. Presumably, in the large industrial centers of Noril'sk and the like, the Dolgans have access to Russian sports.

[17] ENTERTAINMENT AND RECREATION

Children in urban communities enjoy many of the same entertainments that children in the United States do: riding bicycles, watching movies and television, and playing with manufactured toys and games. In rural areas, and especially in the tundra, recreational opportunities are more limited. In villages there are bicycles, manufactured toys, televisions, VCRs, clubhouses (where movies might be shown), and radios. Although a trip to town might produce a store-bought toy, children in the tundra also depend on their imaginations and the games and traditional toys of their nomadic ancestors. The Dolgans have no musical instruments of their own, but at the end of the 19th century began to adopt the Sakha Jew's harp which has become common.

[18] FOLK ART, CRAFTS, AND HOBBIES

Folk arts are represented by the ornamentation of items of traditional material culture. Clothing is often embellished for special occasions with glass beads, metal buttons, embroidery, mosaic designs of fur, and appliqués of various colored skins and furs. Even everyday clothing is decorated with embroidery and beading. Skins are dyed red or black with natural dyes such as ochre, alder bark, and graphite. Reindeer harnesses are decorated with openwork embroidery made by women, and men carve the wooden cheek plates and saddles used for reindeer, inlaying them with tin and pewter. Traditional hunting and special household goods are sometimes inlaid with copper over steel. Wooden sculptures of religious significance were traditionally made in representation of animistic deities.

[19] SOCIAL PROBLEMS

Social problems among the Dolgans are generally related to environmental degradation and related problems as well as discriminatory practices in urban centers. Dolgans living in the Lower Yenisei Valley have experienced serious disruptions in their nomadic lifestyle and have lost most of their domestic reindeer herds due to dramatic changes in the migrations of wild reindeer. The normal movement of wild reindeer herds has been disrupted due to industrial development, and increased shipping traffic which have cut off migration routes. The wild herds steal domestic deer away during the fall breeding season, and they winter unpredictably on pastures previously only used by domestic herds. The industrial city of Noril'sk, where copper and nickel ores are refined, the port cities of Dudinka, Dikson, and Igarka, the mining settlements, and all of the smaller satellite communities of workers that ring these cities have produced pollution of unprecedented scale which expands outward into the rural tundra areas where Dolgans and other indigenous groups continue to practice traditional economic activities. The pollution has serious negative effects on human health, wild and domestic animal communities, and the plant life of Taimyr.

Unemployment, inadequate health care, alcoholism, and poorly developed infrastructure in small villages have all contributed to the serious situation in which the Dolgans and other

Native peoples in Russia find themselves today. Social welfare payments made by the government for unemployment, child care, and pensioners are important in helping support the indigenous population, but they are only short-term solutions to long-term problems. The Dolgans and other indigenous peoples in the Taimyr Autonomous *Okrug* have created an Association of the Indigenous Peoples of the Taimyr Autonomous *Okrug* through which they are demanding the rights to control their own destinies. The Association has declared that indigenous peoples in Taimyr have priority rights to the land and its subsurface resources and hopes to be able to use revenues from mineral exploitation and economic development to fund programs addressing the many social and economic problems facing indigenous peoples today.

[20] GENDER ISSUES

Gender issues among the Dolgan in particular have been little studied. Traditional Dolgan descent groups were patrilineal, although at the same time there was a clear division of labor between the sexes, with women responsible primarily for child rearing and domestic chores. During and after the Second World War Soviet labor policies began to erode this division of labor, accelerated by the sedentarization of the Dolgans, and increasing integration into Soviet society. The collapse of the Soviet Union, and the economic collapse in the Russian Federation in the 1990s probably fell particularly heavily upon Dolgan women, who had to provide for households in the face of severe unemployment and other social problems.

[21] BIBLIOGRAPHY

Anderson, D. "Indigenous Peoples and Development of the Lower Yenisei Valley." INSROP Working Paper No. 18-1995. International Northern Sea Route Programme. Norway: Fridtjof Nansen Institute, 1995.

Forsyth, James. *A History of the Peoples of Siberia: Russia's North Asian Colony, 1581–1990*. Cambridge: Cambridge University Press, 1992.

Gracheva, G. "Dolgan." In *Encyclopedia of World Cultures*. Vol. VI, Russia and Eurasia/China. Boston: G.K. Hall and Company, 1994.

———. "K voprosu o vliianii khristianizatsii na religioznye predstavleniia nganasan," *Khristianstvo i lamaizm u korennogo naseleniia Sibiri*, Leningrad: Nauka, 1979, 29–49.

Great Soviet Encyclopedia. New York: Macmillan, 1983. Trans. from the 3rd eds. of *Bol'shaia Sovetskaia entsiklopediia*. Moscow: 1978.

Latreille, Francis. *Dolgans—derniers nomades des glaces* (Paris: Hors Collection, 2003).

Popov, A. A. "The Dolgans." In *Peoples of Siberia*. Ed. M. G. Levin and L. P. Potapov. Chicago: University of Chicago Press, 1964. (Originally published in Russian, 1956.)

—revised by A. Frank

ENGLISH

LOCATION: United Kingdom (England)
POPULATION: 50.7 million, out of a total UK population of 60.7 million
LANGUAGE: English
RELIGION: Church of England; Protestant; Jewish; Sikh; Hindu; and Muslim

¹ INTRODUCTION

While the English in large part share their national origins with the peoples of continental Europe, their outlook has always been colored by the fact that they live on an island. The surrounding seas have given England a security unknown to other European countries. No one has successfully invaded Britain since the Norman Conquest of 1066, although others have tried—notably the Spanish in 1588, the French in 1805, and the Germans in 1940—but English defenses were aided by the natural barrier formed by the English Channel and the North Sea.

The area that is now called England was first united by the Romans in the 1st century AD. When they withdrew (AD 410), the area was settled by Germanic tribes from continental Europe such as the Angles, Saxons, and Jutes. It is often said that the name "England" is a contraction of "Angle-Land." England was converted to Christianity during the 6th and 7th centuries AD. During the early medieval period, coastal regions were regularly raided by the Vikings, who even came to rule most of the north and east of England. They were ejected by an alliance of nobles, led by the semi-legendary King Alfred.

In 1066, the Normans, from northwestern France, deposed the Anglo-Saxon dynasties, and the new rulers imposed a strong central government with their capital in London. At this point, England's history of expansion into its neighboring countries began. Wales, conquered in the Middle Ages, was incorporated into England in the 16th century. Ireland was first invaded in the 12th century, although it took over 400 years to bring the whole island under English rule. There was recurrent war with Scotland until the time of Henry VIII, but the Scots remained independent until 1603 when the monarchies of the two kingdoms were united. In 1707 Scotland and England were joined politically. From the Middle Ages onward, then, it is difficult to talk about England alone, for its history is inextricably linked to these other nations.

In the 17th century, the first English colonies in America were established. By the mid-19th century, England had become the center of an empire that was eventually to cover a quarter of the globe—28.5 million sq km (11 million sq mi). It was said that the sun never set on the British Empire, because it was always daytime in some part of it. Furthermore, the Industrial Revolution, which began in the 18th century, ensured that England was also the foremost economic, financial, and political power between the fall of Napoleon and the rise of Germany. At the height of the Empire's power, during the reign of Queen Victoria, England controlled an overseas population that was nearly 100 times larger than its own.

World War I (1914–1918) took an enormous toll on the English in terms of lives, resources, and national confidence. Altogether, the nation suffered over a million casualties, and more than 1 in 10 Englishmen under the age of 45 were killed. Soon after the war, the Empire started to disintegrate when Ireland became self-governing. Crippled economically by World War II (1939–1945), Britain withdrew from India and granted independence to most of the remaining colonies over the next 25 years, although almost all of them chose to remain part of the British Commonwealth of Nations. While England's international role is reduced from what it once was, the country is still prominent in world affairs as a member of the United Nations (with a permanent seat on the Security Council), the Commonwealth, the European Union (EU), and the North Atlantic Treaty Organization (NATO).

² LOCATION AND HOMELAND

England is the largest of the four countries that make up the United Kingdom. (The others are Scotland and Wales—located, like England, on the island of Britain—and Northern Ireland.) Wales lies to the west of England and Scotland to the north. England is roughly triangular in shape, with a long, irregular coastline. Its varied terrain consists of rugged highlands in the north, flat plains to the east, lowlands and low hills in the south, and moors in the southwest. England's (and the United Kingdom's) capital city is London.

England has a high population density, with 383 people/sq km (992/sq mi), compared with 114 people/sq km (295/sq mi) for France. About 90% of England's people are city dwellers. Ethnically, the English are descended from a mixture of European groups, including Celts and Romans, various Germanic tribes, Vikings, the Norman French, and others. Immigrants from Scotland, Wales, and Ireland have settled in England, as have more recent arrivals from former British colonies in South Asia and the Caribbean.

³ LANGUAGE

English is the most widely spoken language in the world. It is spoken throughout the United Kingdom and, altogether, by an estimated 500 million to 1.8 billion people worldwide. (There are approximately 300–400 people worldwide who speak English as a first language, and anywhere from 200 million to 1.4 billion people who speak English as a second language worldwide.) English is the international language of business and politics, too.

Derived from the Germanic tongue of Anglo-Saxon and modified by strong Latin, Greek and French influences, modern English has evolved from Old English—spoken until around AD 1100—and Middle English, which was in use from then until the late 1400s. Just as there are many types of English worldwide, so there are also many different dialects and regional accents throughout England itself; for instance, the speech of a person from Liverpool differs considerably from that of someone from Newcastle-upon-Tyne. The "Queen's English," the kind of English that foreigners learn and which BBC newsreaders speak, is a sanitized form of that which is spoken in the southeast of England and London. Furthermore, differences in education and class background can show up between speakers who live in the same region. Class-based speech differences among Londoners were memorably dramatized in George Bernard Shaw's play *Pygmalion* and its musical version, *My Fair Lady*.

Although Americans speak English, in addition to differences in pronunciation, Americans may have difficulty under-

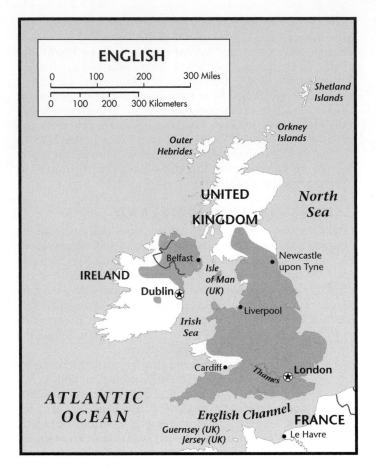

ENGLISH

0   100   200   300 Miles

0   100   200   300 Kilometers

Shetland Islands

Orkney Islands

Outer Hebrides

UNITED

North Sea

KINGDOM

Belfast •

Isle of Man (UK)

• Newcastle upon Tyne

IRELAND

Dublin ☆

Irish Sea

• Liverpool

Cardiff •

Thames

☆ **London**

ATLANTIC OCEAN

English Channel

FRANCE

Guernsey (UK)
Jersey (UK)

• Le Havre

tion pictures (such as *Camelot, Excalibur,* and even *Monty Python and the Holy Grail*) that have been made.

Probably the next most famous legends are those of Robin Hood and his Merry Men. They were outlaws who lived in Sherwood Forest near the city of Nottingham during the reign of King John (12th century AD), and were renowned for stealing from the rich and giving to the poor. Their arch-enemy was the Sheriff of Nottingham, who, like King John, got his comeuppance when the legitimate king, Richard I, was restored to the throne. These tales are full of memorable characters like Little John, Maid Marian, Friar Tuck, and Will Scarlet.

There are many other folk tales, legends, and ghost stories from different parts of England, but their popularity declined after the Industrial Revolution made England more urban than agricultural. However, recent years have seen a revival of interest. Especially noteworthy is the resurgence of the medieval mystery plays. These plays, based upon Biblical stories but incorporating many non-Biblical elements drawn from daily life, were originally performed by ordinary townspeople during religious festivals.

⁵ RELIGION

Although there is almost complete freedom of worship in England, church and state are closely intertwined. The Church of England (or Anglican Church) is an established church. England was Roman Catholic until 1534, when Henry VIII broke with Rome and proclaimed himself supreme head of the Church of England. Today, the head of the church is still the reigning monarch who, upon ascending the throne, pledges to uphold the faith. Until the mid-19th century, a person had to be a church member in order to sit in Parliament or attend the prestigious universities of Oxford and Cambridge. There are approximately 13–17 million members of the Church of England, although only 1 million of those attend services each Sunday. Other Protestant sects, including Methodists and Baptists, are also active in England and are called free churches. The Roman Catholic church is still very strong, partly due to the large numbers of Irish immigrants and Polish or Italian refugees who have settled in England. The country also has one of Europe's largest Jewish populations, numbering 300,000, and many cities have recently become home to large Sikh, Hindu, and Muslim immigrant populations.

⁶ MAJOR HOLIDAYS

Most of England's holidays are those found in the Christian calendar. Others include New Year's Day, May Day and the August Bank Holiday. There is also a great deal of pageantry related to the government and the monarchy. The Queen publicly reviews her regiments of Guards—one of the elite forces of the British Army—at the Trooping of the Colour, which celebrates her official birthday in June. The Guards are the soldiers who perform the daily changing of the guard at the Queen's London residence, Buckingham Palace.

The annual State Opening of Parliament has a lot of complex ceremony built into it. For example, the Queen invites members of the House of Commons to come and hear her speech in the chamber of the House of Lords, but her envoy (known as Black Rod) always has the door to the Commons slammed in his face. He is expected to knock on the door and humbly request that the members come to hear the monarch. On the night before the opening of Parliament, the Tower of

standing the speech of the English because the people of their respective countries refer to many of the same things using different terms. Examples include:

UNITED STATES	ENGLAND
ballpoint pen	biro
car hood	bonnet
car trunk	boot
phone booth	call box
elevator	lift
truck	lorry
baby's diaper	nappy
gasoline	petrol
baby buggy	pushchair
flashlight	torch

⁴ FOLKLORE

England's most famous body of folklore is that made up of the many different tales surrounding the legendary King Arthur and his Knights of the Round Table. Particularly well-known are the stories of the disruption caused by the adultery between Queen Guinevere and Sir Lancelot, Arthur's favorite knight; Sir Gawain's meeting with the Green Knight; and the search for the Holy Grail. These stories have been retold many times. The earliest version is that of Geoffrey of Monmouth, composed in 1135, but Sir Thomas Malory's 15th-century book is probably the best-known. T.H. White's *The Once and Future King* is a very modern view of the legends, as are the many mo-

London guards search the basements of the Houses of Parliament for explosives (a ritual that harks back to the Gunpowder Plot of 1605, a conspiracy to murder King James I as he opened Parliament).

The Gunpowder Plot is also commemorated on Guy Fawkes' Night (November 5) with bonfires, fireworks, and the burning of "guys" (cloth dummies) made from old clothes. Children go from door to door asking their neighbors to give them "a penny for the guy." Chestnuts are roasted in the same bonfire in which the guy is burning. Other historical events are recalled on Remembrance Sunday (the Sunday closest to November 11, the date of the armistice that ended World War I). On this date, the Queen leads a procession of retired soldiers to lay wreaths at the Cenotaph war memorial in Whitehall. At eleven o'clock, two minutes of silence are observed all over the country in honor of those who died in both world wars.

7 RITES OF PASSAGE

England, like the rest of Britain, is a modern, industrialized country. Hence, many of the rites of passage that young people undergo are connected with the education system. Apart from that, getting one's first job, gaining promotion, getting married, having children and retiring in one's sixties are the main signals of change in one's station.

8 INTERPERSONAL RELATIONS

The English are known for their politeness and their respect for law and order. They wait patiently in lines (or, as they call them, "queues") at stores, bus stops, movie theaters, and elsewhere. Hardly anyone dreams of jostling or trying to push ahead of others. Those living in the south are generally more reserved than northerners, who are more likely to greet strangers. The English also pride themselves on their dry humor and are known for their tolerance of other people's views, as well as of eccentric behavior.

It is hard to overstate the importance of class in English society. It has been a long time since England was anything like an absolute monarchy, but the nobility and the landed gentry did enjoy undisputed preeminence in English society until the middle of the 20th century, although the middle classes of businesspeople and industrialists have, for a long time, been far richer. In the 19th and 20th centuries, in fact, middle-class values tended to become the unofficial yardstick by which people's worth was measured. From a different perspective, many of the great philanthropic and reform movements of that time appear to be attempts to make poor people act more like the bourgeoisie. After World War II, many class barriers weakened, as working-class people gained access to better education and hence to better jobs, and society in general became more mobile. In the 1970s and 1980s, the meritocratic views of Margaret Thatcher, the Conservative Prime Minister, gained wide popularity, and a new class of "yuppies" was born. That said, the way in which one speaks, the school one attended, one's parents' occupations, and many other things, still tend to place one in some class or another.

9 LIVING CONDITIONS

In spite of England's high population density, there is less overcrowding than in most European countries. About half the population now lives in dwellings constructed after World War II, usually two-story houses with gardens. More than 80% of England's population live in houses, while the rest occupy apartments (called "flats"). In the 1980s, many tenants were allowed to purchase the low-income housing in which they lived, resulting in a shortage of housing in the low-income rental market. Today, there are a growing number of homeless people in London and England's other major cities.

A comprehensive National Health Service provides health care free, or at reduced rates, to all England's residents. This includes general medical, dental, optical, pharmaceutical, hospital, home health care, and preventive medical services. Average life expectancy in 2007 was 78.7 years. Primary causes of death include cardiovascular disease and cancer. The Department of Health carries out health education campaigns to inform people of the dangers from smoking and the often rather unhealthy English diet. Since 1982, the government has funded measures to control HIV/AIDS, including blood testing and public education.

England's 321,800 km (200,000 mi) of road are its most important means of transportation. Its rail system carries passengers and freight between cities, and high-speed trains provide passenger transport all over the country. England's merchant marine is one of the world's largest and safest. The Channel Tunnel linking England and France boasts the longest tunnel system ever built under water. There are several international airports, and Heathrow in London leads the world in volume of international air traffic.

10 FAMILY LIFE

England's families have gotten smaller over the years. The average household has 2.36 members, compared with 4 at the turn of the 20th century. As housing costs go up and families become more mobile, grandparents often live alone or in retirement homes rather than with the family. An increasing number of couples are living together without being married, and those who marry do so at a later age than previously—26 for men, 24 for women. Often, they try to establish themselves in an occupation or career before they marry and have children. In 2002, approximately 30% of those aged 16 and over were single, with 52% married, 9% per cent widowed, and 8% divorced. The traditional gender roles of men and women are changing both in the home and in the workplace. Equal pay for men and women performing the same work has been the law since 1975.

11 CLOTHING

There is no distinctive national costume for England. The one that is most readily associated with England—a man's dark jacket with striped trousers, bowler hat, and rolled umbrella—is in fact a rather old-fashioned and formal outfit for office-workers, particularly bankers and civil servants. For the most part, the English wear modern Western-style clothing similar to that of people in other industrialized nations. Blue jeans and T-shirts are very popular, heavy coats and mackintoshes (raincoats) and warm woolen clothes are required for the climate's cold, damp winters. Perhaps the best-known traditional costumes in England are the red uniforms and high black hats worn by the Queen's guard at Buckingham Palace. Ceremonial dress is worn by government troops and the royal family on such official occasions as Trooping the Colour. In rural areas, traditional folk costumes are worn for such festivals as May Day. On such occasions, men may appear in "motley"

The Royal Guards are the soldiers who perform the daily changing of the guard at Buckingham Palace, the queen's London residence. There is a great deal of pageantry related to the government and the monarchy. (Cory Langley)

coats featuring swatches of many different colors, knee-length breeches and white hose, and have bells tied around their legs.

12 FOOD

English cuisine, like that of other Northern European countries, does not usually include many herbs or spices, nor elaborate presentations of food. It can therefore seem bland and unimaginative to people from other countries. It seems that many English people agree, given the popularity of food from other countries, especially India and China. However, traditional English cooking relies for its effect upon either the freshness of the ingredients or the taste of the cooking media themselves (which explains the preoccupation with frying food that the English often seem to have).

The English are often believed to eat a large "English breakfast" of bacon, eggs, sausages, mushrooms, grilled tomatoes, fried bread, and, often, kipper, a popular type of smoked herring, every day—and, doubtlessly, some people do so. However, today most families eat a lighter, continental-type breakfast of cereal with milk and sugar, perhaps followed by toast and marmalade. The traditional breakfast, while still widespread, is far too time-consuming to make every morning, when people need to be at work or school on time.

The main meal of the day may be eaten either at midday or in the evening. In either case, it generally consists of a meat dish, vegetables, and dessert. Sunday lunch is the most important meal of the week. Traditional dishes for it include roast beef, mutton, or lamb served with roast potatoes, peas, and other vegetables. Other traditional English fare includes steak and kidney pie; cottage (or "shepherd's") pie, consisting of minced beef with a mashed potato topping; and "toad-in-the-hole," which is made out of skinned sausages baked in pancake batter. Puddings, including rice pudding and bread pudding, are the most common traditional dessert.

Tea is England's national beverage, and the English consume about a third of the world's tea exports. They are known for their custom of afternoon tea, accompanied by cakes and sandwiches. However, in the past, this was mainly a custom of the leisured classes, who were able to take a meal at 4:00 PM when most people were at work. These days, the custom is probably no more common than it ever was, except perhaps on weekends.

13 EDUCATION

Nearly the entire English population is literate, and education is compulsory between the ages of 5 and 16. The education system is divided between state-run schools (which the vast majority of pupils attend) and a much smaller private establishment. State primary education, divided into infant and junior stages, lasts until the age of 11. The state secondary education system is known as the "comprehensive" system, since the state schools—mainly founded in the years following World War II—are designed to give a wide education to those who could not otherwise afford it. There is less "tracking" of students into certain schools, although recently the government has given parents a greater say in which schools their children attend. Students who attend private schools go to "preparatory" school between the ages of 7 and 13. Private secondary schools are known (confusingly to Americans) as "public schools." The best-known of these schools are Eton, Harrow, and Marlborough. The state requires all pupils attempt certain examinations. At the age of 16, pupils sit for exams in several subjects in order to get the General Certificate of Secondary Education (GCSE). Thereafter, one may either leave school to find a job, or continue one's secondary education until the age of 18. At that age, pupils take more specialized, advanced level exams ("A"-Levels). These are usually a way of preparing to attend a university.

The university system is substantially (but not wholly) subsidized by the state. There are about 50 chartered universities in England, established in several historical stages. The "greystones" were founded in the medieval period. These include the world-famous universities of Oxford and Cambridge, which date from the 12th and 13th centuries, respectively. Next oldest are the "redbricks," which were founded in the 19th century, often by philanthropists using money that they had made from industrial or commercial enterprises. During the mid-20th century, many new universities were set up by the government, and are usually called "modern" universities.

14 CULTURAL HERITAGE

England has a distinguished cultural heritage, particularly in literature, where it boasts one of the greatest writers of any time or place, the 16thcentury playwright William Shakespeare. It is traditionally held that his birthday (and also the date of his death) is April 23, which is the feast day of St. George, the patron saint of England. Besides Shakespeare, England can claim great writers and literary works as far back as the Old English epic *Beowulf,* written around the 10th century AD, and Geoffrey Chaucer's 14th-century *Canterbury Tales.* Modern readers are still moved by the works of great Romantic poets such as William Wordsworth and John Keats. The 19th-century clergyman Gerard Manley Hopkins exploited the purely musical potential of the English language perhaps more than any other writer. The 19th century saw a sudden flourishing of the novel, connected with such names as Jane Austen, Charles Dickens, the Brontë sisters, George Eliot, and Thomas Hardy. Only a few of the many great English names in modern literature are D. H. Lawrence, Virginia Woolf, W. H. Auden, and George Orwell. Great English writers born abroad include the Polish-born Joseph Conrad and the American-born T. S. Eliot. The contemporary scene includes Salman Rushdie, Martin Amis, Nick Hornby, Ian McEwan, and Harold Pinter. J.K. Rowling (b.1965) is the author of the wildly famous Harry Potter books.

Great 19th-century English painters include Joseph Turner and John Constable, while Francis Bacon, David Hockney, and Graham Sutherland achieved renown in the 20th century, as did sculptor Henry Moore. From John Dowland, William Byrd and Henry Purcell in the 1500s and 1600s, through Gilbert and Sullivan's popular 19th-century light operas, to the modern works of Ralph Vaughn Williams and Benjamin Britten, English composers have given the world much memorable music. The composer whose name is most inextricably linked to England is Sir Edward Elgar, whose "Pomp and Circumstance" provides the melody for "Land of Hope and Glory," which is something of an unofficial English national anthem. In the 1960s, England became a trend setter in popular music as the home of the Beatles and the Rolling Stones, two of the most successful rock groups ever formed, as well as numerous other successful artists and groups in the 21st century.

15 WORK

The average English work week is 35 to 40 hours long, spread out over five days—half the length of the work week a century ago. About half of England's workers are employed in service sector jobs, a third in manufacturing and engineering, and the rest in agriculture, construction, mining, and energy production. The north is highly industrialized and contains over a third of the country's manufacturing labor force. However, many of the older industries have declined, resulting in unemployment which has led to heavy emigration from the region. About half the workers in the Midlands region are employed in the automobile industry. In the southeast, more than 80% of the labor force works in the service sector, and dairy farming is an important source of employment in the southwest.

16 SPORTS

The most popular spectator and participant sport in England is soccer (usually called "football"), which is played in professional and amateur leagues as well as in schools, colleges, and local boroughs. The ubiquity of the game is such that there are some 100 professional clubs alone. Other favorite sports include cricket and rugby (named for Rugby School, where it began). Soccer, cricket, and rugby all originated in England, and spread worldwide due to the influence of the British Empire. Gambling on sports—which is legal in England—is a popular pastime. Most betting is done on horse racing. Over 90% of the population has gambled at some point, and around half do it regularly. Other popular sports include hockey, cross-country running, tennis, swimming, and other water sports. A famous horse race takes place regularly at the Royal Ascot, in which horses owned by the Royal Family are often entered.

17 ENTERTAINMENT AND RECREATION

Many people in England enjoy spending their leisure time relaxing at home with television or a video. The vast majority are regular newspaper readers, and nearly half read books on a regular basis as well. On weeknights, the hours between 7:00 and 11:00 PM are generally spent watching television or reading. More than 90% of English households own a television set and over half have a VCR or DVD. Until the mid-1980s, only four television stations were available. Since then, however, satellite broadcasting has considerably expanded the alternatives. Second to home recreations is visiting the local pub or club. There are many kinds of drinking establishments, but the most familiar is the quiet, traditional pub which serves not only alcohol but good traditional food.

Angling is the most popular pastime in the country. England has many miles of rivers and canals in which anglers fish for trout, carp, bream, and roach. The English are also very fond of games. Both snooker and darts are played by many people (the latter being especially popular in pubs), and, despite not being very visually exciting events, draw large audiences during televised professional tournaments. Among older people, bingo and cribbage are often taken very seriously.

The English are known for their love of gardening, and even apartment-dwellers without a plot of their own will often rent a piece of land on which to garden, or at least have a window box full of flowers. Fishing, hiking, and horseback riding are other popular outdoor leisure time pursuits. Many adults enjoy taking evening classes in every subject from basket weaving to yoga. Pets are very popular in England and half of its households have one—most often a dog, which is the national favorite.

18 FOLK ART, CRAFTS, AND HOBBIES

England has a history of fine furniture-making dating back to the 18th-century craftsmen Thomas Chippendale and George Hepplewhite, examples of whose art can still be seen today. Their contemporaries Josiah Wedgwood and Josiah Spode made England famous for its ceramics as well, especially the blue-and-white Wedgwood jasperware that England still exports today. The most famous English folk dance is the Morris dance, still seen at local festivals. Male dancers stomp and leap while waving pieces of cloth and jingling bells.

19 SOCIAL PROBLEMS

Class divisions and economic inequality are facts of life in present-day England. Approximately 25% of the nation's wealth is owned by 1% of the population, while unemployment was 5.4% in 2007 and 14% of the population lived below the poverty line. Many immigrants from the West Indies, India, Pakistan, Hong Kong, and other countries have settled in urban areas, where they are often subjected to housing and other types of discrimination and have a high rate of unemployment. Racial tension between the white English community and non-white immigrants has erupted into riots in London, Liverpool, Bristol, and Birmingham. As well, England has been a target of international Islamic terrorists, with bombings on the London public transit system carried out in July 2005, killing 52 and injuring 700. In 2006 controversial Egyptian-born Muslim cleric Abu Hamza al-Masri was jailed for seven years after being found guilty of inciting murder and race hate. Abu Hamza, who is being sought for extradition by U.S. authorities on terror-related matters, preached at the Finsbury Park Mosque, in north London.

20 GENDER ISSUES

Women in England have a long tradition of working for equal rights. The 19th century saw the rise of the suffragettes (the right to vote for English women was won in 1918), and Girton at Cambridge University was founded as England's first women's college in 1869. The number of women in paid work increased substantially after the two world wars, but they generally had low-paid, female-dominated occupations, such as teaching and clerical work. In the late 1980s women made up more than 40% of the workforce in England, and they increasingly took managerial and professional jobs. However, although equal pay for men and women performing the same work has been the law since 1975, few women enjoy parity with men in pay. In 2007 pro-choice British women celebrated 40 years of legalized abortion.

Homosexuality is increasingly being tolerated by a large portion of the British population. However, some gay people still find it difficult to admit their sexuality, especially while at school or university. It is becoming more common for gay men to "come out" openly, but is not common to see gay men showing their sexuality in public (for example by holding hands or kissing). Many older British people still find it difficult to accept homosexuality. The official teachings of most churches in the UK remain hostile to homosexuality. Homosexuality was legalized in the United Kingdom in 1967, and the homosexual age of consent has been reduced since then from 21 to 18 and now to 16 (the same age as for sex between men and women). Since 2003 it is unlawful to discriminate in the workplace against someone on the grounds of his or her sexuality. Gay men and women have been allowed to serve in the military since 2000. Gay marriages are not legal in the UK. However, the Civil Partnership Act (in force as of 2005) created a new legal relationship of "civil partnership," which two people of the same sex can form by signing a registration document.

London, Brighton, and Manchester all have large gay communities. Blackpool, Bournemouth, Edinburgh, Glasgow, and Newcastle also have significant gay communities. The most famous place for gay people to meet is in Old Compton Street in London's Soho area. Every summer (late June or early July) in London there is a Pride London parade and rally. There is an annual film festival in London showing gay and lesbian films.

21 BIBLIOGRAPHY

Abbe Scientist Research Division. *AIDS and HIV in the United Kingdom.* Washington DC: Abbe Publishers Association, 2008.

Díëez Medrano, Juan. *Framing Europe: Attitudes to European Integration in Germany, Spain, and the United Kingdom.* Princeton, N.J.: Princeton University Press, 2003.

England in Pictures. Minneapolis: Lerner Publications, 1990.

Fuller, Barbara. *Britain: Cultures of the World.* London: Marshall Cavendish, 1994.

Gall, Timothy, and Susan Gall, ed. *Junior Worldmark Encyclopedia of the Nations.* Detroit: UXL, 1996.

Greene, Carol. *England. Enchantment of the World Series.* Chicago: Children's Press, 1994.

Helweg, Arthur W. "English." In *Encyclopedia of World Cultures (Europe).* Boston: G. K. Hall, 1992.

James, T. B. *The Story of England.* Stroud, Gloucestershire: Tempus Pub., 2003.

Illustrated Encyclopedia of Mankind. London: Marshall Cavendish, 1978.

Langley, Andrew. *Passport to England.* New York: Franklin Watts, 1994.

—revised by J. Hobby

ESTONIANS

LOCATION: Estonia
POPULATION: 1.3 million total population of country, of which 68% are ethnic Estonians
LANGUAGE: Estonian
RELIGION: Lutheran; Russian Orthodox

¹ INTRODUCTION

After the last Ice Age, the area now known as Estonia was inhabited by people whose ethnic origin was unknown. There are signs of human activity from the middle of the 8th millennium BC. In the middle of the 3rd millennium BC, Finno-Ugric tribes arrived from the east and became mixed with the forerunners of the Baltic people who had previously migrated there. Estonians have thereafter lived on their land for 5,000 years, being one of the longest-settled European peoples. The oldest written record of Estonia was made by an Arab geographer, al-Idrisi, in AD 1154. By the beginning of the 13th century AD, a state had not yet developed, a feudal system was unknown, there were no towns, and the effect of Christianity was minor. There was a population of approximately 100,000 people. Until the end of the 12th century, Estonians had been successful in repelling the attempts of Scandinavians and Old Russians to conquer and dominate the area.

At the end of the 12th century, the militant German religious expansion to the east increased. Warfare commenced at the beginning of the 13th century, when the pagan Estonian society fought against the more advanced European society. German, Danish, Swedish, and Russian conquerors encountered armed resistance. By the year 1227, Estonia had been conquered, tying Estonia's development to that of Europe.

After the conquest, small feudal states were formed. Estonia was divided between the Livonian Order, Denmark (who sold its territory to the Livonian Order in 1346), and the bishops of Tartu and Saare-Lääne. The economy of the towns was based on East–West transit trade. The legal status of peasants deteriorated: by the end of the 14th century, they were attached to the land and by the beginning of the 16th century, serfdom had developed.

In 1558 Prince IV of Moscow invaded Estonia and defeated the divided small states. The rulers sought foreign aid. In 1561 northern Estonia yielded to Sweden and southern Estonia to Poland. By the year 1583, the Russian armies were forced out of Estonia. As a result of the Swedish-Polish wars, all of Estonia became Swedish territory in 1625.

In 1721 Estonia became part of Russia. At the beginning of the 19th century, peasants were granted ownership of their movable property, as well as the right to cultivate their farms in perpetuity. Estonian county schools were established on the farm lands of the manors. Tartu University, which was reopened in 1802, became the most important scientific and cultural center in all of Russia. More peasants bought farms and became independent from the manors. Estonian language journalism began and an Estonian intelligentsia developed. In 1857 the national epic *Kalevipoeg* was published, an Estonian-language school for peasants was established shortly thereafter, the first Estonian national song festival was held in 1869, the collection of folklore began, and national theaters were found-

ed. This politically active period enabled Estonians to become organized, with increasing individualism and self-consciousness. In 1884 the Estonian University Students' Society's blue, black, and white tricolor flag was consecrated. Later, this became the Estonian national flag.

In the late 1800s, Russian nationalism was strengthened in order to tie the peripheral provinces to the center. Local authorities became increasingly under the control of the Russian center. Organizations in the national Estonian movement were closed down, censorship became stricter, and the Russification (Russianizing) of the indigenous population increased. However, Russification policies ended in 1897. Development began in the metal and machinery industries, and cotton and wood processing industries were established. Agricultural cooperatives flourished, and farmers' associations were formed. The towns became more Estonian. A new generation of educated people, including politicians, quickly restored the awareness of a national identity.

In 1918 Estonians finally had the opportunity to create their own state. The subsequent War of Independence was concluded by the Treaty of Tartu, signed in February 1920, whereby Russia recognized Estonia as an independent nation. Soon afterwards, Estonia became a full member of the League of Nations.

Between the two world wars, the Estonian economy grew rapidly. By 1939, national income per capita was approximately equal to that of Finland. At that time Estonia was mainly an agrarian and trading nation. It had also developed an industry well suited to its own needs and quite competitive in international trade.

After the collapse of Germany in November 1918, the Estonian Provisional Government assumed power. Soviet Russia attacked Estonia, and in an attempt to conceal the aggression, the Estonian Working People's Commune was set up in Narva. By the beginning of 1919, two-thirds of Estonia was under Soviet control. The Estonians counterattacked and freed the land in three weeks. In June and July 1919, successful battles were conducted against the Baltic-German Landeswehr army in northern Latvia. The victory at Vonnu on June 23 is commemorated by a national holiday, Victory Day. Military activity against Soviet Russia continued in the autumn, and on 2 February 1920, the Tartu Peace Treaty was concluded, wherein Soviet Russia recognized the Republic of Estonia.

The Molotov-Ribbentrop Treaty signed in 1939, however, consigned Estonia to the Soviet Union's sphere of influence. In 1940 the country was occupied and incorporated into the USSR. The Estonian economy became a supplier to Moscow, and the whole society came under total Soviet control. In the period of July 1940–June 1941, an estimated 1,000 people were arrested and disappeared. On 14 June 1941, mass deportations began: over 10,000 people were sent to Siberia without any legal proceedings. Many went into hiding in forests to escape the terror.

On 5 July 1941, German troops crossed the Estonian border. Around 35,000 people joined the retreating Soviet forces, in addition to the 33,000 Estonian people who had been forcibly conscripted into the Red Army. Approximately 5,500 Estonians were killed in concentration camps. Germans also carried out forced conscription. In February 1944, when the Soviet forces again advanced on Estonia, 40,000 Estonians had joined the German Army and, together with German troops,

ESTONIANS

0   50   150   250 Miles

0   100   200   300 Kilometers

FINLAND

Tampere

Helsinki

Gävle

SWEDEN

Åland
Islands

Tallinn

St. Petersburg

RUSSIA

ESTONIA

Stockholm

Gotland

Riga

LATVIA

Öland

Baltic Sea

LITHUANIA

Vitsyebsk

Bornholm
(DENMARK)

RUSSIA

Vilnius

Kaliningrad

Minsk

Gdańsk

BELARUS

POLAND

Homyel

Poznań

stopped the Red Army. On 22 September 1944, however, the Red Army entered Tallinn and the whole country was conquered again. Some 70,000–80,000 people fled the country by sea.

From 1944, the Sovietization of Estonia continued. Forced industrialization was accompanied by the immigration of more than 240,000 settlers, mainly Russians. Agriculture went through forced collectivization. On 25–26 March 1949, 20,700 Estonians were deported to Siberia. During the Soviet era, the economy became largely urbanized and industrialized. Despite the inefficiencies of the Soviet central planning system, Estonia enjoyed one of the highest standards of living in the former Soviet Union.

In the second half of the 1980s, under the deepening economic and political crises in the Soviet Union, the Estonian Supreme Soviet proclaimed the Estonian Declaration of Sovereignty. This sent a signal of rebellion throughout the Soviet Empire, bringing about the beginning of its eventual collapse. On 20 August 1991, at the peak of the attempted coup in the Soviet Union, the Supreme Council of the Republic of Estonia issued a decision on the reestablishment of independence on the basis of historical continuity of statehood.

On 17 September 1991, the Republic of Estonia was accepted as a full member of the United Nations. In 2004 Estonia officially entered both the North Atlantic Treaty Organization (NATO) and the European Union (EU).

² LOCATION AND HOMELAND

Estonia is located in the northeastern region of Europe, on the eastern shores of the Baltic Sea. It has been inhabited for more than 5,000 years by the Estonians, who belong to the Balto-Finnic group of Finno-Ugric nations. The territory of Estonia is approximately 45,000 sq km (17,300 sq mi). The longest distance from east to west is 350 km (220 mi), and from north to south it is 240 km (150 mi). Estonia's nearest neighbors are Russia in the east, Latvia in the south, and Finland and Sweden across the Baltic Sea to the north and west.

The climate of Estonia is moderate. The mean daily temperature in Tallinn is –5.3°C (22°F) in January and 16.5°C (62°F) in July: the annual average is 4.9°C (41°F). The lowest temperature (–43.5°C or –46°F) was measured in Estonia in January 1941, but as a rule the temperature seldom drops below –25°C (–13°F). The highest recorded temperature is 35°C (95°F), but it is unusual for the temperature to exceed 30°C (86°F). Usually, there is snow cover from December to March.

Estonia has more than 1,500 islands, the largest of which are Saaremaa (2,673 sq km/1,032 sq mi), Hiiumaa (989 sq km/382 sq mi), Muhu (200 sq km/77 sq mi) and Vormsi (92.9 sq km/35.9 sq mi). The length of the coastline is approximately 3,800 km (2,360 mi). There are over 1,400 lakes in Estonia. The largest of them are Lake Peipsi (3,555 sq km/1,373 sq mi), which is the border lake between Estonia and Russia and is therefore divided between the two countries, and Lake Vortsjärv (270 sq km/104 sq mi). The deepest lake is Lake Rouge Suurjärv (38 m or 125 ft deep). The three largest rivers, in order of larger to smaller are the Narva, the Emajogi, and the Pärnu.

There are extensive oil shale deposits in the northeast region of Estonia. These are mainly used for two purposes: production of electricity and as raw materials for the chemical industry. The electricity produced is partially consumed in Estonia and partially exported to the neighboring countries of Latvia and Russia. North Estonia and the islands have deposits of limestone and dolomite rocks used for architectural and building needs, as well as for decorative purposes. In the northern part of Estonia there are also deposits of phosphorite. Cambrian blue clay is used for manufacturing bricks, drainage pipes, and cement. Peat is mainly used for farmers' needs and for the production of pressed blocks that are used as heating material.

Many wild animals and birds live in Estonian woodlands and wetlands. Approximately 48% of Estonia's territory is covered by forests. These have importance not only as hunting areas, but also as a valuable national resource for the relatively well-developed woodworking industry. There are many companies in Estonia involved in fishing, fish processing, and the marketing of fish products.

The total population of Estonia is about 1.3 million, with a density of 30 inhabitants/sq km (78/sq mi). The breakdown of ethnic groups is as follows: Estonians, 68%; Russians, 26%; Ukrainians, 2%; Belarusans, 1%; Finns, 1%; and others, 2%. Some 70% of the population is urban, and 30% is rural. The capital of Estonia is Tallinn (population 395,000). The other largest cities are Tartu (102,000), Narva (66,000), Kohtla-Järve (45,000), and Pärnu (44,000).

In addition to those in the Estonian homeland, there are many Estonians living abroad who fled to the West because of the Soviet occupation in 1944. The largest expatriate Estonian communities are in Sweden, the United States, Canada, Australia, Germany, and Finland.

³ LANGUAGE

The Estonian language is related to Finnish in that it is in the Finnic branch of the Ural-Altaic language family, along with Karelian, Komi, Mari, and Mordvin. Besides Finnish (and, to a lesser degree, Hungarian), no other prominent modern European language is related to Estonian. Although Estonian is a distinct language, it also uses words borrowed from Swedish, German, and Russian. Standard Estonian is based upon the Northern Estonian dialect.

The earliest example of written Estonian dates back to the 13th century, and the oldest known texts are from the 16th century. Estonian grammar was not standardized until the late 1800s, with many revisions taking place in the 1920s and 1930s to reduce the influence of German.

Written Estonian uses the Latin alphabet, with a few added characters: ä, ö, ü, õ, š, and ž. The added vowels are pronounced similarly to German, and the õ is a variant of the German ö. The š carries the "sh" sound, and ž has a "zh" sound. The letters c, q, w, x, and y only appear in words of foreign origin. Spelling is phonetic, so there are no silent letters or consonant clusters. However, there are durations of sounds in spoken Estonian that are not distinguished in written Estonian, as well as some words that are spelled the same but pronounced differently. Estonian uses no articles, noun genders, verb aspects, or prepositions. There is, however, a system of 14 cases, of which 10 act as "prepositions." There is also no future tense, and word order is very flexible.

Estonian first names for males often end in the letter o (as in Finnish). Typical first names include Arno, Eino, Ivo, Jaak, Jaan, Peeter, Rein, and Ülo. Female first name examples include Aime, Ester, Krista, Leida, and Mari. Estonian spellings of many common Scandinavian first names are also typical.

Examples of everyday Estonian words include *Tere* (How do you do?), *palun* (please), *tänan* (thank you), and *head aega* (goodbye). Estonian tends to incorporate newer international words rather than inventing its own equivalents.

⁴ FOLKLORE

The runic folk song is the oldest form of Estonian folklore, originating some 2,000–3,000 years ago as an oral tradition. There are about 3,600 of these runic folk songs known to exist, with about 133,000 variations. The oldest songs are mythic themes and family ballads. When an agricultural society developed, many of the songs dealt with labor and rituals. Most of the songs that originated in the Middle Ages were sung by women and had female-oriented themes, but many of the more modern folk songs are male-centered. Many of the folk stories are legends associated with certain objects or places. As a result, most prominent physical features (large rocks and trees, bodies of water) in Estonia have some sort of legend associated with them.

The national epic *Kalevipoeg* utilizes themes from Estonian folklore. It describes the battles and adventures of Kalevipoeg (Kalev's son), the mythical hero and ruler of ancient Estonia, and ends with his violent death and the country's conquest by foreign invaders. According to Estonian folklore, Kalevipoeg created the Estonian landscape with his own two hands by cutting down the forests to form the plains, uprooting gardens to make the hills, and drawing water to fill in the lakes.

Two popular Estonian legends are based in Tallinn. One legend has it that when Tallinn is completely built, it will be flooded. The flood will happen because Jarvevana, the legendary old man who lives at the bottom of Lake Ulemiste (which is the city's water source), will pull out the plug of the lake. Another legend tells the story of a warrior-maiden who secretly brought in the building stones under cover of night.

⁵ RELIGION

Pagan and totem worship, along with shamanism, were widely practiced in ancient times. Christianity came to the Estonians in the 11th century AD. Over the next two centuries, the majority of Estonians gradually became Christian. During the period of Swedish rule (1629–1710), a state church was established that was based on Lutheran doctrine. Lutheranism is the most widely practiced faith among Estonians today, though there are also Russian Orthodox and Baptist communities within Estonia. From the 1740s until the 1840s, the immense political influence of imperial Russia on the Estonians resulted in a weakened role for the state Lutheran Church and an increase in conversion to the tsar's religion—Russian Orthodoxy. By the early 1900s, however, greater religious tolerance of the Lutheran Church was shown by Russia.

During Estonia's brief period of independence (1918–1940) before the Soviet invasion, the Estonian Evangelical Lutheran Church had a leading role in society. When the Soviet occupation began in 1940, anti-Christian legislation was enacted, and policies were carried out immediately. These policies included banning church activities, shutting down churches and confiscating the property, and limiting religious services to a negligible level. Official antireligious bias and repression by the Soviet government continued to some extent until 1988, but all antireligious legislation was repealed in 1990. Since the end of Soviet rule in Estonia, many Estonians have become interested in religion.

⁶ MAJOR HOLIDAYS

The national holidays are New Year's Day (January 1), Independence Day (February 24), Good Friday (late March or early April), Labor Day (May 1), St. John's Night or Midsummer Day (June 23 and 24), and Christmas (December 25 and 26).

The most beautiful and long-awaited holiday among Estonians is probably Christmas. Winter is the time of the year when there is almost no sunshine, and it is light for only a couple of hours a day. So, people start decorating their homes and often begin lighting candles at the end of November. At the beginning of December there are Christmas decorations everywhere, and soon Christmas trees (fir) are brought into homes. They may be decorated in many ways. During recent years, however, Christmas decorations have become more commercialized. On Christmas Eve many people go to church. It is a tradition in every Estonian family to bake gingerbread. Children look forward to the arrival of Santa Claus, who brings presents. This is traditionally a quiet holiday, which is celebrated with family and close friends. A traditional Estonian Christmas dinner is oven-baked pork with sauerkraut, potatoes, and blood sausage, often served with lingonberry sauce or pickled pumpkin. During the Soviet occupation, celebrating Christmas was prohibited. At home, most Estonians did it secretly anyway.

Another important national holiday for Estonians is St. John's Day. The 24th of June is the peak of summer and the lightest and warmest time of the year. In fact, it never gets com-

Pedestrians pass the Town Hall Square in Tallinn, Estonia. (AP Images/Timur Nesametdinov, NIPA)

pletely dark at night. On June 23, people everywhere light bonfires at night. They drink beer and bake sausages over the fire, sing, and have fun. In the cities people can make small fires in their gardens or in open fireplaces. Real bonfires are made mostly in the country. In times past, children and young people jumped over the bonfires and swung on big village swings.

Another reason to celebrate June 23 is because on that day in 1919, the Estonian national army won the battle of Vonnu, which was decisive in the War of Independence.

7 RITES OF PASSAGE

Rites of passage for Estonians are related to family occurrences like births, deaths, and marriages. A child's first day at school and, especially, the day of graduation from high school are also celebrated. Graduation from university is an important event that may be celebrated for several days among the graduates, as well as with family members and relatives. High school and university reunions are also traditional.

8 INTERPERSONAL RELATIONS

Estonians are generally regarded as shy and withdrawn. They do not communicate with other people easily. However, among friends and family, they are quite friendly and hospitable.

In formal communications, men are referred to as *Härra* (Mr.) and women as *Proua* (Mrs.) or *Preili* (Miss). Usually people shake hands when meeting and departing, and it is polite to look into other people's eyes. The polite form of addressing someone in the Estonian language is *teie,* which is used when meeting someone for the first time or with those one does not know well.

Among good friends and business associates, the informal *sina* is used to address each other. Close friends also greet each other with a wave of the hand and use foreign expressions like *ciao,* "hi," or "bye."

9 LIVING CONDITIONS

The Estonian economy has been growing rapidly since entry into the European Union, resulting in an increased standard of living for many Estonians. Nearly all Estonians now have hot and cold running water, telephones (including land line and cellular), refrigerators, washing machines, and other modern conveniences. There are numerous television stations, and cable is becoming increasingly available, along with internet connections.

The bottom segment of society, however, has experienced a decline in standard of living with a resulting increase in the number of homeless in urban centers. The estimated total number of homeless people in Estonia in the past decade has risen from 100–150 to some 3,500 people.

The number of automobiles in Estonia is growing constantly. However, the importance of a car in the family is not as great as in the United States. Public transportation is quite well developed and covers all areas in major cities and throughout the country. For example, city transportation in Tallinn includes buses, trolleys, and streetcars. There is no subway in Estonia.

The mortality rate is 13.35 per 1,000 people, and the birth rate is 10.28 per 1,000 people.

10 FAMILY LIFE

Most Estonians get married for the first time when they are in their 20s. Usually, people are not engaged before they get married. More than 50% of these marriages end in divorce. In recent years, more couples are choosing to live together without marrying; in 2003 an estimated 58% of all children were born to unmarried couples. A law was proposed in 2008 to register domestic partnerships.

Among Estonians, it is common in that both the husband and wife work full-time. A typical work day ends between 5:00 and 6:00 pm. After that, people do their housework (cook, wash, tidy up, etc.). It is common to watch TV and read books. The role of women is important in Estonia as they are more active in the household than are men. Children normally get home from school earlier and have to spend hours at home alone. As people are not very mobile in Estonia, it is quite typical that several generations live together or close to one another. Grandparents often take care of their grandchildren and help in the household. It is also common that children take care of their parents when they are no longer able to live by themselves.

11 CLOTHING

Clothing in Estonia mostly depends on what type of work one does. As in many other countries, traditional office dress for men is a Western-style suit and tie. Women wear suits, skirts and blouses, or sometimes pantsuits. In some places, people may dress more casually. When not at work, Estonians often wear jeans and sweaters or tee-shirts. In general, however, Estonian people prefer to "dress up" rather than "dress down." For example, Estonians rarely wear jeans and a sweater to the theater or a concert. Most people are quite style-conscious. Wearing gold and silver jewelry is also common. As the climate is rather cold, people need to wear warm and weatherproof clothes. On a cold winter day, women in fur coats are a common sight in the streets of Estonian cities. It has always been characteristic for Estonian women to make clothes for themselves instead of buying what is available at shops. Many women have sewing machines at home. They also knit woolen socks, mittens, and sweaters with traditional Estonian patterns that are admired by foreigners.

Estonian children are not required to wear uniforms to school. The most popular clothes among students are jeans and tee-shirts. On festive school occasions, girls have to wear a white blouse and dark skirt, and boys must wear a dark suit and white shirt. For hygienic reasons, they also have to put on other shoes inside the school building.

12 FOOD

Over the centuries, Estonian cuisine has been influenced by Scandinavians, Germans, and Russians. Estonian eating habits are best characterized by the saying: "Eat your breakfast yourself, share your lunch with your friend, and give your dinner to your enemy." The most typical breakfast would consist of a Scandinavian-style open-faced sandwich (a slice of black or white bread with butter and cheese or sausage, with some slices of fresh tomato, radish, cucumber, etc.) and a cup of rich, good coffee. Coffee is definitely the most popular drink in Estonia. It is served in offices in the morning and during lunch, as well as at home to guests. Children, though, prefer tea, milk, or juice. During recent years, yogurt and cornflakes have become more popular, especially among children.

In Estonia, lunch is the most substantial meal of the day. People try to get out of their offices for an hour between 12:00 and 3:00 pm and have their lunch in cafés, restaurants, bars, or canteens. A typical meal consists of meat and potatoes with gravy and a fresh salad. Some people may have soup, salad, and a light dessert only. Although pizza and hamburgers are becoming increasingly popular, the consumption of fast food is not characteristic of Estonians. Children are served lunch at school.

Dinner is usually eaten at home after work, seldom later than 8:00 pm. In families, dinner may be basically the same as lunch, depending on how much food they have had during the day. For convenience, many people prefer warmed sausages and/or bread and butter and soup. As Estonian people try to avoid heavy food in the evening, yogurt and cottage cheese of all varieties are popular. But, in most cases, women still try to provide warm dinners for their families after work. Going out for dinner is quite expensive and therefore not customary.

In general, Estonians are quite health-conscious and educated. Most people try to supplement their diet with fresh fruits and vegetables that are available throughout the year (mostly imported from Western countries), although they are quite expensive. Snacks like potato chips and popcorn are not popular.

Most Estonian women are skilled at cooking. At home parties (like birthdays), guests are served delicious salads and hors d'oeuvres, homemade pies, and cakes. People also pay attention to how nicely their food is served.

13 EDUCATION

Estonians start school when they are six or seven years old. Primary education lasts for four years. Secondary education, following primary, is divided into two parts: basic education (grades 5–9) and upper secondary education (grades 10–12). Primary and basic education (grades 1–9) is compulsory for all children of Estonia. There are two main options after basic school—upper secondary school or vocational school. Some vocational schools provide secondary education in addition to vocational education. The secondary school certificate gives a student the right to continue his or her education either in universities or in other institutions of higher education.

Estonia has one of the highest levels of education in the European Union, with literacy and school enrollment rates at or near 100%. The rates are approximately equal for males and females.

Many of the graduates from secondary school continue their studies at institutions of higher education, and a large number attend vocational schools. The oldest university in Estonia is Tartu University, founded in 1632. Undergraduate academic studies in universities lasts 4–6 years. The secondary education certificate does not allow a student automatically to enter an institution of higher education or a university. Applicants must pass entrance exams. Most Estonians learn two languages in school, in addition to Estonian. The most common foreign language is English, and the second is usually Russian, German, or French.

14 CULTURAL HERITAGE

Traditional runic folk songs form the basis of Estonian folk music. Although the lyrics are often repetitive, the tunes associated with these folk songs are complex. Estonian folk musicians often play the zither, violin, or concertina when singing traditional songs. Song festivals are popular Estonian cultural events, dating back to 1869. The song festivals nowadays are a major event occurring every five years, with male, female, children's, and boys' choirs all giving performances.

Arvo Pärt, born in 1935, has become internationally renowned for his modern classical compositions based on a method he calls "tintinnabuli" (or "little bells"). Although he now lives in Germany, he is still celebrated in Estonia as a contemporary cultural icon.

The first book in the Estonian language was produced in 1525. Literacy was furthered by the establishment of a village school network. An Estonian edition of the New Testament was published in 1686, and a complete translation of the Bible appeared in 1739. The national epic, *Kalevipoeg* (The Son of Kalev), consists of 19,023 runic verses based on various themes from old Estonian folklore and was written during 1857–61 by Friedrich Reinhold Kreutzwald. Estonian literature of the late 1800s and early 1900s experienced a romantic and then a naturalist phase. The five-volume epic *Tõde ja Õigus* (Truth and Justice) was finished by the revered Estonian novelist A. H. Tammsaare in 1933 and provides an historical overview of Estonian cultural development during the years 1870–1930.

In 1944, most of Estonia's prominent writers and poets fled the country because of the Soviet Union's invasion and occupation. Estonian literature was tightly censored during the Soviet era, and any material that was critical of the Soviet system was not published. Furthermore, some writers whose ideas were seen as threatening by the government were imprisoned. The Soviet government started to relax its control over Estonian literature in the 1960s. A common literary theme since the 1940s has been the injustices committed by the Soviet government against Estonians.

15 WORK

Economic reform and the consequent structural changes have significantly affected the structure of labor demand. Employment in distribution services, catering, and financial services has increased, thanks to the growing number of small private business enterprises. The economy has grown rapidly since Estonia's entry into the European Union in 2004, resulting in one of the highest employment rates and highest per capita income levels in Central Europe.

Most people in Estonia work between 8:00 am and 5:00 pm or between 9:00 am and 6:00 pm. The lunch break usually lasts between 30 minutes to 1 hour and is between 12:00 and 3:00 pm, but most businesses do not close for lunch. Most people in Estonia receive a fixed monthly salary and are not paid for the work they do past 40 hours a week. People are entitled to a paid vacation after they have worked for one year. The length of the vacation varies, depending on the company, from 21 to 35 days. The retirement age is 65 for men and 60 for women.

16 SPORTS

Estonians are especially fond of basketball. Skiing, volleyball, soccer, and motor sports are also popular. Joggers or runners are becoming a common sight in the suburbs, especially in summertime. For years, aerobics has been a popular way of keeping in shape for women. Also, public health clubs with their body-building facilities are widely used by both men and women. Public indoor swimming pools are open to everyone for a moderate fee, and there are swimming pools in some schools. People of all ages can take lessons in tennis, riding, etc., but they are quite expensive. During recent years, bowling, golf, and squash have become popular. As Estonia is a sea country, there are yachting clubs in many seaside places. Spectator sports are not greatly admired by Estonians. On TV, mostly basketball, ice hockey, soccer, and figure skating are watched.

17 ENTERTAINMENT AND RECREATION

One of the most popular forms of entertainment in Estonia is the theater. Many people also go to motion pictures. The TV is still the most accessible form of entertainment at home, especially for elderly people. Nearly all Estonian homes have TV sets, and cable TV has become available for more and more TV fans. In most homes, the radio is nearly always turned on as well.

Many Estonians, especially women, enjoy gardening. Collecting things (like stamps, coins, beer bottles, postcards, etc.) is also widespread. Younger people, though, prefer going out. Discotheques and dancing are popular among young people of both sexes.

Traveling is an increasingly popular form of recreation—during the Soviet occupation the borders of Estonia were closed and it was impossible for the average person to travel abroad. Nowadays, even those who cannot afford more exotic and faraway places still try to make it to the close-by Scandinavian countries or Germany.

18 FOLK ART, CRAFTS, AND HOBBIES

Estonian folk art traditions date back to ancient times when clothes, tools, footwear, utensils, toys, etc., were made by hand. During long and dark winter nights, Estonian women wove fabrics for national costumes. Striped, multicolored skirt fabrics were made of yarn that was colored with herbs. Blouses were made of linen and embroidered by hand. Woolen sweaters, cardigans, mittens, and socks were knitted with elaborate patterns. Each county had its own characteristic patterns. Traditional Estonian jewelry is made of silver. Estonian craftspeople were already known for their skills during the Middle Ages.

Nowadays Estonia is full of shops selling all kinds of national handicrafts. The Estonians excel at leather goods (especially leather-bound notebooks), ceramics, woolens, jewelry, and wrought ironwork. Wicker baskets and wooden beer mugs are also specialties, as are table implements of aromatic juniper wood from the Estonian islands. Also from the islands come tightly woven snowflake-design sweaters with red trim—real Estonian classics. Although most Baltic amber comes from Lithuania, amber jewelry and specimens are also widely sold in Estonia.

Even today, many Estonian women enjoy knitting and embroidering and prefer handmade craft items to those made by mass industry.

¹⁹ SOCIAL PROBLEMS

All people living in Estonia are guaranteed human and civil rights by Estonian legislation. However, there are still some social problems in Estonia, most of which are related to the consequences of more than 50 years of Soviet occupation. During the Soviet occupation, there were tensions between Estonians and ethnic Russians living in Estonia. Although ethnic Russians have been allowed to become full citizens of Estonia since independence, they are required to learn the Estonian language in order to participate fully in society. Many ethnic Russians complain of discrimination and mistreatment.

One serious social problem in Estonia is the lack of financial resources for social guarantees, such as cash assistance for young families, single parents, families with many children, disabled persons, and retired people. In many cases, wages and salaries are very small and barely enable one to make ends meet. The same applies to health care. The rapid economic growth of the 21st century has not benefitted the lowest strata of society; in fact, the increasingly unequal distribution of wealth in Estonia has become a concern for the European Union, which is pushing Estonia to address the problem.

Alcoholism and crime are also major issues in Estonia and efforts are being made by the government to increase security and people's trust in the police. Estonia has become a major transporter of illegal drugs and drug use is increasing among Estonians as well.

²⁰ GENDER ISSUES

Estonia is considerably more advanced than other former Soviet republics in its attitude toward homosexuality. Homosexual acts were legalized in 1992 and, in 2004, Estonia became the first Baltic country to have a gay pride parade. The 2006 parade was marred by violent protests, injuring 15 people, but the parades in other years have met with at least tolerance, if not enthusiastic support.

There are a number of gay clubs in Tallinn that operate openly and attract heterosexuals as well as gays and lesbians. The Gay and Lesbian Information Center (GLIC) opened in 2004 and began to be funded by the Estonian Institute for National Health in 2008. A law was proposed in 2008 to register domestic partnerships, including same-sex couples, granting them some legal rights, though stopping short of recognizing their union as a "marriage."

This is not to say that Estonia is free of homophobia. Physical violence against homosexuals is rare in Estonia, but verbal abuse and other forms of discrimination continue to occur. In 2005 the Estonian Ministry of Justice proposed a new Family Law stating that marriage is exclusive to heterosexual couples, sparking a spirited debate that remained unresolved in 2008.

The 2008 domestic partnership proposal was an attempt to find a middle ground. The Dutch ambassador to Estonia, Hans Glaubitz, resigned in 2006 after only a year in office because of homophobic and racist harassment; Glaubitz is gay and his partner is Afro-Cuban.

²¹ BIBLIOGRAPHY

Baltic States, The. Tallinn, Estonia: Estonian, Latvian, and Lithuanian Encyclopaedia Publishers, 1991.

Estonia in Facts. System of Education. The Estonian Institute, October 1995.

EU Business. "Estonia," http://eubusiness.com/Estonia (12 August 2008).

Grew, Tony. "Estonian Gay Activist to Stand for Parliament." *Pink News,* 6 December 2006, http://www.pinknews.co.uk/news/view.php?id=3190 (12 August 2008).

Estonia. Free and Independent. Estonian Encyclopedia Publishers, 1992, 1994.

Invest in Estonia. Factsheets. Estonian Investment Agency, 1995.

Statistical Yearbook. Statistical Office of Estonia, 2008.

Tallinn-Life.com. "Gay Tallinn," http://www.tallinn-life.com/tallinn/gay-tallinn (12 August 2008).

World Info Zone, http://www.worldinfozone.com/country.php?country=Estonia&page=2 (12 August 2008).

—revised by Dianne De Mott

EVENKI

ALTERNATE NAME: Evenks, Ewenki, Tungus
LOCATION: Russia (central and eastern Siberia), China (Inner Mongolia and Heilongjiang Province), and northern Mongolia
POPULATION: Approximately 66,000 total—35,527 in Russia (2002), 30,505 in China (2000), 1,500 in Mongolia
LANGUAGE: Evenki, Russian, Chinese, Yakut
RELIGION: Eastern Orthodox Christianity, Tibetan Buddhism, native religious beliefs

1 INTRODUCTION

The Evenki are an indigenous people of central and eastern Siberia, Mongolia, and Inner Mongolia. Although there has been a great deal of controversy among scholars regarding their original homeland, the most reliable anthropological, linguistic, and archaeological evidence indicates that the Evenki were formed to the east of Lake Baikal in southeastern Siberia around 1000 BC. They then spread throughout eastern and northern Siberia, mixing and intermarrying with other native Siberian peoples. In addition to the general name *Evenki* (which means simply "person" or "people"), they identify themselves by the names of their clans or tribes: Birat, Ile, Manegir, Mata, Orochen, and so on. Although the word *Evenki* is a singular term in the Evenki language itself, it is used as a plural in Russian, the Russian singular being *Evenk* for a male and *Evenkiika* for a female. In recent decades, the use of *Evenki* as both singular and plural has become common among most non-Russian writers, although one occasionally encounters the form *Evenk/Evenks*. In older Russian and Western ethnographic literature, the Evenki were formerly referred to by the term *Tungus,* which is derived from *Tongus,* the Yakut word for "Evenki."

The Evenki have long been known for their skill at hunting reindeer, bear, moose, sable, squirrel, and other animals, and they rely on hunting for most of their food. The Evenki are divided into two main groups based on the economic activities they perform in addition to hunting. Those of central and northeastern Siberia, herd reindeer, and those of southeastern Siberia, Mongolia, and China, raise horses and cattle. A smaller, eastern group along the coast of the Sea of Okhotsk—often called the "sitting Evenki" because they own no reindeer—has traditionally lived exclusively by hunting forest animals and seals and fishing.

The Evenki have been under Russian and Chinese rule since their conquest during the 17th century by the Romanov and Qing dynasties respectively. Much of the vast territory they originally occupied was gradually taken from them by the government and given to Russian settlers. Nevertheless, with the exception of tax collection (originally in the form of furs), sporadic campaigns by the Russian Orthodox Church to Christianize them, and occasional arrests and trials for theft and other crimes that directly affected the Russian settler community, significant official interference in the day-to-day life of the Evenki came only in the Soviet period. During the 1930s, Evenki hunters and herdsmen were forced into collectives as part of the collectivization of agriculture. Stalin's campaign to rapidly develop Soviet industry simultaneously led to an enormous influx of Russians and other outsiders into Evenki territory to exploit its timber and mineral resources. This resulted in serious environmental damage to ancestral Evenki lands.

2 LOCATION AND HOMELAND

The Russian Federation's Evenki number slightly more than 30,000. The Evenki do not occupy a unified territory and are spread over a wider area than any other native Siberian group—from the Yenisei River in the west to the Sea of Okhotsk and the northern portion of Sakhalin in the east, and from the bottom of the Taimyr peninsula in the north to the Amur River to the south. Evenki settlements are thus scattered over almost 3,000,000 square kilometers (1,800,000 square miles)—an area about three times the size of Alaska. There is an Evenki Autonomous *Okrug* District—sometimes called Evenkia—with its capital at Tura in north central Siberia's Krasnoiarsk Territory (*krai*), but only 3,500 Evenki live there. The rest reside in other parts of Siberia, mainly in the Yakut (Sakha) and Buriat Republics, the area of Krasnoiarsk Territory outside the Evenki Autonomous District, Khabarovsk Territory, and the Irkutsk, Amur and Chita Regions (*oblast*). Outside the Russian Federation, the populations of the northern Mongolian Republic and the People's Republic of China's Heilongjiang Province (formerly known as Manchuria) both contain approximately 30,000 Evenki.

Almost all of Evenki territory is mountainous taiga forest, with larch, birch, ash, fir, pine, and cedar as the most common vegetation. The sparse, scrubby cedar trees, moss, and patches of bare rock typical of the tundra are found at high altitudes and in the northernmost stretches of Evenki settlement, and there is occasionally meadowland in the taiga's river valleys. The Evenki forests have traditionally been rich in fur- and meat-bearing game—wild reindeer, bear, elk, sable, squirrel—as well as wolves, ducks, and geese. Rivers hold salmon, perch, and pike. The climate of the Evenki lands is generally continental. Winters are long and often bitterly cold, with January temperatures averaging –36°C (–33°F) and sometimes falling as low as –80°C (–112°F). Summers are short and warm, with June temperatures averaging 16°C (61°F) and peaking at 36°C (97°F).

3 LANGUAGE

The Evenki language belongs to the Tungusic branch of the Altaic language family, which includes Siberian tongues such as Nanai, Udegei, and Even, as well as the language of the Manchu who conquered China in the 17th century. There are numerous local dialects of Evenki whose pronunciation and vocabulary differ from each other to varying degrees. This is not surprising, as the Evenki have long lived in small groups divided by vast distances. The Evenki did not have a writing system until 1931, when they adopted the Latin alphabet. This was replaced in 1937 by the Cyrillic (Russian) alphabet. The modern Evenki literary language is based on the southern Poligus dialect and is written in the Cyrillic alphabet with additional letters and diacritics used to represent specifically Evenki sounds.

Evenki given names often reflect a geographic feature of a person's birthplace or some natural phenomenon or other event that occurred at the time of his or her birth. For example, a boy born near Lake Kayo might be named *Kayocha*. Girls born at sunrise or the first slushy snow of the year are given the names *Garpancha* and *Libgerik,* which are derived from the words *garpan* ("ray of sunshine") and *libge* ("wet snow"), respectively. Alternatively, a child's behavior at the time of birth might influence the choice of name: *Songocho* (male) and *Songolik* (female) both translate literally as "crybaby." Some Evenki names developed from Russian names that were significantly altered to suit the phonetic norms of the Evenki language. Examples of this type of name are *Ogdo* (female, from *Evdokia*) and *Kostoku* (male, from *Konstantin*). Russian given names in their original forms, such as *Vladimir* (male) and *Aleksandra* (female), as well as fixed surnames based upon the given name of a male ancestor, have become common in the 20th century.

4 FOLKLORE

Although the Evenki did not write in their language until the 20th century, they possess a wide repertoire of centuries-old folk tales and other forms of oral literature. The Evenki tell amusing stories about such human failings as greed, foolishness, and laziness. In addition, there are long epic tales—called in various dialects *nimngakan*, *nimkan*, or *ulgur*—that deal with the feats of mythical heroes. In one such tale, "All-Powerful Develchen in the Embroidered and Decorated Clothes," the hero Develchen makes a long journey through the physical and spirit worlds and fights numerous human and supernatural enemies in order to rescue his betrothed, Kiladii. Develchen and Kiladii then marry, and their children are the ancestors of the Evenki people.

5 RELIGION

The Evenki were largely converted to Eastern Orthodox Christianity by the middle of the 19th century. Shamanism is one of the traditional religious practices of the Evenki. Animals, plants, the sun, the moon, the stars, rivers, forests, and mountains are believed to have spirits, which humans must respect and honor in order to survive and prosper. Animals and plants may be killed for human needs, but needless injury to animals or waste of the products of animal and plant life is forbidden. According to Evenki beliefs, there are three worlds: the upper world, which is inhabited by the spirits of nature and various other deities; the middle world, inhabited by humans; and the lower world, inhabited by the spirits of the dead. Shamans—tribal priests similar to Native American "medicine men"—are men and women who are most able to bridge the gap between the three worlds and communicate with these spirits. The profession of shaman is usually hereditary passed down on the father's side of the family. The rituals of Evenki shamans take the form of chanting, dancing, and beating on the *ungtuvun*, or *nimngangki*—a large, flat drum with a leather head, a cross-shaped handle attached to the back of the frame, and small iron rattles that produce a tambourine-like jingling sound when the instrument is struck. The stick (*gisu*) of the shaman's drum is made either from the wood of a tree that has been struck by lightning or from a bone or tusk from a mammoth preserved in the frozen soil. The deerskin and fur cloaks worn by Evenki shamans are elaborately and colorfully embroidered and festooned with ribbons, bone ornaments, and jingling bells. The rituals of shamans are intended to heal the sick, ease difficult childbirth, foretell the future, send the souls of the departed on their way to the world of the dead, and in general to ensure the people's well-being. The Evenki of Manchuria came under strong influence of Tibetan Buddhism during the Qing era, and many traditional beliefs were integrated into Evenki Buddhist practice.

6 MAJOR HOLIDAYS

Evenki festivals are essentially shamanist rituals performed to ensure success in hunting by honoring the spirits of the animals upon which the Evenki depend for survival. The timing of festivals is tied with the hunt itself, so unlike Western holidays, there is no set date for their observance. One of the most important Evenki festivals is the bear feast, which is held after a group of hunters has killed a bear. On the first day of the festival, the bear is brought back to the hunters' settlement and butchered. A whole series of rules must be observed during the butchering of the bear. For example, its bones must not be cut or broken; they must instead be separated at the tendons, laid on a bed of willow branches, and placed back into the shape of the original skeleton. The meat from the bear's neck is boiled in a cauldron while the young people sing and dance in its honor. At midnight, one of the hunters imitates a crow's call to indicate that the meat is ready. The settlement's inhabitants then walk quietly to each other's homes and wordlessly beckon each other to the feast, which is consumed in silence. On the second day, the bear's heart is cut into small pieces, mixed with bear fat, and boiled in one cauldron while some of the meat is boiled in separate vessels. Again, the young people sing and dance while the meal is cooking, and at midnight a crow's call summons the villagers to the second feast. To trick the bear's spirit into thinking that crows, not humans, have killed him and are eating his body, the participants also caw like crows and call each other *oli* ("crow"). The celebrants each receive a spoonful of the bear's-heart soup and retire with a portion of the meat, which they eat in their own homes. On the third day, the bear's head is placed on a birch-bark mat, combed with a birch-wood comb and decorated with ribbons; earrings made of cedar needles are fastened to its ears. The head is then skinned and boiled, and its brain and flesh are communally eaten. Finally, the skull is taken out from the settlement into the forest and placed high upon a pole. Evenkis in the Russian Federation also observe the major Russian and Soviet holidays, particularly New Year's Day (January 1), Victory Day (May 9) and others.

7 RITES OF PASSAGE

In traditional Evenki society, there were many rules surrounding the birth of a child, and these had to be strictly observed in order to ensure the survival of mother and child. A pregnant woman was not allowed to touch the hook upon which a cooking pot was hung, lest her child be born retarded, or to hang a pot upon it, lest he or she be born mute. She could not step over an axe or saw, for this would lead to an especially painful childbirth. If she looked at a corpse, she would have a difficult delivery. There were taboos for her husband to obey as well. If he dug a grave, his wife would die in childbirth. If he brought a hare into the home, the child would be born with a harelip. If he or his male relatives entered the *khungkingat*—the temporary tent or hut used only for childbirth—the child would be deformed. Certain foods were also forbidden to an expectant mother. For example, she could not eat a bear's peritoneum (the transparent membrane that lines the abdominal cavity), for this would cause her to fall ill during the pregnancy. If she ate a bear's kidneys, liver, or meat from its head, she would suffer from convulsive neck spasms during childbirth. Eating the meat of an old reindeer would result in a long, difficult delivery. When an infant was old enough to eat solid foods but not to speak, its parents could not feed it the gristle from under a reindeer's knee, since this would cause knee injuries, or bear meat, since this would result in muteness. Today, childbirth usually takes place in the special hospitals for expectant mothers and infants that are used throughout the former Soviet Union, and the taboos surrounding childbirth have largely become a thing of the past.

Compared with the maze of taboos that surrounded an Evenki's birth, death was a relatively straightforward affair in traditional society. Immediately after death, the deceased's body was undressed and laid out straight with its arms at its sides and its face covered with a cloth. Depending on which animals were kept by the family, a reindeer, horse, or dog was killed, and the corpse was sprinkled with its blood. The deceased was then washed, laid on a newly dressed fur, and dressed in his or her best clothing (without, however, fastening any laces or buttons). If the person who had died had been married, the bereaved spouse cut off a lock of his or her own hair and laid it on the corpse. To the lock of hair were added items of everyday use—hunting knives or bows and arrows for the men, skin-dressing or sewing implements for women, and tobacco pipes and flints for both sexes. The deceased's family and friends held a feast in his or her honor, and the body was then buried or laid on a raised platform in the forest. Burial in the ground or cremation have become the usual means of disposing of the dead in the 20th century, but items used by the deceased are sometimes still interred with them.

8 INTERPERSONAL RELATIONS

When visiting an Evenki home, it is considered impolite to ride one's horse or reindeer directly up to the entrance of a dwelling and dismount there; one must rather dismount at the side of the home and from there walk to the entrance. It is customary to ask a visitor what he or she has seen on his way to the host's home. Although this is now often a pleasant formality, the original purpose of asking this was to determine whether game is to be found in the area traversed by the visitor. If a guest is older than his or her host, he hands his pipe to the host, who fills it with tobacco, lights it, and returns it to the guest. If the host is older than the guest, it is the host's pipe that is filled and lit by the guest. Guests are always given food and drink, which cannot be refused as this would be interpreted as an intentional insult. It is also customary to give a small gift to the guest, who is expected to reciprocate when possible.

Among the Evenki, dishonesty is considered an especially grievous character defect. Gossip or hypocrisy are seen as forms of deception and are likewise deemed unacceptable. According to the Russian anthropologist Sergei Shirokogorov, this revulsion for dishonesty stems from their traditional reliance on accurate information about the location of game animals and the friendliness or hostility of neighboring peoples. The distaste with which the Evenki view lying and cheating may be deduced from the following anecdote, which Shirokogorov recorded in the early 20th century. An Evenki man was watching some Russian prospectors, who were unaware of his presence, dig for gold. Upon finding a large gold nugget, they agreed to keep silent about it in order to avoid sharing it with their partners. They hid the nugget under a rock and departed. The Evenki emerged from his hiding place, uncovered the nugget, and took it home with him. The local Evenki community refused to tell the Russians what had happened: they considered their compatriot's action to be justified, since he had stolen the gold from men who had conspired to cheat their friends and had thus lost any right to it.

9 LIVING CONDITIONS

The traditional Evenki dwelling is the *dyu*, a large conical tent that is similar in appearance to the tepee traditionally used by some indigenous peoples of the American West, and it is well-suited for the way of life of a people of nomadic hunters and herdsmen. The *dyu* is supported by a framework of wooden poles and covered by reindeer hides or birch bark, which is steamed to increase its toughness and elasticity and then sewn into large sheets. (By the early 20th century, canvas cloth purchased from Russian traders became a common housing material as well.) Fires for cooking and light are built in the center of the floor, and a hole at the top of the *dyu* allows smoke to exit and light to enter. When a family moves from one hunting or herding area to another, they leave the frame of the *dyu* in place and take only the covering with them: it is easier to cut new poles than to drag the old ones along from encampment to encampment. Other types of traditional Evenki dwellings include rectangular log cabins with birch-bark roofs and Mongolian-style yurts, which the Evenki of the Lake Baikal area adopted from the local Buriat Mongols. Since the collectivization of Evenki economic activities in the 1930s, the single-story wooden houses typical of rural housing in the former Soviet Union have largely replaced traditional dwellings; however, the *dyu* is still used by some Evenki, especially during hunting or herding trips.

The Evenki who herd reindeer use the animals for transport as well. Reindeer are saddled and ridden like horses, made to pull sleds, and used as pack animals. The horse- and cattle-breeding Evenki of southeastern Siberia ride horses instead of reindeer, and Evenki who live along the shores of the Sea of Okhotsk have traditionally walked and used birch bark boats or canoes made of hollow logs. Hunters used skis, which they covered with fur in order to muffle their sound and thus enable them to silently approach game. In recent decades, airplanes, helicopters, motorboats, and snowmobiles have supplemented traditional modes of transportation. Automobile and rail transport are not common, due to the vast distances between urban areas in Central and Eastern Siberia and the difficulty of constructing roads and railway lines atop the permafrost.

Prior to the 20th century, medical care among the Evenki was mostly limited to herbal remedies and the incantations of shamans, although pharmaceutical remedies purchased from Russian traders were also used on occasion. (According to traditional Evenki beliefs, illness is often caused by the abduction of the sick person's soul by a spirit, who can be persuaded by the shaman to return the soul to its rightful owner.) Western medicine became much more common than these older methods during the Soviet period, but in the rural Siberian areas inhabited by Evenki, clinics are often many miles away and most offer only the most rudimentary treatments. Health problems caused by the shortcomings of Soviet medical care are exacerbated by widespread alcohol abuse.

10 FAMILY LIFE

Traditional Evenki society was organized into clans that were reckoned on the basis of descent from a common male ancestor and contained from 10 to 100 nuclear families. Clans performed a variety of social functions. For example, they owned communal hunting and herding territory, shared shamans between settlements of clan families, and formed alliances by marriage between their members (it was forbidden to marry someone from the same clan). Clan councils headed by the clan's elder men and women decided on issues such as war with other Evenki clans, punishment of wrongdoers within the clan, and aid to poor clan members.

Within the traditional Evenki nuclear family, men and women performed distinct roles. Men hunted and butchered game and made weapons, tools, and other household items from metal and bone. Women cooked; gathered firewood; herbs, and berries; prepared skins and birch bark; raised children; and cleaned the *dyu* and its surroundings. Women had to observe a wide range of taboos specific to their sex, most of which had to do with menstruation. For example, a menstruating woman was forbidden to touch weapons or wash in running water, and she had to bury the cloth or fur that she used as a sanitary pad far away from the encampment lest misfortune befall the family's hunters. If she was a shaman, she could not practice her profession until her period had passed. To these taboos must be added those mentioned earlier in connection with pregnancy and childbirth. Moreover, an Evenki woman was expected to behave in a reserved and quiet manner around her elders, in-laws, and guests. On the other hand, women had certain rights that could not be violated. Wife-beating was extremely rare, and husbands and wives usually enjoyed har-monious relations characterized practice by a high degree of equality. A woman could leave her husband if he abused her or even summon her male relatives (and sometimes those of her husband) to give him a thrashing. She could also leave her husband if he proved to be a neglectful provider or lover. The taboos restricting women's behavior have passed from observance in the past 50 years or so. The division of labor between the sexes persists in traditional occupations, but men and women interact on equal terms in teaching, administration, and certain other modern professions.

11 CLOTHING

The classic Evenki garment is a knee-length reindeer-skin robe that is fastened in the front by leather laces. The type of reindeer skin used depends on the season. The winter robe—*khegilme*—is sewn from the thick, warm, furry skins of reindeer slaughtered during the winter. The summer robe, or *sun*, on the other hand, is made of the skin of reindeer slaughtered during the summer, when the animals have shed their winter fur. Both sexes wear fur and skin hats and apron-like chest coverings (*khelmi* for men and *nelli* for women) and loincloths (*kherki*) made of cloth or reindeer skin under their coats. Winter boots (*kheveri* in some dialects, *bakari* in others) reach up to the thighs, while summer boots (*khomchura*) barely clear the ankles and are worn with leather or cloth leggings (*aramus* or *gurumi*). Men's and women's clothing is distinguished less by cut than by the degree of decoration: women's clothing is embellished with sophisticated embroidery and fur trimmings, and the clothing worn by shamans of both sexes is particularly elaborate. Traditional Evenki clothing is now worn primarily in the winter. During the summer, Western-style clothing (mass-produced shirts, pants, dresses, undergarments, and shoes) predominates.

12 FOOD

Evenki food has traditionally centered around the meat of the animals that they hunt and herd: reindeer, bear, elk, and in southeastern Siberia, cattle and horses. In the summer and fall, when geese and ducks are to be found in the Evenki lands, these are hunted as well. Blackberries, blueberries, raspberries, wild onions and garlic, edible herbs, cedar nuts, and reindeer or cow's milk are also commonly consumed. Fish also make up part of the Evenki diet, especially along the shores of the Sea of Okhotsk, Lake Baikal, and the Amur River. (The Baikal and Okhotsk Evenki hunt seals as well.) Tea, sometimes mixed with reindeer milk, is the most common drink. Russian vodka is also popular. Traditional Evenki delicacies are *seven*, which is made by mixing roast ground bear meat with fried bear fat, and *meni* (mashed berries mixed with reindeer milk).

Boiling in cauldrons and roasting on spits are the most common methods of cooking Evenki food, which was formerly eaten with hands, knives, and spoons from wooden or birch bark plates. (Ceramics of Chinese manufacture were common among the Evenki of the Amur River basin.) Soup and tea were drunk from wooden cups. The modern Evenki prepare their food in factory-made metal and ceramic pots and pans and eat with metal knives, forks, and spoons. Meat and fish are dried in the sun to preserve them for use during the long, cold winters when the availability of game decreases. Sometimes dried meat is ground into a powder (*khulikta*), which is added to boiling water and the blood of reindeer or other game to make soup.

The heart, liver, and marrow of elk and reindeer are sometimes eaten raw immediately after slaughter. Reindeer blood is also drunk raw as a tonic or boiled as soup. The intestines of game animals are turned inside out, cleaned, boiled, and stuffed with meat to make sausage.

The Evenki have incorporated a variety of influences from neighboring peoples into their cuisine without abandoning their preference for the products of the hunt. Breadmaking was learned from Russian settlers and traders soon after the Russian conquest, and sourdough bread and pancakes have long been staples of Evenki cuisine. The Evenki who live in Buriatia have adopted *süsegei* (a type of sour cream), *eezgei* (a dish similar to cottage cheese), and other milk-based Buriat dishes. Canned vegetables, meat and fish, and other prepared foods purchased from stores entered the Evenki diet during the Soviet period.

13 EDUCATION

During much of the Soviet period, Evenki children were taken from their parents at a very young age and sent to distant boarding schools where the teachers and the language of instruction were usually Russian. As a result, although all Evenki are literate in Russian, many have at best a dim understanding of their own people's history and traditions, and only 30% speak Evenki as their native language. The remainder speak Russian (or, less commonly, Yakut or Buriat) as their first language. Many Evenki in the second group can speak Evenki at levels ranging from the mere command of a few isolated words and phrases to near-total fluency, but the former is far more common. Since the 1980s, native teachers and scholars have had some success in expanding instruction in native folklore, language, and crafts in Evenki schools, but a shortage of personnel and funds (the latter being especially scarce due to the collapse of the post-Soviet economy) has made progress slow in this area.

14 CULTURAL HERITAGE

The folk epics (called *nimngakan*, *nimkan*, or *ulgur*) are among the greatest treasures of the Evenki cultural heritage. Before the Evenki language had a written form, bards (called *nimngakachimni* or *ulguchemni*) learned these epics by heart and recited them aloud before rapt audiences. Some of the epics extend to several thousand lines. Because of their length, they are usually told in a series of sessions spread out over several evenings. A recent recording by Evenki scholars of the recitation of one *nimngakachimni* required 18 hours of tape, and the transcription of another filled 150 typed pages. Today, only a few Evenki bards are still alive. The Soviet practice of sending most native Siberian children to distant boarding schools has robbed young Evenki of the chance to learn the epics from their elders. Nevertheless, many epics have been written down and published in Evenki and Russian, so they will not be lost to future generations. Since the 1930s, oral literature has been supplemented with novels, poetry, and drama in the Evenki language. The best-known Evenki author, Alitet Nemtushkin, has become a passionate champion of Evenki language and culture and the ecology of the Evenki lands.

15 WORK

Because hunting has long played such a central role in Evenki life, the Evenki have naturally become accomplished hunters.

Their main weapons have traditionally been the bow and arrow and, since the 18th century, the rifle. In recent decades, shotguns have become more common, particularly for bird hunting. The Evenki display remarkable skill in luring and catching animals. For example, they manufacture birch bark horns whose sound is similar to that of a male reindeer. When a male reindeer hears one of these horns, he mistakes it for the call of another male reindeer who has found a group of females. When he runs toward the sound of the horn, he is killed. Blinds have been used for centuries: wooden platforms are built in trees overlooking salt springs and surrounded with branches or birch bark walls to hide the hunter. When game animals come to the springs to lap up the salt, they are shot. In another method of luring reindeer, leather straps are attached to the antlers of a tame male reindeer, which is then set loose into a herd of wild reindeer. If it begins to fight another male, their antlers become tangled together in the straps, and hunters can easily approach the pair and shoot the wild reindeer.

16 SPORTS

A number of traditional Evenki sports have survived to this day. Wrestling, tossing heavy stones, reindeer racing, and archery competitions are the most common spectator sports. Foot races are also popular, and sometimes competitors are made to run while holding weights. Kickball is played with leather balls stuffed with reindeer or elk hair.

17 ENTERTAINMENT AND RECREATION

Evenki of all ages have traditionally been fond of conversation and storytelling. Some Evenki stories and jokes are quite bawdy, but they may be told in polite company as long as certain rules are followed: older people may tell them in the presence of younger people, and men may tell them in the presence of women, but not the other way around. It is perfectly acceptable, however, for women and youth to tell these stories in each other's company. Evenki epic poems contain many sung passages, and the audience sings along with the narrator during their narration.

Evenki children's play activities often mimic the work done by adults. Boys are given toy bows and arrows, which provide them with archery practice as well as amusement. Girls typically play with dolls, for which they sew clothing and build cradles. Children of both sexes enjoy playing with puppies and birds. Human and animal figures are cut like paper dolls from birch bark and given to children as toys.

18 FOLK ART, CRAFTS, AND HOBBIES

Evenki arts and crafts, like those of most Siberian peoples that have traditionally practiced nomadism, center around relatively small articles of everyday use that can be conveniently carried from place to place. Evenki men are skilled at engraving and carving wood, metal, and bone into saddle horns and other items relating to reindeer and horse riding, as well as knife handles and tobacco pipes. Women's crafts emphasize the decoration of clothing through embroidery, fur appliqué, and bead work, and common patterns are geometric designs, wave-like swirls, and plant and animal shapes.

[19] SOCIAL PROBLEMS

The foremost social problems facing today's Evenki are ecological and economic. During the Soviet period, the government seized Evenki hunting and herding grounds in order to implement logging and mining projects and build hydroelectric dams. This was done without considering either the wishes of the Evenki or the impact on Siberia's fragile ecosystem. As a result, pollution, overforesting, and flooding have severely damaged the Evenki environment, exacerbating health problems and leading to a decline in the animal population upon which traditional Evenki economic activities depend. During the 1950s and 1960s, small, isolated Evenki settlements were abolished, and their inhabitants were moved into larger villages. The Soviet planners behind this policy hoped that it would improve economic efficiency. Instead, the resulting increased burden on the environment led to declining productivity in meat and fur production, a significant drop in the Evenki standard of living, and a corresponding rise in alcoholism. In the late 1980s, a group of Evenki activists managed to get back a small part of the land that the Soviet government had taken. The result was an improved standard of living and a dramatic drop in alcohol abuse among the Evenki who returned. At about the same time, Evenki ecological activists succeeded in blocking the construction of a dam that would have flooded much of the Evenki Autonomous District.

Cultural survival is another major struggle for the Evenki. Although the Soviet Union's political leaders paid lip service to the official ideal of ethnic and cultural equality, in reality non-Russian cultures and languages (especially those of the numerically small Siberian peoples) were often suppressed. Since Mikhail Gorbachev's liberalization of censorship and minority policies in the 1980s, native journalists, teachers and scholars have worked energetically to increase knowledge of and pride in their cultural heritage among younger Evenki.

[20] GENDER ISSUES

A strong division of labor between genders characterized traditional Evenki society. The effective integration of the Evenkis into the Soviet economy and Soviet society during and after the Second World War and the similar process among the Chinese Evenkis beginning in the 1960s had a particularly strong effect on Evenki women. Particularly in Russia women's increased access to education resulted in women forming a disproportionately large segment of the Evenki intelligentsia and Soviet elite. At the same time Evenki women in the Soviet Union, and later in the Russian Federation, were subject to Soviet gender stereotypes that limited their effectiveness in various ways. Nevertheless, since the collapse of the Soviet Union Evenki women, and particularly women members of the Evenki intelligentsia, have been at the forefront of the movement to revitalize Evenki society along traditional lines.

[21] BIBLIOGRAPHY

Bartels, Dennis A., and Alice L. Bartels. *When the North was Red: Aboriginal Education in Soviet Siberia*. Montreal: McGill-Queen's University Press, 1995.

Bychkov, Oleg, Don Dumond, and Ronald Wixman. "A People Dwindling under Centralized Rule" *Cultural Survival Quarterly* (Winter 1992): 570–60.

Czaplicka, M. A. *Aboriginal Siberia: A Study in Social Anthropology*. Oxford: Oxford University Press, 1914 (reprinted 1969).

Evenki basseina Eniseia (The Evenki of the Yenisei Basin). Ed. V. I. Boiko and V. G. Kostiuk. Novosibirsk: Nauka, Russia: 1992.

Evenkiiskie geroicheskie skazaniia. Khrabryi Sodani-Bogatyr; Vsesil'nyi Bogatyr Develchen v rasshitoi-razukrashennoi odezhde/Nimngakar. So Beie Sodani Mata; Ihardan-deverden tetylken degilter songku Develchen (Evenki Heroic Tales. Brave Sodani the Hero; All-Powerful Develchen in the Embroidered and Decorated Clothes). In Russian and Evenki. Comp. A. N. Myreeva. Ed. N. V. Emel'ianov, E. P. Lebedeva. Novosibirsk, Russia: Nauka, 1990. (Series: Pamiatniki fol'klora narodov Sibiri i Dal'nego Vostoka [Monuments of Folklore of the Peoples of Siberia and the Far East.)

Fondahl, Gail. "Evenki (Northern Tungus)." In *Encyclopedia of World Cultures*. Vol. 6, Russia and Eurasia/China. Ed. Paul Friedrich and Norma Diamond. Boston: G. K. Hall, 1994.

———. "Siberia: Native Peoples and Newcomers in Collision." In *Nations and Politics in the Soviet Successor States*. Ed. Ian Bremmer and Ray Taras. Cambridge: Cambridge University Press, 1993.

———. *Gaining Ground?: Evenkis, Land and Reform in Southeastern Siberia*. Boston: Allyn and Bacon, 1998.

Forsyth, James. *A History of the Peoples of Siberia: Russia's North Asian Colony, 1581-1990*. Cambridge: Cambridge University Press, 1992.

Gorokhov, S. N. "Evenki." In *Narody Rossii: Entsiklopediia* (The Peoples of Russia: An Encyclopedia). In Russian. Ed. V. A. Tishkov. Moscow: Bol'shaia Rossiiskaia Entsiklopediia, 1994.

Khoziaistvo, kul'tura i byt evenkov Buriatii (The Economy, Culture and Way of Life of the Evenki of Buriatia). In Russian. Ed. G. L. Sanzhiev and A. A. Atutov. Ulan-Ude, Russia: Buriatskoe knizhnoe izdatel'stvo, 1988.

Schwarz, Henry, *The Minorities of Northern China: A Survey*. Bellingham, WA: Western Washington, 1984.

Shirokogoroff, M. E. *Social Organization of the Northern Tungus; With Introductory Chapters Concerning Geographical Distribution and History of these Groups*. Shanghai, China: The Commercial Press, 1929.

Ssorin-Chaikov, Nikolai. "Mothering Tradition: Gender and Governance among Siberian Evenki," *Max Planck Institute for Social Anthropology Working Papers*, Working Paper 45. 2002.

Uvachan, V. N. *The Peoples of the North and their Road to Socialism*. Moscow: Progress Publishers, 1975.

Vakhtin, Nikolai. *Korennoe naselenie krainego Severa Rossiiskoi Federatsii* (The Indigenous Population of the Far North of the Russian Federation). In Russian. St. Petersburg: Izdatel'stvo Evropeiskogo doma, 1993.

Vasilevich, G. M. *Evenki: Istoriko-etnograficheskie ocherki (XVIII-nachalo XX v.)* (The Evenki: A Historical-Ethnographic Outline from the Eighteenth to the Beginning of the Twentieth Century). In Russian. Leningrad: Nauka, 1969.

Vasilevich, G. M., and A. V. Smoliak. "The Evenks." In *The Peoples of Siberia*. Ed. M. G. Levin and L. P. Potapov. Trans. Stephen Dunn. Chicago: Univ. of Chicago Press, 1964.

—revised by A. Frank

EVENS

PRONUNCIATION: EH-vens
ALTERNATE NAMES: Ewen, Lamut
LOCATION: Russia (northeastern Siberia)
POPULATION: 19,071 (2002)
LANGUAGE: Even; Russian; Yakut
RELIGION: Russian Orthodox Christianity and native beliefs

¹ INTRODUCTION

The Evens are an indigenous people of Northeastern Siberia. Most Evens are nomadic hunters and reindeer herders, but some Evens along the coast of the Sea of Okhotsk also engage in fishing and seal hunting. They are closely related in language, culture, and physical type to the Evenki (see separate entry). The Evens' name for themselves is *Even* (plural *Evesel*); the origin of this term is obscure. (Some Western scholars write Even as *Ewen*.) The Evens who dwell on northern Kamchatka and along the northernmost coastline of the Sea of Okhotsk also refer to themselves as the *Oroch* (plural *Orochel*) from *oroch* (reindeer). The adjective *Mene*, which means "settled," is sometimes used by the non-nomadic fishermen of the Sea of Okhotsk coast. (A different Tungusic-speaking people of the Amur River region—not to be confused with the Evens—also uses the self-appellation *Oroch*.) Some Evens also identify themselves by the names of their clans or tribes (*Huldacha, Dutki, Kukuin*, etc.). In older Russian and Western ethnographic literature, the Evens who occupied what is now northern Yakutia and Magadan Region (Russian *oblast*) were called *Lamut*: this term is of Evenki origin and is derived from *lamu* (sea). The remaining Evens were not differentiated from the Evenki in ethnographic writing until the Soviet period (when the anthropological and linguistic study of the peoples of Siberia greatly developed) and, like the Evenki, were called *Tungus* (from *Tongus*, the Yakut word for *Evenki*).

Although there is much that is uncertain in the origins of the Evens, it is clear that the Evens were formed over many centuries from Tungusic-speaking tribes that mixed with other native peoples of Siberia (particularly the Yukagir and Yakut) as they migrated through the taiga and tundra of Eastern and Northeastern Siberia. Russian Cossacks and explorers began to move into Even territory in the first half of the 17th century. The Evens put up a fierce resistance and frequently attacked and burned Russian forts. Nevertheless, Russia succeeded in subduing them by 1700. Thereafter, the Evens were required to pay the *yasak* (tax in furs). The Russian government's use of Evens as agents to collect the *yasak* from neighboring Chukchi, Koriak, and Yukagirs facilitated the Evens' expansion onto land previously settled by these peoples.

Russian contact brought diseases such as smallpox, mumps, chicken pox, and influenza, to which the Evens had no immunity. This, coupled with the loss of lands to Russian settlers, a decline in the animal population (caused by overhunting in order to pay the *yasak*), the rise of alcoholism, and economic exploitation by Russian officials and merchants, led to a reduction of the Evens' numbers and a steep decline in their standard of living. After the October Revolution, the Communist government attempted to shield the Evens and other northern groups from the negative effects of Russian contact. This effort was influenced by Russian anthropologists who specialized in the study of the Siberian peoples and idealistic Bolsheviks who shared the anthropologists' concern. To aid them in developing economically and culturally within the framework of their own traditions, 10 Even National Districts (Russian *raion*) and one National Region (*krai*) were established in northern Yakutia and on the shores of the Sea of Okhotsk. Taxes on the Evens were reduced, and Even debts to traders were canceled. State-run trading posts that offered fair prices for Even furs were established, and education and Western medical care began to be provided in at least some Even areas. This relatively humanitarian approach to ruling the Evens was abruptly abandoned upon Stalin's rise to power by the end of the 1920s. During the1930s, Even hunters, fishermen, and reindeer herders were forced into collectives as part of the collectivization of agriculture. At the same time, Stalin's campaign to speedily raise Soviet industry to Western levels brought an enormous number of Russian miners and loggers into Even territory, particularly after the discovery of gold deposits in 1931 and 1932. The proportion of Evens in the population of the Even national areas dropped from 80% to 40%. The eastward evacuation of Soviet industry away from the front during World War II, and the further growth of extractive industries after the war, continued the ecological damage begun in the 1930s. Moreover, increasing official pressure against Even culture (particularly the Even language) from the Stalin years on placed the Evens' survival as a people in jeopardy. Like the other Siberian peoples, the Evens were powerless to criticize policies harmful to their economy and culture until the Gorbachev era.

² LOCATION AND HOMELAND

According to the 2002 Russian census the Evens number 19,071, all of whom live in the Russian Federation. Although they do not form a compact mass and their settlements are located in areas in which members of other nationalities (mainly Russians and Yakuts) form a majority, they are scattered over a very wide territory—almost 3 million square kilometers (1,864,200 square miles). There are 8,700 Evens in the northernmost reaches of the Sakha (Yakut) Republic, particularly its Sarkyryrskii, Ust'-Yanskii, Oimiakonskii, Nizhne-Kolymskii, Sredne-Kolymskii, Verkhne-Kolymskii, Tomponskii, Momskii, Allaikhovskii, and Verkhoianskii districts (Russian *raion*); 1,900 in the Okhotskii and Verkhne-Bureinskii Districts of Khabarovsk Territory (Russian *krai*); 1,300 in the Chukchi Autonomous District (Russian *okrug*); 3,800 in the Ol'skii, Severo-Evenskii, and Sredne-Kanskii Districts of Magadan Region (Russian *oblast*); and 1,500 in the Bystrinskii District and Koriak Autonomous District of Kamchatka Region.

The climate of the Even lands is generally harsh and cold. In northern areas of Even settlement such as the Indigirka River valley, winters last up to nine or ten months, and average annual temperatures do not exceed −13.5°C (7.7°F). Even territory is characterized by mountainous taiga forests of cedar, fir, pine, larch, birch, and spruce, and in the northernmost regions barren or sparsely forested tundra. Reindeer, mountain sheep, squirrel, bear, elk, sable, fox, wolves, ducks, geese, and grouse are the most common animals. Grayling, cod, loach, and freshwater salmon are found in the rivers and streams of the Even lands, and saltwater salmon and seals inhabit the coastal waters of the Sea of Okhotsk.

³ LANGUAGE

The Even language belongs to the Tungusic branch of the Altaic language family, which includes tongues spoken in Siberia and the Far East (for example, Evenki, Nanai, Udegei, and Ul'chi), as well as the language of the Manchus who conquered China in the 17th century. The language most closely related to Even is Evenki. Even is divided into three dialect groups—western, central, and eastern. These three groups are in turn subdivided into 13 or so numerous local forms whose pronunciation and vocabulary differ from each other to varying degrees. The Even language was unwritten until 1931, when the Evens adopted the Latin alphabet. This was replaced in 1936 by the Cyrillic (Russian) alphabet. As was the case among other Siberian peoples who had hitherto used the Latin alphabet, this change was not based on sound linguistic reasons; rather, it took place under pressure from chauvinistic Russian and pro-Russian officials who considered the Russian alphabet inherently superior and did not wish to encourage the use of a "foreign" alphabet by ethnic minorities. The modern Even literary language is based on the eastern Ola dialect and is written in the Cyrillic alphabet with extra letters and diacritical marks that represent Even sounds absent in Russian. Some 44% of the Even speak Even as their native tongue; Russian or Yakut are the first languages of the remainder.

Many Even given names take their origins from the names of animals in the Even environment. For example, the male names *Kabiavchan*, *Giakan*, and *Hingerken* are based respectively on the Even words for "partridge," "eagle," and "little mouse." Of similar derivation are the female names *Hulichan* ("fox"), *Sakla* ("owl"), and *Kachikan* ("puppy"). Some Even personal names were formed by adapting Russian names to the Even phonetic system, for example *N'evde* (female, from Russian *Evdokiia*) and *N'iuku* (male, from Russian Nikolai). Russian given names such as *Vasilii* (male) and *Agaf'ia* (female) are also common. In traditional society, Evens did not use family names unless they were baptized; in that case, they were assigned Russian surnames (e.g., *Lebedev, Nikulin, Trofimov*) by the Russian Orthodox Church. Surnames, usually created by adding Russian suffixes such as -ov and -in to clan names (*Bugach, Dutki, Huldacha*) became universal during the Soviet period, because all families were required to adopt a permanent surname for the sake of bureaucratic convenience.

⁴ FOLKLORE

The Even have amassed a sizeable body of folklore over the centuries. Even folklore includes many genres: *nemkan* (folk tales) about people and animals, which sometimes borrow themes from Evenki, Russian, and Koriak folklore; *teleng* (long epic stories), which are often sung; *ike* (short songs), which often provide humorous glimpses at scenes from everyday life (such as the quarrels of cantankerous elderly couples); and *nenuken* (riddles). The *teleng* usually describe the feats of warrior heroes—for example, Chibdevel, who rescues his bride from enemies who have abducted her—or the Evens' historical conflicts with the Koriak, Chukchi, Russians, and other neighboring peoples.

In one *nemkan*, a young man goes out hunting with his faithful dog. He finds a wild duck but spares its life. On the way home, the dog suddenly becomes fatally ill and asks his master to cut his body up into six parts after he dies; the hunter is confused at this request, but nevertheless honors it. When

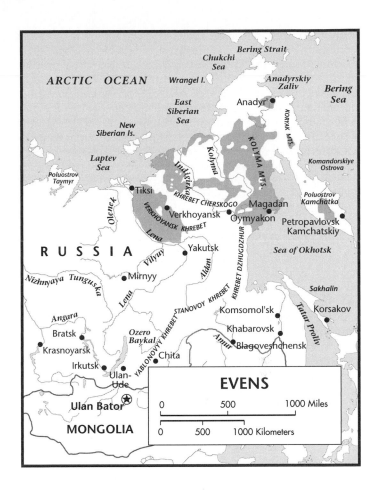

he returns to the dog's dismembered corpse the following day, two bears, two wolves, and two foxes are eating it; they greet him as their master and begin to follow him everywhere as his dog had done. Later, the hunter's evil sister takes up with an iron-toothed, one-eyed, one-legged, one-armed monster called Chölere. She conspires to feed her brother to Chölere, but his animal friends come to the rescue and slay and cremate the monster. The hunter's sister finds Chölere's iron teeth among his ashes and uses them to kill her brother. After his death, the six animals wash his wounds in magic water. He then comes back to life and kills his treacherous sister.

⁵ RELIGION

The Evens' religion is a unique mixture of shamanism and Russian Orthodox Christianity. The Evens were largely Christianized by the middle of the 19th century, and many Evens attend Orthodox church services, wear necklaces bearing crosses, undergo baptism and observe various Christian holidays. It is thought that during the Soviet era anti-religious efforts directed against the Orthodox Church resulted in a revival of traditional beliefs among the Evens. These practices are integrated into a very ancient form of shamanism, which is based on the belief that the forces of nature are ruled by spirits who must be ritually honored in order to ensure man's survival and prosperity. The *togh-muranni* (fire-spirit) is considered particularly powerful, and bits of food are thrown into the fire as an offering at mealtimes. A host of taboos surrounds the use of fire: it is forbidden to spit into a fire, quarrel in front of it, or stick a knife into it. Reindeer are sometimes ceremonially sacrificed to the sun when a person falls ill. Like the shamans of other Siberian peoples, the Even *haman* (shaman) uses ritual prayers, dances, and drum-beating to communicate with the spirits in order to heal the sick, seek advice in personal matters, and foretell the future. The shaman is aided by helper spirits called *ibdiril*, who are described as resembling people, birds, fish, and other animals. The Evens' religious practices were forced underground as a result of the Soviet regime's antireligious policies from the 1930s on. They have begun to reemerge since the end of religious persecution in the 1980s, but the role of the Church and the shaman in everyday life has been much diminished.

6 MAJOR HOLIDAYS

The most important holidays in traditional Even society were clan gatherings that took place every year in either spring or summer (depending on the locality). These often coincided with annual trade fairs established by the Tsarist administration, at which Russian traders purchased furs gathered by Even hunters, and Russian officials collected taxes from the Evens. The most common name for these gatherings was *dalbu* (from the root *dal-*, meaning "friend" or "relative"), but other names were used as well: *khededek* ("the time and place of dancing"), *chakabak* or *sakabak* ("gathering, meeting"), and *munnak* ("the time of sport"). The *dalbu* were marked by reindeer, dog-sled, and foot races; dancing; singing; storytelling; wrestling; and feasting. These activities are now performed at occasional Even folklore festivals, which replaced clan- and trade-based holidays after the 1930s.

7 RITES OF PASSAGE

As was the case among many other native Siberian peoples, pregnancy and childbirth in traditional Even society were accompanied by many rules that the mother-to-be must follow in order to ensure a safe delivery. For example, she could not receive guests, visit other households, keep company with other pregnant women, go out of her home at night, hold broken dishes, touch fishnets, eat fatty foods, or drink strong tea. After the onset of labor, all items in the home that had ties or lids were unfastened or opened to ensure that the child had a clear path into the world. Above all, she was required to keep her home, person, and clothing absolutely clean at all times. Some of these taboos had a practical as well as superstitious, aspect: the ban on socializing and the insistence on a particularly clean environment, for example, protected the expectant mother and her fetus from possible sources of infection. During pregnancy and birth, an older, experienced woman (*atykan*—"grandmother" or "old lady") lived with the expectant mother to help her with household tasks, instruct her in childbirth procedures and parenting skills, and ensure that she followed all relevant rules and taboos. During labor and delivery and for a week after birth, only the *atykan* and the *khevkilen* (midwife) were allowed to be with the mother, whose home was roped off to indicate that no one else could enter. The mother gave birth squatting over the bed while supporting herself on a sturdy wooden frame, which allowed gravity to help the infant through the birth canal; the *khevkilen* continually massaged the mother's belly to relieve pain and move the infant along. For this reason, Even women gave birth quickly and easily. If the child was a boy, its umbilical cord was cut with the mother's knife; if a girl was born, the father's knife was used. Children were named after deceased relatives. Even birth taboos and procedures have largely vanished as a result of modernization.

Prior to Russian contact, the Evens interred their dead in wooden coffins, which they decorated with carvings of crows and raised on tall platforms. The belongings of the deceased were broken or torn (to allow them to be used in the world of the dead) and placed under the platform. Reindeer were sacrificed in the dead person's honor. Platform burial has been replaced by burial in the ground as a result of Russian influence, and graves are now marked with crosses. Yet elements of the Evens' pre-Christian practices remain: the crosses are generally decorated with bird carvings, and broken pieces of the deceased person's possessions, along with the poles of his tent, are scattered around the grave.

8 INTERPERSONAL RELATIONS

Among the Even, it has been customary since time immemorial to share the products of herding, fishing, or hunting with clan members, hunting partners and neighbors. In traditional society, this practice, called *nimat*, was crucial to the community's physical survival, so it was taken very seriously. If an Even repeatedly refused to share his game or fish or the reindeer he slaughtered, he could be put to death by members of his clan or settlement. *Nimat* is still observed by modern Evens, although violations no longer result in death.

9 LIVING CONDITIONS

There are several types of traditional Even housing. The *dyu* (*dyum* in some dialects), like the Evenki dwelling of the same name, is a large conical tent that closely resembles the teepee of nomadic Native American peoples of the Great Plains. The *dyu* consists of a frame of wooden poles covered with reindeer hides or sheets of birchbark made tough and flexible by steaming. A hearth in the center of the *dyu* is used for cooking, warmth, and illumination, and the *dyu* is ventilated by a hole at the top where the tent poles meet. Fur sleeping bags around the edges of the *dyu* serve as beds. The door is made of thick suede decorated with colorful appliqué patterns. Another dwelling, the *chorama-dyu*, is made of the same materials as the *dyu*, but its construction is slightly different. The base of the *chorama-dyu* consists of a set of 8–14 poles about one meter long. These are fastened in pairs into inverted V's, the V-shaped pairs are placed in a circle with the ends fastened to the ground, and horizontal planks are laid across the tops to create a sturdy circular frame. To the top of this frame is attached a conical framework of support poles similar to those of the *dyu*. The entire structure is then covered with deerskin or birchbark. (Travelers to the Even lands in the 17th century reported seeing *chorama-dyu* covered with tanned fish-skins as well). Undressed deer or other animal hides serve as carpets. The *dyu* and *chorama-dyu* were traditionally used by nomadic Evens, who found them convenient to disassemble and reassemble when moving to new grazing or hunting grounds. Settled Even fishermen along the coast of the Sea of Okhotsk lived in *utan* (dugouts) covered with turf in previous centuries; after the 1700s, the dugouts began to be replaced by rectangular log cabins (called *uran*). Many Evens now live in the one-story wooden houses ubiquitous in rural areas of the former Soviet Union. Herdsmen and hunters still make use of the traditional tent-type dwellings, but cloth coverings are often used in place of the former deerskin or birchbark ones.

The reindeer naturally forms the basis of most traditional Even modes of transport. Along with using reindeer as pack animals, the nomadic Evens ride them as well. Evens who live near Yakut, Chukchi, or Koriak settlements have adopted the use of reindeer-drawn sleighs from them. The settled Evens of the Sea of Okhotsk coast also use dogsleds, and less frequently horses, for transportation. Skis are another widespread traditional means of transport, especially among hunters, who use fur-covered skis in order to move silently when stalking game. Although airplanes, tractors, helicopters, and snowmobiles have become common in the 20th century, they have not displaced the traditional modes of transport, which are well-suited to the Evens' environment.

Western medicine was all but unknown among the Evens before the Bolshevik Revolution of 1917; instead, they used a wide pharmacopia of medicinal herbs and barks. Animal substances such as bear's bile and fat and reindeer kidney and blood were also successfully employed as medicines. In the case of frostbite, a reindeer was killed and skinned and the patient was wrapped in its skin in order to warm him gradually. Because illness was traditionally considered to have a spiritual cause, shamans performed prayers and rituals to heal the sick. There has been a significant increase in the use of modern medicines and treatments since the Soviet period, but traditional Even medicine is still widely employed. Hospitals and clinics in Northeastern Siberia are often many miles away, and in some cases Even plant-based medicines are more effective than modern ones.

10 FAMILY LIFE

Prior to the 20th century, the Evens were organized into *ngunmin* (clans) whose members were related to each other by blood. It was forbidden for two members of the same clan to marry each other. Clan members shared hunting and herding grounds and were obligated to help each other in times of need. *Egdengen* (elders) gathered taxes from the clan communities and delivered them to Russian officials, distributed gunpowder from the clan's stores, and judged disputes between members. The clan system was weakened considerably by the Soviet-era forced resettlement of members of different Even clans into the same herding and hunting collectives, and the nuclear family has replaced the clan as the basic Even social unit. Nevertheless, some traits of the clan system—particularly mutual aid and the taboo on marriage between clan members—continue to be observed.

The clans were divided into nuclear families consisting of a man, a woman, and their children, who lived with their parents until marriage. In traditional society, marriages were usually arranged by the parents, sometimes when the pair in question were still minors. The parents of the groom were required to pay a *tori* (bride-price) of reindeer, deerskins, leather tobacco pouches decorated with beadwork, clothing, tea sets, cooking utensils, leather-working tools, knives, axes, or other useful items to the wife's parents, who reciprocated with gifts of their own. After the gifts were exchanged, the bride was taken to the groom's parents' home, which she circled three times on reindeer-back before entering. She then circled the hearth three times and cooked meat there in her own cauldron to signify her entry into the groom's household. Newlyweds usually lived

with the groom's parents until they were able to establish a new household. Wealthy Evens sometimes had two wives, but since polygamy was forbidden by the church, one of the wives had to pose as a servant or blood relative when non-Evens visited the household. Arranged marriages have disappeared during the 20th century. Now men and women marry for love, and polygamy has become a thing of the past.

11 CLOTHING

Traditional Even garments are made of deerskin. Even men and women both wear loose, knee-length deerskin robes called *tety* that are fastened at the throat but otherwise left open in front. They also wear *nel* (leather aprons) that provide warmth for the front of the body, and *kherke* (loincloths) and leggings. The Even *tety* is very similar in form to the *khegilme* and *sun* of the Evenki, but the sides and hems of Even robes, unlike those of the Evenki, are trimmed with fur. *Merun* or *nugdu* (winter boots) are made from skins taken from the legs of reindeer or moose and are decorated with beads or fur strips; *olachik* and *aramra* (summer boots) are made from suede. The typical Even hat is the *avun*, a close-fitting deerskin cap that covers the ears. Women's clothing is of the same cut as that worn by Even men but tends to be more elaborately decorated. At present, traditional clothing is usually worn in winter, while western clothing (factory-made cloth dresses, shirts, trousers, and underclothes, and leather shoes) is worn in summer.

12 FOOD

Most traditional Even cuisine revolves around the meat of the reindeer and various game animals and birds (moose, mountain sheep, squirrel, elk, ducks, geese, and grouse). Meat is usually roasted over a fire or dried, but reindeer kidneys, livers, lungs, and eyes are eaten raw, as this is considered better for one's health. Reindeer blood is used as a tonic and is drunk warm as soon as the animal is butchered. The contents of slaughtered reindeers' stomachs are frozen or dried and mixed with berries. Fish (particularly salmon) and seal meat and fat form the central part of the diet of the sedentary Evens along the coast of the Sea of Okhotsk. Fish is roasted or dried. *Kam* or *niukola* (dried fish) is sometimes kept in special huts to prevent smoke from the hearth and other household odors from spoiling its flavor. Berries, nuts, and edible roots and herbs are also part of the traditional Even diet. During the 20th century, canned foods (vegetables, meat, and fish), bread, potatoes, and fruit have became staples of the Even diet.

13 EDUCATION

With the exception of a handful of missionary schools operated by the Russian Orthodox Church, education was unknown among the Evens prior to the Soviet period. Secular schools began to be established during the 1920s, and the first Even teachers were trained at the Institute of the North (now the Pedagogical Institute of the Peoples of the North) founded in Leningrad (St. Petersburg) in 1926. Now primary and secondary schooling are universal, and many Evens go on to attend universities in Yakutsk, Khabarovsk, Moscow, St. Petersburg, and other cities of the Russian Federation. Alongside these gains, however, the Evens have experienced great cultural losses as the result of Soviet educational policies. Because of the official discouragement of the teaching of "primitive" peoples' languages and cultures during much of the Soviet period, and

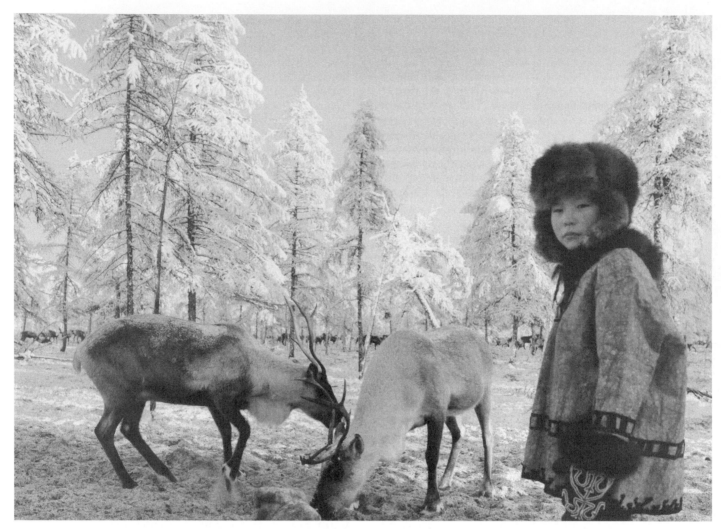

A child of the Evens stands with reindeer in Oimyakon, Russia. Reindeer breeding is the only source of income for these nomadic people. (Ziyah Gafic/Exclusive by Getty Images)

the widespread use of Russian-speaking boarding schools that kept native pupils from their families for many years, many young and middle-aged Evens are ignorant of their own people's cultural heritage, language, and traditional occupations. During the 1980s, native activists and teachers managed to include Even history, language, and folklore, and vocational training in reindeer herding and hunting, in the curricula of some of the schools attended by Evens. Some boarding schools have been replaced by day schools closer to home, thus allowing children to spend more time with parents, and especially grandparents, who are able to teach them the ways of their people.

¹⁴ CULTURAL HERITAGE

Besides the mouth organ used by almost all Tungusic-speaking peoples, the most widespread traditional Even musical instrument is a flat, oval-shaped drum called an *untun*, which is usually used by shamans in religious rituals. In appearance, the *untun* resembles the shamans' drums of many other Siberian peoples (as well as some Native American ones). The *untun* is beaten with a *gisun* (stick) whose striking end is padded with deer-hair and suede to protect the leather drum-head. Small

pieces of bone and iron fastened to the inside of the frame of the *untun* produce a tambourine-like sound when the drum is struck.

Even literature began to develop after the creation of an Even written language in the 1930s. Authors such as Nikolai Tarabukin, Platon Stepanov (who writes under the pen name Lamutskii), and Vasilii Lebedev have published poems, short stories, and novels on themes from traditional and modern Even life. Because these works are published in Russian and Yakut as well as Even, they are accessible to readers belonging to other native Siberian nationalities and to Evens who do not know Even but wish to learn about their people's culture.

¹⁵ WORK

Thanks to their many centuries of experience in herding reindeer, the Evens have become quite skilled at breeding reindeer. Because Even herdsmen and hunters ride their reindeer like horses for long distances, they require animals with specific characteristics: physical stamina; ease of taming and training; and large, heavily muscled bodies. Even reindeer have long been prized among the peoples of Northeastern Siberia for their size, strength, and endurance. Koriak and Chukchi traders traditionally gave two of their own reindeer for one of the Evens'.

16 SPORTS

The most popular Even traditional sports are reindeer and dogsled racing, wrestling, skiing, archery, and jumping contests. Foot races are also commonplace. Even runners have long been renowned among the peoples of Northeast Siberia for their endurance. This is probably a result of the persistence and tirelessness of Even hunters, who often track wounded animals on skis for several days.

17 ENTERTAINMENT AND RECREATION

Dancing is a favorite pastime of the Evens. In one traditional Even dance, the *hed'e*, the participants form a circle facing each other, link arms, and begin to move slowly from left to right. The circle grows to several dozen people as bystanders spontaneously join in. As the speed increases from a shuffle to a near-run, the dancers bend and unbend their knees and move their heads and torsos from right to left and backwards and forwards. At certain points in the *hed'e*, the participants leap high into the air in unison without breaking the rapidly whirling circle! Evens of both sexes and all ages enjoy the *hed'e*, and performances sometimes last for hours, until the dancers collapse from exhaustion.

18 FOLK ART, CRAFTS, AND HOBBIES

Even arts and crafts tend to be similar to those of the Evenki, who also practice nomadic reindeer herding and hunting. Men carve and engrave wood, bone, metal, horn, and leather into saddles and saddle horns, tobacco pipes, knife and tool handles, and other items of everyday use. Women use beads, fur appliqué, and embroidery to embellish articles of clothing with a variety of geometric shapes. Because of the influence from the Yakut, who have long been accomplished metalworkers, the Evens have become skilled at casting iron purchased from Yakut and Russian traders and silver and copper obtained by melting coins into leather-working tools, knife blades, arrow- and spear-heads, and jewelry.

19 SOCIAL PROBLEMS

Contemporary Evens share a number of social problems with other peoples of Siberia: a low life expectancy due to inadequate medical care, alcoholism, and respiratory diseases; widespread poverty; the degradation of their native region's environment; the prejudices of local Russians (and even some Yakuts, who consider the Evens "primitive"); and the threat to their cultural survival posed by Soviet-era policies aimed at eliminating "backward" non-Russian cultures. Representatives of the Evens are active in the Association of the Small Peoples of the North and other native-rights organizations, where they voice their concerns over these issues and fight government plans (for example, for the construction of dams and electric plants in ecologically fragile areas) that, if implemented, would damage their ancestral lands even further.

The Evens of the Sakha (Yakut) Republic have fared better than their compatriots in other administrative regions in recent attempts to gain official support for their cultural and economic needs. Because the Sakha are themselves an indigenous Siberian people who have faced both attacks by officialdom on their culture and way of life and damage to their native environment by extractive industries, their political leaders are particularly sensitive to the problems of native Siberians in general. For example, the Sakha government has founded an Institute of the Problems of the Northern Minorities for the study, preservation, and teaching of the languages, arts, folklore, and history of the Evens and other native groups—that is, Yukagirs, Chukchi, Evenki, and Dolgans—who dwell in the northern reaches of the Sakha Republic. Moreover, in 1989 the Sakha administration established the Even-Bytantaisk District (Russian *raion*)—the first autonomous Even area since its predecessors were abolished in the 1930s.

20 GENDER ISSUES

In traditional Even society a sharp division of labor enforced gender norms. Some scholars have even suggested that women in traditional Even society held a relatively privileged position, especially in economic sector as property holders. During Collectivization, and particularly the period during and after the Second World War, the integration of the Evens into the Soviet economy and society blurred this division of labor, particularly as women gained access to education and industry and Russian migration came to the Even territories. At the same time the imposition of collective property and the abolition of private property had a direct impact on many Even women.

21 BIBLIOGRAPHY

Arutiunov, S. A. "Even: Reindeer Herders of Eastern Siberia." In: *Crossroads of Continents: Cultures of Siberia and Alaska.* ed. William W. Fitzhugh and Aron Crowell. Washington, D.C.: Smithsonian Institution Press, 1988.

Bartels, Dennis A., and Alice L. Bartels. *When the North was Red: Aboriginal Education in Soviet Siberia.* Montreal: McGill-Queen's University Press, 1995.

Bogoraz, V. G. "Igry malykh narodnostei Severa" ["Games of the Small Peoples of the North"] *Sbornik Muzeia Antropologii i Etnografii [Anthology of the Museum of Anthropology and Ethnography]* v. 11 (1949): 237–254.

Dutkin, Kh. I. *Allaikhovskii govor evenov Iakutii [The Dialect of the Evens of Allaikhovskii District in Yakutia].* St. Petersburg: Nauka, 1995.

Fondahl, Gail. "Siberia: Native Peoples and Newcomers in Collision." In: *Nations and Politics in the Soviet Successor States.* Ed. Ian Bremmer and Ray Taras. Cambridge: Cambridge University Press, 1993.

Forsyth, James. *A History of the Peoples of Siberia: Russia's North Asian Colony, 1581–1990.* Cambridge: Cambridge University Press, 1992.

Kocheshkov, N. V. "Eveny" ["The Evens"]. In: *Narody Rossii: Entsiklopediia [The Peoples of Russia: An Encyclopedia].* In Russian. Ed. V. A. Tishkov. Moscow: Bol'shaia Rossiiskaia Entsiklopediia, 1994, p. 419.

Levin, M. G., and B. A. Vasil'ev. "Evens." In: *The Peoples of Siberia.* Ed. M. G. Levin and L. P. Potapov. Trans. Stephen Dunn. Chicago: University of Chicago Press, 1964.

Novikova, N. A. *Ocherki dialektov evenskogo iazyka [An Outline of the Dialects of the Even Language].* In Russian and Even. Leningrad: Nauka, 1980.

Popova, U. G. *Eveny Magadanskoi oblasti: ocherki istorii, khoziaistva i kul'tury evenov Okhotskogo poberezh'ia 1917-1977 [The Evens of Magadan Region: An Outline of the History,*

Economy and Culture of the Evens of the Okhotsk Coast, 1917–1977]. In Russian. Moscow: Nauka, 1981.

Popova, U. G. "Perezhitki shamanizma u evenov" ["Remnants of Shamanism among the Evens"] in *Problemy istorii obshchestvennogo soznaniia aborigenov Sibiri (po materialam vtoroi poloviny XIX-nachala XX v.) [Problems of the History of the Social Consciousness of the Aborigenes of Siberia (From Materials of the Second Half of the 19th and Beginning of the 20th Century)]*. Ed. I. S. Vdovin. In Russian. Leningrad: Nauka, 1981.

Spevakovsky, A. V. "Even" in *Encyclopedia of World Cultures. Volume 6: Russia and Eurasia / China*. Ed. Paul Friedrich and Norma Diamond. Trans. Lydia T. Black. Boston: G. K. Hall, 1994.

The Sun Maiden and the Crescent Moon: Siberian Folk Tales. Coll. and trans. James Riordan. Edinburgh: Canongate, 1989.

Tsintsius, V. I., et al, ed. *Epos okhotskikh evenov v zapisiakh N. P. Tkachika [The Epic of the Okhotsk Evens in the Transcriptions of N. P. Tkachik]*. In Russian and Even (title in Russian only). Iakutsk: Iakutskoe knizhnoe izdatel'stvo, 1986.

Tsintsius, V. I., and L. D. Rishes. *Evensko-russkii slovar' [Even-Russian Dictionary]*. In Even and Russian. Leningrad: Gosudarstvennoe uchebno-pedagogicheskoe izdatel'stvo Ministerstva prosveshcheniia RSFSR, Leningradskoe otdelenie, 1957.

Vakhtin, Nikolai. *Korennoe naselenie Krainego Severa Rossiiskoi Federatsii [The Indigenous Population of the Far North of the Russian Federation]*. In Russian. St. Petersburg: Izdatel'stvo Evropeiskogo doma, 1993.

Vasilevich, G. M., and A. V. Smoliak. "The Evens." In: *The Peoples of Siberia*. Ed. M.G. Levin and L. P. Potapov, trans. Stephen Dunn. Chicago: University of Chicago Press, 1964.

Vitebsky, Piers. *The Reindeer People: Living with Animals and Spirits in Siberia*. Boston: Houghton Mifflin, 2005.

—revised by A. Frank

FINNS

LOCATION: Finland
POPULATION: 5.3 million (2007)
LANGUAGE: Finnish; Swedish
RELIGION: Evangelical Lutheran Church of Finland, Orthodox Church of Finland

1 INTRODUCTION

Politically, Finland is less than 100 years old, having been under the domination of its neighbors, Sweden and Russia, for centuries. However, the Finns are an ancient people and Finland's oldest existing cities date back as far as 1220 (the capital city of Helsinki was founded in 1550). Known for their independence and resilience, the Finns are among the very few neighbors of the former Soviet Union who were not overpowered by it politically and militarily. They repulsed a Russian attack on the eve of World War II, while not actively supporting the Germans, whom they had to remove from their borders in a bitter struggle at the war's end. Relaxing somewhat its perennial concern with guarding its independence, Finland joined the European Union in 1995.

2 LOCATION AND HOMELAND

Finland is one of the world's two northernmost nations (the other is Iceland). It is a flat country slightly larger than the state of New Mexico and dotted with numerous lakes. Most of its terrain is covered by spruce, pine, and birch forests. About a quarter of the country lies above the Arctic Circle; this area is often covered with snow half the year while experiencing brief summers when the sun shines for up to 24 hours a day (giving it the nickname "the land of the midnight sun").

With about 5.3 million people, Finland is one of the world's least densely populated countries. In 2008 the Finns accounted for about 93% of the country's total population. They are thought to be descended from Germanic tribes. About 6% of the population was Swedish. The country had small communities of Russians, Estonians, Roma (gypsy), and Sami (Lapps).

3 LANGUAGE

About 93% of Finns speak Finnish, while approximately 6% speak Swedish, both of which are official languages. Finnish belongs to the Finno-Ugric family of languages and is not related to any of the major European languages. It resembles Estonian and some other languages spoken south and east of Finland and also has a distant resemblance to Hungarian. Finnish is characterized by the use of many vowels and few consonants, and it does not have separate words for articles, prepositions, and pronouns, which are indicated by altered word endings. It is a completely phonetic language.

DAYS OF THE WEEK

maanantai	Monday
tiistai	Tuesday
keskiviikko	Wednesday
torstai	Thursday
perjantai	Friday
lauantai	Saturday
sunnuntai	Sunday

NUMBERS

yksi	one
kaksi	two
kolme	three
neljä	four
viisi	five
kuusi	six
seitsemän	seven
kahdeksan	eight
yhdeksän	nine
kymmenen	ten

⁴ FOLKLORE

Finnish folklore includes many tales tending toward the mysterious and melancholy, such as that of the abandoned foundling Star-Eyes. Charms and superstitions are also plentiful. Someone desiring to find wealth without earning it was traditionally instructed to sit—at Midsummer—on top of a house whose roof had been replaced three times and watch for fires over a swamp or lake. Another Midsummer Night ritual involving the flowering of a fern was said to make a person invisible.

⁵ RELIGION

The Evangelical Lutheran Church of Finland (Finnish Lutheran) and the Orthodox Church of Finland (Finnish Orthodox) are the state churches. In 2007 about 83% of the population was Finnish Lutheran. While rites such as baptism, confirmation, marriage, and funerals are still important for most Finnish Lutherans, it is estimated that as few as 2% attend church regularly. An estimated 1% of Finns belong to the Finnish Orthodox Church. As state churches, both are primary agencies responsible for birth, marriage, and death registrations. Non-members, however, may register at other state agencies. A church tax of up to 2% of personal income is required of members as part of their income tax. Those who are not members of these churches are not required to pay the tax.

Smaller communities of faiths include Roman Catholics, Muslims, Mormons, Jews, and Jehovah's Witnesses. There is also a civil register of individuals not affiliated with any church.

⁶ MAJOR HOLIDAYS

Most Finnish holidays are those of the Christian calendar. Christmas—a bright point of light in the dark of winter—is the most important holiday of the year for Finns. All regular activities come to a halt at noon on December 24 with the ringing of church bells proclaiming "the peace of Christmas," and at sunset families place candles at the graves of their loved ones. Then there is a Christmas Eve sauna, followed by a festive meal. Some of the Finnish Christmas customs—such as the use of decorative straw goats—retain associations from the pre-Christian solstice celebrations that were later merged with the Christian holiday. New Year's Day, Epiphany (January 6), Good Friday, Easter Monday, and Ascension Day are all public holidays as well.

May 1 is actually several holidays rolled into one. It is a celebration of spring, a special day for student celebrations, and the Socialist Labor Day, marked by parades and speeches. Midsummer (*Juhannus*) is celebrated in late June with bonfires throughout the country. Independence Day is celebrated on December 6.

⁷ RITES OF PASSAGE

Finland is a modern, industrialized, Christian country. Hence, many of the rites of passage that young people undergo are religious rituals, such as baptism, confirmation, and marriage. In addition, a student's progress through the education system is marked by many families with graduation parties. At the ceremony for graduation from secondary school, students receive white caps and roses along with their matriculation certificates. Military service for young men could be viewed as a rite of passage. The period of service usually begins after graduation from secondary school and last for a period of 6 to 12 months. Young women have the option of volunteering for military service, but only about 1% actually do so.

⁸ INTERPERSONAL RELATIONS

A famous word used to describe the Finnish character is *sisu*, which connotes a spirit of perseverance and resilience. In addition to *sisu*, autonomy, independence, and respect for the independence of others are inculcated in Finns from childhood onward. Finns are also known for caution, reserve, and silence. According to a Finnish proverb "silence is a person's best friend, for it remains behind after the rest has gone." When Finns do speak, their speech is usually quiet; loud conversation in public will tend to draw stares and interrupting the conversation of others is considered to be extremely impolite. They are typically undemonstrative in public and place great value on privacy. On the other hand, Finnish attitudes toward the body—like those in other parts of Western Europe—make American customs look puritanical by comparison. Small children routinely bathe nude in the sauna with their parents. There are over 1.5 million saunas.

A quick, firm handshake with direct eye contact and a brief nod of the head is customary when greeting a friend or a business associate. Surnames and titles of Mr. or Miss are generally used until one has been invited to use a person's first name.

⁹ LIVING CONDITIONS

There are three basic types of dwellings in Finland: apartment complexes (kerrostalot), single-family homes (omakotitalot), and row-houses (rivitalo). The typical Finnish apartment is smaller than its American or British counterpart—usually only two or three rooms and a kitchen. In many detached homes, a shower and sauna take the place of a bath. Most Finnish homes have been built since World War II. Traditional pre-war homes were wooden and those in the country often constructed by the owner with the help of neighbors, an example of the custom of communal assistance called talkoot. In the cities, many of these older buildings have been demolished and replaced by apartment complexes. Many Finns enjoy the picturesque forests and lakes of their country in summer cottages, usually either rented or borrowed.

Finland has a high level of health care, and the entire population is covered by health insurance. While the nation has one of the world's lowest rates of infant mortality, its mortality rates for men over the age of 25 are somewhat higher than those in most other developed nations due to a high incidence of heart disease. Alcoholism and suicide are also leading causes of death. The sauna has traditionally been associated with medical care; women commonly gave birth in saunas before hospital birth delivery became the norm. In 2008 the average life expectancy was estimated at 78 years, with 75 years for men and 82 years for women.

Every part of the country is accessible by road and the highway system is undergoing constant expansion. However, winter driving is a challenge due to snow and ice. Over 8,850 km (5,500 mi) of rail cover the nation and provide links to Sweden and Russia. Finnair Oy, the national airline, provides both domestic and international service. Finland's merchant marine is one of its lifelines, and the nation is renowned for its shipbuilding.

¹⁰ FAMILY LIFE

While family is important to Finns, the structure of family has changed quite a bit over the years. In 2006 only 32% of all families could be considered traditional, in that the family consisted of a married couple with children (usually two). Another 34% of families were married couples without children. Most couples will live together for a time before making a decision to marry. The percentage of couples opting for common-law marriage (sometimes referred to as a "trial marriage") has been increasing into the 21st century. In 2006 about 21% of all families were formed through common law marriage. While a pregnancy may have once inspired a couple to marry, it is not unusual for a couple to retain their common law marriage sta-

tus while signing a joint custody agreement for the child. Couples expecting a second or third child might be more likely to enter into a formal marriage. Two-income households are the norm whether or not the marriage is common law or legal.

Both mothers and fathers are offered paid leave packages from work in order to care for their newborns, and employers are typically generous in allowing time off to care for children who are ill. By law either parent may stay home to care for their infants (without losing their job) until the child is three years old. During this leave, the family receives an allowance through the Social Insurance program.

Reports indicate that almost half of all marriages end in divorce. Same-sex couples may be legally registered as a couple.

¹¹ CLOTHING

Finns of both sexes sport modern Western-style clothes, including men's suits for work or formal occasions and jeans for casual wear. The traditional national costume has many regional variations but basically consists of a long, full, gathered skirt (often solid black with a red border), white blouse, vest, and cap for women, and a full-sleeved white shirt with stand-up collar, colorful waistcoat, and trousers for men (regional variations might include pointed shoes, a collarless shirt, or gold knife belt).

¹² FOOD

The Finnish diet does not differ a great deal from other Western diets. Seafood plays a large role in the Finnish diet. Milk is also prominent both as a beverage and as a basic ingredient in various curdled, soured, or cultured dairy products. It is also used in soups, stews, and puddings. The Finns eat three meals a day: breakfast (aamiainen), hot lunch (lounas), and dinner (päivällinen), which is eaten at around 5:00 or 6:00 pm. As in other parts of Scandinavia, the "cold table" plays a central role in the Finnish diet. The typical buffet of fish, meat, cheeses, and fresh vegetables eaten with bread and butter—called smørrebrød in Denmark and smörgåsbord in Sweden—is known as voileipäpöytä in its Finnish incarnation. Hot dishes include kalakukko, a pie made with small fish and pork; Karelian rye pastries stuffed with potatoes or rice; and reindeer stew. Popular dishes from Finland's neighbor, Russia, include borscht, beet soup with sour cream, and blini, a type of pancake. A popular delicacy is viili, a cultured dairy product that resembles yogurt. A common breakfast consists of cereals, hot porridges, and cold cuts. Many Finns gather wild berries and mushrooms for meals.

The Finns have the world's highest rate of coffee consumption per person. Coffee drinking in Finland constitutes a ritual that has been compared to the tea ceremony of Japan. Coffee may mark a time of day (afternoon coffee, evening coffee), a place (sauna coffee), or a special occasion (name-day coffee, engagement coffee, funeral coffee). At its simplest, coffee is accompanied by a sweet bread called pulla; more elaborate coffees may include a salty dish as well as a pulla ring or buns, cookies, and cakes. The serving table is often adorned with fresh flowers.

¹³ EDUCATION

Practically all Finnish adults are literate and schooling is compulsory and free. All students complete a basic nine-year program. Formal schooling starts at the age of seven. The school

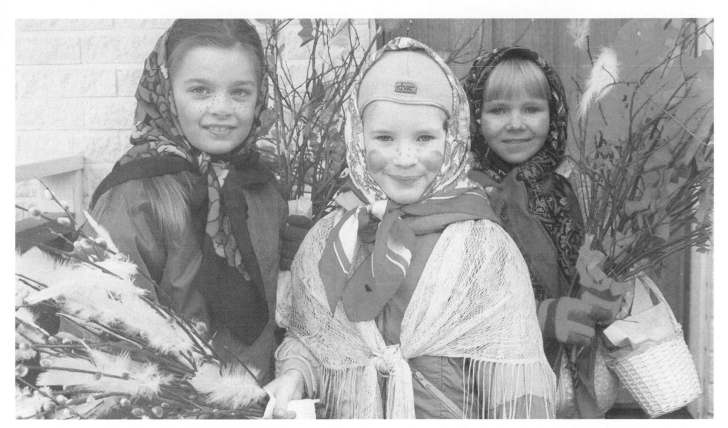

Finnish girls dressed as witches engage in the Finnish version of "trick-or-treat" on Palm Sunday in Helsinki, Finland. The children go door to door offering pussywillow branches as a token of goodwill in exchange for a small payment. (AP Images/Sari Gustafsson)

year lasts from mid-August to the end of May, with a long Christmas break and a one-week skiing holiday in the spring. The Finnish educational system places great emphasis on foreign languages. Two foreign languages are studied in the primary grades and a third added in the seventh grade. Languages studied commonly include English, Russian, French, and German. After the nine years of comprehensive schooling, students may opt for either vocational or secondary (college preparatory) school. In order to enter a university, students must receive their secondary school certificate and pass an exam. There are 20 universities in Finland and many vocational schools.

¹⁴ CULTURAL HERITAGE

Due to its geographic location, Finland's cultural heritage has been impacted by both Eastern and Western influences. Finland's national epic, the *Kalevala*, has made an important contribution to its fine arts. Elias Lönnrot first collected and published the folk tales of the *Kalevala* in 1835. It has inspired numerous musical compositions, including several works by Finland's greatest composer, Jean Sibelius, as well as many sculptures and paintings, notably those of Akseli Gallen-Kallela. Although the great 19th-century writer Johan Ludvig Runeberg wrote in Swedish, a portion of his *Tales of Ensign Stal* was adopted for the Finnish national anthem. The first major author to write in Finnish was Aleksis Kivi, who also lived and wrote in the 19th century. Prominent 20th-century writers include Frans Eemil Sillanpää, who won the Nobel Prize in 1939, Mika Waltari, and Väinö Linna.

Finland is especially known for its great singers and the art of opera has flourished in recent times. Large-scale works are produced at the Savonlinna opera festival held on the grounds of a 15th-century castle every summer. In the classical music world, the best-known Finnish name currently is that of the young composer and conductor Esa-Pekka Salonen.

Linus Torvalds, known worldwide as the man who developed the Linux operating system, was born in Finland, as was Sari Maritta Baldauf, the former head of Nokia Networks. Nokia was founded by Fredrik Idestam, who became known as the father of Finland's paper industry after building his paper mill on the banks of the Nokianvirta River. Eric Tigerstedt was the first person to implement a working sound-on-film technology.

¹⁵ WORK

In 2007 roughly 66% of Finns between the ages of 15 and 74 participated in the labor force—a high percentage in proportion to the total population. As in most Western nations, the trade and service sectors accounted for the greatest number of jobs in 2007 at about 66%. Industry and construction accounted for another 27%. Young people may work at the age of 15 if they have completed the nine compulsory years of comprehensive schooling, but there are laws governing the number of hours and the times during which they may work.

¹⁶ SPORTS

Finns excel at individual rather than team sports, and particularly at activities that require stamina. The primary national sport is skiing, which was invented by the Finns: Finnish skis have been found dating back 3,700 years. While Finns today ski for enjoyment, skiing used to be an important means of transportation, especially for traveling from one village to another. With more than 200 ski jumps in Finland, one can be found in most towns and villages. Long cross-country ski trips are organized on Sundays. Finnish children are introduced to winter sports at a young age, and even in school their classes are punctuated by a recess for outdoor activities every 45 minutes. Besides skiing, hockey is the favorite winter sport. In summer Finnish baseball is popular.

The Finns are also known for their great long-distance runners. Paavo Nurmi (1897–1973), known popularly as "The Flying Finn," was a famous athlete and national hero who won nine Olympic gold medals between 1920 and 1928. Today many of Finland's star athletes are race car drivers. Other popular sports include swimming, skating, and soccer.

17 ENTERTAINMENT AND RECREATION

Finland, with one of the highest literacy rates in the world, is a nation of readers. The libraries are used extensively, and most people are book buyers, even though books are expensive. Helsinki boasts one of the world's largest bookstores, books are sold everywhere in the country, and serious literary works are serialized in popular magazines. For the size of its population, Finland has many newspapers and a high number of book titles published annually. Finns also enjoy the theater and are avid fans of soccer (called football).

Perhaps the favorite leisure-time activity in Finland is relaxing in the sauna. Most private homes have saunas and many city apartments are equipped with them. It is quite common for a Finn to invite a friend over for time in the sauna, which soothes tired muscles and melts away worries. This might be followed by a light meal and/or cool drinks. Finns enjoy entertaining at their homes, whether as dinner parties or simply casual gatherings of friends.

18 FOLK ART, CRAFTS, AND HOBBIES

Finland's tradition of folk poetry, also called rune song, has been preserved in the *Kalevala*, which was assembled and published by Elias Lönnrot in the 19th century. A traditional craft that is flourishing today is the production the woolen *ryijy* rug, which dates back to the 14th and 15th centuries. Originally used to keep warm on boats or sleighs or to keep out drafts, they eventually evolved into decorative hangings which today may combine as many as 100 different colors. These rugs were traditionally produced by women, while men made furniture, harnesses, and the sheath knife (*puukko*) used for hunting and fishing. Other Finnish crafts include ceramics, woodworking, glassware, sculpture, and textiles.

19 SOCIAL PROBLEMS

Alcoholism is a pervasive problem in Finland, as it is in the neighboring countries of Norway, Sweden, and Russia. Some social tension exists between ethnic Finns and minority groups, particularly against Roma and immigrants. Trafficking in persons has been a problem as Finland has been seen as both a destination and a transit spot for trafficking operations that primarily involve women and children. While prostitution is legal in Finland, trafficking and pimping are not. Some foreign women are lured into prostitution rings with the promise of higher wages and better working conditions, but are then forced to work longer hours for little pay under the fear of abuse or deportation. Both men and women have been brought into the country illegally to work in construction, restaurants, or domestic service. The government and various social organizations have taken measures to investigate and prosecute those involved in human trafficking, and to locate and assist victims.

20 GENDER ISSUES

In 1906 Finland became the first nation to give women the vote in national elections. In 2000 Tarja Halonen became the first woman president of Finland. Men and women are legally required to receive equal pay for equal work; however, in fact women receive 18% less pay than men on average. Within the family structure, men and women generally take on equal roles and both often work outside of the home. Both men and women are permitted to take up to three years of leave from work in order to care for their infant children; however, women most often take advantage of this right. Most women enjoy a high level of financial independence. Nearly two-thirds of young women leave their parents' homes before the age of 20 to live independently or with a companion. Young men tend to remain in their parents' home slightly longer, until they have completed their military service. Women and men have equal opportunities in education. Equality in both work and education seems to have resulted in a rising number of adults who choose to remain single or simply live together rather than marry. The average age for marriage is about 30 for both men and women.

Homosexuality was decriminalized in Finland in 1971, but it remained illegal to promote it. Discrimination on the basis of sexual orientation was prohibited by law in 1995. Same-sex unions were made legal in 2002. Finnish support for same-sex marriage stood at about 45% in 2008. There is a significant gay community in Helsinki.

21 BIBLIOGRAPHY

Bird, Tim. *Living in Finland*. London: Thames & Hudson, 2005.

Illustrated Encyclopedia of Mankind. London: Marshall Cavendish, 1978.

Jarvenpa, Robert. "Finns." In *Encyclopedia of World Cultures* (*Europe*). Boston: G. K. Hall, 1992.

Lander, Patricia Slade, and Claudette Charbonneau. *The Land and People of Finland*. New York: Lippincott, 1990.

Maude, George. *Historical Dictionary of Finland*, 2nd ed., Lanham, MD: Scarecrow Press, 2007.

Ministry of Foreign Affairs of Finland. Virtual Finland. http://virtual.finlanf.fi. (23 April 2008).

Moss, Joyce, and George Wilson. *Peoples of the World: Western Europeans*. Detroit: Gale Research, 1993.

Rajanen, Aini. *Of Finnish Ways*. Minneapolis: Dillon Press, 1981.

Taylor-Wilkie, Doreen. *Finland*. Insight Guides. Singapore: APA Press, 1993.

—revised by K. Ellicott

FLEMINGS

ALTERNATE NAMES: Flemish
LOCATION: Belgium (northern region, called Flanders)
POPULATION: 6.2 million
LANGUAGE: Flemish
RELIGION: Roman Catholic; Protestant; small numbers of Jews and Muslims

¹ INTRODUCTION

The Flemings (or Flemish) are Belgium's ethnic majority. They inhabit the northern part of Belgium, which is called Flanders, and speak the Flemish language, which is closely related to Dutch. Present-day Belgium was originally inhabited by Celtic tribes and overrun by the Romans under Julius Caesar in 57 BC. Although Roman rule continued for 500 years, Roman culture was more strongly absorbed by the people in the southern part of the region, who would one day be known as Walloons and speak a dialect of French, a Latin-derived language. In the 5th century AD the Franks, a Germanic people, invaded the region and established control, although they maintained a stronger presence in its northern portion, where early forms of the Dutch language subsequently developed. Frankish settlements in the south were less extensive, allowing the Roman culture and Latin-based dialects already in existence to flourish.

Between the 9th and 12th centuries, both the northern and southern parts of the Belgian region fell under the control of feudal lords, and numerous duchies, principalities, and towns sprang up without any unifying center of power or culture, allowing the Germanic and Latin cultures of the two regions to continue developing along separate lines. Eventually the power of the nobles was challenged by the burghers of the cities, especially in Antwerp, Bruges, and Ghent. As Flemish cities began to play a vital role in European trade, the area entered a cultural golden age in both music and art. However, beginning in the 16th century, both the Flemish and the French-speaking Walloons to their south came under the rule of a succession of foreign powers: Spain, the Austrian Habsburgs, the French under Napoleon, and, finally, the Netherlands. In spite of the Flemings' cultural and linguistic ties to Holland, they joined with the Walloons in revolting against Dutch rule, and the new Kingdom of Belgium was established in 1830.

Throughout the 19th century, the Walloons were the dominant group in Belgium both politically and economically. Their French language and culture were regarded as superior to those of the Flemings, and they led the nation in industrialization, while Flanders remained a primarily agricultural area. Belgium suffered enormous losses in both world wars. After World War II, structural and social problems had a debilitating effect on Wallonia's industries. By the 1930s Flanders had gained sufficient political and economic clout to make Flemish its official language for education, legal proceedings, and government. In the 1960s, the Flemings and Walloons were given political, social, and cultural autonomy over their respective regions. The intervening years have been a period of decline for Wallonia's traditional heavy industries, especially steel and coal, while Flanders has risen in importance as a center for international trade, high-tech manufacturing, and tourism. In 1993, Belgium's constitution was amended, making Flanders and Wallonia autonomous regions within the federal state of the Belgian kingdom, together with the nation's bilingual capital, Brussels, and another autonomous community composed of Belgium's German-speaking population. Belgium was locked in a political stalemate beginning in June 2007 when elections failed to produce a new government. The question arose as to whether or not Belgium should cease to exist as a country, and that the territory would be split into two—Flanders and Wallonia. The crisis was temporarily resolved in March 2008 when a new government was formed, and major reforms of state were planned.

² LOCATION AND HOMELAND

The Flemings live in the northern part of Belgium, above an east-west line dividing the country's Flemish- and French-speaking regions. The Flemish-speaking provinces are East and West Flanders, Antwerp, Limburg, and part of Brabant. One of Belgium's two main rivers, the Scheldt, flows through Antwerp and into the North Sea. The land is mostly low, some of it below sea level, with about 64 km (40 mi) of scenic beaches along the West Flanders coast. Silt deposits have created a rich soil excellent for farming, formerly the economic mainstay of the region and still an important source of income. The Flemings, who account for 58% of Belgium's 10.4 million people, are descended from Celts, who originally inhabited their region, and from the Romans and Frankish invaders who followed. "Vlaanderen," the name for Flanders, is taken from "Pagus Flandrensus," the name of an 8th-century district in the region during the Carolingian era.

³ LANGUAGE

Flemish (Vlaams) is a variant of Dutch that has been spoken for about 1,000 years north of a linguistic dividing line that runs from Aachen in the east to a point north of Lille in the west, skirting the Brussels area. Recognized in Belgium as an official state language, it is distinct from the Dutch spoken in the neighboring Netherlands. Even within Belgium, dialects vary from one region to another, distinguished by differences in pronunciation, individual words, and idiomatic expressions. Flemish does not have its own written language and uses standard Dutch modified by certain specifically Belgian features. The difference between Flemish and Dutch has been compared to that between English as spoken by people in Great Britain and in the United States. However, the difference between Flemish and Dutch may be even greater, as subtitles are sometimes used on Dutch television when Flemish movies are aired. Language differences between the Flemish and the French-speaking Walloons in the south have been Belgium's most divisive political issue.

NUMBERS

one	een
two	twee
three	drie
four	vier
five	vijf
six	zes
seven	zeven
eight	acht
nine	negen
ten	tien

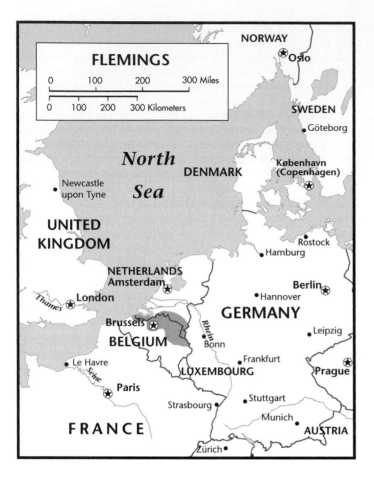

FLEMINGS

0 100 200 300 Miles

0 100 200 300 Kilometers

NORWAY
Oslo

SWEDEN

Göteborg

North Sea

DENMARK

København (Copenhagen)

Newcastle upon Tyne

UNITED KINGDOM

Rostock

Hamburg

NETHERLANDS
Amsterdam

London

Berlin

Hannover

GERMANY

Brussels

Leipzig

BELGIUM

Rhein

Bonn

Le Havre

Frankfurt

LUXEMBOURG

Prague

Seine

Paris

Stuttgart

Strasbourg

Munich

AUSTRIA

FRANCE

Zürich

DAYS OF THE WEEK

Sunday	zondag
Monday	maandag
Tuesday	dinsdag
Wednesday	woensdag
Thursday	donderdag
Friday	vrijdag
Saturday	zaterdag

4 FOLKLORE

The name of Antwerp—the major city in the Flemish part of Belgium—is derived from the name of a Roman hero who is said to have slain a malevolent giant and cut off his hand (the city's symbol is a red hand). Some of the Flemings' colorful pageants and festivals are based on local folklore, such as the Cat Festival of Ypres. This celebration is based on a legend, which exists in different versions, centering on the use of cats to control rodents in this historic city during the Middle Ages and the necessity of disposing of the cats when they became too numerous or were no longer needed. The festivals, held in their original form until 1817, used to involve throwing live cats out of windows. Since their revival in a more humane form in 1938, cloth cats have been used instead. In Belgium's famed marionette theaters, characters from folklore are associated with major cities. The Flemish ones include Schele (Antwerp) and Pierke (Ghent).

5 RELIGION

The vast majority of Flemish are Catholics. While virtually all are baptized and receive a Catholic education, many do not actively practice their religion, and some are even nonbelievers who remain nominally Catholic in order to avoid being cut off from the many social services administered through the Church. Flanders also has a Protestant minority that includes Jehovah's Witnesses, Mormons, and other denominations. There are also Jewish and Muslim communities among the Flemish.

6 MAJOR HOLIDAYS

The Flemish observe Belgium's 10 public holidays: New Year's Day, Easter Monday, Labor Day (May 1), Independence Day (July 21), All Saints' Day (November 1), and Christmas. However, they also celebrate other dates on the Christian calendar (especially those that mark events in the life of Christ), as well as many folk holidays with origins in history and legend. Folk festivals and processions often involve the use of elaborate masks and papier-mâché "giants." The Flemings are especially well-known for their exuberant celebration of the pre-Lenten carnival season, which begins with the *bommelfeesten* in the East Flanders town of Ronse and continues for weeks. The famous Cat Festival takes place in Ypres on the second Sunday in May.

7 RITES OF PASSAGE

Rites of passage include major Catholic ceremonies such as baptisms, first Communions, marriages and funerals. Although most Flemish do not really practice Catholicism, the important events in a person's life tend to be occasions of major family reunions and stress their religious heritage. Special gifts and wishes will be given for baptisms, first Communions, and marriages.

8 INTERPERSONAL RELATIONS

Flemish manners are generally formal and polite, and conversations are marked by frequent exchanges of compliments and repeated handshaking.

9 LIVING CONDITIONS

Most Flemish homes, like those in neighboring Wallonia, are built of red brick. The conservatively furnished interiors are generally crowded with oversized armchairs and other large pieces of furniture, including wall units, or breakfronts, containing dishes, glasses, and other household items. It is also common to see religious artifacts and mementos displayed. Often the house will have a combined living room and dining area; large kitchens are also common. A distinctive feature of Belgian housing, and one especially characteristic of the Flemish, is the location of a shop or other small business at the same site as the family residence (an arrangement referred to as a *winkelshuis* or *handelshuis*).

Like all Belgians, the Flemish have access to modern medical care through private doctors and at state-run hospitals and clinics. The vast majority have most of their medical expenses covered by national health insurance. However, they tend to be negligent about dental care and often lose teeth due to decay. Many believe in alternative medical treatments, especially Oriental ones such as acupuncture. The Flemish port of Antwerp, the second largest in Europe (after Amsterdam), is the center of Belgium's water transport system, and the nation's railway network has its hub in Brussels.

10 FAMILY LIFE

The Flemish generally have larger families than their Walloon neighbors to the south. Nuclear rather than extended families are the norm, and married couples often run small businesses together. Traditionally it was frowned upon for an adult to remain single past his or her mid-thirties, and single adults usually lived with their parents until they married, contributing their earnings to the household income. Today, many young people living at home keep their earnings, which they spend on clothes, cars, and recreation. Also, since the 1970s it has become increasingly common for unmarried couples to live together. The divorce rate among the Flemish, as elsewhere in Belgium and throughout the West, has also risen, not only among young couples married for a year or two, but also among middle-aged couples married for 20 years or longer. The growing gap between generations, as well as the high incidence of dual-career families, has made it increasingly difficult for married couples to care for aging parents at home. The elderly commonly live in retirement communities or homes for the aged, and such facilities often have long waiting lists.

11 CLOTHING

The Flemish, like all Belgians, wear modern Western-style clothing. However, in some rural areas, the traditional dark-colored farmer's garb can still be seen.

12 FOOD

While Flemish cooking does reflect Dutch cultural influences to a certain extent, it has generally developed along its own lines. For example, the Flemish meat-and-vegetable stew (*hochepot*) consists of vegetables and meat in a clear broth, while in the Dutch version (*hutspot*), the vegetables are pureed, and the chunks of meat larger. Fish and shellfish are central to Flemish cuisine, with staples including mussels and herring. Lobster, shrimp, and oysters are also popular. Rabbit cooked in brown beer with stewed prunes is a regional specialty, as is *waterzooi*, a chowder made from vegetables and either chicken or fish. Dinner, the main meal of the day, is eaten at midday. A typical dinner consists of homemade soup, a meat entrée with vegetables, and fruit and pastry. The Flemings are great beer drinkers and brew some of the best beers in the world.

13 EDUCATION

Many Flemish children go to Catholic private schools. Education for all Belgians is compulsory from age 6 through 15, and the national literacy rate is 99%. At the secondary level, students choose between trade-oriented, business, and college preparatory training. Some vocational schools maintain work-study apprenticeship programs, although students enrolled in them still live with their parents.

14 CULTURAL HERITAGE

In the fine arts, the Flemish are particularly renowned for their painting. The works of Jan van Eyck and the other Flemish masters of the 15th century marked an important turning point in Western art by straying from the predominantly re-ligious themes of the Middle Ages to reflect the lifestyles and concerns of the Flemish burghers who were their patrons. Other well-known Flemish painters of the Renaissance included Hieronymus Bosch, Pieter Bruegel the Elder, Pieter Bruegel the Younger, Peter Paul Rubens, and Anthony van Dyck.

Flemish literature began in the Middle Ages with works by authors including Heinrich von Veldeke, Jacob van Maerlant, and a Brabant nun named Hadewijch who wrote mystical dramas. During the hundreds of years of foreign rule that began with the Spanish in the 16th century, Flemish letters fell into decline but were revived after independence was attained in 1830. Established 10 years later, the Flemish Movement advocated the advancement of the Flemish culture and language and was also involved in struggles for political autonomy. Prominent 19th-century Flemish writers include Hendrik Conscience, author of *The Lion of Flanders (De Leeaw van Vlaenderen)* and lyric poet Guido Gezelle.

Well-known modern Flemish authors include novelists Louis Paul Boon and Hugo Claus. In the 16th century, the works of Orlando di Lasso combined the musical traditions of the Netherlands and Italy.

15 WORK

The Flemish are hard workers, often spending long hours running family-owned businesses, sometimes in addition to another source of income. In the 19th century and the first half of the 20th, Wallonia led Belgium in industrialization, while Flanders remained primarily involved in agriculture and trade. However, the lesser-developed Flemish region was able to obtain generous international aid in the years following World War II, and its large labor force and relatively low wages drew increasing foreign investment in the 1950s and 1960s. Its maritime advantages—the busy port city of Antwerp as well as the proximity of the North Sea—rounded out a picture of economic success. Major industries today include textiles, automobiles, and chemicals. Manufacturing in areas such as electronics and computer technology has grown, while the traditional heavy industries, including steelmaking and shipbuilding, have been on the decline.

The fertile, flat land in the Flemish region—of which three-fifths is suitable for farming—remains a source of agricultural income, supporting fruit, vegetables, animal feed, and grains. Today three out of four Belgians work in the service sector, and the Flemish regions have benefited from the growth of tourism to such cities as Antwerp, Bruges, Ghent, and Brussels.

16 SPORTS

The Flemish are enthusiastic players and fans of soccer, Belgium's national sport, and cycling is another favorite sport.

17 ENTERTAINMENT AND RECREATION

The Flemish people enjoy typical leisure time activities such as watching television and reading. Like many Belgians, they are avid gardeners, and nearly every home has a carefully tended garden. Other typical hobbies include stamp collecting and model trains. Popular cultural pastimes include concerts and the theater, and, in Brussels and other major cities, opera and ballet as well. The Flemish also share the general Belgian love of festivals, and their calendar is filled with celebrations of all kinds, both religious and secular.

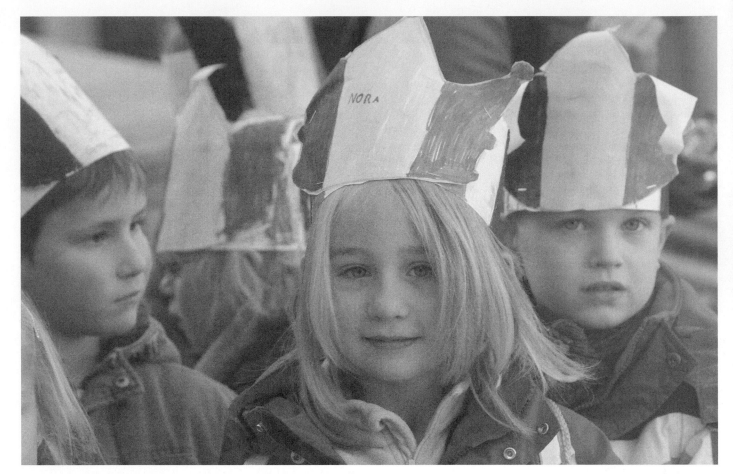

School children wearing paper hats with the Belgian flag wait for the royal family outside Saint Michel's Cathedral to celebrate King's Day in Brussels, Belgium. King's Day is meant to honor the royal family. (AP Images/Thierry Charlier)

18 FOLK ART, CRAFTS, AND HOBBIES

The Flemish are known for their lacemaking, and other crafts include glassblowing, tapestries, and pottery. In recent years there has been a movement to revive folk arts including street singing, folk opera, and the puppet and marionette theaters that once flourished throughout the region, particularly in Antwerp. In the 1970s, Antwerp also became known as a center of women's fashion.

19 SOCIAL PROBLEMS

While the incidence of violent crime in public is relatively low among the Flemish, domestic violence—in which the Belgian police seldom intervene—remains a problem. Spousal and child abuse occur among all social classes, as well as abuse of elderly relatives in a household. Although the fertilizers and crop sprays used by Belgium's farmers result in agricultural yields that are among the world's highest, the country is paying a price in terms of increased levels of river pollution.

Traditionally, ethnic differences between the Flemings and Walloons have been sources of social conflict, and even threatened to divide the country in 2007 and 2008.

20 GENDER ISSUES

Flanders has an old tradition that could be called feminist. Beginning in the 12th century, certain Catholic women in the Low Countries chose to live neither under the care of a man nor the vows of the church. They were called *beguines*—derived from the Flemish word *beghen* (to pray). *Beguinages* were home to generations of religious women who sought to live a more independent life than that of women who married against their will. They made their homes, catered to the sick and poor, and sought to serve God without separating from the rest of the world. They lived simply and wore loose robes and headwear similar to nuns' habits. But they took no religious vows. They could leave and marry, own their own property, and took no alms. Women of all classes were welcomed. They carried on professions, often in the textile industry. They elected women to be leaders—Grand Dames—and each Grand Dame often was assisted by an elected council. Each *beguine* was expected to support herself and make a tangible contribution to the *beguinage*, either through labor or rent income. Eventually many *beguinages* were elevated to parish status and were assigned their own priest. In the 19th century some of the *beguines* retained possession of their homes, while others were taken over by religious orders or transformed into hospices and orphanages. However, many of Belgium's *beguinages* are intact today, as gated or walled communes. In 1998, 13 Flemish *beguinages* were listed as UNESCO World Heritage sites.

Women won the right to vote in Belgium in 1919, and restrictions on the suffrage were dropped in 1948. Abortion was only legalized in Belgium in 1990. As of 2000, women made up 24% of the lower house of parliament, and 28.8% of the upper house. Approximately 55.7% of Belgian women hold a secondary degree, 53.1% hold a bachelor's degree, and 7.6% are in senior management. The government made a concerted effort in the 1990s in involve women in politics.

Belgium decriminalized homosexuality in 1843 and legalized same-sex marriages in 2003—it was only the second country to do so worldwide. Gay and lesbian couples have the same rights as heterosexual ones, including inheritance and adoption. In 2006 the country's first gay church was inaugurated in Ghent.

21 BIBLIOGRAPHY

Blyth, Derek. *Flemish Cities Explored: Bruges, Ghent, Antwerp, Mechelen, Brussels & Leuven.* London: Pallas Athene, 1996.

De Vries, Andreë. *Flanders: A Cultural History.* Oxford: Oxford University Press, 2007.

Flood, Merielle K. "Flemish." In *Encyclopedia of World Cultures (Europe).* Boston: G. K. Hall, 1992.

Fox, Renée. *In the Belgian Château: The Spirit and Culture of a European Society in an Age of Change.* Chicago: Ivan R. Dee, 1994.

Hargrove, Jim. *Belgium. Enchantment of the World Series.* Chicago: Children's Press, 1988.

Hubbard, Monica M, and Beverly Baer, ed. *Cities of the World: Europe and the Middle East.* Detroit: Gale Research, 1993.

Illustrated Encyclopedia of Mankind. London: Marshall Cavendish, 1978.

Lijphart, Arend, ed. *Conflict and Coexistence in Belgium: The Dynamics of a Culturally Divided Society.* Berkeley: University of California Press, 1981.

Moss, Joyce, and George Wilson. *Peoples of the World: Western Europeans.* Detroit: Gale Research, 1993.

Shawe-Taylor, Desmond. *Bruegel to Rubens: Masterpieces of Flemish Painting.* London: Royal Collection Publications, 2007.

Wickman, Stephen B. *Belgium: A Country Study.* Washington, DC: U.S. Government Printing Office, 1984.

—revised by J. Hobby

FRENCH

LOCATION: France
POPULATION: About 60.8 million
LANGUAGE: French; also Breton, Flemish, Spanish, Catalan, Basque, Provençal, and English
RELIGION: Roman Catholic; Protestant; smaller numbers of Muslims and Jews

1 INTRODUCTION

France, which has existed in its present form since the 15th century, is Europe's oldest nation. A leader in intellectual trends, the fine arts, fashion, and cuisine, it is also the world's sixth richest country, a major nuclear power, and Europe's leading agricultural producer.

Originally part of the Celtic region known as Gaul, France became part of the Roman Empire until it was overrun by a Germanic tribe—the Franks—from whom the country's present name is derived. Its greatest early ruler was Charlemagne in the 9th century AD. At the end of the 10th century, Hugh Capet founded the dynasty that was to rule over the French for the next 800 years. Other great figures in early French history include Joan of Arc, who inspired French national feeling during the Hundred Years War and was burned at the stake by the English in 1431, and Louis XIV, the so-called Sun King, who transformed France into an absolute monarchy in the 17th century.

The French Revolution in 1789 was followed by the rise of Napoleon Bonaparte, who conquered much of Europe before his downfall in 1814. In the 20th century, France weathered two world wars and a worldwide economic depression in addition to its own political and social upheavals and the loss of a large colonial empire. However it has survived in the 21st century to become a major political and economic world power and a leader in the European Union (EU). However, in 2005 France's voters rejected the proposed EU constitution in a referendum, dooming the document. France nevertheless is looking to develop the EU's military capabilities to supplement progress toward an EU foreign policy.

2 LOCATION AND HOMELAND

The largest country in Western Europe (Ukraine is the largest country in Europe since the breakup of the Soviet Union), France is located on the extreme west coast of the continent. It is the only country except Spain to have both Atlantic and Mediterranean coasts, as well as direct access to the North Sea. Lowlands make up about half of France's terrain; the other half consists of hills or mountains. The major geographic areas are the Northern Region, the Paris Basin, Normandy, Brittany, the Lower Loire, and the Southwestern Plains. France's principal mountain chains are the Pyrenees, which border Spain, and the Alps, bordering Italy and Switzerland. Its major rivers are the Rhône and the Seine.

France's native-born population has Celtic, Germanic, Latin, and Slavic origins. Its immigrant population of around five million lives primarily in the country's central, southern, and southeastern areas, and immigrants are especially numerous in Alsace. Those from the North African countries of Tunisia, Algeria, and Morocco are called Maghrébins. Other immi-

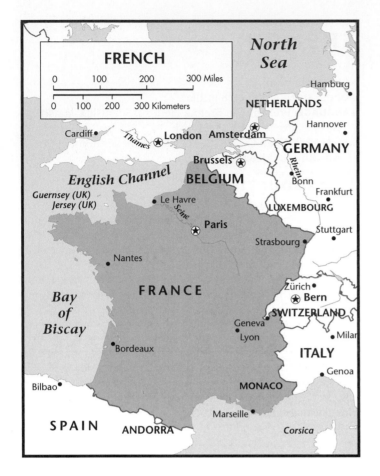

four	quatre
five	cinq
six	six
seven	sept
eight	huit
nine	neuf
ten	dix

4 FOLKLORE

Native folklore varies from region to region. Witches and cave dwellers with supernatural powers traditionally populated Basque legends, and some elderly Basques still fear the evil eye. Ancient Celtic religious sites can still be found in northern Auvergne, together with vestiges of ancient beliefs. The Bretons have many superstitions and rituals accompanying death. Death itself is envisioned as a legendary figure called Ankou, pictured as a skeleton with a scythe, and it is believed that the creaking of the cart he rides in portends the death of a person in the neighborhood. When a person dies, the doors and windows of the house are traditionally left open so that the soul can depart, and mirrors are turned to face the wall.

5 RELIGION

About 83–88% of the French population is Roman Catholic, although less than one-fifth of Catholics attend church regularly. Protestants account for roughly 2%, mostly Calvinist or Lutheran. Anywhere from 5–10% of the population is Muslim, mostly immigrants from North Africa, and Jews make up 1% of the population.

6 MAJOR HOLIDAYS

Religious, historical, and patriotic holidays are observed throughout the year. New Year's Eve is celebrated with a festive dinner; at midnight family and friends wish each other a good year by kissing under mistletoe. For Epiphany on January 6 the custom is to bake a large round pastry with a bean hidden in it; the person who finds the bean becomes "ruler" for the evening. Mardi Gras, on Shrove Tuesday in February, is marked by parades featuring flowers, floats, and giant cardboard figures. Labor Day on May 1 is celebrated by workers' parades. May 8 marks the end of World War II, and France's national holiday (the equivalent of July Fourth in the United States) is Bastille Day on July 14, which commemorates the storming of the Bastille in 1789. It is accompanied by parades, fireworks, and dancing in the streets. The French observe Christmas by attending a midnight mass. France's different regions also celebrate their own holidays and festivals. Many occur at Christmas and Easter, such as Strasbourg's Christmas market.

7 RITES OF PASSAGE

France is a modern, industrialized, Christian country. Hence, many of the rites of passage that young people undergo are religious rituals, such as baptism, first Communion, confirmation, and marriage. In addition, a student's progress through the education system is marked by many families with graduation parties.

8 INTERPERSONAL RELATIONS

The French have a formality and reserve that is often interpreted as rudeness by outsiders. In addition, their pride in their

grants are from Portugal, Italy, Spain, Turkey, and immigrants from Russia and Central and Eastern Europe after the fall of communism in the 1990s.

3 LANGUAGE

French, a Romance language with Latin roots, is the national language not only of France's people but also of some 300 million others throughout the world. It is the first or second language of more than 20 African countries, 6 in Asia and the South Pacific, and 5 in Europe. The original Latin-derived language was modified by the addition of words from Celtic, German, and Greek. Within France itself, other spoken languages include Breton, Flemish, Spanish, Catalan, Basque, and Provençal. English is also spoken by many in France, especially for business purposes.

DAYS OF THE WEEK

Monday	lundi
Tuesday	mardi
Wednesday	mercredi
Thursday	jeudi
Friday	vendredi
Saturday	samedi
Sunday	dimanche

NUMBERS

one	un, une
two	deux
three	trois

taste and culture, which reveres artists and philosophers, is sometimes seen as haughtiness. Money is generally considered something of a taboo topic, and it is considered especially rude to ask the size of someone's salary. When invited to another person's home, a French person will invariably bring along a gift of wine or flowers. Both men and women often greet each other by kissing on the cheek.

9 LIVING CONDITIONS

Long, white-walled, red-tiled farm houses are a typical sight in the French countryside. Most city dwellers live in rented apartments, often a short distance from where they work. While the French like modern homes, many have a taste for antique furniture. Today it is becoming increasingly popular for urbanites to maintain a second home in the country that they can escape to on weekends. Immigrants from North Africa often live in large suburban housing developments called *cités*, which are generally run down and overcrowded.

French life expectancy averages 80.8 years, with heart disease and cancer the major causes of death. France has a comprehensive national health care system that covers both private care and state-operated facilities. Pregnant women receive free prenatal medical care, and infants receive three free checkups during their first two years. Since the 1980s, the trend has been toward outpatient and home care.

France's modern, efficient transportation system is centered in the city of Paris, which can make direct travel between provincial locations difficult. The state-owned railways are punctual, with clean, modern trains. France is known especially for its high-speed train, the TGV (Train de Grand Vitesse)—the fastest train in the world. Placed into service in 1981, it travels at speeds averaging 250 km/hr (150 mi/hr) and connects with the Channel Tunnel ("Chunnel") to England, making it possible to travel from London to Paris in three hours by land. The *Métro*, the Parisian subway, carries 4.5 million passengers per day. The highway system (*autoroute*), which is continually being expanded, is known for its clearly marked expressways and secondary routes. France has many navigable rivers and connecting canals, and its national airline, Air France, operates regularly scheduled flights to all parts of the world.

10 FAMILY LIFE

Traditionally, French households were made up of extended families—grandparents, parents, and children. Today, however, a nuclear family with one or two children is the norm. However, family ties remain strong. College-age children usually attend local colleges and universities, and families get together on birthdays, anniversaries, and holidays. France's divorce rate has doubled since the 1960s, and in 2002 38% of marriages ended in divorce.

11 CLOTHING

Traditional costumes are still worn at festivals and celebrations in regions such as Alsace, where women may be seen in white lace-trimmed blouses, dark bodices, and aprons decorated with colorful flowers, black bonnets, and even wooden shoes. Women's costumes in Normandy include gauzy, white, flared bonnets and dresses with wide elbow-length sleeves and varied types of colorful designs.

For their day-to-day activities, the French, both in the countryside and the cities, wear modern Western-style clothing, for both casual and formal occasions. Perhaps the most typical item of clothing associated with the French is the black beret, which is still worn by some men, particularly in rural areas. French women have long been known for their style and elegance, and France is a leader in the fashion world. The first French *couture*, or fashion house, was founded in 1858, complete with models, fashion shows, salespeople, and designer labels. Today France is renowned for such designers as Coco Chanel, Yves Saint-Laurent, and Christian Dior, whose creations influence fashions around the world. Since the 1960s, French designers have branched out into more affordable ready-to-wear clothing lines, which have become very popular.

12 FOOD

The French are renowned for their elaborate, well-prepared cuisine (a term that comes from the French word for "kitchen"). The diversity of France's terrain and climate and its proximity to both the Atlantic Ocean and Mediterranean Sea provide a wide variety of produce and seafood on which French cooks can hone their culinary skills. Each region of the country has its own specialties. The *choucroute* of Alsace consists of cabbage in white wine with pork and sausages. Central France is famous for *boeuf bourguignon,* beef in red wine sauce. *Saucissons* (dried sausages) are a specialty in the Rhône Valley, and southern France has a typical Mediterranean cuisine that depends heavily on garlic, vegetables, and herbs. One of its characteristic dishes is a vegetable stew called *ratatouille.*

The French typically eat a modest breakfast (*petit déjeuner*) of coffee with milk (*café au lait*) and croissants or bread and butter. In the country, this is often followed by a mid-morning snack of bread and sausages or paté. Lunch (*déjeuner*) is a substantial three- or four-course meal consisting of an appetizer, a main dish of meat, fish, or vegetables, a green salad, and a dessert of fruit or pastry. Dinner (*díner*) is a light meal of soup, cheeses, and sometimes salad or leftovers. The French are famous for their wines, and wine—which plays in important role in French life and culture—is commonly served at both lunch and dinner.

13 EDUCATION

France's literacy rate is above 99%—one of the highest in the world. Education is compulsory between the ages of 6 and 16. Public education is free, and the state also pays for textbooks used in private schools. The school day usually begins at 8:00 am. Between 12:00 and 2:00, the pupils take a long break to go home for lunch (the main meal of the day), and classes end at 4:00 pm. French students spend 936 hours per year in class, compared to an average of 800 in the rest of Europe. As of 2007 two-thirds of children at the primary level attended school on at least one in three Saturdays. However, in September of that year, the French government announced Saturday classes in primary schools would be discontinued in 2008 and that secondary schools could follow suit. After five years of primary school, students spend four years at a middle school called a *collège* for the first part of their secondary education. The next three years are spent either at a general *lycée* for those planning to go on to college or at a vocational *lycée*. After receiving their *baccalauréat* degrees, students may go on to a university or to a *grand école*, which offers preparation for careers in business or government service. France's oldest and most famous university is the Sorbonne, in Paris.

Mounted Republican Guards parade on the Champs Elysees on Bastille Day in Paris, France. (AP Images/Jacques Brinon)

¹⁴ CULTURAL HERITAGE

France has made significant contributions in all of the fine arts, beginning with the great medieval cathedrals at Chartres, Reims, and Amiens, and Notre Dame in Paris. Painting was the dominant French art of the 19th century, particularly that of the Impressionists, including Auguste Renoir, Claude Monet, and Edouard Manet. The most famous French sculptor was Auguste Rodin. Postimpressionists Paul Cézanne, Paul Gauguin, and Henri Matisse painted in new styles that influenced developments in 20th-century French art. France's great musicians include the 19th-century composer Hector Berlioz and the "Impressionistic" composers Claude Debussy and Maurice Ravel, whose new musical styles and harmonies provided a bridge between 19th- and 20th-century musical styles. Currently, Pierre Boulez is an internationally renowned composer and conductor. France is also known as an international center for ballet.

In a nation that places great value on its philosophers and writers, French literature has had a great influence on national opinion. The great 19th-century novelists Victor Hugo, Honoré de Balzac, and Emile Zola wrote about the pressing social issues of their time. Marcel Proust is considered France's great-est 20th-century writer. France also has a rich heritage in film, beginning with the early directors Jean Renoir and Jean Cocteau and continuing through the "New Wave" of the 1950s and 1960s, with award-winning directors including François Truffaut, Jean-Luc Godard, and Éric Rohmer. Louis Malle and Luc Besson are also popular film directors. The prestigious Cannes film festival is held every year in May.

¹⁵ WORK

About 72% of the French labor force is employed in service sector jobs, 24% in industry, and 4% in agriculture. The French work week is a maximum 35 hours, a result of legislation passed in 2000 to deal with the problem of unemployment. There is a lengthy break for lunch, the main meal of the day. Day care is partly funded by the government, and workers receive five weeks of paid vacation per year.

¹⁶ SPORTS

The French are avid football (soccer) fans—there are nearly 8,000 organized soccer clubs in the country. The French national football team won the World Cup as the host nation in 1998 and placed second at the 2006 World Cup tournament.

Other well-attended spectator sports include rugby, horse racing, and auto racing. France's most famous annual sporting event is probably the Tour de France bicycle race, held since 1903. Thousands gather at roadsides to watch the racers cover the grueling 2,000-mile course in three weeks every July. Popular participant sports include fishing, shooting, swimming, skiing, and mountain climbing. In addition, increasing numbers of people are participating in tennis, horseback riding, sailing, and windsurfing.

17 ENTERTAINMENT AND RECREATION

Many people enjoy going out to meet friends at one of France's numerous cafés, but many simply stay home on weeknight evenings and watch television or read. There is now more leisure time over the weekend than there was before the 1960s, when factories were open on Saturday mornings. Domestic activities such as gardening, home improvement, and cooking have become popular leisure-time pursuits: about one-third of the French people spend some of their time gardening. France has one of the world's highest rates of movie attendance. Vacation trips have always been popular among the French, and it has become increasingly common for them to divide their five weeks of paid vacation into several breaks rather than spending the traditional holiday month at the beach (although great numbers of French still flock there in August).

18 FOLK ART, CRAFTS, AND HOBBIES

Folk arts are kept alive in the various regions of France. In Burgundy, artisans produce *sabots* (wooden shoes), *vielles* (stringed musical instruments), and other craft items. Many parts of France have rich traditions of folk music. The music of Brittany shows Celtic influences, with its popular wind instruments, the bagpipe-like *biniou* and the *bombarde*. Village festivals among the Basques feature performances on the drum and *txistu* (a type of flute), which are played simultaneously by a single performer. Traditional folk poets called *bertsolariak* improvise and sing rhymes on any subject. Folk dancing is also extremely popular among the Basques, with a dance troupe in almost every village, and similar groups in the Auvergne have revived the traditional dance of that region, called *la bourrée*.

19 SOCIAL PROBLEMS

Today's France is still a land of sharp class divisions and pronounced income disparity. France is affected by many of the major problems facing other European nations, such as unemployment, pollution, and inadequate housing. In addition, provisions must be made for immigrants and the elderly, whose numbers are increasing. In October and November 2005, France experienced its worst riots since May 1968, which were triggered by the accidental death of two teenagers, Zyed Benna and Bouna Traoré, in Clichy-sous-Bois, a working-class commune in the eastern suburbs of Paris. The unrest spread to poor housing projects in various parts of France. The riots were fueled by the problems of youth unemployment and a lack of opportunities for France's poorest communities, but anti-immigrant and especially anti-Muslim sentiment also played a role. Islam is seen as the most serious challenge to the country's secular model in the last 100 years, and the growing numbers of African, North African, and other Arab immigrants has led to an increase in social and racial discrimination against those groups. In another indication of the growing immigrant population and the government's attempt to deal with it, in 2004 France banned the wearing of Muslim headscarves in schools.

Work stoppages by unions seeking higher pay still occur, and public-sector strikes and protests are a source of instability. Illicit drug use is a problem, and France is a transshipment point for South American cocaine, Southwest Asian heroin, and European synthetics.

20 GENDER ISSUES

The lot of French women has gradually improved since World War II. Although they were granted the vote in 1944, their husbands could still prevent them from having jobs as recently as 1965, and married women were also not allowed to have their own bank accounts. Although many French women today have reached the highest executive and managerial positions in the workforce, women still face open discrimination in their professional lives, both in advancement and in salary levels. Although more than 56% of women have received higher education, they make up less than 5% of senior managers in the largest 200 French companies, and earn on average 20% less than men.

Domestic violence remains a serious problem in France, as was highlighted by the 2003 death of actress Marie Trintignant at the hands of her lover. Studies show that approximately 1 in 10 women are beaten at home.

In a positive development for women, on 28 June 1999 articles 3 and 4 of the French Constitution were amended to promote equal access for men and women to elected positions; the law was adopted on 6 June 2000. Political parties now have to endorse an equal number of men and women candidates in municipal, legislative, and European elections. Parties failing to meet this requirement either have their lists declared ineligible or, for legislative elections, face financial sanctions. France is now able to boast one of the most feminized political leaderships in the world.

A majority of the French are relatively tolerant on the issue of homosexuality: as of 2001, 55% of the population thought homosexuality was an "acceptable lifestyle." There are large gay and lesbian communities in Paris and in other major cities. As of 2008, Paris had a gay mayor, Bertrand Delanoë. Any discrimination on the basis of sexual orientation in employment or service, public or private, has been prohibited since 1985. Gay and lesbian people are free to serve in the armed forces. In 2004 the National Assembly approved legislation which made homophobic or sexist comments illegal. Civil Solidarity Pacts (PACS), a form of registered domestic partnership, were enacted in 1999 for both same-sex and unmarried opposite-sex couples. Couples who enter into a PACS contract are afforded most of the legal protections and responsibilities of marriage.

21 BIBLIOGRAPHY

Bussolin, Véronique. *France. Country Fact Files.* Austin, TX: Raintree Steck-Vaughn, 1995.

Carroll, Raymonde. *Cultural Misunderstandings: The French-American Experience.* Chicago: University of Chicago Press, 1987.

Gall, Timothy, and Susan Gall, ed. *Junior Worldmark Encyclopedia of the Nations.* Detroit: UXL, 1996.

Gilbert, Grant. *Tour de France.* New York: Weigl Publishers, 2008.

Greggio, Simonetta. *One Hundred and One Beautiful Towns in France: Food & Wine.* New York: Random House, 2008.

Moss, Joyce, and George Wilson. *Peoples of the World: Western Europeans.* Detroit: Gale Research, 1993.

Moss, Peter, and Thelma Palmer. *France. Enchantment of the World Series.* Chicago: Children's Press, 1994.

Norbrook, Dominique. *Passport to France.* New York: Franklin Watts, 1994.

Provencher, Denis M. *Queer French: Globalization, Language, and Sexual Citizenship in France.* Burlington, VT: Ashgate Publishing Company, 2007.

Sookram, Brian. *France. Places and Peoples of the World.* New York: Chelsea House, 1990.

Williams, Nicola, et al. *France.* 7th ed. London: Lonely Planet, 2007.

—revised by J. Hobby

FRISIANS

LOCATION: The Netherlands (province of Friesland); Germany; Denmark; North America
POPULATION: 643,000 in Friesland; 50,000 in the North Frisians Islands
LANGUAGE: Dutch; Frisian; English; French; German
RELIGION: Protestant; Mennonite

¹ INTRODUCTION

Frisians, who live in Friesland, a northern province of the Netherlands, value their independence as a unique ethnic group. The only Dutch province to retain its own language, Friesland resisted foreign domination for much of its history, and some Frisians still harbor dreams of regaining their political independence some day. They have their own flag, coat of arms, national anthem, and national drink. However, Friesland shares the basic Dutch struggle to protect its land from the sea. Like other low-lying parts of the Netherlands, it owes its existence to the resourcefulness of its people in fending off the perpetual threat of flooding. Frisians began building the "Golden Hoop" of dikes to extend the length of their coastline as long ago as AD 1000, draining their land with that most quintessential of Dutch symbols—the windmill.

There is archaeological evidence of Frisian culture as early as 400 to 200 BC. The Frisians traded hides to the Romans during the 1st century AD but successfully fended them off when they demanded tribute payments, forcing the Romans to retreat from the region by AD 70. The Frisians' political and territorial power peaked between AD 700 and 900, before the Franks—a Germanic tribe that had resided in Friesland since AD 350—consolidated their control of the region. The Franks brought Christianity to Friesland, although it took several centuries for the new religion to become well established, and even then a body of pre-Christian beliefs survived, intertwined with the symbols and observances of Christianity. During the Middle Ages, many of the scattered Frisian farms were consolidated into villages, and the region's 11 cities, independent of county control, were established.

Continuing their independent tradition, the Frisians resisted domination by the Saxons in the 14th and 15th centuries under the rallying cry, "Free and Frisian, without Tax or Excise." Friesland was one of 17 provinces making up the Low Countries (the Netherlands together with present-day Belgium and Luxembourg) that rebelled against Spanish rule in the mid-16th century, acknowledging William of Orange as their leader. In 1579, under the Treaty of Utrecht, Friesland joined with six other northern provinces—Holland, Zeeland, Groningen, Overijssel, Gelderland, and Utrecht—to form the "Seven United Provinces," the forerunner of the modern Netherlands. The Dutch became a leading commercial and colonial power in the 17th century, establishing settlements and colonies in both the Eastern and Western hemispheres. While Holland's strong economic position made it the dominant member of the union, Friesland maintained a high degree of regional autonomy.

Weakened by naval wars with Britain, the Dutch were defeated by the French revolutionary armies in 1795 and remained under French rule through the Napoleonic period. Supporting the House of Orange, led by King William I, Friesland became part of the kingdom of the Netherlands, which was established at the Congress of Vienna in 1814. (The Netherlands originally included Belgium, which broke away in 1830 to establish its own kingdom.) In the 20th century, the Netherlands remained neutral in World War I and declared neutrality in World War II but was invaded by the German army. The Dutch resistance, in which the independent-minded Frisians played an active role, incurred heavy losses, and the country suffered severe repression until it was liberated by Allied forces in 1945.

2 LOCATION AND HOMELAND

Friesland is one of the northernmost provinces of the Netherlands. It is bounded on the west and north by the Wadden Sea *(Waddenzee)*, on the east by the provinces of Groningen and Drenthe, on the south by the province of Overijssel, and on the southwest by the Zuider Zee *(Ijssel Meer)*. The province has an area of 3,357 sq km (1,297 sq mi), most of which is below sea level. Four of the five Wadden Islands also belong to Friesland. The people of this land, which was reclaimed from the sea some 2,000 years ago, have waged a continuous struggle against storms and flooding. A landmark in that struggle is the 20-mile-long Friesland dike, built in 1934, which connects the province to Noord-Holland to the west and encloses the waters of the Ijssel Meer, essentially turning it into a lake. In addition to the waters of its long coastline, Friesland has some 30 other lakes. The region's soil is a mixture of sand, clay, and peat.

As of 2005, Friesland had a population of 643,000. Frisians are an insular, self-reliant people, proud of their ethnic heritage, which some claim is unique to the Netherlands. Most native Frisians remain in the province throughout their lives, and many can trace their ancestry 200 years or more.

Frisians live in other parts of the Netherlands, as well as in Germany, Denmark, and North America. In Germany, most Frisians live in Lower Saxony, which is near the Netherlands, or in Schleswig-Holstein, which is near Denmark. The Ostfriesland Islands are made up of seven islands (Borkum, Juist, Norderney, Baltrum, Langeoog, Spiekeroog, and Wangerooge). Located in the North Sea, they are popular vacation spots and are home to a national park. The Ostfriesland Peninsula is near the Netherlands border and the Jadebusen Bay. The capital is Emden. Off Schleswig-Holstein, the North Friesian Islands (Nørd Friesische Insel) are home to 50,000 Danes.

3 LANGUAGE

Although Dutch is the official language of Friesland, as elsewhere in the Netherlands, about half of Friesland's 643,000 residents speak both Dutch and Frisian. Frisian is a Germanic language that is similar to Dutch and English. There are three Frisian dialects: Northern, Eastern, and Western. Most Frisian speakers use the language at home but speak Dutch in the workplace and other public settings. It is common to combine the two languages into a hybrid called "Town Frisian." In addition, many Netherlanders speak (or at least understand) English, French, and German, which are taught in the secondary schools. The fishing village of Hindelopen is unusual in that it has its own dialect. With a population of 900, it is believed to be the smallest town in the world to publish its own dictionary.

4 FOLKLORE

Friesland has a substantial body of Germanic folklore that has survived from pre-Christian times. Popular tales and supersti-

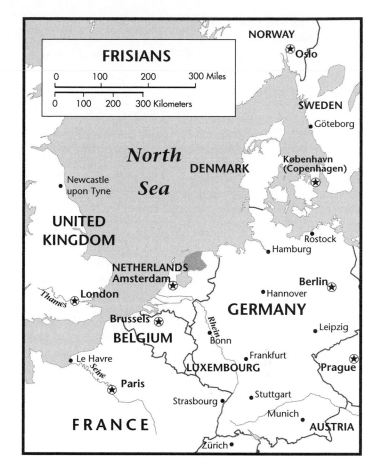

tions feature a variety of devils, ghosts, witches, elves, wizards, and trolls, as well as female spirits who may help or harm travelers. (The dangerous ones, said to live underground and kidnap travelers in the night, are called "white ladies.") According to a popular folk belief, funeral processions should follow a winding path to confuse the spirit of the deceased so that it will not be able to return and haunt the living. For the same reason, the coffin is traditionally carted around the cemetery three times before being interred.

"The Seven Wishes" is a traditional Frisian folktale set at a time when the land was believed to be populated by Little People. It is the story of an old fisherman named Jan and his wife, Tryn. One day Jan caught a magic silver fish that promised him seven wishes, on the condition that he choose wisely. The humble fisherman's only desire was for a new boat because his old one was about to fall apart. However, his wife got carried away by greed, demanding a new house, furnishings, servants, and other luxuries. Finally, she demanded absolute power, and the fish took away everything it had given them. The old woman learned her lesson, the couple realized that what truly mattered to each of them was the other, and they contentedly resumed their modest existence.

5 RELIGION

In the Netherlands, 31% of the population is Catholic and 41% have no religion; however, Protestantism is the majority religion in Friesland. About 85% of Frisians belong to one of two Calvinist churches, the Dutch Reformed Church (Hervormde

Kerk) or the Reformed Church (Gereformeerde Kerk), and 5% are Mennonites. Some Frisians still retain certain pre-Christian beliefs (called *byleauwe*) dating back to the 8th and 9th centuries.

⁶ MAJOR HOLIDAYS

Frisians observe the Dutch legal holidays—New Year's Day (January 1), the Queen's Birthday (April 30), Memorial Day (May 4), National Liberation Day (May 5), and Christmas (December 25–26)—as well as other standard holidays of the Christian calendar, including Good Friday, Holy Saturday, Easter Monday, Ascension, and Whitmonday. Easter is considered an especially important holiday. It is observed with a special dinner and an Easter egg hunt similar to those held in the United States. The Queen's Birthday is another important occasion, marked by flag displays and parades. On this day, girls wear orange ribbons in their hair in honor of the royal family, the House of Orange. Frisians, like other Dutch people, observe Christmas by attending church services. In the Netherlands, the gift giving that people in other countries associate with Christmas takes place on December 6, the day devoted to Saint Nicholas (*Sinterklaes*, the Dutch equivalent of Santa Claus). According to tradition, Saint Nick and his helper, called Black Peter, sail to the Netherlands from Spain to give children candy and other gifts.

⁷ RITES OF PASSAGE

Frisians live in a modern, industrialized, Christian country. Hence, many of the rites of passage that young people undergo are religious rituals, such as the sacraments of baptism, first communion, confirmation, and marriage. In addition, a student's progress through the education system is marked by many families with graduation parties.

⁸ INTERPERSONAL RELATIONS

Frisians, like the residents of the neighboring province of Groningen, are regarded as unsophisticated by Netherlanders living in the southern part of the country. Historically, their perpetual struggle against the sea has given them a strong sense of community, expressed in the concept of *buorreplicht*, or "neighbor's duty." Helping one's neighbors in times of trouble was so crucial to survival that it was actually codified as law under Charlemagne during the Middle Ages. This sense of communal responsibility has survived as a tradition, and relations with one's neighbors have an importance that surpasses even the ties of kinship in holding Frisian communities together.

⁹ LIVING CONDITIONS

The traditional old-fashioned Frisian farmhouse consists of modest-sized living quarters connected to a barn by a narrow section containing a kitchen, milk cellar, and churning area. The living quarters are generally divided into an all-purpose family room and a formal parlor in which visitors are received. Tile roofs have largely replaced the older thatched roofs.

Like other people in the Netherlands, Frisians have access to modern, high-quality health care, and the costs are covered by a national health insurance system. In 2008 the average Dutch life expectancy was 79.25 years. The infant mortality rate was 4.81 deaths per 1,000 live births. Privately funded home nurs-

ing care is provided for children, the elderly, and pregnant women. Frisians enjoy the same extensive road network and state-owned railroad as people elsewhere in the Netherlands and share their passion for bicycling, a favorite form of transportation among the Dutch.

¹⁰ FAMILY LIFE

The nuclear family—called the *gezin*—plays a central role in Dutch life, in spite of the postwar increase in the number of unmarried couples living together. This trend, known as "homing," is as prevalent in Friesland as in other regions, and the divorce rate for Frisians is also on a par with that elsewhere in the Netherlands, as is the growing number of single-parent families. Instead of the elaborate church weddings of the past, many Frisians today opt for civil weddings. The average age at marriage has risen, as young people are choosing to complete their higher education before starting a family.

¹¹ CLOTHING

Like other Dutch people, Frisians wear modern Western-style clothing for both casual and formal occasions. One distinguishing characteristic is their preference for wooden shoes—the modern variety, made of lightweight poplar and generally painted black with leather trim. They use them as functional footwear and not just for tourists or tradition.

¹² FOOD

Like other Dutch people, Frisians prefer wholesome, simply prepared food, often cooked in butter. Dietary staples include seafood and dairy products, including the world-famous Dutch cheeses. Desserts are often served with whipped cream, and popular beverages include tea, coffee, and beer. The Frisian national drink is a potent, heartwarming Beerenburger, an herbal bitter. The Frisians eat a typical Dutch breakfast of sliced bread, meat, and cheese. Lunch generally consists of bread with jam and butter, cold meat, and buttermilk. A large dinner, served at about 6:00 pm, typically includes soup and a main dish containing meat and vegetables. French fries (*patat frites*)—typically served with mayonnaise or ketchup—are popular snacks, as are waffles smothered in whipped cream or caramel sauce.

¹³ EDUCATION

Students in Friesland, as in the rest of the Netherlands, must attend school from the ages of 6 to 16. The Frisian language is taught in public schools but not in Christian private schools. At the age of 12, all Dutch students take an exam that tracks them into a general, pre-university, or vocational school. At the age of 16, they take school certificate exams in a variety of subjects. There is a university in the capital city of Leeuwarden. Higher education is offered at 13 Dutch universities.

¹⁴ CULTURAL HERITAGE

The relative autonomy enjoyed by Friesland for much of its history has given its people a strong sense of ethnic and cultural identity, reinforced by the preservation of their language, folklore, and folk art. The town of Franeker houses the world's oldest planetarium, built in the 1770s by Eise Eisenga in his own home. Accurately demonstrating the movement of the planets (except for Uranus, which had not yet been discovered), Eisen-

Traditional vessels sail during the start of the annual Friese sailing race on the lake of Grou, Friesland, Netherlands.
(© Jaap Schaaf/epa/Corbis)

ga's model, which incorporates 10,000 hand-forged nails, has needed only minor adjustments since it was built more than 200 years ago.

15 WORK

The economy of Friesland is based primarily on agriculture, and many Frisians living in inland areas work on small family farms, raising crops or dairy cattle. The dairy, construction, and tourist industries are important employers.

16 SPORTS

Popular sports in Friesland include cycling, sailing, canoeing, and ice skating. Friesland is home to the famous Elfstedentocht skating race, held every five or six years, when it is cold enough for all the region's canals to freeze over. As many as 20,000 people skate a 125-mile course over the frozen canals connecting Friesland's 11 medieval towns. It is a hypermarathon that began in 1909 and has been run only 13 times since then. Another traditional sport that is popular in Friesland is *fierljeppen*, pole-vaulting across the canals in the warmer months. Sailing is also very popular, and skûtsje sailing is a race conducted in July and August on 65-foot sailing barges.

17 ENTERTAINMENT AND RECREATION

Like other Dutch people, the Frisians enjoy spending much of their leisure time partaking in outdoor activities, including camping, hiking, and a variety of sports. One pastime that is unique to Friesland is *wadlopen,* "mudwalking" across the salt flats and mud of the shallow Waddenzee when the tides go out. This unusual activity is enjoyed both for the vigorous exercise that it entails and for the bird watching that it allows. *Wadlopen* is often undertaken in organized group outings.

Socializing at the weekly livestock market in Tjouwert serves as an informal source of recreation for many Frisians.

18 FOLK ART, CRAFTS, AND HOBBIES

Frisian craftspeople are renowned for their tile work, pottery, and embroidery. Friesland is also noted for the unique folk art that goes into the creation of *ûlebuorden,* elaborately decorated barn gables that feature carved swans and holes through which owls can fly (*ûlebuorden* means "owl boards"). Once a functional creation, *ûlebuorden* are now considered decorative artifacts.

19 SOCIAL PROBLEMS

Frisians experience many of the social problems found in all modern, industrialized countries.

[20] GENDER ISSUES

Women in the Netherlands, including Friesland, make up 44% of the workforce and 37% of the members of Parliament. They enjoy equal rights under Dutch law. Abortion has been legal since 1981, and it is allowed for most reasons. Since 1984, abortion procedures have been provided free of charge.

Homosexuality is very much accepted in the Netherlands. Since 2001, same-sex couples have been allowed to marry. Today, 2% of all marriages in the Netherlands are between same-sex couples.

[21] BIBLIOGRAPHY

Catling, Christopher, ed. *The Netherlands*. Boston: Houghton Mifflin, 1991.

Gall, Timothy, and Susan Gall, eds. *Worldmark Encyclopedia of the Nations*. Detroit: Gale Research, 1995.

Gratton, Nancy E. "Frisians." In *Encyclopedia of World Cultures (Europe)*, edited by Linda A. Bennett. Boston: G. K. Hall, 1992.

Keuzenkamp, Saskia, David Bos, Jan Willem Duyvendak, and Gert Hekma, eds. *Acceptance of Homosexuality in the Netherlands*. Amsterdam: Social and Cultural Planning Office of the Netherlands, 2006.

Mahmood, Cynthia Keppley. *Frisian and Free: Study of an Ethnic Minority of the Netherlands*. Prospect Heights, IL: Waveland Press, 1989.

McDonald, George. *Frommer's Belgium, Holland, and Luxembourg. 10th edition*. Hoboken, NJ: Wiley, 2007.

"The Netherlands." In *Database of Gender Statistics*. Washington, DC: World Bank Group Gender Stats, 2002.

Spicer, Dorothy Gladys. *The Owl's Nest: Folktales from Friesland*. New York: Coward-McCann, 1968.

Spritzer, Dinah A. "Friesland Offers Rural Tranquility." *Travel Weekly's Guide to Europe*, February 22, 1993.

Turner, Barry. *Germany Profiled: Essential Facts on Society, Business, and Politics in Germany*. New York: St. Martin's Press, 1999.

United Nations Population Division, Department of Economic and Social Affairs. "The Netherlands" In *Abortion Policies: A Global Review*. http://www.un.org/esa/population/publications/abortion/index.htm (8 May 2008).

Van Stegeren, Theo. *The Land and People of the Netherlands*. New York: HarperCollins, 1991

—revised by C. Corrigan.

GALICIANS

ALTERNATE NAMES: Gallegos
LOCATION: Northern Spain
POPULATION: 2.7 million
LANGUAGE: Gallego; Castilian Spanish
RELIGION: Roman Catholic

[1] INTRODUCTION

Galicia is one of three autonomous regions in Spain that have their own official languages in addition to Castilian Spanish, the national language. The language of the Galicians is called *gallego*, and the Galicians themselves are often referred to as Gallegos. (The other two regions with their own languages are Catalonia and the Basque region. Like Galicia, they are both in the northern part of the country.) The Galicians are descended from Spain's second wave of Celtic invaders, who crossed the Pyrenees mountains in about 400 BC and settled in the western and northwestern parts of present-day Spain. However, it was the Romans, arriving in the 2nd century BC, who gave the Galicians their name, derived from the Latin *gallaeci*.

Galicia was first unified as a kingdom by the Germanic Suevi tribe in the 5th century AD. The shrine of St. James (Santiago) was established at Compostela in 813, and Christians throughout Europe began flocking to the site, which has remained one of the world's major pilgrim shrines. The Moorish era that began in the 8th century had little effect on Galicia, as the kings of neighboring Asturias expelled the Moors from the region before their culture could gain a strong foothold there. After the unification of the Spanish provinces under Ferdinand and Isabella in the 15th century, Galicia existed on the margins of power as a poor region geographically isolated from the political center in Castile to the south. Prevented from expanding their territory by the proximity of the Portuguese border, the Galicians had to make do with their existing land, and their poverty was worsened by frequent famines. With the discovery of the New World in 1492, large numbers emigrated. Today, there are more Galicians in Argentina than in Galicia itself.

Although Francisco Franco was a Galician himself, his dictatorial regime suppressed the region's aspirations toward political and cultural autonomy. Since his death, however, a revival of Galician language and culture has taken place, and a growing tourism industry has improved the region's economic outlook.

[2] LOCATION AND HOMELAND

Galicia occupies 29,434 sq km in the northwest corner of the Iberian peninsula. Squarish in shape, the region is bounded by the Bay of Biscay to the north, the Atlantic Ocean to the west, the River Miño to the south (marking the border with Portugal), and León and Asturias to the east. Galicia's coastline contains a number of scenic estuaries (*rías*), which are drawing increasing numbers of tourists to the region. The area's mild, rainy maritime climate is in sharp contrast to the dry, sunny lands of southern Spain.

[3] LANGUAGE

Most Galicians speak both Castilian Spanish, the national language of Spain, and *gallego*, their own official language. The percentage of Galicians who speak Gallego is greater than the percentage of Basques or Catalans who speak the languages of their respective regions: 88% of Galicians speak Gallego and 94% understand it. The language has come into much wider use since Galicia attained the status of an autonomous region. Like Catalan and Castilian, Gallego is a Romance language (one with Latin roots). Gallego and Portuguese were a single language until the 14th century, when they began to diverge. Today, they are still similar to each other.

4 FOLKLORE

Galician folkloric tradition is very rich and based in diverse ethnic and cultural components with a predominance of the Celtic and Roman civilizations. Most present-day Christian festivities have a Celtic origin; among them is Saint John's eve in which bonfires are lit, people jump over them and bathe in the sea, reenacting cleansing ceremonies of pagan ancestry. Towns and villages celebrate, usually in summer, their own Patron Saint's Day with different festivities, among them, *romerias*, that usually include Mass, a procession, dining in the open, and folkloric and modern dancing. Paramount among these religious celebrations is el Día de Santiago (Saint James' Day), on July 25, Galicia's Patron Saint, that attracts to the city of Compostela many Galicians living abroad. These are lavish and emotional celebrations with spectacular *fuegos artificiales* (fireworks) in front of the cathedral, religious ceremonies, and folkloric music and dancing.

The *rapa das bestas* takes place in summer and is a popular feast surrounding the cropping of the manes of the horses that had been living wild the rest of year. Galician Shrovetide celebrations (*carnavales*) have ancestral magic and pagan components that make it different from the ones in the rest of Spain.

Celtic culture manifests itself in a number of traditions and beliefs concerning the dead. Ghosts and spirits are believed to live in the forests and the water. Supernatural powers are attributed to a variety of beings, including *meigas* (witches), who provide potions for health and romance; clairvoyants, called *barajeras*; and *curandeiros* or *curandeiras* (healers). To ward off the evil-eye there are amulets made out of coral and *azabache* (jet-black).

Like in the rest of the Celtic world, traditional music has been played by bagpipes that accompany traditional dances like the *muñeira*. Today there is a modern cultural and musical movement, *celtismo*, which promotes cultural links among the peoples of Celtic ethnicity like musical encounters and festivals. There are quite a few bands of new-wave traditional Galician music, the most famous being "Milladoiro," that since the 1970s has lead the revival in Galician music. The Ortigueira Festival has become an essential date on the European music calendar. As far as classical music goes Galicia has two orchestras, the Galician Symphonic and the Galician Royal Philharmonic. There is also the yearly Ourense Film Festival.

5 RELIGION

Like their neighbors in other parts of Spain, the vast majority of Galicians are Roman Catholics, although, on the whole, the women tend to be more religious than the men. Galicia contains numerous churches, shrines, monasteries, and other sites of religious significance, most notably the famous cathedral at Santiago de Compostela in the La Coruña province.

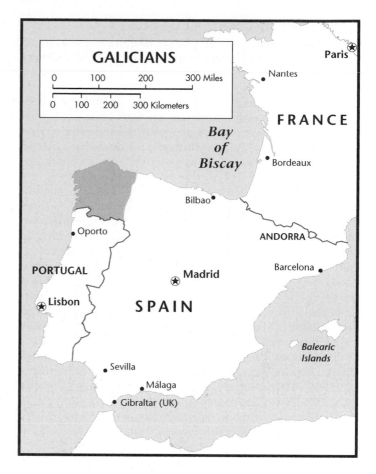

Surpassed only by Rome and Jerusalem as spiritual centers of the Catholic Church, Santiago has been one of the world's great pilgrimage shrines since the Middle Ages. According to local legend, a shepherd discovered the remains of St. James here in the year AD 813, led to the site by a bright star (the name "Compostela" is derived from the Latin words for "bright star," and "Santiago" is Spanish for "St. James"). The trek across the Pyrenees that has drawn millions of people for over a thousand years attracts today a growing number of modern-day pilgrims from around the world. It was declared the first European Cultural Route by the Council of Europe in 1987, and one of UNESCO's World Heritage Sites in 1993.

6 MAJOR HOLIDAYS

(See Section **4 Folklore**)

7 RITES OF PASSAGE

Besides baptism and marriage, the first Communion and military service could be considered rites of passage for Spaniards. The first three of these events are the occasion, in most cases, for big and expensive social gatherings in which the family shows its generosity and economic status. At times, families dig into their savings or borrow money in order to pay for these status shows. Spain abolished compulsory military service in 2001. The armed forces are now all volunteer.

8 INTERPERSONAL RELATIONS

The pervasive temperament associated with Galicia, a mountainous land of ever-present rain and mists and lush greenery, is one of Celtic dreaminess, melancholy, and belief in the supernatural. There is a special term—*morriña*—associated with the nostalgia that the many Galician emigrants have felt for their distant homeland. Galicians are fond of describing the four main towns of their region with the following saying: *Coruña se divierte, Pontevedra duerme, Vigo trabaja, Santiago reza* ("Coruña has fun, Pontevedra sleeps, Vigo works, and Santiago prays").

Since the 1960s, there has been a steady improvement of the economy mainly due to industrial development and tourism, as well as an evolution in customs. Spaniards frequently travel abroad and have adopted customs from other cultures in the last 25 years or so. Although many people living in rural areas have moved to the city, the present generations have preserved the family house in the village and return there at the time of fiestas and for vacation and remain loyal to their community or pueblo. The economic prosperity enjoyed by Galicia has allowed many people to also have a vacation home in the country or an apartment at the beach.

In the cities, office hours begin at 9:00 AM and traditionally include an extended afternoon lunch break beginning at 2:00 PM. Workers then return to their offices from 4:00 to 7:00 PM. The day typically ends with a walk (*paseo*) with friends or family and/or visits to neighborhood bars for a few drinks, appetizers (*tapas*) and conversation. Dinner is often eaten as late as 10:30 PM. Both blue and white collar workers have a paid month vacation, which they usually spend by the sea, the mountains or travelling abroad. Galicians are considered to be friendly and outgoing. It is customary to shake hands and in a social setting women usually kiss their friends on both cheeks. Young groups are formed by co-workers, fellow students or people from the same town that go together to discotheques, organize parties and excursions, and date among themselves. The average citizen spends a great deal of time out of the house. There is an active street life; many people live downtown, frequent bars and restaurants, and go to bed late. Spaniards move from place to place less than Americans and, once they get a job, many aspire to return to their birthplace and settle there. Regional loyalties are usually strong and the new autonomous status of the old provinces has strengthened this feeling. It is not unusual to have lifelong friends known since kindergarten.

9 LIVING CONDITIONS

Like in the rest of Spain, Galicia today is a consumer society that relies on credit cards, loves to go shopping and is interested in cars, gadgets and entertainment. Vigo and A Coruña era both big cities, industrial centers and important Atlantic ports. Galicia has a large fishing fleet with modern boats that work in the African coast and the Northeastern Atlantic. It also has a well-established canning industry and a flourishing tourism industry. Galician towns and cities are linked by bus and rail to the rest of the country, and Santiago de Compostela has an airport with regular flights to Barcelona, Madrid, Seville, and other points in Spain as well as foreign cities including London, Paris, and Amsterdam. There is a National Health Service, cities have both general practitioners and specialists in all medical fields, and the University of Santiago de Compostela has an excellent medical school.

City dwellers typically live either in old granite houses or newer brick or concrete multistory apartment buildings. Outside of the largest cities, most Galicians own their own homes, living in some 31,000 tiny settlements called *aldeas*, which number between 80 and 200 people each. They are usually made up of single-family homes of granite, with animals kept either on the ground floor or in a separate structure nearby. Hemmed in by Portugal, Galicia was historically unable to expand its territory, and its inhabitants were forced to continually divide up their land into ever smaller holdings. According to a popular saying, "Galicians never use handkerchiefs; they till them." Because of these circumstances, Galicia traditionally was a land of emigrants to Spanish America, to Europe and to the industrial areas of Spain. Village farmhouses are distinguished by the presence of granaries, called *hórreos*, granite structures raised on stilts for protection from rodents and dampness. Crosses on their roofs invoke spiritual protection for the harvest.

10 FAMILY LIFE

The nuclear family is the basic domestic unit in Galicia—extended families account for only 10% of all households. Elderly grandparents generally live independently as long as both are alive, and even widows tend to remain on their own as long as they can, although widowers tend to move in with their children's families. However, there are usually not many children one can move in with, as Galicians often relocate from their native villages or leave the region altogether. Galician women have a relatively high degree of autonomy and responsibility, often performing the same kinds of work as men in either agriculture or trade. Over three-fourths have paid jobs. Women also shoulder the bulk of responsibility for household chores and child-rearing, although men do assist in these areas.

Today's Spanish families are much smaller than in the past and usually have two children. Actually the birth-rate is one of the lowest in Europe, and fewer people live in their homes with extended family. Traditional patterns are also changing; young men and women are as independent as the economy allows, and they frequently live together before getting married.

11 CLOTHING

Like people elsewhere in Spain, Galicians wear modern Western-style clothing, although their mild, rainy maritime climate requires somewhat heavier dress, especially in the wintertime, than that worn by their neighbors to the south. Before rubber boots and shoes were made, country people wore wool slippers inside wooden shoes; they are still used today and are also sold as folkloric souvenirs.

In the last decades the Galician fashion industry has greatly developed and some firms, like Zara and Adolfo Domínguez, are known the world over.

12 FOOD

Being a large country with different geographic and climatic areas, Spain also has a wide variety of regional dishes. Galician cuisine is highly regarded throughout Spain. Its most striking ingredient is a plentiful variety of high-quality seafood, including scallops, lobster, mussels, large and small shrimp, oysters, clams, squid, many types of crab, and goose barnacles

A pack of wild horses are gathered together during a round-up in the Galician region of Spain. The round-ups are a traditional event for Galicians during the summer months. (AP Images/Delmi Alvarez)

(*percebes); o*ctopus is also a favorite, seasoned with salt, paprika, and olive oil (*pulpo a feira*, or *pulpo a la gallega*); *empanadas,* a popular specialty, are large, flaky pies with meat, fish, or vegetable fillings; favorite fillings include eels, lamprey, sardines, pork, and veal; *caldo gallego,* a broth made with turnips, cabbage or greens, and white beans, is eaten throughout the region. A hearty dish popular in colder weather is *lacón con grelos,* pork shoulder prepared with greens and potatoes. Popular desserts include almond tarts (*tarta de Santiago*), a regional specialty, and the *churros* (fried pastry) eaten elsewhere in the country. The Galicians drink a strong liquor called *aguardiente,* burned (*queimada*) with lemon peel and sugar. On festive occasions, the queimada is prepared by night, or in the dark, and while the aguardiente burns and it is poured, a magical *conjuro* is recited usually by the person pouring it.

Popular snacks served at *tapas* bars in Galicia include grilled sardines, roasted small green peppers (*pimientas de Padrón*), and the *tetilla* cheese for which the region is famous. Galicia has refined and marketed its white and red wines and today Albariño and Ribeiro wines are highly appreciated.

13 EDUCATION

Schooling in Galicia, as in other parts of Spain, is free and compulsory from the ages of 6 to 14, when many students begin the *bachillerato* course. The adult literacy rate is estimated at 98%. University education is general. Spain has 31 state-run universities and an increasing number of private ones. Students receive a diploma after three years of general study and a *Licenciatura* upon completing a program of specialized study lasting two or more years. Centralized public education depends on the Ministry of Education. Galicia has several universities, the one in Santiago de Compostela being one of the oldest in Europe; its medical school enjoys a well deserved reputation. The Galician language, Gallego, is taught at all levels, from grade school through university.

14 CULTURAL HERITAGE

Compostela is considered a regional shrine. Her poetry has been compared to that of the American poet Emily Dickinson, who lived and wrote at approximately the same time as de Castro. Galician literature begins in 1196, the date of the first known lyric poem written in the Galician-Portuguese language. This lyric poetry, influenced by the troubadours that travelled the Camiño de Santiago (the Road to Santiago), flourished in the 13th and 14th centuries. Among these minstrels were Martin Codax and Pero Meogo. The most famous genres of composition are *cantigas de amigo*, love poems in the voice of a woman, and *cantigas* in praise of the Virgin Mary. Alphonso X, king of Castile and León, wrote the *Cantigas de Santa María* in Gallego, 427 poems to the Virgin, each set to its own music; they are a masterpiece of European medieval music that has been preserved in performances and compact disc recordings up to the present day. Literary Galician was reduced to the oral tradition and a few written texts until the *Rexurdimento*, a cultural and literary revival in the second half of the 19th century to which the names of Rosalía de Castro, Eduardo Pondal, and Manuel Curros Enríquez are attached. Rosalía de Castro's grave is in Santiago. By the end of that century, Emilia Pardo Bazan emerged as one of the greatest fiction writers of the Naturalistic school. In the 20th century, great Galicians included the dramatist and novelist Ramón del Valle-Inclán; fiction writer, poet and playwright Rafael Dieste; and artist, painter, and novelist Alfonso Rodriguez Castelao. Other Galician writers include Alvaro Cunqueiro, Gonzalo Torrente Ballester, and Manuel Rivas, who is the most widely translated Galician writer in history. Camilo José Cela was a recipient of the Nobel Prize in Literature in 1989.

There are several archives, libraries and museums in Galicia, the most important being the Museo do Povo Galego (The Museum of the Galician People) in Santiago, an important research center and home to boats, clothing, furniture, tools, instruments, and artifacts of ethnographic relevance in the cultural ancestry of the Galician people; The Galician Center of Contemporary Art; and the Museum of the Pilgrimage.

15 WORK

Galicia used to be a land of emigrants, and the Galician economy was based mainly in agriculture and fishing. In a process that began in the 1980s it has steadily developed to the point that its economy is one of the best performing in Europe; local companies in sectors such as mining (tungsten, tin, zinc, and antimony), clothing and textiles, pharmaceuticals, canning, agriculture, wood products, and automotives are well known. Services account for more than 62% of gross domestic product (GDP), industry for about 30% and agriculture and fishing for less than 8%. In 2004 there were 172,000 business located in Galicia from small, family owned enterprises to multinational corporations. One of the largest is the giant clothing company Inditex, a global success story, which owns the retail chain Zara. Other companies with an international scope are Group Copo, Pescanova, Zeitia, and Adolfo Dominguez. The infrastructure has also changed and Galicia now has a system of superhighways, and there is a project to bring the AVE (high velocity train) from Madrid.

The fishing industry is a major employer: Spain's fishing fleet is among the largest in the world, and a good part of it is located in Galicia. Spain's economic prosperity attracts a growing work force, some of it made up from people migrating from rural areas to the cities, seeking higher living standards, and others coming from economically or politically unstable foreign countries, mainly from North- and Sub-Saharan Africa, Spanish America and the Eastern Europe. The majority work in agriculture and in construction.

Since the early 1970s Spain has developed a prosperous tourism industry, which accounts for the majority of the country's income. Since the 1970s Spain has been the second most visited country in the world after France. In 2007 almost 60 million foreign visitors arrived in Spain. Along with summer tourism the country offers cultural tours, international conventions, and sports meetings as well as cruises. There is ample hotel space. A network of beautiful de-luxe government-sponsored hotels (*paradores*) have been located in historical buildings. Galicia has beautiful landscapes, beaches, and fjords

(*rías*), and its wonderful food and wines attract each year an increasing number of visitors.

16 SPORTS

As in other parts of Spain, the most popular sport is soccer (called *fútbol*). League matches are played on Saturday and Sunday afternoons from September through May, with tournaments in the summer. Galicia has two teams, Celta de Vigo and Deportivo de A Coruña, home teams of the cities of Vigo and A Coruña, whose rivalry is legendary. Basketball and tennis are also gaining popularity as spectator sports. Participant sports include hunting and fishing, sailing, cycling, and golf.

17 ENTERTAINMENT AND RECREATION

Like people in other parts of Spain, Galicians enjoy socializing at the region's many *tapas* bars, where they can buy a light meal and a drink. The mountains, estuaries, and beaches of their beautiful countryside provide abundant resources for outdoor recreation. In the evenings, they go dancing or have a drink with friends. The mild Spanish climate has fostered an active night life, much of it outdoors in the streets, plazas, taverns, and restaurants. A dinner date may take place as late as 10:00 or 11:00 pm and be followed by a trip to a local club. According to their cultural level, Galicians go to concerts, to the theater, and to movies. People of all ages are fond of television, perhaps the main source of entertainment today.

18 FOLK ART, CRAFTS, AND HOBBIES

Galician handicrafts include traditional silver and gold, coral and *azabache* (jet black) jewelry, as well as world-famous Sargadelos porcelain, besides popular artisanal pottery, musical instruments, and wood artwork.

19 SOCIAL PROBLEMS

Galicia used to be one of the poorest regions in Spain, and, historically, many of its inhabitants emigrated in search of a better life. In the years between 1911 and 1915 alone, an estimated 230,000 moved to Latin America. Galicians have found new homes in all of Spain's major cities, as well as in France, Germany, and Switzerland. So many emigrated to Buenos Aires in the past century that the Argentines call all immigrants from Spain *gallegos* (Galicians). In recent years, due to Galicia's extraordinary prosperity emigration has declined drastically.

This prosperity has attracted foreign emigrants to Galicia, many of them illegal. Because of the peculiar fjord coastal structure (*rías*) of Galicia there is a drug smuggling problem.

20 GENDER ISSUES

Gender issues in Galicia are not different as from the rest of Spain, and women have an ever-increasing role in society. Approximately 15% of Spain's Armed Forces are women and the Defense Secretary (as of 2008) was a woman. Many women hold municipal and government posts as councilwoman, mayor, university professor, and director general and several have been, and are, ministers of the crown or run their own businesses. Evidence of the secular nature of contemporary Spain can be seen in the widespread support for the legalization of same-sex marriage in Spain. In June 2005 a bill was passed to allow gay marriage, making Spain the third country in the world to allow same-sex couples to marry.

21 BIBLIOGRAPHY

Ames, Helen Wattley. *Spain is Different*. Intercultural Press, 1992.

Buechler, Hans, and J.-M. Buechler. *Carmen: The Autobiography of a Spanish Galician Woman*. Cambridge, Mass: Schenkman, 1981.

Casas, Penelope. "A Different Spain (Galicia)." *Travel-Holiday*, June 1995: 35.

Cohn, David. "Pilgrimage to Santiago." *Architectural Record*, October 1994: 102.

Conversi, Daniele. *The Basques, the Catalans and Spain*. Reno: University of Nevada Press, 1997.

Crow, John A. *Spain: The Root and the Flower*. Berkeley: Univ. of California Press, 1985.

Facaros, Dana, and Michael Pauls. *Northern Spain*. London: Cadogan Books, 1996.

Fodor's Spain. Fodor's Travel Publications, 1996.

Hooper, John. *The New Spaniards*. Suffolk, England: Penguin, 1995.

"In Spain's Northwest Corner, Cool and Ancient Galicia." *Sunset,* March 1985: 92.

Lye, Keith. *Passport to Spain*. New York: Franklin Watts, 1994.

Steinberg, Rolf, ed. *Continental Europe*. Insight Guides. Singapore: APA Publications, 1989.

Schubert, Adrian. *The Land and People of Spain*. New York: HarperCollins, 1992.

Tremlett, Giles. *Ghosts of Spain*. New York: Walker and Company, 2008.

Valentine, Eugene, and Kristin B. Valentine. "Galicians." *Encyclopedia of World Cultures (Europe)*. Boston: G. K. Hall, 1992.

Walkup, Carolyn. "Galician Foods Come into Fashion." *Nation's Restaurant News*, 8 August 1994: 29.

—revised by S. Garcia Castaneda

GEORGIANS

ALTERNATE NAMES: Kartveli; Gurji
LOCATION: Georgia
POPULATION: 4.3 million (2002)
LANGUAGE: Georgian
RELIGION: Georgian Orthodoxy

1 INTRODUCTION

The people we know as Georgians call themselves *kartvelebi* and their country *Sa-kartvel-o*, literally, "the land of the *kartvelebi*." The word *Georgia* probably comes from the Turkish word *Gurji,* which is what Turks call Georgians. It is hard to pinpoint exactly where the Georgians came from, but proto-Georgian tribes, such as the Diauhi, the Tabali, and Muskhi, began to make their appearance at the end of the Bronze Age, splinters possibly from the ancient kingdoms of Urartu and the Vannic kingdoms of the first millennium BC. By the 6th century AD, the west Georgian kingdom of Colchis and the east Georgian kingdom of Iberia (unrelated to the Iberian Peninsula) were established.

The inhabitants of what is now Georgia were well known to the Greeks and Romans. The Georgians had a reputation for gold and metalworking, which explains why the Greeks set the myth of the Golden Fleece in the Georgian kingdom of Colchis. Until this century, many Georgians used a fleece to catch gold from mountain streams. Ancient Greeks also set the story of Prometheus in the Caucasus Mountains on Georgia's northern border. After Prometheus gave fire to humans, Zeus punished him by chaining him to one of the highest Caucasian mountains (some say Elbruz, others Kazbegi). An eagle ate his liver, but it rejuvenated overnight, and the eagle revisited to torture him the next day.

Throughout the centuries, because of its strategic location as a crossroads between Europe and Asia, Georgia was invaded and settled by Greeks, Romans, Persians, Turkic tribes, Arabs, Mongols, and Russians. Georgia was also on one of the many branches of the Silk Road, which carried trade from China and India to Europe and back. As a result, the Georgian population was influenced by a multiplicity of cultures both Oriental and European. This is reflected in the country's architecture, language, literature, and cuisine, which draw upon Persian, Arabic, Greek, and Russian sources. Such intermingling over many centuries resulted in a population with both dark and light skin and brown and blue eyes. Physically, Georgians resemble Greeks or Turks and think of themselves as part of Eastern Mediterranean culture.

Georgians probably developed a proto-national identity around the 10th century, when the Bagratid dynasty established an independent and powerful Georgian confederal state uniting both East and West Georgians, along with other ethnic groups including Turks, Armenians, and Persians. The dominant Kartlian tribe gave its name to the new state (*Sakartvelo*), although Georgian regional groupings, such as the Mingrelians, Khevsurs, and Svans, have retained separate identities to this day. Georgians share their country with other nations who have settled in the region over many centuries. Georgians number 3,661,173 and make up 83.8% of the population in Georgia. The largest ethnic minorities are Azeris (6.5%),

Armenians (5.7%), Russians (1.5%), Ossetians (0.9%), Greeks (0.3%), and Abkhazians (0.1%).

Until recently, most ethnic groups in Georgia lived peaceably together. Georgia was cosmopolitan in culture but, since the collapse of the Soviet Union, the country has been torn apart by secessionist wars. Both the Abkhazians (an indigenous Caucasian group related to the Adyghe and Cherkess nations of North Caucasia) and the South Ossetians (who speak an Iranian-based language) wish to secede from Georgia.

² LOCATION AND HOMELAND

The total population of Georgia in 2002 was 4,371,535. In 2002 urban dwellers made up 52.4% of the population. The capital of Tbilisi had a population of 1,081,679 that year, with many people continuing to move there from the villages. This has led to a serious population decline in some rural regions. Fighting in Georgia since 1991 has displaced approximately 400,000 people from Abkhazia and former South Ossetia. Almost 300,000 people are registered as IDPs (Internally Displaced Persons). In 1995 approximately 70,000 of these IDPs (which some call refugees) lived in Tbilisi; the rest were scattered throughout Georgia.

Georgia is between 40°E and 47°E latitude and 41°07'N and 43°35'N longitude and occupies 27,657 square miles, approximately twice the area of Belgium. On its northern border lies the Russian Federation. To the south are Turkey and the Republic of Armenia and to the west and east are the Black Sea and the Republic of Azerbaijan, respectively. Georgia is dominated in the north by the Greater Caucasian Mountain range (Elbruz is Europe's highest mountain at 18,481 feet) and in the south by the Southern Georgian Highlands.

Two-thirds of Georgian territory is mountainous, and between the mountains lie fertile lowlands crisscrossed by some of Georgia's 25,000 rivers, which surge in the spring and summer when the snows melt. Here one finds orchards, vineyards, and in the west, subtropical plantations. Because of the mountains and forests, which make up two-thirds of Georgian terrain, arable land is in short supply, accounting for only about 18% of the total land area. This is made up by its fertility. Most of the population lives in the river valleys, and at least one-third earns its livelihood from the land.

The Georgian climate varies from semi-desert to alpine, but on the whole the climate is hospitable. The Black Sea coast, which forms Georgia's western border, is warm, subtropical, and very rainy, perfect for growing citrus fruit, tobacco, and tea. In East Georgia, the climate is a drier Mediterranean type, similar to that of Greece, and wine, fruit, vegetables, and grain are the major crops.

Georgia is rich in fauna and flora with more than 5,000 types of wildflowers, 100 different mammals, 330 types of birds, and 160 kinds of fish. Indigenous species include Pitsunda pine, Caucasian spruce, Abkhazian hedgehog, Colchis lizard, Caucasian jay, and Caucasian wild goat (ibex), the horns of which are still used for toasting during feasts. The forests provide good cover for deer, boar, bears, and wolves (the latter have been reintroduced). Hyenas and wild leopard are increasingly rare despite hunting restrictions, and environmental degradation includes deforestation (leading to mudslides in the mountains) and serious pollution of the Black Sea.

³ LANGUAGE

Georgian is part of the southwest Caucasian group of languages: Zan (Mengrelo-Chan), Svan, and Georgian proper (Kartuli). It does not belong to any of the world's major language categories (Indo-European, Semitic, etc.) and is incomprehensible to all neighboring peoples. Mingrelians and Svans still speak their own languages at home, although all speak Georgian in public communications. Georgian has its own alphabet, which dates from at least the 5th century AD, influenced by Phoenician-Aramaic and Greek scripts. Since then, there have been two major modifications. The latest alphabet, called *mkhedruli*, has 33 characters and is written from left to right.

Some scholars have suggested Georgian is connected to Basque, but the similarities are superficial. Although there are many word borrowings from Arabic, Turkic, Persian, and Russian, Georgian is quite distinctive. In Georgian, "father" is *mama* and "mother" is *deda*, which can be quite confusing to foreigners. Georgian is particularly rich in indigenous words concerned with agriculture, winemaking, and metalworking—areas in which Georgians have long specialized. For example, all metals have indigenous words: gold is *okro*, silver is *vertskhli*, brass is *titberi*, and copper is *spilenzi*.

For Georgians, language is central to their identity. They are very protective of it. In 1978, when Georgia was still part of the USSR, students organized a major demonstration to defend their language when they felt it was threatened by Russification and diminished legal status. The earliest surviving Georgian literary works date from the 5th century AD. Currently, 98.2% of Georgians consider Georgian their native tongue, and business, political, and cultural activities within the state are conducted in Georgian. Everyday terms in Georgian include *gamarjorbat* ("hello"), *ki* ("yes"), *ara* ("no"), *gmadlobt* ("thank you"), and *nakhvamdis* ("good-bye").

⁴ FOLKLORE

Folklore in Georgia is extremely popular. Its sources are Christian, Greek, Hindu, pagan, and Persian. The Georgian *Visramiani* (mid-12th century), for example, is based on a Persian and (maybe Indian) prose romance, and the "Wisdom of Balahvar" (10th–11th centuries) is a Georgian Christian version of the story of Buddha. *Amiran-darejaniani* (11th century) is a collection of myths based in part on the Greek tales of Prometheus, and the *Rusudaniani* (17th century) borrows extensively from Arab sources, in particular the Arabian Nights. Other sources of Georgian folklore are the tales of surrounding Caucasian peoples such, as the Ossetians and Cherkess, who share pagan Nart epics focused on the earth-goddess Satanei and her offspring. Georgian folklore includes stories of knights, heroes, fantastic battles, chimeras, monsters, and spirits. Many of these stories crossed over into Georgian folk tales where one commonly encounters anthropomorphic animals, *mzetunakhavi* (the most beautiful woman in the world), *modzalade devi* (a beast often with three heads), and *natsarkekia* (a layabout).

Georgian folklore is intertwined with all aspects of Georgian life, from literature and religion, to cuisine, dance, music, and architecture. One of the greatest early 20th century Georgian poets, Vazha Pshavela, depends heavily in his poetry on the semi-pagan world of the Georgian mountain peoples, such as the Pshavs, Khevsurs, and Svans. In his works, he incorporates their magical myths about demons, sorcerers, the underworld, and describes their local deities and demi-gods.

Folklore legends instill in Georgians fabulous versions of their history. One Georgian legend, known by every school child, concerns the location of the capital, Tbilisi. The legend states that the Georgian king, Vakhtang Gorgasali (AD 452–502), was hunting on the site of present-day Tbilisi when he wounded a deer. The deer, bleeding to death, fell into a warm sulfur spring. The spring water healed the wound. The king, impressed with the therapeutic qualities of the water, decided to establish his capital by the spring.

⁵ RELIGION

Georgia's multi-ethnicity is reflected in its multiplicity of religions. The religion of most Georgians is Georgian Orthodoxy, a branch of Eastern Orthodoxy. East Georgia under King Miriam was converted to Christianity by St. Nino of Cappadocia in 330 AD, the third state following Armenia and the Roman Empire to adopt Christianity as its official religion. St. Nino shares with St. George, the patron saint of Georgia, a special popularity among Georgians. She allegedly created the first Georgian cross out of vines tied together with her hair, a relic that is still preserved.

The early influence of Christianity in Georgia is evident from artifacts dating back to the 3rd and 4th centuries. Christianity was introduced to Georgia through contact with local Jews, as well as by Greek and Roman officials. Ancient Greek and Georgian historic sources suggest—though it is unlikely—that St. Andrew may have visited the area. King Rev of Kartli, who ruled during the middle of the 3rd century, was familiar with the scriptures and became a devout Christian. Historically, Georgians have shown a tolerance for other religions.

The adoption of Christianity helped unite Georgians. With a Christian monarchy in place, the state began to promote a separate identity that contrasted with the neighboring Muslim states of Persia and, after the 15th century, the Ottomans. Georgian Christianity was deeply influenced by Byzantium and when the split between the Roman (Catholic) and Constantinople (Orthodox) Churches occurred in 1054, the Georgian Church sided with Eastern Orthodoxy.

The church is a symbol of national unity to Georgians. It held the country together culturally when it was territorially divided in the late Middle Ages. Georgian churches, influenced by Byzantine style, were built in the most inaccessible places to prevent attack by Muslim armies. They date from the 5th century. Perhaps the most famous is *Svetiskhoveli* ("life-giving pillar"), which is located in the old capital of Mtskheta.

Georgians walk in central T'bilisi during a parade marking the Orthodox Christmas. (Karen Minasyan/AFP/Getty Images)

According to Georgians, the original church was constructed from a sacred wooden pillar that grew from the grave of Sidonia, a devout Christian who was buried clutching Christ's shirt brought to Georgia from Jerusalem. The Georgian Orthodox service is similar to that of most other Eastern churches; there are no pews or sermons, but a ritualized liturgy with a choir and much burning of incense. Women still cover their heads. In common with other churches in the USSR, the Georgian church was devastated by the Soviet state's atheist policies, and its more than 2,000 parishes in 1917 were reduced to 80 by the 1960s. The church began to recover with the arrival of Gorbachev's *glasnost* policy of the late 1980s, and since independence in 1991 the Georgian church has revived and played a prominent part in national life. Patriarch Ilia II was elected in 1977.

There are also a small number of Georgian Catholics and larger numbers of Georgian Muslims in Achara in southwest Georgia and along the state's southern periphery. The Ossetians and Abkhazians are mostly Eastern Orthodox; the Azeris, Assyrians, and Kurds are mostly Muslim; and the Armenians, Greeks, and Russians are Gregorian, Greek Orthodox, and Russian Orthodox, respectively. Georgia was noted for its religious tolerance—despite persecution of Western sects like the Jehovah Witnesses in the late 1990s—and the capital of Tbilisi

has two working synagogues, churches of different denominations, and at least one working mosque.

6 MAJOR HOLIDAYS

Georgians venerate tradition, and after the collapse of the USSR, the new government replaced the old communist-inspired holidays with patriotic or religious ones, such as Independence Day (May 26), the day of National Unity (April 9), St. George's Day (November 23), and Mariamoba (August 28). Many Georgians continue to celebrate Christmas and Easter according to the old-style calendar observed by the Georgian Orthodox church. In September and October, the *rtveli*, or grape harvest, is marked by festivals in the villages. Georgian cities also hold celebrations. In the autumn Tbilisi has a *Tbilisoba* festival, which celebrates the life and history of the city. Georgian regions, such as Svaneti and Khevsureti—and even small villages—have their own feast and saints' days.

7 RITES OF PASSAGE

Orthodox baptism and wedding ceremonies serve as important milestones in Georgian life. Since independence, almost all marriages are celebrated in church and almost every child is baptized. High school children consider graduation an important change and celebrate it with mutual congratulatory writing on their school uniforms. Death and funerals are conducted in a highly formalized manner in Georgia. For three days before burial, there is a *panashvidi* (wake), during which people, often in their hundreds, visit the family. Forty days later, a *kelekhi*, or commemorative feast, is organized by the family. A one-year commemorative feast is also considered obligatory.

8 INTERPERSONAL RELATIONS

Georgians are both Middle Eastern and European in manner and share many social attitudes with neighboring Mediterranean cultures. Georgians are shaped by values of honor and shame, and view tradition, loyalty to friends and kin, and generosity toward guests as important values. The words *patiosnoba* ("honesty"), *sitskhvili* ("shame"), and *pativi* ("respect") are commonly heard in Georgian conversation. In contrast to official American values, nepotism—the system by which kin help each other in their careers—is considered mandatory and honorable. This system of mutual help extends to friendships, which in Georgia last for a lifetime. The word for friend in Georgian is *megobari*, which literally means someone who has "shared your drinking bowl." Important relationships might help a child reach university, secure a promotion for a family member, or give a close friend a new business opportunity. Being disloyal to family or friends or failing to provide sufficient help in time of financial and emotional need mark one as a dishonorable person. Neighborliness is highly valued and Georgians, who in the towns and cities traditionally shared common courtyards, often share food with neighbors.

Guests are held in great esteem. A Georgian proverb says that "a guest is sent by God." When a guest visits a Georgian house, he or she is lavishly treated, even if the host cannot afford to do so. An offering of food is mandatory. According to Georgian tradition, an enemy who crosses your threshold must be treated well and not harmed. The best way to show respect for a guest is to honor him or her with a *keipi*, or feast. Feasts are opportunities to invite family and close friends, to exchange gossip, to praise Georgian traditions, and to remember the dead. The *keipi* is a central part of Georgian social life, and on formal occasions, such as marriages and deaths, one can expect hundreds of guests. Feasts are characterized by long toasts. A great deal of wine is drunk. During these feasts men should not get visibly drunk, and toastmasters compete eloquently to show their poetic talents. Guests have obligations too and should bring a symbolic gift, such as flowers or chocolates, when they visit. Relationships between friends and family are close. There are certain important rules of behavior that all Georgians remember: greet a person properly, stand up when someone enters a room, and never sit with your back to anyone.

Georgians are very superstitious, and many pagan customs and beliefs are preserved today. In the countryside you still see trees with ribbons attached to them, each symbolizing a wish (they are known as "wishing trees"). This is connected with the old Georgian belief in wood spirits. Before setting off on a journey, Georgians will sit on their suitcase for a few seconds to ensure a safe journey. If a knife falls off a table, Georgians expect a male guest. No female should sit at the corner of a table, which suggests she will not get married.

9 LIVING CONDITIONS

Sixteen percent of Georgians are 14 years of age and under; 16.6% are 65 and over. The median age is 38.3. Life expectancy in 2004 was 76.51 although there are significant regional and rural differences, and statistics are not reliable in Georgia. Although there are a large number of centenarians in Georgia, the Georgian reputation for longevity has been undermined by modern life. A major killer is heart disease. The infant mortality rate in 2006 was 28 per 1,000 live births, a high figure compared to West European rates. The average family size is 4.1. The percentage of family members living apart from their families (single persons) is 3.1%. The Georgian government is seriously worried about declining birthrates and migration patterns. Between 1989 and 2002, Georgia's total population declined by 1,129,000, almost a quarter of the total population. This is in part because of the loss of Abkhazia and South Ossetia and declining birth rates; however, the greatest factor is emigration due to poor living conditions and unemployment.

When Georgia was part of the USSR, from 1921 to 1991, the economy was state owned. The USSR transformed Georgia into an industrial country with hydroelectric power, coal and manganese mining, and truck and ship-building. Light industries, such as textile production (silk, cotton, and wool), and food processing (tea, fruit, vegetables, and mineral water) were supported by Georgia's local agricultural economy. People lived reasonably well, although their incomes were small. Services, such as health care and education, were free, and people paid very little for rent and utilities. Transportation by metro, bus, or trolley was a few cents. Food was cheap and, if it could not be found in the state shops, (which was often the case) it could be bought at small private markets at a higher price. However, medicines were in short supply, and sophisticated medical equipment was only available for the elite (usually communist party officials). Service for plumbing, electrical repairs, and telephone installation was poor. Some people waited 15 years for a telephone or 10 years to buy a car. Televisions, refrigerators, and washing machines were of poor quality. Many times people had to go to the black market, which was illegal, and pay a high price for things, such as video or tape recorders. Housing was in poor condition, and most families in the cities lived in three- or four-room apartments (two bedrooms, a living room, and a kitchen).

When Georgians gained independence, they believed that things would get better, but switching to a market-based economy has proved very difficult, and for many, economic conditions have worsened. The subsidies for food and services are gone, and the state cannot afford to pay people proper salaries or pensions. Since the Rose Revolution in November 2003, which led to a change of government and major economic changes, macroeconomic figures have improved significantly. Government revenues have quadrupled due to tax reform and improved collection, and annual gross domestic product (GDP) growth rates averaged 8–9% by 2008. Per capita annual income was $591 in 2008, but in reality, despite official figures of just 13.6% unemployment, poverty is widespread. Officially, 31% of the population lives on or below the poverty line, and the average pension is about $30. Inflation is currently about 9.2% and increasing food prices are hurting the less well-off in particular. Higher education and medicine are no longer free, and transportation is increasingly expensive. Georgians now have to be more self reliant. Things are made worse in the winter due to the high cost of oil and gas. Despite all this, most Georgians are aware they have gained important political freedoms, even though it has been at great economic cost, and do not want to return to the communist period. Georgia has great economic potential and is attracting significant foreign investment. When tourists return to Georgia's ski resorts and beaches, things may begin to improve for broader sections of the population.

¹⁰ FAMILY LIFE

Georgian society is patriarchal, patrilocal, and patrilineal. Male culture is dominant, married couples usually move in with the husband's parents, and children adopt their father's name. However, women keep their own surnames when they marry, and there is no longer any real stigma attached to a husband living with his wife's parents. Young couples increasingly choose to live on their own. Social life centers on the family and children. Children are brought up in a structured environment, which inculcates strong respect for family values. Children are expected to respectfully greet older people in the polite form of the Georgian language. (The Georgians, like the French, have two forms of "you"—the familiar *shen,* which is used among friends, and the polite form *tkven,* which is used to address elders or strangers.) Young people are expected to get married and have children relatively quickly. Male children are preferred, although that attitude is changing. In the 1980s, 16% of women married before they were 20, and 55.2% before the age of 25. Divorce was frowned upon. In 1960, there were only 3 divorces per 100 marriages, but that figure rose to 18 in 1992, an indication of changing attitudes and greater pressures on the family. Now it is not unusual to meet divorced parents. Women now marry later than ever before at 25.9 years in 2004, compared to 24.7 in 1990. However, women in Georgia are still expected to do most of the domestic work and child rearing. Women, for example, will always prepare food for guests, clear up afterwards, and do most of the cleaning.

Families are increasingly nuclear (parents and children living in a single unit), with an average of two children, but relatives usually live close by. Grandparents often live physically close enough to take care of the grandchildren. For Georgians, uncles, aunts, nephews, nieces, cousins, and even godparents, are considered close family and should be seen frequently. A person is obligated to help relatives in times of crisis, and it is shameful to neglect family in any way. With unemployment being a major problem in Georgia, the extended family has become important once again as a means of economic survival.

11 CLOTHING

Georgians have always had a reputation for being stylish dressers, and this is still evident today as people stroll down the main boulevard, Rustaveli Prospect, in the capital city of Tbilisi. Although Georgians now wear casual clothes and follow the latest fashions, on special occasions they wear traditional costumes. Georgian men still wear different types of regional hats, such as the *svanuri kurdi,* a round brimless felt hat from the Svaneti mountain region, or the *tushuri kurdi,* a black brimless hat made of wool, which comes from Tusheti. In the mountains, shepherds occasionally wear the *nabadi,* a black felt cloak with stiff wide shoulders that can be used as shelter in winter weather, and the *papakhi,* a large shaggy woolen hat. At festive occasions, one can see other traditional costumes, such

as the *chokha,* a tunic that is usually magenta, black, or white and belted at the waist with decorative cartridge casings on the chest, or the *kartuli kaba,* the traditional female costume made up of a silk veil and an embroidered long dress gathered in at the waist and with wide sleeves. There are costumes associated with various regions and professions. The women in Khevsureti are well known for their *talavari* (intricately patterned, woven tunics) and *tsinda-pachichi* (knee-length, thick socks colored by natural dyes). Traditionally, Khevsur women also wear jewelry of silver and semi-precious stones. People dressed as *kintoebi*—tinkers and traders of the 19th century who wore flat, black peaked caps and baggy black trousers in the Persian style—appear at festivals. Women, particularly in the villages, wear black for a year after a death in the family.

¹² FOOD

Food and wine are a vital part of Georgian culture, and feasting is central to Georgian social life. Georgians eat in abundance and will present guests with dish after dish. The Georgian table, known as the *supra,* is colorful and diverse. It is a mixture of Turkish, Greek, Arabic, and even Indian influences. Food is often spicy, particularly in Samegrelo and Western Georgia, with coriander, tarragon, and *khmeli suneli* (a mixture of spices) being the favorites. Hot and cold dishes are served with side dishes of tomatoes, cucumber, spring onions, *sulguni* (a soft cheese), and *puri* (unleavened bread baked in an open brick oven much like the tandoori). Dishes are brought to the table on small plates, which are often piled up one on top of another. Guests are expected to help themselves. As soon as a guest pauses or a plate is empty, someone will offer another dish.

A typical colorful *supra* might consist of puréed beet and spinach sprinkled with pomegranate seeds, *khachapuri* (a baked cheese bread), *satsivi* (a chicken dish in walnut sauce), *ghomi* (a Georgian version of grits), *chanakhi* (a lamb and vegetable stew), *tolma* (minced meat wrapped in vine or cabbage leaves), and *badrijani nivrit* (eggplant with garlic). Below is a simple *khachapuri* recipe.

Khachapuri (Georgian cheese bread)

2 cups unbleached white flour
½ teaspoon salt
12 tablespoons (1½ sticks) cold butter, cut into pieces
2 eggs, beaten separately
¼ cup plain yogurt
1¼ pounds mixed Muenster and Havarti cheeses
1 egg yolk, beaten

Place flour and salt in a bowl and mix in butter pieces. Stir one beaten egg into the yogurt, and then add the liquid to the flour mixture. Shape the dough into a ball and refrigerate for one hour.

Grate the cheese and combine with the other beaten egg. Preheat oven to 350°F.

Roll out dough to form a 12"x 17" rectangle, trimming the edges. Put the cheese mixture on one half of the dough and fold the other half over the top, sealing the edges

Place cheese dough on a greased baking sheet, brush with egg yolk. Bake for about 30 minutes at 350 or until brown.

Makes 12 to 15 serving pieces. Best served warm.

Other popular Georgian items include *lobio* (beans with grated walnuts and chopped onion) and *chakhokhbili* (chicken stewed with tomatoes). A favorite ingredient in Georgian dishes is walnut, which grows abundantly alongside Georgian highways. Wine, which is sacred to Georgians and has been cultivated in the region longer than most places in the world, is an essential part of any meal. Georgians make a wide variety of both red wines, such as *mukuzani*, and white, such as *tsinandali*, and often store the wine in a *kvevri* (an amphora) buried deep in the ground to keep the wine cool. Regional differences in cuisine are pronounced in Georgia. In Western Georgia, one is more likely to eat *mchadi* (cornbread) and cheese bread, such as *acharuli*, which has an egg baked in the middle of the cheese and dough. Of course, such lavish meals are not a daily occurrence, and Georgians eating at home are more modest, especially in these days of declining standards of living. For sweets, Georgians love to eat extravagantly prepared cakes.

13 EDUCATION

Georgians have a long history of educational achievement. Monasteries and academies have been vital centers of learning from the Middle Ages onwards, preserving Georgia's national heritage in times of occupation. The Soviet period saw a rapid expansion of mass education and today, as a result of compulsory schooling, illiteracy has been largely eliminated. In 1979, 30.7% of Soviet Georgia's working population had completed higher or specialized middle education, which made it a highly educated population. However, the educational approach in the Soviet period was both conservative and narrow, and many subjects, such as sociology, could not be taught due to censorship. In the later Soviet years, higher education institutions were extremely corrupt. After independence, many educational reforms were introduced, but declining revenues and economic chaos led to a decline in school attendance, minimal budgetary support for schools, and increasing corruption. Between 1990 and 1997, total enrollments in educational institutions dropped from 1.242 million to 924,000. This decline affected all age groups. Preschool enrollments in public institutions declined most dramatically from about 200,000 to 83,000. Upper secondary enrollments (grades 10–11) fell from 105,000 to 70,000 and vocational education from 42,000 to 20,000. Some of these declines can be explained by emigration, but other indicators, including poverty, government insolvency, and corruption, are significant factors.

Since the Rose Revolution in November 2003, there has been significant reform of curricula (with more emphasis on a liberal arts approach), teacher training, management of schools (parent-teacher councils have been introduced), and the examination system. A universal entrance exam for higher educational institutions, which replaced university-set entrance exams, eliminated much of the corruption at university level. Investment has increased after a report in 1997 noted that 18% of school buildings were in dangerous or unusable condition, while a further 55% needed significant capital repairs. Under the present constitution, education is compulsory and free of charge up to grade 9, but fees have been introduced for students in grade 10 and 11 and almost all university students now have to pay tuition fees. Higher education is largely private. There are 117 accredited universities in Georgia.

Currently, primary school in Georgia includes grades 1–6, basic education goes up to grade 9, and upper secondary covers grades 10 and 11. The completion of 11 years of schooling in theory qualifies a student for higher education. University usually lasts five years. At the same time, teaching styles are still quite formal, with much learning in school done by rote. Children finish school knowing a great deal of poetry by heart. Final examinations in schools are oral and marked on a scale of 1 to 5, with 5 being the best. An excellent student is known as a *khutosani* (a "fiver"). Children no longer wear uniforms but are generally respectful toward teachers.

14 CULTURAL HERITAGE

Georgian cultural life draws upon European, Middle Eastern, and on its own indigenous traditions. Georgian singing, whether it is secular or ecclesiastical, dates back to the 5th century. Most folk and sacred songs are polyphonic (multiple harmonized voices) and a cappella (without accompaniment). Most performing choirs are male, although female choirs are becoming more popular, and women sing at church services. There are many regional singing styles; the Gurians in West Georgia are well known for their complex use of *krimanchuli* (yodeling). Many Georgians play the piano or guitar, favorite instruments for accompaniment of popular urban songs. Traditional instruments, such as the *duduki* (a double-reeded clarinet-like instrument) and the *panduri* (a three-stringed lute), are used to accompany urban folk songs.

Since the formation of the Georgian State Dance company in 1945, which has toured more than 80 countries, Georgian dance has become a favorite of foreign audiences. The *lezginka*, the *samaia* (a dance performed by three women), and the *mkhedruli* (the military dance), are particular favorites. The men are acrobatic, dancing on the knuckles of their feet, using swords in skillfully choreographed mock fights. The women, in long dresses, glide across the dance floor (on the balls of their feet) using their hands in a symbolic manner reminiscent of Indian and Middle Eastern dances.

Georgians love going to the theater and classical concerts. Georgia has many great classical performers, such as pianists Alexander Toradze and Eliso Virsaladze, violinist Leana Isakadze, bass Paata Buchuladze, *prima ballerina* Nino Ananiashvili, and composer Gia Khancheli. Georgia has its own symphony orchestra, dance, opera, and ballet companies, but the current political and economic crisis in Georgia has put enormous pressure on all arts companies and organizations, and fewer are performing. Under Soviet power, the arts were heavily subsidized, but now they have to be profitable to survive. The Rustaveli Theater Company is widely recognized as one of the most imaginative and talented theatrical groups in the contemporary theater world and continues to tour. Georgian film, with a history going back to the early 20th century (the first Georgian film was made in 1912) and that has produced famous filmmakers, such as Eldar Shengelaia, Giorgi Shengelaia, and Tengiz Abuladze, has been less fortunate. Today, for lack of money, the Georgian film industry has essentially collapsed.

The Georgian literary tradition began with ecclesiastical literature. Early Georgian scholars translated the Bible and other sacred works from Assyrian, Aramaic, Arabic, Armenian, and Greek. Early Georgian literature—hymnography, homilies, hagiography, chronicles—emerged in the 6th and 7th centuries in the Christian monasteries and academies of Greece, Georgia, Mount Sinai, Mount Athosm and Jerusalem. An early chronicle of Georgian history is *kartlis tskhovreba* (*The Life of Kartli*), a collection of histories and tales of Georgian kings originally compiled in the 12th century but continually expanded until the 18th century.

Poetry is considered one of the purest arts in Georgia and is frequently recited at the dinner table or among friends. The greatest classic of Georgian secular literature is a 12th-century epic titled Vepkhistqaosani, or "Knight in the Panther Skin," by the poet Shota Rustaveli. Half pagan, half Christian, and influenced by Persian sources (particularly Firdousi's *Shah-Nameh*), it is about friendship, infatuation, and the search for lost love. Aphorisms from Rustaveli's epic are used like proverbs: "A lion cub is just as good, be it female or male" and "What you give is yours, what you keep is lost." Georgian poetry continued throughout the Middle and late Middle Ages, often from the pens of Georgian kings, such as Teimuraz 1 and Archil, but it was the 19th century that witnessed a major Georgian literary renaissance. For the first time Georgian poets, novelists, and essayists, such as Ilia Chavchavadze, Akaki Tsereteli, Galaktion Tabidze, Vazha Pshavela, and Ana Kalandadze, became popular national figures. In the 20th century, many Georgian poets and writers were executed in the purges of the 1930s. Despite brutal oppression and censorship, Georgian literature remained highly lyrical, being motivated by love of country and nostalgia for the past. Georgian literature has produced brilliant works of both prose and poetry, such as Konstantine Gamsakhurdia's *The Hand of the Great Master*, or Galaktion Tabidze's great poems "The Moon of Mtatsminda" and "The Wind Blows." Georgia's poets and writers have been translated by Russian poets, such as Boris Pasternak and Yevgeny Yevtushenko.

15 WORK

About 2.2. million Georgians are in the labor force. Approximately 35.5% work in services, 8.9% in industry, and 55.6% in agriculture. The self-employed account for about 65% of the workforce (mostly farmers). Most Georgians today survive by working two or three jobs, or, in many cases, rely on help from families and friends. The government is unable to pay living wages, stimulate employment, or pay proper social security benefits. The most vulnerable groups are the quarter million "internally displaced persons," the 700,000–800,000 pensioners, and single mothers. Most of those in state employment receive no more than $300 a month and are forced to seek extra income, usually by working in small commercial operations or by trading on the black market. A new business class, in many cases former communist party officials, has replaced the old communist elite as the most privileged in society. Income and wealth inequalities have increased considerably over the last 15 years. It is estimated the poorest 10% of Georgians share 2.4% of household income and consumption, while the top 10% share 27%.

16 SPORTS

Traditional Georgian sports include wrestling, archery, fencing, javelin throwing, horse riding, *tskhenburti* (a form of polo), and *leloburti* (a field game similar to rugby). Today, the most popular sport in Georgia is soccer, and the best Georgian team until the 1990s was Tbilisi Dynamo, which won the Soviet championship on two occasions and the European Cup Winners' Cup in 1981. Georgian teams now have their own league and have entered UEFA and FIFA (the international soccer association that handles the World Cup). Georgian footballers play on European teams, such as Kakhka Kaladze, Zurab Menteshashvili and Levan Kobiashvili. In addition, Georgians have achieved renown in basketball, rugby, mountain climbing, and skiing (a popular sport in the republic's mountain resorts). As part of the USSR Olympic team, Georgians won 23 gold medals between 1952 and 1980. Since Georgia entered the Olympics in 1994 as an independent state, Georgian athletes have won many medals, mostly in judo and wrestling. In chess, women, such as Nona Gaprindishvili and Maia Chiburdanidze, kept the world championship in Georgian hands for more than 30 years between 1961 and 1991.

17 ENTERTAINMENT AND RECREATION

A favorite Georgian pastime is feasting and singing with friends around a table or at a picnic in the countryside. Some of the most popular songs are "*suliko*," "*mravalzhamier*" ("Be long living"), and "*shen khar venakhi*" ("You are the vine") are heard at the table. The younger generations are keen followers of the Western rock scene, and there are many Georgian rock bands. Since the collapse of communism, bars and clubs have emerged alongside casinos.

18 FOLK ART, CRAFTS, AND HOBBIES

Georgian folk crafts date back more than 2,500 years. The first examples of local pottery come from the 7th century BC. Pottery is still a village craft in Georgia and pots, plates, and all manner of drinking vessels can be bought at the market or even at the roadside. Most pottery is connected with drinking. Simple bowls, known as *pialebi*, are raised to the lips with both hands, and *dokebi* are long-necked pots from which wine is poured. Other crafts include rug making, either woven in traditional Georgian patterns or made from compressed felt with abstract patterns. The colors used most often are deep red, brown, blue, and yellow. Georgians are also very proud of their skills with metal, particularly gold and silver. Their reputation as skilled metalworkers has lasted since the time of ancient Greece. Metal chasing, which Georgians call *chiduroba*, is a treasured craft, as is enameling and jewelry making. Most Georgian women wear jewelry—bracelets, necklaces, and earrings—made of silver and set with semi-precious stones, such as *piruzi* (turquoise) and *dzotsi* (garnet).

19 SOCIAL PROBLEMS

Since independence and the breakdown of familiar economic patterns, Georgians have suffered enormous hardship, job insecurity, and poor health. Mutual support among friends and family is extremely important. In the past, housing, food, transportation, health care, and education were heavily subsidized or free. Women received partially paid maternity leave for a year and a half if they wanted to stay at home with a new baby and could retire at 55 (men at 60). Although the quality of support was poor by Western standards, this rudimentary welfare system has disappeared. The current health system, for example, is no longer free and all hospitals have been privatized. Attempts to introduce private insurance schemes have for the most part failed. Medicines are prohibitively expensive for ordinary people. Except in emergencies, people no longer go to the hospital. Deterioration in health care, poorer diets, greater stress, and inadequate immunization programs have led to a decline in the Georgians' health. This is reflected in increasing death and child mortality rates.

In June 2003 the Georgian government introduced the Economic Development and Poverty Reduction Program (EDPRP), the first comprehensive document outlining a strategy for economic recovery and employment. Poorly implemented, the Rose Revolution leadership quickly abandoned the EDPRP in favor of its own strategy—the Basic Data and Directions (BDD) document in 2006, which outlines its priorities as sustainable economic growth and increased private sector-fuelled employment. However, at the same time, it cut back on state employment, and 30,000 civil servants lost their jobs between 2003 and 2008. By November 2007, when opposition-led demonstrations almost toppled the Georgian government, it was clear the new government strategy was failing politically. The population was angered by increasing joblessness (20–24 year olds are among the most seriously affected), rising prices, and declining services. Life was getting harder for the vast majority of the population and social problems, such as crime, drug abuse, AIDS and fuel costs, were, it seemed, intensifying.

[20] GENDER ISSUES

In the Soviet period, women in Georgia made significant gains in gender equality but still remained unequal in many areas, such as in the home, where traditional patriarchal attitudes remained; at work, where women were paid smaller salaries and concentrated in certain professions, such as teaching and nursing; and in government, where women rarely gained significant posts or power. This situation has continued and worsened in the post-Soviet period. The majority of women employed in the formal sector work in the low-paying fields of agriculture, education, healthcare, and light industry. Vertical and horizontal gender segregation persists in the labor market. According to the State Department of Statistics, in 2004 the average nominal monthly salary of women in all fields of the economy and all sectors was 60% that of men's. Self-employed women in the trade sector earn an average monthly wage that is 68% of men's. As of 2008, women accounted for around 9.4% of members of parliament (MPs), which is indicative of the legislative and internal party barriers to support for women candidates. Women made up 6.4% and 7% of total MPs in the 1995 and 1999 parliaments. There are, however, successful women. In 2008 the foreign minister, Eka Tkeshelashvili, was female, as was the former parliamentary speaker, Nino Burjunadze. Women are well represented in the media, judiciary (44% of judges are women), and in nongovernmental organizations (NGOs). There were 200 women's NGOs registered in Georgia by 2008, but not all are active). Popular attitudes are very supportive of equal employment rights for men and women but the highly respected and influential Georgian Orthodox church supports traditional family values and the domestication of women. Gender equality is not a priority of the government. Despite signing onto the United Nations' *Convention on the Elimination of All Forms of Discrimination against Women* in 1994, there is little concern or focus on legislation on women's issues although two important steps were made in 2006, when legislation on human trafficking and domestic violence against women were introduced in parliament. There is also an Advisory Council on Gender Equality attached to the parliamentary speaker's office.

[21] BIBLIOGRAPHY

Areshidze, Irakly. *Democracy and Autocracy in Eurasia: Georgia in Transition*. East Lansing, MI: Michigan State University Press, 2007.

Jones, Stephen. "Georgia: Nationalism from Under the Rubble," Lowell Barrington (ed.). *After Independence: Making and Protecting the Nation in Postcolonial and Postcommunist States*, Ann Arbor: University of Michigan Press, 2006.

———. "Presidential and Parliamentary Elections in Georgia, 2004." *Electoral Studies*, Vol. 24, Issue No. 2, June 2005, pp.303-311.

———. "The Rose Revolution: A Revolution Without Revolutionaries?" *Cambridge Review of International Affairs*, Vol. 19, No. 1 March 2006, pp.33-48.

Lang, David Marshall. *The Georgians*. New York: Praeger, 1966.

Pitskhelauri, G. Z. *The Longliving of Soviet Georgia*. New York: Human Sciences Press, 1982.

Wheatley, Jonathan. *Georgia from National Awakening to Rose Revolution: Delayed Transition in the Former Soviet Union*. Aldershot, U.K.: Ashgate, 2005.

—by S.F. Jones

GERMANS

LOCATION: Germany
POPULATION: Over 82 million (ethnic German 91.5%, Turkish 2.4%, Italian 0.7%, Greek 0.4%, Polish 0.4%, other 4.6%)
LANGUAGE: Standard German (Hochdeutsch)
RELIGION: Protestant; Catholic; Methodist; Baptist; Mennonite; Society of Friends; Islam, small numbers of Jews; Unaffiliated or other

1 INTRODUCTION

Germany, an independent republic in north central Europe, is one of the continent's largest and most populous nations. Although it has played a pivotal role in European and world history, it has only been a single, unified nation for less than 100 years of its entire history. Originally settled by nomadic tribes, the area that now makes up Germany originally was part of what was called the Holy Roman Empire. It consisted of a cluster of partially independent cities and states. In 1871 the Prussian chancellor Otto von Bismarck succeeded in creating a unified Germany, which subsequently became involved in two world wars (1914–1918 and 1939–1945), both of which it lost. Following the defeat of Nazi-controlled Germany in World War II (1945) and its postwar occupation by the victorious allied powers, the American, French, and British zones were combined in 1949 to create the democratic Federal Republic of Germany (West Germany), while in the same year the Soviet zone became the Communist-controlled German Democratic Republic (East Germany).

Since its inception in 1949, the Federal Republic of Germany has been a strong proponent for European unity. It has been an active supporter of the European parliament and of the various councils that have been formed to integrate the economies and political institutions of the member states. Because of its economic strength, Germany has often been referred to as the "locomotive of Europe."

Both Germanys recovered from the devastation of the war with impressive speed. However, progress was faster and more dramatic in the west than in the east, and nearly three million East Germans fled to West Germany seeking improved living conditions and greater political freedom. Finally, in 1961, the East Germans put up the Berlin Wall and sealed off the nation's borders to prohibit all further emigration to the west. In the late 1980s, Germany became caught up in the changes sweeping over Communist Eastern Europe, and the opening of the Berlin Wall in November 1989 became one of the most memorable symbols of the Communist system's ultimate collapse. In March 1990 the East Germans held their first free elections, and the two German nations were reunified on October 3 of that year. The German Democratic Republic went out of existence, and West Germany's constitution, laws, and currency were extended to the east, as well as its market-based economy.

Today, the Federal Republic of Germany is one of the largest countries in Europe. It is a prominent member of the North Atlantic Treaty Organization (NATO) and a powerful engine behind the European Union integration. Germany advocates for closer political, economic, and defense cooperation among the European countries and strongly supports the Organization for Security and Cooperation in Europe (OSCE). This modern cosmopolitan state actively supports the development of democratic institutions and propagates gender equality. In November 2005 a vote in the Bundestag (House of Representatives or lower house) made Angela Merkel Germany's first woman chancellor.

2 LOCATION AND HOMELAND

Germany's main regions are the Bavarian Alps (which form the boundaries with Austria and Switzerland); the South German Hill Region that contains the Black Forest; the Central Uplands (including the Harz Mountains and the Thuringian Forest); and the North German Plain. Major rivers include the Rhine in the west and the Danube, which flows from west to east. Reunified Germany has the largest population of any European Union (EU) state.

Since the 1950s, significant numbers of foreign workers have immigrated to Germany from countries including Turkey, the former Yugoslavia, Italy, Greece, Poland, and other Eastern European countries. By the end of 1991, Germany harbored a foreign population of close to 6 million. As of 2007, 91.5% of the German population were ethnic Germans, 2.4% Turks, Italians amount to 0.7%, Greeks to 0.4%, Polish comprise 0.4% and others account for 4.6%.

Germany consists of 16 federal states called *Bundesländer*. Federal states have designated governmental powers somewhat similar to those of the United States. Before the unification East Germany had 15 districts. However, they were reconstructed and reduced to five so-called "new states" (*die neuen Länder*). Hence, following unification, western Germany has 11 *Bundesländer* and eastern Germany has five.

3 LANGUAGE

Standard German, or *Hochdeutsch*, is the nation's official language, but many different dialects are spoken throughout the country and have a strong influence in most areas. Low German, spoken along the North and Baltic sea coasts and on Germany's offshore islands, is close to Dutch and even English (examples: Standard German *Wasser* is Low German *Water*, Standard German *Apfel* is Low German *Appel*). Sorbian is a Slavic language spoken by approximately 60,000 people, and a number of different languages, including Turkish, are spoken by Germany's immigrant populations.

Approximately half of all Germans are fluent in English. Many Germans from the former East Germany speak Russian. Also, many Russian Germans who recently returned to Germany speak Russian. About 3% of Germans are fluent in French.

EXAMPLE OF A POEM IN STANDARD GERMAN
Wanderers Nachtlied
by Johann Wolfgang von Goethe
Über allen Gipfeln
Ist Ruh,
In allen Wipfeln
Spürest du
Kaum einen Hauch:
Die Vögelein schweigen im Walde.
Warte nur! Balde
Ruhest du auch.

(Translation follows.)

Over the mountaintops
There is peace,
In all the treetops,
You feel
Barely a breath:
The little birds are silent in the woods.
But wait! Soon
You too will be at rest.

⁴ FOLKLORE

The most famous body of German lore is the *Nibelungenlied*, dating back to AD 1200. Its characters, such as Siegfried, Brunhilde, and Hagen, have become famous to millions through the operas of Richard Wagner's *Ring Cycle*. During World War II, the Allies called the German fortifications along the French border the Siegfried Line. A prominent role in German folklore is played by a set of tales collected by Jacob and Wilhelm Grimm in the 19th-century. The *Tales of the Brothers Grimm* is one of the most frequently translated books in the world.

Another legendary figure in German folklore is Till Eulenspiegel. He was a 14th century peasant, famous for his wit and irreverence. Impudent trickster, Till Eulenspiegel loved to play practical jokes on people in authority exposing their greed and folly, hypocrisy and foolishness. Till's story was first written down in the 16th century. It then became the inspiration for an orchestral work by Richard Strauss and a poem by Gerhardt Hauptmann.

⁵ RELIGION

About 68% of the German population belongs to a Christian Church. An estimated 34% of Germans are Protestants and nearly 34% are Catholics. The Protestants live mainly in the north of the country and the Catholics in the south. Other denominations, some with increasing membership, include Methodists, Baptists, Mennonites, and the Society of Friends. The social and charitable work of the churches is an integral part of German society. Churches provide formidable support for hospitals, assisted-living facilities, nursing homes, schools, and day-care centers. At the same time the German Basic Law guarantees freedom of faith and freedom of religion and declares that no one may be discriminated against due to their faith or religious opinions. Even though religion plays an important role in Germans' daily lives, there is no state church in Germany and no control of the churches by the state.

Before the 1930s, Germany had a Jewish population of around 530,000. However, the great majority fled or was killed in the Nazi Holocaust of World War II. As of 2008 there were approximately 100,000 Jews living in Germany, a number that is expected to increase. Many of them arrived from the countries of the former Soviet Union. The largest Jewish community in Germany exists in Berlin comprising more than 11,000 members. The inflow of workers from foreign countries and their families brought to Germany religious communities that were previously unrepresented. Hence, today approximately 3 million Muslims live in Germany, most of them coming from Turkey

⁶ MAJOR HOLIDAYS

Germany's many holidays include New Year's Day, Good Friday, Easter, Pentecost, Labor Day (May 1), and Christmas. St. Nicolas Day is the Children's most favorite holiday when they

find treats and gifts in their socks in the morning. Many different local festivals are celebrated depending on a region. Similarly, the observance of some religious holidays varies from one region to another. Catholic areas celebrate the Feast of Corpus Christi (11 days after Pentecost) and All Saints' Day (November 1), while Lutheran regions observe Reformation Day (October 31) and Repentance and Prayer Day (the third Wednesday in November).

One of Germans' most favorite holidays without a doubt is Christmas. Many Germans decorate their homes with a Christmas tree. In fact, the Christmas tree tradition is believed to have originated in Germany in the 17th century. German Christmas trees are often decorated with real candles. Germans begin their Christmas festivities a month in advance with Christmas Markets or *Weihnachtsmarkte*. Open each weekend in December in many towns these unique markets sell candles, Christmas trees, seasonal goods, handmade crafts, art, delicious celebration food, warm spiced wine and more. The best Christmas Markets are believed to be in Rothenburg, Nürnberg, Bamberg, Ulm, Augsburg and Munich.

A famous regional German holiday is *Oktoberfest*. This beer drinking jamboree is held in several different cities in Germany, but the true Oktoberfest is the specialty of Munich. Traditionally this festival is celebrated in October, after the harvest is already gathered. This is the time to get together, relax, sing traditional songs and have lots of fun and drink beer.

Another spectacular local festival is *Fasching* or *Karneval* (depending on a region). Except for Oktoberfest, it is the one time of year when many typically sedate Germans loosen up and go a little crazy. Fasching and Karneval celebrations vary from region to region and take place at different times of the year depending on the date of Easter. Some of Germany's best known celebrations are held in Cologne, Mainz, Munich, and Rottweil. But of course Cologne's Karneval is not really the same as Munich's Fasching. Today Fasching and Karneval involve elaborate parades. Marchers often would wear large cartoonish heads lampooning regional and national politicians. Another part of the celebration involves parade royalty (princes, princesses) and a sort of "counter-government" during the season. The highlight of the parade is masks and carnival costumes of all kinds of forest creatures, fairytale characters and such. Participants take great pride in their attire and sometimes spend a year or more to complete their garb. The jolly atmosphere accompanying the parades and intricately crafted masks and costumes with patterns rooted in medieval times, take the observer to the heart of German ancient traditions.

7 RITES OF PASSAGE

Germans live in a modern, industrialized, Christian country. Hence, the rites of passage that many young people undergo are religious rituals. Both Catholics and Protestants have confirmation ceremonies symbolizing rites of passage from youth into adulthood when one is expected to be mature enough to voluntarily assume responsibility for one's religious faith. A secular rite of passage that marks for the German atheists the transition from childhood to adulthood is a specially-designed ceremony known as the *Jugendweihe*, or "youth consecration." This somewhat controversial 150-year-old ritual was mainly celebrated in eastern Germany during the past 50 years and is now introduced to all of the Germany's non-religious teenagers.

In addition, a student's progress through the education system considered to be a rite of passage and is celebrated by many families with graduation parties. Marriage signifies rite of passage in societal status. Moreover military or civil service marks passage from teenage years to responsible adulthood for men. German young men between the ages of 18 and 25 are subject to conscription into the *Bundeswehr*, Germany's armed forces. At present, the length of service is nine months. Training and garrison duty is usually near the young man's home town. Conscientious objectors can engage in substitute service in hospitals, nursing homes, and similar civil protection organizations. Civil service obligation extends to 100 hours each year for six years.

8 INTERPERSONAL RELATIONS

Popular stereotypes cast the Germans as diligent, industrious, efficient, and rather humorless. However, German humor does exist, but it tends toward the farcical and slapstick. Regional differences make it hard to pin down a national character or set of traits. The division between north and south is older and deeper than that between the formerly divided east and west so that the strong sense of regional pride is incorporated into the federal system of German government and often attributed to personal traits of people. The Rhinelanders of the north are said to be easygoing and good-natured, while the Bavarians of the south are characterized as lively and excitable. Frisians, who live between the North and Baltic Seas, have a reputation for being taciturn and tend to be the object of jokes based on

their perceived lack of sophistication. On the whole, however, Germans seem to be more serious and aloof than Americans.

In Germany, it is customary to shake hands when you greet another person. A man waits for a woman to extend her hand before shaking it and in mixed company men shake a woman's hand before a man's. The most common greetings (with regional differences) are *Guten Morgen* (good morning), *Guten Tag* (hello), and *Guten Abend* (good evening). You might also hear the basic hello said as "*Hallo.*" Commonly used *Auf Wiedersehen* means goodbye and *Gute Nacht* means good night. Among friends, relatives, and with young people, the more familiar *Tschüss!* is used in place of *Auf Wiedersehen*.

As tradition has it, only family members and close friends can address each other by their first names. Others are expected to refer to each other using titles and surnames, although this trend is now changing. Pointing and wiggling the index finger to one's own head is an insult to another person. Instead of crossing one's fingers for luck as in America, Germans squeeze their thumbs. Germans greatly value punctuality. For example if guests are invited for dinner at 7:00 p.m., they will arrive sharply at 7:00 p.m. or just a few minutes later. Guests often bring a small gift with them—a box of candies or an odd number of flowers for the hosts.

9 LIVING CONDITIONS

Germans take great pride in their homes, spending about 10% of their income on home furnishings and decoration. The destruction wrought during World War II left Germany with a severe housing shortage, which was addressed more successfully in the former West Germany than in the east, although housing prices in the west were very high. In East Germany, families were often placed on housing waiting lists for years. Although the leaders of unified Germany initially promised that conditions in the east would match those in the west by the mid-1990s, housing conditions in the west are still superior. Throughout the country, families generally live in small houses or apartments with a kitchen, bathroom, living room, and one or two bedrooms. Young children often share a bedroom.

Germans receive high-quality medical care. Based on 2008 data, the average life expectancy is 76 years for men and 82 years for women. Although Germany has a comprehensive health care system, the government imposed spending limits for drugs, doctors' fees, and hospital costs in 1992 to offset rising health care costs. The German love of beer has taken its toll on the nation's health: alcoholism follows smoking as one of the nation's leading causes of death. Another social challenge faced by Germans is a negative population growth rate. Although improved over recent years, the population growth rate is −0.033%.

Germany's transportation system is one of the best developed in Europe. The country's highway system, called the *Autobahn*, begun in the 1930s, was one of the first in the world. Today it contains over 10,900 km (6,500 mi) of roads and, unlike highways in the United States, the Autobahn has no speed limits. However, to combat pollution and traffic congestion, Germans are encouraged to travel by public transportation rather than by car; railways and cross-country buses connect all parts of the country. In fact, most Germans take environmental issues seriously. Public recycling bins can easily be found throughout public spaces. Regular apartment buildings have at least six different garbage containers designated for specific kinds of garbage ranging from glass and plastic to biodegradable garbage allowing people to recycle their waste.

In the past Germany was known to be a conservative state. Now, however, its society is shaped by a plurality of life styles and ethno-cultural diversity. In addition to traditional marriages other forms of coexistence are becoming prominent. Traditional gender roles have eroded. Yet, despite all these social changes, the family remains the most important social unit.

Although the unification of Germany took a toll on its affluent and technologically powerful economy, Germany remains one of the strongest economies in the European Union. After the post-unification period of stagnation with an average economic growth rate of 0.7% and chronically high unemployment reaching 14%, Germany attained stronger gross domestic product (GDP) growth of 2.6 % and a considerable fall in unemployment to about 8%. The modernization and integration of the eastern German economy is still an expansive affair, requiring roughly $80 billion per year. However, a previous comprehensive set of reforms of labor market and welfare-related institutions in tandem with Chancellor Merkel's economic policies gradually improved and strengthened the German economy. Thus, in 2007, the German GDP amounted to an impressive $2.833 trillion or $34,400 per capita. At the same time, similarly to other EU states, the German economy faces long-term challenges of European economic integration and globalization, high oil prices, tighter credit markets, and slowing growth abroad.

10 FAMILY LIFE

Germans generally have small families with one or two children. Although the father is generally conceived to be the head of the family, both parents usually work. German children are taught to be polite and respectful to their elders, although as teenagers they tend to become somewhat rebellious. Most young people prefer to move out from their parents' house as soon as they enter university or become wage earners. Young people usually marry in their late twenties although it is increasingly common for people to live together before or instead of marriage. Some people prefer legal marriages while others favor religious ceremonies.

The Germans referred to the traditional role of women in terms of "three K's": *Kirche* (church), *Küche* (kitchen), and *Kinder* (children). Today, however, German women enjoy legal equality with men. Similarly to women in other countries German women are challenging the restrictions that have traditionally been placed on them. Because of recent laws protecting the rights of unwed mothers and their children, an increasing number of unmarried couples are living together, either with or without children.

11 CLOTHING

German clothing styles are similar to those in United States, but with a distinctively European flavor. It is difficult to designate a specific German fashion, yet it can be said that Germans are distinguished by a classic yet simple style. Cosmetics are worn but sparingly. Sloppy or untidy attire is considered inappropriate in public. Internationally known German clothing brands include Hugo Boss, Willy Bogner, and Strenesse. Among eminent German fashion designers are Karl Lagerfeld, Wolfgang Joop, and Jil Sander. Legendary model Claudia

Schiffer is yet another well-known figure in the world of fashion and design.

Traditional regional costumes are reserved for festivals and celebrations. At festivals such as the popular Oktoberfest in Munich, one still sees traditional outfits such as black feathered hats, white shirts, embroidered suspenders, and *Lederhosen* (leather shorts) for men, and white lacy peasant blouses, black embroidered bodices, and white aprons for women. Regional costumes are especially popular in southern Germany. The traditional journeyman's outfit of the carpenters' guild, for example, may still be seen in some areas. It consists of a felt hat, a black corduroy suit with pearl buttons, bell-bottomed trousers, and a red kerchief worn around the neck.

12 FOOD

The traditional German diet is high in starch (noodles and dumplings in the south, potatoes in the north). *Würste* (sausages)—in hundreds of varieties—are a staple throughout the country, as is bread, which many eat with every meal. While it may be delicious, the traditional German diet, with its cold meats, starches, sugary desserts, and beer, is high in calories and cholesterol, and many Germans are trying to modify their eating habits in order to improve their health.

Most Germans eat their main meal at noon and prefer a lighter, often cold supper. Germans keep knife and fork in their hands while eating. Hands should be kept above the table with wrists resting on the edge and it is considered bad manners to keep hands under the table.

Different regions have their own specialties with every region known for its own kind of *wurst* (sausage). *Weisswurst* and Black Forest cherry cake is a specialty of the south, and *Labskaus* (stew), seafood dishes, and bean soup with bacon (*Bohnensuppe mit Speck*) of the north. A few other renowned German dishes are *Kartoffelsalat* (German potato salad), herring salad, *Sauer und Suess Gedampfter Kohl* (steamed sweet and sour cabbage) and *Kartoffelpuffer* (potato pancakes). German luscious desserts include *Berliner Krapfen* (jelly doughnuts from Berlin), *Marzipankugeln* (marzipan balls), *Apfelpfannkuchen* (apple pancakes) and of course *Lebkuchen* (gingerbread).

In addition, the Germans are famous for their love of beer. German beer gardens date back to the Middle Ages, when brewers planted chestnut trees around their storage areas to protect the beer from the sun. Multiple varieties range from a dark amber, hoppy *Altbier* and strong, dark *Weizenbock* to a pale, malty Bavarian *Helles*, a light, with more prominent hop character *Pilsener* and a full, bitter-sweet and delicately hopped *Spezial*. Furthermore, Germans take pride in their sparkling wine called *Sekt*. This delicious wine is made exclusively from grapes produced in Germany. *Sekt* is typically less austere and lower in alcohol than French sparkling wine.

Also, Germany produces the loveliest, lightest and most delicate white wines in the world. Low in alcohol and exquisitely balanced, German wines are known for their charm and subtle nuances. The wines made in Germany are extremely diverse, although they do have some commonalities. Especially acclaimed varieties are Riesling, Silvaner, Kerner, Scheurebe, Ruländer/Grauburgunder and Müller-Thurgau.

A group of German schoolboys at Steuben Day Parade. The four years of primary school (Grundschule) may be followed by one of several different educational options. (Richard B. Levine, Levine & Roberts Stock Photography)

¹³ EDUCATION

Education in Germany is free and compulsory between the ages of 6 and 18. Although it is administered independently by each of Germany's 16 federal states, the basic pattern is the same throughout the country. The four years of primary school (*Grundschule*) are followed by several different options. Students may spend two years in "orientation grades" and then six years in a *Realschule* in preparation for technical college, or they may spend five years in a *Hauptschule*, followed by a three-year vocational apprenticeship. The other principal option is the nine-year gymnasium education that prepares students for a university. In addition, however, some states offer the comprehensive system (*Gesamtschulen*), a system that had also been used in the former East Germany, where all students attend a single school from the fifth year onward. University attendance is still almost free—students have to pay only a small fee, although this is changing.

Currently, the German education system is undergoing a profound transformation. In this manner, policymakers and university administrations initiated a series of reforms to adapt the university system to new international standards. These innovations involve the switch to staggered degrees such as bachelor's and master's degrees and the introduction of tuition fees and admission tests. Among other changes are the emergence of private facilities for academic training and the development of the stronger strategic alliances between universities and institutes outside the higher education system.

Another important reform in the sphere of education is the "excellence initiative." This initiative is geared toward promoting post-graduate systems, outstanding centers in specific fields of research, and the research portfolios of nine top universities (the LMU and TU in Munich, TU Karlsruhe, RWTH Aachen and the universities of Konstanz, Göttingen, Heidelberg, Freiburg, and the FU Berlin). The goal of the reforms is to strengthen research facilities and to ensure excellence of faculty and high quality of tertiary education. The incentives aim to reestablish Germany's leading position in education on the international level.

¹⁴ CULTURAL HERITAGE

Germany is famous for its great baroque, classical, and romantic composers such as Johann Sebastian Bach, Ludwig van Beethoven, Felix Mendelssohn, Robert Schumann, Johannes Brahms, and Richard Wagner. Well-known 20th-century composers include Paul Hindemith, Kurt Weill, Karlheinz Stockhausen, Carl Orff, and Hans Werner Henze. The Bayreuth opera festival has been a national tradition since its founding by Richard Wagner. In literature, among the greatest German names stand Johann Wolfgang von Goethe, Friedrich von Schiller, Heinrich Heine and Rainer Maria Rilke. Modern German writers include Georg Kaiser, Bertolt Brecht, Nobel Prize winner Thomas Mann, Marie-Luise Kaschnitz, Günter Grass, and Nobel Prize winner Heinrich Böll.

A distinguished name in German art is that of Albrecht Dürer, whose masterpieces embrace both paintings and woodcuts. In the 20th century, German artists have been associated with expressionism and an artistic movement known as Der Blaue Reiter (The Blue Rider), which advocated greater freedom in art. In 1919, German architect Walter Gropius founded the famous Bauhaus school of art and design, which stressed form based on function.

¹⁵ WORK

The total labor force of Germany numbered over 43 million people in 2006. Of these nearly 2 million were foreign workers, including Turks, citizens of the former Yugoslavia, and Italians. The German work day begins early. Many people employed in factories start work at 7:00 AM, and most stores and offices are open by 8:00. On average Germans work 40 hours per week, which is also the average work week for the European Union. German men and women retire around 61 years of age.

The largest proportion of Germans are employed in services (nearly 70% of the economy is composed of service industries), followed by traditional industry, with merely 3% employed in agriculture. Germany's top employer is Deutsche Post (German Postal Service). Employing over 500,000 people, its total revenue amounts to $58.58 billion. The second largest employer is a world known electronics company: Siemens. With total revenue of $90.68 billion Siemens provides employment for 461,000 people. Next in line are two of Germany's auto manufacturers, Volkswagen and Daimler AG. Operating on a worldwide scale, Volkswagen develops vehicles and engines, as well as produces and sells passenger cars, commercial vehicles, trucks and buses. Daimler AG is a producer of the Mercedes-Benz, Maybach (luxury automobiles), and Smart (micro hybrid cars) and is the world's 13th largest car manufacturer.

As the success of the Siemens and German auto-manufacturers demonstrates, Germans can boast superior engineering and technological advances. German inventors are credited with a remarkable number of important items. For example, Felix Hoffmann produced the first aspirin tablet, the creation of modern printing press is attributed to Johannes Gutenberg, and Hans Riegel introduced the world to Gummy Bears. Needless to say, German engineered cars have long been the standard for the auto industry worldwide.

The standard of living of Germans is comparatively high even after the economic challenges caused by unification. There is an extended social safety net that provides German citizens with considerable job security. Wages are reasonably high, making the German labor force one of the best paid in the world. However, there are more than 7 million foreigners living and working in Germany, 1.5 million foreigners who have taken German citizenship, and some 4.5 million repatriates. The integration of foreigners and provision of equitable work benefits and salaries have been an on-going challenge.

¹⁶ SPORTS

Most Germans greatly enjoy sports. In 2007 Germany could boast over 87,000 sport clubs, and approximately 27 million people—or one third of Germany's population—are members of sport clubs. In addition, nearly 12 million Germans engage in sports without belonging to any particular affiliation. Sports are usually run by private regional organizations, but they are also supported by federal government.

Soccer (Fussball) is Germany's most popular sport. Some of its teams have international reputations, and its national soccer association boasts over 4 million members. There are thousands of amateur soccer clubs throughout Germany and more than 6.3 million Germans are members of the Deutsche Fussballbund (German Football Federation). In 2006 Germany proudly hosted the FIFA World Cup.

In addition to soccer, Germany has a tradition of world-class gymnasts. Other popular sports include shooting, handball, golf, horseback riding, and tennis (a sport in which the Germans can claim three of the world's top players: Steffi Graf, Boris Becker, and Tommy Haas). Swimming is very popular too and almost every town has a public Schwimmbad (swimming pool). American football and baseball are not very widespread, but are increasing in popularity.

Recreational sports include hiking, bicycling, camping, sailing, and swimming. The mountainous areas have hundreds of kilometers of picturesque hiking trails. In winter, skiers flock to the German Alps to enjoy both downhill and cross-country skiing. Generally, Germans excel at winter sports, and have won Olympic gold medals for luge, bobsled, and speed skating. Recently, Formula 1 race-car driving has become one of the most popular spectator sports in Germany. Particularly it rose in popularity when Michael Schumacher, the German racer for the Ferrari team, won the World Championship two years in a row.

¹⁷ ENTERTAINMENT AND RECREATION

Many Germans enjoy relaxing around the television set; over 90% of the population owns one, and more than half of all Germans watch television on a daily basis. The use of television and radio is not free—people have to pay a small monthly fee. German teens, like those in other countries, like to buy and listen to the latest pop music recordings. The German people enjoy the scenic forest, mountain, and lake regions of their country while engaging in various outdoor activities, including hiking and jogging (special jogging trails are called Trimmdich-Pfade, or "keep-fit trails"). Cultural entertainment available in all major cities and many smaller ones include museums, concerts, exhibits, and historic sites.

Many Germans have as many as six weeks of paid vacation during the year. And Germans love to travel. Common vacation destinations include the beaches of the North and Baltic Seas, and the mountains, such as Bavarian Alps, the Black Forest, and the Harz Mountains. Since Germans love the sun, Italy, Greece, Spain, and even Egypt have become favorite vacation spots for many families. When vacations begin, the Autobahn, Germany's interstate highway system, is usually plugged up by the mass of cars moving south. The Germans call this "Verkehrsstau"—traffic jam.

¹⁸ FOLK ART, CRAFTS, AND HOBBIES

In their homes or in small shops, German craftspeople still produce traditional works of art and souvenirs. As in many other countries, each German region has its own folk craft tradition. For example Bavarians are particularly known for their wood carvings. As a whole, however, German handwork is famous for its painstakingly crafted intricate decorations and colorful styles. In ancient times German craftsmen used to be organized in guilds and the process of becoming a craftsman involved being a *Lehrling* (apprentice). Apprenticeship involved traveling from town to town getting employed temporarily by different *Meister* (masters). Through this process an apprentice gradually perfected and enriched his skills. The remnants of these practices still survive in some parts of Germany.

German Christmas markets are a perfect place to look for German handicrafts. Choice of crafts ranges from traditional German angels and nutcrackers to smoking men, with all kinds aromatic essences rising from their pipes. Handcrafted clocks (including the cuckoo clocks), beer steins, figurines, Christmas ornaments, wooden dolls, music boxes and other types of woodcarvings don't exhaust the list. The Crystal Road and the Porcelain Road in Bavaria are other important centers of centuries-old glassblowing tradition. Running through the Bavarian Forest they offer a wide variety of traditional glassworks and crystal figurines called Hummel figurines. Zwiesel is yet another great place for delicate glass sculptures.

There is no city in the world that manufactures finer cutlery then Solingen. The Solingen tradition perfected over many generations offers Puma's most prominent knives: Universal Jagdtaschenmesser and the famous Great White Hunter. Several other knife producers operating from Solingen include Kissing Cranes, Richartz, Hen and Rooster, Bulldog Brand, German Eye, Hubertus, Herbertz and others.

The Erzgebirge region in Southeast Germany offers its own tradition of craftsmanship. Working in generations-old, family-based workshops, men and women of Erzgebrige carry on a unique tradition of wood-carving, producing objects of singular beauty and universal appeal. Commonly these items reflect popular folk motifs, but no two craftsmen approach them in the same way. In addition to world-famous *Räuchermännchen* (hand-carved smoking figures), pyramids and nutcrackers and other local crafts, Erzgebirge is also known for ethnic events that include the *Bergparade*, a traditional once-yearly music parade and the Erzgebirge folklore festival.

19 SOCIAL PROBLEMS

The expenses of unification and a worldwide recession weakened the German economy in the early 1990s. The social, political and economic integration of East and West Germany remains an issue. Furthermore, Germany encounters a demographic challenge. The proportion of elderly people in the population mounts while growth rate is at negative 0.03%. Other challenges that Germany continues to confront entail cutting back pollution and resolving the shortage of affordable housing.

Moreover, Germany faces numerous problems caused by the increasing number of immigrants. Discrimination and even violence against immigrants from the Middle East and southern Europe are some of the most prevalent concerns. Returning from the former Soviet Union, repatriates of German descent deepen the problem. To address this challenge, the German government implemented a series of reforms to better integrate immigrants into German society. The reforms made it easier for immigrants to acquire German citizenship. Also, the new immigration law provided for the first time an all-embracing legal framework that considers all aspects of immigration policy.

In addition Germany confronts protracting unemployment at 8 % and inflation in 2%. Since the mid-2000s, the federal government has implemented extensive economic reforms attempting to meet these challenges. Those reforms did address economic stagnation in the short term, but did not completely cure the existing problems. Germany takes a great pride in being a welfare state that considers the social protection of all its citizens to be a priority. However, this comprehensive system of health, pension, accident, long-term care, and unemployment benefits exhibits significant flaws and is in need of fundamental reforms.

20 GENDER ISSUES

For the past several decades, traditional gender roles in Germany underwent significant transformation. If under Hitler, German women were expected to give up work and bear children and were reduced in their social activity to a purely biological purpose, the situation is completely changed now. There has been impressive progress with regard to equal rights for women stipulated in the Basic Law. Based on 2006 data, in the sphere of education girls have outnumbered boys: in elementary schools girls comprise 56% of graduates, and women account for 54% of students in degree courses at universities. Needless to say, more and more women are embarking on professional careers.

German women also established themselves in politics. There is considerable representation of female members in the SPD and CDU, the two main political parties in Germany. Furthermore, the proportion of women in the Bundestag (lower house of the German parliament) is constantly increasing. To compare, in 1980 women amounted to 8% of all members of parliament, while in 2005 this figure had risen to almost 32%. Besides, in 2005 Angela Merkel became the first female German chancellor. Today, Merkel is the leader of a wave of women public servants entering and transforming the local and national political scene.

As of 2008, 67% of women in Western Germany and 73% in Eastern Germany worked. At the same time, men generally have a full-time job, while women, especially those with small children, work only part-time. Although women account for approximately a third of the labor force, men earn higher salaries. Statistics indicate that female workers earn 74% of their male counterparts' pay and salaried staff only 71%. This means that even though women gained power in politics, a large number of women still work in lower-paid positions or are underpaid. And in certain instances women still encounter substantial obstacles. To illustrate, only 15% of university professors are female and only one third of female university students are research assistants.

Furthermore, in a majority of cases women do the prevailing share of housekeeping work. Many fathers enjoy spending time with their children but women, even though employed, dedicate at least twice as much time as their husbands to taking care of their children. In the recent past it was almost exclusively women who have taken parental leave. Yet in the first nine months after introduction of parental support, the proportion of fathers who took leave to concentrate on childcare almost trebled, to 9.6 %.

Although Germany still faces gender inequality issues, the traditional role of a housewife has been very much circumscribed. The German Law provides a firm foundation for German women on their way to true equality. Currently, German women direct their main efforts towards obtaining equality in the workplace and towards achieving equal pay for equal work. And as past experience demonstrates, these efforts have every opportunity to succeed.

21 BIBLIOGRAPHY

Ardagh, John. *Germany and the Germans: An Anatomy of Society Today*. New York: Harper & Row, 1987.

CountryReports.Org. Germany. http://www.countryreports.org/country.aspx?countryid=91&countryName=Germany (11 May 2008).

Eidson, John R. "Germans." *Encyclopedia of World Cultures (Europe)*. Boston: G. K. Hall, 1992.

Eurostat. "EU vs. US Working Hours, Employment, Education & Retirement Statistics." 14 August 2007. http://americaninathens.wordpress.com/2007/08/14/eu-vs-usa-labor-issues/ (11 May 2008).

Facts about Germany. http://www.tatsachen-ueber-deutschland.de/en/society/main-content-08/further-reforms.html (11 May 2008).

Gall, Timothy, and Susan Gall, ed. *Junior Worldmark Encyclopedia of the Nations*. Detroit: UXL, 1996.

German Culture site. "German Women and 3 K's." http://www.germanculture.com.ua/library/weekly/aa080601ahtm (11 May 2008).

Germany in Pictures. Minneapolis: Lerner Publications, 1994.

German Embassy, Washington, DC. "Culture and Life". http://www.germany.info/relaunch/culture/culture.html (26 May 2008).

Hargrove, Jim. *Germany: Enchantment of the World Series*. Chicago: Children's Press, 1991.

Illustrated Encyclopedia of Mankind. London: Marshall Cavendish, 1978.

Lye, Keith. *Passport to Germany*. New York: Franklin Watts, 1992.

My Global Career 500. http://www.myglobalcareer.com/my-global-career-500/ (23 May 2008).

Oppenheimer, Paul. *Till Eulenspiegel, His Adventures*. Oxford University Press, 1995.

—revised by A. Golovina Khadka

GREEKS

LOCATION: Greece
POPULATION: 11 million
LANGUAGE: Greek
RELIGION: Eastern Orthodox Christian Church

1 INTRODUCTION

Of the earliest Greek societies, the most important was the Minoan civilization, which flourished in the Bronze Age on the island of Crete (c.2700–1450 BC). It reached its peak around 1600 BC, and was notable for its magnificent cities, extensive trade, and its use of writing. Second, the mainland Mycenaean civilization, which flourished between 1600 and 1100, imported from the Minoans the first Greek writing and is reflected in the Homeric epics, *The Iliad and The Odyssey*.

Between the 8th and the 6th centuries BC, the Greek city-state, or *polis*, took shape, and the concepts of the rule of law and participatory democracy were conceived. By the 6th century the city-states of Athens and Sparta were rivals for dominance. The classical "golden age" of Athens in the 5th century encompassed great achievements in government, philosophy, drama, sculpture, and architecture. The influence of Greek civilization was expanded through the conquests of Alexander the Great (356–323 BC) before Greece was conquered by the Romans in 146 BC.

After more than 1,000 years as part of the Byzantine (or Eastern Roman) Empire, Greece came under Turkish rule after Constantinople, the Byzantine capital, fell to the Ottomans in 1453. After a 10-year struggle for independence, Greek sovereignty was established in 1831, marking the beginning of modern Greece. Over the next century, the nation's boundaries expanded as it gradually acquired islands and mainland territories. The first half of the 20th century was marked by the two world wars as well as hostilities with Turkey, and a civil war between 1944 and 1949. Greece became a member of the North Atlantic Treaty Organization (NATO) in 1952, and a full member of the European Community in 1981.

After seven years of totalitarian military rule from 1967 to 1974, Greece became democratically governed. Its international concerns since World War II have been dominated by the Cold War and its rivalry with Turkey over the status of Cyprus. Since the break-up of the former Yugoslavia in 1991, Greece has vigorously opposed the use of the name "Republic of Macedonia" by the Former Yugoslavian Republic of Macedonia (FYROM), fearing an expansionist threat to the Greek part of Macedonia—a geographical territory divided among Greece, Bulgaria, and FYROM.

2 LOCATION AND HOMELAND

Located in the southernmost part of the Balkan peninsula, Greece includes over 6,000 islands in the Ionian and Aegean Seas, of which about 227 are inhabited. About 80% of the country is covered by mountains, which form part of the Alpine system. Mt. Olympus, the legendary home of the Greek gods, is the highest peak, rising to 9,573 feet in east central Greece. The nation's coastline—over 14,000 km in length—is one of the longest in the world.

Sunday	Kyriakí
Monday	Deftéra
Tuesday	Tríti
Wednesday	Tetárti
Thursday	Pémpti
Friday	Paraskeví
Saturday	Sávato

⁴ FOLKLORE

The ancient Greeks believed that each person's fate was predetermined. People's lives were a sum of their individual actions and their destiny, from which not even gods could escape. Unlike monotheistic deities, Greek gods were not above human passions and fallibilities. There were priests and priestesses at shrines called oracles, of which the most important was Delphi in the south. The gods were honored publicly at great festivals (including the Olympics) and privately at altars in people's homes with offerings of food and wine. Greek mythology was a way to explain the world, with each god and goddess responsible for a specific aspect of life. It has been tremendously influential in the ways the Western word has configured key ideas, like religion and national identity.

⁵ RELIGION

The Eastern Orthodox Christian Church has played a central role in Greek life. During the 400 years of Ottoman rule, the Church was the main unifying force of the Greek people. Greek history, art, literature, and music were preserved and transmitted partly through the church. Over 98% of today's Greeks belong to the Orthodox Church, which is described in the 1975 constitution as the "established religion" of Greece. Although freedom of religion is guaranteed to all Greeks, the Orthodox Church enjoys a special relationship with the government. The president of Greece must be a member and is sworn into office with church rites. Major religious holidays are also considered civil holidays.

It is common for religious Greeks to keep icons in an area of their homes, together with holy oil, holy water, and a special lamp. Many pray to a particular saint or saints in times of trouble, and pilgrimages are made to shrines considered especially holy. Religious customs have incorporated earlier elements of pagan beliefs.

⁶ MAJOR HOLIDAYS

Many of the major Greek holidays are those of the Orthodox Church. The most important are Easter and the Holy Week preceding it, which occur at a slightly different time from the Western calendar, and the Greeks emphasize the Resurrection rather than the Crucifixion. The New Year is dedicated to St. Basil and celebrated with gift giving and parties. Although Christmas trees have now dominated as the world's commonest festive decoration, the peculiar Greek equivalent was a ship to symbolize the ship that brought St. Basil to Greece. One New Year's tradition consists of hiding a coin in the dough of a special cake spiced with cinnamon, nutmeg, and orange peel. The person in whose piece the coin is found is thought to be blessed with prosperity and health for the year to come. Greeks celebrate both their birthdays and their name-days, the latter on the day dedicated to the saint for whom they are named.

The majority of Greece's 11 million people are of Greek ethnic descent. Minorities include Thrace Muslims, Slavs, Albanians, Armenians, and Vlachs, a people who lived seminomadically in the northern mountains in the 19th century. The massive emigration to North America, northern Europe, Australia, and other destinations in the first half of the 20th century has been offset by incoming immigration from the Balkans and Near Eastern countries at the end of the century. The Greeks travel extensively, and many live and work abroad.

³ LANGUAGE

The language is Modern Greek. Until 1976 a formal, if artificial, version called *katharevousa*, "pure," was used in official business. Originating in Byzantine scholarship, *katharevousa* attempted to imitate classical Greek, against the living language of the people (*demotiki,* "demotic"). Katharevousa received momentum in the 19th century, and the heated debate about which version should be used came down as "The Language Question."

one	éna
two	dío
three	tría
four	téssera
five	pénde
six	éxi
seven	eptá
eight	októ
nine	enéa
ten	déka

7 RITES OF PASSAGE

Greece is a modern, industrialized country with a Christian tradition. Many of the rites of passage that young people undergo are religious rituals, such as baptism, first Communion, and marriage. Unlike Roman Catholics, the first communion is not especially celebrated, and there is no confirmation.

8 INTERPERSONAL RELATIONS

The Greeks are known for their lively, outgoing nature. Spending time in *parëes*, or groups of friends, is a common form of entertainment in private houses and coffee shops, waterfront taverns, and village squares, with people gesturing energetically in conversation. It is acceptable for two heterosexual women, less so of men, to walk in public arm-in-arm as a sign of camaraderie.

9 LIVING CONDITIONS

The bigger the city the more people live in apartment blocks. This widespread European building arrangement is a compound of apartments in a single building. Usually floors vary from two to six. City dwellers comprise more than half the population, with Athens, the capital, approaching 5 million. In smaller towns and villages, the majority of the people live in family-owned one- and two-storey homes. Many Greeks have summer houses.

The sea has traditionally linked Greek cities and towns. As in all of Europe, Greeks rely heavily on public transportation. Athens has an efficient subway. Another one in Thessaloniki, the second largest city, is scheduled to operate in 2013. Nonetheless, the per capita ownership of cars ranks among the highest in Europe.

Health care is provided primarily by the state-run National Health Service. Private facilities are available. The number of doctors is very large (1 for every 450–500 residents), but the bulk of practitioners is concentrated in the bigger cities. However, most towns do have hospitals and/or clinics. Abortion is legal.

10 FAMILY LIFE

The average age at which Greek men normally marry is 28, and the average age for women is 26. Greece has a higher marriage rate and lower divorce rate than the countries of northern Europe. The basic family unit is the nuclear family—a husband, wife, and their children. The bond remains intact even after children marry. It is not considered improper for couples to live with one spouse's family until they are ready to buy their own house. Grown sons and daughters traditionally live with their parents until they marry, and aging parents often join the household when it becomes difficult for them to care for themselves. In January 1983 the Greek parliament legislated changes in the family laws that made divorce easier, abolished the dowry as a legal requirement for marriage, and guaranteed legal equality between marriage partners.

Nowadays rivalries between families and honor-related crimes survive only in a handful of specific rural areas. Westernization, urbanization, and industrialization have modified the traditional ideal of "honorable behavior." Adultery ceased being a penal crime in 1983. Women gained the right to vote in the early 1950s and have dramatically increased their role in the Greek labor force. In the late 1980s women accounted for one-fifth of all industrial jobs and one-third of all jobs in the service sector.

11 CLOTHING

It goes without saying that the traditional 19th-century costume of tunic, vest, and pleated kilt-like skirt is worn only by folk dancers at festivals in the 21st century.

12 FOOD

Greek cooking exemplifies the Mediterranean cuisine, where olive oil predominates. Staples include tomatoes, rice, yogurt, shish kebab, and feta cheese (made from goat's or sheep's milk). Bread is served with every meal. Lamb is used extensively, and so are seasonal vegetables, fruit, and an abundance of native herbs, such as thyme, basil, oregano, rosemary, rue, and sage. An example of a traditional dish is minced meat with spices, rice, and herbs, wrapped in grape leaves or stuffed into vegetables. Greek pastries—many of them extremely sweet and made from a paper-thin dough called *filo*—are eaten not as desserts but as afternoon or late-night snacks. Two typically Greek drinks are *ouzo*, the aniseed residue of winemaking, and *retsina*, a resinated white wine. A toast of *"Yiassas"* ("your health") can often be heard, together with the clinking of glasses, wherever Greeks gather to enjoy food and drink.

13 EDUCATION

Approximately 20.6% of Greeks are high school graduates. One is considered to be illiterate if one has not finished the six-years of primary school (not simply if one cannot read and write). By this (more rigorous) standard, illiteracy is 7%. Education is compulsory for nine years until the age of 15. Students can choose between three more optional years in either high school or technical programs. There is a highly competitive university system, as well as postsecondary technical and vocational schools. The system is state-run and free of charge at all stages, although there exist private schools for those who wish to opt out of the state system.

14 CULTURAL HERITAGE

Even before the great flowering of culture in Athens in the 5th century BC, Greece had already given the world the *Iliad* and *Odyssey* of Homer. With the classical golden age of Athens came the philosophical teachings of Socrates, Plato and Aristotle, the great tragedies of Aeschylus, Euripides and Sophocles, and the comedies of Aristophanes. Greek sculpture progressed from stylization to naturalism, while Greek architecture, which had already introduced the grid town plan and the temple, produced the Parthenon and gave the world the Doric, Ionic, and Corinthian styles.

In the 20th century there was a renaissance of Greek literature that includes the writings of novelist Nikos Kazantzakis and the poetry of C. P. Cavafy, Nikos Gatsos, and Nobel laureates George Seferis and Odysseus Elytis. Modern Greek literature was strongly influenced by such political events as the Greco-Italian war of 1940–41, the German occupation, the civil war of 1944–49, and the military regime of 1967–75. Well-known composers include Mikis Theodorakis, who set Elytis's major work, *To Axion Esti*, to music, and Manos Hadjidakis, who wrote the film score for *Never on Sunday*. Contemporary composers often use the instruments and melodies of Greek

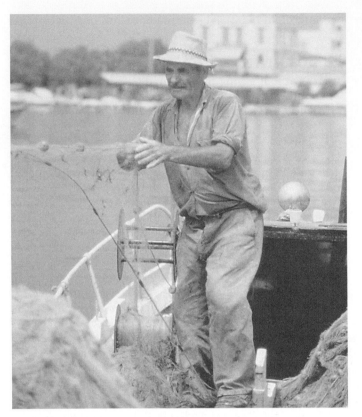

Greek fisherman working his nets from the deck of his boat. Aside from farming, the other major occupations of Greek villagers are fishing and sheep- or goat-herding. (Cory Langley)

folk music, especially the *bouzouki*, a mandolin-like stringed instrument, as well as the *santouri* (dulcimer), clarinet, lute, and drums.

15 WORK

Economic development has increased in services, international trade, shipping and tourism. Greece is among the least industrialized nations of Europe. Food, beverage, and tobacco processing are the foremost industries, followed by textiles and clothing, metallurgy, chemical manufacturing and shipbuilding. An important part of the economy has been family-owned small businesses; in 1990, 85% of Greek manufacturing concerns had fewer than 10 employees. The proportion of Greeks engaged in farming had declined to one-third by 1990. Important farm products include grain, olives, cotton, tobacco, fruits, and wheat. Aside from farming, the other major occupations of Greek villagers are fishing and sheep- or goat-herding.

16 SPORTS

In sports, Greece's Olympic tradition dates back to ancient times. Today, soccer and basketball are the most popular sports. Other favorite sports include volleyball, tennis, swimming and water skiing at the nation's many beaches, sailing, fishing, and mountain climbing.

17 ENTERTAINMENT AND RECREATION

In the country, coffee shops—generally in the village square—are popular gathering places where people congregate after work to socialize. In urban areas, Greeks enjoy television, mov-

ies, theater, and concerts. Forms of traditional entertainment include folk dances performed by dance troupes wearing colorful costumes, with accompaniment led by the bouzouki, and *karagiozi*, a shadow puppet show that is performed live and can also be seen weekly on television. Operas, concerts, ballets and ancient Greek dramas are presented at the Athens Festival each summer. Classical drama is also performed in open-air theaters, the most famous of which is in Epidaurus.

18 FOLK ART, CRAFTS, AND HOBBIES

Craftspeople throughout Greece practice weaving, knitting, embroidery, carving, metalworking, and pottery. Village women are known for their colorful fabrics and carpets and elaborate wall-hangings.

19 SOCIAL PROBLEMS

HIV/AIDS and drug abuse are major problems. The proportion of drug users doubled in the 1980s, with the largest increase among women and the poor. Marijuana is the most frequently used drug. A major domestic problem in Greek society is illegal immigration from the Balkans and the Middle East. Homelessness is exceptionally low, due to strong family ties.

20 GENDER ISSUES

Equality of the sexes has been established by a 1983 law. As everywhere else in the Western world, discrimination on the base of one's sex is something of a thing of the past, although there is always room for improvement. One out of six Greek members of parliament is a woman. Around 60% of each year's college graduates are women. As of the late 2000s, there has been some debate about same-sex marriage, but this remains illegal.

21 BIBLIOGRAPHY

Bennett, A. Linda, ed. *Encyclopedia of World Cultures (Europe)*. Boston: G. K. Hall, 1992.

Cogg, Richard. *A Short History of Modern Greece*. 2nd edition. Cambridge: Cambridge University Press, 1986.

Fodor's Greek Islands. New York: Fodor's Travel, 2008.

Gage, Nicholas. *Hellas: A Portrait of Greece*. New York: Villard Books, 1987.

Gall, Timothy, and Susan Gall, ed. *Junior Worldmark Encyclopedia of the Nations*. Detroit: UXL, 1996.

Hubbard, Monica M., and Beverly Baer, ed. *Cities of the World: Europe and the Middle East*. Detroit: Gale Research, 1993.

Illustrated Encyclopedia of Mankind. London: Marshall Cavendish, 1978.

Leontis, Artemis. *Culture and Customs of Greece*. Westport, CT: Greenwood Publishing Group Inc., 2008.

Moss, Joyce, and George Wilson. *Peoples of the World: Western Europeans*. Detroit: Gale Research, 1993.

Ratto, Stefania. *Greece*. Berkeley; Los Angeles; London: University of California Press, 2008.

Steinberg, Rolf, ed. *Continental Europe*. Insight Guides. Singapore: APA Publications, 1989

—revised by K. Yiavis

HUGARIANS

ALTERNATE NAMES: Magyars (Ethnic Hungarians)
LOCATION: Hungary
POPULATION: About 10 million
LANGUAGE: Hungarian (Magyar); German
RELIGION: Roman Catholic; Reformed Calvinist; Lutheran; smaller numbers of Jews, members of the Eastern Orthodox Church, and other Protestant sects

¹ INTRODUCTION

The western portion of present-day Hungary was conquered by the Romans in 9 BC. The Magyars, who had invaded the Carpathian basin in AD 896, were converted to Christianity at the beginning of the 11th century by King Stephen, who remains a national hero. Turkish rule, beginning in the 16th century, was followed by union with the Habsburgs, which lasted until modern times, although the Magyars gained some autonomy under the dual monarchy from 1867 to World War I.

After 40 years behind the "Iron Curtain," Hungary held its first free elections in 1990 and began transforming its economy, applying for membership in the European Union (EU) in 1994. Hungary joined the North Atlantic Treaty Organization (NATO) in 1999 and the EU in 2004.

² LOCATION AND HOMELAND

Hungary is a landlocked nation in central Europe. While other political boundaries in the region were redrawn in the early 1990s, Hungary's territory remained unchanged: it is bordered by Austria and Slovenia in the w, Slovakia in the n, Ukraine in the ne, Romania in the e, and Croatia and Yugoslavia in the s. Geographically, Hungary consists of four major regions: the Danube River valley, the Great Plain, the Lake Balaton region, and the Northern Mountains. Its highest elevation is Kekes Mountain, which rises to a height of 3,093 feet.

Ethnic Hungarians, or Magyars, make up the vast majority (some 92.3%) of Hungary's population of 10 million. While their cultural ties have always been with the West, particularly Austria, the Magyars were originally a central Asian people who migrated to the Carpathian basin in the 9th century. Hungary's ethnic minorities include Germans, Slovaks, Croats, and Romanians. Approximately 1.9% of the population is Roma.

³ LANGUAGE

The Hungarian, or Magyar, language is universally spoken in Hungary. Since it is a Finno-Ugric rather than an Indo-European language, it has practically no resemblance to such commonly spoken Western languages as English, French, Spanish, or German. The only languages it resembles at all are Finnish, Estonian, and a few others spoken in remote parts of Russia and Siberia. Hungarian is notoriously difficult for non-native speakers to master, with its accent marks, double letters (*cs, gy, ny*), and lengthy words (due partly to the practice of adding prepositions to the ends of words). The most popular second language in Hungary is German, a legacy from the days of the Habsburgs. Despite years of mandatory classes, Hungarians never became comfortable with Russian, which was foreign to them linguistically, as it was not for the Slavic peoples

of other former communist "satellites" such as Poland and Czechoslovakia.

NUMBERS

one	egy
two	kettö
three	három
four	négy
five	öt
six	hat
seven	hét
eight	nyolc
nine	kilenc
ten	tíz

DAYS OF THE WEEK

Sunday	vasánarp
Monday	hétfö
Tuesday	kedd
Wednesday	szerda
Thursday	csütörtök
Friday	péntek
Saturday	szombat

⁴ FOLKLORE

For the most part, the traditional folklore of Hungary is dying out. Even major life-cycle events such as births, weddings, and deaths are commemorated in modern, Western ways. However, some urban dwellers enjoy harking back to their peasant roots with the custom of *disnótor,* a feast that follows the slaughtering of a pig. In addition, the Christmas custom called *Betlehemzés,* in which men and boys perform a nativity play using a model church and manger that they carry with them from door to door, is still alive in some regions. Another religious tradition—revived in some rural areas—is the Eastertime fertility ritual of *locsolkodas,* in which boys and men sprinkle water or perfume on girls and receive a painted Easter egg in return. The traditional wine harvest festival is still held in wine-growing regions in September and October, but these days, as often as not, it includes a rock band and outdoor disco.

⁵ RELIGION

About 52% of Hungarians are Roman Catholic, 16% Reformed Calvinists, and 3% Lutherans, with smaller numbers of Jews, members of the Eastern Orthodox Church, and other Protestant sects. In general, the Hungarians are not a deeply religious people. Historically, the dominant religion of the country changed several times under different rulers, including a period under the Turks when thousands of Hungarians converted to Islam. Thus the Hungarians are known for being more pragmatic—and tolerant—about religion than many of their neighbors.

⁶ MAJOR HOLIDAYS

New Year's, or *Farsang,* begins a season of balls throughout the country that lasts until Ash Wednesday. The *Busójárás* carnival, one of the liveliest celebrations—comparable to the American Mardi Gras in New Orleans—is held in February, on the last weekend before Lent. On March 15, the 1848–49 Revolution is commemorated with speeches, flag-waving, and parades. Large crowds gather in the capital city of Budapest to

HUNGARIANS

emony, takes place in February of the final school year. During a ceremony attended by parents, grandparents, and teachers, members of the junior class perform a solemn ritual of pinning ribbons on members of the senior class. Entertainment follows, and includes both contemporary dancers and traditional folk dancing in costume by members of the senior class. The second ritual, held in May just prior to final exams, involves marching or *ballagas*. The night before the ballagas, the school is decorated with garlands of fresh flowers by members of the junior class. The seniors dress specially for the occasion, often in black and white, and carry embroidered pouches containing some salt, money, and a *pagacsa* or small roll, supplies to support them as they embark on the adventure of life beyond school. Singing, they march through every classroom single file, holding onto the shoulder of the person in front and gathering flowers from onlookers. Other students stand at attention, and family members crowd the halls. Many families continue the celebration with a party at home when the march is finished.

⁸ INTERPERSONAL RELATIONS

Social interaction among Hungarians is formal and polite. A young woman will often have her hand kissed in greeting, especially by an older man, and this custom is referred to in the traditional greeting of young people toward their elders (*Csókolom*—"I kiss it"). Even close friends shake hands when greeting each other. However, at resort areas in the summer it is common for women to appear topless.

Dogs are especially beloved by Hungarians, and many own the popular *puli* or *komondor* breeds.

⁹ LIVING CONDITIONS

After World War II, a severe housing shortage developed in Hungary as workers flocked to the cities from rural villages, attracted by the communist government's industrialization program. Most existing apartments had only one room and a kitchen area and many had been damaged in the war. Lacking resources to build enough low-rent apartments, the government encouraged private housing construction, which improved matters somewhat for higher-income individuals. However, those with less money continued to depend on government-subsidized housing, which had long waiting lists. Housing is still a problem in urban areas, one which has been cited as a prime cause of stress within families.

Work-related stress, smoking, and the heavy Hungarian diet contribute to a high rate of heart disease among Hungarians, who have had the world's highest suicide rate for most of the last century. Average life expectancy was 73 in 2008. Under the communist regime in the 1980s about 99% of the population was covered by national health insurance. Since the collapse of communism, Hungary's health care system became more decentralized and privatized. Employees pay 3% of their income to the social insurance fund, but the population also pays local and national income tax, which helps to finance the health care system. Patients also make co-payments on certain services, including pharmaceuticals, dental care, and rehabilitation. These out-of-pocket payments have increased substantially since 1990, and currently contribute 18% to health care financing.

Hungary's transportation facilities, whose hub is Budapest, have been improving steadily since the 1960s, and the larger

celebrate this event. Easter Monday is the most important religious holiday in Hungary.

Although the spirit of May Day celebrations has changed since the collapse of communism, the day is still celebrated as a workers' holiday. August 20, St. Stephen's Day, is Hungary's national day, celebrated with fireworks throughout the country; in Budapest, a million people gather on the banks of the Danube to watch the display. Proclamation of the Republic Day on October 23, commemorating the 1956 uprising against the communist regime, is marked by torch-lit processions. Christmas and Boxing Day are celebrated privately in family gatherings.

Instead of their own birthdays, Hungarians, like people in other primarily Catholic countries, tend to celebrate the feast day of the saint for whom they are named (special calendars even provide dates for those with purely secular names). The customary gifts are flowers, wine, or cake, all of which can be given any time in the week following the name day.

⁷ RITES OF PASSAGE

Hungary is a relatively modern, industrialized, Christian country. Hence, many of the rites of passage that young people undergo are religious rituals, such as baptism, first Communion, confirmation, and marriage. In addition, a student's progress through the education system is marked by many families with graduation parties.

Two special ceremonies mark students' graduation from high school. The first, known as *szalagavato* or the ribbon cer-

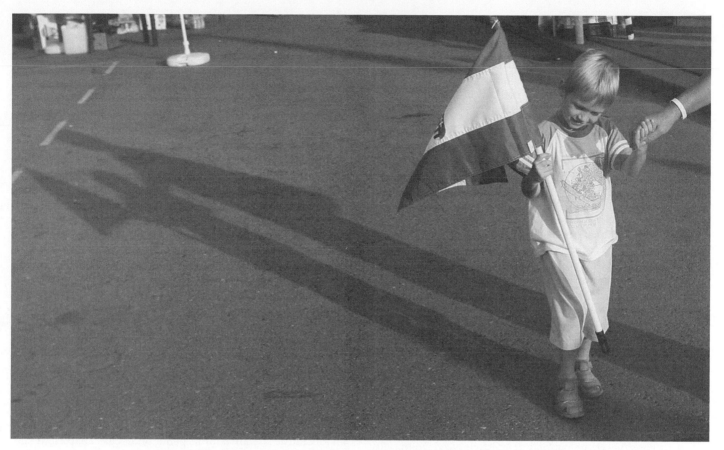

A boy holds a Hungarian flag in Budapest, Hungary. (Joe Klamar/AFP/Getty Images)

cities have good transport systems. The main waterway is the Danube River.

¹⁰ FAMILY LIFE

Traditionally, village households in Hungary were composed of either nuclear or extended families, a pattern which sometimes varied even within a single village. Today, the nuclear family is more prevalent in the country as well as in urban areas. In the past, it was frowned upon for a woman to remain unmarried beyond the age of 22 (27 for a man), but this is changing. The traditional Hungarian wedding is an elaborate and expensive affair. Patterns of family life shifted under the communists, the most notable change being the increased number of women working outside the home. By 1987 around 75% of women had jobs. Although they are still regarded as the head of the household, the traditional dominance of families by men has been reduced. In recent decades the divorce rate has risen; 37.5% of new marriages ended in divorce in 2002.

¹¹ CLOTHING

Hungarians generally wear modern Western-style clothing. Casual wear in the cities includes the jeans, T-shirts, and sweatshirts that might be seen in any industrialized nation. Pantsuits are popular with both men and women for casual and more formal occasions. In rural areas, one can still see women wearing the traditional peasant babushkas on their heads and men wearing hats with floppy brims. The traditional costumes worn for festivals sport much elaborate, brightly col-

ored embroidery. Women wear white embroidered aprons with lace trim, while men wear white plain or embroidered shirts and dark vests, which may also be embroidered.

¹² FOOD

Hungary has long been known for its rich, abundant food. The Hungarian diet is heavily meat-based, with pork the most commonly used ingredient. The most famous dish is probably goulash (*gulyás*), a soup or stew made with meat, onions, potatoes, and, often, other vegetables and seasoned with paprika. Stews with sour cream are called paprikash, and fish soups (called *levesek* or *halászlé*) are also popular. Stuffed cabbages and peppers (*töltött*) are prepared with meat and rice and commonly cooked in tomato sauce or sour cream. The prevalence of the spice paprika in Hungarian cooking has given it a reputation for spiciness, but paprika actually comes in several different strengths and the mildest form is the one used most often. The rich Hungarian desserts resemble those of Germany and Austria; commonly used ingredients include chocolate, various types of nuts, and rich sauces containing cream, more nuts, and more chocolate. Popular desserts include pancakes (*palacsinta*) with dessert fillings (a version of crèpes) and strudel.

¹³ EDUCATION

The Hungarians are a well-educated people: 99.4% of adults are literate, and about 16% of the population have college degrees (approximately 31% of the population was enrolled in college in 2006). Schools provide eight years of primary and four years of secondary education, and education is compulsory until the age of 16. The collapse of communism brought with it major changes in Hungary's educational system. A large percentage of primary and secondary schools are now run by various religious groups, and Russian, once compulsory, is rarely studied now. Hungary is also known for a method of music education devised by the composer Zoltán Kodály.

14 CULTURAL HERITAGE

Hungary has a rich artistic heritage. The arts flourished during the days of the Austro-Hungarian empire and the Dual Monarchy and into the 20th century, although following World War II serious limits were placed on artistic expression by the communist regime. One distinctive feature of Hungarian culture is the interchange between folk art and fine art. Two notable 20th-century examples can be found in the compositions of Béla Bartók and the ceramic sculptures of Margit Kovács.

Notable painters include Mihály Munkácsy in the 19th century and Szinyei Merse at the turn of the 20th. The famous 19th-century composer Franz Liszt spent most of his life abroad but eventually returned to the land of his birth to become the first president of the Hungarian Academy of Music. Other than Bartók, the most prominent 20th-century Hungarian composer was Zoltán Kodály. Much Hungarian literature has been politically inspired. *National Song*, written by the nation's most celebrated poet, Sándor Petofi, became a rallying cry in the mid-19th-century War of Independence. *The Tragedy of Man*, a play written by Imre Madách after Hungary's defeat, is considered the nation's greatest classical drama. Famous 20th-century poets include Endre Ady and Attila József. The works of contemporary writers György Konrád and Péter Esterházy are available in English translation. Imre Kertész is a Hungarian Jewish author, Holocaust survivor, and winner of the Nobel Prize in Literature in 2002.

15 WORK

Employment patterns in Hungary shifted dramatically during the communist industrialization of the 1950s and 1960s. In 1949 only 19% of the labor force was employed in industry; by 2003 that figure had risen to 33.3%. (In the same year, about 5.5% were employed in agriculture, 61.2% in services.) It is not uncommon for Hungarians to hold second and even third jobs in addition to their primary one; in the late 1980s about three-fourths of Hungarian families had income from such economic "sidelines." After the downfall of communism, unemployment rose from about 2% to over 13% by 1993. Although Hungary saw the unemployment level fall to 7.1% by 2007, its labor force participation rate of 57% was one of the lowest in the Organization for Economic Cooperation and Development (OECD). The government implemented an austerity program of tax hikes and subsidy cuts to reduce the large budget deficit, but the reforms caused Hungarians to limit their spending, slowing economic growth to less than 2% in 2007.

16 SPORTS

Soccer ("football") and water polo are both very popular participant sports. Most cities and towns have both indoor and outdoor public pools. Besides soccer, other spectator sports include tennis, skiing, and horse racing.

17 ENTERTAINMENT AND RECREATION

Hungarians like to relax during their leisure hours by reading, watching television and videos, and playing sports. The most popular spectator sport is soccer (called football). Chess is also popular; the young chess master Judit Polgár is a national celebrity. Polgár was the first woman ever to play for the World Chess Championship title, in 2005.

The arts play a substantial role in Hungarian life, especially music. Many cities have symphony or chamber orchestras, theaters, and cultural centers, and there are numerous festivals in the spring, summer, and autumn. Vacation trips are extremely popular among the Hungarians, most of whom head for the country in August. Many own or have access to summer cottages where they can spend time over weekends or during an extended holiday.

18 FOLK ART, CRAFTS, AND HOBBIES

Hungary has a rich tradition of folk art dating back to the 18th century. One famous example is the beautiful, brightly colored embroidery that adorns the traditional costumes of both men and women. The weavers of the Sárköz region produce a distinctive red and black fabric, and simpler cloth is turned out by craftspeople in other parts of the country. The pottery of the Great Plain region is known for its exceptional craftsmanship, and items decorated with writing (usually to commemorate a wedding) are especially prized. Many households are graced by traditional wood carvings, and the art of ceiling and wall painting can be seen in certain parts of the country. Hungarian folk music is known for its pentatonic scale, adapted by such 20th-century composers as Béla Bartók and Zoltán Kodály, and the *csárdás* is a popular folk dance.

19 SOCIAL PROBLEMS

The transition to a market economy caused considerable social disruption and hardship, including spiraling inflation, high rates of unemployment, and the failure of many businesses. In the early 1990s interest rates on loans were as high as 50%. A severe housing shortage continues to be a fact of life in urban areas. Air pollution resulting from industrialization instituted by the former communist regime is a serious problem; the incidence of lung cancer in Budapest has doubled over the past 20 years. Toxic waste dumped by the Soviet military threatens the soil and water supply. While the rights of ethnic minorities are generally respected, there is still widespread discrimination against the Roma in employment, housing, and other areas. Domestic violence is still a problem in Hungary today.

Hungary has an illicit drug problem, being as it is a transshipment point for Southwest Asian heroin and cannabis and for South American cocaine. Chemicals used to make amphetamines and methamphetamines are produced there, and although there are efforts to curb money laundering related to organized crime and drug trafficking, it remains a problem. Hungarians are significant consumers of the drug ecstasy.

20 GENDER ISSUES

Beginning in 1989, many women's and feminist organizations were formed. The Feminist Network, established in 1990, advocates women's equality. Until it turned conservative in the mid-1990s, the Federation of Young Democrats (FIDESZ) was an important political party for liberal young women. The new market economy has affected many women who both provide income and still care for the home and family. While Hungary's abortion laws are relatively liberal, such restrictions as mandated counseling sessions have come into effect in recent years.

Homosexual activity above the age of 20 was decriminalized in 1961, then above the age of 18 in 1978. The age of consent is 14 as of a 2002 Constitutional Court decision. Homosexuals may serve in the military. However, as of 2006, only 18% of Hungarians supported same-sex marriage compared to the EU-wide average of 44%. Budapest has a Gay Pride event every summer, which features a film festival and parade.

21 BIBLIOGRAPHY

Best of Budapest. Oakland, CA: Lonely Planet Publications, 2007.

Biro, Adam. *One Must also be Hungarian.* Chicago: University of Chicago, 2006.

Cartledge, Bryan, Sir. *Will to Survive: A History of Hungary.* London: Timewell Press, 2007.

Dent, Bob. *Budapest: A Cultural History.* Oxford: Oxford University Press, 2007.

Gall, Timothy, and Susan Gall, ed. *Junior Worldmark Encyclopedia of the Nations.* Detroit: UXL, 1996.

Hubbard, Monica M., and Beverly Baer, ed. *Cities of the World: Europe and the Middle East.* Detroit: Gale Research, 1993.

Hungary. London: Dorling Kindersley, 2007.

Hungary: A Country Study. Washington, DC: U.S. Government Printing Office, 1990.

Huseby-Darvas, Eva V. "Hungarians." *Encyclopedia of World Cultures (Europe).* Boston: G. K. Hall, 1992.

Moss, Joyce, and George Wilson. *Peoples of the World: Western Europeans.* Detroit: Gale Research, 1993.

—revised by J. Hobby

ICELANDERS

LOCATION: Iceland
POPULATION: 304,367 (2008 est.)
LANGUAGE: Icelandic
RELIGION: Evangelical Lutheran Church; other Lutheran denominations; Roman Catholic

1 INTRODUCTION

The Republic of Iceland (*Lýdveldidh Ísland*) is a country of dramatic contrasts and contradictions. It is one of the world's most volcanically active regions but also the site of Europe's largest ice-cap—hence its nickname, "the land of fire and ice." An island nation just south of the Arctic Circle, it is considered part of Europe and is a member of NATO, the Nordic Council, and other European organizations. While Icelanders speak the oldest modern language in Europe, their country was the last habitable part of Europe to be settled.

Iceland's first permanent inhabitants were Norwegian settlers who arrived toward the end of the 9th century AD, beginning the Age of Settlement (AD 874–930), when the island's coastal regions were rapidly settled by Norwegians, as well as some Scottish and Irish immigrants. In 930 a central legislative body called the Althing was established and a body of laws created. Following Norway's example, Iceland's inhabitants replaced their pagan religions with Christianity in AD 1000. Following a period of internal strife, Iceland came first under Norwegian control (in 1242) and then—together with Norway—under the rule of the Danish in 1380.

Iceland's allegiance to Denmark lasted nearly 600 years. In 1550, following the Protestant Reformation, Lutheranism replaced Catholicism as the primary religion. From 1602 until 1787, Denmark had a total monopoly on trade with Iceland. In 1800, Denmark abolished the Althing, Iceland's parliament, but a strong nationalist movement later in the century resulted in the granting of home rule in 1903 and independence in 1918 (although Denmark retained control over Iceland's foreign affairs, and Iceland maintained its allegiance to the Danish monarch). In 1944 the people of Iceland voted overwhelmingly in favor of ending the island's union with Denmark, and Iceland became a fully independent republic on 17 June 1944. Iceland joined the United Nations in 1946 and the North Atlantic Treaty Organization (NATO) three years later. In 1970 the nation became a member of the European Free Trade Association (EFTA), and it concluded a trade agreement with the European Community (EC) in 1973. However, as of 2008 Iceland remained opposed to European Union (EU) membership. The country's Scandinavian-type economy is basically capitalistic, yet with an extensive welfare system (including generous housing subsidies), low unemployment, and remarkably even distribution of income. Literacy, longevity, income, and social cohesion are first-rate by world standards. In the absence of other natural resources (except for abundant geothermal power), the economy depends heavily on the fishing industry, which provides 70% of export earnings and employs 6% of the work force. However, Iceland has made efforts to diversify its economy in order to decrease its dependence on fishing: the economy remains sensitive to declining fish stocks as well as to

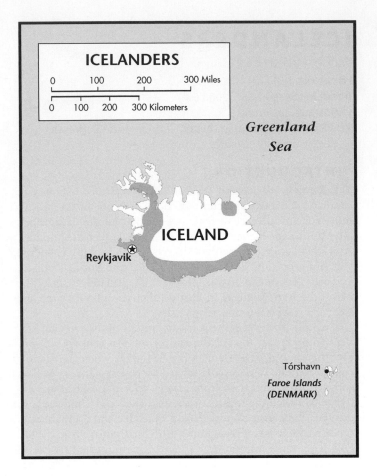

ICELANDERS

0　　100　　200　　300 Miles

0　　100　　200　　300 Kilometers

Greenland Sea

ICELAND

Reykjavik

Tórshavn
Faroe Islands (DENMARK)

fluctuations in world prices for its main exports—among them fish and fish products, aluminum, and ferrosilicon.

2 LOCATION AND HOMELAND

Located in the North Atlantic Ocean between Greenland and Norway, Iceland is Europe's second-largest island (the largest is Greenland) and its westernmost nation. Its total area of 39,769 sq mi (103,000 sq km)—slightly smaller than the state of Kentucky—includes numerous smaller islands off its shores. The interior of the main island consists mostly of a central upland plateau ringed with mountains. Iceland has many active volcanoes (on average, there is an eruption about once every five years), and its terrain is characterized by other volcanic features, including geysers, thermal springs, fumaroles, and lava flows. None of its rivers are navigable (the longest is the Thjórsá in the southern part of the country). However, its coastal fjords provide excellent natural harbors.

Most of Iceland's population lives either near the harbors or in locations where there is sufficient flat land to allow for agriculture or industry. The country's estimated 2008 population was 304,367, of which 90% was urban and 10% rural. The major population centers are the capital city of Reykjavík, Kópavogur, Hafnarfjördur, and Akureyri. Ethnically, Iceland is a very homogeneous society. Almost all its inhabitants are descended from the Norwegians (and a smaller number of Irish and Scots) who settled the island in the Middle Ages. However, in 2006 there were more than 13,000 foreigners living in Iceland. Many men have come to Iceland from the new EU coun-

tries that joined in 2004. Despite the influx, unemployment in Iceland remains around 1%. Anyone from an EU country can come to Iceland without a work permit. They can live in the country for six months if they are looking for work. The majority of foreigners who arrived in the mid-2000s, roughly 64%, work in the construction industry. Polish workers have always been popular in Iceland, and still form the bulk of the foreign workforce. About 7,500 Poles now live in Iceland, 1,394 of them in Reydarfjordur where they make up 75% of the workforce building the Fjardaraal aluminum plant.

3 LANGUAGE

Icelandic is a Germanic language related to Norwegian, German, Dutch, and, most closely, Faroese (the language spoken on the Faroe Islands). Due to the country's isolation, its language has changed little since medieval times compared to other modern languages. The 13th-century Icelandic sagas, written in medieval Icelandic, or Old Norse, can still be read in their original versions by most Icelanders. Today, Icelanders preserve their linguistic heritage by refusing to borrow foreign words for contemporary idioms and modern technologies. A special committee is charged with creating new Icelandic terms for words like "computer" (*tölva*, literally "word prophet").

COMMON WORDS AND PHRASES

men	karlar
women	konur
thank you	takk fyrir
today	í dag
tomorrow	á morgun
meat	kjót
fisg	fiskur
milk	mjólk
water	vatn

NUMBERS

zero	núll
one	einn
two	tveir
three	þrír
four	fjórir
five	fimm
six	sex
seven	sjö
eight	átta
nine	níu
ten	tíu

4 FOLKLORE

Icelandic folklore has preserved elements of Norse mythology, including the belief in the *Huldufolk*, or "hidden people," the descendents of children whom Eve hid from God in the Garden of Eden. Other common features of Icelandic folktales include ghosts, elves, mermaids, and sea monsters. Superstitious beliefs are common among Icelanders, especially in the northern and eastern parts of the country.

5 RELIGION

Over 85% of Icelanders belong to the official state church, the Evangelical Lutheran Church. The entire country makes up a single diocese with 284 parishes. It is headed by a bishop based in the capital, Reykjavík. The church is government supported, but people who do not want their taxes to go for its support may stipulate this on their returns, and their tax money is then used for other purposes. Under 4% of the population belongs to other Lutheran denominations, 2% are Roman Catholics, and about 3% describe themselves as atheists.

6 MAJOR HOLIDAYS

Iceland's legal holidays include New Year's Day (January 1), Good Friday, Easter Sunday and Monday, the First Day of Summer (celebrated on the third Thursday in April), Labor Day (May 1), Whitsunday and Whitmonday, National Day (June 17), Bank Holiday (first Monday in August), Independence Anniversary (December 1), and Christmas (celebrated December 24–26). Icelanders' Christmas customs combine Christianity with Norse mythology, the source of the 13 Santa Claus figures called Christmas Men (or Yuletide lads) who are said to visit every home in the land, leaving gifts but also causing mischief. The Door Slammer disturbs people's sleep by slamming doors, the Candle Beggar steals candles, and the Meat Hooker lowers a hook down the chimney in order to make off with the Christmas roast. The traditional First Day of Summer, celebrated in April, is based on a traditional calendar that divided the year into two seasons, summer and winter, each 26 weeks long. The occasion is still celebrated as a national holiday with parades and festivals.

7 RITES OF PASSAGE

Iceland is a modern, largely Christian country. Hence, many of the rites of passage that young people undergo are religious rituals, such as baptism, first Communion, confirmation, and marriage. In addition, a student's progress through the education system is marked by many families with graduation parties.

8 INTERPERSONAL RELATIONS

Icelanders customarily shake hands when greeting and taking leave of each other. Common greetings include *gódan daginn* (good day), *gott kvöld* (good evening), and *bless* (goodbye). It is considered good manners to take off one's shoes before entering a dwelling.

Icelanders' last names are based on the first names of their parents, with *son* (or *sson*) added for males, and *dóttir* for females. Thus, a boy named Karl, born to a father named Sigurd, will be named Karl Sigurdsson. Other types of surnames are very uncommon and generally belong to persons born outside the country. Icelanders generally call each other by their first names, even in formal situations, and they are listed in their country's telephone directories alphabetically by their first, rather than their last, names (i.e., all the Johanns, followed by all the Jons, and then all the Karls).

9 LIVING CONDITIONS

Icelanders enjoy a high standard of living. Traditionally, Icelanders in rural areas lived in dwellings built of stone and turf, while those in the cities had wooden houses. Today most Icelandic housing is built of reinforced concrete to withstand the country's harsh climatic conditions, which include high winds and earthquakes. Exteriors are generally painted in pastel colors. More and more people are buying condominiums. In Reykjavík, it is common to heat one's house with water from hot springs.

Average life expectancy among Icelanders is among the world's highest: 78.43 years for men and 82.76 for women in 2008. They are physically hearty—among the world's tallest and heaviest people, both at birth and as adults, and they also have a very low rate of infant mortality. Known for their physical strength, Icelanders excel at sports such as weight-lifting, shot-putting, and javelin-throwing. Jon Pall Sigmarsson, an Icelander, won the "World's Strongest Man" title four times and was named "Strongest Man of All Time" in 1987. The robustness of Iceland's people is generally linked to a healthy diet rich in fish, fish oil, and fresh produce; vigorous exercise; clean air; and effective immunization measures.

With no railroads or navigable inland waters, Icelanders depend on road and air transportation. The country's harsh climate is hard on its numerous dirt and gravel roads. Many roads are rutted or filled with potholes, and high winds sometimes blow away entire sections of roadway. Road conditions are better in urban areas, where most main roads are paved. In recent years, domestic air travel has become increasingly popular and inexpensive.

10 FAMILY LIFE

Icelanders tend to have a relatively casual attitude toward marriage, and there are few barriers to divorce. A high percentage of the country's births—some 70% of firstborn children—are illegitimate, and illegitimacy carries no social stigma. It is common for couples to have their own children present at their weddings, often as bridesmaids or pageboys. Married women often keep their original names, and children's last names are commonly based on their fathers' first names, with different endings for a son (*son* or *sson*) and daughter (*dóttir*). Thus, it is possible for all the members of one family to have different surnames. (For example, if a couple named Katrin Magnusdóttir and Hannes Sveinsson had a son and a daughter, the parents would keep their own surnames and their children might be named Gudrún Hannesdóttir and Gunnar Hannesson.) In Reykjavík daycare is readily available for working couples. In smaller towns and in rural areas, parents are more likely to rely on family and friends to assist with child care. In the 1970s, many Icelandic couples adopted Vietnamese orphans.

11 CLOTHING

Icelanders wear modern, Western-style clothing like that worn elsewhere in Europe and in developed countries in other parts of the world. The women's traditional costume that may be worn for festivals or other special occasions consists of a white blouse and ankle-length black skirt, black vest laced in front, long white apron, black shoes, and black cap.

12 FOOD

Fish, mutton, and lamb are staples of the Icelandic diet. Common varieties of fish—often eaten raw—include cod, salmon, trout, halibut, and redfish. Raw pickled salmon is a special favorite. *Hangikjöt* (smoked mutton) is a festive dish served at Christmas and New Year's and throughout the year as well; typically, it is accompanied by potatoes, white sauce, and peas. *Skyr* is a popular yogurt-like dairy food made from nonhomogenized milk and served either at breakfast or as a dessert, often with berries or other fresh fruit. Icelanders seldom

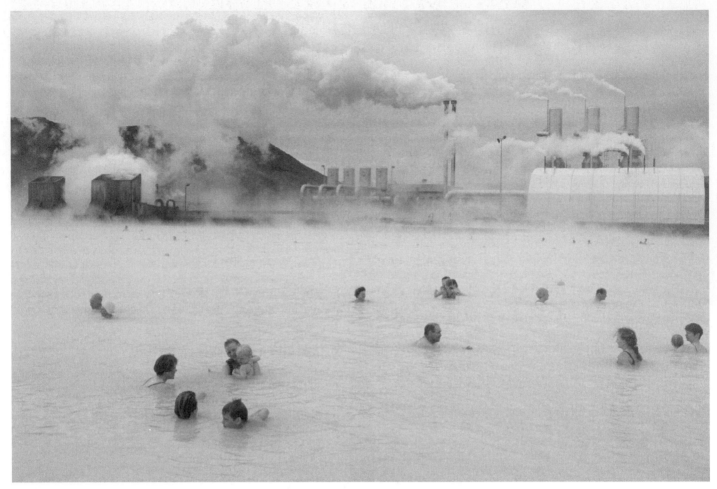

Locals and tourists swim in the Blue Lagoon thermal pool in Iceland. (Tim Graham/Getty Images)

eat salad, and often use sugar to flavor their food. Traditional dishes associated with the mid-winter Thorri feast include *svid* (a sheep's head singed to burn off the wool, boiled, and served with mashed turnips) and *hakarl* (cured shark's meat).

13 EDUCATION

Practically all adult Icelanders are literate—the country's official literacy rate is 99.9%. All levels of education, including college, are free, and school is compulsory between the ages of 6 and 16. Many five- and six-year-olds are enrolled in pre-primary education. Primary school covers all subjects, including vocational guidance, while secondary schools offer either general education, vocational education, or university preparatory study. In 2008 Iceland had eight universities and colleges, including the University of Iceland, located in Reykjavík.

14 CULTURAL HERITAGE

Iceland's literary tradition dates back to the early Scandinavian Eddic and Skaldic poetry brought to the region by Norwegian settlers in the Middle Ages. The nation's most famous early literary works are the Viking sagas, which began in oral form ("saga" means "said") in around the 10th century AD and were then written down in the 12th and 13th centuries. These are mainly family sagas that describe both the important political and military events of their time and the daily lives of the early Icelandic settlers. They also depict life in the foreign lands visited by the Vikings, including Norway and Scotland.

Iceland's contributions to modern literature include late-19th-century children's works by the priest Jón Sveinsson and *Eyvind of the Hills*, a biography of an 18th-century outlaw by Jóhann Sigurjónsson. Iceland's best-known 20th-century author is novelist Halldór Laxness, who won the Nobel Prize for literature in 1955. He is the author of *Independent People*, *The Fish Can Sing*, *The Atom Station*, *A Poet's Time*, and other works. Iceland's theater companies include the Reykjavík Theater and the National Theater. The repertoire of the Icelandic Dance Company includes both classical ballets and works by and about Icelanders. Iceland has a national orchestra and an opera company, and the world-famous classical pianist and conductor, Russian-born Vladimir Ashkenazy, is a naturalized citizen of Iceland. Well-known names in the visual arts include those of sculptor Asmundur Sveinsson, whose concrete statues are found in public places throughout the country, and artists Jon Stefansson, Kristin Jonsdóttir, and Juliana Sveinsdóttir.

15 WORK

Icelanders are hard workers. They value work not only as a means of maintaining their high standard of living but also as a virtue in itself (a concept popularly known—in other countries as well as Iceland—as the "Protestant work ethic"). Their average work week is one of Europe's longest, and many Icelanders hold two or even three jobs. It is common for children to work during their school vacations, and many also have evening jobs during the school year. Fish processing and other industries employ 6% of Iceland's work force, and the fishing industry provides 70% of export earnings. Other major employment sectors include commerce, construction, business services, transportation and communication, and agriculture. Some three-fourths of the work force is unionized, and unemployment is extremely low—at 1% in 2007.

¹⁶ SPORTS

Icelanders, who live surrounded by water, are, naturally, swimming enthusiasts, and heated swimming pools are available for use year round. Soccer is another favorite activity, and a number of top Icelandic players have signed full-time professional contracts with European teams abroad. Icelanders excel, in particular, at sports requiring physical strength, such as weightlifting. Once one of the world's top javelin throwers, Einar Vilhyalmsson, is an Icelander. The country also has a world-class handball team. Other popular sports include golf, basketball, badminton, horseback riding, hunting, fishing, and sailing. While boxing is illegal in Iceland, Icelanders have their own native form of wrestling called *glíma*.

¹⁷ ENTERTAINMENT AND RECREATION

With their high rate of literacy, Icelanders are avid readers. Their country is said to have more bookstores relative to its population size than any other in the world, and most families own good-sized book collections. Writing is also a popular pastime; according to one estimate, one in every 10 Icelanders will have something published in the course of a lifetime. The country's dozen or so periodicals provide additional reading material, and Reykjavík alone has four newspapers. Iceland also has both public and private radio and television stations and an active film industry.

Chess is extremely popular in Iceland. The legendary 1972 world championship match between American Bobby Fischer and Russian Boris Spassky, held in Iceland's capital city of Reykjavík, further increased the nation's passion for the game. Many young Icelanders have won youth-division world championships in recent years. Bridge is another favorite form of recreation in Iceland.

¹⁸ FOLK ART, CRAFTS, AND HOBBIES

Icelandic crafts include traditional hand-knitted woolen sweaters, ceramics, and jewelry.

¹⁹ SOCIAL PROBLEMS

Iceland has an extremely low crime rate, and crimes by Icelanders are often alcohol-related. With the exception of alcohol use, however, Iceland has fewer drug-related problems than most other European countries, and stiff penalties are imposed for drug trafficking. Reykjavík is one of the world's safest capital cities.

²⁰ GENDER ISSUES

The position of women is generally a good one in Iceland, which is traditionally a matriarchal society. The egalitarian nature of Icelandic society with respect to gender is commonly attrib-

uted to the fact that the men have traditionally been fishermen who were required to spend long periods of time away from home, leaving their wives with a high degree of independence and responsibility. In 1980 Iceland became the first country in the world to choose a woman—President Vígdis Finnbogadóttir—as its democratically elected head of state. Three of the country's four most powerful positions—chief justice of the Supreme Court, president of the country's legislature (the Althing), and president of the country—have been simultaneously held by women. Almost 90% of Icelandic women work outside the home, although the average female wage is still lower than that of males. Iceland has the highest percentage of women in the labor market and also has the highest birth rate in Europe.

Iceland, like the Scandinavian countries, takes a liberal position concerning gay rights. The majority of the public is supportive of homosexuality, and gay pride parades are held every August. Laws protecting sexual orientation are in effect. Civil unions between same-sex couples became legal in 1996. There are also adoption laws, which include the right to adopt your partners' biological children. In 2006 same-sex couples became eligible for all adoption and insemination purposes.

²¹ BIBLIOGRAPHY

Bedell, J. M. Hildur, *Queen of the Elves: And Other Icelandic Legends*. Northampton, MA: Interlink Books, 2007.

Byock, Jesse L. *Medieval Iceland: Society, Sagas, and Power*. Berkeley: Univ. of California Press, 1988.

Durrenberger, E. Paul. "Icelanders." *Encyclopedia of World Cultures*. Boston: G. K. Hall, 1992.

——— and Gisli Pallson. *The Anthropology of Iceland*. Iowa City: Univ. of Iowa Press, 1989.

Gall, Timothy, and Susan Gall, ed. *Worldmark Encyclopedia of the Nations*. Detroit: Gale Research, 1995.

Indriðason, Arnaldur. *Jar City: A Reykjavik Thriller*. 1st Picador ed. New York: Picador, 2006.

Lepthien, Emilie. *Iceland*. Chicago: Children's Press, 1994.

Roberts, David. *Iceland*. New York: H. N. Abrams, 1990.

Scherman, Katherine. *Daughter of Fire: A Portrait of Iceland*. Boston: Little, Brown, 1976.

Thompson, Wayne C. *Nordic, Central, and Southeastern Europe, 2007*. 7th ed. Harpers Ferry, WV: Stryker-Post Publications, 2007.

Tomasson, Richard F. *Iceland: The First New Society*. Minneapolis: Univ. of Minnesota Press, 1980.

—revised by J. Hobby

IRISH

LOCATION: Ireland
POPULATION: 4.3 million (2007)
LANGUAGE: Irish Gaelic (official); English (primary)
RELIGION: Roman Catholic; Protestant, and Jewish

¹ INTRODUCTION

The Republic of Ireland, which consists of 26 counties, covers five-sixths of the island of Ireland. The remaining portion is occupied by the six counties of Northern Ireland, which is part of the United Kingdom. The division of the island into two political entities is the legacy of a long period of British rule, dating back as far as 1171, when King Henry II declared himself king of Ireland. Eventually the English controlled most of the island. With the Protestant Reformation of the 16th century, the division between the conquering and conquered peoples took on a religious dimension, as the Protestant English began the suppression of native Irish Catholicism, further aggravating the hostility between the two. When the Republic of Ireland won its independence in 1922, Northern Ireland became a separate political entity, remaining part of the United Kingdom. It was the site of violent conflict between Catholic nationalists and Protestant extremist groups until 1998, when the Good Friday Agreement was negotiated between the Irish and UK governments. The Republic of Ireland became a member of the European Community (now the European Union) in January of 1973. Ireland's economy began to grow rapidly in the 1990s, fueled by foreign investment: it became known as the "Celtic tiger." This attracted a wave of immigrants to a country where, traditionally, mass emigration was the norm. Today, Ireland has been transformed from a largely agricultural society into a modern, high-tech economy. Bertie Ahern, elected prime minister (taoiseach) in 1997, began a record third consecutive term in office in June 2007. However, Ahern in 2006 was criticized over controversial loans he received from friends when he was finance minister in the 1990s. In March 2008 he announced he would resign.

² LOCATION AND HOMELAND

Ireland, which occupies an area smaller than the state of Maine, is bounded by the Atlantic Ocean on the south, west, and northwest, and by the Irish Sea on the east. The country's two main topographic regions are a fertile central lowland and the mountain ranges that surround it. Most of the country is less than 500 feet above sea level. Ireland's population of 4.3 million people is evenly distributed throughout the country. The Irish trace their ethnic origins to the various groups who inhabited and ruled their land over the course of history, including the Celts, Norsemen, French Normans, and English. The people living east of the Shannon River generally have a higher standard of living, with a more advanced level of industrialization and richer farmland. The *Gaeltacht* along the western coast is the nation's Gaelic-speaking region.

³ LANGUAGE

Irish Gaelic and English are the official languages of the Republic of Ireland, and English is more widely used. Only about 30% of the population knows Gaelic well enough to use it in daily conversation, and only about 50,000 people living in the Gaelic-speaking or *Gaeltacht* area on the west coast use it as their primary language. The use and recognition of Gaelic has been taken up as a nationalist cause since the late 19th century. Today Gaelic is a compulsory subject in school, and signs throughout Ireland are written in both English and Gaelic. Irish Gaelic is a Celtic language closely related to Scottish Gaelic. Irish people speak English with an accent known as a brogue.

COMMON GAELIC WORDS
Pronunciation: (æ = a in cat)

man	fear	fær
woman	bean	bæn
yes	sea	shæ
no	ní-hea	nee hæ
hand	lámh	awv
leg	cos	kuss
good-night	codladh sámh	kull-uh sawv

DAYS OF THE WEEK		**PRONUNCIATION**
Monday	Luan	loo-un
Tuesday	Máirt	mawrt
Wednesday	Céadaoin	kay-deen
Thursday	Déardaoin	dayr-deen
Friday	Aoine	een-uh
Saturday	Satharn	sahurn
Sunday	Domhnach	do¯-nukh

NUMBERS		**PRONUNCIATION**
One	Aon	een
Two	Dó	do¯
Three	Trí	tree
Four	Ceathair	kæhir
Five	Cúig	koo-ig
Six	Sé	shay
Seven	Seacht	shakht
Eight	Ocht	ukht
Nine	Naoi	nee
Ten	Deich	deh

⁴ FOLKLORE

The Irish are master storytellers, and their tales and legends date back to Druid priests and early Celtic poets who preserved the stories of Ireland's pre-Christian heroes and heroines. There are tales about the exploits of Cuchulainn, who defended Ulster single-handed, and tales from the era of Cormac Mac Art, Ireland's first king, including the love story of Diarmid and Grania and the exploits of Finn MacCool. Modern authors have helped keep these folk traditions alive: the poet William Butler Yeats wrote five plays based on the legendary adventures of Cuchulainn and James Joyce's final novel, *Finnegans Wake*—whose main character is identified with the mythic figure of Finn MacCool—is filled with Irish legends and mythology. Irish children today still learn tales about these legendary heroes, including MacCool and Saint Finnabar, who is said to have slain Ireland's last dragon.

⁵ RELIGION

Ireland is a staunchly Catholic country. Roman Catholics account for about 88% of Ireland's population, but only 48% of the Irish population in 2006 attended mass every week (down from 81% in 1990). Pilgrimages to shrines and holy places at home and abroad attract tens of thousands annually. Catholicism is strongly woven into the fabric of Irish life, influencing its laws, education, architecture, and daily life. Divorce only became legal in 1997. Abortion is illegal according to the Irish constitution. Catholicism is also deeply intertwined with Irish nationalism: before Irish independence, the British attempted to eradicate Catholicism from Ireland, causing the Irish to cling even more tenaciously to their faith. The non-Catholic minority is mostly Episcopalian, Methodist, Presbyterian, or Jewish.

6 MAJOR HOLIDAYS

Ireland's legal holidays are New Year's Day, St. Patrick's Day (March 17), Good Friday, Easter Sunday and Easter Monday, bank holidays on the first Mondays of June and August, Christmas, and St. Stephen's Day (December 26). In addition to these holidays, a variety of customs and celebrations are associated with various saints' days. St. John's Day (June 24), for example, is traditionally the time to dig up and eat the first new potatoes and on the night before, bonfires are lit on hilltops throughout the west of Ireland. A dish called *colcannon,* made from cabbage, potatoes, and milk, was traditionally served on Halloween with a ring, coin, thimble, and button inserted into it. Whoever found the ring was supposed to be married within a year, while the coin symbolized wealth, the button, bachelorhood, and the thimble, spinsterhood.

7 RITES OF PASSAGE

As in most west European countries, most births occur in hospitals. In Roman Catholic families the child is baptized within a week or so of birth. First Communion and confirmation are important events for Catholic children. Marriage generally takes place in church. Weddings are festive events and in the west may still be attended by "strawboys," uninvited guests dressed in straw disguises who crash the wedding and carouse about in good-humored fashion. Death is a solemn occasion and although the Irish were once known for their wild wakes these are quickly becoming a thing of the past.

8 INTERPERSONAL RELATIONS

The Irish are renowned for their hospitality, which dates back to olden times when it was believed that turning away a stranger would bring bad luck and a bad name to the household. (According to one Christian belief, a stranger might be Christ in disguise coming to test the members of the household.) The front doors of houses were commonly left open at meal times so that anyone who passed by would feel free to enter and join in the meal. While many of the old superstitions are a thing of the past, Irish warmth and hospitality toward strangers remains. Hospitality is practiced not only at home, but also at the neighborhood pub, where anyone joining a group of drinkers immediately buys a round of drinks for everyone at the table. Until 2004 no one smoked a cigarette without first offering the pack to everyone present. But that year Ireland became the first country to have a nationwide ban on indoor smoking in all public spaces, including restaurants and pubs.

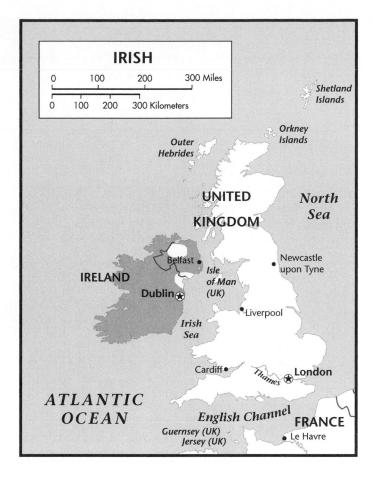

9 LIVING CONDITIONS

The traditional rural home was narrow and rectangular, and built from a combination of stones and mortar (made from mud, lime, or whatever material was locally available), often with a thatched roof. Rural homes and those in some urban areas are commonly heated by fireplaces that burn peat (called "turf" in Ireland) instead of wood. Modern homes have replaced traditional dwellings both in the country and the city, where families generally live in brick or concrete houses or apartment buildings. The large numbers of people emigrating to Ireland's cities since the 1950s have created a great demand for new housing, and developments have gone up around most large towns and cities.

Health care in Ireland is based on a person's ability to pay for services, with low-income persons and those over the age of 66 receiving most services free of charge. Hospital care is free for all children through the age of 16, and the costs of medication are covered for people suffering from infectious or chronic illnesses. Both infant mortality (5.22 out of 1,000 live births) and average life expectancy (77.9 years) are close to the European average.

10 FAMILY LIFE

The Irish have such a strong allegiance to the family that their constitution even recognizes it as "the natural primary and fundamental unit group of Society, and as a moral institution possessing inalienable . . . rights" and guarantees to protect it as "indispensible to the welfare of the Nation." While the nu-

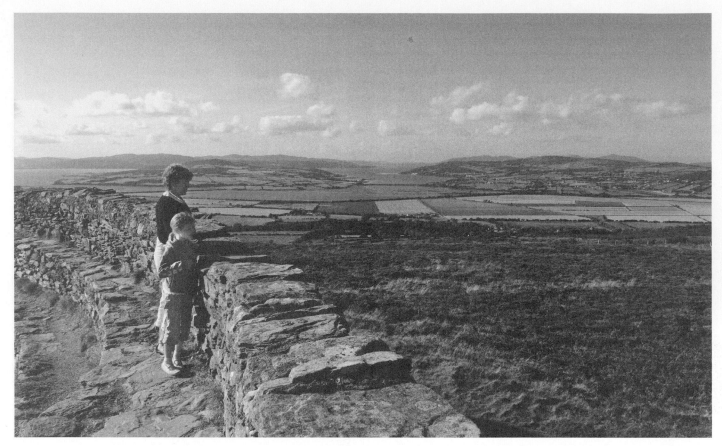

An Irish woman and her daughter stand on top of Grianan of Aileach Fort in County Donegal, Ireland.
(© The Irish Image Collection/Corbis)

clear family is the primary family unit, it expands to include elderly relatives when they become infirm and may also include an unmarried aunt or uncle. Young people have traditionally lived at home with their parents until they married, often after the age of 25 or even 30. Bonds between siblings are unusually strong, especially in the western part of the country, and unmarried siblings often live together, sometimes joined by a widowed sibling later in life. While women are playing an increasingly active role in the work force, traditional gender roles still predominate at home, with the woman doing most of the household chores and child-rearing, and the men fulfilling the traditional role of breadwinner. Before 1972 married women could not be hired for professional positions in the public sector.

11 CLOTHING

People in Ireland wear modern Western-style clothing, with an eye to durability, comfort, and protection from Ireland's often-wet weather. The Irish have been known for their fine cotton lace-making since the early 1800s. Handknitted sweaters are another famous Irish product, especially those made on the Aran Islands, with their high-quality yarn and distinctive patterns. Tweed—a thick cloth of woven wool used for pants, skirts, jackets, and hats—is another type of textile for which the Irish are known. The Irish have adorned (and fastened) their clothing with bronze and silver brooches since the 3rd century AD, and traditional designs have included detailed engravings, animal designs, and enamel inlays.

12 FOOD

The Irish have hearty appetites. Potatoes are the main staple and, together with cabbage, the most popular vegetables in Ireland. Many rural dwellers grow their own potatoes and use them in their meals on a daily basis. Dairy products are a favorite, and milk and butter consumption are both heavy. Irish stew, one of the most common traditional dishes, consists of lamb or mutton, potatoes, onions, herbs, and stock. The main meals of the day are breakfast and lunch. The traditional Irish breakfast (which many have abandoned in favor of lighter fare) includes sausages, bacon, eggs, tomatoes, pudding, other meat dishes (such as liver or chops), and bread, all washed down by plentiful servings of tea. A typical lunch might include a hearty soup, a serving of chicken or beef, and vegetables. Supper usually consists of sandwiches, cold meats, or fish. Soda bread, made with baking soda and buttermilk, accompanies many meals, and popular desserts (called "sweets") include scones, tarts, and cakes.

13 EDUCATION

Adult literacy is nearly universal in Ireland. All children must attend school between the ages of 6 and 15, and most go to single-sex rather than coeducational schools. Both English and Gaelic are taught in primary school (called National School). Secondary school students receive an Intermediate Certificate at the age of 15 or 16 and, following an optional two more years of study, a Leaving Certificate, which is required for admission to one of Ireland's seven universities. Ireland's oldest university is Trinity College, founded in 1591 and also known as the University of Dublin.

14 CULTURAL HERITAGE

The value that the Irish place on the arts can be seen in Ireland's policy of exempting its writers, composers, painters, and sculptors from paying income taxes, as long as their work is recognized as having "artistic or cultural merit." Ireland's greatest contribution has been in the field of literature, and its great writers, include satirist Jonathan Swift, author of *Gulliver's Travels*, the playwrights Oliver Goldsmith and Oscar Wilde, and such giants of 20th-century literature as playwright George Bernard Shaw, poet William Butler Yeats, and novelist James Joyce. Although Joyce left his native land as a young man, Ireland and its people play a central role in all his works, which include the short story collection *Dubliners* and the novels *A Portrait of the Artist as a Young Man* and *Ulysses*, which traces the activities of its characters during the time span of one day in early-20th-century Dublin. Yeats won the Nobel Prize for literature in 1923, as did his fellow Irishman, playwright Samuel Beckett in 1969. Contemporary Irish writers include poets Seamus Deane and Seamus Heaney, who won the Nobel Prize for literature in 1995, and novelist Roddy Doyle, winner of the Booker Prize in 1993. Brian O'Nolan (Flann O'Brien) was an Irish novelist and satirist who wrote many satirical columns in the Irish Times under the name Myles na gCopaleen. There is also a considerable modern literature in Irish Gaelic, including poets Nuala Ní Dhomhnaill and Máirtín Ó Direáin.

15 WORK

In 2006, 67% of Ireland's labor force was employed in service sector jobs, 27% worked in industry, and 6% were in agriculture, forestry, and fishing. Primary industries include meat, dairy, and grain processing, electronics, machinery, beer, shoes, and glassware. Since the 1960s, many small foreign-owned factories have opened in Ireland. Farming takes place on both small subsistence farms where families raise just enough to support themselves, and on large sophisticated commercial farms that produce food for export. Tourism is a mainstay of the service sector, providing restaurant, hotel, and retail jobs as well as expanding the range of government employment. In the decade up to 2006, property values had risen more rapidly in Ireland than in any other developed world economy. Per capita gross domestic product (GDP) is 40% higher than that of the four largest European economies and the second highest in the European Union (EU) behind Luxembourg, and in 2007 surpassed that of the United States. The Irish government has implemented a series of national economic programs designed to cut back on price and wage inflation, invest in infrastructure, increase labor force skills, and promote foreign investment.

16 SPORTS

Ireland's most popular sports are hurling and Gaelic football. Hurling, which is similar to field hockey, is played by two teams of 15 players who attempt to knock a leather ball through their opponents' goalposts with long sticks called *hurleys* or *camans*. The All-Ireland Hurling Championship, held in Dublin every September, is the Irish equivalent of the World Series in the United States. The women's version of hurling is called *camogie*. Gaelic football combines elements of soccer and rugby,

and also culminates in an All-Ireland match in the nation's capital. Another popular traditional Irish sport is road bowling (played mostly in County Cork); its object is to advance a metal ball, called a bullet, over a two- or three-mile course in as few throws as possible. Other widely played sports include soccer, rugby, cricket, boxing, and track and field. Horse racing is a favorite national pastime, and Ireland's famous races include the Irish Derby and the Grand National (the race featured in the movie *National Velvet*).

17 ENTERTAINMENT AND RECREATION

Irish men spend many of their hours in pubs, drinking beer or ale, playing darts, and socializing with their friends. However, a typical rainy evening also finds many Irish people of both sexes at home reading or watching television. In recent years, it has become increasingly acceptable for women to frequent pubs, although the neighborhood pub still remains primarily male turf. Pubs are also the scene of traditional music sessions, which are associated with *craic* (pronounced "crack"), an all-around term for having a good time that can include playing and/ or listening to music, joking around, getting drunk, or flirting with members of the opposite sex. "The craic was mighty" means that someone had a good time. Other popular leisure-time pursuits include chess, bingo, and bridge.

18 FOLK ART, CRAFTS, AND HOBBIES

Traditional crafts include tweed and linen weaving, wool knitting, glass blowing, and wood carving. Belleek china and Waterford crystal are especially famous, and Rathborne, which has been producing candles for over 450 years, is Europe's oldest candle maker. The women of the Aran Islands are known for their distinctive woolen sweaters. (At one time, every family on the islands had its own sweater pattern, which aided in identifying drowned sailors.) Ireland has a rich folk music tradition, and age-old jigs and reels can be heard at local festivals and in informal performances at neighborhood pubs. Since the 1960s, groups like the Chieftains and Planxty have not only revived national interest in traditional tunes and instruments, they have also gained an international audience for Irish music, both live and recorded. Traditional instruments include the fiddle, flute, Celtic harp, accordion, bodhran (a hand-held drum), and uilleann pipes (a bagpipe-like instrument powered by a bellows).

19 SOCIAL PROBLEMS

Ever since the great potato famine of 1845, Ireland has lost a large percentage of its population to emigration, as people leave in search of better opportunities abroad. At one point in the 19th century, the nation's population fell from 8 to 3 million within the space of a single generation. After a period of relative prosperity in the 1960s and 1970s, the worst economic crisis since independence led to a new wave of emigration beginning in the late 1980s, most of it to the United States. Over 100,000 of Ireland's young people left the country. In addition to inflation, high unemployment, and the highest taxes in Europe, the nation had to deal with one of the largest per capita foreign debts in the world. However, fueled by foreign investment, Ireland made a major turnaround in the 1990s, and was dubbed the "Celtic Tiger" for its fast growing economy. In recent years, Ireland has changed from being a country of emigration to a country of immigration. Unemployment is very low and 9% of the labor force in Ireland is foreign born.

Politically, the difficulties in Northern Ireland led to violence that claimed nearly 2,000 civilian lives and injured some 40,000 among the competing Protestant and Catholic factions. However, in 1998 the Good Friday Agreement was signed, which sought to address relationships within Northern Ireland; between Northern Ireland and the Irish Republic; and between both parts of Ireland and England, Scotland, and Wales. In referenda, 71.2% of people in Northern Ireland and 94.39% in the Irish Republic voted "yes" to accepting the Agreement. An Assembly was elected in September that year, and there is an executive composed of a First Minister, Deputy First Minister and 10 further ministers.

20 GENDER ISSUES

With abortion illegal and divorce only becoming legal under certain circumstances in 1997, the lives of Irish women in many respects are circumscribed. The Roman Catholic Church plays a major role in social and family relations. Irish law prohibits discrimination against women in the workplace and provides for protection and redress against discrimination based on gender and marital status. However, inequalities persist regarding pay and promotions. Women constitute approximately 47.5% of the labor force but are underrepresented in senior management positions. The earnings of women average 80% that of men and women work 10 hours a week less.

Homosexuality was decriminalized in Ireland in 1993, and discrimination based on sexual orientation is now outlawed. Ireland also prohibits incitement to hatred based on sexual orientation. A survey conducted in 2008 showed that 84% of Irish people supported civil marriage or civil partnerships for gay and lesbian couples, with 58% supporting full marriage rights. Northern Ireland, as part of the UK, began recognizing same-sex civil partnerships in 2005.

21 BIBLIOGRAPHY

Bew, Paul. *Ireland: The Politics of Enmity, 1789–2006*. Oxford: Oxford University Press, 2007.

Bluett, Anthony. *Things Irish*. Dublin: Mercier Press, 1994.

Fairclough, Chris. *We Live in Ireland*. New York: Bookwright Press, 1986.

Flanagan, William G. *Ireland Now: Tales of Change from the Global Island*. Notre Dame, IN: University of Notre Dame Press, 2007.

Fodor's Ireland. Fodor's Travel Publications, 1995.

Fradin, Dennis B. *England. Enchantment of the World Series*. Chicago: Children's Press, 1984.

Gall, Timothy, and Susan Gall, ed. *Junior Worldmark Encyclopedia of the Nations*. Detroit: UXL, 1996.

Illustrated Encyclopedia of Mankind. London: Marshall Cavendish, 1978.

Ireland in Pictures. Minneapolis: Lerner Publications, 1993.

O'Donnell, Catherine. *Fianna Faÿil, Irish Republicanism and the Northern Ireland Troubles, 1968–2005*. Dublin: Irish Academic Press, 2007.

Pomeray, J.K. *Ireland*. New York: Chelsea House, 1988.

Taylor, Lawrence J. "English." *Encyclopedia of World Cultures (Europe)*. Boston: G. K. Hall, 1992.

—revised by J. Hobby

ITALIANS

LOCATION: Italy
POPULATION: About 58 million
LANGUAGE: Italian, French, Slovene, German, and Fruilian
RELIGION: Roman Catholic; small numbers of Protestants, Jews, and Greek Orthodox

1 INTRODUCTION

Unified Italy is a latecomer among the nations of Europe: its 20 regions did not unify as a single country until 1870. However, its people have wielded great political and cultural influence since the days of ancient Rome. Each year millions of tourists come to view the country's cultural and historical legacy dating back to Rome's Colosseum and the Greek ruins of Sicily and its beautiful landscapes, which range from Alpine peaks to picturesque hill towns and sandy beaches. Today Italy is a modern industrial nation and a leading member of the European Union. In the 1950s economic growth was so rapid that it was called the "Italian miracle." Continuing problems include illegal immigration, organized crime, corruption, high unemployment, slow economic growth, and the low incomes and technical standards of southern Italy compared with the prosperous north. Modern Italy has also had a turbulent political life: in 2008 it elected its 62nd government since World War II.

2 LOCATION AND HOMELAND

Located in southern Europe, Italy is geographically divided into three major regions: the north Italian Plain and the Italian Alps ("continental"); the peninsula south of the plain ("peninsular"); and Sardinia, Sicily, and numerous smaller islands ("insular"). Italy's only major river, the Po, flows from west to east before it empties into the Adriatic sea.

There is a sharp division in temperament, traditions, and socio-economic conditions between Italians living in northern and central regions, and those living in the south. The city of Rome marks the boundaries between the two parts of the country. The more prosperous northern and central regions are more "European," while the poorer, historically neglected south (also called the Mezzogiorno) is more "Mediterranean."

3 LANGUAGE

Italian is the official language and is spoken by the vast majority of the population. Nearly every region has its own dialect, but dialect speakers are rapidly declining—except in Naples and Sicily—due to social mobility, radio, television, and other mass media which use only the standard language. Present-day Italian originated as the regional language of Tuscany. Other languages spoken in Italy include French, Slovene, German, and Fruilian, which is related to the Romansch spoken in Switzerland.

NUMBERS

one	uno
two	due
three	tre
four	quattro
five	cinque

six	sei
seven	sette
eight	otto
nine	nove
ten	dieci

DAYS OF THE WEEK

Sunday	Domenica
Monday	Lunedi
Tuesday	Martedi
Wednesday	Mercoledi
Thursday	Giovedi
Friday	Venerdi
Saturday	Sabato

4 FOLKLORE

According to a myth that probably originated in the 4th century BC, Rome was founded by the twin brothers Romulus and Remus, born to Mars, the god of war. Set adrift to drown in the Tiber River, they came to rest at the future site of the city, where they were suckled by a wolf and later found by a herdsman. After the founding of Rome, Remus was killed by Romulus, who consolidated his power and after his death was worshipped as the god Quirinus.

5 RELIGION

Italy is an overwhelmingly Catholic country: 90% of Italians describe themselves as Roman Catholics, but it is estimated that only about one-third of Italian Catholics attend mass regularly. Catholicism is closely intertwined with many aspects of Italian life, from education to family life. Priests have traditionally taught in Italian schools, although fewer do so since a 1984 law abolishing compulsory religious education. The church's position on such matters as abortion and divorce has had a profound impact on marriage and the family. Italy is also the home of the Vatican, for centuries the international center of the Catholic Church and an independent political entity. In addition, nearly all the Popes through the centuries have been Italians; the current German-born Pope, Benedict XVI (b. Joseph Alois Ratzinger) is a notable exception.

There are about 500,000 Protestants living in Italy, about 30,000 of them belonging to the sect known as Waldensians. Concentrated in the Piemonte region, they practice a French-based Calvinism and, until the late 19th century, held most of their services in French. There are significant numbers of Eastern and Greek Orthodox Christians.

There are about 825,000 Muslims living in Italy, or 1.4% of the population. The Muslim population is diverse, the largest group coming from Morocco. Others are from elsewhere in North Africa, South Asia, Albania, and the Middle East. Most arrived from the 1980s onwards, many of them as students. Up to 160,000 Muslims are Italian born. Most Muslims have the right to reside and work in Italy, but are not citizens. Italy also has about 45,000 Jews.

6 MAJOR HOLIDAYS

Aside from the standard holidays of the Christian calendar, legal holidays in Italy are New Year's Day, Liberation Day (April 25), and Labor Day (May 1). Cities and towns also celebrate the feast days of their patron saints. Colorful traditions mark many observances of religious holidays. In Florence, Easter is

the occasion for the reenactment of a medieval tradition called *scoppio del carro* and on Ascension Day children take part in a "cricket hunt" in the city's largest park. A ritualized secular event is the *Palio,* a famous annual horse race in Siena with competing equestrian teams representing the 17 neighborhoods of that city.

7 RITES OF PASSAGE

Italy is a modern, industrialized, primarily Roman Catholic country. Many of the rites of passage that young people undergo are religious rituals, such as baptism, first Communion, confirmation, and marriage. In addition, a student's progress through the education system is marked by many families with graduation parties.

American influence in Italian society is reflected most conspicuously on the lifestyle of young people, who share with American teenagers the same taste in clothing, music, and entertainment. The factors that motivate such influence are Hollywood films, American television programs dubbed and shown on Italian television, as well as the tens of thousands of students and young tourists who visit Italy every year.

8 INTERPERSONAL RELATIONS

The 19th-century French author Stendhal remarked that "one quickly reaches a note of intimacy in Italy, and speaks about personal matters." Italians are characteristically open, friendly, outgoing, and easily engaged in conversation. Like the people of other Mediterranean nations, they often use a variety of gestures to illustrate or emphasize what they are saying.

The standard form of greeting among acquaintances is the handshake. Italians have fewer inhibitions about personal space than people in some other parts of Western Europe or in the United States. It is common for two grown men to greet by kissing each other on both cheeks, or for either men or women to walk down the street arm in arm. This element of informality, however, is coupled with a traditional respect for the elderly, for instance, young persons often stand up when an older relative or friend enters a room.

⁹ LIVING CONDITIONS

In all Italian regions there is a marked difference in living conditions between large cities and the towns that dot the Italian landscape. In cities, people live in apartments and condominiums; in most towns, the average family lives in two-story homes. The standard of living is comparable to industrialized countries such as France, the United Kingdom, and the United States. Homes in both north and south have such basic creature comforts as refrigerators, color television, and the like. In northern and central Italy, the standards of living tend to be higher than the south. Thousands of middle-class Italians living in large cities own summer homes in the countryside, in coastal areas, or in the mountains. They spend weekends there to avoid the hustle and bustle of city life, as well as the traditional two weeks of vacation in August called *ferragosto* (August holy days).

Italian cities are numerous, historical and attractive. Generally they have a *centro storico* (historical center) corresponding to the center of the town. Here one finds churches, museums, and buildings of esthetic and architectural significance. Southern towns are typically situated on a hilltop with a church, a square or *piazza*, at the center.

Most Italian hospitals are run by regional governments, some by Catholic religious orders. Since 1980 Italy has had a national health plan that covers health care costs for most of its citizens, but facilities in some rural areas are still inadequate. Average life expectancy is 80 years, and the infant mortality rate is below the European average.

Italy's highway system is one of the most modern in the world. The *Autostrada del Sole* (Highway of the Sun) links Milan, Rome, and Naples to the southernmost tip of the Italian "boot." High-speed modern train service is provided between major cities; bus service is generally regional, connecting towns to cities. However, public transportation is often halted by strikes. Italy's only natural inland water route is the Po River, and the national airline is Alitalia.

¹⁰ FAMILY LIFE

The family is the backbone of Italian society. The noted journalist Luigi Barzini has called family loyalty the true patriotism of the Italians. Marriage choices, employment, business relationships, and often political affiliations are all influenced by family ties.

Many aspects of Italian family life have been influenced by the Catholic Church, through both its own beliefs and the influence it has wielded on government policy. The sale and purchase of contraceptive devices was illegal until 1971, bolstering the traditional tendency toward large families, and abortion was not legalized until 1978. Divorce became legal in 1970 and

two-thirds of the voters upheld this policy four years later in a referendum. The divorce rate in Italy jumped 74% between 1995 and 2005, and separations increased 57% during the same decade. There were 82,291 separations in 2005 and 47,036 divorces. Marital break-ups and separations were more common in the industrialized and richer north versus the poorer south, which tends to be more religious and socially conservative. There were 6.2 separations and 4 divorces for every 1,000 marriages in the north in 2005, against 4.2 separations and 1.8 divorces in the south.

¹¹ CLOTHING

Italian fashion had its beginnings more than 150 years ago, when the national hero, Giuseppe Garibaldi, bought up a surplus shipment of bright red butchers' tunics for his 1,000-man revolutionary army. From 1922 to 1942 the black shirt became the official uniform—and the symbol—of fascist forces headed by Benito Mussolini. Today, Italy earns more money from clothing, textiles, and footwear than from any other of its exports, and these industries are Italy's largest employers. Designers such as Versace, Armani, and Nino Cerruti are among the fashion industry's elite, and Benetton clothing is mass marketed throughout the world. Maintaining one's appearance is very important to the Italians. Even their casual clothing is generally of high quality; jeans are popular, but not if they are tattered or frayed. Dress wear includes fashionable silk ties and exquisitely cut suits for men, and elegant dresses or skirts and blouses for women.

¹² FOOD

Italy's national food is pasta, in all its varieties: ravioli in the north of the country, lasagne and tortellini in Bologna, cannelloni in Sicily, spaghetti with tomato or clam sauce in Naples. In general northern Italians eat much less pasta, preferring rice, prepared in various ways, and polenta, a mush made with corn, barley, or chestnut flour. In the north, people tend to use more butter and margarine; in the south, more olive oil. Pasta has been manufactured in the south since the 19th century and pasta dishes are often prepared with such vegetables as zucchini and eggplants. Altogether, Italy has 20 regional cuisines, all at least partially determined by locally available produce. The range of typical dishes includes *fegato alla veneziana* (liver and onions) in Venice; *cotoletta alla milanese* (veal cutlets) in the Lombard city of Milan; *bagna cauda* (a garlic-anchovy sauce for dipping vegetables) in the Piedmont region; and pesto (a basil-and-garlic sauce now popular in the United States) in Genoa and throughout the Liguria region. The Emilia-Romagna region, in central Italy, and the city of Bologna are famous for their cuisine. One regional dish that has become particularly well known worldwide is pizza, which originated in Naples.

Espresso is a standard beverage throughout Italy. Customers at the country's numerous espresso bars can often be heard ordering customized versions such as *lungo* (diluted), *macchiato* (with milk), or *freddo* (iced). Italy is also the world's largest wine producer, and wine accompanies most meals.

¹³ EDUCATION

In 2001 Italy had a literacy rate of around 98%, a substantial improvement over the 1930s, when some 20% of the population was illiterate. However, schools in some rural areas, and in the south generally, lag behind those in the rest of the coun-

A woman hikes past vineyards on a trail near San Gimignano in the hills of Tuscany, Italy. (© Tom Bean/Corbis)

try. Elementary education in Italy is regarded as the most progressive and innovative in the world. Education is free and compulsory between the ages of 6 and 14, and secondary education is offered in either the sciences or humanities, as well as in technical and teacher training schools. A small percentage of students follow their secondary education with study at one of Italy's 77 institutions of higher learning (63 state universities and 14 non-state universities).The university population in 2003 amounted to 1,800,000 individuals. The oldest is the University of Bologna, founded in the 11th century.

¹⁴ CULTURAL HERITAGE

In the visual arts, Italy's cultural legacy dates back to the sculpture and architecture of ancient Rome. The Renaissance, beginning in 15th-century Florence, was the golden age of painting, which saw the production of such works as *The Last Supper* and the *Mona Lisa* by Leonardo da Vinci and Michelangelo's ceiling frescoes in the Sistine Chapel. Other great Italian Renaissance artists included Donatello, Boticelli, Raphael, and Titian. In music, Italy is known for its glorious operatic tradition, from the early works of Monteverdi, the "father of opera," to the great 19th-century achievements of Rossini, Puccini, and Verdi, who is considered the greatest composer of opera. Italy is also known for the compositions of the baroque masters, including Vivaldi, and the makers of great violins such as the Stradivarius. In literature, Italy's great masterpieces

include the Aeniad of the Roman writer Virgil and the 14th-century works of Dante, Boccaccio, and Petrarch, including Dante's *Divine Comedy,* the first great work in the Italian language. Since 1901, there have been six Italian authors who have received the Nobel Prize for Literature.

¹⁵ WORK

In recent years, employment in Italy's service sector has increased rapidly. In 2001, it accounted for 63% of the nation's work force, compared to about 32% for industry and 5% for agriculture. Italian industry expanded rapidly after World War II, especially between the mid-1950s and mid-1960s. The Piedmont region in the north is one of Europe's major auto manufacturing centers and figures in the "industrial triangle" of Turin, Milan, and Genoa, where most of the country's major industries are concentrated. Southern Italy is less developed economically and has a higher rate of unemployment (around 20% in 2008). Many Sicilians now work abroad, and their earnings figure significantly in the island's economy. Labor strikes are common among workers in many areas of the service sector, including the post office, railroads, hospitals, schools, banks, and the media. Italy's economy has approximately the same total and per capita output as France and the United Kingdom. Most raw materials needed by industry and more than 75% of energy requirements are imported.

16 SPORTS

Soccer ("football," called *calcio* in Italy) is by far Italy's most popular sport. In 2006 the Italian national team won the World Cup—its fourth. Nearly all large and medium-size cities have a team in one of the three professional divisions. *Totocalcio* is a very popular betting pool connected with the scores of the soccer games in the three divisions. In addition to its popularity as a spectator sport, soccer is played by many Italians, and games at the village, city, and district level are accompanied by intense competition. Italians also enjoy bicycle and motorcycle racing, basketball, boxing, tennis, and downhill skiing in the Italian Alps. A type of bowling played on clay court called *bocce* is popular in small towns.

17 ENTERTAINMENT AND RECREATION

Like many Europeans, Italians are passionate soccer fans (called *tifosi*), watching games in stadiums and at home on television. The fanaticism surrounding this sport has caused major riots (in which people have died), as well as heart attacks during games (even by fans watching at home). Mammoth traffic jams are commonplace on Sunday afternoons, when games are played. Italians are also avid followers of auto and bicycle racing. Many bicycle races are sponsored by cities and corporations, and crowds congregate at the finish line regardless of the weather.

Many Italians like to spend their leisure hours with friends at a cafe, where they can stay as long as they like. Cafes are also popular spots for such solitary pursuits as reading or letter writing. Even daily meals are a form of recreation in Italy: Italians commonly spend up to two hours eating their midday meal, generally joining their families for food, wine, and conversation. On Sundays, the whole family may gather at an outdoor restaurant for this extended meal and spend the entire afternoon there. Even a night on the town in a sophisticated city like Rome generally means dining late at a *trattoria* (a small restaurant) and lingering over wine as the waiters are closing up for the night.

Beaches are popular recreational spots, especially with young people, who also enjoy "hanging out" at the local piazza, or square.

18 FOLK ART, CRAFTS, AND HOBBIES

Italy's handcrafted products include fine lace linens, glass, pottery, carved marble, and gold and silver filigree work. The sale of these products is important to the Italian economy, and the government provides assistance to the artisans who produce them.

19 SOCIAL PROBLEMS

Bureaucratic red tape and administrative inefficiency affect many aspects of daily life, including transportation, mail and telephone service, health care, and banking, among others. The resulting delays and inconveniences experienced regularly as a result are exacerbated by frequent service-sector strikes. Another traditional problem that still plagues Italy is organized crime, especially in the south of the country. Mafia violence may involve feuds between competing gangs, the kidnapping of wealthy persons or their relatives, or drug-related activities. Mob trafficking in narcotics and other drugs has given Italy a drug problem worse than that in most other European countries. Other problems in the 21st century include illegal immigration, high unemployment, and sluggish economic growth.

20 GENDER ISSUES

Officially, the father is the authority figure in the family, although women wield great power within the domestic sphere, especially in terms of the influence they exercise on their sons—Italian men are said to have an unusually strong lifetime attachment to their mothers. Although many Italian women continue to fulfill traditional roles, more and more work outside the home and pursue professional careers.

Italy, as the home of the Catholic Church, has negative attitudes towards homosexuality in general. Ironically, Italy is one of the few countries in the world that never enacted any specific anti-homosexual legislation. In the poorer south, gays are more stigmatized or discriminated against than in the more cosmopolitan north, especially in the larger cities of Milan and Bologna, where there is much more tolerance and acceptance. Rome and Naples are two exceptions to this rule and both cities have large gay communities. Italian attitudes toward homosexuals are changing, however. A survey taken in 2006 showed that 31% of Italians surveyed supported same-sex marriage and 24% recognized same-sex couples' rights to adopt (compared to the EU-wide average of 44% and 33%, respectively). In February 2007 the Romano Prodi government proposed a new law allowing a restricted version of civil union, which would grant rights to unmarried couples in areas of labor law, inheritance, tax, and medical assistance. The law faced strong opposition from the Catholic church and from Christian members of parliament. The Prodi government fell in 2008, and it was unclear if the legislation would be revived under Silvio Berlusconi.

21 BIBLIOGRAPHY

Barzini, Luigi. *The Italians: A Full-Length Portrait Featuring Their Manners and Morals.* New York: Atheneum, 1965.

Benedetti, Laura. *The Tigress in the Snow: Motherhood and Literature in Twentieth-Century Italy.* Toronto: University of Toronto Press, 2007.

Bennett, A. Linda, ed. *Encyclopedia of World Cultures (Europe).* Boston: G. K. Hall, 1992.

Duggan, Christopher. *Force of Destiny: A History of Italy since 1796.* Boston: Houghton Mifflin Company, 2008.

Fodor's 2008 Italy. New York: Random House, 2007.

Hofmann, Paul. *That Fine Italian Hand.* New York: Henry Holt, 1990.

Locatelli, Giorgio. *Made in Italy: Food & Stories.* New York: Ecco, 2007.

Mignone, Mario B. *Italy Today. A Country in Transition.* New York: Peter Lang, 1995.

Pavlovic, Zoran. *Italy.* Philadelphia: Chelsea House, 2004.

Pojmann, Wendy A. *Immigrant Women and Feminism in Italy.* Aldershot, England; Ashgate, 2006.

Travis, David. *The Land and People of Italy.* New York: HarperCollins, 1992.

—revised by J. Hobby

KALMYKS

ALTERNATE NAMES: Khal'mg (Qal'mg)
LOCATION: Russia (Republic of Kalmykia in the southwest)
POPULATION: 518,500 total, 174,000 in Russia
LANGUAGE: Kalmyk
RELIGION: Tibetan sect of Mahayana Buddhism (Lamaism)

¹ INTRODUCTION

The ancestors of the Kalmyks were originally members of the Oirat (Oyirad) people, a West Mongolian ethnic conglomerate living as nomadic pastoralists in the Dzungarian steppes of the Inner Asian heartland between the Altai and T'ien Shan Mountains. Dzungaria (Djungaria), in Sinkian (Xinjiang) Province of China, is the original homeland of a people known in the West as the Kalmyks (also spelled Kalmucks and Kalmuks), and in Central Asia, particularly among the closely related Mongolian nationalities, as *Idjil Monggol* (the Volga Mongols), *Öröd* (Oirats), or *Dörwn Öröd* (Four Oirat [Allies]). The latter are *Torgűd, Dörböd, Khoshud (Qoshud)*, and *Khöd (Qöd)* or *Qoyid*. The fourth member of this Oirat confederation has been variously referred to as *Qöd (Qoyid)*, *Ölod*, *Dzungar* or *Djungar*, or *Tsoros*.

The self-appellation of the Kalmyks is *Khal'mg (Qal'mg)*. Their Turkic-speaking neighboring peoples and tribes called them *qalmaq*, or *galmuq*, from which the Russian spelling *Kalmyk* has been derived. This name must have come into use at the end of the 16th or the beginning of the 17th century, when the Kyrgyz, Kazakh, and other Turkic peoples first came into direct contact with the vanguard of the ancestors of the Kalmyks, the Oirats (Oyirad). The name *Kalmyk* is not used in Central or Inner Asia. The Chinese historian Chí-yü Wu reports that "throughout the entire Ch'ing Dynasty, in spite of the close relations between the Court and the Oirats, the name Kalmuk never made its appearance in any of either the official or personal works of the period and was not known until very recently, when some of the Western sources began to be used by Chinese scholars."

The ancestors of the Kalmyks initially came into direct contact with the Russians at about the same time. As a result of intertribal internecine dissension, as well as socio-economic and other factors, many of the component tribes of the Oirat confederation (Torigűd, Dörböd, Khoshud) abandoned their ancestral nomadic encampments in Dzungaria and moved westward, finally occupying the steppes between the Ural and Lower Volga Rivers of South Russia in the 1620s. Other Oirat splinter groups joined them afterwards in the then-existing Kalmyk Khanate, and the entire group became known as the Kalmyks.

Under the reign of Catherine the Great (1762–96), Russia became a great European power. It was the policy of the imperial Russian authorities to limit the power and sovereignty of the Kalmyk khans and the Kalmyk fear of eventually being forced to convert to Christianity made them and their nobility discontented and agitated. In January 1771 approximately 169,000 people fled Russia to Dzungaria to avoid being completely subjugated to imperial Russian domination. They left behind, on the west bank of the Volga, one-fifth of their kinsmen, who were unable to join them because that winter

was unusually warm and the river did not freeze over, thereby making it impassable. The flight of the vast majority of the Kalmyks proved disastrous. Only a fraction reached Dzungaria in July 1771 after suffering great losses in human lives, livestock, and property. They became Chinese subjects, while those who remained behind were integrated into Great Russia. The Russians consolidated their rule over the Kalmyks and created three administrative divisions that were attached to the regional governments of Astrakhan, Stavropol, and Don. In the Civil War of 1917–20, most of the Kalmyks adopted a hostile attitude toward the atheist Bolsheviks and sided with the anti-Communist Russian armies. The defeat of these armies in 1920 led some of the Kalmyks to flee Russia. They dispersed into Yugoslavia, Bulgaria, France, and Czechoslovakia. The remaining Kalmyks in the Astrakhan steppe, like other non-Russian nationalities, were allowed to form their own autonomous *oblast'* (region) in November 1920. In October 1935, this region was elevated to the status of a republic and became the Kalmyk Autonomous Soviet Socialist Republic (KASSR) with its capital at Elista. During World War II, the Kalmyks were drafted into the Red Army like all other peoples of the USSR. After the German invasion of the Kalmyk Republic in 1942 and their subsequent expulsion, the Kalmyks were unjustifiably accused of collaborating with the German army. The Soviets took punitive measures with regard to the Kalmyks, not bothering much about the validity of the rumors. They dissolved the Kalmyk Republic, and on 27 December 1943, deported the Kalmyks to Siberia and Soviet Central Asia. After the Twentieth Congress of the Communist Party (1957), at the beginning of the year of the "liquidation of the cult of personality" (i.e., de-Stalinization), the Kalmyks were permitted to return to their former homeland, which on 29 July 1958 again became the KASSR. In 1991 the republic, now one of the 16 autonomous republics within the Russian Federation, changed its name to Kalmykia. It is headed by a popularly elected president for a term of seven years.

² LOCATION AND HOMELAND

The population figures of the Kalmyk people in Russia for the period 1897–1989 present an interesting topic for demographic research. The official census figures of the Kalmyk population in Russia are: 1897, 190,648; 1926, 129,321; 1929, 134,866; 1959, 106,066 (only 64,822 in the KASSR); 1970, 137,194 (of whom 110,264 lived in their native land); 1979, 146,631 (of whom 122,167 lived in the KASSR); and 1989, 174,528 (of whom 146,275 resided in their native republic). In addition, there were 121,531 Russians and 54,773 inhabitants representing 41 different nationalities (i.e., 176,304 non-Kalmyks.) Thus, the total population of Kalmykia comprised 322,579, of whom there were 158,020 males and 164,559 females, and 147,176 urban and 175,403 rural inhabitants. Some 89.9% considered Kalmyk their mother tongue. The significant decreases in population figures between 1897 and 1926 and between 1939 and 1959 are striking. A comparison of the 1897 and 1926 census figures shows that the Kalmyks decreased in number from 190,648 to 134,866. These tremendous human losses should be attributed to the tragic events of the Civil War of 1917–1920 in Russia, the ensuing flight of a sizeable number of people to Turkey and points beyond, malnutrition, and terrible famine in the Volga region in the early 1920s. According to the censuses of 1939 and 1959, the number of Kalmyks declined in 20 years by 28,800, or 21%, if all of these figures are at all trustworthy. There were 91,972 inhabitants in the capital city of Elista (called Steponi between 1944 and 1957) in 1990. The Kalmyk diaspora is made up of about 1,000 Kalmyks residing in the United States, who immigrated in 1951–52 and during the 1960s from various European countries, and between 700 and 750 in Europe, mostly in France, with small numbers in Germany and Bulgaria. A few Kalmyks can be found in Canada, Belgium, and the Czech Republic.

The Republic of Kalmykia is situated in the southwestern part of the Russian Federation, on the west bank of the lower Volga and the northwestern shore of the Caspian Sea. It extends approximately from 41°45' to 47°30' E. and from 48°20' to 44°50' N. The geographic center is at 45°30' E. and 46°30' N. Kalmykia borders on the Rostov-on-Don region in the west, the Astrakhan region in the east, the Volgograd region in the north, and the Stavropol *krai* (territory) and the Republic of Daghestan in the south. It is comprised essentially of a dry steppe or of the vast semidesert flat lowland of the northern Caspian Depression. The climate is markedly continental, with hot and dry summers and very cold winters but with little snow. The average temperature in July fluctuates between 23° and 26°C (73.6° to 78.8°F) and in January from minus 8° to minus 5°C (18° to 23°F).

³ LANGUAGE

Kalmyk is a West Mongolian language, closely affiliated with Khalkha (Qalqa) Mongolian (spoken in Mongolia), various

Mongolian dialects spoken in the Sinkiang (Hsin-chiang) Uighur Autonomous Region of China, Inner Mongolia and Manchuria, and in the Buriat Republic in Russia. They all constitute the Mongolian language group, an important division of the Altaic family of languages. Kalmyk is spoken by the overwhelming majority (89.9%) of the population of Kalmykia and by the older generation of the Sart Kalmyks numbering 3,000 to 4,000 and dwelling in the area of Przhevalsk, near Lake Issyk Kul, in the northeastern part of the Republic of Kyrgyzstan. The younger generation is now almost completely assimilated and speaks Turkic Kyrgyz. The Kalmyk language is divided into three dialects—Torgŭd, Döböd dialect, and Buzâwa. The latter is quite close to Torgŭd and is spoken by the Don Kalmyks, who before the 1920s resided in the Sal'sk District of the Don Cossack region. The Dörböd dialect, spoken by the Dörböd of Astrakhan (Lesser Dörböd) and Stavropol (Greater Dörböd) Provinces, varies in some rather insignificant ways from the Torgŭd and Buzâwa dialects. A few of the characteristic features of the Kalmyk language are as follows: (1) two distinctive inventories of single (short) and geminate (long) vowel phonemes; (2) vocalic harmony, a common feature of the Altaic languages (i.e., in one and the same stem, only front or back vowels may occur, with *I* occurring in stems with any vowels); (3) the absence of any gender categories; (4) ten cases for the declension of nouns, nominal postpositions, pronouns, participles, etc., as well as a singular/plural distinction; (5) verbs having the categories of mood, tense, person, number, voice, and aspect; (6) lack of agreement in gender, case, and number between adjectives and nouns.

Until 1648, the Kalmyks and their kindred Oirates (Oyirad) used the old vertical Mongolian script. In 1648, the learned monk-scholar Zaya Pandiata (1599–662) invented the so-called "clear script" *(todo bichig)*, an improved and phonetically more precise Mongolian script. It came somewhat closer to the actual pronunciation but was never a phonetic one, and thus remained always quite apart from the colloquial Kalmyk language.

The Zaya Pandiata script fell into disuse and was replaced in 1924 by the Cyrillic alphabet, popularly referred to as the Russian alphabet. This was abandoned in 1931, however, when the modified Latin alphabet was introduced in many non-Russian republics and regions, only to be replaced in 1938 once again by the Cyrillic alphabet. The latter has been in use up to this day.

Kalmyk is especially rich in kinship and livestock terminology, forms of polite address with respect to nobility and the secular clergy, and terms of respect when addressing elderly and senior people. The firstborn child is called *uugn* and the youngest one is *otxn*. An ordinary person's photo or picture is *zurg* but that of the ecclesiastic's is *günra*. To die or pass away is *ükx önggrx*, but *taal* or *burxn bolx* for lamas and high secular clergy. To arrive or sit solemnly as applied to princes and high lamas is *zalrx;* otherwise, it is *irx*. Domestic animals such as horses, sheep, goats, cattle, and camels have different names depending on their age, sex, color and, if applicable, whether or not they are castrated. Thus, a one year-old lamb is *xurgn* or *tölg*, a sheep aged two years is *zusg xön*, a ram aged three years is *gunn irg*, a female sheep aged four years or older is *xön*, a ram of the same age is *xuc*, but a castrated one of the same age is *irg*.

⁴ FOLKLORE

The Kalmyk people can justifiably boast of one of the richest oral traditions not only among the Mongolian-speaking peoples but also among Asian peoples as a whole. From time immemorial this tradition has preserved rich and diverse specimens of folklore with loving care. Myths are the most archaic among the specimens of oral literature. Their oldest layer can be traced to the heroic tales and the heroic epic *Janggar*, which states that there are three levels of outer space: the Upper universe (*Tenggrin gazr*) inhabited by dragons, celestial beings, and gigantic birds; the Middle universe (*Zambtiv*), whose inhabitants are the epic heroes, demons, and ordinary mortals; and the Lower universe, which is the realm of various mythological creatures such as gigantic serpents, ghosts of the waters, mountains, and so on.

Legends did not originally differ from the myths either in content or form. The oldest legends reflected mythological and werewolf-like views of the phenomena of nature and primitive society. Quite a few folk legends tell about the origins and the ancestors of the tribes and clans—e.g., a well-known legend about the origin of the Dörböd princes of the Tsoros clan or another tale of Tundutov, the forefather of the Dörböd princes.

The paremiological folklore represented by the proverbs, proverbial phrases, and riddles is especially rich and widespread; these forms clearly reflect the succinct folk wisdom. Benedictions (*yöräl*), glorifications (*magtal*), damnations (*kharal*), incantations (*tarni*), and songs relate to the ancient forms of oral folk poetry. Benedictions are usually rhythmic in nature and are uttered on all kinds of occasions,—for example, weddings, the birth of a child, when greeting guests at the table, in proposing a toast to someone's health, or success, as congratulations, and so on. Damnation (*kharal*) is the complete antithesis to benediction (*yöräl*) because it means misfortune, harm, or disaster to someone else. Glorifications (*magtal*) were an odic form exalting the heroic deeds of epic and war heroes. Incantations (*tarni*) were primarily spoken by women in order to pursue a determinate object producing a particular effect.

The genres of Kalmyk songs are diverse—heroic, historic, ritual, lullaby, drinking, satirical, songs of praise, and so on. They are either short (*axr dun*) or long and drawn-out (*ut dun*). The latter are considered the oldest in the song repertoire of the Mongolian peoples. The folktale is an especially rich and popular genre of Kalmyk oral tradition, and there are four such genres: fairy tales, heroic tales, animal tales, and everyday (morals and manners) tales.

The heroic epic *Janggar's* is the best-known specimen of Kalmyk and Oirate oral literature. It bears the name of the main hero who is surrounded and supported by a dozen of his closest and most trusted heroes. They courageously fight foreign and alien enemies at *Janggar's* side. Each of these heroes is endowed with a specific distinctive attribute. The events in this epic tale take place in the imaginary land of Bumba, a land of boundless happiness and prosperity, of eternal youth and immortality, a land where winter is unknown. Hero worship is an underlying element of this epic.

⁵ RELIGION

The Kalmyks were faithful and fervent Buddhists, following the faith of their forebears. If Kalmykia is classified as a part of Europe, then the Kalmyks would be considered the only Buddhist ethnic group inhabiting Europe. They belong to the Tibetan "Yellow Hat" or *Gelugpa* (Virtuous Way) sect of the Mahâyâna or Northern branch of Buddhism, which is also commonly referred to as Lamaism. It still contains an admixture of indigenous beliefs and shamanistic practices. The Kalmyks were converted from their earlier shamanistic beliefs to Tibetan Buddhism shortly before they reached the Lower Volga area in the early 17th century. Until the exodus in 1771, they were able to maintain direct contacts with Tibetan religious centers, thus enabling the importation of sacred Tibetan texts, religious images and thankas, church plates, and other articles. Many monks went to Tibet and Mongolia for advanced education at the lamaseries. The Dalai Lamas have always been recognized by the Kalmyks and other Mongolian-speaking peoples as the highest spiritual and religious authority.

During the existence of the Soviet Union, religion in the Kalmyk Autonomous Republic was completely suppressed. All Buddhist temples were either closed or destroyed. The last elected religious head of the Kalmyk people, Lama Lubsan Sharab Tepkin (born in 1875), was arrested in 1931, tried, condemned, and exiled to the region of Tashkent in present-day Uzbekistan for a period of 10 years. The date of his death and the place of his burial are unknown. The first sign of the revival of Buddhism in Kalmykia can be dated to January 1989, when the first (albeit small) *khurul* (Kalmyk Buddhist temple) began to function in Elista. In June of that year the first group of 10 Kalmyk boys was selected and sent to Ulan Bator in Mongolia to study Buddhist scriptures and prayers at the local Buddhist academy. In 1991 a Buddhist temple was opened in Buryatia in Siberia, and among its 60 pupils were several Kalmayks. On 5 October 1996 the first large-scale multistoried temple was opened and consecrated. Many other temples have been built throughout Kalmykia, totaling over 20. The Kalmyks in the United States have four functioning temples—three in Howell, New Jersey, and one in Philadelphia.

⁶ MAJOR HOLIDAYS

All holidays celebrated by the Kalmyks are non-secular (i.e., strictly religious) and based on the lunar calendar. As a rule, being Buddhists, the Kalmyks do not observe Christmas, Easter, or other Christian and non-Christian holidays. Six major Buddhist holidays are celebrated and are marked by giving gifts to the temples and money and food for the lamas.

⁷ RITES OF PASSAGE

In the days when doctors or hospitals were not available, Kalmyk women gave birth to their children in their traditional nomadic tents or houses. Midwives were usually unpaid elderly women without any formal training. A midwife (*baabk* in Kalmyk) was highly respected in the household concerned. The birth of a boy always brought joy because it secured the continuity of the patrilineal descent of the family. Childlessness or giving birth only to girls was considered the greatest misfortune that could occur. It was not unusual for a childless woman to return to her parents' home. The childhood and teenage years in Kalmyk families have no distinctive rites of passage. Death and burial are a family matter. It is customary to visit the deceased person's family to express one's condolences. Monks, who consult the sacred Buddhist scriptures, determine the dates of the funeral and the memorial services. During the funeral they let it be known that people born in certain lunar years may not touch the deceased's coffin. At that time or at the requiem, both people present and not present donate money to the bereaved family as a token of their sympathy. It is believed that after death the spirit of a deceased person wanders about for 49 days. On the 49th day the invited monks offer special prayers at the home of the deceased in the presence of his/her family. On this day, the soul of the departed is supposed to leave his/her home and transmigrate into another body or being. In times past, it was customary to cremate the mortal remains of nobility and high ecclesiastics in full view of the people.

8 INTERPERSONAL RELATIONS

The Buddhist clergy occupies a position of high esteem. When commoners meet ecclesiastics, they greet them by bowing and touching their heads against the monks' hands. Formerly, it was not customary to shake hands. Women, especially those who are middle-aged and elderly, usually abstain from handshakes with each other. It is considered to be a sign of piety and courtesy to bow before a host's Buddhist altar if it is within sight. The elderly are highly respected in Kalmyk culture. They are traditionally allowed entry to homes before the younger people and are given the right to lead conversations and not be interrupted. Kalmyks are known to be hospitable. Traditionally, the doors of one's home were always open to everyone, even complete strangers. It was acceptable to enter someone else's abode without ringing the door bell or knocking at the door. Visitors and guests are always served tea, food, and drinks. Refusal of the offer of drink and food is considered rude and pompous, insulting to the host or the hostess. In the past, young unmarried men and women met only at evening parties, as dating was not then socially acceptable. A formerly observed custom was for a bridegroom to meet his bride for the first time on their wedding day. Many customs have since changed, however, and dating, now commonplace, is not significantly different from dating in other countries.

9 LIVING CONDITIONS

Before the 1917 Bolshevik *coup d'état* in Russia, medical care in Kalmykia was virtually nonexistent. The people relied for their medical care on Buddhist monks (*emchi*) who had been trained in Tibetan medicine. The mortality rate was quite high, especially among children. The number of cases of smallpox was substantial because the Kalmyks were afraid of being vaccinated. The introduction of Western medicine in the 1920s significantly alleviated health problems in Kalmykia. At about the same time, the Soviet authorities started to combat the most widely spread diseases—tuberculosis and venereal diseases—just as they did in Mongolia. Tuberculosis was attributed to three causes: an occupational disease among the fishing population along the shores of the Caspian Sea; undernourishment; and the wearing of sleeveless camisoles by Kalmyk girls beginning as early as seven or eight years of age. The tight camisoles prevented normal chest development.

Even though tuberculosis is supposed to have been completely eradicated in Kalmykia, sporadic outbreaks of this contagious disease have been reported in recent years. The Kalmyks seem to be susceptible to tuberculosis. For example, a considerable number of people fell ill with it in prewar Yugoslavia and postwar Germany. Because of negligence on the part of the medical personnel of the Elista city hospital, a mass

outbreak of AIDS occurred in the spring of 1989. The total number of people infected by the AIDS virus in Kalmykia exceeded 100, the overwhelming majority of them children, and some have since died. Teams of medical specialists from New Jersey have visited Kalmykia on half a dozen occasions in order to render assistance and deliver needed medical equipment and instruments to hospitals in Elista.

The population of Kalmykia can be divided into urban and rural. The town dwellers are better off as far as employment opportunities, housing conditions, consumer goods, public education, and medical facilities are concerned. In Elista, for instance, most of the people live in tenement houses in their own multi-room apartments that meet minimum standards of sanitation, safety, and comfort and are usually located near bus stops. Taxicabs are also readily available. The living conditions in most of the rural areas, however, are inferior. Not all of the countryside communities have adequate basic services such as indoor water and sewer facilities, gas, proper housing, transportation, hospitals and clinics. For this reason, many Kalmyks living in villages have decided to migrate to urban areas, either in Kalmykia or further in another part of Russia. The standard of living of Kalmyks living in West European countries and in the United States is predictably higher.

10 FAMILY LIFE

Women were traditionally regarded in Kalmyk society as of lesser standing. To be sure, the Kalmyk women were not blindly subject to their husbands as in India, nor were they strictly isolated as in Islamic tradition. Nonetheless, there was a patriarchal system of rules governing the conduct of women, particularly married women. The practice of taboos against saying men's names resulted in a special women's jargon. All clothing was sewn by women. A woman's daily household routine consisted of preparing food and *arrack* (a type of alcoholic beverage), milking cows and mares, gathering fuel, drying and salting meat, and caring for children. The change from a nomadic to a sedentary way of life alleviated the lives of Kalmyk women as fewer items were domestically manufactured and more were purchased. More women began to attend educational institutions and to receive higher education. Today, many women in Kalmykia hold advanced degrees in a wide range of fields. In the United States, quite a few Kalmyk women have received a college education.

The average family size in Kalmykia consists of about four to five individuals. The strained housing and economic conditions of a sizable proportion of the Kalmyk population significantly affect family size. Previously, it was not uncommon for a family to have six or more children.

Marriage is monogamous; polygamous marriages are unknown. In the past, the only polygamists were khans and high nobility. Until recently, marriages in both Kalmykia and abroad were for the most part endogamous (marrying within one's own ethnic group) unless there were no locally available Kalmyk girls. The number of marriages between Kalmyks of both sexes and non-Kalmyks has been progressively growing. This development has affected the Kalmyk family in many mostly unfavorable ways. Parents strive to have their sons and daughters marry their own kinsmen and co-religionists, but in Kalmyk tradition, marriage between young people of the same *yasun* (kin in the bone) and between distant cousins up to seven times removed is discouraged. This significantly limits the possibilities for in-group marriage. Married sons are customarily expected to live with and care for aging parents. When there are no married sons, married daughters assume this responsibility.

11 CLOTHING

Traditional clothing for men and women was of the same design irrespective of region. Men wore rather long and baggy shirts with low collars made of canvas, coarse calico, or cotton. Trousers were tucked into boots of black goatskin leather. Over their shirts, men wore a Caucasian-type *beshmet* (quilted coat) that fitted at the waist, with a stand-up collar. The preferred color of the *beshmet* was blue. Worn underneath it was a waistcoat made of *nankeen* (cloth). The belt, made of silver, was considered the most valuable item of apparel and a required element of male and female garments. The headdresses of both men and women were diverse. The most widely worn cap was the *toorcg*, with a black lambskin cap band and a quadrangular top trimmed with otter. The top of the cap was made of bright broadcloth edged with white or colored lace. A distinctive red tassel jutted out in the middle. Many men liked to wear Russian-type service caps.

Starting at 14 years of age, girls wore over their underwear a peculiar, tight sleeveless canvas corset (called a *kamzol*) that prevented the natural growth of their breasts. On top of this they wore a special kind of *beshmet* called a *biiz* with a tight waist made of silk, wool, satin or printed cotton. The lace or cloth belt was a required part of the girl's attire. The female headdress was of three main styles. As everyday clothing, married women wore long-sleeved dresses down to their heels. Over their white shirts, they wore a long sleeveless *tsegdeg* embellished with ornamental details sewn from wool or black cotton materials. These were adorned with rich embroidery. Unlike men and unmarried women, married women never girdled themselves. Today, traditional clothing is worn only on special occasions such as religious festivities, major national holidays, weddings, and so on. In the last 80 or so years, Kalmyks have worn clothing similar to that of other modern urbanites.

12 FOOD

The Kalmyk diet is based primarily on meat. By far the favorite meat is lamb, followed by beef, chicken, and pork. In the past, camel and horseflesh were also eaten. Until very recently, the staple of the Kalmyk diet was so-called Kalmyk tea, which was made from crumbled pressed-brick tea, milk, salt, butter, nutmeg, and bay leaves. Brick tea was originally imported from China but in recent years it has been replaced by locally grown tea from Georgia and other southern regions of Russia. This tea is served always at rites and holidays, but regular tea or tea bags and evaporated milk are used for everyday purposes. On ceremonial occasions it is also customary to serve boiled lamb cut up into small pieces and mixed with finely cut fresh onions. Lamb stock is also served on those occasions, and it is believed to have medicinal properties.

A very popular Kalmyk dish is *dotur*. After a sheep is slaughtered, the thoroughly washed large and small intestines, tripe, and stomach are cut into pieces. The lung, liver, kidney, and heart are also washed. All the entrails are boiled and then served. Customarily, relatives and neighbors are invited to eat this *dotur*. An equally popular dish is *böreg*, a counterpart of Chinese boiled dumplings and Russian *vareniki*. This is made of ground lamb or beef that is boiled and sometimes served with sour cream. This dish is also popular in Tibet, Mongolia, Buriatia, and Sinkiang (Xinjiang). Formerly, the common people consumed a soup, *budan*, almost daily. *Budan* consisted of dried lamb or beef with onions and was thickened by adding flour to the broth, and finally sour cream was added. *Kumiss* is a beverage made of fermented mare's or camel's milk. It is not readily available nowadays, but a similar drink prepared from fermented cow's milk is used for medicinal and dietetic purposes. *Chigän*—fermented cow's milk added to fresh milk—is a refreshing drink. *Bulmug*, a gravy-like dish of thick broth, flour, milk, sugar, raisins, and fresh apples and/or pears, is usually prepared in winter. *Borcog* are small flat whorl-shaped cakes made of flour, water, and yeast and fried in oil. These come in various shapes and forms and are served on festive occasions. There are no taboos of any kind insofar as food and drinks are concerned.

Kalmyks today are becoming accustomed to European and Russian food such as *borscht* (soup made of cabbage and beets), *bliny* (thin round pancakes), *xolodec* (jellied minced meat somewhat similar to headcheese), and *vinegret* (salad of cucumbers, potatoes, onions, etc., dressed with oil and vinegar). Kalmyks who have lived in countries outside of Russia (the Balkans, France, etc.) have adopted some of their popular dishes. In the United States, young Kalmyks do not differ from their American counterparts in what they eat and drink.

13 EDUCATION

Until the 1930s, literacy among the Kalmyks was very low. Many parents chose not to send their children to Russian grammar schools out of fear that they might become Russianized and/or baptized. Other parents were unable to educate their offspring because they could not afford to pay the school dormitory expenses in distant locations. The Soviet authorities, realizing that only literate people could be reached by propaganda and be of use for agricultural and industrial development, began massive Soviet campaigns directed at the eradication of illiteracy. According to Soviet sources, by 1940 the literacy rate had risen to 91%, up from 3.8% in 1924. Today, the percentage of Kalmyks who can read and write must be even higher because of considerable progress in education.

Education was sorely neglected in the Kalmyk steppe by the Tsarist government. In 1917, there were only 14 Kalmyks with a higher education. The number of elementary schools was small, and they were far apart. The language of instruction was Russian. Recently, the Kalmyk language has experienced a revival. In 1993, 24 national classes were developed, and national classes and the teaching of Kalmyk language is a priority and continues to be expanded. Teaching of Kalmyk culture and history is also a priority. There are no longer shortages of schools (from grammar to senior high school) or of college-educated teachers. In 1964, the Kalmyk Pedagogical Institute was established in Elista. Six years later, it was reorganized into the Kalmyk State University. It has numerous departments offering undergraduate courses in Kalmyk language and literature, Russian, foreign languages, history, mathematics, agriculture, and so on. In recent years, new courses in marketing, business, and management have been introduced. The establishment of a graduate school is in the initial stages.

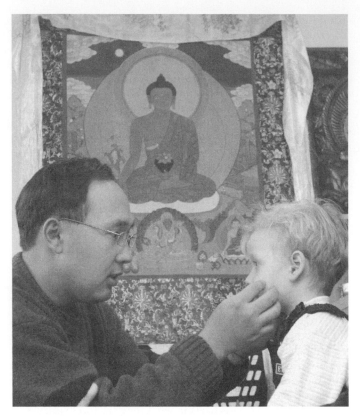

A Kalmyk doctor examines a patient at the Centre of Tibetan Medicine in the Kalmyk capital Elista. Tibetan culture is very popular in the small Russian Republic of Kalmykia. (Tatyana Makeyeva/AFP/Getty Images)

14 CULTURAL HERITAGE

Russian and other foreign travelers who visited the migratory Kalmyks in the 18th and 19th centuries took note of their musical ability. They reported that most of the musicians playing the *dombra*, a two-stringed, triangular-shaped musical instrument, were women. (The instrument's strings were made from sheep intestines.) One of the most prominent foreign visitors was Alexandre Dumas père (1802–1870), a famous French novelist and dramatist, who visited the Kalmyk steppe in October 1859. He was entertained at a dinner in his honor at the mansion of Prince Tseren-Djab Tumen' (1824–1864) by an orchestra of Kalmyk musicians who played overtures by Mozart and Rossini. The great Russian composer and director of the St. Petersburg Conservatory, N.A. Rimsky-Korsakov, immediately recognized the exceptional talent of a Kalmyk student, Dordji Mandjiev (1883–1909), a gifted cellist and violinist. Unfortunately, Mandjiev died of pulmonary tuberculosis in the prime of his life. In general, Kalmyk women are more involved in music and singing than men. Today they are familiar with the violin, cello, accordion, grand piano, and other instruments.

During formal and informal gatherings and various festive ceremonies, Kalmyk singing and dancing take place to the accompaniment of the *dombra*. Dancing involves the stamping and rapid movement of the feet more than the movement of the arms and hands. It is done by same-sex or opposite-sex, individually, in foursomes, or even in a group. Dance partners face each other, but when they turn around they dance back-to-back. Women dance more calmly, easily, and gracefully,

whereas the dancing of the men is notable for its occasional swift movements and for the loud stamping of feet.

Secular literature did not exist until the advent of the 20th century. The only known literary works are three historical chronicles written in the vertical *todo* script during the 18th and 19th centuries. The first Kalmyk writers made their appearance at the end of the 1920s with short stories and poems. The poets wrote their poems in the traditional alliterative metrical verses, which were either consonantal or vocalic—i.e., in a tetrastich (a stanza consisting of four lines) in which initial consonants or vowels were repeated either successively or alternately. In Kalmyk verses, the lines are non-rhyming. The first novels appeared in 1962. In 1957, a new generation of poets and prose writers made their appearance after their return from enforced exile in Siberia and Soviet Central Asia. Some younger writers write their works only in Russian. The works of Kalmyk writers and poets appeared also in Russian translation, particularly in Elista and Moscow. Needless to say, until about 1990, writers had to adhere to the canons of the Communist Party–controlled dominant style of Socialist Realism.

The breeding of horses was traditionally part of the Kalmyks heritage, due to their nomadic past. Today, there is a tendency to return to this tradition, as 28 stud farms operate in the republic. Likewise, the breeding of sheep has been important to the Kalmyks in the past and continues to be important to the Kalmyks.

While Kalmyks are Buddhist, some remnants of older religion and shamanism remain in practice. In some areas, shamans are reported to continue to hold a place of respect. Fire is believed to be sacred and to have cleansing properties. Smoke from juniper branches are also considered to have cleansing properties. Heaps of stones that are believed to have spiritual properties are found in the region.

15 WORK

Until recently, few goods were purchased. Women, who bore the full brunt of domestic housekeeping and were busy from sunrise until late in the evening, made most goods. They sewed all the clothing and, in addition to the daily household work of preparing food and *arrack* (an alcoholic brandy distilled from fermented mare's milk, *kumiss*), they milked the cows and mares, gathered fuel, dried and salted meat, and cared for children. With the abandonment of the nomadic way of life and the rise of a settled agricultural existence, certain changes took place. The evolution of the Kalmyk economy also brought about changes in Kalmyk life. Fewer items were manufactured at home and more were purchased. During World War I and World War II, Kalmyk women had to bear the entire responsibility for the fields and their homes while the men were at the front. In the past, a favorite pastime for men was to visit to their relatives, comrades, or neighbors in order to chat, exchange news and gossip, enjoy some drinks, play cards, or simply lie down out-of-doors either smoking pipes or napping in a shady place. All of this has changed, however, with the radical departure from a nomadic way of life and the advent of secular education. Nowadays, there is no difference between the work habits of Kalmyks of either sex.

16 SPORTS

In the past, Kalmyk-style wrestling, archery, and horse racing were very popular. These took place during folk and religious holidays, weddings, and other festive occasions and attracted throngs of local people as well as guests. Young girls and women competed in archery and horse racing equally with young boys and men. Horse races were conducted over a distance of 6.5 miles to 16.5 miles and involved the participation of 10–20 riders of both sexes. The Kalmyks are very fond of chess and known to be good chess players. In fact, as of 2008 the president of Kalmykia, Kirsan Ilyumzhinov, was the leader of FIDE, the World Chess Federation. He oversaw the building of a multi-million dollar complex called Chess City, located on the outskirts of Elista. By far the most popular sport played and enjoyed by both children and adults is soccer. In the 1930s the Kalmyk soccer team in Prague (consisting of high school and college students) made it to the first Czechoslovak soccer league. In the 1960s a Kalmyk soccer player played for the French national team as its captain. His son also became a famous soccer player.

17 ENTERTAINMENT AND RECREATION

There are theatres and concert halls in Elista and elsewhere in Kalmykia. The former have been experiencing difficult times due to a decline in attendance, a lack of state funding, and a shortage of suitable plays.

Virtually every Kalmyk household has a television, which is very popular among both the urban and rural population. The television station in Elista offers both local and national news and various programs of entertainment and culture. The latter are transmitted from Moscow. In Kalmyk homes in the United States, it is not surprising to find VCRs, DVD players, personal computers, fax machines, and stereo systems.

Teenagers and other young people are fond of American youth culture. American clothing (blue jeans), rock music, and movies are especially popular. Entertainment is usually provided at weddings, dance parties, and other occasions, and musicians perform western-style music. At such functions, native Kalmyk music is also provided for dancing. Elista is home to several discos, which are frequented by young people.

18 FOLK ART, CRAFTS, AND HOBBIES

Traditionally, Kalmykia had a reputation for its bonesetters, who treated both cattle and people. They could set fractures, or broken or dislocated bones, usually quite successfully. Sometimes they resorted to removing certain small shattered bones and replacing them with the bones of a young camel.

The Kalmyks were skilled in almost every imaginable type of handcraft. From head hides they made distinctive large flasks (bortxo) for keeping arrack brandy, and from the hides of legs and bellies of cattle they made hunting bags, buckets, and other vessels, as well as straps for various purposes. From sheepskin women sewed fur coats. Wooden cups of different shapes, sizes, and grades were hollowed out from birch, maple, elm, or walnut wood. These are still used in households for drinking Kalmyk tea. Kalmyks were also skilled goldsmiths and silversmiths.

19 SOCIAL PROBLEMS

In December 1943 the Kalmyks were subjected to the most flagrant violation of their human and civil rights when the entire nation, including front-line soldiers and officers, was deported to Siberia and adjacent regions for alleged collaboration with the German army of occupation. Since their return to their homeland in 1957, they have enjoyed equal rights in every respect. In Kalmykia, Russians enjoy the same rights as the Kalmyks, despite some evidence of tensions. The office of mayor in Elista, the capital city, has been held by a Russian, as has the representative from Kalmykia to the Russian State Duma (parliament).

Drug abuse has as of yet not been a major problem in Kalmykia. Alcoholism is a problem, although numbers of alcohol-related deaths are lower than the average for Russia. Kalmykia has one of the highest infant mortality rates in Russia, and life expectancy is lower.

20 GENDER ISSUES

While in the past there may have been very little equality between the sexes among the Kalmyks, this is a trend that has changed. Today, the situation of Kalmyk women is similar to that of most other women in Russia. Kalmyk women, as women of most ethnicities under the Soviet Union, were actively encouraged to join the workforce. Kalmyk women are known to hold important positions within their community, obtaining success both in business and civil careers.

21 BIBLIOGRAPHY

Bormanshinov, Arash. *Kalmyk Manual.* New York: American Council of Learned Societies, 1961.

Erdniev, U. E. *Kalmyks: Historical and Ethnographical Studies.* 3rd ed., In Russian. Elista, Kalmykia: 1985.

Fagan, Geraldine. "Russia: Few Complaints Over Kalmykia's State Support of Buddhism." *Forum 18 News Service,* 11 April 2003.

Gordon, Raymond G. Jr. (ed). *Ethnologue: Languages of the World.* Dallas, Texas: SIL International, 2005.

———. "The Kalmyks in America, 1952–62." *Royal Central Asian Journal* 50 (1963).

———. "Kalmyks," *Harvard Encyclopedia of American Ethnic Groups.* Ed. S. Thernstrom. Cambridge, MA: Harvard University Press. 1980.

———. "The Kalmyks in the United States 35 Years Later." *The Mongolia Society Newsletter,* n.s. 5 (1988).

———. *The Kalmyks: Their Ethnic, Historical, Religious, and Cultural Background.* Howell, NJ: Kalmyk American Cultural Association, 1990.

Government of the Republic of Kalmykia. Education Section. http://www.kalm.ru/en/education.html (June 2008).

Mydans, Seth. "Where Chess is King and the People Pawns." *The New York Times,* 20 June 2004.

Pridemore, William Alex and Sang-Weon Kim. "Patterns of Alcohol-Related Mortality in Russia." *J Drug Issues.* 2006; 36(1): 229–247.

Rubel, P. G. *The Kalmyk Mongols: A Study in Continuity and Change.* Indiana University Publications, Uralic and Altaic Series, vol. 64. The Hague: Mouton & Co. 1967.

Wu, Chi-yü. "Who Were the Oirats," *Yenching Journal of Social Studies* 3 (1941).

—revised by M. Kerr

KARACHAI

LOCATION: Caucasus mountains between Russia and Georgia
(Karachaevo-Cherkessian Republic)
POPULATION: 169,000 (2002)
LANGUAGE: Karachai; Cherkessian; Russian
RELIGION: Islam

1 INTRODUCTION

The Karachai people live in the Caucasus Mountains. Throughout the history of the Karachai, the mountains have helped to protect them from outside forces. Thus, the Karachai have been able to preserve their language and culture remarkably well.

In 1917, the Karachai supported Soviet power and fought against the Tsarist forces, who had repressed them for decades. For the Karachai, the first 10 years of Soviet power were peaceful and productive. They were granted a shared state status with the Circassian people to form the Karachaevo-Cherkessian Autonomous Region. They were permitted to publish Karachai books and newspapers and to open schools that taught in the Karachai language. However, as Joseph Stalin rose to power in the late 1920s and 1930s, the rights of the Karachai to develop their language and culture were curtailed. The Karachai were pressured to use the Russian language.

During World War II, the Karachai joined the Soviet Army to defeat Nazi Germany. Despite this contribution to the Soviet war effort, Stalin's government suspected the Karachai of secretly supporting the Germans. As punishment, and also to prevent any future betrayal of the Soviet Union, the entire Karachai population was deported in the spring of 1944. In a few days, the Soviet army and secret police rounded up all Karachai citizens, loaded them into boxcars, and shipped them hundreds of miles away to Kazakhstan or Siberia. Families were often separated, and many never saw their relatives again. Many died in transit, and others died of exposure or starvation when they arrived in their new locations, as the government did not provide them with food or shelter. Those living in exile were treated as traitors and suffered severe discrimination. They were not allowed to assemble in groups, participate in local politics, nor engage in their traditional cultural practices. The tragedy of the deportation, combined with the destruction of the Caucasian Wars in the 19th century, fueled a Karachai distrust of Russia that is still evident.

After Stalin's death, Nikita Khrushchev's government reconsidered the decision to deport the Karachai. Thus, in 1956, the Karachai were permitted to return to their homeland in the Caucasus Mountains. They left their places of exile in massive numbers, usually returning to the villages where they had lived prior to 1944. The Karachai spent years rebuilding their local communities and economy, which had suffered during the years of deportation. Although the Soviet government under Khrushchev was considerably less repressive than the Stalinist regime, the Karachai were nevertheless pressured to adopt the Russian language and Soviet culture. Moscow frequently appointed Russians to important political positions in the Karachai territory, and this was resented by many Karachai.

In the last years of Soviet power, under Mikhail Gorbachev, Soviet ethnic groups were given greater freedom to express their language and culture. The Karachai seized this opportunity eagerly. They expanded their publishing houses, developed a new Karachai education program and opened new mosques. Following the collapse of the Soviet Union, the Karachaevo-Cherkessian Republic achieved even greater cultural and economic autonomy from Moscow. The Karachai have continued their cultural development and assumed an active political role in the Karachaevo-Cherkessian Republic. While they retain their own ethnic identity and practices, they are open to modernization, particularly in economic activities.

2 LOCATION AND HOMELAND

The Karachaevo-Cherkessian Republic is located to the south of Russia and north of the Republic of Georgia, in the Caucasus Mountain Range, between the Black and Caspian Seas. The Karachai live in mountainous terrain in the south of the republic with the capital city named Karachevsk. The traditional occupation of the Karachai is sheep farming, and the alpine meadows of the Caucasus provide ideal terrain for grazing. Sheep farming remains a source of employment for many Karachai. Many Karachai have now migrated to the towns and cities to seek modern amenities and work.

According to the 2002 census, the Karachai population was 169,198. They comprise 38.5% of the entire population of the Karachaevo-Cherkessian Republic (Russians account for 33.6%, Circassians for 11.6%, and Abazas for 7.4%), the Karachai population is concentrated in the southern region of the Republic in conditions of relative ethnic homogeneity. Karachai Diaspora still remains in Kazakhstan about 21,000, approximately 10,000 live in Turkey, and 20,000 in the United States (primarily in New Jersey).

3 LANGUAGE

The five official languages of the Karachaevo-Cherkessian Republic are Karachai, Circassian (Kabardian), Russian, Nogai, and Abaza. Most Karachai use their own language and are also fluent speakers, readers, and writers of Russian. Some Karachai have a command of Circassian. The Karachai language is part of the Kipchak Turkic language group. Karachai bears a strong resemblance to Turkish, with a similar structure and many similar words. In the late 1920s, under Stalin, the Karachai were required to change their alphabet from Latin (similar to modern Turkish) to Cyrillic (similar to Russian), and the Karachai still use the Cyrillic alphabet. Since the collapse of Soviet power, Karachai linguists have been working to replace words adopted from Russian with Turkic Karachai variants.

Traditionally, Karachai names were often of Muslim origin, such as the male name Khasan or the female name Zara. During the Soviet period, pressures to assimilate into Russian culture resulted in the frequent use of Russian first names, such as Yuri or Irina. More recently, as the Karachai have been able to express their culture more actively, traditional names have regained popularity. All children take the surname of their father. Upon marriage, most women do change their last names.

4 FOLKLORE

The epic folktale is the central, traditional expression of Karachai folklore. Such tales are lengthy stories of a hero who encounters and defeats obstacles and enemies in order to restore personal or family honor. These tales were usually passed on orally from generation to generation. As the Karachai suffered tragic experiences during the deportations, the epic tales incorporated details of these events. The traditional folktale has become a means of both preserving Karachai history and teaching Karachai values of honor, bravery, and family loyalty. The Karachai retain an ancient set of myths, the Nart sagas.

⁵ RELIGION

The Karachai are almost exclusively Muslim. For most of the 20th century, the Soviet government prohibited the Karachai from openly practicing Islam. Religious celebrations of weddings or funerals were often conducted secretly. Therefore, most Karachai do not adhere strictly to Islamic ritual. For example, most do not participate in prayers five times daily, and many women, especially younger ones, do not wear head coverings. In the late Soviet and post-Soviet years, Karachai began to open and attend mosques. Some Karachai observe major Islamic festivals, such as Ramadan and Eid. During Ramadan, adults fast during daylight hours. Eid marks the end of Ramadan and is celebrated with large feasts.

⁶ MAJOR HOLIDAYS

During the Soviet period, the major holidays were October 7, in recognition of the 1917 revolution, and May 1, the day of international socialism. People did not work or attend school on these days, and local governments often organized displays of music, dancing, and fireworks. Although Soviet power has collapsed, these holidays continue to be observed, and local officials are trying to create non-religious holidays to replace the Soviet celebrations. New Year's Eve is widely celebrated, as people invite guests to their homes to dine.

One of the most respected holidays among the Karachai is the Day of National Resurgence, which the Karachai celebrate on May 3 in honor of the day in 1957 when the first train of Karachai repatriates came from Kazakhstan to Karachaevsk.

⁷ RITES OF PASSAGE

Shortly after birth, boys are circumcised according to Islamic requirements, and this ceremony introduces the baby into the community. Even in the Soviet period, the Karachai adhered to the practice of circumcision. There is no similar ceremony for girls. The birthdate and name of a baby is registered with local authorities.

Traditionally, children would spend time with their parents, learning the tasks that they would be expected to perform as adults. Alongside their mothers, aunts, and grandmothers, girls learned to cook, spin, weave, knit, and run the household. Boys were gradually included in the sheep farming activities of adult males. Children moved quickly into adulthood, with no distinct teenage stage. By the time they entered puberty, most young people had assumed many adult responsibilities and were encouraged to marry by their mid-teens.

In the second half of the 20th century, however, the traditional activities of children and teenagers have changed greatly. Children are required to attend school beginning in grade one, and many also attend nursery school and kindergarten. While children may, occasionally, be kept home from school to help with chores, most parents want their children to receive a good education. Rather than moving straight from childhood to adulthood, teenagers attend high school, a huge percent of Karachai youths continue their education in universities. Although many marry by their late teens, most young people do

have years of relative freedom in their early and mid-teens before moving on to the responsibilities of adult life.

Death is almost always marked by a religious ceremony and burial, practices that were observed even during the Soviet period. The family of the deceased is expected to hold a large feast to which all members of the community are invited.

⁸ INTERPERSONAL RELATIONS

Men usually greet one another with a handshake, and women also often shake hands with one another. Men and women rarely shake hands. According to traditions, a woman is expected to stand respectfully when a man enters a room, even if the man is her brother. This custom, however, is no longer widespread, particularly in towns and cities.

Traditionally, men and women did not dine together. Instead, men ate together in the dining room, and women and children stayed in the kitchen. The women appeared in the dining room only to bring food or clear the table. Although most families no longer observe these formalities, many will observe this segregation on formal occasions when guests have been invited to the house. If all the adult males are absent, which can occur when the sheep are grazing high in the mountains, then the oldest son will sit in the dining room with the guests while the women and other children remain in the kitchen.

The Karachai take great pride in traditions of hospitality toward guests. When important guests arrive in a home, a lamb or sheep may be slaughtered in their honor. The traditional dish with which to honor the guests is a grilled sheep's head. Female guests will usually join the other women in the kitchen, but, if a female guest is not Karachai and is unfamiliar with local customs, she may be invited to eat in the dining room with the men.

9 LIVING CONDITIONS

Until the mid 20th century, most Karachai lived in small mountain communities. Each family had its own enclosed square courtyard that housed a number of buildings, including a barn, a cooking house (for large-scale food preparation, storage, and cooking in the heat of the summer), and a main house for sleeping and daily living. The ideal Karachai house was at least two stories tall, with a long second-floor balcony that extended around the perimeter of the house. Outhouses were located outside the main house, in a discreet spot in the courtyard. Most Karachai now have indoor plumbing.

Over the past 50 years, the Karachai have gradually begun to move to the larger towns or cities to take advantage of educational and employment opportunities. In these urban areas, people generally live in apartment buildings or houses. Despite this migration of Karachai to urban settings, a large proportion of Karachai continue to live in the country, and almost every Karachai person has relatives in rural areas.

During the Soviet period, the Karachai were not permitted to build two-story private dwellings. Even in rural areas, the Karachai were limited to single-floor, bungalow-style homes. After the collapse of Soviet power, these restrictions were removed and a flurry of building activity began in the early 1990s, as Karachai families began to rebuild the traditional, two-story homes.

10 FAMILY LIFE

Among the Karachai, the extended family is the traditional social and economic unit, with grandparents, parents, and children living within a single courtyard or house. When sons married, they would bring their wives home, and the new couple would live together with the son's parents and other family members. When a daughter married, she would leave her home to live with her husband's family. This remains the dominant pattern of family life in rural areas. As urbanization trends continue, more and more young Karachai couples move out on their own. However, urban housing is always in short supply and young urban couples will frequently live with parents for many years. Even urban Karachai adhere to the tradition of living with the parents of the son, since it is considered shameful for a man to live under the support of his in-laws.

Entering the household of her in-laws, a young bride may encounter conflict and tension with her husband's mother and other female relatives. Traditionally, the newest female in the household performs most of the heavy, demanding, or unpleasant household chores, and her opinion carries the least weight in the household. However, young wives may look forward to the day when they are in charge of the household and can rely on daughters and daughters-in-law to help with chores.

Women are responsible for cooking, cleaning, child-rearing, and tending vegetable gardens. If the family possesses livestock other than sheep, such as chickens or a milking cow, the care of these animals also falls to women. Karachai women take pride in hard work. In addition to the household and courtyard chores, many women contribute to the household economy through the cottage industries of spinning and knitting. Shawls, hats, and gloves knitted with the soft wool of Caucasian sheep often bring a good price in urban markets.

11 CLOTHING

The traditional Karachai male costume includes tall, black leather riding boots and loose-fitting trousers. High-collared, long-sleeved shirts are topped with a short-sleeved, vest-like jacket. The jacket is decorated with rows of fabric loops that hold bullets. The jacket is belted, and a highly decorated silver sword is worn at the belt. The outfit is completed with a tall sheepskin hat.

The female costume consisted of a long, wide-skirted, high-necked dress with a fitted bodice and long, flared sleeves. The head covering, which was always worn outside the privacy of the home, included a pill-box style hat, over which was draped a long veil. Although head covering was essential, women did not cover their faces.

Since the last half of the 20th century, the Karachai have adopted Western dress for both informal and formal occasions. Some Karachai women, especially the older ones, still choose to cover their heads with a simple scarf or kerchief, and many men still wear the traditional sheepskin hat.

12 FOOD

The Karachai observe Islamic dietary restrictions. Therefore, they do not eat pork or pork products. The staple meats of the Karachai diet are lamb and mutton, and these meats are always served to honor guests. Only men are permitted to slaughter sheep, while the women perform the tasks of cooking. The Karachai prepare roasted lamb and shish kebab (called *shashlik*). *Shorpa* is a traditional stew made from lamb, rice, and potatoes, and *tursha* are large potatoes that are stuffed with a mixture of ground lamb, garlic, and onion. The organ meats of sheep are ground together with onion and garlic, stuffed into intestinal casings, and served as sausages.

The Karachai also prepare various flatbreads and make their own cheese, which resembles cottage cheese. Tomatoes and green peppers are common vegetables, and such herbs as parsley and fresh coriander are often eaten raw as vegetables. Tea is a favorite Karachai beverage and is consumed in great quantities during celebrations. In the towns and cities, meat may be difficult to obtain. However, as most Karachai have relatives in the countryside, they can usually obtain meat for special occasions.

13 EDUCATION

Until the 1920s, few Karachai received formal education. In particular, girls seldom attended school. The Soviet government made primary education mandatory. Today, education is mandatory for 11 years and children are instructed in both the Karachai and Russian languages.

After graduating from high school, young people have a variety of options. Some choose to receive further education at a trade institute or university. Although the Karachai region has its own university and many institutes, students sometimes attend post-secondary institutions in one of the larger cities within the Russian Federation. Other young people may choose a traditional occupation, living and working on the family farm.

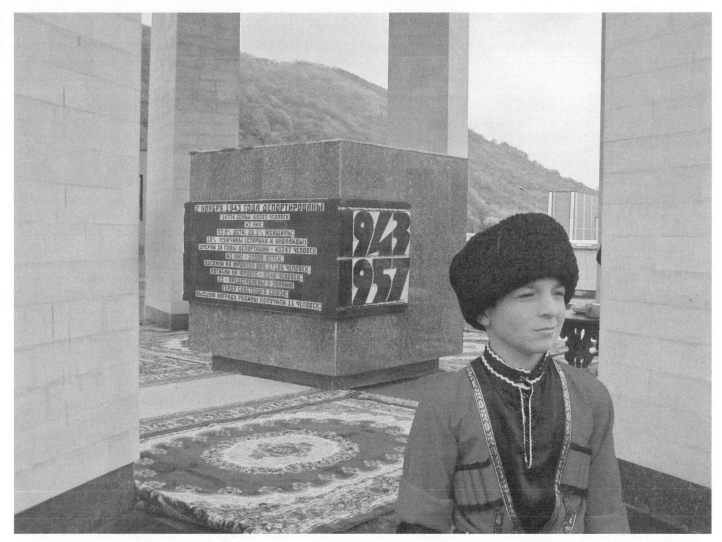

A boy in traditional dress stands in front of the memorial to victims of political repression on the Day of Rebirth of the Karachai people. (© Newspaper Cherkessk/ITAR-TASS/Corbis)

¹⁴ CULTURAL HERITAGE

The deportation and exile of the Karachai from 1944 to 1956, combined with years of cultural repression under the Soviet regime, have had a disastrous effect on the development of Karachai culture. While the Karachai participate in music, dance, and literature, they have been unable to develop these cultural forms fully. Since the late 1980s, liberalization and cultural reform have given the Karachai opportunities to express their cultural identity and record cultural achievements.

The history of the deportations have been of great interest to the Karachai people. Only recently have Karachai scholars been allowed access to the records of these events. They are now permitted to write their histories according to their own interpretation, rather than through the interpretation of the central government. Many projects are underway, including interviews with survivors of the deportations. Other scholars are working to collect and record folklore, as many of the people who know traditional Karachai folktales and practices are very old.

¹⁵ WORK

Traditionally, each Karachai family unit ran its own sheep-farming operation. The sheep were used for wool, milk, and meat. Karachai household income was supplemented by such cottage industries as spinning and knitting, and many families maintained gardens and various livestock for family consumption.

During the Soviet period, employment for each citizen was guaranteed, and urban employment opportunities grew throughout the 20th century. With the availability of higher education, Karachai began to move to towns and cities. However, most families retained ties to the countryside, as many people were still employed in agriculture. The collapse of the Soviet economy meant a decline in state-sponsored jobs. As a more Western-style, market economy has replaced the state-directed economy, people throughout the former Soviet Union have experienced the challenges of a changing work environment. The Karachai, who take pride in their willingness to work hard, have learned many strategies for surviving in new economic conditions. Rural Karachai sell produce and hand-knit garments in cities as far away as Moscow. Others have begun import-export businesses, especially with countries such as Turkey, where many ethnic Karachai reside. Some Karachai have grown wealthy in the post-Soviet era and some have moved into politics.

16 SPORTS

Karachai children enjoy physical activity and informal contests of strength and skill in sports. Girls and boys play together until about age 10, when they begin to develop different interests and are encouraged to learn adult social roles. Soccer is an especially popular sport, both for players and spectators.

Horseback riding, especially jumping and trick riding, is popular among rural youths. Because horses are used to assist with the herding of sheep, youthful riding games help young people gain an important skill.

17 ENTERTAINMENT AND RECREATION

Even in urban areas, there are few restaurants, cafes, or clubs. Although there are theatres and cinemas in larger towns, even these are relatively few. Therefore, the Karachai do not usually go out for dining or entertainment in the evenings. Most entertainment takes place in the home, and neighbors and friends visit each other frequently. Because traditions of hospitality are important to the Karachai, visits are reciprocated.

When the weather is warm, many people take strolls in the early evenings. Along the way, they meet friends and chat. People of all ages enjoy strolling, as it is a way to get outdoors and meet people.

18 FOLK ART, CRAFTS, AND HOBBIES

Many Karachai women are proficient spinners, knitters, and weavers. They produce creative, artistically finished products. Although such woolen goods are unique works of folk art, they are also a form of cottage industry. A proficient craftswoman can make high-quality woolen articles very quickly and receive a good price for each article.

19 SOCIAL PROBLEMS

One of the greatest challenges faced by the Karachai is coming to terms with the deportations of 1944. Many Karachai still bear resentment toward Moscow and Russia for this tragedy. Some Karachai groups feel that the Karachai people have not been fully compensated for the damages that deportation brought upon them. Some have even suggested that the Karachai region should demand autonomy from Russia. Such demands could result in aggressive exchanges between Russia and the Karachai. However, demands to separate from Russia seem to represent the opinion of only a minority of the Karachai population. The advantages of economic partnership with Russia appear to outweigh the difficulties of living within the republic of a historic enemy.

20 GENDER ISSUES

In recent years, Karachai women have received higher education and taken employment outside the home. Although these women may receive salaries equal to those of their husbands, most domestic and childrearing tasks continue to be performed by women. Traditionally, the Western Caucasian women have more freedom, compared to those in the eastern regions of the Caucasus. For example, you will never see a woman driving a car in Dagestan, Chechnya, or Ingushetia. But among Ossetians, Circassians, and Karachai, women have their own cars and it is considered to be prestigious to know how to drive. Nevertheless, gender problems of the Western Caucasian women are in many ways similar to the overall situation of women in the Caucasus.

Karachai women, much like the women of Dagestan, face discrimination in mountain villages. They must perform heavy work at home and simultaneously earn a living by knitting and selling clothes. In mountain villages, girls at the age of five are taught to knit and, for the majority, knitting remains the main source of income during their lives. Each Karachai woman in a mountain village does up to 12 hours of knitting per day. Women bring knitwear things to the cities, where they are sold at the markets. These items are then exported to Siberia, Moscow, and other cold regions of Russia where they are in great demand.

About 86% of Karachai women refer to the lack of jobs as the largest problem that they face. The level of employment of Karachai men is about 40% higher than the level of employment for women. Karachai women are virtually unrepresented in politics. The traditions of Karachai society, where a woman plays the role of an obedient wife for her husband, remain relatively strong in rural areas, while in urban areas it is increasingly possible to observe signs of freer ideas. Some Karachai girls dress similar to like young people in Europe. Scarves and long skirts for women are not required even after marriage. However, the traditional requirements of a strict dress code are still at work for village and elderly women.

21 BIBLIOGRAPHY

Bennigsen, A., and S. E. Wimbush. *Muslims of the Soviet Empire.* Bloomington: Indiana University Press, 1986.

Kozlov, V. *The Peoples of the Soviet Union.* Trans. P. M. Tiffen. Bloomington: Indiana University Press, 1988.

Nekrich, Alexander. *The Punished Peoples.* New York: Norton, 1978.

Wixman, Ron. *Language Aspects of Ethnic Patterns and Processes in the North Caucasus.* Chicago: University of Chicago, 1980.

—revised by J. Colarusso and F. Tlisova

KHAKASS

ALTERNATE NAMES: Abakan Tatars, Minusa Tatars, Kachins, Sagays, Beltirs, Kyzyls, and Koybals
LOCATION: Russia (Republic of Khakassia)
POPULATION: approximately 80,000
LANGUAGE: Khakass; Russian
RELIGION: Eastern Orthodox Christianity combined with native religious beliefs

1 INTRODUCTION

Khakass is an ethnonym used to refer to a number of South Siberian Turkic groups. The term *Khakass* came into use during the Soviet era to refer to a number of Turkic groups, the most numerous of which were the Abakan Tatars and Minusa Tatars, named after the river valleys they inhabited. In fact, the group today known as Khakass is composed of five historically and culturally distinct groups—the Kachins, Sagays, Beltirs, Kyzyls, and Koybals. The origins of these five groups are considerably complex, and although they are all Turkic-speaking, historically they were formed from a number of Turkic, Samoyedic, and Kettic groups.

The homeland of the Khakass, the right bank of the upper Yenisei River, was a central region of the medieval Yenisei Kirghiz Empire, which reached a peak in the middle of the 8th century after its conquest of the Uyghur Empire in Mongolia. The Yenisei Kirghiz state did not last long as an independent state, being conquered already in the 10th century by the Khitay, but Yenisei Kirghiz rulers remained established in Khakasia until the appearance of Russians in the area in the 17th century. By the time of the Russian annexation of the region in the 18th century, the Yenisei Kirghiz had disappeared as a political force and as an ethnic group, and the region remained populated by the five groups previously mentioned as the constituent elements of the modern-day Khakass.

2 LOCATION AND HOMELAND

The homeland of the Khakass is the Republic of Khakasia, located within the Russian Federation, and the capital of Khakasia is the city of Abakan. Khakasia encompasses 61,900 square kilometers (23,900 square miles) and consists of relatively fertile plains, low hills, and woodlands crossed by a series of mountain ranges originating in the Sayan Mountains. The January mean temperatures range from –20°C (–8°F) to –16°C (0°F), and the July mean temperatures range from 18°C (66°F) to 20°C (70°F). Numbering around 71,000, the Khakass are a relatively small Russian minority nationality, although by Siberian standards the Khakass are a numerically substantial group. There is also a large Russian community within the Khakass's ethnic territory.

3 LANGUAGE

The Khakass language is a literary language that was created during the Soviet period to facilitate the integration of the five constituent groups forming the Khakass. In fact, the groups spoke separate, albeit related, Turkic dialects. Linguists commonly classify the language of the Khakass as belonging to the Northeastern group of the Turkic language family, related to Northern Altay, Tuvan and, more distantly, to Yakut. It was

only by the beginning of the 19th century that the Khakass became completely Turkic-speaking. Before that time, certain groups, especially the Koybals, retained some degree of knowledge of their ancestral Samoyedic language. Russian is also widely spoken and used as a literary language among the Khakass, and bilingualism is widespread, although it is estimated that about 64,000 Khakass out of a population of 80,000 retains use of their native language.

The Khakass literary language was created in the 1920s and was based primarily on the Kachin and Sagay languages. The Khakass alphabet, however, has been written in numerous scripts. In 1924 the Soviet authorities introduced a Cyrillic alphabet, but switched to a Latin alphabet in 1929. The Latin Khakass alphabet remained in effect until 1939, when the Soviet authorities mandated yet another change back to a Cyrillic alphabet. This alphabet has remained in use to the present day.

Khakass typically have a first name, a patronymic (taken from the father's first name), and a surname. The Khakass were officially converted to Russian Orthodox Christianity during the 19th century, and as a result, Russian names and surnames became quite widespread, although these Russian names often were phonetically "Khakasized." At the same time, in part as a result of the strength of traditional Khakass culture, the use of Turkic names remained widespread.

4 FOLKLORE

The Khakass, like other South Siberian Turkic peoples, have retained a very rich folkloric tradition, the most prominent element of which is certainly oral epic poetry, much of which was recorded during the Soviet era. While the number of epics in the Khakass's repertoire is considerable, the best-known Khakass oral epic is entitled *Altïn Arïg*. Generally speaking, the Khakas epic tradition has many features in common with the epic traditions of the Northern Altays and the Tuvans. Epics were usually performed by bards who would typically sing in a guttural singing style called *khay*, which was followed by declamatory recitations. The bard would also accompany his recitation with a musical instrument called a *chattagan*. Khakass also play a sort of jaw harp called a *kobïz*. Early observers of the Khakass noted that the Khakass were more musically oriented than their neighbors.

5 RELIGION

Russian Orthodox missionaries converted the Khakass to Christianity in the second half of the 18th century. While the commitment of the Khakass to Christianity is an unresolved issue, there is no doubt that they remained firmly committed to their native religious beliefs and customs even during the Soviet period, when open manifestations of religious life were frequently suppressed. A partial result of the relatively late conversion of the Khakass to Christianity was that the Khakass retained many very archaic religious practices.

Native Khakass religion is characterized by the veneration of clan and family spirits. Likenesses of these spirits were commonly made of wood, fabric, and animal hair and placed within the household. Ritual offerings were made to these spirits in the form of milk and fat, both on a daily basis and during specific rituals.

The most prominent feature of Khakass native religion is the shaman (*qam*), who functioned as an intermediary between the community and the Upper and Lower Worlds. Shamans functioned as healers of the sick, but they also performed important rituals. Shamans were generally respected as possessors of religious power and are also featured as heroes in Khakass folklore.

Since 1991 Western missionaries, primarily of Protestant denominations, have come to Khakassia, although it is unclear to what degree they have succeeded in attracting Khakass converts.

6 MAJOR HOLIDAYS

The most important traditional Khakass holiday was *Tyas Tuyï*, the greeting of spring. This festival usually took place in early June, when the inhabitants of nearby villages would gather to pray to the supreme God *(Quday)* and make offerings of fermented mare's milk. They would also bring sacrificial animals, usually horses, which would be festooned with ribbons. After the sacrifice of the horses and the performance of libations and prayers, the celebration would take on a more festive appearance, with participants taking part in feasting, drinking, contests, wrestling, and horse races.

Another major holiday was the annual Prayer to the Sky, held in early summer. This holiday involved prayers and sacrifices to the Sky to ensure a good harvest of hay and crops. Among the Beltirs, for example, it was performed on a high hill, not by a shaman, but by elders from within the community.

Modern-day Khakass celebrate the Soviet and Russian holidays, including May Day (May 1), Victory Day (May 9), and others.

7 RITES OF PASSAGE

After the birth of a child, the head of the family would name the child after the first thing he laid eyes on. This name would be considered the native name, and six months after birth, the child would receive a Christian name which was in actuality never used in everyday life. Marriage typically involved negotiations between the families of the prospective bride and groom over the size of the dowry *(qalïm)* and the conditions of its payment.

Traditionally, Khakass buried their dead on mountaintops and other elevated areas. The deceased was usually placed in a wooden coffin and oriented on an east-west axis. Shamans, however, were usually buried without coffins, and children were wrapped in birch bark. The dead were usually buried in their best clothes, and with various goods such as saddles, as well as cheese, meat, butter, and fermented mare's milk. On the 3rd and 20th days after a person's death the family gathered at the grave for memorial feasts, and on the 40th day, the deceased's favorite horse was sacrificed. The largest feast was typically held on the 100th day. Most Khakass would hold this feast at home, but the Koybals, for instance, held it at the graveside.

8 INTERPERSONAL RELATIONS

In traditional Khakass culture, women usually stayed at home, and they remained silent when men were present as guests. Men and women were often segregated in traditional Khakass dwellings. Khakass customs generally involved quiet, polite, and reserved relations.

9 LIVING CONDITIONS

The Khakass traditional economy depended to a large degree on nomadic and semi-nomadic stock breeding, and stock breeding remains a major feature of the Khakass's economy. As a result, living conditions were closely tied to the well-being of the herds. Natural disasters, such as spring storms or epidemics among animals, could lead to the sudden impoverishment of entire communities.

Styles of traditional housing varied considerably among the five major Khakas groups. These styles included the *yurt*, the round felt tent characteristic of Inner Asian nomads. The yurt was typically divided into men's and women's halves, with a hearth located in the middle of the earthen floor. There were also numerous shelves and trunks located along the wall. Other common dwellings included teepee-shaped structures made of wood and bark typical of the hunter-gatherer peoples of the Siberian forests, and log structures whose design was borrowed to a large degree from Russian peasant colonists who settled in the Altay lands in the 19th century. There was also some blending between the styles. For example, the Kachins would build hexagon or octagon shaped houses out of logs that mimicked the shape of yurts. The felt and wood structures were usually used as summer dwellings, especially by the more nomadic communities, and the wooden structures were used as winter dwellings.

In general, the standard of living of the Khakass corresponded directly to the well-being and size of their herds. In traditional Khakass society, there was private property, and distinctions existed between rich and poor, but the fluid nature of the stock breeding economy made wealth transitory at best. However, over the course of the 19th and 20th centuries, ag-

Vyacheslav Kuchenov, a Khakass master of throat singing, performs during a festival of ethnic Khakass music in Abakan, Siberia.
(© Ilya Naymushin/Reuters/Corbis)

riculture—especially cereal agriculture—became increasingly widespread among certain groups of Khakass, especially the Kyzyls.

The primary mode of transportation among the Khakass was by horseback, and this continues to be an important mode of transportation today, especially in more remote or mountainous areas. In winter, the Khakass also made use of horse-drawn sleighs and skis.

10 FAMILY LIFE

The Khakass have retained a complex and archaic kinship structure. The five peoples forming the Khakass—the Kachins, Sagays, Beltirs, Kyzyls, and Koybals—are in effect tribal groupings, and each group is further subdivided into clans *(seok)*. Traditionally, the clan was the social unit around which religious rituals were structured, and marriage within one's clan was usually forbidden.

Among many Khakass groups, such as the Beltirs, a father and his married sons held property, such as land and herds, jointly. A father and his married sons lived in separate dwellings but took their meals together. Financial matters were under the authority of the father or should he die, the eldest son. During the Soviet period, this system gradually disintegrated in favor of nuclear family units.

11 CLOTHING

Traditional Khakass clothing varied among the various groups. The Kachins and Sagays, especially the women, retained much of the elaborate traditional dress that was usually reserved for festive occasions. Kachin festive clothing consisted of long robes embroidered with brightly-colored cotton and trimmed with fur. Winter clothes consisted of a sheepskin overcoat, sometimes trimmed with fur or lined with silk. Elaborate and tall fox-fur hats were also worn by women, especially for festivals. Russian-style clothing gradually became more widespread among the Khakass, especially among the more agricultural communities and among the Kyzyls. The clothing of the Koybals, on the other hand, reflected more Mongol influence as a result of their contacts with Tuvans. Modern-day Khakass clothing includes a mix of Westernized and traditional clothing, and completely Russian-style clothing in urban settings.

12 FOOD

The diet of the Khakass was naturally influenced by whether the given community's economy was primarily nomadic or agricultural. The basic sorts of food consumed by the Khakass were meat and dairy products, vegetables, and bread. The staple food was *ayran*, a sort of fermented yogurt made from mare's milk. This product could also be distilled into an alcoholic beverage and the curd dried to be made into cheese. Other sorts of dairy products include cream, sour cream, and butter. Meat, particularly lamb and horsemeat, were made into various dishes, especially soup and sausage. Tea and herbal teas were also very popular among the Khakass. Among the more agricultural communities, who had more contact with Russian peasants, bread, pork, and chicken were more widely consumed (especially by the Kyzyls). The Sagays supplemented their diet with various forest plants as well as wild game.

[13] EDUCATION

No formal educational apparatus existed for the Khakass until the establishment of Russian Orthodox Missionary schools in the middle of the 19th century. However, during the tsarist period, some Khakass were able to take advantage of these mission schools as a gateway to the larger Russian educational system. The best example of this was Nikolai Katanov, a Kachin who eventually became one of Russia's greatest Turcologists and ethnographers, as well as a professor at Kazan University.

With the advent of the 1917 Revolution in Russia, the Soviet government created a formal educational apparatus in the Khakass lands, including primary and secondary schools, as well as a Khakass research institute in the district center of Abakan. The goal of the Soviets was to increase literacy in both Russian and Khakass. The first such schools were opened in 1926, and the research institute opened in 1944. Khakass students can also study outside of the region, in larger institutions in Moscow, St. Petersburg, and Novosibirsk.

[14] CULTURAL HERITAGE

Folklore, particularly the oral epic, remains the richest aspect of the Khakass cultural heritage. During the Soviet era, scholars made considerable efforts to record and publish these epics, both in the Khakass literary language and in Russian translation. In addition to preserving Khakass folklore, the Soviet authorities encouraged the creation of literature, especially fiction and poetry, in the Khakass literary language.

Since the collapse of the Soviet Union in 1991, the Khakass have been freer to express and preserve their religious traditions, which also form an especially rich aspect of their cultural heritage. Despite the conversion of their ancestors to Christianity in the 19th century, modern-day Khakass are expressing renewed interest in their traditional religious life, especially shamanism.

Like other South Siberian peoples, the Khakass have retained the practice of throat-singing, by which one singer can produce two notes in his or her throat at the same time. This tradition is best known among the Tuvans, but it has also been widely recorded among the Khakass, especially within the context of the performance of oral epic poetry.

[15] WORK

Much of Khakass life consists of tending livestock and performing agricultural work. Today, most Khakass live on collective or state agricultural enterprises, whose prosperity depends on the enterprise's resources. Many Khakass are also engaged in hunting and trapping.

[16] SPORTS

The most popular sport among the Khakass is wrestling, and it is widespread during the major holiday celebrations. Another common Khakass sport is horse racing.

[17] ENTERTAINMENT AND RECREATION

Many elements of traditional Khakass life had entertainment and recreational aspects. Most notably, major religious holidays included feasting, drinking, and sports. The performance of oral epics also had a recreational function while at the same time educating the audience about the history of the community, its mythological and religious traditions, and its ethical and moral ideals. Shamanic seances, while intended primarily to heal the sick or to perform a ritualistic function, also served to some degree as a form of popular entertainment.

[18] FOLK ART, CRAFTS, AND HOBBIES

Traditional Khakass clothing is a particularly elaborate type of folk art. Women's festive dress is especially striking, and many objects intended for everyday use bear complex decorations as well. Traditionally, Khakass craftsmen were skilled blacksmiths. The production of religious articles, especially shaman's drums, not only demanded technical skill, but also an understanding of the complex religious ritual that accompanied the manufacture of a drum. Khakass also carved figures out of wood to serve as representations of tutelary spirits of the home or the clan.

[19] SOCIAL PROBLEMS

Drinking has always been an important social and recreational pastime among Khakass men. Traditionally, the most popular alcoholic beverage was fermented mare's milk. Alcoholism became a debilitating social problem, however, with the introduction of distilled grain spirits (i.e. vodka), as a result of large-scale Russian penetration of the region in the 19th century. Today, the Khakass suffer from the general social and economic dislocation affecting all of Russia since the collapse of the Soviet Union.

[20] GENDER ISSUES

In traditional Khakass society there was a sharp division of the sexes in social situations and in terms of the division of labor. Men generally monopolized hunting, warfare, and most aspects of stockbreeding. Women mainly monopolized childrearing, food preparation, and clothing manufacturing.

According to Khakass customary law, women enjoyed certain rights, including the right to divorce, and divorce appears to have been more commonplace among the Khakass than among many of their neighbors. In such cases, the dowry or a portion thereof would be returned by the husband or his family. After the death of a husband, a common custom was for the widow to marry her late husband's brother, thereby ensuring a degree of material support for herself and her children. Monogamy was the rule among the Khakass, although before 1917 polygamy was occasionally practiced by some wealthier members of society.

Following the Second World War, with the expansion of industrial enterprises in Khakasia, women began entering the industrial workforce, and smaller numbers entered the professional workforce as a result of greater access to Soviet education. Nevertheless, the Sovietization of Khakass society did not result in a revolution in Khakass gender roles, particularly within the rural majority of Khakass.

21 BIBLIOGRAPHY

Alekseev, N. A. *Shamanizm tiurkoiazychnykh narodov Sibiri.* Novosibirsk, 1984.

Altyn-Aryg: khakasskii geroicheskii épos. Moscow, 1988.

Butanaev, V. Ia. "K istorii sem'i i semeinogo prava khakasov (XIX-nachalo XX v.)," *Traditsionnye verovaniia i byt narodov Sibiri.* (Novosibirsk, 1987), 155–164.

———. *Etnicheskaia kul'tura khakasov,* (Abakan, 1998).

Diószegi, V. "How to become a Shaman among the Sagais." *Archivum Oriental. Hungar.* 15 1962; 87–96.

Forsyth, James. *A History of the Peoples of Siberia: Russia's North Asian Colony, 1581-1990.* (Cambridge: Cambridge University Press, 1994).

Ivanov, S. V. *Skul'ptura altaitsev, khakasov, i Sibirskikh tatar,* (Leningrad, 1979).

Potapov, L. P. "The Khakass." *The Peoples of Siberia,* (Chicago: University of Chicago Press, 1964), 342–379.

———. "The Origins and Ethnic Composition of the Koybals," *Studies in Siberian Ethnogenesis,* (1962); 144–168.

Radlov, V. V. *Iz Sibiri,* (Moscow, 1989) (Translation of *Aus Sibirien* I-II, Leipzig, 1893).

Troiakov, P. A. "Economic and Magical Functions of Taletelling among the Khakass," *Soviet Anthropology and Archeology,* 14/1-2 (1975), 146–167.

Van Deusen, Kira. *Singing Story, Healing Drum: Shamans and Storytellers of Turkic Siberia.* (Montreal: McGill-Queen's University Press, 2004).

—by A. J. Frank

KORIAK

ALTERNATE NAMES: Koryak; Nymylgu; Chavchyvav
LOCATION: Russia (Kamchatka, extreme northeastern Siberia)
POPULATION: 8,743 (2002)
LANGUAGES: Koriak; Russian
RELIGION: Native version of shamanism

1 INTRODUCTION

The Koriak (also spelled Koryak) are an Arctic people of extreme northeastern Siberia who inhabit the southern end of the Chukchi peninsula, or Chukotka, and the northern reaches of the Kamchatka peninsula across the Bering Sea from Alaska and the Aleutian Islands. The origins of the Koriak are obscure, but archeological evidence suggests that around 1000 AD they inhabited the west coast of Kamchatka along the Sea of Okhotsk, from which they gradually expanded into their present homeland over a period of several centuries. The Koriak who live along the coasts of the Bering Sea and the Sea of Okhotsk have traditionally fished and hunted seals, walruses, sea lions, and whales. Koriak in the interior herd and hunt reindeer. Some Koriak on the Kamchatka peninsula have traditionally both herded and hunted reindeer and hunted sea mammals.

The Koriak officially call themselves the *Nymylgu* (singular: *Nymylgyn*), which means "village-dwellers." This name originally referred only to the seacoast-dwelling Koriak. In addition to this general name, the reindeer Koriak also call themselves *Chavchyvav* (singular: *Chavchyv* or *Chavchu*), which means "rich in reindeer." (The reindeer breeders among the neighboring Chukchi people have also been known to call themselves "Chavchu." The word *Koriak* is probably derived from the Koriak root *kor-*, which means "reindeer."

Russian Cossacks and adventurers first discovered the Koriak in the 1640s, but Russia was still occupied with vanquishing other native Siberian peoples, so it did not begin to conquer the Koriak until the 1690s, when armed parties of tax collectors were sent to demand furs from them. The Koriak fiercely resisted the Russians and, like the Chukchi to their north, often killed their animals, their families, and finally themselves in order to avoid capture. During the second half of the 18th century, the Russian government reduced the *yasak* (fur tax), and conflicts between the Koriak and the Russians came to an end.

2 LOCATION AND HOMELAND

The Koriak number around 8,700. As of 1989 approximately 6,600 lived in the Koriak Autonomous District (Russian: *okrug*), or Koriakia, as it is sometimes called, in Kamchatka *oblast* (region). The capital of the Koriak Autonomous District is Palana. An additional 1,000 Koriak live in neighboring Magadan *oblast*. The remainder of the Koriak population lives in the Chukchi Autonomous District, in the portion of Kamchatka *oblast* outside the Koriak Autonomous District, and in various cities of the former USSR. The territory inhabited by the Koriak includes many different types of landscape—barren tundra, taiga forests, high forested mountains, low-lying swampland, rocky seacoasts, and meadowland—but all of it is characterized by a harsh, cold climate. The average yearly tem-

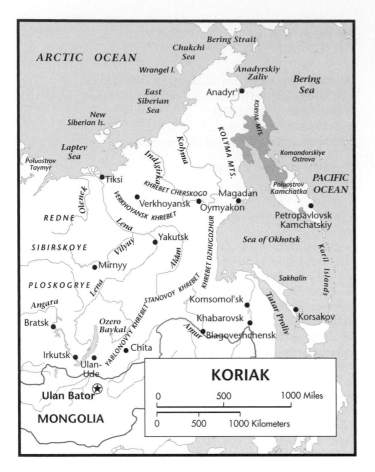

KORIAK

0   500   1000 Miles

0   500   1000 Kilometers

perature in Koriakia is approximately –5°C (23°F). During the winter, temperatures can fall as low as –59°C (–74°F), and in the summer inland temperatures rarely rise above freezing. Temperatures are lowest in the interior of the Koriak Autonomous District, but they are only slightly higher along the damp, foggy coasts of the Sea of Okhotsk and the Bering Sea. Most of the Koriak Autonomous District is covered by tundra mixed with patches of taiga forest. Lichens, moss, grasses (along the coasts), and short, scrubby larches, alders, willows, and cedar are the most common plants here. The more heavily forested areas contain larch, cedar, and birch trees, blackberry bushes, nettles, and grasses. The animal life of the tundra includes polar fox, reindeer, mountain sheep, and more rarely, polar bear. Reindeer, brown bears, crows, foxes and squirrels inhabit the forested regions, and walruses, white whales, killer whales, seals, seagulls, and polar bears are to be found along Koriakia's coastline areas. The most common types of fish are cod, herring, and fresh- and salt-water salmon. Swans, ducks, and geese migrate to the Koriak lands in the summer.

3 LANGUAGE

The Koriak language, along with Itelmen (Kamchadal) and Chukchi, belongs to the Chukotka-Kamchatka (or Chukotic) group of the Paleoasiatic language family. One notable feature of the Koriak language is incorporation. Incorporating languages such as Koriak, Chukchi, and certain Native American tongues have the ability to combine a series of prefixes, suffixes, word roots, and other linguistic units into a single word

to express a concept that would require a whole phrase or even sentence in most other languages. For example, *tymainykap-kantyvatyk* means "I set a large trap." There are nine dialects of Koriak, but with the exception of Kerek (now almost extinct, and considered by some linguists to be a separate but closely related language rather than a dialect), there are very few differences in grammar and vocabulary between them. Koriak was an unwritten language until 1931, when the Koriak adopted the Latin alphabet. Since 1937, the Koriak language has been written in the Cyrillic (Russian) alphabet, with the addition of several extra letters for Koriak sounds that do not exist in Russian. The modern Koriak written language is based on the Chavchyv dialect of the reindeer breeders. Some 53% of the Koriak speak Koriak as their native language, with the remainder speaking Russian as their first language; all Koriak are fluent in Russian.

In traditional society, the Koriak, like the neighboring Chukchi, had only a given name. Surnames (based on the father's given name) were adopted only in the Communist period under pressure from bureaucrats who found the lack of a surname confusing when filling out school registrations, identification cards, and other official forms. Many Koriak have two given names, an "official" Russian one, such as *Konstantin* (male) or *Vassa* (female) used for birth certificates and other documents, and an "unofficial" Koriak one used among themselves. Some common Koriak male names are *Yoltygyingyn, Akket, Talvavtyn, Otap,* and *Pepe;* female names include *Leqqi, Galgangav, Gylvangavyt,* and *Kokok.*

4 FOLKLORE

Although the Koriak did not have a written language until the early 1930s, there is a substantial body of Koriak oral literature. Much of it dates back to deepest antiquity, and many Koriak myths and stories have themes shared by the folklore of the Chukchi, Eskimos, Itelmen (Kamchadal), and even some Native American peoples. The characters of these tales are usually animals—bears, wolves, birds, foxes, and so on—who often change their shape and size and turn into other animals or humans. Koriak historical legends tell of ancient battles between the Koriak and their neighbors. The most widely known Koriak folk tales are about Raven (Quikinnaku), the ancestor of the Koriak who gave them reindeer and dogs, taught them how to domesticate animals, instructed them in the arts of hunting on land and sea, and used his magic powers to help them win battles. In these tales, Raven appears in both human and animal form; he often plays tricks on humans and on his family and has many entertaining adventures.

In one Koriak folk tale, Raven is searching for a suitable wife for his son Ememqut. He flies to a Koriak settlement, alights on a tall tree, and waits for the local maidens to pass by. The first girl to come along is annoyed to see him hanging around aimlessly and speaks rudely of him. The next girl to appear feels sorry for him and feeds him scraps of meat and pudding. Raven decides that the second girl would make a suitable wife for Ememqut. He returns home and tells his son what has happened. Ememqut himself flies to the settlement, repeats the experiment, and has the same experience. He then marries the second girl.

⁵ RELIGION

The traditional religion of the Koriak is a form of shamanism. The Koriak believe that animals, plants, heavenly bodies, rivers, forests, and other natural phenomena have their own spirits, which must be respected and honored. Fire made in the traditional way—that is, by using friction instead of matches or lighters—is considered sacred. In this method of fire-making, a wooden drill is placed into a groove filled with coal dust on a wooden fireboard, which is usually carved into a human shape. The drill is looped into the string of a small bow, which is rapidly turned to produce sparks, which ignite the coal dust. The fireboard is among the most revered possessions of a traditional Koriak family, and it is frequently anointed with the blood and fat of slaughtered animals.

Shamans (tribal priests similar to Native American "medicine men") are men and women who are especially adept at communicating with the spirits. One does not choose to become a shaman; rather, a shaman is chosen by spirits who appear to the shaman-to-be in the guise of an animal—most commonly a wolf, bear, sea-gull, raven, or eagle—and command him or her to become their servant upon pain of death. The rituals of Koriak shamans take the form of chanting prayers and incantations and beating on a drum called a *yayai*. The *yayai*, like the drums of many Siberian and Native American peoples, is large and flat, held by a handle built into its reverse side, and has small iron rattles attached to it that produce a jingling sound similar to that of a tambourine.

During their rituals, Koriak shamans communicate with the spirits and allow them to "speak" through them (Koriak shamans are accomplished ventriloquists). The drums used by shamans are considered to be sacred, and the handling of them is surrounded by many rules and taboos. For example, it is forbidden to take the drum outdoors without its cover, for this will cause a blizzard; the drum belonging to one family may not be used for rituals in another family's dwelling. Koriak shamans, like those of the neighboring Chukchi, sometimes use hallucinogenic mushrooms indigenous to the region to help them fall into the trances in which they perform their rituals.

In addition to the activities of professional shamans, Koriak religion involves ceremonies performed privately within the family. Each family possesses its own drum and various amulets and charms and knows some of the most important chants, which its members use to banish evil spirits and to obtain success in hunting, herding, health, and love. Koriak shamans were severely persecuted by the Communist government; during Stalin's anti-religious campaigns in the 1930s, many of them were imprisoned and executed. Nevertheless, Koriak shamanism, like Soviet shamanism in general, may have suffered less than other religions. Since shamanism lacked the easily identified places of worship and the stable religious infrastructure of Christianity and other organized religions, it was harder for the government to attack it, and so it survived underground with relative ease.

⁶ MAJOR HOLIDAYS

The most important traditional festival of the coastal Koriak was the *Yanyaenacixtitgin* (whale festival), celebrated at the end of the fall hunting season and intended to honor the spirit of the whale so that more whales would return the following year. The dead whale was dragged onto the beach and greeted with sacred fires (made by friction instead of with matches) from the community's households. Branches and sedge-grass were placed into the dead whale's mouth as a symbolic meal. The members of the community, dressed in their dancing costumes—elaborately embroidered coats, trousers, and boots—sang and danced around the whale in its honor, and occasionally sacrificed a dog to it. The whale was then butchered, and its head was taken inside one of the community's homes and hung on a pole so its spirit could join the festivities. There it was "fed" with a pudding-like substance made of whale and seal oil, berries, and roots. After several days, the whale's spirit was urged to return to the sea, tell the other whales of the hospitality it had received, and subsequently come back to the village bringing other whales with it. Seals were also thus honored in places where seals were more commonly hunted.

Reindeer-breeding Koriak celebrated the return of the herd from its summer pasture when the first snows fell in autumn. The returning reindeer were greeted with sacred fires. While drummers beat on their yayais, several fawns were sacrificed, and their blood was smeared onto the sacred fireboards as an offering to Gicholan ("The One on High"), the deity believed to have created reindeer from fire. The inland Koriak also honored Gicholan by holding reindeer races and sacrificing the winning animal to him.

The Soviet government banned these sacrifice festivals because of their religious aspects, but at least one traditional holiday, *Khololo*, managed to survive for reasons that are not clear. *Khololo* consists of several weeks of festivities marked by singing, feasting, drumming, and dancing. All the spirits the Koriak depend on for food, shelter, health, and success in childbirth, economic activities, and so on are thanked for their help in the past year and asked to continue this help in the next year. Since the fall of Communism, interest in traditional Koriak holidays and festivals has grown markedly as the Koriak find themselves free to celebrate their heritage without fear of punishment.

⁷ RITES OF PASSAGE

The Koriak consider each infant born to them to be the reincarnation of a deceased ancestor, and the child is named after this ancestor. In order to properly name a child, it is necessary to discover which ancestor's soul has entered its body. This is done by reciting the names of ancestors as soon as the child is born. When the infant smiles or ceases crying, it is believed that the right name has been spoken, and the child is given this name. Alternatively, a stone tied to a stick is held up by the father and allowed to swing back and forth while ancestors' names are recited; the stone begins to move more rapidly when the correct ancestor's name is mentioned.

In traditional Koriak society, when a person died he or she was dressed in special clothing worn only by the dead and made of the finest materials. Koriak funeral clothing consisted of coats, trousers, and boots sewn by the women of the family from white fawn skin and richly decorated with strips of black and white dog fur and reindeer and seal skin sewn into elaborate patterns. A whole series of rules and taboos surrounded the handling and preparation of these garments. Funeral clothing could not be sold or given away, and it could not be taken into another family's home unless a family member had died there. Funeral clothing had to be prepared well in advance, since it took months to sew it and naturally no one could predict when a person would die. But traditional belief held that once funeral garments were completed, their intended wearer would soon die. Therefore, the clothing was made ahead of time, but with certain stages of the preparation left undone. For example, the soles were not attached to the boots, the fur edge was left off the hood of the coat, and the belt was left without its buckle. After a death, men from the deceased's family and neighbors built a funeral pyre while the women put the last touches on the funeral garments. Some Koriak dissected the corpse to discover the cause of death; if disease was responsible, the corpse was stabbed through the abdomen to prevent the soul's next incarnation from dying of the same illness. When the clothing was ready, the body was dressed, taken out to the funeral pyre, and burned. The cremation was followed by several days of drumming in honor of the deceased.

8 INTERPERSONAL RELATIONS

Like the neighboring Chukchi, who also live in harsh and sparsely populated lands, the Koriak prize hospitality and generosity and have customarily fed and housed strangers who appear among them. In ancient times, visitors to Koriak homes were greeted with fire from the family's hearth as a sign that they were being accepted into the family. Old people among the Koriak are held in great respect. Although the heads of households lose their formal authority over their families when they are no longer able to work, their advice is still highly prized. In the past, old people would have their younger relatives strangle or stab them to death when they became sick or feeble; this practice died out by the 19th century for reasons that are not clear.

9 LIVING CONDITIONS

The traditional dwelling of the nomadic Koriak reindeer herders was the *yayana* (called *rarana* in some dialects), a round reindeer-hide tent with a conical top that was large enough for several families. Each family lived in its own interior chamber separated from that of the other families by dividing walls made of reindeer-skin. Several such tents made up a village. The settlements of reindeer Koriak were limited to the number of families whose herds could be fed by the moss and other edible vegetation in a given area. The coastal Koriak lived in semi-underground houses (also called *yayana* or *rarana*) with walls and ceilings made of logs. A tall, funnel-shaped opening at the top allowed light to enter while preventing snow from drifting in. Each of these houses held two or three families, and the largest held up to forty people. Maritime settlements were much larger than those of the inland Koriak and often had populations of more than 100. Koriak houses were lit by fires or by lamps that burned reindeer or sea-mammal fat. Although traditional Koriak dwellings can still be found, they were largely replaced in the Soviet period by the one-story wooden houses common on collective farms. All Koriak settlements now have electricity, but running water and sewers are far from universal.

The coastal Koriak traditionally used dog-sleds for transportation, while the inland Koriak rode in reindeer-drawn sleds. Reindeer Koriak also occasionally used horses as pack animals in the summer. They made little effort to fully domesticate their horses, however, and left them to find their own food in the winter. Koriak horses were so wild that their owners frequently found it easier to carry heavy loads themselves than to find and catch their horses. Koriak dog- and reindeer-sleds are still used along with airplanes, motorboats, and snowmobiles.

Because few plants or minerals with medicinal qualities are found in the Koriak lands, shamanist rituals were the only medical care available prior to Russian contact. Russians or other native peoples who had been in contact with the Koriak occasionally triggered epidemics of smallpox and measles, because the Koriak had no immunity. Western medicine became much more widespread in the Soviet period. Treatment was either free or inexpensive, but it was often unavailable or of poor quality, especially in rural areas. For this reason, tuberculosis, alcoholism, and other maladies are commonly encountered among the Koriak. The mental disorder known as Arctic hysteria—characterized by sudden fits of rage, depression, or violence that sometimes lead to murder or suicide—is less common among the Koriak than among the neighboring Chukchi and other circumpolar peoples.

10 FAMILY LIFE

The traditional Koriak family was patriarchal. The father had a great deal of authority and his word on important family matters such as choosing the area where the reindeer were to be pastured was final. He also had the right to banish his wife from the household for any reason and to choose his daughters' husbands. Women were allowed to eat only after the men of the family had finished, and men always received the best portions of food. Nevertheless, wife-beating was rare, and most fathers did not force their daughters to marry against their will. Men were generally protective rather than abusive of women. Relationships between spouses were warm and close, and some men were even known to commit suicide upon the death of their wives.

Strict sexual morals (at least as far as women were concerned) were characteristic of traditional Koriak society. Women were forbidden to engage in sexual intercourse before marriage, even with their fiancés. Engaged women were frequently sent off to live with relatives to prevent this, and feuds were sometimes started between families whose unwed children had slept together. Unwed motherhood was considered extremely shameful and was virtually unknown among the Koriak. Modernization has led to freer relations between the sexes over the course of the 20th century.

In order to gain a bride in traditional Koriak society, a man had to work for his future father-in-law for several months or years, herding reindeer or hunting. The groom was intentionally given hard living conditions—little food and sleep, long work hours, and an uncomfortable bed—in order to test his commitment to the bride. The bride was kept well away from the groom and usually moved into a separate tent after the betrothal. During the wedding ceremony, the groom had to chase the bride until he caught her, cut her clothes with a knife to expose her genitals, and then touch them with his hand. The bride was expected to resist as a sign of her chastity prior to marriage and her faithfulness to follow. If she particularly liked the groom, she might run into the bridal tent, since he could overcome her more easily there than outside, but she had to at least pretend to put up a struggle. When the wedding was over, the bride almost always went to live with the groom's family. These traditional Koriak betrothal and wedding practices were replaced by civil ceremonies in the 1920s.

¹¹ CLOTHING

The traditional clothing of both inland and coastal Koriak is made of reindeer skin. Some Russian travelers reported seeing sealskin clothing worn by the coastal Koriak in the 18th century, but they seem to have abandoned it soon thereafter. Women's clothing consists of a *naukei*, a knee-length coverall made from fawn skin and trimmed with fox, wolverine, wolf, or dog fur; the trouser part of the coverall is sometimes made of vertical strips of dark and light fur. A long fawn-skin shirt decorated with beads, embroidery, and fur trimmings is often worn over the coverall. Men wear loose deerskin shirts and trousers. Both sexes wear suede boots and leather undergarments. In cold weather, they wear heavy hooded coats made of fawnskin. A child's *keikei* (coverall) is similar to that worn by women, except that it has a flap between the legs to allow diapers (formerly made of moss, but now made of cloth) to be easily changed. Traditional Koriak clothing is still worn in everyday life, especially during the cold winters for which it is best suited, but Western clothing (cloth dresses, shirts, trousers, as well as underclothes and leather shoes) has also become common in the 20th century.

¹² FOOD

The traditional foods of the reindeer-breeding Koriak are venison and reindeer-blood soup. The liver, gristle, and marrow of the reindeer are eaten raw immediately after slaughtering. The inland Koriak also hunt bears and mountain goats and fish for river salmon. The most common customary foods of the coastal Koriak are fish (particularly salmon and herring); the meat and fat of white whale, seal, and walrus; mollusks; and seaweed. Both reindeer and coastal Koriak traditionally ate cloudberries, cedar nuts, sorrel and sedge-grass roots, and raw or boiled birds' eggs. Each cultural group considered the foods of the other to be great delicacies, and they often traded. The Koriak have drunk tea since they began trading with Russians in the 18th century. In addition to their traditional foods, the Koriak now eat canned vegetables and meats, bread, and other prepared foods purchased in stores. The Koriak formerly cooked meat and fish by boiling them in metal kettles purchased from Russian traders (prior to Russian contact, kettles were made of wood or bark) and ate with their hands and knives from wooden platters. Fish was also eaten frozen or dried. Soup was eaten straight from the kettle with wooden spoons. The modern Koriak prepare their food in mass-produced metal and ceramic pots and pans and eat with knives, forks, and spoons.

¹³ EDUCATION

Until the Soviet government began to establish schools in Koriakia in the 1920s and 1930s, virtually all Koriak were illiterate; only a few were literate in Russian, which they learned from Russian settlers or Russian Orthodox missionaries. Most Koriak teachers were trained at the Institute of the North founded in Leningrad (now St. Petersburg) in 1926, which is now called the Pedagogical Institute of the Peoples of the North. Because most Koriak settlements are too small and widely scattered to permit building schools in each of them, the majority of children receive their primary and secondary education in boarding schools. At first, Koriak teachers used Koriak as well as Russian in the classroom, but the Soviet prejudice against non-Russian cultures soon brought this practice

into official disfavor. In 1954, teaching in the Koriak language was prohibited, and this ban lasted for at least 20 years. Ethnic Russian teachers, many of whom displayed highly negative and racist attitudes toward Koriak schoolchildren, did not attempt to learn Koriak and punished their pupils for speaking the "savage" native language instead of "civilized" Russian on school grounds. For this reason, although all Koriak are now literate in Russian, many are illiterate in Koriak. The use of Koriak in native schools has slowly expanded, however, since the 1980s.

¹⁴ CULTURAL HERITAGE

The Koriak boast a wide repertoire of traditional dances, most of them originally performed in shamanist ceremonies. These dances, and the singing that accompanies them, imitate the reindeer, seals, bears, and other animals whose spirits the rituals were intended to honor. The musical instruments used to accompany these dances are the *yayai* (drum) and the *vaniyayayi* (jaw harp). Koriak songs and dances are usually performed by women. Traditional dance and music are still popular among the Koriak, and the Koriak national dance ensemble "Mengo" has toured throughout the former USSR and has also performed abroad.

¹⁵ WORK

Although ironworking was never a central part of the traditional Koriak economy, Koriak blacksmiths still managed to obtain remarkable results with the simplest tools and methods. Iron tongs and hammers purchased from other native Siberians or Russians were used to shape pieces of iron into knives, axes, spears, saws, and bracelets over fires fanned by sealskin bellows and fueled by homemade coal made from driftwood. The continued existence of native crafts notwithstanding, since the collapse of the Soviet Union in 1991 far-flung Koriak communities have suffered from severe unemployment rates, especially among men.

¹⁶ SPORTS

Dog- and reindeer-sled races and wrestling matches are the most common traditional sports among the Koriak. Another Koriak sport is a walking race in which contestants walk as fast as they can without running to a point up to two miles away and then back to the starting line. There, the winner pulls the prize—a pouch of tobacco—down from a pole upon which it has been hung.

¹⁷ ENTERTAINMENT AND RECREATION

Although the drum (*yayai*) used in shamanist rituals is considered sacred, it is often beaten for entertainment. Despite the subordinate status of women in traditional Koriak society, the best drummers have often been women. The typical plaything of Koriak boys is the lasso; that of girls is the wooden doll. Leather balls, wooden tops, and toy animals carved from wood or bone are enjoyed by children of both sexes.

¹⁸ FOLK ART, CRAFTS, AND HOBBIES

Coastal Koriak craftsmen, like craftsmen among the neighboring Chukchi, have long been adept at carving and sculpting bone, reindeer antler, wood, and walrus tusk. These arts are less developed among the reindeer Koriak; because their way of life demanded constant attention to the herds, they traditionally lacked the leisure time to become skilled carvers and sculptors. Common themes of Koriak art are human figures, particularly drummers and wrestlers; traditional everyday activities such as fire-drilling, sea-mammal and bear hunting, and dogsled riding; and seals, walrus, mountain sheep, shales, bears, fish, worms, birds, dogs, and other animals. The horns of the mountain sheep are carved into tiny human and animal figures. Koriak women are highly skilled at embroidery, and they use fur, beads, silk thread, and reindeer hair to sew detailed geometric patterns and pictures of animals and birds onto clothing and rugs.

19 SOCIAL PROBLEMS

The social problems faced by the modern Koriak are those common to all of Russia's Arctic peoples. These include poor health caused by alcoholism, pollution, and inadequate medical care and diet; low living standards resulting from the inefficiency of the herding and hunting collectives into which the Koriak were forced during the 1930s and 1940s, and the meager selection of consumer goods available in local stores; racial prejudice (attacks by local Russian hooligans are common); and the lingering effects of policies intended by Stalin and his successors to force northern peoples to give up their "primitive" cultures in favor of the more "advanced" Russian one. All of these factors threaten the cultural survival of the Koriak people. As a result of the decades-long ban on speaking Koriak in boarding schools, many young Koriak do not know their own language. There are still few native teachers in Koriak schools, and they are now making great efforts to expand the use of Koriak in the classroom. Dedicated native scholars at the Pedagogical Institute of the Peoples of the North in St. Petersburg are training Koriak teachers and writing new Koriak textbooks, grammars, and dictionaries. Native schools have also begun to instruct their pupils in their people's ancestral art forms—sculpture, sewing, and traditional dance and music. Koriak activists now participate in the Association of the Small Peoples of the North and other organizations that defend the Siberian peoples' economic, political, and cultural interests.

20 GENDER ISSUES

Koriak women currently face many of the same social and economic problems faced by other indigenous women of the Russian Arctic and Subarctic. Koriak women, particularly in rural areas, suffered especially severely from the economic collapse that began in the Russian North in the late 1980s. By 2002 women's life expectancy in some Koriak communities had declined approximately from 64 in 1988 to 51 in 2002, according to some estimates. At the same time, Koriak women's educational levels remained relative high. While unemployment rates among women have been generally lower among women than men, this imbalance places additional burdens upon working-age Koriak women.

21 BIBLIOGRAPHY

Antropova, V. V. "The Koryaks." In *The Peoples of Siberia*. Ed. M. G. Levin and L. P. Potapov. Trans. Stephen Dunn. Chicago: University of Chicago Press, 1964.

Bartels, Dennis A., and Alice L. Bartels. *When the North was Red: Aboriginal Education in Soviet Siberia*. Montreal: McGill-Queen's University Press, 1995.

Czaplicka, M. A. *Aboriginal Siberia: A Study in Social Anthropology*. Oxford: Oxford University Press, 1914 (reprinted 1969).

Fitzhugh, William and Aron Crowell, ed. *Crossroads of Continents: Cultures of Siberia and Alaska*. Washington, DC: Smithsonian Institution Press, 1988.

Fondahl, Gail. "Siberia: Native Peoples and Newcomers in Collision." In *Nations and Politics in the Soviet Successor States*, edited by Ian Bremmer and Ray Taras. Cambridge: Cambridge University Press, 1993.

Forsyth, James. *A History of the Peoples of Siberia: Russia's North Asian Colony, 1581–1990*. Cambridge: Cambridge University Press, 1992.

Jessen, Peter and Inge Larsen, trans., *Indigenous Peoples of the Soviet North*. (IWGIA Document No. 67.) Poul Gustav Pedersen. Copenhagen: International Workgroup for Indigenous Affairs, 1990.

Krushanova, A. I., ed. *Istoriia i kul'tura koriakov (The History and Culture of the Koriak)*. St. Petersburg: Nauka, 1993.

Rethmann, Petra. "Skins of desire: poetry and identity in Koriak women's gift exchange," *American Ethnologist* 27/1 (2000), 52-71.

Slezkine, Yuri. *Arctic Mirrors: Russia and the Small Peoples of the North*. Ithaca, NY: Cornell University Press, 1994.

Turaev, V. A., E. P. Bat'ianova, and Maria Zharnitskaia. "Koriaki." In *Narody Rossii: Entsiklopediia (The Peoples of Russia: An Encyclopedia)*, edited by V. A. Tishkov. Moscow: Bol'shaia Rossiiskaia Entsiklopediia, 1994.

Vakhtin, Nikolai. *Korennoe naselenie krainego Severa Rossiiskoi Federatsii (The Indigenous Population of the Far North of the Russian Federation)*. St. Petersburg: Izdatel'stvo Evropeiskogo doma, 1993.

Vdovin, Inokentii C. and Alexandr P. Volodin. "Koriaks and Kerek." In *Encyclopedia of World Cultures. Vol. 6, Russia and Eurasia/China*, edited by Paul Friedrich and Norma Diamond. Boston: G. K. Hall, 1994.

Zaporotskaia, N. "Zhenshchiny korennykh narodov—v novoi sotsial'noi real'nosti," *Raipon*, (2000) 3.

Ziker, John P. *Peoples of the Tundra: Northern Siberians in the Post-Communist Transition*. Prospect Heights, Illinois: Waveland Press, 2002.

—revised by A. Frank

KOSOVARS

PRONUNCIATION: KOH-soh-vars
LOCATION: Kosovo; Serbia
POPULATION: 2.1 million
LANGUAGE: Albanian (majority), Serbian, Bosniak, Turkish, Roma
RELIGION: Muslim (Sunni and Bektashi), Serbian Orthodox, Roman Catholic
RELATED ARTICLES: Vol. 5: Serbs; Roma; Bosnians

¹ INTRODUCTION

The Kosovars are a predominantly Muslim and Albanian people who come from the young Republic of Kosovo. Although Kosovo only declared its independence in 2008, the ancestors of today's Kosovars have been living in the region for millennia. One of the first peoples to inhabit what is now Kosovo were the Illyrians. Albanian Kosovars claim to be the direct descendants of the Illyrians, but Serbian Kosovars dispute this claim. The Illyrians were conquered by the Romans in the 2nd century BCE. By the 9th century, Kosovo was under the control of the Bulgarian Empire and had become thoroughly Slavicized and Christianized. The Serbs, Bulgarians, and Byzantines fought over Kosovo for the next several centuries, but the Serbs emerged victorious. The Serbian Orthodox Church was created in the 13th century. Many of the Church's most important monuments can be found in Kosovo, and Kosovo is still regarded by Serbs as an integral part of the Serbian homeland.

The armies of the Ottoman Empire moved into Kosovo between the 14th and 16th centuries. The Ottomans ruled Kosovo until the beginning of the 20th century. During the Ottoman period, most of the Albanians living in the Balkans converted to Islam. These Albanians moved into Kosovo in large numbers as Serbs moved out of the province. It was also during this period that Kosovo acquired its Turkish minority.

The province of Kosovo was transferred from the Ottoman Empire to Serbia in 1913. After World War I, Serbia became a province of the Kingdom of Serbs, Croats, and Slovenians. During World War II, Kosovo was briefly annexed into Italian-held Albania. After the defeat of the Axis Powers, Kosovo was returned to Yugoslavia. Communist Yugoslavia was ruled by Josip Broz Tito. Kosovo was one of the poorest regions of post-War Yugoslavia. It was also one of the most volatile, as Kosovo's Albanian population favored greater autonomy while the province's Serb population wished to remain part of Serbia. Over the next several years, the demographics of Kosovo changed greatly. Kosovo Albanians had much higher birth rates than their Serbian neighbors, and by 1960, Kosovo was 67% Albanian and about 23.5% Serbian. In 1968 Albanian Kosovars took to the streets to protest for more autonomy. In 1974 Kosovo was granted autonomous status under a new Yugoslav constitution.

The situation of Albanians in Kosovo became much worse in 1989. The new president of Serbia, Slobodan Milošević, engineered the abolition of Kosovo's autonomous status. His government also purged over 100,000 Albanian Kosovars from their positions in the public sector and restricted the use of the Albanian language in public education and the media. In

response, Albanian Kosovars created their own parallel state institutions. Albanian Kosovars held their own elections and even set up their own underground universities. In 1996 the Kosovo Liberation Army—an ethnic Albanian organization that fought for Kosovo's independence—began a terrorist campaign against the Yugoslav state. The conflict escalated in March 1998 when Yugoslavia sent regular army troops into Kosovo to assist the Serbian police. Within a year, almost 500,000 Kosovars—mostly Albanian—had been displaced by fighting and ethnic cleansing.

The North Atlantic Treaty Organization (NATO) intervened on the side of the Albanians in March 1999. NATO member countries carried out a bombing campaign over Kosovo and Serbia that lasted until June 1999, when President Milošević withdrew his troops from Kosovo. By November 1999, the vast majority of displaced Albanians had returned to their homes (over 800,000 had returned). As Albanians poured in, over 200,000 Serbs and Roma fled Kosovo in response to violence and threats leveled against them by angry ethnic Albanians.

Between 1999 and 2008, Kosovo was administered by the United Nations Interim Administration in Kosovo (UNMIK). Under UN administration, Kosovo saw little development in its infrastructure or economy. The Serb, Roma, and Ashkali communities have also faced violence and harassment. In 2004 interethnic violence displaced 3,600 non-Albanians in Kosovo. Kosovo declared independence on 17 February 2008. The declaration was recognized by a variety of countries, including the United States and many member states of the European Union. The declaration was not recognized by Serbia, which still claims Kosovo. In fact, the Serbian government continues to pay Serbian Kosovars who work in the education, health care, and other sectors in Kosovo. The constitution of the Albanian-led government entered into effect on 15 June 2008, marking the end of UN administration of Kosovo.

² LOCATION AND HOMELAND

Approximately 2.1 million people inhabit the Republic of Kosovo. About 88% of Kosovars are ethnically Albanian, with Serbs making up the largest minority in the country (7% of the population). Other Muslim minority groups include the Turks, Bosniaks, Roma, Ashkali, and Egyptians. The number of Serbs and other minorities in Kosovo has declined significantly since 1999, when Serbia lost control over Kosovo. There are over 200,000 displaced Kosovars of Serbian and Roma background living in Serbia and other countries. There are also approximately 220,000 Albanian Kosovars living outside Kosovo. These ethnic Albanians are dispersed across the world, with especially high concentrations in Albania and Western Europe. Many emigrated during the 1998–1999 conflict in Kosovo, and others emigrated in order to find work. The Albanian share of Kosovo's population will likely increase in coming years due to high birth rates amongst Albanians and emigration of Serbian Kosovars to Serbia.

Kosovo is one of the smallest countries in Europe. The landlocked country covers just 10,887 sq km (4,203 sq mi), making it slightly larger than Delaware. The largest city in Kosovo is Pristina, which also serves as the capital. Prizren, Peć, and Kosovska Mitrovica are the next largest cities. Kosovo's neighbors are Albania, Macedonia, Montenegro, and Serbia.

KOSOVARS

0   25   50   75 Miles

0 25 50 75 Kilometers

³ LANGUAGE

Kosovo has three official languages: Albanian, Serbian, and English. Most Kosovars speak Albanian. Albanian is an Indo-European language that is so different from other Indo-European languages that it belongs to its own linguistic family. Albanian is also spoken in Albania, Macedonia, Italy, Turkey, and a variety of other countries. The language is divided into two main dialects: Tosk and Gheg. Gheg is the dialect that is most commonly spoken amongst Kosovars. However, Standard Albanian, which is based on the Tosk dialect, is used in Kosovo's newspapers, television, and government institutions. There are a variety of Tosk and Gheg sub-dialects, many of which are mutually unintelligible.

Some basic Albanian phrases are listed below:

Hello: *Tungjatjeta*
Yes/No: *Po/Jo*
Good: *Mirë*
I only speak a little Albanian: *Flas vetëm pak Shqip*

Serbian is a South Slavic language also spoken in Serbia, Bosnia and Herzegovina, and other Balkan countries.

Albanian Kosovar children are usually given Muslim or Albanian names. Serbian Kosovar children are given Serbian or Christian names.

⁴ FOLKLORE

The Albanians have a colorful myth that tells of the creation of the Albanian people. According to the myth, an eagle caught a snake in its beak and brought the snake to a nest that sat atop a cliff on the edge of a mountain. A small eaglet began to play with the dead snake once the adult eagle flew off.

As this was happening, a young hunter was climbing that very mountain. He saw the eaglet playing with the snake, but noticed that the snake was not actually dead. The snake opened its mouth and looked as if it were about to strike the small eaglet. At that moment, the young man killed the snake with his bow and arrow. The hunter then took the eaglet and began to make his way down the mountain. The mother of the eaglet returned and approached the hunter. The eagle demanded that the hunter return the eaglet to her. The hunter agreed, but on the condition that the eagle grant him the vision and strength of an eagle. The hunter returned the eaglet, but once it grew, it flew over the hunter and protected him.

The Albanian people were amazed by the exploits of the hunter and made him their king. They named their new king "Son of the Eagle." Albanians refer to themselves as *Shqiptarët*, which is derived from the word "eagle." Although Kosovo's flag does not include an eagle, the flag flown by many Albanian nationalists in Kosovo—including the Kosovo Liberation Army—does have an eagle.

⁵ RELIGION

Islam is by far the largest religion in Kosovo, as it is the religion of the vast majority of Albanian Kosovars. Locally trained imams in Kosovo belong to the Hanafi school of Sunni Islam. Albanians tend to be lax in their practice of Islam. A 2001 survey found that only 12.2% of Albanian Kosovars attended religious ceremonies "several times a month." There are a number of reasons why Albanian Kosovars tend to be less devout than other Muslims. Religious piety was discouraged under the Tito regime. Furthermore, all aspects of Albanian national life were suppressed under Milošević, including Islam.

Sufism, or Islamic mysticism, has a long history in Kosovo. Before the 1998–1999 war, almost every town in Kosovo with a large Albanian population had a *teqe*, or Sufi meeting house. The largest and most famous Sufi group in Kosovo is the Bektashi Order. The Bektashis are affiliated with Shia Islam, although the Bektashi sect differs from Orthodox Shia Islam in a number of ways. For example, Bektashis are permitted to drink alcohol and Bektashi women often lead religious services.

Serbian Orthodox Christianity is the largest Christian sect in Kosovo, although their number has declined dramatically since 1999. Orthodox Christianity in Kosovo has a long history in Kosovo, which is evidenced by the presence of numerous ancient Serbian monasteries throughout Kosovo. Approximately 60,000 Kosovars (3% of the population) belong to the Roman Catholic Church. In Kosovo, the Church is made up of Albanians, Roma, and Croats.

⁶ MAJOR HOLIDAYS

Kosovars celebrate two major secular national holidays. Independence Day is February 17. It commemorates the date on which Kosovo officially declared its independence from Serbia. June 15 has also been designated a holiday. It marks the date in 2008 when Kosovo's new constitution came into effect.

Kosovars also celebrate a number of Muslim and Christian holidays. For Muslims, *Uraza Bayram* (also known as Eid al-Fitr) is one of the most important holidays. It marks the end of the month of Ramadan, during which Muslims are expected to fast from sunrise until sunset. *Kurban Bayram* (the festival of the sacrifice) is a holiday when all Muslim families who are able are obliged to sacrifice a lamb and donate the meat to the poor. Muslim holidays are celebrated at a different time every year because they are determined by the lunar calendar.

In order to accommodate Orthodox and Catholic Christians, Christmas is celebrated on two dates in Kosovo. Orthodox Christmas is celebrated on January 17 and Catholic Christmas is celebrated on December 25. Easter is celebrated on March 23.

7 RITES OF PASSAGE

Circumcision, or *sunet,* is a rite of passage for Muslim Kosovars. Boys are usually circumcised before the age of seven. The *sunet* ceremony is a cause for great celebration in Muslim households. Boys are dressed in special gowns and showered with presents.

Since 1998 it has been difficult for many Muslim Kosovars to access affordable and qualified circumcision services. As a result, some boys have waited until after the age of seven to be circumcised.

Marriage is the principal rite of passage for most women in Kosovo society. In traditional Kosovar families, marriage is the time when women leave the home. Their identity changes from one of daughter and sister to *nusja* (bride). In fact, upon entering the home of a new husband, women are referred to by the term *nusja*, rather than by given names.

8 INTERPERSONAL RELATIONS

Much of social interaction in Kosovo is governed by a set of centuries-old customary law known as the Canon of Leke Dukagjin. Although few Kosovars have actually read the Canon, its tenets are still respected among Albanian Kosovars. The Canon defines honor as extremely important virtue.

Women are expected to maintain their honor through chastity and fidelity to their husbands. Blood feuds sometimes result over insults or attacks on a family's honor. The law also enshrines the value of hospitality, which is still very much alive among Kosovars.

Interethnic tension is a major problem for Kosovars. Human rights organizations have reported numerous instances in which ethnic Albanians have harassed and attacked minorities, especially Serbs and Roma. The homes of many displaced Serbian Kosovars and Roma Kosovars have been appropriated by Albanian Kosovars. The most serious outbreak of interethnic violence since 1999 occurred in 2004, after a clash between ethnic Albanians and ethnic Serbs in the divided town of Mitrovica. At least 19 Kosovars were killed and thousands of Kosovars, most of Serbian and Roma ethnicity, were displaced as a result of the violence.

9 LIVING CONDITIONS

Kosovars face some of Europe's worst living conditions. The homes of many Albanian Kosovars were destroyed by Serbian forces between 1998 and 1999. Poverty has prevented many of these Albanians from rebuilding their homes. As a result, many Kosovars live in clay brick homes that lack insulation and windows. Furthermore, access to electricity is sporadic throughout Kosovo.

Over 200,000 Serbian and Roma Kosovars have been displaced from Kosovo. Most now live in Serbia. Their living conditions vary greatly; many displaced Roma live in shacks built from scrap material, while other displaced persons live in government-run refugee camps.

Kosovo faces a severe shortage of qualified nurses and doctors because Albanians were excluded from higher education during the 1990s. Much of the medical infrastructure remaining from the Yugoslav era is in poor condition. Deficiencies in health care, nutrition and living conditions have caused Kosovo's infant mortality rate to reach 35–49 per 1,000 live births (the highest in Europe).

A parallel health care system exists for Serbian Kosovars. One hospital and a number of clinics are supported by the Serbian government, which does not recognize Kosovo's independence.

10 FAMILY LIFE

Families in Kosovo tend to be large compared to the families of other Balkan and European peoples. The unavailability of contraceptives and the desire of fathers to have sons are the primary reasons for this phenomenon.

In Albanian Kosovar families, a bride leaves home to live with her husband after marriage. The couple may move to a new home or continue living with the husband's family.

Descent is traced patrilineally, and children are thought to derive their personality and "essence" from their fathers. Thus, when parents divorce, the father is usually given custody of the children. Furthermore, if the father of a child dies, the child sometimes goes to live with his father's extended family, even if the child's mother is still alive.

In traditional Kosovar homes, brothers will often share a single household with one another. Paternal uncles, or *axhas*, hold authority over all the children in the household. As many Kosovars have left the country to work, *axhas* provide an important source of parental authority in Kosovar society. On the other hand, the fathers and brothers of female members of the household wield little authority. This lack of responsibility allows maternal uncles, or *dajes*, to be much more warm and loving toward their nephews.

11 CLOTHING

Kosovars wear Western-style clothing. However, some women and girls wear the Muslim headscarf. The headscarf, which is banned in Kosovo's public education system, is a source of contention in the secular republic.

Although traditional attire is not worn on a daily basis in Kosovo, it can be seen during parades and some special occasions. Women wear colorful dresses and headgear that often features ornate flower prints. Men wear pants and shirts, both of which usually have two vertical stripes. Men also wear vests and traditional white Albanian skull caps, known as *plis*.

12 FOOD

The cuisine of Kosovo is similar to that of other Balkan and East Mediterranean peoples. *Qofte* (fried meatballs), *byrek* (filo dough pies filled with spinach, meat, or other vegetables), and grilled meat are all staples of Kosovo cooking.

In recent years a number of foreign cooking styles have been introduced into Kosovo. This is a result of the influx of aid workers and foreign peace keepers. The recipe for spinach *byrek* follows.

Byrek me Spinaq

Ingredients:
25 leaves of filo pasty leaves
1 1/4 pounds spinach, chopped
2 eggs
1/4 teaspoon salt
1 cup olive oil
1 cup diced feta cheese
1/2 cup chopped green onions

Cooking Instructions:

Coat a baking pan with oil and then lay filo pastry leaves on the pan. Coat the leaves with oil and lay down additional leaves over the pan. Make sure the entire pan is covered.

Mix the eggs, onions, feta cheese, oil, and salt. Spread the mixture over the filo pastry leaves and then add spinach on top. Cover the mixture with the rest of the filo pastry leaves. Seal the edges of the pie. Bake at 340 degrees Fahrenheit 45–50 minutes or until light brown.

13 EDUCATION

School overcrowding is a significant problem in Kosovo. Many schools were destroyed during the 1999 conflict. Although many of these have been rebuilt, the lack of schools and teachers is still so severe that children often attend school in shifts. In Pristina children only received 2.5 hours per day of lessons. Education is also a problem in rural areas, because students often have to walk long distances to reach their schools.

There are two public universities in Kosovo. The University of Pristina is controlled by Albanians, while the University of Mitrovica is controlled by Serbs. In 1990 the Serbian government ended the practice of instruction in both Albanian and Serbian. It also removed nearly all Albanian professors and students from Kosovo's universities. During the 1990s Albanian students and professors held informal classes in houses and other private buildings. It was not until 2000 that Albanians gained control of the higher education system and made Albanian, along with Serbian, the languages of instruction.

14 CULTURAL HERITAGE

Kosovo has a rich musical tradition. The *Ciftelia* is a traditional Albanian stringed instrument that originated in Central Asia. Different versions of the *Ciftelia* can be found throughout the Middle East, especially in Iran and in Turkey. The instrument is made of wood and only has two strings. The first string is used to play the melody and the second is used to create harmony.

Pjetër Bogdani is widely regarded as the father of Albanian literature. He lived in the 17th century and wrote the first work of long prose written in Albanian. Bogdani, like most of Kosovo's Albanians, spoke the Gheg dialect. In recent decades, the Socialist Realist literature of communist-era Albania has become popular in Kosovo. The most well known Albanian Socialist Realist writer is the former dissident author Ismail Kadaré. In recent years, Kosovo has produced a number of prominent writers, including novelist Iljaz Prokshi, children's writer Rifat Kukaj, Roma scholar Bajram Haliti, and poet and women's rights activist Flora Brovina.

Kosovo has a small but growing film industry. One of the most famous filmmakers in the country is Isa Qosja. In 2005 Qosja directed *Kukumi*, a politically-charged drama about three mental patients who try to make sense of post-war Kosovo.

15 WORK

In early 2008 the unemployment rate in Kosovo was estimated at 40%. It is difficult for Kosovars to find work within Kosovo because the economy is in such poor condition. The economic situation is aggravated by endemic corruption, poor infrastructure, and the destruction caused by the 1998–1999 war.

Approximately 60% of Kosovars support themselves through agriculture. Agricultural output declined after 1999, but has been increasing ever since. Much of the uptick in agriculture can be attributed to foreign donors who invested in the rebuilding of irrigation networks. Less than a quarter of Kosovars work in mining or industry. A large number of Kosovars work for the numerous international organizations that operate in the small republic. Finally, many Kosovars earn their living through participation in organized crime networks. UNMIK estimates that 15%–20% of the Kosovo economy comes from organized crime.

Many Kosovars leave the country in search of work. Over 200,000 Albanian Kosovars live and work abroad. Many live in Western Europe; Germany and Switzerland are two of the most common destinations. Kosovars of Roma and Serb ethnicity who have left Kosovo tend to live and work in Serbia.

16 SPORTS

Soccer is the most popular sport in Kosovo. In 2008 the Soccer Federation of Kosovo applied to the international soccer association (FIFA) for recognition of Kosovo's soccer clubs. The Kosovo national soccer team played its first games against Germany, Saudi Arabia, and Albania.

Basketball is also quite popular in Kosovo, just as it is in the other former Yugoslav republics. Kosovo has a national basketball federation and a number of regional teams. Kosovo's basketball federation is still seeking recognition from the International Basketball Federation.

In addition to basketball and soccer, Kosovars sometimes play traditional sports dating from Ottoman times. Long jumping, tugs of war, and stone throwing are some of the games played. Turkish wrestling is also popular. The sport has Balkan, Persian, and Turkic influences. Turkish wrestlers grease themselves with oil and wear stitched leather pants called *kisbet*.

17 ENTERTAINMENT AND RECREATION

Kosovars spend a great deal of their leisure time in cafés. In the capital city, Pristina, there are hundreds of small coffee shops that serve Italian-style cappuccinos, Turkish coffee, and other drinks. The unemployment rate is very high and as a result many Kosovars have found that sitting in cafés is a cheap and enjoyable way to pass time.

Young people in Kosovo's larger cities also enjoy nightlife. Although some bars are only for men, many night spots serve both young men and young women. The influx of United Nations personnel and aid workers into Pristina has increased the number of bars, dancing clubs, and music venues in the city.

Satellite television is popular amongst Kosovars. Many watch foreign programs that are dubbed in Albanian or have Albanian subtitles.

Kosovar Bosnian women arrive at a traditional wedding ceremony in the village of Donje Ljubinje. The traditional wedding is viewed by almost all residents with universal pride as a symbol of this village's special identity. (© Vadrin Xhemaj/epa/Corbis)

18 FOLK ART, CRAFTS, AND HOBBIES

Kosovar artisans have a long history of producing ornate wood carvings. Artisans decorate furniture, roofs of buildings, and musical instruments.

Kosovo also has a variety of traditional dances. The performers of these dancers wear their traditional dress. The style of dress and dance varies according to the background of the performers. Albanian Kosovar dance resembles that of other Balkan and Anatolian peoples, although men and women often dance together in the Kosovan versions. Traditional dances are often accompanied by men playing *lodras*, or bass drums, and a variety of other instruments.

19 SOCIAL PROBLEMS

Many of the social problems faced by Kosovars stem from the country's poor economic situation. Industry has been on the decline in Kosovo since the 1990s. The lack of economic activity in Kosovo has contributed to high levels of unemployment and poverty. In 2007 approximately 45% of Kosovars lived below the poverty line.

Poverty contributes to the problem of organized crime. Human traffickers sometimes promise poor women and girls from Kosovo that they will find them legitimate employment in Western Europe. Instead, Kosovars are often trafficked into prostitution rings. Furthermore, Albanian criminal organizations use Kosovo as a distribution point for heroin from Afghanistan. Even Kosovo's prime minister in 2008, Hashim Thaçi, was accused of having once headed up a criminal network involved in a wide range of illicit activities.

20 GENDER ISSUES

Albanian Kosovars tend to be more traditional with regard to gender relations than many other Balkan peoples. In most families, women are expected to raise children and carry out housework. Men are expected to provide for their families financially. The belief that women's responsibilities are in the home often leads to girls leaving school early. Only half of Albanian girls aged 15–18 attend school. Furthermore, Albanian custom dictates that women have no inheritance rights and almost no property rights in the event of a divorce. While Kosovan law provides inheritance rights to Kosovar women, women often come under strong family pressure to forego their legal rights.

Although homosexuality is not illegal, it is viewed as abhorrent in Kosovo's traditional society. Homosexual and transgender Kosovars routinely face violence and harassment. The Canon (Albanian customary law) does not mention homosexuality. However, it places a strong emphasis on honor and masculinity, and homosexuality is regarded as a serious breach of these values.

21 BIBLIOGRAPHY

Di Lellio, Anna, ed. *The Case of Kosovo: Passage to Independence.* New York: Anthem Press, 2006.

Duijzings, Gerlachlus. *Religion and the Politics of Identity in Kosovo.* New York: Columbia University Press, 2000.

Elise, Robert. *A Dictionary of Albanian Religion, Mythology and Folk Culture.* London: Hurst, 2001.

Noel, Malcolm. *Kosovo: A Short History.* New York: HarperCollins, 1999.

Pipa, Arshi. *Contemporary Albanian Literature.* New York: Columbia University Press, 1991.

Schwandner-Sievers, Stephanie and Bernd Fischer, eds. *Albanian Identities: Myth and History.* Bloomington, IN: Indiana University Press, 2002.

—by B. Lazarus

LATVIANS

ALTERNATE NAMES: Letts
LOCATION: Latvia
POPULATION: 2,245,423 [2008 estimate; total population of country, of which 58% are ethnic Latvians]
LANGUAGE: Latvian (Lettish)
RELIGION: Christianity (Lutheran, Roman Catholic, Russian Orthodox, Baptist, Old Believers, Pentecostal, Adventist); Judaism

1 INTRODUCTION

In approximately 2000 BC, Baltic tribes came into the region that is now Latvia and are regarded as the ancestors of the modern Latvians and Lithuanians. These tribes, coming from the south, assimilated into the scattered peoples already living in present-day Latvia. The Baltic tribes first appear in the written records of the Roman historian Cornelius Tacitus around 100 BC. During this period, the early Baltic peoples split up into several tribes. The Latvians, who are sometimes called the Letts (from the German word for "Latvian"), have the largest homeland of the three Baltic republics. Latvia has, like Estonia to the north and Lithuania to the south, been an important trading center and strategic area in the Baltic region.

The various Latvian tribes were loosely self-governing until the end of the 13th century AD when the territory was conquered by German Teutonic knights. The ruling classes during this era were ethnic Germans; and the middle class (mainly artisans and farmers) consisted of Latvians. Even wealthy Latvians were not permitted to integrate into German society. However, in the territory of Prussia to the west, farmers had the possibility of becoming Germans. This is probably the reason why the Baltic peoples, unlike the Prussians, did not lose their unique ethnic identity.

Latvians were subjected to occasional invasions by the Poles and the Swedes until the 18th century. The 1600s were a time of struggle between Poland and Sweden for control over the Baltics, with most of the battlegrounds in present-day Latvia. As a result of the Swedish-Polish war, the northern part of the country (Vidzeme or Livland) and Riga came under Swedish rule. The Swedish period brought new political and cultural changes, and the power of the German feudal lords decreased. The Latvian farmers of Vidzeme were granted the right to voice their concerns directly to the Swedish king, schools for peasants were established in the country, and the shipbuilding and metallurgy industries grew. Latvians also began operating a small colony on the island of Tobago and another inside present-day Gambia.

In 1700, the army of imperial Russia fought Sweden for the sole purpose of acquiring the ice-free harbors on the Baltic Sea. This prolonged war, which lasted for over 20 years, along with a series of plagues, devastated the Latvians. As a result, much of northern Latvia became unpopulated and came under Russian control. Russia gave power back to the local German aristocrats in Latvia. Throughout the 1700s, Latvians were unable to express themselves politically or culturally because of the authoritarian control of imperial Russia.

During the 1800s, an intellectual movement among Latvians began. Latvian scholars wanted political and social equality with the Germans. A sense of Latvian nationalism grew, as many wanted to live in an independent state that was not ruled by foreigners. This Latvian independence movement gained strength and peaked with a national uprising in 1905. The Bolshevik revolution of 1917 marked the end of imperial Russian dominion. At the 1918 Treaty of Brest-Litovsk, Russia agreed to give up its Baltic territories. Although Soviet troops invaded Latvia in 1919, they were defeated and forced out. The Germans were also defeated and forced to leave, as formalized under the Treaty of Versailles. For the first time in six centuries, the Latvians were independent and free to control their own destiny. Politically, Latvia became a member of the League of Nations on 22 September 1921, thus formally joining the family of nations. In 1936, Latvia's minister of foreign affairs, V. Munters, was elected president of the League of Nations.

On 17 June 1940, the Russian Red Army occupied Latvia, in accordance with the secret deal made earlier between Hitler and Stalin to divide Eastern Europe between the two dictators. After the Soviets took over, Latvia was incorporated into the Soviet Union. Immediately after the occupation, the Soviet regime began liquidating the Latvian population. During the first year of the occupation, 35,000 ethnic Latvians and other Latvian citizens (including Jews) were arrested, murdered, or deported to the northern regions of the Soviet Union and Siberia. Some 16,000 alone were sent into exile on the night of 13–14 June 1941. As a result, there are still a few of these exile Latvian communities scattered in the Russian part of Central Asia and Siberia.

The Soviet purges explain why Latvians optimistically welcomed back the German army in 1941. The Latvians hoped that the Germans would get rid of the Soviets and help them reestablish their independent state. That did not happen. For the next three years, the Latvians lived under the Nazi regime as residents of the occupied "Ostland" territory. Many Latvian Jews left Latvia together with the retreating Red Army in July 1941. The loyal Latvian Jews were rounded up, used as laborers, and killed by starvation in the Salaspils concentration camp, or shot in the forest of Rumbula or elsewhere. Latvian men were recruited by both the Nazi and Soviet armed forces, so that they ended up fighting against each other. The Soviets finally regained full control on 8 May 1945, when Germany capitulated. However, many thousands of Latvian soldiers did not capitulate and continued a guerilla war for freedom against the Soviet invaders, hoping for help from the West. They did not get any. The deportation of more than 100,000 farmers on 25 March 1949 destroyed the food supply for the Latvian guerillas and they had to surrender. Many of the soldiers were shot or hanged. The rest were deported to Siberian death camps.

In the mid-1950s, a plan of forced industrialization began, which involved the fusion of a generic "Soviet" culture (which favored things that were Russian) onto the Latvians. However, after Stalin's death, some Latvians were allowed to return from exile in Siberia but were not allowed to live in their own homes because they had been expropriated by ethnic Russians. Harassment of Latvians by Russians continued, and any dissidence was punished with long prison sentences in Siberian camps. Latvian campaigns for democracy and independence did not begin in earnest until October 1988, with the formation of the Popular Front of Latvia. Latvians finally reclaimed their independence in August 1991 after the collapse of Communism and the Soviet government in Moscow.

Latvia joined the United Nations in 1991 and the World Trade Organization in 1999. In 2004, Latvia cemented its ties to Europe and the West by joining both the North Atlantic Treaty Organization and the European Union.

2 LOCATION AND HOMELAND

In 2008 the population of Latvia was estimated to be 2,245,423, of which 58% were ethnic Latvians. About 30% of the population of Latvia is ethnic Russian. At the close of World War II, thousands of Latvians fled their homeland to escape the returning Russian troops. As a result, there are now many ethnic Latvians and their descendants living in the United States, Australia, and elsewhere.

Latvia is on the Baltic coast and borders Estonia to the north, Lithuania to the south, the Russian Republic to the east, and Belarus (Poland before World War II) to the southeast. Latvia covers about 64,100 sq km (24,700 sq mi), making it slightly larger than the U.S. state of West Virginia. The coastline is mostly flat, but inland and eastward the topography becomes hilly, with more forests and lakes present. Reznas Lake is the largest of Latvia's 2,300 lakes. There are also about 12,000 rivers that crisscross Latvia, but only 17 are longer than 100 km (60 mi), the biggest being the River Daugava. The Latvian homeland is traditionally divided into four cultural and historical regions: Kurzeme (the west), Zemgale (the south), Vidzeme (middle and northern Latvia, including Riga—the capital of Latvia), and Latgale (the east).

The climate is generally temperate but with considerable temperature variations. Summer and winter can be intense, but spring and autumn are mild. Precipitation is distributed throughout the year, with the highest amount occurring in August.

³ LANGUAGE

The Latvian language (also called Lettish), along with Lithuanian, belongs to the Letto-Lithuanian branch of Indo-European languages. Modern Latvian also shows the influences of former conquerors, with some words taken from Swedish, German, and Russian. There are three main Latvian dialects: Central (which is used as the basis for written Latvian), East, and Livonian.

Throughout the Soviet period, ethnic Russians settled in Latvia. This immigration caused a massive linguistic shift in the Latvian homeland and resulted in the spreading of Russian words, phrases, and slang into the Latvian language. Today, about 58% of the population in Latvia speaks Latvian. In 1989 the government made Latvian the official language, requiring it in governmental use. Anyone wishing to become a citizen of Latvia must also pass a basic competency test in the Latvian language.

Latvian first names for males always end in the letter "s" and include names such as Andris, Ivars, Jânis, Kârlis, Vilnis, and Visvaldis. Female first names usually end in the letter "a" and include names like Aina, Laima, Mâra, Ausma, Ieva, Inâra, Maija, and Zinta. Examples of everyday Latvian words include *Sveicinati* (How do you do?), *lŭdzu* (please), *paldies* (thank you), and *uz redzçđanos* (goodbye).

⁴ FOLKLORE

The Latvian language finds its most lyrical and expressive use in Latvian folk songs, or *dainas*. The dainas are beautiful and sensitive verses written over many centuries, rich in experience, feeling, and folk wisdom. They cover the total human experience: birth, childhood, love, marriage, death, nature, and the changing seasons; holidays and festivities; work in the fields, pastures, and home; mythology; and the struggle against foreign invaders and oppressors. However, they lose much of their meaning when translated. Here is one daina describing the dawn:

> Sidrabina gailis dzied
> Zeltupítes maliňâ,
> Lai ceďàs Saules meita
> Zîda diegu šíeterçt.
>
> A silver rooster crows
> Beside a golden stream,
> To make the Sun's daughter rise
> To twine her silken yarn.

Some people believe that the oldest dainas perhaps are remnants of ancient riddles and magic incantations, because of their form and structure. When the Latvians started living in villages and towns, a split developed between urban and rural dainas. Modern dainas are typically philosophical and are revered as Latvian lyric poetry. Efforts to preserve traditional Latvian folklore began late in the 19th century, and several volumes of traditional Latvian myths and folk songs were com-

piled and published. Modern scholars have catalogued more than 1.4 million traditional Latvian folk songs.

One of the most famous traditional figures of Latvian myth is Lacplesis the Bear-Slayer. The legend of Lacplesis tells about how he could break a bear's jaw with his fist and even get bears to pull his plow. Although Lacplesis wanted to help others, he often did not know his own strength and would end up breaking peoples' tools. According to legend, Lacplesis was finally defeated by a vicious three-headed ogre. The ogre's mother told her son that Lacplesis would lose his great strength if his ears were cut off. The battling Lacplesis and the ogre plunged into the Daugava River and were swept out to sea.

⁵ RELIGION

Christianity spread through Latvia during the 9th–12th centuries, with Russian Orthodoxy dominant in the east and Roman Catholicism in the west. While the Russian Orthodox Church among the Latvians was adaptive to local culture, the Roman Catholic Church was more rigidly structured. As a result, many Latvians became subordinate to local leaders who were connected with the Roman Catholic Church. By the 1520s, many of the Latvians living in areas of German or Swedish influence were unhappy with the Roman Catholic Church and became receptive to the ideas brought forth by the Protestant Reformation. Lutheranism developed primarily among urban Latvians, especially in Riga. The resulting religious diversity among Latvians meant that Roman Catholicism, Lutheranism, and Russian Orthodoxy were each popular in different parts of the country during the independence years of 1918–40. In 1935, 55.1% of Latvians were Lutheran, 24.4% were Roman Catholic, 8.9% were Orthodox, 5.5% were Old Believers, 4.8% were Jewish, and the rest belonged to other religions. Before World War II, there was a strong Jewish presence in Latvia.

Religious tolerance ended when the Soviet Union annexed Latvia in 1940. All religious activities were discouraged, and the government closed many churches and seized the property. The Russian Orthodox Church was treated less harshly than the others, but only because the Soviet government had a pro-Russian cultural bias. For example, during much of the Soviet period, the identities of Latvians who attended church services on Christmas were recorded. These persons would then later be mocked, harassed, or punished at the workplace or at school. In spite of this psychological tactic, church attendance remained high.

Religious persecution formally came to an end in 1989. Latvians have begun to reopen churches, and attendance at various religious services has grown especially since the collapse of the Soviet Union in 1991. In 2006, about two-thirds of Latvians remained "undeclared" religiously, about 20% of Latvians named themselves as Lutherans, 15% Orthodox, and 1% other Christian sects, with small numbers of Jews, Muslims, and other faiths.

⁶ MAJOR HOLIDAYS

There are three Christian holidays that have become prominent in Latvian culture: Christmas, Easter, and Whitsuntide (the week of Pentecost). At Christmas, Latvians attend church services, decorate spruce trees with ornaments and lights, and exchange presents. Easter traditions include coloring eggs and making decorations from onion skins and herbs. Another popular activity at Easter is to build a swing and swing high, from the traditional belief that such an activity will repel mosquitoes from biting in the summer. Many homes are decorated with birch branches for Whitsuntide. The national holiday of Latvia is on 18 November, to commemorate the proclamation of the republic.

Ligo svçtki is a traditional midsummer festival that celebrates the summer solstice on June 23 and *Jâňi* (St John's Day) on June 24. This is one of Latvia's most popular holidays that has retained most of its pre-Christian flavor. The holiday marks the longest amount of daylight during the year and the shortest nights. The origin of the celebration stems from the time of year when the crops had been planted and farmers were looking forward to the upcoming harvest. The *Ligo svçtki* activities encompass many old customs believed to enlist the aid of good spirits in the home, barn, field, and forest, and shield the crops from witches and devils. It is a night of singing, dancing, light-hearted merriment, and fortune telling. Men, women, and children dress in colorful folk costumes. Fields are weeded, beer is brewed, and a special cheese is made from cottage cheese, milk, cream, and caraway seeds. The *Jâňu* songs are a traditional part of the *Ligo svçtki* celebration. These songs are short four-line verses from *dainas* with the typical refrain of "*ligo, ligo*" (an exclamation of joy). Women wear flower chaplets on their heads, while men (especially those named Jânis) wear wreaths made from oak branches. During the celebration, people go from farm to farm, gathering more flowers and sampling the quality of the cheese and beer. After dusk, fires are lit on hilltops. A wooden barrel is filled with firewood and tar and hoisted as a torch atop a tall pole. A big bonfire is often built alongside. There is much singing, dancing, eating, and drinking throughout the short night, ensuring that no one goes to sleep before sunrise. Similar celebrations also occur among Scandinavian cultures.

Other Latvian traditions include two All Fool's days—one on April 1 and the other on April 30. Every Latvian also celebrates not only a birthday but a namesake day. For an individual's namesake day, specific male and female first names are assigned to each day on the calendar. The *talka* (cooperative harvesting and threshing) is another occasion to celebrate after work is done. Special Harvest Day (Thanksgiving) is celebrated on the first Sunday in October. There are many other celebrations, among them some church festivals, district fairs, monthly market days, 4H Club exhibitions, gigantic open air performances of theater plays, dances, and choir songs, especially the popular *Dziesmu svçtki* (Song Festival).

7 RITES OF PASSAGE

Latvian baptisms are marked by families getting together for a feast. Weddings are celebrated as the preeminent Latvian rite of passage—wedding festivities can go on for as long as three days. Personal autos were rare in Latvia throughout the Soviet years, so learning to drive as a teenager was not common. However, a youth in Latvia could legally only ride a bicycle in the cities with a bicycle driver's license, available at age 16. Universal suffrage is granted at age 18 and passports are issued at age 21.

8 INTERPERSONAL RELATIONS

Handshaking is customary, and most standard European courtesies are observed. Latvians are somewhat reserved and formal in public but are usually very hospitable in private.

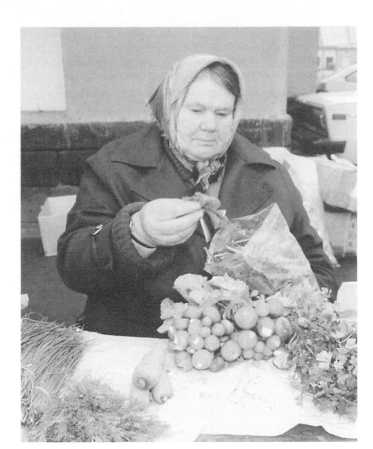

A Latvian woman displaying her vegetables on a table at an outdoor market in Riga, Latvia. (Photo Edit)

9 LIVING CONDITIONS

Many Latvians enjoy local mineral spas. One of the most famous is in Kemeri, near Riga. The local mineral water and mud have been used for medicinal therapy for almost 300 years. Since the winters are cold, housing is built accordingly, with firewood as the main source of heat. Government-operated railroads are the primary way for people to get around in Latvia.

10 FAMILY LIFE

Latvian culture has always emphasized strong familial ties. Men have the role of provider and women are homemakers in traditional Latvian culture. The typical family includes two to four children.

11 CLOTHING

Most Latvians dress in standard European clothes for everyday wear. During folk dances and traditional ceremonies, many women wear the traditional Latvian costume, which consists of a large, colorful, pleated skirt worn with a white blouse and a short, round hat.

12 FOOD

Appetizers are an important part of Latvian cuisine. Traditional Latvian soups include cabbage soup and buckwheat soup (with boiled pork, onions, potatoes, and barley). Traditional dishes include grilled pork ribs, smoked fish (including salmon and trout), gray peas with fried fat, and *piragi* (pastries filled with bacon and onions). A popular sweet pastry is *Alexander Torte,* which is filled with raspberries or cranberries. Other popular national dishes include *zemnieku brokastis* ("peasant's breakfast," a large omelet with potatoes and mushrooms), *maizes zupe ar putukrejumu* (cornbread soup with whipped cream), *skâbe putra* (a drink made in some regions from pearl barley or rye flour and whey), and *sidĭe, biezpiens ar kartupedĭem un krejumi* (salt herring, cottage cheese, potatoes, and sour cream).

Different types of locally brewed beer are popular among Latvians in different parts of the homeland. One of the most famous is a black alcoholic beverage, *Rigas Melnais Balzâms* (Riga Black Balsam), which has been produced in Riga since the 1700s. Its recipe includes many herbs, spices, and cognac as ingredients.

13 EDUCATION

The Latvians' first educational system was operated in Riga by Roman Catholic clergy during the 13th century. Schooling for children began in the 16th century. Russification (Russianization) in the Latvians' educational system was apparent as early as 1789, when instruction began in Russian. During the 1860s, many Latvian schools were prohibited from using Latvian as the language of instruction. During the Soviet era, Latvians had the same type of educational system that existed throughout much of the former Soviet Union, which was based on the Russian model.

During the Soviet years, when children were about 6 months old they started day nursery until age 3, attended kindergarten until age 6 or 7, and went to elementary school until age 10. From ages 10 to 14, children attended a type of school that was like a combination of middle school and junior high school. At the start of the middle school years, students typically studied history, geography, biology, and a foreign language. By the eighth and ninth grades, physics, chemistry, and electives were taught. After ninth grade, a student went either to a vocational school, professional technical school, or preparatory high school. In order to get into a high school, students had to pass an exam in language and mathematics at the end of ninth grade; otherwise, they went to vocational or trade school. Competition for a place at a university was rigorous.

Since 1990, the Latvians have thoroughly changed the organizational structure and curricula that were part of the Soviet system. Primary education still lasts for nine years, and secondary education lasts for three years. There are now private as well as public universities available for those who pass entrance exams. Literacy is 100%.

14 CULTURAL HERITAGE

Latvian folk history preservation is a popular activity. Several folk dance troupes, such as Ilgi, Skandinieki, and Dandari, are well known for their performances that preserve Latvian heritage. Ballet is popular among Latvians, although ballet of Latvian origin dates back only to 1935.

Latvian teenagers outside of Latvia participate in cultural folk dance groups with a special zeal. The well-known *Saules Josta* (Sun Sash) dance troupe of Australia regularly performs world tours. The tradition of singing has no age barriers; Latvian choirs typically include preteens as well as septuagenarians in their ranks.

The *kokle* is the most celebrated of the Latvian folk instruments. A small board zither, the kokle is related to a larger family of similar stringed instruments found throughout the Baltic region and Finland: the *kankles* of the Lithuanians, the Estonians' *kannel,* and the *kantele* of the Finno-Karelians. The kokle was usually played by men to accompany folk dances. It is now favored by young female ensembles and is also played in large modern orchestras—there are soprano, alto, tenor, and bass models available.

The popular *Dziesmu svçtki* (Song Festival) is an event that occurs every four years. The first Song Festival took place in 1873 with 1,003 singers, but by 1938 the event had grown to 16,000 singers with an audience of over 100,000. During the Soviet occupation years, the tradition continued, but with Russian cultural overtones. Latvian Song Festivals are also held every four years in the United States, Canada, Australia, and Europe.

Latvian literature is comparatively new. During the last 100 years, the Latvians have repeatedly struggled against German and Russian invaders to regain their independence. So, Latvian writers during that time focused on describing the Latvian mentality, the history, the attitudes towards the oppressors, and the Latvian way of life in their works as a way of encouraging pride among their fellow Latvians.

Mark Rothko, internationally renowned abstract painter, was born in Latvia in 1903 and emigrated to the United States with his family at the age of 10.

15 WORK

Latvia is an agricultural region, and the Latvians have a very strong work ethic. It is emphasized in their centuries-old folk songs *(dainas),* and it served as a virtue during the independence years of 1918–40. However, the Soviet occupation left a negative imprint that has affected Latvia's current working population.

The Soviet government controlled the economy for decades, during which time the Latvians worked with little incentive under a system of price controls and quotas. Since independence, the Latvian government has adopted a market-based economy to replace the inefficient socialist system. However, the transition toward a market economy was difficult on many workers, since the job market began changing with the economy. As a result, many Latvians (especially women) dealt with unemployment in the first years after independence. The economy has grown steadily since then, though, and unemployment had fallen to 5.7% in 2007. Latvia had the fastest growing economy in the European Union in 2004–2006.

Latvians not in school can begin working at age 16. Compulsory military service was abolished in 2007.

16 SPORTS

Soccer, volleyball, and basketball are popular outdoor activities among Latvians. Latvia has many organized sports clubs and organizations for these and other sports. Bobsled and motor racing are popular spectator sports. Latvian athletes have occasionally won medals at the Olympic games.

17 ENTERTAINMENT AND RECREATION

In 1772 the Riga Opera-Theater house opened. Going to the theater is popular among Latvians. Many productions are dramas, but musicals have become popular in recent years. Circuses are also popular and Riga has had a permanent circus building since 1889.

18 FOLK ART, CRAFTS, AND HOBBIES

Interest in folk arts and crafts is expressed through jewelry-making, intricate sewing, and embroidering of the traditional Latvian folk dress. Workshops in ceramics, woodworking, and leather craft are also common. *Dzintars* (amber)—fossilized pine resin from the Tertiary Period—washes up along the Baltic seashore and is used for making ethnic jewelry and in the manufacture of ornamental objects.

19 SOCIAL PROBLEMS

As in many other places in the world, there is ethnic tension in the Baltics and especially in Latvia, between ethnic Latvians and Russians. In independent Latvia of 1918–40, there was no such ethnic tension, and at that time ethnic Latvians made up over 75% of the population. After 1945, many Latvians were forcefully deported to Siberia, with ethnic Russians settling in their place in confiscated properties in Latvia. After the collapse of the Soviet Union and Latvia's regained independence in 1991, ethnic Latvians accounted for only 52% of the population, and for only 35% of the population in the capital, Riga.

The new Latvian government reinstated Latvian as the official language and permitted Russians to live in the expropriated Latvian properties for seven more years, so that they could have time to find another place to live or to emigrate to Russia. Bitter complaining by the Russians in Latvia resulted, and tensions between the Russian and Latvian governments over the fate of these people have continued to be a source of conflict since then. Latvians feel overshadowed culturally and economically by their powerful Russian neighbors, who have historically dominated nearby ethnic groups. Latvians often consider the ethnic Russians in Latvia as unwanted colonists and part of a well-coordinated expansionist government waiting for the opportunity to reclaim Latvia yet again. The Russian government, however, wants to safeguard the rights of ethnic Russians living in former Soviet republics.

In Latvia there are also some acute environmental problems. In the Soviet era, environmental protection in Latvia did not exist. Air pollution became concentrated in industrialized areas (these were created during the Soviet years), and it is now regularly checked. The rivers and lakes were used as open sewers for sloppy industrial waste disposal methods. As a result, even the Baltic Sea was not safe for swimming. The collective farms *(kolkhozi)*, in order to fulfill Moscow's imposed quotas, abused the use of fertilizers, pesticides, and herbicides. In many places even the groundwater is contaminated. Measures are being taken to reverse the damage; Latvia participates in international efforts to reduce pollution.

Because of its geographical location, Latvia is a transit point for illegal drugs between Eastern and Western Europe. With the destabilization of the economy in 1991, Latvia also become vulnerable to money laundering ventures by organized crime syndicates, a common problem among former Soviet satellites.

20 GENDER ISSUES

Although homosexual activities were decriminalized in Latvia in 1992, homophobia still lingers among the population. The first gay pride parade was organized in 2005 and met with tremendous opposition, so much so that the parade was cancelled in 2006. In 2005, the Latvian parliament approved a constitutional amendment to limit marriage to heterosexual couples by such a wide margin that then-President Vaira Víe-Freiberga felt compelled to sign it into law despite her own disagreement with the legislation.

In contrast to these anti-gay measures, the Latvian government passed a law prohibiting housing and employment discrimination based on a number of factors, including gender and sexuality. In 2007, the gay pride parade was held without serious incident. Latvia's membership in the European Union requires it to recognize human rights and eliminate discrimination based on race, ethnicity, gender, creed, or sexuality, putting pressure on Latvians to overcome their prejudices, be they cultural, ethnic, or religious.

21 BIBLIOGRAPHY

American Latvian Association. *Latvia: Country, People, Liberty.* Rockville, MD: American Latvian Association, 1976.

Andersons, E. *Cross Road Country Latvia.* Waverly, IA: Latvian Book, 1953.

———, ed. *Latvju enciklopçdija.* Rockville, MD: American Latvian Association, 1983.

The Baltic States. Tallinn, Estonia: Estonian, Latvian, and Lithuanian Encyclopaedia Publishers, 1991.

Europa. "Member States of the EU: Latvia," http://europa.eu/abc/european_countries/eu_members/latvia/index_en.htm (18 August 2008).

Latvian Institute. http://www.li.lv (18 August 2008).

Schultz, Gudrun. "Latvian President Insists on Homosexuality Inclusion in Workers' Discrimination Law," *LifeSiteNews.com.* http://www.lifesitenews.com/ldn/2006/sep/06092203.html (18 August 2008).

Simanis, Vitauts. *Latvia.* St. Charles, IL: Book Latvia, 1984.

Šveics, Vilnis V. *How Stalin Got the Baltic States.* Jersey City State College, 1991.

—by Dianne de Mott

LIECHTENSTEINERS

LOCATION: Liechtenstein
POPULATION: 35,200 (2008)
LANGUAGE: Standard German; Alemannic German; English, French
RELIGION: Roman Catholic; Protestant

¹ INTRODUCTION

Liechtenstein is a tiny, picturesque country located in the heart of Europe. The citizens of this politically neutral principality enjoy a peaceful and prosperous existence in the midst of a scenic Alpine landscape. The region now known as Liechtenstein has been continuously inhabited since 3000 BC. After successive periods of rule by the Rhaetians, Celts, and Romans, it was settled by the Alemanni, a Germanic people who arrived in the area in the 5th century AD. In the 8th century the region formed part of Charlemagne's empire, and it was later divided into two separate entities, the Lordship of Schellenberg and the County of Vaduz, both of which later belonged to the Holy Roman Empire. Prince Johann Adam of Liechtenstein acquired Schellenberg in 1699 and Vaduz in 1712, uniting the two domains as the Imperial Principality of Liechtenstein. Except for a brief period of French rule under Napoleon, the principality has been independent ever since that time.

For part of the 19th century, Liechtenstein was an autonomous unit of the German Confederation. Since the 1860s the country has been politically neutral, with no standing army. Under its 1921 constitution, Liechtenstein became a constitutional monarchy with a single-chamber parliament and a prime minister appointed by its prince. Maintaining its neutrality during the First and Second World Wars, Liechtenstein became one of the only areas of western Europe to remain free from warfare during the past two centuries. Economically, Liechtenstein joined with Switzerland to form a customs union in 1924, when it adopted the Swiss franc as its currency. The principality joined the United Nations in 1991. Crown Prince Hans Adam has been Liechtenstein's reigning monarch since 1984; however, on 15 August 2004, Hans Adam transferred the official duties of the ruling prince to his son Alois, retaining his status as head of state. Despite its small size and limited natural resources, Liechtenstein has developed into a prosperous, highly industrialized, free-enterprise economy with a thriving financial service sector and living standards on a par with its large European neighbors. Liechtenstein has been a member of the European Economic Area (an organization serving as a bridge between the European Free Trade Association [EFTA] and the European Union [EU]) since 1995. The government is working to harmonize its economic policies with those of an integrated Europe. Although Liechtenstein has recently adopted anti-money laundering legislation, there are still concerns about the use of financial institutions for money laundering.

² LOCATION AND HOMELAND

Liechtenstein is a landlocked country located in the Rhine River valley between Switzerland and Austria. With an area of roughly 62 square miles (160 square kilometers)—slightly smaller than Washington, D.C.—it is Europe's fourth smallest country. The western part of Liechtenstein, situated on the Rhine's eastern bank, is a flat region covering about 40% of the country, with mountains occupying much of the larger area to the east. A steep Alpine slope called the *Drei Schwestern* ("three sisters") extends across Liechtenstein's border with Austria. The highest point in the country is the *Grauspitz*, at 8,525 feet (2,599 meters).

Liechtenstein has a population of approximately 35,200 people, of whom roughly two-thirds are native-born residents of Alemannic descent. The rest are immigrants from Switzerland, Austria, and other countries. Liechtenstein's population is unevenly distributed among the principality's 11 administrative districts, which are called communes. Vaduz, the capital city, has a population of about 5,250.

³ LANGUAGE

Standard German is the official language of Liechtenstein, used for official purposes and taught in the schools. However, most people also speak a local Alemannic dialect that resembles the German spoken in Switzerland. The people in the mountain region of Triesenberg, whose forebears emigrated from southeastern Switzerland in the 13th century, speak a unique dialect called *Walser*. The principal languages taught in school are English and French.

⁴ FOLKLORE

Some of Liechtenstein's legends date back to the dark days of the 17th century, when a savage wave of witch hunts swept over the principality during the reign of the Count of Hohenems. One concerns a fiddler named Hans Jöri, who unknowingly plays at a party thrown by a group of witches. The witches vanish when he disobeys them by drinking a toast to his own health, after which he suddenly finds himself seated on a scaffold holding a bleeding ox's hoof—a symbol of witchcraft—in his hand. In another tale, a farmer suspects that a witch's spell is preventing his butter from thickening. After he thrusts a red-hot pitchfork into it, it thickens right away. The farmer's suspicions are borne out when he is then approached by a witch who has burn marks on her hands shaped exactly like the prongs of the pitchfork.

⁵ RELIGION

Roman Catholicism is the state religion of Liechtenstein, and as of the 2000 census about 78% of the people were Catholics, while approximately 8% were Protestants, 5% Muslims, and the rest belonged to other denominations. Freedom of religion is guaranteed by the constitution. As of 2008, there were efforts ongoing to disentangle church and state. For instance, in a survey commissioned by the government in 2007, the overwhelming majority of the population was in favor of tolerance and respect toward other religions, called for equal treatment of the religious communities by the state, and tended to support the abolition of the constitutionally guaranteed privileges of the Roman Catholic Church.

⁶ MAJOR HOLIDAYS

Many of Liechtenstein's holidays are holy days of the Christian calendar. These include Epiphany (January 6), Candlemas (February 2), the Feast of St. Joseph (March 19), Easter (observed from Good Friday through Easter Monday), Ascension, Whit Monday, Corpus Christi, the Nativity of Our Lady

(September 8), All Saints' Day (November 1), the Immaculate Conception (December 8), and Christmas, which is celebrated December 24–26. Christmas is the most important holiday of the year, celebrated by putting up Christmas trees, exchanging gifts, and visiting with friends and family. Other holidays include New Year's Day (January 1), Labor Day (May 1), and Liechtenstein's national day (August 15), which is celebrated with speeches and fireworks.

People in rural areas still observe some of the traditional holiday customs passed on by preceding generations. There is the annual Corpus Christi procession, an event for which the entire village turns out, carrying a variety of devotional objects and passing by homes adorned with candles, flowers, and religious paintings. On Bonfire Sunday, the first Sunday of Lent, boys walk through their villages collecting wood for a large bonfire, which they light in the evening. They then perform an age-old ceremony, tracing patterns in the air with torches they have lit from the flames of the bonfire. After the fire dies out, the boys return home to a traditional pancake supper. Another rural Lenten custom is "Dirty Thursday," also called "Sooty Thursday," which is observed on the last Thursday before Lent. On this occasion, boys arm themselves with chimney soot, which they rub into the faces and hair of unsuspecting victims. Another traditional prank carried out on this date is stealing a pot of soup from the kitchen of a village house. Some women have been known to even the score by hiding an old shoe in the soup pot.

7 RITES OF PASSAGE

Liechtensteiners live in a modern, industrialized, Christian country. Hence, many of the rites of passage that young people undergo are religious rituals, such as baptism, first Communion, confirmation, and marriage. In addition, a student's progress through the education system is marked by many families with graduation parties.

8 INTERPERSONAL RELATIONS

Liechtensteiners commonly greet each other by shaking hands. Verbal greetings include *Gruezi* (also used in Switzerland) and the German *Grüss Gott. Hoi!* is a popular informal greeting used among friends.

9 LIVING CONDITIONS

Liechtenstein is a modern, industrialized country whose residents enjoy one of the highest standards of living in the world. Most Liechtensteiners live in single-family homes, although apartment living has become increasingly common for young families who cannot afford their own homes. There is sufficient housing for all of Liechtenstein's inhabitants, and dwellings range from wooden houses scattered across picturesque mountain villages to modern multi-story apartment buildings in the capital city of Vaduz.

Average life expectancy in Liechtenstein is 80 years, and the infant mortality rate is a very low 4.52 per 1,000 live births. Liechtenstein's health care system provides free regular examinations for children under the age of 10. The principality has one public hospital of its own and has also formed agreements with Switzerland and Austria that allow its residents access to hospital facilities in those countries when they are needed. A representative survey conducted in 2006 showed that near-

ly 90% of all respondents were satisfied or very satisfied with medical services in Liechtenstein.

Private automobiles are Liechtenstein's most important mode of transportation, and the principality has a well-developed system of roads and highways. Its main highway runs through the country, linking it with Austria and Switzerland. Low-cost public transportation is provided by postal buses, which carry passengers to destinations within Liechtenstein and also to Austria and Switzerland. Liechtenstein has one railway, operated by the Austrian Federal Railways. There is no airport within Liechtenstein's borders—the nearest one is Kloten Airport in Zurich, Switzerland.

10 FAMILY LIFE

The typical family in Liechtenstein, as in most of its western European neighbors, is the nuclear family, composed of parents and, on average, about two children. Most Liechtensteiners marry in their late twenties, preferring to complete their education before taking on the responsibilities of raising a family. It is not unusual for unmarried couples to live together before (or instead of) marrying. Several distinctive traditional customs are still practiced at weddings in rural villages. When the bride and groom leave the church following the marriage

Sophie, the wife of Prince Alois of Liechtenstein (far right), and other wives of heads of state pose with children in traditional dress in Meersburg am Bodensee, Germany. The women came together for a photograph during an informal meeting of heads of state of German-speaking countries. (Johannes Simon/AFP/Getty Images)

ceremony, they often find their way barred by a rope held by the village children, who must be "bribed" by the best man in order to let the couple pass. Further bribes may have to be paid later, at the wedding feast, if the children manage to make off with one of the bride's shoes. Sometimes the groom's friends even "kidnap" the bride herself, and it is then the groom's turn to pay up. Yet another wedding custom is firing guns into the air, a practice that has been banned for safety reasons, but is still encountered occasionally. Women in Liechtenstein have only had the right to vote nationally since 1984. Many married women work outside the home.

11 CLOTHING

The people of Liechtenstein wear modern, Western-style clothing for both casual and formal occasions. They dress neatly and, in many cases, rather conservatively in public. Their traditional costumes, or *Trachten*, are worn only rarely, for festivals and other special occasions. The women's costume has a gathered waist, a full skirt, and an apron, while men wear knee-length breeches, a flat black hat, and a *loden* (woolen) jacket.

12 FOOD

Liechtensteiners eat three meals a day. Coffee and bread with jam are commonly eaten for breakfast (called *Zmorga*). *Zmittag*, eaten at mid-day, is the main meal of the day and typically includes a main dish, soup, a salad, and dessert. A lighter meal (*Znacht*) is eaten at dinnertime, often consisting of an open-faced sandwich made with various kinds of meat and cheese. Although Liechtenstein is too small to have developed an extensive national cuisine, it does have some distinctive regional dishes. *Käsknöfle* consists of noodles made by squeezing a mixture of flour, water, and eggs through a perforated board. The noodles are then baked with grated cheese and a layer of fried onions and often served with applesauce or a salad. *Hafaläb*, another favorite, is a dish made with a corn- and wheat-flour dough formed into small loaves that are boiled, left out to dry, sliced, and then fried. Corn flour is the principal ingredient of *Törkarebl*, made from porridge that is then fried to create a dumpling-like dish often served with elderberry jam.

13 EDUCATION

Virtually all adults in Liechtenstein are literate. Both primary and secondary education are administered by the central government, and all children must attend school from ages 6 to 15. In addition to government-run public schools, there are also private schools sponsored by the Catholic Church. After completing their secondary school requirements, students either receive vocational training or prepare for the university entrance examination, known as the *Matura*. Liechtenstein has no universities of its own, so its young people go to college in Germany, Austria, or Switzerland (including those studying to be teachers themselves, who are generally trained in Switzerland). Liechtenstein does have an evening technical college that offers courses in engineering and architecture and a music school, as well as a variety of facilities for adult education.

14 CULTURAL HERITAGE

Liechtenstein's great cultural treasure is the art collection of its prince, which dates back to the early 1600s. Housed in the capital city of Vaduz, it is the second largest private art collection in the world (surpassed in size only by that of Britain's royal family) and one of the finest. Its many masterpieces cover a wide range of periods and schools of art, and it includes sculptures, tapestries, silver, and porcelain, as well as paintings by Breughel the Elder, Botticelli, Rembrandt, Rubens, and other masters. Liechtenstein also has a strong musical tradition. Brass bands and vocal ensembles abound in rural areas, while the cities of Vaduz and Balzers both have highly regarded operetta companies.

15 WORK

Since World War II, Liechtenstein has been transformed from an agrarian society into a modern industrial state. Agriculture, which once occupied a majority of the population, now employs 2.1% of the paid work force, and 54% of all employed adults work in service-sector jobs. Liechtensteiners put in a long work day—often from 8:00 am to 6:30 pm with a midday lunch break lasting an hour or longer. About 13,900 of Liechtenstein's labor force of 29,500 people commuted to work from Switzerland, Austria, or Germany in 2001. The greatest proportion of foreign workers are employed in industry. Liechtenstein's major industries include metal finishing, ceramics, pharmaceuticals, and electronic equipment.

16 SPORTS

The majority of Liechtensteiners are sports enthusiasts—45% belong to sports clubs. The principality's downhill ski resorts are world famous, especially those at Malbun and Steg. The Steg resort also has a popular cross-country ski course with a 1-mile (1.7-kilometer) stretch that is floodlit, allowing for night-time skiing. Summer sports include hiking, bicycling, and soccer.

17 ENTERTAINMENT AND RECREATION

The people of Liechtenstein enjoy hiking and other outdoor activities. Cultural pursuits—such as performing in choirs and bands—are also popular, and many people belong to social clubs. Television is a common form of recreation. All television programming is received from abroad, as the principality does not have its own broadcast facilities. Radio broadcasts originating in Liechtenstein began in 1994.

18 FOLK ART, CRAFTS, AND HOBBIES

Historically, Liechtenstein's major crafts included basket weaving, coopering (barrel making), clog carving, and the fashioning of elaborate rakes. Today these activities have largely been replaced by the modern crafts of pottery, sculpture, and woodcarving, all areas in which Liechtenstein's artisans have a distinguished reputation throughout Europe.

Liechtenstein is world famous for its beautiful postage stamps, valuable collector's items that provide a significant source of government revenue. Many are based on paintings found in the prestigious art collection of Liechtenstein's prince.

19 SOCIAL PROBLEMS

Concern about the large number of foreign residents in Liechtenstein—over one-third of the population—has led to restrictive immigration policies, spurred by fears of endangering the cultural unity that distinguishes this tiny nation from its neighbors. However, increased numbers of foreign workers from neighboring German-speaking countries continue to commute to jobs in Liechtenstein, and foreigners still account for approximately 47% of the principality's work force. Some Liechtensteiners fear the growing Muslim population: the Muslim community has grown since the 1990s as a result of an influx of migrants primarily from Turkey and the Western Balkans (Serbia and Bosnia-Herzegovina), many of whom resettled from other Western European countries. The Muslim population increased from 689 in 1990 to 1,593 in 2000. The government grants the Muslim community a residency permit for one imam, plus one short-term residency permit for an additional imam during Ramadan. The government follows a policy of routinely granting visas to the imams in exchange for the agreement of both the Turkish Association and the Muslim community to prevent religious diatribes by the imams or the spread of religious extremism.

20 GENDER ISSUES

The law prohibits discrimination on the basis of gender. The law prohibits all forms of domestic violence and provides for restraining orders against violent family members. Frauenhaus is a women's shelter providing both counseling and refuge for battered women (including nonresidents) and dependent children. Rape, including spousal rape, is a criminal offense. Spousal rape has the same penalties as rape under other circumstances. In 2007 a new provision of the penal code entered into force making stalking a criminal offense. Prostitution is illegal. Sexual harassment is illegal and punishable by up to six months in prison or a fine.

Women enjoy the same legal rights as men, including rights under family law, property law, and in the judicial system. The Equal Opportunity Office and the Commission on Equality between Women and Men works to eliminate all forms of gender discrimination. However, societal discrimination continues to limit opportunities for women in fields traditionally dominated by men. Men earn more than women, and women generally do not receive equal pay for equal work. Implementing a European Union directive, parliament in 2006 unanimously adopted amendments to the labor contract law and the equal opportunity law to combat gender discrimination in the workplace.

In 2007 there were six women in the parliament and one woman in the five seat cabinet.

A recent government-ordered study found evidence of discrimination based on sexual orientation in 2007. In a poll 71%

of homosexuals who responded said that discrimination was widespread in the country; 58% of the overall population expressed the view that homosexuality remained a taboo.

21 BIBLIOGRAPHY

Beattie, David. *Liechtenstein: A Modern History.* London; New York: I.B. Tauris, 2004.

Duursma, Jorri. *Self-Determination, Statehood, and International Relations of Micro-States: The Cases of Liechtenstein, San Marino, Monaco, Andorra, and the Vatican City.* Cambridge; New York: Cambridge University Press, 1996.

Eccardt, Thomas M. *Secrets of the Seven Smallest States of Europe: Andorra, Liechtenstein, Luxembourg, Malta, Monaco, San Marino, and Vatican City.* New York: Hippocrene Books, 2005.

Gall, Timothy, and Susan Gall, ed. *Worldmark Encyclopedia of the Nations.* Detroit: Gale Research, 1995.

Meier, Regula A. *Liechtenstein.* Santa Barbara, CA: Clio Press, 1993.

Nelson, Kay Shaw. *Cuisines of the Alps: Recipes, Drinks, and Lore from France, Switzerland, Liechtenstein, Italy, Germany, Austria, and Slovenia.* New York: Hippocrene Books, 2005.

Paris, Sheldon. "The Principality of Liechtenstein." *Stamps.* 9 October 1993: 40.

"The Principality of Liechtenstein." *Culturegram '95.* The David M. Kennedy Center for International Studies, Brigham Young University. Provo, UT: Brigham Young Univ., 1994.

The Principality of Liechtenstein. http://www.liechtenstein.li/en/portal_fuerstentum_liechtenstein-fremdsprachig/fl-fremdsprachig/fl-fremdsprachig-home.htm (22 May 2008).

Sasseen, Jane, et al. "Europe's Pocket Fortresses." *International Management,* March 1993: 28

—revised by J. Hobby

LITHUANIANS

LOCATION: Lithuania
POPULATION: 3.4 million [total population of country; 85% are ethnic Lithuanians]
LANGUAGE: Lithuanian
RELIGION: Roman Catholicism; Old Believers; Russian Orthodox Church; Lutheranism; Judaism

1 INTRODUCTION

It was long thought that the Lithuanians were descendants of ancient Roman settlers, but it is more likely that the first people to live in the area now known as Lithuania came from Asia around 4,000–10,000 years ago. The modern Lithuanians are closely related in ethnicity and language to the Latvians, but their culture is closer to that of the Estonians because of the Scandinavian and German influences.

The early Lithuanians formed into small self-governing communities organized along family lines. By the 13th century AD, these communities were organized enough to be united by wealthy and powerful Lithuanian dukes. In 1236, these dukes elected Mindaugas as the first grand duke. He unified the Lithuanians into the Grand Duchy of Lithuania as a response to the encroaching Order of Teutonic Knights, a German military organization seeking conquest under the pretext of spreading Christianity. He also led in the defense against the Tatars, invaders from central Asia who conquered much of Eastern Europe during the 13th century.

Under the rule of Grand Duke Gediminas (r.1316–41), the Lithuanians were still trying to repel the Teutonic Knights. As part of this strategy, he invited other knights, as well as merchants and artisans, to come and settle in Lithuania. Many new trade centers were developed during this time, such as the cities of Vilnius and Kaunas. Merchants from across Europe came up the Nemunas River to Kaunas in order to buy amber, furs, and honey. In 1385, the grandson of Gediminas, Jogaila, became the grand duke. With his marriage to Queen Jadvyga of Poland, he converted to Roman Catholicism and decreed Lithuania a Christian nation. Lithuania and Poland then entered into a political and military partnership. Under the leadership of Vytautas the Great (r. 1392–1430), Lithuania's territory spread across present-day Belarus, Ukraine, and western Russia. Under Vytautas, Lithuania's political power reached a new height, and he is often considered Lithuania's most outstanding leader. The military was finally able to drive out the Teutonic Knights from the region. By the 15th century, however, the partnership with Poland was coming apart. Lithuania needed Poland more and more to help drive out invading Russians and became too weak to defend itself. As a result, Lithuania agreed to unite with Poland in 1569.

The union, however, did not prevent the continuing decline of the state over the next 200 years. The principal reason appears to have been a rise of nobility to power without a strong and united central policy. During the 1700s, constant Russian attacks caused famines that killed thousands of Lithuanians. By 1772, the union with Poland had crumbled and Russia began taking over the eastern parts of Lithuania. By 1795, all of Lithuania was under Russian control, and Poland had been taken over by the Prussians and Austrians. The Lithuanians led failed revolts against the Russians in 1795, 1831, and 1863. In 1864, the Russian tsar Alexander II ordered a policy of Russification (Russianization) onto the Lithuanians. Russification involved the forcible imposition of the Russian language, the Russian Orthodox religion, and Russian laws onto the Lithuanian people. The policy was designed to end political unrest among Lithuanians by changing the Lithuanian culture itself. Many Lithuanians, however, refused to cooperate with the intrusive policy. By 1865, only a year after the policy was implemented, the Russian government had exiled or executed around 10,000 Lithuanian dissidents. The occupation of Lithuania by imperial Russia lasted until 1915.

During World War I, the German army occupied Lithuania. The war provided the Lithuanians with the opportunity to get rid of the Russian leadership. Therefore, on 16 February 1918, the Lithuanian National Council declared independence while German troops were still on Lithuanian soil and elected Antanas Smetona as president. The declaration had to be backed up by wars for independence fought against Soviet Russia, Poland, and remnant imperial German troops. Lithuania was recognized as a sovereign state and became a member of the League of Nations in 1922. However, after Smetona left office in 1920, the government became unstable. In 1926 Smetona returned to power in a military takeover. During the late 1920s, Smetona's administration became increasingly authoritarian—he dissolved the parliament in 1927 and banned all opposing political parties in 1930. Despite these actions, Lithuanian society improved. Land reforms made it possible for small farms to prosper. A comprehensive educational system was begun, and Lithuanian literature, arts, music, and theater developed.

In 1939, the Nazi leader Hitler and the Soviet leader Stalin signed a pact in which the two countries promised not to invade each other. A secret part of the agreement permitted the Soviet Union to take over the three Baltic States. On 15 June 1940, the Soviet Red Army invaded and occupied Lithuania, declaring that Lithuania was now Soviet territory. However, in 1941 Germany invaded the Soviet Union and occupied Lithuania. The Germans sent about 160,000 Lithuanians to die in concentration camps. About 130,000 of the victims were Jewish Lithuanians, whom the Nazis had targeted for extermination because of their ethnicity and religion. By 1944, the weakness of the German military gave the Soviet army an opportunity to return to Lithuania. At the close of World War II, many Lithuanians fled the homeland rather than live under Soviet rule, and thousands that remained in Lithuania fought against the Soviets. From 1944 to 1952, well-organized military units of the Lithuanian resistance movement waged a protracted guerrilla war against the Soviet military occupants. About 50,000 lives were lost on each side.

A large Soviet military force and a massive deportation of 10% of the population held the resistance movement in check. The Soviet government sent Lithuanian rebels to labor camps in distant parts of xe Siberia. About 30,000 Lithuanian families were sent away by this process during 1941–52. By the early 1950s, the Soviet Union had firm control over the region and took over all private property. The late 1950s and 1960s were relatively quiet years when Soviet-type institutions were established and the collectivization of agriculture and industrialization were carried out. However, during the 1970s, a national and religious dissent emerged again and revealed deep-seated opposition to the Soviet system. The strict control continued

until the 1980s, when Soviet policy changed to allow peoples within the Soviet Union to speak out against the government without fear of being punished. In February 1990, the Lithuanian Communist party declared that the 1940 annexation into the Soviet Union had been illegal and, by March, there was an independent elected government. The Soviet Union initiated an embargo against Lithuania, to prevent fuel and supplies from reaching the people, but the Lithuanians bartered for goods by trading meat and dairy products. On 13 January 1991, Soviet tanks came into Vilnius, and Soviet troops seized the television and radio stations. When the Soviet Union fell apart in late 1991, Lithuania became the first of the Soviet-occupied republics to declare its independence. After difficult negotiations and a great deal of international pressure, the last foreign army units left Lithuania on 31 August 1993.

Lithuania became a member of the World Trade Organization in 2001 and a member of both the North Atlantic Treaty Organization and the European Union in 2004. Despite multiple turnovers in the government since independence, Lithuania's economy has grown steadily, and conditions in the country continue to improve.

² LOCATION AND HOMELAND

About 85% of Lithuania's 3.4 million people are ethnic Lithuanians. Unlike the other Baltic states, Lithuania did not experience massive immigration of ethnic Russians after World War II, because Lithuania was less industrialized than Estonia or Latvia and did not have the factory jobs that the Russians preferred.

Lithuania is located in the western part of the Eastern European Plain, along the basin of the Nemunas River. The topography of Lithuania is primarily a mix of hilly uplands and lowland plains, with the uplands typically some 80–100 m (260–330 ft) above the plains. The lowest part of Lithuania is the Pajurio Lowland along the Baltic coast, and the highest is Juozapine Hill (294 m/965 ft) in the Medininku Upland near Belarus. Water travel has long been an important means of transportation. There are 758 rivers that are over 10 km (6 mi) long, of which 18 are over 100 km (60 mi) long. The 2,833 lakes in Lithuania occupy about 1.5% of the surface area of the nation. The rivers and lakes are usually frozen over for about three months each winter.

Prevailing winds from the North Atlantic Ocean create a moderate climate for Lithuania. Winter temperatures near the Baltic coast are around –3°C (27°F) and drop to –6°C (21°F) inland. Summer temperatures are fairly uniform throughout Lithuania and typically reach around 16°C (60°F). Rainfall is highest near the coast and in the highlands east of Vilnius, with usually more than 80 cm (32 in) per year. The rest of Lithuania usually gets 60–80 cm (24–32 in) of rainfall annually. About 25% of the precipitation comes as snow. Since Lithuania lies so far north, daylight during the summer can last up to 18 hours per day. In the winter, however, the nights are just as long.

There are thousands of ethnic Lithuanians living outside Lithuania. The rest of Europe has a notable population of ethnic Lithuanians, with communities in London, Rome, Hamburg, Lampertheim-Huttenfeld (Germany), Punsk (Poland), and Paris. There are also small numbers of ethnic Lithuanians living in Switzerland, Belgium, Estonia, Latvia, the Netherlands, and Sweden. A smaller portion of Lithuanians live in Kaliningrad (Russia), Kiev (Ukraine), or Budapest. There are also some ethnic Lithuanians in Russian Siberia and Uzbekistan; these communities are a result of the deportation of Lithuanians from Lithuania during the 1940s.

In North America, there are over a million people claiming Lithuanian heritage living in the United States and Canada. In South America, there are Lithuanian communities in several large cities, including Buenos Aires (Argentina), Rio de Janeiro and São Paulo (Brazil), Montevideo (Uruguay), Caracas (Venezuela), and Medellin (Colombia). There are also Lithuanian communities in the Australian cities of Sydney, Melbourne, and Adelaide.

3 LANGUAGE

The Lithuanian language, like Latvian, belongs to the Letto-Lithuanian branch of Indo-European languages. Some language scholars believe that Lithuanian is related to Sanskrit, the language of ancient India. The Lithuanian and Latvian languages became distinctly different during the 5th–7th centuries AD. Standard Lithuanian is based on the Western Aukštaičiai (High Lithuanian) dialect that was formalized at the end of the 19th century. In addition to the dialect of standard Lithuanian, there are many other dialects spoken throughout Lithuania, although through standardization some of the smaller dialects have vanished over the last 50 years. Although most Lithuanian speakers reside in Lithuania, there are also many living in other parts of Europe (primarily in Russia and Poland), North

and South America (in the United States, Brazil, Argentina, and Canada), and Australia.

Lithuanian first names for males end in the letter *s* (as in Latvian). Typical first names include Algimantas, Jonas, Darius, and Vytautas. Female first names often end in the letter *a* and include Rasa, Daiva, Laima, and Aldona. Examples of everyday Lithuanian words include *Sveiki* (How do you do?), *taip* (yes), *ne* (no), *prašom* (please), *aciu* (thank you), and *sudiev* (goodbye).

4 FOLKLORE

The rich folklore of Lithuania—songs, music, tales, and riddles, as well as traditional architecture and arts and crafts—reflects the life experience of its creators, mostly the tillers of the land. The old Lithuanian *dainos* (songs) are known to scholars of folklore worldwide for their lyric and melodic beauty and variety. The dainos were created by women doing farm work or celebrating festivals (e.g., weddings) or marking mournful occasions. Romantic love and leave-taking are important themes. Many folk songs have been harmonized or used in compositions by modern composers. Massive folk song festivals or performances by individual choral groups are an important part of cultural life. Folk music is played solo or by instrumental groups, using *kankles* (zither), *skuduciai* (panpipe), *lamzdelis* (recorder), *ragas* (horn), *smuikas* (fiddle), *birbyne* (folk clarinet), and *skrabalai* (cow bells).

Folk tales are also numerous and notably original. Some, of course, are based on foreign stories or reflect the influence of neighboring peoples. The first recorded Lithuanian folk tales date back to the 16th century. Lithuanian folklore has much in common with the historical and cultural aspects of Belarusan and Russian folk tales.

5 RELIGION

The ancient Lithuanians worshiped many gods and believed that forests and fires were sacred. The worship of fire may have become common because of the abundance of peat in the region. The most popular gods that they worshiped were Perkűnas (god of thunder), Velnias (the devil, the guardian of wizards), Medeina (goddess of forests), and Zvorűne (goddess of hunting).

In the mid 1200s, Lithuania's leaders began accepting Christianity, and Roman Catholicism soon became the faith of the people as well. Reformationist ideas spread in Lithuania during the first half of the 16th century, but Counter-Reformationist Jesuits in the late 17th century strengthened the position of Roman Catholicism among the Lithuanians. In the late 17th century, many Old Believers came from Russia to escape persecution. When the policy of Russification (Russianization) began after 1863, many Roman Catholic monasteries were closed and the churches handed over to the Russian Orthodox Church. During 1799–1915, Russian Orthodoxy was the official state religion in Lithuania. However, during the independent years of 1918–40, the Roman Catholic Church was revived.

During the half-century of Soviet rule, the government severely restricted all religious activities. Many churches were allowed to deteriorate or were used as museums or warehouses. Many churches and all Catholic monasteries were closed, and believers were often denied access to higher education, lost their jobs, or were sent to prison. After 1988, religious persecution formally came to an end.

About 80% of Lithuanians who profess a religious belief are Roman Catholic. Most of the rest are Old Believers, Russian Orthodox, Lutherans, and Jews.

6 MAJOR HOLIDAYS

Independence Day is on February 16 and commemorates the declaration of independence adopted by the Council of Lithuania in 1918, when the country was still under the harsh occupation and oppressive rule of the German Empire. Restoring independence in reality required armed struggle (the War of Independence, 1918–20) against three enemies: the Red Army invading from the east, Polish troops encroaching from the south, and the Bermondt army (German units and remnants of Russian tsarist forces under German command) invading from the north. Independence Day was the most important civic celebration for Lithuanians until the Soviet occupation in June 1940, when any observance of the holiday was strictly forbidden and had grave consequences (including imprisonment) for anyone ignoring the ban. On the anniversary of the holiday in 1989, Sajudis, Lithuania's largest popular democratic movement, voiced its demand for independence. Before 1990, the February 16 holiday was publicly observed only by Lithuanians abroad.

The Day of Independence Restored is celebrated on March 11 and marks the date in 1990 when the Supreme Council of Soviet Lithuania declared the reestablishment of an independent Republic of Lithuania, formally severing all ties with the Soviet Union.

Easter is the most important religious holiday among Lithuanians. Until World War II, the traditional Easter observances extended over two days, and in some rural areas even longer. Easter Sunday, following attendance before sunrise at Resurrection services and a festive breakfast, was devoted to the immediate family, with even the children's visiting limited to their grandparents and godparents. Beginning in the late afternoon and on Easter Monday, groups of young men would call on their neighbors, singing and asking for *marguciai* (decorated Easter eggs). It was considered the height of inhospitality to refuse the carolers' requests, but that rarely happened. General merrymaking on the second day of Easter included the rolling of Easter eggs, testing one's strength, and swinging on swings "to help the flax grow faster." Adults traveled to visit relatives and friends. On the third day of Easter, the dead were remembered and cemeteries were visited.

Kūcios (Christmas Eve) on December 24 is a day of family reunion with religious significance, associated with the Christmas vigil and day-long fast. The fast is broken with a meatless and milkless evening meal of 12 courses, at which every family member tries to be present. Farm and household help, as well as any travelers, are welcome at the table, which is spread with hay (in memory of the manger at Bethlehem) and covered with a white linen cloth. The meal begins with a prayer for all those present and departed and with the breaking and sharing of blessed wafers of unleavened bread. The singing of a Christmas hymn concludes the meal. Christmas itself in earlier times was celebrated for three days. The first day was the most important but was observed by each family in seclusion at home. Visiting and entertaining were reserved for the second day of Christmas. The popularity of Santa Claus and Christmas trees dates back only to the beginning of the 20th century.

7 RITES OF PASSAGE

A couple who were to be married traditionally participated in a series of pre-wedding rituals and customs. Most of these place great emphasis upon the bride's leaving her parents and childhood home, relinquishing her girlhood by putting aside her carefree days and assuming the mantle of a young matron. Customary ceremonial songs, dances, and verse accompany each of these events, which include *vakarynos* (the last evening) when the bride's friends rebraid her hair for the last time and sing to her of past happiness and future worries. They remind her of the garden of rue (symbol of chastity) that she will soon abandon. *Jaunojo sutiktuves* (greeting the bridegroom) includes the exchange of gifts. Also customary is the *svocios pietūs* (dinner for the bride) during which the bride's wreath is exchanged for a married woman's headdress, and the *nuotakos išleistuves* (taking leave for the parental home) when the bride kisses the table, the crucifix, and a loaf of bread and bids farewell to her parents and other family.

8 INTERPERSONAL RELATIONS

An archaic exchange of greetings still remembered in some rural areas of Lithuania is *Garbe Kristui* (Praise Christ), to which the other replies *per amzius amen* (forever amen). It was also customary to greet someone working in the fields or a garden with *Dieve padek* (may God help you). From long ago until today, Lithuanians have prided themselves on their hospitality. A visit to a Lithuanian home is sure to include a warm response, a richly laid table, and perhaps storytelling and singing.

9 LIVING CONDITIONS

During the Soviet years, medical care was provided by the government. Inadequate treatment and scarcity of medicine and supplies were common, and hospitals were understaffed. The new independent Lithuanian government is developing a health care program to improve facilities and access to services. Cancer is the leading cause of death in Lithuania, and diseases related to alcoholism are also common. The average life expectancy for a Lithuanian born in 2008 was about 72 years.

During World War II, many Lithuanian towns and villages were utterly destroyed. After the war, many uniform and standardized housing projects were constructed, often built in large sections from prefabricated materials. Many of these units today are in poor condition.

The Lithuanian transport sector was isolated from the Western European transport system for decades during the Soviet years. Overall, Lithuania has a relatively good road system as well as maritime, railway, and aviation infrastructure.

10 FAMILY LIFE

Large families, with 10–12 children, were once commonplace in Lithuania. Though traditionally the father was the head of the family, the mother's role was far from diminished. She, too, commanded respect within the family structure. Christianity, more specifically Roman Catholicism, was the fundamental force in family life.

Soviet occupation drastically changed the makeup of the typical Lithuanian family. Because of severe economic crisis throughout the years of occupation, modern Lithuanian families tend to be much smaller, with one or two children being the norm. The mortality rate is now higher than the birth rate.

For quite a few years now, women have outnumbered men in Lithuania, leaving more women unmarried than in the past. Young married couples face many obstacles in securing an ordinary family life. It typically takes a young couple several years to save enough money to buy a house or an apartment due to the difference between average salaries and the cost of living in post-Soviet Lithuania. A young couple must often turn to their parents for financial help. There is also a trend for young people now to wait longer before getting married, and the number of single-parent families is on the rise.

¹¹ CLOTHING

The traditional apparel made in the home and most frequently seen in Lithuania in the middle of the 19th century is now worn only as representative dress by women on major national holidays and by members of folk dance ensembles and choruses. Until the 19th century, all fabric for garments was woven in the home; each household had a spinning wheel and loom. During the second half of the 19th century, homemade clothes began to be replaced by manufactured garments that first appeared in the cities and manors. By the beginning of the 20th century, the wearing of the traditional dress became rare even in villages.

Archaeological excavations and historical sources provide some background for the more ancient fashions from which the now typical national costumes are derived. During the 9th–12th centuries AD, women wore linen tunics with high closed collars over long woolen skirts and somewhat shorter aprons, embellished near the hem with rows of bronze spirals. The main outer garment was a thick woolen shawl decorated with bronze ornaments, secured in the front with large brooches or pins. Jewelry included rings, necklaces, bracelets, chest ornaments with chains, and pendants. Brooches were made of bronze, silver, glass, enamel, and gold. Clothing in various regions differed in form, decorative techniques, color-coordination, and wearing method; distinctions were made not only by tradition and accessibility to materials, but also by the character of the people and their environment. The primary regional classifications of traditional clothing approximated the main dialectal regions of Lithuania.

Men's traditional clothing was similar throughout Lithuania, with regional differences noticeable in certain details. Their garments were generally plainer, grayer, less patterned, and more simply woven than women's clothes. Trousers were the only apparel that had more color, with patterns of stripes or checks. Their other articles of clothing were shirts with embroidered collars and fronts, vests, heavy linen tunics, coats, and fur capes.

¹² FOOD

Food has always been treated with great respect by Lithuanians because it is perceived as a gift from God that is essential to life. Until the early 1900s, eating was regarded as a serious and even holy act; the family dinner table was not the place for banter or children's merriment. In traditional Lithuanian culture, meals were presided over by the male head of the household, who led the family in a short prayer before dividing the bread and meat. Other dishes would then be served by the wife. In recent times, however, meals have become more casual. Dairy products, bread, and potatoes remain mainstays of the diet, with meat, poultry, fish, and vegetables also playing an important part. Old Lithuanian names for beets, carrots, and onions indicate that they have been grown for a long time. Other vegetables such as cabbage, cucumbers, celery, leeks, parsnips, radishes, and turnips are mentioned in 16th-century documents. Potatoes appeared in the 17th century and became more popular among the peasantry than on the estates.

Sour cream is an important condiment or ingredient of Lithuanian dishes. *Varske* (curd or dry cottage cheese) is also important and is used as a filling in such dishes as *varskeciai* (rolled pancakes with sweetened curd), *cepelinai* (airship-shaped large dumplings of potato dough), and *virtinukai* (ravioli-like dumplings). The latter two dishes commonly feature a filling of meat and are topped by a large mound of sour cream or fried bacon bits. Sautéed mushrooms are often used as a filling or are served over boiled potatoes as a main dish. Butter is also important in Lithuanian cooking.

Marinated mushrooms, pickled herring, stuffed pike, a beet and bean salad called *vinigretas,* and Danish-style openface sandwiches are common party appetizers. A very popular summer dish is the refreshing *saltibarsciai,* a cold soup of sour cream and buttermilk or sour milk, with sliced beets, cucumbers, green onions, boiled eggs, and parsley, eaten with a hot boiled potato. Among the large variety of pancakes, potato pancakes form a separate category. Roasts of pork, veal, beef, or poultry, as well as pork chops, are more common on Lithuanian home and restaurant tables than are beef steaks. Generally, the seasoning of Lithuanian dishes is mild.

¹³ EDUCATION

Education is highly valued in Lithuania, and the literacy rate is nearly 100%. Educational instruction at Lithuanian schools starts at age six. There are three types of public schools: elementary (grades 1–4), nine-year (grades 1–9), and secondary (up to grade 12). There are also professional, technical, and specialized secondary schools. Higher education in Lithuania is available at numerous institutions. During the Soviet years, students had the choice of taking classes either in the Lithuanian language, or in Russian or Polish. Since independence, Lithuanian instruction has increased because of the increased importance the Lithuanian language now has in society. Much of the curriculum has been reformed as well—courses in military preparation and communism have been replaced with ones in psychology and sociology.

¹⁴ CULTURAL HERITAGE

The oldest known folk songs are the *dainos,* which were sung during the Middle Ages by Lithuanian women. Traditional Lithuanian folk songs can have either a loose or rigid rhythm. Folk music is played either solo or with an instrumental group. The most popular instruments for playing Lithuanian folk songs are *skrabalai* (cow bells), *dambrelis* (jaw harp), *kankles* (zither), *smuikas* (fiddle), *skuduciai* (panpipe), *lamzdelis* (recorder), *ragas* (horn), *daudyte* (long trumpet), and the *birbyne* (folk clarinet). Musical elements of the traditional folk songs are often incorporated into modern compositions. Choral singing is an important part of cultural festivals in Lithuania. Every five years, Vingis Park in Vilnius is the site of a huge folk music festival, with a stage big enough to hold 20,000 performers. The performers are costumed musicians and dancers who demonstrate ancient Lithuanian folk songs and dances.

The first book in the Lithuanian language was a religious text, *Catechisma Prasty Szadei* (Simple Words of the Catechism), published in 1547. In 1706, Aesop's fables became the first secular work published in Lithuanian. Kristijonas Donelaitis was the first Lithuanian author, though his epic poem about the lives of struggling serfs was only published after his death. Antanas Baranauskas was a famous poet of the mid 19th century, whose lyrical romantic poem *Anykšciu šilelis* (The Forest of Anyksciai) is a milestone in Lithuanian literature. Lithuanian literature has long been linked with nationalism and the liberation movement, especially the literature of the late 19th and early 20th centuries. This was because during 1865–1904, the Russian administration banned the printing of Lithuanian books using the Latin alphabet.

15 WORK

During the decades of Soviet rule, the Lithuanians worked under a system of price controls and quotas, with the government controlling the economy. The independent Lithuanian government has successfully privatized most of Lithuania's industries since independence, and the economy is growing rapidly. After some initial difficulty during the transition, unemployment has fallen steadily while wages have increased.

16 SPORTS

Lithuanians are sports enthusiasts. Riding and hunting are traditional activities. A popular traditional game is *ripkos,* involving the throwing and hitting of a wooden disk. Over 50 types of sports are practiced and played in Lithuania, including rowing, boxing, basketball, track and field, swimming, handball, and table tennis.

Basketball is the most popular sport in Lithuania today, having been introduced by a Lithuanian American named Stasys Darius after World War I. The sport caught on rapidly, and the Lithuanian team won the European basketball championship twice before World War II. During the years of Soviet occupation following World War II until the dismantling of the USSR, Lithuanian players formed the core of the successful Soviet basketball team. Numerous Lithuanian players found success in the NBA. Among the more notable stars that found success playing in America are Arvydas Sabonis, Zydrunas Ilgauskas, and Sarunas Marciulionis. The Lithuanian men's national basketball team won Olympic bronze medals in 1992 and 1996.

Other popular sports in Lithuania include cycling and canoeing. Soccer is also very popular. Most recently, baseball and field hockey have entered the Lithuanian arena of sports as new favorites.

17 ENTERTAINMENT AND RECREATION

From the ancient past until today, Lithuanians have maintained a love of traditional song and dance, often expressing this fondness by either attending or performing in various regional and national folk song and dance festivals, as well as in local folk ensembles. Many Lithuanians also enjoy and avidly support the arts: theater, opera, ballet, and museum and gallery exhibits. The arts are a permanent and varied fixture in all the cities but are especially supported in the capital city, Vilnius.

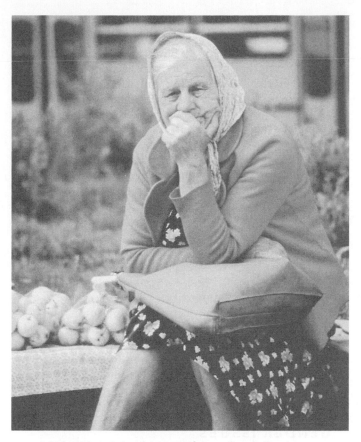

A Lithuanian senior citizen sitting on a bench. Pensions are small in relation to the cost of living increases and are insufficient for maintaining even a minimal standard of living. For young and old alike, it is difficult to secure employment. (Cory Langley)

Family celebrations focus around birthdays, Christmas Eve, Christmas Day, New Year's Day, and Easter. The national independence holidays on February 16 and March 11 are also observed in most households through participation in locally sponsored ceremonies and events.

The people of Lithuania greatly enjoy outdoor life. All summer long, beaches along the Baltic Sea, seaside resort towns, and lakes, forests, and campgrounds in the countryside are visited by vacationing Lithuanians. Health resorts specializing in therapeutic massage and hydrotherapy of all sorts are equally popular. As with many other Europeans, time spent in a sauna or steam bath is considered a necessary luxury by Lithuanians. World travel for the citizens of Lithuania, unheard of during Soviet rule, is briskly increasing in popularity.

Local cafés, movie theaters, and video arcades attract young people of all ages, as do nightclubs and rock concerts. Numerous aerobics studios and health clubs have opened their doors over the last several years and are gaining in popularity.

18 FOLK ART, CRAFTS, AND HOBBIES

Lithuanian folk art frequently involves the decoration of a common household item. Bed and table linens, towels, window treatments, wooden trim, and ceramics are objects that are often decorated. Themes in paintings and sculptures typically focus on religion, work, and everyday life.

¹⁹ SOCIAL PROBLEMS

The aftermath of the 50-year Soviet occupation of Lithuania has had a tremendous impact on its people. There have been continual turnovers in the government since independence due to accusations of corruption and a feeling by voters that their needs are not being served quickly enough. However, despite this rocky start, Lithuania has maintained democratic elections and implemented effective economic policies. Unemployment has dropped significantly while wages have increased. A new middle class is beginning to have a strong voice in Lithuanian decision-making.

Because of the unstable government and initial economic stress during the transition to independence, the crime rate has increased in Lithuania. Mugging, robbery, car-jacking, and murder have become more commonplace. Prisons and juvenile detention centers are overcrowded.

Although health care is provided at no charge in Lithuania, the standard of care is often inadequate. Shortages of medicine and equipment are commonplace. Health insurance is available at an extra cost (as are theft and auto insurance), but due to the financial strain felt by most families, many citizens do not have policies. In a true medical emergency, Lithuanians seek care in one of the many new private medical or dental clinics opened since Lithuania regained independence. However, compared to the average salary, these clinics are considered expensive.

²⁰ GENDER ISSUES

Traditional patriarchal Lithuanian culture, the legacy of homophobic Soviet beliefs during the occupation, and the strong influence of the Roman Catholic Church all contribute to the oppression of women and homosexuals in Lithuania. Women constitute almost two-thirds of the unemployed (70% of the long-term unemployed) and are underrepresented in government and business positions. Despite the passage of laws in recent years guaranteeing equal treatment and prohibiting discrimination on the basis of age, gender, race or ethnicity, disability, religion, or sexual orientation, the actual state of affairs is still marked by deep-seated homophobia and gender inequality.

National programs are being instituted to address issues of discrimination through education and consciousness-raising. Although these programs have succeeded in bringing the issues into the public forum, attitudes and practices have yet to show much improvement. In recent surveys, two out of three Lithuanians stated they would rather live next to a drug dealer than a homosexual and five of seven members of parliament declared that homosexuality is a "perversion." Women continue to be vulnerable to sexual trafficking due to limited economic opportunities in Lithuania, and women greatly outnumber men among the ranks of those in poverty.

Because of harassment or fears of harassment, homosexuals stay underground in Lithuania. No major public figure has come out openly as gay or lesbian and only one gay nightclub exists in the entire country—in the capital city, Vilnius. The Lithuanian Gay League, founded in 1993, continues to work to improve the lives of lesbian, gay, bisexual, and transgendered persons but has yet to receive much real support from the Lithuanian government or general population.

²¹ BIBLIOGRAPHY

Antoine, Prune. "Lithuania: A Fairly Gay Secret," http://p26604.typo3server.info/fileadmin/content/images/Journalist_Award/Articles_2007/Special_Awards/English/FR_SA_Prune_QK.pdf (19 August 2008).

The Baltic States. Tallinn, Estonia: Estonian, Latvian, and Lithuanian Encyclopaedia Publishers, 1991.

Bindokiene, Danute Brazyte. *Lithuanian Customs and Traditions.* Chicago: Lithuanian World Community, Inc., 1989.

European Commission Office of Equal Opportunities Ombudsperson. "2007—European Year of Equal Opportunities for All: Lithuania," http://ec.europa.eu/employment_social/eyeq/uploaded_files/documents/LT_070612_Nati_Strategy.pdf (19 August 2008).

Lithuanian Gay League, http://www.lgl.lt/indexe.php (19 August 2008).

Stasys, Yla. *Lithuanian Family Traditions.* Chicago: Lithuanian Library Press, Inc., 1978.

Stop Violence Against Women. "Lithuania," http://www.stopvaw.org/Lithuania2.html (19 August 2008).

Suziedelis, Simas, and Anatas Vasaitis, ed. *Encyclopedia Lituanica.* Boston: Lithuanian Encyclopedia Press, Inc., 1978.

Tamošaitis, Anatas, and Anastasia Tamošaitis. *Lithuanian National Costume.* Toronto: Time Press Litho Ltd., 1979.

U.S. Department of State. "Background Note: Lithuania," http://www.state.gov/r/pa/ei/bgn/5379.htm (19 August 2008).

—revised by D. de Mott

LUXEMBOURGERS

LOCATION: Luxembourg
POPULATION: 467,000 (2007)
LANGUAGE: Letzebürgesch, French, and German
RELIGION: Roman Catholic; small numbers of Protestants and Jews

¹ INTRODUCTION

The Grand Duchy of Luxembourg is a tiny but prosperous nation in western Europe. While Luxembourg's culture has been strongly influenced by both its French- and German-speaking neighbors, the country retains a distinct identity of its own. The Luxembourgers' pride in this identity and in their national traditions is expressed in their motto: *Mir woelle bleiwe wat mir sin* ("We want to remain what we are").

Luxembourg has been a distinct political entity since AD 963, when Count Sigefroid of the Ardennes built a castle at the present-day site of its capital (also called Luxembourg) and laid claim to the surrounding lands. In 1443 King Philip of Burgundy claimed Luxembourg for France, beginning a 400-year period when Luxembourg was ruled by its powerful neighbors in western Europe, including (in addition to France) Spain and Austria. Luxembourg became an independent, neutral state in 1867 under the Treaty of London, and it has had its own ruling dynasty since 1890, when the crown of the Grand Duchy was transferred to the House of Nassau. With the discovery of iron ore around 1860, the duchy began the transition to a modern, industrialized, and prosperous nation.

In the 20th century, Luxembourg was occupied by the Germans during both world wars. Luxembourgers, who strenuously resisted the Nazi occupiers, suffered the third highest death toll of the war relative to the size of their population, surpassed only by the Soviet Union and Poland. The Battle of the Bulge (1944–45) was to a large extent fought on Luxembourgian soil. After World War II, Luxembourg's government agreed to create an economic union with Belgium and the Netherlands, and full economic union of the Benelux countries was achieved in February of 1958. In April 1963 Luxembourg observed its 1,000-year anniversary. In 2000 Grand Duke Henri became the country's monarch. In addition to the Benelux union, Luxembourg is also a member of NATO, the United Nations, and the European Union.

² LOCATION AND HOMELAND

Luxembourg, with an area of only 998 square miles (2,586 square kilometers), is bordered by Germany on the east and northeast, France on the south, and Belgium on the north and west. The northern third of the country, known as the Oesling, forms part of the Ardennes Mountains, which extend into Germany and Belgium. This forested upland region is dotted with the ruins of many historic castles. Luxembourg's southern two-thirds, called "The Good Land" (*Gutland* in German and *Bon Pays* in French), is home to most of Luxembourg's population and contains its most fertile soil as well as its capital city. The Moselle River, to the south, forms Luxembourg's southeastern border.

Luxembourg's population of 467,000 is approximately three-fourths urban and one-fourth rural, and the rural-to-urban migratory trend is still continuing, especially toward the capital city. Native-born Luxembourgers are mostly of French, German, or Belgian descent. Of all the western European nations, Luxembourg has one of the highest percentage of foreign-born residents. They come mainly from Portugal, Italy, and other southern European countries but also from Luxembourg's neighbors, France, Germany, and Belgium. Many had come to work in the nation's iron and steel mills; others are drawn by jobs in its many international corporations and organizations. As of the 2000s, the industrial sector, initially dominated by steel, has become increasingly diversified to include chemicals, rubber, and other products. Growth in the financial sector accounts for about a third of the country's income, and has more than compensated for the decline in steel.

³ LANGUAGE

Luxembourg has three official languages: French, German, and Letzebürgesch, a national dialect based on German with French elements mixed in. The first language of all Luxembourgers, Letzebürgesch is learned in childhood and spoken at home. Although it is primarily an oral rather than a written language, a Letzebürgesch dictionary and grammar were created in 1950, and the language has been accorded official status since 1984. German, which is taught in primary school, is the language of business and the media, while French, taught at the secondary level, is the language of government, used in the civil service and the courts (although German is used in criminal proceedings). All three of the national languages are spoken in Luxembourg's parliament. In addition to their native languages, many Luxembourgers also speak English.

⁴ FOLKLORE

According to legend, Count Sigefroid, the founder of Luxembourg's walled capital city, married a maiden named Mélusine, ignorant of the fact that she was really a mermaid. She reverted to her natural form every Saturday, a time when she had forbidden her husband to look at her. After he broke his promise and saw her, she disappeared into the stone walls of the city, where she is said to remain, returning every seven years in the form of either a beautiful woman or a serpent with a golden key in its mouth. According to the legend, it would be possible to free her by either kissing the woman or removing the key from the serpent's mouth, but no one has ever accomplished either feat. Mélusine is also said to knit an ever-unfinished garment, completing one stitch every year. It is said that if she completes it before she is freed from the wall, all of Luxembourg will supposedly vanish into the rock with her.

⁵ RELIGION

About 87% of Luxembourg's population is Roman Catholic, although at least a third of these are non-practicing Catholics. Luxembourg's constitution guarantees religious freedom to its people. In spite of the country's overwhelming Catholic majority, the state supports the spiritual leaders of its Protestant and Jewish minorities—the Official Protestant Pastor and the Chief Rabbi—as well as the nation's Catholic priests. The Lutheran and Calvinist Churches are the largest Protestant denominations. There are an estimated 9,000 Muslims, including 900 refugees from Montenegro; 5,000 Orthodox Christians (Greek, Serbian, Russian, and Romanian); and 1,000 Jews. The Baha'i Faith, the Universal Church, and Jehovah's Witnesses

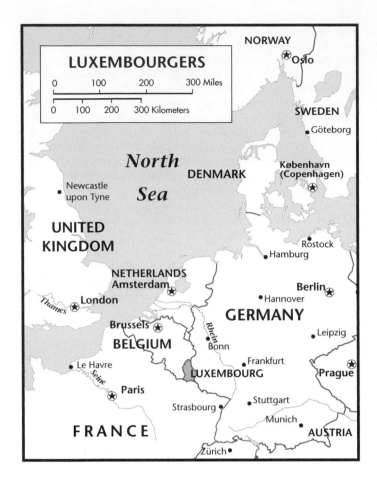

LUXEMBOURGERS

0   100   200   300 Miles

0   100   200   300 Kilometers

progress through the education system is marked by many families with graduation parties.

8 INTERPERSONAL RELATIONS

A casual handshake is considered appropriate when greeting both old and new acquaintances. Close friends, particularly female friends, may hug or kiss each other on the cheek three times. Common greetings include *Moien* ("Good morning"), *Gudden Owend* ("Good evening"), *Wéi geet et?* ("How are you?"), and *Bonjour* ("Good day" in French). On parting, the expression *Addi* ("Goodbye") and the more formal French *Au revoir* are used (as well as the casual *Salut* and *Ciao*, which are popular with younger Luxembourgians).

9 LIVING CONDITIONS

Luxembourg enjoys one of the highest standards of living of any nation in the European Community. Housing ranges from traditional rural cottages with thick walls and heavy beams to the modern apartments rented by many urban dwellers. Luxembourg's national health service covers most doctors' fees and hospital expenses. Average life expectancy is 79 years. The leading causes of death—cardiovascular disease, cancer, and automobile accidents—are typical of those in the world's other developed nations.

Luxembourg's small size spares its residents lengthy commutes to work. The country has an excellent transportation network both within its borders and connecting it to its neighbors. There are approximately 3,000 miles (5,108 kilometers) of state and local roads. In the 1990s its highways were linked to those of Belgium, France, and Germany. However, most travel to and from neighboring countries is by rail. The Moselle River provides water transport, and many international airlines provide service to Luxembourg's Findel airport.

10 FAMILY LIFE

The typical Luxembourg household is composed of a nuclear family with one or two children. The importance of family to Luxembourgers is reflected in a national law requiring adults to take a certain degree of financial responsibility for their aging parents. Families in Luxembourg enjoy a high standard of living. Because of their country's small size, parents generally live near their workplace, allowing them additional time to spend with their families enjoying leisure-time pursuits. The comfortable financial circumstances and cosmopolitan outlook of the country's residents have prompted a number of families to adopt orphaned Vietnamese children since the 1960s. Women account for roughly 44.7% of Luxembourg's labor force.

11 CLOTHING

The people of Luxembourg wear modern Western-style clothing like that worn elsewhere in western Europe and in the world's other developed countries. Luxembourgers are particularly influenced by fashion trends in the neighboring countries of France and Germany, and by Italian fashions as well. Women tend to wear skirts and dresses more often than slacks, and the men favor hats. In public, Luxembourgers are always neatly and carefully dressed, whether for formal or casual occasions. Old, worn clothing is reserved for at-home wear and sporting activities.

are represented in smaller numbers. There is a small Church of Jesus Christ of Latter-day Saints (Mormons) community in Dommeldange, which has been growing since its establishment in 2000. The number of professed atheists is believed to be growing.

6 MAJOR HOLIDAYS

Luxembourg's legal holidays are New Year's Day, Easter Monday, Labor Day (May 1), Ascension Day, Whitmonday, National Day (June 23), Assumption Day (August 15), All Saints' Day (November 1), Christmas (December 25), and Boxing Day (December 26). National Day, a patriotic holiday observed with parades, fireworks, and church services, is also celebrated as the official birthday of the nation's monarch, Grand Duke Henri (although his actual birthday is April 16). Luxembourgers also observe a number of local and regional holidays, including St. Bartholemy's Day (August 24), when sheep are driven through the streets of the capital city, and the Broom Parade, held in the city of Wiltz every May when the broom (a bright yellow plant) blossoms. The pre-Lenten festival of Carnival is celebrated in a number of Luxembourg's cities.

7 RITES OF PASSAGE

Luxembourgers live in a modern, industrialized, Christian country. Hence, many of the rites of passage that young people undergo are religious rituals, such as baptism, first Communion, confirmation, and marriage. In addition, a student's

People sit outside bars enjoying the evening in the Rude de l'Eau, Luxembourg, Luxembourg. (© Franz-Marc Frei/Corbis)

¹² FOOD

The cuisine of Luxembourg, influenced by the culinary traditions of its neighbors, has been called a marriage of French sophistication and German abundance. In Luxembourg, as in Germany, hearty appetites and large portions are the norm. Several of the most popular national dishes are made with ham or pork: Ardennes ham, ham stuffed with beans, smoked pork and beans or sauerkraut (*judd mat gaarde-bounen*), suckling pig in aspic (*cochon de lait en gelée*), and meat pies with minced-pork filling (*fleeschtaart*). Other favorites include liver dumplings (*quenelles de foie de veau*), rabbit served in a thick sauce (*civet de lièvre*), and black pudding (*treipen*) and sausages with mashed potatoes and horseradish. During the fishing season, popular entrees include crayfish, trout, pike, and other fish from the Moselle and the country's other rivers. Luxembourg is also known for its delicious pastries, which fill the counters of special pastry shops throughout the country. Plum tarts called *quetsch* are a seasonal treat in September, and a type of cake called *les penseés brouillées* is traditionally eaten on Shrove Tuesday.

¹³ EDUCATION

Luxembourg's literacy rate is virtually 100%. Education is free and compulsory between the ages of 6 and 15. Students begin with six years of primary school followed by up to seven years of secondary education. Institutions of higher education include the Central University of Luxembourg, the Superior Institute of Technology, the International University Institute of Luxembourg, and Sacred Heart University. Many secondary school graduates attend college in the neighboring countries of France, Belgium, and Germany.

¹⁴ CULTURAL HERITAGE

The arts are supported by the Grand Ducal Institute. In the visual arts, well-known Luxembourgers include 17th-century sculptor Daniel Muller and 20th-century expressionist painter Joseph Kutter. The National Museum of History and Art exhibits both fine and industrial arts and also houses special collections on the nation's history. Luxembourg's literary figures have written in French (Felix Thyes and Marcel Noppeney), German (Nikolaus Welter and "Batty" Weber), and Letzebürgesch (Michael Rodange). Paul Palgen is the country's most famous poet. Luxembourg also has cultural agreements with several other nations, both in Europe and elsewhere, that bring the finest in music and theater to local stages. The Grand Orchestra of Radiotelevision Luxembourg is world famous. Internationally acclaimed photographer Edward Steichen was a native of Luxembourg.

¹⁵ WORK

About 86% of Luxembourg's labor force is employed in the service sector, which includes government, trade, tourism, and financial services. About 13% work in industry, construction, and transportation, and the remainder (about 1%) are engaged in agriculture. In 2007, 121,6000 of the total work force of 205,000 were foreign cross-border workers commuting primarily from France, Belgium, and Germany. Most of them are employed in the banking and insurance industries or in the offices of the European Union. Many Portuguese have worked in the iron and steel industry. Unemployment, which was virtually nonexistent in Luxembourg until the mid-1980s, was around 4.4% in the 2007.

16 SPORTS

Popular sports in Luxembourg include jogging, tennis, volleyball, and soccer. Pursuits such as hunting, fishing, cycling, and boating allow Luxembourgers to spend their leisure time enjoying their country's scenic landscape. The route of the world's most famous bicycle race, the *Tour de France*, passes through Luxembourg. The country has 25 national hiking routes (5,000 km) as well as countless other paths and trails, and organized walking tours are a popular activity. Favorite winter sports include cross-country skiing and ice skating.

17 ENTERTAINMENT AND RECREATION

The people of Luxembourg enjoy socializing in their country's many cafés and pastry shops, and one can often find them engaged in informal chess matches in restaurants and cafés. Luxembourgers enjoy many types of music, including choral and band music and musical theater. The capital city has a folk club, a jazz club, and a society for new music. Virtually every household has a television, and movie theaters show foreign films—including American box office hits—with French or Dutch subtitles. Gardening, hiking, camping, and other outdoor activities are also very popular.

18 FOLK ART, CRAFTS, AND HOBBIES

Pottery and other traditional crafts are practiced in Luxembourg. In addition, the Fonderie de Mersch manufactures cast-iron wall plaques that portray local coats-of-arms, scenery, and historic castles. Luxembourg's scenic landscapes are also reproduced on porcelain plates.

19 SOCIAL PROBLEMS

Luxembourg is free from many of the social problems that plague other developed nations. In spite of its lack of natural resources, the country enjoys a healthy, stable economy and a high standard of living and has very low unemployment. It is also among the most generous nations in terms of social spending.

However, in the mid-1990s, the country received thousands of asylum seekers from the former Yugoslavia, which made Luxembourg less welcoming to all immigrants. Although political integration—in the form of local voting rights for foreigners—has been rather successful, immigrant children generally perform poorly in school. Also, the country has yet to consider a broad integration program for new arrivals. In 2006, approximately 181,962 foreigners lived in Luxembourg —39.6% of the country's total population. Most of the foreigners are white, European, and Catholic, and of these, Portuguese constitute the majority. About 13% of foreigners are from the former Yugoslavia, the United States, and the former Portuguese colony Cape Verde. Among the foreigners there are about 5,000 Muslims, most of them from the former Yugoslavia. The tightening of border controls since the attacks of 11 September 2001 on the United States had effects in Luxembourg as well. On the eve of the attacks, Luxembourg's small Muslim community was close to obtaining both formal recognition and public financing— already granted to the Catholic, Protestant, Orthodox Christian, and Jewish communities—when the weekly magazine *Le Jeudi* accused the country's Muslims of being connected to radical Islamists. There were no openly anti-Islamic reactions, but suspicions developed concerning supposed links between the Luxembourgian Muslim community and radical Islamist organizations.

20 GENDER ISSUES

Luxembourg law prohibits domestic violence. The law is gender neutral and provides that a batterer will be removed from the house for 10 days; this can be extended an additional three months. There is a hot line for battered women. Government-sponsored nongovernmental organization (NGO) shelters provide refuge to women and children. In addition, the government provides financial assistance to domestic violence victims. The government funds organizations that provide shelter, counseling, and hot lines. The law specifically prohibits rape, including spousal rape. The penalties are five to 10 years' imprisonment. Prostitution is legal. The law prohibits sexual harassment.

Under the law, women enjoy the same rights as men, including rights under family law, property law, and in the judicial system. The law mandates equal pay for equal work; however, women are paid 20% to 30% less than men for comparable work. The Ministry of Equal Opportunity is responsible for protecting the legal and social rights of women; in 2005 it began a gender mainstreaming program, which is to assess all government policies in order to determine whether they result in any gender-based disparities. In 2006 the parliament introduced the principle of non-discrimination in the country's legislation. In 2006 there were 13 women in the 60-member Chamber of Deputies and 3 women in the 14-member Council of Ministers. There were 15 women in the 32-member Supreme Court.

21 BIBLIOGRAPHY

Clark, Peter. *Luxembourg.* New York: Routledge, 1994.

Delibois, John. *Pattern of Circles: An Ambassador's Story.* Kent, OH: Kent State Univ. Press, 1989.

Eccardt, Thomas M. *Secrets of the Seven Smallest States of Europe: Andorra, Liechtenstein, Luxembourg, Malta, Monaco, San Marino, and Vatican City.* New York: Hippocrene Books, 2005.

Lepthien, Emilie U. *Luxembourg.* Chicago: Children's Press, 1992.

"Luxembourgeois." *Encyclopedia of World Cultures (Europe).* Boston: G. K. Hall, 1992.

Sheehan, Patricia, and Sakina Dhilawala. *Luxembourg.* New York: Marshall Cavendish Benchmark, 2009.

Triandafyllidou, Anna, and Ruby Gropas, eds. *European Immigration: A Sourcebook.* Aldershot, Hants, England; Burlington, VT: Ashgate, 2007.

—revised by J. Hobby.

MACEDONIANS

LOCATION: Macedonia
POPULATION: 2,050,000 [total population, of whom 65% are
ethnic Macedonians, and 25% ethnic Albanians]
LANGUAGES: Macedonian and Albanian
RELIGIONS: Eastern Orthodox and Islam

¹ INTRODUCTION

The following text attempts to delineate the cultural characteristics of the people of the Republic of Macedonia, also known as Vardar Macedonia, so-named after the principal river which originates in, and runs through practically the entire north–south length of, the country.

As a historical and geographical entity, Macedonia's name figures centrally in both European and world history from even pre-Biblical times. The region's early recorded past is inextricably connected with the names of Philip II, who ruled from 359 to 336 BC, and Alexander the Great, Philip's son, who ruled from 336 to 323 BC. Historians count Alexander among the most important and successful military conquerors of all time, insofar as his dominion stretched from central Europe to north Africa and all the way to India. Immediately following Alexander's death, in 323 BC, his territorial holdings were divided up by his most accomplished generals into four sections (with, ironically, the smallest of the four being comprised of Macedonia and Greece). Less than three centuries later, at the end of a series of wars against the emerging Roman Empire, Macedonia and the rest of the Balkan Peninsula were subdued and turned into a corridor for the Roman legions marching to the Near East.

Unaffected by the collapse of the western realm of the Roman Empire, including the city of Rome itself, Macedonia continued as part of Rome's eastern realm, or the resultant Byzantine Empire. By the end of the 6th century and throughout the 7th century AD, migrating Slavs from beyond the Carpathian Mountains began to settle in the Balkans. In the face of all the ethnic and linguistic differences, the Byzantine Empire eventually began to break down into various feudal kingdoms, and Macedonia came under the control of the Bulgarian crown. Later on, sensing that the days of Bulgaria's power were numbered, Samuil, a statesman and military leader, managed to free Macedonia and to have himself declared tsar by the Roman pope. But Samuil's state lasted only from 976 until 1018, when it was again subjugated by Byzantium and relegated to the level of a province.

During the latter half of the 14th century, the Byzantine Empire crumbled at the persistent attacks of the Ottoman Turks, and Macedonia was plunged into a lengthy struggle for the preservation of its Slavonic literacy and religious identity. This is, arguably, Macedonia's most traumatic historical period, for, though not enslaved, its population was considered and treated as *raja* (pronounced rah-yah), which in Turkish means "people without rights." Rather astonishingly, though challenged by numerous rebellions and insurrections, the Ottoman Empire's grip on Macedonia and all of southeastern Europe did not come to an end until as recently as the Balkan Wars, in 1912–1913. With the 1913 Treaty of Bucharest, Macedonia was unequally divided among Greece, Serbia, Bulgaria, and Alba-

nia. Following World War I, the Serbian section of Macedonia became the southernmost part of the newly formed Kingdom of Serbs, Croats, and Slovenes—later known as the Kingdom of Yugoslavia—and remained as such until 1941. The socially and economically restless climate in Europe between about 1910 and 1940 prompted, among other historically seminal events, a large-scale emigration from all over Macedonia to North and South America, with the greatest number of newcomers finding their way to such industrial cities in the north as Detroit, Gary, Buffalo, and Toronto.

At the conclusion of World War II, the Kingdom's Macedonia was transformed into one of the six autonomous Republics of the Socialist Federal Republic of Yugoslavia, whose harsh economic and political conditions during the 1960s and 1970s incited a second, large wave of emigration from Macedonia to North America and Western Europe. Not surprisingly, when during the late 1980s it became increasingly evident that socialism throughout the world was largely on its way out, Macedonians seized the initiative and on 8 September 1991 approved a referendum on their country's independence. On 17 November 1991, the voters further adopted a new constitution which, for the first time ever, turned Macedonia into a parliamentary democracy with strictly defined executive, legislative, and judicial branches of government. Accordingly, Macedonians are today guaranteed religious, economic, and political freedoms similar to those of Western democracies. In April 1993, the Republic of Macedonia became a member of the United Nations, and in 2008 a majority of European Union member nations offered support for Macedonia's acceptance into the EU.

² LOCATION AND HOMELAND

Macedonia is situated in the south-central area of the Balkan Peninsula in Europe, and its capital city is Skopje (pronounced skop-yeh). It covers an area of roughly 25,900 sq km (10,000 sq mi) and borders with Serbia and Kosovo to the north, Albania to the west, Bulgaria to the east, and Greece to the south. Its landlocked status notwithstanding, Macedonia holds a central geopolitical position, which makes it a crossroads linking Europe, Asia, and Africa. It is thus hardly surprising that various neighboring powers have during the past 2,000 years attempted to annex either the whole or at least a part of this largely mountainous region. Since most of its territory lies between latitudes 40° and 42° north, Macedonia's climate is a transition between temperate Mediterranean and moderate continental, with maximum summer temperatures climbing up to about 38°C (100°F), and lowest winter temperatures falling to about –23°C (–10°F).

According to its 2002 census, the Republic of Macedonia's total population stood at about 2,023,000, with a roughly even male/female ratio. Reflective of Macedonia's Western lifestyle, the life expectancy for the average citizen is about 75 years, or 73 years for males, and 77 years for females. The country's ethnic composition includes about 1,298,000 Macedonians, 509,000 Albanians, 78,000 Turks, 54,000 Roma (or Gypsies), and 36,000 Serbs. This census did not, of course, take into account the almost 400,000 (republican) Macedonians of all ethnicities who have settled as permanent residents mainly in North America, Australia, and Western Europe. It is pertinent to note here that the preceding figure is increasing daily, for—still dealing with publicly obvious lingering difficulties in the wake of its shift from socialism to a free market economy, dif-

MACEDONIANS

0   100   200   300 Miles

0   100   200   300 Kilometers

ficulties such as corruption on probably every social and governmental level, and underemployment for most of those who still work in federal government jobs—Macedonia is (as of this writing) experiencing a third wave of emigration.

³ LANGUAGE

Within the past decade, the Macedonian government has allowed the use of the Albanian language in Albanian minority-run schools, newspapers, and radio stations, especially in the north-west section of the country. Still, the prevalent and semi-official language in Macedonia is Macedonian, a distinct Indo-European language of the Slavonic family. While its modern codification occurred no earlier than 1944, the development of the Macedonian literary language dates back to the 9th century AD—the time when the educators (and brothers) Sts. Cyril and Methodius created the first Slavonic alphabet, the Glagolitic. As with most Slavonic languages, Macedonian is today written in the Cyrillic alphabet, named after Cyril but invented by St. Clement of Ohrid. As with all Western vocabularies, Macedonian is primarily a derivative of the Latin and Greek languages. Through historical and trans-cultural osmosis, the Macedonian language has also acquired thousands of Turkish, German, and, since the 1970s, even variations of American English words. Most of the last, however, are internationally recognized musical terms ("folk," "hit," "pop," "rock and roll," etc.) and expressions adopted by those who resort to a bit more urbane type of speech ("photo finish," "controversy," "polemics," "business," etc.).

Traditional Macedonian names are of two types: (1) Christian—such as, for males, Petar, Jovan, and Tomislav, or for females, Petranka, Jovanka, and Tomka; and (2) wish-based—such as, for males, Zdravko (Healthy), Stojan (Stay [Alive]), and Spase (Saved), or the female forms, Zdravka, Stojanka, and Spasija. Since World War II, many newborns have been given rather nondescript names like Zlatko (Golden), Tsveta (Blossom), and Blaga (Sweet); and since the 1960s, parents have been increasingly deciding on English-sounding names as, for example, Robert, Edvard, Meri, Suzana, etc. It is foreign (and especially English) linguistic encroachments such as these that have recently prompted many Macedonian academicians and members of parliament to call for the passage of legal measures that would protect their mother-tongue, and with it their culture itself.

⁴ FOLKLORE

Macedonia's folk wisdom comprises a number of such legendary heroes as King Marko, whose larger-than-life deeds wreaked terror in the hearts of the occupying Turks, and whose horse could leap from one mountaintop to another, and satirical figures like Clever Pejo (pronounced Pe-yo), who exposed and ridiculed the vices and abuses of local Ottoman officials and Islamic religious leaders. It is, however, aphorisms and tales that stand as Macedonia's most colorful treasure. The following several aphorisms formulate some of the more popular conceptions Macedonians have maintained for many generations: "Falsehoods have short legs"; "Children and dogs you should never trust much at all"; "Nothing is sweeter or more bitter than one's own children"; and "Begin a task, but always have its conclusion in mind."

Similarly, many (and particularly older) Macedonians frequently resort to telling folk tales and parables to emphasize some moral, didactic, or philosophical message that would likely not carry the same weight if communicated in any other manner. To illustrate, the maxim in the succeeding story encapsulates the essence of no less than existence itself: In ancient times, a tsar's daughter fell ill, but none of the royal medical personnel could help her. At last, an old healer took on the persistent problem. He fashioned for the patient a ring on whose band he wrote the axiom: "Everything that ever was has passed, and everything that ever will be will pass." One morning he took the ring to the princess, put it on her finger, and said that her illness would go away if she read aloud the ring's axiom every night right before going to bed, and every morning immediately after waking up. And, eventually, she did indeed become well again, encouraged as she was by the hope that her illness would pass as does everything else in life.

⁵ RELIGION

The predominant religion in Macedonia is Eastern Orthodoxy, one of the three principal faiths comprising Christianity as a whole. Unlike Catholicism and Protestantism, Eastern Orthodoxy is an association of 15 nationalistic, autocephalous churches, each governed by its own head bishop, with the Ecumenical Patriarch of Constantinople holding honorary primacy. This is why one frequently hears of the Greek Orthodox Church, the Russian Orthodox Church, the Bulgarian Orthodox Church, etc. The Eastern Orthodox Church began its independent existence in 1054, when it irrevocably rejected the authority of the Roman See. Until this event, which historians and theologians frequently refer to as the Great Schism, the nouns Catholicism and Christianity were, for all practical purposes, used interchangeably.

Since the Orthodox Church follows the Old Style (or Julian) Calendar, Macedonians normally celebrate the main holy days of Christianity several days—and, in the case of Easter, sometimes even several weeks—later than do Catholics and Protestants. For example, while both of the latter observe Christmas on December 25, Orthodox adherents celebrate it on January 7 according to the New Style (or Gregorian) Calendar. Correspondingly, New Year's Day falls on January 14. Moreover, aside from recognizing all principal Christian saints and martyrs, every nationalistic Orthodox church venerates its own, more "regional" saints and martyrs. Thus, the Macedonian Orthodox church pays homage to Sts. Cyril and Methodius; to their most important successor and founder of the Ohrid Literary School, St. Clement; his brother, Naum; and dozens of other less historically important canonized personages. Actually, Cyril and Methodius have come to be known as the "Apostles of the Slavs," which means that they are revered by Orthodox churches worldwide.

6 MAJOR HOLIDAYS

Aside from commemorating their national holidays, Macedonians honor the Day of the Woman, on March 8, which is in essence identical with Mother's Day in the US; the Day of the Laborer, on May 1, a remnant of the worldwide socialist observance of May Day, also referred to as the Day of the Proletariat; and the Ilinden (St. Elijah's Day) Uprising, on August 2. Whereas socialist Macedonia looked upon May 1 as a day of revolutionary rededication, punctuated by parades, demonstrations, and interminable political speeches, Macedonians today regard the same holiday as primarily a day of rest and recreation. In contrast, the Ilinden Uprising, on 2 August 1903, is widely seen as the beginning of the Macedonian national movement and, as such, the country's most noteworthy cultural and historical landmark. During this rebellion, the city of Kruševo (pronounced Khru-shevo) was liberated from Ottoman rule, and with that the first democratic republic on the Balkans was established. Ultimately, however, the Kruševo Republic lasted a mere 10 days, before Turkish armies recaptured the town and indiscriminately slaughtered a great number of its citizens alongside all of the Uprising's leaders.

Prior to Macedonia's cessation from Yugoslavia, public celebrations of religious holidays were invariably discouraged, and for the younger generation even proscribed. In keeping with Karl Marx's notion that religion of all stripes is simply "opium" of the people, dissuading the younger generation from attending church was thought of as essential, if the revolutionary spirit requisite for energizing the movement from socialism to communism was to remain vital and focused. Nowadays, following socialism's demise, Macedonia's churches tend to be filled to capacity with people of every age during Christmas, Easter, and other holidays honoring regional saints recognized by the Macedonian Orthodox Church.

7 RITES OF PASSAGE

Insofar as most city and many village families in Macedonia own the latest instruments for mass communication, including cellular telephones and personal computers, some of the more-recently acquired cultural values and practices seem identical to those of people in other Western nations. This is especially evident in the lifestyle of young adults, who wear the same style of clothes, listen and dance to the same music as do other Westerners, and have taken up the practice of piercing and tattooing their bodies. Still, there are two significant differences between Macedonian teenagers and their American counterparts. Though probably most Macedonians are sexually active well before getting married, childbearing out of wedlock is rare and socially frowned upon. Also, a large number of Macedonian teenagers speak rather fluently at least one other language, usually, but not only English.

Like people in so many other societies, Macedonians regard the birth of a boy as the most momentous familial event. While this tradition may be traced to the time when men were needed to work in the fields and vineyards, nowadays a male child simply continues his father's family name. Irrespective of gender, however, most babies, in accordance with the Eastern Orthodox faith, are baptized before their first birthday. A new mother is expected to stay at home and, except for her immediate relatives, receive no visitors for at least six weeks.

The ceremonies and rituals concerning death are no less important than are those concerning birth. While a deceased person's children and siblings are expected to wear dark clothes for at least a few months following his or her passing, the same individual's mother and (especially older) spouse might dress so for the rest of their lives. Memorial services are held on the ninth day, the fortieth day, six months, one year, and three years after one's death. On these anniversaries, family members go to church and/or to the deceased's graveside, and they distribute homemade bread, black olives, feta cheese, and small cups of wine to those attending. These are consumed in memory of the deceased's soul. To some of his or her surviving friends, many families also give such items as shirts, socks, and/or towels. Observing the first two anniversaries is particularly significant, since it is believed that the soul does not leave the terrestrial realm until or shortly after the fortieth day of its "release" from the body.

8 INTERPERSONAL RELATIONS

Macedonians usually greet one another with the customary *zdravo* (pronounced zdrah-vo), which is a variation of the word "health," and inquire about each other's family members' well-being and their more recent undertakings and achievements. The exchange is generally friendly, and one is rarely thought of as rude for asking personal questions. On the contrary, those who do not care for this type of conversation are often characterized as cold, distant, or arrogant. Children and teenagers refer to older men as *chichko* (pronounced tchitch-ko) or *striko*, meaning "uncle," and address almost all older women as *tetko* or *strino*, meaning "aunt." Men and women show their love for their nieces and nephews, and their approval and acceptance of the children of friends and acquaintances, by occasionally giving them modest sums of money. These little gifts are usually made during visits to someone's home.

Mostly a village custom, when passing by someone or a group of people engaged in harvesting or tending a large vegetable garden, one normally exclaims, *Ajrlija rabota!* (pronounced ayr-li-yah rah-bo-tah), translated "May your work meet with goodness and profit!" The recipients of this greeting normally respond with: *Ajr da imaš!* (pronounced ayr dah ihmash), or "May you, also, have goodness and profit (in your life)."

Raised with the idea that an individual's humaneness is partly revealed in the kind and number of people visiting his or her home, most Macedonians regard social calls as a sign of respect; and attending an open house on the host's name day—traditionally held by males on the feast day of the saint after whom they are named—is a great honor to any man. Major patron saints' days are so special that they are also celebrated on the communal level, with almost every village having one of its own. Accordingly, on the day of, say, St. George, the citizens of any village observing that day take off work and, usually the men, freely visit each others' homes, wherein food and drinks of all sorts are served in abundance.

Dating in Macedonia normally begins somewhere between 14 and 16 years of age. In the villages, a young adult simply "throws an eye" on his or her intended one, and, providing the "look" is reciprocated, the lovers meet informally whenever and wherever they can. In the cities, teenagers and younger adults meet either at promenades or at the remarkably large number of coffeehouses and pubs one finds on most main streets. Importantly, any prolonged dating is seen by friends and families as a manifest signal of impending marriage.

9 LIVING CONDITIONS

Living standards in Macedonia vary. The federal health care industry is barely adequate, which explains the sudden rise of private medical practitioners. Even so, whereas physicians are highly trained in medical theory, studying from translations of the latest books used in American and Western European medical schools, some medications and imaging instruments are in short supply. Macedonia's bloodless secession from Yugoslavia (which caused the latter to take most of the government-owned instruments back to what is now the Republic of Serbia), its unfinished move toward privatization, and the high cost of medical care have all contributed to the country's poor health conditions. Most Macedonians have come to expect that seriously ill friends or relatives would travel abroad in search of medical help, assuming such a trip is financially feasible.

Consumer goods, on the other hand—most of them imported from all over the globe—are readily available. Durable appliances such as automobiles, TVs, VCRs, refrigerators, washers, dryers, and personal computers may be found in virtually every household. Similarly, housing is no longer the major problem it used to be under socialism. Not only is it no longer difficult to find an apartment or a condominium anywhere in the country, but with the relatively easy loan terms from federal banks and remittances from abroad, many families have built villas in the country or in villages near resort areas.

10 FAMILY LIFE

The typical Macedonian family is nuclear in structure, with usually two children. Single-parent families are becoming more common, as divorce is on the rise even though it is still socially disapproved of, and especially so after a woman has given birth. However, the number of extended families in Macedonia is one of the highest in Europe. Taking up at least temporary residence with the husband's parents is a widespread practice for newlyweds, while accepting into the household a widowed in-law of either side is expected. The majority of older individuals live out their last years in such a familial arrangement.

The wife in any Macedonian family tends to wield an unusually strong influence. It is true that most older and some younger men still regard themselves as the "boss" of the family, but this is more of a traditional boast than fact. The wife's influence is so pervasive that a husband often takes her attitude toward individuals or families in deciding who would qualify to become his friend(s). On the domestic front, few women ask their husbands to help with any but the most uninvolved household chores. Even younger professional women insist on preserving the kitchen as their virtually undisputed domain.

Relatively few families own pets, and those that do have either a cat or a dog but rarely both at the same time.

11 CLOTHING

Whether city- or village-dwellers, Macedonians wear clothes of the type and quality that are similar to those in the US; in fact, a host of styles designed and manufactured in Macedonia have been sold in the West. Macedonian businesspeople wear suits, sport jackets, and dresses, skirts, or pantsuits for women. Looking respectable is important, but a small but steadily growing number of younger professionals are beginning to dress in a more casual manner.

The traditional, intricately embroidered style of dressing, varying in design from region to region, includes garments made of coarse, tightly woven wool yarn. When dressing in the national costume, men wear caps, mostly of the type that resembles the fez often worn by older Muslim men, vests, white linen shirts, a *pojas* (pronounced poh-yahs), that is, a wide cloth belt long enough to wind several times around one's waist, and tight-fitting pants closely resembling English riding breeches (wide around the hips and thighs but fitting snugly just below the knee). Women wear ankle-length, wide-hemmed dresses, a long and wide apron that ties just below one's chest, a white linen shirt, a pojas, and a headscarf that covers not only the head but almost the entire back of a woman's body. The predominant color in men's traditional attire is black, while in women's, red and white. Both men and women wear *opinci* (pronounced oh-pin-tsi), leather slippers that usually end in a hard, curved frontal tip.

12 FOOD

The principal as well as traditional food on the Macedonian menu is stew, a mixture of meat and vegetables cooked by simmering. To derive just the right flavor, however, this mixture must be a proper matching of the products. Thus, for example, beef is normally mixed with potatoes, pork with beans, and lamb with rice or spinach. Stews are prepared spicy, combined with roux (a cooked mixture of flour, red pepper, and fat, used as a thickening agent), and are practically always consumed with bread, which explains the surprisingly large, commercially produced variety of the latter. Other main staples are feta cheese, black olives, peppers of all types, which are usually either roasted, or stuffed, or pickled; *zelnik*, a flat pastry made of several layers of sheet dough, filled with cheese or leek or spinach; and its close culinary relative, burek (pronounced boo-rek). Because in most families both parents work outside the home, and children are expected to be at school by 8:00 am, supper is the most important meal of the day, often eaten less than two hours before retiring for the night.

Macedonians dressed in traditional costume celebrating the day of uprising against the Ottoman Empire in Meckin Kamen, Macedonia. (AP Images/Boris Grdanoski)

Many city-dwellers and almost all villagers make wine and brandy legally, with most of the brandy being distilled from lees, or the sediment of wine which results from the fermentation and aging process. Both drinks are rather heavy in taste and high in alcohol content; indeed, the brandy is so strong that many people drink it boiled hot as a kind of medicine against the flu. Brandy is usually drunk at any time, but especially before a main meal or with a salad, while wine is primarily consumed during the winter months, with fried smoked *kolbasi* (homemade kielbasa), made mostly of pork mixed with some beef and a generous amount of leeks.

13 EDUCATION

Having a good education is very important to Macedonians. The literacy rate in 2002 was 96%. Parental and cultural expectations encourage higher education. An individual with only a high school diploma often has a difficult time finding a decent job.

Since its independence from Yugoslavia in the early 1990s, Macedonia has allowed the establishment of dozens of privately run schools, including branches of US universities. The University American College Skopje offers undergraduate programs in business administration, political science, and foreign languages, while New York University Skopje makes available programs in language and literature, international relations, and politics and European studies. Still, the country's main university is the University of Sts. Cyril and Methodius, founded in 1949, which has granted over 100,000 bachelor's degrees and over 10,000 masters and doctoral degrees.

14 CULTURAL HERITAGE

Folk music and dance are two of the most valued and colorful aspects of the Macedonian culture. While music has in the preceding 20 years become modernized with the use of instruments like electric guitars and synthesizers, the traditional beat and the flavor of the melody remain. The traditional music group, once heard at village weddings and other social functions, is comprised of a clarinet, or *gajda* (pronounced gahy-dah)—a bagpipe made of lambskin; a bass-sized drum, which hangs from the player's shoulder; an accordion; and a violin. The tempo of the songs and dances ranges from slow to quite fast, depending on what the singer is describing or the mood the instrumentalists wish to capture. Most Macedonian folk songs are ballads concerning everyday problems and happy events, though many also depict the people's sufferings at the hands of the Ottoman Turks. Paralleling these compositions is the symbolism conveyed by a profusion of different dances, ranging from the slow *teškoto* (pronounced tesh-ko-to), or the "heavy" dance—performed generations ago by mournful bands of young village men on the day of their departure for foreign lands—to the exuberant *sitnoto*, or the "tiny-stepped dance."

Modern Macedonian literature made its appearance during the late 1800s with the poetry of the brothers Dimitar and Konstantin Miladinov, whose works are still recited by students from primary school through college. The growing literary collection grounded in the current standard of the Macedonian language marks its beginning with the 1939 publication of Kosta Racin's (pronounced Rah-tsin) programmatic collection of poems entitled *Beli Mugri* (*White Dawns*). While most of the distinguished 19th- and early 20th-century literary figures were poets, since World War II there has been an increase in the number of prose writers and playwrights. Compilations of Macedonian poetry and prose, including the novels and short stories of Meto Jovanovski, have been translated into dozens of foreign languages.

15 WORK

Macedonia has a fairly healthy manufacturing sector, but most of the currently available jobs are in the service industry. A major part of Macedonia's economy is sustained by small, family-owned businesses such as grocery stores, restaurants, cafés, service garages, clothing boutiques, etc. Unemployment and under-employment are problems. In fact, underemployment is even more of a problem today than it was during socialism, as often workers at many private businesses as well as government enterprises go home at the end of the month with only a promissory note instead of a paycheck.

On the other hand, a relatively small number of teenagers or college students in Macedonia hold summer jobs. Aside from the fact that such jobs are few and thus hard to find, it is culturally accepted that after nine months of studying, every student deserves a summer of relaxation and recreation. This is why within a few days after the end of every academic year, beaches, resorts, mountain retreats, and camps of all types—and for about two weeks between semesters, ski slopes—become primarily occupied by students.

16 SPORTS

Unquestionably, the most popular sport played by practically all Macedonian children is soccer. Of course, the number of players, the size of the playing field, and the width of the makeshift goals—usually two stones representing the goal posts—vary from pickup game to pickup game. Games are normally played with such energy and infectious enthusiasm that they often attract small audiences of all ages. Young adults also play soccer, though basketball, tennis, table tennis, and chess are also enjoyed. In fact, basketball in Macedonia is almost as well-liked as it is in the US., while American football and baseball are scarcely known at all. In 2008, hoping to cultivate a generation of tennis players who would duplicate the success of American, Russian, and Serbian tennis players, the Macedonian government authorized the building of over 100 tennis courts throughout the country.

Professional and semi-professional soccer and basketball organizations have abounded in Macedonia ever since World War II. Not only do such teams flourish in almost every city and sizable town, but prior to the large-scale emigration of the 1960s, many villages had their own regional or inter-village soccer leagues. Since most of the soccer and basketball players are either teen-agers or in their early twenties, these sports are commonly regarded as a young person's diversion.

17 ENTERTAINMENT AND RECREATION

Macedonia boasts 15 active professional theater groups that average over 1,700 total performances per year, a Philharmonic Orchestra (founded in 1944), 6 chamber ensembles, a host of annual folk music festivals held in different cities, hundreds of amateur rock and roll bands, and at least one professional pop group, Leb i Sol (Bread and Salt), which has been performing its own compositions throughout Europe and North America for over two decades. Since gaining independence, Macedonia has also produced some promising film directors whose pictures have acquired international recognition and praise. Most notably, in 1994 the American Academy of Motion Pictures nominated the film *Before the Rain*—which incorporated Macedonian dialogue and featured Macedonian actors in starring roles—for the Best Foreign Language Film Award. By then, the film had already won the Golden Lion award at the Venice Film Festival.

Every year Macedonia hosts several world-renowned cultural events, such as the Struga Poetry Evenings, begun in 1961, which has bestowed its Golden Wreath upon such eminent poets as Allen Ginsberg (US), Pablo Neruda (Chile), and Ted Hughes (UK); the Skopje International Jazz festival; and the World Cartoon Gallery. Most Macedonians also love to visit the beaches of their two favorite lakes, namely, Prespa and Ohrid, while many of the younger generation crowd the ski slopes on Mount Pelister and Mount Šar.

18 FOLK ART, CRAFTS, AND HOBBIES

The bulk of traditional Macedonian arts and crafts output comes from the hundreds of old-time master craftsmen's shops, normally found in the old commercial sections of larger cities such as Skopje, Bitola, and Ohrid. These sections are old literally and stylistically, in that most of the buildings and even the manner of production date back to the time of the Ottoman Empire. Serving as more than tourist attractions, these areas serve as shopping centers for the local populace. In the narrow and winding cobblestone streets of the old bazaars, one comes across an array of small goldsmith and silversmith shops selling intricate filigree rings, bracelets, and necklaces; tinsmith shops where one finds baking utensils of all sorts; *stomnari*, or jug-makers, who still produce glazed terra cotta vessels like jugs, urns, pitchers, cups, and bowls; and kilimari, or Oriental-style carpet shops. Villagers in Macedonia are famous for their weaving of colorful blankets, carpets, and traditional attire. However, village craft items are becoming increasingly difficult to find, since so many villagers have moved either to the city or abroad.

Aside from small establishments making jewelry and household implements, whether in bazaars or in other, more modern parts in cities and larger towns, one may step into any of the numerous slatkarnitsi (pronounced slaht-kharnitsi), or patisseries, which feature such delicacies as tulumbi (a ridge-surfaced, doughy pastry about three inches in length, ideally hollow inside, and soaked in syrup), *baklava* (made from layers of phyllo dough, filled with ground-up walnuts or pistachios and drenched in syrup), *kataifi* (thin-stranded pastry, filled with chopped nuts and served drenched in syrup), *boza* (a sweet, fermented drink made from wheat or millet), and *salep* (a similarly sweet drink made from salep flour).

¹⁹ SOCIAL PROBLEMS

While it was part of Yugoslavia, Macedonia had a poor human and civil rights record. Because the Communist Party was the only legally recognized political organization, any known challenge or opposition to its authority met with swift imprisonment and even torture. Today, Macedonia has over a dozen political parties of various sizes—a sharp reduction from the 64 officially registered parties that cropped up within a year after the country's declaration of independence—and political prisoners are officially nonexistent. Party leaders are calling for further reductions in the number of parties, so the number is expected to be brought down in the future.

Alcoholism and nepotism are longstanding social problems, while spouse abuse appears to be on the decline. Since the early 1990s, the divorce rate has risen. Other problems such as truancy, drug addiction, juvenile delinquency, and violence in general have arisen since the country's political and economic reconstruction. Drug addiction, rare prior to the early 1990s and punished by lengthy prison sentences, has now reached epidemic proportions. Ethnic relations between the Macedonian majority and the Albanian minority have been tense, and in the 1990s there was widespread fear that violence between the two might culminate in a civil war. However, following the government's concession to the minority's demands for the right to establish their own schools and a university, relations seem to have improved somewhat.

20 GENDER ISSUES

The treatment and status of women in Macedonia must be divided into two different periods, the pre-socialist and the socialist/post-socialist. In the former, women fared pretty much the same way they did in any patriarchal society. The husband stood as the head of the household, while the wife served as its caretaker. Since World War II, women in Macedonia have become equal to men in many respects. They are represented in every facet of the country's economy and political structure, from the factory floor to the halls of parliament. Many women are teachers and physicians and there are few women who do not work outside the home.

Spurred by the freedoms guaranteed by Macedonia's current constitution, the same kind of recognition has within the past two decades been extended to homosexuals and transsexuals. It is true that, whether gay or lesbian, one runs into an undercurrent of social resistance, if not hostility; yet it is also true that gay meeting places are becoming less of a novelty.

²¹ BIBLIOGRAPHY

Apostolski, M., et al. *Istorija na Makedonskiot Narod*. Skopje: Prosvetno delo, 1972.

Buckland, Theresa Jill, ed. *Dancing from Past to Present: Nation, Culture, Identities*. Madison, WI: University of Wisconsin Press, 2006.

Jakimovski, L., and V. Andreev. "Macedonia." In *Makedonski Iselenički Almanak '97*. Skopje: Redakcijata na Ilustriranoto Spisanie "Makedonija," 1997.

Konstantinov, D. H. "Prosvetiteli na Slovenite: Kiril i Metodie." In *Makedonski Iselenički Almanak '97*. Skopje: Redakcijata na Ilustriranoto Spisanie "Makedonija," 1997.

Laity, Mark. *Preventing War in Macedonia: Pre-emptive Diplomacy for the 21st Century*. London: Royal United Services Institute, 2008.

Madgearu, Alexandru. *The Wars of the Balkan Peninsula: Their Medieval Origins*. Lanham, MD: Scarecrow Press, 2008.

Penušliski, K. "A Prolific Collector of Macedonian Folklore." *Macedonian Review* (1997).

Rossos, Andrew. *Macedonia and the Macedonians: A History*. Stanford: Hoover Institution Press, 2008.

Tammer, P., and A. Tammer. *Macedonian Folk Songs*. Vallejo, CA: 1981.

Wroclawski, K. *Makedonskiot Naroden Raskažuvač Dimo Stenkoski*. Skopje: Institut za folklor, 1984.

—by T. Jovanovski

MALTESE

LOCATION: Republic of Malta (short form: Malta; in Maltese: *Repubblika ta' Malta*)
POPULATION: 420,000 (2008 estimate)
LANGUAGE: Maltese (or Malti) and English are official languages; Italian is widely spoken
RELIGION: Roman Catholic (98%); small number of residents belong to other religious communities—Christian, Muslim, Jewish and Buddhist

¹ INTRODUCTION

Malta, officially known as the Republic of Malta, is a parliamentary republic, and a full member of the European Union since 1 May 2004. Its house of representatives is made up of 65 members of parliament. The president of the republic is elected every five years by the house of representatives. The main political parties are the National Party (a Christian democratic party) and the Malta Labor Party (a social democratic party). There are several smaller political parties with no current parliamentary representation. The country's de facto capital is Valletta, situated on the eastern shore of the island of Malta. Malta's currency is the euro; before 2008, and since independence from Great Britain, the currency was the Maltese lira. Since 1993, the country has been organized into 68 local councils, which represent the elementary form of local government.

The origin of the country's name is not certain. Some scholars argue that it derives from the Phoenician word for harbor or refuge, *malat*; others claim that its roots lie in *meli*, the Greek word for honey, and the fact that in antiquity the Maltese islands were known for this product (the island of Malta was called Melita or "land of honey"). Today, the name of Malta is used either in reference to the entire country or merely to the largest of its islands.

Malta's history reflects its crucial strategic position in the center of the Mediterranean, between the continents of Europe, Africa, and Asia. Human life in Malta goes back to 5200 BC when the islands were settled by farmers from the nearby island of Sicily, although some archeological evidence points to the possibility that they were inhabited as early as 7200 BC. Between 3600 and 3000 BC, the early Maltese built a series of temples made out of large limestone slabs arranged in circular patterns. The economy of the islands at that time was based mainly on agriculture and stock-breeding, and some trade with other Mediterranean peoples; the population of Malta was peaceful. The temple period and the so-called civilization of the Temple Builders came to an abrupt end in 2000 BC, soon after it had reached its peak. Around that time, the islands were invaded by an unknown people known as The Destroyers, who dominated the islands until approximately 1400 BC, when another Bronze Age people, originating in Sicily, invaded the Maltese archipelago. They occupied it for five centuries, until the arrival of the Phoenicians, a Semitic-speaking people from the eastern Mediterranean. Lacking the population to establish large colonies in the Mediterranean, the Phoenicians used Malta's harbors as staging posts and anchorages on their trading routes.

By about 600 BC Greeks had established large settlements in southern Italy and Sicily and were looking for new territories for their growing population. The Carthaginians, inhabitants of the prosperous city-state that the Phoenicians had founded in 814 BC on the coast of North Africa, fought as supporters of the Phoenicians in their conflicts against the Greeks for control of Sicily and the western Mediterranean and occupied Malta in 480 BC. Under the Carthaginian rule, the population of the islands increased and settlement moved inland on Malta and Gozo. In that same period, the northeastern port of Grand Harbor was developed. During the last Punic War between the Carthaginians and the Romans in 218 BC, the Maltese rebelled against Carthaginian rule and declared their loyalty to Rome. The islands, famous for honey and cloth production, prospered under Roman rule. The Romans called the main island Melita and used the same name for its inland capital (today's Mdina). In the year 117, under the Emperor Hadrian, Malta and Gozo were granted the official status of *Municipium* and were allowed to have an autonomous local government. In year 60, the Christian apostle Paul was shipwrecked on the northern coast of Malta, initiating Malta's long history of Christianity and eventually becoming the country's patron saint, with the Feast of the Shipwreck of St. Paul celebrated as a public holiday on February 10.

After the Roman Empire split in two in 395, Malta is believed to have been occupied by either the Goths or the Vandals, or perhaps even both of these tribes. In the 6th century, the islands fell under the control of the Byzantine Empire and its capital Constantinople. Byzantine rule of Malta lasted for the next four centuries. In 836, the Aghlabid Arabs of North Africa began to carry out raids into the Maltese islands. In 870 Malta succumbed to repeated Arab invasions, remaining under Arab rule for the next 220 years. The Arabs introduced new ways of irrigation, citrus fruits and cotton, and left an indelible mark on the culture of Malta by bringing with them their language, the Siculo-Arabic language spoken by the Arabs of Sicily, which became the foundation of modern Maltese.

In early 11th century, the Normans, returning from their pilgrimage to the Holy Land, passed through Calabria in southern Italy, many settling there. In 1061 they invaded Sicily, defeating Arab rulers of the island in 1090. That same year, they landed in Malta. While at the beginning the Muslim population was allowed to remain on the islands, in 1122, King Roger I of Sicily had all Arabs deported and established the feudal system in Malta, which marked the birth of Maltese nobility. Malta became part of the Kingdom of Sicily, which also included parts of southern Italy. Catholicism was reinstated as the religion of Malta, and King Tancred of Sicily made the islands of Malta and Gozo into a fief under the rule of the Count of Malta. Because of the great strategic importance of the islands, most early counts were Genoese corsairs. When in 1194 the rule of Malta passed from the Normans to the Swabian dynasty of Hohenstaufens, Malta became part of an immense empire stretching from the north to the south of Europe. The most prominent of Hohenstaufen rulers, Frederic II, was tolerant of Muslims, but did not hesitate to expel any Arabs seen as fomenting rebellion. In Malta, his most important act was to allow the people to elect local residents to help with the administration of the island. This group of Maltese, elected annually, was known as the Consiglio Popolare and represented the people of Malta to their ruler.

After 1266 and the end of the Hohenstaufen rule of Malta, the islands briefly passed on to the French House of d'Anjou, which never became popular among the Maltese. Exorbitant taxes were imposed on the population of the islands, but the people never felt sufficiently protected by the garrison of French soldiers based in Malta. After the island of Gozo was sacked by the Genovese in 1275, there was a large revolt against French rule in Sicily, and the Kingdom of Sicily, including Malta, fell under the rule of the Spanish House of Aragon. The Aragonese ruled Malta from 1283 to 1412. Until 1350, the Aragonese kings of Sicily gave Malta, and the title of Count of Malta, as a feudal grant to highly-born individuals, who then frequently abused their privilege to tax the Maltese. When in 1350 the local population complained to King Louis, asking him to return the islands to his own direct rule, the request was granted, but this was reversed in the 1390s, and the practice of granting out Malta was resumed. Heavy taxes, failing crops, and raids of the islands by Arab corsairs all contributed to the dissatisfaction of the Maltese, who in 1425 rose in revolt against Count Gonsalvo Monroy. In 1428, King Alphonso decreed that the government of the islands should remain in the hands of its inhabitants, and that all government officials are to be elected from among the Maltese. An assembly, divided into nobles, clergy, and commoners, was founded, and it was decided that it should meet annually.

In 1530, in spite of the royal pledge made in 1507 not to cede Malta, Charles V of Spain granted the islands to the Sovereign Military Order of the Knights of St. John (known during the Crusades as the Hospitallers) in perpetual fiefdom, in exchange for an annual fee of a single Maltese falcon. With the arrival of the Knights of St. John on the islands, the history of Malta took a different, independent course. The Knights Hospitaller was founded in Jerusalem in the 11th century to provide care for sick pilgrims to the Holy Land in an infirmary near the Church of Holy Sepulcre. It was a religious order divided into military brothers and those dedicated to the care of the sick. The Knights were required to show proof of noble birth. The Order was organized into national chapters called *Langues*. After the withdrawal of the Christian forces from the Holy Land in the late 13th century, the Knights Hospitaller were forced to look for a new home. They found it on Rhodes, where they became a more militarized Order, but in 1522 the Ottomans forced them to leave the island. After Charles V gave them the Maltese islands and the North African port of Tripoli, the Knights continued their actions against the Barbary corsairs and the Arabs. In 1565, the Ottoman Sultan Suleiman the Magnificent sent a force of 40,000 to besiege the 500-700 knights and 8,000 soldiers in Malta and expel them from the Maltese islands. The Knights and the population of Malta endured one of the bloodiest and most difficult sieges in history, which lasted almost four months. The Ottoman defeat marked the turning point in the Turkish naval domination in the Mediterranean. After the siege, the Knights embarked on building a series of fortifications throughout Malta and built the new city of Valletta, named after their Grand Master Jean de la Valette.

The rule of the Knights Hospitaller (now also known as the Knights of Malta) on the islands remained strong until 1798 and brought prosperity to the islands, in spite of the numerous incidents demonstrating the discontent of the native Maltese with taxes, the Maltese nobles, and local clergy. Nevertheless, with the decline of the Ottoman threat in the Mediterranean, and the loss of many of its European holdings following the rise of Protestantism in Europe, the Order saw its revenues and its prestige decline. Additional sources of the Order's revenue were lost during the French revolution of 1789. Finally, after Napoleon captured Malta in 1798, during his expedition to Egypt, the Knights were forced to leave Malta. When the Maltese rebelled against the French occupation of the islands, Great Britain blockaded the islands, and in 1814, as part of the Treaty of Paris, Malta was declared to be a part of the British Empire. Positioned mid-way between Gibraltar and the Suez Canal, the islands were valued as a British naval base. Malta became prosperous as a refueling and restocking station on the way to India, and in World War I it was used as a large hospital. In the 1930s, Great Britain's role in Malta came under scrutiny among the native Maltese population. During World War II, the islands became the most bombed place on earth, and in 1942 the people of Malta were awarded the George Cross for their heroism.

Malta was granted independence from Great Britain on 21 September 1964. Under the 1964 constitution, Queen Elizabeth II remained the queen of Malta, with a governor-general exercising authority on her behalf. On December 13, the country became a republic within the Commonwealth, with a president heading the state. Nevertheless, Maltese association with the British has had a long-term cultural impact: the Maltese are still a bilingual nation, where English continues to be one of the two official languages. Maltese politics continue to reflect the traditional historical and cultural affiliations of its population, generally divided between the supporters of pro-Italian and pro-British policies and cultural orientation.

² LOCATION AND HOMELAND

The Republic of Malta is an archipelago situated in the almost exact center of the Mediterranean, with the total area of only 316 sq km (122 sq mi) and consisting of three inhabited islands—Malta, Gozo (Għawdex) and Comino (Kemmuna)—and several small, uninhabited ones—Filfla, Cominotto (Kemmunett), Fungus Rock (Il-Ġebla tal-Ġeneral), Manoel Island, and the Islands of St. Paul. Malta is situated 93 km (60 mi) south from the Italian island of Sicily, 296 km (185 mi) east of Tunisia, and 320 km (200 mi) north of Tripoli in Libya. There are no permanent lakes or rivers on Malta. The country's population is estimated to be 420,000 (including approximately 30,000 residents of foreign origin), with a density of 1,282 inhabitants per square kilometer (or 3,339 per sq mi). The largest island in the archipelago is Malta, with an area of 246 sq km (95 sq mi). Most of the country's important harbors are on this island. The next largest island, Gozo, has a land area of 67 sq km (26 sq mi). It is predominantly rural and is probably the first of the Maltese islands to have been settled. The third inhabited island, Comino, has an area of only 2.5 sq km (1 sq mi) and less than ten residents. Its name derives from the herb cumin, introduced by the Romans and grown on the island. Small-scale farming and tourism are the main sources of income on Comino. While Malta is a member of the European Union, it has historically been strongly influenced by the cultures of North Africa.

The Maltese climate is Mediterranean, with two, rather than four seasons: hot, dry summers and mild, rainy winters. The rainiest time of the year is December, with the average temperature of 16°C or 61°F, and the hottest month is July (33.2°C or 92°F). Malta has low rainfall; some of its water is produced by desalination, and some of it comes from wells. Malta's soil is quite fertile, but prone to erosion. Its terrain is mostly low and rocky, boasting many beautiful coastal cliffs. The Maltese islands are composed of sedimentary rock, with the western halves of the two largest islands higher than the eastern. The highest elevation in the country, Ta'Dmejrek, is only 253 m (83 ft) high.

³ LANGUAGE

Malta has two official languages: Maltese (or Malti) and English. While the ancient Maltese spoke Phoenician, this language was replaced in the 9th century by another Semitic tongue: Arabic. Modern Maltese is descended from Siculo-Arabic, a variant of Arabic spoken in Sicily and southern Italy. It is also strongly influenced by its centuries-long contact with various Romance languages (Sicilian, Italian, French and Spanish) and, starting from the early 19th century, English. Maltese is written in the Maltese alphabet, which has 29 letters and is based on the Latin alphabet, but uses several peculiar diacritically altered letters.

The Maltese islands have always been characterized by diglossia, a parallel use of one high-prestige language of the government and the elite (one of the Romance languages), and another, low-prestige language of the people, i.e. the spoken vernacular tongue (Maltese). The earliest known literary work in Maltese is *Cantilena*, a 15th-century poem composed by Pietro Caxaro. Other writings in Maltese date to the 17th century, but many more have been found from the 18th and 19th centuries. For many centuries, Malta's ruling classes, most often of foreign origin, preferred the use of Romance languages (Italian, French, and Spanish) or Latin. The members of the Order of the Knights of St. John, for example, many of whom were French, preferred to use French and Italian in their written records and correspondence. Italian, with its strong literary tradition, was for many centuries the recognized cultural language of Malta. Maltese writers living in the islands, but composing their work in Italian, constituted a literary movement that flourished until the second part of the 20th century; until the early 1900s, in fact, most literary works in Malta were written in Italian. The standardized written form of the Maltese language was established only under the influence of the Romantic movement in the early 19th century and particularly its emphasis on the national and the folkloric, when the celebrated Maltese linguist and writer, Mikiel Anton Vassalli composed a Maltese-Italian dictionary, a Maltese grammar, and a book of proverbs. After centuries of foreign domination and the successive use of Siculo-Arabic, Latin, Sicilian, Spanish, French, and Italian as languages of the administration and the educated classes, in the 1930s Maltese was recognized as an official language, alongside English, in an effort by the British to diminish the strong Italian influence in Malta.

Today, Maltese and English are both official languages of Malta. Virtually all native residents are bilingual and fluent in Maltese and English, and most of them understand or speak Italian. English and Maltese are languages of instruction in all public primary and secondary schools, while in the private schools all teaching is done in English. Most departments at the University of Malta also prefer to teach in English. The National Council for the Maltese language sets the usage standards for the Maltese language. There are approximately 500,000 speakers of the Maltese language in the world, including Maltese emigrants on all continents.

⁴ FOLKLORE

The most popular traditional Maltese folk instrument is a type of bagpipes known as *iż-żaqq*. Other known old Maltese musical instruments are: *iż-żummara* (reed pipe amplified with a cow's horn bell), *il-fifra* (cane whistle flute), *it-tanbur* (a frame drum made with a goatskin head), *and iż-żafżafa* (a friction drum made of ceramic and goatskin).

Maltese folksong, a form of oral poetry, is called *l-għana*. It is sung by village bards, often accompanied by a guitar, and it has traditionally been the most popular form of folk entertainment. It is similar in its melancholy to Sicilian folk ballads and the traditional Arab wailing tunes, expressing the passion or the sadness of love. *L-għana* has generally developed in these three styles: *Spirtu Pront* (quick wit), an improvised form of a song duel, traditionally sung by a group of two or more singers; *Tal-Fatt* (a story of an event), a narrative song based on tragic or humorous real events or fiction; and *Fil Gholi* (high-pitched), a high-register song also known as *il-Bormliża*, short in form, with repetitive and highly-allusive lyrics. Maltese country dance, locally known as *il-Kuntradanza*, and a dance known as *il-Parata* (sword-dance) are two well-known forms of traditional dance in Malta. Nursery rhymes are another traditional form of Maltese folk art transmitted through generations.

The most characteristic garment in the traditional dress for women used to be the long veil called *faldetta*, or *ghonnella*, a part of Maltese costume that has now completely disappeared in Malta. It was made of cotton or silk and was black or blue in color. This veil is thought to have its origin in the Arab veil or in an ancient Spanish form of traditional dress. Maltese folk costumes, now practically disappeared from everyday life, can still be seen at many local *festas* throughout Malta, when folk-dancing and singing is performed in traditional dress.

In the villages of Malta and Gozo, each family has their own nickname. The nickname or *laqam* identifies a person, a family, and even a social group or a town by what is perceived to be their most expressive characteristic ("giant," "hedgehog," etc.; occasionally nicknames refer to occupations). Nicknames given by inhabitants of Maltese and Gozoan villages to other towns and villages on the islands often reflect animosities that once existed between them (*Tar-Redus* or "manure" is, for example, a nickname for the town of Tarxien). Some towns or villages owe their names to legends.

The island of Gozo is considered by many to be the island of Ogygia Homer described in the Odyssey and where the poem's hero, Ulysses, spent seven years. According to this belief, Ramla Bay was the meeting place of Ulysses and the enchanting nymph Calypso, queen of the island.

Luzzus are the traditional brightly painted fishing boats, the design of which is said to go back to the times when the Phoenicians ruled the Maltese islands. The Eye of Osiris, an ancient symbol of protection against evil, is painted on every prow.

⁵ RELIGION

There are hundreds of churches in Malta, the majority of them Roman Catholic. Roman Catholicism is the state religion in Malta, and it is estimated that 98% of the population is Roman Catholic. Most residents belonging to the Protestant churches are not native Maltese, but British and Northern European expatriates, retirees, and tourists. There are small Anglican, Church of Scotland, Greek Orthodox, Methodist, Jewish, Muslim, and Buddhist communities in Malta.

Pre-Christian religious heritage in Malta includes some of the oldest surviving free-standing buildings in the world, built on Gozo of coralline limestone during the Ġgantija and Tarxien eras (3600-3200 and 3150-2500 BC respectively): Ħaġar Qim and Mnajdra temples.

The patron saints of Malta are St. Paul, St. Agatha, and St. George. The most revered religious figure in Malta by far, St. Paul is thought to have been shipwrecked on the northern coast of Malta in AD 60 and to have converted the local population, and the Roman Governor Publius, to Christianity. According to a legend, St. Agatha hid from her Roman persecutors in a cave in Rabat.

In 870 Malta was occupied by the Sicilian Arabs. They exerted strong influence on every aspect of life on the islands, and Islam was a dominant religion in Malta for the next 220 years. Christians and Jews were not forced to convert, but they had to pay additional taxes and could not serve in the government or military. Muslims remained a strong presence in Maltese society until the 14th century, long after the conquest of the island by the Norman rulers of Sicily in 1090.

An important religious figure in Malta is St. John the Baptist, patron saint of the Knights Hospitaller (Knights of Saint John), who received the Maltese Islands and the North African port of Tripoli as a gift from Charles V in 1530.

The most important churches in Malta are St. John's Co-Cathedral in Valletta, boasting a painting by Caravaggio of "The Beheading of John the Baptist " (1608), and a museum; St. Paul's Shipwreck Church in Valletta, containing a fragment of the pillar on which the saint was beheaded and a relic of his wrist bone; Church of St. Lawrence in Vittoriosa, where the Knights celebrated the end of the Great Siege of 1565; Our Lady of the Assumption in Mosta, and Xewkija Church in Gozo.

The Jewish population in Malta goes back to 1500 BC. It reached its greatest numbers in the Middle Ages, under Norman rule. Avraham Abulafia, a renowned Jewish mystic, lived on Comino from 1285 until his death in 1290. In 1492, shortly after the beginning of the Aragonese rule in Malta in 1479, all Jews were forced to leave the country, most of them eventually settling in the Levant. A number of Jews remained in Malta and converted to Christianity. Under the rule of the Knights of Malta, the position of the Jewish population was not significantly improved. Today's small Jewish community dates back to the French and British rule of Malta, and to the arrival of a number of Jewish refugees in the years preceding World War II, when Malta was one of the few countries not to require visas of Jews fleeing Nazi persecution.

6 MAJOR HOLIDAYS

Malta is the country with the greatest number of holidays in the European Union. National holidays are: Freedom Day (March 31, the anniversary of the withdrawal of British troops from Malta in 1979), Sette Giugno or Maltese National Day (June 7, commemorating the anti-British riots of 1919, the forming of the national assembly and the demand for self-government), Victory Day (September 8, in remembrance of both the end of the Great Siege of 1565 and the 1943 withdrawal of the Italian troops), Independence Day (September 21, marking Malta's 1964 independence from the Great Britain), and Republic Day (December 13, the anniversary of the substantial revision of Malta's Constitution in 1974, and its transformation from a Commonwealth Realm into a republic within the Commonwealth).

Public holidays are: New Year's Day (January 1), Saint Paul's Shipwreck (February 10), Feast of Saint Joseph (March 19), Good Friday, Worker's Day (May 1), Feast of Saint Peter and Saint Paul (June 29), Feast of the Assumption of Our Lady (August 15), Feast of the Immaculate Conception (December 8), and Christmas Day (December 25).

Malta is a Catholic country, and many Maltese holidays and festivals are based on the holy days of the Christian calendar. One of the highlights of the Christmas season is carol singing in the Co-Cathedral of St. John, and in other, mostly Baroque, churches in Malta. Cribs (*presepju*), some very ornate in design, are placed everywhere, both in Maltese homes and churches, and a very popular pastime of the Christmas season is going around and visiting as many of them as possible. Another popular pastime of the season is visiting the Manoel theatre in Valletta, where the annual satirical pantomime can be seen.

Carnival is a tradition that came to Malta with the Knights of St. John in the 16th century. It takes place in a week preceding Ash Wednesday. It is celebrated across the Maltese islands with parades of outrageous, multi-colored floats, dressing up in fancy costumes, and late-night dancing and drinking in the clubs and bars of Paceville. While the biggest celebrations take place in Valletta, each town in the country has developed its own way of celebrating the Carnival. Nadur, on Gozo, for example, is known among the Maltese for its unusually macabre version of celebrating this tradition.

On Holy Friday, parades of scenes from the Passion of Christ can be seen on the streets. On Easter Sunday, a procession with the statue of the risen Christ takes place around and inside of churches. The Maltese celebrate Easter with a large family lunch, visits to relatives and friends, and the exchange of gifts: chocolate eggs and rabbits are common, as well as *figolla*, traditional almond-filled pastry covered with icing. The Maltese are fond of fireworks, and sometimes include them in the celebration of Easter.

The feast of San Grigor (or St. Gregory) takes place on the Wednesday following Easter Sunday. A religious procession, first held in the 17th century as a thanksgiving for the end of the bubonic plague, starts at the chapel of St. Clement on the outskirts of Zejtun. After the procession, the Maltese celebrate with picnics and family outings in the fishing village of Marsaxlokk on the south-east coast of Malta.

Another opportunity to celebrate with fireworks is the annual Maltese Fireworks Festival, taking place in the first four days of May, with spectacular fireworks organized for three consecutive nights in Valletta's Grand Harbor, along with many concerts, shows, colorful street entertainment, and a variety of food events.

L-Imnarja (a festival of light, from the Italian Luminara) is a summer folk festival, once considered (along with the feast of St. Gregory) as a central feast for the Maltese. It coincides with the feast of Sts. Peter and Paul on June 29 and goes back to the time before the arrival of the Knights of St. John on the islands. The main area of celebration is Buskett Gardens, Malta's largest area of natural woodland, where families can picnic all day and night, drink wine and eat *fenkata* (rabbit feast), which is a traditional rabbit dish, and engage in the traditional singing called *l-għana*. The following day the celebrations continue with bareback horse and donkey races organized near Mdina.

September 8 is a day dedicated to remembering three events: the birth of the Holy Virgin (Maria Bambina), the end of the Great Siege of 1565, and the capitulation of the Italian navy to the British forces in the Second World War. A rowing regatta competition is held in Valletta's Grand Harbor to commemorate the end of the Great Siege.

Festival Mediterranean takes place in the autumn on the island of Gozo and is a mix of local food and wine tastings, concerts, art exhibitions, plays, conferences, and lectures, with walks led by scholars around archeological sites.

Village parish *festas* are a Maltese tradition that is thought to go back to the 16th century. The *festas* offer the village inhabitants an opportunity for a community celebration and a spiritual renewal. The celebrations are usually preceded by three days of prayer, vespers and masses with special hymns dedicated to the patron saint of the village.

7 RITES OF PASSAGE

Most of the rites of passage typical of Malta are linked to Catholic traditions and customs. Baptism and the first Holy Communion (around the age of seven or eight) are two important occasions followed by festive gatherings of extended family, with everyone bringing gifts for the child, including tokens of a religious nature or even monetary gifts. Following the christening of the child, hot chocolate and oval-shaped almond macaroons called *biskuttini tal-maghmudija* are served at the home of the child's parents. In the past, it was considered prudent to have the baby baptized as soon as possible, within only 24 hours after the birth. Such speedy christening, it was believed, freed the soul from purgatory. Traditionally, children were named after their grandparents, on the father's side if it was a boy, and on the mother's side if it was a girl. Today, little attention is paid to tradition in naming children.

The ceremony known as *quccija* (choosing) is a Maltese tradition linked to a child's first birthday. A basket is filled with various small objects representing different professions and trades; the first object that the child's hand touches is believed to be the sign of its future occupation.

Confirmation, which usually takes place in early adolescence, is the Catholic rite of initiation bestowing on a young person a full membership in the Church and represents another occasion for organizing festivities with the extended family. Maltese weddings are usually celebrated in churches, followed by large (300 guests are not an oddity at a Maltese wedding), lavish parties for extended family and friends. January, April, and August are traditionally considered to be the best months to get married. It is an old custom that the weddings are usually celebrated in the bride's parish. Instead of riding to church in a car, the more romantically-minded couple often chooses an *Il Karrozzin* (horse-drawn carriage), introduced in mid-19th century by the British. Wedding souvenirs wrapped in small boxes called *qoffini* (or souvenir baskets) are distributed to all guests. Most Maltese families have a particular place where the wedding souvenirs are displayed.

Some of the secular rites of passage for young Maltese include completing secondary education or receiving a university degree. Both occasions are marked with parties for family and friends, with presents or money given to the graduate. Sometimes such occasions are celebrated with a trip abroad.

8 INTERPERSONAL RELATIONS

Malta is a country marked by contrasts, and the Maltese, easy to befriend, are often described as having a Mediterranean personality of extremes. They quickly and readily express their strong opinions in most political and personal matters and have little understanding for those who refrain from taking sides in an issue, or choose the middle ground. This passion in taking sides is reflected in the country's political life.

Strangers are quickly welcome as friends and are expected to voice their opinions as passionately as the Maltese. Family and friends are welcome for unannounced round-the-clock visits. Malta's hospitality to visitors is legendary and marked by great warmth, and the culture of friendship based on loyalty and sharing strong opinions has a long history in Malta.

9 LIVING CONDITIONS

Most people in Malta live in the urban agglomeration of Valletta, the Grand Harbor, and Sliema, on the northeastern coast of the island of Malta. Marked differences exist in values, dress, and speech between city and village dwellers. With rare exceptions, most highly-educated Maltese professionals do not live in villages. This is one of the reasons why there are few social differences in Malta's villages, and why the church is still felt to be the center of the community life. The village priest is still seen as the religious leader, family counselor, and legal advisor. Exposure to international tourism and modern media has, nevertheless, already penetrated the fabric of the close-knit village life, and eroded the sense of unity and closeness that the villagers historically enjoyed.

Malta's urban population enjoys an excellent level of education and a lifestyle similar to that of urban dwellers throughout southern Europe. Many members of Malta's upper-middle classes and aristocracy have been educated abroad (often in Great Britain and Italy) and have a sophisticated, cosmopolitan outlook.

Malta has an excellent public health system, ranked by the World Health Organization as the fifth among the world's health systems, and every resident is entitled to free use of public health institutions. While real-estate prices have risen significantly in the recent decade, housing is still relatively affordable. Family ties are strong in Malta, and many young Maltese continue living with their parents for some time following the graduation from the university. At the same time, many new graduates rely on the strong extended family network when looking for suitable employment.

The Maltese are seen as enjoying a slower and more pleasant pace of life than that of their counterparts in other European countries, especially those of Northern Europe. The average life expectancy in Malta is 79.3 years, with 81.6 years for women and 77 years for men. Infant mortality rate is low at 3.79 deaths/1,000 live births.

There are approximately 130,000 Internet users in Malta, and 90% of all Maltese own a mobile phone.

Voluntary military service in Malta starts at the age of 17, and lasts 6 months. There is no conscription in Malta.

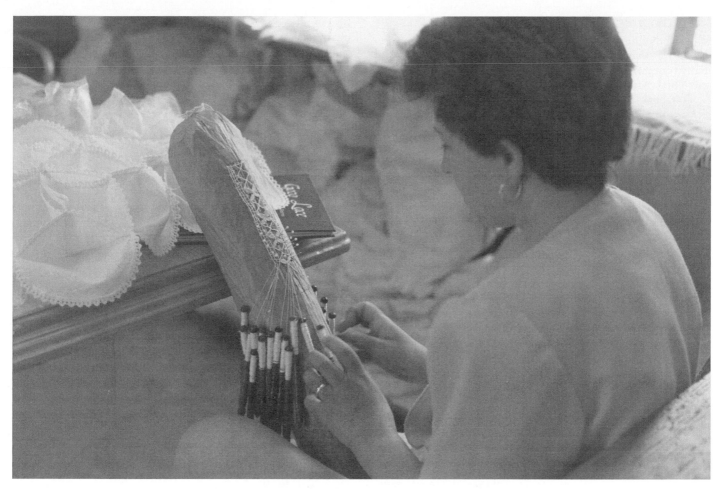

A woman making lace in Malta. (© Michelle Chaplow/Corbis)

¹⁰ FAMILY LIFE

Maltese culture is strongly family-oriented, and the degree of devotion the Maltese show to their immediate and extended family is remarkable. The traditional Maltese family is close-knit, extending into a network of relatives and in-laws, where family members rely on each other for material, social, and emotional support across the generations. The relatively traditional concept of Catholic family still prevails in Maltese society, although the long multicultural history of the islands has made the Maltese tolerant and open toward other kinds of communal values. In Maltese society the solidarity is strongest within the extended family, seen as the most important of all social networks in Malta. Rather than relying on friends and neighbors, the Maltese traditionally turn to close and distant relatives for support. This is why poverty in Malta is generally seen as being a consequence of the alienation of the individual from kin and family network.

The Maltese pay great attention to child-rearing and openly show their love for their children. Although the Mediterranean preference for the first-born male remains, Maltese families are as devoted to the education and rearing of female children as to that of the males. Young people in Malta usually live with their parents until graduation from university, and sometimes afterwards; often several generations of a family share a house. Such arrangements are less common then they used to be, but are not considered unusual. Ties between parents and children continue to be strong throughout their lifetime, and grandparents are often directly involved in raising grandchildren. While Maltese families are thought to be led by the strong father figure, this belief only serves to obscure the crucial role of the mother of the family, seen as its true center and de facto decision-maker. While large families used to be the rule in this Catholic country, most Maltese couples today have one or two children and are as inclined to use modern contraception as their counterparts in other areas of European Union.

¹¹ CLOTHING

Most Maltese dress similarly to their neighbors to the north, Italians, with some influences coming from the British style of dress, noticeable especially in formal clothing for men. Dress codes range from casual to traditionally elegant, and smart and fashionable. Casual beach-style clothing has recently gained in popularity.

Topless bathing is not allowed on public beaches, but it is often tolerated on private ones. Visitors to churches must dress respectfully (shorts or strappy tops are not allowed). Shoes with sharp, pointed heels are also not allowed in many churches, because they might damage the floors.

¹² FOOD

Malta's cooking is typically Mediterranean, based on locally-grown fresh vegetables, herb cheese, fish, and game. It shares many traits with the cuisines of its neighbors in southern Italy and North Africa.

Slow-cooking, favored in Malta in the past because of the lack of fire-wood ovens, remains the preferred food-preparation technique. Throughout the centuries, food in Malta was placed in an earthenware pot over a small stone hearth, or *kenur*, and allowed to simmer for a long time. Maltese meals still traditionally begin with a soup, but a soup may also form a meal in itself. Some of the most popular Maltese soups are *minestra* (thick vegetable soup) and *ġbejnil-armla* (widow's soup), a lighter version of minestra with a piece of fresh *ġbejniet* cheese melted in the soup and raw eggs added at the end. *Aljotta* (fish and garlic soup), spiced with mint or marjoram and tomatoes and containing rice or fine pasta, is another favorite of the Maltese.

Maltese and Sicilian cuisines have a lot in common. *Ravjul* (Maltese ravioli) is often prepared at Maltese homes from scratch. It was originally eaten on Fridays, when eating meat was forbidden by the Church.

Lampuka (dolphin fish) is the preferred fish of the Maltese, eaten with typical Mediterranean spices, such as rosemary, garlic, marjoram, olives, tomatoes, lemon, and capers, or in a *lampuki* pie (*Torta Tal-lampuki*). Salt cod stew, *stuffat tal-Bakkaljaw*, combining cod with potatoes and other diced vegetables is a winter favorite. *Fenek* (rabbit) is the most popular meat in Malta, often eaten marinated and browned with herbs and garlic and then simmered in red wine or tomato sauce; sometimes roast rabbit is served with a bitter chocolate sauce.

Malta is famous for its many kinds of excellent bread, ranging from a crusty sourdough eaten with fresh tomatoes or tomato paste and *ġbejniet*, to a less crusty bread called *ftira*, ring-shaped and resembling the Italian *ciabatta*. *Ġbejniet* are small, round cheeses made from sheep's or goat's milk and produced in three varieties: fresh, sun-dried (traditionally eaten with Maltese biscuits, or *galletti*, and served with red wine), or peppered. *Hobz biz-zejt*, a thick slice of bread dipped in olive oil and rubbed with ripe tomatoes or tomato paste, then covered with tuna, capers and onions, is a favorite snack in Malta. Other traditional snacks favored by the Maltese are *pastizzi*, diamond-shaped flaky pastries filled with ricotta cheese or mushy pea mixture and sometimes meat and anchovies. They can be bought at *pastizzerias* (small neighborhood shops selling baked goods), or virtually everywhere, in countless variations. Quassatat are somewhat lighter pastries, round in shape. Maltese pastries are often eaten with tea or weak coffee.

Favorite sweet dishes are *kannoli* (crispy, tube-shaped fried pastry filled with ricotta cheese), *imqaret* (pastries filled with date-mixture and deep-fried), *figolla* (an Easter-time biscuit, made with almonds, prepared in many different shapes), *helwa tat-tork* (Turk's Sweet, or locally made halva, made with sesame seeds, sugar, and almonds). *Qubbajt* is a nougat dating back to the time of the Arab domination, and it is traditionally bought at food stalls at *festas*.

Maltese wines are unjustly not as renowned as Italian or French wines, but they are inexpensive and of excellent quality. Some of indigenous wine varieties are *Gellewza* and *Ghirghentina*. Gozo wines tend to be stronger than the wines from the island of Malta. Excellent beers and ales, a British tradition, are also produced in Malta. Maltese coffee is typically drunk weak and milky, and the influence of Great Britain in the islands has made tea drinking very popular. *Anisette*, a flavored liqueur, is a specialty of Gozo and an ingredient in many sweets. *Bajtra* liqueur is a sweet liqueur made of prickly pears, honey, and herbs. Most Maltese prefer bottled water to drinking tap water (mostly produced by desalination).

The Maltese eat their main meal of the day at lunchtime (around 1 p.m.). The lunch often has five to six courses and lasts several hours. Dinner is usually eaten around 7 p.m.

¹³ EDUCATION

About 92.8% of the population of Malta is considered literate (92% men and 93.6% women). Malta's public school system has been strongly influenced by the British system, and formal education is mandatory for all Maltese children between the ages of 5 and 16. Day care is free of charge for all children over three years of age. Mandatory education is divided into a six-year primary cycle (from the ages of 5 to 10) and secondary education (11 to 16). Children with special learning needs are integrated into mainstream classrooms. All primary schools are free of charge and co-educational, with textbooks and transportation to school free of charge. At the end of primary school, all children take the nationally standardized Junior Lyceum Examination. Students then enroll into Junior Lyceums, which offer a more challenging, academically-oriented curriculum; Area Secondary Schools, for students who failed the examination; or the so-called "opportunity schools" for low-achieving students. Students attend secondary schools between the ages of 11 and 16; most of the schools are single-sex and years (grades) are called "forms."

Upper secondary education can be received at the pre-university Junior College, which is part of the University of Malta, or in other secondary-education institutions, administered by the Church or a private organization. There students spend two years preparing for their future university studies. All students receive a monthly scholarship, with both State and Church educational institutions funded; private institutions charge tuition fees. An alternative to Junior College is Vocational Upper Secondary Education, where students enroll full-time, or part-time, in combination with an apprenticeship, acquiring professional and vocational education in the fields of electronics, business, art and design, agribusiness, etc., and preparing to enter the workforce early.

The University of Malta, which traces its origins to the Jesuit Collegium Melitense, was founded in 1592. It is organized into 11 schools (faculties) and several interdisciplinary institutes and centers, and offers undergraduate and graduate education to approximately 10,000 students, with 2,500 graduates annually. Students usually enroll into the university at the age of 17 or 18. Local students study tuition-free, and if they are below the age of thirty they also receive stipends. Foreign students pay tuition. Classes are normally held between October and May. At the end of three or four years, students receive a Bachelor's degree, with some courses of study (medicine, dentistry, engineering, law) lasting up to five or six years. Most instruction is based on credit system. Graduate degrees require between one to four years of part-time or full-time study (master's degrees); doctoral degrees are awarded based on research.

14 CULTURAL HERITAGE

Malta's cultural heritage reflects its fascinating, multicultural history. Valletta, the country's capital, is home to numerous museums. Among them is the National Museum of Archeology, housed in the former Auberge de Provence, which once belonged to the Order of Knights Hospitaller. The National Museum of Fine Arts is home to a number of works by Mattia Preti (1613–1699), a Baroque painter from Calabria, who worked in Italy and Malta, and was a Knight in the Order of St. John. It also houses sculptures by the Maltese sculptor Antonio Sciortino (1879–1947) who studied and worked in Rome. Museum of St. John's Co-Cathedral in Valletta has on display many portraits of Grand Masters of the Order of St. John, as well as various treasures once belonging to the Knights. Lascaris War Room (located in the World War II military operation rooms in the bastions of the capital) and National War Museum are dedicated to preserving the memory of World War II in Malta. St. James Cavalier Centre for Creativity in Valletta hosts film performances, theatre and music events, and workshops.

Manoel Theatre in downtown Valletta is a jewel of 18th century architecture and one of the oldest surviving enclosed theatres in Europe. It was built in 1731 by António Manoel de Vilhena, Grand Master of the Knights of Malta, who commissioned and personally funded the building of the theatre, in order to satisfy the growing demand among the Maltese for opera and dramatic productions, and to provide the people of Malta with "honest entertainment." The first performance, in January of 1732, was a classic Italian tragedy, Scipione Maffei's *Merope.*

The Museum of Archeology in Rabat/Victoria on the island of Gozo is located in an old aristocratic mansion, and is home to ancient Gozitan artifacts. Cathedral Museum in Malta's ancient capital, Mdina, boasts a collection ranging from Roman tombstones to 16th century art and the works of Albrecht Dürer. The Folklore Museum in Rabat/Victoria is located in three houses. Its displays recreate the life in traditional rural houses of Malta and Gozo.

A unique example of Baroque architecture, Valletta was built by the Knights of St. John, following the Great Siege of Malta in 1565. The first major buildings in Valletta are works of the noted Italian architect from Lucca Francesco Buonamici (1490–1562). Francesco Laparelli da Cortona (1521–1571) was a prominent engineer in the employ of Pope Pius IV, who sent him to built Valletta as a fortress to defend Christendom. Laparelli was assisted in his work by the Maltese Gerolamo Cassar (1520–1592), who built the Grand Masters' Palace in Valletta and St. John's Co-Cathedral. Matteo Perez d'Aleccio (1547–1616) was an Italian painter from Lecce and pupil of Michelangelo who introduced Mannerism to Malta. He painted 13 frescoes in the Great Masters' Palace showing the Great Siege of Malta, and the "Baptism of Christ," originally a titular painting of the Co-Cathedral of St. John.

Cathedrals in Mdina and Gozo were designed by Lorenzo Gafa (1638–1703), a noted Maltese baroque architect.

Perhaps the most well-known 18th century Maltese artist is Antoine de Favray (1706–1791), a French-born painter who came to live in Malta in 1744 and spent the rest of his life there, devoting himself to portraiture and genre painting. He enjoyed the patronage of two grand masters, which resulted in a number of historical portraits. His portraits and island scenes show native Maltese in their traditional costume, and they earned him fame in France. Portraits made for his wealthy Maltese clientele were of a more conventional nature. His first picture painted in Malta is a "Portrait of Maltese Lady" (1745), now housed in the Louvre Museum.

Maltese literature, written mostly in Italian until the 20th century, has after 1900 been defined by two major literary movements: The Academy of Maltese Writers (founded in 1920 and still active) and The Movement for the Revival of Literature (founded in 1967, short-lived but radical in its esthetic orientation and very influential). Poetry and narrative have dominated the Maltese literature, while theatre in Maltese, in the modern sense of the word, represents a recent development. Its predecessor is a form of popular Maltese theatre called *tijatrin.* Anton Manwel Caruana's (1838–1907) historical novel *Inez Farrug* is widely considered to be the first novel in Maltese. Oliver Friggieri (1947–), who writes in Maltese, English, and Italian, is renowned as Malta's best contemporary poet. Francis Ebeyer and Oreste Calleja are the most respected modern playwrights. Children's fiction is represented by Trevor Zahra. One of the most popular women poets are Maria Grech Ganado, and Simone Inguanez, while Clare Azzopardi is known for her innovative prose, where the protagonists are strong women who refuse to be dominated by anyone. The most popular author of the new generation is Immanuel Mifsud (1967–), author of short stories, poetry, and stories for children.

15 WORK

Per capita gross domestic product (GDP) in Malta is estimated to be approximately $23,000. The largest sector of Maltese economy is that of services (75% of GDP, with tourism as the most important source of revenue). Industry (22.5%) produces semi-conductors, pharmaceuticals, communications technology, rubber, and plastic products; shipbuilding and repair are also important sources of revenue in Malta. Agriculture accounts for 2.5% of Malta's GDP with products such as typical Mediterranean fruits and vegetables and potatoes. Malta's entry into the European Union also increased the emphasis on the outward orientation of its economy. Most of Maltese exports go to the European Union, Singapore, and the United States. Recently, Malta has been also showing great interest in developing medical tourism. An important source of revenue for the country's public and private sector is the international film industry, with many English-language, big-budget productions filmed in Malta every year.

Malta has a highly educated, multilingual workforce of 149,000, and the unemployment rate was at 5.8% in 2008, lower than the average EU unemployment rate of 6.8%. Services employ 47% of Malta's labor force, the public sector employs 29%, manufacturing 16%, and construction and quarrying 8%. In recent years, the government has been introducing a policy of gradual economic liberalization. Malta is one of the smallest and most densely populated countries in the world (1,160 inhabitants per sq km, or 3000 per sq mi), and finding work is not always easy. Since the country's entry into the European Union, any citizen of the Union is entitled to live and work in Malta. Australian citizens under 30 years of age are also entitled to work on Malta for a year (significantly, this country is also home to a very large Maltese immigrant community). Citizens of other countries generally find it difficult to obtain a work permit. Job vacancies are advertised, but most are filled by word of mouth, and go to Maltese citizens.

Malta's working day is traditionally divided in two by a long siesta, when many shops and small businesses remain closed.

16 SPORTS

Malta's Mediterranean climate makes many outdoor sports attractive year-round, and the country boasts a wide variety of land and water sports facilities. Horseback riding is a favorite Maltese recreational activity, and horse-racing, with races being held every Sunday between October and May, is Malta's preferred spectator sport. Other sports popular among the Maltese are lawn bowling (or bocci, played in almost every village), tenpin bowling, and clay pigeon shooting competitions, held every Sunday morning. The Maltese are also passionate about water polo and soccer, and soccer teams are numerous on the Maltese islands, with the regular season running between October and May, and most fans supporting either Italy or England in international competitions. Each February, the country hosts the Malta Marathon, a 42 km (26 mi) race from Rabat to Sliema, attracting runners from the entire world. In April the Malta Archery Federation holds the International Archery Tournament at the Marsa Sports Club.

Visitors will find some of the best opportunities for recreation available in the Marsa Sports Club, a large sporting complex with first-rate sports facilities and membership available on a daily or weekly basis. Water sports, such as scuba diving (with a full range of diving courses available on Malta and Gozo), water-skiing, windsurfing, and paragliding are popular among the locals and the tourists alike, and the clear waters of Malta are ideal for snorkeling. No fishing license is required in Malta. Sailing races are popular events between late spring and mid-fall. The most attractive are the Comino Regatta in June, the Malta-Syracuse (Italy) race in July, and the Rimini (Italy)-Malta-Rimini yacht race in August. September 8 is a day dedicated to remembering the end of the Great Siege of 1565, and a rowing regatta competition is held in Valletta's Grand Harbor.

Sports facilities are plentiful throughout Malta and available at most hotels. A number of hotels also have their own facilities for tennis and squash. Excellent boat and yacht rental facilities are also available on Malta.

The Maltese islands lie on the central bird migration route, and shooting and trapping birds for trophies and display is still one of Malta's favorite and most notorious pastimes. This has attracted much negative attention from the local Ornithological Society, the conservation group BirdLife Malta, bird-lovers, and animal protection agencies in Malta and internationally. Malta has more than 16,000 hunters, and despite the legislation to curtail hunting, they often ignore the rules governing hunting seasons and protected areas, killing around 30,000 birds in Malta each year, including those belonging to the endangered species.

17 ENTERTAINMENT AND RECREATION

During the day, the capital of Malta, Valletta, offers a wide array of attractions, ranging from the numerous museums to shopping and people watching. A city bursting with locals and tourists during the day, Valetta shuts down early by European standards, and has few late-night bars and clubs. Entertainment can be found in its Mediterranean Conference Centre, which regularly hosts music and theatre events, and in Manoel Theatre, one the oldest surviving enclosed theatres in the world.

Northwest of Valletta is a coastal district of Paċeville, considered to be Malta's nightlife capital. Paċeville has a great number of pubs, bars, clubs, and restaurants, especially popular with young Maltese and tourists on Saturday nights. The nearby St. Julian's and Spinola Bay are more appealing to middle-aged and older residents and tourists.

On Sundays, a favorite outing for many Maltese families is a visit to the old fishing village of Marsaxlokk, on the southwestern coast of Malta. They visit the famous fish market, take a stroll, and then sit down for a long lunch in one of Marsaxlokk's seafront restaurants.

Maltese *festas* are the most widespread and traditional form of entertainment in Malta; in their present form, they date back to the 19th century, when they emerged as a fusion of several local traditions. Every village and town in Malta and Gozo celebrates the day dedicated to its patron saint with processions, colorful street decorations and lights, parades, food and wine, music, and fireworks. Folk dances are performed in traditional dress and traditional and modern-day foods are sold at market stalls. The *festa* season lasts from May and September, and approximately 90 *festas* are celebrated in this small country every year. *Festas* are popular among the young and the old alike, and the forms of entertainment available have been successfully adapted to modern times.

There are five major TV channels in Malta, and their funding is provided mostly by the state and political parties. Italian radio and TV stations enjoy wide popularity in Malta among all age groups. Newspapers are published in both English and Maltese. The most widely read English-language newspapers are *The Times* and *The Independent*. *In-Nazzjon* and *L-Orizzont* are main Maltese-language papers.

18 FOLK ART, CRAFTS, AND HOBBIES

The Maltese art of lacemaking has been renowned since at least the 16th century, descending probably from the Genoese lacemaking tradition (which, in turn, came to Italy from the East, through Venice). It reached its peak in the 18th century. The craft of lacemaking became almost extinguished in the first years of the British rule, due to the economic crisis on the islands, but was revived in 1833 by the great demand for lace in England. At the same time, lacemaking spread throughout the island of Gozo. Malta's lace (*bizzilla*) is noted not only for its exceptional beauty, but also for its remarkable durability. It is made by women on the islands of Malta and Gozo, where lacemakers often practice their craft seated in front of their houses, attracting the attention of residents and visitors alike. One of the most recognizable characteristics of Malta and Gozo lace is its creamy or honey-colored thread, made of Spanish silk and used to make exquisite tea towels or table-cloths. Black silk was also widely used until the 20th century, when its popularity diminished. British missionaries spread the art of Maltese lacemaking by copying its patterns and introducing them in China and India. Modern-age boom in tourism and the related souvenir trade has been an important factor in the survival of this ancient art. Lacemaking is nowadays taught in public trade schools for girls in Malta, and its history and techniques are subject of regular exhibitions and academic studies of Maltese national heritage.

[19] SOCIAL PROBLEMS

Malta is a very low-crime rate society (this is especially true of the island of Gozo), and many social problems typical of large, highly-urbanized countries are not present in Malta. At the same time, high population density and the small size of the country represent a challenge to the Maltese economy and job creation.

Malta has the highest traffic accident rate in Europe, and drivers often ignore speed limits and the rights of pedestrians. Drivers employed in public transportation are sometimes equally disrespectful of those sharing the roads with them. Parking space is very difficult to find in Valletta.

Malta is a melting point of cultures. This fact, together with a high density population and Malta's geographical position between Africa, the Middle East, and Europe, has made Malta a tolerant society, where the downside has been be a laissez-faire response to alcohol abuse. The medical profession and the government still do not feel sufficient urgency to call for effective laws and regulations, specialized treatment services, or educational programs related to alcohol abuse.

Illegal immigration from Africa, with approximately 2,000 persons arriving to Malta each year, mostly on fishing boats, is one of the biggest concerns of the Maltese. In spite of the rich, multi-cultural history of the Maltese islands, the arrival of growing numbers of illegal immigrants has resulted in open expressions of racism in the country, giving rise to concern among church officials, who continue to appeal for solidarity, and humanitarian organizations. Illegal immigration has also been perceived as placing a degree of strain on Malta's health and social services, and on its labor market. Around 45% of immigrants to Malta have been granted refugee or protected humanitarian status.

Malta is also home to a large hunting population, which openly disrespects legislation governing hunting seasons and protected natural areas. Maltese hunters regularly shoot and trap a great number of birds enjoying international protection as endangered species.

A serious problem in the Maltese islands is the lack of water resources. Water in Malta is scarce and much of the country's water is obtained by the process of desalination, bringing up the problem of fossil fuel use and pollution.

Drug trade and the related delinquency are not a significant problem in Malta; the country is considered to be only a minor point of hashish trade between North Africa and Western Europe. There are fewer than 500 people living with HIV/AIDS in the country.

[20] GENDER ISSUES

Women in Malta voted for the first time in the general elections of 1947. Women are present in many spheres of Malta's labor force, ranging from banking, media, and journalism, to academia, legal and medical professions, and small business ownership. Since 1992, Malta has adopted several laws intended to eliminate all sex-based discrimination. In January 2000, for example, the country promulgated a law on equal treatment, which entered into force in October of that year. However, a 2003 follow-up report stated that further progress was still needed in this area, and recommended that the Maltese government should reinforce the existing, and implement additional, regulations in the area of gender equality. The government of Malta has adopted a policy of having at least one women member in each one of its committees, and in recent years made considerable efforts to help achieve gender equality in the workplace, such as the 2003 adoption of the Equality for Men and Women Act and the creation in 2004 of the National Commission for the Promotion of Equality for Men and Women. Nevertheless, large-scale workplace equality between Maltese men and women still remains a goal to be achieved, and equality issues do not yet figure prominently in collective bargaining in Malta's labor market. While the past years have seen many legal and social achievements for Maltese women active in the work force, the employment rate of 37% for women is still low by European standards, and women's presence in the labor market remains concentrated in specific sectors and levels of occupation, while being noticeably absent in others. Moreover, most women often do not enjoy the same working conditions as men, and they tend to participate in continuous training and education at a significantly lower rate.

The National Council of Women of Malta, established in 1964, is a non-governmental and non-partisan organization whose objective it is to promote equal rights for women in every sphere of Maltese society. The Department for Women's Rights was established in 1989.

Divorce does not exist in Maltese legal system. A foreign divorce can be registered in Malta, after which both parties are free to remarry. The only other way to end a marriage in Malta is marriage annulment. Legal separation (consensual or contentious) releases both parties from the obligation to live together, but the obligations to fidelity and support continue. The complications associated with divorce and separation has prompted many modern Maltese to seek alternative living arrangements, such as co-habitation. Pre-nuptial agreements are also growing in popularity.

Female writers, such as Claire Azzopardi, focusing on non-traditional themes of lesbianism and oppressive patriarchy, are contributing to a shift in perception of woman's role in the Maltese society.

Male homosexuality has been legal in Malta since 1973, while laws against female homosexuality were never introduced. The overall attitude of the Maltese towards gay tourists is generous and open, but in spite of several gay bars, clubs, and a gay hotel, there is no strong gay scene in Malta. The Malta Gay Rights Movement is a non-governmental organization fighting for the social and legal equality of gay people in Malta, while the Maltese society remains fairly traditional.

In 1981 all abortions were banned in Malta. This represented a change from a prior law, which allowed for therapeutic abortions when the life of the mother was in danger. In spite of the United Nations' urging the Maltese government to review its legislation on abortion in cases of rape or incest, or in case of therapeutic abortions, the laws governing abortion had not changed as of 2008. Together with Ireland, Malta is the only EU member state that bans abortion in cases of rape or incest.

The age of consent for sexual activity in Malta is 18, and for civil marriage 16.

[21] BIBLIOGRAPHY

Atauz, Ayşe Devrim. *Eight Thousand Years of Maltese Maritime History: Trade, Piracy, and Naval Warfare in the Central Mediterranean.* Gainesville: University Press of Florida, 2008.

Buhagiar, Mario. *Christianization of Malta: Catacombs, Cult Centers and Churches in Malta to 1530*. Oxford: Archaeopress, 2007.

Castillo, Dennis. *The Maltese Cross: A Strategic History of Malta*. Westport, CT; London: Praeger Security International, 2006.

Goodwin, Stefan. *Malta, Mediterranean Bridge*. Westport, CT: Bergin & Garvey, 2002.

Gregory, Desmond. *Malta, Britain and the European powers 1793-1815*. Madison, NJ; London: Farleigh Dickinson University Press; Associated University Presses, 1996.

Luttrell, Anthony. *The Making of Christian Malta: From the Early Middle Ages to 1530*. Aldershot (England): Burlington (Vt.): Ashgate/Variorum, 2002.

Mallia-Milanes, Victor, ed. *The British Colonial Experience, 1800-1964: The Impact on Maltese Society*. Msida, Malta: Mireva Publications, 1988.

Sagona, Claudia. *Archaeology of Punic Malta*. Leuwen; Sterling, VA: Peters, 2000.

Sant, Alfred. *Malta's European challenge*. Malta: SKS, Information Department, Malta Labor Party, 1995.

Spiteri, Edward. *Island in Transition: The Economic Transformation of Malta from a British Crown Colony to an Independent Democratic Republic*. Valletta, Malta: Progress Press, 1997.

Trump, David H. *Malta, Prehistory and Temples*. Malta: Midsea Books, 2002.

Vassallo, Carmen. *Malta Chamber of Commerce, 1848-1979: An Outline History of Maltese Trade*. Valletta: Malta Chamber of Commerce, 1998.

Wettinger, Godfrey. *The Jews of Malta in the Middle Ages*. Valletta, Malta: Midsea Books, 1985.

—by K. von Wittelsbach

MARIS

ALTERNATE NAMES: Cheremis (former)
LOCATION: Mari El Republic Volga-Ural region of Russia)
POPULATION: 660,000
LANGUAGE: Mari; Russian; Tatar
RELIGION: Eastern Orthodox Christianity, Mari Native Religion

¹ INTRODUCTION

The Maris, formerly known as the Cheremis, are a Finno-Ugric people who inhabit the Middle Volga region of the Russian Federation. They are divided into three groups—Highland, Lowland, and Eastern Maris. The origins of the Maris are disputed, but there is little doubt that they migrated to their current homeland from the west. In Jordanes' 6th-century chronicle, he mentions the "Sremniscans" as subjects of the Ostrogoths, and this is probably a reference to the Maris (i.e. Cheremis). In any case, the Maris are more positively identified in the Russian *Primary Chronicle* (a 12th-century collection of history). In the medieval period, the Maris were subjects to the Muslim Volga Bulgarians, and later they were subjects of the Golden Horde and the Kazan Khanate. During the time of Russia's conflicts with the Kazan Khanate, to which they were in close proximity, the Maris were divided in their loyalties. The Maris on the western bank of the Volga—the Highland Maris—provided troops to the Russians, while the Lowland Maris, in closer proximity to Kazan, supported the Tatars. Lowland Maris not only helped defend Kazan in 1552, but they were also involved in a series of revolts against Russian rule in the second half of the 16th century.

In response to the Russian policy of Christianization, many Maris fled their homeland, and in the 17th and 18th centuries migrated to the Ural Mountains and the trans-Kama lands in what is today northern Bashkortostan. These communities eventually came to be known as the Eastern Maris. In addition to migration, Maris would occasionally resist Russian policies more forcefully, and they were actively involved in the major Cossack and peasant revolts of the 18th century, most notably the Pugachev rebellion of the 1770s. During the late 19th century, the Maris were especially afflicted by poverty, and 98% of Maris were rural dwellers.

With the advent of the 1917 Revolution, a small Mari national movement emerged among the Eastern Maris, but it was soon crushed by the Bolsheviks. In the 1920s, however, the Soviets authorized the creation of a Mari autonomous region, which soon after became the Mari Autonomous Soviet Socialist Republic (ASSR), a constituent part of the Russian Soviet Federated Socialist Republic (RSFSR). However, this republic included only the Highland and Lowland Maris; the Eastern Maris were left in other jurisdictions.

During the Soviet era, Mari autonomy was in political terms a fiction, and it was not until the era of *perestroika* (1985–91) that the Mari republic began to test its autonomy. At this time, Mari intellectuals became especially active in calling for measures from the government to better protect Mari culture especially concerning the Mari language. Meanwhile, the name of the Mari ASSR was officially changed to Mari El, meaning the Mari land. However, no serious independence movement emerged among the Maris as among some of their neighbors such as the Tatars.

² LOCATION AND HOMELAND

According to recent population estimates there are about 660,000 Maris in the Russian Federation about half of whom live in the Mari El proper. The largest concentration of Maris outside the Mari El are the Eastern Maris, who inhabit northern Bashkortostan as well as the districts of Perm and Ekaterinburg (formerly Sverdlovsk) in the Ural Mountains area. In addition, large communities of Maris are also found in jurisdictions adjacent to the Mari Republic, especially Vyatka (formerly Kirov) district, Nizhnii Novgorod (formerly Gorki) district, Tatarstan, and Udmurtia.

The Mari Republic is divided by the Volga River. The "highland" side, corresponding to the western bank, possesses the best agricultural land, and the population there is relatively dense. The opposite bank of the Volga, the "lowland" side, constitutes the lion's share of the republic's territory, but this area is covered by very dense evergreen and birch forest, and much of the land is swampy. The settlements there are much sparser, the land is poorer, and much of the traditional economy depended on hunting, trapping, and gathering forest products. The Mari republic itself consists of 23,200 square kilometers (about 8,960 square miles), and its capital is Ioshkar-Ola (previously known as Krasnokokshaisk, and in tsarist times, Tsarevokokshaisk), located on the Kokshaga River. The climate is a cool continental one, with an average January temperature of –13°C (4°F) and an average July temperature of 19°C (68°F).

³ LANGUAGE

The Mari language is part of the Volga Finnic branch of the Finno-Ugric language family. It is most closely related to the Mordvin languages, but Mari and Mordvin are not at all mutually intelligible; Mari is more distantly related to Finnish and Estonian. Mari is further divided into two separate literary languages, Highland Mari *(kuryk Mari)* and Lowland *Mari (olyk Mari)*, and it would be more precise to speak of Mari languages, as these two languages are generally not mutually intelligible. Lowland Mari speakers account for approximately 90% of Mari speakers, while Highland Mari speakers, numbering only 66,000, account for about 10%. The Eastern Maris speak a form of the Lowland dialect, but their own dialect is distinguished by a large number of Tatar loan-words. According to the 1989 Soviet census, 80.9% of Maris considered themselves fluent in their native language. Nearly all Maris are fluent in Russian, often at the expense of Mari. Among the Eastern Maris, nearly all are very fluent in Tatar as well as Russian.

Mari names are rather varied, and they include native Mari names as well as Russian and Tatar names. In fact, native Mari names are relatively rare. Native Mari male names include *Kugerge* (meaning elder son) and *Shumbat* (Saturday), and female names include *Iziudir* (younger daughter) and *Unay*.

⁴ FOLKLORE

During the first half of the 18th century, most Maris became Eastern Orthodox Christians, although large communities of Maris, especially Eastern Maris, have never become Christians and have remained adherents of Mari native religion. As a result, native religious features remain important elements in Mari folklore, even among Christian Maris. The Maris have re-

tained numerous myths, especially concerning tutelary spirits such as Sultan Keremet, Akpatyr, and Kugu Jeng. Maris venerate shrines connected with these heroes, who are said to have been past leaders of the Mari people who protected them from foreign conquerors. Mari mythology, which in some cases displays strong CHRISTIAN influences and in others strong Muslim influences, includes not only native figures, such as Jumo, the supreme God, but also figures such as Shaytan (the Devil) and biblical and Koranic prophets. In addition, the Maris have retained a rich tradition of songs, historical legends, and other oral traditions.

⁵ RELIGION

Of all the peoples of the Middle Volga region, and arguably in all of Russia, the Maris have been the most successful at retaining their native religion while at the same time resisting the pressures of Islamization. Not only has the adherence to native religious traditions deeply influenced Mari folklore and cultural life in general, but it has also remained an important factor in Mari history and, in the current period, in Mari politics as well.

In any case, most Maris were converted to Eastern Orthodoxy during the first half of the 18th century, and today roughly two-thirds of religious Maris are Orthodox Christians. Christianity took especially deep roots among the Hill Mari, who were all Christians by the beginning of the 19th century. Similarly, the vast majority of Lowland Mari were also Christian by the beginning of the 19th century, although many communities both formally and informally retained their native religion, which they termed *chi marla vera* (the genuine Mari faith), as opposed to the *rushla vera* (Russian faith) of the Christianized Maris. Finally, the vast majority of Eastern Maris, both in Bashkortostan and the Urals region, have remained staunch adherents of the *chi marla vera*. As a result of their long contact with Tatars, many Mari communities, especially Lowland Maris, became Muslim, but these groups became assimilated into Tatar society, and their descendants came to consider themselves Muslims and Tatars, rather than Maris.

Native Mari religion has been in a process of transformation since it was first described by European travelers in the 18th century. Nevertheless, certain fundamental features endure. The focus of Mari religion is the community, and the rituals and offerings characteristic of Mari religion are intended to preserve the health and prosperity of the community. As a result, rituals are closely bound with the agricultural calendar, especially since the majority of Maris today remain rural dwellers. Rituals include sacrifices of livestock at sacred groves to ensure that the spirits protect the community. In addition, special attention is devoted to ancestral spirits, who are considered among the most important supernatural guardians of the community.

In recent times, native Mari religion has become a political force through the creation of a political organization for the adherents of the *chi marla vera*. This organization, called *Osh Mari Chi Mari*, seeks to legitimize Mari native religion and, against the protests of the Russian Orthodox Church, revitalize it.

6 MAJOR HOLIDAYS

Among Christian Maris, the most important holidays are *Kugeche* (Easter), and *Shoryk Yol* (Christmas), which involve church services, prayers, and feasting. Many Maris also observe *Aga Pairem*, a festival usually held in June after the spring planting and celebrated with offerings to the field spirits as well as feasting, dancing, and sports, especially horse racing. Despite the religious origins of this festival, many Maris celebrate it simply as a national or ethnic festival. Among the Eastern Mari, the most important festival is *Küsoto Payrem*. This usually involves the gathering of a number of villages over a two- or three-day period, and each day a specific number of animals is offered to the spirits for the protection of the community. Maris, especially those in urban areas, also celebrate the secular holidays of the Russian state, including New Year's Day (January 1), May Day (May1) and Victory Day (May 9).

7 RITES OF PASSAGE

The main life-cycle rituals are closely connected with native Mari religious traditions. Among Christian Maris, baptism is naturally an important moment in the life of a child, as it inaugurates the child into the Mari and Christian community. Traditional Mari weddings were typically complex affairs, and each community had its own traditions and its own variants in the rituals. Often the groom or his family would pay a bride-price to the bride's family, and the bride would move in with her husband or in-laws. Despite the difficulties for the bride of leaving her home, weddings were usually festive occasions and involved much feasting and drinking. Today, traditional weddings have become scarce, in favor of simpler Soviet-style civil weddings.

Burial rituals and memorial feasts are perhaps the rites of passage that changed the least over the Soviet period, because they are so closely connected with the veneration of ancestors so central to Mari religious life. Traditionally, Mari burial ceremonies included the placing of grave goods (such as food, household goods, tools, and so forth) in the grave. This practice is rarely encountered among Christian Maris, but it is still encountered among non-Christian Maris. In addition to the burial ceremony, funeral repasts are commonly held for the dead, especially on the 3rd, 7th, and especially the 40th day after death. The 40th-day repast is called *nylle* in Mari. Eastern Maris believe that, on the 3rd day, the soul of the deceased goes from the house to the cemetery. On the 40th day, they lead the soul back to the house, offering it vodka, pancakes, and eggs, and the family offers prayers that the deceased should be released to the land of the ancestors. Among the Christian Highland Maris, the *nylle* is observed by the family reading prayers, lighting candles, and holding a feast for the soul of the deceased.

8 INTERPERSONAL RELATIONS

Maris typically greet one another with the words "*salam lijzhe*," and they commonly shake hands or embrace. Guests, especially those from far away, are generally respected and honored. Hospitality is considered an important obligation among Maris.

In traditional Mari life, young people socialized during specific festivals, and there was no dating in the modern sense of the term; rather, matches were usually arranged through matchmakers or parents. In modern times, these customs have been largely eroded, especially in urban areas.

9 LIVING CONDITIONS

Traditionally, Mari standards of living were low. Mari communities were remote and often afflicted with poverty as well as periodic famines and epidemics, including throughout much of the Soviet period. Currently, Mari rural poverty continues to be a problem, and living conditions in rural areas are generally not good, while in urban areas they are somewhat better. In rural areas, Mari houses tend to be built out of wood, moss, and clay. The houses generally have two or three rooms, and around the house there are usually various outbuildings such as barns, storage sheds, and bath houses. Such Mari houses usually have electricity, but almost never running water. Water is usually obtained from wells, communal pumps, or nearby streams. Houses are heated with wood, and in the center of every house there is a large brick or clay stove that functions as a furnace, stove, and oven. Maris in rural areas usually have their own fowl, livestock, and gardens, and much of their food is derived from these sources. In urban areas Maris usually live in small apartments that have running water and electricity, but, as throughout the former Soviet Union, the shortage of apartments is a serious problem.

In urban areas, health care is usually available, although the quality can be extremely variable. In rural areas, especially in remote areas, health care can be difficult to access, if not lacking outright. In both rural and urban areas, Maris still make use of herbal medicine and traditional healers, and Mari folk medicine can at times be both effective and sophisticated.

10 FAMILY LIFE

Traditional Mari families were large and organized into extended families. There was no formal clan or tribal system as such, as there was among the Maris' neighbors, the Udmurts and the Bashkirs. However, the Maris did form groups of extended families descended from common ancestors. These "clans" and extended families maintained small shrines for their ancestral spirits where family members would go and pray either individually or collectively. Today Mari families are small and typically include only one or two children.

In traditional Mari society, much of the agricultural work fell on the shoulders of women, in addition to their child-rearing and domestic duties. Marriages were usually arranged by matchmakers acting as intermediaries for the parents, and the groom or his parents were obligated to pay a bride-price to the bride's family. After the wedding, the bride would move in with her husband, thus being forced to leave her family and village.

11 CLOTHING

Maris traditionally wove their own cloth and made their own clothing. Mari clothing, especially in summer, was made of linen and was usually white. In winter, the Maris would wear garments made of wool and reversed sheep-skin. In the past, the Eastern Maris often dressed in the Tatar fashion, with longish buttoned gowns and Muslim skull-caps. Women's traditional clothing was elaborate, usually made of white linen with extensive embroideries. Traditional clothing is still worn to some degree, especially in the villages of the Eastern Maris, where women can still be seem wearing the traditional Mari headgear. Today, however, most Maris dress in clothes typical of modern Russian society as a whole.

12 FOOD

The traditional Mari diet consisted of cereals and vegetables supplemented by meat (especially poultry and pork), fish, and forest products such as berries and honey. The main staples of the Maris diet are rye bread, groats, and milk. More recently, an important staple crop is potatoes, which are grown both in rural areas and in the suburban gardens of city dwellers. Beverages include tea and vodka, as well as home-made alcoholic beverages such as beer.

Mari cooking was traditionally done in iron pots on the large brick stove located in the middle of the house. Eating utensils (especially spoons, cups, and plates) were carved out of wood. There are usually three meals a day, with the main meal in the early afternoon.

13 EDUCATION

Today, literacy among Maris is very high and nearly universal. Before World War II, and especially in pre-Soviet times, illiteracy among the Maris was high, especially among the Lowland and Eastern Maris and among Mari women in general. This high rate of illiteracy was the result of several factors, including the remoteness and isolation of many Mari settlements and the fact that a Mari literary language had only been marginally developed. The schools that did exist in pre-Soviet times were primarily administered by Russian Orthodox missionaries and were most numerous among the Highland Maris. The Eastern Maris, among whom the Russian missionary presence was very low, had only limited access to the Islamic education offered by their Tatar neighbors, and in these areas it was not uncommon for Maris to make use of Tatar as a literary language.

During the Soviet period, and especially after World War II, education became more widely available among the Maris, although much of this education used Russian as the language of instruction, thereby accelerating the assimilation of the Maris into Russian society and Russian culture. At this time, higher education also became available to Maris, leading to the development of a small Mari intelligentsia.

14 CULTURAL HERITAGE

Before 1917, there was virtually no written Mari literature, with the exception of bible translations and other religious literature translated from Russian. The formal creation of a Soviet Mari intelligentsia led to the creation of Mari literature, which included both journalistic prose and fiction, as well as poetry and, to a limited extent, drama. Since the advent of *perestroika* and the collapse of the Soviet Union, Mari writers have been able to openly discuss national and social issues.

15 WORK

In traditional Mari life, labor was organized to some degree along the lines of the clan and extended family. However, with the violent collectivization of the Mari peasantry in the 1930s, this kinship-based labor structure was replaced with a government-organized collective system, which essentially remains in place today.

16 SPORTS

In the past, Mari religious festivals included sporting events such as horse racing and wrestling, and to some extent this remains the case today. In addition to these traditional sports, hockey and soccer are the main recreational sports among young people and are the main spectator sports among the population in general.

17 ENTERTAINMENT AND RECREATION

Religious festivals, weddings, and other gatherings were important sources for entertainment and recreation in traditional Mari life. Today, television and movies are important sources of entertainment.

18 FOLK ART, CRAFTS AND HOBBIES

Since the Maris inhabit a densely forested region, they are especially skilled in woodworking, especially wood carving. A popular hobby in rural areas is beekeeping, which is also an important supplementary economic activity.

19 SOCIAL PROBLEMS

One of the most serious social problems facing the Maris today is alcoholism, which is rampant, especially in rural areas, where recreational opportunities are few. Alcoholism is common among both men and women. Alcohol is readily available in shops and also prepared in homes. Mari society is also adversely affected by the unemployment and low wages characteristic of Russia's current overall economic crisis during the 1990's. Since 2000 economic conditions have improved to some degree, although rural poverty remains a significant problem.

[20] GENDER ISSUES

In traditional Mari society, particularly up until World War II, women and men had sharply divided social, economic and religious roles. Women were mainly responsible for child-rearing, domestic duties, and a portion of agricultural production. Before the 1940's Mari women had only the most limited access to education, and as a result literacy was extremely rare among Mari women. World War II brought large numbers of Mari women into the industrial and urban workforce, and into the Soviet educational system, after which they largely remained in the workforce, while retaining their traditional roles in child-rearing and domestic duties. Their limited access to education also made Mari women particularly culturally conservative, especially in terms of native language use and religious activities. Certain religious ceremonies excluded either men or women, but more generally it was women who retained religious ceremonies and practices, despite official anti-religious pressure from the authorities during the Soviet era. Since 1991 Mari women have largely maintained their access to education.

[21] BIBLIOGRAPHY

Frank, Allen. "Traditional Religion in the Volga-Ural Region: 1960-1987." *Ural-Altaische Jahrbücher* 63 (1991): 167–184.

———. "Mari Language Sources on Mari Religious Practices in the Soviet Period." *Eurasian Studies Yearbook* 66 (1994): 77–87.

Lallukka, Seppo. *East Finnic Minorities in the Soviet Union: An Appraisal of the Erosive Trends.* Helsinki: Suomalainen tiedeakatemia, 1990.

———. *From Fugitive Peasants to Diaspora: The Eastern Mari in Tsarist and Federal Russia.* Helsinki: Suomalainen tiedeakatemia, 2003.

Sanukov, K. N. *Problemy istorii i vozrozhdeniia finno-ugorskikh narodov Rossii.* Ioshkar-Ola, 1994.

Toidybekova, Lidiia, *Mariiskaia izycheskaia vera i etnicheskoe samosoznanie.* Joensuu, 1997.

Vuorela, Toivo. "The Cheremis." In: *The Finno-Ugric Peoples.* Indiana University Uralic and Altaic Series, No. 39 Bloomington, IN, 1964, 237–264.

Werth, Paul. "Big Candles and 'Internal Conversion': The Mari Animist Reformation and its Russian Appropriations." *Of Religion and Empire: Missions, Conversion, and Tolerance in Tsarist Russia.* Ithaca: Cornell University Press, 2001, 144-172.

— by A. J. Frank

MOLDOVANS

LOCATION: Moldova
POPULATION: 4.3 million, total population of country; 78% are ethnic Moldovans
LANGUAGE: Moldovan (Romanian); Russian
RELIGION: Russian Orthodox Church; Judaism

[1] INTRODUCTION

The ancient Dacians are believed to be the first people to set up communities in the area now known as Moldova. The Dacians were farmers who organized themselves in family groups and settled in the land between the Dniester and Danube Rivers around 2000 BC. By the 7th century BC, the Dacians had established commercial trading posts on the coast of the Black Sea and were trading with the Greeks. In the first century BC, the Dacians were conquered by the Roman Empire, and their homeland became part of the province known as Dacia.

The Romans lost power in AD 271 because of the steady immigration of people into the region from the north and east, making the province too difficult to control. After the Romans left, a free-for-all began as Slavic invaders came from the east. The territory was divided, with the eastern part dominated by the Kievan Rus state. Several groups occupied the area over the next few centuries, including the Huns, Ostrogoths, Slavic Antes, the Bulgarian Empire, Magyars, and the Pechenegs. Mongol dominion lasted from the mid-13th to mid-14th centuries. Hungary was also moving into the area, building fortifications along the Siretul River. In 1349, Prince Bogdan established an independent Moldovan principality, which was under the power of Hungary. The new principality, originally called Bogdania, stretched from the Carpathian Mountains to the Nistru River. It was later renamed Moldova, after the Moldova River that flows through present-day Romania.

By the 15th century, there was enough unity among the people for the emergence of the Principality of Moldavia. This realm consisted of all of Bessarabia (the land between the Prut and Dniester rivers) and part of present-day Romania. It was during this time that Stephen the Great (Stefan cel Mare, 1457–1504) fought against the encroaching Ottoman Empire. Stephen the Great has become a revered national hero and a symbol of Moldovan unity and sovereignty. He built many churches and monasteries to commemorate his victories over the Turks. Most of them still exist and are visited by large numbers of people. A statue of Stephen the Great stands in the main square in Chisinau, and the main boulevard of the city bears his name.

Independence for the principality was fleeting, and Moldova fell to Ottoman control in 1512 and remained an Ottoman territory for the next three centuries. During the 1700s and 1800s, the Russian Empire battled against the Ottoman Turk Empire for control over the region. In 1711, imperial Russian troops under Peter the Great first occupied Bessarabia but eventually had to give up the territory to the Ottoman Turks. This pattern of conquest and retreat by the Russians happened three more times during the 1700s. In 1812, the Treaty of Bucharest finally forced the Turks to formally hand over Bessarabia to the Russians.

In 1856, after Russia lost the Crimean War, it had to give back Bessarabia to Moldavia, which at the time was operating as a self-governing principality within the Ottoman Empire. In 1858, a union of the Moldovan territory west of the Prut River with Walachia formed the foundation for the modern state of Romania. The de facto union of Romania was accomplished with the election of Alexandru Ioan Cuza as single prince of Moldova and Walachia in January 1859. When Russia won the Turkish War in 1878, it again reclaimed the territory and held on to it until the collapse of the Russian imperial government in 1917.

When the Bolsheviks toppled the Russian imperial government in 1917, an independence movement sprang up in Bessarabia, and the National Moldavian Committee (NMC) was formed. The NMC sought to unite the region with Romania and implemented policies of land reform and official use of the Romanian language. On 9 December 1918 the Bessarabian independent government voted for a total union with Romania, which was recognized by the Treaty of Paris. The Soviet Union, however, never recognized Romania's sovereignty over Bessarabia. In 1924, the Soviet Union created the Moldavian Autonomous Soviet Socialist Republic on the left bank of the Dniester River (which was Ukrainian territory), even though its population was only 30% ethnic Romanian.

In 1939, Hitler formally accepted that Bessarabia was Soviet territory as a concession to appease the Soviet dictator Stalin. The Soviet government formally created the Moldavian Soviet Socialist Republic on 2 August 1940. During World War II, Romania fought against the Soviet Union to regain control over the region. By 1944, however, Soviet troops were occupying Bessarabia and all of Romania as well. Since Romania had no allies, it had to submit to Soviet demands. As a result, the Soviet Union reestablished the territorial arrangements of 1940. One of the most detrimental consequences of the Soviet regime was the forced collectivization of agriculture (the transformation of private farming into state agricultural enterprises). The refusal of many farmers to give their land and cattle to the state resulted in mass deportations to Siberia. Only the strongest managed to survive the long trip and the rough conditions of the Siberian wilderness. The ones who stayed in Moldova had to cope with a wave of severe famine in 1945–47, caused by drought, crop failure, and poor government policies.

The Soviet authorities changed the name of the Romanian language, spoken by the majority of the population, into Moldavian and its alphabet from Latin to Cyrillic (the alphabet of Russia). For approximately 45 years, Moldovans had limited access to their history and culture.

At the end of the 1980s, a new independence movement called the Popular Front of Moldavia (PFM) arose. The PFM demanded the end of Communist rule, propagated the revival of the Romanian language and culture, and wanted to again unite the republic with Romania. In 1989, the government restored the use of the Latin alphabet, abolished the official use of the Cyrillic alphabet of Russian, and officially changed the name to the Republic of Moldova. In 1991 Moldova was one of the first republics of the former Soviet Union to declare its independence.

However, the Russian-speaking minorities felt threatened by a possible unification with Romania, even though a new Moldovan law guaranteed equal rights to all ethnic minorities. As a result, two self-proclaimed, breakaway republics, the

Trans-Dniester on the eastern bank of the Dniester River, and Gagauzia in the south, were formed in 1990. The situation in the Trans-Dniester erupted in violence in 1992. Eventually the Gagauz region obtained local administrative independence, while the Trans-Dniester has not yet been recognized either by the government of Moldova or by any other government or international organization.

In 2000, the Moldovan parliament passed a law making Moldova a parliamentary republic with its president elected by parliament rather than by popular vote. The people of Moldova voted the Communist Party into power in 2001, but in the years since the Communists have steadily lost ground to opposition parties. Most of the economy and agricultural land has been successfully privatized.

2 LOCATION AND HOMELAND

The tradition of the Moldovan homeland is really that of historic Bessarabia—the land between the Prut and Dniester rivers in the southwestern corner of the former Soviet Union. One of the smallest of the former Soviet republics, Moldova's entire landmass amounts to only about 33,670 sq km (13,000 sq mi), making it only slightly larger than the U.S. state of Maryland. Most of the terrain consists of hilly plains with many rivers and streams. In the west, the Prut River forms the boundary with

Romania, and the Dniester River marks part of the boundary with Ukraine in the east. The Stepa Balti (Balti Plain) is in northern Moldova. The highest point is Mount Balenesti (in the west-central part of Moldova), which rises to 430 m (1,400 ft) above sea level. About 75% of Moldova is covered by a highly rich type of fertile black soil known as *chernozem*. Much of the rich soil lies in the lower elevations and plains of the Budzak Steppe in the south. The climate is continental, with summer temperatures averaging around 20°C (68°F) and winter temperatures averaging –4°C (25°F). Annual precipitation can fluctuate widely in the north, averaging around 40–60 cm (16–24 in). Flash-flooding often occurs in summer because of the uneven topography.

Today, about 78% of Moldova's 4.3 million inhabitants are ethnic Moldovans. Moldova has historically been home to a large number of ethnic groups, such as Russians, Ukrainians, Gagauz (a Turkish group of the Christian faith), Gypsies, Jews, Poles, and Germans. Although Moldova was the most densely populated of all the former Soviet republics, its people are traditionally rural, and there are few large cities.

³ LANGUAGE

The language spoken in Moldova is Romanian, though it is called Moldovan by an amendment to the Moldovan Constitution. Romanian is similar to Italian, Spanish, French, and Portuguese, as a member of the eastern division of the Romance languages of the Indo-European family. Moldovan was written in the Cyrillic alphabet during the Soviet era in order to legitimize the claim that it was a separate language from Romanian. Many archaic and obsolete words that had Russian origins were reintroduced, along with modern Russian slang and phrases. Names of persons and places were also Russianized during the Soviet years. After independence, however, the Moldovans named the official language as "Moldovan," to be written in Latin script. The Russian language is still heard in Chisinau, the capital, almost as often as Romanian.

Mihai, Ion, Mircea, Octavian, and Andrei are common boys' names, and Elena, Angela, Diana, Christina, and Liliana are common girls' names. Examples of everyday Romanian words include *noroc* (hello), *buna ziua* (good afternoon), *da* (yes), *nu* (no), *poftim* (please), *multumesc* (thank you) and *la revedere* (goodbye).

⁴ FOLKLORE

Moldova has an extensive history of folklore, consisting of ballads, songs, tales, jokes, riddles, dances, and games. The ancient folk ballad "Miorita" is the most prominent of all in traditional Moldovan culture. It provides an insight into the philosophical and moral values of the Moldovan people. Its rhyme reveals the melodiousness and beauty of the Romanian language.

Ileana Cosinzeana and Fat Frumos are the romantic couple present in a number of fairy tales, in which the brave Fat Frumos frees the beautiful and kind Ileana Cosinzeana from the evil dragon and they live happily ever after. Pacala and Tindala are two funny men that are the characters of hundreds of jokes.

⁵ RELIGION

Because of the influence of Romanian culture, most Moldovans (98%) associate with the Orthodox Church, although there are also some Uniates. Before the Soviet era, most ethnic Romanians in Moldova belonged to the Romanian Orthodox Church, but the Russian Orthodox Church maintains jurisdiction over the area today. The Orthodox Church in Moldova today conducts liturgies in Russian, Romanian, and Turkic (Gagauz). Moldova has over 1,000 Orthodox churches and dozens of Orthodox monasteries. There are also 15 Old Believers churches (a breakaway Orthodox sect dating from the 17th century). In 1992, the Moldovan government guaranteed freedom of religion but required that all religious groups be officially registered with the government. The registration process has prevented many groups from practicing freely, and the international community continues to urge the Moldovan government to reform the situation.

A pogrom (an organized persecution or massacre) against Moldovan Jews in 1903 severely reduced the urban Jewish population. Jews in Moldova were also harassed during the Soviet era. In the early 1990s, many Jewish newspapers were started, and a synagogue and Jewish high school opened in Chisinau. Also, the Chisinau State University created a Department of Jewish Studies. Current estimates place the Jewish population of Moldova at about 24,000.

⁶ MAJOR HOLIDAYS

The major holidays celebrated widely in Moldova are the traditional Christian holidays, such as Christmas and Easter. Christmas is celebrated in much the same way as in Western countries, although it is less commercialized. Easter is a family holiday, when women bake a special kind of bread called *pasca* and paint eggs red.

Each village has its own holiday once a year, called *hram* (church). It celebrates the establishment of the village church. By now it has lost some of its religious character, becoming a special day when each family prepares a lot of delicious food and receives guests from other villages or towns. It is the day of family reunions, fun, and friendship.

Independence Day is on August 27, when Moldova declared its independence from the Soviet Union. It is a national holiday. *Sarbatoarea Limbii Noastre* (National Language Day) is on August 31 and marks the day when Romanian became the state language of Moldova and changed back to the Latin alphabet. During this day, people go out to attend outside concerts and book fairs.

⁷ RITES OF PASSAGE

Christian baptism is an important rite of passage for Moldovan children and their parents. High school graduation usually marks a turning point where a young Moldovan is faced with a dilemma: either to begin work or to continue school in preparation for the university. Many also begin to consider marriage after graduation, because the completion of high school marks the end of childhood and the beginning of adulthood. As with many other cultures, the wedding ceremony formally distinguishes the union of the couple and the joining of their families.

⁸ INTERPERSONAL RELATIONS

Social relations in urban and rural areas differ from each other. In villages, even people who do not know each other are supposed to say "Buna ziua" (Good day) to each other. In big towns and cities, only acquaintances greet each other. In formal settings, adults greet each other with "Buna ziua." Men shake hands and may also kiss the women's hands. Kissing a woman's hand, when introduced to her or when meeting on formal and semiformal occasions, is an old custom that has survived in Romania and was reintroduced to Moldova after it became independent.

Young people usually greet each other with "Salut" or "Noroc," which are the Romanian equivalents of "Hi" and "Hello." Close friends may hug and kiss each other on the cheek. Family and relatives greet each other with hugs and kisses. It is very common for parents to kiss and hug their children.

⁹ LIVING CONDITIONS

The instability following the end of the Soviet Union has significantly affected public health in Moldova. The birth rate in 2008 was 11.01 per 1,000 people (down from 16.1 in 1992), and the death rate in 2008 was 10.8 per 1,000 people (up from 9.2 in 1992). Infant mortality was 13.5 deaths per 1,000 live births in 2008. There is a lack of modern medical facilities and equipment. The leading causes of death among Moldovans are cardiovascular diseases, cancer, respiratory diseases, and accidents. Major health problems include high levels of alcohol consumption and both respiratory and digestive illnesses related to the overuse of herbicides and pesticides.

The rural culture of Moldova has always placed a high value on private housing. During the Soviet years, much of the housing stock was in fact held by private citizens. Most of the urban housing units were built in the years immediately following World War II, because the cities had been heavily bombed. When Moldova became independent in 1991, there was a severe shortage of building materials and an unreliable delivery system. Private builders accounted for only 26% of construction in urban areas, but for 95% in rural places. During 1993–95, most state-owned housing was privatized through a system of vouchers in order to create an open housing market. Today, about 80% of housing units are privately owned.

Railroads are an important means of transportation for many Moldovans. Tracks link most of the cities within Moldova, and railroads also connect with Odessa (in Ukraine) on the Black Sea and with several Romanian cities. Highways link most of the cities and are the primary means of getting around Moldova. However, poor road maintenance and an unreliable gasoline supply often make it difficult to drive from one city to another. Most Moldovan towns have at least 1,000 inhabitants and are connected to public utilities. Chisinau offers an extensive public transport system, and the city is serviced by an international airport and train station. In Chisinau's older sections, narrow, winding streets and alleys are lined with bungalow-style houses that are more reminiscent of Bulgaria and Romania than of the former Soviet Union.

¹⁰ FAMILY LIFE

At the beginning of the 20th century, families with 5–9 children were common in Moldova, but that is not the case anymore. Most couples decide to have only one or two children. This can be explained by economic insecurity and by the fact that usually both parents work full-time and are not able to take care of more children. Family connections are quite strong due to longstanding traditions, but also because of financial dependence. Children depend on the support of their parents for a long time, even after they get married. Parents

A Moldovan man fishes on a frozen lake on the outskirts of Chisinau, Moldova. (AP Images/Vadim Ghirda)

count on the help of their children when they retire. Quite often grandparents dedicate themselves to babysitting.

The distribution of family duties between men and women is uneven, as women have more responsibilities. Most women work full-time, take care of their children, and do most of the shopping, cooking, laundry, and cleaning. Men usually spend most of their time at work. It is not common for men to cook or do the dishes or the laundry. In spite of all difficulties, a lot of women manage to build careers by finding a balance between their jobs and household chores.

¹¹ CLOTHING

The traditional national costume has become obsolete. It can only be found in museums, as well as in some families that passed the costumes from generation to generation. The female's traditional garment consists of a white embroidered blouse, a vest embroidered and furnished with sheep fleece on the edges and a white skirt with lace on the hem, usually covered by a black embroidered overskirt.

The male costume consists of a white embroidered shirt, a vest similar to the women's, white pants, a hat decorated with peacock feathers or flowers, or a sheep fleece cap, and a wide belt. The belt can be made of leather or cloth and is usually embroidered. Both men and women wear a special kind of shoes, called *opinci*. They are made of pieces of leather, wrapped around the feet, with leather laces tied around the ankles.

The costumes used to be entirely handmade. Every young girl was supposed to be able to weave cloth and to do elaborate embroidery. Now, only folk music and dance groups wear national costumes, but most of them are mass-produced. Some elements of the costume, such as the handmade embroidery, periodically come into fashion.

People who live in cities and towns dress like other Eastern or Western Europeans. Jeans and tee-shirts are popular with teenagers and young people. It is common to dress up when going out to the theater, or on other formal occasions.

The everyday clothes of people who live in villages are fit for farming work. Women wear flowery cotton or flannel dresses, depending on the season, and flowered kerchiefs on their heads. Men wear shirts and pants made of durable cloth, and caps or hats.

12 FOOD

To most former Soviet citizens, the mention of Moldova immediately brings to mind *Moldavskoe vino* (Moldavian wine). Moldova's mild climate and fertile land is home to many well-known vineyards in the hills. Moldovans take great pride in their tradition of wine-making, and homemade wines are common. Sparkling wines and brandies are also produced.

The local bazaar is the distribution method used for supplying fresh fruits and vegetables. The availability of fruit and vegetables depends on the season. Most of the ingredients used for typical meals grow in Moldova. A typical breakfast may consist of a sandwich, a piece of cake, an omelet, or porridge, with tea, coffee, or milk. Lunch is an important meal of the day, consisting of a starter, soup, and a hot dish. Dinner may also be a hot meal, or may be lighter than lunch.

Traditional Moldovan dishes resemble the cuisine of the neighboring countries. Stuffed cabbage or grape leaves are considered part of the national cuisine, as well as *placinte,* a special pastry filled with cheese, potatoes, cherries, cabbage, etc. *Coltunasi* resembles ravioli. *Mamaliga* is a hard corn porridge, eaten with sheep cheese, farm cheese, an omelet, fish, fried meat, sour cream, or milk.

13 EDUCATION

During the Soviet years, ethnic Russian and Ukrainian students were given educational preference, which meant that there were few Moldovans in higher education at that time. Since independence, the Moldovan government has put in place reforms to promote higher education for all citizens. Moldova has an extensive system of primary and secondary schools, and most children go to a preschool before entering the primary grades. Literacy is nearly universal (99%). Moldova's educational system requires students to complete 10 years of basic education. After that, students may choose from either a technical school or a university preparation track.

Since independence, the Moldovan government has restored the Romanian language as the language of instruction and has added classes in Romanian literature and history to the curriculum. There are also student exchange programs with Romania, and several thousand Moldovans are now enrolled in Romanian schools. The government has also replaced old Soviet textbooks with new ones donated by the Romanian government. Ethnic minorities have the right to education in their own languages, and there are many schools with instruction in Russian and other languages. Perhaps the most unique

educational institution in Moldova is the 150-year-old College of Wine Culture, which graduates about 300 students from all over Eastern Europe each year.

14 CULTURAL HERITAGE

Moldovan music, dance, and arts share many traits with their Romanian counterparts. For example, Moldovans often play the *cobza,* a wooden stringed instrument similar to the lute that is common in traditional Romanian music.

The Moldovan government has a leading role in the promotion of folk culture through Joc, the national dance company, and Doina, the national folk choir. There are numerous semiprofessional and amateur dance and music groups that perform around the country as well. There are a number of professional theaters, most of which perform in Romanian.

During the Soviet era, Soviet authorities split Moldovan culture along urban and rural lines, with the urban culture influenced by ethnic Russians and the rural culture influenced by ethnic Romanians. The Soviet government encouraged the cultural arts in Moldova but sometimes distorted certain aspects to camouflage the Romanian heritage.

Moldova shares most of its literary heritage with Romania, and sometimes it is difficult to draw a dividing line between Romanian and Moldovan literature. The 19th century produced many outstanding Romanian authors, such as the poet Mihai Eminescu; the storyteller Ion Creanga; the linguist, writer, and historian Bogdan Petriceicu Hasdeu; the literary critic Titu Maiorescu; and many others. World-renowned Romanian writers and philosophers such as Mircea Eliade and Lucian Blaga are widely studied and respected by Moldovans.

15 WORK

Moldova remains largely an agricultural country, with over 40% of workers employed in agricultural jobs. Service jobs now account for almost 50% of the labor force, however, with industry employing only 12%. The official unemployment rate in 2007 was 2.1%, but 25% of the labor force was employed abroad.

In villages, children begin to help their parents around the house, or on the farm, at an early age. In the city, high school graduates start working when they are around 17 and college graduates at around 22. Many students, however, have part-time jobs.

During the Soviet regime, there was an extensive system of social welfare that provided good pensions for retirees. Because of inflation since independence, the pensions became insufficient for meeting basic needs. The Moldovan government has put programs in place to improve the situation.

A working day lasts 8–9 hours, and the work week is from Monday through Friday.

16 SPORTS

Soccer is popular with youths and adults, both for playing and watching as spectators.

17 ENTERTAINMENT AND RECREATION

Attending family and friends' reunions, the theater, concerts, movies, and discos are typical forms of recreation. The numerous public parks of Chisinau are wonderful recreation spots. On vacations many people travel to the Romanian or the

Ukrainian seaside or mountains. Traveling abroad, however, is affordable only to a small percentage of the population.

¹⁸ FOLK ART, CRAFTS, AND HOBBIES

Pottery, woodcarving, carpet-weaving, and metalwork are the most famous Moldovan handicrafts.

¹⁹ SOCIAL PROBLEMS

Moldovans face many of the same economic problems as the other former Soviet republics in the transition to a market-oriented economy. The economic transformations brought with them inflation, price deregulation, unemployment, and the weakening of the social welfare system. Wages could not keep up with the increase in prices, plunging many people of Moldova into poverty. Moldova is now one of the poorest countries in Europe, with almost one-third of the population falling beneath the poverty line in 2008. Retirees, single parents, and the unemployed have been the most vulnerable groups. Black-market activities brought fast wealth to some Moldovans, and caused a deep sense of unfairness about the present wealth distribution. The roads suffer from long-term neglect, and the telephone system is inadequate and unreliable.

There is still some tension with the two regions within the country that have declared their independence from Moldova. The Gagauz region in the south declared the "Gagauz Republic" as a separate nation in 1990. The Gagauz are Turkic-speaking Orthodox Christians who live mainly in and around the southern cities of Comrat, Ciadîr-Lunga, and Vulcanesti. The other region that broke away consists of a large number of Russian-speakers living on the eastern bank of the Nistru River who proclaimed the establishment of the "Dniester Republic" in 1990. In 1994, the Moldovan Constitution gave both groups more political freedom and granted them home-rule. This autonomy has eased tensions in the Gagauz region. However, the Trans-Dniester government is supported by the military presence of Russian troops, who agreed to withdraw but have yet to do so. Conflicts over the Trans-Dniester region continue to cause problems for Moldova.

Environmental problems in Moldova are a legacy of Soviet mismanagement. The liberal use of pesticides, herbicides, and artificial fertilizers was designed to increase crop output despite the ecological repercussions. Today, Moldova's groundwater and soil are contaminated with chemicals, some of which (such as DDT) were shown to be harmful long ago. In addition, deforestation has contributed to the ongoing soil erosion problem. Moldova has ratified a number of international agreements to address environmental problems, including the Kyoto Protocol.

As elsewhere in the former Soviet Union, crime has become more frequent in Moldova. Crimes motivated by money or drugs have become the most prominent, and it is believed that many more of these crimes go unreported. Opium poppies and cannabis (marijuana) are grown illegally in Moldova and exported to other former Soviet republics through the black market. Moldova has also become an important transfer point for illegal drugs headed for Western Europe.

²⁰ GENDER ISSUES

Because of its entrenched poverty, Moldova is a major source of sexual trafficking in women and children, as well as illegal trafficking in children and men for forced labor. Lack of economic prospects makes Moldovans vulnerable to offers of jobs or marriage in other countries, only to find themselves sold into slavery of one form or another. Trafficking even occurs within Moldova's own boundaries, between the destitute rural areas and Chisinau, the capital city. In recent years, the Moldovan government has begun to put in place programs to confront and reduce illegal trafficking, but with the persistence of Moldova's economic woes, the root cause of trafficking will take some time to eradicate.

Although homosexual acts were legalized in Moldova in 1995, there are no laws specifically against discrimination or harassment of homosexuals. Homophobia remains rampant, and both verbal and physical abuse of homosexuals is not uncommon.

²¹ BIBLIOGRAPHY

Amnesty International. "Eastern Europe: Crucible of Hate," http://action.web.ca/home/lgbt/databank.shtml?x=106123 (25 August 2008).

Fedor, Helen, ed. *Belarus and Moldova: Country Studies.* Lanham, MD: Federal Research Division, Library of Congress, 1995.

Moldova.org, http://www.moldova.org/index/eng (25 August 2008).

U.S. Central Intelligence Agency. "Moldova." *The World Factbook,* https://www.cia.gov/library/publications/the-world-factbook/print/md.html (25 August 2008).

U.S. Department of State. "Background Note: Moldova," http://www.state.gov/r/pa/ei/bgn/5357.htm (25 August 2008).

World Health Organization. "Highlights on Health, Republic of Moldova," http://www.euro.who.int/eprise/main/who/progs/chhmda/home (25 August 2008).

—revised by Dianne de Mott

MONÉGASQUES

LOCATION: Monaco
POPULATION: 34,000
LANGUAGE: French (official), also Monégasque, Italian and English
RELIGION: Roman Catholic; small number of Jewish and Church of England residents

¹ INRODUCTION

Next to Vatican City, the Principality of Monaco (*Principauté de Monaco* in French and *Principatu de Múnegu* in the native *Monégasque* tongue) is the world's smallest independent state. It is located on the northern coast of the Mediterranean, surrounded on three sides by France, and on the fourth side by the sea, only 8 km (5 mi) from the French-Italian border. Monaco is a Constitutional Monarchy and Principality with Prince Albert II as the head of state. Monaco's defense is the responsibility of France, and its foreign policy is aligned with that of the French Republic. The principality is the smallest of all French-speaking countries and the world's most densely populated state. Its climate is Mediterranean, with mild, wet winters and hot, dry summers.

There is ample evidence of Stone Age settlements on the territory of today's Monaco but its first known inhabitants were probably the ancient Ligurians. Throughout antiquity, this area was called "Port Herakles" for an ancient god known in Greek as "Herakles Monoikos" (or "Herakles of the Single House") and a temple that was dedicated to him there. The Greek geographer Strabo describes the place as "The Port of Monoikos." In the Roman Empire Monaco was part of the Province of the Maritime Alps and after the fall of the Empire it was invaded by various tribes of barbarians, among them the Saracens. In 1215 the Genoese Ghibellines, supporters of Emperor Henry VI, attracted by the strategic advantages of Monaco's harbor, lay the first stone of the fortress, the foundation of today's Prince's Palace. Eager to attract residents, they granted the new arrivals exemptions from taxes and important land privileges. In the next three centuries Monaco would become a site of continuous strife between the Ghibellins, supporters of the Emperor, and the Guelphs, supporters of the Pope. One of the most prominent Genoese Guelph families were the Grimaldis. In 1296 the family was expelled from Genoa and settled in Provence. From there, in 1297, with their small army, the Grimaldis seized the fortress and captured Monaco. They lost control over it in 1301 only to return in 1331. Charles Grimaldi, considered to be the real founder of the principality, then bought the neighboring lordships of Menton and Roquebrune; they would remain part of the principality until 1861. Yet, it took the Grimaldis nearly two centuries to establish their indisputable sovereignty over Monaco in 1489, when Charles VIII of France and the Duke of Savoy recognized its independence. In 1524 Monaco was placed under the protection of Spain, with grave financial consequences for the principality's treasury. The reign of Honoré II (1587–1662) marked the most brilliant period in Monaco's history. Honoré II firmly allied himself with France and in 1641 the French king Louis XIII signed a treaty placing Monaco under the friendly protection of France, but recognizing the independence of the country

with all its rights and privileges. The Spanish garrison was expelled and a French one installed in Monaco. In addition, the prince significantly enlarged and embellished the Palace and added art by the greatest European masters to its collections. Life at the court flowered, with numerous balls and ceremonies throughout the year.

After Honoré's death, the splendor of Monaco's courtly life greatly diminished and in 1731 the male line of the Grimaldis died out. Jacques-François-Léonor de Matignon, heir of one of the most illustrious families of Normandy, who had married into the Grimaldi family, was in 1731 named Prince of Monaco Jacques I, only to abdicate in 1733 in favor of his son, Honoré III. Honoré ruled Monaco until 1795, but spent more time in his Paris residence and in Normandy than in the principality. In 1789, after the outbreak of the French Revolution, Monaco's rulers, whose income largely depended on their fiefs in France, found themselves cut off from the considerable part of their financial resources. In February 1793 the principality was incorporated into France and the Palace—its works of art dispersed or sold—became a hospital and a home for the poor. Members of the prince's family were imprisoned and then freed; some even served in the French army. Following the abdication of Napoleon in 1814, sovereignty was restored in the principality. In 1815 the second Treaty of Paris placed it under the protection of the King of Sardinia, and the financial resources of the country were considerably diminished. In 1848 the communes of Menton and Roquebrune declared their independence and in 1861 Prince Charles III gave up his rights over these territories to France, reducing thus the principality to one-twentieth of its territory, in exchange for a large indemnity and guaranteed independence. Forced to find additional sources of revenue, in 1863 the prince established a gaming house under the name the *Société des Bains de Mer* (The Sea Baths Company). The revenue generated by the Company and the number of visitors exceeded even the most optimistic expectations, especially after 1868, following the construction of the railway line between Nice and Ventimiglia. It is indeed to Charles III and to his son Albert I that Monaco owes its most striking economic development. Albert I, who succeeded his father in 1889, was a world-famous oceanographer and paleontologist, one of the founders of modern oceanography, and a great pacifist. Arts prospered once again in the principality and in 1911 Albert I gave Monaco a constitution. His son, Louis II, succeeded him as the prince of Monaco in 1922. In 1943 the Italian army occupied Monaco, establishing a Fascist administration. After the fall of Mussolini's Italy, Germany occupied the principality and started to deport the resident Jewish population. Soon after the end of World War II, in 1949, Louis II was succeeded by his grandson Rainier III, issue of the marriage of Louis's only daughter Charlotte to Prince Pierre de Polignac, who adopted the name of Grimaldi upon his marriage.

Rainier III (1923–2005) was to be, with his 56-year long reign, one of the longest ruling monarchs of the 20th century. He drew international attention by his 1956 marriage to the American motion picture actress Grace Kelly. After ascending the throne of a country with a practically empty treasury, Rainier III worked assiduously on promoting Monaco as a tax haven and a sophisticated commercial and international tourist center. In 1962 he introduced a new constitution that reduced the power of the sovereign, abolished capital punishment, and granted voting rights to women. He became popularly known as "The Builder Prince," working tirelessly to transform Monaco into a thriving international business, sports, tourism, and culture center, and launching in 1965 the land reclamation project to increase his country's small territory. Rainier was equally dedicated to establishing Monaco's status in the international community and in 1993 the principality become the 183rd member of the United Nations. With the contribution of Princess Grace, Monaco became an international cultural center, attracting visitors and celebrities from all over the world. After the princess was killed in a 1982 car accident, her eldest child, Princess Caroline, assumed her mother's official duties. Rainer III died in April 2005 and the enthronement of Prince Albert II took place in July of the same year. Princess Caroline of Hanover (as she has been officially known after her 1999 marriage to Prince Ernst-August of Hanover, grandson of the last German Emperor) continues to represent Monaco in her country and abroad and is UNESCO's goodwill ambassador for the education of young girls and women. Through AMADE (World Association of Children's Friends), founded in 1963 by Princess Grace, she continues to promote children's rights around the world, especially in Africa and Asia. Princess Stéphanie, the youngest of the three children of Rainier III and Princess Grace, after pursuing a career as a pop singer and fashion designer, became involved in the battle against AIDS as a UNAIDS ambassador. She is also the founding president of "Fight Aids Monaco," an organization she established to help people living with HIV. The Foundation Prince Albert II of Monaco, created by Prince Albert II, has as its goal the protection of the environment and funding research on sustainable development at the international level.

2 LOCATION AND HOMELAND

Monaco is situated at France's southeastern-most corner, near the Italian border. With an area of 1.97 sq km (0.76 sq mi) it is roughly the size of New York City's Central Park. Its coastline is 4.1 km (2.5 mi) long. The principality is divided into four traditional quarters. Monaco-Ville, the oldest section, is the site of the prince's palace, which is located on a promontory called *le Rocher* (the Rock), the gardens, Saint Nicholas Cathedral, and the Oceanographic museum. The Condamine is the second oldest area of Monaco, situated in the northwest corner of the principality. Monte-Carlo, created in 1866 and named by Prince Charles III, is the main luxury resort area and home to Monaco's famous gambling casino. Fontvieille is the newest of the four traditional quarters and is built on the land reclaimed from the Mediterranean Sea since the 1970s. Its waterfront area features an industrial zone consisting mainly of light, non-polluting industries, the Louis II soccer stadium, a heliport with links to Nice airport in France, and the International University of Monaco. Administratively, Monaco is divided into 10 wards. They are: Monte-Carlo, Saint Roman, Larvotto, La Condamine, Monaco-Ville, Fontvieille, La Colle, Les Révoires, Moneghetti, Saint Michel. The 11th ward, Le Portier, is to be created from land reclamation and settled from 2014.

The people of Monaco are called Monégasques or Monegasques. Of Monaco's estimated population of 34,000 only approximately 16% claim Monégasque descent. The remainder of its residents are foreigners (among which 47% are French, 16% Italian, and 21% Swiss, Belgian, British, and other, with some 125 countries represented), attracted by its glamorous lifestyle and—on a more practical level—its liberal tax policies. Non-

French residents pay no personal income, capital gains, housing, or real estate tax. With 15,000 residents per sq km (40,000 per sq mi), the tiny principality is one of the world's most densely populated countries.

3 LANGUAGE

French is Monaco's official language, but the language of daily communication among its Monégasque residents is often Monégasque (natively Munegascu or Munegu). It is a Romance language and a dialect of the modern Ligurian language, currently spoken in the Italian region of Liguria and parts of the Mediterranean coastal zone of France. Monégasque is most similar to the language spoken in the nearby Italian city of Genoa, and it has been strongly influenced by the Proven al (also known as Occitan), a Romance language very similar to modern Catalan, and spoken in Southern France and some parts of Italy and Spain. Because the Monégasques are a minority in Monaco, in the 1970s the Monégasque language was considered threatened. Strong efforts have been made since to prevent its disappearance. Monégasque is now taught in schools and its survival among the new generation of Monégasques is considered certain.

The most important literary work in Monégasque is widely considered to be the poem "The Legend of Saint Dévote" ("A Legenda de Santa Devota"), sung in 1927 by the Monégasque poet Louis Notari (1879–1961). Before Notari, only oral literature existed in Monégasque. His writing, mostly religious in its inspiration, represents the starting point of the revival of the

Prince Albert II (third from left) and Princess Stephanie (center) pose with Monegasques at the Red Cross headquarters in Monaco. The Prince and Princess often attend several events before Monaco National Day on November 19. (Valery Hache/AFP/Getty Images)

Monégasque language in the principality and the flowering of its literature. Notari also wrote Monaco's national anthem.

Because of the large number of foreign nationals residing in the principality and many visitors, English is frequently used as a *lingua franca* (vehicular language). Italian is also widely spoken.

⁴ FOLKLORE

A colorful legend surrounds Monaco's patron saint, St. Dévote, who was born in the island of Corsica in the 3rd century AD. Persecuted by the Romans for her religious beliefs, she died a martyr's death before reaching the age of 20. Obeying the instructions they had received in a vision, a priest and his deacon put the martyr's body in a boat and set out to sea. The boatman, following the dove that he saw flying out of the dead woman's mouth, landed in Monaco, where her body was buried at a chapel. St. Dévote's martyrdom is commemorated every year on January 27, a national holiday. As part of the observance, in the evening of January 26 the Grimaldi family and other government officials set fire to a wooden boat in front of the church of St. Dévote near the harbor. On January 27 a religious service at the Saint Nicholas Cathedral is held, and there is a procession of the relics and the blessing of the Palace, the town, and the sea. The service is followed by fireworks and receptions in the Monte Carlo Opera House.

National Day (November 19) festivities typically are: a Thanksgiving Mass, a conferring of honors and decorations at the Palace, a gala evening at the Opera House, gifts and treats for children and the elderly, and fireworks. Monégasque Christmas typically means a family meal consisting of *brandamincium*, a Monégasque dish of salt cod with garlic, oil and cream; *cardu*, cardoon in white sauce; *barbagiuan* (literally "Uncle John"), fritters stuffed with vegetables and cheese; and flat, crunchy biscuits called *fougasses*. A Christmas loaf (*u pan de Natale*), with an ornament in the shape of a cross, made of walnuts and olive twigs, decorates the table. Before Christmas dinner, the youngest or the oldest guest soaks an olive branch in a glass of old wine. He or she then approaches the fireplace, makes a sign of a cross with the branch, and pronounces a few words on the virtues of the olive tree.

On a darker note, another legend claims that a woman wronged by Rainier I, an ancestor of the current monarch, placed a curse on his family, casting a shadow on any happiness they might enjoy in marriage. The Grimaldi family has certainly had its share of unhappy events in the recent past. In 1982 Princess Grace was killed in a car accident and in 1990 Stefano Casiraghi, the first husband of Grace's eldest daughter Caroline, died while competing in a boating race, leaving his young wife a widow with three small children.

⁵ RELIGION

The official religion of the principality is Roman Catholicism (approximately 90% of residents are Roman Catholic), but freedom to practice other religions is guaranteed by the Constitution. There are five Catholic churches in Monaco and one cathedral. Monaco also belongs to the Church of England's Gibraltar diocese. There is one Anglican church, with membership of 135, but serving also a large number of visitors and tourists. The Jewish community numbers 1,500 and congregates in the Association Culturelle Israélite de Monaco, a house converted into a synagogue, Hebrew school, and a kosher shop.

⁶ MAJOR HOLIDAYS

Most national holidays in Monaco are holy days of the Christian calendar, including Easter, Saint John's Day (June 24), the Day of Saint Roman (August 9), who is, after Saint Dévote, the most venerated saint in the Principality, the feasts of the Assumption (August 15), and the Immaculate Conception (December 8), Ascension, Pentecost Monday, All Saints' Day (November 1), and Christmas. The martyrdom of Monaco's patron saint, St. Dévote, is commemorated on January 27. Other holidays include New Year's Day and Labor Day (May 1) and the Monégasque National Holiday (or Saint Rainier's Day, November 19; before 1857, the Day of Saint Dévote was celebrated as the National Holiday).

⁷ RITES OF PASSAGE

Monégasques live in a modern European country, where Roman Catholicism is nominally the faith of the majority, but where religion, like in the rest of Western Europe, is not widely practiced. Many of the rites of passage that young people undergo are based on religious rituals, such as baptism, first Communion, confirmation, and marriage, but the emphasis is placed significantly less on the religious than on the social aspect of the ritual. In addition, a student's progress through the education system is marked in many families by graduation parties, culminating with the celebration of the successful passing of the *baccalauréat*, a demanding comprehensive examination taken at the end of the last year of high school.

⁸ INTERPERSONAL RELATIONS

The people of Monaco interact with each other in ways similar to those of people in sophisticated cities worldwide. Relationships between sexes are marked by complete equality and cohabitation (either before or, increasingly, instead of marriage) is common. The customary greeting is a handshake while the embrace and kisses on both cheeks are reserved for friends and relatives. The usual form of address is "Mr." or "Mrs." (*Madame*, used with all women except with very young girls), followed by the last name. Some of the more traditional ways of interaction and courtesy (opening a door for a woman or an elderly person, or offering them a better seat in a restaurant or in public transportation) are still widely observed. In daily interactions with strangers and casual acquaintances, great importance is attached to a courteous and cordial, but unintrusive mode of communication, where spirited remarks are exchanged and appreciated, but where questions of a more personal nature are generally discouraged until a much closer relationship has developed. In conversation, strong and straightforward opinions about politics and culture are expected. Invitations to dinner are usually reciprocated by a small gift of chocolates for the hostess. In restaurants with friends, acquaintances or business partners, most Monégasques do not split the cost of a meal, instead taking turns in paying for meals on different occasions.

⁹ LIVING CONDITIONS

Monaco's residents enjoy a high standard of living that includes one of the greatest per capita incomes ($70,670) in the world. The demand for residential space in the tiny principality is so great that lawns are built on the roofs of some new residential dwellings. Architectural styles range from the ornate grandeur of 19th-century villas to the modern lines of concrete high-rise apartment buildings. Meeting the high demand for luxury housing is a high priority for both the government and the construction industry. Apartments rent for as high as $25,000 a month or more, and the cost of a square meter (10.7 sq ft) in a new building varies between $10,000 and $20,000. Nationals of any country may buy real estate in the principality.

Monaco's residents can afford the best in health care and enjoy excellent health. There is no governmental or societal discrimination against persons with disabilities. The average life expectancy is close to 78 years, and the country has a low infant mortality rate of 4 deaths for every 1,000 live births, with one physician and over 100 nurses for every 700 people. The principality has frequent bus service, and rail service is provided by the French national railroad system, which has about 1.6 km (1 mi) of track in the country. The international airport at Nice is only 10 km (6 mi) from Monaco, and the principality's harbor provides sea access.

Though not a member of the European Union, Monaco uses the single European currency of the euro. About 45.9 out of 100 residents are cellular phone users, and 49.4 are Internet users. The majority of Monaco's restaurants and hotels are pet-friendly. Public cleaning service employees keep Monaco's streets and green areas outstandingly clean and beautiful at all times of the year.

¹⁰ FAMILY LIFE

The typical family in Monaco is the nuclear family composed of parents and their children, where close relationships are maintained with grandparents, cousins and in-laws. Most Monégasque women have one or two children during the course of their childbearing years. Like in the neighboring France, cohabitation is increasingly replacing marriage, and the number of children born out of wedlock is consequently rising. Because of the small size of their country, the residents of Monaco have an unusually personal relationship with their ruling family, the Grimaldis. All adult Monégasques are invited to the palace to celebrate major events in the lives of the Grimaldi family, such as engagements, weddings, and christenings. All Monégasque children under the age of 12 are invited to an annual palace Christmas party that includes refreshments, entertainment, and a gift for every child.

¹¹ CLOTHING

Monégasques wear modern, stylish clothing typical of Western and Mediterranean Europe, especially France and Italy. Monaco's residents can be seen sporting the best in fashion (formal or casual), especially in the evening, at Monaco's restaurants, casinos, and other entertainment spots. While topless bathing is common and accepted in Monaco as in other parts of the French Riviera, multilingual signs posted throughout Monaco warn: "Apart from the immediate vicinity of the beaches and bathing facilities it is forbidden to walk around bare-chested, wearing only a swimming costume, or barefoot. Failure to comply with these regulations could result in prosecution." Visits to local churches require modesty in dress, banning bare shoulders for women and shorts for both sexes.

12 FOOD

Monaco's cuisine, like that of the neighboring cities on the French Riviera, is essentially Mediterranean in nature, with plenty of olive oil, fresh tomatoes, onions, garlic, black olives, and anchovies. Fresh fish—including sea bass, red mullet, and *daurade*—are, naturally, plentiful and popular, as is the famous fish stew, *bouillabaisse*. The region is also known for its abundance of fresh vegetables, savored both in salads and dishes such as *ratatouille*, a vegetable stew made from tomatoes, onions, peppers, and eggplant (called *aubergine* on the Mediterranean coast). A local favorite for a warm snack is *barbajuan* (or *barbagiuan*), a fried pastry filled with chard, spinach, leek, oregano, and cheese. Wine is drunk with lunch and dinner. The Hôtel de Paris has the world's deepest hotel wine cellar, with a special section boasting champagnes that are almost 200 years old.

13 EDUCATION

Education in Monaco is compulsory between the ages of 6 and 16, and literacy is practically universal (99%). The school curriculum is based on that of France, but students are also taught the history of Monaco and, increasingly, there is formal instruction in Monégasque (natively *Munegascu* or *Munegu*), a small Romance language spoken in the principality. Students attend *école élémentaire* (primary school) between the ages of 6 and 11, *collège* (junior high or secondary school) and *lycée* (high school) between the ages of 11 and 15, and 15 and 18, respectively. Monaco has 10 public schools, among which seven are nursery (*école maternelle*) and primary schools, one *collège*, and two *lycées*, in addition to two denominational private schools and one international school. About 80% of students in public schools are not Monaco nationals, and one-third of these students are not domiciled in the principality.

The International University of Monaco is an English-language private institution founded in 1986. It offers undergraduate and graduate degrees in business.

14 CULTURAL HERITAGE

The lively interest that the Grimaldi family has always demonstrated for the arts, and their continuously strong patronage of resident and visiting artists, set the tone for the principality's cultural life. The Monte-Carlo Philharmonic Orchestra is a permanent orchestra established in 1863. It found its home in the Salle Garnier Opera House in 1879, and in 1953 it was renamed the National Orchestra of the Monte-Carlo Opera, becoming finally in 1979 the Monte-Carlo Philharmonic Orchestra. Among its past conductors are many great names, from Richard Strauss and Arturo Toscanini, to Leonard Bernstein, Lovro von Matacic and Lorin Maazel. Its Artistic Director and Conductor-in-Chief in 2008 was Marek Janowski, scheduled to step down in 2009. Another one of Monaco's cultural attractions is its opera. Since its creation, the Opera of

Monte-Carlo has attracted the world's best singers, and composers such as Bizet, Franck, or Massenet wrote some of their best works for the Opera. At one time the Opera was also home to the Ballets Russes, a ballet company of the famous Russian impresario Serge Diaghilev. Today, Monaco has its own ballet company. In 1985, following the wishes of her mother, the late Princess Grace, Princess Caroline of Hanover established the new Monte-Carlo Ballet, the official national company of the principality. The company is housed at The Princess Grace Academy of Classical Dance, a ballet school that the late Princess Grace established in 1975. The youngest Monégasques are represented by The Little Singers of Monaco, a world-renowned children's choir, established by Prince Antoine I in the early 18th century. Monaco's Music Academy was founded in 1956, under the patronage of Prince Rainier III. In memory of his father, in 1966 Prince Rainier also established the Foundation Prince Pierre, which assigns the Prince Pierre Literary Prize, the Musical Composition Prize, and the Contemporary Art International Prize. In 1964 the Princess Grace of Monaco Foundation was created to support the performing arts. The Foundation, now chaired by Princess Caroline of Hanover, has three permanent activities: The Princess Grace Academy of Classical Dance, the *Boutiques du Rocher,* and The Princess Grace Irish Library, established by Prince Rainier in 1984 as a tribute to the Irish heritage of his late wife. The library houses a collection of rare Irish books and music sheets, and its staff promotes Irish culture through conferences, readings, and fellowships.

The Oceanographic Museum and Aquarium, located at the water's edge and towering over a cliff, was inaugurated in 1910 by Prince Albert I, grandfather of Prince Rainier III, and an internationally recognized scientist and oceanographer. It houses an impressive aquarium and a display of whales' skeletons, as well as both historical and modern exhibits dealing with oceanographic study. In 1902 Prince Albert I founded Monaco's Museum of Prehistoric Anthropology, and in 1913 he established the basis for today's Exotic Garden, devoted to the preservation of the flora of the world's arid zones.

15 WORK

Monaco has practically no unemployment. It is the only country in the world in which the labor force exceeds the total population. Over two-thirds (28,000 French and 6,000 Italians) of its labor force of 44,200 commutes to work from France or Italy. All non-French citizens wishing to work in Monaco must obtain a work permit from the Department of Employment. Every employee in Monaco is entitled to 12 legal paid public holidays and a minimum of 30 days annual paid vacation days. Commerce represents 40% of all economic activity in the principality. Banking and financial sector account for 15% of its economy. Tourism is a major employer in this nation that welcomes over 6 million visitors from abroad every year, with 700,000 overnight stays and 700 conferences (2005), and it represents 13% of the economy. Monte-Carlo's casino enterprise, the Société des Bains de Mer (S.B.M.), provides numerous jobs in its restaurants and hotels, as well as in the casino itself. Industrial activity represents approximately 8% of the total economy in the principality. Many workers—especially those who commute from neighboring countries—are employed in new real-estate projects and in the low-polluting, but high-added-value light industries that have been established in Monaco since the 1970s through the efforts of Prince Rainier III. Products include perfumes and cosmetics, pharmaceuticals, precision instruments, jewelry, leather goods, radio parts, textiles and garments, with the emphasis on high-tech production. The rest of Monaco's economy is based on real-estate development, shipping, transportation and other services. Most recently, discussions about the future of Monaco's economy have been directed toward attracting businesses based on information technology services. The total turnover of the private sector in 2005 was approximately Û11 billion.

¹⁶ SPORTS

Monaco is connected with several world-famous sporting events. The first Monégasque sports association was founded in 1888, eleven years after the Tennis Master Series had begun in Monte-Carlo. 1904 saw the first speedboat meeting, and 1929 saw the first automobile Grand Prize race. Today the race is named Monaco Grand Prix and is widely considered to be the most challenging Formula One track in the world. The Grand Prix is a unique event whose circuit lies totally within Monaco's modest borders. Its 100 laps include both uphill and downhill stretches, hairpin turns, and passage through a tunnel. Residents gather at strategic spots throughout the principality to view the race, and some lucky ones can even see part of the route from their own houses. Other well-known sporting events include the Monte-Carlo Golf Open, which was held at Monte Carlo Golf Club at Mont Agel (France) between 1984 and 1992, and the prestigious Monte-Carlo Masters (until the early 1990s known as the Monte-Carlo Open), an annual tennis tournament for male professional players, held in Roquebrune-Cap-Martin (France). The tournament is played on clay courts, every year in April/May, and is part of the ATP Masters Series. Additionally, a number of world's top professional tennis players have made Monaco their primary residence.

In addition to their status as top spectator sports, both golf and tennis are also popular participatory sports in Monaco. The Monte-Carlo Country Club's clay tennis courts overlooking the Mediterranean Ocean are some of the most scenically located in Europe. Monégasques also enjoy a variety of water sports. The Monaco Yacht Club runs a sailing school and also rents out boats for big-game fishing.

¹⁷ ENTERTAINMENT AND RECREATION

Monaco residents and visitors enjoy a variety of opera, ballet, and concert events all year round. In addition to high culture, Monaco hosts International Circus Festival, Monte-Carlo Television Festival and Market, Monte-Carlo Spring Arts Festival, Monaco International Dogs Show, International Fireworks Festival, Monaco Yacht Show, and International Fine Art and Antiques show.

Monaco has been known as a gambling mecca since the opening of the Casino at Monte-Carlo in 1863. Residents and visitors alike enjoy its beaches, its numerous museums and other cultural events, and its beautiful gardens, including the Princess Grace Rose Garden that boasts 150 different varieties of roses. The yearly Rose Ball and Monte-Carlo Red Cross Gala Ball are two of Europe's most glamorous charity events, bringing together many international celebrities, and benefiting the Princess Grace Foundation and the Red Cross. The annual film festival in nearby Cannes, France, is one of the most famous in the world of entertainment. Monaco's residents receive numerous foreign and locally produced radio and television programs.

¹⁸ FOLK ART, CRAFTS, AND HOBBIES

In 1964 the Princess Grace of Monaco Foundation was established to support local craftsmen and women. In 1960s, the princess opened shops in Monte Carlo and Monaco-Ville where potters and other local artisans could sell their work. The two shops, known as the *Boutiques du Rocher,* continue to sell Monégasque and Provençal hand-made wares, gifts made of porcelain, wood and textiles, toys and dolls. Their income benefits hospitalized children, and their entire costs of operation are underwritten by the Foundation.

¹⁹ SOCIAL PROBLEMS

With its high level of per capita income ($70,670 in 2007), high employment, and efficient government, Monaco is free of the social problems encountered in most countries. A watchful police force sees to it that street crime is virtually nonexistent. Some 500 police officers patrol the streets of the tiny principality, and close to 100 surveillance cameras allow the officers at police headquarters to further monitor any suspicious activity. Concern has been voiced in some quarters about the impact of the country's industrial development and residential construction boom on the quality of daily life for its residents.

²⁰ GENDER ISSUES

Life expectancy for women in Monaco in 2007 is 83.85 years (compared to 75.99 for men). The median age of Monaco women residents is 47.5 (compared to 43.5 for males). The fertility rate for 2007 was 1.75 children born/woman; the birth rate is 9.12 births/1,000 residents. The literacy rate for women in Monaco is 99% (same as for men).

The new Constitution of Monaco was proclaimed on 17 December 1962, establishing the Supreme Court of Monaco, abolishing capital punishment, and providing for women's suffrage. The Constitution declares all Monaco nationals to be equal before the law. While the percentage of women in politics and government still does not correspond to their percentage of the population, women are very active in public service. Some remnants of legal discrimination are still present, particularly with regard to the transmission of citizenship: women who acquire Monégasque citizenship by naturalization cannot transmit it to their children, while naturalized male citizens can. Only male nationals between the ages of 16–49 are considered available for military service. On a historic note, a treaty between Monaco and France, signed in 1918, contained a clause providing that, should the Grimaldi dynasty become extinct, Monaco would become an autonomous state under French protection. A revision to the Constitution in 2002 added females and their legitimate children to the line of succession, making Princess Caroline second in line for the throne of the principality.

Women are generally represented well in the professions. although somewhat less well in the business. They receive equal pay for equal work. In 2008 the Dean of the International University of Monaco was a woman, as were two out of the seven members of Monaco's Physicians Association Council, and one of the three members of Monaco's Attorneys Association Council.

Reported occurrences of violence against women are rare, and there are no reports of sexual harassment. Domestic violence is illegal, and any wife who is a victim of marital violence may bring criminal charges against her husband. The Monaco government provides mandatory, free and universal education for children up to the age of 16.

Monaco shares very liberal French attitudes towards sexuality. Cohabitation is increasingly replacing marriage. Homosexuality, male and female, enjoys wide social acceptance, and is legal under the Monégasque Penal Code, all criminal penalties for homosexual behavior having been eliminated in 1973. The legal age of consent is set at 16 years. At present, Monaco provides no civil unions, or recognition of same-sex partners. There are, so far, no exclusively gay public clubs or gathering places in Monaco.

The Grimaldi family has demonstrated firm commitment to promoting equal rights for women and homosexuals. Princess Caroline of Hanover, appointed as UNESCO's Goodwill Ambassador for the education of young girls and women, is active in lending Monaco's financial support to women's welfare in developing countries, especially in Africa and Asia. Her younger sister Princess Stéphanie has dedicated considerable efforts to the fight against AIDS, and to removing the stigma surrounding the disease. She created the foundation "Fight Aids Monaco" in support of people living with HIV and is an UNAIDS (Joint UN Programme on HIV/AIDS) ambassador.

21 BIBLIOGRAPHY

Bernardy, Françoise de. *Princes of Monaco: The Remarkable History of the Grimaldi Family.* London: Barker, 1961.

Conniff, Richard. "Monaco." *National Geographic.* May 1996, pp. 81–94.

Eccardt, Thomas M. *Secrets of the Seven Smallest States of Europe: Andorra, Liechtenstein, Luxembourg, Malta, Monaco, San Marino and Vatican City.* New York: Hippocrene Books, 2004.

Edwards, Anne. *The Grimaldis of Monaco.* New York: Morrow, 1992.

Gall, Timothy, and Susan Gall, ed. *Worldmark Encyclopedia of the Nations.* Detroit: Gale Research, 1995.

Glatt, John. *The Royal House of Monaco: Dynasty of Glamour, Tragedy and Scandal.* New York: St. Martin's Press, 1998.

Grinda, Georges and Jorri C. Duursma, trans. *The Principality of Monaco: State, International Status, Institutions.* Hague: T.M.C. Asser Press, 2006.

—by K. von Wittelsbach.

MONTENEGRINS

LOCATION: Montenegro
POPULATION: 620,000
LANGUAGE: Montenegrin or Serbian
RELIGION: Orthodox Christian, some Catholics and Muslims

1 INTRODUCTION

The name Montenegro is from the Italian phrase *monte nero*, or "black mountain." The native name *Crna Gora* has the same meaning, an apt name for a small, rugged, entirely mountainous country. While it is one of the most recent countries to gain independence, the national identity has a long history. The land reaching up into the mountains from the steep east coast of the Adriatic Sea was part of the ancient Roman Empire. Slavic speakers, the linguistic forebears of the present Montenegrin population, arrived from the 6th century AD on. These early medieval newcomers settled in small villages forming a patchwork pattern with those of the Romance speakers and those of the Albanian speakers, all engaged in sheepherding and small-scale agriculture. This pattern persisted until a century ago with elements of it remaining to the present. In the medieval period the land was also dotted with small fortified towns, some of which were church centers.

In the early Middle Ages coastal cities, such as Ulcinj, Bar, and Kotor related to the culture of the Adriatic Sea and of Italy just across the sea, while they related politically to the inland, paying tribute to Serbian kings and feudal nobles there. Later, they were ruled by Venice.

From the late 10th through the 12th century the lands comprising much of Montenegro but extending farther south to include all of the environs of Lake Skadar was known as Doclea or Duklja. This was a period of swiftly shifting boundaries and allegiances.

The area then came to be known as Zeta and was ruled first by Serbian kings from the late 12th century until 1356. However, in the 14-15th centuries the larger shepherds' camps gave rise to tribes and clans that were the basis of society until a century ago. In 1356 Zeta became an independent entity under one of these clans or great families, the Balšić family. It was subsequently ruled by Serbian rulers called despots from 1421 to 1451. The Crnojević family took it over for the remainder of the 15th century.

In the 14th century mention of Crna Gora or Montenegro begins in historic sources, especially in reference to the area between Cetinje and Lake Skadar. The Turkish Ottoman Empire's conquest of Serbia in 1389 and Bosnia in 1463 was the defining moment for Montenegrin identity. Montenegro, for a time a smaller area than Duklja and Zeta, fell technically to the Turks in 1496 but was never fully conquered by them, although they took over the coastal cities of Ulcinj and Bar in 1571. From 1516 on the name Montenegro became official, and hereditary rule was consolidated in the bishops of Cetinje, who became the prince-bishops, gaining more power in the 17th century, consolidating it into an effective monarchy in the mid 19th century, and continuing until World War I. As the once seemingly unstoppable Ottoman Empire declined in the 19th century, neighboring Croatian Dalmatia, Herzegovina and Bosnia were taken over by Austria-Hungary; Serbia became an independent kingdom. Montenegro was not conquered except for a brief surrender to the doomed Austro-Hungarian Empire during World War I.

Throughout the five centuries of Ottoman rule over the Serbs, the Montenegrins prided themselves in being the only Serbs remaining independent. This was the essence of their identity. They might be impoverished, but their clan-dominated warrior culture of fighting and guns, united by the Orthodox Church, kept them free of outside domination. However, when Serbia gained full independence in 1878, the Montenegrins were faced by a contradiction. Which part of their identity was essential? The Serb aspect implied that they should unite with Serbia, de facto becoming subordinate to it. The independent aspect suggested that Montenegrins should stay apart, but that put them in opposition to the Serbs in Serbia.

After World War I, when the maps of Europe were redrawn and numerous nationalities became independent nations, Montenegro did not. It was swallowed up in the newly-created Yugoslavia, the Kingdom of the Serbs, Croats, and Slovenes (1918–1941).

During World War II, Italy, which had swiftly taken the length of the Croatian Adriatic coast to the northwest and Albania to the southeast, found separatist collaborators and took over inland Montenegro as well in 1941. The Communist Party of Yugoslavia led an uprising that left the Italians holding only the cities of Cetinje, Podgorica, and Nikšić, but in 1942 the Italian fascists took back the hinterland. Guerrilla partisans continued the struggle to drive them out. Italy surrendered in 1943 only to be replaced by German troops, and the resistance continued. After heavy fighting in late 1944, Montenegro was liberated on 6 January 1945.

Montenegro then became the smallest of the six republics of the Federal People's (later Socialist Federal) Republic of Yugoslavia. Typically called simply Yugoslavia, this was a maverick Communist country. Within three years it broke with the Soviet Union, soon opening its borders to the West and finding its place in the world as a leader among the non-aligned nations. While the government, dominated by the Communist Party, never allowed democracy, it did modify the economic system to one of worker self-management. It also granted the republics broad decentralized powers in economic affairs and administration, especially following the constitution of 1974.

In 1992, after Slovenia, Croatia, Bosnia and Herzegovina, and Macedonia had broken away from the SFRY, the Republic of Montenegro joined together with the much larger Republic of Serbia to form the Federal Republic of Yugoslavia. In 2003 the state was reorganized and renamed Serbia and Montenegro.

In 2006 the Montenegrin population voted to declare independence from Serbia, and Montenegro became a separate country. It is now working hard to become a member of the European Union.

Montenegrins are very aware that their old royal capital was Cetinje. In 1946 Yugoslavia moved the capital of the newly-formed Republic of Montenegro to newly-named Titograd. In 1992 the old name of this city, Podgorica, was restored, but it has remained the capital.

² LOCATION AND HOMELAND

Montenegro is a small country in the western part of the Balkan Peninsula. It is roughly diamond shaped, with the east

coast of the Adriatic forming its southwestern edge, lying between Croatia in the north and Albania in the south. The border with Croatia extends northward from the sea for only about 20 km (12.4 mi); from there Bosnia and Herzegovina lie to the north and west of Montenegro. From the northernmost point of the Montenegrin diamond on, the land to the northeast of the border is Serbia. From the easternmost point, the land to the southeast for about 60 km (37 mi) is Kosovo, technically still a part of Serbia. Albania forms the southeastern border of Montenegro. The coastline is about 100 (60 mi) km long as the crow flies, but nearly 300 km (180 mi) if the deep indentations are counted.

Winters are harsh and snowy in the mountains, but the Mediterranean climate of the coast is very mild. Mimosas bloom in late January in Hercegnovi.

The country had a population of 620,000 according to the 2003 official census. There were an additional 50,000 people in the country, apparently refugee or immigrant Bosnians and Albanians. Among the population of citizens and permanent residents, self-declared Montenegrins are 43%, Serbs 32%, Bosniaks 8%, and Albanians 5%. However, Montenegrins have a long tradition of considering themselves Serbs, so these are not two clearly distinct groups.

Thus, earlier Montenegrin emigrants to the United States organized and identified themselves as Montenegrin-Serbs; only since the late 1990s have they called themselves specifically Montenegrin. There are perhaps 260,000 Montenegrins in Serbia. There are also self-identified Montenegrins in Croatia, Canada, Australia, Cyprus, Argentina and other Latin American countries. Such emigrant populations number in the thousands.

It has been estimated that a few thousand Montenegrins live in Albania, not as immigrants but remaining since medieval times.

³ LANGUAGE

Most of the inhabitants of Montenegro speak one or the other of two dialects out of the many that make up Serbo-Croatian, a South Slavic language. In terms of the oldest and deepest dialect divisions, both fall within the Štokavski group that forms the basis of all the standard languages, and both fall within the Ijekavski group that was favored by Vuk Karadžić, the 19th century pioneer in the standardization of Serbo-Croatian, but was adopted as the Croatian standard, not the Serbian one. The dialect of the northern half of Montenegro is in essence that of Vuk Karadžić, while the dialect of the southern half including the coast and the past and present capitals has various archaic and less usual sound features and shares some changes in the case system with the southern Serbian dialects. Publishing in the past used the same Cyrillic alphabet as the Serbs of Serbia, but unlike them, they used the Ijekavski spelling system. However, Montenegrins called their language Serbian.

At present both the Cyrillic and the Latin alphabet are used.

The constitution adopted after Montenegro declared independence in 2006 states that the official language of Montenegro is Montenegrin. Its standard has not yet been defined, but the Latin alphabet in the form used by Croatians seems to be favored. A few scholars call for a more radical break with Serbian and Croatian and want to add three new letters to each alphabet. Some citizens declare their languages to be the mutually intelligible Serbian, Bosnian, or Croatian. Some citizens speak Albanian, which is a very different language.

Montenegrins typically have a first (given) name and a surname. Many typical first names are Orthodox saints' names, such as Aleksandar, Petar, Jelena (Helen), and Marija. Others are meaningful Slavic names, such as male Predrag, "most dear," or female Milena, "beloved." Names that originally were nicknames like Stanko can also be used as given names. Surnames were frequently derived with the suffix -ić 'son or daughter of' added to the root of a personal name, although now these surnames are passed on through the generations. Other surnames go back to old clan names. Some are of Romance or Albanian origin.

⁴ FOLKLORE

Industry, mass communications, and even widespread literacy came relatively late to Montenegro. A rich orally-transmitted folk tradition has remained alive until the recent past. It is famous for the heroic, often bloody epic poems that are performed to the accompaniment of the *gusle*, a one-stringed instrument played time with a bow. They are not memorized but improvised; the plot and the phrases are learned, but they are composed anew with each performance.

The small seaside town of Perast has a legend that in 1452 fishermen found a miraculous healing icon of the Virgin on a small offshore reef. A church was built on the spot. The "*fašinada*" is now held annually on July 22 . A procession of decorated boats row out to the church in the early evening bearing rocks that are dropped to shore up the church.

⁵ RELIGION

The coastal areas stretching inland to include Doclea (near today's Podgorica) were Christianized in Roman times, from Rome, not Byzantium, and Roman influence persisted into the Middle Ages. For centuries after the Great Schism divided Orthodox Christianity from Roman Catholicism, both coexisted in Montenegro or rather were not really distinguished from one another. Subsequently, the Orthodox Church, supported by Serbian princes, grew stronger, spread to the coast, and supplanted Roman Catholicism. In the era of the struggle against the Turks, and until recently, Montenegrins identified strongly with the Serbian Orthodox Church. With the impetus for national independence in recent years came the establishment of an independent Montenegrin Orthodox Church. It is controversial, for the Serbian Church still claims authority over all of Montenegro and discourages other Orthodox churches from recognizing that of Montenegro.

⁶ MAJOR HOLIDAYS

Public holidays are New Year's Day (January 1), Labor Day (May 1), Independence Day (May 21), and Statehood Day (July 13), each celebrated with two days off. Other important religious holidays are Christmas on January 7 and Good Friday, Easter, and Easter Monday, on whatever date they fall in the Orthodox Church calendar. The Montenegrin Church also honors the death of St. Peter of Cetinje, the prince-bishop credited with founding the modern state, on Lučindan, or St. Luke's Day,

There is also an important private holiday, the *slava*, or celebration of the family's patron saint. Relatives and friends are invited or drop in for a feast that includes a traditional cake *slavski kolač*.

⁷ RITES OF PASSAGE

The birth of a son was signaled with gunfire, while the birth of a daughter was not considered an occasion for rejoicing.

Marriage was a ritual reinforcing the patriarchal system. It was seen not as the union of the couple but rather the union of two families. Hitherto, the girl had been in the care of her paternal family; henceforth, she would be protected by her husband's family. On the wedding day a party consisting of the groom's brothers and a flag bearer and other males went from the groom's home to that of the bride. Lunch was at the bride's parents' home, with toasts, gifts and numerous rituals. Then, the groom's party took the bride with them. Both families fired guns in celebration. Dinner was at the groom's home, the future home of the couple. The marriage was performed in a church in the groom's village. People danced the *oro*. The new family saw to it that at first the bride did not sleep with her new husband, but rather with other members of his family—even the brothers-in-law, who, however, remained fully clothed and did not touch her. Only when the family judged it to be time,

Supporters of Montenegrin independence celebrate in Podgorica, Serbia, Montenegro, after an independent monitoring group said Montenegro voted for independence in a 2006 referendum. (© Koca Sulejamovic/epa/Corbis)

the new wife began sleeping with her husband. While many aspects of marriage and weddings were similar among Orthodox Montenegrins, Slavic Muslims, Albanian Muslims, and Albanian Catholics, all of whom live in Montenegro, the unusual custom of first sleeping with the in-laws rather than the groom was practiced only by Orthodox Montenegrins. Already on its way out in the early 20th century, it was sometimes still done as late as World War II.

Funerals traditionally included laments that commented on the life of the deceased and called for revenge if he had died violently. While laments in surrounding areas were performed by women, in Montenegro there was a special kind sung by men.

8 INTERPERSONAL RELATIONS

When people meet for the first time, each person introduces himself or herself; as they shake hands in pairs, each repeats his or her own name.

Traditions of hospitality are strong. A host expects to treat a guest lavishly with food, coffee, and drink.

The two traditional virtues among Montenegrins are *čojstvo* and *junaštvo*. The second means "bravery" or "heroism" while the first, a local pronunciation of the word for "humanity," implies magnanimity and self-restraint towards others—protecting others from oneself.

9 LIVING CONDITIONS

Long known as one of the most impoverished and backward areas of Europe, Montenegro has made breathtaking progress in recent decades. Thus, an unimpressive infant mortality index of 11 per 1,000 in 2006 must be compared with the 84.7 infant mortality in 1951. Life expectancy is 72 years for men and 77 years for women. The number of physicians per 100,000 population reached 191 in 2003, comparable to that of the United States and increasing yearly.

The consumer goods that are standard elsewhere, including electric ranges, refrigerators, and televisions, are standard here too. Estimates of Internet access range from 20% to over 40% of the population. The number of cell phones in the country exceeds the population.

10 FAMILY LIFE

The traditional Montenegrin marriage was an arranged marriage. If the man and woman lived nearby, they might have known each other before, but in most cases they were strangers when they married. The groom's family scrutinized the bride's family more than the individual young woman for suitability. Then, the family asked the girl's father for her; if he agreed, the bride was asked for consent, but girls did not feel they had any option to refuse. A woman was taken from the family in which she grew up (*rod*) and brought to live with her husband's family (*dom*).

The household was an extended family in which all the brothers lived and brought in their wives.

It is only since World War II that people, particularly in urban areas, have begun to live as nuclear families. In the past half century household size has been decreasing, judging by figures in the Statistical Yearbook of Montenegro 2007.

The extended family still functions, even though they do not all live in the same household. People tend to know the names of even distant ancestors. They stay in touch with distant cousins and may ask them for help.

Many households in the countryside would move between the summer herding camp, or *katun,* and the winter home. In recent decades the *katun* has transformed seamlessly into the summer home, a popular feature of life throughout the countries of former Yugoslavia.

11 CLOTHING

People dress as do any Europeans or Americans, whether it's suits for formal business, jeans, shorts, t-shirts, or sleeveless blouses on the street, or bikinis on the beach. The folk costumes are still an option for special occasions. Thus, a recent photo from a blueberry festival in Podgorica shows men in suits and ties but women in the long straight skirt, vest, and headscarf of the national costume.

The historic male costume had a characteristic cylindrical brimless cap with a flat top, white shirt, belt, blue pants down to the knees, sometimes baggy, white knee boots, and a red vest or jacket. The jacket might have a unique type of sleeves sewn on in the back but not the front, so that the arms could be withdrawn in warm weather while the vest was still on, leaving the sleeves to hang loose. Costumes were often surprisingly lavish considering the poverty of the people, adorned with gilded threads and silver plates called *toke*, themselves decorated with filigree work and gilt patches.

12 FOOD

Traditional foods of Montenegro emphasize milk, buttermilk, cheese, *kajmak* (a rich soft cheese that has not aged), sheep cheese, meats, *pršut* or smoked dried ham, wheat, buckwheat, corn, potatoes, cabbage, and honey. These are the foods of a mountain region better suited to herding than extensive farming. There are regional wines and brandies, often made from grapes. In earlier times, especially in times of war, food was scarce. Now, the economy has improved to the point where there is plenty to eat. Still, Montenegro is a net importer of food.

13 EDUCATION

A country that was 77% illiterate in 1900 now has only about 2.3% illiteracy in those aged 10 years or over. Primary education lasts from four to nine years. Secondary education may be in academic schools or in specialized vocational schools. The University of Montenegro, founded in 1974, now has 14 faculties and one higher school, most located in Podgorica, but some in Nikšić, Cetinje, Kotor and Hercegnovi. By 2009 all education at the university will be conducted in accord with the Bologna Declaration, the European standard. Nearly half of university students have their education financed by the government, but a swiftly growing number are financing it privately.

14 CULTURAL HERITAGE

Aside from the rich traditions of epic folk poetry and folk music and dance, which are still alive there, one author stands out as the embodiment of the spirit of Montenegro. Petar II Petrović Njegoš was born in 1813 (possibly 1811; records are sparse) in a family nearly as impoverished and illiterate as all the others in the country at that time. His uncle, Bishop Petar, saw to it that several nephews were educated as potential successors, and upon the uncle's death in 1830 seventeen-year-old Njegoš became bishop. The duties of the bishop also included rule of the secular affairs of the country, primarily mediation among the rival tribes. Over the years he became ever less the mediator and more the absolute monarch. A lifelong poet, Njegoš's greatest work is *The Mountain Wreath*, an apocryphal account of how the Montenegrins rose against the Ottoman Empire in the late 17th century and slaughtered all those compatriots who had opportunistically converted to Islam. The poem is in the form of a drama in the ten-syllable style of folk epic poetry. Scenes of discussion and depictions of folk life lead to the poet's conclusion that the massacre was inevitable and necessary.

An important World War II Partisan fighter and later government official, Milovan Djilas, got into trouble for his political writings in the early 1950s. He later turned to writing memoirs and historical and literary works about Montenegro and was widely published outside Yugoslavia.

15 WORK

Out of 150,800 Montenegrins employed in 2008, nearly one fifth worked in retail and wholesale commerce, nearly as many in diverse manufacturing. Significant numbers also worked in transportation and communications as well as in hotels and restaurants.

There are bauxite mines and an aluminum plant, now in Russian hands, but the latter consumes half of the country's supply of electricity and may be closed down.

Tourism, especially on the coast, is a swiftly growing industry. Montenegro was one of Lonely Planet's seven Top-Pick countries to visit in 2008. Tourism was already well-developed in the Yugoslav years. Sveti Stefan, a tiny island city with traditional clustered red tile roofs, was renowned as a luxury resort. The tourist industry is now attracting extensive foreign investment.

Unemployment, which had reached a peak of 32.7% in 2000, has been steadily falling and was down to 10.81% as of the end of July 2008.

It is estimated that nearly 50,000 Montenegrins, mostly age 20 to 30, work illegally in the informal economy, especially in tourism and construction, which means that their employers do not pay into the social insurance system. Montenegro is inspecting workplaces and has been able to convert many such jobs into regular, legal ones.

16 SPORTS

Clearly football (soccer) is the leading sport for participation, followed by various martial arts (judo, karate, wrestling), basketball, and general fitness. Not only football but also water polo makes the headlines, thanks to a successful team. The women's handball team is on the front page when it is in an international match.

The old and dangerous economic activity of floating logs downriver to market has in recent decades been turned into a tourist attraction: rafting on the Tara.

17 ENTERTAINMENT AND RECREATION

Judging by the number of sports clubs and the specialized daily newspaper devoted to sports, both participation and watching are important parts of recreation. Television is in all households; many shows are from the U.S. or other countries. Young people follow the same movie and TV stars and popular music groups as elsewhere in Europe and North America.

18 FOLK ARTS, CRAFTS, AND HOBBIES

The folk art belongs to the Dinaric Zone that encompasses not only Montenegro but also Bosnia, Herzegovina and the mountains of Croatia to the northwest and north, and western Serbia to the northeast. An isolated, mountainous region, it preserves forms rooted in Roman and even prehistoric times. Geometric motifs predominate in all media. Traditional unglazed pottery with simple patterns is archaic in style. Wool is woven, often in striped or geometric designs. Utilitarian wooden objects, such as chests, distaffs, water jugs, cradles, and one-stringed *gusle* may be elaborately carved and sometimes painted as well. Metal work was more highly developed, for daggers, swords and guns are prized possessions and can be lavishly decorated with beaten silver, filigree, and inset stones. Silver jewelry may be done in filigree shaped into balls for a necklace. A well-to-do woman could have a belt decorated with large silver plates, either embossed or covered with extensive and surprisingly intricate filigree.

19 SOCIAL PROBLEMS

Montenegro has a murder rate that is more like that of the United States than the much lower rate of surrounding European nations. One-third of killings are by guns. Some appear to have political motives, e.g. the assassination of prominent newspaper editor Duško Jovanović in 2004.

Poverty remains a problem despite some vigorous recent development. Per capita Gross Domestic Product is similar to that of other Balkan countries but far behind neighboring Croatia and even Serbia.

Violence against women is a tradition and now a recognized problem.

20 GENDER ISSUES

Traditional Montenegro was a warrior clan society, a patriarchy in the purest sense of the word. A woman was subordinated, first to her parents and then to her husband and his family. Her purpose was to bear sons, not daughters. However, with men frequently away at war, be it five hundred years of fighting against the Turks, blood feuding among clans, or the four wars of the twentieth century, women were in fact responsible for much of the agricultural and herding work as well as all household work and child rearing. They carried supplies to the fighters, buried the dead, and in some cases bore arms and participated in the fighting. Such women were celebrated in song.

Nowadays women have jobs and can put their children in daycare while they work. Typically, they still have the double duty of household work. As their economic independence has increased, particularly in the past two decades, some have begun to keep their own surnames when they marry or use both maiden and husband's surname.

21 BIBLIOGRAPHY

Alexander, Ronelle. *Bosnian, Croatian, Serbian, a Grammar: With Sociolinguistic Commentary.* Madison, Wisc.: The University of Wisconsin Press, 2006.

Djilas, Milovan. *Montenegro.* Translated by Kenneth Johnstone. New York: Harcourt, Brace & World, Inc., 1963.

———. *Njegoš: Poet Prince Bishop.* Translated by Michael B. Petrovich. New York: Harcourt, Brace & World, Inc., 1966.

Milich, Zorka. *A Stranger's Supper: An Oral History of Centenarian Women in Montenegro.* New York: Twayne Publishers, 1995.

Montenegro. Statistical Office. *Statistical Yearbook 2007.* Podgorica, Montenegro: MONSTAT, 2007.

Pantelić, Nikola. *Traditional Arts and Crafts in Yugoslavia.* Photographs by Miodrag Djordjević. Belgrade, Yugoslavia: Jugoslovenska Revija, 1984.

Roberts, Elizabeth. *Realm of the Black Mountain: A History of Montenegro.* London: Hurst & Company, and Ithaca: Cornell University Press, 2007.

—By T. Alt and W. Browne

MORDVINS

ALTERNATE NAMES: Erzias; Mokshas (self-references)
LOCATION: Russia (Moksha and Sura rivers region)
POPULATION: 1.15 million
LANGUAGE: Mordvin (Moksha and Erzia); Russian

¹ INTRODUCTION

The Mordvins are a Finno-Ugric nationality inhabiting the Russian Federation. The term *Mordvin*, however, is not used by the Mordvins themselves, who consider themselves to be two separate groups—the Erzias and the Mokshas. The first mention of the Mordvins in historical sources may reach back to the 6th century, when the historian Jordanes mentions the "Mordens" as subjects of the Ostrogoths, then inhabiting the South Russian steppe. The Mordvins are identified with more certainty in the Russian *Primary Chronicle* (a 12th-century collection of history) as inhabiting their present homeland in the 10th century. The Russian chronicles, our earliest sources for Mordvin history, relate that the Mordvins, before the Mongol conquest of the 13th century, lived under their own "princes." Some Mordvin communities paid tribute to Russian princes, while others paid tribute to the Muslim rulers of Volga Bulgaria, centered to the east of the Mordvins at the confluence of the Volga and Kama Rivers. As a result of the Mongol conquest, the Mordvins found themselves subjects of the Golden Horde. In fact, the Mongols established a local administrative center known as Navrochat in the middle of Mordvin ethnic territory. After the collapse of the Golden Horde in the early 15th century, the Mordvins again found themselves straddling the border between the powerful Russian principality of Moscow and the Kazan khanate, a successor state of the Golden Horde roughly corresponding to the geographical location of Volga Bulgaria. With the Russian conquest of Kazan in 1552, the Mordvin ethnic territory as a whole fell under Muscovite control.

Under Russian rule, the Mordvin peasants were gradually enserfed (immobilized) and Christianized, although these processes only began in earnest at the beginning of the 18th century, during the reign of the Russian tsar Peter the Great. As a result of these pressures, the Mordvins took part in the periodic peasant and Cossack rebellions against Russian rule, most notably in the Pugachev uprising in the 1770s. During the 17th, 18th, and 19th centuries, many Mordvin communities migrated out of their traditional homeland along the Oka and Moksha Rivers to the newly conquered steppe lands on both the western and eastern banks of the Volga River. In the 19th century, Mordvin peasants also migrated to the more distant regions of the Transcaucasus, Siberia, Central Asia, and even California.

One result of these migrations was to disperse the Mordvin population, making them more susceptible to Russification, and many Russian observers of the Mordvins before 1917 noted that they were among the most Russified of all Russia's minority nationalities. Although the Mordvins have defied, and continue to defy, the frequent predictions of their total Russification, this dispersal may be one among several reasons for the Mordvins' failure to articulate any political demands as Mordvins during the Russian revolutions of 1905 and 1917.

The Mordvins' apparent indifference to the political articulation of ethnic issues continued into the early Soviet periods, and it was only in 1936 (more than a decade after neighboring ethnic groups) that the Soviet authorities granted the Mordvins an autonomous region, which came to be known as the Mordvin Autonomous Soviet Socialist Republic (ASSR), a constituent region of the Russian Soviet Federated Republic (RSFSR). However, most Mordvins lived outside of the republic. During the Soviet period, the Mordvin ASSR was closed to foreigners, largely because of the presence of numerous forced-labor camps in the territory of the republic. The republic's Communist administration was notoriously severe, and during the Gorbachev era conservative.

During the era of *perestroika* (1985–91) and soon after the collapse of the Soviet Union in 1991, a small Mordvin national movement emerged called "Mastorava" after the pre-Christian Mordvin earth spirit. However, the Mordvin republic remained a notoriously conservative and pro-Communist region within the former Soviet Union, and by 1992 the Mastorava movement had ceased to function.

² LOCATION AND HOMELAND

According to recent estimates, there are approximately 1.15 million Mordvins in the Soviet Union, making the Mordvins one of the largest ethnic minorities in Russia. The traditional homeland of the Mordvins is the Moksha and Sura River Valleys and their tributaries (these rivers are themselves tributaries of the Oka River). This area corresponds in broad terms to the territory of the current Republic of Mordovia, which occupied 26,200 square kilometers (10,100 square miles) and whose capital is the city of Saransk. The Republic of Mordovia and the immediately adjacent regions are located within the forest-steppe zone, with broadleaf forests interspersed with isolated areas of grasslands and fields. The climate is very much continental, with January temperatures averaging –12 to –11°c (about 16 to 18°F) and July temperatures averaging 20°c (about 70°F).

Most Mordvins, however, live outside their titular republic, either in the neighboring districts of Penza, Nizhnii Novgorod (formerly Penza), or in areas further to the east, such as Tatarstan or the districts of Simbirsk (formerly Ul'ianovsk), Saratov, Samara (formerly Kuibyshev), and Orenburg, or even in the more distant region of Siberia. Outside of the Russian Federation, Mordvin communities can be found in Kazakhstan and Armenia.

³ LANGUAGE

The Mordvin language actually consists of separate but closely related languages called Moksha and Erzia. Moksha and Erzia belong to the Volga Finnic branch of the Finno-Ugric language family. These languages are most closely related to Mari, another member of the Volga Finnic branch, and are more distantly related to Finnish and Estonian. Moksha and Erzia constitute two separate literary languages as well and, for the most part, these two languages are not mutually comprehensible, making Russian the language of communication between Erzias and Mokshas. Moksha speakers number approximately 300,000, and Erzia speakers approximately 500,000.

Virtually all Mordvins are fluent in Russian, often at the expense of their native language, and both Moksha and Erzia are heavily influenced by Russian, especially lexically. However, there also exists a small community of Mordvins in Tatarstan, known as Karatais, who long since abandoned the use of Mordvin, and speak only Tatar while retaining a strong sense of Mordvin identity.

Mordvin names consist of a first name, a patronymic (the father's name), and a surname. Since their Christianization in the early 18th century, Mordvin first names, patronymics, and often surnames are identical to common Russian names. However, some Mordvin surnames are derived from Mordvin words, such as *Vergazov* (*vergaz* meaning wolf) and *Atiakshev* (*atiaksh* meaning rooster).

⁴ FOLKLORE

The Mordvins have retained a rich body of oral literature and music, much of which was recorded in the Soviet era. Of particular interest are Mordvin historical songs, which some scholars have tried to identify as the remnants of a now-lost Mordvin national epic. Whether or not this is the case, a number of Mordvin historical songs (which in fact, are extensive narrative poems), have been passed down. These include narratives of the Russian conquest of Kazan, as well as accounts of Christianization in the 18th century.

In addition to the many songs, riddles, folk tales, and fairy tales that constitute the body of Mordvin oral literature, the Mordvins, despite their conversion to Christianity, have retained much of the mythology describing the spirits of their native religion. To be sure, Christian motifs are evident in many of the narratives, but at the same time much of the native tradition was retained and recorded by ethnographers. This mythology includes accounts of the creation of the world. In these accounts, the Erzia supreme deity is *Paza*, or *Chama-Paz*, and the Moksha one is called *Shkai*.

⁵ RELIGION

Mordvin communities as a whole were converted to Russian Orthodox Christianity in the first half of the 18th century, but some communities and individuals had adopted the new religion in the 17th and even 16th centuries. Although the Russian missionaries involved in the conversion of the Mordvins often made use of violence (and occasionally used troops to subdue Mordvin resistance), by the end of the 18th century, Russian observers often noted with satisfaction that the Mordvins were not only the most Russified of the region's minority nationalities, but also the most thoroughly Christianized. In fact, while Russian Orthodox Christianity as well as non-Orthodox sects sank deep roots in the Mordvin communities, the Mordvins retained much of their native religious orientation, which coexisted with Christian traditions. Not only did Mordvins retain their native mythology, but they continued to venerate native spirits, shrines, and their ancestors. Their activities included communal prayers and animal sacrifices for various field spirits, tutelary spirits known as *keremed'*, and ancestral spirits. This aspect of Mordvin religious life survived the Soviet period and is still evident today. Various Old Believer sects were also prevalent among Mordvins before 1917, and since 1991 many Mordvins have been attracted to Protestant sects that have been introduced.

⁶ MAJOR HOLIDAYS

The major holidays of the Mordvins correspond to the Russian Orthodox calendar, with the chief religious holidays being

Easter, and Orthodox New Year (January 6, by the Gregorian calendar). Traditionally, however, Mordvins observed most other Christian holidays and festivals as coinciding with the agricultural calendar. Equally important, if not more important, among modern-day Mordvins are the secular holidays that were promoted during the Soviet period and that continue to be observed today. These include New Year's Day (January 1), May Day (May 1), and Victory Day (May 9).

⁷ RITES OF PASSAGE

The major rites of passage among the Mordvins are closely connected with religious life. These include birth, baptism, marriage, and burial rituals. Birth rituals were typically performed by a religious specialist, usually an old woman, and included rituals to protect the newborn from harmful spirits. Baptism, although discouraged during the Soviet period, was nevertheless seen by many Mordvins not as a religious ritual, but rather as a Mordvin national custom. Mordvin weddings, at least in traditional society, were elaborate and complex rituals that differed widely from village to village. They included a specific repertoire of songs and other traditions and included feasting and other entertainments. Before the conversion to Christianity, Mordvin funeral rituals involved the inclusion of grave goods in the tomb of the deceased, but this tradition was largely abandoned by the late 18th century. However, the Mordvins did retain the tradition of funeral feasts for the dead, as well as the practice of holding communal prayers and making offerings at the tombs of ancestors.

[8] INTERPERSONAL RELATIONS

Interpersonal relations among the Mordvins (such as greeting, body language, and gestures), do not differ substantially from those of Russians. In both Erzia and Moksha, the typical greeting upon seeing someone for the first time on a given day is *"Shumbrat."*

[9] LIVING CONDITIONS

The bulk of the Mordvin population today continues to live in rural areas—that is, in villages. In Mordvin villages, the houses tend to be made out of wood. Typically, the house forms part of a courtyard, to which is attached sheds, barns, and other outbuildings. In addition, nearly every house has its own sauna or bathhouse. Most villages have electric power, but very few houses have any indoor plumbing, and water is usually obtained from a well or a communal pump. By American standards, the standard of living is rather low. Wages are usually very low, and there is little disposable income available for consumer goods. Similarly, health care in rural areas is of poor quality and not always available. However, Mordvins often make use of herbal medicines and other traditional remedies.

Very few Mordvins own their own cars, and most rely on public transportation. In urban areas, this includes buses and trains. In rural areas, bus transportation is not always reliable, and Mordvins, like others in Russia, must hitch rides with passing vehicles or rely on horse-drawn transportation.

[10] FAMILY LIFE

Women have traditionally played a special role in Mordvin society as the preservers of Mordvin cultural tradition. Historically, women were more confined to the home and rarely traveled far from their village, so they were less likely to speak Russian or be exposed to Russian culture. As a result, Mordvin women played a large role in the preservation of not only the Mordvin languages, but also of oral traditions and customs. In traditional Mordvin society, when a girl married she would leave her home and move in with her husband's family. As a result, a Mordvin family had an interest in delaying a daughter's wedding as long as possible, so as not to lose her labor, and there was a corresponding interest in marrying a son as soon as possible so as to bring an extra worker into the family. As a result, Russian observers noted the frequency of marriages between 11- or 12-year-old Mordvin boys with 25-year-old (or older) Mordvin women. During the Soviet period, this custom gradually disappeared, and today Mordvin marriage patterns are similar to those for Russia as a whole. A typical couple today will have only one or two children, whereas before World War II, family sizes were much larger, and the infant mortality rate was also much higher.

[11] CLOTHING

Traditional Mordvin festive clothing was typically white and decorated with elaborate embroidery. The most elaborate and artistic clothing was worn by women. By the 19th century, Mordvin men were already dressing in the Russian manner. Summer clothes were often woven out of linen in winter, woolens and reversed sheepskin coats were common. Currently, everyday clothing is identical to the clothing typical of Russian society as a whole.

[12] FOOD

The basis of the Mordvin economy was cereal agriculture, and the staples of the Mordvin diet were bread made from rye flour, as well as oats and barley. During the Soviet period, potatoes also came to form an important part of the Mordvins' diet. The main vegetables include cabbages, carrots, beets, and onions. The main types of meat are pork, chicken, and mutton. Beverages include tea, beer, and vodka. Traditionally, Mordvin eating utensils, with the exception of knives, were made out of wood. Mordvins also carved elaborate ladles and spoons out of wood for religious rituals.

[13] EDUCATION

Before the Soviet period, Mordvins had some access to religious schools established by church officials in their villages, and the most educated members of Mordvin society were often priests. However, access to higher education was extremely limited for Mordvins. Illiteracy rates were very high; among women, illiteracy was nearly universal.

In the Soviet period universal education was applied to Mordvins, as it was to the rest of Soviet society. The medium of instruction was often Russian, however, few Mordvins, especially in the later Soviet period, were educated in their native language. Typically, Mordvins achieve the equivalent of a high school education.

[14] CULTURAL HERITAGE

The creation of the Mordvin ASSR in 1936, in keeping with Leninist nationality policy, also necessitated the creation and sponsorship by the Soviet State of a Mordvin intelligentsia and a formal Mordvin national culture. Before the Soviet period, the only written Mordvin documents intended for Mordvins were prayer books and Bible translations published by the Russian Orthodox Church. By the 1920s, the standardization of the Mordvin languages into two separate literary languages, Erzia and Moksha, was already underway. Subsequently a Mordvin national literature emerged along Soviet lines, with poetry, prose, and drama being produced and performed in the two Mordvin literary languages, and published both in journals and as separate books. Similarly, the Mordvin intelligentsia created formal folk dance ensembles. Among the most well known Mordvin artists is the painter and sculptor Stepan Erzia (1876–1959), who was active before 1917, but is best known as a Soviet artist.

[15] WORK

Throughout their history, Mordvins have been primarily engaged in agricultural labor, and this would traditionally involve the entire family. During the Soviet period and since the collapse of the Soviet Union, Mordvin agriculture has been collectivized, with Mordvins either working as part of a collective farm (*kolkhoz*) or as paid employees on a state-owned farm (*sovkhoz*). Before the Soviet period, it was common for Mordvin laborers to belong to a cooperative organization, known as an *artel*, and during the Soviet period many Mordvin peasants moved into urban areas for industrial work.

[16] SPORTS

Numerous sports and games are played at the religious festivals of the Mordvins, especially foot races and horse races, and other contests. The most popular sports are soccer and hockey, which are not only spectator sports but played by children and young adults alike.

[17] ENTERTAINMENT AND RECREATION

The lack of recreational outlets in rural areas has limited the recreational opportunities of rural Mordvins. In larger urban areas, however, common recreational activities include the theater, movies, sports events, and television.

[18] FOLK ART, CRAFTS, AND HOBBIES

Mordvins are skilled at woodcarving, and this forms an important element of their folk art. Another folk art which is especially well-developed is weaving. Beekeeping is an economic activity that is also common among the Mordvins, but it is not practiced by every household, and it is often approached as a hobby.

[19] SOCIAL PROBLEMS

Among the most severe social problems of the Mordvins is alcoholism, which is endemic throughout the Russian Federation. The problem is especially severe in rural areas, where recreational opportunities are limited, if not entirely absent. In those areas, drinking alcohol is in effect the main form of recreation. In addition, the current economic crisis affecting all of the former Soviet Union is also a problem for Mordvins, who are suffering from low and erratic wages and a severely diminishing standard of living.

A different sort of problem facing the Mordvins is Russification. Historically, the Mordvins have managed to maintain some sense of separateness from Russians while being one of the most acculturated nationalities in Russia. The isolation of the Mordvins and their lack of access to Russian educational establishments ensured the survival of the Mordvin language, at least before 1917. However, the integration of the Mordvins into Soviet society and the access to Russian education coupled with limited access to Mordvin-language education has resulted in a rapid assimilation of Mordvins into Russian society. In fact, Russia's Mordvin population has gradually been declining.

[20] GENDER ISSUES

In traditional Mordvin society, particularly up until World War II, women and men had sharply divided social, economic and religious roles. Women were mainly responsible for child-rearing, domestic duties, and a portion of agricultural production. Observers of Mordvin communities commonly reported on a common practice among Mordvins of delaying marriage for girls as long as possible, so as not to lose an important source of labor for agriculture. As a result it was common for young Mordvin men to take much older brides. Before the 1940's literacy was extremely rare among Mordvin women due to their limited access to education. World War II brought large numbers of Mordvin women into the industrial and urban workforce, and into the Soviet educational system, after which they largely remained in the workforce, while retaining their traditional roles in child-rearing and domestic duties. Their limited access to education also made Mordvin women particularly culturally conservative, especially in terms of native language retention and religious activities. Since 1991 Mordvin women have largely maintained their access to education. Certain religious ceremonies excluded either men or women, but more generally it was women who retained religious ceremonies and practices, despite official anti-religious pressure from the authorities during the Soviet era.

[21] BIBLIOGRAPHY

Belitser, V. N. *Narodnaia odezhda mordvy*, Moscow, 1973

Frank, Allen. "Traditional Religion in the Volga-Ural Region: 1960-1987" *Ural-Altaische Jahrbücher* 63 (1991); 167–84.

———. "Resolutions of the First All-Union Congress of the Mordvin Mastorava Society for National Rebirth" *Ural-Altaische Jahrbücher* 64 (1992):153–55.

Kreindler, Isabelle. The Mordvinians: a Doomed Soviet Nationality? Jerusalem, 1984

Lallukka, Seppo. East Finnic Minorities in the Soviet Union: An Appraisal of the Erosive Trends. Helsinki, 1990.

Makarkin, P. N. (ed.) Mordva: Istoriko-kul'turnye ocherki. Saransk, 1995.

Maskaev, A. I. *Mordovskaia narodnaia epicheskaia pesnia*, Saransk, 1964.

Mel'nikov, P. I. *Ocherki mordvy* (Saransk, 1981) [originally written in 1867].

Vuorela, Toivo. "The Mordvinians," in: *The Finno-Ugric Peoples*, (Indiana University Uralic and Altaic Series, No. 39), Bloomington, IN, 1964, 221-236.

—by A. J. Frank

NANAIS

ALTERNATE NAMES: Hezhen, Goldy
LOCATION: Russia (extreme southeastern Siberia), China (Heilongjiang Province)
POPULATION: 12,160 in Russia (2002), 4,640 in China (2004)
LANGUAGE: Nanai, Russian, Chinese
RELIGION: Shamanism

¹ INTRODUCTION

The Nanais are an indigenous people of extreme southeastern Siberia (also called the Russian Far East) who inhabit the shores of the Amur River and its tributaries. Anthropological, linguistic, and archaeological data suggest that people similar to the Nanais in ethnicity, language, and culture have continuously inhabited the Amur region and supported themselves by fishing and hunting since the Neolithic era (that is, for more than 3,000 years). The Nanais were formed from a mixture of these local groups with migrants who gradually arrived from the north, west, and south (i.e., from Siberia and Manchuria).

The Nanais' name for themselves is *Nanai* (plural: *Nanaisal*), which means "local dweller" and is derived from the words *na* (place, land) and *nai* (person). The Nanais were previously called *Gol'dy* in Russian ethnographic literature. This term is the word for "Nanai" in the language of the Ul'chi, another Amur people who are closely related ethnically and linguistically to the Nanais. (The name *Nani* has also been used by both the Nanais and the Ul'chi to refer to themselves.)

For several centuries prior to their absorption by the Russian empire in the mid-19th century, the Nanais maintained trade relations with the Russians, Chinese, and the Manchus who conquered China in 1644 and established the Qing Dynasty. They exchanged fur, ginseng, and reindeer antlers (used in a powdered form as an aphrodisiac by the Chinese) for guns, iron, tea, flour, tobacco, vodka, grain, and textiles. Russian explorers probably made contact with the Nanais as early as the 1640s, but the Manchus claimed the Amur region as their own because it was adjacent to their homeland. In any event, the border drawn between the Russian and Chinese empires in 1689 left the Nanais under the latter's control. The Manchus levied taxes upon the Nanais and the other Amur peoples, appointed elders for their villages, and formed marriage alliances between Manchu officials and local clan leaders; many Nanai village and clan leaders became very wealthy in this way. After Russia gained control of the Amur region from China in the 1858 Treaty of Aigun and the 1860 Treaty of Peking, the Nanais became Russian subjects. Tens of thousands of Russian colonists began to pour into Nanai territory; this process was encouraged by the tsarist government, which considered the Amur River basin to be a strategic area and feared Chinese encroachment on it if it were left sparsely populated by non-Russian aborigines. These colonists settled on Nanai hunting grounds, seized the best fishing areas, and used both dishonest commercial methods and the threat of violence to cheat the Nanais out of land and other property. The Nanais became a minority in their own land, and their standard of living greatly declined. By the early 20th century, the ratio of colonists and their descendents to Nanais was 90 to 1. The Amur peoples suffered greatly from the destruction and bloodshed of the Civil War that followed the Bolsheviks' seizure of power in October 1917. The Amur River basin was the scene of intense fighting among the Communist Red Army, the anti-Communist White Army, and Japanese troops who hoped to take advantage of the chaos to extend Japan's influence in the region.

Conditions among the Nanais improved in the 1920s after the end of the Civil War. Bolshevik-sponsored cooperatives allowed Nanai fishermen and hunters to pool their scarce resources, and the new government took steps to develop education and Western medical care. The Nanais' fortunes worsened, however, after Stalin's rise to power in 1929. They were forced out of their widely scattered traditional villages and crowded into a smaller number of large settlements, which the government's economic planners considered more efficient. Moreover, Stalin and his successors intensively developed mining, logging, and industry in the Amur region without taking environmental consequences into account. This resulted in serious ecological damage to Nanai territory.

² LOCATION AND HOMELAND

As of 2002 there were slightly more than 12,640 Nanais in the Russian Federation, and almost all of them live in the Russian Far East near the Chinese border. As of 1989 about 11,600 Nanais resided in Khabarovsk Territory (Russian *krai*), chiefly in its Khabarkovsk, Nanai, and Komsomol'sk Districts (Russian *raion*). Some 400 more Nanai lived along the Ussuri River in the neighboring Primorskii (Maritime) Territory, and an additional 170 dwelt on the island of Sakhalin off the Russian Federation's eastern coast. In addition, as of 2004 there were about 4,600 Nanais in the northeastern reaches of the People's Republic of China, primarily in Manchuria, where they are known as the *Hezhen*.

The climate of the Nanais' territory is somewhat different from much of Siberia and the Russian Far East. For example, its summers are relatively warm, with July temperatures averaging between 16° and 20°C (60.8° and 68°F). Monsoon winds from the Pacific bring heavy rainfall in late summer and early fall and sometimes result in severe flooding. Winters are severe: heavy snows and high, chilly winds are typical, and January temperatures range between –28° and –20°C (–18.4° and –4°F). Most of the territory inhabited by the Nanais consists of low-lying valley lands along a 700-kilometer(420-mile) stretch of the Amur River. Marshlands, sometimes containing larch groves, are common at the lowest elevations, and the banks of the Amur and other rivers are dotted with small islands separated by rivulets. The northernmost reaches of Nanai settlement are more mountainous the further one goes from the Amur. Larch, yew, birch, maple, lilac, honeysuckle, and swamp grasses are the most typical forms of vegetation in low-lying areas. Mountains are mostly covered with mixed forests of larch, spruce, fir, ash, lime, maple, and walnut (with larch predominating in the foothills). At the highest elevations, cedar and lichens are the most common plants. Rivers have traditionally been rich in aquatic life, particularly salmon and otters, although overfishing has seriously reduced stocks in recent decades. Squirrels, foxes, bears, sables, hares, boars, Siberian tigers, elks, grouse, and deer are the most widespread fauna on dry land.

³ LANGUAGE

The Nanai language belongs to the Altaic language family's Tungusic, or Tungus-Manchu, branch. Its closest relatives are tongues spoken by other peoples of the Amur region (Oroch, Ul'chi, and Udegei), Manchu, and the language of the Xibei people of northwestern China's Xinjiang Province (who are the descendants of Manchu frontier troops). The languages of the Evenki and Evens of eastern and northeastern Siberia are also closely related to Nanai. In addition to borrowings from other Tungusic languages, the Nanai vocabulary includes loan words from Russian and Chinese as well as Nivkh (an unrelated language spoken in the Amur Region and on the island of Sakhalin). Nanai is divided into several regional forms that differ from each other to varying degrees. The classification of these forms of Nanai as dialects or subdialects (minor variants of dialects) has long been a matter of controversy among linguists specializing in the study of the Tungusic languages, and there is still no scholarly agreement on this issue. Prior to the Soviet period, the Nanai language did not have a written form except for the academic transcriptions of linguists. A Nanai writing system based on the Latin alphabet was adopted in 1931; five years later, it was replaced by the Cyrillic (Russian) alphabet, which is still in use. The modern Nanai literary language is based on the Naikhin dialect (the most widely spoken form of Nanai). Diacritics and special letters are used to reflect Nanai sounds that are absent in Russian, but their use is not always consistent. For example, Nanai, like other Altaic languages, differentiates between "long" (stressed) and "short" (unstressed) vowels. In some writings, a diacritic shaped like a short line is written over a vowel letter to indicate that it is a long vowel, but in other books, double letters are used. (See the titles of the two Nanai dictionaries in the bibliography for examples of variant spellings.)

Some Nanai personal names are very ancient, and their sources and original meanings remain a mystery to ordinary Nanais and linguists alike. This is the case with the male names *Bamba* and *Gibi* and the female names *Dekhe* and *Iaota*. The etymologies of other traditional names are clearer. Some, such as *Orokto* ("grass," male) and *Sunke* ("beetle," female) are the words for plants and animals in the Nanai environment Others—for example, the male name *Aka* ("strong or brave man") and the female name *Bulke* ("gentle")—refer to positive characteristics that parents wish a child to possess. During the 20th century, Russian personal names such as *Anna* (female) and *Fyodor* (male) have become widespread.

The use of surnames based upon the name of a given family's clan (*Kilen, Gair, Oninkan*, etc.) has been common since the 1930s. It is interesting to note that the spelling of many clan-based Nanai surnames often differs from the actual Nanai pronunciation of these names: this is most likely due to mistakes made by Russian bureaucrats while filling out personnel forms and other paperwork when the use of surnames was first required. Thus, the surname of the Nanai cultural anthropologist and native-rights activist Evdokiia Gair is written *Gaer*; the surnames of the linguists Sulungu Oninkan and Nikolai Kilen are spelled *Onenko* and *Kile*, respectively.

⁴ FOLKLORE

Nanai folklore includes legends and stories (*telungu* or *ningman*) about the origins of the universe, the earth, humans, animals, and local mountains, rocks, and lakes. Some *telungu* and

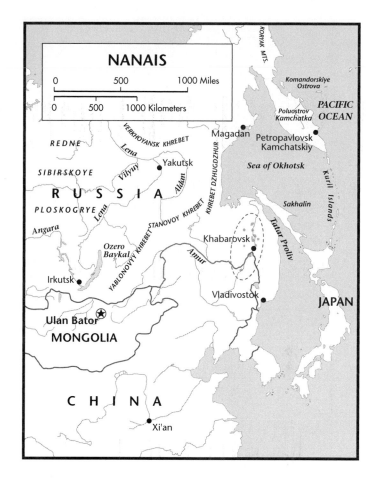

ningman narrate the feats of shamans and the exploits of hunters and warriors; others tell the histories of the various Nanai clans and the animals or plants (tigers, bears, hawks, birches, etc.) from which they descended. Generally speaking, a legend or story is called a *telungu* if its events are believed to have occurred in remote antiquity; otherwise, it is called a *ningman*. There are also numerous tongue twisters (*deuruen*), and riddles (*nambokan*).

In traditional Nanai society, folklore was not only a form of entertainment, but also an important tool of socialization. Many works of oral literature indirectly taught the young proper behavior, useful hunting and fishing techniques, and the mythology and religion of the community. Given Nanai folklore's didactic aspect, it is not surprising that many tales concern human shortcomings such as laziness and vanity. One *ningman* tells the story of Aioga, a beautiful but extremely vain girl. One day, Aioga's mother asked her to go fetch some water, but Aioga refused, preferring instead to sit admiring her own reflection in a shiny copper pan. A neighbor girl offered to go in Aioga's place, and Aioga's mother rewarded her with a scone, but did not give one to Aioga. Enraged, Aioga fled from her mother in a rage and sat down to pout on the bank of a nearby stream. Aioga stared at her reflection in the water, now and then glaring at the neighbor girl, who sat on the opposite bank eating her scone. Suddenly, Aioga's neck began to grow. Noticing this, she flapped her arms in anger, and they turned into wings. She then fell into the stream, where she turned into a swan. She forgot how to speak Nanai and could only remem-

A storyteller of the Siberian Nanai tribe.
(© Viviane Moos/Corbis)

ber her name, which henceforth became the call of the swan: "Ai-oga-ga-ga! Ai-oga-ga-ga!"

⁵ RELIGION

Traditional Nanai religion includes shamanistic practices. Nanai shamanists believe that fire, mountains, stars, constellations, forests, and rivers have spirits *(endur)* that humans must respect in order to survive and prosper. The most revered nature-spirit is the sky-god, whose names are Sangiia and Boaendurni. Certain animals, such as bears and Siberian tigers, are also considered spiritually powerful and are eaten only at ritual meals. Lesser spirits or ghosts, called *seven* or *busyu*, are capable of helping or harming humans. The Nanai shaman *(saman)*, like the Native American "medicine man," is a man or woman skilled at communicating with all these spirits during rituals that involve chanting and singing prayers and beating an *ungchukhun* (a large, flat, round drum). Nanai shamans use their rituals to heal the sick, improve believers' fortunes, and foretell the future. The most powerful shamans, called *kasaty-saman*, accompany the deceased to Buni, the World of the Dead. (A *kasaty-saman* must always be a man.) Although the profession of shamanism is hereditary, not all sons and daughters of shamans follow the path of their ancestors: they must be chosen by the spirits themselves. Each shaman is guided and protected by a personal helper-spirit, or *aiami*. If the shaman is a man, his *aiami* is a woman; the *aiami* of female shamans are always male. A shaman's *aiami* is considered his or her spouse, and the two have sexual intercourse during the shaman's dreams. The shaman is respected but never envied. It is believed that a shaman's life does not belong to him or her, but rather to the *aiami*. Therefore, no Nanai wishes to become a shaman, and a person chosen by the spirits often resists the call for years. After the Nanais' homeland passed under Russian control, missionaries from the Russian Orthodox Church effected their conversion to Christianity. Although many were formally baptized, they continued to practice their ancient religion along with Russian Orthodox practices. Nanai shamans, like those of other Siberian native peoples, suffered imprisonment and execution during Stalin's anti-religious campaigns and as a result shamanism was driven underground. Since Soviet leader Mikhail Gorbachev ended the Soviet government's persecution of religion during the 1980s, the Nanais have begun to practice shamanism more openly.

⁶ MAJOR HOLIDAYS

Most traditional Nanai "holidays" are not celebrated at the same time every year, as they are essentially shamanist rites performed for specific purposes. Among these are the ritual blessings of hunting and fishing gear by shamans and the monthly wakes held by bereaved relatives and friends for several years after a person's death. Some holidays do, however, have a more or less set date. The most important of these is the *nengnemeni enei*, a spring gathering held in the last days of April and the first few days of May to celebrate the breaking up of the river ice and the beginning of the spring fishing season. During the *nengnemeni enei*, dozens of members of related families set up camp together on the riverbank and celebrate the end of winter with dancing, games, storytelling, singing, and feasting. Ritual offerings of food, drink, and tobacco are made to the water and fire spirits. Centuries-long contact with Chinese traders and settlers has led the Nanais to adopt the Chinese New Year, which is marked by family feasts. During the Soviet period, the Nanai celebrated communist holidays such as May Day (1 May), the anniversary of the victory over Nazi Germany (9 May), International Women's Day (8 March), and the anniversary of the Bolshevik Revolution (7 November).

⁷ RITES OF PASSAGE

In traditional Nanai society, childbirth was surrounded by numerous rules that had to be observed to ensure the child's survival. As soon as a Nanai woman discovered that she was pregnant, she had to observe certain taboos. For instance, she could not sew or use glue in her housework during the last stages of pregnancy or the fetus would be "stuck" to the womb and the delivery would be difficult. She could not attend funerals or she would have a miscarriage. (If she could not avoid attending a funeral, she had to first gird her loins with a protective rope or net). Chopping tree branches could cause deformities or induce an expected boy to be born as a girl. A pregnant woman was also forbidden to eat certain foods. If she ate the hearts of large game animals, her heart would not withstand the delivery. Consuming the eyes of roast fish might cause the child to be born with a sore on its eye, while squirrel's brains could cause hyperactivity. Husbands of pregnant women also had to observe certain taboos. For example, they could not hunt on the eve of a birth or the child might be born with a harelip. Activities that required driving stakes into the ground (for example, building fences) were also to be avoided close to the expected date of birth, since they too could harm the fetus. Delivery took place in a temporary shelter near the house, access to which was forbidden to all save the birthing mother, a midwife, and female relatives or friends. After the child was born, special measures were taken to conceal its identity from malevolent spirits by confusing them in various ways. No public celebration was held, and family members spoke vaguely when informing others of the fact of the birth. Additionally, the child was ritually given to a couple from another clan or even another nationality, against whom the spirits were harmless; In addition, it was temporarily given a name intended either to disgust harmful spirits, such as *Polokto* ("moldiness") or *Lebe* ("vomit or trash"), or to frighten them—*Nekte* ("wild boar") or *Kachakta* ("prickly salmon"). For the last few decades, delivery has taken place in hospitals, and many traditional taboos relating to childbirth are no longer observed.

The most ancient means of disposing of the dead among the Nanais and other Amur peoples is internment in wooden or bark coffins raised on platforms. Infants who died before their first birthday have traditionally been wrapped in cloth or birch-bark and placed in the hollows of trees. As a result of Russian influence, burial in the ground has replaced platform and tree burial. After a person has died, he or she is placed on a flat board called a *dirkinche*. The corpse's face is covered with a cloth, and its feet are tied with a white braided string and held in place by a stone, lest the soul of the deceased kick the souls of his or her relatives. Food, drink, a pipe, and tobacco are placed next to the body. After several days have passed, the body is dressed in fine clothes that have been kept for the occasion, put into a coffin, and taken to a cemetery, where it is buried. (Personal possessions that have been broken or torn to allow their owner's spirit to escape from them are placed into the coffin along with the body. Men are buried with hunting and fishing tools, and women with sewing pouches containing needles and thread.) On the seventh day after death, a shaman performs a ritual to lead the soul of the deceased to the World of the Dead *(Buni)*. Traditional Nanai burial practices have been preserved to a much higher degree than birth rituals.

⁸ INTERPERSONAL RELATIONS

Among Nanais who follow traditional rules of behavior, it is a sign of respect to bow upon meeting someone. There are certain protocols that must be observed when deciding whether or not to bow. For example, one never bows to a younger person or to a person of the same age. Men always bow to older men and older women, but women do not bow to older members of either sex. There are no special rules for bowing to shamans: one bows to them only if they are male and older than oneself.

⁹ LIVING CONDITIONS

The ancestors of the Nanais originally lived in dugouts with log frames and roofs, but for centuries the most typical Nanai dwelling has been the *dio*, a large, one-room rectangular house whose design shows strong Chinese and/or Manchu influence.

The walls of the *dio* are formed by a lattice-type frame of willow or alder branches; this frame is then covered on both sides with thick layers of clay. The *dio* is heated by several adobe stoves. Benches around the walls of the *dio* serve as both seats and beds, and a large platform in its center is used for storing hunting, cooking, and fishing tools and other items of everyday use. The windows were formerly covered with fish skin or Chinese wax paper, but now glass is more common. Wealthy Nanais furnished their homes with lacquered cupboards and chests-of-drawers manufactured in China. Although the *dio* has not entirely vanished, most rural Nanais now live in the one-story Russian-style wooden houses characteristic of collective farms throughout the former Soviet Union. Nanais in Komsomol'sk and other urban areas dwell in typical Soviet concrete apartment buildings.

Since fishing has long been the chief occupation of most Nanais, boats have naturally been the most important means of transport. Canoes are made either by hollowing out logs or by attaching panels of birch-bark or wood to a wooden frame. Nanai canoes are usually propelled by double-headed paddles (similar to those used with kayaks), although sometimes long poles are used to push the canoe along from the river bottom in shallow water. Skis and dogsleds are the most common means of traditional transport on dry land; certain groups of Nanais have also traditionally used horses for riding, carrying loads, and pulling sleds. Motorboats, trucks, bicycles, and motorcycles—along with buses and automobiles in urban areas—have become commonplace in recent decades, but they have not entirely crowded out customary Nanai means of transportation.

In traditional society, the Nanais relied almost exclusively on herbal remedies and the incantations of shamans, although they occasionally purchased pharmaceutical remedies from Russian or Chinese traders. Western medicine has become widespread during the 20th century, as the Soviet government provided free or low-cost universal health care to all its citizens. Still, Western medicine has not eliminated traditional Nanai forms of treatment. Clinics are sometimes too far away, and they usually offer only the most rudimentary forms of medical assistance. Moreover, Nanai herbal medicines are often quite effective, as they are the products of hundreds, (perhaps thousands), of years of investigation and practice.

¹⁰ FAMILY LIFE

Traditional Nanai society was based on small households consisting of a man, a woman, several children, and perhaps a few elderly parents. Wealthy Nanais often had more than one wife; this practice was abolished during the Communist period, although anthropologists encountered a few elderly polygamous families as late as the 1950s and 1960s. Each household belonged to one of 20 or so clans *(khala)* that varied considerably in size: the smallest clans had only a few dozen members, while the largest had more than 900 members. Marrying a member of the same clan was forbidden. Small clans sometimes formed inter-clan alliances by the marriage of a member of one clan to a member of another clan; these alliances were called *dokha*. Custom forbade marriage between members of the same *dokha*, although exceptions were occasionally made on grounds of economic hardship (for example, when a widow needed to remarry in order to survive and could not find a suitable partner outside her *dokha*). Members of the clans and inter-clan alliances aided each other in times of need, held courts that judged members accused of wrongdoing, and took revenge upon other *khala* and *dokha* whose members had caused harm to their people. The social functions of the clans and *dokha* in everyday life have lessened in importance over the course of the 20th century, although certain features (for example, the ban on intermarriage) are still observed.

The work of men and women in traditional Nanai economic activities is strictly defined by custom, although the contributions of each are equally valued. Men's work includes fishing, hunting, and making and repairing the weapons and tools used in these activities. Women cure meat and fish, prepare animal and fish skins, sew, clean, care for children, and cook. Women also fish when their husbands are absent. Since the Soviet period, men have also worked in forestry, while medicine, teaching, and work in the service sector has largely been performed by women.

11 CLOTHING

The traditional Nanai garment for both men and women is the *tetue*, an ankle-length robe fastened on one side with buttons or hooks. Winter *tetue* are made of fish skin that when cured produces a soft, and light but warm leather; summer garments are made of boar skin. (In the prerevolutionary period, wealthy Nanai men and women also wore silk robes, hats, and shoes imported from China.) Both sexes wear the *tetue* with a belt *(omol)*, short trousers *(peru)* and leggings *(garon)*. Women wear a breastplate *(lele)* festooned with metal pendants. Low boots *(ota)* made of fish or boar skin lined with soft grasses are worn with cloth or leather stockings *(dokton)*. The most distinctive type of Nanai headgear is the men's rounded cap *(korbochi)* worn with earflaps *(siapton)* and a white cloth veil *(garmaso)* that falls over the neck and shoulders from the back of the head. (This design was originally conceived to protect hunters from the gnats and mosquitoes common during the damp Amur summers.) Present-day Nanais usually wear Western clothing (cloth dresses, shirts, trousers, stockings, socks, and underclothes, and leather shoes), except on holidays and other special occasions.

12 FOOD

The most common food in traditional Nanai cuisine is fish, particularly salmon. The Nanais usually prepare fish by boiling, smoking, freezing, or drying. Salting fish and other meat was unknown prior to Russian contact but is now a common method of preparation. Fish is sometimes eaten raw as well. Favorite Nanai dishes include *boda*, a porridge made of salmon roe and millet; *taksan*, which is made by boiling a mass of fish in their own oil and fat; and *tala*, thin chips of frozen fish. Berries, mushrooms, and edible grasses are eaten fresh or preserved for later use by drying them in the sun and wind. Flour is used to make scones and pancakes. Squirrel, elk, venison, pork, and boar, although consumed less frequently than fish, are also part of the traditional Nanai diet. Prior to the 20th century, most Nanais ate with their hands or wooden spoons from bark, horn, or wood plates and bowls. (Wealthy Nanais used porcelain dishes of Chinese manufacture). Traditional dishware and utensils have largely been replaced with Russian mass-produced metal knives, forks, and spoons, enamel pots and pans, and porcelain dishes. Canned vegetables and meats, bread and pastries, vodka and other alcoholic beverages, and sweets have become established ingredients of the Nanai diet.

13 EDUCATION

After the Russian acquisition of the Amur region in the mid-19th century, Russian missionaries established schools that combined the teaching of the Russian language and general educational subjects with instruction in Russian Orthodox Christianity, but their influence on the Nanais was slight. The Soviet government began to establish public schools among the Nanais in the 1920s. These initially used only Russian textbooks, as linguists did not perfect a Nanai alphabet until 1931. Today all Nanais attend primary school and at least some secondary school, and many attend college. However, alongside these indisputable benefits, the manner in which education developed among the Nanai has threatened their cultural heritage, because Soviet policies toward minority peoples after the 1920s tended more and more to suppress their cultures and languages. Between the 1950s and the 1980s, the use of Nanai in the classroom both as a means of instruction and as an academic subject was all but eliminated, and Nanai culture in general was disparaged in favor of Russian culture. As a result, although all Nanais are fluent in Russian (a prerequisite for higher education), many have at best a dim understanding of their own people's history and traditions, and only 44% speak Nanai as their native language. Since the 1980s, native teachers and scholars have achieved some success in expanding instruction in native folklore, language, and crafts in Nanai schools.

14 CULTURAL HERITAGE

Although the Nanais did not possess a written language until the 20th century, oral literature has been a highly prized part of the Nanai cultural heritage since time immemorial. Folklore was customarily recited by male and female bards called *ningmanso (ningmasu* in some dialects). Men's performances *(khuse nai ningmani)* often included singing passages, but tradition forbade women to sing in the presence of men, so the female bards' performances *(ekte nai ningmani)* consisted entirely of spoken recitations. The *ningmanso* have all but disappeared from Nanai society, due not least to Soviet officialdom's policies aimed at suppressing non-Russian cultures, which it viewed as "backward" and "anti-Soviet." Nevertheless, scholars managed to collect and publish valuable folklore materials both in Nanai and in Russian translations during the Soviet period; this work has continued since the fall of communism, although in extremely difficult conditions. The growth of Nanai literacy has allowed a creative intellectual class to form during the 20th century. The poems, short stories, and novels of Grigorii Khodzher, Kisa Geiker, Vladimir Zaksor, Akim Samar, Andrei Passar, and Georgii Bel'dy have been published in both Nanai and Russian. On a worldwide level probably the best known Nanai figure is Dersu Uzala, the hero of the 1975 film of the same name by Japanese director Akira Kurosawa. Kurosawa's film was based on the memoir by early 20th century Russian explorer Vladimir Arsen'ev, whose book *Dersu the Trapper* describes his Nanai guide who accompanied Arsen'ev during his explorations of the Maritime Province.

15 WORK

Fishing and, to a lesser degree, hunting have been the mainstays of the Nanai economy for thousands of years. The phenomenal richness of the Nanai language's vocabulary in terminology relating to fishing tools and techniques attests to the important place fishing has occupied in Nanai daily life.

The Nanais obtain fish by hooking, netting, trapping, and spearing. Most salmon fishing is done between July and September, when the salmon are spawning; carp, pike, and catfish are caught year-round. Otters, foxes, lynxes, and martens are hunted for their fur, which has traditionally been used in trade and clothing manufacture. These animals are caught by deadfalls, nets, and small self-firing bows and arrows called *dengure* that are rigged to shoot animals that disturb them. Meat is obtained from elk, deer, and boars, while squirrels provide both meat and fur. Game animals are either trapped by the same methods used to catch fur-bearing animals or are killed with spears or bows and arrows. Traditional Nanai economic activities greatly changed during the Soviet period: individual hunters and small hunting groups were replaced by state-run fishing and hunting enterprises. The use of firearms, which became common after Russian colonization began in the 19th century, has become universal in the 20th century, although rifles and shotguns have not eliminated traditional weapons.

16 SPORTS

Many traditional Nanai sports are based on fishing and hunting. For example, boat and ski races not only provide entertainment, but also teach young Nanais the skills necessary to travel to fishing spots and to pursue game animals. (Such races also allow older Nanais to maintain and refresh these skills.)

In one children's winter sport, *khasigboan* ("catch"), a small boy chosen for his speed and cunning plays the role of "deer," while three to five older boys pursue him on skis in the capacity of "hunters." (If there are more than five "hunters," there must be two "deer.") The "deer" sets off from the starting point alone, and the "hunters" follow 15 or 20 minutes later. The "deer" must return to the starting point without being caught by the "hunters," who attempt to find him and "shoot" him by symbolically touching him with a ski pole. The first "hunter" to thus shoot the deer is declared the winner and receives the title of "*bongo khasigboan*" or "best pursuer."

17 ENTERTAINMENT AND RECREATION

Nanai children of both sexes enjoy playing with dolls. Girls' dolls are made of birch-bark and paper and represent people; boys' dolls are made of animal bones and hair and birds' beaks and represent bears and other animals. A popular form of entertainment among adult Nanais is *arakap*, a board game similar to chess. *Arakap* uses a wooden board (*undene*) upon which are drawn five vertical and three horizontal "roads" (*pokto*) or lines. The game's two players move five "soldiers" (*pikte*) around the board in an attempt to outmaneuver each other. (Unlike chess, the "soldiers" in *arakap* are placed on the intersections between the "roads" rather than inside the squares formed by them.) If a "soldier" belonging to one player is backed into a corner and surrounded by two or more "soldiers" belonging to the other player, it is removed from the game. The player who loses all his "soldiers" first is the loser.

18 FOLK ART, CRAFTS, AND HOBBIES

Nanai women are skilled at decorating items of clothing with appliqué and embroidery and fashioning containers from birch bark. Men carve decorations into knife handles, door posts, window sills, and other items of daily use. The clothing of shamans is particularly elaborate; it is usually decorated with pictures of trees, dragons, humans, birds, insects, snakes, and other animals. Spirals and waves are the most common geometric designs in Nanai folk art. Dragons (a result of Chinese influence) are also quite common. Wood is carved into statues representing spirits and amulets intended to bring their bearer good fortune. During the 20th century, secular wood sculpture, usually of human and animal figures, has also become common.

19 SOCIAL PROBLEMS

The modern Nanais face a variety of social problems that are shared by all native Siberian peoples. For example, many Nanais suffer from poor health brought about by heavy drinking, inadequate medical care and diet, and air and water pollution caused by Soviet-era mining and industrial practices. Nanai living standards are often low, due not only to the Soviet system's economic inefficiency (particularly in the distribution of consumer goods), but also to ethnic and racial prejudice as well: indigenous Amur peoples are often either paid less than Russians for equivalent work (even in fishing and other traditional economic activities) or confined to the lowest-paid jobs. The wasteful harvesting of the Nanais' natural resources by Soviet industry has resulted in the depletion of fish and other animal stocks and the destruction of more than 30% of the Amur region's forests. Issues of Nanai cultural survival have also come to the fore in recent years as a result of the lingering effects of policies intended by Stalin and his successors to force the Nanais and other non-Russian peoples to give up their "primitive" cultures in favor of the more "advanced" Russian one. Since the Nanais' arts, oral literature, folkways, and language were excluded from the local mass media and Nanai schools for decades, many young Nanais have been robbed of their cultural heritage. Nanai scholars, both in local teachers' colleges and in St. Petersburg's Pedagogical Institute of the Peoples of the North, are now making great efforts to expand knowledge of the Nanai language by training Nanai teachers and writing new textbooks and dictionaries for Nanai children. The relaxation of Soviet nationality policy under Mikhail Gorbachev allowed the Nanais to express pride in their cultural heritage without fear of being labeled "anti-Soviet," and Nanai music and dance festivals began to be held more frequently during the late 1980s. Nanai political activists, led by the cultural anthropologist Evdokiia Gaer, now participate in the Association of the Small Peoples of the North and other organizations that defend the Siberian peoples' economic, political, and cultural interests before the Russian government and the public.

20 GENDER ISSUES

A strong division of labor and defined gender roles characterized relations between the sexes in traditional Nanai society. During and after the Second World War Russian Nanai society became strongly integrated in Soviet society and the Soviet economy. Among the Chinese Nanais, or Hezhens, their integration into the People's Republic of China began already in 1945, as the Nanais were one of the first minority nationalities to come under Communist control. For Soviet Nanai women traditional gender roles eroded quickly, and many Nanai women were able to benefit from educational possibilities the Soviet integration afforded. As a result among the Nanais, as among several other small Siberian peoples, women constitute a particularly active force in the preservation of Nanai culture and in advocating for the interests of Nanai communities.

²¹ BIBLIOGRAPHY

Arsen'ev, Vladimir K. *Dersu the Trapper.* Kingston, NY: McPherson & Company, 1996.

Avrorin, V. A. *Materialy po nanaiskomu iazyku i fol'kloru* [Materials on Nanai Language and Folklore]. In Russian and Nanai. Ed. S. N. Onenko. Leningrad: Nauka, 1986.

Bartels, Dennis A,. and Alice L. Bartels. *When the North was Red: Aboriginal Education in Soviet Siberia.* Montreal: McGill-Queen's University Press, 1995.

Forsyth, James. *A History of the Peoples of Siberia: Russia's North Asian Colony, 1581–1990.* Cambridge: Cambridge University Press, 1992.

Gaer, Evdokiya A. "Birth Rituals of the Nanai." In: *Culture Incarnate: Native Anthropology from Russia.* Ed. Marjorie Mandelstam Balzer. Armonk, NY: M. E. Sharpe, 1995.

———. *Traditsionnaia bytovaia obriadnost' nanaitsev v kontse XIX-nachale XX v.* [Traditional Everyday Rituals of the Nanai at the End of the Nineteenth Century and the Beginning of the Twentieth Century]. In Russian. Moscow: Mysl', 1991.

———. "Nasha sila v edinstve" [Our Strength is in Unity]. In: *Narodov malykh ne byvaet* [There Are No Small (e.g. "Minor") Peoples]. Moscow: Molodaia Gvardiia, 1991.

Kile, N. B. "Antroponimiia u nanaitsev" [Personal Names among the Nanais]. In: *Proiskhozdenie aborigentsev Sibiri i ikh iazykov* [Origins of the Aborigines of Siberia and their Languages]. In Russian. Ed. E. G. Bekker, et al. Tomsk: Izdatel'stvo Tomskogo Universiteta, 1973.

———. "Problemy izucheniia i publikatsii fol'klora nanaitsev" [Problems of the Study and Publication of Nanai Folklore] in vol. 1 of *Aborigeny Sibiri: Problemy izucheniia ischezaiiushchikh iazykov i kul'tur* [The Aborigenes of Siberia: Problems of the Study of Vanishing Languages and Peoples]. In Russian. 2 vols. Novosibirsk: Rossiiskaia Akademiia nauk, Sibirskoe otdelenie, 1995.

Kile, Pongsy Konstantinovich. "Igry nashego detstva" [Games of Our Childhood]. In: *Severnye prostory* [Northern Expanses] 42 (June 1991): 35–37.

Malygina, A. A. "Mir detstva u narodov Sibiri" [The World of Childhood among the Peoples of Siberia]. In: *Ekologiia etnicheskikh kul'tur Sibiri nakanune XXI veka* [The Ecology of Ethnic Cultures of Siberia on the Eve of the Twenty-first Century]. In Russian. Ed. V. B. Kurylev and V. A. Koz'min. St. Petersburg: Nauka, 1995.

Onenko, S. N. *Lotsa-naanai khesengkuni/Russko-nanaiskii slovar'* [Russian-Nanai Dictionary]. In Russian and Nanai. Moscow: Russkii iazyk, 1986.

Pisateli malykh narodov Dal'nego Vostoka: biobibliograficheskii spravochnik [Writers of the Small Peoples of the Far East: A Biographical and Bibliographic Guide]. In Russian. Comp. S. Zaitseva. Ed. A. Maslova. Khabarovsk: Khabarovskoe knizhnoe izdatel'stvo, 1966.

Schwarz, Henry. *The Minorities of Northern China: A Survey.* Bellingham, WA: Western Washington, 1984.

The Soviet Empire: Its Nations Speak Out. Ed. Oleg Glebov and John Crowfoot Intro. by Ernest Gellner. New York: Harwood Academic Publishers, 1989.

Smoliak, A. V. "Nanaitsy" [The Nanais]. In: *Narody Rossii: Entsiklopediia* [The Peoples of Russia: An Encyclopedia]. In Russian. Ed. V. A. Tishkov. Moscow: Bol'shaia Rossiiskaia Entsiklopediia, 1994.

———. *Traditsionnoe khoziaistvo i material'naia kul'tura narodov Nizhnego Amura i Sakhalina* [Traditional Economy and Material Culture of the Peoples of the Lower Amur and Sakhalin]. In Russian Moskva: Nauka, 1984.

———. "Nanai." In: *Encyclopedia of World Cultures. Vol. 6: Russia and Eurasia/China.* Ed. Paul Friedrich and Norma Diamond. Trans. Lydia T. Black. Boston: G. K. Hall, 1994.

Spravochnik lichykh imen narodov RSFSR [Handbook of Personal Names of the Peoples of the RSFSR]. 4th ed. In Russian. Ed. A. V. Superanskaia and IU. M. Guseva. Moscow: Russkii iazyk, 1989.

The Sun Maiden and the Crescent Moon: Siberian Folk Tales. Coll. and trans. by James Riordan. Edinburgh: Canongate, 1989.

Vakhtin, Nikolai. *Korennoe naselenie krainego Severa Rossiiskoi Federatsii* [The Indigenous Population of the Far North of the Russian Federation]. In Russian. St. Petersburg: Izdatel'stvo Evropeiskogo doma, 1993.

Van Deusen, Kira. *The Flying Tiger: Women Shamans and Storytellers of the Amur.* Montreal: McGill-Queens University Press, 2001.

—revised by A. Frank

NENTSY

ALTERNATE NAMES: Yurak, Samoyed
LOCATION: Russia (Northwestern Siberia)
POPULATION: 41,302 (2002 Census)
LANGUAGE: Nenets
RELIGION: Eastern Orthodox Christianity, Native beliefs

¹ INTRODUCTION

For thousands of years, people have lived in the harsh arctic environment in what is today Russia. In prehistory, people relied exclusively on what nature provided and on what their ingenuity allowed them to use and create. The seas provided seals, walrus, and whales, and the rivers provided fish. The tundra abounded with reindeer, fox, and other animals as well as edible plants and berries. The land and all of these resources provided human groups with food, shelter, clothing, transportation, and the basis for a rich spiritual life. Today the land and seas and their plant and animal life also provide food, shelter, clothing, and transportation to the Nentsy people. Although many aspects of their lives have changed, the Nentsy continue to respect the land, and they rely on their traditional livelihoods of hunting, reindeer herding, and fishing, as well as on employment in the industrial world.

In the years following the Russian revolution in 1917, the Nentsy went from being considered subjects of the Russian Czar to being an ethnic minority within the Soviet Union. As members of a socialist society, they were expected to participate in the social and economic policies of the new government. These policies began in the 1930s and included collectivization, universal education, and assimilation. Collectivization meant turning over rights to land and reindeer herds to the Soviet government, which reorganized them into collective *(kolkhoz)* or state farms *(sovkhoz)*. The Nentsy were expected to assimilate into the dominant Russian society, which meant changing the way they thought of themselves. They would no longer be an ethnic group called the "Nentsy" but instead would belong to a larger group, the "Soviet people," a change in identity made through education, new jobs, and close contact with members of other (mainly Russian) ethnic groups.

The Nentsy are one of five Samoyedic peoples, which include the Nentsy (Yurak), Entsy (Yenisei), Nganasany (Tavgi), Sel'kups, and Kamass (who became extinct as a group in the years following World War I). None of the names generally cited in the literature for the Nentsy people (such as Samoyed or Yurak) are ethnonyms (names that they would use for themselves). As is true of many northern peoples, names based on territorial groupings were common among the Nentsy. For example, in the western tundra, the Tundra Nentsy traditionally referred to themselves as *nenei nenets'* (real men), and in the eastern regions they used *khasava* (person, or man). The Forest Nentsy used the ethnonym *neshcha'* (men).

² LOCATION AND HOMELAND

The Nentsy are generally divided into two groups, the Forest Nentsy and the Tundra Nentsy. The Tundra Nentsy live in a territory that extends from the Kanin peninsula in the west to the western part of the Taimyr peninsula in the east. To the south, their territory covers the forest tundra zone along the northern tree line. The northern boundary of the Tundra Nentsy territory is the arctic coastline, although some islands in the Kara and Barents seas are also included. Forest Nentsy territory lies within the taiga zone in the basins of the Pur and Nadym rivers and reaches the northern tributaries of the Vakh river. The Tundra Nentsy are found in three administrative areas. The Taimyr' (Dolgano-Nenets) Autonomous *Okrug* covers 862,100 sq km (332,400 sq mi) in its Krasnoiarsk *krai*; its administrative center is Dudinka. The Nenets Autonomous *Okrug* covers 176,000 sq km (67,900 sq mi) in Archangel'sk *Oblast'*; its administrative center is Nar'ian-Mar. The Yamalo-Nenets Autonomous *Okrug* covers 750,300 sq km (289,700 sq mi) in Tiumensk *Oblast'*; its administrative center is Salekhard. The territory of the Forest Nentsy is split between the Yamalo-Nenets Autonomous *Okrug* and the Khanty-Mansi Autonomous *Okrug*. In all of these administrative units, the Nentsy are a minority living among a majority immigrant (primarily Russian) population. The Russian census of 2002 recorded 41,302 Nentsy in the Russian Federation, the majority of whom (33,458) live in rural areas and follow a "traditional" way of life. When discussing Nenets lifestyles today, the Nentsy can be divided into three groups based on where they live: larger towns and cities, small rural villages, and the tundra and taiga.

A variety of animal and plant species are important to the traditional Nentsy economy because they provide food, clothing, building materials, transportation, and cash income. Seals (several species), walrus, and whales are all important along the arctic coast. Fish (saltwater and freshwater), polar fox, squirrel, wild reindeer, hare, ermine, bighorn sheep, geese, ducks, and other birds (such as ptarmigan) are also important resources found throughout the territory of the Nentsy. Many of these same resources are important in the contemporary Russian economy as well, where fish (Atlantic salmon, nelma, whitefish, herring, navaga) and furs, for example, have commercial value. The arctic zone has few lichens and shrubs and only sparse mosses and liverworts. The tundra area generally has willows and arctic birch trees, lichens, mosses, liverworts, and grasses. The northern boundary of the forest-tundra zone has forests of dahurian larch, spruce, and burch. Vast expanses of this area are covered with the lichens that both wild and domestic reindeer depend on for food.

Climatic conditions vary somewhat across the vast territory inhabited by the Nentsy. Winters are long and severe in the far north, with the mean January temperature ranging from –12°C (10°F) in the southwest of the Nenets Autonomous *Okrug* to –30°C (–22°F) in Dudinka. Summers are short and cool with frost. Temperatures in July range from a mean of 2°C (36°F) in Dudinka to 15.3°C (60°F) in southern parts of the Yamalo-Nenets Autonomous *Okrug*. Humidity is relatively high, strong winds blow throughout the year, and permafrost is widespread.

³ LANGUAGE

Nenets is the language of the Nentsy people. It is part of the Samoyedic group of Uralic languages and has two main dialects: Forest and Tundra. Each of these main dialects is further divided into sub-dialects. In 1932, a Latin-based alphabet was created for the Nenets language, which had previously been unwritten. In 1937, the Latin alphabet was replaced by an alphabet based on the Russian language. In 1989, 77.7% of Nentsy said that Nenets was their native language; 17.6% considered

NENTSY

ARCTIC OCEAN

SWEDEN
FINLAND • Murmansk
Barents Sea
Severnaya Zemlya
Kara Sea
New Siberian Is.
Laptev Sea
Kol'skiy Poluostrov
KARELIA
Poluostrov Taymyr
Poluostrov Yamal
• Arkhangel'sk
RUSSIA
Gydanskiy Poluostrov
SEVERO SIBIRSKAYA NIZMENNOST'
REDNE
Olenek
• Nizhniy Novgorod
ZAPADNO
Khanty Manisysk
SIBIRSKOYE
SIBIRSKAYA
Nizhnyaya Tunguska
Kazan'
Kama Perm'
Ob'
Ob'
PLOSKOGRYE
Lena
Ufa • Yekaterinburg
RAVNINA
Angara
Samara
Irtysh
Yenisey
URAL MOUNTAINS
• Chelyabinsk
• Omsk
• Krasnoyarsk
• Novokuznetsk
Irkutsk
• Qaraghandy
KAZAKSTAN
Ulan Bator ⍟
MONGOLIA
UZBEKISTAN
Alma Ata
KYRGYZSTAN

0 500 1000 Miles
0 500 1000 Kilometers

Russian their native language. People who live in rural areas and are engaged in traditional economic activities use the Nenets language at home and work and thus consider it their native language. People who have moved to towns and cities spend more time among Russians and thus tend to use Russian more and forget their native Nenets language.

⁴ FOLKLORE

Oral history is very important, not only as entertainment, but also as a means of preserving the world view of the Nentsy, their rules for behavior, their past glories, their knowledge of the natural world, and their place in it. The oral tradition also explains the roles of men and women in Nenets society. The Nentsy have a rich and varied folklore that includes many different forms. Long heroic epics *(siudbabts)* are told in the third person about giants and the heroes who battle them for control of reindeer or a woman. Short personal narratives *(yarabts)* are told in the first person about the trials and triumphs of individual heroes. Legends *(va'al)* relate the history of clans and the origin of the world and its people. In fairy tales *(vadako)*, mythical events occur in which the physiological and behavioral characteristics of certain animals are explained. Riddles *(khobtsoko)* are told in the form of short tales. Some types of stories are spoken, others chanted, and still others sung by the Nentsy.

⁵ RELIGION

Traditional Nentsy religion is a type of Siberian shamanism. The natural environment, animals, and plants were all viewed as having their own spirits. The earth and all living things were created by the god Num, whose son, Nga, was the god of evil. Num would help humans in their efforts to protect themselves against Nga only if they asked for help and made the appropriate sacrifices and gestures either directly to the spirits or to wooden idols made to give human forms to animals as gods. Shamans of different varieties acted as mediators between the spirit world and humans, conveying requests for help and the replies of Num to supplicants. Both men and women could be shamans. A second benevolent spirit, Ya-nebya (or "Mother Earth") was a special friend of women, aiding, for example, in childbirth. Worship of certain animals such as the bear was common. Reindeer were considered the embodiment of purity and accorded great respect. In some areas, elements of Christianity (especially from the Russian Orthodox church) were mixed with the traditional pantheon of gods. Although it was discouraged to conduct religious rituals during the Soviet period, the Nenets religion seems to have survived and is enjoying a strong revival today. Nenets religion stresses respect for the land and its resources. Spirits that protect and guide in both the household and the tundra are still provided with gifts of food and asked for aid and advice.

Another important religious tradition among the Nentsy is Eastern Orthodox Christianity. The Nentsy probably came into contact with Orthodox Christianity by means of Komi traders already before their incorporation into Russia. The Russian Orthodox Church began missionary activity among the Nentsy in the 18th century, but it was not until the 1820s that Russian missionaries succeeded in converting Nentsy communities in any lasting manner.

⁶ MAJOR HOLIDAYS

Traditional clothing worn on holidays is the same as daily wear, but much more ornate, with leather fringe, beads, and leather and metal ornaments.

Prior to the Socialist revolution, Nentsy who had been baptized into the Orthodox church celebrated such Christian holidays as Easter, but did not necessarily attach the same significance to these holidays as their Orthodox benefactors. After the Socialist revolution, religious beliefs and practices were forbidden by the Soviet government. Secular holidays were expected to completely replace those of both the Orthodox church and traditional Siberian shamanism. International holidays of special Soviet significance such as May Day and Victory in Europe Day were celebrated by Nentsy and all peoples throughout the Soviet Union.

⁷ RITES OF PASSAGE

Birth and death were always accompanied by special shamanic rituals. Births were accompanied by sacrifices, and the *chum* (tent) where the birth took place would be purified after the woman's confinement. Children were tended by their mothers until the age of 5 to 7 years, at which time gender roles began to be defined. Girls would then spend their time with their mothers, learning how to take care of the *chum*, prepare food, sew clothing, and so on. Boys would go with their fathers to learn how to tend reindeer, hunt, and fish.

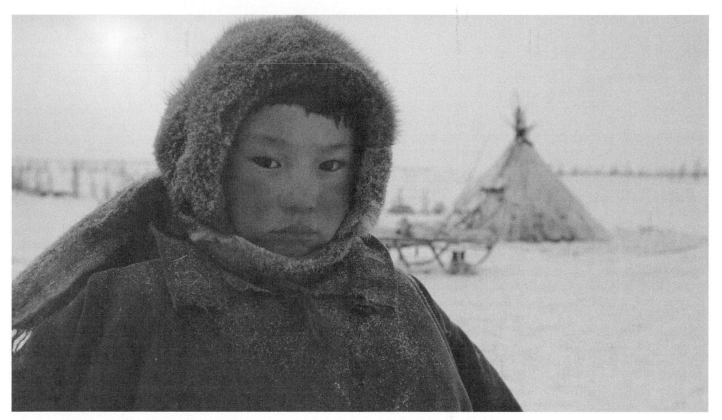

A young Nentsy boy stands in the sub-zero Arctic cold near his home in the Siberian Arctic, Russia.
(Steven L. Raymer/National Geographic/Getty Images)

8 INTERPERSONAL RELATIONS

Marriages were traditionally arranged by the heads of clans and served to strengthen the relationship between two clans, who often depended on each other in times of need. Family size varied, with as many as 15 or more individuals living in one household. Herders with large herds were able to afford more than one wife. "Bride price" might include reindeer, furs, money, or other goods and was paid to clan leaders. A bride brought a dowry to the marriage, including such things as household goods, clothing, sleds, and her own reindeer. All of these things were her property (as was anything she herself produced during her marriage), and if she divorced, she kept them. Only men inherited goods and animals, however. Marriages today are generally personal matters between adults.

There are strict divisions between the activities of men and women in traditional Nenets society. Women have the power and ability to both give life (through childbirth) and assure death. For example, in some Nenets folklore, women are called upon not to actually fight enemies but to assure their death by breaking male/female taboos in their presence.

Taboos that governed the relationships between men and women were observed, especially with regard to childbirth and menstruation. Although women were generally considered subordinate, the strict division of labor between men and women in the arctic made relations more equal than not.

9 LIVING CONDITIONS

Reindeer herding is a nomadic occupation, requiring herders and their families to move with the reindeer across the tun-dra to find new pastures throughout the year. Herding families live in tents made from reindeer hides or canvas and take their personal possessions with them as they travel, in some cases as many as 1000 kilometers in a year. Although official Soviet policy was to force people to settle in permanent, Russian-style homes in villages and towns, reindeer breeding makes this difficult, and many people still live nomadic lives. On the Yamal peninsula, for example, 51% of the indigenous population were nomadic in 1994, and more than half of this nomadic group was female, indicating that whole families, not just men, still lead somewhat traditional lives. These nomads are administratively attached to certain villages and towns, but they travel throughout the year with the reindeer herds. Nentsy engaged in non-traditional occupations live in Russian log houses or elevated apartment buildings, as do the non-Native residents of their territory. These Nentsy shop, attend school, and live in much the same way as non-Natives in their territory.

Transportation in the tundra is often by sleds pulled by reindeer, although helicopters, airplanes, snowmobiles, and all-terrain vehicles are also used, especially by non-Natives. The Nentsy have different types of sleds for different purposes, including traveling sleds for men, traveling sleds for women, and freight sleds.

10 FAMILY LIFE

Patrilineal clans were traditionally the basic units of Nenets society. Each clan had its own specific pastures, hunting grounds, fishing grounds, burial places, and sacred sites. Today there are still approximately 100 Nenets clans, and the clan name is used as the surname of each of its members. Although most Nentsy have Russian given (first) names, they are one of the few Native groups to have non-Russian surnames. Clan affiliation today is being used as the basis for legal claims to land and the protection of sacred sites. Kinship and family units continue to be the main organizing features of society in both urban and rural settings and often serve important functions in linking urban and rural Nentsy. Social behavior is focused on family and community, not on the individual. Rules regarding appropriate behavior are observed and often punished according to traditional guidelines handed down from elders to young.

11 CLOTHING

Clothing is most often a combination of traditional and modern. People in towns and cities tend to wear modern clothes made of manufactured cloth, perhaps with fur coats and hats in winter. There are also modern clothes in rural villages and in the tundra, but traditional clothes tend to predominate as they are more suitable for the lifestyles of people in these areas. In the tundra, traditional clothing is generally worn in layers. The *malitsa* is a hooded coat made of reindeer fur turned inside-out. A second fur coat, the *sovik,* with its fur turned to the outside, would be worn on top of the *malitsa* in extremely cold weather. Women in the tundra might wear the *yagushka*, a two-layered open coat made with reindeer fur on both the inside and the outside. It extends almost to the ankles, and has a hood that is often decorated with beads and small metal ornaments. Fur boots *(pimy)* were worn by all. Generally speaking, there are no special traditional summer clothes. Older winter garments that are wearing out are used, and today lighter-weight manufactured garments are often worn. Each woman also has a reindeer-skin purse uniquely decorated to carry her personal belongings. Reindeer skins are the primary source of traditional clothing, but domestic dog, polar fox, and seal are also used, especially in collars, hoods, and decorative elements. Today many manufactured items are also used.

12 FOOD

Reindeer are the most important source of food in the traditional Nenets diet. Russian bread, introduced to the Native peoples long ago, has become an essential part of their diet, as have other European foods. Tundra Nentsy rely on reindeer for food, whereas Forest Nentsy rely on reindeer primarily for transportation and rely instead on fishing and hunting for food and clothing. Nentsy hunt for wild reindeer, rabbits, squirrels, ermine, wolverine, and sometimes bears and wolves. Along the arctic coast, seal, walrus, and whales are hunted as well. Tea is a preferred beverage and is usually purchased on trips to villages, although traditionally it was made from cranberry leaves or the roots of various plants. Many foods are eaten in both raw and cooked forms. Fish, for example, can be eaten fresh, frozen, boiled, or dried. Meat is preserved by smoking and is also eaten fresh, frozen, or boiled. In the spring, reindeer antlers are soft and grisly and may be eaten raw or boiled. A type of pancake is made from frozen reindeer blood dissolved in hot water and mixed with flour and berries. Gathered plant foods were traditionally used to supplement the diet. Beginning in the late 1700s, imported foodstuffs such as flour, bread, sugar, and butter became important sources of additional food. Reindeer meat, antlers, and game are readily available in small villages, whereas non-traditional, imported foods are predominant in cities and towns.

13 EDUCATION

When the Soviets came to power, Nentsy children were sent to school, sometimes in their village, but often to boarding schools far from their parents and other relatives. The Soviet government believed that by separating children from parents, they could teach the children to live in more modern ways, which they would then teach their parents. Instead, many children grew up learning the Russian language rather than their own Nenets language and so had difficulty communicating with their parents and grandparents. Children were also taught that traditional ways of living and working were bad and should be abandoned in favor of life in a modern industrial society. Thus, they learned little about their cultural traditions and the land on which their families depended. Settling families in permanent homes in villages was another means of educating children, and today most small villages have nursery schools and "middle" schools that go up to eighth grade and sometimes tenth. After the eighth (or tenth) grade, students must leave their village to receive a higher education, and such a journey for 15- and 16-year-olds can be quite daunting. Today, attempts are being made to change the educational system to include studies of Nentsy traditions, language, reindeer herding, land management, and so on. Educating children of herders, who spend most of the year away from any village, is still a difficult task. Traveling teachers who could move with the herding groups are one possible solution to this problem, but even this system would have limitations, especially as children grow older and require more specialized instruction. Educational opportunities at all levels are available to the Nentsy, from major universities to special technical schools where they can learn modern veterinary practices regarding reindeer breeding.

14 CULTURAL HERITAGE

The territory now inhabited by the Nentsy had long been inhabited by other non-Samoyedic people. These people hunted wild reindeer on the tundra, fished in the numerous lakes and rivers, and hunted seals, walrus, and whales along the arctic coast. Archaeological and linguistic evidence has shown that Samoyedic peoples and their languages came north, mixing with and eventually assimilating peoples who had been in those areas previously. The Nentsy seem to have first been concentrated around the mouth of the Ob' river, and from there they moved north approximately 1000 years ago. The first mention of Samoyedic people in Western sources is in the Nestor Chronicle, where they are mentioned in connection with events that took place in the year 1096. Samoyedic peoples, have, therefore, long had some contact with Europeans. The Nentsy and other Samoyedic peoples did not willingly accept the interference of either Czarist Russia or the Soviet government in their affairs, and beginning in at least the 14th century they often put up fierce resistance to attempts to conquer and control them. Today they continue to struggle for control of their own lives.

15 WORK

Nentsy have traditionally been reindeer herders, and today reindeer are still a very important part of their lives. Oral traditions from the early 1900s tell of Nentsy clans in Yamal whose livelihood focused on coastal sea-mammal hunting, and evidence exists of Nentsy involvement in commercial hunting and fishing in the arctic seas in the 1700s. Today, sea-mammal hunting is secondary to reindeer herding in the overall economy of the Nentsy. In traditional Nentsy society, the basic social unit was the individual family; in reindeer herding, however, the basic unit was the herding camp, composed of two to five families, each related to the other by blood, marriage, or other partnership ties. Although collectivization and forced sedentarization often seriously disrupted this system, herding groups today continue to be formed around a family core or group of related people.

Reindeer herding among the northern Tundra Nentsy is characterized by the year-round pasturing of reindeer under supervision of herders and the use of herd dogs and reindeer-drawn sleighs. Herds are kept in well-defined pasture areas and moved at specific times of year. Seasonal migrations cover great distances, as much as 1000 kilometers (more than 600 miles). In winter, herds are grazed in the tundra and forest-tundra. In the spring, the Nentsy migrate north, some as far as the arctic coast; in the fall, they return south again. Herding dogs are important in helping herders control and move herds, which may number in the thousands of animals.

The Forest Nentsy who live to the south have smaller herds, which are grazed in the forest. Their winter pastures are only 40 to 100 kilometers (25 to 60 miles) from their summer pastures. In the summer, the Forest Nentsy turn their reindeer loose while they fish along the rivers. In the fall, the herds are gathered back together and moved to winter grounds. These herds usually number twenty or thirty animals. Reindeer-herding families among the Forest Nentsy also make extensive use of forest and river resources, including hunting and fishing, to supply food and other products for their families.

In addition to food and clothing, reindeer provide transportation (pulling sleds) and additional income (from the sale of antler velvet, or *panty*, which is used in Korea for medicinal purposes). Some families have herds large enough to support themselves independently of the state economy, but others combine work for the state with herding to make a living. Families with few reindeer often live close to rivers and lakes, where they can focus on fishing and hunting while giving their reindeer to a relative to tend. A fairly strict division of labor between men and women is characteristic of Nenets society. Men are primarily responsible for subsistence activities, and women are responsible for the dwelling, clothing, food preparation, and children. There are, of course, times when women gather plants foods and fish, and when men supervise children and cook. Nentsy living in urban areas work as: teachers, nurses, doctors, store clerks, and so on. In rural areas, most Nentsy are engaged in at least some aspects of traditional livelihood, although some are teachers, cooks, or store clerks as well. In villages or the city, women are still responsible for children and the home in addition to working outside the home.

16 SPORTS

There is little information on sports among the Nentsy. Recreational activities such as bicycle riding occur in the villages.

17 ENTERTAINMENT AND RECREATION

Children in urban communities can enjoy riding bicycles, watching movies, or television, and other modern forms of recreation, but children in rural settings are more limited. In villages, there are bicycles, manufactured toys, televisions, radios, VCRs, and sometimes movie theaters. In the tundra, there might be radio and an occasional store-bought toy, but children also depend on their imaginations and the games and toys of their nomadic ancestors. Balls are made of reindeer or seal skin. Dolls made from felt with heads made from birds' beaks are not only toys but important items in Nentsy tradition. These dolls play the roles of: father and mother, host and guest, bride and groom, and in such play children learn the roles of males and females in their societies. The destiny of a doll is said to be the destiny of its owner, so a doll is a special part of a child's world.

18 FOLK ART, CRAFTS, AND HOBBIES

There is generally little spare time to devote to hobbies in Nentsy society. Folk arts are represented in the figurative art that adorns traditional clothing and some personal items. Other forms of expressive arts include carving on bone and wood, inlays of tin on wood, and wooden religious sculptures. Carvings are sometimes used to decorate sleds, smoking pipes, and *kolotushki* (scrapers to remove snow from fur), but this practice is not widespread. Among some Nentsy, tin and sometimes lead were used to decorate wooden objects such as the handles of knives and tobacco boxes. Wooden sculptures of animals or humans as representations of gods took two basic forms: wooden sticks of various sizes with one or more crudely carved faces on their upper portions and carefully carved and detailed figures of people, often dressed with real furs and skins. The ornamentation of women's clothing was especially widespread and continues to be important. Medallions and appliqués are made with furs and hair of different colors and then sewn on to the clothing.

19 SOCIAL PROBLEMS

The economic basis of Nentsy culture—the land and the reindeer herds—are threatened today by the development of natural gas and oil. Economic reforms and democratic processes in Russia today present both new opportunities and new problems for the Nentsy. Natural gas and oil are critical resources that Russia's economy desperately needs to develop. On the other hand, the reindeer pasture destroyed by resource development and the construction of pipelines is critical to the survival of the Nentsy culture. These two land use strategies compete with each other, and complex negotiations are needed to ensure that pasturage is protected and resource development is environmentally safe and not without limits.

Unemployment, inadequate health care, alcohol abuse, and discrimination all contribute to declining standards of living and increased morbidity and mortality among the Nentsy (and other northern indigenous groups). Social welfare payments for children, pensioners, and the disabled are essential to the well-being of many families unable to support themselves entirely through jobs or traditional means. Native peoples throughout the Russian North have begun to organize and discuss solutions to these problems and to assert their rights as distinctive ethnic groups in a multiethnic society. In Yamal, for example, the Nentsy have formed *Yamal Potomkan* ("Yamal for Future Generations"), an organization through which they can work with legislative and political bodies in their region to improve social, economic, and political conditions for the Nentsy.

[20] GENDER ISSUES

Within the family, work is divided along gender lines. Women are responsible for the home, food preparation, shopping, and child care. Some men follow traditional occupations, and others choose professions such as medicine or education. They might also take jobs as laborers or serve in the military. In towns and villages, women may also have non-traditional jobs as teachers, doctors, or store clerks, but they are still primarily responsible for domestic chores and child care. Extended families often include some individuals engaged in traditional occupations and some engaged in non-traditional work. Communication and exchange in such families is important in helping to maintain cultural traditions in the villages and in ensuring that manufactured goods are sent to the tundra. Among the traditional Nentsy women had strong property rights with respect to reindeer. During the Soviet era, especially following Collectivization, women's property rights, together with private property as a whole, were strongly degraded. Since the collapse of the Soviet Union traditional women's property rights with respect to reindeer herds have begun to make somewhat of a comeback.

[21] BIBLIOGRAPHY

Anderson, D. *Indigenous Peoples and Development of the Lower Yenisei Valley*. INSROP Working Paper No. 18 (1995). (International Northern Sea Route Programme.) Norway: Fridtjof Nansen Institute, 1995.

Chance, N. and E. N. Andreeva. "Sustainability, Equity, and Natural Resource Development in Northwest Siberia and Arctic Alaska." *Human Ecology* 23, No. 2 (1995): 217–240.

Golovnev, Andrei V. and Gail Osherenko, Siberian Survival: The Nenets and their Story. Ithaca, NY: Cornell University Press, 1999.

Great Soviet Encyclopedia. New York: Macmillan, 1983. (Trans. from *Bol'shaia Sovetskaia entsiklopediia*. 3rd ed. Moscow, 1978.)

Hajdu, P. *The Samoyed Peoples and Languages*. Bloomington, IN: Indiana University Press, 1963.

Krupnik, I. *Arctic Adaptations: Native Whalers and Reindeer Herders of Northern Eurasia*. Hanover, NH: University Press of New England, 1993.

Osherenko, G. "Property Rights and the Transformation of Russia: Institutional Change in the Far North." *Europe-Asia Studies* 47, No. 7 (1995): 1077–1108.

Pika, A., and N. Chance. "Nenets and Khanty of the Russian Federation." In *State of the Peoples: A Global Human Rights Report on Societies in Danger*. Boston: Beacon Press, 1993.

Prokof'yeva, E. D. "The Nentsy." In *Peoples of Siberia*. Ed. M. G. Levin and L. P. Potapov. Chicago: University of Chicago Press, 1964. (Originally published in Russian, 1956.)

Ziker, John P. *Peoples of the Tundra: Northern Siberians in the Post-Communist Transition*. Prospect Heights, IL: Waveland Press, 2002.

—by D. L. Schindler; revised by A. Frank

NETHERLANDERS

ALTERNATE NAMES: Dutch
LOCATION: The Netherlands
POPULATION: 16.6 million
LANGUAGE: Dutch
RELIGION: Roman Catholic; Protestant (including the Dutch Reformed Church); small populations of Muslims, Hindus, and Jews

[1] INTRODUCTION

The Netherlands is a small, flat country located on the shores of the North Sea in western Europe. The whole country is often referred to as Holland, although this term is actually the name for certain provinces in the northwestern part of the country. Over many centuries, the Dutch people literally built their nation by shoring up its lowlands against the sea with dikes, dunes, and windmills. Its coastal location has historically made it an important trading center. Through the efforts of the Dutch East India and Dutch West India companies in the 17th century, the Netherlands acquired colonial territories on every continent to become one of the world's most powerful nations.

In the 20th century, the Dutch recovered from the devastation of World War II and helped found the European Community (EC) in 1957. In the 1990s, this institution became the European Union, offering the Netherlands, like its fellow members, new opportunities as part of a single trading bloc with enhanced economic powers. Meanwhile, the nation's lowlands are sinking at the rate of 45 cm (1.5 ft) per century, and the North Sea is rising, meaning that the Dutch will have to continue waging their ongoing struggle against the sea.

[2] LOCATION AND HOMELAND

The name "Netherlands," meaning "lowlands," derives from the fact that much of the western part of the country is low-lying land (called *polders*) that has been reclaimed from the sea by dikes and dunes. In addition, windmills, called polder mills, pump excess underground water to keep these areas dry and farmable. Other geographic areas include sand dunes along the western coast and higher land in the eastern and southeastern areas.

Most of the 16.6 million Dutch people belong to the same ethnic group, descended from Frankish, Saxon, and Frisian tribes. A measure of diversity has been added by the arrival of immigrants from the former Dutch colonies of Indonesia and Suriname and foreign workers from Turkey, Morocco, and southern Europe. Throughout history, the Dutch have been known for tolerance of different ethnic and religious groups. They welcomed Jews and Huguenots (French Protestants) in the 16th and 17th century, and played a role in aiding Jews fleeing Nazi persecution in World War II. The most famous of these Jewish refugees was Anne Frank, whose family hid for several years in a secret annex in Amsterdam, aided by their Dutch employees. Tragically, the Franks' hiding place was discovered in the final year of the war, and the whole family except for Anne's father, Otto, died in concentration camps. However, the famous *Diary of a Young Girl*, kept by Anne during the war years, bears witness to the courage of ordinary Dutch citizens who risked their lives attempting to save this German Jewish family.

³ LANGUAGE

Dutch, a Germanic language, is the official language in all 12 provinces of the Netherlands and the language in everyday use everywhere but in Friesland, where ancient Frisian is spoken. Dutch dialects can vary enough to make it difficult for speakers from different regions to understand each other.

COMMON WORDS

Man	Man
Woman	Vrouw
Mother	Moeder
Father	Vader
Yes	Ja
No	Nee
Right	Rechts
Left	Links
Breakfast	Ontbijt
Lunch	Middageten
Dinner	Avondeten
Milk	Melk
Beer	Bier

⁴ FOLKLORE

Dutch mythology is strongly linked to the sea and characters associated with it, such as mermaids and pirates. There is also a tradition of tales about devils who tempt people with riches in order to gain their souls; one of the popular subjects of these tales is the devil Joost. Many popular Dutch tales, riddles, and rituals were suppressed over time by wealthy burghers promoting high culture in their stead, but some survived as part of the country's Christian traditions. The Dutch Father Christmas (named, like the American Santa Claus, for Saint Nicholas) is called *Sinterklaas* and has a dark-faced assistant called Black Peter who is said to carry disobedient children to Spain in a sack.

⁵ RELIGION

An estimated 31% of the Dutch people are Roman Catholics, while 20% belong to six major Protestant groups, of which the largest is the Dutch Reformed Church. There are smaller populations of Muslims, Hindus, and Jews. Approximately 40% of Netherlanders claim no religion. Traditionally, the northern and eastern parts of the country have been Protestant, while the south has been Catholic. Since the mid-19th century, the Dutch have practiced a kind of religious "apartheid" known as *verzuiling* (in English, "columnizing" or "pillaring"), that mandated the establishment of separate Protestant and Catholic schools, newspapers, political parties, radio stations, and other institutions. This system has weakened somewhat since the 1960s, but it still controls many facets of life in rural areas.

⁶ MAJOR HOLIDAYS

Legal holidays include New Year's Day, the Queen's birthday (April 30), Memorial Day (May 4)/Liberation of the Netherlands (May 5), and the Christmas holidays. In addition, many Dutch people observe the other standard holidays of the Christian calendar. The Dutch are great celebrators of birthdays. On their birthdays, the Dutch stay in bed late and family

members come into the bedroom singing "Lang Zal Hij Leven" ("Long May He Live"—for females, "Lang Zal Zij Leven"). Gifts are presented, and the festivities continue at school or work, and, in the evening, with a party for family and friends. The Queen's birthday is considered an especially important occasion, marked by flag displays, parades, and girls wearing orange ribbons in their hair in honor of the royal family, the House of Orange. The Memorial Day holiday in the spring has two contrasting parts. At eight o'clock on the evening of May 4, people throughout the country stop whatever they are doing to remember the Dutch war dead and pray for peace. The next day, May 5, is a time of festivals and celebrations.

⁷ RITES OF PASSAGE

The Netherlands is a modern, industrialized, traditionally Christian country. Hence, many of the rites of passage that young people undergo are religious rituals, such as baptism, first Communion, confirmation, and marriage. Religious minorities observe their own rituals. In addition, a student's progress through the education system is marked by many families with graduation parties.

⁸ INTERPERSONAL RELATIONS

On the whole, the Dutch are a reserved people who do not speak readily to strangers. Public interaction, usually marked by close eye contact, is direct but formal. (Close friends, however, do greet each other with a kiss on the cheek.) Restraint and moderation can be seen in many aspects of Dutch life, from cars (medium-sized and -priced) to clothing (casual and unostentatious). The primary Dutch focus is on the family and on being *gezellig thuis*, or "cozy at home."

Popular Dutch sayings include:

"You'll face the wind" (Je krijgt de wind van voren)—comparable to the American phrase "face the music"

"I'll row with the oars I have" (Ik roei met de riemen ik heb)—i.e., I'll make the best of the situation

"God's mills grind slowly" (Gods molens malen langzaam)

9 LIVING CONDITIONS

Traditionally, the Dutch have striven to make their homes *gezellig*, which means "homey" or "cozy." They favor knick-knacks such as colorful tiles and blue-and-white Delft porcelain. Most homes have colorful flower gardens in front, typically featuring the tulip, the Dutch national flower. With the nation's high population density, Dutch cities suffer from overcrowding and housing shortages. Many of the tall, gabled traditional houses in cities like Amsterdam have been divided into apartments. One popular response to the scarcity of dwellings is living in a houseboat, generally a converted barge. By 2008 there were approximately 2,400 such boats anchored on the canals in the center of Amsterdam.

The Dutch receive modern, high-quality health care. While most health-care facilities are privately operated, costs are covered by a national health insurance system. In 2008 the average life expectancy was 79.25years, and the major causes of death were heart disease, cancer, and traffic accidents. Privately funded home nursing is provided for children, the elderly, and pregnant women. Home birth has always been popular in the Netherlands; the government finances a 16-month training program for midwives, who assist doctors with delivery and provide postnatal care for mother and infant.

The Netherlands has an extensive network of highways. Dutch cities and suburbs have good public transportation, although a major expansion is slated for completion by the year 2010 in order to reduce pollution. Bicycles are a favorite form of transportation, and the country has about 9,920 km (6,200 mi) of bicycle paths. A state-owned railway system links most Dutch cities and also offers daily express service to cities in Belgium and France. Rotterdam, in the heart of one of Europe's major industrial centers, is one of the busiest ports in the world.

10 FAMILY LIFE

The Dutch place great value on family life. A traditional Dutch saying is "Your own hearth is worth gold" (Eigen haard is goud waard). The nuclear family—called the *gezin*—has traditionally been at the center of Dutch life, especially since the 19th century. Since World War II, there has been an increase in the incidence of unmarried people living together, and the divorce rate has risen as well. The Dutch tend to have small families and to lavish care and attention on their children. The concept of *deftig*, or respectability, is important to the Dutch family and is related to an age-old custom known as *schmeren*. At sundown, the Dutch traditionally leave their curtains open with the lights on low, leaving themselves visible to neighbors or passersby behind their large front windows. This practice is often interpreted as a symbolic attempt to show their neighbors that all is *deftig* within, although some have attributed it to the desire to check up on what is going on outside, or even as a thrifty way to make use of all available daylight.

11 CLOTHING

In everyday life, the Dutch wear typical modern Western-style clothing for both formal and casual occasions, although people who work outdoors may still wear the wooden shoes (klompen) popularly associated with the Dutch. Due to the efforts of animal rights activists, fur coats have become unpopular. Traditional folk costumes vary from region to region, but most feature baggy black pants and wide-brimmed hats for men and full black dresses with embroidered bodices and lace bonnets for women. The popular image of the Dutch people often includes a woman wearing wooden shoes and the white cap of the Volendam region with its high peak and wing-like folds at the sides. Traditional costumes may still be seen in Volendam and Marken, where they are a tourist attraction.

12 FOOD

Dutch food is wholesome and simply prepared, often with butter but not thick sauces or strong spices (although the spicier Indonesian *rijsttafel* dishes have gained popularity in recent years). Seafood is widely eaten, especially herring, which are traditionally lifted by the tail and dropped head first into one's upturned mouth. Dairy products are a dietary staple, and the Dutch are known worldwide for their cheeses, the most popular being Gouda, which is round and flat, and Edam, which is shaped like a ball. Many desserts come with whipped cream, and popular beverages include tea, coffee, beer, and *Jenever,* a Dutch gin made from juniper berries.

The Dutch breakfast is generally a cold meal of sliced bread, meat, and cheese. This is followed by a modest midday meal, also cold, and a large dinner, served at about 6 PM, which typically includes soup and a main dish containing meat and vegetables. Popular snacks include french fries—*patat frites*—often served with mayonnaise or ketchup, and waffles, smothered in whipped cream or caramel sauce.

13 EDUCATION

The Dutch are a well-educated people with virtually no illiteracy. Schooling is compulsory between the ages of 5 and 16. At the age of 12, students take an exam which tracks them into either general, pre-university, or vocational school, although it is generally possible to change schools at a later time. At the age of 16, school certificate exams are taken in a variety of subjects. Students in the pre-university, or gymnasium, track can advance automatically to a university at the age of 18, while others must take an exam. Higher education is offered at nine universities and four technical institutes. The oldest university, which is at Leiden, dates back to 1575.

14 CULTURAL HERITAGE

The 17th century was the golden age of Dutch painting, marked by the work of such masters as Rembrandt van Rijn, Jan Vermeer, and Jacob van Ruisdael. Supported by the rich burghers and merchants of the upper middle class, these works are known for their depiction of everyday scenes showing middle-class life. The great 19th-century painter Vincent van

Netherlanders selling cheese in a market in Alkmaar, The Netherlands. (© Benoit Roland/The Image Works)

Gogh was born and lived most of his life in the Netherlands before moving to Arles, France, two years before his death in 1890. The 20th-century *De Stijl* movement, which advocated simplicity, is represented in the works of Piet Mondrian and Theo van Doesburg. The Netherlands was home to two great philosophers, Desiderius Erasmus in the 15th century and Baruch Spinoza in the 17th. The 19th-century novel *Max Havelaar,* by Edouard Douwes Dekker, caused a public outcry over Dutch treatment of the people in its colonies and led to eventual government reforms. In music, the Renaissance composers Jan Sweelinck and Jacob Obrecht were renowned throughout Europe. Twenty-first century Dutch popular music has African and Middle Eastern influences.

¹⁵ WORK

The Dutch economy expanded from World War II until economic growth slowed in 1973 due to rising world oil prices. Over the next decade unemployment skyrocketed from 3% to 17%. In 2007 it stood at 4.1% of the work force. The main industry of the 20th century was the production of petrochemicals. Agriculture, which accounts for only 3% of workers, is still an important part of the national economy, with many Dutch specializing in dairy farming and flower-growing. Industrial activity in the 2000s is predominantly in food processing, chemicals, petroleum refining, and electrical machinery. Many people in the Netherlands go into the family business,

eventually taking it over from the older generation. Foreign workers, who first entered the country in large numbers in the 1960s, perform low-paying, unskilled work.

¹⁶ SPORTS

At least 4 million people belong to sports clubs. The largest is the Royal Netherlands Football (i.e., soccer) Association, which claims about a million members. The Dutch won the European soccer championship in 1988. Other popular sports are tennis, swimming, and hockey.

¹⁷ ENTERTAINMENT AND RECREATION

The Dutch enjoy many forms of outdoor recreation. Fishing is extremely popular, as are boating, sailing, and camping. Throughout the country, bicycles are used for recreational outings and races, as well as transportation. Winter sports include skating, curling, ice boating, wind-assisted skating (performed wearing a kite-like triangular sail on one's back), and many kinds of races and endurance tests. As many as 16,000 people compete in the 200-km (124-mi) Elfstedentocht skating race over frozen canals connecting 11 towns in Friesland. (However, in many years temperatures do not drop low enough for this event to be held.) Another traditional sport popular in Friesland is *fierljeppen,* a form of pole-vaulting.

18 FOLK ART, CRAFTS, AND HOBBIES

Traditional Dutch crafts include pottery, tile work, glassware, and silver. The famous Delft pottery has been produced in the city of that name since 1653. Plates, vases, pitchers, and a multitude of other decorative pieces are still made by workers who enter the trade at ages 16 or 17 and receive eight years of training. Over a thousand different types of objects are produced, and no two pieces are the same. The designs were originally copied from fine Chinese porcelain that entered Holland during the 17th century.

19 SOCIAL PROBLEMS

The generous Dutch program of social benefits has been abused by a multitude of persons claiming sickness or disability: in the early 1990s one-fourth of Amsterdam's population was living on welfare. Absenteeism at work is also a problem. Overcrowding in the cities has resulted in the illegal occupation of buildings by squatters. The position of Amsterdam as one of Europe's main entry points for illegal drugs has led to a drug problem, which the government has addressed with strong anti-drug laws. However, the number of addicts using hard drugs in the Netherlands is low compared with the rest of Europe and considerably lower than that in France, the United Kingdom, Italy, Spain, and Switzerland. Dutch rates of drug use are lower than US rates in every category.

20 GENDER ISSUES

Progress on women's rights issues has been realized in the Netherlands in the last 50 years. In the mid-20th century, women still needed their husbands' consent to enter into employment contracts. The percentage of women in the labor force jumped from 22% in 1960 to 56% in 2006; just 10% of women leave the workforce after having their first child. The Netherlands has a goal of having 65% of all women working at least 12 hours per week by 2010. Still much remains to be done to fully achieve gender equality in government and society. A Law on Child Care entered into force in January 2005. The Netherlands has invested considerably in child-care facilities. There were 200,000 child-care facilities in 2007 and all schools were required to provide child care from 7:30 AM to 6:30 PM. Child care has been made affordable for all income groups. Parents pay no more than one-third of child care costs. Working parents are entitled to parental leave and tax breaks during that leave.

The Netherlands is also taking steps to combat domestic violence, sexual violence, honor-related violence, and human trafficking. Prostitution in the Netherlands is legal. Eighty percent of women working as prostitutes are foreigners, and 20% are of Dutch origin. The Dutch Parliament, citizens, and Dutch non-governmental organizations broadly support the legalization of brothels. The government asserts that that policy protects sex workers, with the government having more control over the sex industry and combating human trafficking. Local authorities can issue work permits for brothels and can thus control safety, health, and working conditions.

The Netherlands is known for its liberal policies on gay rights. The public widely supports tolerance and equal rights for homosexuals, although conservative Christians and Muslim immigrants tend to be more conservative in their beliefs about gender and sexual norms. The 1993 Equal Rights Law prohibited discrimination on the grounds of sexual orientation. In 1998 the Dutch parliament granted same-sex couples domestic partnership benefits and in 2001 the government legalized same-sex marriages. The Netherlands was the first country in the world to do so. A 2006 European Union member poll showed the Dutch to be the strongest supporters of same-sex marriage at 82%.

21 BIBLIOGRAPHY

Bennett, A. Linda, ed. *Encyclopedia of World Cultures (Europe)*. Boston: G. K. Hall, 1992.

Frank, Anne. *Anne Frank: The Diary of a Young Girl*. Translated by B.M. Mooyaart. New York: Bantam Books, 1993.

Gall, Timothy, and Susan Gall, ed. *Junior Worldmark Encyclopedia of the Nations*. Detroit: UXL, 1996.

Goodfriend, Joyce D., et al, eds. *Going Dutch: the Dutch Presence in America, 1609-2009*. Leiden, Boston: Brill, 2008.

Hubbard, Monica M. and Beverly Baer, ed. *Cities of the World: Europe and the Middle East*. Detroit: Gale Research, 1993.

Kristensen, Preben, and Fiona Cameron. *We Live in the Netherlands*. New York: Bookwright Press, 1986.

Moore, Bob, and Henk van Nierop, eds. *Twentieth-Century Mass Society in Britain and the Netherlands*. Oxford: Berg, 2006.

Moss, Joyce, and George Wilson. *Peoples of the World: Western Europeans*. Detroit: Gale Research, 1993.

Netherlands in Pictures. Minneapolis: Lerner Publications, 1991.

State, Paul F. *Brief History of the Netherlands*. New York: Facts On File Inc., 2008.

van Stegeren, Theo. *The Land and People of the Netherlands*. New York: HarperCollins, 1991.

—revised by J. Hobby

NIVKHS

LOCATION: Russia (Siberia, Sakhalin Island, Amur Estuary region)
POPULATION: 5,162 (2002)
LANGUAGE: Russian, Nivkh
RELIGION: Traditional form of shamanism, Eastern Orthodox Christianity

¹ INTRODUCTION

The Nivkhs are an indigenous people of extreme southeastern Siberia (also called the Russian Far East) who inhabit the island of Sakhalin and the Amur River Valley. Their traditional economic occupations are fishing and, to a lesser extent, hunting. It is believed on the basis of archaeological, anthropological, and linguistic evidence that they are the descendants of the earliest inhabitants of the region. Archaeologists have found evidence of ancient settlements on Sakhalin dating from the Neolithic era (5,000 BC–1,000 AD) and is quite possible that their inhabitants were the ancestors of the Nivkhs. The Nivkhs' affiliation, if any, to other ethnic groups of northeastern Asia has long been a matter of speculation. Some scholars have concluded that the Nivkhs may be ethnically and linguistically related to the Koriaks and Chukchi of far northeastern Siberia and perhaps some native peoples of Alaska. Other researchers have tentatively suggested possible links between the Nivkhs and the ancient inhabitants of Southeast Asia.

The Nivkhs call themselves *Nivkh* (plural *Nivkhgu*), which simply means "person." The term *Nivkhi*, which is the Russian plural of *Nivkh*, is often used as both a singular and plural form in Western ethnographic literature. Russian and Western ethnographers formerly called the Nivkhs the *Gilyaks* or *Giliaks*. There has been considerable disagreement among scholars as to the origin of the name *Gilyak*. Some suggest that it is derived from *Kile*, the name of a nearby Tungusic-speaking group whom early Russian explorers may have mistaken for Nivkhs, while others believe that it may be an obsolete Tungusic name for Nivkh.

Although linguistically isolated from their neighbors, the Nivkhs maintained trade and marriage relations for centuries with the Nanais and other Tungus-speaking peoples of the Amur and the Ainu of southern Sakhalin. Contacts with the Ainu were sometimes hostile; the two groups occasionally raided each others' settlements and took slaves. Contacts between the Nivkhs along the Amur and the Chinese began as early as the 12th century AD: Nivkhs exchanged furs for Chinese cloth (mainly silk, cotton, and brocade), alcohol, tobacco, beads, and metal disks that were fashioned into jewelry. During the 18th century, Chinese officials claimed control over Nivkh territory and appointed headmen in the Nivkh village communities to serve as liaisons between the Nivkhs and the Chinese government and to collect taxes from their compatriots. These headmen had no real authority among the Nivkhs, however, as they merely served as ceremonial figureheads in dealings with Chinese officials. Nivkh-Japanese trade, which became extensive in the early 19th century, involved the exchange of sea-eagle feathers gathered by the Nivkhs and used by the Japanese in certain religious rituals for Japanese metal goods such as cooking pots and knives. Nivkh blacksmiths often melted down metal trade items into various tools, arrowheads, spear and harpoon points, hooks, and earrings.

The first Russian-Nivkh contacts began in the 17th century, when Russian explorers encountered Nivkh settlements along the Amur; these meetings were not always cordial, and the Nivkhs earned a reputation among the Russians as ferocious warriors. During the 19th century, the Nivkhs became Russian subjects: treaties between Russia and China in the late 1850s and early 1860s gave Russia control over the Amur River valley, and several decades of conflicts and negotiations between Russia and Japan resulted in Russia's acquisition of Sakhalin in 1876. (Russia ceded the southern half of Sakhalin to Japan in 1905, when it lost the Russo-Japanese War; southern Sakhalin did not return to Russian/Soviet control until Japan's defeat at the end of World War II.) Henceforth, Nivkh territory was flooded by tens of thousands of Russian colonists, and the Nivkhs became a minority in their own land. The Russian government encouraged the colonization of both areas of Nivkh settlement—the lower Amur and Sakhalin—but for different reasons. Since the Amur River basin bordered on China, it was considered an area of strategic significance, and the Russian government did not wish to leave it sparsely populated by non-Russian natives. Sakhalin's damp, cold climate and poor soil provided little attraction for colonists, but it was geographically isolated not only from Central Russia but also from the Far Eastern mainland, so it presented a suitable location for a prison colony. By the end of the 19th century, the Russian population of Sakhalin included almost twice as many prisoners and exiles as free colonists.

Both along the Amur and on Sakhalin, Russian newcomers seized Nivkh lands and cheated the Nivkh out of their furs and other goods; at the same time, extensive commercial fishing by Russian and Japanese firms caused fish stocks to decline. As a result, poverty and hunger became widespread in Nivkh communities. The Nivkhs on Sakhalin faced additional dangers from escaped prisoners and ex-convicts, who often robbed Nivkh households, beat or killed Nivkh men, and raped Nivkh women. Some Sakhalin Nivkhs were forced by economic necessity to work as prison guards or to track escaped prisoners for the Russian prison administration; this naturally caused friction between Nivkhs and local Russians, many of whom were themselves former prisoners. During the Civil War that followed the Bolsheviks' seizure of power in October 1917, the Nivkhs were drawn into bloody conflicts between supporters of the Communist Red Army and the anti-Communist White Army and Japanese forces who saw in the prevailing chaos an opportunity for Japan to gain territory and influence in Russia's eastern borderlands.

During the 1920s, the Nivkhs' situation improved somewhat. The Bolshevik government provided economic relief and basic Western medical care and established a few schools in Nivkh territory. (Nevertheless, the Nivkhs had little influence on local government, which was, as before, dominated by Russians.) Economic exploitation of Nivkh lands by Russians—particularly the overfishing that had led to Nivkh famines before the Revolution—lessened during the first decade of Soviet rule. Ethnographers and Bolsheviks sympathetic to the Nivkhs and other numerically small nationalities persuaded the central government to put native needs before the state's interest in developing the area economically. After Stalin's rise to power in 1929, however, this policy was abandoned. Many

NIVKHS

² LOCATION AND HOMELAND

According to the 1989 Soviet census, the Nivkhs numbered 4,631, practically all of whom live in the Russian Far East. There were 2,008 Nivkhs living on the island of Sakhalin, and an additional 2,368 Nivkhs inhabited the lower Amur River valley in the Nizhne-Amurskii and Takhtinskii Districts (Russian *raion*) of Khabarovsk Territory (Russian *krai*). The remaining 255 Nivkhs lived scattered throughout the Russian Federation. As of the 2002 Russian census, the number of Nivkhs topped 5,000.

In the territory of the Amur Nivkhs, winters are characterized by high winds and heavy snows. January temperatures usually range between –28° and –20°C (–18.4° and –4°F). Summers are damp and moderately warm, averaging between 16° and 20°C (60.8° and 68°F). Rains are heavy in late summer and early fall, thanks to Pacific monsoon winds, and flooding along the Amur is common. Larch, yew, birch, maple, lilac, honeysuckle, and swamp grasses predominate in low-lying areas; at higher elevations, mixed forests of larch, spruce, fir, ash, lime, maple, and walnut are the most common forms of vegetation. (The tops of the highest mountains are covered by cedar and lichens). Rivers have traditionally teemed with fish (particularly salmon) and otters. Foxes, bears, squirrels, sables, hares, boars, Siberian tigers, elks, grouse, and deer are the most typical animals along the lower Amur.

The climate in which the Sakhalin Nivkhs live is quite harsh. Winters are long and cold, with average temperatures of –19.6°C (–3.3°F) in the north and –13.2°C (8.2°F) in the south. Summers are much warmer—median temperatures are 15.2°C (59.4°F) in the north and 17.8°C (64°F) in the south—but the climate is unstable, so temperatures often drop significantly without warning. The northernmost part of the island consists of barren tundra with sparse stands of larch and birch trees and various grasses; rugged mountainous taiga forests of larch, birch, spruce, and fir predominate further to the south. Sakhalin is very damp and windy, and violent hurricanes and blizzards frequently lash the island. Bears, foxes, otters, lynx, and reindeer are Sakhalin's most typical forms of wildlife; its rivers, particularly the Tym' and Poronai, are rich in fish, especially salmon. Seals and sea lions are found along Sakhalin's coastline.

³ LANGUAGE

The Nivkh language is sometimes classified together with Chukchi, Koriak, Kamchadal, and several other Siberian languages in the Palaeoasiatic language family, but in reality it shares few features in common with them. In fact, Nivkh is an isolate—a language that cannot be proven to be related to any other known tongue. The grammar of Nivkh is quite complex. For example, numerals can take more than 20 different forms depending on the characteristics of the items being counted. Small, round objects; long objects; large, round objects or objects with an indeterminate shape; thin, flat objects; animals and insects; humans and spirits with human-like forms; objects that occur in pairs; and so on—all of these use different words for the same number. Thus, one person (*nivkh*) is *nivkh nin*; one dog (*kan*) is *kan n'yn'*; and one tree (*tig'r*) is *tig'r nekh*. The Nivkh language is divided into two dialects: the Amur dialect, which is spoken along the Amur River and on northern Sakhalin; and the Eastern Sakhalin dialect, which is spoken by the remainder of the Sakhalin Nivkhs. The Nivkh language

Nivkhs were forced out of their widely scattered settlements and shipped to a handful of larger villages. The government's economic planners assumed that this form of centralization would render fishing and hunting more efficient and productive; instead, it resulted in the depletion of fish and other natural resources (besides disrupting Nivkh communities). The Nivkhs suffered, along with the other peoples of the USSR, from the widespread political hysteria and mass arrests of the Stalinist purges. Local agents of the NKVD (the forerunner to the KGB) filled their arrest quotas by seizing Nivkhs on false charges of espionage for Japan (particularly among the Sakhalin Nivkhs), anti-Soviet sentiments, and economic sabotage. Forestry, mining, oil-drilling, and industry were developed in the Amur region and on Sakhalin without considering the economic consequences, which caused serious environmental damage to Nivkh territory.

The 1930s policy of resettlement was resumed with increased vigor in the 1960s, when government officials embarked upon a campaign of closing settlements they considered lacking in economic potential. However, the towns to which the Nivkhs were relocated offered few economic opportunities; dispersed among Russian majorities and denied instruction in Nivkh language and culture in local schools, many young Nivkhs were robbed of their cultural heritage. The Nivkhs had to bear in silence the economic and cultural damages wrought by the resettlements until Soviet leader Mikhail Gorbachev's relaxation of censorship allowed them to air their grievances.

was unwritten (except for the academic transcriptions of linguists and ethnographers) until 1931, when Soviet linguists created a Nivkh writing system based on the Amur dialect and written in the Latin alphabet. Publications in the new alphabet (chiefly schoolbooks) soon began to appear, and literacy in the native language began to spread. However, the new alphabet was banned five years later: the Russian chauvinism typical of the Stalinist regime had led the government to oppose the use of the "foreign" Latin alphabet. A new alphabet based on the Cyrillic (Russian) alphabet was to have been adopted in 1936, but for reasons that are unclear, it does not seem to have come into widespread use until the 1940s or 1950s. (The Stalinist suspicion of non-Russian peoples and their cultures and languages may have in some way been behind this delay). Nivkh is now written in the Cyrillic alphabet, with numerous extra letters and diacritics to represent specifically Nivkh sounds. Until 1979, only the Amur dialect of Nivkh had a written form. In that year, a separate writing system (also based on the Cyrillic alphabet augmented with special letters and diacritics) was developed for the Eastern Sakhalin dialect; this form of written Nivkh is used mainly in textbooks for Nivkh children.

Nivkh personal names are usually formed by adding special suffixes to nouns, verbs, and adjectives or their roots. Male personal names use suffixes ending in -*n*, while female names are formed by adding suffixes that end in -*k*. Many Nivkh personal names reflect the Nivkhs' natural surroundings, such as the male names *Kharkhin* (derived from *khar*, "wasp") and *Tutin* (from *tu*, "lake"), and the female names *Chryguk* (from *chry*, "river bank, beach") and *Chngyruk* (from *chngyr*, "grass"). Some names refer to a pleasant item or reflect a physical or moral characteristic that the parents wish the child to have—e.g., the female names *Aisik* (from *ais*, "gold") and *Iazruk* (from *iazrud'*, "to respect"), and the male names *Pilgun* (from *pila*, "big") and *Smedun* (from *smod'*, "to love"). Other names refer to a person's behavior or appearance in infancy: examples of this type of name are *Togun* (male) and *Toguk* (female), which are based on the verb *tod*, "to cry"; *Vadun* (male) and *Vaduk* (female), which are derived from *vad'*, "to fight"; and *Ngokhtik* (female, from *ngokh*, "fat"). A child may be named in reference to an event that took place at the time of his or her birth. Thus, if a dogsled broke down when a girl was born, she might be named *Myiguk* (from *myid'*, "to go to ruin, to fall down"). It is for this reason that there are many Nivkh names of otherwise inexplicable origins—for example *Taligun* (male, from *tali*, "bag, sack") and *Chvark* (female, from *chvar*, "chain"). Russian personal names such as *Vladimir* (male) and *Zoya* have become common in the 20th century. The Nivkhs did not use surnames until the Soviet period, when the government demanded that they, along with the other Siberian and Far Eastern Peoples, adopt surnames in the interest of bureaucratic convenience: Nivkh surnames are based on the personal name of the male who was the head of the family at that time.

4 FOLKLORE

The Nivkhs possess a rich heritage of oral literature that has been passed on from generation to generation since time immemorial. Besides riddles, songs, and short folk tales, there are longer, more elaborate forms of folklore, such as the *t'ylgund* and *ngastund*. *T'ylgund* (singular *t'ylgu*, *t'ylgursh*), or myths, describe the creation of the universe and man, the origins of

the Nivkh clans and ancient wars between them, and the adventures of fantastic heroes, spirits, and beasts. In traditional Nivkh society, the *t'ylgund* were considered to be true. The *t'ylgund* have a fixed form and are not subject to improvisation or embellishment. (Some scholars, such as the Russian ethnographer Lev Shternberg, have compared the Nivkh *t'ylgund* to the mythological stories of the ancient Greeks and Romans on these grounds.) The *ngastund* (singular, *ngyzit*), or mythological tales, also center on mythical heroes. In some of the *ngastund*, the protagonist is a hunter who defeats evil spirits, cold, and hunger to survive and prosper; in others, he is a warlike hero who avenges wrongs done to his relatives or rescues women taken as brides against their will. Unlike the *t'ylgund*, the *ngastund* were not considered to be accurate representations of prehistoric events, even in traditional Nivkh society. They were told for amusement, not enlightenment, and were consciously embellished and altered by adding and changing details and plots.

5 RELIGION

The traditional Nivkh religion is a form of shamanism. Nivkh shamanists believe that fire, mountains, stars, constellations, forests, and rivers have spirits, and that man's survival and prosperity require that these spirits be respected. Certain animals, such as bears, dogs, and whales, are also considered sacred and are eaten only at ritual meals. The Nivkhs divide the universe (*kurng*) into three parts: the Upper World (*Tly Vo*) is the domain of the Master of the Heavens (*Tly Nivukh*). Humans, animals, and various deities such as the Master of the Mountains and Forests (*Pal Ys*) and the Master of the Waters (*Tol Ys*) dwell in the Middle World (*Mif*, or "Earth"). The Lower World (*Mly Vo*) is inhabited by the dead and is believed to more or less exactly resemble the world of the living. The Nivkh shaman (*ch'am*) communicates with the spirits by chanting and singing prayers while dancing and beating a large, flat, round drum called a *k'as* during rituals intended to ward off bad fortune and heal the sick. Nivkh shamans can be either men or women, but they must be chosen by the spirits. Shamans are respected but feared, because they are believed to have the ability to use magical powers for evil purposes if they so choose. During the imperial Russian era Russian Orthodox missionaries were active among the Nivkhs, converting a portion of the population. However Orthodox Christianity continued to coexist with the older beliefs. Many Nivkh shamans were imprisoned and executed during Stalin's anti-religious campaigns; as a result, shamanism was driven underground. The Nivkhs have practiced their religion more openly since Soviet leader Mikhail Gorbachev ended the Soviet government's persecution of religion during the 1980s.

6 MAJOR HOLIDAYS

The most important Nivkh holiday is the Bear Festival (*Chkhyf-Lekherno*; literally, "bear game"), a shamanist ceremony held to honor the bear-spirit and the memories of departed ancestors. The Bear Festival does not have a fixed date, but in pre-Soviet society it was usually held in January or February and was celebrated separately by each clan. Preparations for a Bear Festival sometimes took several years. Each celebration required a live bear, which was sometimes captured or purchased while still a cub. The bear was held in captivity in a small log building and fed by the clan's members. (Traditional Nivkh villages usually had several such cages, each holding an animal to be used in future Bear Festivals). A few months before the festival was to take place, the participants gave the bear's master food and money to be used in preparing a feast. On the day of the ceremony, the bear was tied between several elaborately carved poles or trees, killed with a bow and arrow, and butchered in a lengthy and complex ceremony. Dogs were also sacrificed at this time. The clan feasted on the bear's meat and celebrated with games, music, and dancing. Observance of the Bear Festival sharply declined during the Soviet period as a result of anti-religious persecution and the dispersal of Nivkh communities, but it was revived in the 1980s. The Bear Festival is celebrated by modern Nivkhs less as a religious ceremony than as an expression of Nivkh cultural identity.

7 RITES OF PASSAGE

In the traditional societies of the Nivkh and other Amur-dwellers, all couples wished to have many children, since this was considered a sign of prestige, especially for men. At the same time, pregnancy and childbirth were viewed as dangerous. (This is understandable, given the absence of medical care beyond shamanist rituals and certain herbal medicines.) For this reason, there were a host of taboos intended to ensure a safe delivery. Pregnant women were forbidden to sew clothing and footwear, repair fish nets, set animal traps, or perform any other activity that involved "tying" or "closing." In the last few months of pregnancy, this prohibition extended to other members of the household. Childbirth took place in a small temporary lean-to called a *lanraf*, from which men were barred. (Menstruating and birthing women were considered to bring bad fortune; they were forbidden to touch fishing and hunting equipment, and their husbands were not allowed to hunt or fish). Upon delivery, mother and child remained in the birthing hut for several days before returning to the family household. Both parents were forbidden to work for the time it took the child's umbilical cord to wither and drop off.

Cremation is the traditional form of burial among the Nivkhs. (In pre-Soviet society, Nivkhs who died in infancy were not cremated; instead, they were placed in coffins in the forks of trees in the hope that their spirits might fly off, to return one day to the clan.) Soon after death, the deceased is dressed in fine clothing (usually white), and a white cloth band called a *niakh tiakh* was used to cover their eyes. Food, drink, and tobacco are placed next to the body and periodically consumed by the mourners. After several days have passed, the body is removed from the house and cremated outdoors. The ashes and remaining bones are collected and placed in a *raf*—a small raised house a few feet square—in the settlement's graveyard.

8 INTERPERSONAL RELATIONS

In view of the harsh environment of the territory occupied by the Nivkhs, it is not surprising that hospitality has long been an esteemed trait. In traditional society, it was expected that any Nivkh experiencing economic hardship could receive food and shelter at any home for an indefinite time and that the favor would be returned when needed. Travelers to the Nivkh lands in the 19th century reported that this practice was often extended to strangers as well, even though the Nivkhs regarded outsiders with a certain degree of suspicion. (Nivkhs who abused this system of mutual aid were, however, roundly

despised.) Elderly people, especially old men, were held in high esteem. Although they held no special positions in the community (there was no traditional post of "elder") and enjoyed no special privileges, their advice was often sought on important personal and community matters. The forced dispersal of most Nivkh communities in the Soviet period has undoubtedly done much to lessen the influence of these values on everyday behavior.

9 LIVING CONDITIONS

Because of the Nivkhs' reliance upon fish for most of their food, their settlements were traditionally established along rivers or seashores. High ground was chosen to provide protection from tides and floods. Most villages contained five or fewer extended-family households, although some had as many as 20. In addition to residential buildings, Nivkh villages contained doghouses; elevated sheds for storing weapons, tools, and preserved food; platforms and racks for drying fish; and raised log houses called *lezng* that held the skulls and bones of bears sacrificed during the Bear Festival. The Nivkh were semi-nomadic and had separate winter and summer settlements. Winter houses (*t'ulf tyf*) were built near hunting grounds and occupied from October until April or May. There were two basic types of winter dwelling. The most ancient was called a *to ryv* in the Amur dialect, and a *to* in the Eastern Sakhalin dialect. The *to ryv* was a round dugout about 23 feet in diameter shored up by wooden poles and covered with packed earth and grass. Wide, low benches along the walls also served as beds. A fireplace in the center of the *to ryv* provided heat and light, and a smokehole in the center allowed smoke to escape and light to enter. The other type of Nivkh winter house was the *chad ryv*. The *chad ryv*, like the Nanai *dio*, was modeled after Chinese or Manchu houses of the Amur region. It was a large, rectangular house of dried earth with wooden supports and a grass or bark roof. Adobe stoves on either side of the door provided warmth, and the inhabitants sat and slept on benches lining the walls. The windows of the *chad ryv* were covered with fishskin. Summer houses, or *ke ryv*, were built along fishing grounds and were occupied from May until September. The *ke ryv* were rectangular wooden buildings between 36 and 45 feet long that were raised several feet above the ground on poles. Entry was by way of a notched log used as a ladder. Virtually all Nivkhs now live in one-story Russian-style wooden houses or prefabricated concrete apartment buildings.

Prior to the 20th century, dogsleds and skis were the most common form of Nivkh winter transportation. In summer, journeys were made on foot, in light bark boats (*hivmu*), or in long, flat-bottomed wooden boats (*kylmr mu*). Dogsleds, skis, and traditional boats are now used much less frequently than motorboats, automobiles, trucks, and buses.

10 FAMILY LIFE

Traditional Nivkh society was divided into several dozen clans (*k'al*) of related nuclear families that took part in the Bear Festival and other religious rituals, avenged wrongs done to their members by members of other clans, and shared hunting and fishing grounds. Two clans often formed *pandf*, marriage alliances according to which each agreed to give wives to, or receive wives from, only the other clan. Because this practice resulted in a high degree of interrelatedness among the Nivkhs, there were strict and very complex rules on the degree

A Nivkh family rest at home in the village of Nogliki on Sakhalin Island, Russia. The main businesses of Sakhalin people are fishing and the oil industry. (Laski Diffusion/East News/Liaison/Getty Images)

and type of blood relationship permitted between marriage partners. Although the complex obligations and rules surrounding the clan system are no longer observed, the Nivkhs are still conscious of their clan affiliations and the locations of traditional clan territories. Since the Second World War Nivkh family life has generally followed the same patterns as Soviet and Russian family life.

11 CLOTHING

The traditional Nivkh garments for both men and women were robes (*siky* for men, *hukht* for women) that fastened on the left side of the body with three buttons and were worn with trousers (*varsh*). Winter garments were made of fish-skin, seal-skin, sable, otter, lynx, fox, and dog furs; summer garments were sewn from cotton and silk cloth purchased from Japanese, Russian, and Chinese traders. (Only wealthy Nivkhs wore silk.) Women's *hukht* extended below the knee and were made of light or multicolored furs, skins, or cloth, while the *siky* worn by men were slightly shorter, used dark materials, and had pockets built into the sleeves. The collars, hems, and sleeve ends of women's robes were elaborately ornamented with beads, Chinese coins, or other metal disks, glass trade beads, embroidery. and appliqué. Men's robes were decorated more modestly and only on the sleeve ends and the left lapel. Boots (*myn'd'kh*) were made of fish-skin, seal-skin, or deer-skin; stockings (*kanyng kamys*) were made of dog fur. Fur hats

(*hak*) were worn in winter. Women were particularly fond of *tlyhi hak*, hats whose crown and back were decorated with, respectively, the ears and tail of the animal that had provided the fur. In summer, Nivkhs wore conical birch-bark hats called *hif hak*. Men always wore seal-skin belts from which hung knives, tools, amulets, and pouches for tobacco, flint, and tinder. (Although women also wore belts on occasion, belts were generally considered a sign of manhood.) Men's *siky* were protected from water damage while hunting and traveling by dog-sled by a loose kilt called a *kosk*. Underclothing consisted of skin loincloths or cloth undershorts and undershirts; in winter, women wore richly embroidered fur and cloth chest coverings for additional warmth. Today, the Nivkhs usually wear Western clothing (cloth dresses, shirts, trousers, stockings, socks, and underclothes, and leather shoes), but traditional clothing is worn on holidays and other special occasions. Modern Nivkh women sometimes sew traditional patterns onto store-bought cloth dresses.

12 FOOD

Fish, particularly salmon, is the mainstay of the traditional Nivkh diet and is usually eaten raw, dried, or boiled. Dried fish (*ma*) is prepared by hanging fresh fish in the wind and sun. Seaweed, wild garlic and onions, caviar, wild apples, cedar nuts, hazel nuts, cranberries, cloudberries, whortleberries, and edible roots, fungi, and grasses add variety to Nivkh national cuisine. In traditional society, meat was consumed much less frequently than fish and usually consisted of deer, elk, seal, sea lion, and dolphin; bears and dogs were almost never eaten outside of shamanist rituals. A favorite Nivkh dish is *mos'*, which is made by pulverizing dried fish and mixing it with fish skins, water, seal fat, and berries until the mixture has the consistency of sour cream. Salt, sugar, rice, millet, legumes, liquors, and tea entered the Nivkh diet within the last few centuries as a result of contacts with Chinese, Japanese, and Manchu traders; Russian/Soviet influence has led the Nivkhs to adopt bread and flour, vodka, potatoes, butter, and canned vegetables, fruits, and meats. Prior to the Soviet era, the Nivkhs stored food in birchbark or wooden containers, cooked in iron kettles of Chinese manufacture, and ate from wooden platters and bowls with wooden spoons; now, they use mass-produced metal, plastic, china, and enamel vessels, utensils, and plates.

13 EDUCATION

Education and literacy were unknown among the Nivkhs until the Soviet government began to establish public schools in the 1920s; these schools used Russian textbooks and teachers and operated in Russian until the creation of a Nivkh alphabet in 1931. Primary schooling is now universal among the Nivkhs; almost all attend at least some secondary school, and many go on to college. All Nivkhs are fluent in spoken and written Russian, knowledge of which is essential for entry into institutions of higher learning. Because teaching in native Siberian languages was neglected, and often officially discouraged, during much of the Soviet period, many young and middle-aged Nivkhs have little or no understanding of their own people's language. According to information from 2006 only 23.3% of the Nivkhs speak Nivkh as their mother tongue. (In some Nivkh communities, fewer than one in ten speak Nivkh as their first language). The remainder speak Russian as their first language, although at least some in this group know Nivkh at varying levels of fluency.

14 CULTURAL HERITAGE

The cultural heritage of the Nivkhs includes thousands of songs, most of which have yet to be recorded or written down. Some Nivkh songs are of great antiquity and have been sung for centuries. The ability to improvise new songs is also highly valued among the Nivkhs. Nivkh women are considered especially talented at composing beautiful and poetic songs on a moment's notice. The most popular Nivkh songs are the *alkhtund* (singular: *alkhtursh*), or love songs. The *alkhtund* usually concern the tragic consequences of an ill-fated love: a typical theme is the suicide of two lovers who cannot marry either because they are members of the same clan or because the woman has been given in marriage to another man.

Nivkh songs are often accompanied on the *t'yngryng*, a violin-like one-stringed instrument with a round, hollow birchbark body and a fish-skin soundboard. The *t'yngryng* is played with a bow made of wood and horsehair. Another Nivkh instrument is the *kangga*, a copper, iron or wooden mouth instrument that resembles a jaw harp. A log was sometimes suspended between two trees and beaten like a drum during the Bear Festival. During the Soviet period, these instruments were largely replaced by European instruments (guitars, wind instruments, accordions, etc.), but they are still played at public performances by Nivkh folklore ensembles.

15 WORK

Fishing has traditionally been the Nivkhs' primary economic activity, and they have developed a variety of skillful methods of netting, hooking, and trapping fish, particularly salmon. Nets were formerly made by hand from nettle fiber but now mass-produced rope or plastic-filament nets are purchased in stores. Nets are sometimes used in conjunction with an L-shaped trap called a *myr*, or *chkhyl'*. The *myr* is placed in a river or stream at a right angle to the riverbank in such a manner as to force schools of fish to run into it; when they attempt to turn, they are caught in a net. By using this combination of trap and net, a fishing expedition of three to ten men can catch four or five thousand fish in the space of a few days.

16 SPORTS

Nivkhs have long enjoyed dogsled racing, boat racing, archery contests, and fencing with sticks. These sports are an integral part of Bear Festival celebrations. Children play tug-of-war and ball games (for example, one player tosses a grass ball to another player, who attempts to catch it on a stick). Curiously, although the Nivkh have traditionally lived near rivers and other bodies of water, swimming did not become popular in the Soviet period.

17 ENTERTAINMENT AND RECREATION

Most Nivkh households now own televisions and radios with which they receive news and entertainment broadcasts in Russian from both Moscow and local stations. Nivkh cultural activists have recently begun to suggest that local studios also produce native-language programs on Nivkh cultural themes. Modern Nivkhs also enjoy attending concerts of classical, popular, and Nivkh traditional music and Russian and Nivkh plays.

18 FOLK ART, CRAFTS, AND HOBBIES

Nivkh men have traditionally been skilled at engraving intricate decorations on wooden spoons, storage trunks, knife handles and sheaths, and metal knife blades and spear tips. Women's artistic skills find expression in embroidery and appliqué, with which they adorn clothing and blankets. Common themes of Nivkh engraving and sewing are symmetrical spirals and other abstract geometric designs, fish, dragons, deer, bears, birds, snakes, and turtles. Sculpture in wood and bone originally centered around the representation of shamanist spirits, such as the "Master of the House" *(Tyv ys)* that protected each family. In the 20th century, its repertoire has expanded to include animal and human figures as well as hunting scenes and other themes from traditional life.

19 SOCIAL PROBLEMS

The modern Nivkhs face a number of problems shared to one degree or another by all of Russia's Siberian and Far Eastern Peoples. Alcoholism, pollution, and a low standard of living exacerbated by late Soviet and post-Soviet economic upheavals have resulted in poor health and a low life expectancy. Nivkhs are sometimes subject to economic discrimination in the areas where they live; that is, they are paid less than Russians for equivalent work or find it more difficult to obtain well-paying employment. Overfishing and ecologically unsound fishing, logging, and industrial practices have caused significant environmental damage to the Nivkh lands. Issues of cultural survival, too, present a formidable challenge. Soviet policies toward minority peoples after the 1920s tended more and more to suppress their cultures and languages in favor of Russian culture and language. The "small peoples" of Siberia and the Far East in particular saw their histories, cultural achievements, and languages steadily and inexorably removed from educational institutions and public life. By the 1970s, the Nivkh language was no longer even taught as an elective subject in local schools, as Soviet officials had decided that such a "backward" people's language was not worthy of preservation. Since *perestroika*, Nivkh teachers, activists, journalists, and scholars have achieved some success in expanding knowledge of Nivkh history, language, folklore, and arts. A small but vigorous native rights movement led by Nivkh author Vladimir Sangi emerged during the *glasnost'* era with the long-term goal of a Nivkh autonomous territory inside the Russian Federation; it has already obtained the return of some Nival lands to communities dispersed during the 1960s resettlements. Perhaps the most prominent Nivkh cultural figure today is the novelist Vladimir Sangi, who in the late 1990s was openly critical of Russian cultural and economic policies regarding the Nivkhs, including issuing a call for reparations from the Russian government to the Nivkh community.

20 GENDER ISSUES

Men and women had separate economic roles in the Nivkh community, and children were taught early on how to perform the activities suitable for their sex. Women processed skins and furs, cleaned fish and game, sewed clothes, and cleaned house; men hunted, fished, built homes, carved household items from wood, and made various weapons and tools. Boys and girls were considered of marriageable age at puberty. Young men and women were often sexually active before marriage, although this was often frowned upon (at least as far as the behavior of young women was concerned).

During the Soviet era, particularly following collectivization and during the Second World War, the full incorporation of Nivkh economic life into the Soviet system resulted in the gradual integration of Nivkh women into the Soviet workforce. In addition, Nivkh women were granted access to Soviet educational opportunities.

21 BIBLIOGRAPHY

Austerlitz, Robert. "Nivkh." In: *Encyclopedia of World Cultures. Vol. 6: Russia and Eurasia/China.* Ed. Paul Friedrich and Norma Diamond, Trans. Lydia T. Black. Boston: G. K. Hall, 1994.

Bartels, Dennis A., and Alice L. Bartels. *When the North was Red: Aboriginal Education in Soviet Siberia.* Montreal: McGill-Queen's University Press, 1995.

Black, Lydia. "Dogs, Bears and Killer Whales: An Analysis of the Nivkh Symbolic System," Ph.D. Dissertation: University of Massachusetts, 1973.

———"The Nivkhi (Gilyak) of Sakhalin and the Lower Amur." *Arctic Anthropology.* 10 (1973); 1–110.

Chekhov, Anton. *A Journey to Sakhalin.* Trans. Brian Reeve. Cambridge, England: Ian Faulkner, 1993.

D'iakonova, V. P. "Zhilishche narodov Sibiri" [Housing of the Peoples of Siberia".] In: *Ekologiia etnicheskikh kul'tur Sibiri nakanune XXI veka* [The Ecology of Ethnic Cultures of Si-

beria on the Eve of the Twenty First Century]. In Russian. Ed. V. B. Kurylev and V. A. Koz'min. St. Petersburg: Nauka, 1995.

Forsyth, James. *A History of the Peoples of Siberia: Russia's North Asian Colony, 1581–1990.* Cambridge: Cambridge University Press, 1992.

Gaer, Evdokiya A. "Birth Rituals of the Nanai." In: *Culture Incarnate: Native Anthropology from Russia.* Ed. Marjorie Mandelstam Balzer. Armonk, NY: M. E. Sharpe, 1995.

Grant, Bruce. *In the Soviet House of Culture: A Century of Perestroikas.* Princeton, NJ: Princeton University Press, 1995.

Ivanov, S. V., M. G. Levin, and A. V. Smoliak. "The Nivkhi." In: *The Peoples of Siberia.* Based on data by A. M. Zolotarev. Ed. M. G. Levin and L. P. Potapov. Trans. Stephen Dunn. Chicago: University of Chicago Press, 1964.

Malygina, A. A. "Mir detstva u narodov Sibiri" [The World of Childhood among the Peoples of Siberia]. In: *Ekologiia etnicheskikh kul'tur Sibiri nakanune XXI veka* [The Ecology of Ethnic Cultures of Siberia on the Eve of the Twenty-first Century]. In Russian. Ed. V. B. Kurylev and V. A. Koz'min. St. Petersburg: Nauka, 1995.

Nivkhi Sakhalina: sovremennoe sotsial'no-ekonomicheskoe razvitie [The Nivkhs of Sakhalin: Contemporary Socio-Economic Development]. Ed. V.I. Boiko, et al. Novosibirsk: Nauka, 1988.

Panfilov, V. Z., "Remarks on Nivkhi (Gilyak) Proper Names (Anthroponyms)." In: *Popular Beliefs and Folklore Traditions in Siberia.* Ed. V. Dioszegi. Bloomington: Indiana University; The Hague: Mouton; Budapest: Akademiai Kiado, 1968.

Semeinaia obriadnost' narodov Sibiri: opyt sravnitel'nogo izucheniia [Household Rituals of the Peoples of Siberia: A Comparative Study]. Ed. I. S. Gurvich. In Russian. Moscow: Nauka, 1980.

Shternberg, L. and Bruce Grant. *Social Organization of the Gilyak.* New York: American Museum of Natural History, 1999.

Smoliak, A. V. *Traditsionnoe khoziaistvo i material'naia kul'tura narodov Nizhnego Amura i Sakhalina* [Traditional Economy and Material Culture of the Peoples of the Lower Amur and Sakhalin]. In Russian Moskva: Nauka, 1984.

Taksami, Ch. M. "Nivkhi" [The Nivkhs] in *Narody Rossii: Entsiklopediia* [The Peoples of Russia: An Encyclopedia]. Ed. V. A. Tishkov. In Russian. Moscow: Bol'shaia Rossiiskaia Entsiklopediia, 1994.

———. *Nivkhi (sovremennoe khoziaistvo, kul'tura i byt)* [The Nivkhs (Contemporary Economy, Culture, and Way of Life)]. In Russian. Leningrad: Nauka, 1967.

Taksami, Ch. M. *Osnovnye problemy etnografii i istorii nivkhov* [Basic Problems of the Ethnography and History of the Nivkhs]. In Russian. Leningrad: Nauka, 1975.

Vakhtin, Nikolai. *Korennoe naselenie krainego Severa Rossiiskoi Federatsii* [The Indigenous Population of the Far North of the Russian Federation]. In Russian. St. Petersburg: Izdatel'stvo Evropeiskogo doma, 1993.

Working, Russell. "Nivkh Novelist Wants Reparations, " *Vladivostok News,* 21 August 1998.

—revised by A. Frank

NORWEGIANS

LOCATION: Norway
POPULATION: 4.7 million
LANGUAGE: Norwegian in two forms: Bokmål and Nynorsk
RELIGION: Evangelical Lutheran Church of Norway;
  small numbers of Roman Catholics, Greek Orthodox,
  Methodists, Baptists, Anglicans, Muslims, and Jews.

¹ INTRODUCTION

The Kingdom of Norway is part of Scandinavia in northern Europe, together with its neighbors Denmark and Sweden. Norway is bounded on the west by the Atlantic Ocean for most of the country's length, on the southwest by the North Sea, and directly to the south by the Skagerrak, an arm of the North Sea. To the east, Norway shares a long border with Sweden, and for a short distance in the north with Finland and the Russian federation.

Most Norwegians live within a few kilometers of the sea, which has played a pivotal role in their country's history. Norway's great Viking era took place during the 9th century AD, when the Vikings extended their territory as far afield as Dublin and Normandy. Their leader, Harald Fairhair, unified the country around the year 900, and King Olaf converted the Norwegians to Christianity. The Vikings were the first to cross the Atlantic Ocean, a feat accomplished with Erik the Red's voyages to Iceland and Greenland. According to tradition, Erik's son, Leif Erikson, landed on the coast of North America in the year 1001. The year 1380 began Norway's long period of union with Denmark, which lasted over 400 years, until 1814, when the Norwegians adopted their own constitution. Their short-lived independence ended as Norway was united with Sweden under one head of state until 1905. That year marked Norway's peaceful secession and installation of its own monarchy. Since Norway, long a subject people, had no royal family of its own, it chose Prince Carl of Denmark to become the new nation's first king, as Haakon VII, an ancient Viking name like that given to his son, Olav.

Norway remained neutral during World War I, but was invaded by Germany early in World War II. Norwegian resistance to German occupation resulted in severe reprisals as the Nazis attempted to destroy the underground movement. The Norwegian merchant fleet played a vital role in aiding the Allies. Although it lost half of its fleet, the country recovered quickly after the war. In 1957, King Haakon died and was succeeded by his son, Olav V, who died in January 1991. In June of that year, Olav's son was crowned king of Norway as Harald V. Although Norway joined the European Free Trade Association (EFTA) in 1960, it rejected membership in the European Community (EC) in 1972, and decided against joining the new European Union (EU) in 1994. In 1992, however, Norway became a member of the newly created European Economic Area (EEA), through which it participates in the European single market and contributes to the budget of the EU.

² LOCATION AND HOMELAND

Norway stretches across the north and west of the Scandinavian peninsula. It is a long country with bulges at the north and south, while its mid-section is as narrow across as 6.28 km

(3.9 mi) at one point. It has an area of 323,882 sq km (125,051 sq mi)—roughly the same size as the state of New Mexico. Norway is the longest country in Europe and one of the most mountainous: only one-fifth of its total area is less than 152.4 m (500 ft) above sea level. Almost one-third of the country lies within the Arctic Circle. In this so-called "land of the midnight sun," the sun shines almost continuously through every 24-hour period at the height of summer and never sets at all on Midsummer's Day (June 23), a date celebrated with bonfires throughout the country. Overseas territories claimed by Norway include: the Svalbard islands, the volcanic island of Jan Mayen Peter I Island and Queen Maud Land, both north of the Arctic Circle.

With 4.7 million people, Norway has the lowest population density of any country in Europe—15 people per sq km (38 people per sq mi). Ethnically, it has a largely homogeneous population of Nordic, Alpine, and Baltic origin. However, there are also minority populations of some 30,000 Sami (Lapps), some of whom still maintain the traditional reindeer-herding life of their people. Norway also has about 7,000 residents of Finnish origin, and, more recently, immigrants from southern Europe and a variety of Third World countries, many of whom first arrived as guest workers.

³ LANGUAGE

Norwegian is a Germanic language closely related to Swedish and Danish. There are actually two forms of Norwegian, both of which are considered official languages and can be understood by all Norwegians. *Bokmål*, the more common of the two, was developed from Danish during the nineteenth century, while *nynorsk* grew out of nationalistic impulses at the same time. *Nynorsk* is a combination of rural dialects intended to be a distinctly Norwegian language, one not influenced by Danish. Today, *bokmål* is mostly spoken by people living in cities and towns. A third form of Norwegian, *samnorsk*, which was earlier proposed as a way of simplifying language use in Norway by combining elements of *bokmål* and *nynorsk*, has now been abandoned.

EXAMPLES
(B= bokmål; N= nynorsk)

one	en (B); ein (N)
two	to
three	tre
four	fire
five	fem
six	seks
seven	sju (N and B); syv (B)
eight	åtte
nine	ni
ten	ti
church	kirke (N); kyrkje (B)
breakfast	frukost (N); frokost (B)
open	open (N); åpen (B)
closed	stengd (N); stengt (B)

⁴ FOLKLORE

Norwegian mythology originated from the ancient religion of the region, whose chief god, Odin, lived in a walled city called Valhalla and was escorted into battle by nine warrior maidens called the Valkyries. Norway has a strong tradition of storytelling, and its folklore is full of odd, sometimes grotesque, creatures. The *hulder* is a woman with the tail of a cow which will only disappear if she marries; thus these beings are always chasing after men to marry. Others include the *fossegrimen,* a benign water spirit found at the base of waterfalls; the *nøkken,* a mischievous water spirit who lures boys and men to their death; and the *nisse,* a small white-bearded man with a red cap and wooden shoes. Probably the most famous feature of Norwegian folklore are the trolls—large, powerful, grotesque creatures. Some trolls are considered friendly, while others delight in plaguing human beings. Trolls appear as mascots, in Norwegian place names, in folk art, and in many folk tales.

5 RELIGION

Norway's official religion is the Evangelical Lutheran Church of Norway. While 83% of the population are members, fewer than 10% are regular churchgoers. Norway also has small numbers of Roman Catholics, Greek Orthodox, Methodists, Baptists, Anglicans, Muslims, and Jews.

6 MAJOR HOLIDAYS

Constitution Day on May 17 is the Norwegian equivalent of the Fourth of July in the United States. It is celebrated with parades and other gala events throughout the country, often with traditional folk costumes. In Oslo a parade of schoolchildren is greeted by the king. Midsummer's Eve on June 23 is another major holiday. It marks the longest day of the year and is celebrated with bonfires along the country's lakes, rivers, and fjords. Celebrants continue eating, drinking, and dancing throughout the night. All Saints' Day is celebrated on November 1, but Christmas is Norway's major winter holiday. On Christmas Eve, families celebrate with a traditional festive dinner that often includes pork and *surkål,* a cabbage dish. Afterwards they sing carols around the tree, which is decorated with white candles, and open the Christmas presents. Traditionally, the Norwegians perform a thorough housecleaning before Christmas, which actually extends until January 2, the end of the holiday season. Other religious holidays include Easter, Maundy Thursday, Good Friday, and Ascension Day.

7 RITES OF PASSAGE

Most Norwegian babies are born at hospitals or at special lying-in clinics *(fødestuer).* Although Norwegians are not particularly religious, the overwhelming majority of parents have their children christened as infants. Norwegian children engage in a lot of unsupervised play, as the crime rate is very low and even the larger cities are very safe environments. Most teenagers go through confirmation, the primary rite of passage for young men and women in Norway, at approximately age fifteen. Military service is compulsory for males starting at the age of nineteen.

8 INTERPERSONAL RELATIONS

Norwegians are a hard-working and self-reliant people, with an independence fostered by their harsh climate, with its long dark winters. Emotionally reserved, they avoid direct confrontations in their relationships with other people. They are courteous and polite, and their social encounters are marked by repeated handshaking, by both men and women. A common greeting when shaking hands is *"Takk for sist."* Norwegians are

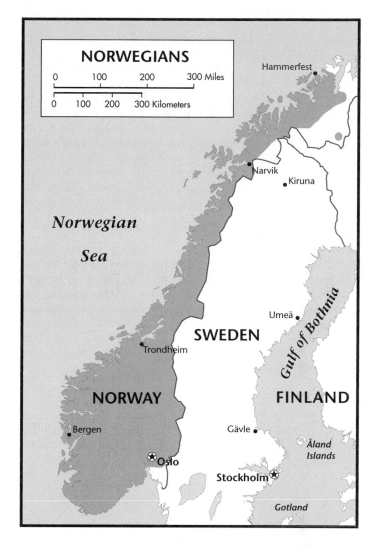

also known for their hospitality, especially during the Christmas season. Guests in a Norwegian home do not touch their drinks until the host offers a toast using the word *"skål."*

9 LIVING CONDITIONS

Norway has one of the highest standards of living in the world, enhanced by the discovery of petroleum and natural gas in the Norwegian section of the North Sea in the late 1960s. Norwegian houses are typically of stone or wood, with one or two stories. Many farm homes include a detached wooden building called a *stabbur,* a general storage facility, as well as the requisite barn.

Norway's state-supported health-care system covers most medical expenses for its residents. Average life expectancy in 2007 was 79 years, up from 56 years a century earlier. Like those in other industrialized nations, Norway's leading causes of death include cancer and heart disease. As the average life span of Norwegians has increased, a shortage of nursing and retirement homes has developed.

In spite of Norway's rugged terrain, the country has a modern, efficient transportation network. The best-developed roads are found in the southeast, where there are fewer natural barriers. Most of Norway's roads are paved. Although most Norwegians own cars, good public transportation is available, with express service provided between large cities and towns. Shipping is a mainstay of the Norwegian economy.

10 FAMILY LIFE

The typical marriage age for men is 25–30, for women 20–25. Norwegian families are getting smaller, and it is not unusual for women to decide not to have any children. The parent or parents of one spouse generally live with the family, often in a separate suite of rooms in the house or a nearby separate apartment. Husbands and wives generally share decision-making responsibilities. The divorce rate, while low, is rising, with incompatibility and alcoholism cited as the primary causes.

11 CLOTHING

Norwegians wear modern Western-style clothes for casual, business, and formal wear. At festivals, one may still see traditional costumes. Women's costumes include high-collared white blouses with embroidered or plaid bodices and ankle-length skirts, often in blue or red. This outfit may be completed by a hat of lace or other fine cloth. Men wear broad-brimmed hats, white shirts, colorful embroidered vests with dressy buttons, and tight black knee-length breeches with white hose and silver-buckled shoes.

12 FOOD

Norwegians eat four meals a day, of which the main one is *middag*, a hot meal usually eaten between 4:00 and 6:00 PM. A typical *middag* meal would be fish served with boiled potatoes and vegetables. The remaining meals are cold meals featuring the typical Scandinavian open-faced sandwich, called *smørbrød* in Norway, and consisting of ingredients including cheese, jam, salmon spread, cucumber, boiled eggs, and sardines, served with bread and crackers. While fish is often served in mildly flavored forms such as fish loaf and fish balls, the more pungent smoked salmon (*røkelaks*) and aged trout (*rakørret*) are popular as well. Commonly eaten meats include mutton and meat balls. Lingonberry jam is a popular accompaniment to meals, and for dessert one may be served fresh berries, *rømmegrøt* (cream pudding), or fruit soup. Coffee is the most commonly served beverage. In recent years American-style fast food has become very popular.

13 EDUCATION

Literacy is nearly universal in Norway. School is compulsory between the ages of 7 and 16. After this point, students choose between vocational and college preparatory training. Higher education, which is free, is offered at seven universities and a number of other institutions. In 2007, 208,000 students were enrolled in higher education, which is equivalent to more than 4% of the population. Opportunities for vocational education also abound, and it is the policy of the government that all youth have the right to education up to the age of 18.

14 CULTURAL HERITAGE

Norwegian literature begins with the Sagas and Eddas of the medieval Vikings, written in Old Norse and found mainly in Icelandic texts. Norway's most illustrious writer during the period of Danish rule was the 18th-century playwright Ludvig Holberg, whose comedies are still performed in Norway and Denmark (and to whom the composer Edvard Grieg dedicated a suite of pieces). Norway's liberation from Danish rule in 1814 marked the beginning of the country's modern literary tradition. Its most famous author is the playwright Henrik Ibsen, whose works of realism and social criticism—including *A Doll's House, An Enemy of the People,* and *Peer Gynt*—are known and performed throughout the world. Other prominent 19th-century authors included Henrik Wergeland and Bjørnstjerne Bjørnson (a 1903 Nobel laureate). In the 20th century, Knut Hamsun's novels have explored social problems, and Sigrid Undset—who won the Nobel prize for literature in 1928—portrayed the Norwegian past in sweeping historical novels, the most famous being the trilogy *Kristin Lavransdatter*.

In the visual arts, the painter Edvard Munch—known worldwide for his famous painting *The Scream*—pioneered expressionism in Norway during the late 19th and early 20th centuries, and Gustav Vigeland is known for his sculptures. Norway's most famous composer is Edvard Grieg, who incorporated elements of Norwegian folk music, culture, and history into his compositions.

15 WORK

Much of Norway's formerly agricultural employment has shifted to both small industries (paper, textiles, and food and beverage processing) and larger ones, such as shipbuilding, shipping, as well as North Sea oil development. Today only about 4% of the workforce is engaged in farming, while industry employs 22% and the service sector 74%. Government regulations limit the work week to 38 hours, prohibit more than 200 hours of overtime in one year, and require employers to provide workers with job security.

16 SPORTS

Skiing—which was once a means of transport—is the Norwegian national sport. Children learn to ski at an early age; downhill, cross-country, and slalom skiing are all popular. Other winter sports include ice-skating and a game called bandy, which is similar to hockey. Soccer is the most popular summer sport, and tennis is widely played as well.

17 ENTERTAINMENT AND RECREATION

Norwegians enjoy watching televised competitive skiing and speed skating events. Hunting and fishing, including ice-fishing, are popular outdoor activities, as are hiking, boating, and white-water rafting. Many people take skiing vacations in the mountains during Easter week. Summer vacations are often spent either in cabins in the mountains or along the coast, especially in the south. Vacationers can enjoy swimming, sailing, relaxing on the sandy beaches, and viewing waterfalls. Many Norwegians also vacation in warmer climes, with Spain, Greece, and Thailand as popular destination.

18 FOLK ART, CRAFTS, AND HOBBIES

Norwegian craftspeople turn out knitted and woven goods and wood products including utensils, bowls, and furniture. Another leading craft is the production of traditional Norwegian costumes. Folk dancing and singing are enjoying a revival, and are practiced at festivals throughout the country.

¹⁹ SOCIAL PROBLEMS

Traditionally, binge drinking and the resulting alcoholism have been Norway's most important social problem. Since the 1960s, drug use has been a significant problem as well. Drugs have not been legalized in Norway, and liquor and wine are only available through state-operated liquor stores. Human trafficking has become a problem as women from Eastern Europe and Africa have been forced into prostitution in many Western European countries, including Norway.

²⁰ GENDER ISSUES

The struggle for women's rights has deep roots in Norway, going back to the 1850s. A number of women's organizations had been founded before 1900, and women were given the right to vote in 1913. The Equality Act, first passed in 1978 and revised in 2005, prohibits both direct and indirect discrimination. Compensation levels must be established according to the principle of comparable worth, governing boards must have at least 40% women and 40% men among its members, and both men and women have the right to paid leave to care for newborns. It is very common for women to serve in high government positions and as members of parliament. Abortions up to the end of the twelfth week of the pregnancy were made available on demand in 1978 and are paid for with public funds. Discrimination based on sexual orientation is illegal, and as of 2008 it seemed likely that the marriage law would be changed to remove any difference between the legal status of heterosexual and same-sex marriage.

²¹ BIBLIOGRAPHY

Bendure, Glenda, et al. *Scandinavian and Baltic Europe.* Hawthorn, Australia: Lonely Planet Publications, 1995.

Charbonneau, Claudette, and Patricia Slade Lander. *The Land and People of Norway.* New York: HarperCollins, 1992.

Gall, Timothy, and Susan Gall, ed. *Junior Worldmark Encyclopedia of the Nations.* Detroit: UXL, 1996.

Illustrated Encyclopedia of Mankind. London: Marshall Cavendish, 1978.

Larson, Karen A. "Norwegians." In *Encyclopedia of World Cultures (Europe).* Boston: G. K. Hall, 1992.

Maagerø, Eva, and Birte Simonsen, eds. *Norway: Society and Culture.* Kristiansand, Norway: Portal Books, 2005.

Norway in Pictures. Prepared by geography department, Lerner Publications Company. Minneapolis: Lerner Publications Company, 1990.

Selbyg, Arne. *Norway Today: An Introduction to Modern Norwegian Society.* Oslo: Norwegian University Press, 1986.

Sjåvik, Jan. *Historical Dictionary of Norway.* Lanham, Maryland: Scarecrow Press, 2008.

Statistical Yearbook of Norway. Oslo: Statistisk Sentralbyry, 2006.

—revised by J. Sjavik

OSSETIANS

LOCATION: Caucasus Mountains between Russia and Georgia (Ossetian territory)
POPULATION: 680,000 (2001)
LANGUAGES: Ossetian; Russian; Georgian
RELIGION: Orthodox Christian; Muslim

¹ INTRODUCTION

The Ossetians, who live in the Caucasus Mountains between the Russian and Georgian Republics, are the descendents of an ancient people, the Alans, who occupied this territory as early as the 5th century AD. This ancient people spoke a language belonging to the Iranian branch of Indo-European and were distantly related to today's Iranians and Afghans. Even during the 20th century, Ossetians have defended their right to live in the territories of Ossetia by tracing their roots in the region back to the ancient Alans. In the 1990s, to honor these origins Moscow renamed North Ossetia as North Ossetia–Alania.

Throughout the 20th century, the Ossetian nation has suffered from interference with its territorial boundaries. In 1918, following the collapse of the tsarist Russian Empire and the rise of the Soviet regime, the Ossetian territory was divided into North and South Ossetia. North Ossetia was defined as part of the Russian state, while South Ossetia was considered to be part of the Georgian Republic. Ossetians still protest the division of their territory, preferring a single, united Ossetia. Some consider the division of Ossetia to have been an attempt on the part of the Soviet government to weaken the culture and national identity of Ossetians.

In 1989, the government of the Georgian Republic dissolved the separate territory of South Ossetia and declared the citizens of South Ossetia to be merely "settlers." The Georgian government urged Ossetians to leave South Ossetia and settle in the North. The Ossetians resisted the Georgian attempts to destroy South Ossetia. The resulting conflict between Georgia and South Ossetia lasted for almost four years, and erupted into war from 1991–92. North Ossetia assisted the South Ossetians in their struggle. During the war, more than 80,000 Ossetians were forced to flee South Ossetia and live as refugees in North Ossetia. Many young men from North Ossetia volunteered to fight on the Ossetian side in South Ossetia. Although the war ended formally in 1992 with a series of peace agreements, relations between South Ossetians and neighboring Georgians remain tense. Occasional armed clashes continue to break out.

North Ossetia had its own territorial difficulties. In 1944, the North Ossetian state was expanded, receiving territories that had formerly belonged to the Ingush, a neighboring people to the east. The Soviet regime had suspected the Ingush of betrayal during World War II. In the spring of 1944, the entire Ingush population was forcibly deported to areas of Central Asia and Siberia. North Ossetia was granted a portion of territory formerly occupied by the Ingush. When the Ingush were permitted to return in 1956, they received most of their former territories. However, a portion of the territories remained within North Ossetia, in the Prigorodnyi region. Thus, some Ingush families who returned to the Prigorodnyi region some-

and culture have been very well-preserved. The mountainous terrain and alpine meadows help to support sheep raising, the most common rural occupation. Most of the territory is mountainous, but the plains in the North of the Ossetian territory allow for farming of vegetable and fruit crops.

Although North and South Ossetia share a border, North Ossetia–Alania is a state within the Russian Republic, and South Ossetia lies within Georgia. In 1989, 164,000 Ossetians lived within the Georgian territory and approximately 400,000 in North Ossetia. As of 2007, there are 445,000 Ossetians in North Ossetia–Alania and perhaps 45,000 remaining in South Ossetia, the changes being due in part to refugees who have moved north.

The largest city in Ossetia is Vladikavkaz, in the North. Since the 19th century, Vladikavkaz has been an important administrative center for the entire North Caucasus region. Administrators and politicians from the central government in Moscow have been sent to Vladikavkaz. Therefore, most Ossetian residents of Vladikavkaz have a fluent command of Russian. A southern suburb of the capital has been reassigned its ancient Ossetian name of Dzaudzhikau.

The capital of South Ossetia is Tskhinvali, and most residents speak both Ossetian and Georgian. The war with Georgia has resulted in the devastation of Tskhinvali. Many buildings remain destroyed, and many people fled to claim refugee status in North Ossetia. However, since the conflict has lessened, the former residents of Tskhinvali are returning to help rebuild the city.

3 LANGUAGE

The Ossetian language is in the Iranian family of languages, although Ossetian and Iranian (Farsi or Persian) are not mutually comprehensible. There are three main dialects of Ossetian: Digor, Iron, and Tual. The Digor speakers live mainly in North Ossetia, the Tual in the South, and the Iron in both North and South Ossetia. The Iron is the largest dialect group, and many Digor and Tual speakers can also speak the Iron dialect.

In North Ossetia–Alania, the two official languages are Ossetian and Russian. Most North Ossetians can speak Russian competently, although often with a distinct accent. The two official languages of South Ossetia are Ossetian and Georgian. Both official languages are taught in school, as are Ossetian and Russian in North Ossetia. However, many South Ossetians also have a command of Russian.

Perhaps the most popular name for Ossetian males is Alan. This name honors the Alans, the ancient ancestors of the Ossetians. The name Ossetian itself reflects that of the ancient As, a group even older than the Alans.

4 FOLKLORE

For hundreds of years, Ossetians have told a series of epic folktales called Narty. The stories tell of the exploits of the giant heroes (the Narts) and also feature magical animals with mysterious powers. To this day, the Narty are popular and well-known among Ossetians. The Narty tales have been published in Ossetian and Russian editions for folklore specialists, in collections for interested adults, and also in illustrated children's versions.

times found that the land they had occupied prior to the deportation was now settled by Ossetians, who refused to leave.

The conflict between North Ossetians and neighboring Ingush was relatively quiet until the early 1990s. With the collapse of Soviet power, the Ingush became more vocal in their demands for the restoration of their former territories. The Ossetians continued to resist these demands. The dispute escalated into armed conflict in October–November 1992. Russia attempted to resolve the conflict, and the two sides reached an agreement in 1994. However, feelings of mutual hostility between the Ingush and Ossetians remain and occasional fighting continues to occur.

Historically, Ossetia's relationship with Russia has been peaceful. The South Ossetian government has declared its wish to leave the Georgian Republic and join North Ossetia in Russia. However, in 1994 the North Ossetian government threatened to separate from Russia because of Russian interference in the conflict between North Ossetians and the Ingush. North Ossetia also demanded greater autonomy in economic affairs. In 1995 Russia granted North Ossetia considerable autonomy, and the conflict between Russia and North Ossetia appears to be resolved.

2 LOCATION AND HOMELAND

The Ossetian territory is located between the Black and Caspian Seas, in the Caucasus Mountains. The mountains have helped to isolate Ossetians from contact with others. Therefore, despite the small size of the population, the Ossetian language

⁵ RELIGION

Prior to the adoption of Christianity or Islam, Ossetians celebrated an active and ancient pagan faith. Khitsau, the God of Gods, can be traced back to the ancient Alan people. One of the most important gods, whose name is used even in the late 20th century, is Wastyrji. He is considered the patron of men and warriors. Aside from these gods, who were acknowledged throughout Ossetia, many families had totem animals, such as deer or wolf. Families would try to protect their totem animal and celebrate yearly feasts in the animal's honor. Ravens were significant animals for some families, and snakes were the totem animal of others. To this day, some rural families remember their totem animal and avoid killing such animals. Most of the totem animals also play roles in the Nart folk tales.

Contemporary religion was adopted by Ossetians relatively recently, in the mid-19th century. Most Ossetians adopted the Orthodox Christian faith. However, a significant minority, between 15% and 20%, adopted Islam, the faith of many neighboring ethnic groups. While both Christians and Muslims celebrate the major holidays of their religions, many pagan customs have remained part of the religious practices of both groups. Thus, Ossetian Christians and Muslims have similar, uniquely Ossetian celebrations surrounding the events of death and marriage.

Both Christians and Muslims celebrate St. George's Day on November 10. However, the Ossetians call St. George by the name of Wastyrji, the pagan god of men and warriors. Thus, the Ossetian religious culture transforms St. George into Wastyrji, a uniquely Ossetian figure who can be recognized by both Muslims and Christians. Roadside shrines, dedicated to the saint and bearing his picture, are found along the highways of North and South Ossetia. A large pile of stones marks the shrine, and the picture of Wastyrji is housed in a small lean-to or shack. Traditionally, passing motorists would stop at the shrine, throw a stone on the pile, remove their hats, pray for a successful journey, and leave some silver or money as a dedication to Wastyrji. It is considered bad luck to pass a shrine without stopping, and many Ossetians still pay their respects at the shrines. Sometimes, families will slaughter a lamb or sheep at the shrine in honor of Wastyrji. Most villages have similar shrines.

Sacred groves remain important. The trees therein are decorated with ribbons tied around their trunks.

⁶ MAJOR HOLIDAYS

A traditional festival honoring Wastyrji takes place in July, at the site of a shrine. Because Wastyrji is the patron of men, women do not attend this celebration for fear of offending the saint. The men—Christians and Muslims alike—drink beer, which is the traditional celebratory drink of the Ossetians. They sing songs, dance around the shrine, and dine together. Although the women are prohibited from celebrating the holiday, they cook the food for the celebration and bring the food to the shrine. Although some Ossetians, especially those living in the city, have ceased to observe this holiday, the celebration is still held in many rural areas.

In the spring two clans, the Alægætæ and the Borætæ, stage a mock battle. The significance of this ritual warfare has been forgotten, but the ritual itself seems to be very ancient, since the first name reflects a form of the name Alan, while the second is the same name as used in the ancient Indian epic, the *Mahabharata,* or *Bharata.*

During the years of Soviet power, the major national holidays were the Day of the Revolution on October 7 and the Day of International Socialism on May 1. Since the collapse of Soviet power in 1991, the Ossetian governments have tried to create new holidays, with significance for Ossetians, to replace the Soviet holidays.

New Year's Day is celebrated throughout Ossetia, and most people receive a few days off from work and school at this time. Like North Americans, Ossetians have summer holidays, and schools are closed. Children may attend summer camp, vacation with their families, or work on the farm. Most adults, except for those working on their own farms, are able to take some weeks of vacation in the summer.

⁷ RITES OF PASSAGE

Many of the traditional Ossetian rites of passage are pagan in origin and were later incorporated into the Christian and Muslim faiths. When a child is born, families and friends will celebrate the baby's first time in the cradle and first haircut. Males are particularly valued, and special celebrations attend the birth of a boy. For instance, a celebration is held on the day that the boy's name is chosen, and another takes place on his first birthday. At one time, the entire village would have attended these celebrations. Many families still celebrate these occasions, but the festivities are more private and modest.

Males remain the focus of many rites of passage. A boy's initiation into adult male society was celebrated when he first went out to work in the pastures. More recently, the occasion of choosing a career is celebrated as an initiation.

In traditional Ossetian society, children moved quickly into adulthood without an interim teenage stage. As soon as children were old enough to work, they were initiated into adult responsibilities. Traditionally, girls were expected to marry at age 13 or 14, and boys at age 15 or 16. Now, because of mandatory high school education, young people have several years in their teens before they are expected to assume adult roles. Entry into adulthood is celebrated as the young person graduates and takes up a career, or when he or she marries.

Death is marked with a funeral rite and a series of wakes. Although funerals are conducted according to Christian or Muslim rites, some pagan practices are included in the funeral service. In mountain regions, Ossetians still celebrate the ritual of dedicating a horse to the deceased. In ancient times, the horse was sacrificed and buried with the dead man. In a contemporary version, the horse is decorated with a fancy bridle and saddle and led three times around the grave. Finally, a small cut is made on the horse's ear and the horse is led away. In the towns and cities, this custom is not practiced. However, it is common to bury some favorite personal belongings with the deceased.

A wake is held on the two days following the funeral. The family of the deceased holds a large feast. According to folklore, the food does not strengthen those who eat it, but the strength is transferred to the spirit of the dead person. Another wake is held a year later. This wake usually includes the lighting of a fire (either a candle or a bonfire), at the home of the deceased, as fire is associated with renewal and rebirth.

A South Ossetian woman stands ouside her home in the North Ossetian village of Kombileyevskoye, Georgia. Women fleed the South Ossetian territory for North Ossetia which is within the borders of Russia. (Kazbek Basayev/AFP/G,etty Images)

8 INTERPERSONAL RELATIONS

Male friends and acquaintances greet one another with handshakes. Traditionally, women were expected to behave modestly and deferentially in the company of men, keeping their eyes lowered. They did not shake hands, either with each other or with men. In contemporary life, however, women will shake hands with co-workers in a professional setting and interact with men in a direct, professional manner.

Ossetians take pride in their customs of hospitality to guests. A guest in an Ossetian home can expect to receive good meals, friendly company, and comfortable accommodation. Ossetians frequently visit one another, and guests are expected to return invitations.

Dating became a traditional part of Ossetian social life. Marriages between young men and women were customarily arranged by the families, usually when the couple was quite young. In contemporary times, this has changed. Most young people choose whom they will marry, although many ask for parental approval. By North American standards, dating among Ossetians is very restrained and conservative. Young men and women will get to know each other in public settings, such as school or with friends, and may go out with groups of friends. Taking walks together is the most common dating sce-

nario, and young couples have little opportunity for privacy. Premarital sexual relations are discouraged.

9 LIVING CONDITIONS

Until recently, part of Ossetians lived in isolated mountain villages. They built large, three-story stone houses to accommodate large extended-family groups. In the North, on the plains, the villages were larger, people lived with fewer family members and, therefore, built smaller, single-story wooden dwellings. According to the last census data 225,500 Ossetians live in the villages and 454,500 live in cities. In particular, the populations of the larger cities, such as Vladikavkaz and Tskhinvali, have risen sharply since the mid-20th century. Most city dwellers live in small bungalows or apartment buildings.

Living conditions in Ossetian homes can be challenging, as they lack many of the conveniences that North Americans take for granted. Some rural dwellings do not have indoor plumbing. In the cities, the supply of hot water is not always guaranteed, and some homes may have hot water for only a few hours each day. Dryers and dishwashers are very rare. However, most homes have refrigerators, washing machines, televisions, and DVD players, and many people have cars. Fresh meat and vegetables are common at any time of a year.

Because of the war with Georgia, living conditions in South Ossetia have been extremely harsh. The dangers of war forced many people to flee to North Ossetia. Some South Ossetian refugees were able to live with friends or relatives, but others were housed in army barracks and summer-camp facilities. The destruction of much of South Ossetia meant that shelter was inadequate, and consumer goods were in short supply. Water, heat, and electricity were cut off in many areas. After 1992, the Ossetians began to repair the devastation of the war. However, the reconstruction process remains incomplete, as the economy is unable to support an efficient, large-scale effort and tensions with Georgia remain high.

10 FAMILY LIFE

In the mountainous regions, Ossetian families traditionally lived in large, extended family units. The sons, and their wives and families would often live with the parents in a single large home. The farming activities of a mountain family required much labor. If a family was not large enough to provide its own labor, it would be forced to hire workers. Thus, an Ossetian proverb states: "To live alone is to live poorly."

Since the mid-20th century, few families have lived in the traditional, large family groups. Sons are still encouraged to start their own families in their father's house, moving out only after several years of marriage or after the birth of the first child. One son, usually the youngest, is expected to remain at home and raise his family in the house of his parents. A couple will rarely live with the wife's family. Even now, Ossetian men consider living under the roof of the wife's father to be dishonorable.

According to traditional custom, marriages were arranged by extended families. Women were expected to provide a dowry, and men paid a bride price, of similar value to the dowry, to the bride's family. If two young people wished to marry but could not obtain parental consent, they would arrange with the friends of the groom to stage a mock "kidnapping" of the bride. The couple would be whisked off to be married. Sometimes, if a man wished to marry a woman, he would arrange to kidnap her without her consent. If the man was of lower wealth or social standing than the woman, these marriages could result in a feud between his and her relatives.

In contemporary society, arranged marriages are rare, although most couples will obtain parental permission before marrying. If the parents will not give consent, a couple may resort to the traditional mock kidnapping. A couple who has married without parental consent will often choose to live in a different town or city for a few years until the parents accept the marriage.

In earlier times, relations between family members and in-laws were governed by "avoidance customs," taboos that restricted contact between various family members. Avoidance customs were practiced as soon as a couple announced their engagement. Once engaged, a couple was not permitted to appear together publicly and was discouraged from meeting prior to the wedding. During the wedding ceremony, the bride and groom were separated. The bride would sit quietly in a corner, surrounded by other women. The groom would not be present for much of the festivity. On the wedding night, the groom would sneak into the bride's bedroom. The next morning, the couple was considered officially married and was permitted to appear together. In contemporary conditions, couples rarely observe avoidance customs, although displays of intimacy prior to marriage are discouraged.

Other avoidance customs limited the relations of a son-in-law with his mother-in-law. A son-in-law was not allowed to speak to, or even see, his mother-in-law. Although this custom is no longer strictly observed, sons-in-law are not expected to have close relationships with their mothers-in-law. Similar customs restricted contact between a daughter-in-law and her father-in-law. Traditionally, a new wife, who would be living with her in-laws, was expected to veil her face and did not speak directly to her father-in-law. These restrictions were lifted after an unveiling ceremony. Although these customs are no longer observed, a woman is expected to behave respectfully and deferentially toward her father-in-law.

11 CLOTHING

The traditional costume of Ossetian women was modest but elaborate. Women wore a long dress with a flowing skirt and sleeves. The bodice was tight-fitting and high-necked, with elaborate embroidery. The head, but not the face, was covered with a long veil of fabric or lace. The veil was draped over top of a tall, pillbox-shaped hat. Gold or silver jewelry, with detailed metalwork, was worn for special occasions.

Men wore a jacket, tightly belted at the waist, with a flared hem and a high stand-up collar. The breast of the jacket was decorated with bullets, which were sewn on, and a silver sword was worn at the belt. For ease on horseback, men wore loose trousers tucked into black leather riding boots. The hat, which was made of Persian lambs' wool and dyed black or dark grey, was worn almost all the time.

Contemporary everyday clothes bear little resemblance to the traditional national costume. Men dress in the North American style, wearing suits to office jobs and preferring jeans or work pants for casual occasions. Some old men in the villages continue to wear the woolen hats, and men who work on horseback wear traditional riding boots. Women have also adopted Western clothing, although women almost always wear skirts or dresses, rarely trousers or jeans. Few women wear head coverings, and most women use make-up and wear contemporary Western hairstyles.

12 FOOD

The staples of the everyday Ossetian diet are bread, milk products, vegetables (particularly beans and tomatoes), and lamb or mutton. In the winter, pickled vegetables and preserved fruits are common. Dried fruits, especially prunes and apricots, are common throughout the year and are often used to make desserts. The Christian Ossetians have no food taboos. Ossetian Muslims, like all Muslims, do not eat pork or pork products.

Stuffed flatbread (*fidjin*) is a unique Ossetian dish. The bread may be stuffed with white cheese, cooked beans, or a mixture of lamb, garlic, and onion. Nearly every Ossetian homemaker is a proficient baker of these stuffed breads, and they are sold at most bakeries and cafeterias.

In traditional Ossetian families, men and women dined separately. The men would eat together in the dining room as the women cooked and served the food. Women and children ate in the kitchen. Most families no longer observe this segregation, although older women may refuse to eat in a room with the men.

Beer is the traditional drink of Ossetians. Even Muslims, who are prohibited from drinking alcoholic beverages, drink the traditional beer. Ossetians take great pride in their unique brewing methods, which are said to have been passed down from the 5th-century Alans.

13 EDUCATION

Under the Soviet regime, education to grade 10 was mandatory for both boys and girls. Universities and trade institutes throughout Ossetia, and in both Russia and Georgia, offer further career training to high school graduates. Because virtually all Ossetians receive an education, literacy is high. Most Ossetians graduate from high school, and many go on to post-secondary education.

Parental expectations vary according to the occupations of the parents. City dwellers usually want their children to receive the best education possible. Furthermore, most parents encourage their children to improve their career prospects by learning either Russian or Georgian. Rural parents may have entirely different aims for their children, as they will likely encourage at least one child to live and work on the family farm. In South Ossetia, education was interrupted by the war with Georgia. Many children did not attend school on a consistent basis for the four years of the war.

14 CULTURAL HERITAGE

The Ossetians take great pride in the preservation of their culture. The national folk epic, the Nart epic, appears in various editions for both children and adults. During the years of Soviet power, the central government controlled both the educational curriculum and the writing of national histories. Ossetians were forced to teach the history of their nation according to the Soviet government's version of events. Since the collapse of the Soviet government in 1991, Ossetians have developed a new school curriculum with greater instruction in the Ossetian language. History books describe the Ossetian, rather than Moscow's, interpretation of national history.

Traditional Ossetian music and dance are still enjoyed by Ossetians. During dances, couples do not touch. They play out a kind of courtship scene in which the man performs bold, athletic movements to display strength and honor while the woman keeps her eyes modestly lowered and sways gracefully. Occasionally, a street musician, often playing accordion in a city park, will attract a throng of passers-by who dance to the music.

15 WORK

The traditional occupation of Ossetians was farming, particularly sheep farming. In the 20th century, opportunities for urban employment have grown, and many people choose to leave farming, obtain higher education, and work in towns or cities.

After the collapse of Soviet power, many jobs that had formerly been sponsored by the government were no longer funded. The post-Soviet years have been difficult for many, especially the elderly, who have had difficulty fitting into a market economy. However, there are many opportunities for new types of work, especially in business, computer technology, and import/export. Because most North Ossetians are comfortable speaking and working with Russians, they are able to take advantage of economic opportunities with Russia.

The employment situation in South Ossetia is difficult, however. Because of the war with Georgia, the destruction of South Ossetian cities and towns, and on-going tensions, many people can no longer return to their former occupations. South Ossetia has experienced financial problems as a consequence of the war. However, with reconstruction, the economic situation of South Ossetians is slowly improving, though problems persist. South Ossetia seeks unification with North Ossetia–Alania and hopes that this will provide security and better conditions.

16 SPORTS

Soccer is one of the most popular sports in Ossetia. Children may play with teams organized at school, and teenagers and adults can join amateur teams. Ossetians also enjoy watching televised soccer or attending games.

Wrestling and contests of strength are popular with boys. Such activities are usually informal and incorporated into games. However, some Ossetians undertake rigorous training in sports, such as wrestling and weight-lifting, and Ossetia has produced a number of world-class athletes in these events.

17 ENTERTAINMENT AND RECREATION

In towns and cities, cinemas and theatres offer evening entertainment. There are also a lot of cafes and restaurants. Spending time in the cafes in the early evening is a favorite pastime. In the summer, most people will go out for a walk after dinner, to meet friends and socialize.

Most Ossetian homes have television. Ossetians receive programs from their own local stations, as well as from national Russian or Georgian stations. DVDs are very common and a variety of videos, including North American and European movies, are available.

Most people have iPods and CD recorders, and classical, folk, and rock music are widely available. Young people enjoy Russian, European, and North American rock, as well as traditional Ossetian music.

18 FOLK ART, CRAFTS AND HOBBIES

Traditional crafts and folk art include pottery, metalworking, weaving, and knitting. Because fashionable clothing was often difficult to obtain during the Soviet period, many women became proficient at sewing. In school, children have opportunities to learn music and visual arts.

19 SOCIAL PROBLEMS

The most pressing social problems in Ossetia have arisen because of Ossetian conflicts with neighboring peoples. Although the war between South Ossetia and Georgia and the clashes between the North Ossetians and the Ingush have subsided, tensions in these areas remain high. Especially for South Ossetians, many of whom lived as refugees in North Ossetia, the war brought instability, loss, and poverty. Lingering conflicts in both North and South Ossetia create difficult conditions for establishing a stable, secure way of life.

20 GENDER ISSUES

The traditional role of women was to maintain the household and raise the children. Few women attended school, and women rarely had their own careers. This has changed, however. The status of women in modern Ossetia is in many ways similar to the overall gender picture in the North Caucasus, but at the same time it has some significant differences, which are determined by objective factors. First, in the past decade Ossetia has experienced two wars: with Georgia for the independence of South Ossetia and with Ingushetia over the land border. The problems of refugees, poverty, unemployment, and depression, were the consequences of this war. Secondly, in Ossetia there is a religious division—83% of the Ossetian population is orthodox Christian, 17% is Sunni Muslim. Ossetian women must find a balance between religion, tradition, and the need to survive in the face of economic instability.

Many laws, that sometimes prescribe a woman to total isolation from public life, now cease to be relevant. Ossetian women have access to higher education and are on equal terms with men. They are officially unlimited in the choice of profession. However, they suffer discrimination in hiring and firing practices and, in general, women receive lower wages than men with the same qualifications. The involvement of women in politics and business remains miserable. In 2008, there was one female minister and two women in parliament.

The women's social activism movement was most evident in connection with the tragedy in Beslan, where hundreds of children became victims in a school seized by terrorists. Ossetian women were united in two human rights organizations: Beslan Mothers and Voice of Beslan. Women, who at the beginning were only trying to investigate the tragedy, soon found themselves in stiff opposition to the regime of the Kremlin. The women from Voice of Beslan may be remembered throughout history of Russia as citizens of the country who sued the ex-president of Russia, Vladimir Putin, for the murder of their children.

Permanent fear of war or terrorist attacks and the feeling of insecurity increased after Beslan. In the years after the tragedy, Ossetia has experienced the lowest number of births. According to the statistics of the Ministry of Health in Ossetia, the idea of having children whom they are powerless to protect from the government or terrorists is frightening to many women. This indicates that the overall social depression in the Caucasus is deeply felt by Ossetian women.

Working hard on building a career does not free women in Ossetia from their everyday routines. Even though many women spend as much time at work as do men, women are still expected to run their households and raise children with little help from their husbands.

[21] BIBLIOGRAPHY

Bennigsen, A., and S.E. Wimbush. *Muslims of the Soviet Empire.* Bloomington: Indiana University Press, 1986.

Kozlov, V. *The Peoples of the Soviet Union.* Trans. PM. Tiffen. Bloomington: Indiana University Press, 1988.

May, Walter, Tamerlan Salbiev, and John Colarusso. The *Nart Sagas of the Ossetians.* Washington, DC: Institute for the Study of Man, monograph series.

Wixman, Ron. *Language Aspects of Ethnic Patterns and Processes in the North Caucasus.* Chicago: University of Chicago, 1980.

State Committee of Information, Statistic data on Ossetia, Vladikavkaz, 2007–08.

Panorama of life in RSO-Alania, Russian State Library, Moscow, 2002

Sarah Mikle, *The Youths of the North Caucasus.* World Bank, 2006.

—revised by J. Colarusso and F. Tlisova.

PEOPLES OF DAGESTAN

LOCATION: Dagestan in the Caucasus Mountain region between Russia, Azerbaijan, and Georgia
POPULATION: 2,600,000 [total population; see Introduction for each ethnic group]
LANGUAGE: Languages of each ethnic group; Russian
RELIGION: Muslim (majority); Christian; Mountain Jews

[1] INTRODUCTION

The name Dagestan refers only to the territory of Dagestan. The territory of Dagestan is shared by numerous ethnic groups, 14 of which are officially recognized ethnic groups. The mountainous terrain of Dagestan, in the Caucasus range, has isolated many of its ethnic groups from outside influences.

The most recent official census in Dagestan was taken in 2002. At that time, the list of officially recognized ethnic groups and their populations was as follows:

ETHNIC GROUP	POPULATION
Avar	758,000
Agul	23,000
Azeri	88,300
Chechens	92,200
Dargin	426,000
Kumyk	366,000
Lak	140,000
Lezgin	337,000
Mountain Jews	13,000
Nogai	38,000
Rutu	24,000
Russians	150,100
Tabasaran	101,000
Tsukhur	20,000

Many of these groups are quite small in population, yet they have been able to retain their distinct languages and cultures. The Agul, for instance, comprise only 21 villages. The Mountain Jews are a small group that has managed to preserve their distinct religion, although they are surrounded by Muslims.

The large Caucasus region of the former Soviet Union has a long history of conflict and bloodshed among its peoples. In this context of ethnic tension, Dagestan is remarkable for its stability. Although many ethnic groups live within one relatively small republic, the peoples of Dagestan have little history of fighting among themselves. This is especially striking in the late 20th century, when many ethnic groups throughout the world are trying to separate from larger, multiethnic state structures and form their own sovereign states. For the most part, separatist groups in Dagestan have attracted very little support, and most citizens seem content with a multiethnic state governed by a parliamentary system.

The peoples of Dagestan are drawn together by years of common history. During the 19th century, most of the peoples of Dagestan fought against Russia in the Caucasian Wars. Although badly outnumbered, the Caucasian mountaineers managed to engage Russia in a war that lasted nearly 100 years. Russia subdued the mountain people with great difficulty after years of violence. The Caucasian Wars are legendary in Dagestan and are the basis for many folk-tales and stories of heroism and suffering. Shamil, the great leader of the Caucasian mountaineers, was an Avar, one of the peoples of Dagestan. He is still regarded as a national hero by many. One of the political parties in Dagestan, the Shamil Popular Front, is named after this leader. The main street in a capital city Makhachkala is named after Shamil.

When the Tsar fell from power in 1917, the Soviet government took over and began to make changes throughout the newly founded Soviet Union. In the 1920s, the Soviet government discouraged religious expression and ethnic identity and tried to encourage people to embrace communist ideas and join the party. Many of the peoples of Dagestan resented the intrusion of the Soviet regime and joined a large-scale, armed rebellion in the early 1920s. The Avars, known in Dagestan for their aggressive and militaristic values, led the rebellion. Although the rebellion was quelled by the mid 1920s, Dagestan groups continued to show resistance to Soviet power. Thus, Dagestan was the last area in the former Soviet Union to adopt the collectivized, socialized agricultural practices of the 1930s.

The peoples of Dagestan are predominantly Muslim. This religious unity has contributed to the peaceful coexistence of the various ethnic groups in Dagestan. Dagestan is an important center of Islam in the Caucasus and former Soviet Union. Makhachkala, the capital city of Dagestan, is the seat of the Muslim Spiritual Board of the North Caucasus and Dagestan. Since the 19th century, Dagestan has housed many religious schools for training new Muslim clergy. Religion is a strong force among most of the peoples of Dagestan, and multiethnic political movements and parties have attracted considerable support.

The few peoples of Dagestan who are not Muslim include the Mountain Jews, who follow Judaism rather than Islam, and the Cossacks, who are Christians. Cossacks are not identified in official census data but live as a distinct ethnic group in Dagestan. Despite their religious differences, the various groups appear loyal to Dagestan. Another basis for this loyalty is the common history and the large number of common customs shared by the various ethnic groups, such as clothing (both traditional and contemporary), social values, and economic activity.

As Soviet power weakened in the late 1980s, and eventually collapsed in 1991, the peoples of Dagestan became increasingly interested in their own cultural and religious self-expression. Although some independence movements sprung up in the early 1990s, most of these were short-lived as people remained loyal to the multiethnic state. Indeed, after the collapse of Soviet power, the peoples of Dagestan endeavored to create a state in which all native ethnic groups would be treated fairly. Thus, electoral districts were reorganized to ensure that no single ethnic group would be able to dominate. In 1993 citizens of Dagestan held a referendum opposing the creation of a presidency in Dagestan. Instead, the people expressed a strong preference for a parliamentary system to better reflect the special, multiethnic character of Dagestan.

2 LOCATION AND HOMELAND

Dagestan is located in the Caucasian mountain range. It is nestled between Russia to the north, Azerbaijan to the south, Georgia to the west, and the Caspian Sea to the east. For the most part, the terrain is very mountainous. The high mountain regions are cold, with alpine meadows, forests, and rocky outcroppings. The spaces between the mountains are more temperate, consisting of wide basins and flat valleys. The coastal land on the Caspian sea is warm, with many resorts and beaches. Historically, the coastal border has given the peoples of Dagestan the opportunity to engage in trade with other countries, particularly Muslim neighbors.

The ethnic groups of Dagestan live in neighboring mountain villages, which are isolated and protected by the mountains. The mountains have also provided important military refuge so that the relatively small population of Dagestan has managed to mount tough resistance to Russian and Soviet encroachment.

3 LANGUAGE

Each officially recognized ethnic group in Dagestan has its own distinct language. While some of these languages belong to the same linguistic families (either Turkic or Caucasian), many are not mutually understandable. In the 19th and early 20th centuries, Arabic was a common language spoken by educated peoples of Dagestan and was used to relay messages between various ethnic groups. In addition, Avar, the language of the largest and most powerful Dagestani ethnic group, was spoken by many other people.

Most of the peoples of Dagestan did not have an official written language until the 1920s, when the central Soviet government sponsored the creation of written national languages. Some of the smaller groups, however, still do not have their own written languages. The Agul language, for example, is closely related to the language of the Lezgins, a much larger group. Thus, Aguls used the Lezgin written language. Similarly, the Rutuls and the Tsakhurs used the written language of Azeri. In the late 1990s Agul, Rutul, and Tsakhur were elevated to literary status.

In the 1920s, when the Soviet government consolidated power throughout the territories of the former Soviet Union, Russian became another official language in Dagestan. Instruction in Russian became mandatory in schools, and a policy of Russification (Russianization) in Dagestan was pursued throughout the Soviet years. In the 20th century, Russian has replaced Arabic as a common language. Despite Soviet efforts to promote Russification and curtail education and publication in the native languages of Dagestan, the peoples of Dagestan have managed to retain and use their languages. The remoteness of their mountain villages has been a factor, and the relatively peaceful conditions in Dagestan have provoked little active interference from Russia in educational and cultural issues.

4 FOLKLORE

Each ethnic group has its own particular folkloric tradition. Folk tales are passed orally from generation to generation, and some themes common to the peoples of Dagestan emerge. The tales are usually epic in nature, emphasizing heroism in battle, bravery, and loyalty to clan, village or family. In particular, the history of the Caucasian Wars has captured the imagination of many ethnic groups, and the themes of the struggles with Russians often enter the folkloric narrative. Only in the late 1990s did much interest develop in gathering these folk tales into written collections. Also, biographies of national historical heroes, such as the Imam Shamil, have been published.

In addition to epic bravery and historical detail, religious themes find expression in folkloric form. The Muslim peoples tell of events from the life of Muhammad and histories of local Muslim figures. Similarly, the Mountain Jews tell stories from their own religious tradition.

5 RELIGION

Aside from the Mountain Jews and the Christian Cossacks, the peoples of Dagestan are almost exclusively Muslim. Islam has an ancient history in Dagestan, some historical accounts suggesting that Islam was introduced to Dagestan in medieval times. Islam remains a very strong force in Dagestan, and state efforts throughout the Soviet years to curtail the practice of Islam and enforce atheist ideas were not successful. In the capital of Makhachkala, most demonstrations are of a religious, rather than ethnic, nature. Dagestanis of various ethnic groups will often join together to work toward a common goal related to Islam. For instance, the peoples of Dagestan have joined together to demonstrate in favor of diverse Islamic causes ranging from protesting Russian and American interference in the Middle East to objecting to the rising costs of airplane tickets for the pilgrimage to Mecca.

Although the Mountain Jews and the Cossacks do not observe Islam, they have been treated respectfully by the Muslim majority. These two groups have been able to observe their religious beliefs relatively free from interference by Muslim peoples. In particular, the Mountain Jews have retained an ancient Jewish faith featuring a unique blending of Caucasian Mountaineer practices and Jewish religious traditions. Fundamentalist Islam had made inroads, especially among some highlanders. Russia is seeking to discourage the spread of this form of Islam.

6 MAJOR HOLIDAYS

Many of the Muslim peoples celebrate the Muslim festivals of Eid al-Fitr and Ramadan. During Ramadan, adults fast during the daytime, abstaining from both food and water as long as the sun is up. Children, the sick, and pregnant women are not obliged to fast. The festival of Eid al-Fitr marks the end of Ramadan and is celebrated by sumptuous feasting.

During the Soviet period, official holidays were introduced. These included the celebration of the 1917 Revolution (November 7) and the Day of International Socialism (May 1). Schools and workplaces were closed on these days, and the state sponsored cultural events and fireworks displays. The officially atheist Soviet government also sponsored a New Year's holiday, which was acceptable because of the lack of religious significance. While the other Soviet holidays were not of great cultural significance to most Dagestan peoples, New Year's Day was, and still is, widely celebrated.

7 RITES OF PASSAGE

For the peoples of Dagestan in general, the birth of a boy is celebrated with greater festivity and enthusiasm than that of a girl. For all ethnic groups but the Cossacks, the ceremony of circumcision marks the initiation of a baby boy into the family and community. There is no similar ceremony for girls. However, babies of both sexes are registered with local authorities, and relatives, friends, and neighbors visit and bring gifts of welcome for the baby. Traditionally, young boys and girls spent most of their time with their mothers, learning the basic expectations regarding social behavior. Girls would work alongside their mothers, grandmothers, and other female relatives

to learn the skills of cooking, spinning, weaving, and household maintenance. Boys developed many skills by playing and rough-housing with each other. Once a boy was able, he would join his father and other male relatives to learn the farming skills of their mainly agricultural way of life. Many Dagestani peoples view a boy's first trip to the pastures as a rite of passage and mark this development with a celebration in recognition of the boy's approach to manhood. The start of formal schooling for both boys and girls at age seven marks another transition in a child's life.

Traditionally, Dagestani teenagers did not have the opportunity to enjoy a period of youthful freedom. Young men were expected to marry by their mid-teens, and girls even earlier, so that young people quickly assumed the responsibilities of adult life. Furthermore, as the youngest adults in the family group, they were expected to behave deferentially and respectfully toward parents and elders. Today, young people usually complete their education before marrying, and thus do not enter into adult life directly from childhood. However, by Western standards, young people in Dagestan marry young, usually by their late teens or early twenties. Young people are expected to treat their elders with great respect and live up to traditional expectations.

As young couples have children, and as their younger siblings marry, they acquire greater authority in the household. The couple gains even further status as elder members of a household when their children marry.

Particularly in the mountain villages, the death of a community member is observed by the entire community. Despite attempts of the Soviet regime to develop and encourage atheist funeral rites, religious observance of funerals and wakes is well-established and practiced throughout Dagestan. While the different peoples observe various customs surrounding death, burial, and remembrance, in almost all cases the family of the deceased holds a large feast, to which all extended family and community members are invited. Such feasts are usually very expensive undertakings because a skimpy funeral is regarded as a sign of disrespect to both the deceased and the guests.

8 INTERPERSONAL RELATIONS

Generally, men greet each other with handshakes. Women rarely shake hands, either with each other or with men. This is especially so in rural regions. In larger cities, women involved in professional careers will shake hands as a form of greeting and professional courtesy.

Social life in Dagestan follows traditional patterns, and children and young people are expected to assume responsibilities at home. Between household obligations and school, especially in families involved in agriculture, young people in Dagestan have relatively little time for leisure and socializing with peers. In the teenage years, young women and men are not encouraged to spend time in each other's company unless they are in a large group or accompanied by an adult. In formal circumstances, many families observe gender segregation, with women and men socializing and dining separately from one another. Young people tend to be more flexible, spending more time in groups with both genders.

Throughout the Caucasus, traditions of hospitality are firmly rooted and observed. This is true for the peoples of Dages-

People unload items from a truck at a market in Kubachi, Dagestan, Russian Federation. Villagers enjoy life here with pure air, magnificent views, and plentiful jobs in silver handiwork. (Stephen Boykewich/AFP/Getty Images)

tan, who are known for their hospitable reception of guests. Guests are expected to reciprocate any invitations, however.

9 LIVING CONDITIONS

Traditionally, the peoples of Dagestan lived in villages with others from the same ethnic group. The enclosed courtyard, which houses all the family buildings behind a high fence, is a traditionally Caucasian type of dwelling and is found throughout Dagestan. The family courtyard and living arrangement is almost always patrilocal, meaning that family members always lived under the roof of male, rather than female, relatives. Each family usually had its own plot of land, but pastures and meadows, where the sheep grazed, were considered the common property of the entire village.

In contemporary times, rural conditions remain fairly traditional, and people continue to live with their extended families in courtyards. While most villages have electricity, many homes lack central heating and running water. Some mountain villages are quite remote, and villagers may have a difficult time getting to the city for medical attention, supplies, or services, especially during the winter.

In the course of the 20th century, the Dagestani peoples have gradually begun to move into urban areas to take advantage of educational, economic, and professional opportunities.

In the cities, conditions more closely resemble European or North American life. Many people live in apartments. While newlyweds and young couples will often share the apartment of the groom's parents, most aspire to move into a place of their own.

After the collapse of Soviet power, many essential services in Dagestan declined. In the cities, water and electricity supply can be irregular and unreliable. In 1994, Dagestan faced a serious medical crisis during a cholera epidemic. The cholera was suspected to have originated in Saudi Arabia and carried back by Dagestani pilgrims returning from Mecca. A decaying water purification system allowed the cholera to spread quickly. The government lacked the medical and technical resources necessary to control the spread of the disease and was forced to apply to Moscow for assistance. Repairs of the decaying infrastructure are dependent on a strengthened Dagestani economy during the transition from a Soviet, state-run economy to a stable free-market system. Until such time as Dagestan can sustain a strong economy, it will rely on heavy subsidies from Moscow, as it did during most of the 20th century.

10 FAMILY LIFE

Traditionally, for most of the peoples of Dagestan, the paternal extended family was the basic social and economic unit. Grandparents, parents, and children lived within a single courtyard, either in the same dwelling or in separate dwellings, depending upon the local customs of the particular village or ethnic group. Generally, the father of the household's sons was considered the elder of the household and had the ultimate decision-making power. The wife of the elder man presided over the running of the household and of the younger women. Rural families still organize their households according to these traditions, but many urban families live in nuclear family units, consisting only of parents and young, unmarried children.

In marriage, the wishes of the elders played a strong role in the choice of a spouse, although young people sometimes made their preferences known to their parents. A couple who wished to marry against the wishes of their parents might carry out a mock kidnapping, with the young man and his close male friends abducting the bride and taking her off to be married. Sometimes the mock kidnapping would be arranged in advance by the couple. Less frequently, a young man who was unable to obtain the consent of the girl he desired might kidnap her forcibly.

Most of the ethnic groups of Dagestan strongly encourage young people, particularly girls, to marry within their ethnic group. Young people have been willing to comply with this stipulation, and have thus helped to ensure the survival of their particular ethnic group. Traditionally, a woman would enter marriage with a dowry, which included household supplies, livestock, foodstuffs, and even land. The groom's family would pay a cash bride-price to the family of the bride. Dowries and bride prices were outlawed during the Soviet period, but continue to be part of the wedding arrangements of many peoples of Dagestan.

For most of the peoples of Dagestan, a bride would go to live in the household of her husband's parents. As the junior woman in the household, she could expect several years of hard work, until a younger woman or new bride joined the household and assumed the unfortunate role of junior female. In the cities, however, conditions have changed, and most young couples try to move out on their own, especially after having children.

In cases of divorce, Muslim law held that the children of the marriage should remain in the custody of the father. The Mountain Jews are the exception to this, and children traditionally remain with the mother. In recent times, Soviet and state laws have favored maternal custody of children. Traditionally, women were allowed to retain the value of their dowries upon divorce.

Although urbanization and modernization have brought some changes to the structure of family life in Dagestan, most of the peoples of Dagestan, particularly those in remote mountain villages, have remained loyal to traditional values. Since the collapse of Soviet power, traditional values have grown more popular among young people, who are often even more conservative than their parents.

11 CLOTHING

The traditional attire of men in Dagestan was similar to that worn by men throughout the Caucasus. High-collared shirts, usually white, with long, full sleeves were worn under a short-sleeved, tunic-like garment. Belted tightly at the waist, this tunic was otherwise full and flared, and usually made of black or dark grey cloth. The jacket was decorated with bullets, which were held in special fabric loops. The number of bullets traditionally increased with a man's battle experience, local prestige, age, and alleged bravery. Long, black leather boots and loose trousers tucked into the boots were suitable for horseback riding. Men usually wore a head covering—a tall, pillbox-shaped sheepskin hat.

The traditional female dress featured a fitted, lined bodice with full sleeves that could be cuffed at the wrists or left hanging loose, and a long wide skirt. For formal occasions, the dress featured a decorated insert sewn into the front of the bodice. Women wore slippers indoors and leather boots outdoors. The boots were similar to the men's, but were more highly decorated and made in brighter colors. Women also wore head coverings, usually kerchiefs or headscarves made of various fabrics, with woolen or simple cotton fabrics for everyday use, and silk for ceremonial occasions. Generally, older women wore darker colors like black, dark grey, or brown, while younger women wore brighter scarves. For funerals or somber occasions, darker scarves were worn. Women also wore gold or silver jewelry, often highly ornamented.

Today, both men and women have adopted conservative Western-style dress. Most women wear skirts and rarely wear jeans or trousers. Both men and women continue to wear head coverings, particularly older people in rural regions. Jewelry continues to be popular, and Dagestani metalworkers produce highly decorative gold and silver jewelry.

12 FOOD

The Muslim peoples of Dagestan and the Mountain Jews observe similar traditional dietary restrictions. Meat is slaughtered according to a prescribed ritual that is common to both the Muslims and Mountain Jews. Pork is not consumed by either Muslims or Jews, and Muslims traditionally do not drink alcohol.

Throughout Dagestan, the staple meat is lamb or mutton. *Shashlik,* or shish-kabob, is one of the most popular ways of preparing lamb. In addition to *shashlik*, popular lamb dishes include roast lamb, peppers or tomatoes stuffed with lamb, and lamb stew. Many of the peoples of Dagestan prepare a dish of boiled dumplings, stuffed with a mixture of lamb, garlic, and onions. Another traditional dish is made of grape or cabbage leaves rolled in cigar-like shapes, stuffed with a mixture of lamb, rice, and onions.

Rice or wheat porridge is a common breakfast food, as is bread and cheese. Side dishes for lunches and dinners include potatoes, rice pilaf, tomatoes, and stewed beans. Desserts are usually simple, featuring fresh fruits in season, jams and preserves, dried fruits, and sweet breads. Tea and coffee are imported and frequently served, especially after the evening meal.

13 EDUCATION

Traditionally, most children did not receive formal education, but were educated at home in the tasks of running the household. Some boys were sent for religious training and received their education in clerical academies. After the Soviet government came to power, primary education became mandatory. Throughout the 1920s, schools were built in both rural and urban areas, and families were required to send their children to school. At first, many families were reluctant and did not see the value of formal education, especially for girls. However, this resistance was overcome.

Although some children in urban areas may attend nursery school or kindergarten, most children start school in the first grade at age seven. Children are educated in both Russian and their own ethnic language. Graduation from the eleventh grade, the highest grade of basic education, marks a point of transition as young people must decide whether to pursue further education, a trade, or, in many cases, to remain in the village to work on the family farm. For rural families, it is expected that at least one son will choose to remain on the farm. Although Dagestan has various institutes and a university, ambitious and exceptionally bright students may apply to prestigious universities in Moscow or St. Petersburg. Some young women may elect to marry and raise a family rather than pursuing a career or higher education.

14 CULTURAL HERITAGE

The peoples of Dagestan take great pride in their ethnic and cultural identities and customs. They strongly resisted government attempts to promote the adoption of Russian and European culture and values during the Soviet period. Each particular ethnic group adheres to its own customs, encouraging each successive generation to marry and raise a family within the ethnic community. Since the collapse of Soviet power, the peoples of Dagestan have made efforts to improve education and popularization of traditional customs and practices.

The peoples of Dagestan are also loyal to the common, multiethnic state of Dagestan. Because each ethnic group is protective of its own customs and traditions, separatist movements have made little headway in Dagestan. The common experiences of war, repression by Russian and Soviet governments, and many common cultural values have created a harmonious multiethnic state.

15 WORK

Agriculture is the traditional occupation of the peoples of Dagestan. While most families kept gardens, and wheat was grown in some of the lowland areas, sheep farming was the main form of agriculture. The high mountain pastures and alpine meadows were well-suited for sheep farming, and men lived a seminomadic life, taking the sheep to various pastures and returning home on a regular basis.

Many rural families continue traditional agricultural employment. Although the Soviet government tried to nationalize agriculture, turning the farmers into land-users and state-farm workers, the nationalization of agriculture met with limited success. For the most part, traditional patterns of agricultural activity persisted, although farmers were obliged to give a quota of their produce to the state.

With urbanization and modernization, more career opportunities have become available for citizens of Dagestan. The Caspian coast offers opportunities to engage in import/export businesses with other countries.

16 SPORTS

Horse-racing and trick riding are traditional sports common to many Dagestani ethnic groups. Children learned to ride at a very young age and competed with peers. Aside from its function as recreational activity, the equestrian sports helped boys develop the riding skills that they would need later in life as herdsmen.

Boys in particular are encouraged to engage in sports. Displays of strength and speed are valued, making both wrestling and soccer popular. In rural areas, horseback riding continues to be a popular sport.

17 ENTERTAINMENT AND RECREATION

Home entertainment is one of the most common forms of recreation. Because there are few restaurants or cafés, people usually visit each other's homes. Hospitality is an important social value in the Caucasus, and hosts consider themselves responsible for a guest's pleasure.

Young people socialize at school or at work. They may visit each other's homes, although these are rather formal occasions presided over by parents. In warm weather, people of all ages enjoy going for strolls, especially in the early evening. For young people, this provides a welcome opportunity to get together free of parental company.

18 FOLK ART, CRAFTS, AND HOBBIES

A variety of arts and crafts are practiced among the peoples of Dagestan. Commonly practiced crafts include spinning, weaving, and knitting. Some men excel in woodworking and carpentry. While these crafts are common to peoples of the Caucasus Mountains generally, some other arts are unique to Dagestan.

Metalworking, especially the creation of ornaments and jewelry in silver and gold, is a traditional Dagestani craft. A certain ornate style, combining gold and silver with an oxidized black design and textured ornamentation, is unique to Dagestan and is sold throughout the former Soviet Union. Ceremonial daggers, ewers, rings (for both men and women), earrings, and bracelets are among the more commonly-produced items.

Another craft practiced in Dagestan is carpetmaking. Dagestani carpets are of unique design. They resemble Persian or Turkish carpets, except that the Dagestani artists tend to make greater use of earth-tone colors and animal shapes. Dagestani carpets rival the more famous Turkish and Persian carpets for quality of workmanship and artistry of design.

19 SOCIAL PROBLEMS

The most pressing social problems have been brought on by the transition from the state-run, Soviet system to the present, free-market system. While most people are pleased to have gained greater political and cultural freedom, many aspects of life have grown more difficult. Unemployment is high, especially in cities, and citizens have little knowledge of how to cope in such conditions. Many people who formerly held prestigious or powerful positions now find themselves out of work. The elderly are often impoverished, their pensions rendered nearly valueless by severe inflation. The general impoverishment and financial difficulties of Dagestan have resulted in declining maintenance of basic sanitation, water supply, electricity, and medical services. Thus, social anxiety, cynicism, and sense of hopelessness can be felt in many sectors of society. The new oil wealth that flows through Russia proper to the north and through the Azerbaijani south has yet to trickle through Dagestan.

Another social problem involves the rise in violence in the region. While Dagestan has been relatively free of conflict, wars and armed clashes in neighboring regions have resulted in the ready availability of weapons. Thus, in Dagestan, such crimes as armed robbery and vandalism are rising. With the increase of import/export opportunities, smuggling has also increased. Occasional political violence erupts as assassinations or bombings in Makhachkala.

20 GENDER ISSUES

The results of modern research suggest that, in Dagestan, there is discrimination of women and infringement of women's rights in all spheres of private and public life. The unemployment rate, the incidence of severe disease, and the mortality rate among women of Dagestan are traditionally higher than among men. About 92% of the women of Dagestan call unemployment their main problem. In cities, women have the opportunity to study and work, but take only minor jobs and service posts. Business and politics are closed spheres for the Dagestan women. According to Islam, which is practiced in Dagestan more strictly than in other parts of Northern Caucasus, a woman cannot be considered equal to a male business partner in a transaction and cannot even participate in the negotiations. In the mountains, women are deprived not only of work but also of basic necessities for life, such as health care.

The leader of a charitable fund for women, Ayshat Magomedova, describes the lives of modern women in the mountains of Dagestan: "In mountain villages there is no gas, light or water. A woman in a mountain village works for a full light day. She is the main instrument for carrying weights. During the day, one woman takes the brunt of all the needs for water, firewood to cook food and warm the house, and hay for the animals. To see a doctor, a woman must also undergo a long walk of 50 kilometers to get to a district centre, because the villages do not have a paved way, so they cannot travel by transportation. It often happens that a seriously ill or pregnant woman takes the road and simply dies halfway."

The state is indifferent to the problems of Dagestani women. The only charity hospital in the capital of Dagestan, supported by foreign funds, has been closed in 2007 by the authorities after the tightening of a law in Russia on non-governmental organizations, banning foreign funds to carry out its activities on the Russian territory.

[21] BIBLIOGRAPHY

Bennigsen, A., and S. E. Wimbush. *Muslims of the Soviet Empire*. Bloomington: Indiana University Press, 1986.

Chenciner, Robert, Gabib Ismailov, and Magomedkhan Magomedkhanov. *Tattooed Mountain Women and Spoon Boxes of Daghestan*. London: Bennet & Bloom. 2006.

———. *Daghestan: Tradition and Survival*. New York: St. Martin's Press, 1997.

Gammer, Moshe. *The Lone Wolf and the Bear*. London: Hurst & Co., 2006.

———. *Muslim Resistance to the Tsar*. London: Frank Cass, 1994.

Job, D. Michael, and Rieks Smeets, ed. *The Northeast Caucasian Languages*. Part 1. Delmar, NY: Caravan Books, 1994.

———. *The Northeast Caucasian Languages*. Part 2. Delmar, NY: Caravan Books, 1998.

Kozlov, V. *The Peoples of the Soviet Union*. Trans. by P. M. Tiffen. Bloomington: Indiana University Press, 1988.

Nichols, Johanna. *The Chechen Language. Noxchiin mott* http://socrates.berkeley.edu/~chechen/

Russian Federation. *Census of the Population* (Vsesoiuznoi perepis naseleniia). Moscow: 2002.

Schulze, Wolfgang. *Caucasian Albanian (Aluan)*. http://www.lrz-muenchen.de/~wschulze/Cauc_alb.htm

van den Berg, Helma. *Dargi Folktales*. Leiden: Research School of Asian, African, and Amerindian Studies, 2001.

———. *A Grammar of Hunzib*. Munich: LINCOM-Europa, 1995.

Wixman, R. *Language Aspects of Ethnic Patterns and Processes in the North Caucasus*. Chicago: University of Chicago Press, 1980.

—revised by J. Colarusso and F. Tlisova

PEOPLES OF THE CAUCASUS

LOCATION: Caucasus Mountain region that includes Armenia, Azerbaijan, Georgia, and Russia
POPULATION: See Location and homeland
LANGUAGE: Five language families, see Language
RELIGION: Christianity; Islam; Judaism; Sufism; traditional beliefs

[1] INTRODUCTION

Between the Black and Caspian Seas rise the Caucasus Mountains, stretching in a line 1,000 km (600 mi) long from the northeast corner of the Black Sea, near the Sea of Azov, southeastward to Baku, the capital of Azerbaijan, near northwestern Iran. The region has traditionally been considered the southeast corner of Europe. As such, it contains the highest mountains in that continent: Mount Elbruz, whose twin peaks rise to heights of 5,621 m (18,441 ft) and 5,642 m (18,510 ft), and Mount Kazbek at 5,047 m (16,512 ft), all of which are higher than Mount Blanc in the Alps, 4,810 m (15,781 ft). In the north, the region extends into the plains of southern Russia and is bordered by the Kuban and Terek rivers. In the south, it runs into the highlands of eastern Turkey and northern Iran, where it may be thought of as ending at the borders of these two nations, which in part follow the Aras River. The region is a meeting place for European, Central Asian, and Middle Eastern civilizations and exhibits a mixture of features from these cultures as well as some that are strictly its own.

There are roughly 50 languages indigenous to this region, and the ethnic complexity of the Caucasus is unequalled in Eurasia, with nearly sixty distinct peoples, including Russians and Ukrainians. The Trans or South Caucasus is home to three new nations that formed at the breakup of the Soviet Union: Georgia, Armenia, and Azerbaijan. Georgia has a history dating back to the 2nd century AD. It was annexed by Russia in 1801. Armenia is the sole surviving fragment of the Armenian nation, which at one time occupied most of eastern Anatolia (Turkey). It was annexed by Russia in 1828. Azerbaijan was once a part of Iran called "Aran." It has emerged as a mixture of Turkic peoples who have mixed with and assimilated the earlier Caucasian Albanians or Alwanians. Azerbaijan was also annexed to Russia in 1828. The North (or Cis) Caucasus has seven republics, all part of the Soviet legacy and located within what is now the Russian Federation. From west to east, they are: Adygheya, Karachay-Cherkessia, Kabardino-Balkaria, North Ossetia-Alania, Ingushetia, Chechnya (Ichkeria), and Daghestan. In addition, the southern portion of Krasnodar *kray* (district) extends south of the Kuban. The central region of the North Caucasus traditionally looked to Moscow for protection against raids from the Krim Khans (Crimean Tatars) and formed political links early (1774 in the case of Ossetia). The northwest region traditionally turned to the Ottoman Empire for trade and hence saw Russia as an enemy. It was only annexed in 1864 after prolonged and bitter warfare. The northeastern region traditionally looked south to the Middle East and hence also saw Russia as an adversary. This area was annexed by Russia in 1859 after prolonged resistance led by the famed Imam Shamyl. To some extent, this threefold west- to-east division crosses over into the south as well and in many ways rivals the customary north-south division in its social and political importance.

The region is potentially wealthy. Gold, iron, zinc, molybdenum, copper, lead, aluminum, tungsten, oil and coal deposits exist. Semi-precious stones, fine mineral springs, hot baths, and ski resorts also can be found. Agriculture is well developed. Tea, tobacco, cotton, walnuts, melons, apples, peaches, pears, and citrus fruit are grown; cattle, oxen, sheep, and fine horses are raised. Most important, however, are vast reserves of oil and natural gas; particularly, it was known to exist in Chechnya's case but during the last few years oil was found in Kabardino-Balkaria and Ingushetia as well. The crude oil from the latter is the finest known, emerging from the earth nearly clear.

Political stability could bring prosperity, but the Caucasus is the most unstable region of the former Soviet Union. Since 1989, the region has witnessed six wars: Nagorno-Karabakh (Armenia-Azerbaijan) (1989–1995), South Ossetian–Georgian (1991–1992), Abkhazian-Georgian (1992–1993), North Ossetian–Ingush (1992), and two Chechen-Russian (1994–1996, 1999-present). Not only have these wars been ruinous in terms of loss of lives and property, but also they have occurred in a region whose economic collapse was abrupt. Furthermore, nearly every area has some serious conflict over borders or land rights that stem from Communist patterns of abuse and manipulation. The two wars in Chechnya have been exceptionally destructive, with the second war still simmering as sporadic guerrilla action. Tensions have spread from Chechnya out across most of the North Caucasus. Uprisings and terrorist attacks erupt with tragic consequences, as with the school attack in Beslan, North Ossetia–Alania on 1–3 September 2004; the uprising in Nalchik, Kabardino-Balkaria, on 13 October 2005; or with ongoing turmoil in and around Nazran, Ingushetia, and tension in Karachay-Cherkessia. Further turmoil can be expected in what the West has only just begun to realize is a geopolitically crucial region.

² LOCATION AND HOMELAND

The Caucasus region is roughly the size of Spain (approximately 388,498 sq km/150,000 sq mi). The South Caucasus is arid in portions that constitute the eastern extremity of the Anatolian highlands, primarily Armenia. Azerbaijan is arid toward its Iranian border, but becomes lusher as it rises into the foothills of the Caucasus. Georgia, by contrast with these two, is lush and well watered. Even in its highlands, it enjoys substantial rainfall from the winds off the Black Sea. This verdant landscape is semi-tropical along the Abkhazian coast of the Black Sea and becomes colder but still verdant across the mountains in the north. Only in the east, in Dagestan, does this pattern alter and the land become dry, all the rain having been taken by the high summits. The lowlands along the Caspian Sea coast are arable, but the Dagestani highlands can vary from alpine pastures to alpine deserts.

The ethnic makeup of two of the three southern states is relatively simple. Armenia and Nagorno-Karabakh are almost wholly Armenian (nearly 3 million), with a few enclaves of Kurdish speaking Yezidis (1.3%). Azerbaijan (8.1 million) consists almost wholly of Azeri Turks, close kin of the Turks of Turkey and the Turkmens of Central Asia. A few Dages-

tani peoples spill over into it, but these will be treated with the North Caucasians. At the extreme eastern end of the mountain chain (the Apsheron peninsula) are the Iranian-speaking Tats (10,900). Adjoining Iran at the extreme southeast is an Iranian-speaking people called the Talysh (400,000), most of whom (1 million) live across the border.

Georgia (4.6 million) is by far the most ethnically complex of the southern states. Recently 18 ethnic groups could be found there, but three have either been driven out or emigrated. In the southwest, there are Ajars, Mingrelians, and Laz, the last extending well across northern Turkey to the city of Trabzond. The Ajars are Muslim and inhabit the eastern tip of a large Georgian-speaking region in eastern Turkey. These Muslim Georgians and the Ajars form a cultural continuum, but the Laz and Mingrelians stand apart from the rest of Georgia both in language and customs. In this southwestern region dwelt a Turkish-speaking group called Meskhetians, who were deported to Central Asia in 1944. In 1989, following riots against them in Uzbekistan, most of them relocated to Azerbaijan. In addition, there are in the south large groups of Armenians, Greeks, and Azeris. In the center of Georgia are the Georgians proper (formed from four earlier groups: the Gurians, Imeretians, Kartlians, and Kakhetians). In the highlands are found Georgian-speaking peoples so distinctive as to form separate ethnic groups. These are the Khevsurs (who wore chain mail and fought with broad swords and bucklers until World War I), the Pshavis, and the Tushetis. A Georgian-speaking Shiite Muslim people, the Ingiloi, who wear Maltese crosses on their clothing, reside across the border in western Azerbaijan. Also located in the Georgian highlands is one village of people who speak a language related to Chechen and Ingush, the Batsby or Kists. A few Dagestanis (Avars) were driven from their highland villages in 1991. By contrast, only recently have the Udis found refuge from religious turmoil in Azerbaijan among their kin in the village of Oktomberi in eastern Georgia. The Udis, a Dagestani people, were the central ethnic group around which the old Christian kingdom of the Caucasian Albanians, or Alwanians, was formed. The central highlands are home to the South Ossetians, who fought a war of secession (1992-3) in an effort to unite with their kin in North Ossetia–Alania. To their west live the Svans, a people only distantly related to the Georgians but who are nevertheless content to be part of this nation. Along the northwest coast, however, live the Abkhaz, who fought a war (1992-3) to establish their own state. Finally, Georgia was once home to a distinctive community of Jews who now dwell in Israel.

The northwest Caucasus was home to five ethnic groups, the first three of which are related: Circassians, Abazas (northern Abkhaz), Ubykhs, Mountain Turks, and the distinctive Caucasianized Kuban Cossacks. In 1864, after more than 150 years of warfare, the Russians, aided by the Cossacks, expelled nearly all of these people into the Ottoman Empire. At most 10% remained, with the exception of the Ubykhs, who were all expelled. Today the remaining Circassians are scattered in and around three republics: Adygheya (116,000), Karachai-Cherkessia (49,600), and Kabardino-Balkaria (500,000). The 32,000 Abazas are located in Karachai-Cherkessia. Population figures are suspect, but a total of about 658,000 is possible if the numerous Circassian villages to the west of Adygheya are counted. This should be contrasted with roughly 3 million Circassians, 0.5 million Abazas, and 50,000 Ubykhs in Turkey. The tendency to distinguish the ethnic groups Adyghey, Cherkess, and Kabardian has some basis in dialect diversity and some political motivation (the Kabardians, being in the center of the North Caucasus, tended to have good relations with Moscow). Nevertheless, they themselves do not recognize these divisions, referring to themselves simply as Adyghey. A small population of Circassian-speaking Jews is also considered to be Adyghey. Similarly the Mountain Turks are now called Karachay (169,000) and Balkar or Malkar (105,000), but here, too, the latter are distinctive merely in their proclivity to see in Moscow an ally because they fall in the center of the North Caucasus as opposed to the Karachay.

Although one can speak of the Kabardian Circassians and the Balkar Mountain Turks as being Central North Caucasians, the North Ossetians (445,000) are the only people largely treated as such by the Russians. There is a distinctive western group, the Digoron, and an eastern, the Iron. The southern Ossetians are called *tuallaeg*, which simply means "mountain men."

To their east are the Ingush, but this too is case of political proclivities splitting an ethnic group in two. Together with the Chechens (1.1 million) further east, the Ingush (361,000) form the Vai Nakh peoples (which include the 5,000 Kists or Batsby of Georgia) and are relatives of the Dagestanis of the Northeast Caucasus. Prior to the Chechen-Russian War, there was a small population of Chechen-speaking Jews, but these have fled to Israel. The northern reaches of Chechnya are also home to the distinctive Terek Cossacks, old Russian-speaking settlers who have adopted many local ways.

Dagestan (2.6 million) is unquestionably the most complex of the Caucasian republics, with 32 indigenous ethnic groups. Turkic nomads are found in the lowlands: Kumyks (366,000), Noghays (38,000), and a few displaced Turkomans (18,000). In the northern highlands are the Akhka Chechens (88,000), the Avars (758,000), and higher still are the Andis (9,000), Karatas (5,000), Chamalals (4,000), Bagwalals (4,000), Akhwakhs (5,000), Botlikhs (3,000), Godoberis (2,500), and Tindis (5,000). Still in the high valleys, but going south toward the Georgian border, are the Tsez ([Dido] 7,000), Hinukhs (200), Hunzibs (400), Khwarshis (1,000), and Bezhitas ([or Kapuchis] 3,000). South of the Avar are the Laks (140,000), Dargwas (426,000), Kubachis (3,000), and Khaidaqs (28,000), all forming a closely related group of peoples. In one high village, standing apart from them, are the Archis (1,000), whose links lie further south with the so-called Lezgian peoples, the Aghuls (23,000), Tabasarans (101,000), and Rutuls (24,000). A part of the Lezgis (337,000) and most of the Tsakhurs (8,000) spill over into Azerbaijan in the south. Other Dagestanis who are restricted to northern Azerbaijan are the Kryz (6,000) in one mountain village and three coastal ones, Budukhs (1,000), Udis (formerly 6,000), and Khinalugs (2,000). There is in Dagestan a group called "Mountain Jews" ([Givrij or Dagchifut] 13,000), who speak an Iranian language. They are sometimes called "Tats," but are not to be confused with the Muslim Tats of Azerbaijan. In addition, there are a few Dagestani Cossacks who are strongly assimilated to indigenous patterns.

It must be emphasized that all of these groups are distinct peoples, however small they may be. Many are further subdivided by tribes, clans, and blood lines. Conversely, most traditionally form larger units for self-defense when threatened. This is particularly true of the smaller peoples of Dagestan. In

ethnographic, social, and political terms, the Caucasus is like a miniature continent.

In physical appearance, the people in the South Caucasus tend to be Mediterranean, with dark hair and olive complexions. The Dagestanis often have olive complexions that are suffused with a ruddy undertone, an adaptation to cold mountain air in the form of enhanced blood flow to the skin. The Armenians tend to have marked aquiline features, while the Azeris have features typical of Persians. The Georgians exhibit features also seen among the northern Caucasus. Georgians and North Caucasians often have dark hair with light skin, though individuals who are almost brown-skinned can be seen. Aquiline profiles are also common. Most Georgians and North Caucasians look much like central Europeans or northern Italians, with facial features that often have a fine, chiseled quality. The Ingush are the tallest people in the Caucasus, while the Circassians and Karachay-Balkars are famous for their beauty, tall stature, and graceful movement. Among the Ubykhs and Circassians are many individuals with blond or red hair and pink complexions. The variety of its people reflects the region's complex history.

³ LANGUAGE

Known as the Mother of Tongues, the Caucasus is home to five language families, three of which are indigenous. In the north, four Altaic languages are spoken: Karachay, Balkar, Noghay, and Kumyk. :These belong to the Kipchak Turkic branch. In the south, two Turkic languages, Meskhetian and Azeri, are found, both belonging to the Ghuzz branch, to which Turkish and Turkoman belong. These Altaic languages show rich verbal inflection (person, tense, mood), and elaborate case systems (alternation of the nouns to reflect their roles in a sentences), but are very regular and transparent in their formation. They have a pleasant, mellifluous sound. Only Azeri is a written language, and it now uses a Latin-based script. Turkic Karachay and Malkar/Balkar use Cyrillic.

Of the Indo-European family, the Slavic branch is represented by Russian and Ukrainian. The Kuban and Terek Cossacks speak Russian. These complex languages have large case systems that extend both to their nouns and adjectives, with many irregularities. Further, nouns come in three categories, called genders: masculine, feminine, and neuter. The Slavic verb is highly sensitive to "aspect," the degree of completion of an action. There are more than a dozen verbs of motion that reflect subtle differences in movement. The languages are mellifluous, having unusual sustained intonation patterns that give them a song-like quality. One of their hallmarks is palatalization, raising of the tongue to produce a y-like sound along with the main consonant. The Iranian branch is represented by Tat, Talysh, and Kurdish in the South, and by Ossetian in the North. This last is the sole surviving form of the language of the ancient Alans, Sarmatians, and Scythians, nomadic horsemen of classical antiquity. While retaining verbal aspect, much as does Slavic, the grammars of these languages have lost most of their case systems and have leveled out most irregularity. Only Ossetian has kept an elaborate case system due to neighboring Ingush and Chechen influence. Iranian languages make abundant use of fricatives (s- sh- and kh-like sounds). Armenian forms a distinct branch of Indo-European in the south. In grammatical complexity, it stands midway between Iranian and Slavic. It is remarkable for its elaborate consonant clusters.

Russian, Ukrainian, Ossetian, and Armenian are written languages. The first three use a Cyrillic-based script, while Armenian has its own distinctive national writing.

The Southern Caucasian or Kartvelian language family consists of Georgian, Mingrelian, and Laz (collectively called Zan or Chan), and distantly related Svan. Only Georgian is written, using its own national alphabet. These languages have complex sentence formation (syntax), with Georgian and Svan being "ergative." Ergative languages mark the person (or thing) undergoing an action by the absolutive case, whether it is done by the person alone (intransitive) or brought upon it by another (transitive). The person or thing that brings the action upon another is marked by a special case, the ergative. For example, (using English), a Georgian would say the boy (absolutive) sleeps, but the teacher (ergative) scolded the boy (absolutive). If the action is incomplete, then the case marking switches with the subject in the absolutive and the object in a sort of geometric role (dative case): the teacher (absolutive) is scolding/will scold at the boy (dative). Word formation is highly irregular and highly unusual in that material is added both to the front and end of a root (circumfixation). The noun exhibits a large number of cases, while the verb inflects not only for person, but also for intentions, distinguishing between accidental, purposive, direct, and self-serving actions. The sound systems show enormous and difficult consonant clusters, as in *mtskheta* (a place name), Tbilisi (the name of the capital, which means "of the warm spring"), *tqbili* (sweet), or *prtkhili* (careful). Long strings of vowels are also possible. A contrast between regular (k) and back (q) k-sounds occurs. Glottal ejectives, characteristic of the Caucasus, also occur. These are consonants made with a slight popping sound by shutting the vocal cords and causing a momentary smothering sensation.

The Northeast Caucasian languages are also ergative. Most word modification is by means of attaching material at the end of a root (suffixation). The verb is relatively simple, in most cases not even inflecting for person, though some, as in Archi or Chechen, can be elaborate. Most complexity resides in the noun system, where large numbers of cases are used to denote almost every conceivable grammatical role or spatial relationship. Cases even have cases and can express, for example, not only whether something crosses something else (the "translative"), but whether the crossing took place either horizontally, or from above to below, or from below to above. Some languages, such as Lak and Tabasaran, have nearly 50 cases, the largest such systems known anywhere. These systems are suited for the geometric complexity of their mountainous environment. The nouns further belong to class systems. These are gender systems like those found in Slavic, but with as many as nine categories: male, female, neuter, animal, plurals, mass objects (sand, water, etc.), long objects, edible objects, and so on. The sound systems have a profusion of fricatives (s-, sh-, or kh-like sounds), many of them gutturals (made in the back of the mouth or in the throat). One form of Aghul makes such sounds in more places than any other known language: at the soft palate (velars), at the back of the mouth (uvulars), at the back of the mouth with the throat contracted (pharyngealized uvulars), in the upper throat (pharyngeals), in the lower throat (epiglottals or adytals), and in the voice box (laryngeals). Prolonged consonants also occur, as do glottal ejectives, and rounded consonants (simultaneous kw or tw, for example). Many languages show a profusion of laterals (l-like) sounds,

(Archi has 11), some of which are made in the back of the mouth. Elaborate vowel systems occur, with ordinary vowels (oral), vowels made with the nose open (nasalized), with the throat constricted (pharyngealized), or with the epiglottis lowered (adytalized). Some languages, such as those of the Andi group (Andi, Botlikh, Godoberi, Chamalal, Bagawalal, Karata, Akhwakh, and Tindi), have tone (like Chinese), as well as breathy voiced vowels, and "stiff" vowels. Chechen and Ingush are written languages, as are Avar, Lak, Dargwa, Tabasaran, and Lezgi. In the 1990s, Aghul, Rutul, and Tsakhur were raised to literary status. All languages use a modified Cyrillic script.

As complex as the South and Northeast families are, the Northwest family is more complex still, approaching what may be some sort of maximum. The family consists of Circassian, Abkhaz, Abaza, and Ubykh. Their syntax is ergative, but shows a wide range of alternative patterns depending upon the exact relationship of actor and object. The verb inflects for every noun in the sentence, as well as expressing a plethora of geometric information by the unusual means of attaching material to the front of the root (prefixation). Some sentences have two objects (ditransitives), while others have two subjects (causatives). In fact, the verb is so expressive that conversations in these languages often turn into a series of verbs once the speakers know the nouns they are talking about. The case system on the noun is simple (Circassian, Ubykh) or absent (Abkhaz and Abaza). The vast majority of nouns are made up of simpler terms. For example, *na-pa* (literally "eye-nose") means "face," *sh'ha-pq* ("head-bone") means "skull," *wuna-pq* ("house-bone") means "frame of a house," and *woradi-pq* ("song-bone") means "melody." The sound systems, however, are the most unusual feature of the family. All the languages have enormous consonantal systems, with rounded, labialized (simultaneous p-, b-, f-, or v- made with the sound), palatalized (raised tongue), and pharyngealized (constricted throat) consonants made at almost every possible point in the mouth and throat. Kabardian has the fewest with 48 consonants, while Ubykh has the most with 81. (For example, Ubykh has 14 guttural fricatives and 27 s-, ts-, sh-, and ch-like sounds.) These sounds also occur in elaborate clusters, especially in Abkhaz and Abaza. As hard as the consonants are, the vowels are harder. This family is known for its "vertical vowel system," in which vowels contrast only in degree of openness. By some analyses, these languages have four, three, or only two vowels. Some linguists have even argued that the vowels of Kabardian are all predictable and therefore not really part of its sound system (phoneme inventory). Two dialects of Circassian serve as written languages: Chemgwi (West Circassian) and Kabardian (East Circassian). Both Abkhaz and the closely related Abaza are literary languages, while Ubykh, still spoken by a handful of people in Turkey, has been extensively documented by linguists and folklorists. The literary languages use highly modified Cyrillic scripts, while Ubykh has been recorded in an elaborated Latin one. Many families across the North Caucasus have rune-like symbols, *tamghas*, as emblems of identity. Many of these reach back to old symbols used by nomadic hordes in antiquity.

In the Northwest, special membership in hunting bands carried with it knowledge of a special language for its male members. In old Circassian, this was *she-ko-bza* ("hunting-go-language"). In Abkhazia, a woodsman language is still used. There are spotty reports of a women's language that seems to have been spoken until recently across the entire North Caucasus. One old Ossetian related how his mother and sister would speak in a monosyllabic language with tone (like Sumerian of ancient Mesopotamia).

Scholars have tried to find links between various Caucasian languages and some of the languages of the Ancient Middle East and Anatolia, such as Hattic (with Northwest Caucasian), Sumerian (with Georgian or Dagestani), Urartean and Hurrian (with Dagestani). One such proposal that has attracted much interest and some support is that linking Proto-Indo-European with the Northwest Caucasian family.

Bilingualism is virtually universal among Caucasians. Nearly everyone speaks Russian in addition to his or her own language. The only people to be predominantly monolingual are the Russians, who tend to dominate in urban centers. The villages and countryside remain bastions of the native languages.

In the North as opposed to the South Caucasus, the family name comes first and then the given names. In Russian, practice this is reversed, but the original order is retained in the social practices of the individual peoples.

4 FOLKLORE

The Caucasus is rich in folklore. In the southern highlands, tales of a mountain sorceress, Dal, are widespread. Dal is beautiful and glowing and a protector of the alpine wildlife, but she can lure hunters to their doom. Other tales show strong Zoroastrian influences from ancient Iran. In the North, there are tales that recount battles with the ancient Goths, Huns, and Khazars, the last a Turkic people who ruled the Caucasus and adopted Judaism wholesale. One of the most noteworthy traditions is that of the Nart sagas, dramatic tales of a race of ancient heroes in which the figure of the all-wise and all-fertile Lady Satanaya is pivotal. Other figures include a villainous shape changer (Sosruquo), a mighty hero who is resurrected from the dead and returns to annihilate his enemies (Pataraz or Batradz), a giant or hero who, like the Greek Prometheus, is chained to a mountain top as a punishment for trying to return fire to humankind (Nasran), and a cyclopean giant (Yinizh). There are numerous links to the myths of ancient Greece, ancient India, and Norse Scandinavia. There is even a sort of Christmas-tree figure, Lady Tree, and a "Forest Mother," Amazan, from which the Greeks took the figure of their women warriors, the Amazons.

There is widespread belief in the western Caucasus of wild men in the high mountain forests, especially among people who dwell in the upper villages. These hairy people are reputed to be about five feet tall and to travel in small family groups. Occasionally, they are said to come into the lowland fields at harvest time and feed on the ripening ears of corn. Men are said to be very brave if they can go into the high forests and trade with these wild men, because after having met with one or two of them in a clearing to offer trinkets, they run the risk of being ambushed by the whole band as they return through the high, dense rhododendron forests. It is worth noting that in 1991 and 1992 fossils of small early humans were found at Dmanisis in Georgia. Perhaps these Wildman tales are based on encounters with relic forms of Homo georgicus.

5 RELIGION

The nation-states of Georgia (Georgian Orthodox Christian), Armenia (Armenian Orthodox Christian), and Azerbaijan use religion as central components in their identity. The first two claim to be the oldest Christian nations and have nationalist churches. Azerbaijan is Shi'ite Muslim (Azeri Turks and Georgian-speaking Ingiloi), Sunni Muslim (southern Lezgi Dagestani peoples), and Alwanian Christian Orthodox Christian, now a branch of the Georgian patriarchate (the small Udi community). These nations-states feel a sense of privilege in comparison with the smaller peoples of the Caucasus and have used their religion as a part of their pride. The Nagorno-Karabakh war (1989–1995) involved serious ethnic clashes between Azeris and Armenians that resonated with religious and ethnic hatred.

By contrast, religious tolerance is one of the strongest features of the North Caucasus, where Christians (Orthodox), Muslims (Sunni), and Jews can be found living side by side. Even during the recent wars in the North, religious hatred never emerged as a motive. The highlands also had mystical traditions of meditation and martial arts that in the east have become Sufi practices. In Dagestan, holy men often have shrines, usually placed at the highest point of the village. Pagan elements persist throughout the Caucasus, and many Abkhaz are avowedly pagan. The Abkhaz even had women shamans. Religion is always socially and conceptually subordinated to ethnic identity throughout the Caucasus.

There are enigmatic relics of older beliefs. For example, Ossetia preserves "beehive" mortuaries made of flat stones, which must reflect an older, local religion of unknown character. Dagestan shows many old beliefs surrounding animals, such as snakes, horses, and especially bears. This last totemistic animal is associated with sacred rocks and even a half-bear/half-man creature. Sacred rocks of heaven are also mentioned in some of the Nart sagas of the Northwest Caucasian Abazas. These are considered the heaviest stones and might even have been nickel-iron meteorites.

Islamic societies, *jama'at,* are appearing across the North Caucasus. Many of these have fundamentalist Salafi leanings, unlike the usually Hanafi form of Sunni Islam. Given the turmoil and economic stress in the North Caucasus, Islam seems to be emerging once again, as it did in the 18th and 19th centuries, as a unifying principle.

6 MAJOR HOLIDAYS

Major holidays are those of the Orthodox Christian and Sunni Muslim faiths. The Northwest Caucasians (Circassians, Ubykhs, Abazas, and Abkhaz) in the diaspora mark deportation day (21 May 1864), the anniversary of their expulsion from the Caucasus. In Dagestan, the "first plowing" in the spring is widely celebrated with a ritual plowing of a furrow by a bull and with festivities, races, and tests of strength.

7 RITES OF PASSAGE

Apart from Muslim and Orthodox Christian rites of circumcision and christening, there are no rites of passage into adulthood. Both boys and girls are considered mature between the ages of 16 and 18. Marriage is the chief change in life for both men and women.

Funeral rites vary, but almost all groups set out a place setting at the table to mark the missing dead at feasts. After three months a monument is erected and a day of remembrance observed. In Abkhazia the next of kin gather when an elder lies dying and sing to her or him.

⁸ INTERPERSONAL RELATIONS

In all Caucasian societies, siblings were supposed to be married in order from oldest to youngest. In all cases, the bride went to live in the extended family of her husband (patrilocal marriage). Whether arranged or through love, marriage was viewed as the linking of two families. Accordingly, matters of social rank between them were always a concern.

Marriage was by abduction among the Northwest Caucasians. These were often prearranged by the couple in love, and mock abductions are still performed. A leather corset with many knots was worn by the bride for those prearranged abductions. After the first night, the man had to present this corset with its thongs intact to both families as a sign of his courtesy to his new wife and of his restraint. Marriages often took place when the couple was in their thirties, which is extraordinarily late for a traditional society. Premarital life was filled with decorous and discrete romance. Young girls had a room in their family homes in which they were free to entertain their suitors. Trysts were arranged for an amorous young couple by the youth's maternal uncle, while a young woman's well-being was the responsibility of her brothers. In Ossetia, marriage was generally for love, with couples marrying in their twenties, but family rank was still an important factor. In the Northeast Caucasus, marriages were usually arranged, with young people marrying in their teens. Among the Chechens actual abduction of a woman still takes place. Brides were subservient to their in-laws. In the South Caucasus, a similar pattern was followed in Armenia, where family negotiations and an engagement of their teenage children were begun as early as two years before the marriage. Brides were subservient to their mothers-in-law and had to observe a ritual silence in their new families, often for years. In public, their faces were veiled or even tightly wrapped until they had a child. Among the Georgians, young people marry by mutual consent in their twenties, with civic and church ceremonies. The bride is supposed to have an agreeable, but respectful relationship with her in-laws. Among the Azeris, couples marry in their twenties. Rural marriages are usually arranged, but even those urban marriages that are motivated by love are expected to take place between families who are known to one another or even related. The latter case is unique in the Caucasus, where strict exogamy (marriage outside a clan or lineage) is otherwise the rule.

Throughout the Caucasus, hospitality to strangers is one of the foremost social imperatives. Lavish feasts are given for guests and, in theory, a host would even give his life to defend a guest. In return, a guest is expected to act discretely and respectfully to his host and so bring honor to the host's family. Even a prisoner of war or an enemy could be treated hospitably if he had shown great valor. In the midst of a duel, it was possible for one adversary to seek a suspension of hostilities for a period of time as long as several days. The combatants would then resume their struggle at an agreed upon time and place. This chivalric code has been eroded by modern warfare, however.

People who are strongly attracted to one another or who admire one another can declare themselves to be "milk" sisters or brothers. Such a bond can cross gender lines. To be chosen as a milk sibling is one of the greatest honors that can be bestowed upon someone by a Caucasian. Such bonds last for life and have all the force of true kinship. Often a man and a woman who cannot marry for some reason will instead form a lifelong bond in this way.

Four other marked features are found throughout the Caucasus. First, elders are revered. The old are expected to have full and passionate lives, although women are cautioned that "a man past one hundred is no longer much of a man." The elderly also have economic roles in the community, sorting fruit or tending gardening, which permit them to contribute without taxing their powers. Young people are greatly honored to wait upon or care for an elderly member of their clan or their community. Many groups have choruses or dance troupes in which all the members are 100 or more years old. These have special dances and distinctive songs.

Second, almost all peoples have clan structures of one sort or another. These play a vital role in their societies. Social support, kinship bonds, economic support, socializing, and vengeance obligations are or were defined by clan affiliation. In some cases, as with the Chechen clans, called *teips*, war has weakened their role, and warlord-like allegiances have come to dominate. In other cases, as among the Circassians and their kin, expulsion has also weakened these old links, reducing them to matters of family pride rather than active social organizations.

Third, vengeance was a dominant theme in the Caucasus, especially the north. Even the accidental death of a clan member forced upon all its males an obligation to seek revenge from the offending clan, even by taking the life of someone who had no role in the incident. Only males were involved in such vendettas.

Fourth, dance was a central social activity of every people. Men and women entered into joint dances, although single gender dances, and solo performances, also existed. Dance is still important, even among Diaspora communities.

Two features found in the Northwest Caucasus, among the Circassians and their kin are the high social prestige and sexual freedom that women enjoy. Among these peoples women are seen as the sources of fertility, social grace, and intellectual knowledge. Until recently, a woman could halt the most vicious fight simply by tossing her scarf between the two men. Women have the right to initiate altruistic friendships with men or even embark upon sexual ones if they do so discreetly. Such overtures are difficult for a man to reject, because he would be rejecting her whole family, so women do not make such overtures lightly. One opener is for a woman to ask to borrow a pen or other small item even when it is obviously not needed. To comply is to show interest. In Dagestan, sexual prerogatives of women can be more circumscribed, with the prowess of men being important. This can be shown when the men set water buckets out on their porches in the evening for nocturnal ablutions after sexual intercourse: the bigger the bucket, the greater his presumed sexual prowess. Some men even set out two. The somewhat lower rank of women in Dagestan correlates with a greater economic burden of toil on their part. Women remain subservient in Dagestan. Efforts to promulgate traditional Muslim norms in Chechnya are met with resistance from women. As in Russia, older women in the Caucasus, especially in the North East and South, often cover their heads with scarves.

A man drives his cattle across a snowy mountain outside of Vladikavkaz. This road through Russia's Caucasus Mountains has been shut down many times because of heavy snowfall. (Kazbek Basayev/Getty Images)

⁹ LIVING CONDITIONS

Living conditions are relatively good in the South and Northwest, where the land is verdant, but life is difficult in the Northeast where mountain deserts dominate. Life in the high reaches of Dagestan is especially harsh due to the prolonged winters and barren land. Men go on long outings to earn money in the lowlands, while the women remain behind to maintain the households through strenuous work. One advantage to living in the highlands is that every step is either up or down, and the resulting exercise contributes to many people being long-lived. Whatever their age, people are often extremely strong and youthful looking.

The typical Northwest Caucasian house is long with one floor, much like a ranch-style home. It is made of wattle covered in clay daub. Villages were formed of compounds containing a main house and several outbuildings, including guest housing, that were originally strung out like necklaces along riverbanks. Tower fort homes were common in the highlands of Svan territory (Svanetia), Ossetia, and the Circassian and Abkhazian highlands. These striking buildings, sitting within a walled yard, were made of stone, with a first floor for livestock, a second floor for humans, and a high tower in which all could take refuge when under siege from a blood feud. The Northeast Caucasian stone houses run on top of one another, the roof of the lower serving as the porch of the upper, as they cling to hillsides to form compact villages called *auls*. Andi aul of Muni is so compact that it forms one giant building with enclosed streets. Houses in such auls were usually made of local

stone and had two floors; the first for livestock, and the second for people (also to be above the snows).

The cities, many of which were founded as Cossack forts, have a blend of older 19th-century housing and modern Soviet high-rise apartments. Most of these cities are attractive, with large parks and tree-lined boulevards.

¹⁰ FAMILY LIFE

Extended patrilocal families are the norm across the Caucasus. In highlands, people often live to be very old, so great-grandparents or (even great-great-grandparents) are part of the family. Children must respect elders and older siblings. Brothers have very close, protective relationships with their sisters. Boys have very close ties with their maternal uncles, while they have relatively formal relationships with their fathers. This is part of the Circassian kinship system, where the husband's relationship to his wife is formal, and the wife's bond to her brother is spontaneous and deep. The eldest man is master of the extended family unit insofar as he rules over disputes or regulates social relationships with the outside world. Within the confines of the home, however, the eldest woman is supreme and runs the details of the household. Often she works hard to organize feasts, supervising her daughters-in-law or even poor female relations who may come to help, but she can be rewarded after the dinner by having her family and guests gather outside the kitchen to applaud her while she takes a bow.

Family life is further integrated into the community by tight networks of clans and blood lines. These are centered around villages in Dagestan, where such clans will have their own tea houses for their members to gather. Clan houses are merely meeting houses among the Chechens and Ingush. With the Ossetians, Northwest Caucasians, Mountain Turks, and Armenians, clans are vital to social organization and have local "seats," but clan houses do not exist. In Georgia, a loose network of noble families serves a similar function, with clans being absent. In Azerbaijan, clans and wider social structures are lacking. Even there, extended families are a social reality and define family matters, such as marriages.

The clans were also the basis for the blood feud or vendetta. Customary law, called *adat*, stipulated that if a member of one clan killed or even accidentally brought about the death of a member of another, then every man in the offended clan had the obligation to restore "the balance of life" by killing the man responsible or, if that was too difficult, another male from the killer's clan. This obligation passed down the male line for seven generations. There were only fours ways to stop the bloodshed. First, one clan eventually killed all the males of the other, which sometimes happened. Second, a blood price was stipulated, usually in livestock, and the offending clan was able to meet this demand. Third, an exalted social figure, an elder or an imam (Muslim cleric), forced the offended clan to renounce their obligation or risk taking the blame for humiliating him in turn. Sometimes this peacemaker would have to threaten suicide to force such a renunciation. Fourth, the killer could sneak up on a woman from the victim's clan, seize her, tear off her blouse, and place his lips to her breast. Such an act, however fleeting, would suffice to create a kinship bond between the two clans that precluded further bloodshed. This was not an easy feat, because many Caucasian women will fight and are sometimes armed with small daggers. During war, vendetta was suspended so that men could form an army and fight beside their blood enemies. In recent decades, Soviet courts had begun to assume the role of arbiters of justice in such cases, but with the collapse of Soviet authority, vendetta has reemerged.

In the Northwest Caucasus, princely and noble families practiced fosterage: they would give their sons to trusted retainers to be reared. This was nearly the highest honor a retainer could know because it linked his family to that of the nobility by fictive kinship bonds. The highest honor was when the foster child refused to return to his natural family at 16 years of age, but chose instead to remain in the household of his foster parents.

¹¹ CLOTHING

Distinctive to the Caucasus and borrowed by the Cossacks is a man's garment called a *cherkesska*. This is a robe-like suit, tightly fitting on the upper torso, and flaring out from the waist, with long flaring sleeves. On either side of the chest cylindrical pockets were sewn on in a row for cartridges or to hold cases of measured powder charge for a musket. A long-sleeved, collarless shirt is worn under it, together with fitted trousers. In the Cossack variant, the trousers are baggy. As the name suggests, this dashing outfit originated among the Circassians (the "Cherkess" in Russian). Over it can be worn a heavy, rectangular sheepskin cape, the burka, which can even serve as a makeshift tent. In Dagestan, sheep's wool leather coats with long sleeves dangling below the hands were common as well. Lamb's wool hats are worn, some high and cylindrical, others shorter and flaring or shaggy and spherical,

depending upon the region. Footwear consisted of a boot that resembled a leather knee sock. No man was considered dressed without a long dagger, the *kinjal*, hanging from a narrow leather belt. The belt itself was adorned with hanging weighted straps that served to balance a dagger or sword.

In the Northwest and South Caucasus the traditional woman's garment is a long, flowing gown with pendant sleeves and either a high, crown-like hat, or a pillbox hat with a trailing scarf attached to it. Shoes are pump-like slippers, but in older times noble women wore platform shoes. Northeast Caucasians had woolen sweater-like tunics and heavy socks and mittens to ward off the winter cold. Dagestani women often wore baggy trousers and tunics. Dagestani, Chechen, Ingush, and Karachai-Balkar women often wear head scarves, sometimes hanging far down their backs, but they did not wear veils. Women often wear pendant earrings, necklaces, and bracelets. Some Dagestani women wear large broach-like pieces of silver on their foreheads attached to their head scarves. Outside Dagestan modern dress is now the rule except for parties or festivals when the traditional costumes are worn.

¹² FOOD

Outside Dagestan, food is relatively plentiful and varied in the Caucasus. Common foods include chicken, mutton, cornmeal, and millet mush, all seasoned with garlic or, in the South, with hot spices, as well as yogurt, a walnut paste, fruits, watermelons, wine, cognac, and millet beer. One popular dish that has spread beyond the Caucasus is "chicken Circassian," which consists of cornbread served with ground chicken that has been mixed with onions and walnuts and topped with a cream garlic sauce. Traditional diets were low in fat, and people were slender. Now, the diet is high in fat and starch and people thicken with age. One item eaten nowadays that reflects such dietary changes is ground liver spread in a layer and then topped with a layer of lard. The whole thing is rolled up and sliced like a jelly roll. Even though feasting could last for days and drinking was heavy, overeating and drunkenness were considered disgraceful lapses in etiquette. The clan or community feast was an important affair and was run by the *tamada*, a Circassian word, *t'hamata*, that has spread across the Caucasus, up into Russia and down into Iran. Invariably a man was elected, and he determined seating and set the tempo for courses and drinks. A person was judged by the eloquence of his or her toasts; even women were permitted to offer them among many groups. Only the Aghuls of Dagestan stand apart in that no toasting takes place at their feasts. Dagestanis are noted for grinding grains that have begun to sprout, a practice that enhances the vitamin content of the flour.

¹³ EDUCATION

All children were reared from an early age to observe formal etiquette, to honor elders, and to dance. In the highlands, training in hunting and stalking was important. In lower lands, training in the details of horse breeding was often vital. Formal education is conducted in local languages up to high school, but then is usually in Russian. Up until the Russian conquest, the religious universities (Medrassas) of Dagestan were renowned throughout the Muslim world. The Russians discouraged such institutions, but they did introduce widespread literacy in both Russian and many of the native languages, and they opened up the Caucasus to modern urban culture and science. In the South Caucasus and in parts of Chechnya, Russia is giving way to English and German as the preferred second language. The Caucasus region has a high percentage of scientists, intellectuals, and artists.

14 CULTURAL HERITAGE

The Caucasus is a refuge for many peoples who were driven from the steppes of Eurasia. The region has preserved many values and customs that seem ancient. Since the Russian conquest and with the advent of modernity, Caucasians have faced many challenges to their heritage and sense of identity. The issue of heritage is difficult for the Circassians, Abazas, Abkhaz, and Ubykhs because their expulsion from the Caucasus in the 19th century, when Circassians lost 90% of population during the war with Russia and deportation. Internal deportations play a similar vexing role for the Karachai-Malkar and for the Chechen-Ingush. These peoples were deported to Siberia and Central Asia by Stalin in 1944 and were allowed to return under Khrushchev only in 1956-7. Many died and much was lost. One dominant theme, however, emerges from the array of local concerns. All Caucasians wish to be a part of modern culture in some sense, even those who are otherwise staunchly Muslim. Theirs is a desire to enter upon the stage of world culture as a respected and distinct form of civilization. They feel that they have much to offer, but they have trouble sorting out the details and finding new roles for old values.

Caucasians face a range of difficulties in finding a modern identity for their warrior heritage. They are still outstanding fighters, but urban culture offers them roles and goals that are new. Furthermore, the Diaspora and the home populations have differing needs. The former seek to retain or revive aspects of identity in their new homelands, chiefly Turkey, while the latter try to find viable roles for older customs in the new urban centers established by the Russians. Despite these challenges certain core traits still form part of the heritage of most Caucasians: honoring of elders, keeping of one's word, showing hospitality, showing restraint, feeling the imperatives of vendetta and vengeance if not often acting upon them, forming fictive kinship bonds (milk siblings), avoiding a mercenary attitude toward money, adhering to old home territory if in the Caucasus, observing proper conduct and etiquette, and cultivating good humor and a sharp wit.

Other aspects of Caucasian heritage are dance and music. Music was played at one time on violins and oboe-like instruments, but now clarinets and accordions are preferred. Drums, gourd rattles, and wooden clackers form the rhythm section. Long horns (like Swiss alp horns) were used in Ossetia to communicate between valleys. Poetry recitals are another important cultural element. Women as well as men can be bards in the Northwest. In times past, in Dagestan, bards (only males) would hold contests in eloquence, with the loser reputedly losing his head.

Another vital heritage that has been carried down to modern times is an elaborate tradition of herbal medicine. This is especially active in Dagestan among the men and in the Northwest highlands among the women. It has spread to Russia with Caucasian immigrants and is a highly valued service among the population at large. Its practice is open only to the initiated, and scholars or doctors have yet to study these remedies and techniques.

15 WORK

Labor is specialized by gender across the Caucasus. Men work with livestock and in the open fields, whereas women tend gardens, thresh grain, do household chores, and tend to sewing. Men do metal working and leather tooling. In Dagestan, women both young and old can often be seen carrying enormous loads of hay or kindling on their backs or large jugs of water on their heads. Children and the elderly are also given tasks suitable to their abilities that contribute to the prosperity of the village. Despite the gender-based specialization, both sexes accord mutual respect to their roles.

Some Caucasians engage in careers that carry on older cultural specialties. For example, many diaspora Caucasians have become military leaders in Russia, Turkey, and the Middle East, following the earlier example of the Circassian Mamelukes (hired warriors) who ruled Egypt in the 13th to 15th centuries. The Mongols were finally defeated in their onslaught by the Circassian Sultan Kutuz. The same name was borne by General Kutuzov of the imperial Russian army who defeated Napoleon 500 years later. The name "Kutuz(ov)" is still common among the Chechens. One effect this warrior heritage has on modern society is that one cannot offer to help a Caucasian man without offending him, since such an offer implies that he is incapable of accomplishing his task. He must ask for help. Another effect is the heavy emphasis throughout the Caucasus on etiquette and proper conduct in order to curb the excesses of the warrior code in normal social life.

Other diaspora Caucasians have become skilled machinists, pharmacists, or physicians. The Ubykhs, for example, who were reputed for their healing skills back in the Caucasus, are frequently doctors in Turkey. Others raise horses, and others are merchants.

16 SPORTS

A popular reworking of the old warrior ethic appears to be the sport of soccer, the most popular sport in the Caucasus. A close second is wrestling, which combines a kick-boxing-like manner of fighting, perhaps descended from the older martial traditions of hand-to-hand combat. Caucasian dance has the quality of a sport, demanding enormous strength in jumps and leaps and attended by a pervasive grace. The men twirl, strut, and leap with a proud bearing, while the women glide and swirl in a demure manner. Arm motions are an important part of the dance, with the arms often held straight upward and then brought downward while flexing the hands at the wrists. Chechen dance adds to these features one that exemplifies the Caucasian virtue of self-control. While the woman glides about, the man whirls around her, moving in and out. At unexpected moments, he will shout abruptly and loudly into her face or ear, and if she is a skilled dancer, she will neither flinch nor even bat an eye. Skill at horseback riding and horse racing are valued. One of the most spectacular feats on horseback is to lean over and cut through 21 oranges (the product of two magical numbers, 3 and 7) with a saber without moving even one of them. It is achieved by pulling the razor-sharp saber toward you while you sweep it through the lined up oranges. The nobles of the Circassians, Ubykhs, and Abkhaz still practice a martial art form. From the age of 12 they toughen their hands by thrusting them into huge bags of clay. In close combat, they were said to have been able to thrust their hands into an enemy's body and rip out his heart. The rule was "in a fight, don't get close to a noble."

17 ENTERTAINMENT AND RECREATION

Many of the cities have national museums, theatres, and dance troupes based upon local ethnic customs, and these are well attended. Music, dance, and bardic recitations are still popular forms of entertainment. The arrival of a guest is an opportunity for such entertaining, as well as for feasting with a *tamada*. In the highlands, hunting boars, badgers, stags, and bears is a popular pastime.

18 FOLK ART, CRAFTS, AND HOBBIES

The peoples of Dagestan are famous for their woven rugs, tapestries, and textiles, with each ethnic group having its own distinctive repertoire of forms. The peoples of the Northwest Caucasus make felt rugs and folk costumes. Their favored decoration is a pleasing open exfoliate pattern (resembling leaves and vines). Poetry is an active folk art, with some groups, such as the Abaza, producing volumes of popular poetry by hundreds of amateurs. Some groups, such as the Kubachis of Dagestan, are famed for their metal working. Kubachi metal goods, including swords and daggers, are considered among the best examples of Islamic metal working in the world. Many Dagestani peoples supplement their meager incomes with home knitting of socks, mittens, and sweaters. These are often done by hand in a matter of hours or days by the women and then sold in Georgia or in Russia by the men.

19 SOCIAL PROBLEMS

The problems faced by Caucasians, both in the Caucasus and among the diaspora, are numerous and acute. In the Caucasus, endemic violence, dislocations in social structure, high youth unemployment, new and seemingly arbitrary borders, sharp ethnic rivalries, the recovery of lost practices and identities, and a coming to terms with the communist legacy are all problems that must in some sense be solved. In the damaged hierarchical Northwest Caucasian societies, where there were once princes, nobles, freemen, and slaves, there is now a chronic struggle for prestige and rank, as former princes and noble no longer command deference from former freemen or slaves. In North Ossetia–Alania, problems center around ethnic identity and union with the South Ossetians. North Ossetians are highly Russified, but have been brought up short in this evolution by the influx of conservative South Ossetian refugees. Northeast Caucasian societies are also hierarchical except for Chechen-Ingush and Lezgi. In this region, the major problem is balancing the competing claims of the numerous ethnic groups. The Chechens face the acute problem of rebuilding after the disastrous wars with Russia and of normalizing their relations with vastly more numerous former imperial masters. These tasks are made even more difficult by the horizontal organization of Chechen society in clans. Chechens are not accustomed to following a hierarchical authority, even when it is their own. Georgian society has endured acute economic collapse, which was exacerbated by South Ossetia and Abkhazia having fought wars of secession. The role of the old Georgian noble families are being revived and reappraised in an effort to enhance social cohesion. Armenia and Azerbaijan are locked in a stalemate over Nagorno-Karabakh, with Armenian forces holding more than one-third of what was Azerbaijani territo-

ry. Azerbaijan has embarked upon a strategy of ethnically and religiously homogeneous social identity that seems ill-suited to accommodate the Lezgi, Tsakhur, Kryz, Budukh, Khinalug, Ingiloi, or Udi peoples who live within its borders, not to mention the Armenians of Nagorno-Karabakh.

Wars have devastated Georgia, Abkhazia, South Ossetia, Ingushetia, Chechnya, Azerbaijan, Armenia, and Nagorno-Karabakh. Preventing renewed or future hostilities and rebuilding in the aftermath of those past will be a major challenge for the future of the region. Russian policies under President Putin have aggravated many local problems. Chief among these irritants has been Moscow's policy of appointing regional governors and heads. Often such individuals are corrupt and indifferent to local needs. They have frequently failed to restore the confidence of their populaces.

These same wars have reawakened ethnic identity among the diaspora Caucasians in a vivid and abrupt way, and these people face their own array of social problems. The foremost problem is to find ways to accommodate their newly revived ethnic identities within their host countries, and to find tangible forms of expression for these identities after six generations in exile. Most recently younger members of the Caucasian diaspora have used the internet to establish electronic forms of identity, even going so far as to devise ways of writing their languages in Latin script. This is tied in with another problem among the diaspora: native language literacy. There is a renewed desire both to publish in the languages of their heritage and to learn and preserve those languages. The last few Ubykh speakers in Turkey, for example, are making an effort to revive this language. Ubykhs have emerged as visible components of most diaspora communities, having regained a sense of identity.

Turkey has shown political tolerance and innovation by permitting its large Caucasian minority to establish a North Caucasus Studies Center and to record the languages. A limited amount of publishing in the Caucasian languages is allowed. Jordan and Israel have long allowed their Caucasians language rights. The diaspora offers the promise of assisting other Caucasians through trade and investment.

20 GENDER ISSUES

The role and status of women in the traditions of the North Caucasus in the past and current times differs substantially from Islamic norms. Despite the fact that the peoples of the Caucasus profess Islam, the behavior of women, their status in the family and society is increasingly governed by ethnic laws, which are more liberal than Islamic laws. In the culture of Dagestan, Vai Nakh, (Chechen and Ingush) and others it is *adat*, for the Ossetians, *aeghdau*, and for the Circassians, *habze*.

Women of almost of any nation in the Caucasus have largely similar rights, responsibilities, and privileges. But, there are significant differences. For example, a woman of Dagestan, in the past, had the right to choose her husband. The selected man had no right to refuse, but had to marry, even if he did not like the woman. In the tradition of the Circassians, a woman submitted to the will of her father (or a senior in age) in the choice of a husband. On the other hand, a Dagestan woman was responsible for much manual labor, because it was a disgrace for a Dagestan man to carry anything on his back or shoulder. Often, women gather everything that is needed for the household, including wood and hay. This tradition is still observed in the mountains and in the cities of Dagestan, where you can observe a man and a woman walking together, while he is freely waving hands and she is carrying heavy bags. In Circassian and Ossetian societies, however, such things are not allowed. Traditions do not permit a woman to lift heavy weights if there is a man nearby.

In today's Caucasian society many of the most severe restrictions on women are not as urgent as in the past. There is a freer European style of dress. The ban on women visiting cafes, restaurants, and discotheques was removed. Family members are more or less equal, although the strict adherence to traditional primacy of men is still shown in public life. In Chechnya, a strong tradition of a father's privileges still remains. After a divorce, the children stay with their father and the mother is prohibited for life in seeing her children.

The ban on jobs is no longer widely practiced and modern Caucasian women have the opportunity to get an education and make a professional career in various fields. Nevertheless, the range of occupations remains fairly narrow. Feminine professions are considered school teachers, doctors, university professors, and government employees of average level. Rarely or never are Caucasian women in politics or leading positions in governments.

After Gorbachev's time the market became one of the ways of survival for many families in the Caucasus. Women are actively engaged in buying and reselling items and products. They go to various countries, mostly to Turkey, from where they import large quantities of clothing to the Caucasus. Many trade in the market themselves from 6 am to 4 pm outdoors in all seasons. That business, by local standards, is considered is very profitable, although it only helps families make ends meet, and women pay their health for it. Meanwhile, a major financial, constructional, and tourist or oil businesses remain a closed zone for women in the Caucasus.

In a region that was a hot spot for many years, human rights movements are one of the most dangerous political occupations and, strangely enough, it is women in the Caucasus who play a dominant role in these movements.

21 BIBLIOGRAPHY

Abdurakhmanov, A. M. "Totemistic Elements in Rituals and Legends about Animals." *Caucasian Perspectives* (1992): 392-405.

Aronson, Howard. *Georgian: a Reading Grammar.* Columbus, Ohio: Slavica, 1990.

Babchenko, Arkady. *One Soldier's War.* Nick Allen, translator. New York: Grove Press, 2006.

Baddeley, John F. *The Rugged Flanks of the Caucasus.* 2 vols. Ayer, NH: 1973.

Benningsen-Broxup, Marie, ed. *The North Caucasus Barrier.* London: Hurst and Co., 1992.

Bitov, Andrei. *A Captive of the Caucasus.* New York: Farrar, Straus, Giroux, 1992.

Blanch, Lesley. *The Sabres of Paradise.* New York: Carroll and Graf, 1960.

Burney, Charles, and David Marshall Lang. *The Peoples of the Hills: Ancient Ararat and Caucasus.* New York: Praeger, 1971.

Chenciner, Robert. *Daghestan: Tradition and Survival.* New York: St. Martin's Press, 1997.

Chenciner, Robert, Gabib Ismailov, and Magomedkhan Magomedkhanov. *Tattooed Mountain Women and Spoon Boxes of Daghestan.* London: Bennet & Bloom. 2006.

Chorbajian, Levon, Patrick Donabedian, and Claude Mutafian. *The Caucasian Knot.* London: Zed Books, 1994.

Colarusso, John. *Kabardian (East Circassian).* Munich: LINCOM-Europa, 2006.

———. *Nart Sagas from the Caucasus, Myths and Legends from the Circassians, Abazas, Abkhaz, and Ubykhs.* Princeton: Princeton University Press, 2002.

———. "Abkhazia." *Central Asian Survey* (1995): 75–96.

———. "Chechnya: the War without Winners." *Current History* 94 (October 1995): 329–36.

———. "Myths from the Forest of Circassia." *The World & I* (December 1989): 644–51.

———. "Prometheus among the Circassians." *The World & I* (March 1989): 644–51.

———. "A Wild Man of the Caucasus." *Manlike Monsters on Trial, Early Records and Modern Evidence.* Vancouver: University of British Columbia Press, 1980.

———. "The Woman of the Myths: the Satanaya Cycle." *The Annual of the Society for the Study of Caucasia* 2 (1989): 3–11.

Comrie, Bernard. *The Languages of the Soviet Union.* Cambridge University Press, 1981.

Dumas, Alexandre. *Adventures in Caucasia.* Trans. and ed. A. E. Murch. Westport, CT: Greenwood Publishers, 1962.

Edwards, Mike. "The Fractured Caucasus." *National Geographic* 189, (February 1996): 126–31.

Friedrich, Paul, and Norma Diamond, ed. *Encyclopedia of World Cultures.* Vol. VI: *Russia and Eurasia/China.* Boston: G. K. Hall and Co., 1994.

Gammer, Moshe. *The Lone Wolf and the Bear.* London: Hurst & Co., 2006.

———. *Muslim Resistance to the Tsar.* London: Frank Cass, 1994.

Goldenberg, Suzanne. *Pride of Small Nations.* London: Zed Books, 1994.

Grant, Bruce and Lale Yalçin Heckmann, ed. *Caucasus Paradigms. Halle Studies in the Anthropology of Eurasia,* vol. 13. Berlin: Lit Verlag Dr. W. Hopf, 2007.

Harris, Alice C., ed. *The South Caucasian Languages.* Delmar, NY: Caravan Books, 1991.

Henze, Paul B. *Chechnya, a Report.* London: International Alert, 1992.

———. *The North Caucasus: Russia's Long Struggle to Subdue the Circassians.* Santa Monica, CA: The Rand Corporation, 1990.

Hewitt, B. George, ed. *The Northwestern Caucasian Languages.* Delmar, NY: Caravan Books, 1989.

Hill, Fiona, ed. *The Caucasus and the Caspian.* Cambridge, MA: Strengthening Democratic Institutions Project, John F. Kennedy School of Government, Harvard University, 1997.

Hill, Fiona. *Russia's Tinderbox.* Cambridge, MA: Strengthening Democratic Institutions Project, John F. Kennedy School of Government, Harvard University, 1995.

Hunt, Kathleen. *Repatriation in Georgia.* New York: Forced Migration Project, Open Society Institute, Soros Foundation, 1995.

Iskander, Fazil. *Sandro of Chegem.* New York: Random House, 1983.

———. *The Gospel According to Chegem.* New York: Random House, 1984.

Job, D. Michael, and Rieks Smeets, ed. *The Northeast Caucasian Languages.* Part 1. Delmar, NY: Caravan Books, 1994.

———. *The Northeast Caucasian Languages.* Part 2. Delmar, NY: Caravan Books, 1998.

Karpov, Y. Y. *The Place of Woman in Culture of the Peoples of the North Caucasus,* S-Peterburg, 2001.

Khadikova, A.K. *The Ossetian Etiquette.* Vladikavkaz, 2006.

King, Charles. *The Ghost of Freedom, a History of the Caucasus.* Oxford: Oxford University Press, 2008.

Kumakhov, M. A. ed. *Adygskaja (Cherkesskaja) Énciklopedija.* Moscow: The Akbashev Foundation, 2006.

Lang, David Marshall. *The Armenians.* London: Unwin Paperbacks, 1981.

———. *The Georgians.* New York: Praeger, 1966.

Maier, Frith. *Trekking in Russia and Central Asia.* Seattle, WA: The Mountaineers, 1994.

Nekrich, Aleksandr M. *The Punished Peoples.* New York: W. W. Norton, 1978.

Ragimova, B.R. *The Role of woman in Dagestan.* Nalchik, El-Fa, 2001.

Said, Kurban. *Ali and Nino.* New York: Random House, 1971.

Shah-Kazemi, Reza. *Crisis in Chechnya.* London: Islamic World Report, 1995.

Tolstoy, Leo. *Hadji Murat.* Virginia: Orchises Press, 1996.

———. *The Raid.* Virginia: Orchises Press, 1996.

van den Berg, Helma. *Dargi Folktales.* Leiden: Research School of Asian, African, and Amerindian Studies, 2001.

———. *A Grammar of Hunzib.* Munich: LINCOM-Europa, 1995.

Wixman, Ronald. *Language Aspects of Ethnic Patterns and Processes in the North Caucasus.* Chicago: Department of Geography, University of Chicago, 1980.

Yagan, Murat. *I Come from Behind Kaf Mountain.* Putney, VT: Threshold Books, 1984.

—revised by F. Tlisova

POLES

LOCATION: Poland
POPULATION: 38.2 million
LANGUAGE: Polish
RELIGION: Roman Catholicism (94%)

¹ INTRODUCTION

In AD 966, under the reign of Duke Mieszko, the Poles embraced Christianity and formed their first state. During the first seven centuries of its history, Poland steadily expanded to become one of Europe's largest countries. After union with Lithuania in the 14th century, it was the center of a multiethnic commonwealth. The 16th and 17th centuries are considered the Golden Age of Polish history, when the nation pushed eastward to take over its Slavic neighbors, dreaming of a kingdom that stretched from the Baltic to the Black Sea. By the end of the 18th century, neighboring countries destroyed Poland, and its territories were divided among the Austrian, Prussian, and Russian empires in three successive partitions—1795 marked the disappearance of Poland as a political entity for more than a century. Although separated politically, the Poles held fast to their cultural unity and were able to preserve their national identity without the framework of a nation-state.

Reunited and restored to independence after World War I, the country was able to sustain a parliamentary democracy for only a few years before Marshal Józef Piłsudski, a figure of heroic proportions in modern Polish history, seized power in 1926 and introduced authoritarian rule. Overwhelmed by Nazi Germany and the Soviet Union in 1939, Poland entered into the darkest period of its long history, suffering the deaths of more than six million of its population during World War II.

After the war, Poland's fate was determined by the victorious Allies. Its borders were shifted westward and the Soviet Union transformed Poland into a satellite state, the Polish People's Republic, founded in 1948. Although they were forcibly integrated into the Communist system, the Poles retained a spirit of independence, strengthened by their deep-rooted ties to Roman Catholicism. Membership in the Warsaw Pact did not mean that all aspects of the Soviet system were implemented in Poland. Agriculture, for instance, was never collectivized; instead, all farms were small. Protests against economic conditions and against violations of human rights were mounted in the late 1970s by a coalition uniting workers and peasants, the intelligentsia, and the church.

In 1980 and 1981 the independent trade union movement Solidarność (Solidarity), under the leadership of Lech Wałęsa, demanded recognition as an organization operating outside the control of the state or Communist party. In December 1981, however, Solidarity was disbanded, and its leaders were arrested. Martial rule was imposed by the prime minister and first secretary of the Communist Party, General Wojciech Jaruzelski, who assumed virtual dictatorial power as the head of a military junta. Personal freedoms were drastically curtailed, universities were closed, activities of all organizations (including Solidarity) were suspended, and over 5,000 activists, among them Wałęsa, were interned. In 1983 Wałęsa was awarded the Nobel Peace Prize.

Renewed labor unrest in 1988 prompted Jaruzelski to begin negotiations with the outlawed Solidarity movement, which resulted in far-reaching reforms of the political system. In the June 1989 elections, Solidarity won the majority and formed a coalition government with the Communists. In 1990 Solidarity leader Lech Wałęsa was elected president. The new government's radical plans to transform Poland's centrally planned economy into a free-enterprise economy —collectively known as "shock therapy"—quickly led to sharp price increases and high unemployment, creating discontent among the population and dissension within the government. Four different prime ministers held office in 1992 and 1993, and former Communists made impressive gains in the 1993 parliamentary elections. The government continued the transition to a free-market economy but at a slower pace. There are now multiple parties. More recently, conservative parties have regained the upper hand. Never apathetic, many Poles are opposed to siting U.S. missile defenses on their territory and are actively protesting rising food prices.

As early as 1989, Poland signed an agreement on trade and trade cooperation with the then European Community. On 1 May 2004 Poland became a member of the European Union. The currency is still the złoty, which is keeping up its value relative to the euro and thus gaining on the dollar. By 2012, however, Poland is slated to adopt the euro.

2 LOCATION AND HOMELAND

Poland is bordered on the east and northeast by Ukraine and Belarus, on the northeast by Lithuania and Russia, on the south by the Czech Republic and Slovakia, on the west by Germany, and on the northwest by the Baltic Sea. The capital city is Warsaw.

Poland consists primarily of lowlands belonging to the North European Plain. The climate is transitional between maritime and continental, with cold, snowy winters and warm summers. There are mountains in the south. Forests occupy more than one-fourth of the total land area.

Poland's population of 38.2 million is highly homogenous, both ethnically and linguistically, although the country does have minority groups, including Ukrainians, Germans, Belarusians, and Roma.

3 LANGUAGE

Polish is a Slavic language that uses the Roman alphabet but has a number of extra characters and diacritical marks (ć, ł, ń, ś, ż, ź, ą, ę, ó). It also uses digraphs to express certain sounds; much as English uses the letter h to modify preceding consonants, Polish uses the letter z to do something similar in the combinations cz, rz, and sz. Spelling is a nearly-reliable guide to pronunciation, with the stress usually on the second-to-last syllable of a word.

Some common everyday words are: *tak* (yes), *nie* (no), *jak* (how), *dobrze* (OK), *dzień dobry* (good day), *cześć* (hello), and *proszę* (please).

4 FOLKLORE

There are many legends associated with Easter and Christmas, which are very important holidays in Poland. For example, a legend of the Christmas spiders tells of when Jesus was a little boy and came upon a poor farmhouse. He heard a family of spiders crying because there was not enough money to buy

decorations for the Christmas tree. The spiders let him in, and he blessed the tree. Within minutes it was decorated in silver and gold webs. This is why tinsel is used to decorate Christmas trees to this day.

A limestone cavern in the bluffs below the Wawel Castle in Cracow inspired the many legends of the Wawel Dragon. The dragon, it is said, was ravaging the countryside and, in particular, devouring young girls. Many knights failed to overcome it. Finally, a cobbler's apprentice stuffed a lamb with sulfur and laid it before the entrance to the dragon's cave. The dragon swallowed the lamb, began to burn inside, dashed down to the Vistula, drank half the river, and burst. The young hero went on to marry the king's daughter and founded the city of Cracow.

5 RELIGION

The Poles are a deeply religious people. Roman Catholicism is the religion of some 94% of Poles, and it exerts an important influence on many aspects of Polish life. Since the introduction of the Catholic Church in AD 966, it has remained a pillar of strength in Poland. The Polish church had a rather distant relationship with Rome until 1978, when a Pole, Cardinal Karol Wojtyła, was chosen to become Pope John Paul II, the first Polish person to be so honored. Poland has 2,500 convents with 28,000 nuns and over 500 monasteries. The Catholic university in Lublin and the Academy of Catholic Theology in Warsaw are the leading church-controlled institutions. Częstochowa, with its Black Madonna, is one of the most important pilgrimage centers in Europe. Other Christian denominations besides Catholicism include Russian Orthodox, the Uniate faith, which combines aspects of Catholicism and Orthodoxy, and a variety of Protestant churches. There are a few Jews left from a community that was large before the Holocaust.

⁶ MAJOR HOLIDAYS

There is a famous Polish saying, "Every day is good for celebration," and this is certainly true in Polish culture.

Important public holidays in Poland include New Year's Day, Good Friday, Easter, All Saints Day (November 1), Corpus Christi Day, and Worker's Day (May 1). Once a constant reminder of Communist power, Worker's Day is now a commemoration of solidarity's triumph over communism. Constitution Day (May 3) and Independence Day (November 11) are also important holidays in Poland.

Polish Catholics have an interesting annual tradition of pledging their vows to the Blessed Virgin Mary. The Mother of God, or Bogurodzica, is the patron of the Polish Crown. People usually come to Częstochowa, to the shrine of the Black Madonna, to renew their vows to her. The church calendar is based on two cycles, which culminate in the two biggest religious celebrations: Christmas (*Boże Narodzenie*) and Easter (*Wielkanoc*). There are also many saints' feast days, which are especially numerous for the Virgin Mary.

St. John's Eve, a few days after the summer solstice, is one of the most popular holidays. Originally a pagan celebration designed to drive out devils, it is now celebrated with great bonfires, around which young people dance and over which boys try to leap, carrying buckets of water with which to douse the girls.

⁷ RITES OF PASSAGE

Occasions such as baptism, first communion, and marriage are cause for festive celebrations.

A Polish wedding always promises a good time. Some traditional rituals associated with a Polish wedding included long blessings by the parents before the actual ceremony and greenery on the bride's headpiece symbolizing her virginity. Large weddings remain mainly in the countryside. Old customs are not always practiced today, and urban Poles have adopted Western-style wedding traditions, with generally smaller, simpler weddings. Wedding anniversaries are very special among Polish couples. The tenth wedding anniversary is the occasion for a major celebration.

Lively wakes are held after Polish funerals, with toasts and tributes to the deceased. In the past, Poles wore black for a year following the death of a family member; today, a black armband is worn instead.

⁸ INTERPERSONAL RELATIONS

Poles greet each other by shaking hands. Men and women often shake hands, but usually the man waits until the woman has extended her hand first. In general, Poles are more conservative and formal than Westerners, but they are known for their hospitality. When responding to a dinner invitation, it is considered polite to bring a bouquet of flowers for the lady of the house.

In any sort of business, tourist, or social situation outside the family, titles (i.e. *Pan* 'Mr.', *Pani* 'Mrs., Ms.', *Pan Doktor* 'Dr.') and occupational titles are used in greetings and in reference to others.

Poles often gesticulate enthusiastically when they talk. In rural areas, it is common to see women crossing themselves as a sign of faith when they come to a crossroads. The Polish good luck gesture (comparable to crossing one's fingers in the U.S.) is a thumb tucked into the palm of one's hand and covered with the other four fingers.

Common Polish civilities include *przepraszam* (excuse me), *Jest pan/pani bardzo uprzejmy/uprzejma* (Sir/madam you are very kind), and *dziękuję* (thank you).

⁹ LIVING CONDITIONS

The average life expectancy for Poles is 75.3 years, and the infant mortality rate is 6.0 per 1,000 live births. Government-funded medical care is no longer available to all Poles. Reforms in 1999–2000 made the system more complex, with 17 insurance funds, and left some people uninsured. Facilities are poor by OECD standards, while spending on medical care is low for an OECD country but rising fast. The availability of modern diagnostic equipment like MRIs and CTs has been growing rapidly. There is one doctor for every 400 patients and one hospital bed for every 179 people. Private medical care is available but very expensive. People express great dissatisfaction with the reforms. The number of smokers has fallen, although it is still somewhat higher than in comparable countries. Obesity has risen, though not to the level of other OECD countries. Alcoholism is a major health problem in Poland.

Poland faces a serious housing shortage, and young couples often live with one or the other set of parents for the first years after they marry. The shift to a market economy led to slowed housing construction, although the pace has picked up in recent years. Housing may be in short supply, but rents are only a small part of living expenditures, since subsidies have not been altogether abolished. Still, the 1991–92 reforms brought a steep rise in housing costs for most families. In urban areas, large tracts of apartment buildings are the norm, but one-family homes are becoming fashionable. In the villages, masonry structures with fireproof roofs have replaced the traditional wooden houses with thatched roofs.

Nearly half of all households own cars, and car ownership has nearly doubled in a decade and is on the rise. The classic Polish Fiat has not been produced since 2000. Poles are now buying Toyotas and many other world brands. To cope with a scarcity of parking spaces, many Poles park half-on-half-off the sidewalk. Hitchhiking used to be not only legal but actually encouraged in Poland through coupons that hikers could buy and give to drivers. It is still popular; there are now internet ride boards. Warsaw has a subway. Most cities have efficient bus and streetcar systems, and there are air and rail links to major cities.

While refrigerators are nearly universal, dishwashers are rare. Virtually every home has a television set and, by 2006, 73% had mobile phones.

¹⁰ FAMILY LIFE

Families in this predominantly urban country typically (88%) have one child; a few have two children; even among rural families it is rare for a couple to have more than two children. Traditionally, the Polish father is a stern authority figure, with the mother mediating between him and the children. The nu-

Villagers wearing traditional dress in Lyse, Poland, participate in a Palm Sunday procession between old and new village churches.
(Wojtek Laski/Getty Images)

clear family is the norm, although aged parents or unmarried brothers and sisters may be part of the household. Single-parent households are becoming more common. In most families, both parents work, and children assume considerable responsibility for themselves at an early age, helping cook, clean, and care for younger siblings. However, grandparents also play a significant role in childrearing. Mother's Day is a big occasion for Polish children, who often put on performances for their mothers at school.

11 CLOTHING

Poles wear modern Western-style clothing and generally dress elegantly, but conservatively. Clothing is very expensive, so wardrobes tend to be small, and it is still common to wear handmade clothing. Young people favor jeans and sweatshirts with American slogans or logos. Jeans are also popular among academics and people in the arts. In rural areas, older women can still be seen wearing full skirts, thick stockings, and head scarves.

Traditional costumes are reserved for Sundays or special occasions in the villages. Costumes vary considerably in the different regions, but some features are typical everywhere. A woman's costume has a blouse, a full skirt (often brightly striped), an apron, and perhaps a vest or jacket. Unmarried women may wear elaborate and varied headdresses. Men too may wear highly decorated headdresses. Pants vary regionally from wide in the north to narrow in the south and are tucked into boots. The southern mountaineers wear moccasins.

Polish women are very fond of amber from the Baltic and coral beads, which are believed to bring many healthy children.

12 FOOD

Meat is integral to Polish cuisine. Beef, pork, ham, and sausage make up many national dishes, such as *bigos* (sauerkraut with spicy meat and mushrooms), *flaki* (tripe boiled or fried), *golonka* (pig's leg), and *pierogi* (dough filled with cheese, meat, or fruit). Common fish include pike, carp, cod, crayfish, and herring. The Poles are known for their thick, hearty soups. Soups such as *borsch* (beet soup), *botwinka*, *chłodnik* or *krupnik* are preludes to Polish main courses. Sour cream and bacon bits are condiments necessary for almost every dish. Typical desserts include stewed fruit, fruit dumplings, pancakes with fruit or cheese, and jam donuts called *pączki*.

Poland has several varieties of vodka—a favorite drink that Poland claims to have discovered. Local bottled beers are popular as well as soft drinks made of strawberry and apple. Pepsi and Coke are everywhere, and tea, especially, is consumed with everything.

13 EDUCATION

Poland has an over 99% adult literacy rate and a near-universal attendance level in its schools. In 1773 a national education commission was established. The system this commission set up lasted for over 200 years, although in periods of partition and occupation it operated underground. The system was reformed in 1999. Compulsory primary school starts at age six or seven and lasts six years, followed by three years of compulsory lower secondary school, called *gimnazjum*. For upper secondary school there are choices: three years of *liceum* or four years of *technikum* both ending in an equivalent examination that is the key to entering higher education, or else two or three years of vocational technical school. In addition to the traditional focus on Polish history and culture, today there is a strong emphasis on foreign languages and computer skills. Rural schools, however, are having a hard time attracting qualified teachers. Students who have good grades or pass an entrance exam may attend one of Poland's 18 universities or many more technical institutes or other types of postsecondary institution. Higher education is in theory free, but there are not enough scholarships to go around. Poland has 466 institutions of higher education. The Jagiellonian University in Cracow, founded in 1364, is the second-oldest university in Central Europe.

14 CULTURAL HERITAGE

In the 19th century when Poland was split among three empires, art, literature, and theater were media through which Polish identity and protest against the state were voiced. Under Nazi Germany (1939–45), clandestine literature flourished and continued during Communist control, joined by theater and film as means of free expression of ideas. Polish movie posters became known internationally as a separate branch of graphic art.

Music is well represented in Poland. Such greats as composers Frederic Chopin and Witold Lutosławski, and pianists Ignacy Jan Paderewski and Artur Rubinstein are known throughout the world.

Poland has over 20 symphony orchestras; even small cities have their own. Conservatories and music high schools make training for the talented publicly available. There are now also private music schools. In Warsaw, nightly operas, ballets, chamber concerts, and recitals are a popular recreational activity. Warsaw is also the home of the Jazz Jamboree festival—the oldest and biggest jazz show in Eastern Europe.

Village musicians often play at weddings and festivals. Their sound is a combination of the fiddle, wooden flutes, accordion, and a single-reed bagpipe.
The polka, known around the world, is not a real Polish folk dance, but the polonaise and mazurka are distinctively Polish.

Writers are considered important people in Poland. Adam Mickiewicz, a 19th-century poet, is the national bard. Many streets and squares are named after him. The following Polish-born writers have won Nobel Prizes for literature: Henryk Sienkiewicz for *Quo Vadis*, a story about the times of Roman emperor Nero; Władysław Reymont for *Chłopi (The Peasants)*, an epic novel of Poland; and Czesław Miłosz and Wisława Szymborska for their poetry. Twentieth-century poets, such as Julian Przybos and Julian Tuwim, have celebrated Polish uprisings and written both experimental verse and poetry with political messages.

The first Pole to win a Nobel Prize (1903 and again in 1911) was Maria Skłodowska (Madame Curie), who with her French husband studied radioactive elements. Poland was a world center in mathematics and logic before World War II. Jan Łukasiewicz found a way to write all logical formulas without using parentheses; it is now called "Polish notation" in his honor.

15 WORK

Poland has a long history as an industrial nation, beginning in the 19th century and intensively developed in the Communist period.

By 2004 most Polish industry was in private, overwhelmingly Polish hands. Manufacturing predominates with metal processing in first place, followed by clothing and fur, furniture, and other wood processing. In the past 15 years, the service sector has grown greatly. Industry has become a smaller part of the total economic output but, nevertheless, has been modernized and has grown at a far higher rate than in the rest of Europe. Electrical and machine products are important exports. Manufacturing accounts for 20% of employees, while agriculture has 16%.

There are large deposits of coal, including hard coal and lignite, which together provide most of the country's electricity. Copper and salt are also extracted.

Poland has been attracting foreign investment by offering a highly-skilled workforce at relatively low wages for Europe. Nevertheless, unemployment remains high at nearly 15%, and many Poles are working abroad, notably in Ireland.

Close to 4 million Poles belong to unions including a union of small farmers and farm workers that has been known to conduct militant protests.

16 SPORTS

For many years a big emphasis was placed on sports activities in Polish schools. Today, there is less funding for equipment, and parents often cannot afford to pay membership fees at private sports clubs.

Some popular sports include swimming, gymnastics, hockey, volleyball, and soccer. Streetball, similar to basketball, is played by children in the parks. On some Saturday mornings, part of a street may be closed off for a soccer game. Soccer, which is played at every school, is also the biggest spectator sport. Skiing is Poland's most popular winter sport. The beautiful ski resort of Zakopane (which means "a place buried in the ground") is the most popular ski getaway for Poles. "When life gets unbearable, there is always Zakopane," is a Polish saying.

Poles have taken new interest in Formula One automobile racing now that there is a Polish driver, Robert Kubica, in world competition. With cars ever more available, Poles have also become involved in typically illegal drag racing. The city of Łódź has taken this on by occasionally closing streets for legal drag racing.

17 ENTERTAINMENT AND RECREATION

Popular family activities include traveling, watching TV, listening to Polish, European, and American pop music, and in recent years shopping. Poland's cities are famous for theater and cinemas, opera houses, jazz and classical concerts, and discos. Outdoor activities include hiking, motorcycle racing, horseback riding, and hunting. Poland's spas are also popular leisure-time venues. The largest is Ciechocinek.

¹⁸ FOLK ART, CRAFTS, AND HOBBIES

Among folk art specialties from particular regions are paintings on glass by the Zakopane mountain folk; red sequined Cracow folk costumes; the black pottery of Kielce; lacework from Koniaków; rainbow-colored cloth from Łowicz; and paper cutouts from Kurpie. The small village of Zalipie is famous for the flower paintings on its wooden houses, wells, wagons, and chairs.

Highly decorated Easter eggs are a folk art that is still used in holiday celebrations. So are Christmas tree decorations, as well as traditional Christmas carols.

In 1948 the government initiated a company called Cepelia to buy Polish folk arts and crafts and sell both small souvenir items and more valuable goods in local stores and internationally. The selection is unusually tasteful, and the project has helped to keep folk art viable in a changing economy. The company continues to this day, making Polish craft items available to Poles, tourists, and on the world market.

¹⁹ SOCIAL PROBLEMS

Social tensions are caused by the disparity in income between the poor and the wealthy, exacerbated by the fact that under the Communist regime wealth was associated with corruption. Inequality increased sharply between 1990 and 1993; since then the class lines have hardened. Other problems include housing shortages and inadequacies in the health care system.

Lustration is a Polish term for vetting or background checking. Specifically it means making former Communist officials, and anyone who collaborated with the Communist-era secret police, ineligible for responsible jobs in government, education, and media. How far such people should be kept out of public life continues to be highly controversial, even two decades after the end of communism. The surviving secret police files can contain false information accusing someone of having been an agent. Courts have declared several lustration laws unconstitutional.

While there are few speakers of minority languages in Poland, there are also few protections for their rights. Roma in particular face discrimination and violence.

A new social problem has been dubbed "Euro-orphanhood." Now that Poland is part of the European Union, Poles can leave freely to take work in other European countries. Some leave spouses and children behind; such marriages may be heading for divorce. In some cases children are left behind with no parents, and grandparents, siblings or neighbors care for them.

²⁰ GENDER ISSUES

The advent of political democracy in Poland in 1989 actually reduced the rights of women. Previously, abortion had been readily available. With the influence of the Roman Catholic Church now dominant, an extremely restrictive law against abortion passed in 1993. In 1996 it was liberalized somewhat, then made somewhat more restrictive again in 1997. The present law allows abortion when the life or health of the woman is threatened, when the embryo is seriously and irreversibly damaged or incurably ill, or when the pregnancy is the result of an illegal act. However, practice has turned out to be more restrictive than the law, and many women whose pregnancies met the legal criteria have still been unable to get legal abortions. Most turn to illegal ones or, if they can afford it, go abroad. This is exacerbated by a complete lack of sex education and by expensive contraceptives.

In addition, the United Nations Human Rights Committee noted in 2004 that women are paid less than men for their work and rarely promoted to senior positions. There is now little in the way of subsidized child care to help women who work. Domestic violence is another problem, with little training of police and inadequate shelter resources.

The Polish government has begun to address such issues by appointing the Government Plenipotentiary on the Equal Status of Women and Men.

The UN report also noted lack of protection from discrimination based on sexual orientation.

²¹ BIBLIOGRAPHY

Benet, Sula. *Song, Dance and Customs of Peasant Poland.* London: Dennis Dobson, 1951.

Curtis, Glenn E. *Poland: A Country Study.* 3rd ed. Washington, D.C.: Federal Research Division, Library of Congress, 1994.

Heale, Jay. *Cultures of the World. Poland.* New York: Marshall Cavendish, 1994.

Meras, Phyllis. *Eastern Europe: A Traveler's Companion.* Boston: Houghton Mifflin, 1991.

Otfinoski, Steven. *Poland.* New York: Facts on File, 1995.

Poland, Republic of. Central Statistical Office. *Statistical Yearbook of the Republic of Poland 2007.* Warsaw: Statistical Publishing Establishment, 2007.

Polish Federation for Woman and Family Planning. http://www.federa.org.pl/english/english1.htm. (October 2008)

Shoemaker, M. Wesley. *Russia, Eurasian States and Eastern Europe 1993.* Washington, D.C.: Stryker-Post Publications, 1993.

Slomczynski, Kazimierz M., and Sandra T. Marquart-Pyatt (ed.). *Continuity and Change in Social Life: Structural and Psychological Adjustment in Poland.* Warsaw: IFiS Publishers, 2007.

Taras, Ray. "The End of the Walesa Era in Poland," *Current History,* March 1996, pp. 124–28.

—revised by T. Alt and W. Browne

PORTUGUESE

LOCATION: Portugal
POPULATION: 10.6 million (2007)
LANGUAGE: Portuguese
RELIGION: Roman Catholic; small Muslim, Jewish, and Protestant populations

¹ INTRODUCTION

Portugal is located in the southwestern portion of Europe. Due to colonization and emigration, there are Portuguese-speaking peoples living in North and South America, Asia, Africa, and Australia.

Portugal was among the first European nations to be unified into a single entity, gaining independence with the accession of Alfonse I in 1143. The Portuguese Age of Discovery began in the 15th century, marking the beginning of a vast overseas empire which expanded for over three centuries. Portugal's prosperity and influence declined after the loss of Brazil in 1822. In 1910 the monarchy was eliminated and a republic was declared, only to be replaced by the authoritarian rule of António Salazar in 1926. The Salazar regime was finally overthrown in 1974, a democratic government was established, and a new constitution was adopted in 1976. During this period Portugal granted independence to its remaining colonies, including Angola and Mozambique. In spite of continuing poverty, especially in rural areas, the nation has seen numerous advances, most notably the consolidation of the first successful democratic system of government in its history.

² LOCATION AND HOMELAND

Portugal occupies about one-fifth—and most of the western coast—of the Iberian Peninsula, bounded on the south and west by the Atlantic Ocean and on the north and east by Spain, its only neighbor. The two principal geographic areas are the mountainous interior *(meseta)* and the plain that lies along the Atlantic coast. Portugal's four major rivers are the Minho, Tagus, Guadiana, and Douro. North of the Tagus, the land reaches elevations of 396.2 m (1,300 ft) or more, while it is lower to the south.

Portugal's population of 10.6 million people is ethnically homogeneous, as the country had virtually no ethnic, tribal, racial, or cultural minorities for much of its history. There is a small Muslim population of guest workers from North Africa and small Jewish and Protestant communities composed mainly of foreigners. There may also as many as 100,000 Roma, mostly in the Algarve region. About 200,000 immigrants are from Eastern Europe.

³ LANGUAGE

The official languages are Portuguese and Mirandese. Portuguese is a Romance language that is most closely related to the Spanish dialect Galician. Over time it was modified by the Mozarabic language of the Muslim Moors living in lands taken over by Portugal. Mirandese is also a Romance language most common in Mirando do Douro in northeast Portugal. Mirandese has been given official status for local use.

COMMON WORDS AND PHRASES IN PORTUGUESE

Good morning	bom dia
Good afternoon	boa tarde
Good evening	boa noite
Yes	sim
No	não
Please	por favor
Thank you	men say obrigado; women say obrigada
Goodbye	adeus

⁴ FOLKLORE

The Portuguese are a deeply superstitious people whose formal Catholicism is profoundly intertwined with pre-Christian lore and beliefs. Votive offerings to saints—intended to promote healing—hang on strings near many church altars, with images depicting whatever is to be (or has been) healed, including hands, heads, breasts, babies, and animals. Popular superstitions involve the phases of the moon, the healing power of fountains, and the evil eye, which is feared in a number of situations. Ceremonies surrounding death and the occult abound. Portuguese widows are expected to wear black for about seven years and many wear it for the rest of their lives. The loss of a parent is mourned for up to three years.

⁵ RELIGION

The overwhelming majority of Portuguese (85%) are Roman Catholics and Catholicism is at the center of Portuguese life. Although church and state were formally separated in the 1976 constitution, Portugal's holidays, its moral and legal codes, health and educational systems, and even many aspects of the national character are intertwined with its Catholic heritage. By a special arrangement between the Church and the government, Roman Catholic citizens may designate that 0.5% of their income tax be allocated to the Catholic Church. While only about a third of the population attends church regularly, almost all Portuguese are baptized and married within the church and receive its last rites when they die. Religious observance is greater in the northern part of the country than in the south.

Churches occupy a prominent physical location in almost every Portuguese village. However, many religious folk practices and beliefs are centered outside the church itself. Many Portuguese make pilgrimages *(romarias)* to religious shrines, of which the most famous is the one at Fátima where the Virgin Mary is said to have appeared before three children in 1917. The cult of the Virgin is very powerful in Portugal, and images of Mary and Christ are commonly seen even in such secular places as labor union offices. While the Virgin is the most popular religious mediator, belief in personal intercession by a variety of saints is also widespread, accompanied by direct offerings of gifts as well as alms for the poor.

Portuguese folk religion also contains elements of witchcraft, sorcery, and superstition, which are intertwined with Catholicism in the popular imagination, although frowned on by the church. In general, however, Catholicism in Portugal has the character of a benign and humanizing force: whereas saints and martyrs are depicted with agonized expressions in Spain, in Portugal their pictures are calm and peaceful.

6 MAJOR HOLIDAYS

Most holidays celebrated in Portugal are those of the Roman Catholic calendar. Those with the status of national holidays are Shrove Tuesday, Good Friday, Corpus Christi, All Saints' Day (November 1), the Immaculate Conception (December 8), and Christmas. Secular holidays include New Year's Day; Liberty Day (April 25), which commemorates the death of the national poet, Luiz Vaz de Camões, in 1580; Portugal Day (June 10), which celebrates the 1974 Revolution; Proclamation of the Republic Day (October 5), celebrating the founding of the Republic in 1910; and Restoration of Independence Day (December 1).

In rural areas, villagers honor their patron saint during the annual *festa,* a celebration that is both religious and secular. There is a procession, and people fulfill their religious vows *(promessas)* for the occasion. The festivities may last several days and often include such secular elements as picnics, dancing, fireworks, and bullfights.

7 RITES OF PASSAGE

Portugal is a modern, industrialized, Christian country. Hence, many of the rites of passage that young people undergo are religious rituals, such as baptism, first communion, confirmation, and marriage. In addition, a student's progress through the education system is marked by many families with graduation parties.

8 INTERPERSONAL RELATIONS

When the Portuguese greet each other, they generally expect to be kissed on both cheeks. Those who live in the northern part of the country, which has historically been isolated from foreign influences, are formal, conservative, and reserved among strangers, while attitudes in the south are generally more casual, relaxed, and friendly. In the north, many people are referred to by nicknames *(alcunhas),* which are an important part of their identities.

9 LIVING CONDITIONS

Over 60% of the Portuguese own their own homes. However, according to a 2001 census, over 70% of all families lived in substandard housing. Rural villagers often live without electricity or running water. Migration to the cities intensified an already existing shortage of urban housing, resulting in the growth of shantytowns *(bairros da lata)* with substandard housing that often lacks sewage systems. Government housing programs have not been able to keep up with the demand for adequate housing.

Almost all sectors of Portuguese society have access to modern medical care. Portugal's national health service was inaugurated in 1979. While infant mortality rates were cut nearly in half between the mid-1970s and mid-1980s, the government program is still insufficient to meet the nation's health care needs and it is supplemented by church-supported services. While home birth was common as recently as the 1960s, as of 2008 almost all Portuguese women had their babies in hospitals. Life expectancy in 2008 was estimated at about 78 years (75 for men and 82 for women).

Bus service links all Portuguese cities, towns, and principal villages. Most road travel is on paved but winding roads. There are few highways, and many back roads are inaccessi-

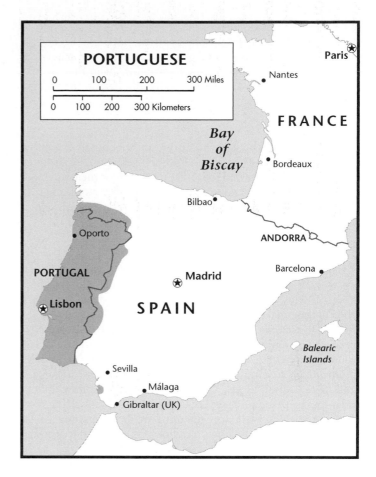

ble to traffic. Like the roads, the state-owned rail system runs mainly north/south, branching eastward into Spain in places. The main ports are Lisbon, Setubal, and Porto.

10 FAMILY LIFE

While the patriarchal nuclear family is the cultural ideal throughout Portugal, actual family dynamics vary considerably according to class and region. Middle- and upper-class Portuguese and those in the southern part of the country are more likely to adhere to the patriarchal model, with women staying home to raise children and to run the household while men engage in business or the professions. Among the peasantry, especially in the northwest, the relationship between marriage partners is a more equal one. Households are headed jointly by the husband and wife, referred to as *o patrão* and *a patroa.* In farming families, women may work the fields alongside their husbands; fishermen's wives may help repair nets or sell the day's catch. Due to high rates of male emigration, a relatively large number of women in the north never marry and many have traditionally managed their own farms, remaining financially independent, as women in Portugal can both inherit and bestow property.

Much political and economic influence in Portugal is wielded through networks of extended family, in what is essentially a system of patronage. Many marriages are still determined by what kinds of advantages—in terms of land, property, or prestige—will result for the families of the bride and groom. Especially among the country's elite, it is considered important to have kinship connections in the government and the political parties. Low-income groups, by contrast, have few ties outside the nuclear family. Among all groups, the relationship between children and their godparents *(padrinhos)*—who may or may not be actual relatives—is especially important throughout one's lifetime.

11 CLOTHING

Western-style clothing is the norm, and people in the cities, especially Lisbon, dress well. However, vestiges of traditional garb—such as berets and loose-fitting shirts for men and black shawls for women—may still be seen in some rural areas, in addition to the *capucha,* a hooded cape, and the *patocas,* a rain cape of reeds.

12 FOOD

Fish is the main staple of the Portuguese diet. Cod *(bacalhau)* is universally popular—the average person in Portugal eats about 45 kg (100 lbs) of it every year. Over the years, dried and salted cod, nicknamed *o fiel amigo*—faithful friend—has saved the lives of thousands of poverty-stricken Portuguese. *Bacalhau* is prepared so many different ways in Portugal that there is said to be a different recipe for every day of the year. Other commonly eaten seafoods include sardines, salmon, sole, sea bass, and hake, as well as eel, squid, octopus, and lamprey. Practically every Portuguese meal is accompanied by soup. The most popular is *caldo verde* (green soup), made with *couve galega* (Galician cabbage), sausage, potatoes, and olive oil. Another popular soup is *sopa alentejana,* simmered with bread, garlic (another staple of the Portuguese diet), and other ingredients. *Caldeirada,* a fish stew, is another popular national dish.

Portugal's varieties of succulent fruit, which vary regionally, provide some of its best desserts, including peaches, strawberries, oranges, figs, plums, pineapples, and passionfruit. Of the sweet dessert offerings, the most common is *arroz doce,* a cinnamon-flavored rice pudding. Flan, a custard with caramel topping, also graces most dessert menus.

13 EDUCATION

Although education is free and compulsory to the age of 15, traditionally some children drop out after primary school to begin working. Enrollment and completion rates have been increasing since the 1990s. In 2006 primary school enrolment was at 98% for all children, while secondary school enrollment was at about 86% for girls and 78% for boys. Secondary education is completed either at state-run high schools or at a choice of technical and professional institutes. The twelfth grade (at age 18) consists of preparatory study for university or technical college. Portugal's main universities are located in Lisbon, Porto, Aveiro, Coimbra, and Braga. There is also a government-supported adult education program, as well as hundreds of private schools, most supported by the Catholic Church.

14 CULTURAL HERITAGE

Portugal's most famous poet was Luiz Vaz de Camões (1524–1580), who wrote during Portugal's Age of Discovery and was also an explorer himself. His epic poem, *Os Lusiadas (The Lusiads),* is based on the life of Vasco da Gama. Gil Vicente, the "father of Portuguese theater," is known for *autos* (religious dramas) and farces. In modern times, Fernando Pessoa (1888–1935) has been acclaimed for his poetry. Freedom of expression has thrived in the period since the 1974 Revolution, which has seen the publication of formerly censored works as well as new ones by women writers such as novelist Olga Goncalves and Portuguese-Africans, including Angolan Jose Luandino Viera.

The Age of Discovery also produced the Manueline style in architecture, which expressed the national passion for exploration and the sea through flamboyant ornamentation with marine motifs, such as mariners' knots. Famous examples of this style include the Tomar and Batalha convents. Also unique to Portugal are the decorative tiles known as *azulejos.* Adopted from Spain, they were modified by the Portuguese, who added a variety of colors, most notably the blue, or azure *(azul),* from which they get their name.

In music, Portugal is known for its *fado* songs, the plaintive popular art form said to reflect the fatalistic Portuguese spirit of melancholy and nostalgia known as *saudade.* Performers of *fado* (which, roughly translated, means "fate") are known as *fadistas.*

15 WORK

Portuguese workers are known for being adaptable, hard working, and frugal. Industry employs about a third of the country's labor force, while nearly 60% work in service jobs, a figure partially accounted for by the rapid growth in civil service employment since 1974. Employment varies by region. The main occupation in the Azores and Madeira is agriculture. Madeira's embroidery industry employs about 70,000 women. In the south, the people of the Algarve find employment in agriculture, fishing, and the tourist industry. Fishing predominates in the coastal villages and cash-crop agriculture (wheat, corn, rice) in the Alentejo. Heavy industry, including steel working, shipbuilding, and iron production, is concentrated in the Lisbon-Setubal region to the south. Other occupations include forestry, furniture making, food processing, winemaking, and pulp and paper production. In 2005 the minimum monthly salary was about $450. In 2007 the unemployment rate was 8%.

16 SPORTS

Soccer ("football") is the foremost sport in Portugal, as in much of Europe. Golf has grown increasingly popular, and the country now boasts more than 20 world-class golf courses. Tennis is widely played as well and auto racing becomes the focus of attention during the annual Grand Prix of Portugal held in September.

17 ENTERTAINMENT AND RECREATION

One of the most popular recreational activities in Portugal is bullfighting *(Tourada),* with *cavaleiros* dressed in 18th-century costumes that include tricornered hats, silk jackets, and riding breeches. In contrast to the violent bullfights in Spain and parts of Latin America, in Portugal the bull's horns are sheathed to avoid injuries, and bulls are not killed at the end of the event. Another well-known national pastime is dancing; the fandango and other popular folk dances are enjoyed throughout the country. Other forms of recreation include horseback riding, fishing, hunting, skiing, and water sports.

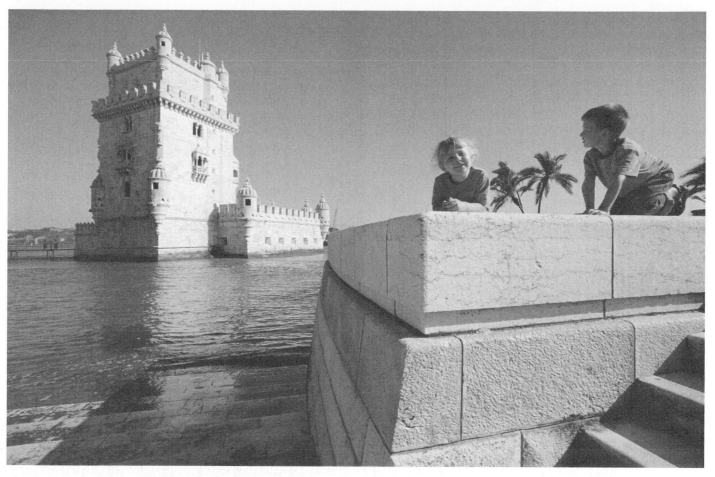

Children play near Torre de Belem in Lisbon, Portugal. (© John and Lisa Merrill/Corbis)

18 FOLK ART, CRAFTS, AND HOBBIES

Traditional craft industries can be found throughout Portugal. The people of Arraiolas in the south are renowned for their rug making, while fine embroidery is associated with Guimares, black pottery with Vila Real, and basket weaving with the Algarve. Characteristic folk art is also seen on floats carried in religious pageants.

19 SOCIAL PROBLEMS

Violent crime is rare in Portugal; murders generally occur in the context of personal conflicts rather than during the commission of other crimes, such as robbery. Emigration has served as a release for social tensions and discontent, helping to keep the crime rate low.

Poverty is a primary concern in Portugal. In 2006 about 18% of the population was below the poverty level. In 2006 unemployment was at about 8% of the labor force and minimum wages were not generally considered to be sufficient to support a family. Many families live in substandard housing. Approximately 30% of all youth drop out of school before completing high school, often for the purpose of seeking employment to help their families.

Portugal has a problem with illicit drug use. In facing such a challenge, the government passed a law in 2001 that essentially decriminalized the personal use and possession of many illicit drugs, including heroin and marijuana. Under the new law, those found to be in possession of small amounts of drugs are not sent to prison but are referred to a panel consisting of a psychologist, a social worker, and a legal adviser who question the individual and decide upon sentences that include mandatory counseling or treatment, fines, and in some cases community service. While many have criticized the new approach, the government maintains that the move toward treatment instead of punishment should have a positive effect in the long run. Drug sales and trafficking are still considered criminal offenses.

20 GENDER ISSUES

The position of women in Portugal improved greatly after the ouster of the military dictatorship in 1974 and the drafting of the 1976 constitution, which guaranteed women full legal equality. By the early 2000s, women accounted for 55% of all persons enrolled in higher education. In 2007 women made up about 62% of the work force; however, the average salary for women was estimated to be about 23% lower than that of men. A 2004 study estimated that one in three women in the work force have experienced sexual harassment on the job. While sexual harassment is considered to be a crime, most cases are not reported by women who fear losing their jobs. Pregnant women and new mothers have faced discrimination in the work force.

Violence against women, particularly domestic violence, has been a cause for concern. The government has issued a number of laws against rape and domestic violence and generally enforces the laws with strict penalties. Unfortunately, many women do not report incidents of violence and only about 10% of all domestic violence cases are ever brought to trial. A majority of cases are mediated by lawyers outside of the court system.

[21] BIBLIOGRAPHY

Ballard, Sam, and Jane Ballard. *Pousadas of Portugal.* Boston: The Harvard Common Press, 1986.

Bennett, A. Linda, ed. *Encyclopedia of World Cultures (Europe).* Boston: G. K. Hall, 1992.

Birmingham. David. *A Concise History of Portugal,* 2nd ed. Cambridge: Cambridge University Press, 2003.

Gall, Timothy, and Susan Gall, ed. *Junior Worldmark Encyclopedia of the Nations.* Detroit: UXL, 1996.

Hubbard, Monica M., and Beverly Baer, ed. *Cities of the World: Europe and the Middle East.* Detroit: Gale Research, 1993.

Illustrated Encyclopedia of Mankind. London: Marshall Cavendish, 1978.

Moss, Joyce, and George Wilson. *Peoples of the World: Western Europeans.* Detroit: Gale Research, 1993.

Ortiz-Griffin, Julia L. and William D. Griffin. *Spain and Portugal Today.* New York: Peter Lang, 2003.

Porter, Darwin. *Frommer's Comprehensive Travel Guide (Portugal'94–'95).* New York: Prentice Hall Travel, 1994.

Solsten, Eric. *Portugal: A Country Study.* Washington, DC: U.S. Government Printing Office, 1994.

Stone, Glyn A. *Spain, Portugal and the Great Powers, 1931–1941.* New York: Palgrave Macmillan, 2005.

—revised by K. Ellicott

ROMA

ALTERNATE NAMES: Self-ascriptive names: Roma, Rom, Romanichals, Cales, Kaale, Kawle, Sinti/Manouches. Also known as Gypsies.
LOCATION: Dispersed population in Europe; parts of Asia, North, Central and South America, Australia, New Zealand, North and South Africa, the Middle East, and elsewhere.
POPULATION: 12–15 million (estimate)
LANGUAGE: Romani dialects; also the language of the host country
RELIGION: An underlay of Hinduism with an overlay of either Christianity or Islam (host country religion)

[1] INTRODUCTION

The Roma people originated in India. By the 11th century AD they were located in the area called Gurjara, in what was then the Rajput Confederacy. The Rajputs were a group of clans. Each had its own ruler, a caste of military landowners, and a population belonging to the lower castes, composed of animal drovers, artisans, entertainers, blacksmiths, weapon smiths, and persons in other modest but necessary occupations. Among these supportive castes was a group called *Dom,* who belonged to the aboriginal peoples of India but had adopted the Hindu religion and an Indo-Aryan language derived from Sanskrit. Some groups of *Dom* were nomadic entertainers and artisans. The Hindus defined the word *Dom* as a lower-caste person who did jobs forbidden to higher-caste Hindus; however, to the *Dom* themselves, the word simply meant "man" and, in the plural, "the men," or "the people."

In the 10th century, a Muslim kingdom arose in what is now Afghanistan, with its capital at Ghasni. This was called the Ghaznavid Empire, and in 1017, its ruler, Mahmud Ghazni, launched a series of massive raids into India. He and successive rulers entered India, plundering and massacring the people, carrying off thousands of slaves, and laying waste to the countryside. The Rajputs contested these raids, and many battles took place, during which groups of people were displaced or forced to move out of desolated areas. At some point during the 11th century, the ancestors of the Roma made their way into the Upper Indus Valley from Gurjara and spent some time in this region, whose inhabitants spoke Dardic languages, which had an effect on their own.

The ancestors of the Roma then left India via the Shandur or Baroghil pass and entered Xinjiang in northwestern China. From there they followed the Silk Road, which led them to ancient Persia, then through Southern Georgia to an Armenian-speaking region around the city of Trebizond, and finally to the Byzantine Empire, borrowing words from these linguistic regions as they slowly migrated over many generations. From Constantinople (now Istanbul) they traveled up the Balkans and reached the Romanian Principalities of Wallachia and Moldavia by at least the 14th century. Some groups remained in the Balkans below Romania but many moved through Romania, traveling both west and east. By the end of the 15th century, Roma could be found as far west as the British Isles and Spain and as far east as Poland and Lithuania.

ROMA

At some point during their migration from India, scholars believe, their original name, *Dom,* or *Domba* in the plural, was altered phonetically to *Rom* (singular) and *Roma* (plural), while the caste structure of the group gradually disintegrated until they intermingled and became one people culturally.

Millions of Roma now live in the post-communist countries of Central and Eastern Europe. The post-World War II communist governments of countries, such as Hungary, Romania, and Bulgaria, attempted to assimilate their Roma populations into economic and ethnic mainstreams. These efforts were, for the most part, unsuccessful. The political and economic turmoil that followed the fall of communism has harmed the position of millions of Roma in Eastern and Central European countries. Roma in Slovakia have faced forced residential segregation. Roma communities in Kosovo and other territories of the former Yugoslavia have faced ethnic cleansing from majority communities. In other countries, such as Bulgaria and Romania, Roma have been turned into scapegoats for the economic ills of the post-communist transition. The recent accession of many Central and Eastern European countries to the European Union has brought a new focus to issues of inclusion and human rights for European Roma communities.

² LOCATION AND HOMELAND

Since the 15th century, Roma have been a dispersed ethnic population in Europe. Roma in the Romanian-speaking principalities, later including Transylvania, were enslaved. These Roma are known as Vlach Roma (the "ch" in Vlach is pronounced as *k*). After their emancipation in 1864, large numbers promptly departed and made their way into Central and Western Europe and the Balkans, eventually reaching North, Central, and South America by the 1890s. Today, they are the most numerous and most widespread group of Roma. In Western Europe, because of persecution in most countries, Roma were forced to become highly mobile nomadic groups, giving rise to the tradition in popular literature of the semi-mythological, footloose, vagabond "Gypsy." In Spain, Roma were forcibly settled and their language and culture destroyed, surviving only in Flamenco music and in the Calo dialect. In Eastern Europe and the Balkans, Roma were tolerated but were considered to be outcasts at the bottom of the social ladder.

By now Roma from many groups have migrated from Europe into the Americas, Australia, New Zealand, North and South Africa, and elsewhere. They assume the nationality of their host countries and consider themselves American Roma, Canadian Roma, Australian Roma, or South African Roma, depending on where they live. In the past, the colonial powers deported or transported Roma to their colonies in Africa, the West Indies, the Americas, and Australia, while Portugal even sent some to its colony in Goa, India, where they found people speaking a language closely related to their own. Since the fall of communism, hundreds of thousands of Roma have migrated from Central and Eastern Europe to Western European countries, such as France and Italy.

Accurately estimating the number of Roma is a difficult task, because official censuses often undercount Roma communities. Turkey is home to about 2 million Roma, making it the country with the largest Roma population. Current estimates put the number of Roma in Europe at approximately 10 million, making the ethnic group the largest minority in Europe. Of these 10 million, 1.8–2.5 million live in Romania, 600,000–800,000 live in Bulgaria, 500,000–1 million live in Hungary, 480,000–520,000 live in Slovakia, and 250,000–300,000 live in the Czech Republic. In Western Europe, France and Spain have the largest Roma communities. The French Roma population numbers between 500,000 and 1.2 million, while the Spain's Roma population is estimated to be about 700,000. The countries of the former Yugoslavia are home to over 750,000 Roma. The United States is home to approximately 1 million Roma.

³ LANGUAGE

The original language (proto Romani) spoken by the Roma when they arrived in Europe has evolved into numerous dialects. The speakers normally refer to the language as *Romani*, *Romani chib* (Romani language), or by the adverb *Romanes*, which means "like a Roma"; thus, they say *Vakiarel Romanes*, he speaks like a Roma (i.e. speaks Romani). The Romani dialects of some splinter groups have different names, such as Romnimus (in Wales), Kaale (in Finland), or Calo (in Spain). Most Romani speakers speak what is called inflected Romani, which has its own unique grammar, as opposed to adopting the grammar of the country in which they live. As an example, note the following comparative sentences:

ENGLISH
I am going into the village to buy a horse from the non-Roma man.
Inflected Romani
Jav ando gav te kinav grast katar o gadjo. (These are all words of Sanskrit/Indian origin)

ENGLISH ROMANI
I'm jall in' into the gav to kin a grai from the gorjo.

SPANISH ROMANI
Voy en el gao para quinelar un gras del gacho.

In the English and Spanish versions, the Romani grammar has disappeared and been replaced by the grammatical structure of English and Spanish, into which the original Romani vocabulary has been inserted. (How this happened is not clear and is disputed by scholars.) The inflected Romani example could belong to many different dialects, while the English and Spanish versions would be understood only by other people who spoke the same dialect.

While English makes use of prepositions, such as *with*, *from*, *to*, etc., inflected Romani dialects replace these by varying the endings of the words themselves (referred to as post-

positions). Below are examples of the inflection of the word *manush* (man).

Nominative	The man is coming	*O manush avel*
Accusative	I see the man	*Dikav le manushes*
Instrumental	I went with the man	*Gelem le manushesa*
Ablative	I heard from the man	*Ashundem le manushestar*
Genitive	It's the man's	*Le manushesko si*
Dative	I did it for the man	*Kerdem le manusheska*
Vocative	Listen, man!	*Ashun, manusha!*

There are only two genders in inflected Romani. Male persons and animals are masculine, female persons and animals are feminine, and inanimate objects are either masculine or feminine. A chair is feminine, while the house is masculine in Vlach Romani. As commonly spoken, Romani uses many idiomatic expressions, proverbs, and sayings, often with metaphorical qualities. For example, "He is retiring" in English would be expressed in Romani as: *Beshel lesko kam* (His sun is setting). This makes it difficult to write dictionaries of Romani with word-for-word equivalents, leading to the erroneous belief that Romani is not a complete language. For example, there is no verb for *to think*. All dialects employ a word borrowed from another language. However, in Romani itself, "What are you thinking?" is expressed as *So si tut ando shoro*, which means "What do you have in your head?"

Romani employs an English alphabet except for the letter *x* (pronounced like the Spanish *jota*) and *zh* (as in *azure*).

Roma in Christian countries usually take Christian names like those of the people around them, such as Milano, Yanko, or Zlatcho for men, and Mara, Tinka, or Pavlena for women. The last name is the genitive inflexion of the father's Christian name. Thus, a name is *O Milano le Yankosko*—the Milano, son of Yanko (Yanko's Milano), or *E Mara le Zlatchoski*—the Mary, daughter of Zlatcho (Zlatcho's Mary). When Vlach Roma meet they ask each other, *Kasko san tu*—"Whose son are you?" The Vlach Roma have no surnames. Other groups adopt last names similar to those of the people among whom they live. The Vlach Roma also do this for identity papers, driver's licenses, and other documents, but do not use these names among themselves. Many of these "non-official" Roma names are quite colorful. It is possible to find Roma named after famous politicians or celebrities from the entertainment industry. Some Roma names are also derived from distinguishing physical characteristics of the name's owner.

⁴ FOLKLORE

Roma have a rich folklore, which is contained in the *paramichia,* or folktales and legends. Stories would be told around the campfires at night while the adults, teenagers, and children sat around listening to their elders recite them. They later passed them on to the next generation. Like most other groups, the Roma have their ethnic hero. Among the Vlach Roma this is Mundro Salamon or Wise Solomon. Other Roma groups call this hero O Godjiaver Yanko. Among the Wels Kawle, he is Merlinos (the Wizard), taken from Celtic folklore. Essentially, Mundro Salamon is the archetypal wise man who uses his mental powers and cunning to escape from those who would harm him or to save others from danger. Since the Roma always lived in small groups surrounded by strangers who outnumbered them and had the law on their side, they were unable to resort to force of arms to defend themselves. Their defense mechanisms were wisdom and "the smarts," which Mundro Salamon exhibits to the "nth degree."

A typical Mundro Salamon story runs as follows: One day Mundro Salamon learned that the Martya, or Angel of Death, was about to come and claim the soul of the village miller who was his friend. He went to the Martya and asked her to spare the miller's life because he had small children to support and the people of the village needed him to grind their corn. She refused, so Mundro Salamon tricked her. "How could you take his soul," he asked her, "if he locked himself in a room?" "I would simply dissolve into smoke and slip under the door," she told him. "Rubbish," Salamon replied. "You mean you could slip inside this peashooter I am whittling for the miller's son?" To prove it, the Martya dissolved into smoke and entered the peashooter. Salamon then plugged both ends of the peashooter, trapping the Martya inside. He locked the peashooter inside a metal box, rowed out to the sea in a boat, and dumped the box over the side. For seven years nobody died, until one day two fishermen casting their nets caught the metal box and retrieved it. They smashed it open, found the peashooter, and unplugged it, allowing the Martya to escape.

Now she began to search for Salamon to get her revenge. But Salamon had anticipated she might escape and had taken precautions. He had shod his horse backwards so that the prints of the horseshoes led the Martya to look for seven years in the wrong direction. She then realized her blunder and spent another seven years looking in the right direction. She finally found Salamon, now an elderly man. "Now I'm going to make you suffer," she told him. "For seven years I will freeze you in ice. Then, for another seven years I will roast you in fire. Then, for seven years I will turn you into rotten pulpwood and you will be nibbled on by maggots. Only after this will I put you out of your misery and take your soul." "Rubbish," Salamon said mockingly. "How can you take my soul? You don't have the power. You're bluffing me." "I'll show you," the Martya screamed, and blew three times on his face. Salamon died smiling. He had outwitted the Martya even in death!

Roma folklore often impacts the daily lives of ordinary Roma in very significant ways. For example, many Roma believe that diseases are caused by evil spirits (Hungarian Roma refer to these spirits as *beng*, or *bizuze*). According to some Roma traditions, these sprits can take the forms of a shepherd, a dog, a rabbit, or some other animal or human form.

5 RELIGION

As Roma tend to adhere to the religion of the country in which they reside, the vast majority of Roma are Christian. Roma in the United States tend to be either Protestant or Catholic Christians. In Europe, the majority of Roma are Catholic, although large numbers of Orthodox Roma live in Bulgaria, Greece, Ukraine and elsewhere. About 10–15% of the world's Roma are Muslim. Most Muslim Roma live in Turkey, Bulgaria, and Albania. Evangelical Christianity is growing rapidly amongst Orthodox and Catholic Roma, as it allows for more accommodation of traditional Roma beliefs and practices.

Traditional Roma religious beliefs are rooted in Hinduism. Roma believe in a universal balance, called *kuntari*. Everything must have its natural place: birds fly and fish swim. Thus, hens, which do not fly, are considered to be out of balance (and

therefore bad luck), as are frogs, which can go into the water and also walk on land. For this reason, many Roma will not eat hens' eggs and are afraid of frogs. The Roma also believe it is possible to become polluted in a variety of ways, including breaking taboos involving the upper and lower halves of the body. A Roma who becomes polluted is considered out of balance and must be restored to purity through a trial before the Roma tribunal of elders (called *Kris Romani* among the Vlach Roma). If declared guilty, he is usually given a period of isolation away from other Roma and then reinstated after a specified time. In severe cases of pollution, a Roma can be outlawed from the group forever, but this is rare today. Children are exempt from these rules and from pollution taboos until they reach puberty.

The surrounding host-culture religions are used for ceremonies like baptisms or funerals for which the Roma need a formal religious institution. Except for the elders who are the spiritual leaders, there are no Roma priests, churches, or Bibles except among the Pentecostal Roma, who are a growing minority. Despite a 1,000-year separation from India, Roma still practice shaktism, the worship of a god through his female consort. Thus, while most Roma worship the Christian God, they pray to Him through the Virgin Mary or St. Ann, his female consorts, just as they once prayed to one of the Hindu gods through his consort *Sat-Sara,* or *Kali/Durga/Sara.* In France, there is a shrine at the village of Les Saintes Maries de la Mer in the Camargue. Tradition says that the Virgin Mary, Mary Magdalene, and Mary Jacobee landed there after the death of Jesus, having come from Palestine in a small boat with their Egyptian servant, Sara. The three Marys then preached the Gospel among the local people and converted them to Christianity. Every year, in May, large numbers of Roma from Spain, France, and other European countries take part in a pilgrimage to the shrine, where they pay homage, not to the three Marys but to the servant girl, Sara, who does not exist as an official saint in the Catholic Church. In Romani Saint Sara is called *Sara E Kali* and identified with the *Kali/Durga/Sara* of Hinduism. In France the Roma carry a statue of Saint Sara on a large platform into the nearby Mediterranean Sea.

In Canada, at Sainte Anne de Beaupré in Québec, there is a shrine where Roma of the Vlach Roma group make annual pilgrimages late in July during the Novena. The Roma women offer flowers and rice cakes to the statue of Saint Anne, the men prepare a feast table with a roasted lamb, and the Roma celebrate Saint Anne, whose statue appears on the feast table. The ceremonies the Roma perform differ radically from those of non-Roma Catholics, who also attend in large numbers.

6 MAJOR HOLIDAYS

Roma in different countries celebrate different holidays, and different holidays are observed by different groups of Roma as well. The Vlach Roma and many other groups celebrate Christmas, Easter, and All Saints' Day. They have no specific Roma holidays except in Romania, where there are holidays commemorating the emancipation of Roma slaves. In Muslim countries Roma often observe Muslim religious holidays. In some countries Roma take part in the national holidays and play an integral part in religious festivals. In Canada and the United States some families travel to Sainte Anne de Beaupré for the annual pilgrimage just to see friends and relatives and to socialize. Others do the same thing in Europe at Les Saintes

Maries de la Mer. Here they can celebrate their group culture, playing music, dancing, singing, and socializing. It also gives the teenagers a chance to meet other young people from different groups and sometimes meet someone they want to marry.

Christmas and Easter among the Vlach Roma are always celebrated by feasts. The head of each extended family will prepare a lavish table and invite all the Roma in the community. Sometimes family heads will get together and pool their resources to hold one large feast for the entire community. There will be music, dancing, singing and socializing. At Easter, each family will dye Easter eggs a special color and place them in a large bowl. These are given, one each, to every guest. There is also a ceremony called *chognimos,* or egg-whipping, where the visitor or guest will bring one of his own eggs and hold it in the palm of his hand. The host will do the same, and they will slap their palms together, usually cracking or crushing both eggs. This is believed to bring *baxt,* or good karma. Many Balkan Roma also celebrate St. George's Day, which they call *Ederlezi.* The holiday celebrates the spring season and is usually observed with feasts and picnics. Some Roma believe that wishes come true on the night of *Ederlezi.* Many also believe that *Ederlezi* is a time when people receive cures for their ailments and good luck.

7 RITES OF PASSAGE

Birth is a happy event among the Roma. They believe in fecundity, and large families are the norm. When the baby is born, the mother and her baby are considered agents of pollution and are separated from the rest of the household and from other Roma for a predetermined period, which varies among clans and groups. Once this period is over, godparents are selected from the Roma community. They take the baby to a church for the actual baptism ceremony. They also give the baby a small gold cross. When the godparents return with the baptized baby there is a feast called *bolimos.*

Children are pampered and protected by the Roma. When they reach puberty, they become *shave* (boys) and *sheya* (girls) and are initiated into the world of adults. Boys are taught to drive and to work with their adult male family members at the family trade. Girls are instructed by female adults in women's work and strictly chaperoned when they go to movies or shopping. Teenagers enter adulthood when they marry, which is generally at 15 or 16 for girls and from 16 to 18 for boys. The young married person becomes a *Rom* (male adult Roma) or a *Romni* (female adult Roma). The bride, or *bori,* must serve a period of apprenticeship in the home of her in-laws until the mother-in-law is satisfied that she is following the laws of respect and pollution to the family's satisfaction.

When adults become middle aged, they graduate to the ranks of the elders: men become spiritual leaders of the community and sit as judges on the tribunal of elders. Women, once they pass through menopause, can no longer pollute men and are then "sanctified" among the Vlach Roma. They too become spiritual elders who advise the younger women. Some gain a reputation for white magic and herbal remedies.

Death among the Roma is a serious affair. There is a one-year mourning period called *pomana,* with feasts for the dead at 3, 6, 9, and 12 months, as well as the actual funeral feast. Deceased Roma join the ranks of the ancestral dead who watch over the actions of the living and are called as witnesses at solemn events like the swearing of oaths at the tribunal of elders, where they are assumed to be spiritually present and able to send a *prekaza,* or jinx, to any Roma who perjures himself. Roma do not discuss their dead. They say simply *Mek les le Devleste*—"Leave him to God to be judged."

Roma traditions have proven remarkably durable. They have survived repeated cultural assimilation campaigns in many of the countries in which Roma live. Furthermore, the phenomenon of Roma conversion to Evangelical Christianity has done little to change the traditional rites of passage of the Roma.

8 INTERPERSONAL RELATIONS

Roma greetings are respectful. When a guest arrives, the host will say "Welcome! God has sent you!" The guest or guests must also be served food and drink. Not to do so would be a sign of disrespect. The usual greeting is a handshake, although Roma men often embrace relatives and close friends and kiss them on the cheek. Women also embrace and kiss when they meet. The guest or guests must be shown the utmost in politeness, served food on clean dishes, and offered whatever they might require. Family members and friends are usually received more casually than adults from another clan or an unrelated family group. When such people visit, the host will often provide entertainment and ask his sons to play music and his eldest daughter to dance. Women must appear modestly dressed before guests and at group gatherings. Roma girls do not go on dates and must be chaperoned outside the home. Boys have more freedom and are allowed to go to dances and socialize with non-Roma teenagers.

Roma body language varies in different countries but most Roma are very expressive and impulsive. They make use of gestures, use their hands when talking, wink, snap their fingers, and indulge in mimicry. When talking about somebody else, they will imitate his or her voice or mannerisms. Among the Vlach Roma, behavior toward other members of the group, including the beliefs that govern taboos, is codified in the *Romaniya.* Whereas most modern cultures have two concepts of cleanliness (clean and dirty), the Roma have three: *wuzho,* or clean; *melalo,* dirty with honest dirt; and *marime,* which means polluted or defiled among the Vlach Roma (other groups use different words). Where Westerners regard a person who showers twice a day, even if he is a plumber, as clean, a Roma man who worked as a plumber would be defiled or polluted no matter how many showers he took, while a man who sold horses for a living might not take any showers but would be considered unpolluted. While non-Roma are concerned with visible dirt, Roma are concerned with invisible pollution.

Another central belief regarding cleanliness involves the upper and lower halves of the body. Roma do not take baths but shower standing up, since the lower part of the body is considered an agent of pollution. The body above the waist is considered clean, and the head is the cleanest and purest area of all. Clothing worn above the waist must be washed separately from clothing worn below the waist (also, men's clothing cannot be washed with women's clothing). This demarcation between the halves of the body accounts for another Roma custom that often amazes outsiders. Since the female breast is above the waist, it is not seen as a sex object. Many Vlach Roma women carry money, cigarettes, and lighters in their brassieres. It is not unusual for the husband to reach over and help himself to a pack of cigarettes and lighter concealed in his wife's low-cut blouse. Women's legs, however, can only be visible below the knees, hence the traditional long skirts of Roma women.

Sometimes a Vlach Rom man will experience a string of *bibaxt,* or bad luck, and will assume that he has inadvertently done something that has placed him out of balance. Believing that God is punishing him, he will throw a lavish feast, or *slava,* to some saint, usually Saint Mary or Saint Ann or, among some groups, Saint George. He will rent a hall and prepare a long table, inviting all the local Roma in the town or in his *kumpaniya* (an economic unit of Roma occupying a specific geographical area). He hopes that the saint he honors with his feast will intercede with God to change his bad karma (*bibaxt*) and remove the *prekaza,* or jinx, from him, and provide him with good karma (*baxt*). This belief in *baxt* is fundamental to most Roma groups. One gets *baxt* by being in balance and one stays in balance by following the *Romaniya* (cultural taboos) and adhering to the *potchiyaimos Romano* (Roma code of respect).

The *Romaniya* affect many aspects of Roma life. Dishes cannot be washed in the sink or in pans used to wash clothing. The floor is considered defiled, so food or anything connected with the intake of food, like dishes, cannot be placed on it. Anything that does has to be destroyed, because detergent cannot remove pollution. Roma wash their hands constantly—after touching their shoes or doorknobs, or doing anything considered necessary but potentially defiling. Menstruating women have the potential to pollute men.

If a Roma person is declared to be polluted, he or she may not socialize with other Roma nor have any dealings with them, since Roma believe that the pollution can spread from one person to another and contaminate the entire community.

The relationship between Roma communities and non-Roma communities is often strained. Since the fall of communism, the level of anti-Roma discrimination and violence has increased in Central and Eastern Europe. Discrimination and hostility towards Roma has fueled the social segregation of Roma from majority populations. Roma beliefs about cleanliness, along with a traditional aversion to *Gadje* (non-Roma people), also leads to the alienation of Roma from other communities.

9 LIVING CONDITIONS

The living conditions of Roma vary enormously, from the wealthier, technologically advanced countries like the United States and Canada to poor Balkan countries. In any society, Roma usually live at a somewhat lower standard than the non-Roma—in Albania, where the non-Roma have next to nothing, the Roma have even less. Roma are usually industrious and are always able to earn enough to feed and clothe themselves except in circumstances where they are prevented from doing so, such as under the former Communist regimes in Eastern Europe, where free enterprise was a crime against the state.

Roma fit well into societies where there is a surplus of consumer goods that they can buy and sell, or where there is scrap they can collect to recycle. While many Roma are nomadic, especially in Europe, others are sedentary. They might settle in trailer camps, living in horse-drawn wagons or travel trailers, or in modern apartments. Others live in shantytowns or *bidonvilles* in France and Spain, which are often bulldozed into oblivion by the town councils while the occupants are at a local feast. Many Roma in Western Europe are squatters, occupying condemned buildings while trying to find more suitable accommodations. In the United States many Roma own their own homes or rent decent living accommodations. In Central and South America many are still nomadic and live in tents. In Portugal Roma travel with horses and wagons and sleep in tents.

The settled Roma of Eastern and Central Europe tend to live in ethnically homogenous villages or ghettoes. In some cases, residential segregation is a choice of Roma families. In other cases, it is forced upon Roma. For example, in many Slovak towns, Roma have been forced from city centers and herded into crowded ghettoes. In most of Europe, the infrastructure and social services available in Roma ghettoes is of much lower quality than what is available to members of the majority-communities.

Nomadic Roma are often healthier than those who lead sedentary lives. The Roma diet was evolved for a nomadic and active people, and when they settle down and still eat the same types of foods, they often become overweight and suffer from health problems. Women generally live longer than men, who often pass away in middle age from heart attacks. Roma life can be stressful because of constant problems arising from their lifestyle, which is often misunderstood by the law enforcement agencies who move them on when they are traveling or, when they are sedentary, harass them over by-laws, work permits, and licenses. In Eastern Europe, there is a high mortality rate among Roma children and infants, and it has been reported that 80% of the orphans in Romania are Roma children suffering from diseases like AIDS (often caused by infected medical syringes).

Except in rural areas of the less developed countries, where they still use horses and wagons, most Roma have made the transition to cars, trucks, and travel trailers. In countries like the United States they fly to visit relatives or to attend weddings. In Europe they travel by train, bus, or in their own cars and trailers. The Roma in the United States and other developed nations see the car as a status symbol and try to own an impressive vehicle. Usually the interior sports torn upholstery and stains caused by children, but from the outside the vehicle reflects pride of ownership. The Roma have adopted the conspicuous consumption of their fellow Americans and love to show off their purchases to visitors. They often buy expensive jewelry, watches, home furnishings, and appliances as well as luxurious carpets and other furnishings. In Europe, Roma caravans are often full of expensive china dishes. They also buy tapestries and brass decorations. In general, Roma like to live in comfort. Even if they live in substandard housing, they will try to fill their homes with attractive furnishings and decorations.

Discrimination and poverty tend to the limit the access to health care of most Roma. One effect of poverty and lack of health care access has been an increase in the HIV rate amongst Roma. In Bulgaria one study found that Roma intravenous drug users were several times more likely than non-Roma intravenous drug users to contract HIV. Lack of information about safe sex and the increasing prevalence of sex work amongst impoverished Roma also leads to higher HIV rates.

Roma family selling flowers in Bucharest, Romania. (AP Images)

10 FAMILY LIFE

Roma families are usually large and extended. The nuclear family is rare and unmarried adults are looked upon with suspicion. To be unmarried means to be out of balance according to the Roma beliefs. Among the Roma women are equal to men, but each sex has its own traditional role. The men go out to work and earn the larger sums of money, which tend to come in sporadically, while the women earn the day-to-day expenses needed to run the household. This is somewhat reversed in the United States, where the main income in many families comes from the reader/adviser parlors of the women. Here the husband acts as a manager/agent as well as working for himself in some trade or profession. This applies primarily to Vlach Roma, however. Other American Roma groups differ. Among the Bashalde, or Hungarian musician group, the men play music while the women generally remain at home and fulfill the role of wife and mother. Among the Romanichals the men earn most of the money, but the women also contribute by selling items or operating a tea room. The Roma woman, or Romani, is the absolute ruler of the home and plays a very matriarchal role. The eldest daughter, or *she bari*, also has a special role in the family. She replaces the mother in the role of housekeeper when the mother is sick or absent and is responsible for the meals, housecleaning, and the care of her younger siblings. Men do cook and do housework but their role is often limited to doing the dishes and cooking the lambs for a feast. Generally they clean the house only if their wives are unable to do so.

Pets are rare among the Roma since animals can pollute the Roma environment. Watchdogs are kept outside, while cats, which can jump and climb, are taboo. However, some groups are more relaxed toward pets. Horses are considered clean animals and many Roma like to own them even if they no longer need them to travel. Some families even own racehorses.

Since the fall of communism labor migration has become a common phenomenon for Roman males from Central and Eastern Europe. Labor migration often weakens familial ties in normally tight-knit Roma families, leading to higher divorce rates in Roma communities.

11 CLOTHING

There is no traditional male Roma costume. Women among the Roma wear a traditional costume composed of a voluminous ankle-length skirt tied on the left side at the waist, a loose, low-cut blouse, a bolero vest, and an apron. In the United States the bandanna of the married woman is often replaced by a thin strip of ribbon. In Europe the full traditional female costume is still in common use among the Vlach Roma and other more traditional groups. Roma men like to dress well and often adopt a particular style. In the United States during the 1980s the "J.R. look" from *Dallas* was popular: the Stetson, cowboy boots, and Western suit of the Texas oil tycoon. Roma men wear expensive suits but seldom wear ties, except for Western-style string ties. In Europe men in some groups, like the Romanichals of Britain and the Sinti of Western Europe, wear a *diklo*, a type of neckscarf, around the neck, often with an ornate ring that they slip over it to tighten it. Most Roma men like fancy belt buckles and lots of jewelry. Women also wear jewelry. Traditionally they wore gold coins, or *galbi*, on a gold chain around their necks. In modern societies too many have been mugged and their chains stolen. Nowadays they seldom wear them outdoors unless accompanied by men.

For everyday wear Roma dress casually. When working men wear a business suit without a tie, unless they are doing manual labor like sandblasting or spray painting, for which they will wear jeans and an old shirt. Hats are still popular among older Roma men and they also wear them indoors, at feasts and even just sitting in the living room. Teenagers and younger men adopt the local styles, such as baseball caps, sneakers, and windbreakers. Girls can wear jeans at home, but when guests arrive, they have to rush off and change into something more traditional. Miniskirts and other revealing garments are forbidden by the parents.

12 FOOD

Roma food differs from one country to another. The roasted lamb of American Roma feasts becomes the roasted pig at Hungarian Roma feasts. The Vlach Roma love stuffed cabbage rolls, which also appear among the foods eaten by Roma of some other groups. Stews are popular among most Roma groups and in the past nomadic Roma always kept a stewpot simmering in the camp, where the hungry members of the group could help themselves. Many items of small game were baked in clay in the fire, especially hedgehogs, which are a delicacy among some nomadic Roma.

The two basic dietary staples of the Roma are meat and unleavened bread, called *pogacha*, augmented by salads and fruit. Roma drink a lot of tea specially prepared their own way, not with milk, but with slices of fruit in glasses with sugar. Tea is often made in a large silver samovar among the Vlach and Russian Roma. Most prefer cast-iron or copper pots for cooking and try to avoid modern aluminum pots and pans. Lambs are roasted outdoors on revolving spits and sprinkled with beer. The crusty skin of roasted lamb, called *chamb*, is considered a delicacy.

There are many taboos surrounding food. Certain foods like peanuts can only be eaten at a *pomana,* or funeral feast. Bread cannot be burned, and any food that falls on the floor is polluted and must be destroyed. Horsemeat is taboo to all Roma. Food served at a funeral feast must be eaten before sundown or given away to total strangers. Pregnant or menstruating women among the Vlach Roma and the other more traditionally minded groups cannot prepare food to be eaten by others, especially guests, and all foods must be washed and cooked in special containers used only for this purpose. Roma generally do not have set mealtimes. The biggest meal of the day is in the early evening when all the family is home. Food prepared by *Gadjes* is considered unclean. The inability of Roma to eat food prepared by non-Roma reinforces the cultural and social separateness of the Roma from majority-populations.

13 EDUCATION

Until the 20th century a formal education was virtually unheard of in the Roma community. Traditionally parents taught their children the skills they needed to survive as Roma. In the modern world, however, even the traditional Roma occupations, as well as the newer ones they are entering, require literacy. In Eastern Europe under Communism a fair number of Roma were educated and some have become doctors, journalists, teachers, nurses, and technicians. The Vlach Roma and other traditionalist groups tend to see education as assimilating their children, and the schools are viewed as dangerous places and agents of pollution. In Spain the illiteracy rate amongst Roma is 15%, and in Hungary the illiteracy rate amongst Roma is 23%. High Roma illiteracy rates are common in almost all countries where Roma live.

Once children of both sexes reach puberty, they are usually taken out of school and the boys begin to work with their male elders. The Roma would like schools where their children can be taught their own language, culture, and history, preferably by Roma teachers or non-Roma who are sympathetic to and familiar with Roma culture. In Europe most schools aim at assimilating Roma children into the dominant culture of their country. Today, the Roma have a flag, an anthem, and an educated elite that is growing among the younger generation. The concept of the Romani nations, rather than isolated groups of traditional Roma, is emerging. Many young Roma want to help educate their fellows but mass education for Roma belongs to the 21st century. Roma want the right to define themselves in education, not to be defined by outsiders.

In addition to cultural issues, discrimination often limits the access of Roma to educational opportunities. Many Roma children who live in post-communist European Union (EU) states are forced into remedial schools from an early age. These schools often serve as a means of segregating Roma children from the children of the dominant ethnicity. The combination of poverty, Roma culture, and outside discrimination has created a situation in which the number of Roma who complete higher education is miniscule.

14 CULTURAL HERITAGE

The Roma have a strong cultural heritage, which is expressed mainly in music and dance. The roots of Roma music go back to India and show traces of all the musical cultures to which the Roma have been exposed in their migrations. Roma music from certain countries has become world renowned. Foremost is the Flamenco of the Spanish Roma, who are called Cales. Developed in Andalusia, the former Moorish kingdom of Spain, Flamenco displays Roma, Moorish, and Spanish influences. The Roma Flamenco differs from the non-Roma Spanish Flamenco; it has always been performed and developed by a small number of interrelated families.

Equally well known is the Hungarian Roma music, played on violins and cimbaloms, which can be heard in many Hungarian restaurants, even in the United States and Canada. Russian Roma music has also become famous. Under the czars Roma choirs performed for the royal family and the nobility, while other musicians played for army officers and businessmen at restaurants and inns. In France the Sinti musician Django Reinhardt popularized Sinti swing, which became very popular worldwide. The tradition has been continued by other Sinti musicians. Roma music is also popular in Turkey. Roma musicians can be found serenading couples in many of the fashionable cafes of Istanbul. One import from Roma music is the Gypsy Kings, who play a mixture of traditional Flamenco and Salsa. More recently the rock group Gogol Bordello has gained international success. The group mixes traditional Roma melodies with punk rock, creating a new genre which is now known as Gypsy Punk

Roma dancers are also world famous. Usually it is women like Carmen Amaya who are best known, but many male Flamenco dancers, such as Vicente Escudero, have also emerged on the popular scene. In the 1990s, Flamenco dancer Joaquin Cortes received wide acclaim in Europe and was labeled "the Demon of Dance." Music among the Roma has always been divided into the music of the professional musician class—clans and families whose vocation has always been entertainment—and the simpler folk music of the Roma in general, which until recently was never recorded or made available to outsiders. The songs are usually in Romani, and there are songs and dances for specific cultural events, like marriages, feasts, and other gatherings.

Among the Vlach Roma the fast step dance *baso* is performed by both men and women. It is a dance of respect, and at a feast, men will dance singly, calling out "I honor you (name of host)." Women can dance in groups or singly. There is also a folk dance called the *kolo* where Roma dance in a circle. Folksongs are traditional and exist in many versions. The melodies can be ancient from now-forgotten sources or might be taken from modern popular music and given Romani words.

15 WORK

Since their arrival in Europe Roma have been self-employed artisans, entertainers, and middle men dealing in various commodities. There have always been Roma horse trainers, animal dealers, rat catchers, and other lines of work too numerous to list. The Roma economy has been built around self employment and the perpetuation of old skills, plus the acquisition of new skills to adapt to new technological developments. In the past, and to a large extent today, this involves commercial nomadism. Even in slavery, in the principalities that later became modern Romania, each group of slaves had its own skill, from gold panners to ironsmiths, musicians, coppersmiths, brick makers, and bear trainers. Thus, work to the Roma not only served as a survival strategy but also defined to which group or class the individual Roma man belonged. Of course, musicians might trade a few horses and coppersmiths might temporarily switch to some other trade, as most Romas were multifaceted and able to turn their hand to different occupations as the economy demanded.

Roma men usually work in groups, either with relatives or with other Roma skilled in their profession. The profit from any work done is divided equally among all the partners who worked on the job, whether buying and selling automobiles or plating vats for a jam factory. Women also share the profits when they work in groups. An adult man or woman receives a full share of the profits, while unmarried members of the group receive half a share. Today, Roma have adapted to the modern marketplace and can be found dealing in real estate, selling diamonds, and buying and selling automobiles, trailers, antiques, clothing, and other items. Some are professional entertainers; others are scrap collectors. Wherever there is an economic niche, the Roma will find it and try to make a living as new work strategies become viable.

Since the early 1990s millions of Roma have migrated to Western Europe in search of work. Unemployment is a very serious problem amongst the Roma of Eastern and Central Europe; in Prague, one of the most prosperous cities of the post-communist world, the unemployment rate of Roma is estimated to be 70%. In contrast to previous movements of Roma, some of the current migration wave is made up of lone adult males. The destination of labor migrants often depended on which country they were leaving. For example, Roma labor migrants from Albania often moved to Greece. Roma from Romania often left for France or Italy in search of work. Roma men who work abroad often send home remittances to support their families.

16 SPORTS

While there are individual Roma who participate in mainstream athletic events, sports in general do not appeal to the Roma, although certain regional games can be found, such as Roma wrestling in Romania. Many Roma enjoy horse racing and will patronize local racetracks. Roma men and teenagers also like to play billiards, often for money with non-Roma. It is a status symbol among American Roma teenagers to be a good billiard player. Children play games, usually those of the surrounding culture. Nomadic Roma children make catapults and learn to hunt wild game. In Europe Roma participate in mainstream rather than Roma sports, and there are a few Roma soccer teams. Since they have always been a culture geared strongly toward survival, Roma have had little time or inclination to develop an ethnic sport.

17 ENTERTAINMENT AND RECREATION

Roma, especially children and teenagers, enjoy going to the movies. Roma do not care much for live theater, although some Romas have become actors, notably the late Yul Brynner, whose mother was Roma.

In a Roma home, the television, if there is one, is usually left on so that the children may watch it. Adults seldom have time for television. Roma are exposed to popular culture on televi-sion but most adults take no part in it. Since Roma have little to do with non-Roma, except for business, many form their ideas of non-Roma culture from what they see on television. Teenagers may adopt the slang they hear from teenagers on television or copy their way of dressing, but for the most part the surrounding mainstream culture contravenes Roma taboos.

Some families, tired of the local routine, will decide to travel around for a while just to meet relatives, attend a social function in some other city, or camp out in a camper van like the Roma used to do when they were nomadic. Local fairs like Appleby Fair in Britain also attract many Roma, not only those who still deal in horses. Some will go to sell seconds of fine china or to hawk other wares. Some go just to be there and to socialize and perhaps turn a little business their way.

In recent years European Roma have begun to enjoy Romani-language television, radio, news and Internet publications. However, illiteracy and poverty have limited access to these media outlets. In addition most Romani media is produced by highly educated Roma elites, leading to a disconnect between ordinary Roma and the Romani media.

18 FOLK ARTS, CRAFTS, AND HOBBIES

While some individuals have excelled as painters or sculptors, and in other art forms, the majority of Roma practice few handicrafts. Some Roma men make belts or leather clothing and women may do elaborate embroidery work, while both sexes create artifacts, such as baskets, for sale.

The carving and fretwork designs seen on the Roma wagons in England became world famous and were later copied by European Roma in some countries. The original Romanichal caravans appeared around 1860 and were a Roma adaptation of the original English showman's wagon. These *vardos,* or caravans, were adorned with intricate carvings and fretwork designs, painted and even highlighted with gold leaf in some expensive versions. The last type to survive the automobile and the freeway was the bow top made from birch planks bent into a semicircle inside a wagon base, covered with canvas, and painted green to help hide it among the trees and away from the police. Today, some of the ornately carved versions are made for European collectors by Roma craftsmen, while some Romanichals build or buy one, not to travel with, but simply to own as a matter of nostalgia and prestige.

In Eastern Europe, Roma woodcarvers also make wooden bowls and trenchers. Others manufacture wooden flutes and other musical instruments. Among the Vlach Roma the *Kalderash*, or coppersmiths, make intricate copper objects of artistic merit, usually on order for some prestigious hotel or restaurant. Before the age of plastic, Roma also made wooden clothes pegs.

A new European Union push to foster Roma inclusion has led to renewed interest in traditional Roma crafts. Crafts are seen as a way of providing employment opportunities in Roma communities.

19 SOCIAL PROBLEMS

European Roma today are survivors of the Nazi Holocaust in which Roma, like Jews, were singled out as an ethnic group to be completely exterminated. At least a million Roma died in Nazi Germany and in the occupied countries. Others were annihilated by Nazi collaborationist regimes, such as Croatia under the Ustashi. Postwar Communism in Eastern Europe tried to assimilate the Roma into the general populations, and in all countries they became an unwanted, surplus population denied their identity as a people.

Since 1977 Roma have been recognized by the United Nations as a legitimate people with rights to their own identity, language, culture, lifestyle, and religion. The challenge now is to have the governments of the former Communist countries of Eastern Europe recognize these rights. In most of these countries, as reports by Helsinki Watch, Human Rights Watch, and other organizations have attested, the official government policy toward Roma is ethnocide—the destruction of their language, culture, and identity in order to assimilate them. In Slovakia, the Czech Republic, Romania, and Hungary, Roma have become the new scapegoats and the target of skinheads and other lawless elements of society. In Slovakia Roma have been forcefully expelled from city centers and sent to squalid ghettoes. In 2008 Roma communities in Naples, Italy were attacked by violent mobs and entire neighborhoods were burned to the ground. In other parts of Central and Eastern Europe Roma face routine violence and acts of discrimination. Part of the problem in Romania is that when Roma were slaves between the 15th and 19th centuries, they were stigmatized and regarded as inferior. The myth of the half-human, dangerous, dirty, uncivilized, and lazy Roma slave became part of the Romanian psyche, in much the same way that the myth of the racial inferiority of African Americans became part of the communal psyche in the southern United States. In other countries folk mythology reduced the Roma to the level of romantic misfits or backward savages who should be civilized and assimilated into the general population.

Large numbers of Roma have fled to Western Europe, where they have created a refugee problem. They are entitled to apply for asylum but many countries deport them for lack of documents or for false documents sold to them by underworld "people smugglers" who have helped them enter the country. The Roma in the Americas, Canada, and other countries outside Europe have much greater freedom and protection under the law, although still subject to ethnic stereotyping and discrimination and conflict with authorities over aspects of their lifestyle and economic practices.

Next to discrimination, poverty is the greatest challenged faced by most Roma. In 2006 the $4.30/day poverty rate amongst Roma was over 45% in most countries of Southeast Europe. High unemployment rates, high levels of discrimination, and low levels of education attainment all create a vicious circle that leads to the continuation of poverty for Roma.

Alcoholism and drug abuse exist among Roma, although drugs are taboo under the pollution code of the Vlach Roma and other groups. While Roma used to drink only at feasts and on special occasions such as a betrothal ceremony or a funeral, today it is not uncommon for them to turn to alcohol as a temporary escape from their problems. The disease of alcoholism is not understood among the Roma. If a Roma gets drunk, the blame tends to fall on the alcohol, not on the person. The Roma say *Lya les e rakiya*—"The whiskey took hold of him"— as if it were some kind of malevolent spirit that entered and possessed him. Although forbidden, drug use has also taken hold amongst many young Roma. Intravenous drug use is increasing the spread of disease, such as HIV and hepatitis.

Traditionally Roma have not been dangerous criminals. Their crimes are generally of a petty nature, consisting of confidence games, shoplifting, or other types of pilfering. Offenses like selling drugs, organized prostitution, arson, murder for hire, and loan sharking are all forbidden to them by their own code of laws. That said, abject poverty has led many Roma to commit such serious crimes. Crimes like these are thought to bring bad karma and place the criminal "out of balance."

[20] GENDER ISSUES

In traditional Roma households the roles of men and women are strictly defined. The duty of men is to provide for the family. Women may also contribute to the household income but their primary duty is to cook, clean, and raise children. Many Roma girls leave school early to help their mothers with housework. This has led to an imbalance in the literacy rates and levels of educational attainment between many Roman males and females. Roma tradition dictates that girls remain virgins before marriage. The consequences for girls suspected of premarital sex can be quite severe. It is uncommon for males to be seriously punished for similar activity.

Most Roma view homosexuality as an extremely negative phenomenon; homosexuals are regarded as unclean. If outed, gay and lesbian Roma are usually banished from their community. In many Roma communities, women and young people are challenging traditional values that pertain to gender and sexuality. However, change is difficult, because most Roma are quite resistant to transforming their culture to conform to that of the *Gadje*.

[21] BIBLIOGRAPHY

Acton, T. *Gypsy Politics and Social Change*. London & Boston: Routledge & Kegan Paul, 1974.

Bancroft, Angus. *Roma and Gypsy—Travellers in Europe: Modernity, Race, Space and Exclusion*. Burlington, VT: Ashgate Publishing, 2005.

Brown, I. *Gypsy Fires in America: A Narrative of Life Among the Romanies of the United States and Canada*. New York & London: Harper Brothers, 1924.

Gropper, R. C. *Gypsies in the City: Cultural Patterns and Survival*. Princeton, NJ: The Darwin Press, 1975.

Guy, Will. *Between Past and Future: The Roma of Central and Eastern Europe*. Hertfordshire, UK: University of Hertfordshire Press, 2001.

Hancock, I. *A Grammar of Vlax Romani*. London & Austin: Romanestan Publications, 1993.

———. *The Pariah Syndrome: An Account of Gypsy Slavery and Persecution*. Ann Arbor: Karoma Publishers, Inc., 1987.

Leblon, B. *Gypsies and Flamenco: The Emergence of the Art of Flamenco in Andalusia*. Hatfield, England: Gypsy Research Center, University of Herfordshire Press, 1995.

Lee, R. *Goddam Gypsy, An Autobiographical Novel*. Montreal: Tundra Books, 1971.

Liegeois, Jean-Pierre. *Roma in Europe*. Strasbourg: Council of Europe Pub., 2007.

McDowell, Bart. *Gypsies: Wanderers Of The World*. Washington, D.C.: National Geographic, 1970.

McLane, M. *Proud Outcasts: The Gypsies of Spain*. Carderock Press, MD, 1987.

Nicolae, Valeriu and Hannah Slavik, eds. *Roma Diplomacy*. New York: International Debate Education Association, 2007.

Ringold, Dena. *Roma in an Expanding Europe: Breaking the Poverty Cycle.* Washington, D.C.: World Bank, 2005.

Salo, M. T. *The Kalderash of Eastern Canada.* Ottawa: The Canadian Center For Folk Studies, R.O.M. 1977.

Stauber, Roni and Raphael Vago, ed. *The Roma: A Minority in Europe: Historical, Political and Social Perspectives.* Budapest: Central European University Press, 2007.

Thompson, J. *Making Models of Gypsy Caravans.* Fleet, Hampshire, U.K.: John Thompson, 1978.

Tong, D. *Gypsies: A Multidisciplinary Annotated Bibliography.* New York & London: Garland Publishing Inc., 1995.

———. *Gypsy Folktales.* New York and London: Harcourt Brace Jovanvovich, 1989.

Yates, D. *A Book of Gypsy Folktales.* London: Phoenix House, 1948.

Yoors, J. *The Gypsies.* New York: Simon & Schuster, 1967.

———. *Crossing.* New York: Simon & Schuster, 1971.

—revised by B. Lazarus

ROMANIANS

LOCATION: Romania
POPULATION: 22 million, of whom 91% are ethnic Romanians
LANGUAGE: Romanian
RELIGION: Christianity (Romanian Orthodox Church; Greek Catholic Church; Protestantism)

¹ INTRODUCTION

Romania has a long and heroic, but tragic history. The ancient historian Herodotus writes that the territory that comprises Romania today was inhabited by the Dacians and Getae as early as the 6th century BC. The ancestors of the Romanians organized a separate country known as Dacia, which developed and prospered to the time of King Decebalus (AD 87–106). Dacia increasingly became a menace to the expanding Roman Empire. After a few futile attempts to subdue the Dacians, the Roman emperor Trajan fought two fierce battles with them between AD 101–106 and finally conquered Dacia in AD 106. The victory over the Dacians was considered so important in Roman history that a monument was erected in the Forum at Rome to commemorate the event. Known as "Trajan's Column," it depicts battle scenes in bas-relief of Dacians in their native dress and habitat. It still exists today and is considered "the birth certificate of the Romanian nation."

From 106 to 271, Dacia was a Roman province. Besides the indigenous Dacian population, a growing number of colonists from throughout the Roman Empire settled in this area. The province became one of the most prosperous in the Roman Empire and was known as "Dacia Felix" (happy and flourishing Dacia). As a border province, however, Dacia became increasingly difficult to defend against the barbaric invasions from the East. Therefore, Emperor Aurelian decided to retreat from Dacia with his armies in 271, ceding the country to the invading Goths. Most of the native population, which by this time was developing into a new nation, remained in Dacia. The use of the Latinized Daco-Roman language persisted in the region as a means of communication, commerce, and administration. This new language eventually evolved into the distinctive Romanian language. The language, religion, customs, dress, beliefs, behavior, techniques, tools, ideas, and many other vestiges of the early civilization prove without a doubt the Romanians' Latin origin.

The drama of Romanian history is that of a people blessed with a beautiful and rich country, but also situated at the crossroads of invasion routes for the first millennium of its existence. Fortunately, most of the invaders came and left. After the Goths left in 375, and the Huns left in the 6th century, there was a slow but steady infiltration of Slavs among the Romanians. Though most of them proceeded on south of the Danube, some of them remained and were assimilated by the native Romanians, adding some of their linguistic, cultural, and social influences to the cultural mix.

Beginning in the 10th century, there was a gradual but steady penetration of Hungarians, especially among the Romanians of Transylvania, the cradle of the Romanian nation, which became a Hungarian province and remained so until it finally reverted to Greater Romania in 1918.

Romanian political units were formed in territories inhabited by them beginning in the 11th century, including Moldova and Wallachia. They eventually became principalities in the 13th century. Muslim Turks had a firm hold on Romanian territories. Nevertheless, Michael the Brave, after a number of victories, was able to unite briefly all the Romanians under one rule in 1601. Though short-lived, this unification contributed to the strengthening of Romanian identity.

The Ottoman Empire imposed its rule over the Romanian principalities for nearly 300 years. In the 18th century, the Turks sent Greek Phanariots to rule the Romanian principalities, from which they extracted considerable sums. To get back the money they had invested, the peasants were heavily taxed and harshly oppressed.

With the help of Russia, which defeated the Turks, the Romanians were given more freedom and granted a new constitution in 1829. Finally in 1859, Wallachia and Moldova were united into one country, with Prince Alexandru Ioan Cuza as ruler. Antagonizing some of the Romanian leaders, he was forced to resign, and in 1866 Prince Carol of Hohenzollern was invited to head the country. In 1881 Romania became a monarchy, and the new King Carol I ruled for over 30 years. After his death in 1914, he was succeeded by his nephew, King Ferdinand, who married Princess Marie, the granddaughter of Queen Victoria of Great Britain.

Romania fought on the side of the Allies during World War I and was rewarded the Austro-Hungarian provinces of Transylvania, Banat, and Bucovina in 1918, thus uniting most of the Romanians in one country for the first time in its history.

In 1940, General Ion Antonescu's government signed an alliance with Germany, which lasted until 23 August 1944 when the Romanians joined the Allies and the Russians entered the country. Two provinces (Bessarabia and present day Moldova) were taken by the Russians as spoils of war, and attached to the Russian Federation (the former USSR). With the forced abdication of King Michael, the few Romanian Communists gradually took control of the government, the educational system, and the economy. In 1965 a new constitution along communist lines was adopted and Nicolae Ceaușescu became president of the country, which was known as the Socialist Republic of Romania. Under his harsh regime, the country faced a dramatic economic crisis with many shortages of foods and consumer goods.

With a single-party political system completely controlled by the Communist Party, the living standard of the average citizen eroded noticeably and the national debt rose abruptly. Citizens were summarily arrested, tried, and imprisoned. Many fled the country. It is believed that over 500,000 Romanians emigrated to Western Europe, the United States, and elsewhere throughout the free world. Most of the Jews and German-speaking citizens also left for Israel, Germany, the United States, and other countries.

Those who remained behind, especially the young people, showed their opposition by antigovernment demonstrations calling for changes. When the security forces opened fire on demonstrators in Timișoara on 16 December 1989, a state of emergency was declared, but the protests continued to spread and grow in Bucharest and throughout the country. As a result, Ceaușescu was arrested, tried, summarily judged, and found guilty of genocide. He was hastily executed on 25 December 1989.

After the execution of Ceaușescu and the ousting of many Communist officeholders, a hastily garnered government made up mostly of former Communists and headed by Ion Iliescu took over the reins. The situation did not improve much; in some respects, it even worsened. Inflation rose, living standards suffered, and corruption continued. Nevertheless, Ion Iliescu was reelected for a second term. He was finally voted out by a coalition of democratic parties in November 1996; Emil Constantinescu was elected as the first non-Communist president in over 50 years. The coalition government that took over power in 1996 was made up of former dissidents, intellectuals, and members of historical Romanian parties that survived Communist rule. While they were well intentioned, and openly tried to implement ambitious reforms, they were not seasoned politicians. Consequently, their four-year term was marked by internal power struggles, frequent cabinet changes, and a worsening of the economic, political, and social situation. Only towards the end of their rule, when Mugur Isarescu (president of the National Bank of Romania) was installed as prime minister did the situation improve slightly. In 2000 elections were held and power was won again by the former-Communists (christened under a new name—the Socialist Democratic Party). Ion Iliescu became president (for what some called an unlawful third term), and Adrian Nastase became prime minister. Although their rule was plagued by accusations of corruption, Romania enjoyed strong and sustained economic growth, and a general improvement of living conditions. In 2002 Romania was invited to join the North

Atlantic Treaty Organization (NATO), and finally did so in March 2004.

Following the 2004 elections, a coalition government (dominated by the Democratic Party and the National Liberal Party) took power, and Traian Basescu was elected president for a five-year term. This government was fraught with internal disputes, and split in 2007. As of 2008 Romania had a minority government headed by Calin Popescu Tariceanu of the National Liberal Party. Tariceanu and Traian Basescu (of the Democratic Party) openly criticized each other's policies, creating a tense political climate. Despite the contentious political situation, the Romanian economy continues to expand, and living standards are increasing rapidly. In January 2007, Romania joined the European Union (EU).

² LOCATION AND HOMELAND

Romania is located in Eastern Europe at the mouth of the Danube River as it flows into the Black Sea. Situated west of Russia, east of Hungary, north of Serbia and Bulgaria, and south of Slovakia and Poland, it is slightly less than 238,000 sq km (92,000 sq mi), about the size of New York State and Pennsylvania combined.

The majestic Carpathian Mountains run from north to south through the middle of the country. Giving way to sub-Carpathian hills and finally to vast fertile fields, the mountains divide Transylvania, the largest province, from the Old Romanian Kingdom.

Romania has a population of about 22 million people with a density of 97 persons per sq km (252 persons per sq mi). Ethnic Romanians comprise 91% of the population. The remaining population includes Hungarians (6.7%) and various other minorities. Before World War II, Romania had a large Jewish population, most of whom have since emigrated to Israel, the United States, and Western Europe. It also had a sizeable German minority—mostly Saxons and Swabians—who had been in the country since the 13th century and who emigrated in large numbers to Germany, the United States, and elsewhere during and after World War II.

Romania is made up of about 200 cities and 15,000 villages, divided administratively into 42 counties. The capital is Bucharest, with a population of over 2 million people.

Romania is in the North Temperate Zone, with hot summers, cool autumns, and cold winters with snow and winds. It is primarily an agricultural country with 45% arable land. Among the natural resources are oil, gas, and coal, much of which has dwindled since Germany and the USSR siphoned them off during and after World War II. There is a growing industrial and commercial base, which employs about one-third of the labor force.

³ LANGUAGE

The Romanian Orthodox Church helped to formulate and promote the Romanian language and culture. The first schools were opened and the first books written and published in Romanian Orthodox monasteries.

The Romanian language is one of the major modern Romance languages of the world, alongside Italian, French, Spanish, Portuguese, and a few other minor ones. It is closest in structure to the Latin spoken in the first centuries AD by the average Roman citizen on the street. Romania's very name,

deriving from "Romanus," as the Roman colonizers of Dacia were known, is an indication of its Latin heritage.

In spite of attempts by foreign rulers—Turks, Greeks, and Hungarians—to impose their respective languages and cultures upon the Romanian people, its fundamental Latin origin emerged practically intact. Latin-derived Romanian is the language spoken and written by the overwhelming number of Romanians today.

⁴ FOLKLORE

Romanian culture is defined by a unique blend of folklore and learned culture. Up to World War II, Romania was a predominantly agrarian society, and even today, more than 40% of people still live in the country side. Folk creations were the main source of inspiration for early Romanian writers, and they remained the main literary genre until early 18th century. The best known folklore creation is the ballad *Miorița*, which describes Romanian spirituality.

Another popular folk tale is that of *Meșterul Manole* (roughly: The Master Builder Manole), which tells the story of a craftsman who was hired to build a monastery for the prince of Wallachia, Negru Vodă. The walls that Manole and his workers built during the day would crumble during the night. This caused Manole to pray to God for help and guidance. The response came in the form of a vision that showed Manole the only way he could finish his work: by walling his wife Ana inside the church walls. He reluctantly proceeded to do so and completed his masterpiece—the Curtea de Argeș Monastery. When he saw the finished work, Prince Negru Vodă became fearful that Manole might build another masterpiece that would be as—if not more—magnificent than his. He thus decided to leave Manole and his team stranded on top of the church. To escape, the workers built themselves wings out of shingles and attempted to fly to safety. All of them failed. The place where Manole fell to his death caused water to burst forth, and according to myth, the spot is marked by an actual fountain on one side of the church.

Many of the folk traditions have survived to this day in rural communities, and are carefully preserved by the Romanian Academy and the Museum of the Romanian Peasant. Traditional folk arts include wood carving, ceramics, weaving and embroidery, household decorations, dance, and folk music. Constantin Brâncuși (one of the most well known modernist sculptors in the world) drew his inspiration from Romanian folk art, and many of his masterpieces are throw-backs to traditional Romanian wood carving. Professional and amateur dance groups are trying to keep alive the rich variety of dances encountered throughout Romania, and some of these dances (such as *Călușarii*) have been declared by UNESCO to be "Masterpieces of the Oral and Intangible Heritages of Humanity."

Some of the Romanian folklore myths that have become part of international culture are the myth of the vampire (or *strigoi*—the undead), and the myth of the werewolf (vârcolac).

⁵ RELIGION

Religion has always played an important part in the life of the Romanians. Aside from the years during the Communist domination of Romania after World War II through 1989, there was a close relationship between the state and the church. The state funded the church, and religion was taught in schools.

After forsaking the pagan religion of their Dacian forbears, the new Daco-Romanians gradually adopted the Christian religion, establishing churches dependent upon the Eastern Orthodox Patriarch of Constantinople. Even though there was a Slavonic influence in the Romanian Orthodox Church beginning in the 9th century when the two Greek missionary brothers, Cyril and Methodius, introduced the Cyrillic alphabet into the country, and later when the Greek Phanariots also exerted their influence, the Romanian Orthodox Church never lost its Latin character.

When Romania finally became one unified country in 1918, over 80% of Romanians belonged to the Romanian Orthodox Church, while 10% belonged to the Greek Catholic Church (also known as the Uniate Church). The rest of the population belonged to various Roman Catholic or Protestant Churches.

The Romanian Orthodox Patriarchate was established in 1925 with metropolitans, archbishops, and bishops to oversee the 15 million members of over 15,000 churches, served by over 18,000 priests, thus making it the second-largest Orthodox Church in the world, after the Russian Orthodox Church. There are about 250 Romanian Orthodox churches (with about as many priests) outside of Romania proper in adjacent countries, as well as in Western Europe, the United States, and Canada.

⁶ MAJOR HOLIDAYS

The major Church holy days, besides their religious aspects and significance, are also occasions for rest and relaxation. No doubt, Christmas has more customs and observances than any other Church holy day. Beginning on 15 November, when Advent begins, the villagers prepare not only spiritually, but also socially, for the celebration of the Nativity of Christ. Adults slaughter and dress the hog, and bake and prepare goodies for the season, while children learn carols and their roles in the pageant of Christ's birth. Dressed in their best clothes, groups of carolers go from home to home on Christmas Eve, spreading the news of the coming of Christ in word and song. There is no other form of popular poetry more prevalent than the traditional carols, which have been passed down from one generation to the next. Christmas celebrations last for two weeks until the Epiphany on 6 January and take on many variations, such as family gatherings, reunions, visiting friends, dances, and social events.

New Year's Day is a secular holiday, but also a Saint's Day—Saint Basil. As in the world over, Romanian revelers ring in the New Year with partying, singing, and drinking at restaurants, social establishments, and in their homes. It is customary among the Romanians to go to the homes of friends and acquaintances, wishing them a happy, healthy, and prosperous new year. Some New Year's Day customs have prevailed throughout the centuries, dating from pagan Roman times, such as the *plugusotul* (plow). Boys dressed in sheepskin outfits pull a small plow through the village, wishing everyone a prosperous new year. Likewise, there are groups leading a *capra* (goat) or beating drums, reciting New Year's greetings in rhythmic verse.

Easter is the greatest religious holiday. With its six-week Lenten preparatory season, solemn Holy Week rituals, and bright midnight resurrection service, everyone rejoices in the renewal of spiritual life and of the spring weather. The coloring of Easter eggs in decorative Romanian designs is an art in itself and reveals the artistic talents of the Romanians. Households are cleaned, repainted, and refurbished. New clothes are made or purchased. Soup, roasts, and casseroles of lamb are prepared. Nut and raisin kuchen are baked. Merrymaking abounds after church services. After the Lenten restriction on dancing for six weeks, the village dances are resumed and a happier atmosphere prevails.

Secular holidays change according to the political regime in power. During the 50 years of Communist government control, some of the traditional national holidays were not observed, such as 10 May, when Romania gained its independence and eventually became a monarchy. Instead, 23 August became the most important holiday during the Communist reign. It commemorated the "liberation of Romania from the German fascists by the Romanian Communist troops." When Communist control ended in 1989, this holiday was discontinued and the Romanian people reverted to the traditional 10 May day. The Communists also introduced May Day, which is observed by all Communists throughout the world, and Labor Day, honoring all workers. Ceauşescu's birthday was celebrated as his cult grew but celebrations were discontinued when he was overthrown.

⁷ RITES OF PASSAGE

When an infant is baptized, there is always a celebration at the home of the child's parents, with godparents, relatives, and friends present. Godparents become spiritual parents to the newly baptized and maintain a special relationship with them throughout their lives. If anything should happen to the parents of the godchild, the godparents would usually take over some of the responsibilities to see that the child is brought up properly until maturity. At baptism, children are given the name of a saint, usually one whose feast day is nearest to the date of birth. In Romania, as in other Orthodox countries, the name-day of the person is often celebrated with more festivity than the birth date. It is an occasion of congratulations and socializing among friends and relatives.

Children are taken to Sunday church services from a young age and participate in the social life of the parish, such as parties, outings, and dances. Young people participate at village dances held on Sunday afternoons after Vespers. They are held in the church yard, school auditorium, village square, or in more spacious barns of prosperous peasants. They are occasions to socialize and meet other young people. Friendships are usually formed, which can result in dating and closer relationships, eventually leading to marriage.

Marriage is a very important time in a Romanian's life and is not to be entered into lightly. When young people decide to marry, they ask for the blessing of their parents. The girl usually has a dowry that her parents start when she is very young and to which she adds periodically. It consists of household linens, rugs, tablecloths, personal items, kitchen utensils, and family heirlooms.

After the marriage date is set and arrangements are made for the religious ceremony, the groom sends out emissaries to personally invite friends and relatives to the wedding. The invitation is sealed with a mutual sip of plum brandy, which means acceptance of the invitation. Weddings are held mostly on Sunday afternoons after church services. The male members of the bridal party, bedecked in their finest peasant clothes, usually come to church on horseback, while the bride is brought in a carriage bedecked with flowers and peasant embroideries. After the nearly one-hour church ceremony, during which they declare their mutual love and exchange rings in token thereof, and after prayers asking for God's blessings, the bride and groom drink wine from the "common cup," signifying their sharing from now on, for better or for worse. Finally, they are crowned and encircle the front of the altar, venerating the icons as a symbol of their spirituality. With the joyous hymn wishing them many happy years, they leave the church and are accompanied by a band to the place where the festivities are to be held. The groom is very attentive to the new bride so that she will not be "abducted" by former buddies and have to be "redeemed" with a round of drinks.

The social celebration of the wedding lasts into very late hours of the night. It is probably one of the most lavish and generous events in the couple's life. Food is plentiful and drinks—usually wine, plum brandy, and beer—are available all evening, sometimes ending in overindulgence. Monetary gifts are given to the couple to start them off on their new conjugal life. Sometimes weddings last two or three days, with time out for some sleep and rest, but most are limited to a few hours.

Funerals also offer occasions for socializing in a more somber way and abound with many local customs and practices. When someone dies, he or she is properly "prepared" without being embalmed After being washed and deodorized, the body is laid in a simple wooden coffin and is brought to his or her home, where there is a wake. Often "wailers" lament and in cadence review the life of the deceased. Two or three evenings before the funeral service in church, prayer services are held before the open coffin. On the day of the funeral, the coffin is brought to the church in a horse-drawn wagon and is carried inside on the shoulders of friends or relatives. After an hour-long ceremony, emphasizing the Resurrection and the positive aspects of death, the closed coffin is taken to the cemetery, which is usually next to the church, and is interred. The mourners return to the deceased's home, where a requiem meal is served. Food is provided by relatives and friends. After mourning, there is a period of relaxation and a return to the world, signifying the peasant's philosophy, "the living with the living, and the dead with the dead" and "life goes on."

⁸ INTERPERSONAL RELATIONS

Romania's greatest asset is the people themselves. After centuries of foreign domination and corruption, Romanians emerged as a self-reliant and intelligent people. From their Church, they learned to be humble, loving, and forgiving. They are noted for being kind and caring, which is reflected in their warm greetings and willingness to be of service to others. When visiting a Romanian, he or she is likely to offer you the best bed in the house, and the best food they can provide. As Romania is becoming more westernized, so are the customs of the people—especially in large urban centers. City dwellers nowadays are always on the run, always pressed for time, and less likely to engage in extensive interpersonal relations the way they used to during Communist rule.

In rural areas, interpersonal relations are nurtured and centuries-old customs are respected. When visiting a village, people will great you with a nod of the head and a smile, even if they do not know you. Women are respected. A man tips his hat, offers his seat, kisses the hand, and offers to help women. The elderly are also respected. When encountering an elderly person or a woman, the greeting *sărut mâinile* (kiss hands) is customary.

⁹ LIVING CONDITIONS

Romania developed a distinctive architectural style, known as the Brâncoveanu style, in which many churches and public buildings were built. A specific Romanian style was developed in Transylvania with wooden churches, characterized by a steep shingled roof and tall, sleek spire. In northern Moldova and southern Bucovina, a distinctive church style developed in the time of Stephen the Great. The nave was in the shape of a ship, with an overhanging roof and frescoes on the inside and outside.

After their liberation from serfdom, the Romanian peasants were able to build modest homes, which they lavished with Romanian decorations and motifs. Peasant architecture throughout Romania varies from the impressive two-story houses (*cula*) of the more-prosperous Romanians to the simple thatched-roof cottage. The more elaborate houses were surrounded by a terrace with an overhanging roof.

The typical one-story Romanian house usually includes an anteroom with an oven for cooking. In the rear is a pantry. Some homes have a living room with a fireplace and at least one bedroom with a large bed and a wooden chest to store linens, clothes, and personal belongings. The room may have a wooden bench and beams across the ceiling. The more prosperous peasants have a large enclosed yard with a garden, hay barn, stable, pigsty, chicken coop, corncrib, and outhouse.

In 1935, representative houses, churches, and other buildings from all regions of the country were disassembled and then reassembled in a large area outside Bucharest for a permanent display known as the museum of the village.

Romania has undergone many changes in the last 50 years, especially during the Communist regime. There was a large migration from villages to cities. Because of political persecution, many Romanians fled the country. The population in villages has decreased considerably. There was a tendency at one time to reduce the number of villages and to house the population in public housing. During the Communist regime, some villages were obliterated as inhabitants moved to the cities, where nondescript high-rise apartments were built to accommodate them. They can be seen on the outskirts of most of the major cities, but they lack the comforts, facilities, and amenities for more gracious living. This trend has stopped.

With the collectivization of farmlands, even though modern equipment was used, production decreased because of the uncooperative attitude of the peasants.

Young people between the ages of 9 and 14 belonged to the Young Pioneers, while those over 14 were enrolled in the Union of Communist Youth. They were expected to help out in workshops and collective farms. Communist youth organizations have been done away with, and most youth activities take place in schools and voluntary organizations in urban areas. American films, music, social behavior, and dress have had a marked influence on the youth of Romania. In the villages, however, life is more sedate and still revolves to a great extent around the family and the Church, which teaches restraint and modesty.

Life expectancy is 68 years for males and 77 years for females. Infant mortality is 25 deaths per 1,000 births. There is 1 hospital bed per 100 persons, and 1 doctor per 559 persons.

A father and child walk through a neighborhood in Bucharest, Romania. Romania still struggles with widespread poverty. Despite these problems, Romania has made headway in fighting corruption and modernizing infrastructure to meet stringent EU standards. (Spencer Platt/Getty Images)

Though the state is supposed to offer free health care to the citizens, there is a scarcity of hospitals, clinics, and other facilities. Doctors are poorly paid and lack much of the necessary equipment and medicine to adequately meet the health needs of the population. Because of poverty, some children are abandoned and end up in orphanages, which have a difficult time caring for them. Some of the orphans are adopted locally and others by families abroad. Though there are medical schools, which graduate a number of doctors, many of the graduates try to emigrate elsewhere for higher pay and better facilities. With the end of Communist rule, there is more private practice and conditions have improved somewhat, but there are still many pressing needs. It will be some time before the health care system will reach western standards throughout the country.

Following the economic boom of the new century, living conditions for most Romanians have improved dramatically. People have higher wages and access to a large assortment of consumer and household goods. A real estate boom has been witnessed in most major urban centers, as developers try to cover the rising need for new housing. There are more than 2 million Romanians working outside the country and most of them send remittances back home. This money is usually used for purchasing a new home and household goods.

Significant investments in infrastructure and the public sector have also lead to a betterment of living conditions.

10 FAMILY LIFE

Romanians are family-oriented and try to bring up their families in the highest moral Christian spirit. Traditionally, Romanians had large families. Many hands were needed to work the fields. The patriarchal system predominated. The elderly were respected and were usually the head of the extended family. Much of this tradition was done away with when peasants migrated to towns and were alienated from the more intimate village life.

Children are considered to be blessings from God and are brought up in the Romanian national tradition, greatly fostered by the Church. Respect for parents is a cornerstone of this philosophy. The family spirit is very strong, and relationships with relatives are quite close. Traditionally, promiscuity was rare, and abortion was frowned upon. One of the social problems was alcoholism among men, even though the average Romanian man could carry on his daily workload in spite of it. Divorce in the villages was at a minimum but was more prevalent in the cities.

Life in the villages is more tranquil and there are fewer social problems than in the city. The Church also has a greater influence over its believers in the village than in the city. Much of village social life revolves around the Church holy days and various religious events in the believer's life—at baptisms, marriages, and funerals.

City life is increasingly defined by western culture. Women are more mobile in the labor force and less likely to be dependent on a husband. Consequently, fertility rates are going down (1.38 children born to each woman in 2007), and divorce rates are going up. Many city dwellers are professionally oriented and family life often takes a secondary role.

11 CLOTHING

Among the most visible and attractive articles of clothing are the Romanian traditional costumes, especially the blouse, which varies greatly from one district to another. Each one is different and has its beauty, being lavished with intricate embroidery. They are much appreciated throughout the world.

The traditional Romanian male costumes were just as varied as the women's, but less elaborate. The trousers and the long shirt were mostly white. The men wore a leather belt. In cold weather, they wore sheepskin jackets. Footwear was usually leather moccasins, and the headgear was a rounded black hat with a narrow brim, or a lambskin cap in the winter.

In recent years, many new clothing stores have sprung up in most Romanian urban centers. Western fashion (especially Italian and American) defines the way people dress in cities. In rural areas, traditional costumes are seldom encountered any more. Peasants are more likely to wear second-hand clothes bought in the cities, or utilitarian clothes they take to the fields. Traditional garb is still worn for major celebrations.

12 FOOD

Romanian cooking was influenced by those nationalities living within the same areas, especially Hungarian and Serbian. Old Kingdom Romanians were influenced by Turkish, Russian, and other ethnic cooking. In all cases, the Romanians added their own touch and varied it to suit their taste. The more sophisticated Romanians availed themselves of French, Viennese, and other Western European ways of cooking.

Mamaliga (cornmeal mush) is one of the staples of the Romanian diet and, in a sense, is the national dish. It is easy to prepare, is very digestible, and is served in as many ways as the imagination can dream up. It is usually served as a side dish and sometimes in place of bread. Besides being used for cooking, corn is also used to feed the livestock.

Pork is the favorite meat of the Romanians. Almost every village household raises a few pigs for their own use and for sale. They are usually slaughtered before Christmas, smoked, made into sausage, and preserved for use throughout the year. Peasants working in the fields can make a meal out of a slab of smoked bacon, a generous portion of hard-crust black bread, and wine. Dishes using pork products, such as bacon or ham and eggs, stuffed cabbage, spare ribs, pork chops, sausage, and various cold cuts are favorites for the Romanians, much more so than beef.

For appetizers, Romanians prefer chopped chicken liver, eggplant spread, carp roe paste, and aspic. Soups include thick cream soups with sour cream, sauerkraut juice, lemon juice, or vinegar, to which are added various chunks of meats, vegeta-bles, and potatoes. The Sunday meal is usually chicken soup with noodles or dumplings and roast chicken from the family's own back yard.

Romanians especially enjoy broiling meat. Aside from pork chops, spare ribs, flank steak, and lamb chops (especially during the Easter season), the undisputed favorites are the traditional *mititei*—small sausages made of ground pork, beef, and lamb, marinated and then broiled. Stews, roasts, and casseroles with vegetable, salads, sour pickles, and sauerkraut make up the usual main course.

Many Romanians observe the four Lenten seasons prescribed by the Orthodox Church and shy away from all meat and dairy products then. There is a whole array of foods that can be prepared to meet these Lenten requirements, such as Lenten bean, caraway seed, lettuce, mushroom, tomato, vegetable, and potato soups, to which are added vegetable dishes, such as mushroom stew, braised cabbage, Spanish rice, vegetable *ghiveciu,* and baked beans. Others are mashed beans, Lenten stuffed cabbage, potato stew, Lenten spaghetti, and fresh beans with tomato sauce.

Traditional Romanian desserts are made of raised dough, such as kuchen, Moldavian rolls, sweet dough, nut squares, *lichiu,* cheese cake, crescents, horns, strudel, water twists, and puff pastry, with crepes suzettes being the most common.

The art of Romanian cooking was passed down from generation to generation by word of mouth and by example. Eventually recipes were collected and published, the most popular being the cookbook of Sanda Marin, which became a sort of standard. Today, there are many Romanian cookbooks, some of which are published in other languages, including English. Romanian cooking is appreciated in many parts of the world.

13 EDUCATION

A good education is prized by every Romanian. People with a high educational achievement and intellectuals are highly respected. The education sector itself went through several reform processes, the boldest of them being implemented by Andrei Marga—the former Minister of Education, and currently the rector of the Babes-Bolyai University in Cluj-Napoca. Most of these reforms (which among others include curriculum changes, student assessment, teacher training, finance, and governance) need to be continued to improve education outcomes.

Now that Romania is part of the EU, its education sector needs to be revamped to satisfy the demand for a more skilled labor force. The most difficult challenge will be to bridge the divide between education in urban areas and education in rural areas. Without a centralized placement system, it is increasingly difficult to find teachers that are willing to work in remote villages.

As of 2008 the literacy rate was nearly 98%, with compulsory education for 10 years. The Babes-Bolyai University in Cluj-Napoca is, at over 60,000 students, the largest multi-cultural university in Europe. It offers programs of study in Romanian, Hungarian, German, English, and Roma.

14 CULTURAL HERITAGE

The first printing presses were brought to Romania and Transylvania by the Saxons in the 16th century. With the introduction of the printing press, Romanian books, still with Cyrillic letters, were published. The Romanian deacon Coresi published the first book of the Gospels in Romanian at Bras,or in 1561. Metropolitan Varlaam of Moldova published the famous *Cazania* (explanation of the New Testament) in 1643, and Metropolitan Simeon Stefan published the New Testament in 1648.

Thereafter, a growing number of other Romanian books were published but still with Cyrillic letters. It was only after some Orthodox Churches in Transylvania united with the Roman Catholic Church in Rome (1698), and with the establishment of Romanian schools in the 19th century, that the Latin alphabet was reinstated officially. By the middle of the 19th century, a veritable educational and literary revival began. Romanian universities and other schools of higher learning were opened. Grade schools appeared in the villages, cultural organizations sprang up everywhere, and literary magazines and books started to be published in growing numbers.

Many poets, novelists, historians, essayists, and other writers flooded the market with their literary works. They enriched Romanian literature in all fields, and their number is legion, including such well-known poets as Vasile Alexandri, Grigorie Alexandrescu, George Cos,buc and Duliu Zamfirescu; novelists such as Costache Negruzzi and Alexandru Odobescu; storytellers such as Ion Slavici, Liviu Rebreanu, Mihail Sasoveanu, and Ion Agarbiceanu; dramatists such as L. Caragiale, Barba Delavraucea, and Victor Eftimiu; historians such as Alexandra D. Xenopol, Nicolae Iorga, Titus Maiorescu, Sextil Prescariu; and many others too numerous to mention.

Music has always been a significant factor in the life of the Romanian peasant. Peasants sing when they are happy or sad, when they are spiritually moved, or when they want to express their patriotic, romantic, and pastoral feelings. There are different types of music for different moods.

Almost every village has at least one musical group to play at village dances and other occasions. The basic Romanian musical instrument is the violin. Others include the wooden saxophone and the cymbalon. Later, orchestras added the bass fiddle, the piano, the clarinet, and the accordion. Romanians are among the few people who have preserved the ancient "pipes of Pan."

Among the most popular styles of folk songs are the *doina*, love songs, and pastoral and patriotic songs. During the Christmas season, the Romanians sing a great variety of carols. There are many religious hymns and songs for various feast days, which are familiar to all Romanians. On special occasions, there are ballads, lamentations, wedding songs, and a variety of others.

One of the most common and generalized folk dances is the *hora* (circle dance), danced by men and women holding hands. A popular dance is the *Sârba*, with dancers holding each other by the shoulder in a semicircle. There is also the *Brâul* (straight line). The most popular dances in Transylvania are the *invârtita* and *hategana*.

15 WORK

Once Romania was known as the breadbasket of Eastern Europe, exporting large quantities of wheat and corn. Nearly half of Romania's arable land is given over to agriculture, but because it is divided into so many small plots, with a lack of fertilizers and modern farming equipment, the output is poor. At times not enough food is produced to meet domestic needs, much less to export.

Nevertheless, villagers with their small plots raise enough food for their own needs. Since there is not much of a surplus, they do not bother to sell any produce at markets in nearby cities. In this respect, villagers are more or less self-sufficient and not lacking in the bare necessities of life, whereas urban dwellers, who must buy all their food, have a more difficult time because of scarcities, inflation, and low salaries. The new democratic government is trying desperately to reverse this trend and to make agriculture once again one of the main sources of income for the Romanian people.

Romania, with its beautiful mountains, quaint towns with ancient architecture, picturesque villages, seaside resorts, and many other tourist attractions, always afforded vacations at reasonable prices. Foreigners flocked to Romania for good monetary exchange rates and the country's many attractions. Some of this luster wore off during the Communist regime, and the number of foreign tourists decreased considerably, but it is now picking up again. With new airlines, railroads, and other new services, Romania's tourism industry hopes to regain some if its former polish and sophistication offered by warm and friendly hosts.

With increased wealth, the work ethic of Romanians has improved. A profitable career is often the main goal of young urban dwellers. Enrollment levels within universities have increased substantially, and private and public investments have driven up salaries in most economic sectors. In addition, more than 2 million Romanians are working abroad. In 2007 they sent nearly $7 billion to families and relatives back home. These remittances are an important source of economic growth, driving up consumption rates and development even in the most remote villages.

16 SPORTS

Romania is not especially known as a sports-minded nation, even though the people indulge in various kinds of sports. After working hard and long in the fields and factories, many are content to be mere spectators rather than participants. As in many European countries, the preferred sport is soccer. It is easy to lay out a playing field, and all one needs is a soccer ball. Aside from amateur teams and informal tournaments, Romania has a number of professional teams, which compete favorably with other countries. Each larger town has its own stadium, and some of them accommodate tens of thousands of spectators.

Besides soccer, Romanians also enjoy basketball, boxing, rugby, tennis, volleyball, and a few other sports imported from abroad. Sports such as hiking, swimming, mountain climbing, camping, hunting, and fishing are also popular.

Calisthenics, exercising, and other gymnastics are a part of the school curriculum. Some of the best students are specially trained to compete in international events. Nadia Comenici is a world-renowned Romanian gymnast, and Ilie Nastase is a top-level tennis player. Some of the Romanian trainers who have produced Olympic winners have found more profitable employment abroad in their fields.

17 ENTERTAINMENT AND RECREATION

Most Romanians are addicted to *promenade* (or *corso*). On any Saturday or Sunday afternoon in good weather, one will meet most of the villagers and small townspeople out for a leisurely walk, stopping to chat with friends and acquaintances, window-shopping, and just relaxing, ending up in a restaurant or open-air eating place for a drink and snacks.

Romanians also enjoy folk dance groups, amateur theatrical groups, music ensembles, and a host of other entertainers. The entertainment business is bustling. There are movie houses galore for local productions, as well as imported films with Romanian subtitles. Solo entertainers and any number of groups tour the country and present all kinds of entertainment to enthusiastic audiences.

Romania has many radio stations, television stations, live theaters, opera houses, cabarets, and entertainment establishments. Western influence, especially American and Italian, is noticeable in the music, dancing, films, dress, and behavior of present-day Romanians.

18 FOLK ART, CRAFTS, AND HOBBIES

Before the age of industrialization and commercialism, peasants made most of their own apparel, textiles, and domestic and household articles by hand, using materials that they grew, raised, or happened to have on hand. They purchased very few manufactured commodities.

The handmade articles were not only utilitarian, but also decorative. The Romanian peasants embellished not only their clothing and domestic utensils with colorful and intricate designs, but also the interiors and exteriors of their homes, their yards, their churches, and their cemeteries.

The basic textiles used by the peasants were made of hemp and wool. Cotton goods, linen, and silk were purchased. The hemp was cut, soaked, dried, beaten to free the fibers, tied to a distaff, and finally twisted into yarn on a spindle. After being bleached or dyed with vegetable colors readily available in the garden or the fields, the yarn was woven into a rough fabric on a loom. A similar procedure was followed to prepare and weave woolen fabrics. From these fabrics, a variety of garments, household articles, and decorative pieces were made, such as bed sheets, blankets, pillowcases, tablecloths, towels, shawls, and doilies.

Most of the tedious and intricate needlework was done at "spinning bees" during the long winter evenings at the homes of villagers. While the women sewed, knitted, and crocheted, the men were busy carving geometric designs or painting wooden articles and ceramics. These spinning bees were veritable cultural events, when epic stories were told, traditional songs were learned and sung, new folk dances were rehearsed, poems were recited, and personal experiences were exchanged.

Besides crafting textiles and wooden articles, Romanian peasants also wove rugs with unusual designs and pleasing colorful schemes. The rugs of Oltenia and Moldova are especially appreciated by connoisseurs of folk art. The floor rug, bench rug, and the wall rug are variations. Rugs are one of Romania's most prized and expensive exports.

Besides beautifully embroidered native costumes, rugs, and scarves, the artistic talents of the Romanian peasant were manifested in ceramics. Most peasant households had a variety of decorated plates, pots, vases, and jugs. Unglazed red pottery was used mostly for cooking and glazed pottery mostly for storing and carrying liquids. The more decorative pieces, varying in design, color, and shape, were hung on the wall or displayed on carved wooden shelves. Pottery was usually decorated with circles, spirals, stylized flowers, and other imaginative patterns.

Romanian peasants usually carried around a pocket knife, which had many uses, such as whittling and carving. Chip-carving is a specific Romanian art. The handiwork of these chip-carvers can be seen in their homes, such as carved picture frames, walking canes, ornamented boxes, distaffs and spindles, ladles, ax handles, cupboards, shelves, hope chests, chairs, tables, beams, window frames, doors, and gates. Along the roadside are to be found wayside shrines and, in cemeteries, many carved crosses and monuments. Various pieces of furniture and wooden items used in church are also carved with folk designs. Besides chip-carving, in some parts of Romania, peasants were adept at the art of pyrography, the process of burning designs into wood or leather.

A most unusual form of Romanian folk art is that of icons painted on glass. This art came to Transylvania from Bohemia in the 17th century and flourished for over 150 years before it nearly died out. It has been lately revived. The icon was painted backwards on a piece of glass, so it could be seen correctly when viewed from the front side. Rather amateurish, but flashy and unique, they originally sold mostly at local marketplaces.

Secular painting in Romania grew out of ecclesiastical art in the beginning of the 19th century, especially through the efforts of George Tatarescu, Theodor Aman, and Constantin Lecca. Nicolae Gregorescu, who started as an iconographer, became one of Romania's greatest painters with his rural scenes and landscapes. Many others followed, and their works are to be found in various galleries, museums, and private collections throughout Romania.

19 SOCIAL PROBLEMS

Though Romania had to endure barbaric invasions, foreign domination, political upheavals, serfdom, suppression, and persecution, the population remained optimistic and had a vision of a brighter future. Sadly, Romanians' hopes were darkened by the Communist philosophy that was imposed on the people in the 20th century.

The transition period that followed 1989 was not easy, and incidents of civil unrest (such as miners' strikes in 1990 and 1991, or the 1990 inter-ethnic clashes in Târgu Mureş) made headlines in the years to follow. However, with the advent of better economic conditions in 2000, most social problems have been resolved. Romania now has one of the lowest crime rates in Europe.

20 GENDER ISSUES

In the 1950s, Romania's newly laid socialist foundations created a desire for more independence for women. In 1957, abortion was legalized and an increasing number of women started to join the work force, albeit in predominantly feminized sectors. However, in 1966 abortion became illegal, which was an attempt on the part of the Communist regime to raise birth rates and rapidly increase the size of the population. These pro-natalist measures were unique in the region.

In the 21st century, equal opportunity legislation has been enacted to protect the rights of women and of ethnic and sexual minorities. However, men continue to earn on average more than women do.

President Traian Basescu took a bold stance in favor of gay rights. Although much progress has been made in the area of gay rights, much remains to be done. The 2007 Gay Parade in

²¹ BIBLIOGRAPHY

Augerot, Joseph E. *Modern Romania.* Columbus, Ohio: Slavica, 1993.

Baerlin, H. ed. *The Romanian Scene.* London: F. Muller, 1945.

Basderant, Denise. *Against Tide and Tempest: The Story of Romania.* New York: R. Speller, 1966.

Boia, Lucian. *Romania.* New York: Reaktion Books, 2004.

Carran, Betty. *Romania.* Chicago: Children's Press, 1988.

Fischer-Galati, Stephen A. *Romania.* New York: Published for the Mid-European Studies Center of the Free Europe Committee by F. A. Praeger, 1957.

Feffer, John. *Shock Waves: Eastern Europe after the Revolutions.* Boston: South End Press, 1992.

Hall, D. J. *Romanian Furrow.* London: G. Harrap, 1939.

Hupchick, Dennis P. *The Balkans: From Constantinople to Communism.* New York: Palgrave Macmillan, 2002.

Kaplan, Robert D. *Balkan Ghosts: A Journey Through History.* New York: Picador, 2005.

Klepper, Nicolae. *Romania: An Illustrated History.* New York: Hippocrene Books, 2003.

Logio, George C. *Rumania, Its History, Politics, and Economics.* Manchester: Sherratt & Hughes, 1932.

Markham, Reuben H. *Romania Under the Soviet Yoke.* Boston: Meador Publishing Company, 1949.

Matley, Ian M. *Romania: A Profile.* New York: Praeger, 1970.

Patmore, Derek. *Invitation to Roumania.* New York: Macmillan, 1939.

Pittaway, Mark. *Brief Histories: Eastern Europe 1939–2000.* London: Arnold, 2004.

Roberts, H. L. *Romania: Political Problems of an Agrarian State.* Hamden, CT: Archon Books, 1969.

Seton-Watson, R. *A History of the Roumanians.* Cambridge: University Press, 1934.

Zderciuc, G. *L'Art Populaire Roumanie.* Bucarest: Editions Meridiane, 1964

—revised by Marcel Ionescu-Heroiu.

RUSSIANS

LOCATION: Russia
POPULATION: 142.9 million [Russian 79.8%, Tatar 3.8%, Ukrainian 2%, Bashkir 1.2%, Chuvash 1.1%, other or unspecified 12.1%]
LANGUAGE: Russian (official); more than 140 other languages and dialects.
RELIGION: Russian Orthodox, Roman Catholicism, other Christian, Islam, Buddhism, Judaism, other

¹ INTRODUCTION

The Russians are a people of mixed origins. Although they are primarily eastern Slavs, many Russians have a Finnish, Siberian, Turkish, or Baltic heritage. Since the Russians' domain has historically covered such a large territory, many culturally distinct subgroups have developed. These subgroups formed because of ethnic mixing, cultural assimilation, or isolation and include the following: Meshcheryak, Kerzhak, Bukhtarman, Semeisk, Polyak, Starozhil, Russkoustin, Markov, Yakutyan, Kamchadal, Karym, Kolymchan, Zatundra Peasants, Pomor, Polekh, and Sayan groups. Many of these smaller groups are Russian Orthodox Old Believer communities or mixed Cossack-Siberian peoples.

The Slavic ancestors of the Russians are believed to have first settled in the area north of the Black Sea. The ancient Greeks and Romans made mention of these ancient Slavic tribes in their writings, but little was known about them. By the 7th century AD, there were many Slavic tribes in the region between the Baltic Sea and the Black Sea, living in autonomous villages that cooperated in areas such as defense. The "Varangians" (the old Slavonic term for Vikings) came to rule over the Russians in Novgorod, and the Rurik dynasty was established as the first ruling family of Russia as head of the Kievan Rus state. Trade between the Kievan Rus state and Constantinople exposed the Russians to Byzantine culture and religion. Eastern Orthodox Christianity was introduced during the mid-900s, but it was not until 988 that the largest conversion to Christianity happened.

An event that had a profound effect on the development of Russian culture was the Mongol occupation (c. 1240–1480). For over two centuries, the Mongols used threats and force to make the Russians pay them tribute and taxes, but the Mongols let the ruling princes and the Russian Orthodox Church remain in power. At that time a very strong Tatar/Mongol admixture began with the Russians. Some scholars think that the occupation helped unify local leaders against a common foe, which led to the strong tradition of autocracy in later centuries. Other historians believe that the period of Mongol rule disrupted cultural links with the rest of Byzantium and Eastern Europe and is part of the reason why Russia was not influenced by the Renaissance, Reformation, or Industrial Revolution when those events occurred in Western Europe. By the end of the occupation, the village of Moscow had positioned itself as an important political and religious center.

The Rurikovich dynasty that claimed its Viking origin ended in 1598 when Fedor died with no heir. Then, a period of tumultuous power struggles ensued, which the Russians call the "Time of Troubles." In 1613, order finally returned to the throne as the nobility elected Michael Romanov as the new tsar (a term taken from the Roman title "Caesar," meaning "emperor"). During the 1600s, the Russian conquest of Siberia began. Out of the Romanov dynasty came the man who is usually considered to have been the greatest tsar in Russian history, Peter I (1672–1725), called Peter the Great. Peter instituted many policies to change or modernize Russian culture so that it would be more like that of Western Europe. During the reign of Catherine II (r.1762–96) the Russian Empire added substantial territory through conquest, and there was a mass migration and heavy presence of Germans in Russia.

For centuries, serfdom was a way of life for most Russian peasants who did not own any land. Serfdom was a feudal form of bonded servitude similar to slavery, except that a serf belonged to the master's land. Whenever land was sold, the serfs who worked on that land became the property of the new owner. The victory over Napoleon's army in the War of 1812 was one of the most important events to consolidate the Russian people in the early 1800s. Throughout much of the 1800s, the Russians (especially the nobility) held a passion for French culture and language. After the French retreated, the tsar, Alexander I (r.1801–25), tried to return to business as usual but eventually abolished serfdom in a few small areas near the Baltic Sea.

In 1825, the first organized revolt against the imperial government was instigated by a group of army officers called the Decembrists, who wanted to abolish serfdom and set up a constitutional government. Although the revolt was small and unsuccessful, its memory served to rally the people in later years. In 1861 Alexander II (1855–81) emancipated the serfs. By the late 1870s, however, there were already revolutionary stirrings present within Russian society that grew out of the nihilist and populist movements. In 1881, Alexander II was assassinated by terrorists. Industrialization helped improve the economy, but a financial crisis in 1899, crop failures, and a humiliating defeat in a 1905 war with Japan led to more civil unrest and strikes by organized labor. Millions of Russian peasants were moving from the country into cities. The urbanization made it possible for Russians to mobilize. At the turn of the 20th century, many Russians had come to believe that the imperial government was incompetent.

Relations with Germany and Austria had been tense in the 1880s and 1890s, and problems flared up again in 1908. A complex system of treaties and alliances caused the unrest in the Balkans to inflame tensions throughout Europe, which led to World War I. By 1914, the Russians found themselves fighting in a useless war that plunged the nation into economic turmoil and chaos. Nicholas II (r. 1894–1917) abdicated the throne. A provisional government was formed to be replaced by the Bolsheviks, led by Lenin (r. 1917–24). In 1918, Lenin had the entire royal family executed.

The Soviet era lasted from 1917 to 1991. During the Soviet years, there was a massive mixing of Russians with Ukrainians, Belarusans, Jews, Finno-Ugric peoples, etc. In the 1920s and 1930s, the Communist Soviet government under Stalin (r.1924–53) instituted policies of terror and persecution to consolidate its power. The government tried to control all property and access to information in order to keep people in line. Millions of Russians were eventually imprisoned, exiled, or executed on fabricated charges and suspicion. It has been estimated that as many as 20 million Soviet citizens died during the period of 1928–38 from Stalin's reign of terror and a series of famines that Stalin could have prevented.

The most profound event to unite the Russian people during the Soviet years was World War II, which Russians call "the Great Patriotic War." An estimated 27 million Soviet citizens died in the war, half of which were civilians or prisoners. After World War II, the Soviet Union quickly rebuilt its military and became a leading ideological and military rival of the United States. During the 1950s and 1960s, the Soviet Union, under the leadership of Nikita Khrushchev (r.1953–64), and the United States began stockpiling nuclear weapons to use against each other in the event of warfare. However, the horror of mutual destruction served to prevent either nation from starting such a war.

The losses from World War II and the focus on the military afterwards deeply affected modern Russian culture. During the 1970s, political and economic stagnation in the Soviet Union became rampant, and daily life for many Russians reflected the spirit of those times. In the mid-1980s, widespread reforms began under the leadership of Mikhail Gorbachev (r. 1985–91), and these reforms ushered in a new optimism among the Russian people that eventually challenged the very existence of the authoritarian Soviet government.

When the Soviet Union ceased to exist in 1991, the Russian people (as well as those from the other republics) were filled with hope for a glorious future. The Russian people now had their first chance in history to freely choose their own leadership through democratic elections. During the 1990s, however, the naive expectations for many Russians disappeared when it became apparent that the transition from central planning to a market economy would not be quick and painless.

President Boris Yeltsin's era brought Russia a democratic constitution and economic reforms resulting in a deep financial crisis and regional disintegration. Vladimir Putin came to power in 2000 just in time to implement a series of liberal economic reforms that rescued a faltering economy and stopped the spiral of hyperinflation. Putin achieved wide popularity among the Russian population by stabilizing the government. The economy grew both due to Putin's reforms in banking, taxation, labor, and private property and rising oil prices. Putin's political and economic policies were predicted to continue with his successor, Russian president Dimitry Medvedev.

In 2002, the North Atlantic Treaty Organization (NATO)-Russia Council was established, giving Russia a voice in NATO discussions. Russia is also a permanent member of the United Nations Security Council, the leading nation of the Commonwealth of Independent States, a member of the Group of 8, and other international organizations as well. Recently, Russia moved closer politically to the United States, especially after the 11 September 2001 terror attacks. At the same time recent consolidation of presidential powers, certain nationalistic movements, and instances of violation of human rights and freedom of expression prompt the West to question Russian democracy.

2 LOCATION AND HOMELAND

The Russian homeland traditionally extended from the easternmost parts of Europe to the Ural Mountains. Beginning in the 1500s, Russia experienced a massive acquisition of territory. By 1600, Russia was already larger than any other country in Europe and extended eastward all the way to the Pacific

Ocean. By 1800, Russia consisted of much of Eastern Europe, extended well into Central Asia, and even had territorial claims in North America.

As of 2008, Russia is the largest country in the world. It occupies about 17,075,000 sq km (6,592,700 sq mi), covering nearly 12% of the world's land surface. Russia shares land borders with Norway, Finland, Estonia, Latvia, Lithuania, Poland, Belarus, Ukraine, Georgia, Azerbaijan, Kazakhstan, China, Mongolia, and North Korea. It is in near proximity (by Russian standards) to the United States, Sweden and Japan. Stretching from Europe to Asia, Russia envelops 11 time zones.

Russia is divided into a complex system of 83 distinct administrative units. This includes 46 *oblasts (provinces)*, 9 *krais* (territories), the metropolitan cities of Moscow and St. Petersburg, 16 self-governing autonomous republics, 5 autonomous regions, 1 autonomous province (the Jewish Autonomous Oblast) and 4 autonomous *okrugs* (autonomous districts). Until recently, Russia had more units, but after several subsequent merges beginning in 2005 the number of units shrank to 83. Russia's population is about 140 million, and it has been estimated that about 80% of the population consists of ethnic Russians. There are also approximately 3 million people in the United States who claim Russian ancestry. About 74% of the population lives in urban areas.

For many decades, most Russians were not permitted to freely emigrate from the Soviet Union. Many Russians did settle in the other republics of the Soviet Union, especially in urban or industrial areas. Since the end of the Soviet era, there has been a massive movement of Russians to and from the homeland. Many ethnic Russians in the other former Soviet republics chose to go back to Russia because some of those new governments were pressuring them to leave. At the same time, large number of Russians left and continue to leave Russia for the United States and Europe. Educated but unemployed or underpaid Russians (such as scientists) are now emigrating to the West in search of jobs to match their expertise.

³ LANGUAGE

Russian is the official language of Russia. In addition, Russia has more than 140 other languages and dialects. Modern Russian is an Eastern Slavic language. During the 10th century, two Orthodox monks, Cyril and Methodius, wanted to translate the Bible into the Russians' native language. This older language later came to be known as Old Slavonic, and it is still used by the Russian Orthodox Church. Since the Russians had no written language, the monks created a new alphabet from parts of the Latin, Greek, and Hebrew alphabets to represent the sounds of Old Slavonic. The Cyrillic alphabet, as it is called, is used in Russian and some other Slavic languages (such as Ukrainian, Bulgarian, Serbian, etc.). During the Soviet era, many of the other languages used within the Soviet Union were changed to the Cyrillic alphabet (and now many have changed back), and so there are many other ethnic groups familiar with the Cyrillic alphabet.

Common male first names include Aleksander, Boris, Dmitri, Ivan, Leonid, Mikhail and Sergei. First names for women typically end with an "a" or "ya" sound and include Anastasia, Maria, Natalya, Olga, Sophia, Tatyana, and Valentina. Most of those names come to Russia with Christianity and therefore of Jewish, Greek or Roman origin. Furthermore, there are a few Slavic Russian names dating back to thousand years ago. Among them are Svetlana (of light), Lubov (love), Vera (hope, faith) and Ludmila (beloved by people) used by women and Vladimir (one who owns the world), Svyatoslav (holy glory), Vechelsav (eternal glory), Bogdan (given by God) used by men.

Examples of everyday Russian words include *Kak delah?* (How's it going?), *da* (yes), *nyet* (no), *pozhaluistah* (please), *spaseebo* (thank you), and *do sveedanniya* (goodbye).

4 FOLKLORE

Russian oral folklore fall into several categories: *bylinas*, legends, fairy tales, animal tales, and tales of everyday life.

Traditional Russian fairy tales are just as likely to have a sad ending as a happy one. A fairy tale hero is usually a prince such as Ivan Tsarevich or a simpleton, such as Emelya Durak (Emelya the Fool). Prominent evil figures include Baba Yaga, a witch who lives in a house on chicken legs; and Koshchey the Immortal, a dragon that can only be killed if the egg that holds the essence of its death is found. More often than not, Russian fairytale is a story about a young man's or a young women's venture into the outer world, often dangerous and unpredictable. As a quest, this venture may take spiritual, intellectual or physical forms. Along the way, the hero or heroine is required to perform various tasks ranging from the trivial to the breathtaking. Russian fairy tale heroes often overcome a dangerous quest through the help of magical animals or objects.

Russian heroic tales narrate the epic deeds of *bogatyrs* (mighty warriors). This genre consists of epic songs, known as *bylinas and legends. Bylinas* were sung by peasants and date back to before the 16th century. Some of the *bylinas* and legends such as those about Svyatogor the Giant or Volk Vseslavich (Wolf the Almighty) are probably over 1,000 years old. Many of heroic tales are set in an idealized vision of the Kievan Rus age or in Novgorod.

The heroes and heroines of bylinas and legends are diverse. Yet they have many commonalities in their goals including the main goal—to defeat the insidious and formidable adversary and liberate the homeland. As a rule, bogatyrs from their very birth demonstrate excessive physical strength and innate intelligence. Since their childhood they are local favorites and acclaimed community leaders admired by both men and women.

In the well-known story "Ivan Tsarevich and Storm Bogatyr" three identical heroes are born at the same moment

as a result of their three mothers drinking a fine soup made of golden-finned pike: Ivan Tsarevich, Ivan the Maid's son, and Storm Bogatyr, who is also known as Ivan the Cow's son. They have adventures, such as the mighty struggle on Kalinov Bridge with three Dragons who devastated the county side. All struggles are won by Storm Bogatyr. The dragons' mothers and wives, powerful witches, try to work the ruin of bogatyrs, but Storm Bogatyr outsmarts them and destroys their plots.

Exaggeration of physical strength in Russian heroic tales is typical not only for male, but also for female personages. Thus, women-warriors, such as the sisters Polyanitsas, easily beat male bogatyrs in multiple contests. No bogatyr except for the main hero can withstand Polyanitsas. In addition to distinguished strength, the woman-bogatyrs are known for their loyalty, extraordinary beauty, and intelligence

Animal tales often deal with humorous interactions among animals that possess human qualities. Two of the most popular animal characters are Lisa Patrikeevna, a smooth-talking and cunning fox, and Mikhail Ivanych, a sometimes clumsy, sometimes wise bear. Through these anecdotes, Russian people convey absurdity of certain situations; laugh at foolishness; praise wisdom and kindness; and address other situations common in life.

More recent in folklore history are tales of everyday life. Such tales often incorporate practical jokes and satire. They illustrate people's daily troubles and concerns and reveal their hopes and aspirations. It is common for these stories to see an underdog succeed despite great odds.

5 RELIGION

Initially followers of paganism, Russians converted to Christianity in the 10th century. In AD 988, Prince Vladimir of the Kievan Rus state proclaimed Christianity as the official religion of the realm in order to ally his kingdom with the powerful Byzantine Empire. Although keeping close connection with Byzantine canons, Russian Orthodoxy developed its own distinct features and traditions. A typical Russian Orthodox Church is adorned with many icons (images of persons who are revered as holy). Most icons are of biblical characters or saints, but some are of prominent clergy or leaders. Large churches often display an iconostasis (a wall of arranged icons) between the sanctuary and the rest of the church.

Lavish ceremonies on holy days (such as Epiphany and Easter) are well incorporated into Russian Orthodox tradition. Russian Orthodox worship services follow a liturgical format with heavy usage of choirs. The congregation typically stands for the duration of the service (many churches have no pews) and move to various stations around the sanctuary. It is common to see a person of the Russian Orthodox faith cross himself or herself using three fingers, touching first the forehead, then the abdomen, followed by the right shoulder, and ending at the left shoulder (because it is closest to the heart).

During the Soviet era, religious intolerance became official policy. It has been estimated that 85% of all churches were shut down and the property seized. Communist leaders were atheists who perceived the Russian Orthodox Church as a player in the corrupt imperial system of the tsars. The tsars had claimed rule by divine right and were endorsed by the Russian Orthodox Church. To eradicate the Church's influence, the Soviet government encouraged discrimination against Russians with religious beliefs, and some Russians were imprisoned or killed

Nesting dolls in front of the Church of the Resurrection of Christ in St. Petersburg, Russia. (© Bo Zaunders/Corbis)

for their faith. Ironically, the Soviet regime tried to establish its authority by manipulating and utilizing many of the traditional Russian religious symbols, customs, and beliefs to give them a new, Soviet-style meaning. For example, the people represented on icons changed from religious to ideological and political figures (such as Marx, Lenin, and Stalin).

However, the Soviet era did not eradicate religion completely. Many religious activities were conducted secretly. For many people religious and spiritual matters became a strictly personal rather than public affair. After the disintegration of the Soviet Union many of the closed churches reopened. Today, with nearly 5,000 religious organizations, the Russian Orthodox Church accounts for over half the total number of religious groups registered in Russia. Next in numbers come Muslim communities amounting to 3,000. Other religious organizations include Baptists, 450; Seventh Day Adventists, 120; Evangelicals, 120; Old Believers, over 200; Roman Catholics, 200; Krishnaites, 68; Buddhists, 80; Jews, 50; and Unified Evangelical Lutherans, 39.

Muslims are the second largest religious community in Russia. Current estimates indicate that Russia has over 19 million Muslims. They have over 800 parishes and mosques, mostly in Bashkortostan, Dagestan, Kabarda-Balkaria, North Ossetia, Tatarstan, Ingushetia, and Chechnya. Most prominent organizations include the Muslim Board for Central European region and the Moscow Muftiyat. Additionally, Russia has 42 Jewish communities. Moscow alone accounts for over 10% of Russian Jews, and has three synagogues, one of which is Hasidic.

In recent decades, Buddhism has risen in popularity among Russians. Pockets of newly initiated Buddhists are spread across the whole country, while traditional Buddhism is re-establishing its prominence in Buryatia, Kalmykia, Tuva, and the Irkutsk and Chits regions. The Russian Federation currently has ten datsun monasteries and multiple Buddhist centers, with the total monastic body approaching 200. Another 10 monasteries are under construction.

Despite several decades of Soviet pragmatism and atheism, superstition and mysticism have long been an integral part of Russian spiritual culture. The Russians today are often more open than other people to the possibility of paranormal activities, such as psychic experiences, mental telepathy, and extra-terrestrial life.

6 MAJOR HOLIDAYS

There are several religious holidays that have been celebrated in Russia for centuries. Among them are Orthodox Christmas, Epiphany and Easter. The origin of one of the world's most famous Christmas traditions began with St. Nicholas of Myra, a patron saint of Russia. For centuries, St. Nicholas was honored in the Russian Orthodox Church with dignity and devotion, playing a central role in Christmas festivities. On Christmas

Eve it was customary to fast until after the first service in the Russian Orthodox Church. With the appearance of the evening star on Christmas Eve, the fast was over. Following the meal, families would walk around the neighborhood singing carols, dressed as the stable animals present at Bethlehem. Meanwhile, St. Nicholas would reward good children with presents.

However, under the Soviet regime, many religious holidays were lessened in importance or forgotten, while new holidays were created. New Year's Day became a major holiday among Russians. It adopted the St. Nicholas tradition replacing St. Nicholas with Grandfather Frost. Marked with conviviality, wonderful meals with friends and family, and songs and fireworks, this holiday is equally loved by children and adults. On New Year's Eve children eagerly await for the Grandfather Frost and the Snow Maiden. The two weeks preceding January 1 and a few days after are full of festivals. Crowds flock to the city square to celebrate with each other the end of the year and to enjoy illuminations, ice sculptures, ice slides, New Year skits, free concerts, champagne, food, and everything else that the festival has to offer.

February 23 or the Day of the Protector of the Motherland honors Russian men. All men receive presents, cards and appreciation. Children make handmade gifts for their fathers and grandfathers. Women's Day, another holiday remaining from Soviet times, is celebrated on March 8. This holiday celebrates women. Mothers, daughters, girlfriends, wives—all women—receive gifts and flowers. Loving husbands and fathers try to grant any wish their wives and daughters might have. First of May is no longer International Workers' Solidarity Day as it was during the Soviet era, but is now a festival known as Labor and Spring Day. Victory Day on May 9 commemorates the end of World War II in Europe and is usually observed as a time to solemnly honor those who died during that war. During that day each city holds numerous parades. The highlight of the day is fireworks. November 4, the Day of National Unity, is the newest Russian holiday. It allows Russians to celebrate their country and pride in their culture and traditions.

Recently, church feasts also have been revived. The Orthodox Christmas is gaining in popularity. It occurs on January 7 (the Russian Orthodox Church still follows the old Julian calendar, which differs from the modern Gregorian calendar by 13 days). Involving church rituals, Christmas is especially honored by the Christian community, but being an inseparable part of Russian culture for centuries, it is currently recognized nationwide. Often a day off, Christmas became another holiday to spend with family and friends. The Russian Church of course honors this day with elaborate rituals and extravagance. Epiphany, which occurs 12 days after Christmas, is another major holy day in the Russian Orthodox Church and is celebrated with much pageantry and symbolism. Easter (in March or April) is the most popular religious holiday. It was celebrated even under the Soviet regime, but now people try to revive Easter customs and traditions that were abandoned after the revolution. Importantly, Muslims, Jews and Buddhists also celebrate their holidays without fear of secular authorities.

7 RITES OF PASSAGE

Completion of high school or university are important moments that mark the passage into independent live. Entrance into military service is regarded in the same way. Weddings symbolize path into adulthood and are usually followed by a trip in a special black limousine (crowned with two large interlinked rings on the top) to pay homage and leave flowers at a local memorial. The birth of one's first child and one's first professional job are other events that indicate a change of social status.

8 INTERPERSONAL RELATIONS

Generations of authoritarian influence have helped form a distinct division between public and private behavior in Russian society. This contrast came about because, until recently, people were often hesitant to speak freely in public because of what the government might do to them. In public situations, Russians are often very reserved and formal. However, in private and informal settings, Russians are very cordial and sincere. They often openly show deep feelings of affection when guests arrive and depart.

In public, (i.e. in the street, on the bus), Russians might appear cold and reserved. However, once the ice is broken—for example when a passerby asks for directions, Russians instantly display friendliness and eagerness to help. Russians place a great value in friends. People enjoy visiting each other. It is common to drop by unannounced and share a meal with the host. It is customary for Russians to treat their guests with tea and pastries, cookies, preserves, jams etc. Russians are especially hospitable to the foreigners. For centuries, foreigners and travelers have been revered in Russia. Foreign guests are sure to get the best meal and best possible accommodations.

Russians use patronymics (where the father's first name forms the root of the child's middle name) in formal and business situations. For example, the patronymic for the son of Pavel (Paul) is "Pavlovich," and "Pavlovna" for a daughter. Among adult acquaintances, even casual friends will usually address each other using the first name combined with the patronymic. Among family and friends, many common first names are shortened. For example, a man named Aleksander is often called "Sasha" by his friends and family. Sasha's parents or wife may sometimes call him "Sashen'ka," which would be a term of endearment. However, if they called him "Sashka," it would indicate anger or disappointment with him.

When one Russian asks another "How are you?" there is a genuine and sincere interest; it is not done merely as a courtesy. When asked such a question, it is not customary for Russians to feel compelled to give a short and positive response. To ask someone how they are doing and then to ignore or trivialize their response is considered rude.

War veterans are extremely revered in Russia, particularly anyone who defended or aided Russia during World War II. Along with handicapped persons and expectant mothers, veterans are commonly given preferential seating on public transportation. It is not unusual to see elderly Russian women and men wearing their medals in public, especially on national holidays.

Flowers are an important token of admiration or affection. Flowers are often given as presents when visiting friends, either in a bouquet or as a single blossom. Visiting a local monument or memorial to leave flowers has become a tradition among newlyweds. After an opera or dance performance, Russians often shower the stage with flowers as a sign of delight.

9 LIVING CONDITIONS

During the Soviet years, Russians received health care from a large state-run system that provided service free of charge. In theory, this socialist system supposedly served everyone equitably, made use of the most recent technology, promoted preventive medicine, and was open to recommendations from the population. In reality, however, resources were distributed unequally, with political elites receiving the best care and rural citizens served with the least adequate equipment and undertrained personnel. Although medical care was free, many health care professionals moonlighted to make some extra money because official health care usually involved long lines and waiting lists. Although the number of doctors doubled from the 1960s to the 1980s, health indicators such as illness rates, mortality rates, and life expectancy worsened during that time. After the 1990s the situation changed. Now people have to pay for almost all medical care and the system of medical insurance is being established. The visit to renowned specialist is the most expensive. There are still some free services offered for the poorest population, but those serves are of inferior quality.

Pregnant Russian women go to special maternity homes for delivery. Newborns are wrapped in swaddling clothes because of the traditional belief that it will help the infant's fragile bones to grow straight. Russian women receive two months of paid maternity leave before delivery and two months of paid leave afterwards, in addition to another year of leave at half-pay.

The communal *banya* (bathhouse), where bathers soak and sweat together, has been a mainstay of Russian culture for centuries. The banya is like a large sauna and is especially popular in the winter. Some banyas may be open only to either men or women on certain days of the week, while others may have some separate and some combined facilities for both sexes. Russians often carry small birch brooms in the banya and will lightly swat themselves and others (if asked) with the birch because they believe that it helps improve circulation and draws out toxins from the body.

Standing in long lines to buy consumer goods was a fact of daily life during the Soviet era. Russians became used to the idea of on-the-go shopping, constantly keeping alert for anything they might need. Some families would even rotate the responsibility of a designated shopper—someone who spent the day standing in lines and looking for available items. Now things are changing. Many supermarkets and new stores are open. They operate 24 hours a day 7 days a week and carry all possible goods. However, not everyone can afford to shop in such stores. The average price for certain foods and other consumer items is higher than in the United States while the household income is much lower.

Today, Moscow is one of the most expensive cities in the world. In 2008, 7 out of the 25 wealthiest people in the world lived in Russia. Still 15% of the population lives below the subsistence level and very few have savings. The gap between rich and poor is rapidly growing and experts estimate that the middle class ranges from one-fifth to one-third of the population. That said, statistics indicate that in 2006 there were 112 fixed-line and mobile subscribers per 100 people in Russia. Purchase of clothes and footwear and other consumer goods has grown. In short, in contemporary Russia people put a lot of value in material things and work very hard to get them.

10 FAMILY LIFE

Russian women typically get married between the ages of 19 and 22, while men are usually between 20 and 24 years old at marriage. Marriages traditionally involved high ceremonies in the Russian Orthodox Church. During the Soviet era, celebration in the church was largely abandoned. Civil marriages became common, and new Soviet marriage customs developed. Couples who decided to marry would have to register at a local office, where they would be assigned a wedding date in advance with enough time to let them reconsider. These new marriage customs included a brief civil ceremony at a town "Wedding Palace," officiated by a woman from the local political council. Today many people include in their wedding a ceremony in the church. Although honeymoons are not a tradition among Russians, due to Western influence they have gained in popularity.

Despite the general lack of housing, Russian society highly reveres parenthood and large families. During the Soviet era, women who gave birth to five or more children were awarded medals and given special titles by the government. Although Russian society favors large families, the birth rate among Russians has been low since the 1970s, as a result of economic uncertainty and a high frequency of abortions among Russian women. This was especially true during the Soviet years, when contraceptive devices were often unavailable. Most urban Russian families have only one or two children, but rural families frequently have more. Recent governments have attempted to ameliorate the low birth rate by giving special rewards and privileges to parents with newly born babies. However, the birth rate is still low.

Russian society often focuses on children, who have a privileged role of honor. Russian adults typically do not hesitate to assist any child in need, and parents will often make tremendous personal sacrifices for their children. It is also common for Russian adults to scold any misbehaving child, regardless of relation.

11 CLOTHING

Most Russians wear European-style clothing on a daily basis and for special occasions. Jeans and other types of practical work clothes are often preferred as well. Russians usually try to appear as neatly groomed and dressed as possible when out in public. It is considered important, especially among women, to have clothes of the newest fashion. Many Russians cannot afford an extensive wardrobe, and demonstrate resourcefulness and creativity in getting and wearing garments of high quality. Well made, fashionable shoes are praised both by men and women.

During the winter, it is customary for Russian men and women wear the *ushanka* (fur hat), which has ear flaps that can be tied up or down depending on how cold it is. Many Russians wear fur in the winter—not as a status symbol but because of the harsh climate and the practicality of available fur. Today though, more and more Russians, especially teenagers, wear lighter sporty jackets and winter coats made of synthetic fabrics.

Traditional costumes are usually seen during cultural performances. For young girls costume items include colorful ribbons in the hair and for older women large kerchiefs. Other female garments comprise a long, loose, usually white robe and a bright colored tsarafan (dress) worn over the robe. Often

An older Russian woman sells hand-knit goods in an open-air market in Zaraysk, Russia. (Melanie Stetson Freeman/The Christian Science Monitor/Getty Images)

times robe and dress would have elaborate embroidery or lace on them. For men, a traditional outfit consists of a white or red spacious hip-long robe tied on the waist with rope and voluminous pants. Today, traditional headscarves are still widely worn by elderly women. Ethnic patterns are becoming increasingly incorporated into modern clothes. Also, in a recent Miss Russia beauty pageant, there was a traditional dress contest, for which the women had to appear in ethnic attire.

12 FOOD

Russians greatly enjoy drinking *chai* (hot tea). A typical Russian meal consists of *pervoye* (first), *vtoroye* (second), *zakuski* (side dishes), and *sladkoe* (dessert). Zakuski usually include salads, fish, cold cuts and pickles. Bread is an essential indigent of every meal. "No dinner without bread," goes the Russian saying. There are multiple varieties of wheat loaves, rye bread, and other types of bread. Also, Russians eat more rye bread than any nation in the world—a peculiarity of the Russian diet. *Kartoshka* (potatoes) are often served at meals, either boiled, mashed, as pancakes, or as a *kugel* (baked pudding).

Russians can boast an extensive list of traditional soups. *Borshch* is just one of the everyday Russian soups, made with red beets and beef, usually served with a dollop of sour cream. *Shchee* is another popular Russian soup, made from cabbage and meat stock. Another favorite soup is *solyanka,* which is tomato-based and has pieces of fish or meat, olives, and lemon. *Okroshka* is an exquisite cold soup with chopped-up meat, vegetables and broth made of *kvass* (traditional Russian drink made from rye).

Bliny, also a part *of the national cuisine,* are thin crepes served plain or with different types of fillings, and *pirozhki* are fried or baked pasties that usually have a meat or vegetable filling. Russians are great lovers of *pel'meni*—small Siberian meat pies boiled in broth and many enjoy *varenniki*—pot stickers with vegetable feeling. Often times pel'meni and varenniki are served with mustard, horseradish, and/or sour cream. *Ikra* (caviar), a famous Russian appetizer made from harvested sturgeon eggs, is also a part of formal Russian cuisine. *Morozhenoye* (ice cream) is a popular year-round treat.

As the Russian custom has it, a festive table is not worth much without a bottle of good vodka. It is considered that Russian wheat vodka is the world's best. Vodka varieties range from the clear, colorless Moskovskaya and Stolichnaya to all imaginable flavored kinds with herbs and spices. Of ethnic Russian soft drinks, kvass is the best-known. Made of brown bread or malted rye flour, it is particularly appreciated on a sultry summer day.

13 EDUCATION

After Russian children are about 1 year old, they go to a day nursery called a *yasli* until they are about 3 years old. From ages 3 to 6 or 7, Russians attend *detski sad* (kindergarten). Elementary school (grades 1–4) is called *nachalnaya shkola*. At age 11, Russian children enter the fifth grade and stay in *srednaya shkola* (high school) through the tenth grade, usually at age 17. At the start of the middle school years, students typically study history, geography, biology, and begin a foreign language. In the eighth and ninth grades, physics, chemistry, and electives are taught. After the ninth grade, a student may follow one of three educational paths: vocational school, professional training at a *tekhnikum* (secondary specialized school), or two years of general high school as preparation for university studies. In order to go to a high school, students need to pass an exam in language and mathematics at the end of the ninth grade. In addition to advanced studies of subjects taught in the middle-school years, Russian high school students study information systems and computer technology, social studies, and astronomy.

Attending a university or science institute is difficult because there is much competition just to get in. There are a series of special examinations, and many students will spend an entire year studying for those tests. A college program takes five years for a masters degree (there is no equivalent to a bachelor's degree in Russian universities) or six years for a medical degree.

Children are often exposed at an early age to systems that stress or value collective efforts. For example, young children in nurseries are typically toilet-trained in large groups. Students in schools often perform in groups and are graded as a team rather than as individuals. Oral and written examinations are given frequently. Teachers will often tell students their grades out loud, so that each person knows what grade the others received. Schools are often open 12 hours per day, but classes only take up about half of that time. The rest of the time, the school acts as a community youth and recreation center. Russian education emphasizes history, science, and math, and frequent homework assignments usually keep students busy in the evenings. Students are responsible for keeping the classrooms and hallways clean. Extracurricular activities that are not sports (such as clubs, bands, and drama groups) are usually sponsored by the community and not by the school.

14 CULTURAL HERITAGE

Russian cultural heritage goes back over 1,500 years. One of the typical Yuletide observances by Russians is the singing of *kolyadi,* carols that have their roots in pagan culture. The verses usually have no connection to the Nativity but come from old sacrificial songs to the sun, moon, and stars. The themes relate to various gods and goddesses, and typically express the hope for abundant crops. When Russians converted to Christianity, some of the kolyadi incorporated Christmas words.

Russian folk music is often played with a variety of instruments. The most well-known folk instruments are probably the *balalaika* (a triangular guitar with three strings) and the *garmon'* (concertina). Some instruments, such as the *gusli* (psaltery), *gudok* (similar to a *rebec,* a primitive violin), *rog* (horn), wooden spoons and *treshchotka* (rattle) have been a part of Russian folk music for centuries.

During the Soviet years, the government tried to control and direct the types of music available. Popular Soviet music featured hundreds of ideological songs for youths, workers, and soldiers. In the 1970s and 1980s, official control over popular Soviet culture began to decrease and some imports of Western music were allowed. Jazz, which had been officially denounced in the past, saw a revival and is very popular among today's Russians. Since the collapse of the Soviet Union, there has been a surge in the amount of shocking and provocative music in Russian popular culture. This trend is probably a consequence of the decades of censorship that suppressed erotic, religious, and nonconformist artistic expressions.

Classical Russian literature plays a significant role in Russian culture. Poetry recitals, going to plays, and discussing novels are all popular activities for Russians. These activities are enjoyed by Russians of all social levels, not just by an educated elite. Russians usually refer to Alexander Pushkin (1799–1837) as the single most influential poet of the Classical era. Other important writers of the Classical era include Ivan Turgenev (1818–81), Fyodor Dostoevsky (1821–81), Leo Tolstoy (1828–1910), and Anton Chekov (1860–1904). Russians revere their poets, playwrights, and authors as popular celebrities.

Each city and town has an impressive array of theaters and cultural centers. The country's most renowned theaters are of course located in Moscow and St. Petersburg. Thus, the Bolshoi Theater in Moscow and the Mariinsky Theater in St. Petersburg are two centers that have always been and remain the major cultural symbols of the Russian nation. Being centers of the Russian and international traditions of opera and ballet, the Mariinsky and Bolshoi bring the Russian classical heritage into the context of changing cultural demands of Russian society.

St. Petersburg's Hermitage Museum and Moscow's Tretyakov Gallery are among the world's greatest art centers. While the Hermitage offers an impressive collection of world art, the State Tretyakov Gallery is the national treasury of Russian fine art. The Tretyakov's collection consists entirely of Russian art and artists who have made a contribution to the history of Russian art or have been closely connected with it. The Gallery is home to over 130 000 works of painting, sculpture, and graphics, created throughout the centuries by successive generations of Russian artists.

15 WORK

During the Soviet years, the government controlled the labor market by setting wages and conditions of employment. Individuals, however, did have the freedom of choosing where they wanted to work in later years. The Soviet labor market in the early years was focused on the rapid growth of heavy industries (such as coal mining and steel production) and the collectivization of agricultural production into *kolkhozy* (huge collective farms). Most workers were members of trade unions. The problems that came with bureaucratic control over the labor market, however, were immense. The system was such that workers had no incentive to be productive, while factory managers had little motivation to operate efficiently. A popular saying by workers during the Soviet years that summarizes the situation was, "We pretend to work, and they pretend to pay us." If there was one good thing about the Soviet system it was that it gave almost equal employment opportunities for women and men.

With the collapse of the Soviet Union, many workers found themselves without an employer. As a result, unemployment and destitution became visible in post-Soviet society. However, private business and entrepreneurial enterprises blossomed. The transition to a market-oriented economy greatly impacted the work ethic and working style of the Russian population. If before Russians would often work inefficiently and sluggishly, now many employers require their staff to be efficient, detail-oriented, punctual, and hardworking

Since 2000 the Russian economy has undergone continuing expansion and growth with the annual gross domestic product (GDP) growth averaging at 6.4% per year. However, this growth is mainly due to the development of the oil and gas sectors. Construction is the fastest growing sector of the economy, expanding by 14%. The main private sector services, including wholesale and retail trade, banking and insurance, and transportation and communications, amount to about 10% of economic growth. In contrast, public sector services such as education, health care, and public administration suffer low investment and low growth.

In general the Russian population is highly educated and skilled. Yet it is largely mismatched to the rapidly changing needs of the Russian economy. Official unemployment has dropped in recent years to 6.9%. At the same time, unemployment remains high with many Russian workers being underemployed. Unemployment is particularly felt among women and young people.

16 SPORTS

About one-fourth of all Russians participate in some kind of sport. Soccer and hockey are popular team sports that Russians (primarily men) enjoy playing as well as watching. Russians usually do not have to look very hard to find a soccer or hockey match on television. Sports societies and organizations were prominent in the Soviet years, and the government liberally advocated public participation in a wide variety of sports. Many of the former "sports palaces" built by the Soviet government have been converted to health clubs. The role of sports in Russian life makes international competitions, such as the Olympics, very important social rallying events.

Skiing and ice skating are popular recreational activities. Tennis has become increasingly more popular since the mid-1950s. Gymnastics and acrobatics are also prominent, perhaps due to the influence of ballet and the circus on popular culture. Baseball, basketball, and golf have been growing in popularity as well. Women's boxing has attracted its share of fans in recent years.

Physical activity is stressed as a part of education. When a student is about 11 years old and shows special ability in a particular sport, he or she is often encouraged to switch over to a "sports school." This type of school has regular academic classes in the mornings and special sports classes in the afternoons.

Russian society is known for its penchant for *shakhmahty* (chess), qualifying it as a sport. The Soviet government began promoting chess in the 1920s as a way to emphasize discipline and training. As its popularity grew, chess masters became highly respected members of society and often received special privileges and honors. Chess instruction starts in kindergarten, and children study the strategies and techniques of champions before they begin serious competition at around age 10. There are thousands of Russian children who have achieved the International Chess Federation's rank of chess master.

Although Russians are in general avid sport lovers and strive to participate and win gold medals in all possible world contests, such as the Olympics and World Cup, in recent years there has been a shortage of funds for sport clubs and other athletic activities. As a result, many of the best Russian hockey and soccer players take contracts with professional teams abroad.

17 ENTERTAINMENT AND RECREATION

Russians are fond of outdoor activities. It is not unusual to see people outdoors playing chess or musical instruments and singing, even during the cold winters. The circus is traditionally a popular form of entertainment enjoyed by Russian families. Russia has hundreds of circus schools, where performers train for up to four years to develop and perfect their acts.

Russians also have a strong ballet tradition, which started in 1738. During the reign of the tsars, ballet schools became prominent and were patterned after the classical French style. During the 1800s, many new ballets were choreographed using traditional Russian themes and compositions. Russian ballet is known for its elaborate choreography and stages.

18 FOLK ART, CRAFTS, AND HOBBIES

Traditional Russian folk art often utilizes elaborate designs on everyday objects such as wooden spoons, bowls, magazine tables, plates, cutting boards, jewelry boxes, brooches—the list goes on. Ornate designs placed on wooden objects are typically covered with lacquer to ensure the longevity of colors. The patterns sometimes resemble whimsical spirals or other nonrepresentational shapes from fantasy land, but they might also be scenes from fairy tales or of famous people or places.

Some regions and villages in Russia developed their distinct craft tradition. Over the centuries, a given location would perfect the craftsmanship it is known for. Thus, the most popular handcrafts in present-day Russia are named after the region they originated from. For example, the vivid and fanciful gold and red drawings on wood (spoons, bowls, jars etc.) are called Golden *Khokhloma* (after the village of *Khokhloma*). *Gzhel* village gave its name to artistic ceramics of blue and soft pink patterns on white surfaces. Ethnic clay toys are called *Dymkovo* and *Filimonovo* after their respective towns.

Perhaps the best-known lacquered Russian folk art piece is the *matryoshka,* a series of wooden dolls that nest inside each other. The dolls usually depict a woman in traditional dress, but in recent years other themes have become popular, such as political figures and holiday motifs.

Lacquer painting on jewelry boxes and chests portraying various scenes from Russian fairytales and legends is known as *Palekh, Mstera* and *Kholui.* The colors employed by Palekh artists are so vivid and drawings are so elegant and magical that one can easily perceive the centuries of Russian soul invested in this art. The harmony of colors, cheerfulness, and creative patterns found their way into the decorative tray painting of *Zhostovo* and *Troitskoe.* Then there are of course some regions, including Vologda, Vyatka, and Yelets, that are renowned for their lace making and some that are acknowledged for their imaginative embroidery, golden thread needlework, pattern weaving, and rug making.

Russians also take pride in their artistic metalworking. The most famous metal crafts include *Veliky Ustiug* silver, *Rostov* enamel and *Kazakovo* filigree. Mountain regions in Russia have first-class masters in stone work. Tyva is recognized for carved sculpture while the Ural region can boast its jewelry, sculptures and other articles made of malachite, garnet, and other semiprecious stones. The Ural stonework impresses with its grace and lightness. When one looks at this sculpture long enough, it seems that it is coming to life.

In sum, the expanses of land and centuries of history allowed Russia's regions to create and master their unique craft traditions, whether they be wood carving, earthenware, artistic ceramics, metalwork, stonework, or lace making. Whatever kind of folk art is regarded, it reflects the richness and diversity of Russia's soul and the splendor of the works crafted by Russian hands.

19 SOCIAL PROBLEMS

Since the collapse of the Soviet Union, Russians have been forced to confront many of the old social problems that existed during the Soviet era, as well as a new set of problems brought about by the rapid changes in opening up the society. Privatization across Russia has created new opportunities but has also resulted in high unemployment in many areas. Because of high inflation and economic instability, many elderly persons who live off of a government pension are now impoverished. Life expectancy and health rates have plunged as well. Reduced funding for road maintenance and rehabilitation over the last few years and the poor quality of roads and bridges have caused deterioration in Russia's road network and a growing backlog of needed repairs.

Ethnic hostilities have begun flaring up in some parts of Russia that were either taken over by the Soviet government or conquered during the imperial Russian era. When the Soviet government collapsed, it provided the instability for some areas to distance themselves or even try to break away from the Russian government. The fiercest fighting of this type so far has occurred in Chechnya, a region in the Caucasus Mountains near Georgia. Thousands of Russian troops have been sent into the area, and many people on both sides have been killed.

Alcohol abuse has traditionally been a problem for the Russians. Temperance movements were not prominent in Russia's history. Family violence in households is often a consequence of alcoholism. Crime rates have risen rapidly in Russia since the end of the Soviet Union, which has made the economic situation even worse. Much of the crime problem is due to the extortion and violence caused by organized crime, which has considerable power in some areas. Organized crime is also aided in some places because of corruption among local politicians and officials. Decades of socialism have encouraged a manner of thinking where class envy is common. Russians, therefore, often scorn the "new rich," who are assumed to be racketeers. Vladimir Putin put significant constraints on oligarchs and the "new rich," but organized crime and corruption remain significant problems.

Right after the breakdown of the Soviet Union prostitution become a popular way for women to make money. Many teenage girls believe that a career in prostitution will pay more than most legitimate professions ever would, regardless of education. About one-fourth of Russia's prostitutes have received some sort of higher education. Although since 2000 the economic situation has improved, female unemployment is still high. The number of girls going into the hospitality business is gradually decreasing, but not very significantly.

Furthermore, currently Russia faces a serious demographic crisis. Russia's population of 142.9 million is rapidly falling. Births lag far behind deaths, the population is aging, and the average male hardly lives to age 60. Cardiovascular disease, cancer, traffic injuries, suicide, alcohol poisoning, and violence are some of the major causes of death. In 2007 life expectancy at birth was only 59 years for men and 73 years for women. In the past 20 years, lower birth rates and higher death rates have reduced Russia's population at nearly 0.5% per year. A substantial increase in HIV/AIDS infections and tuberculosis worsens the problem. Some reports indicate that Russia has one of the highest growth rates of HIV infection in the world, with the estimated number of HIV-infected persons at approximately 3 million.

The Russian government acknowledged that Russia is facing a demographic crisis. President Putin initiated a series of reforms attempting to improve the situation. Reforms included measures to improve birth and mortality rates and increase population through immigration, primarily the return of Russian-speaking foreigners.

20 GENDER ISSUES

The Soviet ideology promoted equal rights for all, opening the doors for women to enter higher education and professional careers. Continuing this trend, in the period from 1992 to 2000, the number of female students at higher educational establishments rose by 50%. In fact, in 2008 approximately 57% of university students were women and 43% men.

However, despite possessing a higher average level of education, women in Russia earn less than men, averaging 60–70%

of men's wages. Women are underrepresented in legislative bodies and are not represented in the government at all. Female workers face discrimination in employment-related matters, including promotion. Furthermore, most women have to combine professional work with the lion's share of work at home.

At the same time, the unemployment rates of women and men have been roughly equal, standing at 6.7% and 6.5% respectively in 2006. In 2006 women comprised over 48% of the economically active population. In the face of recent political and economic change, men have retained their economic advantage, but women have maintained their presence in the labor market. In fact, some men were experiencing greater problems in adapting to the new Russia than women. Meanwhile, the gender restructuring of employment during transition favors men in a sense that men increased their presence in the now-lucrative, but once female-dominated, spheres of banking and commerce, while women continue to make up the overwhelming majority of employees in the poorly-paid "budget sector" areas of health care and education.

Although women are in a disadvantaged economic position, they appear to be healthier and emotionally happier than men. Data indicate that in 1989 male life expectancy was at 64.3 years of age while in 2008 it barely reached 59. However, female life expectancy proved to be more constant, declining from 74.4 years in 1989 to 73 in 2007. Bearing the main responsibility for the well-being of a family binds women to a web of on-going relations with family members and female acquaintances. By contrast, men's social networks tend to revolve around their workplace. While this undoubtedly has positive effects in terms of job search and promotion prospects, it entails that men's safety networks can be endangered in the face of changes in employment status. Men who become unemployed or marginalized at work can find themselves cut off from their contacts causing men great mental distress. Distressed men often turn to drinking which further intensifies the problem. *Alcohol consumption in Russia is 10 times higher among men than among women.*

In sum, women in Russia are more likely to live in poverty, but it seems that men are more vulnerable to its effects. Women have to cope with the double burden of work and household management, but this has turned out to have hidden benefits in a period of economic crisis, while men's freedom from domestic responsibilities and license to drink have proved very dangerous to their health. Women and men have almost equal opportunities for education, and women have increasingly higher prospects of career advancement, yet men still earn more and dominate in certain positions, including positions in administration and government. Women still have to confront negative gender stereotyping. However those trends are gradually changing. While competition for top jobs and other opportunities is always fierce, the right mindset combined with an excellent education and good contacts can be and is the hammer in women's hands that shatters the foundation of a traditionally patriarchal society.

21 BIBLIOGRAPHY

Afanas'ev, Aleksandr Nikolayevich. *Russian Fairy Tales.* New York: Random House, 1980.

Ashwin, Sarah, (ed.). *Adapting to Russia's New Labour Market: Gender and Employment Behavior.* London and New York: Routledge, 2006.

Ashwin, Sarah. *Adapting to Russia's Transformation: Women and Men Compared.* United Nations Development Program: Gender in Transition, 2007. http://www.developmentandtransition.net/index.cfm?module=ActiveWeb &page=WebPage&DocumentID=666 (1 May 2008).

Bolshoi Theater Website. http://www.bolshoi.ru/en/theatre/mission/ (11 May 2008).

Brown, Archie, Michael Kaser, and Gerald S. Smith, ed. *The Cambridge Encyclopedia of Russia and the Former Soviet Union.* Cambridge: Cambridge University Press, 1994.

Brumfield, William Craft, and Blair A. Ruble. *Russian Housing in the Modern Age: Design and Social History.* Washington, D.C.: Woodrow Wilson Center Press, 1993.

Embassy of the Russian Federation in the United States. http://www.russianembassy.org/ (9 May 2008).

Euromonitor International 2008. "Russia." http://www.euromonitor.com/factfile.aspx?country=RU (5 May 2008).

Goskomstat. *Demografic Yearbook of Russia, 2002* (Demograficheskii ezhegodnik Rossii, 2002). Moscow: Goskomstat Rossii. 2002.

———. *Russian Federation Statistics Yearbook, 2003* (Rossiiskii statisticheskii ezhegodnik, 2003).

Mezentseva, Elena. *Gender Inequality in Today's Russia: Who Bears the Social Costs of Reforms?* http://www.indiana.edu/~reeiweb/events/2005/mezentseva%20paper.pdf (1 May 2008).

National Geographic Magazine. "Russia." http://www3.nationalgeographic.com/places/countries/country_russia.html (1 May 2008).

Russia Profile Online Magazine. http://www.russiaprofile.org/page.php?pageid=MainPage (1 May 2008).

US Department of States, Bureau of European and Eurasian Affairs. "Russia." http://www.state.gov/r/pa/ei/bgn/3183.htm (11 May 2008).

World Development Indicators. "Russian Federation Data Profile." World Bank. http://devdata.worldbank.org/external/CPProfile.asp?CCODE=RUS&PTYPE=CP (1 May 2008).

—revised by A. Golovina Khadka

SAKHA

ALTERNATE NAMES: Yakut
LOCATION: Russia (Eastern Siberia)
POPULATION: 443,852 (2002 census)
LANGUAGE: Sakha (Yakut), Russian
RELIGION: Eastern Orthodox Christianity and native religious practices

[1] INTRODUCTION

The people who call themselves Sakha are termed *Yakut* in some European literature. An older term derived from legends is *Urangkhai Sakha.* The Sakha are the farthest north of the Turkic language speakers. They live in the Sakha Republic of the Russian Federation, in the far east of Siberia. Their territory was called Yakutia, or the Yakut Autonomous Republic, when it was part of the former Soviet Union.

The Sakha claim that their ancestors once lived farther south, and ethnographic and archeological data confirm an area near Lake Baikal for an aboriginal homeland where Sakha predecessors, identified in some theories with the Kuriakon people, may have been part of the Uighur state bordering China. By the 14th century, Sakha ancestors came north, perhaps in small refugee groups, with herds of horses and cattle. After arrival in the Lena valley, they fought and intermarried with the indigenous Evenk and Yukagir nomads.

When the first parties of Russian Cossacks arrived at the Lena River in the 1620s, the Sakha received them with hospitality but also wariness. Several skirmishes and revolts followed, led by the legendary hero Tygyn. By 1642, the Lena Valley was under tribute to the czar. Peace was won only after a long siege of a formidable Sakha fortress. By 1700, the fort settlement of Yakutsk (founded in 1632) was a bustling Russian administrative, commercial, and religious center and a launching point for further exploration into Kamchatka and Chukotka. Some Sakha moved northeast into territories they had previously not dominated, further assimilating indigenous neighbors. Most Sakha, however, remained in the central meadowlands, sometimes assimilating Russians. Sakha leaders cooperated with Russian commanders and governors, becoming active in trade, fur tax collection, transport, and the postal system. Fighting among Sakha communities decreased, although horse rustling and occasional anti-Russian violence continued. For example, in the 19th century, a Sakha Robin Hood named Manchaari led a band that stole from the rich (usually Russians) to give to the poor (usually Sakha).

By 1900, a literate Sakha ("Yakut") intelligentsia was influenced by Russian merchants and political exiles. A party called the Yakut Union resulted. Leaders such as Oiunsky and Ammosov led the revolution and civil war, along with Bolsheviks such as the Georgian Ordzhonikidze. The 1917 revolution took several bloody years to consolidate, with extensive opposition to Red forces by Whites (czarists) under Kolchak lasting until 1920, and unrest until 1923. After relative calm during Lenin's New Economic Policy, a harsh collectivization and anti-nationalist campaign under Stalin ensued. Intellectuals such as Oiunsky (founder of the Institute of Languages, Literature and History) and Kulakovsky (an ethnographer) were persecuted in the 1920s and 1930s.

Traditionally, kinship and politics were mixed in a hierarchical council system that guided various levels of Sakha social organization. Sakha ideas of themselves as a people were conveyed by their word *dzhon*, which means "community" or "tribe" in a territorial sense. Councils were composed of ranked circles of elders, usually men, whose leaders, *toyons*, were called nobles by the Russians. Lineage councils decided major economic issues, inter-family disputes, and questions of "blood revenge" for violence committed against the group. Full tribal councils were infrequent, dealing with issues of security, revenge, alliance, and (before Russian control) war. In war, prisoners were captured to serve as slaves in the wealthiest households.

By the 20th century, councils were rare, although the demise of the Soviet Union has led some Sakha to argue for a return of community councils. Under a Sakha constitution passed in 1991, an elected Sakha parliament, called *Il Tumen* ("meeting for solidarity") has become influential, in addition to an elected Sakha president. A bilateral treaty with Russian Federation leaders signed in 1995 outlined the terms of the republic's political and economic relationship to the central government.

2 LOCATION AND HOMELAND

The Sakha Republic covers 3,100,000 square kilometers (1,200,000 square miles), or more than four times the area of Texas, in eastern Siberia. Located at approximately 56°–71°N latitude and 107°–152°E longitude, it is bounded by Chukotka to the northeast, Buriatia in the south, and the Evenk region to the west. Its northern coast stretches far above the Arctic Circle, along the East Siberian Sea, and its southern rim includes the Stanovoi mountains and the Aldan plateau. Its most majestic river, the Lena, flows north along cavernous cliffs into a long valley, and past the capital, Yakutsk. Other key river systems, where major towns have developed, include the Aldan, Viliui, and Kolyma. About 700,000 named rivers and streams cross the territory, which has some agricultural land, but is primarily non-agricultural taiga with vast resources of gold, minerals, gas, and oil. Tundra rims the north, except for forests along the rivers.

Notorious for extremes of long, cold winters and hot, dry summers, the republic has two locations residents claim to be the "coldest on earth"—Verkhoiansk and Oimiakon, where temperatures have dipped to -79°C (-110°F). More typical are winters of 0° to -40°C (32° to -40°F) and summers of 10° to 30°C (50° to 86°F).

Spread throughout the republic, the Sakha are no longer a minority in their own republic. The 2002 Russian census recorded a total population of 949,280 for the Sakha Republic. The Sakha totaled 443,852 (432,290 in the republic) in 2002. The proportion of Sakha in their republic has been gradually increasing. In 1989 they made up 35%, and by 1996 they made up approximately 40%. In 2002 they constituted the single largest ethnic group in the Sakha Republic, making to 45.5% of its population. By contrast in the 1920s, Sakha constituted about 82% of their republic's population. Sakha outside their republic are mostly in the Far East and the major cities of Russia.

The Sakha have become increasingly urban over the past 20 years, although at a slower rate than the majority Slavic population. Whole villages in central and northern regions remain solidly Sakha, while the major cities of the republic are heavily Russian. The republic population was 65% urban in 1989. In-terethnic marriages between the Sakha and other groups were as high as 10% in the 1970s, but this percentage had halved by the 1990s. As of 2002 Sakhas were approximately 65% rural dwellers and 35% urban dwellers.

3 LANGUAGE

The Sakha, more than 90% of whom speak Sakha (or Yakut) as their mother tongue, call their language *Sakha-tyla*. A Northeast Turkic language of the Altaic branch of Ural-Altaic, it is divergent from most other Turkic languages, although related to Dolgan. The current Sakha written language, developed in the 1930s, uses a modified Cyrillic script. Before this, several written forms were tried, including a Latin script developed in the 1920s and a Cyrillic script introduced by missionaries in the 19th century. The first books in the Sakha language were published in 1862.

Many Sakha names are variations on Russian, for example, *Iuban* (Ivan). Names sometimes derive from folklore—for girls, for example, *Tuiaarima* (a heroine), *Aisa* (a good spirit), and *Sardana* (a kind of lily), and for boys, *Niurgun* (a hero), *Aisin* (a good spirit), and *Ellei* (an ancestor).

4 FOLKLORE

Sakha folklore includes legends of a written language lost after they traveled north to the Lena valley. Oral histories begin well before first contact with Russians in the 17th century. *Olonkho* (epics) date at least to the 10th century, a period of inter-ethnic mixing, tensions, and upheaval that may have been a formative period for Sakha tribal affiliations. Today, few young people memorize the sung epics, which rival in size the Greek *Iliad* or Finnish *Kalevala*, but parts of the epics are performed in contests. Other folklore includes stories of benevolent or malicious animal spirits and the feats of traditional spiritual leaders or shamans.

5 RELIGION

Sakha religion derives from Turkic, Mongolic, Tungusic, and Russian ideas. Labels such as "animist," "shamanist," or "Russian Orthodox" do not suffice. Ideas of sin are syncretized with concepts of contamination and taboo. Saints are seen as shamanic spirit-helpers, as are bears. Christ is identified with the Bright Creator Elder God Aiyy-toyon. A pantheon of gods, believed to live in nine hierarchical eastern heavens, was only one aspect of a complex traditional cosmology that still has meaning for some Sakha. Sakha also believed in the spiritual power of blacksmiths, because iron-working was an important part of traditional Sakha culture.

A crux of belief is the *ichchi* (spirit-soul) of living beings, rocks, trees, natural forces, and objects crafted by humans. Most honored is the hearth spirit, *yot ichchite*, and it is fed morsels of food and drink by believers. Deep in the forest, *al lukh mas* (giant trees) are especially sacred; their *ichchi* are given small offerings of coins, scarves, and ribbons. Belief in *ichchi* is related to ancient ideas of harmony and equilibrium with nature and to shamanism.

Sakha shamanism is a Turkic, Mongolic, and Tungusic blend of belief in the supernatural with emphasis on the ability of "white," or benign, shamans to intercede through prayers and séances with eastern spirits for the sake of humans. "Black" shamans, communing with evil spirits, can both benefit and harm humans. Shamans can be male (*oiuun*) or female

SAKHA

0   500   1000 Miles

0   500   1000 Kilometers

(udagan), with debate over which gender is more powerful. Shamans use drumming to enter into a trance during séances to ascertain the cause of illness or other problems.

In the 19th century, Russian Orthodox priests spread through Siberia, but their followers were mainly in the major towns. A few Sakha leaders financed the building of Russian Orthodox churches, and many Sakha declared themselves Christian, but this did not mean they viewed Christianity and shamanism as mutually exclusive.

Although shamans with full powers are rare, in the 1990s, urban as well as rural Sakha have adapted shamanic rituals. Current Sakha shamans combine medical and spiritual practice. Despite centuries of Russian Orthodox and Soviet discrediting of shamans as greedy charlatans, some Sakha maintain belief in shamans and supernatural powers. Others, struggling to recover spirituality after rejecting Marxist-Leninist materialism, accept aspects of shamanic philosophy. Still others, influenced by Soviet education and science, reject all religion as superstition.

6 MAJOR HOLIDAYS

The most important Sakha ceremony, associated with founding ancestor Ellei, is the annual summer *yhyak* festival, a celebration of seasonal change, of *kumys* (fermented mare's milk), and of kin solidarity. It was declared a national republic holiday in 1990. Once religious, and led by a shaman, the ceremony has become a mostly secular celebration of Sakha traditions. Practiced in villages and towns, it features opening prayers *(algys)*

and libations of *kumys* to the earth. Although some debate its "authenticity," the festival still includes feasting, horse racing, wrestling, and all-night line dancing to improvised chants. It lasts three joyous days in Suntar, where it is especially famed. Other major holidays include New Year's, (1 January) and World War II Victory Day (8 May).

7 RITES OF PASSAGE

Traditional rituals of birth that involved supplicating the goddess of fertility *(Aiyyghyt)* are rarely observed today, and some Sakha women mock the restrictions once associated with beliefs about female impurity. New rituals marking weddings, anniversaries, and graduations at all educational levels involve *serge,* or sacred marker posts, on which names of those honored are carved.

Sakha beliefs accord each person three souls. Before burial, the deceased's spirit is thought to visit every place traveled in life. Family members dress the deceased in finery. On the third day, bearers take the body to the graveyard, where a grave is prepared deep enough to touch permafrost yet shallow enough to be seen by escort spirits. A horse, steer, or reindeer is sacrificed, to help the deceased travel to the land of the dead and to provide food for family and grave preparers. One of the deceased's three souls is believed to travel skyward for life in a lush greenery-filled heaven until possible return in reincarnation. Some Sakha fear that souls, especially those of shamans, can stay on earth and haunt kin. Burial symbolism is observed more in villages than cities and a combination of shamanic and Russian Orthodox ritual prevails.

8 INTERPERSONAL RELATIONS

Travelers from afar once greeted each other with the request "Tell me what is new" and with a discussion of kin connections if the people did not know each other. Variations of this occur today, although most Sakha greetings have become Russified, with handshakes and kissing on both cheeks. To show a more traditional style of affection, people greet and part with a small sniff to the cheek. Couples are restrained in public, but warm and considerate at home. Visiting across considerable distances is common for special family and seasonal occasions. Couples usually meet through friendships of their families or through school, and dating takes place both in groups and more privately.

9 LIVING CONDITIONS

With the decline of shamans, most Sakha rely on Western medicine administered in hospitals and clinics. Folk medicine, however, including extensive use of herbal knowledge, is also prevalent. Traditional healers have long periods of apprenticeship and are specialized. There are herbal experts, bone setters, shaman's assistants, as well as various grades of shamanic power.

Housing is Russian in style, often rough-hewn log huts with broad, raised stoves. Many families, even in large towns, rely on outhouses and outdoor water pumps. Some collectives, however, let workers build more substantial individual family homes with modern amenities. Another style of housing is low concrete apartment buildings with indoor plumbing. The largest city is Yakutsk (187,000 in 1989), and the towns of Viliusk, Olekminsk, Neriungri, and Mirny are growing rapidly.

As horse and cattle breeders, the Sakha had a transhumant pattern of summer and winter settlements. Winter settlements comprised as few as 20 people, members of several closely related families who shared pasture land and lived in nearby yurts *(balagan)* with surrounding storehouses and corrals. The yurts were oblong huts with slanted earth walls, low ceilings, sod roofs, and dirt floors. Most had an adjoining room for cattle. They had substantial hearths and fur-covered benches lining the walls, with sleeping arrangements made according to social protocol. Yurts faced east, toward benevolent deities. In summer, families moved with their animals to larger encampments. The most ancient summer homes, *urasy*, were elegant conical birchbark tents, some of which could hold one hundred people. Their ceilings soared above a circular hearth at the center point and around the sides were wide benches placed in compartments that served as ranked seating and sleeping areas. Every pole or eave was carved with symbolic designs of animals, fertility, and lineage identities. By 1900, however, *urasy* were rare; summer homes became yurts or combination yurt-log cabins. By 1950, yurts too were obsolete, found only in a few museums. In the 1990s, new versions of collectives still send workers to summer sites to graze cattle away from large villages, and some families are returning to homestead-style cattle breeding.

10 FAMILY LIFE

Key kin relations are based on a patrilineage *(aga-usa)* that traces membership back as far as nine generations. Within this, children born to a specific mother are distinguished as a group *(ye-usa)* and may form the basis for different households *(korgon)*. Historically, more distant kin were recognized on two levels, the *aimak* (or territorial *nasleg*), with 1 to 30 lineages, and the *dzhon* (or territorial *ulus*), composed of several *aimak*. These larger units were united by common defense alliances and economic relations and reinforced by councils and festivals. A lineage head was *bis-usa-toyon*, while respected warriors and hunters were *batyr*. Kin terms reflect gender and age distinctions, marking senior paternal lines from junior ones. All relations are called *uru*, which is also the term for wedding.

Wedding rituals, pared down from previous eras, center around carved memorial posts, with couples honored by blessings, special food, and dancing. Earlier (and sometimes today), a dual celebration would go from the bride's household to the groom's, where the couple traditionally lived. Since the 1970s, interest in aspects of ritual and gift exchange has been revived, although few couples are paired through matchmakers as previously. Multi-generational families often live together, although the movement of young families to cities has made smaller, less-extended families a more recent norm.

Traditionally marriage could be polygamous for wealthy Sakha. Monogamy was more common, however, with occasional remarriage after the death of a spouse. Arranged marriages were sometimes politically motivated. Patrilineage exogamy (marriage of a Sakha man to a non-Sakha woman) was reckoned with strictly; those one could marry were called *sygan*. Until the 1920s, marriages had many stages involving financial, emotional, and symbolic resources of the bride's and groom's extended families. This included a matchmaking ritual; several formal payments of animals, furs, and meat to the bride's family; informal gifts; and extensive dowries. Some families allowed poor grooms to work in their households as replacement for "bride wealth." Occasionally bride capture occurred and may have been more common in pre-Russian times.

By customary law, land, cattle and horses were controlled by the patrilineage although used by households. Inheritance or the sale of animals or land had to be approved by elders. Men owned most of the wealth, and passed it down to sons, especially elder sons, although the youngest son often inherited the family yurt. Mothers could pass on dowries to daughters, unless the dowry had been forfeited by bad behavior. In theory, dowries included land as well as goods, jewelry, and animals, although in practice elders rarely gave land to another lineage. Soviet law limited inheritance, but new land laws have made families with small plots more secure. In addition, most apartments and summer houses are kept in families.

Children were reared to be good workers, with boys racing, hunting, playing games of strength while girls learned domestic tasks. Girls were expected to be shy, learning taboos that would become important in a husband's household. With education, however, youth, especially girls, have more freedom. After training, many opt to live away from their rural homes. Even so, the values of Sakha pride, language fluency, and the advisability of endogamy (marriage to other Sakha) are strongly instilled.

11 CLOTHING

Sakha women are fashion conscious, with a strong sense of style and access to European magazines. However, for weddings and the annual *yhyakh* holiday, women are returning to versions of traditional flowing gowns with ribbons and appliqué. Fur appliqué on coats and strong colorful designs on vests (especially with green and red) merge old and new styles. Long silver and gold earrings and elaborately carved breast and headdress jewelry are popular, especially since the resurgence of traditional Sakha crafts in the republic. Men usually wear European-style casual and more formal clothing. Both genders prefer beautifully made fur hats, coats, and boots during the cold winters.

12 FOOD

Dairy products and meat from cattle and horses are especially valued. Diet is augmented by hunting (deer, elk, squirrel, hare, bear, ferret, and fowl) and fishing (salmon, carp, *muksun*, and *mundu*). Because of Russian influence, agricultural products (cereals and vegetables) are grown or bought in stores and markets. Mildly alcoholic fermented mare's milk, *kumys*, varies in processing and taste, with one bubbly style considered the "champagne" of this traditional Turkic drink. A heavy whipped cream with berries called, *kerchek*, is labor-intensive and therefore a special treat. Horse-meat kabobs cooked over an open fire are served at holidays, and when the horses have been raised for their meat, the kabobs are tender. Bread and waffles have become popular through Russian influence.

Utensils are store-bought and European-style, although traditional carved wooden bowls and spoons are valued as serving implements. Carved wooden *kumys* cups, called *choron*, come in many sizes. With a single stem or three carved legs, they are said to be the shape of a woman's breast and symbolize fertility.

Klaudia and German Khatylaeva are a husband and wife team of professional performers from the Sakha Republic. They performed at the Tibet House in New York, New York, on this their first visit to the United States. (© Viviane Moos/Corbis)

¹³ EDUCATION

Before the Russian Revolution, a few Sakha children attended missionary schools, but most were illiterate. Literacy campaigns for both children and adults in the 1920s and 1930s improved basic education. The turmoil of Stalinist policies and World War II left many Sakha without their traditional homesteads and unused to salaried industrial or urban work. Education improved their chances of adaptation and also stimulated interest in the Sakha past.

By the 1980s, the intelligentsia of the republic was dominated by indigenous men and women in prestigious cultural, scientific, and political jobs. A Sakha man was director of the gold ministry, and a Sakha woman was head of the republic legislature. The Yakutsk State University was a main mechanism for advancement, as were various Russian Academy of Sciences institutes. In the 1990s, not every Sakha child who wants higher education can obtain it, but most Sakha have a high school education and know Russian. Technical schools and on-the-job training improve career chances, but republic leaders recognize that educational reform is needed. There are debates over the goals of education and the level to which training should continue in the Sakha language.

¹⁴ CULTURAL HERITAGE

Sakha linguists proclaim that the Sakha language, in oral and written form, has metaphoric flexibility that lends itself to poetry. Continuity of folk arts is strongest in exuberant improvisational poetry that accompanies a type of line dancing, called *ohuokhai*. A leader sings out a line of verse, which other dancers repeat in unison, giving the leader a chance to think of the next line. This rhythmic dance goes on for hours, traditionally during weddings and the seasonal summer celebration, but recently also at clubs. Similarly, a revival of the twanging mouth harp, *khomus*, has spread beyond its original familial and shamanic ritual context onto the Sakha stage.

Filmmakers, theater groups, opera, and dance companies enrich Sakha cultural life with performances that build on traditional themes in new ways. Tension between Russian influence and pride in Sakha identity is clear in many works. Sakha novelists and playwrights, such as Suoron Ommolon, have adopted Sakha pseudonyms, though their readers usually know their Russian family names. Sakha ethnographers explore their roots in widely read works.

15 WORK

In such a harsh climate, pastoralism requires homestead self-reliance, with intense devotion to calves and foals. Before 1917, rich families owned hundreds of horses and cattle while poor ones raised a few cattle or herded for others. Wealthy Sakha hunted on horseback using dogs. The poorest Sakha, without cattle, relied on fishing with horsehair nets and, in the north, herding reindeer like their Evenk and Yukagir neighbors. Sakha also engaged in the fur trade, relying on squirrel by the 20th century when luxury furs (ermine, sable, and fox) were depleted. Sakha merchants and transporters spread throughout the entire Northeast, easing communications and trade for natives and Russians. Staples such as butter, meat, and hay, plus luxuries such as silver and gold jewelry, carved bone, ivory, and wood crafts, were sold. Barter, Russian money, and furs formed the media of exchange. Guns were imported, as was iron for local blacksmiths.

Although occupations within a household were divided by gender and status, the atmosphere was usually one of productive group activity. Haymaking, cattle herding, and milking were done by all, although horses were more a male preserve and cattle a female responsibility. Women tended children and fires, prepared food, carried water, and made clothing and pottery. Men handled firewood preparation, house building, sled making, hunting, fishing, and mowing. Ivory carving and wood and metalworking were male tasks.

16 SPORTS

Horse racing is one of the most popular sports, and it is featured at the annual summer *yhyakh* festival. Traditional male sports of wrestling, balancing across poles, rock lifting, hurdles and foot racing hone important skills and remain popular at festivals. Victors are awarded legs of cooked meat as well as more modern commercial prizes.

17 ENTERTAINMENT AND RECREATION

On dark winter nights, long epics were the most valued form of entertainment. A single traveling tale singer would take the parts of all the characters in a given drama, and families would cluster around a hearth for several nights running. Traditional tales have recently been transformed onto the stage and into movies by skilled Sakha artists. Other traditional entertainment included songs (*lada*), riddles, and comic, fast-paced tongue-twister dialogues.

There is television in nearly every Sakha home, introducing Sakha viewers to international films, news, and soap operas. But a Sakha language channel also offers home-grown popular songs and comedy, programs on nature, and critical commentary on issues of the day.

18 FOLK ART, CRAFTS, AND HOBBIES

Iron-working from marsh ore preceded imported iron, just as ceramics from local clay preceded Russian pottery. Most homemade crafts are for household use, and include birchbark containers, leather bags, dairy-processing equipment, horsehair blankets, fur clothing, benches, hitching posts, and elaborately carved wooden containers. Sakha art takes many forms, sometimes rooted in ritual life, although since the Soviet period, it is often secular and commercial. Silver and gold jewelry, once considered talismanic, is now enjoyed for its aesthetic value.

The Sakha were once famous for their bone carvings, which included boxes, pipes, chess pieces, and dagger hilts. The most famous carvings were made from ancient mammoth bones and tusks that had been found in ice. Famed for ivory and wood carving, Sakha artists have recently branched out into graphic art, painting, and sculpture. A group of young artists called Flagiston brings traditional shamanic themes into new mediums.

19 SOCIAL PROBLEMS

During most of the Soviet period, crime was covered up with false statistics by Soviet officials engaged in corruption. In addition, elite Sakha helped kin obtain jobs and political positions that built on traditional obligations and were not defined by locals as corrupt. Bad Soviet management, nuclear testing, and disastrous mining practices have left the republic with serious social and economic problems. An environmental movement has formed in response, as well as some political reform agitation. Demonstrations erupted on Yakutsk streets several times in the 1980s, mostly by young Sakha protesting police inaction over violent incidents involving Russians and Sakha. Tensions exist between newcomers and natives, developers and environmental activists, and "internationalists" and "nationalists." Alcoholism and unemployment rates have increased since the Soviet collapse, thus aggravating already existing problems.

Non-Sakha indigenous minorities, such as the Evenk, Even, and Yukagir, have demanded greater cultural and political rights. In response, a national district, Eveno-Bytantaisk, was established in 1989 in the republic, and local self-rule councils are developing.

20 GENDER ISSUES

In traditional Sakha society the subsistence economy and its division of labor strongly affected gender roles. With the establishment of collective and state farms during the Soviet era women were integrated into the Soviet labor force and the Soviet workplace, particularly during and after the Second World War. While child-rearing and household duties generally remained the realm of women, Soviet Sakha women also gained access to educational opportunities. Divisions of labor continued through the 20th century in households of rural collectives, although possibilities for both sexes have expanded. Women now hunt, fish, and engage in crafts once associated with men. They have become doctors, nurses, teachers, engineers, bookkeepers, and politicians, and some work in the growing industrial sector. Men are engineers, tractor drivers, geologists, teachers, doctors, managers, and workers in the lucrative energy, metallurgy, gold, diamond, and building industries.

Since the collapse of the Soviet Union, in some rural Sakha communities the lines between division of labor have blurred to some degree, with men sharing household duties and also being involved in herding activities that beforehand had largely been the realm of women.

21 BIBLIOGRAPHY

Bychkova Jordan, Bella and Terry Jordan. *Siberian Village: Land and Life in the Sakha Republic*. Minneapolis: University of Minnesota Press, 2001.

Crate, S. "Sakha," in Carol and Melvin Ember, eds. *Encyclopedia of Sex and Gender*. New York: Kluwer, 2004.

Gogolev, Anatoli Ignatevich. *Istoricheskaia etnografiia Iakutov*. Yakutsk, Russia: Yakutsk University Press, 1983, 1986.

Gurvich, Ilya Samoilovich. *Kul'tura severnykh Iakutov-olenevodov*. Moscow: Nauka, 1977.

Jochelson, Waldemar. "The Yakut." *Anthropological Paper* 33 (American Museum of Natural History), 1933.

Okladnikov, Aleksei Pavlovich. *Yakutia Before its Incorporation into the Russian State*. Trans. Stephen and Ethel Dunn. Ed. Henry Michael. Montreal: Anthropology of the North series, 8, 1950, 1970.

Tokarev, S. A., and I. S. Gurvich. "The Yakuts." *Peoples of Siberia*, M. G. Levin and L. P. Potapov, ed. Chicago, IL: University of Chicago Press, 1956, 1964.

—revised by A. Frank

SAMI

ALTERNATE NAMES: Lapps, Samer
LOCATION: Norway, Sweden, Finland, and Russia
POPULATION: About 100,000
LANGUAGE: Sami language in many dialects; also language of country in which they live
RELIGION: Lutheran

¹ INTRODUCTION

While the Sami (also spelled Saami), or Lapps (as they were formerly called), are commonly thought of as the inhabitants of Lapland, they have never had a country of their own. They are the original inhabitants of northern Scandinavia and most of Finland. Their neighbors have called them Lapps, but they prefer to be called *Samer* or *Sami* (pronounced "Sa-mee"). (They refer to their land as *Sapmi* or *Same eatnam*.)

The Sami first appear in written history in the works of the Roman author Tacitus in about AD 98. Nearly 900 years later, a Norwegian chieftain visiting King Alfred the Great of England spoke of these reindeer herders, who were paying taxes to him in the form of furs, feathers, and whale bones. Over the centuries many armed nations, including the Karelians, Swedes, Danes, Finns, and Russians, demanded their allegiance and taxes. In some cases, the Sami had to pay taxes to two or three governments, as well as fines imposed by one country for paying taxes to another.

The Sami are now citizens of the countries within whose borders they live, with full rights to education, social services, religious freedom, and participation in the political process. At the same time, however, they continue to preserve and defend their ethnic identity and traditional cultural values. Until the liberalization instituted by the Gorbachev government in the late 1980s, the Russian Sami had almost no contact with those in other areas. Sami living in Finland, Sweden, and Norway formed the Nordic Sami Council (Nordisk Samerad) in 1956 to promote cooperation between their three populations. In 1992, the Russian Sami joined the organization, which then changed its name to the Sami Council (Sameradet). The Sami Council secretariat, based in Utsjoki, Finland, has had advisory status within the United Nations since 1989.

In 1973 the Nordic Sami Institute at Kautokeino, Norway, was founded to promote the study of the Sami language and culture and, in 1989, a Sami College was established there as well. The universities of Tromsø in Norway, Umla in Sweden, and Oulu in Finland have Sami departments in which Sami topics are taught, both separately and as part of established disciplines.

² LOCATION AND HOMELAND

The Sami live in tundra, taiga, and coastal zones in the far north of Europe, spread out over four different countries: Norway, Sweden, Finland, and the Kola peninsula in Russia. They live on coasts and islands warmed by the Gulf Stream, on plateaus dotted by lakes and streams, and on forested mountains. This land area inhabited by the Sami is referred to as the Sampi.

Sami territory lies at latitudes above 62° north, and much of it is above the Arctic Circle, with dark, cold winters and warm, light summers. It is often called the land of the midnight sun, which, depending on the latitude, may be visible for up to 70 days in the summer. The far north sees almost three months of continuous daylight. Balancing this out, however, is an equally long period of darkness in the winter, which may last from October to March. Beginning in November, the sun disappears for weeks. Much of the Samis' land is at high altitudes, rising to over 1,829 m (6,000 ft) above sea level. The highest point is Kebnekajse, at 2,121 m (6,960 feet).

Traditionally, the Sami lived in a community of families called a *siida,* whose members cooperated in hunting, trapping, and fishing. While exact numbers are not available, the Sami population in the four major countries of Finland, Sweden, Norway, and Russia has been estimated at 70,000 and 100,000 (or more). It is thought that between 60,000 and 100,000 live in Norway, 15,000 to 25,000 live in Sweden, over 6,000 live in Finland, and about 2,000 live in Russia. However, some think the actual number is considerably higher, perhaps up to 200,000. For many years, the Sami culture and way of life were disparaged by their neighbors, causing many to conceal their true identity. Thus, it is difficult to know how many Sami there actually are.

³ LANGUAGE

Sami is a Finno-Ugric language that is most closely related to Finnish, Estonian, Livonian, Votic, and several other little-known tongues. While it varies from region to region, it does so based on the lifestyle of the Sami people rather than on the

national boundaries of the lands in which they live. In fact, the present official definition of a Sami is primarily a linguistic one. There are several distinct dialects; however, the language is usually grouped into three main categories: Eastern Sami, Central Sami, and Southern Sami. Today, almost all Sami also speak the language of their native country.

Sami is rich in words describing reindeer, with words for different colors, sizes, antler spreads, and fur textures. Other words indicate how tame a reindeer is or how good at pulling sleds. There is actually a separate word describing a male reindeer in each year of his life. A poem by Nils-Aslak Valkeapää, recipient of the Nordic Council prize, consists mainly of different Sami words for different kinds of reindeer. There are also hundreds of words that differentiate snow according to its age, depth, density, and hardness; terms exist for powdery snow, snow that fell yesterday, and snow that is soft underneath with a hard crust.

The availability of schooling in the Sami language has become an important issue to those concerned with the preservation of the Sami culture and way of life. In 1995, the Norwegian government issued the Sami Language Act, allowing for the use of Sami as an official language in several municipalities. Finland and Sweden have since passed similar acts. Sami may be used as the language of instruction throughout primary and secondary school. Sami is taught and studied at the university level as well.

⁴ FOLKLORE

Traditionally, the Sami believed that specific spirits were associated with certain places and with the deceased. Many of their myths and legends concern the underworld. Others involve the Stallos, a race of troll-like giants who ate humans or sucked out their strength through an iron pipe. Many tales involve Sami outwitting the Stallos.

Some of the Sami epics trace Sami ancestry to the sun. In the mid-19th century, a Sami minister, Anders Fjellner, recorded epic mythical poems in which the Daughter of the Sun favored the Sami and brought the reindeer to them. In a related myth, the Son of the Sun had three sons who became the ancestors of the Sami. At their deaths they became stars in the heavens, and can be seen today in the belt of the constellation Orion.

⁵ RELIGION

The traditional Sami faith contained elements of animism, shamanism, and polytheism. The Sami believed that both living beings and inanimate objects, such as trees, had souls. A priest or shaman, called a *noaidi*, acted as an intermediary between the spiritual and material worlds. He would consult with the dead while in a trance, induced by beating on a magic drum and performing a special kind of chanting called *yoik*.

Over the course of time, all of the Sami were converted to Christianity, either by choice or by force of assimilation through the governments of the countries in they live. One major move toward Christianity was brought about through the efforts of Lars Levi Laestadius, an evangelical Congregationalist who was the founder of the Laestadian Lutheran Church in the 19th century. Today, most Sami practice the dominant Lutheran religion of the Nordic countries in which they live.

⁶ MAJOR HOLIDAYS

Sami observe the major holidays of the Christian calendar. Every Easter, a big festival is held at Kautokeino in northern Norway, complete with typical Sami entertainments, including sledge races and *yoik* singing. Many couples choose this setting for their weddings. Many Sami observe Finland's "little Christmas" (*Pikkujoulu*) early in December, marking the beginning of festivities that last through the twenty-sixth of the month. On Christmas Eve, special "midday trees" are adorned with candles, silver, and gold ribbons, and other decorations. After readings from the Gospels, a festive meal is eaten, typically consisting of salmon, ham, vegetables, and rice pudding. Boxing Day on December 26 is marked by sledge rides, lasso throwing, and other traditional games.

Secular holidays include the large spring celebrations held by the Sami every year, occasions on which they don their best clothes and gather with friends to mark the end of winter. Since 2004, Sami National Day has been celebrated on February 6 in Norway, Sweden, Russia, and Finland. The day commemorates the establishment of the first Sami congress in Norway in 1917. In Norway, Sami National Day is observed as a flag day by the government, meaning that both the Norwegian flag and the Sami flag are flown from the Government Administration Complex and the Storting (parliament building) on that day.

⁷ RITES OF PASSAGE

The Sami observe major life cycle events within the Christian tradition.

Sami weddings are festive affairs and are primarily the responsibility of the bride's parents. In one traditional secular courtship ritual, a man circled the *lavvo* (tent) of his lover with his reindeer and sledge; if the woman regarded his suit favorably, she came out and unharnessed the reindeer.

Sami funerals and burials are generally conducted according to Lutheran customs. The Sami have little interest in an afterlife.

⁸ INTERPERSONAL RELATIONS

Sami society is traditionally open and egalitarian, and the Sami are known for their courtesy and hospitality to outsiders. They willingly accept other Sami who may not be full-blooded; a person's attitude toward the treasured Sami language and traditions are more important than bloodlines. A knowledge of the Sami language is considered one of the main ways of identifying someone as a Sami.

⁹ LIVING CONDITIONS

As a nomadic people, the reindeer-herding Sami traditionally maintained permanent dwellings, sometimes more than one, and spent part of their time living in tents. The permanent homes were either frame buildings or sod huts. The Sami tent, called a *lavvo*, has a circular framework of poles leaning inward like the teepee or wigwam of Native Americans and a floor of birch twigs covered with layers of reindeer fur. Both tents and huts are arranged around a central fire. Today, most Sami, who are no longer reindeer herders, live in typical Scandinavian houses with central heating and running water. Family life typically centers on the kitchen.

The Sami receive the same level of health care as other citizens of the countries in which they live. Like their Scandinavian neighbors, they have a high rate of heart disease. However, Sami are often active and well into their 80s. They sometimes supplement Western-style medical care with home remedies or treatment derived from old beliefs in the curing power of the word of the shaman, or medicine man.

¹⁰ FAMILY LIFE

Traditionally, the Sami lived in a group of families called a *siida*. Today, the nuclear family is the basic social unit among the Sami, and families are close-knit with lavish attention paid to the children. The Sami language contains an unusually large number of words that refer to family relationships. Traditionally, the males of the family were occupied with herding, hunting, and making boats, sleds, and tools, while the women cooked, made clothing and thread, and cured the meat. Each family had its own mark (and children had their own marks as well). Herding families use these marks to distinguish their reindeer from those of other families.

¹¹ CLOTHING

Some Sami still wear the group's brightly colored traditional costume, known as a *kolt*. It is most easily recognizable by the distinctive bands of bright red and yellow patterns against a deep blue background of wool or felt. These bands appear as decorations on men's tunics (*gaktis*), as borders on the women's skirts, and on the hats of both sexes. Men's hats vary from region to region; some are cone-shaped while others have four corners. Women and girls may drape fringed scarves around their shoulders. Warm reindeer-skin coats are worn by both sexes. The traditional Sami might wear moccasins of reindeer skin with turned-up toes, fastened with ribbons. However, they wear no socks. Instead, they stuff their moccasins with soft sedge grass to protect their feet against the cold and dampness. Today, many Sami wear the styles of clothing typical to their home country, saving the kolt for special ceremonies.

12 FOOD

Reindeer meat has been a traditional dietary staple. Even the reindeer's blood is used for sausages. Fish caught in the many lakes of the Sami's homelands are eaten boiled, grilled, dried, smoked, or salted. Wild berries are another mainstay of the Sami diet, especially the vitamin C–rich cloudberry. To help them stay warm and alert in their cold environment, the Sami drink coffee throughout the day. Supper is the main meal of the day.

13 EDUCATION

Traditionally, Sami children learned what they would need to know as adults by observing and helping their parents. The goal of education was not simply to acquire more knowledge but to become a better citizen. In modern society, many Sami still maintain this attitude toward education and prefer an experiential approach to learning. Sami often attend the schools in the countries in which they live. However, there are now schools within Norway and Sweden where most of the subjects are taught in the Sami language. Sámi Allaskuvla, a Sami university, was established in Norway in 1989.

14 CULTURAL HERITAGE

The Sami have a rich tradition of oral storytelling. A Sami tradition that has recently been revived is the singing or expression of the *yoik*. The *yoik* might be considered as both a form of poetry and of song; however, the melody is based on non-Western scales and what might be considered as non-melodic vocalizations. Traditional *yoiks* are typically unaccompanied. They do not generally tell a narrative story, as the typical Western song might. Instead, a *yoik* presents an idea, a memory, or an emotion through the use of melody, rhythm, facial expressions, and gestures, as well as words. The *yoik* resembles the Native American practice of "melodizing" a feeling or mood. As new generations of Sami and their European neighbors have rediscovered the *yoik*, they have added to and reshaped the tradition. Musicians of pop, rock, and folk music have added *yoik* techniques and melodies to their music. An annual Sami Music festival is held in Kafjord, Norway.

The earliest Sami literature dates back to about the 17th century, with the earliest texts relating to religion and the Sami language, such as alphabet books. In 1991, Nils-Aslak Valkeapää of Finland became the first Sami writer to win the Nordic Council prize for literature with his book *Beaivi, Áhcázan* (*The Sun, My Father*).

The revival of the Sami language in recent years has also opened the door for the creation of Sami language theater productions, films, and newspapers.

15 WORK

About 10% of the Sami population in Sweden is still nomadic reindeer herders, making treks of up to 220 miles to provide pasture for their herds, which average about 500 animals. In 1947, Sami reindeer breeders formed the National Association of Norwegian Reindeer Breeders, which today plays an important role in the development of modern reindeer breeding. Handicrafts are a major source of income for some Sami, who find eager markets among tourists. While some Sami still work in the traditional occupations of fishing and hunting, a growing number of Sami live in urban areas and work in a wide variety of common occupations.

16 SPORTS

Outdoor recreation for the Sami is closely linked to the activities that provide their sustenance. They enjoy competing to see who can throw their reindeer lassos the farthest and with the greatest precision. Reindeer-drawn sledge races are another popular leisure-time activity, especially at the Easter festivals in the heart of Sapmi, which many tourists also frequent. Skiing is a popular sport among the Sami, who believe that their own ancestors were the inventors of skis. Soccer has also become a popular sport among the Sami.

17 ENTERTAINMENT AND RECREATION

Sami entertainment is provided both by expressive activities, including storytelling and *yoiking*, and physical contests such as sledge racing, skiing, lasso throwing, and soccer matches. The Sami also participate in the wide variety of entertainment options enjoyed by their fellow Scandinavian citizens.

18 FOLK ART, CRAFTS, AND HOBBIES

The traditional style of Sami arts and crafts is known as *duodji*. Sami crafts usually had a very practical purpose in daily living, such as tools and utensils that are made from bone, wood, and reindeer antlers. However, these items are often highly decoration, designed to be pleasing to the eye as well as useful. *Duodji* has a spiritual aspect as well as a material one. Items are usually made from natural materials, with the expectation that they will be worn down and even destroyed through repeated use, perhaps to remind the user that all natural life is only temporary. Modern art in the Sami tradition is known as *Dáidda*, and includes items that are generally meant for display, rather than use. The Sami have also perfected a special kind of ribbon weaving. Their crafts are popular tourist purchases, although the Sami save many of their creations for their own use, and much of their artistic talent goes into the elaborate braided designs of their costumes.

19 SOCIAL PROBLEMS

In recent years, the Sami homelands have been affected by the encroachment of mining and logging concerns, hydroelectric power projects, communication networks, and tourism. A controversy that received particular attention was the building of the Alta hydroelectric dam in Norway, which flooded reindeer pastures important to the region's Sami herders. A group of Sami protesters traveled to the capital city of Oslo, where they set up *lavvos* (tents) in front of the Norwegian parliament and began a hunger strike. While their cause was unsuccessful, their actions drew worldwide attention to their threatened way of life.

Since 1968, the National Association of Norwegian Sami (NSR) has been working actively for Sami political rights, as well as improvements in cultural, social, and economic conditions. Norway, Sweden, and Finland all have separate Sami parliaments addressing issues of concern for the Sami.

The Sami were also affected by the 1986 nuclear accident at Chernobyl in Ukraine, which contaminated some of their grazing areas, making their reindeer potentially unsafe for them to market or eat themselves. Fish, berries, and drinking water in the affected areas were poisoned as well. Another problem for the Sami has been the increase of tourists from the south, who deplete important Sami resources, such as gamebirds, fish, and berries, without actually bringing much money into their community.

Besides displacement by roads and other forms of development, the livelihood of the Sami herders is also threatened by overgrazing and uncontrolled breeding, which results in smaller, less healthy animals, and it is hard for the migrant Sami to find alternative forms of employment.

[20] GENDER ISSUES

There has been some evidence to indicate that the traditional Sami embraced a matriarchal culture, in which women held a high level of authority in both the community and in the family. The tasks of raising children and providing food and clothing for the family were considered to be of great importance. Since women were the ones trained in accomplishing these tasks, women were held in high esteem. Traditional Sami religion, which included a number of female deities, may have also supported a culture in which men and women were viewed as equals. However, the introduction of Christianity and the influence of more dominant cultures resulted in a loss of authority to women. New Christian men and women were taught that women should be submissive to men. Assimilation into other Scandinavian societies also inspired a shift toward a more patriarchal attitude.

A Sami feminist movement began in the 1970s at the initiation of female reindeer herders who expected equality with their male herders. In 1988, Sami women formed the organization known as Sarahkka, which works to resolve issues important to Sami women. The group became a central force in the formation of the World Council for Aboriginal Women in 1989. Sarahkka continues to focus on projects that lead to greater education and social development among women.

Many Sami women still consider raising children and passing along the traditions and beliefs of their culture as their most important roles. These roles are also generally respected within Sami society. The creation and sale of *duodji,* traditional Sami handicrafts, has been taken up by some women as a primary or secondary source of income. Some Sami women, particularly in urban areas, have taken jobs typical of their female counterparts from their home countries. Sami women have also been elected to seats in the Sami parliament.

[21] BIBLIOGRAPHY

Gaski, Harald. "The Sami People: The 'White Indians' of Scandinavia." *American Indian Culture and Research Journal* 17, no. 1 (1993): 115–28.

Illustrated Encyclopedia of Mankind. London: Marshall Cavendish, 1978.

Irwin, John I. *The Finns and the Lapps: How They Live and Work.* New York: Praeger, 1973.

Lander, Patricia Slade, and Claudette Charbonneau. *The Land and People of Finland.* New York: Lippincott, 1990.

Moss, Joyce, and George Wilson. *Peoples of the World: Western Europeans.* Detroit: Gale Research, 1993.

Rajanen, Aini. *Of Finnish Ways.* Minneapolis: Dillon Press, 1981.

Reynolds, Jan. *Far North.* New York: Harcourt Brace, 1992.

"Saami." *Encyclopedia of World Cultures (Europe).* Boston: G. K. Hall, 1992.

Sami Culture in Nordic Countries. University of Texas, http://www.utexas.edu/courses/sami (September 2008).

Sápmi: Samiskt Informationscentrum

Sametinget. http://www.eng.samer.se/servlet/GetDoc?meta_id=1001 (September 2008).

Taylor-Wilkie, Doreen. *Finland.* Insight Guides. Singapore: APA Press, 1993.

Vitebsky, Piers. *The Saami of Lapland.* New York: Thomson Learning, 1993.

—revised by K. Ellicott

SAMMARINESE

LOCATION: San Marino
POPULATION: 29,973 (2008 est.)
LANGUAGE: Italian; Romagna
RELIGION: Roman Catholic

¹ INTRODUCTION

The tiny nation of San Marino, located completely within the borders of Italy, is Europe's third-smallest country and its oldest independent republic. The people of San Marino are called Sammarinese. For hundreds of years, their country's mountaintop fortifications helped it maintain some distance from the recurrent power struggles that engulfed their region until the unification of Italy in the 19th century. Since then, a mutual defense treaty has guaranteed San Marino's continuing political independence from Italy, and the two nations have also formed a customs union. Today San Marino's primary sources of income are tourism, light manufacturing, and the sale of postage stamps to collectors throughout the world.

The only one of Italy's historic city-states to survive as an independent nation, San Marino had its beginnings in AD 301 when a Christian stonecutter named Marinus, fleeing persecution by the Roman Emperor Diocletian, founded a monastery atop Mount Titano. He was later canonized as Saint Marinus (San Marino in Italian). In the succeeding centuries, the population of the region grew, and its people remained independent of any outside civil or religious authority, eventually erecting fortifications consisting of walls and towers. A document from AD 885 called the *Placito Feretrano* establishes the existence of San Marino as an independent political entity prior to AD 1000. By the 11th century, it had developed a system of government that still survives today in a modified form, and by the 13th century, it had formed a militia to keep its territory free of foreign domination.

For hundreds of years, the tiny state fended off attempts by a succession of popes and ruling families to seize control of its territory. As part of a power struggle involving one of its popes, the Catholic Church excommunicated all the Sammarinese between 1247 and 1249, and tensions in the region erupted into open warfare in the 14th and 15th centuries. For a time San Marino allied itself with the Duke of Urbino, but eventually faced new threats when the surrounding states formed a papal union. In 1739, Cardinal Giulio Alberoni from the neighboring province of Romagna seized control of San Marino using troops under the church's command, but he was eventually forced out by the religious authorities. San Marino, as a political entity, remained separate from the 19th-century struggle for unification of the Italian states, although it provided a haven for many of the combatants, including the national hero, Giuseppe Garibaldi. In 1862, the new Kingdom of Italy signed an agreement recognizing the sovereignty of its tiny neighbor, finally ensuring San Marino's independence.

At the beginning of the 20th century, San Marino underwent a governmental reform that resulted in the establishment of an elected parliament, the Grand and General Council. The country's first democratic election took place in 1906. Although San Marino remained neutral in both world wars, it couldn't avoid being affected by the turmoil of the era. Be-

tween the wars, the Fascism that was sweeping Italy also gained a number of converts within the borders of its smaller neighbor. However, the government of San Marino remained neutral, and the country harbored thousands of refugees during the war, putting an enormous strain on its resources. However, the greatest suffering inflicted by the war occurred on 26 June 1944, when 63 people were killed and hundreds of others injured by the "friendly fire" of an ally: The British Royal Air Force inexplicably dropped 243 bombs on San Marino, although there were no enemy troops present at the time. The country later received financial compensation for the incident from the British government. During the postwar period, political control of San Marino has alternated between right- and left-wing parties. The nation established diplomatic ties with the European Community in 1983 and became a member of the United Nations in 1992. Before then, it had maintained permanent observer missions in various U.N. organizations. San Marino's foreign policy and social and political trends track closely with those of Italy. In 2006 more than 2.1 million tourists visited San Marino.

² LOCATION AND HOMELAND

San Marino lies completely within the country of Italy, in the central Apennines about 22 km (13 mi) southwest of the city of Rimini on the Adriatic coast. Located on the summit and lower slopes of Mt. Titano, San Marino has an area of 60 sq km (23 sq mi) and a total boundary length of 39 km (24 mi). About one-third the size of Washington, D.C., the tiny republic is only 13 km (8 mi) long, and 9 km (5.5 mi) wide at its widest point. Mt. Titano, whose three main peaks—with fortresses atop each one—are pictured in the San Marino coat of arms, has an elevation of 750 m (2,460 ft). Two rivers, the Marano and the Ausa, flow through San Marino.

In 2008 San Marino had a population of nearly 30,000, making it one of the world's most densely populated countries. The capital city, also called San Marino, had a population of 4,500. Other population centers include the town of Dogana and the following locales, each with its own castle: Serravalle, Borgo Maggiore, Faetano, Domagnano, Chiesanuova, Acquaviva, Fiorentino, and Montegiardino. The Sammarinese are mostly of Italian ancestry, and most new immigration to the country is from Italy. The main destinations for those emigrating from San Marino are Italy, the United States, France, and Belgium.

³ LANGUAGE

Italian, the official of language of San Marino, is spoken by all its people, although many also speak the regional dialect of Romagna, the part of Italy where San Marino is located. Even the standard, or Florentine, Italian of the Sammarinese contains certain words and idioms unique to San Marino.

⁴ FOLKLORE

Mt. Titano, on which San Marino is located, is named for the Titans, characters from Roman mythology who tried to dethrone Jupiter by piling one mountain on top of another in order to reach the sky.

⁵ RELIGION

Roman Catholicism is both San Marino's official religion and the faith of almost all its residents. Ceremonies marking many

SAMMARINESE

ITALY

0   1   2   3 Miles

0   1   2   3 Kilometers

Marecchia

Barigello

Falciano

Serravalle

Torello

Ranco

Domagnano

Acquaviva

Borgo
Maggiore

Corianino

San Marino

Albereto

CaChiavello

Poggio di
Chiesanuova

Montemaggio

Chiesanuova

Montegiardino

Gaiano

Castello

ITALY

state occasions are held in the country's churches. San Marino has nine parishes, all belonging to a single diocese. Some areas that are actually in Italy, such as the town of Rimini, belong to the diocese of San Marino.

6 MAJOR HOLIDAYS

In addition to the standard holidays of the Christian calendar (including Epiphany, Assumption, Easter Monday, Ascension, Immaculate Conception, and Christmas), legal holidays in San Marino include New Year's Day (January 1), Labor Day (May 1), August Bank Holiday (August 14–16), and All Saints' Day and Commemoration of the Dead (November 1 and 2).

San Marino also has five national holidays that commemorate important historical or political events. February 5 is celebrated both as the Anniversary of St. Agatha, the republic's second patron saint, and as the date on which San Marino was liberated from occupation by Cardinal Alberoni in 1740. The Anniversary of the Arengo, observed on March 25, marks the date in 1906 on which the first democratic elections to the Grand and General Council were held. April 1 and October 1, the two days of the year when San Marino's Captains Regent, its joint chief executives, are installed, are also celebrated as national holidays. Finally, on September 3, the feast day of its patron saint (Saint Marino), the republic celebrates the anniversary of its founding.

7 RITES OF PASSAGE

San Marino is a relatively modern Roman Catholic country. Hence, many of the rites of passage that young people undergo are religious rituals, such as baptism, first Communion, confirmation, and marriage. In addition, a student's progress through the education system is marked by many families with graduation parties.

8 INTERPERSONAL RELATIONS

The Sammarinese show the same basic openness and friendliness found among the neighboring Italians, a quality that has been important in the success of their nation's busy tourist industry. Respect toward the elderly is an important social tradition.

9 LIVING CONDITIONS

Nearly all dwellings in San Marino have electricity and indoor plumbing. All Sammarinese are covered by a comprehensive national health care plan, which pays for both private treatment and care at the public state hospital. In 2008 the average life expectancy was 81.9 years. Although it is near the Adriatic Sea, San Marino is a landlocked nation and accessible only by motor vehicle or helicopter. The railway that once connected it to Rimini has been inoperable since being badly damaged by bombing in World War II, but there is regular bus service between the two locations.

10 FAMILY LIFE

San Marino's government provides family supplement payments to families with children. Until 1982, Sammarinese women who married citizens of other countries lost their San Marino citizenship. In 1973 women won the right to be elected to any political office in the land, including the highest one—Captain Regent.

11 CLOTHING

The Sammarinese wear modern Western-style clothing like that worn in the other countries of Western Europe. However, colorful ceremonial costumes are connected with some of their traditions. The corps of young flag-bearers, who continue a tradition that dates back to ancient times, wear brightly colored tights, black boots, and loosely fitting colored shirts with black belts. The honor guards for the Captains Regent—the nation's chief executives—wear black uniforms with gold trim, including a gold stripe down the trousers, and high plumed hats with blue and white feathers.

12 FOOD

Homemade pasta is one of the most popular foods prepared by the Sammarinese. *Fagioli con le cotiche*—a hearty bacon soup with bacon rind—is a special holiday dish traditionally eaten at Christmastime. *Nidi di rondine* (literally, "swallow's nest") consists of hollow pasta filled with smoked ham, cheese, and a meat-and-tomato sauce and baked in a white sauce. Other favorites include *pasta e cece,* a chickpea soup seasoned with garlic and rosemary and served with noodles; snails cooked with tomatoes, red wine, and fennel; and roast rabbit. Popular cuisine from the Italian province of Romagna, which surrounds San Marino, includes *tagliatelli* (a type of pasta that consists of thin strips), as well as *ravioli* and *lasagna,* two dishes popularized in the United States by Italian-Americans.

Favorite desserts include *zuppa di ciliege* (cherries soaked in red wine and sugar and served with a special bread); *bustrengo* (a traditional carnival dish made with milk, eggs, sugar, raisins, corn flour, and bread crumbs); and *cacciatello* (a milk-and-egg dessert served cold). San Marino is known for its local wines, especially a red wine called *Sangiovese.*

13 EDUCATION

San Marino has a literacy rate of about 96%. Its educational system is based on that of Italy, and school is compulsory between the ages of 6 and 16. High school graduates, after taking a qualifying examination, may attend colleges and universities in Italy, or at the Università degli Studi della Repùbblica di San Marino which offers graduate and postgraduate studies.

14 CULTURAL HERITAGE

San Marino's long history has produced an impressive heritage of visual art, showcased in the republic's museums and churches, as well as in its outdoor public sculptures. The Valloni Palace, rebuilt after falling victim to "friendly fire" from the British in World War II, houses many of the nation's cultural treasures (although many others were destroyed by the bombing). Famous paintings kept there include *Saint Philip Neri* and *Saint Marino Lifting Up the Republic,* both by Guercino, and *Saint John* by Strozzi. The 14th-century Church of St. Francis, itself an architectural treasure, houses more historic paintings.

San Marino's national anthem is probably the oldest of any country in the world. Derived from a medieval chorale, it is unusual in that it is a purely instrumental composition with no words. San Marino has a military band, which performs at ceremonial and other events.

15 WORK

While agriculture provides a smaller percentage of San Marino's income than it did in the past, many Sammarinese are still farmers, growing barley, corn, vegetables, grapes, and other fruits, and raising livestock. The main agricultural products are wine and cheeses. Most of the wage labor force is employed by the tourist sector or in manufacturing, which includes textiles, ceramics, leather goods, and metalworking. The per capita level of output and standard of living are comparable to those of the most prosperous regions of Italy, which supplies much of its food. San Marino has a very low level of unemployment. In 2004 the unemployment rate was 3.8%.

16 SPORTS

The traditional national sport of San Marino is archery, practiced as an art of warfare in the distant past and as a recreational pursuit today. The tiny republic is known for the strength and skill of its champion crossbowmen, demonstrated every September in a competition in the palace square. Marksmanship also figures in two other favorite sports, pistol- and rifle-shooting. San Marino's location near Italy's Adriatic coast—at some points the distance is as short as 10 km (6 mi)—allows its residents to enjoy such water sports as swimming, sailing, and deep-sea diving. The Italian sport of *bocce,* lawn bowling with heavy metal balls, is a popular pastime that can be played on almost any moderately flat surface. The Sammarinese also enjoy soccer, baseball, tennis, and basketball. In addition, their country sponsors a Grand Prix Formula One auto racing event, although it must be held over the border in Italy due to the lack of a suitable racetrack within San Marino's own borders. San Marino's National Olympic Committee manages all the nation's sports facilities.

17 ENTERTAINMENT AND RECREATION

In addition to a variety of sports and other outdoor activities, the Sammarinese enjoy socializing at cafés (including outdoor cafés in summertime) and attending movies, concerts, and plays. In addition, those with a taste for the visual arts may view fine art and sculpture in their museums and churches.

18 FOLK ART, CRAFTS, AND HOBBIES

San Marino's tourist industry has created a thriving market for its craftspeople, whose work is sold in a number of shops. A special association monitors the quality of all crafts sold in the country. The work of San Marino's potters encompasses both medieval designs and contemporary styles, and the region's white sandstone has been quarried and carved into statues, building stones, friezes, and other objects since ancient times. Other traditional crafts include painting, jewelry, wood carving, tilework, leather goods, and textiles.

Like Liechtenstein, another tiny European country, San Marino is famous for its stamps, internationally prized collectors' items that provide the republic with an important source of income. Designed by respected artists, they are known for their wide variety of themes, which has even included a Walt Disney series with such cartoon characters as Mickey Mouse, Donald Duck, and Goofy. San Marino's Philatelic and Numismatic Museum houses all stamps issued by San Marino since it began to produce them in 1877 under a postal agreement with Italy. San Marino's coins show the same artistic creativity as its stamps, and few circulate because, like the republic's stamps, they are usually snapped up by collectors. A series of coins minted in 1985 had as its theme the war on drugs, and the coins—ranging in value from 1 to 500 lira—depict nine stages of drug addiction. (Today most money circulating in San Marino is the euro).

19 SOCIAL PROBLEMS

With its small size, low rate of unemployment, and extensive social programs, San Marino has relatively few of the social problems that affect other modern nations.

20 GENDER ISSUES

Women enjoy the same rights as men, including rights under family law, property law, and in the judicial system. In 2007 there were eight women in the 60-seat Great and General Council and two women in the 10-member Congress of State.

Rape, including spousal rape, is a criminal offense. The penalty for rape is two to six years' imprisonment. In the case of aggravating circumstances, the penalty is 4 to 10 years' imprisonment. The law also prohibits violence against women. The penalty for spousal abuse is two to six years' imprisonment. In the case of aggravating circumstances, the penalty is 4 to 10 years' imprisonment. Prostitution is illegal and is not common. Sexual harassment is prohibited.

In 2001 San Marino's parliament voted for the repeal of part of its criminal code. Until this time homosexual contacts could be punished with imprisonment from three months up to one year, if they had been engaged in "habitually" and thereby caused "public scandal." A conviction under this law resulted in loss of political rights and removal from public office for a period from nine months to two years.

²¹ BIBLIOGRAPHY

Carrick, Noel. *San Marino.* New York: Chelsea House, 1988.

Catling, Christopher. *Umbria, the Marches, and San Marino.* Lincolnwood, IL: Passport Books, 1994.

Duursma, Jorri. *Self-Determination, Statehood, and International Relations of Micro-States: the Cases of Liechtenstein, San Marino, Monaco, Andorra, and the Vatican City.* Cambridge; New York: Cambridge University Press, 1996.

Eccardt, Thomas M. *Secrets of the Seven Smallest States of Europe: Andorra, Liechtenstein, Luxembourg, Malta, Monaco, San Marino, and Vatican City.* New York: Hippocrene Books, 2005.

Gall, Timothy, and Susan Gall, ed. *Worldmark Encyclopedia of the Nations.* Detroit: Gale Research, 1995.

The Marche and San Marino. New York: WW Norton, 2006.

Paris, Sheldon. "San Marino is Europe's Oldest Independent Republic." *Stamps.* (8 April 1995): 19.

—revised by J. Hobby

SCOTS

LOCATION: United Kingdom (Scotland)
POPULATION: Over 5 million
LANGUAGE: Scottish dialect of English (also called Scots); Gaelic
RELIGION: Church of Scotland, a Presbyterian sect; Roman Catholic; small numbers of Baptists, Anglicans, and Methodists

¹ INTRODUCTION

Scotland is one of four nations that make up the United Kingdom of Great Britain and Northern Ireland (the other three are England, Wales, and Northern Ireland). A small country—only 442 km (275 mi) long—it covers the northern portion of the island of Great Britain, which it shares with England and Wales. The name Scotland, first used during the 11th century, is derived from the name of a Celtic tribe from Ireland, the Scotti, who settled western Scotland during the 6th century. The Romans called the area Caledonia.

For centuries, social and political life in the northern (Highland) area of Scotland was organized around clans, communities of people with strong family ties, whose powerful chieftains commanded their loyalty in exchange for protecting them from invasion. (Today, the cultural tradition of clans such as MacGregor or MacDonald survives at ceremonial gatherings such as weddings.) The southern areas of the country were much more affected by English patterns of organization. Repeated disputes with the English sometimes led to war, and before the early 14th century, the Scottish were dominated by English monarchs. In 1603 a new era of cooperation began when James VI of Scotland became James I, King of Great Britain. In 1707 the Act of Union made Scotland, together with England and Wales, part of the United Kingdom, sharing a single parliament.

Scotland saw difficult times in the 20th century. The depression of the 1930s wrought havoc on its economy and began an era of unemployment which forced thousands to emigrate in search of a better life. However, the discovery of North Sea oil in the 1960s created as many as 100,000 new jobs, and emigration slowed. As a part of Britain, Scotland joined the European Community (now European Union—EU) in 1973. Since the late 1980s there has been a resurgence of Scottish national sentiment in favor of separation from England. In September 1997 Scotland voted in favor of establishing its own parliament. The 129-seat Scottish Parliament, which saw its first elections in 1999, has the power to increase or cut income taxes by up to 3%. The vote marked the most profound change in Scotland's relationship with the rest of Great Britain since the Act of Union in 1707. As of 2007 there were calls for television production and broadcasting to be devolved to the Scottish parliament, as some saw Scotland as being marginalized by the British broadcasting industry. For example, the British Broadcasting Corporation (BBC) had decreased its investment in Scotland by £30 million.

² LOCATION AND HOMELAND

Located in the northern part of the island of Great Britain, Scotland can be divided into three principal areas: the Southern Uplands, a hilly region noted for its sheep-raising industry; the more densely populated Central Lowlands, consisting of flatter, more fertile land; and the Highlands, which account for the northern two-thirds of the country and include lochs (lakes), glens, mountains, and numerous small islands.

Scotland has a population of over 5 million, about three-fourths of whom live in the central Lowland area. Two hundred years ago, almost half the Scottish population lived in the Highlands. Ethnically, most Scots are descended from Celtic tribes that were the original inhabitants of their lands, as well as the Viking, Norman, and English invaders who followed each other in succession. There are fundamental population divisions between Highland and Lowland Scots, as well as between mainland dwellers and those living on the small islands off the coast, such as the Shetlanders and Hebrideans.

³ LANGUAGE

Scotland's official language is English, but it is spoken in distinctive dialects and with a unique Scottish accent, or "burr," that is especially prominent in words containing "r" sounds. Scottish English (also called Scots) contains words borrowed from Gaelic, French, Dutch, and Scandinavian languages, and its grammar sometimes differs from that of standard English, as in expressions like "Are you no going?" and "I'm away to bed." Some examples of Scots dialects are Doric, spoken in the northeast, and Lallans, spoken in the southwest (and the dialect of poet Robert Burns). Gaelic is spoken as a second language by less than 2% of the population, mostly in the Highlands and Hebridean islands, although all Scots recognize at least a few words of Gaelic.

COMMONLY USED SCOTS TERMS

dinnae, cannae, willnae	don't, can't, won't
wee	small
aye	yes
ken	know
greet	weep
kirk	church
breeks	pants
lassie	girl
bairn	child
bonny	pretty
bide	stay

TYPICAL SCOTS PHRASES

Ah'm fair farfochen.	I'm exhausted.
The bairn's a wee bit wabbit.	The child's a little tired.

⁴ FOLKLORE

The oldest Gaelic songs recount legends of warrior heroes battling Norsemen, magic rowan trees, and monstrous old women living in the sea. There is also a rich folk tradition revolving around belief in fairies and other supernatural forces. The most famous character in Scottish folklore is the dinosaur-like Loch Ness monster. Although this creature has supposedly been seen swimming in the deep by hundreds of people, no scientific evidence of its existence has ever been produced.

The "border ballads" of the southern regions and a wealth of urban folk songs, especially in the Glasgow region, comprise another segment of Scottish folklore.

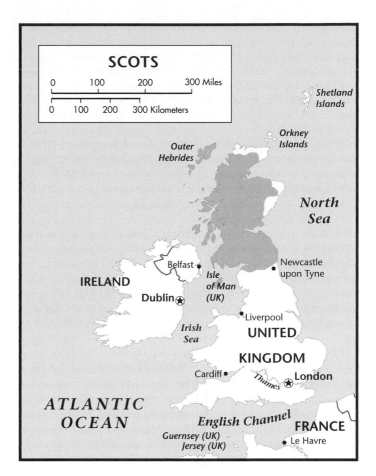

⁵ RELIGION

With about 587,000 members, the Church of Scotland, a Presbyterian sect founded in the 16th century by John Knox, is the country's dominant religion. Commonly known as "the Kirk," it has been Scotland's official religion since 1690. The Roman Catholic Church has about 212,500 members and other trinitarian churches have about 164,000 members. Catholics live mainly on the west coast. Scotland also has smaller populations of Baptists, Anglicans, and Methodists, as well as more modern evangelical sects. Church attendance in Scotland is very low with less than 10% of the population attending regularly.

⁶ MAJOR HOLIDAYS

Aside from the major holidays of the Christian calendar, the Scots celebrate the commemoration of Saint Andrew, patron saint of Scotland, on November 30.

Another unique holiday is the Hogmanay (New Year's Eve) celebration. Until the 1960s, this holiday far outpaced Christmas as the major winter celebration. It involves the ceremony of "first footing," the custom of visiting the homes of friends, neighbors, and even strangers, in the "wee sma' hours" of New Year's Day. Christmas, which was formerly frowned on by the Scottish church and only became a public holiday in 1967, resembles a modern Christmas in England or the U.S., with fir trees, carols, and gift-giving. Scots gather for dinner on Burns Night, January 25, to honor the Scottish poet Robert Burns. Traditionally, the Scottish national dish, haggis, is served as Burns's poem, "Address to a Haggis," is recited. Scottish Quarter Day (40 days after Christmas) was a holiday celebrated widely until the 1950s; it is rarely celebrated today.

Interestingly, one of the most important celebrations of the Scottish year is Halloween, on October 31. Like "trick-or-treaters" in the United States, Scottish "guisers" go from door to door in costumes asking for candy or money. However, unlike their counterparts in the United States, they must perform a song or poem before receiving their treat. Another possible feature of the Halloween celebration is a party with supernatural themes and decorations such as the Scottish version of the American "jack-o'-lantern": a scooped-out rutabaga called a "neep lantern."

7 RITES OF PASSAGE

The Scots live in a modern, industrialized, Christian country. Although Scots are relatively casual about the practice of religion, many of the rites of passage that young people undergo are religious rituals, such as baptism, first Communion, confirmation, and marriage. In addition, a student's progress through the education system is marked by many families with graduation parties.

8 INTERPERSONAL RELATIONS

The Scottish are known for their taciturn and reserved manner. It is unusual for Scots to be seen holding hands, kissing, or touching in public. Within the household, however, family members maintain close relationships that include many "inside jokes." The humor of the Scots tends toward the deadpan and ironic, and they tend to minimize direct expressions of enthusiasm. However, it is also considered unacceptable to criticize others in public, or to discuss personal problems with anyone other than close associates. As a form of greeting, the handshake is less common than in other parts of Britain.

9 LIVING CONDITIONS

Most Scottish houses have a small garden, and many are built in rows called terraces. Homes built before World War I were generally made of stone (single-story cottages of this type can still be found in some highland areas as well as urban areas), while most newer dwellings are built of brick or concrete blocks. Slate roofs are common, and many houses are covered by a painted coating of cement. Many Scottish houses are protected from harsh winters by the traditional "double door" arrangement: a heavy outer door, a vestibule, and a lighter inner door. Over half of all Scots live in "council houses," low-cost housing built by local authorities. These generally consist of high-rise apartment complexes with small rental units. In the late 20th century, complexes of this type began to give way to terraced housing.

Scotland's National Health Service has significantly raised the country's level of medical care since it was instituted following World War II. However, as of 2007 Scotland was the worst performing small country in Western Europe in terms of health and other factors. The Federation of Small Businesses' annual Index of Wealth compared 10 countries on economic performance, employment rates, health and education. Scotland also fell by one place, to 17th, in the Organization for Economic Co-operation and Development (OECD)'s table of the world's 24 most developed countries. Scotland had the lowest life expectancy in the UK for both men and women in 2007. The figures were 74.2 for men and 79.3 for women, compared

to the UK average of 76.6 and 81 years. As well, the gap between rich and poor is widening. In 2007 Glasgow City was the worst performing local authority area in Scotland, with the poorest record in three of the four indicators: mortality, education, and employment. The leading causes of death in Scotland are heart disease, strokes, and cancer. The Scots smoke more and eat more sugar and fats than any other nationality in Europe.

Scotland has a modern system of highways and two-lane roads totaling some 88,500 km (55,000 mi) of paved roads altogether. In the western Highlands, however, many of the roads are single lanes with periodic passing places. Double-decker buses with an extra passenger level above the normal one are a common sight in cities and towns. The government-run railway system operates both diesel and electric trains and serves all major cities, linking Glasgow and Edinburgh to each other and to London. The mainland and the islands are linked by ferries and air service. Glasgow has a major international airport and Edinburgh and Aberdeen are served by both national and international air services.

10 FAMILY LIFE

The traditional role of women as laborers in the textile, jute, and fish-processing industries can be traced as early as the 19th century—and the economic independence it brought them has given them a relatively high degree of authority within the family. While traditionally male skilled trades like steelmaking and mining still do not hire female employees, increasing numbers of women are entering the professions, and there are nearly as many women as men at Scotland's colleges and universities. Scots are legally allowed to marry by the age of 16, and many do marry as teenagers, although the early 20s are still the most typical marriage age. Although the divorce rate has risen in Scotland, it is still low relative to the American rate of divorce.

11 CLOTHING

When people throughout the world think of the Scots, most probably picture them in their famous traditional costume, the kilt. However, this skirtlike garment is only worn on ceremonial occasions by Scottish regiments of the British army, by ordinary citizens on formal occasions such as weddings and black-tie dinners, and for traditional festive events such as the Highland Games. Otherwise, the Scots wear standard Western-style clothing. Because of the climate, Scottish clothing tends to be made of heavier fabrics such as wool, including the native *tweed*. Each of Scotland's clans has its own tartan (or plaid) developed over the centuries—there are at least 300 different designs in all. Women's ceremonial costumes include tartan skirts and white blouses worn under snug black button-down bodices. Between 7 and 10 m (7–10 yds) of wool tartan are required for the average kilt.

12 FOOD

The Scottish national dish is *haggis,* a sausage-like food made from chopped organ meat of a sheep or calf mixed with oatmeal and spices and traditionally boiled in the casing of a sheep's stomach (although today a plastic bag is often used). Dietary staples include oats (in porridge, oatcakes, and other forms) and potatoes, or "tatties." These are commonly eaten as french fries ("chips"), as well as boiled, baked, or mashed. A

Scottish pipers take to the parade ground at Redford Barracks in Edinburgh, Scotland. Military bands braved the Scottish rain and gathered for a final rehearsal of the 55th Edinburgh Military Tattoo. (Chris Furlong/Getty Images)

side dish of mashed potatoes and rutabaga, called "clapshott," is sometimes served with haggis. The main meal of the day is tea, served at dinnertime, usually around 6:00 PM (the midday meal is called "dinner"). However, in rural areas, the midday meal is still the main one. Besides oatcakes, typical Scottish desserts include shortbread, a rich fruitcake called "Dundee cake," and a New Year's specialty called "black bun."

13 EDUCATION

Despite the information seen in "Living Conditions" above, the Scots remain a well-educated people. Universal education has been an institution in their country for centuries, and Scots read more newspapers than any other European people. About 95% of adult Scots are literate. Their educational system is operated separately from England's. After seven years of primary school, Scottish children attend secondary school for six years. The school day generally ends at 4:00 PM. Many private schools require students to wear uniforms, but they are optional at most other institutions. After secondary school, students can attend one of Scotland's 20 institutions of higher learning, including universities and vocational schools. A great value is placed on higher education, and the universities of St. Andrews, Edinburgh, Aberdeen, and Glasgow are especially prestigious.

14 CULTURAL HERITAGE

Of all the arts, the Scots have particularly distinguished themselves in the realm of literature, especially poetry and novels. Scotland's most famous poet, Robert Burns, lived and wrote at the end of the 18th century, dying at the age of 37. Writing both poems and songs, he popularized the dialect of his homeland both at home and in England. The poet Lord Byron was born and educated in Aberdeen. Scotland produced the famous philosophers Thomas Carlyle and David Hume, as well as the renowned economist Adam Smith, who became famous for his work, *The Wealth of Nations*. Scotland's other important writers include two authors of adventure novels, Sir Walter Scott, whose romantic tales often dealt with Scottish history, and Robert Louis Stevenson, author of *Treasure Island* and *The Strange Case of Dr. Jekyll and Mr. Hyde*. Arthur Conan Doyle, another Scot, created the famous fictional detective Sherlock Holmes, and his countryman J. M. Barrie authored the play *Peter Pan*, which has delighted generations of audiences throughout the 20th century. A contemporary Scottish author is fiction writer A.L. Kennedy (born in Dundee, 1965), who is also a stand-up comedienne and an Associate Professor with the Warwick University Creative Writing Program.

15 WORK

Since the 1960s there has been a marked shift in the economy from manufacturing to service industries—including tourism, with the service sector accounting for nearly four times the number of jobs as the manufacturing sector. Private services contribute about two-fifths of Scotland's gross domestic product (GDP), while public services account for more than one-fifth. Retail trade also creates many jobs in Scotland. Agriculture, forestry, and fishing make up a very small percentage of the economy. However, Scotland has a unique agricultural tradition, primarily in the Highlands, called crofting. Farmers living on crofts (a term that refers to both their land and to the family home) raise grains or vegetables individually on their own plots of land, and animals communally on a larger grazing area. Today, crofting rarely serves as a primary source of income or food, although some still rely on it for supplementary income. Most manufacturing is concentrated in the Central Lowlands. Important industries include textiles, chemicals, steel, electronics, whiskey, and petroleum products.

16 SPORTS

The Scottish national sport, soccer (called football), is associated with fierce rivalries between Catholic and Protestant teams that sometimes erupt into violence. The most famous pair of rival teams both belong to Glasgow: Celtic and Rangers, collectively referred to as the "Old Firm." Competition between the Scottish and English teams also arouses a high level of national feeling. The nation's second most popular sport (which it claims to have invented) is golf, which is on record as having been banned by the Scottish king, James II, in 1457. Present-day Scotland boasts over 400 golf courses. Scotland's third favorite sport is rugby, which is similar to American football. Tennis, lawn bowling, skiing, and curling are other popular sports.

17 ENTERTAINMENT AND RECREATION

Many Scots relax after work by watching television programs broadcast by Great Britain's government-owned broadcasting service, the BBC (British Broadcasting Corporation). Others visit local bars called pubs (short for public houses), where they can eat, drink, and socialize with friends. Popular outdoor recreation includes fishing, hunting, hiking, and mountain-climbing.

Scottish teenagers have many interests in common with other Western teenagers, such as popular music, clothes, and dating (according to local customs). The presence of fast food restaurants and U.S. television shows and movies are helping to narrow the gap between Scottish teens and their American peers.

18 FOLK ART, CRAFTS, AND HOBBIES

Crafts such as pottery (especially in the Celtic tradition), hand-knitting, jewelry-making, and weaving are widely practiced.

Scotland has two main traditions of folk song, Gaelic and Lowland Scots. Traditionally, each clan had a bard (a sort of poet/composer) to sing its praises and preserve its musical traditions. Bards commonly memorized as many as 350 different stories and poems. Many Gaelic work songs that were sung as accompaniment to such tasks as milking and harvesting have survived up to modern times. Women cloth-makers traditionally sang "waulking songs" around a narrow table, providing a steady beat for the music by thumping on the table. The most famous feature of Scotland's traditional music is its national instrument, the bagpipe, which is played at weddings and other celebrations, in military marching bands, and as a hobby.

19 SOCIAL PROBLEMS

Scotland has a high rate of alcoholism, particularly on the islands of Lewis and Harris. Scots also have the United Kingdom's highest rate of hospitalization for depression. Another problem confronting Scotland is its dwindling population. Unemployment has traditionally been well above the British average, and thousands of people have emigrated to England and other countries in search of better job opportunities. As a result, the birthrate has fallen. In an effort to stem the tide of emigration and its attendant "brain drain" of many of the country's best and brightest, government and industry are cooperating to create new industries.

20 GENDER ISSUES

Women in Scotland have made great gains in equality with men since the 1960s. However, as of 2008 Scotland had one of the highest rates of unwanted pregnancies in Europe. Women made up 89% of single parent families in Scotland and 53% of single parent households are in poverty. In Scotland women in full-time employment still earn on average 75% of the average of their male counterparts.

Regarding homosexuality, the first International Gay Rights Conference was held in Edinburgh in 1974. In 1980 male homosexuality was decriminalized in Scotland (female homosexuality had not previously been criminalized in Scotland). In 2004 the UK passed the Civil Partnership Act, giving same-sex couples the same rights and responsibilities as married heterosexual couples. The first civil partnerships took place in Northern Ireland on 19 December 2005, followed by Scotland on 20 December and then England and Wales on 21 December 2005. Glasgow, Aberdeen, and Edinburgh have large gay communities.

21 BIBLIOGRAPHY

Cumming, Elizabeth. *Hand, Heart and Soul: The Arts and Crafts Movement in Scotland*. Edinburgh: Birlinn, 2006.

Fuller, Barbara. *Britain. Cultures of the World*. London: Marshall Cavendish, 1994.

Grant, Neil. *Clans and Tartans of Scotland*. New York: New Line Books, 2006.

Gratton, Nancy E. "Lowland Scots." *Encyclopedia of World Cultures (Europe)*. Boston: G. K. Hall, 1992.

Knipe, Ed. "Highland Scots." *Encyclopedia of World Cultures (Europe)*. Boston: G. K. Hall, 1992.

Meek, James. *The Land and People of Scotland*. New York: Lippincott, 1990.

Montgomerie, Norah. *The Folk Tales of Scotland: The Well at the World's End and Other Stories*. Edinburgh: Birlinn, 2008.

Moss, Joyce, and George Wilson. *Peoples of the World: Western Europeans*. Gale Research, 1993.

Porter, Darwin. *Frommer's Comprehensive Travel Guide (Scotland '94–'95)*. New York: Prentice Hall Travel, 1994.

Scotland in Pictures. Minneapolis: Lerner Publications, 1991.

Walking in Scotland. Melbourne, Australia: Lonely Planet, 2001.

—revised by J. Hobby

SERBS

LOCATION: central and western part of the Balkan Peninsula (Southeastern Europe), Serbia, Bosnia and Herzegovina, Montenegro, Croatia, Kosovo
POPULATION: 12.5 million (est.); 6.7 million in Serbia
LANGUAGE: Serbian
RELIGION: Serbian Orthodox (85%), Catholic (5.5%), Muslim (3.2%), Protestant (1.1%), Other (5.2%)
RELATED ARTICLES: Bosnians, Montenegrins, Croats, Kosovars

¹ INTRODUCTION

The Serbs are a South Slavic people primarily inhabiting Southeastern Europe (commonly referred to as the Balkans) and Central Europe. Present day Serbs are said to have descended from Slavic tribes who migrated to the Balkans from the area of present day Poland, called White Serbia. Their movement to the area began in the 6th century through raids, but by the beginning of the 7th, century they began to settle. The point at which the Serbs emerged as an ethnic group distinctive from other neighboring Slav tribes, such as Croats, is disputed. Although the area on which future Serbs settled in the Balkans was Christianized by Byzantine missionaries before their arrival, the Slavic ruling class was converted to Christianity in the late 9th century, at which point there was still no distinction between Roman Catholicism and Eastern Orthodoxy. The rest of the population slowly converted from paganism to Christianity from that point on. Until the 11th century, Serbs were largely dominated by the Byzantines and neighboring Bulgarians. After the Great Schism in 1054, Serbs remained largely under Byzantine influence, resulting in the strengthening and consolidation of Orthodoxy among Serbs.

Serbia reached the height of its power during the Nemanjić dynasty, which ruled for 200 years and significantly expanded the Serbian state, achieving both political and religious independence from Byzantium. Stefan Nemanja, the founder of the Nemanjić dynasty, came to power in the mid-12th century in the area of present-day Montenegro. The Serbian Kingdom was established in 1217 and the Serbian Orthodox church became autocephalous in 1219. For the first time in history, the Serbs became a unified people. The Serbian state steadily declined from this point, and with the death of Stefan Uroš Dušan in 1355, it began to disintegrate.

By the late 14th century, Serb territory began to be invaded by the Ottoman Empire. Their first major defeat of the Serbs occurred in 1371 at the Maritsa River. In 1389 the Serbs were defeated in the Battle of Kosovo, which marked a turning point in the war, ensuring the eventual ultimate defeat of the Serbs. By 1459 Serbia was overrun by the Turks. Serbia was ruled by the Ottoman Empire for the next three centuries. During this period, thousands of Serbs were enslaved through the Ottoman practice of Devşirme, in which non-Muslim children were taken from their families and converted to Islam in order to later join the janissary corps—the Sultan's personal soldiers—in the Ottoman army. Under the Ottoman Empire, the Serbian Orthodox church was the only independently functioning Serbian institution. This contributed to the close relationship between the Serbian Orthodox religion and Serbian national identity that still exists today.

Serbian territory was also subsequently invaded by Hungarians, Venetians, and Habsburgs. It was not until the Serbian Revolution, which lasted from 1804 to 1815, that Serbs were able to establish an independent Serbian principality.

In 1914, Gavrilo Princip, a Bosnian Serb and member of the pan-Slavist secret society the Black Hand, assassinated Austrian Crown Prince Franz Ferdinand in Sarajevo, the capital of Bosnia. Austria then declared war on Serbia, which marked the beginning of World War I. By the end of World War I, both the Austro-Hungarian and Ottoman Empires had collapsed, paving the way for the creation in 1918 of the Kingdom of Serbs, Croats, and Slovenes. Its name was changed to Yugoslavia (literally "land of the Southern Slavs") in 1929.

Yugoslavia experienced great turbulence during World War II, for while some factions fought against Nazi occupation and division of Yugoslavia, interethnic violence raged throughout the duration of the war. In 1945, the partisans, lead by Josip Broz Tito, defeated the Nazis and the Croatian fascist separatists known as Ustaše, taking complete control of Yugoslavia and establishing a Communist government. Throughout its Communist period, Yugoslavia remained independent from the influence of the USSR and the Warsaw Pact nations.

In 1991, the dissolution of Yugoslavia began when Slovenia, Croatia, and Macedonia declared independence. In 1992 Bosnia followed suit. Later that year, under the leadership of Slobodon Milošević, Serbia and Montenegro declared a new Federal Republic of Yugoslavia and began several military programs aimed at uniting the ethnic Serbs left on the territories of Yugoslavia's now independent neighbors. Serbs in Croatia formed the state of Republika Srpska Krajina. During "Operation Storm," the Croatian government expelled more than 250,000 of these Serbs, resulting in thousands of deaths. Serbs in Bosnia-Herzegovina formed the state of Republika Srpska, which still exists today as an official political entity of Bosnia and Herzegovina. Territorial disputes over sections along the Drina River still exist between Bosnia-Herzegovina and Serbia.

As a result of the Milošević government's military campaigns, Yugoslavia was dismissed from the United Nations (UN), and violence continued until the ratification of the Dayton Peace Accords in 1995. Violence resumed in 1998, however, when Yugoslavia began a counterinsurgency campaign in the autonomous Serbian province of Kosovo against the ethnic Albanian majority. Western powers responded in 1999 with the North Atlantic Treaty Organization's (NATO) bombing of Serbia. Serbian military and police forces withdrew from Kosovo in June 1999 and the UN, in conjunction with NATO forces, created a secure environment and established various self-governing institutions for the inhabitants of Kosovo. After the war, more than 200,000 Serbs left Kosovo. These and the other Serb refugees from Croatia and Bosnia-Herzegovina settled primarily in central Serbia and in the autonomous Serbian province of Vojvodina. In 2000 Milošević was replaced as president by Vojislav Kostunica, a democratic reformist representing the coalition known as the Democratic Opposition of Serbia. Milošević was arrested in 2001 and tried at an international criminal tribunal for crimes against humanity. He died in 2006 before his trial was completed.

In 2001 Yugoslavia rejoined the UN and, in 2003, its name was officially changed to Serbia and Montenegro. In 2006 Montenegro peacefully seceded from Serbia. In 2008 Kosovo declared independence from Serbia. As of mid-2008, Serbia, along with several other states, such as Russia, Bosnia-Herzegovina, Romania, Moldova, Georgia, Azerbaijan, and more, had either officially refused to recognize Kosovo as an independent state or remained silent. Kosovo was officially recognized as independent by the United States and 45 other UN member states. Ethnic Serbs still inhabit areas along Kosovo's northern borders, although Serbs make up less than 5% of the population of Kosovo. Several thousand NATO peacekeepers, known as Kosovo Force (KFOR), continued to keep peace between the ethnic Albanian majority and the Serb minority within Kosovo as of 2008.

² LOCATION AND HOMELAND

The majority of Serbs inhabit Serbia, which was settled by Serbs in the 7th century. Serbia is located in Southeastern Europe, on the southeastern section of the Balkan Peninsula. It is bordered by Hungary, Romania, Bulgaria, Macedonia, Kosovo, Montenegro, Bosnia-Herzegovina, and Croatia. It covers an area slightly smaller than South Carolina. Its terrain is extremely varied, with rich fertile plains in the north, limestone ranges and basins in the east, and ancient mountains and hills in the southeast. Its winters are cold, with heavy snowfall in some places, and its summers are hot, humid in some areas and dry towards the south.

In total, there are over 12.5 million Serbs in the world. The population of Serbia is approximately 8 million, of which ethnic Serbs comprise roughly 83%. The rest of the population of Serbia is made up of Hungarians, Romany, or Gypsies, Bosnians, Montenegrins, Albanians, Bulgarians, Germans, Russians, Ruthenians, Slovaks, Slovenes, Ukrainians, Croats, and Czechs. Roughly 1% of Serbia's population still identifies itself as "Yugoslav." Its two largest cities are Belgrade, the capital of Serbia, and Novi Sad, the capital of the Serbian autonomous province of Vojvodina. Although the historic core of the Serbian homeland was originally located further south, the domination of the Ottoman Empire in the south prompted mass movements of Serbs in the 17th and 18th centuries towards the more Christian north. These population movements are known as the Great Serbian Migrations. They resulted in the permanent relocation of the Serbian center in the north.

The majority of Serbs who live outside Serbia live in Montenegro and Republika Srpska in Bosnia-Herzegovina. Until the exodus of August 1995, caused by the Croatian government's "Operation Storm," a large number of Serbs also lived in Republika Srpska Krajina in Croatia. Smaller numbers of Serbs can be found in Macedonia, Slovenia, Romania, Hungary, Kosovo, and Italy. Many capital cities of the former Yugoslav Republics, such as Zagreb, Skopje, Ljubljana, Sarajevo, and Podgorica, contain large Serbian minorities.

Large Serbian Diaspora communities also exist outside of Southeastern Europe, although exact numbers cannot be determined since census takers use varying criteria to identify Serbs abroad. Some counts reflect numbers of individuals who either still possess Serbian citizenship or have emigrated from Serbia, while other counts include individuals of Serbian descent. The most notable Serbian Diaspora communities can be found in Germany, Austria, Switzerland, France, Sweden, Brazil, Canada, the United States, and Australia. Many of the Serbs inhabiting regions in Central Europe today, such as Romania, and Hungary, and other former territories of the Habsburg Empire, are descendents of Serbs who migrated there to escape the Ottomans. Several thousand also immigrated to Russia and settled the areas now known as Nova Serbia and Slavo-Serbia.

³ LANGUAGE

The Serbian language is a member of the South Slavic group of languages. Like other Southern Slavic languages, Serbian received a number of formative characteristics from the Glagolithic alphabet and other standardizing initiatives developed by Byzantine missionaries Cyril and Methodius during their efforts to Christianize the Slavs. The oldest documents written in the Serbian language date from the 11th century. Largely due to the work of Vuk Stefanović Karadžić, the Serbian language was standardized in the 19th century based on its vernacular form. In addition to its other variants—Old Serbian and Russo-Serbian, a type of Church Slavonic—the Serbian language has three dialects that are distinguished by the pronunciation of the Old Slavonic sound "yat."

Serbian names derive primarily from the Christian tradition, but many also have meanings in the Serbian language. Names often reflect character traits, such as Miroljub from *mir*, peace, and *ljubav*, love. Many names are also nature-inspired and have origins in words for animals, flowers, and other natural phenomena. Most Serbian surnames contain the suffix –ić, which originally functioned to designate paternal lineage, much like "son" or "sen" in Nordic languages. The suffixes –ov and –in are also common and tend to correspond with certain regions. They derive from Slavic possessive case endings, thus also originally functioning to form patronymics. Combinations of these endings in one surname often occur as well.

Serbian is written using both the Cyrillic and Latin alphabets, and in spoken form, it is mutually intelligible to standard Croatian and Bosnian. Before the breakup of Yugoslavia, these languages were considered to be one, Serbo-Croatian. Since then, however, the differentiation of these languages has become a highly contentious issue, in part due to the historic role that language has played in the formation of identity for the peoples of the former Yugoslavia. In the 19th century, the Balkan intelligentsia argued that Serbs, Croats, Balkan Muslims, and Montenegrins were the same people since they spoke a very similar language to one another. Beginning in 1878 with the invasion of Bosnia-Herzegovina by the Austro-Hungarian Empire, this sense of unity through sameness of language was consolidated against the dominant languages of the occupying forces. The notion that a shared language indicated a shared ethnicity and identity eventually became one of the central pillars of the argument for the creation of a southern Slavic State, Yugoslavia. This notion still exists in the former Yugoslavia today. As a result, as groups have broken off from one another, they have made concerted efforts to differentiate themselves through systematic language reform efforts. Embracing existing linguistic differences, or creating new ones, has become a way for groups to distinguish themselves as nations separate from their fellow former Yugoslavs. The Croats made the greatest efforts to do so under Franjo Tuđman, the first president of Croatia after the breakup of Yugoslavia. Croats drew from pre-Yugoslav Croatian dictionaries to introduce new, distinctly Croat words for use by their population. As such, Serbian and Croatian are considered to be separate languages today, although some Croats are still learning a new, distinctive Croat vocabulary.

⁴ FOLKLORE

Much of Serbian folklore is rooted in pre-Christian, pagan belief and practice but was adapted into a Christian framework with the conversion of Slavs to Christianity. For example, the pagan belief in household gods was recast into the custom of *slava*, by which each family has its own saint that it celebrates and passes down from generation to generation. Similarly, the pagan notion of a cult of ancestors today takes the form of the custom of *zadusnice*, in which families hold feasts at the graves of their deceased, lighting candles for them and making offerings of food and drink. This practice now largely follows the Orthodox religious calendar and corresponds to larger Christian events, such as Easter, Christmas, and various saints' feast days. Many religious processions, such as *lazarice*, a procession of virgins and *koledari*, a masked procession at Christmas, originate from pagan rituals. Many of the rituals surrounding Serbian religious icons, such as special veneration, processions, and belief in their healing powers or animation, also originate from paganism.

Superstition and belief in magical powers still persists among some groups. Some still believe in the power of the evil eye—that an individual can be harmed by the envious look of another—and take various precautions to ward it off. Serbian folk beliefs about magical beings, such as witches, vampires, fairies and dragons, have been largely relegated to children's games and fairytales, but have left marks on Serbian culture in various ways. Dragons, for example, were believed to have protected people from evil and misfortune. Many of the heroes of Serbian folktales and poetry were said to have gotten their extraordinary powers from being part dragon. During the wars that accompanied the breakup of Yugoslavia, the trauma caused a resurgence of superstitious belief among some Serbs, who turned to modern-day commercial psychics for relief.

One of the most popular stories in the Serbian folk tradition is that of their defeat by the Ottomans at the Battle of Kosovo Polje (field) in 1389. Folk tales and poetry cast this event in Christian language, giving it a religious meaning for the Serbs, who it portrayed as martyrs. This event, and the stories surrounding it, proved to still resonate widely with Serbs over 600 years later when it was used by Slobodan Milošević and others after the breakup of Yugoslavia to mobilize Serbian nationalism with regard to events surrounding the then autonomous province of Kosovo.

5 RELIGION

The majority of Serbs are Serbian Orthodox. They were converted to Christianity from paganism beginning in the late 9th century, before Serbs had emerged as a distinct group from the southern Slavic tribes. Their conversion took place before the break between Orthodoxy and Catholicism in 1054, but because Serbs were largely aligned with the Byzantine Empire, they developed into an Orthodox people. The Serbian Orthodox Church became autocephalous in 1219. After the invasion of the Ottoman Empire in the 14th and 15th centuries, some southern Slavs converted to Islam.

Under communism, religion was largely repressed. Religion in Serbia today faces different problems. Because the Communist legislation on religion from Yugoslavia has been repealed but not been fully replaced, many religious communities face a great deal of institutional limitations. Attempts to adopt an Act on Religious Freedom failed because many critics opposed the fact that it named seven specific historical, traditional religious communities of Serbia, the most important being the Serbian Orthodox Church. Many believed that despite the law's intention to guarantee freedom of religion and separation of church and state, its recognition of the traditional religions of Serbia gave those religions special legal advantages over others. Although the law was never passed, for many reasons the Serbian Orthodox church nevertheless occupies a privileged position in Serbia.

6 MAJOR HOLIDAYS

National holidays in Serbia include New Year's Day (Nova Godina, January 1 and 2); Christmas (Božić, January 7, celebrated by the Orthodox, or Julian, calendar); Day of Saint Sava, the founder of the Serbian Orthodox church (Savidan, January 27), also commonly known today as the Day of Spirituality (Dan Duhovnosti); Day of Statehood (Dan Državnosti, February 15), to mark the First Serbian Uprising in 1804; May Day, or Labor Day (Dan Rada, May 1 and 2); Victory Day (Dan Pobede, May 9); and St. Vitus' Day (Vidovdan, June 28), which functions as a sort of memorial day, specifically in relation to the 1389 Battle of Kosovo Polje (field). Other national holidays include Good Friday (Veliki Petak), Holy Saturday (Velika Subota), Easter (Vaskrs), and Easter Monday (Veliki Ponedeljak), but their dates are tied to the Orthodox calendar and are determined by the movable Pascal Cycle each year. Other Christian religious feasts occurring on the holidays, such as Epiphany, Visitation, Palm Sunday, Ascension, and more, also play a large role in Serbian society.

Christmas in Serbia is surrounded by many traditions, most with Slavic pagan roots. Customarily, on the morning of Christmas Eve, the head of the house would cut down a young, dry oak tree, called a *badnjak*, and bring it to church for a blessing. Churches at this time of year will still cover their floors with hay on Christmas Eve in reference to the manger where Jesus Christ was born. Later, the blessed piece of oak would be stripped of its branches and burned as a sacrifice to God along with various grains in the hopes that the coming year would bring prosperity. Today, Serbs still receive small pieces of oak trees bundled with grains at church to be taken home and burned on Christmas Eve. Serb families prepare large meals of Lenten foods, avoiding certain animal products, on Christmas Eve. The traditional Christmas Eve meal includes beans, walnuts, and a special Christmas Eve cake. Christmas Day also has its own special feast, comprised usually of roasted pork, *koljivo*, a sweet wheat cake, and *česnica*, a special traditional bread with a coin hidden in it. The family member that finds the coin is thought to have a fortunate year ahead of them. Serbs traditionally exchange presents not on Christmas but on New Year's Day, although this is changing due to Western influences.

In addition to these general Christian feasts, Serbs also have their own particular religious celebrations, such as *slava*, the celebration of the patron saint of an individual family, *zavetine/litije*, a procession on the day of a particular community's saint, and *zanatlijske slave*, the celebration of the patron saint of a professional guild. There are approximately 150 patron saints in the *slava* tradition, the most popular of which include St. Dmitri, St. George, St. John, St. Michael, St. Nicholas, and more. Families celebrate the day before, *navece*, and the day after, *okrilje* or *sutradan*, the saint's feast day, as well as the feast day itself. Ritual objects involved in the celebration include icons of the saint, candles, and dried basil. Ritual dishes include *Slavsko Zito*, a sort of boiled wheat, and *Slavski Kolac*, a specially blessed bread. Family elders, friends, relatives, and neighbors are all invited to *slava*, and during the celebrations, guests sing folksongs and tell folktales.

7 RITES OF PASSAGE

Most Serbs observe major life events, such as birth, marriage, and death, according to the religious traditions of the Serbian Orthodox Church, although some of the traditions surrounding these events have their roots in pre-Christian practices. For example, many rituals are carried out during weddings, such as sprinkling the couple with grains, are meant to ensure the couple's fertility and prosperity.

⁸ INTERPERSONAL RELATIONS

Shaking hands and kissing cheeks (most commonly three kisses) are standard forms of greeting among Serbs, depending on closeness. Standard salutations include *dobro jutro* (good morning), *dobar dan* (good day), and *dobro vece* (good evening). *Dovidjenja* means "good bye," and *daku noc* means "good night." When leaving for a journey, travelers are told *drecan put* (lucky journey). In rural areas, some older residents still greet each other with *pomaze Bog* (God helps). The traditional response is *Bog ti pomogao* (may God help you).

As in many other languages, modes of expressing respect and courtesy are built into Serbian grammar. Serbian has a second, more formal case for the second person. For example, in addressing a close or familiar acquaintance, Serbs use the word *ti* for "you." When addressing someone unfamiliar, or to convey a more formal, respectful relationship, Serbs use the word *vi* for "you."

Serbs enjoy entertaining at home. It is customary for guests to bring to their hosts a gift, such as a bottle of wine or some sort of alcohol, coffee, or flowers. The gesture for wishing someone good luck (the equivalent of crossing one's fingers in the U.S.) is to squeeze the thumb between the index and third finger. Hitting the bent elbow of the left arm with the right hand is a very offensive gesture.

⁹ LIVING CONDITIONS

Since the mid 20th century, Serbs have steadily migrated from rural areas to industrial and cultural centers within the former Yugoslav Republics and today within Serbia. Wars have also contributed to the flux of migrants into cities. This has resulted in the general depopulation and aging of the Serbian countryside. Many Serbs, especially those that live in cities, keep small weekend and vacation houses in the country. Historically, lodging in Serbia varied greatly—ranging from stone to mud to wood—because of the country's extremely varied terrain and because of the varied historical experiences of different areas, but now, lodging is much more uniform and is made primarily of brick and concrete.

During the early 1980s, Serbs enjoyed a generally adequate standard of living and productive agricultural and mineral resources. In the late 1980s and early 1990s, Serbia's economy began to worsen. This general trend was largely exacerbated by the economic sanctions imposed on Serbia by the West because of its actions during the breakup of Yugoslavia. Subsequently, a great deal of damage was done to Serbia's infrastructure during the 1999 NATO bombings. This, in addition to the problems Serbia has experienced in transitioning from a state-run, centrally planned economy has also set back modernization and the standard of living in Serbia significantly. The impact on daily life, levels of pay, and employment opportunities has been catastrophic. Educational, cultural, and scientific exchange with the rest of the world ceased for several years. As medical, educational and other professionals were either recruited into the military or fled from war, the quality of medical care, education, and other public goods suffered greatly.

Since 2000 living conditions in Serbia have begun to improve. Serbia is still struggling to modernize, as its growing telecommunications network still ranks below those of its neighbors. In 2006 it was estimated that only 1.4 million inhabitants of Serbia had internet connection, although this number too, is rapidly growing. Roughly 6.5% of Serbia's population lives below the poverty line. Life expectancy for Serbs averages 75 years. Healthcare has greatly improved in the past decade, and immunization and other forms of preventative medicine are common practices. Medication, however, still remains unaffordable for many families.

¹⁰ FAMILY LIFE

Serbian society is very family-oriented. The most common family unit in Serbia is the nuclear family, although extended family is also very important and remains in close relation. Historically, Serbs lived in a large extended family community called a *Zadruga*. The Serbian language reflects this importance, for it has a number of specific terms for various familial relationships. For example, the word used to denote an uncle who is a father's brother is *Stric*, whereas the word used to denote an uncle who is a mother's brother is *Ujak*.

¹¹ CLOTHING

Serbs wear modern Western-style clothing, including business attire for work, and jeans and T-shirts for casual wear. Until the end of the 19th century, clothes were largely homemade. On special occasions, or during festivals or holidays, some Serbs still wear traditional dress. For women, this includes embroidered wool knee socks, gathered, linen, embroidered skirts, aprons decorated with floral motifs, and shirts decorated with silver thread and other kinds of cording. In some areas, the female Serbian national dress consists of either a red or blue sleeveless, knee-length dress that was richly decorated and buttoned in the front. The traditional costume also includes a headdress of scarves and caps trimmed with cording and often decorated with metal coins or flowers. Women would also wear gold coin necklaces, earrings, and bracelets. For men, traditional Serbian dress includes leather shoes, upturned at the toes and decorated with leather strips that fasten the shoes to the legs, knitted, decorative socks, pants that stop and gather at the calf, a wide, woven, decorative sash around the waist, an embroidered white linen or silk shirt, and either a short, sleeveless vest or a long-sleeved jacket with ornate cording. The traditional Serbian men's costume also includes either a fur cap or a military cap from a later period, which became known as the Serbian national cap. Such costumes are usually very colorfully embroidered with thread and cord and adorned with silver and gold buttons and other ornaments. Traditionally, they were made of homespun cloth and sheepskin, but this is rarer today. Styles, colors, and accessories historically varied depending on region.

¹² FOOD

Typical Serbian cuisine has been greatly influenced by Turkish, Mediterranean, and Austro-Hungarian traditions. Serbs generally eat three meals a day—breakfast, lunch, and dinner. The traditional main meal of the day in Serbia is lunch, but more Serbs are increasingly making dinner their main meal rather than lunch. Traditionally, Serbian families produce various foods and beverages in their own homes. They distill alcoholic beverages, preserve jams, and pickle peppers, cucumbers, cabbage, and more. Some even make their own sausages. Serbian cuisine is rich in spices and herbs, such as pepper, paprika, co-

A Serbian folk dancer wearing traditional clothing at the Edmonton Heritage Festival in Alberta, Canada. (© Richard Cummins/Corbis)

riander, cloves and more. *Ćevapčići,* seasoned, grilled meat, is the Serbian national dish, although Serbs also eat meat of all kinds, prepared a variety of ways. *Podvarak,* roasted meat with cabbage, is also a very popular dish. Fish is popular in communities near the Danube River. Serbian cuisine includes cheeses, such as *Kajmak,* boiled eggs, smoked or cured ham, soups, such as *Backa*—a four meat soup, potatoes, cabbage, and beans. Peppers or cabbage leaves are often stuffed with ground meat, rice, and various spices. These are called *Sarma.* Peppers can be filled with cheese and yogurt. Serbian salad usually consists of tomatoes, peppers, onions, oil and vinegar, and a soft white cheese. *Pita* is a Serbian dish that comes from Turkish influence. Pita dough is light, flaky and crispy and can be filled with both savory and sweet fillings. The most common kind of *pita* among Serbs is *Gibanica,* which consists of a cheese, cream, and egg filling.

Bread is one of the most pivotal elements of Serbian food culture and is tied to many traditions and rituals. Serbs welcome guests by offering them bread and salt. Some breads, such as *Koljivo* and *Moussaka Česnica,* are used in religious rituals on various Christian feasts. Because of bread's connection to ritual, in the past, Serbian households were wary of discarding old bread. Serbian bread is mostly made of wheat, both with and without yeast, but it is also sometimes made of barley and rye. *Pogaca,* for example, is a bread without yeast that is prepared for special occasions.

The Serbian national drink is *Slivovitz,* a plum brandy. It is also often served warm in colder months. *Slivovitz* is a type of *Rakia,* or distilled fruit brandy. Many other types of *Rakia* exist as well, such as pear and grape. Many Serbs distill their own *Rakia.* Domestic wines are also widely drunk, mainly from the famous wine region of *Vrsac.* Beer is also popular. Popular non-alcoholic beverages include homemade fruit juices, *Boza,* a corn-based drink, and *Kvas,* a fermented drink made from rye or black bread. Turkish coffee (*Turska Kafa* or *Crna Kafa*) is very popular and drunk very often. It is served when guests make visits and also at the end of large meals.

13　EDUCATION

Serbia has a literacy rate of 96.4%. Since the breakup of Yugoslavia, Serbia's poor economic situation has decreased investments in culture and in education in general. When Yugoslavia began to dissolve in the early 1990s, 10% of its population had no education, 50% had either an incomplete or a full primary education, 32% had a secondary education, 4% had a college degree, and only 5% had a university diploma. Today, roughly 6% of the population have had no schooling, 16% have an incomplete primary education, only 24% have a full primary education, 41% a secondary education, 24.5% a college degree, and 6.5% a university diploma.

In recent years, with the resurgence of the Serbian Orthodox church, religious instruction in public schools has become a central issue in education. The push to have religious instruction in public schools began immediately after the fall of Milošević in 2000. The issue was highly debated due to the implications it had for larger church-state relations. Today, legislation makes religious instruction in public schools an alternative subject that is taught for one hour per week. Religious instruction is not compulsory, and students have the option to attend civic education classes instead. The Serbian government provides finances for religious instruction on the seven recognized religious communities of Serbia (Serbian Orthodoxy, Catholicism, Islam, Judaism, Slovak Lutheranism, Serbian Lutheranism, and Hungarian Reformed Protestantism), but other religious communities are allowed to organize and fund their own religious instruction in public schools if students request it. The content of religious instruction is decided by the Minister of Education and Sports, who works with members of the various religious communities.

While lack of investment in education harms Serbian society as a whole, children with special needs, as well as children of refugees, migrants, and returning nationals have suffered disproportionately. Economic constraints have increased the level of educational exclusion these groups experience. Many Serbs believe that future economic improvement, combined with the government's drive to meet standards for accession into the European Union, will improve this situation and education in general. In the meantime, however, Serbian higher education suffers as well. As the world trend continues to favor knowledge and innovation-based economies more strongly, there is a need in higher education to develop new, modern research areas and to provide more interdisciplinary and more topical programs, such as management and computer sciences, for students. The number of students interested in these areas has increased, however study programs cannot respond to these societal and market needs because they still reflect the traditional background of higher education staff. Higher education institutions are financed by the Serbian government and by private funds granted for various research projects. Both of these sources have been stifled by the economic situation of Serbia, and as a result, institutions of higher education cannot provide high enough salaries to attract qualified scholars of newly emerging research areas. Consequently, Serbian students of higher education can only choose from professions with increasingly slim employment prospects.

¹⁴ CULTURAL HERITAGE

Orthodox Christianity has played a significant role in formation of the Serbian culture. Medieval Serbia was under the Byzantine sphere of influence, and when it emerged as a strong, independent kingdom under the Nemanjić dynasty, the Serbian Orthodox Church was its central institution. This cultural heritage can be most strongly seen in Serbia's rich medieval church architecture, icon painting, and manuscript illumination, which were directed largely by state patronage. Serbian churches boast domed ceilings, Byzantine-style frescoes, extensive sculptures, and numerous icons. Serbian church art benefited greatly from the Fourth Crusade on Constantinople in 1204, when many Byzantine artists sought refuge in Serbia and brought their artistic influence with them. Serbian epic poetry also flourished during the medieval period. Much of it was based on historic events, such as the battle of Kosovo in 1389. Although Orthodoxy has had the most extensive influence on Serbian culture, elements of Catholic and Ottoman culture are also perceptible, in some areas more than others. Throughout the history of the Serbs, Catholic influence penetrated Serbian culture through Austrians and Venetians, primarily in Vojvodina and along the coast of the Former Yugoslavia. Once Serbia gained autonomy and eventually independence in the 19th century, there was an increase in Serbian cultural activity, which included a resurgence of Serbian epic poetry and songs.

Despite the resurgence of the Serbian Orthodox Church, the primary capsule of Serbia's cultural heritage, Serbian culture experienced a decline during the Milošević era, when traditional Serbian culture was recast and used to bolster Milošević's power. This phenomenon became most widespread in the form of widely popular "Turbo-Folk" music—pop music inspired by traditional Serbian folk songs (with Russian, Turkish and Greek influences) but set to a techno beat, most often by scantily dressed women. Just as Serbs in the 1980s embraced Belgrade Rock in their attempt to break from Communism and open to the West, Turbo-Folk functioned as the soundtrack for the aggressive nationalistic politics of the 1990s. Its lyrics both glorified traditional Serbian culture and promoted the glamorous lifestyle of the new Serbian elite, consisting of powerful politicians, businessmen, war-profiteers, and individuals involved in organized crime. This manipulation of traditional Serbian culture undermined the morality and civil order of Serbian society by spreading a problematic system of values, lifestyle, and emotional nationalism. Turbo-Folk's popularity spread throughout Serbia contemporaneously with crime, disorder, and fear, offering to Serbs the government's official façade of wealth, glamour, power, and attractiveness during a time of poverty, war, chaos, international isolation, and despair in Serbia. The occurrence and spread of Turbo-Folk was initiated by the changes in social conditions in Serbia as Yugoslavia dissolved. These social changes were precipitated by the long-lasting economic crisis, the wars in Croatia and Bosnia, the great numbers of war victims and refugees, Serbia's isolation from the world community, and later, the 1999 NATO bombings. To aid in the spreading of this new interpretation of Serbian culture, the government harnessed television programming. Television stations specializing in "folk" music and dance emerged in the early 1990s, bringing considerable changes to Serbia's cultural climate. These trends coincided with expansion of mass media in Serbia. It was in this period that television began exerting a growing influence on Serbian society. This spread of television and its use by the government combined with the economic hardships being experienced by rock and pop producers, and a shortage of material for television left an empty space for Turbo-Folk. Following the cultural isolation of the Milošević era, new musical styles, such as rap, have gained popularity in Serbia. Influences from the West are increasing. Serbian rappers and punk bands are now widespread. The Serbian city of Novi Sad hosts the annual Exit Festival of alternative music, which draws crowds from all over Europe. Turbo-Folk today is widely associated with the brutal nationalism of the 1990s, yet, it is still played in popular clubs and on radio and television.

¹⁵ WORK

Serbs were traditionally very heavily involved in agriculture. Like other Eastern European countries, Serbia became more industrialized during the Communist era, creating manufacturing jobs in the production of agricultural machinery, electrical and communication equipment, paper and pulp, and transportation equipment. Since the end of the Communist era, the Serbian economy has undergone a major shift in composition. Today, over 63% of Serbia's GDP comes from the service industry, as compared to industry at 24% and agriculture at 12%. The majority of Serbia's workforce, however, is still employed in the industry sector. Only 24% of Serbia's labor force works in services, and 30% works in agriculture. Serbs grow wheat, corn, sugar beets, sunflowers, and raspberries, and raise livestock such as cows and pigs. The unemployment rate in Serbia in 2007 was almost 19%. It has consistently increased since the dissolution of Yugoslavia for a number of reasons. Economic activity and capital investment decreased as a result of war and instability, and the skills of the labor force do not meet the needs of the new market economy. Serbia's education system has not been adapted to train workers to respond to these changes, and as a result, the majority of people who are unemployed are under the age of 30. Alternately, Serbia has compulsory military service for men ages 19 to 35. During wartime, conscription can begin at age 16. Conscription is set to be abolished in 2010.

As a result of the high unemployment rate, many Serbs choose to move abroad in search of better work opportunities. Serbia is also experiencing a phenomenon known as the "internal brain drain," whereby trained professionals remain in the country but chose not to utilize their skills in formal careers. This occurs because of very low wages, slow career promotion, poor research facilities, lack of project funding, and restricted communication with professionals in other countries. A social element is also involved, for in Serbia's transitioning society, businessmen and politicians who earn more money tend to be perceived as having a higher social standing than scientists or academics.

16 SPORTS

Soccer is one of the most popular sports in Serbia. It came to Serbia at the end of the 19th century via students who had studied in Switzerland. The first soccer clubs of Serbia, such as Soko (the Falcon), Srpski Mac (the Serbian Sword) were founded in the early 1900s. In 1991, a Serbian team won both the European and the World championships in soccer. In addition to team sports, Serbs also like wrestling, boxing, and judo. Serbs are also known throughout the world for being excellent tennis players. Some Serbian tennis players include Novak Djokovic, Ana Ivanovic, Jelena Jankovic, and more. Monica Seles is ethnically Hungarian but from the Serbian autonomous province of Vojvodina.

17 ENTERTAINMENT AND RECREATION

Television has become the main source of entertainment for Serbs, exercising enormous influence on Serbian family and social life. Serbs also often go to the cinema. More traditional forms of entertainment include folk festivals, which every town has each year over several days. Serbs also like to visit family and friends in their homes. Musical concerts are also a popular sort of entertainment. Younger Serbs often go to dance clubs.

18 FOLK ART, CRAFTS, AND HOBBIES

Serbian folk music dates from the medieval period and has been strongly influenced by Serbian Orthodoxy. During the Ottoman period, Serbian Christian peasants developed a small, single-string instrument, called a *Gusle,* so that they could play religious music easily and undetected. Traditional Serbian folk music, as well and more modern forms like the Turbo-Folk mentioned previously, remains popular today, especially in rural areas.

Serbian culture also has a strong tradition of folk dance. The most common folk dance is a *Kolo,* in which dancers form a ring by holding on to each others hands, waists, arms, or shoulders. Such dances have various rhythms and steps. Depending on which direction dancers move in, the dance can take on different meaning. A reverse circle is made when the dance is being performed in memory of the dead, called a *Mrtvacko Kolo.* The *Kolo* is still danced at parties today. Several other folk dances, once ritualistic, still exist in various forms, but primarily for entertainment.

Serbs also have a strong tradition in various kinds of handicrafts, such as pottery and other ceramics, rug weaving, jewelry making, metalwork, leatherwork, hand-knitting of clothing, embroidery, wood carving, and stonecutting. Traditional Serbian folk art decorates items used in everyday life, such as gravestones, ceilings and doors of homes, furniture, musical instruments, and other household objects.

19 SOCIAL PROBLEMS

The social problems that Serbs currently face are a reflection of Serbia's long-lasting economic crisis due to the Milošević administration's mismanagement of the economy, the civil wars endured at the dissolution of Yugoslavia, the great numbers of war victims, refugees, and internationally displaced persons,

Serbia's economic and cultural isolation from the rest of the world during war, and the damage done to its infrastructure by the 1999 NATO bombings. All of these factors have led to the general impoverishment of the population and to widespread crime.

As Yugoslavia has continued to dissolve, Serbia has taken in more than half a million refugees, primarily from Croatia, Bosnia-Herzegovina, and Kosovo. This has aggravated the ongoing problems of unemployment and lack of housing and has led in many cases to the destabilization of familial relationships. In search of relief from these conditions many Serb refugees have attempted to return to their homes in surrounding countries, but all ex-Yugoslav republics, especially those, such as Croatia and Bosnia, that were involved in war, went through similar processes of social disintegration and have fallen into similar impoverished and chaotic conditions. Despite government directed programs that are meant to aid in the process of returning, returnees often face many obstacles. Many of their homes have been destroyed or occupied by others, unemployment is high, and there is little infrastructure in the rural areas where most Serbs lived. Additionally, the majority of Serbs who attempt to return are older, and thus the youth and reproduction needed to regenerate these areas are largely absent. Moreover, ethnic tensions still linger and Serbs are largely discriminated against by titular nationalities.

Other Serbs have sought relief by emigrating to foreign countries, leading ultimately to what experts call a "brain drain," or the loss of intellectual and professional capital that society has developed over several years, through education, training and development of its young population. Because of a shortage of jobs in Serbia, the best Serbian professionals are moving mainly to Canada, the United States, and Australia. Previously, the outflow of Serbs with a university education was not very significant. Most Serbs who left went to Western Europe and were skilled workers, craftsmen, and technicians. This movement of population initially had a positive effect on the economy, for it decreased the rate of unemployment within Serbia and provided a steady inflow of remittances, or funds sent back by workers to their family members remaining in Serbia. As more educated Serbs leave, and as these movements become permanent rather than temporary, Serbian society as a whole is being negatively impacted.

This trend of emigration contributes to Serbia's extremely low population growth rate, which was actually registered to have been negative in 2001. The fertility rate in Serbia is 1.69 children per woman. The population of Serbia is growing older and the demographic and educational distributions will probably worsen as the small number of young university-educated individuals continues to leave. In the coming years, this will not only negatively impact Serbia's economy, but as work force and age distributions of the population change, Serbia's already weak social security system, infrastructure, educational system, and other systems will face even greater pressures and become more unsustainable. These trends comprise the greatest long-term social threat to Serbs.

20 GENDER ISSUES

Some of the main social and economic problems of the post-Communist transition of Serbia have had a disproportionately negative impact on female Serbs. During the Second World War and the Serbian fight for national liberation, Serb women experienced a sort of emancipation themselves. Through their involvement in the national effort of supporting Serb partisan fighters, women emerged from their closed, traditional, patriarchal families. After the war, it became more common for women to move to cities, get jobs in factories, and receive an education. During the Communist period, women were no longer limited to simply getting married, having children, and remaining in the domestic sphere. In retrospect, however, scholars believe that the advancements made in gender equality during this period have been exaggerated, much to the detriment of the feminist movement today. On a practical level, despite the rights and liberties attained under Communism, Serb women remained largely subordinate to men and segregated as a group in society. On a theoretical level, the declaration that women and men were made equal under the Communist system produced in Serbian society a false comfort that the problem of gender inequality was solved. This general belief continues to diffuse and undermine the feminist movement by making gender equality a non-issue for society, which is problematic today since women's rights have continued to erode in Serbia with the fall of the Communist system for a number of reasons.

With the dissolution of Yugoslavia, war has proven to be the single most detrimental force to the female gender. In war-torn Yugoslavia, interpersonal and familial relationships were destabilized, and domestic violence grew substantially. The effects of economic hardships of war on Serb women were two-fold. First, unemployment, economic instability, and impoverishment made conditions within families very tense, causing domestic abuse to be more prevalent and more readily accepted by society. Additionally, the bad economy did not afford women who were being abused the chance to escape their situations and become monetarily self-sufficient, forcing them to remain reliant on their existing domestic relationship for economic security. Domestic abuse spiked in wartime Yugoslavia for other practical reasons as well. In addition to the tense family conditions it created, war also increased the number of weapons available. This did not necessarily increase instances of domestic abuse, but accessibility of dangerous weapons made it more brutal and deadlier than usual. Finally, institutional help for women experiencing domestic abuse was generally absent during this time, since attention and resources were allocated to more immediately pressing dangers. All of these factors made women the unseen victims of the civil wars of Yugoslavia.

The refugee crisis in Serbia caused by the wars of the 1990s has also had an extremely negative impact on women. Serbia's refugees in general went largely unacknowledged by the rest of the world, and as such suffered from insufficient international aid and received fewer chances for asylum or emigration. Many of the refugee women are from broken homes; some were widowed during the war or were separated from their husbands by various other social pressures. Many of the refugee women either act as single mothers or as the sole provider for their families. Possessing no valid citizenship, protection of rights, or secure employment opportunities, many refugee women began practicing prostitution, for it became one of the only possibilities for earning money. Others also work in smuggling. Some women have been able to get jobs outside of the shadow economy, but since they still do not have citizenship, their rights are not guaranteed and they receive no welfare, no healthcare, and no pension plan. Because they have not been fully integrated into society, and because they are often single, refugee women also experience widespread sexual harassment.

Finally, the dissolution of Yugoslavia was accompanied by a strong surge in nationalism, and while such periods tend to effect ethnic minorities most greatly, recent nationalist efforts in Serbia have also translated into the restoration of traditional expectations about the role of women in society in general. This has resulted in gender discrimination against women both socially and civically. Increasing numbers of women choose to remain in the domestic sphere and not to venture into business or politics, and the gender gap in Serbia is becoming more visible. Regardless, the feminist movement among Serbs remains quite weak. The number of women's organizations in Serbia has grown since the beginning of the new democratic regime in 2000, but there are still very few. The concept of feminism is still generally rejected by mainstream Serbian society. Men tend to stereotype feminists and women's organizations, viewing them as enemies of the Serbian society and nation. Women largely distrust women's organizations and hesitate to become involved. Thus, while women's organizations are legal in Serbia, they still encounter both institutional and social hurdles.

[21] BIBLIOGRAPHY

Ćopić, Sanja. "Wife Abuse in the Countries of the Former Yugoslavia." *Feminist Review*, No. 76 (2004): 46-64.

"Country Report: Yugoslavia (Serbia-Montenegro)." *The Economist Intelligence Unit*, 1998.

Funk, Nanette, and Magda Mueller. *Gender Politics and Post-Communism Reflections from Eastern Europe and the Former Soviet Union*. New York: Routledge, 1993.

Gettelman, Elizabeth and Vedran Horvat. "Serb Refugees Return to their Homeland." *Christian Science Monitor*, July 26, 2004.

Glenny, Misha. *The Balkans: Nationalism, War, and the Great Powers—1804-1999*. London: Penguin, 1999.

Ilić, Angela. "Church and State Relations in Present-Day Serbia." *Religion in Eastern Europe*. Vol. 25, Issue 1 (February 2005): 8-33.

Itano, Nicole. "Turbo-Folk: Serbia's Political Soundtrack." *Christian Science Monitor*, May 5, 2008.

Kronja, Ivana. "Politics, Nationalism, Music, and Popular Culture in 1990s Serbia." *Slovo*. Vol. 16, Issue 1 (Spring 2004): 5-15.

Milić, Andjelka. "The Women's Movement in Serbia and Montenegro at the Turn of the Millennium: A Sociological Study if Women's Groups." *Feminist Review*, No, 76 (2004): 65-82.

Mazower, Mark. *The Balkans: a Short History*. New York: Random House, 2000.

Nikolic-Ristanovic, Vesna. "Refugee Women in Serbia: Invisible Victims of War in the Former Yugoslavia." *Feminist Review*, No. 73 (2003): 104-113.

Okey, Robin. "Serbian? Croatian? Bosnian? Language and Nationality in the Lands of Former Yugoslavia." *East European Quarterly*, XXXVIII, No. 4 (January 2005): 419-441.

Radoman, Vesna, Virxhil Nano, and Alison Closs. "Prospects for inclusive education in European countries emerging from economic and other trauma: Serbia and Albania." *European Journal of Special Needs Education*, Vol. 21, Issue 2 (May 2006): 151-166.

Ramet, Sabrina P. *Balkan Babel: The Disentigration of Yugoslavia from the Death of Tito to the Fall of Milošević.* Cambridge, MA: Westview, 2002.

———. *Gender Politics in the Western Balkans: Women, Society, and Politics in Yugoslavia and the Yugoslav Successor States.* University Park, PA: Pennsylvania State Press, 1999.

Ramet, Sabrina, and Vjeran Pavlakovic. *Serbia since 1989: Politics and Society under Milošević and after.* Seattle, WA: University of Washington Press, 2005.

Stanford, Elanor. "Culture of Serbia and Montenegro." Countries and their Cultures. http://www.everyculture.com.

Stevanović, Bosiljka. "Serbian Americans." *Multicultural America.* http://everydayculture.com.

Turajilic, Srbijanka. "Staff Recruitment in Higher Education: Country and Institutional Experiences-The Case of Serbia." *Higher Education in Europe.* Vol. 31, Issue 3 (October 2006): 295-302.

Wachtel, Andrew Baruch. *Making a Nation, Breaking a Nation: Literature and Cultural Politics in Yugoslavia.* Stanford, CA: Stanford University Press, 1998.

Wolff, Robert Lee. *The Balkans in Our Time.* New York: Norton, 1978.

Woodward, Susan L. *Balkan Tragedy: Chaos and Dissolution after the Cold War.* Washington, DC: Brookings, 1995.

Zindović-Vukadinović, Gordana. "Serbia and Montenegro: the Catalytic Effects of Higher Education." *Higher Education in Europe,* October 2004, Vol. 29, Issue 3, p. 329-341.

—by Sarah Dixon Klump

SLOVAKS

LOCATION: Slovakia, United States, Czech Republic, Serbia, Canada, United Kingdom, Hungary
POPULATION: 6 million (4.7 million in Slovakia)
LANGUAGE: Slovak
RELIGION: Roman Catholicism (69%); Protestantism (11%); Other (20%)
RELATED ARTICLES: Czechs, Hungarians

¹ INTRODUCTION

Slavic peoples first settled on the territory of present-day Slovakia in the 5th century AD. The original territory inhabited by proto-Slovaks also included parts of present-day southeastern Moravia and approximately the entire northern half of present-day Hungary. A Slavic state was formed there under Samo, a Frankish merchant, in the 7th century. At this point, Slovaks were still indistinguishable from other Slavs. In the 8th century, the group of Slavs that would later become the Slovaks inhabited the Principality of Nitra, which eventually became a part of the Moravian Empire in the 9th and 10th centuries. It was during this period that the Byzantine missionaries Cyril and Methodius traveled to this region to convert pagan proto-Slovaks to Christianity. To aid in conversions, Cyril and Methodius developed Glagolithic, a precursor to Cyrillic, and provided Slavs with their first written alphabet. Great Moravia reached its peak during the reign of King Svatopluk between 870 and 894. In 907, Great Moravia was defeated by the Magyars, or Hungarians, in the Battle of Bratislava. Slovakia would continue to be under Magyar rule of some form until the beginning of the 20th century.

In 1526, Hungarians came under the rule of the Habsburg Empire. In 1867, Hungarians and Austrians struck a compromise and transformed the empire into a dual monarchy, but this changed very little for Slovaks. In the wake of the fall of the Austro-Hungarian Empire in World War I, Czechs and Slovaks united in 1919 to create the independent state of Czechoslovakia. Throughout the union of the two ethnic groups, the more numerous and powerful Czechs exercised greater political power than the Slovaks, and tensions between the two groups finally resulted in the dissolution of Czechoslovakia by 1939, when Slovakia declared its independence and allied itself with Hitler's Germany. The Slovak puppet government operated under German control during World War II. However, in 1944 Slovaks from the central and eastern parts of the country rebelled against the Nazis, but their revolt was quickly put down and an estimated 30,000 Slovaks were killed.

After the war, Czechoslovakia was reunited, and the Communists seized control of the country in 1948. Under Communist rule, as in the post–World War I era, the Slovaks were once again subordinate to the Czechs. In the 1960s, President Alexander Dubček, a Slovak, attempted to combine Communist ideology with democracy, an effort that culminated in the "Prague Spring" of 1968, which was crushed by military intervention from the Soviet Union, which occupied the entire country and abolished the democratic reforms of the preceding years. Twenty-one years later, through the peaceful "Velvet Revolution" led by dissident playwright Vaclav Havel and the Civic Forum party, the old order collapsed and Communism was overthrown. After the first democratic elections and the departure of the Soviet troops, old ethnic enmities resurfaced, with the Slovaks demanding separation from the Czechs. Prime Minister Havel and Slovak leader Vladimir Meciar agreed to dissolve the union of the two peoples, and on 1 January 1993, in an event known as the "Velvet Divorce," the Slovaks declared their independence, establishing their own parliament in Bratislava. In 1991, Slovakia joined the Czech Republic, Hungary, and Slovakia in the Visegrad Group, an alliance for the integration of these countries into greater Europe. In 1992, Slovakia joined the United Nations. Since 2004, Slovakia has been a member of the North Atlantic Treaty Organization (NATO) and the European Union (EU).

2 LOCATION AND HOMELAND

Slovakia is a small, landlocked country located in Central Europe. It is about the size of Vermont and New Hampshire combined. Slovakia's neighbors are Poland (to the north); the Czech Republic (to the northwest); Austria (to the southwest); and Hungary (to the south). It also shares a short eastern border with Ukraine. Much of Slovakia consists of unspoiled mountains and forests. The High Tatras, a part of the Carpathian Mountains, are the second-highest mountain ranges in Europe after the Alps. The Kriváň mountain peak, a Slovak national symbol, is located in the High Tatras. The land of the Slovaks slopes down from this high mountain range into lakes and fertile river valleys, which are traversed by several tributaries that drain into the Danube River. The Danube forms part of the southern boundary of the country. Other rivers that flow through Slovak territory include the Váh and the Hron. Slovakia has fertile farmland. Its winters are cold, cloudy, and snowy, and its summers warm.

In total, there are over six million Slovaks in the world. The population of Slovakia is approximately five and a half million, of which ethnic Slovaks comprise roughly 86%. The rest of the population of Slovakia is made up of Hungarians, Czechs, Ukrainians, Carpatho-Rusyns, and Romany, or Gypsies. Just under half of Slovakia's population lives in rural areas, although significant migration from rural to urban areas is steady. The two largest cities in Slovakia are Bratislava, its capital, and Košice, in the east.

It is estimated that between 1.5 and 2 million Slovaks live outside of the Slovak homeland. Exact numbers cannot be determined since census takers use varying criteria to identify Slovaks abroad. Some counts reflect numbers of individuals who either still possess Slovakian citizenship or have emigrated from Slovakia, while other counts include individuals of Slovak ethnic descent. The largest numbers of Slovaks outside of Slovakia can be found in the United States, the Czech Republic, Serbia, Canada, the United Kingdom, and Hungary. Hundreds of thousands of Slovaks emigrated to North America in the late 19th and early 20th centuries, making the number of Slovaks and those of Slovak descent range today between 800,000 and 1.2 million in the United States and 50,000 and 100,000 in Canada. An estimated 200,000 to 375,000 Slovaks live within the borders of the Czech Republic. Because of centuries of Magyar rule, a sizeable Slovak population could be found in Hungary until the beginning of the 20th century. Since the fall of the Austro-Hungarian Empire, the number of Slovaks living in Hungary has steadily declined. Currently, roughly 20,000 Slovaks can be found in Hungary.

Historically, a considerable number of Slovaks could be found in the Balkans, primarily in Serbia and Bulgaria. After World War II, thousands of Slovaks left Bulgaria for Czechoslovakia in a state-run initiative to repopulate the Czech and Slovak lands. As such, a very small number of Slovaks remain in Bulgaria today. Roughly 60,000 ethnic Slovaks remain in northern Serbia today, primarily in the autonomous province of Vojvodina. Slovaks are the third largest of over 26 ethnic groups in Vojvodina. Slovak is one of the province's six official languages. Most Slovaks in Vojvodina are the descendants of the late 18th and early 19th century Slovaks who settled in the region when it was still under Hungarian rule, after the retreat of the Ottoman Empire from the area. Since religion was a primary stimulant for many of the original Slovaks who immigrated to Vojvodina, one of the distinguishing factors of the Slovaks of Vojvodina today is that the majority of them are Protestant rather than Roman Catholic.

3 LANGUAGE

Slovak is a member of the Western Slavic language group. Of all other languages, Slovak is most similar to Czech. Although the two languages are clearly distinct from one another, they are mutually intelligible. Like other Western Slavic languages, Slovak received a number of formative characteristics from the Glagolithic alphabet and other standardizing initiatives developed by Byzantine missionaries Cyril and Methodius during their efforts to Christianize the Slavs. The present Slovak alphabet has 43 letters and is written using Roman characters.

This reflects the early change in religious orientation from the Greek Orthodox East to the Latin Catholic West and remains a distinguishing factor between the Western Slavic language group and the Eastern Slavic language group, which uses Cyrillic characters. There are three major Slovak dialects: Eastern, Central, and Western. The Western dialects of Slovak shade onto the Moravian dialects of the Czech language. Slovak words have an accented first syllable, and words with more than three syllables have a secondary accent as well. Like those of other East European languages, Slovak words feature many clusters of consonants. Some Slovak words, such as *smrt'* (death), *srdce* (heart), *slnko* (sun), and *yrt* (to drill, or bore), have practically no vowels at all.

Efforts to standardize the Slovak language began as early as the 17th century, primarily in the form of literature. The two main individuals credited with contributing the most to the standardization of the Slovak language were Anton Bernolák in the 18th century and Ľudovít Štúr in the 19th century. While Bernolák worked with the western Slovakian dialect, Štúr's use of the central dialect has become the basis of standardized Slovak today. The Slovak political experience, however, has proven to curtail the development and standardization of Slovak during the last three centuries. Under the Hungarian Empire, the Hungarian language was privileged over Slovak and Slovaks experienced heavy Magyarization efforts in education and other public spheres. During the existence of Czechoslovakia, the Slovak language was considered an official language of the country, but Czech was privileged over Slovak in politics, professions, education, and other public spheres. As a result, the Slovak language was heavily influenced by Czech and took on many Czech borrowings.

The Slovak Language is the official language of Slovakia, but both Czech and Hungarian are also widely spoken. Those who speak Hungarian primarily populate the southern region of Slovakia. Because of the rapid pace of globalization, borrowing from both Czech and other languages still occurs.

⁴ FOLKLORE

Slovaks possess a very rich oral history that deals, like most peoples' folklore, with all aspects of life and nature. Because of Slovakia's predominantly agrarian history, however, themes of love, marriage, health, and agricultural bounty are particularly common.

Almost every ruined castle in the Slovak Republic has its legend. Sometimes these legends are extremely violent, like the story of Csejte, a ruthless countess who murders three young girls and bathes in their blood in an effort to renew her youthfulness. There are also many stories about Janosik, a well-known folk hero whose adventures date back to the Turkish invasions of the 16th and 17th centuries. These kinds of folk tales provided a great deal of inspiration for later Slovak literature. In the mid 19th century, Pavol Dobšinský worked to collect and publish anthologies of Slovak folk fairy tales like these. Such activities were closely related with the Slovak National Awakening.

Belief in witches, ghosts, and other supernatural beings persists as a remnant of pre-Christian paganism. One such figure is Morena, a goddess of death who is the object of a springtime custom by which young girls ritually "drown" a straw doll in waters that flow from the first thaw. In rural areas, some Slovaks still believe that illness and misfortune can be caused by witches, demons, or the "evil eye" and seek the services of traditional healers who use folk remedies and rituals to protect or exorcise villages and homes.

Slovak folklore also includes a number of means by which individuals can determine and try to control their futures, most occurring around Christmas and the New Year. On November 30, lead is poured into boiling water, and the shape it takes is used to make predictions about the coming year. Young women have many ways of trying to discover who their husbands might be, such as peering upside-down at the water's surface in a well. On Christmas Eve, nuts are cracked and their contents are examined to determine what the coming year will bring. Additionally, food from the Christmas Eve feast is given to livestock in hopes that they be granted good health.

⁵ RELIGION

Most Slovaks (about 70% of the population) belong to the Roman Catholic Church and are closely affiliated with their church communities. Slovak Catholicism is generally more traditional than the more liberal Czech version. The next largest group, 13% of the population, consists of those who claim either atheism or no religious affiliation. This is quite small compared to the 59% of neighboring Czechs in this category. Roughly 11% of the population identifies itself as Protestant and roughly 4% as Greek Catholic, a Christian religion that acknowledges the Catholic Pope but whose liturgical traditions follow those of Eastern Orthodoxy. Others include Calvinist Reformed, Eastern Orthodox, and Baptist. Slovakia's once populous Jewish community was destroyed in the Nazi Holocaust.

Churches and religion presented a strong obstacle to the Communists after World War II. The government banned religious activity and closed all private religious schools. In 1989, with the fall of Communism, churches were restored and religious schools reopened. Although most Slovaks have returned to the traditional Slovak religion of Roman Catholicism, the Protestant Evangelical movement in Slovakia, as in other former Communist countries of Eastern Europe, continues to grow in order to fill the religious vacuum created by the Communist ban on organized religion.

⁶ MAJOR HOLIDAYS

National holidays in Slovakia include New Year's Day (January 1), Liberation Day (May 8), Cyril and Methodius Day (July 5), Slovak National Uprising Day (August 29), Constitution Day (September 1), Independence Day (October 28), and Day of the Struggle for Freedom and Democracy (November 17), which simultaneously commemorates Slovak demonstrations against the Nazis in 1939 as well as the demonstrations in 1989 that are said to have triggered the Velvet Revolution.

In late October, Slovakia hosts the Bratislava music festival, which attracts national and international performers. Many towns and villages host annual folk festivals in the late summer or fall, with plentiful singing, dancing, and drinking.

Most Slovaks also observe the major feast days and holidays of Roman Catholicism, such as Easter and Christmas. The Slovak celebration of Easter extends to the Monday after Easter Sunday as well. September 15, the Day of Our Lady of Sorrows, is an important holiday for Slovaks since the Virgin Mary is considered to be the patron saint of Slovakia. The largest of Slovak celebrations culminates around Christmas, over a period of three days. On Christmas Eve, Slovaks attend church services. Christmas trees are decorated, gifts are exchanged, and there is a traditional Christmas Eve dinner called *vilija*, consisting of mushroom soup, fish, peas, prunes, and pastries. December 26 is the Feast of Saint Stephen and is called "Second Christmas Day" by Slovaks. Slovaks usually celebrate birthdays with their families, and name days, days dedicated to the saint for which one is named, with friends and co-workers.

7 RITES OF PASSAGE

Most Slovaks observe major life events, such as birth, marriage, and death, according to the religious traditions of the Roman Catholic Church.

8 INTERPERSONAL RELATIONS

Shaking hands is a standard form of greeting; men generally wait for women to extend their hands first. Upon parting, a man may hug a woman or kiss her on both cheeks. Standard salutations include *Dobrý den* (good day), *Velmi ma tesi* (pleased to meet you), and the more informal *Ahoj* (the equivalent of "hi"). *Dovidenia* means "good-bye," and the more casual terms *Ciao* and *Servus* mean either "hello" or "good-bye." In rural areas, some older residents still greet each other with *S Bohom* ("God be with you").

When not among family or close friends, Slovak forms of address are very formal and courteous, including both *Pán* (Mr.) or *Pani* (Mrs.) and any professional title, such as doctor, professor, or engineer. As in many other languages, modes of expressing respect and courtesy are built into Slovak grammar. Slovak has a second, more formal case for the second person. For example, in addressing a close or familiar acquaintance, Slovaks use the word ty for "you." When addressing someone unfamiliar, or to convey a more formal, respectful relationship, Slovaks use the word vy for "you."

Slovaks enjoy entertaining at home. It is customary for guests to bring to their hosts a bottle of wine or some sort of alcohol. Upon entering a Slovak home, guests generally remove their shoes; their hosts often provide them with slippers. Fresh flowers are often given, and when they are presented, they are always unwrapped and in odd numbers, since it is the custom to bring even numbers of flowers to funerals. The gesture for wishing someone good luck (the equivalent of crossing one's fingers in the United States) is to fold the thumb inward and close the other fingers around it.

9 LIVING CONDITIONS

Roughly 21% of Slovakia's population lives below the poverty line. Life expectancy for Slovaks averages 75 years of age, and the rate of infant mortality is 7 deaths for every 1,000 live births. The adult prevalence rate of HIV/AIDS is less than 0.1%, and it is estimated that fewer than 200 people in Slovakia are HIV positive. There is virtually universal access to medical care and a high rate of immunization for infants in the first year of life. Slovakia's health spas are known around the world and have many international visitors.

Most city dwellers live in modest-sized apartments built during the Communist era. Varied types of housing are found in rural Slovakia, ranging from two-room detached dwellings to two-story apartment buildings with up to six units. Indoor plumbing has been standard in rural areas for the past 40 years. Common building materials are cinder blocks and fired bricks. In the wake of the fall of Communism, Slovakia

experienced a serious housing shortage as housing units were recovered from state control. The privatization of state housing units resulted not only in the slowing of new construction, but also in the increase in the amount of owner-occupied housing. Both of these trends have affected the rental market, causing the creation of a rental black market and making housing unaffordable for many. Additionally, the shift of maintenance responsibility from public to private has caused repair and upkeep of lower income rental properties to be neglected. The Slovakian government is addressing these problems by building new rental properties. Now, approximately two million housing units exist in Slovakia, but it is estimated that over 150,000 units are still needed.

Most Slovak families own a car, but public transportation, including buses, trolleys, and trains, is widely used due to the high price of gasoline. There are rail links and highways between major cities. Because of the growth in cellular services and access to the internet, communication technology in Slovakia has expanded dramatically in recent years and is widely accessible.

10 FAMILY LIFE

The most common family unit in Slovakia is the nuclear family, although extended families can still be found in rural areas, where houses may have extra rooms to accommodate the family of a grown son or daughter. The average Slovak family has one to two children. Women receive paid maternity leave and a cash allowance when each child is born. Most women work outside the home (women account for 47% of the Slovak labor force.) Women and men have equal rights under the law, including property and inheritance rights.

11 CLOTHING

Slovaks wear modern Western-style clothing, including business attire for work, and jeans and T-shirts for casual wear. On special occasions, or during festivals or holidays, some Slovaks still wear traditional dress. For women, this includes puffed-sleeve blouses, vests, full skirts, aprons, boots, and a bonnet or headscarf depending on marital status. For men, this includes hats, shirts, vests, boots, and either form-fitting or flared pants. Such costumes are usually very colorfully embroidered. Traditionally, they were made of homespun cloth and sheepskin, but this is rarer today. Styles, colors, and accessories historically varied depending on region.

12 FOOD

Pork is the most common meat consumed in Slovakia, although beef, poultry, fish, and game, such as boar, rabbit, and venison, are also regularly eaten. Slovaks also make various types of spiced sausages, primarily from pork. The Slovak national dish is *bryndzové halušky*, dumplings made with potatoes, flour, water, eggs, and salt and served with processed sheep's cheese, and occasionally, bits of pork. In some regions, *halušky* is also served with cabbage and onions. Other Slovak favorites include *Kapustnics*, or cabbage soup, and *rezen*, or breaded steak. Fresh fish and wild game are often served in Slovak homes, and fresh-baked bread and soup are dinnertime staples. Favorite desserts include *tortes*, frosted, multilayered cakes, and *koláč*, or rolls with a nut or poppy seed filling.

Pilsner beer and dry, white wine are both produced and regularly consumed in Slovakia. The vineyards of Slovakia are

A Detva bride. On special occasions, people in the hill country still wear traditional dress, including dark woolen suits and knitted hats for men and full skirts, aprons, blouses, and scarves for women. (Helen Cincebeaux)

primarily located in the southern part of the country, in the Male Karpaty region near Hungary. As in the Czech Republic, *slivovice* (plum brandy) is also very popular.

The traditional main meal of the day in Slovakia is lunch, but more Slovaks are increasingly making dinner their main meal.

13 EDUCATION

Slovakia has a literacy rate of over 99%. Schooling is compulsory for 10 years, from ages 6 through 16. As in the United States, students go to school for five days a week, Monday through Friday. There are many secondary schools in Slovakia that prepare children for a higher education, as well as a variety of vocational schools. Most schools are still owned by the state, although since the fall of Communism there has been an increase in church-run schools and other types of private schools. There are over 30 schools of higher education in Slovakia, several of which opened after the fall of Communism. The oldest Slovak university is Comenius University in Bratislava, founded in 1919. Despite pending plans to implement tuition fees, there is still no charge to attend a university. Admission,

however, is limited and highly competitive. The grading system in Slovakia uses a scale ranging from one to five, with one being the highest grade and five being the lowest.

Since the fall of Communism, public schools and universities have struggled to overcome a lack of adequate funding. Instructors are underpaid and a great deal of the teaching material is outdated. As a result, corruption has become widespread as educational administrators and instructors are more prone to turning to illegal bribes in exchange for giving students entrance to schools, better grades, and more. Additionally, the quality of teachers has diminished since schools cannot compensate better qualified professionals and experts.

Regardless, Slovakia's secondary education is ranked as thirtieth in the world, just behind the United States, which is ranked twenty-ninth.

14 CULTURAL HERITAGE

Folk music is one of the most important elements of Slovakian culture. Slovakian national music was greatly strengthened and popularized in the early 19th century, although the origins of traditional Slovakian music are located in early Christian liturgical music. The Slovaks' pride in their musical tradition is expressed in the saying *Kde Slovák, tam spev* ("Wherever there is a Slovak, there is a song"). Villages have amateur musical groups that perform at school graduations and harvest festivals. Characteristic Slovak folk instruments include the bagpipes (*gajdy*), pipes (*píst'ala*), the *fujara*, a large shepherd's flute held vertically in front of the body, and native instruments similar to the fiddle and dulcimer. One popular series of folk songs, *Janosik* songs, are based on the exploits of a well-known folk hero. A common theme in many Slovak folk songs is Slovak subjugation to other national groups, such as Hungarians and Turks. Immigrants from Romania, Germany, and Hungary have also brought varying music styles to Slovakia. More recently, contemporary composers have begun to incorporate Slovak folk melodies into their works. Slovaks also have a strong folk-dance tradition, with dances such as the *Kolo, Hajduch, Verbunk, Czardas,* polka, waltz, a shepherd's dance called the *Odzemok*, and the *Chorodový*, a communal women's dance. Although popular music began to replace folk music after World War II, folk music remains an important element of Slovak culture and is celebrated, along with other folk arts, at a major folk festival every year in July.

Slovak literature began to experience great vibrancy in the early 19th century, when talented poets, such as Andrej Sladkovic and Jano Kral, produced some of the most original Slavic Romanticism. Such writing was heavily inspired by Slovak folk tales. Slovak literature came of age after World War II, but during the four decades of Communist rule after World War II, Slovak writing underwent a general decline.

15 WORK

Slovakia has more or less completed its transition from a centrally planned economy to a market economy. Like other Eastern European countries, Slovakia became highly industrialized during the Communist era, creating manufacturing jobs in steel, chemicals, glass, cement, and textiles. Since the end of the Communist era, the Slovakian economy has undergone a major shift in composition. In 1991, for example, 43% of the labor force was employed in heavy industry. In 2003, however, 56% of the labor force was employed in the service

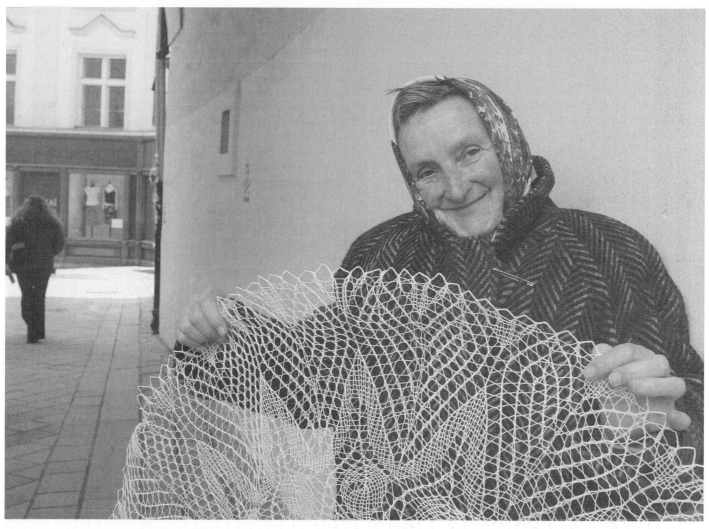

A woman in Bratislava, Slovakia, displays her needlework. (AP Images/Rudi Blaha)

industry, with 29% in heavy industry, 9% in construction, and 6% in agriculture. Workers in Slovakia have benefited from the country's sustained, strong economic growth, which has occurred even during a more general European slowdown. In the midst of privatization, the rate of unemployment went as high as 19.2% (in 2001). By the beginning of 2008, it had dropped to 8%. Despite its generally successful transition to a market economy, however, Slovakia is still in need of greater investment in research and development in order to cultivate a modern knowledge-based economy and remain competitive with the rest of Europe and the world.

16 SPORTS

Popular sports among Slovaks include soccer, tennis, and skiing, although Slovakia is known best around the world for ice hockey. Ice Hockey became popular in Slovakia in 1925 when the European Ice Hockey Championship was held in the High Tatras in 1925. This established the beginning of the Tatra Cup, which is now the second oldest tournament in Europe. In 2002, Slovakia won the world hockey championship.

17 ENTERTAINMENT AND RECREATION

In their leisure time, Slovaks enjoy attending movies, local festivals, and cultural events and participating in outdoor activities including hiking, swimming, and camping. Slovakia also has over 1,000 mineral and hot springs. In rural villages, men meet after work at the local bar to drink, play cards, and socialize.

18 FOLK ART, CRAFTS, AND HOBBIES

Folk arts and crafts, which include pottery, porcelain sculpting, woodcarving, metalworking, toy making, and glass painting, have a long and popular tradition in Slovakia, especially in rural areas. Many women knit, sew, embroider, and make lace. Popular patterns are handed down from generation to generation. Slovakia also possesses very rich folk architecture in the forms of wooden churches, brightly painted houses, and more.

19 SOCIAL PROBLEMS

Despite the large improvements in the economy over the last several years, Slovakia still has the highest unemployment rate of any country in the European Union. Many Slovaks have moved abroad in search of employment, and Slovakia's accession to the European Union has aided in such movement. This trend of emigration contributes to Slovakia's extremely low population growth rate of 0.14%. The fertility rate in Slovakia, 1.33 children per woman, is one of the lowest in the European Union. In the coming years, this may not only negatively impact Slovakia's economy, but as work force and age distributions of the population change, Slovakia's social security system, infrastructure, educational system, and other systems may become unsustainable. These trends comprise the greatest long-term social threat to Slovaks.

Two of the larger immediate social problems facing Slovaks are drugs and prostitution. Both drugs and humans are trafficked through Slovakia. Synthetic drugs are produced in Slovakia and distributed throughout Eastern and Central Europe. The drug ecstasy is also used in Slovakia.

[20] GENDER ISSUES

Women and men in Slovakia are roughly equal when it comes to literacy, education levels, employment, and civic and political rights. Some of the main social and economic problems of the post-Communist transition, however, have had a disproportionately negative impact on the female gender. Generally, the Communist period is thought by experts to have had a negative impact on the feminist movement. Under Communism, women and men in Czechoslovakia were officially declared equal by law, but this did not translate into practice beyond the most visible public spheres. The Communist government's version of equal rights was simply ensuring that women were employed at a comparable rate to men. They did little to address the other domestic and societal conditions, expectations, and stereotypes of women. Often, gaining employment outside the home actually worsened conditions for women, who were still largely expected to perform all of their domestic tasks, such as cooking, cleaning, and child-rearing, in addition to their work outside the home. Many experts argue that the Communist rhetoric of equality among men and women produced a false comfort among Slovaks, as among other peoples under Communism, that the gender imbalance had been solved. This sense diffused and undermined the feminist movement by making women's rights a non-issue in society.

The feminist movement in Slovakia does not have much strength and it is not a part of mainstream Slovak culture. Inequality, at least in societal expectations of women, still exists when it comes to reproductive issues, family life, work, political affairs, and public life. Slovak women themselves, however, do not consider their situation to be inappropriate or in need of being changed. Studies show that only 30% of women in Slovakia have positive or neutral views on the idea of feminism, while 24% have a negative view and 46% are not even familiar with the concept. Even more Slovak men are ignorant or possess a negative view of feminism. In both men and women, social demographics seem to affect awareness levels of feminist issues, but not attitudes. The more highly educated men in Slovakia are actually more negative toward the feminist movement, which poses problems for educated Slovak women attempting to pursue women's rights.

The post-Communist period has also taken its toll on certain groups of women in a very concrete way. High unemployment, the rising cost of living, and increased contact with larger markets since the fall of Communism have caused an increase in prostitution activities of Slovak women, both in Slovakia and abroad. Within Slovakia, authorities have done little to regulate prostitution, which has been detrimental to both women practicing prostitution and inhabitants of areas where prostitution activities occur. Before the fall of Communism, prostitution was prohibited in the streets, making many of these problems new to Slovak society. The lack of regulation or restriction leaves women who practice prostitution with no rights or protection and has led to the increase in other problems connected to prostitution, such as violence and drug abuse. These problems penetrate broader portions of Slovak society because they occur in residential areas. Since no official laws exist to regulate prostitution, police are often not able to respond until other crimes surrounding the activity, such as pimping, drug distribution, and theft, are committed. Often, it is the female prostitutes who are punished by law enforcement rather than the male perpetrators. Official regulations have still yet to be put into place, leaving only non-governmental organizations to address the issue. Such organizations focus on health education, social and legal issues, the provision of contraceptives, and widespread preventative activities in an effort to alleviate the problem. Such organizations are few and lack sufficient state support for their activities. Additionally, due to the nature of prostitution, many of the women who need to access these services cannot since they are outside of the mainstream social system. Prostitution is highly stigmatized in Slovak society, making it even harder for these women to break away from their situations.

Prostitution is equally, if not more dangerous for Slovak women outside of Slovakia's borders. Since the fall of Communism, the illegal trafficking and prostitution of women from former Eastern Bloc countries in Western Europe has grown immensely. The European Commission estimates that over 2,000 Slovaks per year are trafficked as prostitutes to France, Spain, Italy, Greece, and Germany. Young Slovak women are most often told by traffickers that they will be employed in high-paying jobs as waitresses and au pairs in their new country of residence. Upon arrival, their personal identification and travel documents are stolen and they are forced to work as prostitutes on streets or in brothels against their will. Such women are not only limited by not knowing the local language, but are also beaten and threatened. These women become susceptible not only to heavy drug use, but to murder as well. Contrary to the call for regulation of prostitution at home, some experts believe that legalization and toleration of prostitution in Western Europe has only aided human traffickers in seeming more legitimate. Police and various non-governmental organizations are working to create a system for locating and retrieving victims, but due to widespread Slovak social attitudes toward prostitution, many of the victims who do make it back to Slovakia are ostracized from their communities.

Legitimate agencies that seek to employ young Slovak women abroad as au pairs do exist, but when Slovak women arrive in foreign countries, they are often treated not as au pairs on a cultural exchange but as live-in migrant domestic workers, making them vulnerable to exploitation. Both forms of exploitation are made possible by the unemployment rate in Slovakia and by the economic disparity between Slovakia and its richer western neighbors.

21 BIBLIOGRAPHY

Alexander, June Granatir. *Slovak Americans. Countries and their Cultures.* http://www.everyculture.com.

Bogatyrev, Petr. *The Functions of Folk Costume in Moravian Slovakia.* The Hague: Mouton, 1971.

Bútorová, Zora, ed. *She and He in Slovakia: Gender Issues in Public Opinion.* Bratislava: FOCUS, 1996.

European Commission. "Eurostat." http://www.ec.europa.eu/eurostat.

Faltan, Lubomir and Richard A. Dodder. "Privatizing the Housing Sector: The Case of Slovakia." *Public Administration and Development*, vol. 15, issue 4 (2006): 391-396.

Fila, Lukáš. "Oldest Profession is Risky Business in Slovakia." *The Slovak Spectator*, 28 April 2003.

Funk, Nanette, and Magda Mueller, eds. *Gender Politics and Post-Communism: Reflections from Eastern Europe and the Former Soviet Union.* New York: Routledge, 1993.

Hess, Sabine and Anette Puckhaber. "'Big Sisters' are Better Domestic Servants?! Comments on the Booming Au Pair Business." *Feminist Review*, no. 77, (2004): 65-78.

Kiliánová, Gabriela, and Eva Krekovičová, eds. *Folklore in the Identification Process of Society.* Bratislava: Ústav Etnológie SAV, 1994.

Kirschbaum, Joseph M., ed. *Slovak Culture through the Centuries.* Toronto: Slovak World Congress, 1978.

Kirschbaum, Stanislav J. *A History of Slovakia: The Struggle for Survival.* New York: St. Martin's Press, 1995.

Kucekova, Eva Susan. "Slovak Folklore: An Anthology." PhD diss., University of Massachusetts, Amherst, 1982.

Leff, Carol Skalnik. *The Czech and Slovak Republics: Nation vs. State.* Boulder, Colo.: Westview Press, 1997.

Mikuš, Joseph A. *Slovakia and the Slovaks.* Washington, D.C.: Three Continents Press, 1977.

Oddo, Gilbert Lawrence. *Slovakia and its People.* New York: R. Speller, 1960.

Pollak, Janet. "Slovaks." *Encyclopedia of World Cultures.* Boston: G. K. Hall, 1992.

Republicki Zavod za Statistiku. "Statistical Yearbook of Serbia: 2007." Republic of Serbia. http://webrzs.statserb.sr.gov.yu/axd/en/god.htm.

Reynolds, Matthew P. "Aiding Women Sold into Prostitution." *The Slovak Spectator*, 14 May 2001.

Toma, Peter A. and Dušan Kováč. *Slovakia: From Samo to Dzurinda.* Stanford, CA: Hoover Institution Press, 2001.

—by Sarah Dixon Klump

SLOVENES

ALTERNATE NAMES: Slovenci; Slovenians [both forms, Slovene and Slovenian, are used as noun and adjective]
LOCATION: Slovenia and regions of Austria, Italy, and Hungary along their Slovenian borders
POPULATION: 2,003,358 million, of whom 83.1% are Slovenes (2007 census)
LANGUAGE: Slovenian; in nationally mixed areas, also Italian and Hungarian and others
RELIGION: Roman Catholic, Muslim, Orthodox, other Christian, other or unspecified, none

1 INTRODUCTION

Slovenes, a distinct South Slav people, originally located in the area northeast of the Carpathian Mountains, settled in the eastern Alpine region of Central Europe in the 6th and 7th centuries AD. Although they established a short-lived political entity, Karantania, in the 8th century, they obtained their own independent state only in 1991. For over 1,000 years, Slovenes lived under mostly German rule as part of the Holy Roman (962–1806), Austrian (1804–1867), and Austro-Hungarian (1867–1918) empires. During centuries of foreign rule, the Slovenes preserved their language and, in the last 200 years, formed a modern nation with a rich culture and aspirations for political independence.

In 1918, following the collapse of the Austro-Hungarian Empire, the Slovenes joined with other South Slavs to form the Kingdom of Serbs, Croats, and Slovenes (in 1929 renamed Yugoslavia, meaning "the land of South Slavs"), but one-third of Slovene ethnic territory remained outside its borders. Within this new state, the Slovenes acquired institutions crucial for national development, among them a university and the Slovene Academy of Sciences and Arts.

World War II (1941–1945) was a traumatic experience for the Slovenes. Their territory was divided among three occupying powers: Germany, Italy, and Hungary. Many Slovenes died during the wartime liberation struggle, but many more—thousands—were killed in a bloody civil war, fought during World War II. Victorious Communists massacred over 10,000 anti-Communists in the spring of 1945. The Communist takeover triggered massive emigration from Slovenia and left deep political divisions, which persist to this day. In federally organized Communist Yugoslavia (after 1945), Slovenia, as a constituent republic, acquired its own constitution, as well as cultural and some political autonomy. With the demise of Communism in Europe, Yugoslavia fell apart in June 1991, after two of its constituent republics, Croatia and Slovenia, proclaimed their independence.

Since then, Slovenia has been an independent state and a republic with a parliamentary democracy. Slovenia joined the North Atlantic Treaty Organization (NATO) and the European Union (EU) in 2004. In January 2008 Slovenia became the first of the ten 2004 EU newcomers to hold the EU's rotating presidency.

2 LOCATION AND HOMELAND

The Republic of Slovenia borders on four countries: Austria in the north, Hungary in the northeast, Italy in the west, and tional symbol, featured on the national coat of arms and the flag.

Slovene archeological sites attest to several prehistoric and Roman settlements and to the strategic importance of the Slovene ethnic territory as a crossroads between northern and western Europe, and Europe's east and the south. The land originally settled by the Slovenes, south of today's Vienna, Austria, and east of Venice, Italy, was three times the size of the present Slovene ethnic territory. Not all Slovenes live within the boundaries of the Republic of Slovenia: Slovene minorities exist in neighboring Austria, Italy, and Hungary. Also, an estimated 2.5 million Slovene emigrants and their descendants live throughout the world, around 300,000 of them in the United States. Slovenes emigrated for various historic reasons. Poverty was the most prevalent reason before World War I, and fear of political persecution after World War II.

About 50% of Slovenes live in cities: in Ljubljana, the capital, with approximately 276,000 inhabitants; in Maribor, with 106,000 inhabitants; and in several smaller cities, each with under 50,000 inhabitants. Ljubljana is a unique city that maintains the friendliness of a small town, while possessing all the characteristics of a metropolis. It is considered to be a meeting point of the cultures of the east and west, where the old interlaces in harmony with the new.

In the past, the Slovenes were mostly peasants and, before World War II, over 50% of Slovenes made their living from farming; in the 1990s, however, the number of peasant farmers had dwindled to 7%. After World War II, Slovenia rapidly industrialized, but did not become urbanized. Many Slovenes still live in the country while commuting to work in the cities. Preserving the countryside helps people to maintain close bonds with nature, Slovenian culture, customs, and habits. While being a very modern society, Slovenes place a great value in delicious home cooked meals, homemade wines and brandies, the traditional ceramic heating stove, and the captivating scent of new-mown hay. Both in the city and in the countryside people are hospitable and welcoming.

³ LANGUAGE

The language of Slovenes is Slovenian, which is the official language of the Republic of Slovenia. However, Hungarian and Italian are spoken in the border regions, and German fluency is common near the Austrian border. Bosnian, Croatian, and Serbian are spoken by a sizable (6% of the population) minority.

Slovenian is a South Slavic language, closely related to Croatian and similar to other Slavic languages, e.g., Czech. Similarly to many other Slavic languages, it uses the Latin alphabet. It is spoken by approximately 2 million people in the Slovene ethnic territory, and by emigrants around the world. Natural boundaries (mountains and rivers) and the proximity of other language groups (Croatian, German, Hungarian, Italian) influenced the development of Slovenian and its division into several distinct dialects. In the past, spoken Slovenian, particularly that of uneducated people, borrowed many words from German, such as *štumfi* (from the German *Strumpf*) for *nogavice* (stockings). At present, slang, especially of youth, and technical language of professional groups are heavily influenced by English. In teenagers' talk, the English words "full" and "cool" are staple expressions of emphasis, e.g., *To je ful dober!* (This is very good!). Another often-used English expression is "OK".

Croatia in the east and south. It occupies a small (20,256 sq km or 7,821 sq mi, about the size of the US state of New Jersey) but geographically diverse area: the Alpine region in the west and north, the Subpannonian hilly terrain with large fertile basins in the northeast and east, the Dinaric Karst in the south and southeast and the fertile Slovene Littoral, with 46 km (29 mi) of Adriatic coast, in the southwest. Also, despite its small size, this eastern Alpine country controls some of Europe's major transit routes.

Slovenia's climate varies with its geographical makeup. The Alpine region has long, cold winters and short, cool summers; the Subpannonian area has a continental climate with cold winters, hot summers, and fluctuating daily temperatures; while a Mediterranean climate, with mild winters, is characteristic of the Slovene Littoral. Slovenia, half of its land covered with forests and enhanced by sufficient rainfall, is considered "green country on the sunny side of the Alps." Although mountains and karst areas are poorly suited for agriculture, they are beautiful, unique regions, which offer wonderful possibilities for tourism and sports. In fact, tourism is one of the most important branches of the Slovene economy.

Additionally, Slovenia can boast over 26 000 km of permanent and torrential water courses, about 6,500 karstic caves, thousands of springs, waterfalls and gorges, and its natural and artificial lakes. There are the karst-limestone regions with their reservoirs of subterranean water, as well as the remains of once formidable glaciers below the peaks of Triglav and Skuta. Triglav is the highest mountain in Slovenia. Its name means "three-heads." The mountain is 2,864 m high and is a true na-

Slovenes are proud of their language, but at the same time they are aware of the need to learn foreign languages to be able to communicate with their neighbors and the rest of the world. Thus, the majority of Slovenes speak at least one foreign language. In elementary school, all children begin to learn a foreign language in the fifth grade; in secondary school, students often study two or even three languages. The most-frequently taught foreign language is English, followed by German. In the border areas, with Italian and Hungarian and other minorities, those respective languages are also taught.

People are most often named after Catholic saints (Ana, Andrej, Joxe, Marija, Matevx). Also popular are old Slavic names, such as Iztok (source) or Vesna (spring). Family names are derived from people's occupations, e.g., Kmet (farmer), or Kovaȟh (blacksmith); from locations where they live, e.g., Dolinar (one who lives in a valley), or Hribar (one who lives on a mountain); and from animals, e.g., Medved (bear), Petelin (rooster), or Volk (wolf).

Impressively, statistics indicate that over the centuries Slovenians accumulated 42,889 different first names (20,366 male names and 22,523 female names) and 88,157 different last names. Although some names are disappearing (such as Karol, Vilko, Radoslav, Hilda, Leopoldina, Fanika), other first and last names are being created or acquired from other countries.

Despite the extensive list of names to choose from, half of the population of Slovenia has one of the top 50 names. Two female and five male names are so popular that more than 20,000 people have one of this seven names. Thus, every eighth person in Slovenia (about 12% of the population) has one of the following names: Franc, Janez, Anton, Ivan, Jožef, Marija, or Ana.

4 FOLKLORE

Many Slovene folk traditions are associated with seasonal celebrations, dating to pre-Christian times. They were adopted, modified, and perpetuated by the Catholic Church. Slovene Carnival celebrations with parades, carnivals, and masquerade balls vary from region to region. Among them, *kurentovanje* in Ptuj is the most famous tourist attraction. The central figure is the *kurent,* whose fur clothing and unusual masks with horns, representing human and animal traits, evoke images of another planet. Always happy, the kurent is considered a harbinger of spring, fertility, and new life. Accompanied by a ceremonial plowman, he visits farms and wishes their owners a prosperous year. Adults and children enjoy the spring Carnival season, called *pust* (Mardi gras). The traditional pastries *krofi* and *flancati* (similar to doughnuts) are prepared. Costumed children, wearing masks, go from house to house, asking: "Do you have anything for Pusta, Hrusta?" People give them sweets and fruits. Adults attend masquerade balls. This tradition is similar to Halloween in the United States.

Slovene heroes are usually optimistic, wise, and cheerful. Stories about Kralj Matjax (King Mathias), Martin Krpan, and Miklova Zala, for example, are introduced to children early in their lives. The story about Kralj Matjax goes back to the difficult times of the bubonic plagues, Turkish invasions, and famine in the 16th and 17th centuries. People elected a good king who would protect them from danger and never die. However, he and his army are said to be sleeping under Mt. Peca. When needed, they will awaken and protect their people. Another popular hero is Martin Krpan, a common Slovene person from a small village who is strong, wise, and cunning, who saved Vienna and the Austrian emperor from a Turkish ogre.

One of the most beautiful stories is of a Slovene woman, Miklova Zala, and also dates from the time of Turkish invasions. She epitomizes love and fidelity. Captured by the Turks, she was taken to Constantinople where she was sold to a pasha who wanted to marry her. Refusing to abandon her Christian beliefs and her husband, she succeeded in escaping. After long and challenging travels that lasted seven years, she was reunited with her husband. This story celebrates true love, the faith and beauty of Slovene women, love for homeland, courage, and strength.

5 RELIGION

Slovenes are mostly Roman Catholic. In the 8th century AD, Slovene worshipers of Slavic gods were Christianized by Irish missionaries. Since then, the Catholic Church has played a major role in preserving and cultivating Slovene language and culture. Although 90% of Slovenes claim to be nominally Catholic, considerably fewer practice their religion (go to mass regularly and receive the sacraments). But Slovene culture is inseparable from Catholicism.

Small numbers of people belong to other religious groups. The Evangelical Protestant Church (Lutheran), established during the 16th-century Reformation movement, is the oldest. Of recent groups, some are non-Christian, such as Hare Rama Hare Krishna. In the last decade, there has been more interest, especially among young people, in various spiritual movements. As of 2008, 38 other religious communities, spiritual groups, societies and associations were registered in Slovenia.

6 MAJOR HOLIDAYS

Religious holidays, such as Christmas, New Year's Day, Easter, Assumption Day (August 15) and All Saints Day (November 1) are recognized as national holidays. A few secular holidays are also observed. Since gaining independence in 1991, Slovenes celebrate Statehood Day (June 25), and Independence Day (December 26). Besides official celebrations with political speeches, cultural programs, fireworks, and receptions for diplomats, families and friends gather, light bonfires, picnic, and sing.

Since 1945, Prešeren Day (February 8) has been celebrated as a Slovene cultural holiday honoring the great Romantic poet France Prešeren. Cultural programs of all kinds (concerts, poetry readings, theater performances, and the presentation of the most prestigious national award for artists) take place in schools, cultural institutions, and the media.

Although the majority of Slovenes are Catholic, Reformation Day is also observed as a national holiday on October 31 to recognize the important role the Protestants played in establishing the identity of the Slovene nation. In 1550, they published the first book, *Cathechismus,* in the Slovene language, followed by other books, among them a translation of the Bible.

7 RITES OF PASSAGE

Major life transitions are marked with religious ceremonies and celebrations appropriate to the Roman Catholic tradition followed by the majority of Slovenes. Such events as baptism, First Communion, and confirmation are considered important rites of passage in a child's life.

Slovenes wear traditional costumes of fur and bells during the Pust or Carnival parade. The carnival dates back to old Europe when people would celebrate spring and the end of winter's dark and cold. (Melissa Farlow/National Geographic/Getty Images)

8 INTERPERSONAL RELATIONS

When meeting, Slovenes exchange various greetings, depending on the time of day. Until approximately 10:00 am it is customary to use "*dobro jutro!*"; during the day, *dober dan* (good day); and after dark, *dober vecer* (good evening); to all of which the traditional reply is "*Bogda!*" (May God grant you). Slovenes, especially the young, often greet each other with "*zivijo!*" (long life). At parting, various expressions are used. The most common are "*nasvidenje!*" (so long), "*adijo!*" (goodbye) and, in the evening, *lahko noc* (good night). When Slovenes meet or part, they often shake hands.

In addressing a person, Slovenes use either the informal or the formal form. A friend or a close relative would be addressed with *ti* (informal for "you") and the verb in corresponding form; an older person, a teacher, or a stranger would be addressed with *Vi* (formal for "you"). Teachers in school are never addressed by their first name but rather with *Gospod* (Mr.) and *Gospa* (Mrs.). For example one would refer to a teacher as *Gospod Kovac (or Mr. Smith)*. Students in elementary schools are addressed informally with *ti*, while in high schools and universities they are addressed formally with *Vi*.

Slovenes are courteous visitors and when invited to dinner will always bring small gifts: flowers for the hostess, a bottle of wine for the host, or candy for the children. It is considered rude to refuse what is offered, but, usually, it is good manners to decline politely once or twice before taking it. *Hvala* (thanks) is the word used to express gratitude, to which *prosim* (please) is the polite response. *Prosim* is also used when a request is put forward, or when a listener did not hear or understand what was said.

Slovenes tend to appear reserved at first, but are very friendly on acquaintance. Slovenes, usually friendly and hospitable, are eager to help a foreigner with information. They are quick to invite him or her home to share a meal. Among themselves, they value friendship, spend time together, and help each other build houses, move, or bring in the harvest.

It is not unusual to see Slovenes express their emotions, especially affection, in public places. This is especially true of teenagers, who can be seen in the streets and parks holding hands and kissing. Many old courting and dating customs, once popular particularly in villages, have died out, but a few are still observed. Just before young people marry, they organize pre-wedding parties: the *dekliščhina* (maiden party) is organized by a bride for her women friends, and the *fantovščhina* (bachelor party) by a groom for his men friends.

9 LIVING CONDITIONS

Statistics show that the quality of life in Slovenia is relatively good. Life expectancy for men is 72 years and for women 80 years. Mothers are entitled to one year's maternity leave so that they can stay with their babies and nurse them. Maternity leave could also be a "parental" leave, since half of it can be used by fathers.

With recent improvements in medicine, only 5 out of 1,000 newborn infants die. All children are vaccinated against the most common diseases and undergo regular medical checkups. Infectious diseases have been practically eradicated. Most Slovenes have public health insurance and reasonable pension plans. Slovenes die primarily of cancer and heart diseases; the latter account for 50% of all deaths. Cigarette smoking is less popular than in the past, however it remains a little below 30% of the population. Consequently, respiratory illnesses and problems associated with smoking and air pollution are common.

Public transportation (train and bus service) is well organized. Also, many families own a car. Young people can obtain a driving license when they turn 18. Owning a car in Slovenia is a status symbol. Hence, people spend a lot of money on cars. According to survey results from 2006, only 5% of households were not able to afford a car. Poor roads and inclement weather conditions contribute to fatal traffic accidents, which are commonplace.

Historically, there is a shortage of housing in cities; apartments are small and modest. Very few children have their own rooms and are bound to share them with other siblings, sometimes even with parents. However, many people living in cities have small cottages, called *vikendi*, in the countryside or resort areas where they spend their weekends.

Although statistics indicate longevity and the general good health of population, many Slovene families still face economic and financial constraints. Approximately 13% of households cannot afford decent meal every second day and 34% of households cannot afford a week of annual holiday away from home. At the same time every family owns at least one television. Computers are somewhat less common but over one million people possess mobile phones (2001 census).

10 FAMILY LIFE

The majority of young people get married in their 20s and establish a family with one or two children. Families with three or more children are rare. Because of the shortage and relatively high cost of housing, newlyweds often live with their parents for years before they are able to acquire their own home. Slovenes maintain close relations with their parents, siblings, and extended families. Even though Slovenes love their family, many marriages end in divorce, and most children are left with their mothers. In general, divorce is easily obtained.

According to 2the 2007 census, there were approximately 670,000 mothers in Slovenia. About 10% of women over 40 have never given birth. Throughout the years the role of mothers has changed significantly. If 50 years ago more than half of Slovenian women stayed home and took care of the family and household, today typical Slovenian mothers pursue professional careers. In fact, mothers in Slovenia are more active in their professional pursuits than mothers in other EU member states. At the same time employed mothers still perform the lion's share of the household chores. Recently, husbands began to share with their wives responsibility for housework and education of children. Yet credit for the family well-being is mainly due to Slovene women. A Slovene proverb says, "The wife supports three corners of the house."

Traditionally, women had their first child soon after getting married. However, today the average age of a woman at the first childbirth is 28 years. Women increasingly try to finish their education, get a good job, and purchase a place to live before they have a child. Thus, the tendency to have a first child after 30 is growing. Furthermore, more and more mothers give birth outside marriage. The share of children born to unmarried women has grown by significantly. The number of unmarried couples is growing too. If 50 years ago consensual unions were socially unacceptable, now they are commonplace, so that as many as 38% of second children are born to unmarried parents (2006 census).

On weekends, especially on Sundays, and in the evenings, families spend their time together. There are no shopping malls, and only a very few stores are open on Sundays. Thus, families go to church, take trips, hike, ski, collect mushrooms, visit each other, and enjoy long conversations. Many families visit relatives in the countryside on weekends and help them with work in the fields, orchards, and vineyards. This is especially true at harvest time. An increasing number of families own pets: dogs, cats, or birds are the most common.

11 CLOTHING

Similar to other Europeans, Slovenes wear contemporary Western clothing. Young people prefer jeans and tee-shirts. Women like to dress up and especially favor Italian fashion, while men dress informally, even at the office: short-sleeved shirts in summer and woolen sweaters in winter. Recently it has become very popular to wear jewelry. Extreme body-piercing and tattooing are rare.

In the past, people wore hand-sewn garments. They were made from linen or wool and varied from region to region. Roughly, there were Alpine, Pannonian, and Mediterranean styles of clothing. However, regional differences in everyday attire disappeared in the late 19th century. At the same time, the Slovenes adopted the modified traditional costume of the Gorenjska region as their national costume. Since then, this traditional outfit was worn at public events and celebrations to emphasize national identity. Today, Slovenes wear the national costume only at folk festivals or traditional celebrations.

A woman's apparel consists of a long, dark brocade skirt, a white petticoat and underclothes, a bodice, a richly decorated headdress, colorful silk scarves, hand knit socks, and an ornate metal belt. A man's costume consists of a dark velvet vest, often embroidered, suede shorts worn over long white underwear, boots, a silk scarf, and a hat.

12 FOOD

Most of the Slovene land is not suited for agriculture, thus not enough food is produced at home. While there is sufficient production of poultry, dairy products, and potatoes (the staple food since the 19th century), Slovenes import many basic foods such as oil, wheat, sugar, and meat. Food is expensive, costing most Slovenes at least half of the family budget.

In the past, *mocnik*, a dish similar to porridge made from wheat, buckwheat, or corn flour, was the most popular staple food among farmers, eaten twice a day. Meat was available rarely, the major source of protein being legumes. Vegetables and fruits varied with the season; sauerkraut and dried fruits were the source of vitamin C during the long winters. With the rise in the standard of living and new technologies (refrigeration, quick transport), Slovenes began to change their eating habits: meat became an everyday food, and regional and seasonal differences were no longer as distinct.

Slovene cooking has three major influences: Alpine, Mediterranean, and Pannonian. There are 30 recognized regional cuisines, each for example, serving its own type of bread. Famous regional foods include Primorska's fish and seafood and Karst's pršut (cured ham). Slovenes everywhere enjoy bread and potatoes. Potatoes are served boiled, sautéed, deep-fried, or roasted, and are used in various dishes including dumplings, soups, and stews. Breakfast consists of coffee, tea, or hot chocolate, and rolls with butter and jam. *Zemlja,* a special kind of hard roll, is especially popular. Salami, cheese, and soft-boiled or fried eggs are also served for breakfast. Some people do not take breakfast and drink only strong coffee.

The main meal in the Slovenian diet is lunch. A typical Slovenian lunch begins with soup before moving on to the main course. The most popular Slovenian soup is *Goveja juha z rezanci,* a beef or chicken broth with noodles. Some other soups are *Grahova juha* (pea soup), *Gobova kremna juha* (creamed mushroom soup) and *Zelenjavna juha* (vegetable soup). The main course, accompanied by a side dish and salad, is followed by a dessert. Lunch is usually prepared by working mothers and is eaten in the mid-afternoon. Supper is a light meal with salads, yogurt, and leftovers from lunch.

One recent eating trend in Slovenia is the "slow food movement." A typical "slow food" meal takes place in a restaurant or at a private home among a group of family members or close friends. There are usually eight or more courses, the emphasis being on local produce, old-style recipes and a relaxed pace, with a different wine to accompany each course.

Slovenes have many delicious traditional dishes that they cook for holidays. One of the most genuine festive Slovene foods is a rolled yeast cake, called *potica,* with sweet (walnuts, tarragon, raisins) or salty (cracklings) fillings. Potica is usually made for Christmas and Easter. Among traditional meat dishes, *kranjske klobase* (sausages, similar to Polish kielbasa) are well known, as are pork dishes *(koline)* in winter.

Many restaurants offer a wide range of traditional national dishes, as well as international dishes like pizza, pasta, and oriental dishes. The coast offers excellent seafood, including shellfish and the Adriatic bluefish. Although eating out is expensive, Slovene *gostilnas,* traditional taverns, serve as popular gathering places, particularly in the country. They offer homemade dishes and pastries. The typical Sunday lunch menu in a Slovene gostilna includes beef or chicken soup with homemade noodles, pork or veal roast, sautéed or roasted potatoes, salad, and potica or strudel for dessert. Young people like pizza and adore eating in a newly opened American McDonald's.

Of alcoholic drinks beer and fruit brandies (e.g., *sadjevec, slivovka*—plum brandy) are served today, while in the past, *medica* (mead) was a common alcoholic drink. Above all, Slovenia is known for its great red and white wines. Winemaking has a long history in Slovenia. Its origins can be traced back to the 6th century BC. Popular nonalcoholic beverages are fruit juices and drinks made with fruit syrups (*malinovec*—with raspberry syrup), herbal teas, and, lately, Coca-Cola, especially among young people.

13 EDUCATION

The Slovene literacy rate is almost 100%. Compulsory eight-year elementary education has been a legal requirement since 1869. All school-age children (6-14 years old) attend elementary school. At age 14, students take a lower-level comprehensive exam *(mala matura),* whose results influence students' further schooling. Some 90% of students who finish elementary school continue their education at the secondary level. Some go to four-year schools to prepare for higher studies, but many enter two- and three-year vocational schools. A school year lasts 190 days. Not all students graduate. Those who finish take the upper-level comprehensive exam *(velika matura),*

which enables them to enroll in the university. About 33% of them continue their studies, but only 9% graduate. Social studies, e.g., law, business, and economics, are more popular than natural sciences. There is no tuition in the public school system at any level for full-time students, but parents have to pay for the students' textbooks and other supplies. Since 1991, the law allows home-schooling and private schools, which are few in number.

Education has long been the only channel of social promotion for Slovenes and is highly valued by parents, who expect their children to do well in school. Many students follow in their parents' profession. School attendance and studying are the major responsibilities for most students, and almost no elementary or high school students work during the school year. They do have summer jobs, some out of need, and others just to earn pocket money.

The educational system in Slovenia is almost fully financed by the state budget. The Slovene school system has undergone a number of changes in recent years. In light of the reforms, children enter elementary school at the age of six. Beginning in 1999, the length of elementary education has been increased from eight to nine years. Thus primary or elementary school now consists of nine-year program, and is divided into three three-year periods.

Upon completion of their elementary education children are expected to pursue secondary education, either in vocational schools, technical schools, or in gimanzija. Gimnazija is a four-year general education program designed to prepare students for university. Children of foreign residents can also receive education at all levels. Approximately 84% of secondary school graduates pursue further studies. In fact, the profile of Slovenia's population enrolled in higher education is improving. The number of students in vocational colleges and higher education institutions is increasing. In the academic year 2007/08, 115,445 students were enrolled in post-secondary vocational and higher education studies. This means that in the 2007/08 academic year 50% of all persons aged 19 to 23 were enrolled in post-secondary vocational and higher education institutions, while 10 years ago the share was below 30%. Large numbers of female students major in commerce, business administration, and accounting while the majority of men study mechanical engineering, electronics, computer science, and civil engineering. More than 85% of all university students are enrolled in the University of Ljubljana and the University of Maribor.

14 CULTURAL HERITAGE

Music has always been an important part of the Slovene culture. Vocal and instrumental music has ritual and entertainment functions. Folk songs, usually sung in three- or four-part harmony, are simple in form, lyrics, and music, and deal with love, patriotism, war, work traditions, changes of season, and religious and family holidays. In the past, folk singing was part of everyday life, closely associated with group work, e.g., harvesting or spinning. Today, it plays an important role in churches, in traditional celebrations, and at social gatherings. For centuries, Slovenes have spent their free time singing in choirs, and choral singing has been an important hobby. At present, there are hundreds of choirs established in schools, organizations, and churches, wherever Slovenes live. Choral singing is also alive in Slovene emigrant communities, for example in Cleveland, Ohio. Choral performances include folk songs as well as works of Slovene classical and contemporary composers.

Instrumental music was traditionally performed on simple wind, string, and percussion instruments, made by local craftspeople employing materials at hand. The accordion, introduced in Slovenia in the late 19th century, quickly replaced more traditional instruments and became the most popular folk instrument of the 20th century. Today, the electric guitar is a popular instrument among young people. Music education is part of the elementary school curriculum.

Slovene history and culture are reflected in folk arts and literature. Many folk poems, fairy tales, short stories, proverbs, and riddles have been recorded and preserved for future generations. Old fairy tales (such as *The Golden Bird*), stories, and poems are still very popular among children and adults. Motifs in folk literature are often used by poets and writers as the inspiration for their literary work.

France Prešeren is considered Slovenia's most celebrated writer and poet. He is regarded to be a great leader of Slovenian culture, nationality and independence. His poetry modernized the Slovenian language. A portion of his poem "The Toast" is used as the national anthem. February 8, the day of Prešeren's death, is a national holiday celebrated by the entire country.

Slovenes have built hundreds of churches, wayside shrines, and towns with numerous art galleries, which speak of a rich and high-quality arts tradition throughout history. Although influenced by specific Slovene cultural characteristics, literature, music, visual arts, architecture, and theater have been part of Central European art movements, appearing approximately at the same time as anywhere else in that part of Europe. Slovene artists worked in the European art centers, and European masters came to Slovenia. The same is true today. Slovenes have had many important artists, some of whom they have honored by putting their likenesses on the new bank notes in 1992.

In short, modern Slovenia has a rich cultural life bustling with a myriad of theatres, cinemas, libraries, and educational facilities, and is well known abroad for its cultural exports.

15 WORK

Most employed people in Europe work a 40-hour week. Industrious Slovenes usually work much longer. Besides holding jobs in factories and offices, many moonlight, run their own businesses, and/or work on small family-owned farms. Under socialism, everybody had the right to work; hence, the state created jobs even if they were not needed. These policies were a double-edged blessing. While they provided some social security and minimal means for living, they also brought about economic conditions incompatible with a market economy, such as a lack of competition, inefficiency, and the high cost of goods. After 1990, several industrial plants were scaled down or closed, and thus unemployment became a serious social problem.

Post-independence economic reforms were implemented to mend unemployment and economic instability. Current data indicates that in December 2007 there were 864,361 employed persons, 43.3% of whom were women. The Employment Service of Slovenia reported 68,411 unemployed persons, 53.7% of whom were women. At the end of 2007 the unemployment rate was 7.3%: 8.9% for women and 6.1% for men.

16 SPORTS

Slovenes enjoy sports: hiking, mountain climbing, biking, swimming, rafting and rowing, tennis, horseback riding, fishing—the list goes on. In winter people ski and skate. Almost every child and adult owns a bike, and many ride it to school or the office every day. Skiing has a long history in Slovenia, and is probably the most popular sport. Skis were invented in Slovenia independently at the same time as in Scandinavia and were once a major means of transportation. Today, there are a few hundred thousand recreational skiers, from whose ranks competitive skiers are recruited. They compete internationally in all skiing disciplines: downhill, slalom, jumping, and cross-country, and have won medals at Winter Olympic Games.

Davo Karničar is one of the most renowned alpine skiers in Slovenia. In 2000 he became the first person to ski nonstop down Mount Everest. He has also skied Mont Blanc and Annapurna in the Himalayas. Another famous Slovenian athlete is a marathon swimmer Martin Strel. Strel's records include swimming the entire length of the Danube River in 2000, and swimming the length of the Mississippi River in 2002.

International athletic events held in Slovenia include World Cup downhill skiing in Kranjska Gora and Pohorje, World Cup ski jumping in Planica, and biathlon competitions in Pokljuka.

17 ENTERTAINMENT AND RECREATION

Many schools organize dances for their students on weekends. Proms (*maturitetni plesi*) are traditional in elementary and secondary schools and are organized for graduates every year in the spring. Adults dance on various occasions: weddings, traditional celebrations such as *Martinovanje* (Celebration of New Wine) in the fall, and masquerade balls (*pustovanje*—Mardi gras) in the Carnival season. The polka and waltz are very popular, but Slovenes dance all major known dances from the tango to the macarena.

Slovenes enjoy strolling, often in attractive old town centers, meeting people, chatting with them, and having a coffee or a drink in small coffee shops, or *kavarnas*. Trips on weekends to neighboring mountains are also very popular. Slovenes enjoy walking in the woods and picking mushrooms to prepare them as culinary specialties.

Movies, concerts, and theater performances are enjoyed by many people. In Slovenia, concerts are attended by more people than are soccer games. Young people enjoy listening to various jazz, rock, and techno groups. Although there are several local rock groups, young people listen mostly to popular American, English, and German groups. The Beatles, the Rolling Stones, and Bob Marley are known to every Slovene teenager. Television-viewing has increased in the last decade. Besides Slovene TV programs, Slovenes can also watch Italian, Austrian, English, and American TV shows, including news on CNN.

18 FOLK ART, CRAFTS, AND HOBBIES

Folk arts were mostly associated with crafts and decorating peasants' or, later, workers' homes. Painters often decorated furniture (e.g., chests, bed headboards, and cribs). Painting on glass was popular in the 19th century. Talented but unschooled folk artists often portrayed religious motifs, motifs from popular folk stories, and events from everyday life. Geometric patterns were also popular.

Many traditional Slovene crafts are unique and deserve attention, among them pottery, woodenware, embroidery, and lace-making, and crafts related to candle-making, gingerbread pastries, glass-making, wrought iron, and clock-making, to name a few. As the conditions of life vary from region to region, so do the crafts. With the development of industrial production after World War II, many crafts almost died out. Some were kept alive, and others have been revived in the last few decades to preserve Slovene cultural traditions.

Pottery-making, among the oldest of traditional crafts, has developed in various Slovene regions. In some of them potters are still active today. Potters produce many useful objects: pots, baking and roasting dishes, jars, pitchers and goblets for wine and drinks, whistles, toys, musical instruments, and ceramic tiles for stoves. Beautifully shaped and decorated, they are still popular in Slovenia today. Woodenware (spoons, various kitchen utensils, toothpicks, and sieves) was produced in several centers, the best-known of which, the Ribnica valley, is still active. In the past, Ribnica artisans traveled throughout the Austro-Hungarian Empire, selling their handmade products.

19 SOCIAL PROBLEMS

Alcoholism is an old, persistent, and serious problem among Slovenes of all ages and both genders. It is disturbing that the consumption of alcohol increased by about 25% during the 2000s. Yearly, the average Slovene drinks 11 liters (3 gallons) of hard liquor and 60 liters (16 gallons) of wine. Drug abuse has also increased, especially among young people. The number of smokers has decreased for the past decade, but still a sizable 29% of the population smokes.

Except for the 50 years under Communist rule, unemployment has always been a problem for Slovenes. Usually it was solved by emigration. In the late 19th and 20th centuries, thousands of Slovenes emigrated to industrialized Europe and the United States. Economic emigration continued after World War II. Due to the world recession in the 1980s, many emigrants returned home. With the change in the economic and social systems in Slovenia in the early 1990s, unemployment began to rise, reaching 14% of Slovenes out of work in 1996. In 2008 unemployment had been reduced to 7%, but still remains a major social problem.

Although since the 1990s the standard of living improved, 12% of the population in Slovenia remains below the poverty threshold. The share for young people aged 16–24 amounts to 12.4%: 11.4% for men and 13.6% for women. The unemployment rate is the highest among young people aged 15 to 24.

20 GENDER ISSUES

Today the position of women in Slovenia is not ideal, but it is better than in some other European countries. The majority of young women choose to postpone getting married and having children, focusing instead on education and professional careers. The share of women in vocational colleges and higher education institutions is continually growing, amounting to 58.3% of tertiary students in 2008. Furthermore, in Slovenia the female employment rate is 61.8%, while in the EU it is 57.2%. In the past, prestigious universities clearly favored male applicants. Now this trend is changing. It is true that among doctoral candidates men still prevail, but probably not for long. Although men and women have equal opportunities for education, certain disciplines are particularly popular among women, while others are reserved for men. Thus in 2006, 68.7% of student enrolled in the fields of social science, business, and law were women. Yet, the fields of natural science, mathematics, and computer technology are dominated by men, with women representing only 2.6% of graduates. Similarly, the fields of engineering, manufacturing, and construction are dominated by male students, while women represent the highest share of graduates (80%) in the fields of education, health care, and social work.

According to EU data, since 2000 women took 7.5 million new jobs out of the total of 12 million available. Since 2000 there has been a steady increase in female employment. Male employment increased as well but at a significantly lower rate.

At the same time, even though the majority of women have a university education and are often better educated than men, their employment rate is on average 10 percentage points lower than that of men. Women earn 15% less per hour than men do and it is quite challenging for them to achieve high positions in administration, management, and government. The share of women managers is growing very slowly; in 2008 they accounted only for 33% of managers. In sum, while the Slovenian constitution includes provisions for anti-discrimination laws, women and minorities regularly face inequality and bias. Though laws exist to protect women from harassment and violence, women are still subject to abuse due to the remnants of the patriarchal nature of Slovenian society.

21 BIBLIOGRAPHY

Benderly, Jill, and Evan Kraft. *Independent Slovenia*. New York: St. Martin's Press, 1994.

Discover Slovenia. Ljubljana: Cankarjeva zaloxba, 1995.

Gams, Ivan. "The Republic of Slovenia—Geographical Constants of the New Central European State." *GeoJournal* 24, no. 4 (1991): 331340.

Plut-Pregelj, Leopoldina, and Carole Rogel. *Historical Dictionary of Slovenia*. Lanham, MD: Scarecrow Press, Inc., 1996.

Republic of Slovenia. Government Communication Office. www.ukom.gov.si/eng/slovenia/background-information/waters/ (May 2008).

Republic of Slovenia. Statistical Office of the Republic of Slovenia. www.stat.si/eng/tema_demografsko_prebivalstvo.asp (May 2008).

"Slovenia." *The Europa World Year Book, 1996*. Vol. 2. London: Europa Publications Limited, 1989.

Slovenia. Ljubljana: Izseljeniška matica, 1988.

"Slovenia." *Country Reports*. www.countryreports.org/Slovenia.aspx (May 2008).

"Slovenia Cultural Profile." Visiting Arts Cultural Profile Program, www.culturalprofiles.net/slovenia/Directories/Slovenia_Cultural_Profile/-6800.html (May 2008).

StaniƗh, Stane. *Slovenia*. London: Flint River Press, 1994.

Statisticni Letopis 1995/Statistical Yearbook. Vol. 34. Ljubljana: 1995.

Susel, Rudolf. "Slovenes." In *Harvard Encyclopedia of American Ethnic Groups*. Cambridge, MA: Harvard University Press, 1980

Vode v Sloveniji/Waters of Slovenia. text by Dr. Dušan Plut, photographs by Matevž Lenarčič, (Nazarje): EPSI, 1995.

—revised by A. Golovina Khadka

SPANIARDS

LOCATION: Spain
POPULATION: 40 million
LANGUAGE: Castilian Spanish; Catalan; Galician; Basque
RELIGION: Roman Catholic

¹ INTRODUCTION

Spain, the second-largest nation in Europe (after France) is a country of large geographical and cultural diversity, a land of contrasts and extremes. Its terrain includes Mediterranean beaches and snow-capped Pyrenees, dry plains and coastal rice paddies, volcanic islands and rolling hills. Its people have strong regional identities forged by this diverse geography and by the events of their history. After colonization by the Greeks and Romans and invasion by Germanic tribes, Spain was conquered by the Muslim Moors, who seized control in the 8th century AD and maintained it for nearly 800 years, introducing many cultural innovations. Isabel and Ferdinand, called the Catholic monarchs, conquered Granada, the last city held by the Moslems. They sponsored the discovery of America (1492) by Christopher Columbus. Spain became the greatest world power during Europe's Age of Discovery, reaping tremendous wealth for an empire that extended to virtually all areas of the globe.

After becoming a republic in 1931, the nation was torn apart by a Civil War (1936–1939), the end of which marked the beginning of General Francisco Franco's repressive 36-year regime, until his death in 1975. Since then, Spain has been a parliamentary monarchy under King Juan Carlos, joining the European Community (now European Union) in 1986. For administrative purposes, Spain is divided into seventeen Autonomic Regions (Autonomías), and two autonomous cities (Ceuta and Melilla) on the Northern Moroccan coast; each one of these regions is made of one or several provinces (Provincias). In 1992 Spain hosted the Olympic Games in Barcelona and the International Exposition in Seville.

² LOCATION AND HOMELAND

Spain comprises approximately four-fifths of the Iberian peninsula (with Portugal accounting for the remainder). Its most outstanding geographic feature is its average elevation of 660 m (2,165 ft), the second-highest in Europe after Switzerland. In addition to its portion of the Iberian mainland, Spain also includes the Canary Islands in the Atlantic and the Balearic Islands in the Mediterranean. Altogether, its total area of 504,739 sq km (194,880 sq mi) is slightly less than the combined area of Utah and Nevada. Three-fifths of the Spanish mainland is a broad plateau, or tableland, called the Meseta, located in the center of the country. Spain's other topographical regions are the northern coastal belt, Andalucía in the south, the Mediterranean coastal belt, and Catalonia and the Ebro Valley in the northeast.

Spain has a population of 44,708,964 people (as of January 2006), with a much lower population density than most other European countries. Geographic barriers have helped preserve a keen sense of identity in all six of Spain's major ethnic and local groupings. The Castilians, who live in the central meseta, are the nation's ethnically dominant group, and Castil-

ian Spanish is Spain's national language. The other groups are the Galicians, who inhabit the northwest region of the country; the independent-minded Basques, their neighbors to the east; the Catalans, known for both commerce and in connection with artists such as Pablo Picasso and Salvador Dalí; the Levante, known for its oranges and paella; and the southern region of Andalucía, famous for its flamenco music and Moorish architecture.

³ LANGUAGE

According to the 1978 Constitution, Castilian Spanish is the national language. It is spoken by a majority of Spaniards and used in the schools and courts. Castilian derives from Latin as well as the regional languages which include Catalan and Galician, which is similar to Portuguese. Basque is a pre-Roman language whose origin has not been clearly determined. Together with Castilian, Catalan, Galician, and Basque are co-official languages in these autonomous regions.

NUMBERS

one	un, uno
two	dos
three	tres
four	cuatro
five	cinco
six	seis
seven	siete
eight	ocho
nine	nueve
ten	diez

DAYS OF THE WEEK

Sunday	domingo
Monday	lunes
Tuesday	martes
Wednesday	miércoles
Thursday	jueves
Friday	viernes
Saturday	sábado

⁴ FOLKLORE

Spanish folkloric tradition is very rich and one finds elements with origins as diverse as Celtic, Roman, Germanic, Jewish and Moorish. Spain's ancient musical heritage is diversified with bagpipe music in Galicia and Asturias, *sardanas* in Catalonia, flamenco dancing accompanied by the guitar in Andalucia, or the lively Aragonese dance called the *jota*. Bullfighting is the most widely known Spanish tradition and some historians trace it to a cult of bull worship.

⁵ RELIGION

Historically, Spain has been one of Europe's most staunchly Catholic countries. Currently, about 76% of Spaniards are Roman Catholics and Catholicism is the country's established religion, although about 19% do not declare any religion. While observing baptism and other important Catholic rites many Spaniards do not participate regularly in religious services. Religious Spaniards, like the Catholics in other countries, believe strongly in intercession by the saints and especially by the Virgin Mary. Cofradías, Catholic lay societies devoted to particular saints, play an important role in religious life in many areas of the country. A 1967 law guarantees freedom of reli-

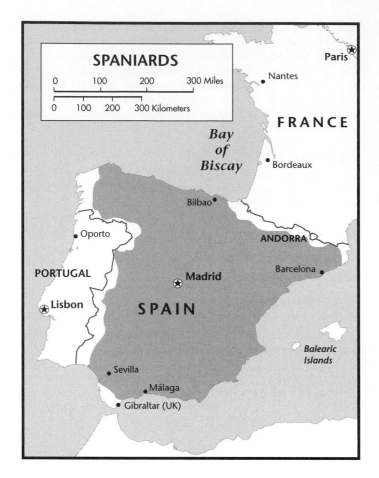

SPANIARDS

0   100   200   300 Miles

0   100   200   300 Kilometers

FRANCE

Paris

Nantes

Bay of Biscay

Bordeaux

Bilbao

ANDORRA

Oporto

Barcelona

PORTUGAL

Madrid

Lisbon

S P A I N

Balearic Islands

Sevilla

Málaga

Gibraltar (UK)

gion. The recent waves of immigration, especially during the 1990s, have led to an increasing number of Muslims—currently there are approximately one million Muslims living in Spain. Islam is today the second largest religion in Spain, after Roman Catholicism.

6 MAJOR HOLIDAYS

In addition to New Year's day and the major holidays of the Christian calendar, Spain's other national holidays include St. Joseph's Day (March 19), the Day of St. Peter and St. Paul (June 29), St. James's Day (July 25), and a National Day on October 12. Every city or town also celebrates its local saint's days with processions, dancing, and bullfights. Joseph, the patron saint of Valencia, is commemorated with fireworks and the burning of wood and cardboard figures of satirical character and monumental size called *fallas*. Bonfires are lit on the Night of Saint John's Day, following ancestral pagan traditions. Pamplona is known for its celebration of San Fermin, when bulls are turned loose in the streets. Barcelona's town fiesta, the Feast of La Merced, is marked by a week of celebrations that include fire-breathing dragons. Madrid's Festival of San Isidro involves three weeks of parties, processions, and bullfights. The celebrations of Holy Week in many cities and towns of Spain include floats with scenes of the Passion and Death of Christ, and likenesses of the Madonna, each one sponsored by a different religious society. Among the civilian holidays are the celebrations of Carnival, that begins a week before Lent; Fiesta del Trabajo, equivalent to Labor Day, on May 1; Hispanidad Day or Día de

la Raza on October 12; Constitution Day on December 6; and each autonomous community celebrates its own Autonomy Day at different dates.

7 RITES OF PASSAGE

Traditionally, besides baptism and marriage, the first Communion and military service were considered rites of passage for Spaniards. The first three of these events are the occasion, in most cases, for big and expensive social gatherings in which the family shows its generosity and economic status. At times, families dig into their savings or borrow money in order to pay for these status shows. Spain abolished compulsory military service in 2001. The armed forces are now all volunteer.

8 INTERPERSONAL RELATIONS

Since the 1960s there has been a steady improvement of the economy mainly due to industrial development and tourism, as well as an evolution in customs. Spaniards frequently travel abroad and have adopted customs from other cultures in the last 30 years or so. Although many people living in rural areas have moved to the city, the present generations have preserved the family house in the village and return there at the time of fiestas and for vacation and remain loyal to their community or pueblo. The economic prosperity enjoyed by Spain has allowed many people to also have a vacation home in the country or an apartment at the beach.

In the cities, office hours begin at 9:00 AM and traditionally include an extended afternoon lunch break beginning at 2:00 PM. Workers then return to their offices from 4:00 to 7:00 PM. The day typically ends with a walk (*paseo*) with friends or family and/or visits to neighborhood bars for a few drinks, appetizers (*tapas*) and conversation. Dinner is often eaten as late as 10:30 PM. In some locales, such as Barcelona, however, the traditional afternoon siesta is no longer the rule. Both blue and white collar workers have a paid month vacation which they usually spend by the sea, the mountains or travelling abroad. Travel to faraway or exotic places has become quite popular due to the affordable travel packages offered by travel agencies. Spaniards are considered to be friendly and outgoing. It is customary to shake hands and in a social setting women usually kiss their friends on both cheeks. Young groups are formed by co-workers, fellow students or people from the same town that go together to discotheques, organize parties and excursions, and date among themselves. The average citizen spends a great deal of time out of the house. There is an active street life; many people live downtown, frequent bars and restaurants, and go to bed late. Spaniards move from place to place less than Americans and, once they get a job, many aspire to return to their birthplace and settle there. Regional loyalties are usually strong and the new autonomous status of the old provinces has strengthened this feeling. It is not unusual to have lifelong friends known since kindergarten.

9 LIVING CONDITIONS

Spain today is a consumer society that relies on credit cards, loves to go shopping, and is interested in cars, gadgets and entertainment. Cars are commonplace and have become a problem in big cities (parking, pollution, congested traffic, car theft). The public transportation system in Spain is excellent and thus many people who work in cities have moved to towns in the periphery that are now part of suburbia. In the 1970s

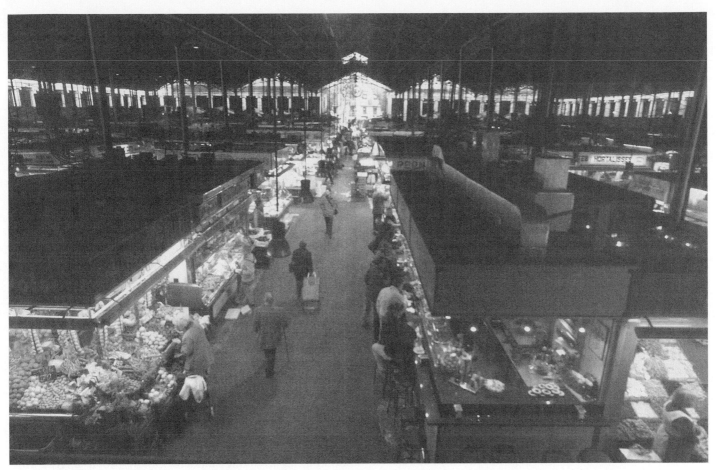

An elevated view of La Boqueria fish and vegetable market off Las Ramblas Boulevard in Barcelona, Spain. Las Ramblas is full of activity day and night. (AP Images/Denis Doyle)

and 1980s there was a building boom and although rents and the price of apartments are high, there is no housing problem.

The average life expectancy in Spain is 78 years. There is a National Health Service and cities have both general practitioners and specialists in all medical fields. Madrid and Barcelona have modern subway systems. Today, Spain has an excellent system of highways. RENFE, Spain's national rail network, provides service between all major cities and is developing a service of ultrarapid trains, called AVE. The first of this kind was the Madrid-Sevilla line started for the 1992 World Expo, followed by the Madrid-Barcelona. Major ports include Barcelona, Tarragona, and Cartagena on the Mediterranean, Algeciras on the Strait of Gibraltar, and Cádiz, La Coruña, Santander, and Bilbao on the Atlantic.

10 FAMILY LIFE

Today's Spanish families are much smaller than in the past and usually have two children. The mother has most of the responsibility for rearing them, while a father's relationship with his children can be formal and remote. In general, when children reach adolescence, their relationship with their families diverges based on gender. A teenage male, while continuing to revere his mother, begins spending much of his time with other young men, while teenage daughters and their mothers grow closer than ever. Even after a daughter is grown and married, her mother continues to play a prominent role in her

life. Yet these traditional patterns are also changing and young men and women are as independent as their economy allows it. Today people live longer lives, have fewer children than before (actually the birth rate is one of the lowest in Europe), and fewer people live in their homes with extended family. Spanish people usually marry within their own social class. Only church marriages were recognized in Spain until 1968, when civil ceremonies were first allowed by law. Divorce has been legal since the 1980s.

11 CLOTHING

Both in town and in the country, Spaniards conform to the average European fashion standards, and boutiques and ready-to-wear shops can be found all over the country. Although many young people wear sports clothes and blue jeans, the average Spaniard pays more attention to personal appearance than his or her American counterpart. Businessmen wear a suit and tie, businesswomen dress fashionably in suits or dresses and high heels. The Spanish fashion industry has greatly developed and some firms, like Zara, Mango, and Camper, are known the world over. Children who attend some private schools wear school uniforms.

12 FOOD

Being a large country with different geographic and climatic areas, Spain also has a wide variety of regional dishes. As in other Mediterranean countries, they make liberal use of olive oil, fresh vegetables, and garlic. Originally from the South, gazpacho is a cold soup made from tomatoes, peppers, cucumbers and onions. Galicia is known for its seafood and stews, Catalonia for its fish casseroles and for cured and smoked meats, such as *butifarra,* a type of sausage. The regional dish *paella,* which originated in Valencia, has become a national delicacy. It consists of a rice-and-saffron base and commonly it can include mostly seafood *(a la marinera),* or several kinds of meats *(mixta).* Spaniards love cured ham *(jamón serrano),* several kinds of sausage, including *chorizo* and *salchichón,* and cheese, especially the variety called *queso manchego.* Popular seafood includes squid, crab, shrimp, fresh sardines and tuna, salmon, trout and dried and salted codfish. Spanish wine and champagne *(cava),* sherry and brandy are excellent and are exported both to Europe and the Americas. There are several areas in the country where different varieties of wine are produced like la Rioja, la Mancha, Rivera del Duero, and several zones in Andalucía. Spanish-made beer is also very good. Both wine and beer are drunk together with *tapas* or at mealtimes. For breakfast Spaniards usually take coffee with sweet rolls, and sometimes hot chocolate with strips of dried dough called *churros.* Fruit juice and a bowl of cereal are becoming popular for breakfast among young people.

Lunch in Spain, eaten between about 2:00 and 4:00 PM is a leisurely meal comparable to dinner in the U.S. *Tapas,* appetizer-like snacks, are served in bars together with drinks, and are usually eaten before lunch and dinner. Popular tapas include seafood such as small fried fish, *boquerones* (pickled fish), *berberechos* (cockles), *calamares* (squid), olives and almonds, in addition to cheese, ham and sausage. A tortilla in Spain is an egg omelette and not, like in Mexico, a flat and thin piece of corn bread.

13 EDUCATION

School is free and compulsory from the ages of 6 to 16, with secondary education or vocational training available for students aged 14 to 16. Private schools, mostly run by the Roman Catholic church and subsidized by the government educate nearly one-third of Spain's children. The adult literacy rate is estimated at 98%. University education is general and students must sit for an entrance examination *(selectividad)* to enter the university system. Spain has 31 state-run universities and an increasing number of private ones. Students receive a diploma after three years of general study and a *Licenciatura* upon completing a program of specialized study lasting two or more years. Centralized public education is administered by the Ministry of Education.

14 CULTURAL HERITAGE

Spain enjoyed a Golden Age of literature in the 16th and 17th centuries. Widely regarded as the first great novel, *Don Quixote* by Miguel de Cervantes eventually became the most widely translated work other than the Bible. In modern times, poet and dramatist Federico Garcia Lorca won international acclaim. Several Spanish authors including playwright José Echegaray, poet Vicente Aleixandre and novelist Camilo José Cela have been recipients of the Nobel Prize. Musically, Spain gave the world the guitar, developed from a four-stringed instrument of the 12th-century Moors. Great Spanish composers have included Isaac Albéniz, Enrique Granados, Manuel

de Falla and Joaquín Rodrigo and virtuoso performers such as Pablo Casals and Andrés Segovia.

Spain is particularly known for its contribution to painting, which can be said to have begun with the prehistoric cave paintings at Altamira. El Greco and Diego Velázquez were among the artists of Spain's Golden Age, and the passionate works of Francisco Goya communicated an intensely personal vision at the end of the 18th and early 19th centuries. In the 20th century innovators in painting include Pablo Picasso, perhaps the single most powerful influence on 20th-century art, as well as Joan Miró, Salvador Dali, Antoni Tapies, Antonio Saura and others. Some of the best architects internationally are Spanish, such as Rafael Moneo, Ricardo Bofill, and Santiago Calatrava. Spanish films are at the avant-garde of the film industry. Movie director Pedro Almodovar is internationally known, as are Spanish actors Penélope Cruz and Javier Bardem.

15 WORK

In the past, agriculture, livestock, and mining were the mainstays of the Spanish economy. Under the regime of General Franco industrial expansion was emphasized, and the bulk of Spanish employment shifted to industry. More recently, the service sector has expanded greatly. Farmers may work on large estates or small farms. Typical crops in the north are potatoes, beans, corn and vegetables; in the central areas, wheat, soybeans, sunflowers, lentils, chickpeas, grapes and other fruits. In the Mediterranean area, vegetables, rice and fruits, especially citrus, are grown. The fishing industry is also a major employer: Spain's fishing fleet is the largest in the world. Seeking higher living standards, many people migrate from rural areas to the cities. Spain's economic prosperity attracts a growing work force (some workers enter the country illegally) coming from economically or politically unstable areas. The new immigrant workers come mainly from North- and Sub-Saharan Africa, Spanish America, and Eastern Europe. The majority work in agriculture and in construction.

Since the early 1970s Spain has developed a prosperous tourism industry. Since the 1970s Spain has been the second most visited country in the world after France. In 2007 almost 60 million foreign visitors arrived in Spain. Parallel to summer tourism the country offers cultural tours, international conventions, and sports meetings as well as cruises. There is ample hotel accommodation and a network of beautiful de-luxe government-sponsored hotels *(paradores)* located in historical buildings.

16 SPORTS

The most popular sport is soccer (called *fútbol*). League matches are played on Saturday and Sunday afternoons from September through May, with tournaments in the summer. Madrid has two teams in the top division, and Barcelona's team, known as Barsa, is world-famous. It forms the basis of a sporting club with over 100,000 members, one of the oldest such clubs in Europe. Membership passes from father to son, and some 80,000 members have permanent seats for matches in the Camp Nou stadium, the largest in Europe and the second largest in the world. The 1992 Olympics were hosted in Barcelona. Basketball and tennis are also gaining popularity as spectator sports. Spanish world class champions today are cyclist Miguel Induráin, winner of the Tour de France five times, golfer Steve

Ballesteros, tennis players Arancha Sánchez Vicario and Conchita Martínez, and motorcycle champions Sito Pons and Angel Nieto. In September 2007 Spain won Europe's Volleyball Championship in Moscow. Participant sports include hunting and fishing, sailing, *fútbol*, cycling, golf, horseback riding, and skiing.

17 ENTERTAINMENT AND RECREATION

The most characteristically Spanish form of entertainment is the bullfight (*fiesta brava),* whose history can be traced back to the Middle Ages. Popular throughout the country, this ritualized fiesta involves grace, courage, and spectacle. Bullfights take place in three stages, called *tercios,* or thirds. First comes the *tercio de capa,* when the matador tests the bull with his cape, becoming familiar with the animal. In the next part, the *tercio de varas,* the picadores and banderilleros weaken the bull with lances and brightly colored darts. Last comes the *tercio de muleta,* the final life-and-death confrontation between matador and bull. In an afternoon of bullfighting, six bulls are usually killed by three different matadors.

However, not all Spaniards today are fond of bullfighting. Many, especially the young, prefer to go to the beach in summer and to the countryside and the mountains for hikes and picnics. In the evenings, they go dancing or have a drink with friends. The mild Spanish climate has fostered an active night life, much of it outdoors in the streets, plazas, taverns, and restaurants. A dinner date may take place as late as 10:00 or 11:00 pm and be followed by a trip to a local club.

According to their cultural level, Spaniards go to concerts, to the theater, and to movies. People of all ages are fond of television, perhaps the main source of entertainment today.

18 FOLK ART, CRAFTS, AND HOBBIES

Spanish handicrafts include lace and leather goods, gloves, basketry, tapestries, carpets, wrought iron, ceramics, and products of gold and silver. Each region has specialties, including leather in Cordoba, lace and carpets in Granada, pearls in the Balearic Islands, jewelry, swords and knives in Toledo and ceramics and pottery. The Spanish government has taken steps to assure that traditional crafts, or *artesanía,* survive against competition from mechanized industry. Spain is also known for its handmade musical instruments, especially guitars.

19 SOCIAL PROBLEMS

Terrorism by separatist groups, particularly the Basque ETA, has plagued Spain in recent years. On 11 March 2004 Spain suffered its most horrific terrorist attack: 191 people were killed and 1,400 were injured in bombings at Madrid's railway station; al Qaeda was responsible. A few days later, Prime Minister José María Aznar's Popular Party experienced a stinging defeat, and José Luis Rodríguez Zapatero of the Socialist Party became the new prime minister. After four decades of violence, responsible for more than 800 deaths and for terrorizing Spanish society with its bombings, ETA announced a permanent ceasefire on 24 March 2006; however, in June 2007, it renounced the ceasefire and vowed to begin a new offensive.

Another growing social problem is caused by illegal immigration (see **Section 15 Work**). Finally, like the rest of the developed countries, Spain has an illicit drug problem and a high rate of crime in the big cities.

20 GENDER ISSUES

Women are playing ever-increasingly important roles in Spanish society. Approximately 15% of Spain's armed forces are women. For the first time, Spain's prime minister José Luis Rodríguez Zapatero, upon being reelected in 2008, announced a 17-member cabinet that had more women than men. One of them was Spain's first female defense minister, Carme Chacón, who was also seven months pregnant when she was appointed. Many other women hold municipal and government posts as councilwoman, mayor, university professor, director general. Several Spanish women are ministers of the crown, manage businesses, and a large percentage go to the university.

Evidence of the secular nature of contemporary Spain can be seen in the widespread support for the legalization of same-sex marriage in Spain. In June 2005 a bill was passed to allow gay marriage, making Spain the third country in the European Union to allow same-sex couples to marry.

21 BIBLIOGRAPHY

Ames, Helen Wattley. *Spain is Different.* Intercultural Press, 1992.

Bennett, A. Linda, ed. *Encyclopedia of World Cultures (Europe).* Boston: G. K. Hall, 1992.

Conversi, Daniele, *The Basques, the Catalans, and Spain.* Reno: University of Nevada Press, 1997.

Hooper, John. *The New Spaniards.* Suffolk, England: Penguin, 1995.

Illustrated Encyclopedia of Mankind. London: Marshall Cavendish, 1978.

Leahy, Philippa. *Discovering Spain.* New York: Crestwood House, 1993.

Moss, Joyce, and George Wilson. *Peoples of the World: Western Europeans.* Detroit: Gale Research, 1993.

Steinberg, Rolf, ed. *Continental Europe.* Insight Guides. Singapore: APA Publications, 1989.

Tremlett, Giles. *Ghosts of Spain.* New York: Walker and Company, 2008.

—revised by S. Garcia Castañeda

SWEDES

LOCATION: Sweden
POPULATION: 9.2 million
LANGUAGE: Swedish; Sami; Finnish
RELIGION: Church of Sweden (Lutheran)

¹ INTRODUCTION

The Kingdom of Sweden is part of the Scandinavian Peninsula in northwestern Europe. With an abundance of natural resources, it is a leading industrial nation, and its people enjoy one of the highest living standards in the world. The first written reference to Sweden is by the Roman historian Tacitus, who called the Swedes "mighty in ships and arms" in AD 98. Sweden represented a major European power during the 17th century, with its territories including Finland (1000–1805), parts of Germany, the Baltic States, and even an American colony. Christianity was introduced from the 9th through the 11th centuries. An age of territorial expansion during the 1500s and 1600s ended in defeat by Russia in 1709 and the loss of most overseas possessions by the early 19th century. Norway was united with Sweden from 1814 to 1905.

In the 20th century Sweden remained neutral in both world wars, serving as a haven for refugees in World War II. The country joined the United Nations in 1946, although it did not join the North Atlantic Treaty Alliance (NATO). In 1953 it joined with Denmark, Norway, and Iceland (and, later, Finland), to form the Nordic Council. Carl XVI Gustaf has been king since 1973, though his sphere of power is limited to only ceremonial practices today. In 1986 the nation was shaken by the assassination of Prime Minister Olof Palme, a crime that has never been satisfactorily solved. In 1991, Sweden applied for membership in the European Community, although many in the nation remained opposed to this move. However, Sweden became a member of the European Union in 1995.

² LOCATION AND HOMELAND

Sweden is the largest country in Scandinavia and the fourth largest in Europe. With a total area of 449,966 sq km (173,732 sq mi), it is close in size to the state of California and is one of the more sparsely populated countries, with a mere 21 persons per sq km (55 persons per sq mi). It is bounded by Norway on the north and west, Denmark on the southeast, and the Gulf of Bothnia, the Baltic Sea, and Finland on the east. One-seventh of Sweden lies within the Arctic Circle, the "land of the midnight sun," where the sun never really sets for three months during the summer, beginning with the Summer Solstice on June 20. The country has about 100,000 lakes and many rivers, and more than half its terrain is forested. Most of its 9.2 million people live in the south of the country.

The Swedes are a Scandinavian people descended from Germanic tribes who emigrated to the region in ancient times. Ethnic minorities include about 200,000–300,000 Swedish Finns living in the northeastern section of the country and approximately 35,000 Sami, a traditionally nomadic group of reindeer herders who live in northern portions of Sweden, Norway, Finland, and Russia. Since World War II, Sweden has also accepted immigrant workers from Greece, Germany, Turkey, Great Britain, Poland, Italy, and the former Yugoslavia, as well as political refugees, mostly from the Middle East, Asia, and the Latin American countries of Chile and Argentina.

³ LANGUAGE

Swedish is a Germanic language closely related to Norwegian and Danish. There are also similarities between Swedish and English, and most Swedes speak English as a second language. The Sami have their own language, and there is also a large Finnish-speaking population in the country.

EVERYDAY IDIOMS INCLUDE

Hello	Hej/ Hej då
Goodbye	Adjö
Yes/ No	Ja/ Nej
Please	Var Snall Och or Varsagod
Thank you	Tack
Breakfast	Frukost
Lunch	Lunch
Dinner	Middag
One	Ett
Two	Två
Three	Tre
Four	Fyra
Five	Fem
Six	Sex
Seven	Sju
Eight	Atta
Nine	Nio
Ten	Tio

Popular boys' names which are distinctly Swedish are Anders, Hans, Gunnar, Ake, and Lars, while girls are commonly named Margareta, Karin, Birgitta, Kerstin, and Ingrid.

⁴ FOLKLORE

Rural dwellers have traditionally believed in the existence of a variety of supernatural beings. Every province of Sweden has its own customs and local lore. For example, there is a legend about the difference between the lush, fertile land of Skåne in the south and the neighboring northern province of Småland, which is rocky and barren. While God was making Skåne so beautiful, the devil supposedly sneaked past him and turned Småland into a harsh and desolate place. It was too late for God to change the land, but he was able to create its people, and he made them tough and resourceful enough to survive successfully in their difficult environment.

⁵ RELIGION

Until 2000, Sweden's state religion was Lutheranism, and about 76% of the population belongs to the Church of Sweden, the country's Lutheran church. In the past, all Swedes automatically became members of the church at birth but had the right to withdraw from it. Church membership until 2000 was only achieved through baptism, but then Sweden enacted reforms of church and state. Although most people mark major life-cycle events such as baptism, confirmation, marriage, and burial within the church, the majority do not attend services regularly. Of the 87% Lutheran population, only 2% of these Swedes attend church. Minority religions include Roman Catholicism, the Pentecostal church, the Mission Covenant Church of Sweden, and the Greek Orthodox Church. In addition, there is a solid concentration of Jews in Sweden, as well as a tremendous growth in the Islamic population, which has spurred much racial tension.

6 MAJOR HOLIDAYS

Sweden's legal holidays are New Year's Day, Epiphany (January 6), Good Friday, Easter Monday, May Day (May 1), Ascension Day (May 31), Whit Monday, Midsummer (June 23), All Souls' Day (November 3), and Christmas. At midnight on New Year's Eve, ship horns and factory sirens usher in the New Year and, following a century-old tradition, Alfred Tennyson's poem, "Ring Out, Wild Bells," is read at an open-air museum in Stockholm and broadcast throughout the country. The feast of St. Knut on January 13 is the time when Christmas decorations are taken down. Shrove Tuesday, the last day before Lent begins, is traditionally observed by eating a bun filled with cream and marzipan. As Easter approaches, Swedes decorate twigs with colored feathers and place them in water to sprout new leaves in time for the holiday. Young boys and girls dress up as the Easter Hag and visit their neighbors, from whom they receive small gifts similar to the Halloween festivities observed in the United States.

Among the most important secular holidays, *Valborgsmassoafton,* observed on April 30, celebrates the coming of spring with bonfires and other festivities which are performed both publicly and privately. The Swedish flag is honored on June 6, a day on which all cities and towns fly flags and hold ceremonies in the flag's commemoration. Finally, the Summer Solstice is observed on June 21 and June 22 through the raising of the Maypole, around which celebrants dance, sing traditional songs, and eat.

7 RITES OF PASSAGE

Sweden is a modern, industrialized, Christian country. Hence, many of the rites of passage that young people undergo are religious rituals, such as baptism, first Communion, confirmation, and marriage. In addition, a student's progress through the education system is marked by many families with graduation parties.

8 INTERPERSONAL RELATIONS

The most common Swedish greeting is *hej!,* to which the response is usually *hej, hej!* The usual farewell is *hej då!* A handshake with either a *hej* or the more formal *god dag* is used between businessmen and acquaintances. Greetings among family depends on how close the family is, and Swedes, in contrast to Americans, are much more reserved in their interpersonal relationships. Therefore, they are not very demonstrative in their gestures, and refrain from touching others when communicating, as it is considered poor manners.

A very common practice among Swedes, when they are invited to another's home, is to bring flowers which are of an odd number (usually a single flower, or three or five). When hosting a group of less than 12 guests, the Swedish host demonstrates his or her etiquette in the art of toasting, which is performed according to a rigid, complex set of rules. For example, the host will lift his glass close to the third button of his shirt as he separately acknowledges each guest with a glance and a nod of the head; the glass is then sipped and returned to the third button position.

9 LIVING CONDITIONS

Except for brick-and-clay farm houses in southern Sweden, most dwellings were traditionally built of wood. In the past, the style of rural dwellings varied by region, with five main types. Contemporary housing is basically similar throughout the country, and it features building materials and styles similar to those in the United States. Many empty country houses are now used as summer homes.

Sweden's extensive system of social insurance pays for medical and dental care. The nation's infant mortality rate—2.75 deaths for every 1,000 live births—is one of the lowest in the world. Maternity leave with 80% pay begins from 60 days before the expected birth of a child until 6 weeks after birth, and lasts until the child is 18 months old. This legitimate leave of absence is termed "parental leave," as it can be chosen by either mother or father. The average life expectancy in Sweden is 78.5 years for men and 83 years for women.

Sweden has over 96,000 km (60,000 mi) of highways and more than 11,200 km (7,000 mi) of nationalized railroads. In 1967 the country changed from the left-hand traffic common to most European countries to a right-hand system like the one in the United States. Shipping has always been important to Sweden; its three largest ports are Göteborg, Stockholm, and

Sofia Lillemae (l) and Maja Hansson pick flowers in preparation for the annual Midsummer holidays in Hassleholm, Sweden. Swedes traditionally celebrate Midsummer with dancing and feasting. (AP Images/Pressens Bild/Patric Berg)

Malmö. Sweden operates the Scandinavian Airlines System (SAS) jointly with Denmark and Norway.

10 FAMILY LIFE

Most Swedish families have only one or two children. During the past 30 years, it has become so common for unmarried couples to live together that the people have coined a name for this arrangement: *sambo* (*sam* means together; *bo* means live). In 1988 legislation extended the legal rights of persons involved in such relationships, making them almost the legal equal of spouses. Nevertheless, *sambo* relationships often lead to marriage. Sweden's divorce rate has doubled since 1960. The older Swedish generation views the husband's role as that of the breadwinner, and still relegates the wife to domestic tasks within the home. However, as in the United States, the younger Swedish generation considers marriage more as a partnership with shared responsibilities extended to the children family members, since both spouses work. Swedish women are guaranteed equal rights under the law, and the vast majority work outside the home. Because Swedish women today feel an acute need to be in the work force, and excellent day care services are available, about 75% of mothers with preschoolers work. Four times as many women hold upper-level government positions than U.S. women, jobs which include parliament and the governing cabinet. Almost half of all working women have children under the age of 16.

11 CLOTHING

Modern, Western-style clothing is worn in Sweden and, as in the United States, the Swedes' casual wear is typically slacks, shorts, and T-shirts. Likewise, suits are worn by both men and women in the typical place of business, and tuxedos and evening gowns appear at formal affairs. All clothing is costly in comparison to the standard prices of the United States. Swedish folk costumes, which were introduced as late as the 1890s as a means of glorifying the cultural richness of the nation, are worn for special festivals such as Midsummer's Eve, and consist of white blouses, vests, and long dark skirts (often worn with aprons) for women and white shirts, vests, dark knee-length breeches, and white hose for men. Only a small segment of the population even owns such a costume, and the costumes vary dramatically from region to region.

12 FOOD

Swedes typically wake up to a breakfast of hard or soft ryebread smothered with butter and cheese, sandwich meat, or *filmjolk,* which is similar to yogurt, with a soup-like consistency. Because lunches interrupt the work day, they are light in Sweden. In contrast, dinners almost always abound in fish, sausage, and meat, though the latter is less often purchased because of its high cost. This main course is typically accompanied by potatoes and vegetables—the most common being peas, carrots, or salad. While the Swedish main meal was traditionally earlier in the day as a result of the wife's confinement within the home, dinner is now largely extended to the hours of early evening.

The Swedes savor rich sauces in their food, which is heavily influenced by the French. The Swedish name for the open-faced sandwich meal universal throughout Scandinavia—*smörgåsbord*—is the one by which this buffet meal is known in the United States. In Sweden it commonly includes herring, smoked eel, roast beef, tongue, jellied fish, boiled potatoes, and cheese. Favorite hot dishes include meatballs *(köttbulla)* served with lingonberry jam *(lingonsylt); pitty panna,* fried meat, potatoes, and egg; and *Janssons frestelse* ("Jansson's temptation"), a layered potato dish with onions and cream, topped with anchovies. The Swedes love fish, especially salmon, which is typically smoked, marinated, or cured with dill and salt. Fresh fruits and vegetables, including all kinds of berries, are also very popular. Favorite beverages include milk, *lättöl* (a type of beer with almost no alcohol), and strong coffee.

13 EDUCATION

Sweden has a literacy rate of virtually 100%. School is mandatory between the ages of 7 and 16. During the first nine years, students attend a "comprehensive school," where they study a variety of subjects. Grades one through three are called the junior grades, four through six the middle grades, and seven through nine the senior grades. There is a three-week Christmas vacation and a summer vacation that extends from early June to late August. Free hot lunches are provided to all students. English is taught as a second language from the third grade on, and crafts such as woodworking and textile-making are also part of the curriculum. While immigrant children receive education in their own language a few hours each day, there are also special English classes for these students from countries such as Germany and Turkey.

Beginning in the seventh year, instruction varies based on students' interests and abilities; about 30% choose the college-preparatory curriculum, while others opt for more vocationally-oriented training. Swedes maintain the Scandinavian tradition of giving ceremonial white hats to secondary school graduates. Sweden has a number of universities, including those in Stockholm, Linköping, Göteborg, Uppsala, Lund, Umeå, Växjö, Karlstad, Luleå, and Örebro.

14 CULTURAL HERITAGE

The arts receive strong support from the government in Sweden. The Swedish National Council for Cultural Affairs approves subsidies for theater, dance and musical groups, literature, public libraries, museums, and other cultural institutions. It also helps inaugurate new artistic activities and educate the public about the arts. County councils, under the authority of the national council, oversee regional activities. Performers in Sweden enjoy a level of job security unknown in most other countries, including the United States. They are hired by the year, drawing a regular salary and receiving pension, insurance, and vacation benefits. However, even the most successful Swedish performers do not receive the astronomical levels of pay accorded to "superstars" in some other countries, particularly the US.

Sweden's best known writer was August Strindberg, who wrote novels, short stories, essays, and plays that influenced the course of modern drama. Selma Lagerlof, the first Swede to win the Nobel Prize, is known for both her novels and her children's classic *The Wonderful Adventures of Nils.* Another world-famous Swedish children's author is Astrid Lindgren, creator of the Pippi Longstocking books. In the visual arts, prominent Swedish names include the sculptor Carl Milles and the jewelry maker Sigurd Persson. The Swedish film industry has gained a worldwide audience for its films, notably those of its world-famous director Ingmar Bergman. Famous Swedish film stars include Ingrid Bergman and Max von Sydow. The creator of the Nobel prize itself was a Swede—Alfred Nobel, the inventor of dynamite.

15 WORK

Sweden has achieved an enviable standard of living under a mixed system of high-tech capitalism and extensive welfare benefits. Sweden's labor force is divided almost equally between men and women. About 74% are employed in the service sector, 24% in industry, and 2% in agriculture. Unemployment in Sweden has been low compared to other European countries (under 4.5% in 2007). About 85% of the Swedish work force is unionized. The minimum age for employment is 16; persons under that age may be hired during school vacations for easy jobs that last five days or less.

Though Sweden has some of the highest taxes in the world, it generously pays a pension which is two-thirds of the worker's pre-retirement salary. Swedish retirees enjoy other benefits, such as instant health insurance and price reductions on prescriptions.

In September 2003 Swedish voters turned down entry into the European Union's euro system, concerned about the impact on the economy and sovereignty.

16 SPORTS

There are about 40,000 sports clubs throughout Sweden. The most popular sport is soccer (called *fotboll).* Favorite winter sports include cross-country and downhill skiing and long-distance skating. Popular water sports include swimming, rowing, and sailing, and many Swedes also enjoy cycling. Major annual events for amateur athletes include the Vasa cross-country ski race, the Vättern Circuit two-day bicycle race, the Vansbro swim meet, and the Lidingö cross-country running race. In 1987, the Swedish tennis team won the Davis Cup for the fourth time. Outstanding Swedish athletes include alpine skier Ingemar Stenmark, tennis great Björn Borg, and golfer Annika Sörenstam.

17 ENTERTAINMENT AND RECREATION

Many of the Swedes' leisure hours are devoted to outdoor activities that enable them to enjoy their country's beautiful natural scenery. It is common to retreat to rural areas during weekends and vacations. The summer cottage by the lake is a common sight; altogether there are about 600,000 summer homes in Sweden, many in abandoned rural areas. The islands near Stockholm are especially popular sites for these retreats. In recent years, it has also become popular to take winter vacations in Mediterranean resort areas. Walking is a favorite pastime in Sweden, and marked walking paths can be found throughout the country. Sailing on Sweden's rivers and lakes is also very popular.

[18] FOLK ART, CRAFTS, AND HOBBIES

The Swedes are known for their high-quality handicrafts. Handmade utensils have been produced since the beginning of the 19th century; the primary textiles are wool and flax. Swedish crystal and glass—of which 90% is produced at the Orrefors factory—are famous worldwide and half of the country's production is exported, much of it to the United States. The Dalarna region is known for its distinctive wooden horses with their brightly painted designs. Folk influences are evident in modern Swedish ceramics, woodwork, textiles, furniture, silver, and other products.

[19] SOCIAL PROBLEMS

Like several neighboring countries, Sweden has a high rate of alcoholism, and organizations devoted to helping people deal with this problem have around 6,000 local chapters altogether. Another—and possibly related—problem is absenteeism from work, which rose sharply in the late 1980s. One of out every four workers called in sick on any given day. There has also been some discontent with the high taxes necessary to fund Sweden's extensive network of social services.

A relatively new and sweeping social problem in Sweden is that of racism. A neo-Nazi group similar to the "skinheads" of the United States is the "VAM" ("Vit Ariskt Motstand"—or, "White Aryan Resistance"), which in the 1990s experienced an increase in membership. In the 2000s the Svensk Hednisk Front (Swedish Heathen Front—SHF) is an emerging Nazi organization of increasing importance.

[20] GENDER ISSUES

Gender equality issues in Sweden are dealt with at the Ministry for Integration and Gender Equality, where the Division for Gender Equality has among its tasks the processing of gender equality matters. Governmental policy is to ensure that "women and men shall have equal power to shape society and their own lives." Women and men are to enjoy the same opportunities, rights, and obligations in all spheres of life. The government promotes equal pay between women and men, an equal distribution of unpaid care and household work, and an end to men's violence against women. Sweden has done much to accomplish these goals.

Sweden is considered to be one of the most liberal countries in Europe and indeed the world when it comes to laws pertaining to homosexuality. A 2006 European Union member poll showed 71% of Swedes support same-sex marriage, although as of early 2008 it was not legal in Sweden. However, civil unions are considered to be marriage according to Swedish law. Homosexuality was legalized in 1944. In 1987 a law against sex in gay saunas and prostitution was created to prohibit the spread of HIV, but this was repealed in 2004. Homosexuals are not banned from military service. The Swedish constitution bans discrimination on the grounds of sexual orientation.

[21] BIBLIOGRAPHY

Barton, H. Arnold. *The Old Country and the New: Essays on Swedes and America*. Carbondale: Southern Illinois University Press, 2007.

Gall, Timothy, and Susan Gall, ed. *Junior Worldmark Encyclopedia of the Nations*. Detroit: UXL, 1996.

Gerholm, Lena. "Swedes." In *Encyclopedia of World Cultures* (*Europe*). Boston: G. K. Hall, 1992.

Hintz, Martin. *Sweden. Enchantment of the World Series*. Chicago: Children's Press, 1994.

Illustrated Encyclopedia of Mankind. London: Marshall Cavendish, 1978.

Keeler, Stephen, and Chris Fairclough. *We Live in Sweden*. New York: Bookwright Press, 1985.

Scobbie, Irene. *Historical Dictionary of Sweden*. 2nd ed. Lanham, MD : Scarecrow Press, 2006.

Svallfors, Stefan, ed. *The Political Sociology of the Welfare State: Institutions, Social Cleavages, and Orientations*. Stanford, CA: Stanford University Press, 2007.

Sweden in Pictures. Minneapolis: Lerner Publications, 1990

Thompson, Wayne C. *Nordic, Central, and Southeastern Europe, 2007*. Harpers Ferry, WV: Stryker-Post Publications, 2007.

—revised by J. Hobby.

SWISS

LOCATION: Switzerland
POPULATION: About 7.5 million
LANGUAGE: Schwyzerdütsch (Swiss-German dialect), French, Italian, Romansh, English
RELIGION: Protestant; Roman Catholic

¹ INTRODUCTION

Switzerland is located at a crossroads in Europe and is known for its stability, multiculturalism, neutrality, and prosperity. The country's central location in the heart of Europe and the right mix of features has helped to link Switzerland with the rest of Europe in many ways—culturally, economically and politically. Although a small country, it is the meeting point for three of Europe's major cultures—German, French and Italian. This, along with a unique history and political institutions, contributes to the belief that Switzerland is a special case (*Sonderfall*), incomparably different from other countries.

The area that is now Switzerland was inhabited as early as 40,000 BC as shown by archeological evidence. Various Celtic tribes—among them the Helvetii and Rhaetians—settled in the region around 1,000 BC. For almost 500 years—from 58 BC to AD 400—Switzerland was part of the Roman Empire. Starting in AD 260 a number of Germanic tribes—the Alemanii and the Burgundians being the most important—started to make their way onto the scene.

The development of modern Switzerland can be traced back to a confederation of several Alpine valley communities and a number of city-states in the Middle Ages. These original communities have given their names to the present cantons (provinces) of Switzerland of which there are 26 (20 full cantons and 6 half cantons). The official (Latin) name of the country—*Confoederatio Helvetica*—bears witness to its old confederate past and can be seen in the "CH" decal on cars in Switzerland. Swiss history is unique in Europe since the Swiss never had a monarchy. Instead, the different members of the confederation governed political affairs. Today, the Swiss political system is federal, with many powers left in the hands of the cantons.

Switzerland's present boundaries were fixed and its neutrality guaranteed in 1815 at the Congress of Vienna. In the 20th century, its neutral stance kept it out of both world wars and dictated its refusal to join the United Nations, although it houses such UN agencies as the International Labor Organization and the World Health Organization (as well as the International Red Cross).

The Swiss live in a democracy where the average citizen can have greater influence than in other countries. This is accomplished through two institutions—the referendum and the initiative. A referendum allows the Swiss electorate to vote on laws passed by parliament, constitutional amendments and important international treaties. An initiative lets Swiss citizens make suggestions for either constitutional amendments at the national level or regular laws at the local level. A truly fascinating example of direct democracy is also found in parts of Switzerland—the *Landsgemeinde* (People's Assembly) where the electorate gathers under the open sky on a Sunday in spring to pass laws and elect of officials with a show of hands.

² LOCATION AND HOMELAND

One of Europe's smallest countries in terms of both territory and population, Switzerland is roughly equal in size to the combined area of Massachusetts, Connecticut, and Rhode Island. It is also a place of contrasts—of plains, lakes, rivers and mountains. Still when one thinks of Switzerland, one thinks of mountains, since approximately 70% of the country is covered by them.

Switzerland's three natural geographic regions are: the Jura Mountains in the northwest, making up 10% of the Swiss landscape; the Alps—which cover three-fifths of the country—in the south; and the central plateau, or Mittelland, which comprises 30% of the country. This central plateau contains all larger towns and most major cities, the most highly developed agriculture area and three-fourths of the total population of Switzerland. This last condition leads to a very high population density since three-fourths of the population is forced to live in only one-third of the country's entire geographical space.

The Alps have inspired poets and artists across Europe. It was this attraction of the mountains for sport and nature enthusiasts which originated the modern tourism industry. Sometimes called "a nation of hotel keepers," the Swiss welcome some 20 million international visitors annually, many of whom continue to be drawn to the Alps. The most famous of the Swiss Alps is the Matterhorn, rising 4,478 m (14,692 ft) above sea level. Two of Europe's principal rivers, the Rhine and the Rhone, have their sources in the Swiss Alps.

A unique feature of the Alpine climate is the *föhn,* a special Alpine wind. This occurs mainly in spring and autumn, when a depression north of the Alps draws air from south of the Alps. This air falls into the northern valleys as warm, dry and cloud-free wind. Its effects are many: average temperatures rise, fruit ripens faster, and a number of ailments occur in humans, such as migraine attacks, blood circulation problems, and mood swings.

Switzerland's population of almost 7.5 million people is very diverse, being composed of four major ethnic groups: German (65%), French (18%), Italian (10%), and Romansh (1%). There are also over a million foreigners, accounting for about 22% of the total population. The country is becoming increasingly urban, with significant internal migration from the mountains to the cities of the plateau. This is particularly intense in the five largest Swiss cities—Basel, Bern, Geneva, Lausanne, and Zurich—which combined account for one-third of the total Swiss population.

³ LANGUAGE

Switzerland has four national languages. In 2008 speakers of *Schwyzerdütsch,* a Swiss-German dialect, accounted for about two-thirds of all Switzerland's people. Another 20% spoke French, about 6.5%—mostly in the Ticino region—spoke Italian, and less than 1% spoke Romansh, a Rhaeto-Roman dialect that is found mostly in the Grison region. The remainder of the population consisted of foreigners who spoke the languages of their homelands, particularly Albanian, Portuguese, Spanish, and Serbo-Croatian. Most native Swiss are bi- or multi-lingual and many speak English. While *Schwyzerdütsch is* clearly distinct from ordinary German (which is used in formal contexts such as books and newspapers), the French and Italian spoken by the Swiss are basically similar to those languages as spoken in their home countries.

the Swiss to reevaluate their past in the hope of helping them think more about the present.

The *Rütli Schwur* (Rutli Oath) is another powerful symbol in Swiss folklore. This oath refers to an agreement made on the Rutli meadow between several Swiss valley communities in the Middle Ages to create an alliance for common protection and defense. Popular opinion sees this oath as the founding of Swiss freedom and democracy—in other words, the founding of Switzerland itself. Historians question whether or not this event ever took place. Still, the story of the *Rütli Schwur* is a powerful illustration of the role that national myths can have. For example, during World War II when Switzerland was surrounded by Nazi Germany, the Swiss army commander, General Guisan, gathered his officers on the Rutli meadow as a symbol of Swiss determination to fight for their freedom. People today still remember this act by General Guisan as a sign of the special position of the Rutli legend in Switzerland.

The traditional folk beliefs of German-speaking Alpine dwellers invested natural forces such as avalanches, landslides, and storms with malevolent qualities. More important has been the key position that the mountains have played in shaping the beliefs the Swiss have about themselves. For a long time the Swiss saw themselves linked to the mountains, with special qualities that made them different from other people. The mountains were associated with simple living, self-reliance and innocence. An example of this is the story of Heidi, written by Swiss author Johanna Spyri. Heidi and her grandfather represent the simple and wholesome qualities the Swiss saw in themselves.

5 RELIGION

At the 2000 Swiss Census, about 42% of the population was Roman Catholic and 35% Protestant. The predominantly German-speaking cantons are divided nearly equally between the two religious affiliations. Catholicism is the predominant religion of the French-speaking cantons and the Italian-speaking canton of Ticino is mostly Catholic as well. Religious tensions have historically been a source of unrest and even today Switzerland's religious division between Protestant and Catholic remains significant. This can be seen in all aspects of life. There are both Protestant and Catholic youth organizations, labor unions, and women's associations and the Swiss political parties have been shaped by the religious differences of the past.

In the history of Swiss Protestantism, two figures stand out—Huldrych Zwingli and Jean Calvin. Zwingli began the Reformation in Switzerland from his pulpit in Zurich's main cathedral. He helped spread the new faith throughout Switzerland and debated Martin Luther on a number of issues in a famous debate that almost turned violent. Calvin is responsible for bringing Geneva into the Protestant fold. Calvin formalized Protestant thought into a more systematic doctrine and governed Geneva with a strict moral code. Other parts of Switzerland maintained close ties with the Catholic Church, which can still be seen today in the Swiss Guards at the Vatican. They once protected the Pope but now serve as an honor guard with their colorful uniforms and shiny helmets.

6 MAJOR HOLIDAYS

Switzerland's legal holidays are New Year's Day, Good Friday, Easter Monday, Ascension Day, Whitmonday, *Bundesfeier* (which resembles the American Fourth of July) on August 1,

Schwyzerdütsch is itself not a single language, but a term used to describe the various German dialects spoken in Switzerland. In other words, the dialects spoken in Basel, Bern, and Zurich, while mutually intelligible, have their differences. In contrast, people in a couple of places in Switzerland speak a dialect that most other Swiss-German speakers have difficulty understanding. Likewise, Romansh consists of five major dialects. Attempts have been made to preserve Romansh, while other efforts to create a single Romansh language from the five dialects have met with resistance. The balance of languages in Switzerland is reflected in its political system, with each canton bearing the responsibility of language policy.

4 FOLKLORE

The national hero of Swiss legend is William Tell, supposed to have lived in the early 1300s shortly after the Habsburgs came to dominate Switzerland. Forced to shoot an apple off his son's head as punishment for insubordination toward the Habsburg governor Gessler, Tell later escaped from his Austrian captors to slay the foreign tyrant. This legend, which inspired popular ballads during the 15th century, provided the subject for a drama by the German poet Friedrich Schiller in 1804 and has been made even more famous by the overture to Gioachino Rossini's opera *Guillaume Tell*. In 1970 Swiss author and social critic Max Frisch wrote an essay entitled, "William Tell for the School." In this essay Frisch questioned the truth of this legend and portrayed a less heroic Tell. Frisch's purpose was to force and Christmas. The German-speaking Swiss mark the seasons and many religious days with festivals, which vary with each canton (province) and commune (locality). Altogether, over 100 different festivals—pagan, Christian, and patriotic—are celebrated in Switzerland. The most famous celebration is Basel's *Fastnacht,* or carnival, marking the final days before Lent (and similar to the Mardi Gras festivities held in New Orleans). For three days, masked and costumed revelers parade through streets filled with decorative floats to the strains of pipe-and-drum bands.

⁷ RITES OF PASSAGE

In Switzerland many rites of passage are similar to those found in the United States. These include religious rituals such as baptism and first communion and events in the family such as births, deaths, and marriages.

For men, one of the most important aspects of life in Switzerland is military service. The Swiss army is a militia army, which means there is no professional military force. Instead, all male citizens serve a compulsory period of military duty throughout their lives, keeping all of their equipment, including weapon and ammunition, at home. Until recently, conscientious objectors were subject to imprisonment. Nevertheless, military service is required of all Swiss males between the ages of 20 and 50. Military training is conducted regularly throughout one's lifetime until age 50. First is a four-month basic training program. Then between the ages of 21 and 32 there are eight refresher courses which are each three weeks long. Between the ages of 33 and 42, three additional training courses of two weeks each are required. Finally after age 42, two more weeks are necessary before the age of 50. This adds up to one full year of service. Swiss military duty is a rite of passage because serving in the army is seen as a sign of true citizenship. An individual is seen as a full citizen through defending the country. The Swiss army is also called a citizen army to reflect the ideal that the Swiss citizens protect and defend their rights and freedom themselves. This equation of military service with the values of citizenship has been challenged by both women and the younger generation. Women are not required to perform military service and many women criticize their exclusion from the army and the consequences this has for them in society. Many younger Swiss citizens are also questioning the need of mandatory military service for everyone—they see it no longer as a patriotic obligation but as a nuisance and inconvenience.

⁸ INTERPERSONAL RELATIONS

With its combination of ethnic, linguistic, and religious affiliations, Switzerland has historically fostered tolerance, politeness, independence, and reserve in its people. Relationships between the Swiss reflect these differences of language, religion and region. In a country with four languages, communication between people can lead to problems and a number of stereotypes exist between the various regions. An example of this is the tension between the French- and German-speaking parts of Switzerland, referred to as the *röstigraben*—or hash brown chasm. The German-speaking Swiss see themselves as hard working and efficient, while they see their French-speaking countrymen as easy-going, friendly, and open. The French-speaking Swiss see the German speakers as arrogant, pushy, and too serious. According to recent polls, the German speak-

ers tend to like the French speakers more than the other way around.

In a social setting between individuals, a handshake is normal between men and women unless you are familiar with the person. In this case, a triple-kiss on the cheeks—first one kiss on one cheek, then the next cheek and finally back to the first cheek—is appropriate between men and women and among women. Men continue to shake hands. Another feature of social interaction that may seem unfamiliar to many Americans is the use of a person's name and formal speech. In Switzerland it is customary to greet and say goodbye to a person using their name. This makes it important to pay attention when meeting people for the first time, since you will be expected to remember names. Formal speech refers to the use of special forms of addressing people in the languages spoken in Switzerland (e.g. in German: *Sie* versus *Du;* in French: *vous* versus *tu*). Formal speech is used in less intimate situations, such as in business settings.

⁹ LIVING CONDITIONS

The Swiss enjoy one of the highest per capita incomes in the world and a correspondingly impressive standard of living. The Swiss, especially those living in the Alpine or forest regions, have traditionally lived in wooden houses with shingled or tiled roofs and carved gables. Corners and roofs have often been reinforced with stone, and kitchens encased in stone or masonry to prevent fires. Fewer and fewer houses of this type are constructed. Even in remote rural areas, newer houses are commonly of brick or block. However, mountain chalets built by urbanites as vacation homes often imitate the older rustic styles. In general, most Swiss live in apartments while fewer live in houses that they own.

Switzerland's standards of health and medical care are excellent. Over 84% of men and women consider their health to be good or very good. In 2008 the average life expectancy was estimated at about 79 years for men and 84 years for women. A law providing medical insurance to most citizens has been in effect since 1911. The nation's pharmaceuticals industry is a world leader in the production of specialized pharmaceutical products.

Situated at the center of Europe, Switzerland is both a center for international air traffic and a crossroads for road and rail travel. The renowned Swiss efficiency is evident in the nation's excellent transportation network. Within each community, there are excellent bus and metro-train systems. The government-run Swiss Federal Railways is one of Europe's best rail systems, connecting all of the country's major cities. Cog railways, cable cars, and chairlifts transport people to popular resort towns and Alpine summits, including the Jungfrau near Interlaken. A network of expressways includes several tunnels through the Alps, such as the Great Saint Bernard and Saint Gotthard tunnels. Inland waterways are also an important means of transportation. The Rhine river is navigable to Basel, the only river port, by barge traffic.

Due to this extensive transportation system, many people can get around quite easily without an automobile—it takes only three to four hours to get from one end of the country to the other by train. Also in order to get a driver's license, an individual must be 18 years old and pass an expensive driver education course. Thus, many choose to rely on public transportation.

Switzerland, with its high standard of living, is a consumer society like many others. There is an increasing enthusiasm for American products in Switzerland. Items like Levi's jeans, Coca-Cola, pop music, and Marlboro cigarettes are popular. McDonald's and other American fast-food restaurants, like Subway and Pizza Hut, are becoming more widespread. Not only are American brands popular with Swiss consumers, but Swiss companies use the image of America and the American way of life to sell their own products. As a result, "American" theme restaurants are becoming more common, as is the use of English in advertising.

10 FAMILY LIFE

The traditional family household—a married couple with children—is still the predominant lifestyle among the Swiss. At the 2000 Swiss Census, about 63% of all households were family households, with about 48% of family households consisting of a married couple with children and another 24% consisting of a married couple without children.

Traditionally, the family structure has been male-dominated, with the husband working outside of the home and the wife taking care of the home and the children. However, more and more women are finding greater opportunities in the workforce and a greater number of men and women are choosing to remain single or to marry later in life. In 2000 approximately 35% of all households were single person households. The size of the average Swiss household dropped from 3.3 people in 1960 to 2.3 in 2000. The number of marriages has decreased from 7.6 for every 1,000 people in 1970 to 5.4 per 1,000 in 2005. It has also been estimated that about 53% of all the marriages that took place in 2005 will end in divorce. In general, the German-speaking Swiss tend to marry among themselves.

11 CLOTHING

Western-style clothing is the norm, although traditional costumes, many displaying the Swiss art of fine embroidery, can still be seen at local festivities and parades. Herdsmen in the Gruyère region wear a short blue jacket of cloth or canvas called a *bredzon* with sleeves gathered at the shoulders. On special occasions, women in this region wear silk aprons, long-sleeved jackets, and straw hats with crocheted ribbons hanging from the brim. Other traditional women's costumes include gold lace caps in St. Gallen and dresses with silver ornaments in Unterwalden. Traditional male dress common to many Alpine Swiss includes the leather shorts called *lederhosen*, often worn with sturdy leather boots.

12 FOOD

Swiss cuisine combines the culinary traditions of Germany, France, and Italy and varies from region to region. Throughout the land, however, cheese is king. The Swiss have been making cheese for at least 2,000 years and today produce hundreds of varieties (of which the hole-filled Emmentaler popularly dubbed "Swiss cheese" is only one). Switzerland's most characteristic national dish is fondue, melted Emmentaler or Gruyère cheese—or a combination of both—in which pieces of bread are dipped, using long forks. The cheese is often melted in white wine and commonly seasoned with garlic, lemon juice, pepper, and other ingredients. Also popular is another melted-cheese dish called *raclette*, traditionally made of cheese from the Valais region, although other varieties are also used. A quarter or half a wheel of cheese is melted in front of an open fire and scraped off into onto the diners' plates using a special knife. The cheese is traditionally eaten with potatoes, pickled onions or other vegetables, and dark bread.

A popular dish in German-speaking regions is *rösti*, hash-browned potatoes mixed with herbs, bacon, or cheese. Typical dishes in the Italian-speaking Ticino region are a potato pasta called *gnocchi*; *risotto*, a rice dish; and *polenta*, which is made from cornmeal and is something like American grits. Gallic specialties such as steaks, organ meats, and wine-flavored meat stews are prevalent in French-speaking parts of the country. Besides cheese, the other principal food for which the Swiss are known is chocolate.

13 EDUCATION

Education at all levels is the responsibility of the cantons, so Switzerland actually has 26 different educational systems, with varying types of schools, curricula, length of study, and teachers' salaries. However, all require either eight or nine years of schooling beginning at age six or seven and track students into either academic or vocational programs in secondary school. At this point those students entering an academic track take a course of instruction to prepare them for university study. Other students in a vocational program continue to take classes while also entering into an apprenticeship—after which students receive certification in a specific trade and are ready to enter the work force. Post-secondary education is offered at nine cantonal universities and two federal institutes of technology at Zurich and Lausanne. In 2004 about 30% of all persons between the ages of 25 and 34 had obtained a higher education degree.

Swiss schools tend to be more oriented toward academics and less toward extra-curricular activities. Activities such as sports—like in the United States with football and basketball teams, pep rallies, homecoming, etc.—are found more in a private club setting rather than in the schools. Besides the cantonal schools mentioned above, there are many private boarding schools in Switzerland. Swiss boarding schools attract students from abroad and many of these schools have a well-known reputation.

14 CULTURAL HERITAGE

From 18th-century philosopher Jean-Jacques Rousseau to psychologist Carl Jung and child psychologist Jean Piaget in the 20th century, Switzerland's cultural achievements have been wide-ranging and profound. In addition to a number of native intellectual and artistic figures, Switzerland has made a unique contribution to world culture by providing a neutral haven for leading intellectuals from Voltaire to Lenin. Significant Swiss artistic personages include playwright Friedrich Dürrenmatt, novelists Gottfried Keller and Max Frisch, sculptors Alberto Giacometti and Jean Tinguely, architects Le Corbusier and Mario Botta, and painter Paul Klee. The International Committee of the Red Cross owes its founding to Swiss humanitarian Henri Dunant from Geneva, where today many other international organizations have their offices.

The number of foreign intellectuals and artists that have called Switzerland home at one time or another is many. Fleeing the communist regime of the former USSR, Alexander Solzhenitsyn first emigrated to Switzerland where, appropriately, he wrote a novel about Lenin. Other distinguished emi-

A yodel club from Thun sings at the 24th federal yodeling festival in Frauenfeld, Switzerland. (AP Images/Walter Bieri)

grés welcomed by the Swiss include authors Hermann Hesse, Thomas Mann, James Joyce, and Erich Maria Remarque, film star Charlie Chaplin, scientist Albert Einstein, philosopher Friedrich Nietzsche, and composer Richard Wagner.

15 WORK

The percentage of Swiss people engaged in agriculture has declined sharply since the 19th century, when 60% were farmers. This figure had dropped to 22% by World War II and fell to about 4% in 2005. Almost 23% of Switzerland's labor force is employed in industries, particularly machinery, electronics, and metallurgical industries. The chemical, pharmaceutical, and textile industries are also major employers. In 2005 about 73% of the labor force was employed in services. One traditional type of labor for which the Swiss are famous is watchmaking, begun by French refugees in the 16th century. Mass production had begun by 1845, and today Switzerland produces over 70 million watches and watch parts annually. The quartz watch was developed by the Swiss in the 1960s, and the most recent advances in the industry include a watch that is responsive to the human voice. More than half of those employed work in the expanding service sector. In this area, tourism and banking are important providers of employment.

Switzerland and the Swiss economy benefit from a comparatively low level of strikes due to what are popularly called "industrial peace treaties"—special collective bargaining ar-rangements—between labor and management. Employers and employees agree to cooperate with each other and strikes and lockouts are forbidden. The first of these no-strike agreements was signed in 1937 in the watch and metal industry and has been renewed over the years and copied in practically all other Swiss industries as well.

Many young Swiss spend a period of apprenticeship outside the country before entering the labor force. A unique Swiss practice is the *Welschlandjahr,* in which young Swiss from the German-speaking part spend time in the French-speaking part in order to learn French and become familiar with the way of life in this part of Switzerland.

16 SPORTS

Both summer and winter sports are extremely popular among the Swiss. The country's Alpine peaks provide a setting for skiing, bobsledding, tobogganing, mountain walking, and climbing. After skiing, ice skating is Switzerland's favorite winter sport, and the team sport of curling is gaining increasing popularity. Summer activities include tennis, hiking, golf, cycling, fishing, and a variety of water sports.

Two popular sports are handball and soccer. Handball in Switzerland is played with two teams and a ball slightly smaller than a volleyball that is easily held in the hand. Each team attempts to score against the other team by trying to get the ball into a guarded goal smaller than a soccer goal but larger than a hockey goal. The ball can be thrown directly into the goal or can be bounced in to get around the goalie. Soccer enjoys even greater popularity, especially as a spectator sport. In 1994 the Swiss National Team qualified for the World Cup Soccer Championship. This created a wave of enthusiasm and support across Switzerland.

17 ENTERTAINMENT AND RECREATION

Relaxing after hours is important for the Swiss, who have one of the longest work days in Europe—usually 8:00 am to 5:00 pm—and average between 2,000 and 2,300 hours of work per year. Much of their recreation is family oriented and they often entertain at home rather than going out. One of the most universal leisure-time activities is simply reading the newspaper, either at home or at a cafe, over a cup of coffee or glass of wine. Extremely popular is a card game—*Jass*—played with 36 cards and a variety of rules which vary from region to region. Concerts and the theater are also enjoyed by many Swiss. The youth scene is dominated by parties and music.

At their many festivals, the Swiss still enjoy traditional activities, including dancing and yodeling, and local sports such as the baseball-like *Hornussen,* or farmer's tennis, stone-putting *(Steinstossen)* where the object is to throw a stone weighing 80 kg (184 lbs) as far as possible, and Swiss wrestling *(Schwingen)* in which each wrestler wears a pair of canvas-like shorts over his pants and tries to throw his opponent to the ground by grabbing hold of these shorts.

Each region of Switzerland has its own festivals and special events. Some important ones include the *Tellspiel* at Interlaken and Altdorf where the heroic story of William Tell is reenacted for audiences; the world famous Montreux Jazz Festival which hosts jazz performers from around world; and the well-known and popular Locarno Open Air Film Festival. Across all of Switzerland, shooting dubs and tournaments are very popular, even among teenagers.

18 FOLK ART, CRAFTS, AND HOBBIES

Switzerland's traditional decorative arts include weaving, embroidery, dressmaking *(Frauentracht)*, wood carving, and painting. A unique form of Swiss folk art is *Senntumsmalerei,* or herd-painting, which originated among Alpine dairy farmers as far back as the early 18th century with carved and painted farm implements. Characteristic forms include *Fahreimebödeli,* wooden pails with decorated bases, *Sennenstreifen,* long boards or strips of paper picturing cattle drives to the high Alpine pastures (traditionally hung in the living room or above the door to the cowshed), and *Wächterbild,* large-scale paintings of cow herders traditionally found on window shutters. *Senntum-Tafelbilder,* small, brightly colored, stylized paintings of cattle drives and other pastoral scenes, were especially popular in Eastern Switzerland from the mid-19th to the mid-20th centuries and can be seen in the many Swiss folk museums today.

19 SOCIAL PROBLEMS

The influx of foreign, or "guest" workers *(Gastarbeiter)* from southern Europe and North Africa since World War II—who made up a quarter of the labor force in 2006—has produced a backlash and a fear of *Überfremdung* (over-foreignization). The Swiss have voted three times on the question of expelling much of the foreign work force, defeating such a measure all three times, although immigration laws have been tightened. Many foreign workers also returned to their home countries in the 1970s due to recession. However, anti-immigrant feeling persists against some *Ausländers* (foreigners), who are subject to discrimination and social isolation.

Drug use and alcoholism are the biggest challenges facing Swiss youth. Many view this as a rejection of society or as a sign of youth's inability to cope with social pressures. Therefore, there is a need, which is slowly being met, to provide youth with positive outlets—such as cultural centers, or movements to get the younger generation interested in social issues.

A very important area of consideration is the issue of European integration. Switzerland is not a member of the European Union and in December 1992 voted not to join the European Economic Area—a step towards joining the European Union. The vote was very close, 50.3% against membership and 49.7% in favor. This has sparked what many have referred to as an identity crisis within Switzerland. Since the majority of those in favor of integration with Europe lived in the French-speaking part, questions were raised over whether or not the division between French- and German-speaking Swiss—the *Röstigraben*—was widening. Fears over European integration focus on the consequences for Swiss neutrality, federalism, and democratic institutions. Many believe that these will be done away with membership in the EU. Still, a good portion of the Swiss populace favors greater links with Europe.

There are a range of other problems which, like other countries, Switzerland is now facing—air pollution from trucks and automobiles resulting in the government encouraging greater reliance on rail travel; unemployment and economic restructuring; and political reform in order to make government more efficient and responsive to the needs of people.

20 GENDER ISSUES

The status of Swiss women, who were only granted suffrage in 1971, is below that of women in most other European countries. By law they have traditionally needed their husbands' permission to get a job, open a bank account, or run for political office (although they were allowed to volunteer for military service). Husbands have also had the last word on such important matters as where a family would live and, in case of a disagreement, what they would name their children. In 1981 a constitutional amendment was passed giving women equal rights, especially in the areas of work, education, and family matters, and in 1985 a law mandating equal rights in marriage was passed by a slim majority of the voters (54.7%). In situations of divorce, women are more likely than men to end up as single parents relying on public assistance. This is a result of a divorce law dictating that the primary wage earner in a divorce must be left with finances sufficient enough to remain above the poverty level. Since the primary wage earner is generally a man, a divorced woman is not always entitled to spousal support or sufficient child support and is more likely to fall below the poverty level.

Swiss women in general must still overcome attitudes that their place is in the home or only in certain kinds of jobs—like salesclerk, office worker, waitress, teacher, or nurse. The difficulties Swiss women must confront include the belief that working women neglect their children, find self-fulfillment at the expense of the family, and steal jobs from men who have to support families. Thus, women in Switzerland continue to meet the challenge of combining roles—in the workplace and at home.

²¹ BIBLIOGRAPHY

Bennett, A. Linda, ed. *Encyclopedia of World Cultures (Europe)*. Boston: G. K. Hall, 1992.

Birmingham, David. *Switzerland: A Village History*. Athens, OH: Swallow Press, 2004.

Bouvier, N., G. Craig, and L. Gossman. *Geneva, Zurich, Basel: History, Culture & National Identity*. Princeton: Princeton University Press, 1994.

Church, Clive H. *The Politics and Government of Switzerland*. New York: Palgrave Macmillan, 2004.

Coordinating Committee for the Presence of Switzerland Abroad. *Switzerland As We See Ourselves*. Zurich: Der Alltag/Scalo Verlag, 1992.

———. *Switzerland Through the Eyes of Others*. Zurich: Der Alltag/Scalo Verlag, 1992.

Flüeler-Grauwiler, Marianne, ed. *Switzerland*. Insight Guides. Singapore: APA Publications, 1992.

Gall, Timothy, and Susan Gall, ed. *Junior Worldmark Encyclopedia of the Nations*. Detroit: UXL, 1996.

Hilowitz. Janet. *Switzerland in Perspective*. Westport, CT: Greenwood Press, 1990.

Hughes, Christopher. *Switzerland*. London: Ernest Benn Ltd, 1975.

Hubbard, Monica M., and Beverly Baer, ed. *Cities of the World: Europe and the Middle East*. Detroit: Gale Research, 1993.

Illustrated Encyclopedia of Mankind. London: Marshall Cavendish, 1978.

Levy, Patricia. *Switzerland*. New York: Marshall Cavendish, 1994.

Moss, Joyce, and George Wilson. *Peoples of the World: Western Europeans*. Detroit: Gale Research, 1993.

Porter, Darwin. *Frommer's Comprehensive Travel Guide: Switzerland and Liechtenstein '94-'95*. New York: Prentice Hall Travel, 1994.

Steinberg, Jonathan. *Why Switzerland?* 2d edition. Cambridge: Cambridge University Press, 1996.

Steinberg, Rolf, ed. *Continental Europe*. Insight Guides. Singapore: APA Publications, 1989.

Swiss Federal Statistics Office. http://www.bfs.admin.ch (22 April 2008).

—revised by K. Ellicott

TATARS

LOCATION: Russia
POPULATION: 6.6 million
LANGUAGE: Tatar; Russian; Ukrainian
RELIGIONS: Islam (Sunni Muslims, majority); Christianity; Sufism; Old Believers; Protestantism; Judaism

¹ INTRODUCTION

Of all the Turkic ethnic groups living within the former Soviet Union, the Tatars historically lived farther west than any other Turkic nationality. It is believed that the name *Tatar* came either from a term of contempt applied by the Chinese to the Mongols or from the Mongol term for "conquered." Later, the name *Tatar* itself became synonymous with Mongol.

After the death of Atilla the Hun in the middle of the 5th century, the Great Hun Empire started disintegrating into several smaller Turkic kingdoms, out of which the Kingdom of Great Bulgaria emerged in the 7th century. This kingdom did not last long and split into two nations upon the death of its ruler, Kubrat Han. His youngest son, Asparuh Han, moved into present-day Bulgaria, allied with the Slavic people already there, and established the Bulgarian Kingdom in AD 681. The two older sons, Batbay and Kutrag, favored an alliance with the Khazar and Alan tribes and remained in the eastern part of the European Plains. By the 8th century, some of these people had moved to what is now Tatarstan and Bashkirtistan, began to accustom themselves with other Turkic and Finno-Ugric peoples, and formed the Bulgar realm in the 9th and 10th centuries.

The Bulgars traded goods with the peoples of Central Asia and China and converted to Islam in 922. They established an urban culture and became skilled in agriculture and commerce. Bulgar society had potters, blacksmiths, coppersmiths, carpenters, stonemasons, jewelers, and tanners. However, in 1236 the Bulgars were conquered by the Mongolian ruler Batu, and they were made provincial subjects of the new Bulgar Khanate. Power struggles within the Bulgar Khanate prompted many people to move west to the more stable area of Kazan. As Mongolian control dissipated in the 1430s and 1440s, several Tatar states emerged, including the Kazan, Crimean, Kasym, Siberian, and Astrakhan Khanates. During the 15th and early 16th centuries, the Kazan Khanate became the most prominent, and its people became known as the Tatars (named for the Turkic tribes forced to fight in the vanguard of Genghis Khan's armies).

The Kazan Tatars were conquered by imperial Russian forces during the reign of Tsar Ivan IV in 1552, thus giving Russia control over the middle part of the Volga River. In 1556, Russian troops conquered the Astrakhan Tatars, thus securing control over all the Volga River and access to the Caspian Sea. To celebrate the victory of Russia over the Tatars, the tsar ordered the construction of St. Basil's Cathedral in what is now Red Square in Moscow. The Tatars became the first Muslim subjects of the Russian Empire. In 1593 Tsar Fedor ordered the destruction of all Kazan Tatar mosques. In 1708 the region was officially organized by the Russian Empire as the Kazan Province, and the construction of mosques was allowed in 1766.

During the late 19th and early 20th centuries, a renewal in Tatar national identity began. This cultural awakening included increased interest in religion, education, publishing, and political activity. When the Russian Empire collapsed in 1917, the Tatars were encouraged by the Bolsheviks to pursue their ethnic identity within a communist setting. The Tatars took advantage of the chaos and formed the Idil-Ural State in November 1917. This territory encompassed about 220,000 square kilometers (85,000 square miles), an area about as large as Utah, in what is now Tatarstan and Bashkirtistan. The Soviet government, however, did not tolerate the independence movement and declared the formation of the Bashkir Autonomous Republic in 1919 and the Tatar Autonomous Soviet Socialist Republic in 1920. When the Soviet government annexed these regions, it redrew the boundaries to give neighboring Russian provinces preferential treatment. By altering those boundaries, about 75% of the Tatar population found itself living outside the borders of Tatarstan.

In the 1920s, members of the independent Tatar government and most of the educated Tatar population were eliminated through execution or exile. This policy against the Tatars continued to some extent until the early 1950s. Tatar culture was also affected until the 1970s through the policy of Russification, where the Russian language, alphabet, and culture were legally imposed on the Tatars and other ethnic groups. During the Soviet era, economic hardship and job preference given to Russians in industrial areas caused many Tatars to leave their homeland.

A distinct group of Tatars known as the Krym (Crimean Tatars) once inhabited a certain part of the Crimean peninsula (during the Soviet era, the region was called the Crimean Tatar Autonomous Soviet Socialist Republic and was located within Soviet Ukraine). The Crimean Tatars had occupied the peninsula for more than 1,000 years as a result of intermarriage and mixing with other peoples present. The independent Crimean Khanate was abolished in 1783 when the Crimea was annexed by the Russian empire. Afterward, the Crimean Tatars suffered from repressive policies that limited their control over political, economic, cultural, and religious affairs; violence was often used to enforce imperial policy. The Crimean Tatar population declined from around 2.5 million in 1783 to 130,000 in 1921 while its territory was thoroughly settled by colonists. In 1944–45, the Soviet government forced them to leave, because Crimean Tatars had been accused of supporting the Germans during World War II. As scapegoats, the Crimean Tatars were deported to various regions of Central Asia, Kazakhstan, the Urals, and Siberia. The deportation served as a type of genocide, because 194,000 (about 46% of all Crimean Tatars) died in the process due to violence, starvation, and destitution. Their property and lands were confiscated as well. In 1989 the Soviet government began a repatriation program that allowed for the return of some 50,000 persons per year. Since gaining independence in 1991, Ukraine has administered this program, and over 200,000 of the estimated 550,000 Crimean Tatar population have returned, but many have suffered from discrimination and poverty. The Crimea is officially an autonomous region within Ukraine, but the government is controlled by ethnic Russians. Many Tatars want more political power, but not necessarily autonomy.

After the breakup of the Soviet Union, many Tatars agitated for an independent Tatar nation-state. In August 1990, the Tatar parliament declared Tatarstan's sovereignty and in April 1991 declared that Tatar law had dominance over Russian law whenever the two were in conflict. Tatarstan functioned as an independent state until 1994, when the leaders of Tatarstan and Russia signed a treaty bringing Tatarstan into the Russian Federation. Since the rise to power of Vladimir Putin, Tatarstan has lost even more of its autonomy. That said, Tatars have maintained their linguistic and cultural rights within Tatarstan.

² LOCATION AND HOMELAND

The Tatars are a very diverse group, both ethnically and geographically. The Tatars formed the second largest non-Slavic group (after the Uzbeks) in the former Soviet Union. There are more than 6.6 million Tatars, of whom about 26% live in Tatarstan, an ethnic homeland of the former Soviet Union that is located in present-day Russia. Tatarstan, with about 3.8 million inhabitants, is about the size of Ireland or Portugal and considered the most northern frontier between Muslim and Orthodox Christian cultures. The capital of Tatarstan is Kazan (sometimes referred to as "the port of five seas"), a city of more than a million people and the largest port on the Volga River. Tatarstan is a secular republic with political stability, official support for two languages, and a high percentage of mixed marriages.

After Russians and Ukrainians, the Tatars are the most populous ethnic group in the Russian Federation. About 15% of all Tatars live in Bashkiria, another ethnic homeland that lies to the east of Tatarstan. There are also smaller Tatar populations in Kazakhstan, Kyrgyzstan, Tajikistan, Turkmenistan, Turkey, Uzbekistan, Romani and in the regions to the north and west of Tatarstan. Small Tatar communities are also scattered all across Russia. A unique group of Tatars are the Krym (also called the Crimean Tatars), with a population of around 550,000. The Krym are from the Crimean peninsula of present-day Ukraine. Along with the Russians, Armenians, Estonians, and Latvians, the Tatars were the most urbanized ethnic group of the former Soviet Union, especially among those who lived outside of Tatarstan.

There are numerous subgroups within the Tatar population. The Bukharlyk Tatars are descended from 15th- and 16th-century fur traders who lived in Central Asia and western Siberia. The Kasymov Tatars are descended from the refugees of the Kazan Khanate who settled in Riazan in the 15th century. Lithuanian Tatars (also called Polish or Belarusian Tatars) are the Polish-speaking Muslim descendants of the Nogai Horde warriors who helped the Lithuanians fight against the Teutonic Order. The Volga Tatars (also called the Kazan Tatars) are the largest of all the Tatar groups and are descended from Turkic-influenced Eastern Finns, and range from Scandinavian to Mongol in appearance. The Mishars are also Turkic-influenced Eastern Finns who are Finnish in appearance. The Teptiars are Volga Tatars who fled to the east after the Russian Empire took over the Kazan Khanate. The Kryashans are Volga Tatars who converted to Christianity during the 16th and 18th centuries.

Since the fall of the Soviet Union, over 200,000 Crimean Tatars have returned to Ukraine. In addition, thousands of Crimean Tatars have immigrated to Russia and the European Union in search of work.

³ LANGUAGE

Tatar is a Turkic language. Like other Turkish languages, it is agglutinative, meaning suffixes are added to the ends of words to form sentences. Tatar is closely related to Kazakh and Kyrgyz. It is a more distant relative of the Turkic languages spoken in Azerbaijan, Turkey, Turkmenistan and Uzbekistan. Tatar has three main dialects. Western Tatar is spoken by the small Tatar minority in Finland. Middle Tatar, by far the most widely spoken dialect of the language, is spoken in Russia and Ukraine. Finally, Siberian Tatar is spoken by the Tatar ethnic groups of Siberia. Tatar borrows a large number of words from Russian and incorporates some English words as well.

In 922, the Bulgars converted to Islam, and the old Turkic script was replaced by the Arabic alphabet. Tatar is now written using the Cyrillic alphabet.

A famous old Tatar saying is *"Kilächägem nurlï bulsïn öchen, utkännärdän härchak ut alam,"* which means "To make my future bright, I reach for the fire of the past." Another well-known Tatar proverb is *"Tuzga yazmagannï soiläme,"* which means, roughly, "If it's not written on salt, it's wrong to even mention it." The proverb refers to the ancient method of keeping records on plaques made of wood and salt and commends the practicality of keeping written records.

⁴ FOLKLORE

There are many Tatar legends about how the new city of Kazan (which means "cauldron") was built. The origin of the city's name goes back to Tudai-Menghe, who ruled the city in the late 13th century. One of his servants was said to have dropped

a golden cauldron into the river, and the town was later founded nearby.

Another Tatar legend about Kazan tells of a rich man who was a beekeeper and would often take along his daughter to visit his hives in the woods near Jilan-Tau ("snake hill"). When the daughter got married, she lived in the old part of Kazan, where it took a long walk to get water. She complained about the poor planning of the town to Ali-Bei, the ruler of Kazan. She suggested that Jilan-Tau would be a better place for the city, because it was at the mouth of the Kazanka River. The khan ordered two nobles to take 100 warriors to the site and to then open his sealed orders. According to the orders, they were to cast lots and bury the loser alive in the ground on the spot where the new city was to be built. However, when the khan's son lost, they buried a dog in his place. When the khan heard the news, he was happy for his son but said that it was an omen that the new city would one day be overtaken by the "unholy dogs"—a term referring to those of a different religion.

Waterfowl are an important symbol of life in Tatar culture. Ducks especially are significant because, according to ancient Bulgar mythology, the Earth was formed when a duck dove to the bottom of an ancient sea, brought up a piece of mud, and set it afloat on the water's surface.

⁵ RELIGION

Most Tatars are Sunni Muslims, with the exception of the Kryashan Tatars, who are Christian. In Tatarstan, along with Islam and Orthodoxy there are some other religious communities such as Old Believers, Protestants, Seventh-Day Adventists, Lutherans, and Jews. Islam has played an important role in solidifying the Tatar culture, because the imperial Russian government repeatedly tried to limit the spread of Islam from the Tatars to other peoples. This approach, however, usually pushed Tatar Muslims closer to their faith, and there is generally a devout observance of rituals and ceremonies among Muslim Tatars. Sufism (Islamic mysticism) also has a long history with the Tatars and is appealing for many because of its emphasis on ascetics. While observance of some Islamic rituals was common, it was very uncommon for Tatars to have a deep knowledge of their faith or to practice all the tenets of Islam. For example, Islamic clergymen would often preside over Tatar weddings. After the clergyman would leave, family and friends would celebrate the wedding by drinking vodka (alcohol is forbidden to Muslims).

Islam has enjoyed a resurgence among Tatars since the fall of the Soviet Union. In 1990, there was only one mosque in Kazan. Now there are dozens. A number of *madrasas*, or religious schools, have also been established in order to educate Tatar Muslims about their faith.

⁶ MAJOR HOLIDAYS

Tatars typically observe some of the Soviet-era holidays and also Muslim holidays that, to a large degree, are the same as those elsewhere in the Muslim world. The Soviet celebrations include New Year's Day (January 1), International Women's Day (March 8), Labor Day (May 1), and Victory Day (May 9—commemorates the end of World War II). Since the Tatars are widely scattered across Russia and Central Asia, different communities may observe regional holidays as well. Many Tatars celebrate the new year holiday of Nowruz, which is celebrated throughout the Persian and Turkic world.

Russian singers of the Tatarstan capital Kazan peform during a celebration of the capital's 1,000 anniversary. Tens of thousands of Tatar, Russians, and others packed in Kazan to celebrate the millennial anniversary. (Maxim Marmur/AFP/Getty Images)

The Islamic holidays include *Milad al-Nabi* (the birth of the Prophet Muhammad), *Id al-Adha* (celebrating the ancient account of Abraham offering his son for sacrifice), and *Id al-Fitr* (celebrating the end of the Ramadan fast). The dates of these holidays are not fixed due to the rotating nature of the lunar calendar. Russian influence has led many Tatars to incorporate the drinking of alcohol into their traditional celebration. The Kryashan Tatars celebrate Christian holidays such as Easter and Christmas. These religious celebrations were observed in secret during the Soviet era but are now held in the open. As a result, the number of Tatars who celebrate Islamic and Christian holidays has increased considerably since the fall of the Soviet Union.

7 RITES OF PASSAGE

Circumcision and other rituals associated with birth, death, and marriage are practiced by many Tatars today.

Since the fall of the Soviet Union, the number of Tatars performing the Hajj—pilgrimage to Mecca—has increased greatly. Every Muslim is expected to make the pilgrimage to Mecca at least once during his or her lifetime.

8 INTERPERSONAL RELATIONS

For centuries, there was tension between ethnic Russians and Tatars. As a result, the Tatars suffered from discrimination, which affected how they came to interact with Russian society.

The Tatars of today typically live in small communities and often utilize a network of friends and business contacts from within the Tatar community.

In the early 1990s, the hundreds of thousands of Crimean Tatars who returned to Ukraine faced hostility from their Russian and Ukrainian neighbors. Over time, these tensions have eased considerably.

9 LIVING CONDITIONS

Health care is provided by the state, although not all Tatars have adequate access to it. The government of Tatarstan is in the process of moving to an insurance-based health care delivery system. The high rate of new HIV infections affects Tatars, just as it affects the other peoples of the Russian Federation.

Most Tatars live in the Soviet-style apartment blocks found throughout Russia. Tatars live relatively well, as Tatarstan is one of the most prosperous republics in the Russian Federation.

10 FAMILY LIFE

Urban Tatars often promote endogamy (marriage to other Tatars) out of the belief that it will help keep the Tatar identity from being assimilated. However, since the 1960s, intermarriage with Russians and other ethnic groups has become more common. Family size is usually larger than that of neighboring populations. Traditional Tatar households are comprised of three or more generations.

11 CLOTHING

Tatars, as one of the most urbanized minorities, wear European-style clothing, and occasionally, mostly in rural areas, include fragments of traditional clothing such as the headscarf for women and skullcaps for men. In 2003 Muslim Tatar women won the right to wear headscarves in their passport photographs.

12 FOOD

Lamb and rice play a prominent role in the traditional Tatar diet, as in those of many other central Asian peoples. The Tatars are known in particular for their wide array of pastries, especially their meat pies, which, besides beef or lamb and onions, may include ingredients such as hard-boiled eggs, rice, and raisins. Another traditional dish is *chebureki*, or deep-fried lamb dumplings. Following is the recipe for the basic Tatar meat pie called *peremech*.

Peremech

Dough ingredients:
2 eggs
½ cup sour cream
6 tablespoons of light cream or half-and-half
a pinch of salt
2½ cups flour

Filling ingredients:
1 pound slightly fatty boneless beef chuck
1 onion
1 clove garlic
1 teaspoon salt
vegetable oil for frying

Dough: Beat eggs, then add sour cream, light cream, sugar, salt, and flour. Knead until smooth and pliable. Wrap the dough in wax paper and chill overnight before making into pies.

Filling: Add salt and garlic to meat and grind together with onion in a meat grinder or food processor.

To make the pies: Take only a quarter of the dough out of the refrigerator at a time. Roll each quarter of dough into a 12-inch cord. Slice each cord into six pieces, rolling these smaller pieces between the palms of the hands to form balls, then flatten the balls slightly. On a surface dusted with flour, roll each into a 3½ to 4 inch round disk. Spread 1 tablespoon of the meat mixture on each disk, leaving a 1 inch border around the edge. Gather the dough upward all the way around each patty, forming a round, flat pastry and leave a hole about 1 inch across on top. As each pie is made, cover with a cloth to prevent uncooked dough from drying. Heat the pies in ½ inch of vegetable oil in a large skillet, a few at a time, with the hole side down. Cook for approximately 15 minutes, or until golden brown. Makes 24 pies.

13 EDUCATION

During the Soviet era, the prerequisite Russian language examination served to keep many Tatar youths out of institutions of higher learning.

Since the end of the Soviet period, Tatar-language education has increased in popularity. In 1998 there were 38 Tatar language schools in Kazan alone. Tatar-language schools differ from Russian-language schools in that the purpose of the Tatar schools is to inculcate students with a sense of Tatar national identity. Many of these schools actively seek to create a new Tatar intelligentsia.

14 CULTURAL HERITAGE

It is believed that Tatar prose dates back to the 12th century, but scholars disagree about its origin. Jakub ibn-Nogman, who wrote "The History of Bulgaria," lived in the first half of the 12th century. The scholar Burchan ibn-Bulgari wrote about rhetoric and medicine. The 13th-century poem by Kol-Gali called "A Tale about Yusuf" was well-known far from Bulgar lands and greatly influenced the development of Bulgarian and Tatar literature.

Professional Tatar theatre began in December 1906 with the premiere of Galiaskar Kamal's play, *Wretched Child*. Modern Tatar literature began around the same time period. The poet Gabdulla Tukay is credited with founding modern literary Tatar. During the early part of the Soviet era and immediately after World War II, Tatar literature was largely confined to praising communist ideology. Since the 1960s, however, Tatar literature has often emphasized the role of the artist in voicing the ideals of the Tatar people. Prominent modern Tatar writers include R. Faizullin, R. Gäray, R. Mingalimov, R. Kharisov, F. Shafigullin, M. Agliamov, and Zöl'fat. Famous Tatar artists include actress Chulphan Khamatova, ballet dancer Rudolf Nureyev, and composer Farit Yarullin.

15 WORK

Traditional occupations of the Tatars include agriculture, hunting, fishing, crafts, and trade. Under Soviet rule, many jobs were based on collectivized agriculture and industrialization. The Tatars have held an increasing number of white-collar and professional jobs since World War II.

Heavy industry makes up a large share of employment in Tatarstan. Many Tatars work in mining, automobile manufacturing, chemical production, and oil refining.

16 SPORTS

The Tatars enjoy many traditional and Western-style sports. Soccer became popular during the Soviet years and is perhaps the most widely played sport among young men. Horse racing is also very popular, as the horse has long been a prominent part of traditional Tatar culture.

A traditional form of wrestling known as *koresh* is still practiced by Tatars. *Koresh* wrestlers wrestle standing up and attempt to throw their opponent to the ground. The most points are awarded to wrestlers who can throw their opponents on their backs. Wrestlers who throw their opponents on their sides or buttocks receive fewer points. The recent Tatar national revival in Russia has led to greater interest in *Koresh*.

17 ENTERTAINMENT AND RECREATION

Tatars enjoy many of the same leisure activities as neighboring populations in the former Soviet Union, such as watching television and visiting with friends and neighbors. Prominent among the traditional entertainments in rural areas is the week-long Festival of the Plow, or *Sabantui*, held in spring, which ends with a day of singing, dancing, and sporting events.

18 FOLK ART, CRAFTS, AND HOBBIES

The ancestors of the modern Tatars were skilled in crafting jewelry of gold, silver, bronze, and copper. They also were known for making pottery with engraved ornaments, metal decorations, and bronze locks in the shape of animals.

The Tatars who have returned to the Crimean Peninsula are fueling a resurgence in traditional Tatar crafts. Traditional Tatar embroidery is now practiced in Ukraine. Traditional Tatar craftsmen use gold thread to embroider images of fruits and grains.

19 SOCIAL PROBLEMS

The Tatar suffered discrimination under the imperial Russian dominion as well as during the Soviet era. Massive deportations of Tatars fragmented the culture, and the loss of lives and property from those days still has an impact on contemporary Tatar society.

Problems with Crimean Tatars are much more complicated because of forced deportation from the Crimean peninsula. Now that almost half of the Crimean Tatars have returned from Central Asia, they are facing problems with employment, housing, and schooling.

Social problems that affect many communities in the Russian Federation affect the Tatars. Since the collapse of the Soviet Union, the number of sex workers and drug users in Russia has risen drastically. These dynamics have led to an increase in the number of HIV cases in Tatar communities. Although the Russian economy in the 2000s was growing at a fast pace, many Tatars still face poverty and unemployment.

20 GENDER ISSUES

Tatar women who live in the countries of the former Soviet Union have legal equality with men. However, Tatar women, like women in nearly every country around the world, still face disadvantages because of their gender. Women's participation in politics has decreased drastically since the fall of the Soviet Union. Wage discrimination is a particularly acute problem for Tatars in Russia; in 1998, women in Russia earned only 70% of what men earned, even though women tended to have higher levels of education. At the same time, gender discrimination may be less prevalent among Tartars than among ethnic Russians. A 2004 study found that 44% of Tatar men believed that women should work outside the home, while only 25% of ethnic Russians held the same opinion.

Until the 1980s, it had been common for homosexual Tatars, along with every other ethnic group of the Russian SFSR, to be sent to mental hospitals. Homosexuality was decriminalized in Russia in 1993. Leaders of the Tatar Muslim community are staunchly anti-gay, and there is little public acceptance of sexual minorities amongst ordinary Tatars.

21 BIBLIOGRAPHY

Fisher, Alan W. *The Crimean Tatars*. Stanford, CA: Hoover Institution Press, 1978.

Johnson, Juliet, Marietta Stephaniants, and Benjamin Forest. *Religion and Identity in Modern Russia: The Revival of Or-thodoxy and Islam*. Burlington, Vermont: Ashgate Publishing, 2005.

McCann, Leo. *Economic Development in Tatarstan: Global Markets and a Russian Region*. New York: RoutledgeCurzon, 2005.

Pope, Hugh and Joanne Myers. *Sons of the Conquerors: The Rise of the Turkic World*. New York: Overlook TP, 2006.

Rorlich, Azade-Ayse. *The Volga Tatars: A Profile in National Resilience*. Stanford, CA: Hoover Institution Press, 1986.

Smith, G., ed. *The Nationalities Question in the Post-Soviet States*. New York: Longman, 1996.

Shnirelman, V.A. *Who Gets the Past?: Competition for Ancestors among Non-Russian Intellectuals in Russia*. Washington, DC: Woodrow Wilson Center Press; Baltimore: Johns Hopkins University Press, 1996.

Uehling, Great Lynn. *Beyond Memory: The Crimean Tatars' Deportation and Return*. New York: Palgrave MacMillan, 2004.

—revised by B. Lazarus

TUVANS

ALTERNATE NAMES: Tuvinians, Tyva; Uriangkhais; Urianghais; Tannu-Uriankhaitsy; Soyots
LOCATION: Russia (southern Siberia), China (northern Xinjiang province), northwestern Mongolia
POPULATION: 243,442 (2002, in Russia), 70,000 in Mongolia, 2,400 in China
LANGUAGES: Tuvan; Russian, Mongol
RELIGIONS: Native religious practices; Tibetan Buddhism

¹ INTRODUCTION

The Tuvans are a native people of southern Siberia mainly found in the Tuvan Republic (also known as Tuva) of the Russian Federation. Substantial Tuvan communities are also found in western Mongolia and in the Altai Mountain region of western China. The Tuvans' name for themselves is *Tyva*. They have also been referred to in ethnographic writings as the Uriangkhais, Urianghais, Tannu-Uriankhaitsy, and Soyots. Archeological, linguistic, anthropological, and historical evidence indicates that the ancestors of the modern Tuvans were formed during the first millennium AD from a mixture of Turkic-, Mongol-, Ket-, and Samoyedic-speaking tribes. Most Tuvans have traditionally been nomads who raise cattle, horses, sheep, yaks, and goats, although some Tuvans in the mountainous forests of northern and eastern Tuva have customarily bred reindeer instead. Tuva was conquered by the Mongol armies of Chinggis Khan around AD 1207 and was subsequently administered by a series of Mongol rulers. In the 1750s, Tuva's Mongol rulers were defeated by the Manchu Qing dynasty that had conquered China during the previous century, and the area passed under Manchu rule until the fall of the Qing dynasty in 1911. The Russian Empire declared Tuva its protectorate in 1914 and allowed Russian settlers to move into Tuva, much to the dismay of the Tuvans, who occasionally attacked them. In 1921, Russia's new communist government proclaimed that the protectorate declared earlier by the Russian monarchy was illegal and that, henceforth, Tuva was to be independent. In reality, the "Tannu-Tuva People's Republic" that existed from 1921 to 1944 was a Soviet puppet state. During the 1930s, its government engaged in policies identical to those of the Soviet government—for example, religious persecution and the imprisonment and execution of suspected political opponents. At this time, steps were also taken toward the collectivization of animal husbandry. In 1944, the Soviet Union annexed Tuva; soon thereafter, thousands of Russian settlers arrived to work the land and construct factories and coal and gold mines. The Tuvans were forced into herding collectives similar to agricultural collective farms. Many Tuvans slaughtered their animals in protest and engaged in anti-Soviet uprisings.

² LOCATION AND HOMELAND

The total Tuvan population is about 310,000, slightly more than 200,000 of whom dwell in the Russian Federation's Tuvan Republic. The geographical center of the Asian continent has been calculated to lie just outside the Tuvan capital Kyzyl, and this spot is marked by an obelisk. The Tuvan Republic borders on the Gorno-Altai Autonomous Region (Russian, *avtonomnaia oblast*) to the west, the Khakass Autonomous Region to

the northwest, Krasnoyarsk Territory (Russian *krai*) to the north, Irkutsk Region (Russian *oblast*) to the northeast, the Buriat Republic to the northeast, and Mongolia to the south and southeast. About 9,000 Tuvans live scattered throughout the rest of the former Soviet Union's territory. An additional 70,000 Tuvans dwell in the northwest of the Mongolian Republic, and 2,400 more are to be found in the People's Republic of China's Xinjiang Province. The Tuvans are divided into two distinct ethnographic groups. The first are the western Tuvans, or Tuvans proper, numbering about 305,000. The second is a much smaller group, the Tuja Tuvans (Tuvintsy-todzhintsy in Russia), who live in Tuva numbering 4,442 in 2002. In 2002 approximately 55% of Tuvans were rural dwellers, and 45% were urban.

Because more than 80% of the Republic of Tuva is covered by mountains (even the lowest points are 500 meters [1640.4 feet] above sea level), the most typical landforms are naturally alpine ones—mountain meadows and taiga forest—although valleys contain some steppe and semi-desert areas as well as a limited amount of arable farmland. The climate is dry and sharply continental: winters are long and very cold, with January temperatures sometimes dropping as low as –61°C (–78°F). Summers are short and hot, with June temperatures reaching 43°C (109°F). Tuva is rich in wildlife, particularly bear, fox, mountain goat, snow leopard, wild reindeer, wolf, squirrel and antelope. Vegetation varies widely. Grasses and wormwood trees are common in the mountain meadows and steppe valleys inhabited by cattle-breeders. Larch, cedar, fir, and birch forests appear in the northern and eastern areas occupied by hunters and reindeer herders. Sparse grasses and shrubs are found in the semi-desert areas south of the Tannu-Ola mountain range.

³ LANGUAGE

The Tuvan language belongs to the Turkic family; its closest living relative is the language of the Tofalars (also called the "Karagas" or "Toba") who live to the north of Tuva. The four dialects of Tuvan are classified according to the parts of Tuva in which they are spoken: Central, Western, Northeastern, and Southeastern. The modern Tuvan literary language is based on the Central dialect. The Tuvan dialects differ from each other mainly in vocabulary and pronunciation, and the differences between them are not significant enough to prevent speakers of different dialects from understanding each other. Until the 20th century, the few Tuvans who could read and write did so in Classical Mongolian, a literary language that uses a flowing vertical script in which words are written from top to bottom in columns of text read from left to right. The use of Classical Mongolian, along with centuries of continual contacts between Tuvans and Mongols, has had a significant influence upon the development of the Tuvan language, especially its vocabulary. Many Tuvan words are identical to Mongolian words with the same meaning: for example, *mal* means "cattle" or "livestock," and *nom* means "book" in both Tuvan and Mongolian. *Chettirdim* means "thank you."

The Tuvan language did not have a written form until the late 1920s, when Soviet linguists created a Tuvan writing system based on the Latin alphabet. This alphabet was replaced by the Cyrillic (Russian) alphabet in 1941. Although the form of the Cyrillic alphabet used to write Tuvan includes several extra letters for Tuvan sounds that do not exist in Russian, many

Tuvan scholars feel that the present writing system is still inadequate for representing the sounds of spoken Tuvan and is in need of reform. Because Tuva was not formally annexed by the Soviet Union until 1944 and the Tuvans make up a larger percentage (70%) of their officially recognized homeland's population than any other native Siberian people, and they tend to live in compact groups separate from the local Russians, they have a higher degree of native-language retention than any other indigenous Siberian group. A full 99% of Tuvans speak Tuvan as their mother tongue, and only 1% speak Russian as their first language. Young and middle-aged Tuvans are also proficient in Russian, which is taught in all Tuvan schools.

Many Tuvan personal names are based on common Tuvan words that have a pleasant meaning. *Chechek* (female) means "flower," *Maadyr* (male) means "hero," and *Belek* (both sexes) means "gift." Suffixes are often added to such words to specify male or female names: the male ending *-ool* and the female ending *-kys* are added to words such as *chechen* ("eloquent"), *mergen* ("wise"), and *aldyn* ("golden") to produce the male names Chechen-ool, Mergen-ool and Aldyn-ool and the female names *Chechen-kys, Mergen-kys,* and *Aldyn-kys.* Because most Tuvans practice the Tibetan form of Buddhism, many Tibetan names have been adopted, including *Seren-Chimit* (male) and *Dolgarzhaa* (female).

A child might even be called by the Tibetan word for the day of the week on which he or she was born: *Baazang* ("Friday"), *Davaa* ("Monday"), and so on. Russian names such as *Nikolai* (male) and *Maria* (female) have also become common in the

last few decades. Family names are based on the surname of a male ancestor; for that reason, many surnames end in the suffix *-ool.*

4 FOLKLORE

Although the Tuvan language was unwritten until this century (except for the scholarly transcriptions of linguists and ethnographers), the Tuvans have long possessed a rich heritage of oral literature. Tuvan folklore contains a variety of genres—fairytales, stories about animals, riddles, songs, folk sayings, and long epic tales about the battles and exploits of heroic warriors that are very similar to the epics of the Mongols. There are also myths about the origins of the constellations. For example, *Chedi khan* (The Seven Khans), a myth of the reindeer-breeding Tuvans, tells how the constellation Ursa Major was formed. According to the myth, Ursa Major's seven stars are actually seven khans. They were journeying separately through the Upper World where the spirits dwell when they happened to meet. The seven khans decided to have a meal together, but none of them knew how to cook. To this day, they are standing there deciding how to prepare the meal. Tuvan folklore was formerly passed down orally from generation to generation and recited by *toolchus* (bards). Scholars at the Tuvan Scientific Research Institute of Language, Literature and History *(Tyvanyn Dyl, Literatura, Bolgash Töögünün Ertem Shinchilel Institudu)* in Kyzyl have worked together with the *toolchus* to collect and publish Tuvan folklore to ensure that it will be available to future generations of Tuvans.

5 RELIGION

The ancient religion of the Tuvans is shamanism. According to Tuvan shamanism, mountains, forests, rivers, animals, and the sky all possess their own spirits that must be honored in order for man to survive and flourish. Most Tuvan shamanists believe that the universe is divided into three worlds: the Upper, or Heavenly World *(Üsütüü-oran),* where the spirits of nature and various other deities dwell; the Lower, or Earthly World *(Ortaa-oran),* which is inhabited by humans; and the Subterranean, or Dark World *(Aldyy-oran),* which is inhabited by the spirits of the dead. (Some Tuvans believe that there are only two worlds—the Upper and Lower—and that the dwelling place of the dead is located at the edge of the Lower World.) The shaman, a tribal priest similar to the Native American "medicine man," is a man or woman who is adept at traveling between the worlds and communicating with spirits through rituals that involve dancing, chanting, and beating on a large, flat round drum called a *dünggür.* The shaman's prayers are believed to heal the sick and improve the luck of those who have lost cattle to disease or experienced other misfortunes. The shaman also foretells the future and presides at sacrifices *(ydyk-kylyr)* during which young bulls are killed in honor of holy mountains. The profession of shamanism is usually hereditary. Most shamans are therefore the sons and daughters of shamans, although men and women without shamans as ancestors may also become shamans if they feel that they have been chosen by the spirits.

The Tuvans' belief that animals have spirits that must be respected has led to the development of many taboos concerning hunting. For example, Tuvan hunters may not refer to certain animals directly by their usual Tuvan names, but must instead allude to them by a host of elaborate euphemisms. (This cus-

tom is shared by some other Siberian peoples—for example, the Buriats.) Thus, a bear is not spoken of using the ordinary Tuvan word for "bear" *(adyg)* during the hunt, but is instead referred to as *khaiyrakan* ("the sovereign"), *kara chüve* ("the black thing"), *choorganyg* ("the one who has a blanket [i.e., fur]"), *irei* ("grandfather"), or *daai* ("uncle"). The Tuvans consider trees with oddly twisted trunks or other unusual features to contain spirits; they call such trees "shaman-trees" *(kham-yiash),* and when passing by them, they leave bits of food, brightly colored ribbons, drops of milk, tea, or vodka, and strands of horsehair as offerings.

The Tibetan variety of Buddhism was brought to Tuva by Mongolian lamas (Buddhist monks or priests) during the 18th century and soon claimed many converts. Instead of abandoning shamanism, however, the Tuvans continued to practice it along with the new religion. Besides filling religious needs, the Buddhist monasteries *(khürees)* of Tuva served important cultural functions as well. They provided literacy in Mongolian and Tibetan and contained libraries of religious and secular works in these languages. During the 1930s, the Tuvan government, in imitation of its Soviet model, destroyed the monasteries and imprisoned or killed many Tuvan lamas and shamans. Tuvan religious practices emerged from underground in the 1980s when the Soviet leader Mikhail Gorbachev put an end to the Soviet government's war on religion. Since then, several young Tuvans have gone to Mongolia's Buddhist monasteries for religious training, and Tuvan Buddhists have made plans to rebuild some of the destroyed monasteries.

⁶ MAJOR HOLIDAYS

The most popular Tuvan holiday is *Shagaa*, the New Year's Festival. Because the Tuvans formerly used the lunar calendar, *Shagaa* falls on a different day each year in the Gregorian calendar. Tuvans also celebrate the Western New Year's Eve and New Year's Day on 31 December and 1 January. In Tuvan, the new year is welcomed by saying *"Chaa Chyl-bile"* ("happy new year"). *Shagaa* is celebrated by feasting, wrestling matches, archery contests, and horse racing. While under Soviet rule, Tuvans celebrated Soviet holidays such as May Day (1 May), the anniversary of the Soviet victory over Nazi Germany (9 May), International Women's Day (8 March), and the anniversary of the Bolshevik seizure of power in 1917 (7 November). Most Tuvans undoubtedly stopped observing these Soviet holidays after the collapse of the communist regime.

⁷ RITES OF PASSAGE

In traditional society, childbirth took place at home and was assisted by a midwife. As soon as the infant emerged from the womb, the midwife washed it with strong tea in order to strengthen it. The afterbirth was wrapped up in the sheepskin upon which the mother had given birth and buried. The umbilical cord was tied with string; when it fell off, it too was buried. The practice of burying the afterbirth seems to have passed from observance, although the umbilical cord is still buried.

A Tuvan child is given his or her first haircut at three years of age. This is an occasion for celebration by the child's family and relatives, because he or she has now survived infancy. The parents take the boy or girl to the homes of relatives, who each cut off a small lock of hair and present the child with gifts. Before the Soviet ban on arranged marriages, girls underwent an additional rite of passage involving hair. Young girls' hair was kept short like that of small boys until they reached eight or nine years of age, at which time the hair was allowed to grow out. When a girl's hair had grown long enough for it to be woven into a braid, she was considered old enough for her parents to choose a husband for her.

The oldest son held a privileged position in traditional Tuvan society. According to the Buddhist patriarchal social organization of the Tuvans, the oldest son was always given to the temple to become a lama (Buddhist monk). Also, the flocks (animal breeding was the basis of the economy) were not divided among surviving children, but always inherited entirely by the oldest son. Needless to say, this privileged group never worked, and this situation limited the society's economic opportunities because a large number of potential workers remained idle. It was also hard on younger sons, who often resented their subordinate role in society. With Soviet support, these younger sons formed the core of a revolutionary organization that overthrew the power of the lamas in 1926.

In traditional Tuvan society, the dead were either buried in the ground or placed in a wooden casket that was then raised on poles or placed in a tree. Food and drink or items of everyday use were placed in the casket along with the corpse. Shamans were laid to rest with their drums. Sometimes, corpses were wrapped in cloth and laid on the ground to be devoured by vultures. This practice is similar to a traditional Tibetan method of disposing of the dead and was especially widespread among Buddhist Tuvans, although some Buddhist clergymen chose to be cremated instead. Tuvans now bury their dead in the ground in caskets or cremate them.

⁸ INTERPERSONAL RELATIONS

Over the centuries, the Tuvans have adopted the Tibetan and Mongolian practice of presenting respected guests with a *khadag*—a band of silk that is about one yard long and a little under a foot wide. When presenting the *khadag* to a guest, a Tuvan host lays the *khadag* across his or her outstretched arms, which are bent at the elbow. The guest also places his arms in this position, and the host transfers the *khadag* from his or arms to those of the guest.

⁹ LIVING CONDITIONS

The most common traditional dwelling of the Tuvans is the *ög*, or yurt, which is covered with felt cloth stretched over a wooden frame. The frames of Tuvan *ögs* have customarily been imported from Mongolia. An iron stove in the center of the *ög* is used to cook food and provide warmth. A flap in the center of the roof is opened to allow light to enter, and an iron stovepipe removes smoke. The *ög* is well-suited for a nomadic way of life, because it can be quickly taken apart and reassembled when a family drives its herds from pasture to pasture. Tuvans of the mountainous northern Todzh region, who herd reindeer and hunt instead of raising livestock, have traditionally lived in *chadyrs*, conical tents similar to the teepees of some Native American peoples of the Great Plains. The wooden frame of the *chadyr* is covered with reindeer skins in the winter and birchbark in the summer. In traditional Tuvan society, the homes of two or three related families that shared herding and hunting grounds were grouped into a small settlement called an *aal*. After Tuvas' annexation by the Soviet Union, *aals* were abolished and their members moved to large collective farms. Since the 1950s, traditional Tuvan dwellings have largely been replaced by the one-story wooden houses common on Soviet collective farms. Tuvans in Kyzyl and other cities live in prefabricated concrete apartment buildings that are indistinguishable from those in urban areas of the former Soviet Union.

Tuvans have ridden horses and used them as pack animals for as long as there has been recorded information about them. Because of Russian influence, Tuvans have begun to use horses to pull carts and sleighs as well in recent decades. Reindeer-breeding Tuvans ride domesticated reindeers and use them to carry loads. Yaks and oxen are also occasionally ridden in the southern areas of Tuva where they are bred, although they are used for transport far less frequently than horses. Automobiles, bicycles, taxis, and buses are common in cities and towns, but Tuva's rugged mountainous terrain has severely limited road construction between cities. For the same reason, there are no railways in Tuva. There are still many rural areas that can be reached only by airplane, horse, or reindeer.

Herbal medicine and the incantations of shamans were the chief forms of medical treatment in traditional Tuvan society. Lamas trained in Tibetan medical practices at Buddhist monasteries also served as doctors before the anti-religious campaign of the 1930s. Western medicine first became available to Tuvans in the first decade of the 20th century when Russian doctors moved into Tuva to serve Russian farmers who had settled in the region. It has become much more common since Tuva's incorporation into the Soviet Union (a large modern hospital was constructed in Kyzyl during the first years of direct Soviet rule). The Soviet government provided medical care either free or at low cost, but it was not always available in remote areas, and most rural clinics provided only the most basic care. To these existing problems must be added the dire economic conditions in which post-Soviet medical facilities now find themselves.

10 FAMILY LIFE

For many centuries, related Tuvan families were grouped into clans (sööks) that shared hunting lands and helped each other in time of need. Members of a söök were forbidden to marry each other. Although the clan system's rules (such as the prohibition on marriage among members) have passed from observance during this century (and in some places even earlier), many Tuvans are still aware of their clan affiliation and feel a vague sort of kinship with other members of the same clan. The Tuvan language has also preserved elements of the clan system. The word aky means both one's own elder brother and the younger brother of one's father (uncle), and the word ugba refers to both one's own elder sister and the younger sister of one's father (aunt).

The small nuclear family consisting of a man and woman and their unmarried children has been typical among modern Tuvans throughout the 20th century. Wealthy Tuvans formerly had two or more wives, but polygamy was relatively rare and there have apparently been no cases of it since the 1920s. In traditional Tuvan society, marriages were arranged, with the average age of marriage 15 or 16 for girls and between 18 and 20 for boys (although marriages sometimes took place with one partner as young as 13). The legal age for marriage in Tuva is now 18, and marriages are no longer arranged.

11 CLOTHING

Tuvan traditional clothing is very similar to that worn by Khalkhas, Buriats, and other Mongolian-speaking peoples. The typical garment for men and women is the ton, an ankle-length robe fastened on the right side with buttons or hooks. Light cloth shirts and trousers are worn under the ton. Summer tons are made of calico, silk, velvet, thin felt, or deerskin. Those worn in winter are made either from sheepskin or from felt lined with the thick skins of reindeer slaughtered in the winter. Both sexes wear fur and cloth hats of various cuts and boots. Stiff boots with thick, multilayered soles, felt linings, and toes that curl upward are called kadyg idiks. High, soft boots made of thin leather, reindeer, or goatskin are called chymchak idiks. There is little difference between the traditional clothing of men, women, and children, although men usually wear a belt over their tons to hold pouches for tobacco, fire-lighting flints, and various small tools used in herding and hunting work. Underclothing for both sexes was formerly limited to undershirts and underpants made of cloth in the summer and leather in the winter, but these have been replaced by cloth shorts and undershirts for men and cloth bras and panties for women since the mid-20th century. Mass-produced items of Western outer clothing—cloth dresses, shirts, trousers and suits, and leather shoes—have also become common, especially in urban areas. Traditional clothing is still widely used in daily life in the countryside, however, and it is worn on holidays and other festive occasions by both rural and urban Tuvans.

12 FOOD

Many traditional dishes of the cattle-breeding Tuvans are made from milk and are identical to those of the Mongols. Curds (aarzhy) are dried during the summer and eaten year-round. Sour milk (khoitpak) is either drunk, whipped into a sweet, creamy substance called eezhegei, or pressed into a sour, hard cheese (kurut). Mare's milk is fermented to make a drink called khymys (called kumys by other Turkic-speaking peoples) and distilled into arak, a vodka-like alcoholic beverage.

There are a number of taboos regarding the handling of milk. For instance, it is forbidden to spill milk on the ground. If one does inadvertently spill it, one must cover it with a sprinkling of soil. One may not take milk outside after dark. It is generally considered amiss to take milk away from one's household; if someone cannot avoid giving another person milk to take away, he must pour the first few drops into one of his own containers before giving away the remainder.

In addition to beef, the cattle-breeding Tuvans consume mutton, camel, yak, and goat meat. Boiling is the usual method of preparation. The traditional fare of reindeer-breeding Tuvans centers on reindeer meat and milk. Reindeer milk is drunk fresh and added to tea; it is also dried and stored in leather bags for later use, or else made into cheese. In the fall, reindeer meat and milk are frozen in the open air to be thawed and boiled during the long, bitter winters. Hunting is a common occupation for both cattle- and reindeer-breeding Tuvans, so the meat of wild reindeer, bear, and squirrel often graces Tuvan tables. Millet, barley, oats, and wheat are grown in the fertile river valleys. Common traditional dishes from these ingredients include millet soup, noodles, and pancakes. Russian influence has made fruit, vegetables, pork, bread, and various canned goods an integral part of the Tuvan diet in the last 50 years.

13 EDUCATION

Before the 20th century, the Tuvans' only educational institutions were Buddhist monasteries. The languages of the religious rituals students were made to memorize and the texts they used were Mongolian and Tibetan. Because these languages (especially Tibetan) are very different from Tuvan, some students memorized their lessons without understanding their content. During the 1920s, a few secular schools were founded by the Tuvan government. Buddhist monks, who were practically the only literate Tuvans, were employed as teachers, and textbooks and homework were written in Classical Mongolian. In the 1930s, the creation of a Tuvan written language and the return of young Tuvans who had studied to become teachers in the Soviet Union significantly aided the growth of education. Still, only half of Tuvan school-age children attended school until Tuva's annexation by the USSR in 1944, when funds from the Soviet government allowed the development of a modern educational system. All Tuvans now attend primary and secondary schools, and many go on to study at technical institutes, teachers' colleges, and universities in both Tuva and the rest of the Russian Federation.

14 CULTURAL HERITAGE

The aspect of the Tuvan cultural heritage best known outside Tuva is its music. Tuvan singers are famous for a special type of singing called *khöömei*, known in English as "overtone," "throat," or "harmonic" singing. A *khöömei* singer produces two tones at once: a low, droning tone that produces the melody and a higher "overtone" that has been compared to the sound of a flute. The "overtone" is produced by vibrations in the throat and mouth caused by the lower tone. *Khöömei* is a very difficult art that requires years of training to coordinate the muscles of the vocal cords, throat, soft palate, tongue, and lips. There are several styles of *khöömei* singing: *sygyt* has a whistling overtone, whereas *kargyraa* has a very deep lower tone and hoarse overtone and is similar to the harmonic chanting of Tibetan Buddhist monks. The *ezengileer* and *borbannadir* styles use overtones that have a pulsing rhythm similar to a galloping horse. *Khöömei* singers such as Kaigal-ool Khovalyg have performed in many countries, including the United States.

15 WORK

Tuvans have long been skilled metalworkers. The profession of blacksmith is a highly respected one, and in traditional society only the sons of blacksmiths could enter it. Tuvan blacksmiths produce items of everyday use, such as knives, ploughshares, arrowheads, locks, trivets, axes, nails, and even rifles from scrap iron. Another type of metalwork widespread among the Tuvans is casting. Copper, bronze, lead, and a silver-tin alloy called khola are poured into stone or clay molds to make bridles, stirrups, chains, chess pieces, and decorative plaques that were fastened to saddles. Mass-produced metal goods have become more common since the 1950s, but items custom-made by Tuvan metalworkers are still highly sought for their attractiveness and durability.

16 SPORTS

The Tuvans' favorite sports are horse racing, archery, and wrestling. Tuvan wrestling (*khüresh*) is very similar to Mon-

gol wrestling. The rules are the same, and Tuvan and Mongol wrestlers even wear the same type of uniform. The uniform of a Tuvan wrestler (*mögö*) consists of heavy, knee-high leather boots; a leather or silk "shirt" that covers only the shoulders, upper back, and arms; and leather or silk shorts similar in cut to men's briefs. During a traditional Tuvan wrestling match, the two competitors square off and grab each other by the shoulders. They grapple with each other in a standing position until one of them is forced to touch the ground (usually with his knee or elbow). The wrestler who forces the other to the ground is declared the winner.

17 ENTERTAINMENT AND RECREATION

Tuvans have enjoyed chess for centuries. Some scholars believe that chess was brought to Tuva by Chinese settlers after the Manchu conquest of Tuva. The chess pieces used by Tuvans have more or less the same functions as those in other cultures, but they have been modified to depict camels, kings and princes in traditional dress, and other themes from traditional Tuvan daily life. *Daaly*, a game similar to dominoes, is another favorite pastime.

18 FOLK ART, CRAFTS, AND HOBBIES

Stone carving has long been practiced by Tuvan craftsmen. Pyrophyllite, a substance similar to soapstone, is carved into chess pieces and small sculptures. Common themes are wild and domesticated animals, Tuvans in traditional dress, and everyday activities such as hunting. Wild animals are often depicted in complicated poses that show them hunting or fighting each other.

19 SOCIAL PROBLEMS

Some of the most pressing issues facing modern Tuvans are ecological ones. The ecology of Tuva, like that of the other native Siberian peoples' homelands, has been damaged by Soviet economic projects that did not take into account their effects on the environment. Hydroelectric dams have flooded river valleys traditionally used for agriculture. The replacement of the small *aals* by collective farms has concentrated livestock into excessively large herds that overtax Tuva's grass and water resources. Gold, uranium, and coal mines have scarred the landscape and polluted Tuva's once-pristine air and water, and the absence of environmental safeguards at the open-pit asbestos mines dug since the 1970s has led to fears that cancer rates will soon rise sharply.

Ethnic conflicts between Tuvans and Russians have increased sharply since the relaxation of censorship in the 1980s. All Tuvans are now keenly aware that their annexation by the Soviet Union took place without their consent, and they blame the Russian-led Soviet government, the native political leaders whom they view as traitors, and the uninvited Russian settlers for the present damage to their homeland's environment and economy and the destruction of Tuvan religious and secular traditions. There have been interethnic fights and even murders. In 1990, three Russian fishermen were murdered at an isolated mountain lake, and many local residents suspect that Tuvans killed them for fishing at a place sacred to Tuvan shamanists. The result has been the flight of thousands of Russian colonists: between 1989 and 1992, the proportion of Russians and other non-Tuvans in Tuva's population dropped from 36% to 30%. Some Tuvan nationalists have advocated the formation of an independent Tuvan state. Although it is very unlikely that the government of the Russian Federation will allow Tuva to secede, Tuvan political leaders have managed to gain greater autonomy in economic matters and have succeeded in increasing the use of the Tuvan language in education and government.

²⁰ GENDER ISSUES

Tuvan women and men now have equal legal rights, but this has not always been the case. A woman's role in the family was in some ways subordinate to that of men in traditional society. A woman was forbidden to speak the names of her father-in-law or mother-in-law and could not appear before them with her head or feet uncovered. She could not inherit property from her husband, as this was a privilege reserved for male family members. Still, a woman possessed that property (including the family dwelling) which she had brought to the marriage and to which neither her husband nor her in-laws had any right. Although men and women performed different economic tasks—men usually herded and hunted, while women milked the cattle or reindeer, cooked the family's meals, and cleaned house—a woman's work was highly valued, and her husband often sought her advice on matters affecting the running of the household. Tuvan gender roles changed considerably after Tuva's annexation into the Soviet Union, with the integration of the Tuvans into the Soviet economy and Soviet society, and with the increased educational opportunities from which many women were able to benefit.

²¹ BIBLIOGRAPHY

Balzer, Marjorie Mandelstam. "From Ethnicity to Nationalism: Turmoil in the Russian Mini-Empire." In *The Social Legacy of Communism*. Ed. James R. Millar and Sharon L. Wolchik. Cambridge: Cambridge University Press, 1994.

Fondahl, Gail. "Siberia: Native Peoples and Newcomers in Collision." In *Nations and Politics in the Soviet Successor States*. Ed. Ian Bremmer and Ray Taras. Cambridge: Cambridge University Press, 1993.

Forsyth, James. *A History of the Peoples of Siberia: Russia's North Asian Colony, 1581–1990*. Cambridge: Cambridge University Press, 1992.

Istoriia Tuvy [The History of Tuva]. In Russian. 2 vols. Ed. L. P. Potapov et al. Moscow: Nauka, 1964.

Krueger, John. *Tuvan Manual: Area Handbook, Grammar, Reader, Glossary, Bibliography*. Bloomington: Indiana University, Research Center for Language and Semiotic Studies, 1977.

Leighton, Ralph. *Tuva or Bust! Richard Feynman's Last Journey*. New York: W. W. Norton, 1991.

Leighton, Ralph, and K. A. Bicheldei. "The Tuvans." In *Encyclopedia of World Cultures. Volume 6: Russia and Eurasia/China*. Ed. Paul Friedrich and Norma Diamond. Boston: G. K. Hall, 1994.

Levin, Theodore, and Valentia Suzukei, *Where Rivers and Mountains Sing: Sound, Music, and Nomadism in Tuva and Beyond*, Bloomington, Indiana, Indiana University Press, 2006.

Potapov, L. P. *Ocherki narodnogo byta tuvintsev* [An Outline of the Folkways of the Tuvans]. In Russian. Moscow: Nauka, 1969.

Potapov, L. P. "The Tuvans." In *The Peoples of Siberia*. M. G. Levin and L. P. Potapov, eds. Stephen Dunn, trans. Chicago: University of Chicago Press, 1964.

Spravochnik lichnykh imen narodov RSFSR [Handbook of personal names of the peoples of the RSFSR]. In Russian. Ed. A. V. Superanskaia and Iu. M. Guseva. Moscow: Russkii iazyk, 1989.

Tuva: Voices from the Center of Asia [Sound recording]. Recordings and notes by Eduard Alekseev, Zoya Kirgiz, and Ted Levin; performed by Fedor Tau et al. Washington, D.C.: Smithsonian/Folkways Records, 1990.

Vainshtein, Sevyan. *Mir kochevnikov tsentra Azii* [The World of the Nomads of the Center of Asia]. In Russian. Moscow: Nauka, 1991.

———. *Nomads of South Siberia: The Pastoral Economies of Tuva*. Ed. and intro. by Caroline Humphrey. Trans. Michael Colenso. Cambridge: Cambridge University Press, 1980.

———. "Tuvintsy" [The Tuvans] in *Narody Rossii: Entsiklopediia* [The Peoples of Russia: An Encyclopedia]. In Russian. Ed. V. A. Tishkov. Moscow: Bol'shaia Rossiiskaia Entsiklopediia, 1994.

———. *Tuvintsy-todzhintsy: istoriko-etnograficheskie ocherki* [The Tuvans of the Todzh Area: An Historical-Ethnographic Outline]. Moscow: Izdatel'stvo vostochnoi literatury, 1961.

Van Deusen, Kira. *Singing Story, Healing Drum: Shamans and Storytellers of Turkic Siberia*. Montreal: McGill-Queens University Press, 2004.

———. *Woman of Steel: A Tuvan Epic*. Vancouver, Canada: Udagan Books, 2000.

—revised by A. Frank

TYROLESE

ALTERNATE NAMES: Tyroleans
LOCATION: Tyrol (Tirol); western Austria and northern Italy
POPULATION: 1,708,000
LANGUAGE: German, Italian, Ladin (or Ladinian)
RELIGION: Roman Catholic

1 INTRODUCTION

Tyrol (or Tirol) is a name for a historical region in Western Central Europe, covering the area in the eastern Alps in western Austria and northern Italy. It includes the Austrian state (Bundesland) of Tyrol, which is divided into North Tyrol and East Tyrol; the Italian region known as Trentino–Alto Adige; and three communes in the Italian region of Veneto (Livinallongo del Col di Lana, Colle Santa Lucia, and Cortina d'Ampezzo). The name of the region derives from a family name linked to a castle near Meran (now Merano in Italy).

In prehistoric times (the late Bronze Age and the Iron Age), the most prominent cultures of the region were the Laugen-Melaun (Luco-Meluno) and the Urnfield, succeeded by the Fritzens-Sanzeno (also known as the Rhaetics). In 15 BC the region was conquered by the Romans and incorporated into the Roman Empire. From the 6th to the 9th century, the region was settled by the invading tribes of Bavarians, whose southernmost territory was the area of today's Bolzano (Bolzen) and the Longobards (who ruled in the area of today's Trentino). After it became part of the Frankish Empire and later the Holy Roman Empire, the region was considered to be of great strategic importance as a bridge between Italy and Bavaria. Tyrol became part of the Duchy of Bavaria in the Early Middle Ages. Its territory consisted predominantly of properties belonging to the bishops of Brixen (Bressanone) and Trento. In 1248 the scions of the Tyrol family, residing in a castle near Merano, acquired extensive lands from the bishop of Brixen. By 1271 the Tyrol family had effectively replaced the ecclesiastical power in the region. In 1342, Margaret Maultasch, heiress to the Tyrol, married the son of the Holy Roman Emperor, Louis IV. When she died childless in 1363, the Tyrol came under the rule of the Habsburgs, which lasted until 1918 (with the exception of the time period between 1805 and 1814, when Austria was forced to cede it to the Kingdom of Bavaria and later Italy). In the 16th century, Tyrol prospered largely because of its mines and the production of weapons. It adopted the Reformation movement, but it then reverted to Catholicism after a large peasant revolt of 1525 had been crushed. In 1867, Tyrol was declared the Crown Land of Cisleithania, the western half of Austria-Hungary. After World War I, and following the dissolution of the Austro-Hungarian Empire and the Treaty of Saint-Germain, northern Tyrol became part of the First Austrian Republic. Today, it is one of Austria's nine federal states, with Innsbruck as its capital. The state of Tirol is divided into eight districts (*bezirke*) and one statutory city (Innsbruck). The southern Tyrol region, in spite of the region's overwhelmingly German-speaking population, became part of Italy and was known, until 1947, under the name of Venetia Tridentina. In 1948 it was granted a special regional autonomy within the Republic of Italy. The provincial capitals in Trentino–Alto Adige alternate biennially as the site of the regional parliament.

In addition to denoting a historical region, the name of Tyrol is sometimes also used simply to refer to the Austrian federal state of Tirol.

2 LOCATION AND HOMELAND

The Austrian part of the historic region of Tyrol, known in Austria as Tirol, is bordered by Germany to the north, by the Austrian federal states of Salzburg and Carinthia (Kärnten) to the east, by Vorarlberg to the west, and by Italy to the south. Its area covers 12,647 sq km (4,883 sq mi). The region is entirely Alpine in character. The highest peak, the Wildspitze, is 3,744 m (12,382 ft) high. The largest rivers in North and East Tyrol, respectively, are the Inn River and the Drava (Drau).

The Italian part of the historic Tyrol is known as Trentino–Alto Adige (in Italian), Trentino-Südtirol (in German), or as Trentin–Adesc Aut and Trentin-Sudtirol (in Ladinian). It is bounded by Austria (and its federal state of Tirol) to the north, by Switzerland (the canton of Graubünden) to the northwest, and by the Italian regions of Lombardy (Lombardia) and Veneto to the west and south, respectively. Its area covers 13,619 sq km (5,256 sq mi). The entire region is extremely mountainous, with most regions over 900 m (3,000 ft); the mountain peak called Palla Bianca (Weisskugel) reaches 3,738 m (12,264 ft). The main rivers in this region are the upper Adige (Etsch), the Isarco (Eisack), the Noce, and the Avisio, all of which are tributaries of the Adige River, flowing south through the cities of Bolzano and Trento to the Italian city of Verona in the Veneto region.

Winters in the Austrian part of Tyrol are cold and snowy, but summers are moderately warm, despite much precipitation. Average temperatures for December range from -4°C to 2°C (25°F–36°F), and average June temperatures range between 11°C and 24°C (52°F–75°F). The climate in the province of Bolzano is very similar to the climate in Austrian Tyrol and significantly colder than Trentino's climate.

3 LANGUAGE

Three languages have traditionally coexisted in Tyrol: German, Italian, and Ladin (or Ladinian), a Rhaeto-Romance language. While German prevails in North, Eastern, and West Tyrol, in South Tyrol the Italian and German languages have been spoken side-by-side since the Early Middle Ages. Ladin is spoken in the Dolomite Mountains of Italy between Trentino–Alto Adige (Südtirol) and Veneto. This regional language is related to the Swiss Romansh, Surselvan, and Friulan. It is officially recognized in Italy and has official rights in the region of Trentino–Alto Adige but not in the region of Veneto.

The agglomerations around the towns of Bolzano and Merano have always attracted speakers of all three language groups, but for a long time they lived side-by-side, with only a limited interest in multilingualism and communication beyond their linguistic community. In the feudal system, the ruling elites were not preoccupied with the languages spoken by their subjects; their own languages of communication were French and Latin. The predominantly rural way of life in the region did not promote contact between the language groups, especially in the case of German- and Ladin-speaking populations living in the alpine valleys. This linguistic situation changed at the beginning of the 19th century, when cultural and national movements equating language with national identity created an interest in the vernaculars. After World War I, when South

Tyrol became part of Italy, and following the rise of fascism in the peninsula, the use of the German dialects and of German was banned in South Tyrol. Many German-language speakers left Italy at that time, some returning only after World War II. The conditions for the peaceful coexistence of the Italian and the German language groups in the region were not promising at that time, and their mutual unease culminated in political clashes and even bomb attacks. In 1969 a set of laws was passed between the Italian and the Austrian governments that made possible the intensive program of protecting the German language in the region of Trentino–Alto Adige, where the German language prevails in the cities of Bolzano and Trento. The debate on the future of minorities in Europe, opened in the 1960s, gradually led to the implementation of a set of protective measures for the members of German- and Ladin- speaking minorities in the region. Moreover, interethnic relations improved significantly in the 1980s, during the years of the economic boom in the region. All this has led to an important degree of bilingualism, especially in the area of Bolzano. With the appearance of a new model of open, multilingual European identity, the privilege of bilingualism has been especially attractive to the young South Tyrolese.

4 FOLKLORE

Some folklore and traditions among the Tyrolese vary by region, but there are traditions that all parts of the Tyrol share.

According to an old courtship tradition, for example, if a young woman presents a young man with a bottle of spirits, she intends to say that he has found favor with her and may visit her at home. If her parents look upon the young man with disfavor, she might lower the bottle at night from her bedroom window. In parts of Eastern Tyrol, invitations to a wedding are conveyed by a best man or "wedding-inviter," about a fortnight before the event. He goes around the village inviting the people in each house; if he is offered food, it is taken to be an acceptance of the invitation; if he is denied food, the likelihood is that the invited will not attend the wedding. In the Unter Innthal, the bride is often stolen away by a few wedding guests after the ceremony and sometimes taken to the next village or to an inn where the group eats and drinks until the groom appears to pay the bill. In South Tyrol (Ampezzo), weddings usually take place about a fortnight after the betrothal. During this time, the bride is guarded by a chaperon known as "the growling bear" (brontola). In West Tyrol, the parents inspect each other's houses shortly before the betrothal, in order to evaluate the property of the other family. Today, these customs are largely symbolic.

The traditional Christmas market takes place in most German-speaking towns in Tyrol every year, typically from the last Friday of November to December 23. Visitors can buy traditional food and mulled wine and walk along stands selling Christmas wares, inexpensive toys, and souvenirs.

The emblem of Tyrol is edelweiss ("noble white"), a simple flower that grows spontaneously only at high altitudes. Its image is often embroidered or pinned on clothing produced in Tyrol, as a symbol of regional pride.

5 RELIGION

Tyrol is a region where Roman Catholicism, the dominant religion of the Habsburg Empire, prevails among all three language groups. Although in the early 16th century a large part of Tyrol accepted the teachings of the Reformation, the region reverted to Catholicism following the crushing of the large peasant revolt in 1525. Roman Catholic churches can be found in even the smallest Tyrolese hamlets. Wooden outdoor sanctuaries adorned with images of the Virgin Mary, Jesus, or different saints are a common sight on Tyrolese roads.

The presence of Jews in Tyrol was documented as early as the beginning of the 14th century; in 1520 a decree was issued expelling all Jews from the region. Some returned, numbering by the end of the 18th century only eight families, living in Innsbruck and Bolzano. The center of Jewish life in today's Tyrol is the city of Innsbruck.

6 MAJOR HOLIDAYS

Most major holidays in Tyrol are based on the Catholic calendar. The feast day of St. Nicholas on December 6 is the traditional beginning of the Christmas season. Christmas and Easter, mark the high points of the Tyrolean year. In Tyrol, Christmas is celebrated on December 24, with a large family dinner. A midnight mass on December 24 is an age-old custom, followed in all parts of Tyrol. December 26 is celebrated in Tyrol as St. Stephen's Day. New Year's Day is celebrated. Epiphany (January 6), also known as Three King's Day, is the day that closes the Christmas season.

Other holidays include All Saints' Day on November 1, a religious holiday during which Tyrolese typically bring flowers to the graves of deceased family members. The time preceding Lent is marked in Tyrol by Carnival festivities. On Easter Monday, many Italian-speaking Tyrolese traditionally have a picnic in the countryside to celebrate the beginning of spring. Festa della Liberazione (April 25) marks the end of World War II in the Italian part of Tyrol. Another spring holiday is Labor Day on May 1, celebrating the international workers' movement. Whit Monday, the day following Pentecost, is a Catholic holiday celebrated at the end of May or the beginning of June. In the Italian part of Tyrol, June 2 marks the day of the Italian Republic. A holiday marking the height of the summer vacation season is the feast of the Assumption of Mary on August 15, when many Tyrolese take time to relax with family and friends during a long weekend. In the Austrian parts of Tyrol, October 26 is celebrated as the Austrian National Day (marking Austria's Declaration of Neutrality made in 1955).

In addition to these national holidays, towns and villages throughout Tyrol celebrate the feast day of their patron saint.

7 RITES OF PASSAGE

Rites of passage in the traditionally Roman Catholic region of Tyrol have generally coincided with the rites of passage in the Catholic Church: baptism, first Holy Communion, and confirmation are some of the steps in the life of young Tyrolese that are celebrated by a gathering of a large extended family. In the rural areas of Tyrol, traditional marriages still form the basis of communal living; in the urban areas, marriages have often been replaced by cohabitation, although this is still a more common phenomenon in the Austrian part of Tyrol than it is in the Italian part. Another important rite of passage in the life of young Tyrolese is completing secondary school; passing the secondary-school leaving examination called Matura (or Maturità) is often a reason for a large celebration with family and friends, marking the entry of a young person into the adult world.

8 INTERPERSONAL RELATIONS

From the times of the Habsburgs, the Tyrolese inherited a respect for authority. This has included respect for the traditional family, based on the principles of the Roman Catholic faith. Large rural families were, in the past, an essential source of labor on the family's farmstead. While the trend of large families continues in the most isolated areas of Tyrol, families with more than two children have become rare in urban areas and among the population employed in economic sectors other than farming. In a relatively harsh climate, a sense of community and a feeling of solidarity among members are valued very highly and cherished across the generations. Considering that, in many areas of Tyrol, geographical mobility was traditionally low, it is not surprising that the feelings of neighborly common interest and friendship that have bound families to one another for decades, if not centuries, are still attributed great importance. Increased demographic mobility in more urban areas has weakened such attachments, but lasting friendships are still valued very highly in all of Tyrol.

Honesty and directness are highly valued in all personal relationships among the Tyrolese. In family life, older generations are typically shown great respect and afforded deferential treatment.

There are many interethnic marriages in Tyrol now, a phenomenon that was not always approved of in the past.

9 LIVING CONDITIONS

In the Italian part of Tyrol, the cities of Trento and Bolzano have enjoyed a reputation as being among the best cities in Italy in which to live. In the entire region of Tyrol, the absence of crime, the general neatness, the efficiency and reliability of public services, the high quality of education, and the pleasant pace of life, have all contributed to making the area very attractive, among both travelers and those looking for a permanent home.

Strict regulations protect the wildlife and vegetation in the region, and they seem to be very effective. Cleanliness of public and private spaces is a tradition and a norm in Tyrol, and recycling is both highly diversified and efficient. Both private gardens and public parks are maintained lovingly and carefully. Public transportation in the region is excellent, with trains and buses connecting cities with the many valleys of the region.

10 FAMILY LIFE

In rural areas of Tyrol, families tend to be more traditional, cultivating a division of labor that runs along gender lines. Fathers are still seen as heads of the family, and traditional marriages prevail, with a very low divorce rate. Childcare and housekeeping are typically women's duties, but the work on the farm is often shared between women and men. In urban areas, a different family model prevails, with single-parent families and cohabitations on the rise.

In keeping with an old tradition, the names that are recorded in the parish registers of births, deaths, and marriages by Tyrolean peasants often differ from the names by which these people are known in the community. The appellation given to the owner of a farmstead is often transferred from one owner to the next, so that whoever acquires the land, also acquires a nickname for the rest of his life.

11 CLOTHING

Although traditional Tyrolese clothing is still displayed at tourist venues and folk festivals, in daily life it is mostly a thing of the past. In urban areas, the Tyrolese are wearing clothing similar to many urban Western Europeans, incorporating traditional pieces of clothing such as *loden* coats, hats, and jackets for women, men, and children. *Lederhosen* (leather knickerbockers) are a traditional outfit for men; however, they are no longer seen in everyday life very often but remain a symbol of regional pride. *Dirndl*, a simplified version of the traditional Alpine dress for women, consisting of a colorful bodice, blouse, full skirt, and apron, can still be seen in Tyrolese cities, worn by young urban settlers as a wink to their local traditions. Showing pride in one's region and one's origins by wearing a *dirndl* at formal occasions has also been a favorite among the noble women in the Austrian part of Tyrol.

12 FOOD

Tyrolese food, similarly to other cuisines of cold mountainous areas in Europe, is high in calories derived from fat. *Crafuncins da ula verde*, or *schlutzkrapfen* (also known as "lean Tyrolese ravioli") is a type of pasta filled with spinach, parsley, and onion, and eaten during Lent, when meatless dishes prevail. Another traditional meatless dish is *nioch da patac* (potato gnocchi), dumplings made with barley flower, potatoes, and eggs. *Speckknoedel* (bacon dumplings) and *spinatknoedel* (spinach dumplings) are an important part of local cuisine that started out as a way to use stale bread. They are a mixture of dried bread soaked in milk, chopped onion sauteed with bacon, parsley, and eggs, slowly cooked in boiling water, and served with a stew or in hot broth. Similarly prepared are *bales de furmenton* (buckwheat dumplings) and *bales da fuia* (liver dumplings). *Schüttelbrot* is a type of Tyrolese crispbread typically eaten with cheese, ham, or cold cuts, and a favorite in local ski resorts. The spices used in the dish vary, but it can consist of fennel seeds, caraway, fenugreek, coriander, dill, or anise, according to local or individual preferences. *Grosti* are deep-fried pastries that can be prepared savory or sweet and dusted with sugar. They are typically served at Carnival time. Sometimes they are prepared with mashed potatoes and served with sauerkraut in the winter or boiled vegetables in the summer.

Traditional Tyrolese soups include *panicia cun cern sfumieda y bales* (barley soup with smoked pork and dumplings), *panicia da venderdi* ("Friday soup" made with dried beans), and *tiroler suppe* (Tyrolean split-pea soup with onion). *Golasc* is a Tyrolean-style goulash, a heavy beef stew spiced with marjoram, caraway, cloves, and paprika. The Tyrol *gröstl* is a traditional food containing potatoes and pieces of cut pork, onion, and butter browned in a pan, and spiced with marjoram, caraway, salt, pepper, and parsley. It is often served with fried eggs or beetroot salad. Another traditional meat dish is *herrengröstl*, or *herrengroschl* (sauteed veal ragout with crunchy potatoes, often served with a side dish of green salad). *Tiroler Leber* (calf liver Tyrolean style) is sliced and fried liver, served with fried chopped onions, capers, lemon, and heavy cream. Polenta is a cornmeal dish traditionally eaten in the rural areas of South Tyrol for breakfast, lunch and dinner; in today's restaurants it has become a side dish served with meat, fish or other dishes, but not as flavorful as the slowly-cooked traditional polenta. Tyrol is also rich in edible mushrooms, and its cuisine reflects that.

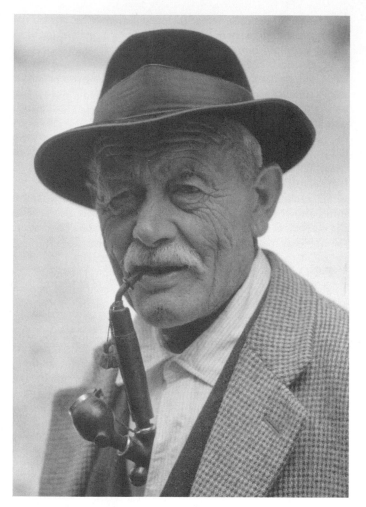

A gentleman wearing a Tyrolean hat in Vaduz, Liechtenstein.
(© Jim Sugar/Corbis)

Some of the popular sweet dishes are: *crafons* (poppyseed doughnuts traditionally made in Val Gardena), *fanzieutes da leva* (another traditional fried doughnut), and *fanzieutes da meiles* (apple-fritters).

South Tyrol is a region renowned for its production of Cabernet Sauvignon and Pinot Grigio wines. The best known Tyrolean wine is *Kalterersee (Lago di Caldaro)*, which should be drunk no later than a couple of years after harvesting.

13 EDUCATION

In the Austrian parts of the Tyrol, all public schools are subject to the educational laws and regulations governing education in the Republic of Austria. Austria has a free and public school system, with nine years of mandatory education. The Federal Ministry of Education funds all primary, secondary, and tertiary (higher) education. Primary and secondary educations are administered on the state level. Private primary and secondary schools (approximately 10% of all primary and secondary educational institutions) are mostly run by the Roman Catholic Church. *Gymnasium* is a secondary school that focuses on general education, as opposed to the specialized education students receive in vocational or professional secondary schools. The series of demanding final written and oral examinations in the last year of *Gymnasium* is called *matura;*

it gives students who successfully pass it access to university. Austria has no tradition of private universities, but this has been changing since 2001, with the law on accreditation of private universities (11 existed in Austria in 2008). Until recently, the only degree in the Austrian university system was a magister (a four- to five-year degree with a substantial thesis), but recently, in keeping with the Bologna process of educational reform, some universities have introduced a bachelor's degree. The University of Innsbruck was founded in 1669 and remains one of the best universities in Austria and in Europe. Innsbruck is also home to an important and prestigious Medical University, one of the three medical schools in Austria, and a world center for treatment of ski-injuries.

Educational institutions in South Tyrol are governed by general rules and regulations pertaining to the Italian educational system, with a significant bilingual component (German-Italian, especially in the area of Bolzano), and they are granted a considerably greater degree of regional autonomy than their counterparts in other regions of Italy. The Italian school system starts with primary (five years) and continues with secondary school (divided into two stages: middle school, lasting three years, and secondary school, lasting between three and five years). Any secondary school that lasts five years grants access to the final exam called *maturità*, which grants students who pass it access to university education. Most Italian universities, and the best, are public; they grant university degrees called *laurea* (after three years of study), or *laurea specialistica* (also known as *laurea magistrale)* after 5 years of study and a thesis. The University of Trento (founded in 1962) is considered to be among the very best in Italy (and consistently top ranked in science) and among the most open to international exchange of students and researchers and scientific collaboration. The Free University of Bolzano (founded in 1997) is a private university, and offers free, practice-oriented, multilingual education, oriented towards the local labor market.

14 CULTURAL HERITAGE

The region of Tyrol has traditionally been a mediator between two great European literary traditions: the German-language and the Italian-language literature. An abundance of literature in Latin (clerical texts, inscriptions, letters, scientific writings, and a variety of texts used in daily life) has been found in Tyrol dating from the beginning of its existence as a political unit in the 13th century, until the late 17th century. The birth of literature in Italian and German has generally followed the gradual decline of writing in Latin and started to flourish in the 18th century.

Goswin von Marienburg (14th century), a Benedictine monk and a historian, is particularly known for his chronicles in Latin. Another important representative of the German-speaking group in Tyrol was 15th century theologian and philosopher Nicolaus de Cusa (1401–1464), the bishop of Brixen and one of the most renowned personalities of early Renaissance, a lover of literature from antiquity, and a promoter of religious tolerance. While de Cusa's writings were in Latin, his native German was in his time in Tyrol mostly a vehicle for the oral tradition, folktales, and legends. Aeneas Silvius Piccolomini (1405–1464), later Pope Pius II, was of central-Italian origin, but he spent a significant part of his life in Trento and northeastern Italy and is widely seen as one of the most important representatives of Humanism in Europe. Astronomer

Christoph Scheiner (1573 or 1575- 1650) was a Jesuit, physicist and astronomer famous for discovering sunspots. Jakob Balde (1604–1668), also a Jesuit, was a poet and author of many epic, satiric, dramatic, and lyric verses in Latin and, less famously, German. His contemporary Diego Tafuri de Lequile (1604–1673), Italian court chaplain at Innsbruck, wrote treatises in Italian and Latin, ranging from a noted study on the happy disposition of Austrians to the chronicle of Queen Christina of Sweden's visit to Innsbruck.

With the decline of writing in Latin in the 17th century, Tyrolese intellectuals began to show a more pronounced interest in the vernacular. Simon Pietro de Bartolomei (1709–1763), born near Trento, wrote with particular interest about the many dialects of all language groups of Tyrol and about their history. Karl von Güntherode (1740–1795) dedicated his life to the study of theology and metaphysics and wrote verses and satiric dramas. Yet, only the 18th century saw renewed cultural vitality in the region, for the first time since the advent of Humanism. In the mid-century, poet Bianca Laura Sailente and her husband Giuseppe Valeriano Vannetti found the *Accademia degli Agiati*, where Italian-speaking Tyrolese secular intellectuals and writers could gather, converse, and read their works. Sailente's and Vannetti's son, Clementino Vannetti (1754–1795), never attended university but spent his relatively short life writing and translating from Latin into Italian, writing essays, poems and satirical works, studying different national literatures of his time, and writing treatises on education and the regionalist sentiment in Trentino. Girolamo Tartarotti (1706–1761) from Rovereto, an important center of Italian-language culture in Tyrol, was another representative of the new Tyrolese literature in Italian, and composed works ranging from verses to essays on history and philosophy. Among German-speaking Tyrolese writers of the time, Ignaz Weitenauer (1709–1783) was a philologist and Orientalist, who also wrote lyric and dramatic works, and is widely considered to be one of the best Jesuit dramatists of the 18th century. He also wrote one of the first scientifically based manuals of German orthography. A poet associated with the Romantic movement and the movement for the unification of Italy is Giovanni Prati (1814–1884). In the last hundred years, Tyrolese literatures in Italian and Ladin have been marked by both regional and ethnic themes and the strong interest in the revival of the dialectal. Among the best known modern Tyrolese writers in German are: Anita Pichler (the first South Tyrolean postwar author to become known outside her country, and whose writings mark a formal breakthrough in Tyrolese literature), Helene Flöss, Sabine Gruber, Joseph Zoderer, Norbert Conrad Kaser (who was strongly influenced by Italian poetry, and wrote both in German and Italian), and Gerhard Kofler (also a bilingual writer of essays and poetry).

15 WORK

The estimated population in the Austrian part of Tyrol is 700,000, but its distribution is uneven, with the highest concentrations in the Inn and Drava river valleys and around the cities of Innsbruck, Schwaz and Kufstein. Most inhabitants of the rural areas are engaged in pasture farming, dairy farming, forestry, and cattle and livestock raising. Wheat and rye are grown in the Inn valley, while the city of Innsbruck is a traditional center of textile industry. The size of industries is relatively limited; goods include pharmaceutical and chemi-cal production and electrical appliances. The population in the Italian part of Tyrol is estimated to be 1,008,000, with the highest concentration around the city of Trento, and in the area between the cities of Bolzano and Merano. Italian speakers constitute a majority with about 60% of the total population, German around 35%, and 5% speak Ladin.

The economy of the region is based on tourism (especially in winter and summer), excellent wine production, dairy products, timber, and fruit. Its industries are concentrated around the production of metals, chemicals, and paper. The region is also a major producer and exporter of hydroelectric power.

Tourism is a major source of employment and revenue in the region. Medical University in Innsbruck and the University of Trento are internationally renowned for their innovative scientific work and consistently attract a highly educated international workforce to the region.

The Tyrolese are renowned for being honest and loyal business partners and for cultivating high ethical standards in all professions; in international collaboration, they expect to find the same qualities in their counterparts from other countries.

16 SPORTS

Tyrol is known for some of the best ski slopes in the world. Famous ski resorts in the region are Cortina d'Ampezzo, Kitzbühel, Ischgl, Wilder Kaiser, and St. Anton (where the world's first ski school was founded). Skiing represents not only a popular pastime, but is also a significant source of income in the highly developed Tyrolese tourist industry. The skiing season at the famous five glaciers (Kaunertaler, Pitztaler, Stubaier, Hintertuxer and Sölden-Ötztal) starts as early as mid-October and is open-ended, with excellent powder-snow. More than 30 ski areas feature monoskiing facilities, ski lifts, and expert service, with a wide range of slopes for monoskiers and the disabled. Mountain guides and mountaineering instructors provide instruction in winter sports, such as snowshoe hiking, icefall climbing, glacier crossing, and ski mountaineering. Tyrol is renowned for its excellent and highly skilled ski guides. In the summertime, mountain trekking and climbing are the most popular sports, both among the Tyrolese and the tourists.

17 ENTERTAINMENT AND RECREATION

Alpinism and winter sports are a favorite pastime of both the Tyrolese and the visitors to the area. Tyrol's many mountain shelters are generally open from May/June to October. Visitors may obtain temporary hunting and fishing licenses. Mushroom-picking is allowed in some parts of Tyrol and not in others because fungi are considered to be an integral part of the Alpine biosphere and essential nourishment for the animals. Merano was a popular 19th century spa town, and today the town of Brixen is known for its weight-loss clinics, hydrotherapy, and fashionable health tourism.

18 FOLK ART, CRAFTS, AND HOBBIES

The tradition of woodcarving is old in Tyrol, largely thanks to the abundance of forests in the region, and the need for the Tyrolese to while away the many long winter evenings, while talking and telling legends and tales to one another. The artwork produced includes statues of biblical figures and saints, toy animals, pretty household objects, ornaments for crèches, and picture frames. In some areas of the region, woodcarving has become a real industry, with carvings sold all over Europe.

¹⁹ SOCIAL PROBLEMS

Many social problems developing in other, highly urbanized areas of Europe and the world are almost absent in Tyrol. Overdevelopment in recent decades, along with the greatly increased traffic and large tourist population year-round are widely seen as the biggest threats to Tyrol today. The heavy traffic on the highway through the mountain pass of Brenner (Brennero) has been at the center of environmentalists' concerns. Many local families now own several cars, and commercial traffic between northern Europe and the Italian peninsula continues to increase. Environmentalists in Tyrol have lately gained strength, denouncing air and water pollution, projects that include more asphalt and concrete roads, as well as golf courses and other large sports installations.

The crime rate is very low in all parts of Tyrol, making it a very attractive residential area for people of all ages.

²⁰ GENDER ISSUES

Laws and regulations pertaining to women's and gay rights differ in the parts of Tyrol belonging to Austria from those in the parts belonging to Italy.

In 1918, women were given the right to vote in the newly founded First Austrian Republic. The University of Vienna first started accepting women in 1900. In 1976 a law established the principle of equal rights and responsibilities for married men and women, and equal rights and responsibilities in caring for children. The Equal Treatment Law of 1979 made various forms of discrimination against women illegal, establishing the principle of equal pay, and making it possible for women to receive compensation if they have been victims of sexual harassment in the workplace. Another goal of this law was to increase the number of women employed in government agencies. In 1925 Italy granted limited, and in 1945, full voting rights to women. Strong Italian feminist movement of the 1970s and 1980s stressed the demand for the complete equality of women in the workplace and other areas of public life, mobilizing both women and men in the issues of equal pay, reproductive rights and violence against women. When it comes to university education, the number of women in Italy who attend university now exceeds the number of men. Women in northern Italy (e.g. Tyrol) have a higher rate of employment than women in southern Italian regions. In spite of these legislative improvements, traditional roles prevail in the homes of many rural Tyrolese, with men still considering the majority of household and child-drearing tasks to be "women's work." This situation is different in urban areas, where more progressive attitudes towards sharing household tasks are the norm.

Abortion in the Austrian part of Tyrol is available upon request up to 14–15 weeks of pregnancy. Beyond that time, and up to 24 weeks of pregnancy, the abortion is possible only if the mother can show that there is risk to her mental or physical health, or to the health of the fetus. In the Italian part of Tyrol, Italian abortion laws govern reproductive rights. There, abortion became legal in 1978, and is performed free-of-charge in public hospitals and private clinics authorized by public health authorities. Surrogacy and egg donation are banned in Austria. In 2003, Italy banned use of donor sperm, eggs, or surrogate mothers, and restricted assisted fertilization to heterosexual couples in long-term relationships.

Gay rights are slowly gaining strength in Austria, a country generally seen as moderate when dealing with gay rights. Homosexuality in Austria was legalized in 1971, and homosexuals are not excluded from military service. While the first parliamentary debates on the issue took place in the mid-1990s, at the federal level, anti-discrimination laws pertaining to sexual orientation were introduced in 2004, and there is now discussion in Austria to provide a possibility for gay couples to register their partnership. Austria recognizes the right of the person not to testify against their same-sex partner. In 2006 the first legal same-sex marriage came into being when a transsexual who became a female was allowed to switch gender while remaining married to his wife. 49% of Austrians support gay marriage. The gay scene is particularly strong in Innsbruck, with numerous gay-friendly cafés and clubs, while rural areas remain generally more conservative. In the Italian-speaking part of Tyrol, public support for gay rights remains somewhat more subdued (only 31% of all Italians support same-sex marriages). Since the late 19th century, there have been no laws against homosexual practices in Italy, although homosexuals were often persecuted by the Fascist regime and during World War II. Homosexuals are not excluded from serving in the Italian military forces. Since 2003, discrimination based on sexual orientation has been illegal, but same-sex couples still have no shared rights regarding property, inheritance or social benefits. Although many Italian regions have since 2005 passed resolutions in support of same-sex civil unions, Trentino–Alto Adige is not among them. The gay scene in Trento and Bolzano is relatively strong, while in the countryside more traditional attitudes prevail.

²¹ BIBLIOGRAPHY

Foster, Charles Robert. *Nations without a State: Ethnic Minorities in Western Europe.* New York: Praeger, 1980.

Gregston, Brent. *Drive around Bavaria & The Austrian Tyrol,* 2nd ed. Peterborough, U.K.: Thomas Cook Publishing, 2006.

Hofmann, Paul. *The Sunny Side of the Alps.* New York: Henry Holt and Co., 1995.

Levy, Miriam J. *Governance and Grievance: Habsburg Policy and Italian Tyrol in the Eighteenth Century.* West Lafayette, IN: Purdue UP, 1988.

Steininger, Rolf. *Sunny Tyrol: A Minority Conflict of the Twentieth Century.* Edison, N.J.: Transaction Publishers, 2003.

Toscano, Mario. *Alto Adige, South Tyrol: Italy's frontier with the German world.* Baltimore: Johns Hopkins UP, 1975.

Walsh, Edmund. *The Woodcarver of Tyrol.* New York and London: Harper and Brothers Publishing, 1935.

White, Walter. *Holidays in Tyrol.* London: Chapman and Hall, 1876.

Wildner, Sigrun. *Words in Place: Contemporary Literature in South Tyrol.* Rutgers, NJ: Transaction Publishers, 2006.

Woelk, Jens, et al., eds. *Tolerance Established by Law: Self-Government and Group Rights in South Tyrol.* Leiden/Boston: Martinus Nijhoff/Brill, 2008.

Wolff, Stefan. *German Minorities in Europe: Ethnic Identity and Cultural Belonging.* New York: Berghahn, 2000.

—by K. von Wittelsbach

UDMURTS

ALTERNATE NAMES: Votyaks (former)
LOCATION: Russia
POPULATION: 637,000 (2002)
LANGUAGE: Udmurt; Russian, Tatar
RELIGIONS: Eastern Orthodox Christianity; native Udmurt religion

1 INTRODUCTION

The Udmurts are a Finno-Ugric people inhabiting the Russian Federation. In many sources, especially those dating from before 1917, the Udmurts are commonly referred to as *Votyaks*. The traditional homeland of the Udmurts is bordered to the south and east by the Kama River, a major tributary of the Volga River, and to the west by the Vyatka river, a tributary of the Kama. It is unclear when the ancestors of the Udmurts migrated into this area, but it appears that the Udmurts preceded not only Turkic and Slavic groups in the area, but even other Finno-Ugric groups such as the Maris.

The Udmurts have never lived within their own state, and throughout history they have been the subjects of numerous empires and other states. It is likely that the Udmurts became the subjects of the Volga Bulgarians, a Turkic group who in the early 8th century formed the first state in the Volga region to appear in historical sources. Udmurts first appear in historical sources only in the 12th century, in a travel account of the Arab traveler Abu Hamid al-Gharnati. With the conquest of Volga Bulgaria by the Mongols in the 1230s, the Udmurts found themselves subjects of the Mongol empire, and later the Golden Horde. After the collapse of the Golden Horde in the early 15th century, the Middle Volga region came under the domination of the Kazan Khanate, a Tatar and Muslim state. It was during the late 14th and early 15th centuries that groups of northern Udmurts came under Russian rule, first under the rule of Vyatka, and later under Muscovite rule. It was only in 1552, after the Russian conquest of Kazan, that the entire Udmurt ethnic territory came under Russian domination, and the Udmurts have remained under Russian rule to the present day. After the Bolshevik Revolution of 1917, the Soviet authorities, in keeping with the policy of granting at least the appearance of cultural and territorial autonomy to the national minorities of the former Russian empire, created the Udmurt Autonomous Soviet Socialist Republic (UdASSR), which was subordinate to the Russian Soviet Federative Socialist Republic (RSFSR). With the collapse of the Soviet Union in 1991 and the emergence of the former RSFSR as the newly independent Russian Federation, the former Udmurt ASSR remains dependent upon Russia but was renamed the Republic of Udmurtia.

2 LOCATION AND HOMELAND

According to the Russian census of 2002, there were 647,000 Udmurts in the Russian Federation, of whom 460,500 inhabited the Republic of Udmurtia. Some 120,000 Udmurts inhabit the neighboring regions of Tatarstan, Bashkortostan, the Mari Republic, as well as the Russian *oblasts* of Kirov, Perm', and Sverdlovsk. In addition, smaller Udmurt communities are located in Siberia (Krasnoiarsk *krai*), Kazakhstan, Central Asia, and the Ukraine. In the Republic of Udmurtia, Udmurts actually form a minority, numbering about 30% of the population. Russians account for about 60% of the population, and Tatars for 7%.

The Republic of Udmurtia covers a territory of 42,100 square kilometers (16,250 square miles). Before World War II, most of Udmurtia was covered in evergreen and deciduous forests. As a result of severe deforestation that took place in the later Soviet period, Udmurtia's forests have greatly diminished, yet they still cover much of the republic. The average temperature in January is –15° to –14°C (0° to 2°F) and the average July temperature is 17° to 18°C (64° to 66°F). Udmurtia can be categorized as having a cool continental climate.

The capital of Udmurtia is the city of Izhevsk, with a population of around 700,000. Izhevsk was and continues to be a predominantly Russian city and an important center for the Russian armaments industry.

The Udmurts' traditional economy consists of cereal agriculture, supplemented by hunting, fishing, and gathering forest products. Cereal and other agriculture continue to be the mainstays of the economy in rural Udmurt communities, although manufacturing plays an important role in the overall economy of Udmurtia.

3 LANGUAGE

The Udmurt language belongs to the Permian subgroup of the Finno-Ugric language family. It is closely related to the Komi language spoken in the Russian Federation's Komi Republic and more distantly related to Finnish and Estonian. Udmurt is divided into northern, central, and southern dialect groupings, but all dialects are mutually comprehensible, with the exception of the so-called Besermian dialect spoken in northern Udmurtia by approximately 3,000 people as of 2002. This dialect, which some linguists consider a separate language, differs substantially from the other Udmurt dialects. The origins of the Besermians themselves, like their dialect, is also puzzling. They do not consider themselves Udmurts, and it appears that they are descended from Turkic Muslims who settled the region both before and after the Mongol conquests of the 13th century.

Most Udmurts are fluent in their native language, and nearly all are fluent in Russian as well, if not actually native speakers of Russian. Fluency in Tatar is also common in the Udmurt communities located in Tatarstan and Bashkortostan.

Udmurts typically have a first name, a patronymic (the father's first name), and a surname. Since the imposition of Christianity on the Udmurts in the 18th century, most Udmurts have Russian names such as *Ivan*, *Grigorii* and *Sergei*. However, especially among the southern Udmurts, who remain "unbaptized" to the present day, Muslim and Turkic surnames (such as *Gabdulla*, and *Mukhammed*) and given names are frequently encountered, as well as Udmurt "pagan" names.

4 FOLKLORE

The Udmurts have a rich folklore tradition consisting of heroic legends, folktales, and an especially rich body of songs. A significant part of Udmurt folklore consists of specifically religious genres such as incantations, spells, and prayers. Similarly, many Udmurt songs are associated with specific religious ceremonies as well as specific festivals and other events such as weddings and funerals.

UDMURTS

0   500   1000 Miles

0   500   1000 Kilometers

Of particular interest is the cycle of legends surrounding the heroic figure Eshterek, who typically appears as an Udmurt hero who defends his people from the Tatars. An older layer of historical legends also describes the battles of Udmurt heroes against Mari invaders. Udmurt folklore has retained many mythological features, and many spirits and deities from Udmurt native religion appear in the folklore of both "unbaptized" and Christian Udmurts.

5 RELIGION

Today the majority of Udmurts professing religious belief are Eastern Orthodox Christians, although a significant minority of Udmurts, especially those inhabiting southern Udmurtia, Tatarstan, and Bashkortostan, have retained their formal adherence to native Udmurt religion and commonly refer to themselves as "unbaptized" Udmurts. Over the centuries Udmurt native religion has by no means remained static, and in fact has proven itself to be rather dynamic. Nevertheless, certain fundamental features can be identified as permanent features of Udmurt native religion. Udmurt native religion had and continues to have a communal orientation, and many of the ritual prayers and sacrifices are held in conjunction with the gathering of the village. Furthermore, Udmurt beliefs and rights are closely connected with both agriculture and the agricultural calendar and the veneration of the spirits of the community's ancestors.

At the summit of the Udmurt pantheon is Inmar, the supreme god. Today, the Christian Udmurts use this term to refer

to the Christian God as well. Traditionally, Inmar is conceived of as inhabiting the sky. Inmar's counterpart for the earth is Mu Kyldysyn. Similarly, there are a host of other spirits associated with numerous natural features and phenomena, such as wind, water, forests, and so forth.

Traditionally, Udmurt society itself was structured along religious lines. Udmurt society was divided into approximately 70 clans, and a clan was united not only by kinship but also by the veneration of tutelary spirits known as *vorshuds*. A *vorshud* was both a spirit and a shrine at which the members of the clan performed ceremonies and offered sacrifices.

6 MAJOR HOLIDAYS

Traditional Udmurt holidays were closely tied to the agricultural calendar and involved feasting, singing, and dancing, as well as prayers and offerings to the ancestors and other spirits. This characterization is equally valid for "unbaptized" Udmurts, and the Christianized ones, because the Eastern Orthodox holidays were themselves closely connected to the agricultural calendar; on that level, the transition from native to Christian holidays did not significantly alter their celebration by the Udmurts. Similarly, Udmurts in Bashkortostan and Tatarstan continue to celebrate the agricultural festivals of their Turkic and Muslim neighbors, such as the Tatar festival of *Sabantuy*. In Udmurtia, an especially important Udmurt festival is *Gerber*, the plow festival, which takes place in late June. Among "unbaptized" Udmurts, this festival, involves a sacrifice of a sheep to the field spirits, as well as feasting, dancing, and games, especially horse racing.

During the Soviet era, authorities discouraged the Udmurts' traditional religious holidays, both Christian and native, and the observation of the sanctioned Soviet holidays became widespread among the Udmurts. Since the fall of the Soviet Union, Udmurts have continued to celebrate some of these holidays, especially New Year's Day (January 1) and Victory Day (May 9).

7 RITES OF PASSAGE

Udmurt rites of passage and life-cycle rituals were closely bound with native religious beliefs. These rituals and rites continue to be widely observed among both Christian and "unbaptized" Udmurts. In villages, childbirth usually took place in the family's bathhouse and was attended by a midwife. When the childbirth was successful for both mother and child, the midwife performed a prayer of thanks and gave the child a provisional name, which was changed as the child grew older. Udmurts typically used amulets to protect the child, which was believed especially prone to illnesses borne by harmful spirits.

The most elaborate of the Udmurt rites of passage is the wedding ceremony, which traditionally involved very complex rituals and extensive feasting and other festivities. Of all the native rites of passage, wedding rituals continue to be the most widely observed, especially in rural areas, although civil ceremonies of Soviet origin, especially in urban areas, are also widely observed. Traditional Udmurt wedding rituals varied considerably from region to region. Not only was there specific clothing and specific foods for the rituals, but also a rich repertoire of songs reserved specifically for weddings.

Udmurt burial rituals involved not only the burial of the deceased, but also a series of memorial feasts to ensure the secure transition of the deceased from the realm of the living to the realm of the ancestral spirits. Among "unbaptized" Udmurts, and to a lesser degree among Orthodox Udmurts, the deceased was buried with grave goods, such as food, drink, household articles, and tools.

In addition to these major life-cycle rituals, another important rite of passage for males were ceremonies relating to military conscription. These ceremonies involved prayers for the health and safety of the young man about to be inducted into the Russian or Soviet army, and they obviously took on special significance in wartime.

8 INTERPERSONAL RELATIONS

Udmurt interpersonal relations, including greetings, body language, and gestures, do not substantially differ from those of Russian society as a whole. Both in traditional Udmurt society and in modern times, Udmurts place a strong emphasis on showing hospitality to guests, and between Udmurt guests and hosts there was even a repertoire of songs to be sung.

9 LIVING CONDITIONS

Traditional Udmurt society was both isolated and relatively impoverished, and during both the pre-Soviet and Soviet periods, Udmurt communities were periodically affected by famine and epidemics. Northern Udmurt were traditionally poor and continue to be so today as a result of the shorter growing season and poor soil of northern Udmurtia. In urban areas, especially in Izhevsk, living standards approximate those of Russian society in general. Very few Udmurts own their own automobiles, and salaries remain low. In rural areas, the standard of living is especially low, and consumer items are both expensive and often inaccessible.

In Udmurt villages, the inhabitants typically live in one- or two-room wooden houses and to a large degree depend on their gardens and family livestock for food. Nearly all villages have electric power, but almost no houses have indoor plumbing. As a rule, water is obtained from wells or streams.

Because very few Udmurts possess their own automobiles, they depend on public transportation. Larger cities are served by an extensive rail and bus system, but in rural areas bus service is very erratic, and many small or remote villages are not served by any sort of public transportation. In these cases, villagers hitch rides with passing trucks or cars, ride horses or horse-drawn wagons, or simply walk from one village to another. All travel in rural areas is exceedingly difficult in winter.

10 FAMILY LIFE

Before World War II, family size was large. Although infant mortality was very high, a woman could frequently have six or more children survive into childhood. In rural areas, child-rearing was to a large degree a communal matter, and children usually found themselves in a large extended family. Beginning in the later Soviet period continuing to the present day, the birth rate among Udmurts has been relatively low, averaging less than two children per family. In modern society, marriage and divorce involve simple civil procedures, and both are easily obtainable. First marriages occur around the age of 20, but there is also a high divorce rate.

Traditionally, and in many rural areas today religious rites, including sacrificial rites, remain an important element in both family cohesion and religious tradition. Families in rural areas retain their own family shrines and ceremonies, which exist alongside larger communal and even regional shrines.

11 CLOTHING

Traditional Udmurt clothing was functional and designed for both agricultural work and harsh winters. Summer clothes were usually made of linen, but wool garments were also worn year-round. In winter, woolen garments, as well as reversed sheepskin coats were worn. Udmurt folk costumes were worn on festive and ceremonial occasions, and these varied considerably from region to region. Typically, the folk costumes of the northern Udmurts were mostly white in color, and featured intricate embroidery. The southern Udmurts wore more colorful clothing and, in terms of fabric and design, their clothing was influenced to a degree by Tatar folk dress. One interesting feature of Udmurt folk costumes was the use of silver coins, which were fastened together as chest ornaments and on headgear, to display the wealth of a woman's family. Elements of traditional clothing are still occasionally worn, especially by older women in rural areas, but the clothing of most Udmurts today differs in no way from that of Russian society as a whole.

12 FOOD

The main staples of the Udmurt diet were, and continue to be, cereals such as rye, oats, barley, and to a lesser extent, wheat, all of which were usually baked into bread. In addition, during the Soviet era, potatoes became an important feature of the Udmurt diet. Vegetables such as cabbage, carrots, and onions also played an important role in their diet. The most common types of meat are pork, chicken, mutton, and to a lesser extent, beef. Furthermore, the famous Russian dumpling dish, *pelmeni*, is said by Udmurts to be of Udmurt origin, coming from the Udmurt words *pel'* (ear) and *nian'* (bread). Among common beverages are tea, beer, vodka, and a home-made liquor called *kumyshka*, which is a necessary element in festive occasions.

Modern-day eating utensils differ in no way from those used in Russia as a whole. Traditional utensils were typically made of wood, and of special note were large spoons, or ladles, which were elaborately and artistically carved, and which were also used in religious libation rituals.

There are usually three meals a day, with the mid-day meal being the heaviest.

13 EDUCATION

Before the Soviet era, the only kind of education afforded Udmurts was what was offered in Russian Orthodox religious institutions; there was no formal educational apparatus for "unbaptized" Udmurts, although there is evidence that some Islamized Udmurts in the 19th century were studying in *madrasas* of Bukhara. As a result, illiteracy was widespread in Udmurt communities. During the Soviet period, literacy increased substantially, and Udmurts were granted access to Soviet education institutions. Instruction in the Udmurt language, however, was limited to primary schools. In the later Soviet period, Udmurt was dropped as a medium of instruction in Udmurtia itself, and it came to be taught only as a separate subject in an otherwise Russian curriculum; however, Udmurt was retained as a medium of instruction in the Udmurt villages of Tatarstan and Bashkortostan. Most Udmurts have the equivalent of a high school education. As Russian citizens Udmurts study in the larger universities outside of the republic in Kazan, Ufa, St. Petersburg, and Moscow. More recently Udmurt scholars have been able to study in Finland and Estonia as well.

[14] CULTURAL HERITAGE

The richest element of the Udmurts' cultural heritage is their folk culture, which has an amazingly rich collection of music, songs, and other oral traditions. However, in keeping with Soviet nationality policies, after 1917 the Soviet government encouraged and funded the creation of a formal "cultural" apparatus, which included the creation of formal literature, including poetry, prose, and drama, as well as music and visual arts. Thus, in Izhevsk there is an Udmurt theater as well as substantial publishing in the Udmurt language.

[15] WORK

In rural areas, the vast majority of Udmurts are engaged in agricultural work, which tends to be organized along the collective system. These collectives are known by the Soviet term *kolkhoz*. However, because of the limited access to consumer goods, much energy is expended on private plots, where families grow their own potatoes, fruits, and vegetables. Much of the summer is spent preserving fruits, vegetables, and meat for the winter. Urban Udmurts commonly have smaller plots located in the suburbs or in nearby rural communities and likewise expend considerable energy growing and preparing food for the winter and spring.

[16] SPORTS

Traditionally, sports such as wrestling and horse racing took place during festivities. Today spectator sports such as soccer and hockey are popular among Udmurts.

[17] ENTERTAINMENT AND RECREATION

In rural areas, religious festivals and weddings not only fulfilled religious requirements, but they were also important sources of entertainment and recreation. Winter sports such as skating and cross-country skiing are popular recreational activities today, and in urban areas movies, theater, and concerts are also popular forms of entertainment.

[18] FOLK ART, CRAFTS, AND HOBBIES

Udmurts are especially renowned for their skill in woodworking and in weaving. Although most examples of woodworking and weaving are of a functional nature, the artistic level evident in many works remains very high.

[19] SOCIAL PROBLEMS

Many of the social problems that plague Russian society as a whole are especially severe in Udmurtia. One of the main social problems is alcoholism, which is endemic throughout Russia, but which is exacerbated in the rural areas of Udmurtia by poverty and the lack of recreational diversions. In addition, Udmurtia's suicide rate is one of the highest in the Russian Federation. Besides these social pathologies, the economic crisis following the collapse of the Soviet Union has affected Udmurts no less than the rest of Russian society, resulting in high unemployment and wages that are both low and erratically paid.

Another problem facing the Udmurts collectively is the issue of population decline; the population declined from 746,000 in 1989 to an estimate of 637,000 in 2002. While cultural assimilation is certainly a factor, it appears likely that collectively Udmurts are affected particularly severely by the same sorts of social and health problems causing population decline in the Russian population as a whole.

[20] GENDER ISSUES

The role of women in Udmurt society differs in certain ways from the role of women in the neighboring Russian and Tatar communities. Udmurt clans are matrilineal, and therefore some observers of Udmurt family life have suggested that this in some way elevates the status of women. In any case, in both rural and in urban settings, Udmurt women bear the double burden of both agricultural or wage work and child-rearing and domestic duties. In this respect, the position of Udmurt women is equivalent to that of women in Russian society as a whole.

The role of women in Udmurt society changed most drastically after World War II when a large proportion of Udmurt women were mobilized into the industrial workforce. At the same time, Udmurt women began to gain better access to educational opportunities.

[21] BIBLIOGRAPHY

Egorova, L. I., ed. *Udmurtiia: Bibliograficheskii ukazatel.'* Izhevsk, 1991.

Frank, Allen. "Traditional Religion in the Volga-Ural Region: 1960–1987." *Ural-Altaische Jahrbücher* 63 (1991): 167–84.

Khristoliubova, L. S., et al., ed. *Udmurty: istoriko-etnograficheskie ocherki.* Izhevsk, 1993.

Khristoliubova, L. S. and T. G. Minniiakhmetova, *Udmurty Bashkortostana.* Ufa, 1994.

Lallukka, Seppo. *East Finnic Minorities in the Soviet Union: An Appraisal of the Erosive Trends.* Helsinki, 1990.

Sanukov, K. N. *Problemy istorii i vozrozhdeniia finno-ugorskikh narodov Rossii.* Ioshkar-Ola, 1994.

Trofimova, E. Ia. "Gostevoi etiket udmurtov (k postanovke problemy)," in: *Folklor i etnografiia udmurtov: obriady, obychai, pover'ia,* Izhevsk, 1989, 18–27.

Vikar, Laszlo, and Gabor Bereczki. *Votyak Folksongs.* Budapest, 1989.

Vladykin, V. E. *Religiozno-mifologicheskaia kartina mira udmurtov.* Izhevsk, 1994.

Vladykin, V. E. and L. S. Khristoliubova, *Etnografiia udmurtov.* Izhevsk, 1991.

Vuorela, Toivo. "The Votyaks," in: *The Finno-Ugric Peoples.* Indiana University Uralic and Altaic Series, no. 39: Bloomington, 1964.

—by A. J. Frank

UKRAINIANS

LOCATION: Ukraine
POPULATION: Over 45 million [total population of country; 77.8% ethnic Ukrainians, 17.3% Russian, 0.6% Byelorussians, 4.3% others]
LANGUAGE: Ukrainian
RELIGION: Ukrainian Orthodox – Moscow Patriarchate, Ukrainian Orthodox—Kiev Patriarchate, Ukrainian Autocephalous Orthodox, Ukrainian Greek Catholic, Roman Catholic, Protestant, Jewish, Muslim, others

¹ INTRODUCTION

Ukraine has had three periods of national statehood. The first period existed from the 9th to 14th centuries AD and was known as Kievan Rus', with its capital in Kiev. The second was the Cossack period, lasting from the middle of the 17th to the end of the 18th centuries. The third period began with the fall of tsarist Russia and the establishment of a sovereign Ukrainian state in the form of the Ukrainian National Republic on 22 January 1918; this state lasted only a few years before it was partitioned among Russia, Poland, Czechoslovakia, Hungary, and Romania. During the German occupation in June 1941, the Ukrainian people made an unsuccessful attempt to reclaim their sovereignty in Lviv, the capital of Western Ukraine. As a result of peace treaties signed at the end of World War II, all the Ukrainian territories were integrated into the multinational Soviet Union in the form of the Ukrainian Soviet Socialist Republic.

With the spread of Gorbachev's *perestroika* and *glasnost* policies across the Soviet Union in the 1980s, people in Ukraine and other republics began demanding more freedom and ultimately independence. In August 1991 Ukraine became independent; elected Leonid Kravchuk (a former Communist) as its president; and began implementing democratic, free enterprise policies as well as gradual economic reforms and nuclear disarmament. In 1994 Leonid D. Kuchma, former director of the world's largest rocket factory and prime minister under President Kravchuk was elected president. President Kuchma developed friendly political and economic relations with the West and enacted economic reforms to improve the country's growth prospects. On 29 June 1996, the Ukrainian Parliament approved the first Constitution of Ukraine, just a few weeks before the fifth anniversary of its independence.

Tensions between ethnic Ukrainian and Russian populations in Ukraine compounded by political pressures from Russia and the United States reached a peak during the campaign leading up to the 2004 presidential elections. Prime Minister Viktor Yanukovych, supported by Russia, and opposition leader and former Prime Minister Viktor Yushchenko, supported by the West, came out in a tie. The ensuing runoff election on November 21 designated Yanukovich as the winner. However, many Ukrainian citizens felt that this result was fraudulent. Hundreds of thousands of people took to the streets of Kiev and other cities to protest the election of Yanukovich and to express their support for Yushchenko. As a result of these demonstrations, now called the "Orange Revolution," a re-vote took place in which Yushchenko received a majority of votes and took presidential office on 23 January 2005.

Following his inauguration, the country's new president appointed Yulia Tymoshenko as his prime minister. One of the major figures in the Orange Revolution, Tymoshenko brought strong leadership into the heart of Ukrainian government. Opposed to some of the Yushchenko's reforms and incentives, Tymoshenko left the government. However she returned for the 2006 parliamentary elections. Although the Party of Regions won a plurality of the vote, President Viktor Yushchenko's Our Ukraine—People's Self Defense Bloc and former Prime Minister Yulia Tymoshenko's Bloc formed a coalition and established a government with Tymoshenko as the prime minister. Prime Minister Tymoshenko is considered a possible candidate for president of Ukraine in 2010.

Today Ukraine enjoys a wide range of active political parties and blocs, from leftist to center and center-right to ultra-nationalist. Occupying a strategic position at the crossroads between Europe and Asia and possessing rich farmlands, a highly trained labor force, and a good education system, Ukraine has the potential to become a major European economy.

² LOCATION AND HOMELAND

Ukraine, commonly referred to as the "breadbasket of Europe," covers about 604,000 sq km (233,000 sq mi) of land in Eastern Europe. Territorially, Ukraine is the second-largest country in Europe after France. It is bordered by the Black Sea to the south; Moldova and Romania to the southwest; Hungary, Slovakia, and Poland to the west; Belarus to the north; and Russia to the north and northeast. Approximately 65% of the soil is *chornozem (chornozem in Ukrainian simply means fertile, black soil). Traditionally an agricultural area, Ukraine* grows wheat, maize, buckwheat, all kinds of vegetables, fruit, melons, and berries. Ukraine is also known for its plentiful mineral resources.

Almost the entire country of Ukraine is a vast flat plain, bounded by the Carpathian mountains in the southwest, the Black Sea and the Sea of Azov in the south, and the Crimean Mountains on the southern end of the Crimean Peninsula. The highest point in Ukraine is Mt. Hoverla in the Carpathians, with an elevation of 2,061 meters. The Dnieper is the main river that runs through Ukraine. One of the longest European rivers, the Dnieper is the republic's most important source of hydroelectric power.

In general, the country's climate is temperate continental, except for the southern Crimea, which has a sub-tropical climate. The typical Ukrainian winter is rather mild, with no severe frosts but with regular snowfalls everywhere except in the south. The average winter temperature reaches –20°C in the north and –3°C in the south. Summers tend to be hot and dry with occasional showers and thunderstorms.

Kiev, with over 2 million inhabitants, is the capital of Ukraine. It boasts numerous beautiful churches and is known as the Golden Domed City. The Monastery of the Caves (*Pecherska Lavra*) is one of the brightest of Kiev's gems. The Lavra was founded in 1051 and is now part museum and part functioning monastery. Its 40 buildings represent eight centuries of art and architecture. Other major cities in Ukraine include Zaporozhye, Dnepropetrovsk, Dnyeprodzerzhinsk, Odessa, Kharkiv, Lviv and Nickolayev. Crimea is an autonomous republic within Ukraine. It was annexed by Russia in 1783 and transferred to Ukraine in 1954.

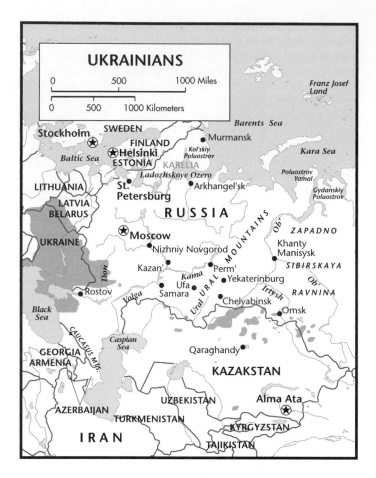

UKRAINIANS

0   500   1000 Miles

0   500   1000 Kilometers

³ LANGUAGE

Ukrainian is the official state language of Ukraine. Belonging to the East Slavic subgroup of the Slavic languages, Ukrainian employs its version of the Cyrillic alphabet with 33 characters. It shares some vocabulary with the languages of the neighboring Slavic nations, including Russia, Byelorussia and Poland. Ukrainian is the most ancient living Slavic language, as it is the most closely related to Old Slavonic, the common language of the ancestors of modern Slavs. It is also the language that was spoken in the medieval Kievan Rus' kingdom.

Ukrainian is the native language of nearly 40 million people, which makes it the second most widely spoken in the Slavic group of Indo-European languages. It is used particularly widely in central and western Ukraine. In cities such as Odessa and in eastern Ukraine, where there are large concentrations of ethnic Russians, both Ukrainian and Russian are widely spoken. In areas of eastern Ukraine located near the border with Russia, Russian often dominates.

Although during the Soviet regime the Ukrainian language underwent some Russification, there were no profound changes. Ukrainian is presently undergoing a revival and has become the language of choice for television shows, films, science, newspapers, computers, and the Internet in Ukraine.

At present, Ukrainian has nine distinct dialects: Volhynian, Podillya (Podole), Galician, Kiev-Poltava, Southern, two Carpathian dialects (Hursul and Boyko), and two Pokutya (Bokovynian) dialects. Examples of everyday Ukrainian words include *dobryj den* (hello), *tak* (yes), *nee* (no), *bood laska*

(please), *dyakooyoo* (I thank you), *dyakooyemo* (we thank you) and *do pobachenya* (goodbye). Other useful expressions of everyday speech are: *vybachte* (excuse me), *pereproshuyu* (pardon me!), *neobkhid'no* (it is necessary), *skil'ky?* (how many/much?) and *pravyl'no* (right).

Among most commonly used exclamations (or *vyhuky*) by Ukrainians are the following:

> *Os'!*—Here you are!
> *Hey!*—Hey!
> *Hayda'!*—Let's go! Come on!
> *Oy! Oy-yoy!*—expression of surprise
> *Okh!*—expression of being tired
> *Harazd'!*—Okay! Deal!

⁴ FOLKLORE

Ukrainian culture is rich with beliefs and rituals stemming from pre-Christian times. Folk beliefs are primarily associated with major life events such as birth, marriage, and death and are also connected with nature (clouds, earth, fire, water, etc.). Through the centuries, these ritual and verbal customs have been incorporated into Christian rites.

Legends passed on from generation to generation include tales of the founding of the city of Kiev by the three brothers Kyi, Scheck, and Khoryv and their sister Lybed. A monument in their honor can be found in the capital city of Kiev. Other legends tell of the magical steppe plant called *yevshan zillia* that has the power of bringing lost souls back to their homeland. Children are often reminded of the mythical dragon-slayer Kyrylo Kozhumiaka, who was endowed with tremendous strength and ultimately freed the people of Kiev from the vicious grasp of a dragon. There is also the tale of Oleksa Dovbush. This Ukrainian Robin Hood lived in the Carpathian Mountains, stealing from the rich and giving to the poor. A number of different sites in the Carpathians are named after him.

Furthermore, Ukraine has a rich folk music tradition. Ukrainian folk songs reflect its people's spirit, philosophy, perspective on life, historical events, and regional diversity. Some of the songs were created thousands of years ago. These ancient songs are often dedicated to peasant rituals and agricultural cycles.

Moreover, Ukrainians can boast their own musical instruments, including the *bandura*, *tsympaly* (hammer dulcimer), and *trembita*. The *bandura*, a lutelike instrument with 50 or more strings, is Ukraine's national instrument. The origin of the *bandura* dates back to the 7th century AD, when it was used mainly to accompany epic ballads and folk dances. Beginning in the 15th century and lasting until the 18th century, *Kobzars* (traveling musicians) made the *bandura* into one of the most popular folk instruments. Wandering from village to village, *Kobzars* used the *bandura* to accompany their songs about Cossack (Ukrainian warrior) exploits. Over the centuries, the *bandura* acquired more and more strings and became a fully chromatic instrument with switches for changing tonalities. The *tsympaly* is a Ukrainian hammer dulcimer that originated in the Middle East. It was first brought to Ukraine during the Crusades by wandering Gypsy and Jewish musicians. The earliest mention of the Ukrainian term *tsymbaly* dates back to the 17th century.

Another folk instrument called the *trembita* is the Ukrainian version of the alpine horn. It is typically made of spruce that has been split, with a central bore dug out and then glued together and bound with birch bark. Its length ranges from three meters (10 feet) to half a meter. Traditionally, the *trembita* was used to signal events such as the coming of visitors, enemies, or death in the mountain regions of Ukraine. Consequently, a system of elaborate signals was devised. Over time, the *trembita* was adapted to play Christmas carols.

Modern Ukrainian music has come a long way since the *Kobzars*, and Kolomiya rap and Polissia pop enjoy great popularity among Ukrainian youth. Nevertheless, Ukrainian music embedded in ancient traditions is still appreciated. There also has been a revival of Cossack songs and poetry.

In addition to oral folklore, Ukrainians have preserved various forms of folk dances and dancing games. Many dances originated in rural Cossack villages while some of them are rooted farther back in ancient cults. In one of the most popular folk dances called the *hopak,* male dancers compete against each other in performing acrobatic leaps. Although initially many of the folk dances were performed solely by males or females, today more often than not men and women perform these dances together. It is customary for dancers to wear colorful costumes. Folk dancing is performed for special occasions, such as weddings, festivals, and other functions. Folk dance ensembles can be found not just in Ukraine, but in Ukrainian communities throughout the world.

5 RELIGION

Because of the geographical proximity of Ukraine to the Black Sea and the Near East, Christianity was found in the present territory of Ukraine as early as the 1st century AD. The Primary Chronicles mention the missionary St. Andrew, who preached the gospel in Kievan Rus' and blessed the hills on which the Lavra Monastery was later built. In the 9th century, the missionary brothers Sts. Cyril and Methodius came from the West and spread Christianity throughout the region. However, Ukrainian Orthodox Christianity came from Byzantium due to the strong ties between Kievan Rus' and Greece. In 954 Olga, the grand princess of Kievan Rus', was baptized, becoming the first Christian ruler of the region. Because of her efforts in spreading Christianity, she was canonized after her death. Her grandson, Prince Vladimir, believing that the new faith would strengthen the state and increase its prestige among its Christian neighbors, adopted Christianity and converted all of his people to the Christian faith in 988. Thereafter, Christian writings and culture spread throughout Kievan Rus'. Vladimir established religious schools and built churches, where the liturgy was given in the Slavonic tongue.

Ukraine's years spent under a communist regime dealt a substantial blow to the Ukrainian Orthodox Church. In the 1930s, the Ukrainian church lost three metropolitans, over 30 archbishops and bishops, and many thousands of priests due to imprisonment and persecution. Finally, the Church was forcibly incorporated into the Russian Orthodox Church. The Ukrainian Catholic Church met a similar fate soon after its abolition by the Soviet government in 1946. There were mass arrests and assassinations, and many priests were exiled to Siberia. Although in 1974 a Council on Religious Affairs was created by the Soviets to abolish religious activity, underground Catholic churches continued to operate. The future cardinal of the Vatican, Yosyf Slipyj, spent 18 years incarcerated in Siberia. Because of the intervention of U.S. President John F. Kennedy and Pope John XXIII, Cardinal Slipyj was allowed to emigrate to the West. He died in Rome in 1984.

Despite such hardships, the Ukrainian Orthodox Church survived communism. In 1988 Ukrainians throughout the world celebrated the 1,000-year anniversary of Ukrainian Christianity. Famous religious sites in Ukraine include the St. Sophia Cathedral in Kiev, built in 1037 by Prince Yaroslav the Wise; the Pecherska Lavra Monastery, an underground labyrinth of monastic caves in Kiev dating back to the 11th century; St. George's Cathedral in Lviv, a notable baroque monument; a 17th-century wooden church in Yaremcha (Lviv district), and the Pochaiv Lavra Monastery in the Volyn district of western Ukraine, one of the most revered holy sites in Ukraine.

At present the dominant religions in Ukraine are the Ukrainian Orthodox Church and the Ukrainian Greek Catholic Church (which practices Orthodox rites but recognizes the Roman Catholic Pope as head of the Church). The Ukrainian Orthodox Church is further divided between a Moscow Patriarchate and an independent Kiev Patriarchate.

6 MAJOR HOLIDAYS

The Ukrainians enjoy celebrating a number of holidays. Christmas, Easter, New Year's, and festival of Ivana Kupala are among the most favorite holidays. The most important holiday in the Ukrainian church is Easter, followed by Christmas. Easter Sunday does not have a set date but changes every year to fall on the first Sunday after the full moon that occurs on or right after the spring equinox. Both Christmas and Easter are celebrated in accordance with the Julian (old style) calendar, resulting in Christmas Day being celebrated on January 7. Some Ukrainian communities abroad, however, celebrate these holidays according to the newer Gregorian calendar.

Many of the Ukrainian holiday traditions can be traced back thousands of years. New Year's carols *or shchedrivky,* spring songs and dances *(vesnianky, hahilky),* the old pagan midsummer festival of Ivana Kupala, marriage rites with their ritualized dramas, and celebrations of birth involving godparents and christening linen all stem from pagan beliefs, symbols, and images. Even the Easter egg dyeing that has its roots in Ukraine is a thousand-year-old tradition that predates the arrival of Christianity in the country.

7 RITES OF PASSAGE

Traditional Ukrainian rites of passage mark significant life transitions or celebrate milestones in the lives of a group of people. Marriage is one of the most important events in one's life and symbolizes a transition from one social status to the next. Rooted in folk customs, Ukrainian wedding traditions are rich and elaborate. An important component of the marriage ceremony is the special nuptial service in the church. Bearing a child (especially the first one) is another event that marks a significant change in a family's life. There are special puerperal ceremonies that accompany the delivery of a child. Families in some parts of Ukraine consider the one-year anniversary of a child's birth to be a rite of passage. This ancient custom, called *postryshyny*, revolves around cutting the child's hair. Family members and friends gather together to celebrate the child's life. This custom is primarily preserved and practiced in the territory of Ukraine's central lands.

Ukrainians attend a rally to mark the Day of Unity in Kiev, which is the day the Union of Ukrainian People's Republic and West-Ukrainian Republic happened in 1919. (Sergei Supinsky/AFP/Getty Images)

Ukrainians also consider funerals to be important rites of passage. Funeral rites ensure not only the easy transition of the souls of deceased persons into the world of ancestors but also the protection of the living from the negative influences of dead spirits. These rituals include burial ceremonies and commemorative gatherings in honor of the deceased person.

One Ukrainian custom that celebrates young people's wish to find true love is the Ivan Kupalo festival. In pagan mythology, Kupalo was the god of love and fertility. In his honor, young men and women gather around streams and ponds, where they build fires and sing songs. Some of them jump over the fire and braid field flowers into wreaths that they send floating on the water. If the wreath floats, they will be lucky in love; if it sinks, they will be unhappy.

8 INTERPERSONAL RELATIONS

Ukrainians are very warm and affectionate people. It is common to greet visitors with three kisses on the cheek. Hugging is another way Ukrainians greet one another, often followed by a hearty handshake. During the early 1990s a popular salutation among Ukrainians was "*Slava Ukraini*" (Glory to Ukraine). Toasting is also a popular custom among Ukrainians. Often in a group, one person will announce a toast, followed by the words "*na zdorovia*" (to your health), or "*day Bozhe*" (glory to God).

Ukrainians often put their heart and soul into enjoying a hearty meal, a fine drink, and a good laugh. They love having company, often turning a simple visit into a large party, and even outsiders easily become part of the family. It is not unusual for friends at such gatherings to get into heated debates over politics and to openly express their feelings. Ukrainians are also known for their legendary hospitality. Ukrainian hosts will go out of their way to treat their guests to delicious and elaborate meals. When invited to a Ukrainian home, one must be prepared to stay for several courses. It is expected that the guest will at least try every dish offered. Refusing food is considered an insult to the host's generosity. It is common for guests to compliment food and the company. Often times parties, celebrations, and other informal gatherings involve singing. Even in mixed company there are a few songs that everyone knows how to sing.

9 LIVING CONDITIONS

Health is a major issue being discussed in Ukraine since its independence. It was always very difficult for people in Ukraine and other former Soviet republics to get proper medical care.

Soviet-era hospitals lacked funding and equipment, and often even simple procedures like cataract surgeries were impossible, and basic medicines such as aspirin were not available. Doctors would take bribes from families desperate to help their loved ones in the hospital. Today, the health industry is undergoing scrutiny in Ukraine. With the help of Western physicians and pharmaceutical companies, Ukrainians are learning about advanced medicine and surgical procedures.

Another great concern for many people in Ukraine is environmental pollution. Fallout from the 1986 Chernobyl disaster in conjunction with continuous industrial pollution has had a damaging effect on air quality and drinking water. During the 1986 explosion at the Chernobyl nuclear power plant near Kiev, Ukraine and other Eastern European countries were saturated with radioactivity. Once known as the "breadbasket of Europe," some of Ukraine's regions are still radioactive and will remain so for decades. At the same time, an environmental movement known as "Green World" has made major progress in fighting pollution and has spread awareness of the problem of Chernobyl throughout Europe. Furthermore, in accordance with its agreement with the Group of 7 and European Commission in 1995, Ukraine permanently closed the Chernobyl plant in 2000. Also, in 2007 Western nations provided the Ukrainian government with funds for construction of a new shelter to be built around the closed plant.

In addition to challenges in the environmental arena, Ukraine since independence has faced major problems with its transportation system. The lack of diversified energy sources, due partly to Ukraine's disagreements with Russia over oil, has caused numerous delays and inconveniences. Ukraine's highways consist of about 146,000 km (91,000 mi) of paved road; however, many roads, especially in rural areas, are unpaved or in need of repairs. Only about a third of people in Ukraine own cars, in part because gasoline prices have skyrocketed. Buses and trolleys can be seen in cities but they are not very punctual. However, the subway systems in Kiev, Kharkiv and other major cities are relatively good, and major cities and industrial centers are well connected by railway. Ukraine's major ports—Kerch, Kherson, Lviv, Odessa, Sevastopil, and Yalta—are also connected by water.

Approximately two-thirds of Ukraine's population (68%) lives in cities, where high-rise apartments ("*Khrushchovki*") built during the Soviet era are dominant. Many of these buildings are poorly constructed and overcrowded. About one-third of Ukraine's population (32%) still lives in rural areas, where there are small villages and homesteads, and the primary occupation is farming. Here the standard of living is lower than in the cities, which is why Ukrainians from rural areas continue to leave their villages to go to the cities.

Ukraine's annual economic growth rate in 2007 was 6.9%, and its real gross domestic product (GDP) growth amounted to 5.68%. Personal incomes are rising and the level of unemployment is lower than in many other European countries. Yet Ukraine's economy remains burdened by excessive governmental regulation, corruption, lack of law enforcement, and mounting inflation. In 2006 the inflation rate was 9.08%; in 2007 it reached 12.8%; and in the first part of 2008 it has jumped to 21.9%. The Ukrainian government has taken measures against corruption, and small and medium enterprises have been largely privatized; however, key sectors such as energy and telecommunications remain under governmental con-

trol and require restructuring and partial privatization to be able to compete in world markets.

10 FAMILY LIFE

Matriarchy was dominant in prehistoric times in the territory of Ukraine, and women enjoyed full authority in historic times during the rule of Ukrainian princes and Cossacks. Over the centuries the position of women deteriorated, with women becoming inferior to men. However this trend is gradually changing.

Traditional Ukrainian families are large and familial ties are strong, although now most city families can only afford to support one or two children. It is common for family members to help each other so that people place great value in family networks. Young people generally respect their parents and grandparents and are expected to take care of the older folk in the family. Weddings are grand affairs in Ukrainian society, with many associated customs and beliefs. Even though many marriages in recent years suffered divorce, family remains the most important unit in Ukrainian society.

11 CLOTHING

Ukrainians generally wear Western-style clothing. Young Ukrainians enjoy following Western trends and fashions and especially like to wear clothing with popular labels like Nike, Levi's, Guess, Reebok, Adidas, etc. However, on special occasions or holidays, many people dress in national costume.

The earliest known dress worn in the territory of Ukraine dates back to the Scythian and Sarmatian tribes, with men wearing cloth or fur trousers, jackets, and pointed caps. Women dressed in loose shirts, coats with armhole slits, and caps similar to a man's cap but covered by wraps. As evidenced by archaeological finds, embroidery was used as a Scythian art as far back as the 5th century BC. Learning the art of embroidery from Scythians, Ukrainians made it into a fundamental element of folk costume.

Today, Ukrainian folk costumes come in many varieties depending on a region of Ukraine and could be roughly divided into five regional styles: that of the Middle Dnieper Region, originating in the Hetman period; Polisia; Podilia; central Galicia and Volhynia; and the Carpathian Mountains and Subcarpathia, including Pokutia, Bukovyna, Hutsul, Boiko, and Lemko. In addition to regional differences, costumes differ according to sex, with women's dress more elaborate and colorful than men's dress. Time of the year also influences the dress. Despite these differences each costume demonstrates a high degree of sophistication, elegance, and artistry.

12 FOOD

Ukrainian cuisine is varied and rich in taste and is an integral part of Ukrainian customs and religious rituals. The ritual breads baked for Christmas and Easter, weddings, and funerals have special meanings and uses. The Easter *paska* bread, wedding *korovai*, delicious *pyrohy* (baked pies with fillings) and intricate *holubtsi* (stuffed cabbage rolls) are all part of the Ukrainian cuisine. *Varenyky* (dumplings) is another quintessential Ukrainian food. They are considered a Ukrainian specialty and have many fillings such as potatoes, meat, cottage cheese, and berries.

Among everyday dishes are soups, stews, sausages, smoked meats, and rye bread. Meals made with beef, lamb, pork, poultry, and fish dishes are usually eaten with vegetables and salads. One of the most preferred Ukrainian soups is *borshch*. This red beet soup made with vegetable and meat is usually served for lunch. Ukrainians also eat large amounts of potatoes, cooked buckwheat *(kasha),* and varieties of rye and wheat bread. Dairy products, such as cream, cottage cheese, and eggs, have their prominent place in the Ukrainian diet as well.

The most popular meat is pork and its products, such as ham, sausage *(kovbasa)* and blood sausage *(kyshka). Salo,* salted pig's fat, is a traditional food and is used in Ukrainian cooking in a variety of ways. Other authentic Ukrainian dishes include herring a la Kiev and jellied veal roll.

Some popular drinks are tea, coffee, honey liqueur, *kvas*—a special sour drink, and vodka, or *horilka* in Ukrainian. Favorite desserts include pancakes, cakes and fruit dishes with blueberries, cherries, plums, and strawberries. More elaborate desserts that are typically prepared for festive occasions include torts (such as Kyivsky torte) and all sorts of sweet rolls. Ukraine is also known for its high quality honey.

Ukrainians abroad have preserved Ukrainian cooking as part of their cultural heritage. This is particularly true of their festive or ritual foods.

13 EDUCATION

Ukrainian children are required to attend school for 11 years, from about the age of 7 to the age of 15. After grade nine, students can continue a general academic program, or they can enroll in technical or trade schools to further their education. In Ukraine there are around 150 schools of higher education, including 9 universities. There are about 80 research institutes. The largest and most popular universities are the Kiev State University, Lviv State University, and Kharkiv State University. Ukrainian parental expectations are no different from those of parents in the West. Education was always considered a vital part of Ukrainian life, and children are encouraged to excel and achieve a higher education. Many young people in Ukraine enroll in medical universities, while other popular practices are law, engineering, and communications.

Education is free and universal; however, the public education system continues to suffer from chronic under-funding. Teachers are paid relatively low salaries. Children from poor families tend to drop out of school. Over 3% of school-aged children are not able to attend school for various reasons. Additionally, a lack of schooling remains a significant problem among the rural population.

14 CULTURAL HERITAGE

Ukrainian music is firmly rooted in the rich, mystical folklore of the country. Of the prominent composers or classical music, Mykola Lysenko (1842–1912) is regarded as the first to infuse the genre with a distinct national character. During the 1860s Lysenko collected an impressive assortment of Ukrainian folk songs, many of which he later arranged and published. His original classical compositions are instilled with Ukrainian folk themes and motives. Although Lysenko introduced a Ukrainian flavor in classical compositions, it is Borys Lyatoshynsky (1895–1968) who is considered to be the "father" of modern Ukrainian classical music. His works are strikingly original, conceptually profound, and technically sophisticated. A highly regarded professor at the Kiev and Moscow Conservatories, Lyatoshynsky taught some of the leading Ukrainian

composers of his time. His influence stimulated a progressivism in Ukrainian music, which culminated in the early 1960s with the "Kiev avant-garde," a movement spearheaded by Valentin Silvestrov and Leonid Hrabovsky. Today, Ukraine is blessed with a sizable group of first-rate composers, including (along with Silvestrov and Hrabovsky) Volodymyr Huba, Ivan Karabyts, Oleh Kyva, Myroslav Skoryk, Yevhen Stankovych, and many others.

Ukrainian pop music also traces its origins to folk music. In particular, its folklore roots are evident in the predominantly strophic structure and propensity of minor mode in pop melodies. The most important Ukrainian pop composer of the late 1960s, 70s, and 80s was Volodymyr Ivasiuk (1949–1979), whose songs were characterized by impulsive rhythmic patterns, rapidly changing harmonies, and sweeping vocal lines tinged with Bukovinian folk motifs. Ivasiuk's compositions were recorded and performed by leading Ukrainian pop artists such as Sofia Rotaru, Kobza, and Smeritchka.

After the disintegration of the Soviet Union in 1991, Ukrainian pop songs became one of the primary vehicles of social consciousness and expression. Independence spawned a number of new pop genres in Ukraine, ranging from rap to jazz and beyond, many of them highly imitative of Western models. At present, the freeing of the Communist grip on the popular music industry has been something of a double-edged sword. What has been gained from the resulting freedom of expression has been offset by lower production standards, the disintegration of marketing mechanisms for recorded music, piracy, and rampant copyright violation.

Beside rich musical traditions, Ukrainians take pride in their literature. The earliest Ukrainian literature was composed in Church Slavonic and dates back to Kievan Rus' (11th–13th centuries). After the Mongol invasion in the 13th century, Ukrainian literature was in decline until the 16th century, when it experienced a revival. Ukrainian literature in the 19th century reflected the rapid development of national consciousness under Russian rule.

At the heart of modern Ukrainian literature lies Ivan Kotliarevsky. His creative *Eneida* (1798), a travesty of Virgil's *Aeneid,* transformed the *Aeneid's* heroes into Ukrainian Cossacks. Following Kotliarevsky's lead, in 1830 the city of Kharkiv became the center of Ukrainian Romanticism. Meanwhile, western Ukraine gave birth to the "Ruthenian Triad" of Shashkevych, Holovatsky, and Vahylevych, who became the leading writers of Kiev Romanticism. Romanticism found its highest expression among the literary circle, the Writers' Brotherhood of Sts. Cyril and Methodius (1846).

Without a doubt, the most famous Ukrainian poet is Taras Shevchenko. A bard of Ukrainian literature, this 19th century poet portrayed in his works Ukraine's history and satirized Russia's oppression of Ukraine. Next to Shevchenko stands the greatest realist of the late 1800s, Ivan Franko. A poet and novelist whose naturalistic novels chronicled contemporary Galician society, Franko is particularly appreciated for his long narrative poem, "Moses," that marks the height of his literary achievement. Lesia Ukrainka is a female poet and dramatist who made her unique imprint on Ukrainian literature of the late 19th century, with her poetic dramas and dialogues.

In the first three decades of the 20th century, Ukrainian literature experienced such literary movements as realism, symbolism, neoclassicism, and futurism. After the Russian

Revolution, during a short period of relative freedom, a host of talented writers became critical of Soviet policies, but in 1932 the Communist Party began enforcing socialist realism as the required literary style. During Stalin's great purges of 1933–38, many talented writers were imprisoned or executed, or fled into exile. The post-Stalinist period saw the emergence of a new generation that rejected socialist realism, but they were silenced in the 1970s by repressive measures from the Soviet government. With Ukraine's independence in 1991, many young talented writers have emerged, beginning a new chapter in the history of Ukrainian literature.

15 WORK

Ukraine is now in the process of transitioning to a market economy, a move that has been socially and politically difficult due to inflation, unemployment, and general economic uncertainty. Most of Ukraine's population is employed in the agricultural and metalwork industries, machine building, construction, chemical, food, and light industries.

Typically Ukrainians work 40 hours per week and enjoy at least 24 days of paid vacation per year. There are also 10 official holidays in Ukraine. That means that each employee has a minimum of 31 days of paid holidays per year. In accordance with the Labor Law, the minimum employment age is 17 years. Although a monthly wage minimum has increased, as of 2007 it was only $90 (460 *hryvnia*). Evidently, the minimum wage does not provide a decent standard of living for a worker and his or her family. Consequently, many people have a second job or are engaged in some kind of entrepreneurial activity, such as small family business. This is where family networking and family support plays an important role.

The Constitution of Ukraine in conjunction with the Labor Law both preclude discrimination based on race, color of skin, political, religious and other beliefs, sex, ethnic and social origin, property status, place of residence or other characteristics. In practice, however, men do have more opportunities than women. Very few women in Ukraine hold top managerial positions in the government or private industry. Ukraine has only 8.7% female representation in parliament. Yet, Ukrainian women are present in politics and these women politicians are often extremely powerful—for example Prime Minister Yulia Tymoshenko, who currently heads her own parliamentary bloc.

Additionally, women are granted generous maternity leave. Women enjoy up to 70 calendar days of paid leave before childbirth and up to 56 calendar days after. The payment is provided by the Social Security Fund and is based on levels of income used for social security contribution purposes. To encourage families to have more children, additional paid leaves are granted to women who have two or more children under the age of 15 or a disabled or adopted child and to single parents. Workers who are engaged in part-time studies may also be considered for additional vacation leave.

16 SPORTS

Ukrainians play many sports, including soccer, volleyball, track and field, basketball, hockey, skating, and swimming. Soccer is undeniably the most popular sport in Ukraine, with the most popular team being Dynamo Kiev. It is common to see youngsters playing soccer and rugby in the streets of Ukraine. Impressively, the Ukrainian team was the first soccer team to qualify for the 2006 World Cup Finals in Germany. In addition to soccer and rugby, many Ukrainians play cricket. Numerous cricket clubs include Kiev Cricket Club, Kharkiv Cricket Club, Crimea Cricket Club, Vinnytsya Cricket Club, Ternopil Cricket Club, Donetsk Cricket Club, and Luhansk Cricket Club.

Ukrainian athletes do very well in the summer and winter Olympic Games and have participated in the Olympic Games since the 1950s. Famous Ukrainian medalists include Larysa Latynina, the gymnast awarded a record 18 medals (nine gold), swimmer Yana Klochkova (two gold medals, 2000), and pole-vaulter Sergey Bubka (gold, 1988). At the 2004 summer Olympic Games in Athens, Ukrainian competitors won a total of 23 medals (nine gold medals, five silver, and nine bronze), finishing 12th in overall team standings. Ukrainian athletes also compete in the Winter Olympics. The 1994 Winter Olympics brought Ukraine two medals; in the 1998 Winter Games, Ukrainians won one medal, and in the 2006 Winter Olympics Ukrainian athletes took bronze medals in ice-dancing and the women's 7.5 kilometer biathlon sprint.

Recently, outdoor sports and activities such as diving, mountain climbing, mountain biking, swimming, trekking, and horse riding have become increasingly popular. Skiing is another sport enjoyed by many. Mountain skiing and snowboarding are rapidly gaining popularity among young people. The Carpathian Mountains are especially good for winter sports. Spectacular all year round, the Carpathians are particularly picturesque in winter, offering families and professional athletes a range of winter sports facilities. The Ukrainian government is supportive of professional winter sports and is bidding for Ukraine's popular Bukovel ski and snowboard resort to host the 2018 Winter Olympic Games.

Chess is another popular sport in Ukraine. The 2002 World Chess Championship tournament in Moscow started with 128 of the best chess players in the world and came down to a head-to-head eight-game match between two Ukrainians, Vasily Ivanchuk and Ruslan Ponomariov. Ponomariov (who at 14 had become the youngest grandmaster in history, although the record is now held by Bu Xiangzi of China) won the title in seven games, winning two games and drawing the other five. On his way to victory Ponomariov defeated a chess player from China, one from Bulgaria, one from the Netherlands, and three from Russia.

17 ENTERTAINMENT AND RECREATION

The liberating policies of *perestroika* and *glasnost* relieved previously existing constraints inspiring artists for creative expression. Since then the arts movement gained momentum. However, the new democratic government lacks funds to support the arts, and many well-known artists, performers, and composers are trying their luck in the West, where they continue to perform and gain prominence. Nevertheless, in spite of these difficulties, one can find numerous art exhibits, concerts, literary evenings, and plays being performed in most Ukrainian cities.

Kiev is the vibrant national and cultural capital of Ukraine and boasts the National Fine Arts Museum, Taras Shevchenko Museum, National Museum of Decorative Arts, and other galleries that host new and exciting exhibitions. The Shevchenko National Opera Company, Ivan Franko National Theater, and State Operetta add to the wealth of the Ukrainian cultural palette. Life in large cities and smaller towns bustles with opera and ballet performances, philharmonic concerts, and other cultural events. Lviv's Ivan Franko Opera and Ballet Theater, Ukrainian Drama Theater, the Kharkiv Opera and Ballet Theatre, the Odessa State Academic Opera and Ballet Theatre, the Symphony Orchestra of the National Philharmonic Society of Ukraine, and scores of anthropological and history museums ensure that Ukrainian culture continues to flourish.

[18] FOLK ART, CRAFTS, AND HOBBIES

Ukrainian folk art is an integral part of Ukrainian culture, reflecting the spiritual and artistic values of Ukrainians. The art forms that were developed in ancient times still exist today, both in Ukraine and in Ukrainian communities around the world. Ukrainian folk art is primarily known for its ceramics, decorated Easter eggs (*pysanky),* embroidery, woodcarving, weaving, tapestry, carpeting, and leatherwork. *Pysanky,* or Ukrainian Easter eggs, date back to pre-Christian times, when they were believed to have magical powers. With Christianity the *pysanka* took on a spiritual, religious meaning, and the eggs began to be decorated with crosses, geometric designs, and miniature churches.

Over the centuries, Ukrainians have developed a unique pottery tradition. Pottery flourished in all regions of Ukraine, utilizing plant and animal designs and other patterns. The Hutsul region of the Carpathians is particularly known for its ceramics. In this region ceramic decoration took a variety of forms, including plates, pitchers, pots, and toys.

The art of embroidery (*vyshyvannia)* is yet another popular Ukrainian folk art and hobby. Through a variety of thread colors, complex stitches, and design intricacies, the Ukrainian *vyshyvka* is applied to all items of folk dress, as well as to pillows, aprons, towels, and other household articles. Many of the oldest *vyshyvkas* can be viewed in museums around Ukraine.

[19] SOCIAL PROBLEMS

As a newly independent country Ukraine faces a number of growing social problems including alcoholism, unemployment, prostitution, the spread of the AIDS epidemic, and negative population growth. A growing crime rate adds to Ukraine's woes, with 149,000 convicts serving their sentences in 2008.

Similarly to many European countries, Ukraine is challenged by a serious demographic crisis. As estimated in 2006, the population growth rate stood at –0.6% and in 2008 had declined further to –0.651%. Not only is the birth rate declining, but life expectancy at birth for the total population is only 68.06 years, with 62.24 years for men and 74.24 years for women (2008 est.). Each year since 1990 the United Nations has published a Human Development Index (HDI), which looks beyond GDP to a broader definition of well-being in a given country. In 2007 the HDI for Ukraine was 0.788, which gives the country a ranking of 76th out of 177 countries. To compare, Ukraine's ranking places it behind all of the European Union (EU) member-countries, including its closest neighbors (and former Soviet satellites), Hungary (36), Poland (37), Slovakia (42), Bulgaria (53), and Romania (60), which joined the EU in 2004 and 2007. Some of the factors that HDI takes into account include the fact that Ukraine has the lowest birthrate in Europe. With deaths currently almost twice the number of births, the population of 47.4 million people (as of 1 October 2004) is projected to decrease by up to 40% by 2050.

Deaths caused by HIV/AIDS are another grave problem confronting the Ukrainian population. The prevalence of HIV/AIDS infection has already crossed the 1% threshold and has surpassed levels across all countries of Europe and Central Asia as well as India and China. Sadly, the scale of the crisis is so extensive that the current budget of both domestic and international donor-supported programs is not sufficient to reverse the present trend. The Ukrainian government is well aware of the situation but is concentrating on economic transformation and has not allocated enough attention and funds to the socio-demographic sphere. As a result, the HIV/AIDS problem becomes increasingly daunting every day.

To exacerbate these social problems even further, a great number of Ukrainian women have recently fallen victim to international sex traders. A chain of "employment" and "marriage" agencies recruit young women and girls for work abroad in photo modeling or domestic service. "Marriage," "employment," and "visa" agencies capitalizing on the difficult economic situation in Ukraine promise their recruits secure employment, good working conditions, and reasonable benefits. Often women who struggle to find an adequate job in Ukraine are attracted to newspaper ads advertising jobs in foreign countries. However, once these women accept the jobs and arrive in the foreign countries, they are often forced to work in the local sex industry. The UN Office in Ukraine has been publishing these findings, attempting to draw the attention of the country's policy-makers and civil society to the issue. Since the publication of a recent National Human Development Report (NHDR), Ukrainian civil organizations have put forward several initiatives to alleviate this problem, which still remains largely unresolved.

[20] GENDER ISSUES

Today, Ukraine is a modern nation that strives for gender equity. Yet gender relations in Ukraine are complex. Historically, during the Soviet period, Ukrainian men and women enjoyed equal access to education and employment. Women were granted generous maternity leave and other child-related benefits and rights to early retirement and pension. For the most part, legislation treated women and men equally; however, protective labor legislation excluded women from "dangerous" but also highly paid positions with good benefits, and widespread conservatism pressured women to continue to bear primary responsibility for the family and housework. A number of women took high positions in government, but their representation in politics remained limited, with men clearly dominating in the higher echelons of power.

Although since 2000 there has been some improvement in gender issues, strongly entrenched stereotypes of men as leaders, managers, and primary breadwinners, and stereotypes of women as wives and mothers first, workers second, continue to limit actual gender equality in Ukrainian society. Women still face gender-based job discrimination in certain areas of employment. Some employers flatly refuse to hire younger women likely to become pregnant or women over 35. Loss of state support for child care, poor maternal health, limited political representation, gender-based violence, incidents of rape and a dramatic increase in prostitution and trafficking have also emerged as serious issues. According to the Bureau of Democracy, Human Rights, and Labor, spousal abuse is illegal but common. Based on 2006 data provided by Amnesty International 50% to 70% of all women have been subjected to physical violence or psychological abuse at home. To deal with this problem, the law requires the regional governments to operate shelters for victims of domestic violence and crisis centers in every major city, but in practice, they do not.

At the same time, male underemployment and unemployment have undermined men's traditional role, thereby affecting the structure of authority and relative bargaining power of men and women within the household. Greater opportunities in the areas of education and employment for females have prompted women to become more independent. There has been an increase in the numbers of female-headed households and number of women focusing on their careers. Also, recent labor laws establish the legal equality of men and women, including equal pay for equal work. A burgeoning civil society sector and the emergence of many organizations addressing gender issues (whose existence was formerly ignored or denied) provide a strong platform for addressing and promoting all aspects of gender equality.

21 BIBLIOGRAPHY

Bench, Olha. *Ukrainian Folk Music.* The Kiev Municipal Chamber Choir Website. http://www.cck.kiev.ua/en/cd/d18ukr_nar_muz2/text.htm (25 May 2008).

Euromonitor International. "Ukraine." http://www.euromonitor.com/factfile.aspx?country=UK (25 May 2008).

Fechbach, Murray and Cristina Galvin. "HIV/AIDS in Ukraine: An Analysis of Statistics." Demography Matters Network. http://demography.matters.googlepages.com/ukraine (1 June 2008).

Filipenko, Inna. "On the Verge of a Society: Ukraine Ranks Eighth in the Number of Convicts per 100,000 Citizens." *The Day,* #16. http://www.day.kiev.ua/201413/ (20 May 2008).

Hodges, Linda. Ed. "Ukrainian Language, Culture and Travel Page." http://pages.prodigy.net/l.hodges/ukraine.htm#Language (1 June 2008).

International Women's Rights Centre La Strada-Ukraine. http://www.brama.com/lastrada/about.html (1 June 2008).

Kardash, Peter. *Ukraine and Ukrainians.* Australia: Fortuna Co., 1991.

Kubijovyc, Volodymyr, and Danylo Husar Struk, ed. *Encyclopedia of Ukraine.* Toronto: University of Toronto Press, Inc., 1993.

Mizynec, Victor. *Folk Instruments of Ukraine.* Australia: Bayda Books, 1987.

Owechko, Iwan, ed. *A Pocketbook Guide to Ukraine and Ukrainians.* 2nd ed. Colorado: Ukrapress, 1985.

Subtelny, Orest. *Ukraine: A History.* Toronto: University of Toronto Press in association with the Canadian Institute of Ukrainian Studies, 1988.

Szporluk, Roman. *Ukraine: A Brief History.* Detroit: Ukrainian Festival Committee, 1979.

Ukraine and the Ukrainian People. New York: Ukrainian Congress Committee of America, 1980.

Ukraine.com. http://www.ukraine.com/corporate/ (1 June 2008).

Ukrainian Information Collective. *Geography of Ukraine.* Akron, OH: AlexSon Publishing, 1985.

U.S. State Department. Bureau of European and Eurasian Affairs. "Ukraine: March 2008." Background Notes, http://www.state.gov/r/pa/ei/bgn/3211.htm (25 May 2008).

U.S. State Department. "Ukraine: 2007." Country Reports and Human Rights Practices, http://www.state.gov/g/drl/rls/hrrpt/2007/100590.htm (25 May 2008).

World Bank Group. "Gender Statistics: Ukraine." http://devdata.worldbank.org/genderstats/genderRpt.asp?rpt=profile&cty=UKR,Ukraine&hm=home (25 May 2008).

Zakharii, Roman. Ukrainian Language Resources Website. http://www.personal.ceu.hu/students/97/Roman_Zakharii/ukrainian.htm (4 June 2008).

Zinkewych, Osyp, and Volodymyr Hula, ed. *Ukraine: A Tourist Guide.* Kiev: Smoloskyp Publishing, 1993.

—revised by A. Golovina Khadka

VLACHS

LOCATION: Romania, Moldova, Ukraine, Serbia, Greece, Albania, Macedonia, Bulgaria, Hungary
POPULATION: 23.5 million Romanians, 500,000 Aromanians, 20,000 Megleno-Romanians, 1,200 Istro-Romanians
LANGUAGE: Romanian and Romanian dialects (Aromanian, Megleno-Romanian, and Istro-Romanian)
RELIGION: Christianity (Eastern Orthodox, Roman Catholic)

1 INTRODUCTION

The history of the Vlachs is inexorably linked to the history of the Romanians, although some specialists think that they more generally represent the descendants of romanized Dacians, Thracians, and Illyrians. Throughout history, the term Vlachs was used both to describe all people of Romanian origin, and particular groups scattered throughout the Central and Western Balkans. Nowadays it is used mainly to describe people of Romanian origin living outside Romania.

At the start of the 2nd century AD, the Roman emperor Trajan conquered and colonized Dacia (roughly the territory of present day Romania), expanding the Roman Empire territory to its largest size in history. The Roman legions that were sent there mingled with the local population, and by the time the Roman army retreated in 271 AD, the seeds of a new people were laid.

In the 11th century AD, the population living on the territory of present day Romania formed political units, which became principalities in the 13th century—Moldova and Wallachia. People from Wallachia, Moldova, and Transylvania have migrated and settled in different parts of the Balkans throughout the years, bringing their customs and language with them. The main Vlach groups outside Romania are the Aromanians, the Megleno-Romanians, and the Istro-Romanians.

There are only a few remnants of the Vlach populations today (an estimated 500,000), and their numbers are dwindling. The spread of universal education in even the most remote villages and the effects of modern civilization have often blended them together with the surrounding populations. Between the two World Wars, some Vlachs have migrated into Romania and they have been rapidly assimilated. Despite their relatively small numbers, Vlachs have played an important historic role in all of the Balkan states where they were found. Prominent Vlachs include Ioannis Kolettis (prime minister of Greece), Georgios Averoff (Greek magnate), Andrei Şaguna (Romanian Orthodox Metropolitan of Transylvania), and the Ghica family (Romanian prime ministers and *voivodes*).

The words Vlach and Romanian have been used interchangeably throughout history, and the principality of Wallachia was also known as Ţara Românească (The Romanian Country). In Greek, the word Blachos means shepherd. More commonly, it is assumed that the word Vlach is derived, via the Slavic medium, from the Germanic. A similar root is used in Welsh and Walloon and it is used to denominate a stranger.

2 LOCATION AND HOMELAND

Vlachs are for the most part found in the Balkans, although small groups can be found further north, in countries like Austria, Hungary, Poland, Slovakia, and the Czech Republic. Romanians and Moldovans constitute the largest Vlach populations, and they are concentrated in their respective countries. Aromanians and Megleno-Romanians can be found in Romania, Macedonia, northern Greece, Albania, Serbia, and Bulgaria. Istro-Romanians constitute a particular and fairly small group (around 1,200 people), concentrated in the northwestern part of Croatia.

In 1941, when Greece was under Nazi occupation, a group of Aromanian nationalists established, for a short time, an autonomous Vlach state under the control of Fascist Italy—The Principality of Pindus and Voivodship of Macedonia.

3 LANGUAGE

What distinguishes Vlachs living outside Romania today is not as much their culture, religion, or their consciousness of a separate identity. Their defining feature is the language they speak. One of the reasons why the Vlach language has survived this long is the remoteness of the areas where it is spoken, and the fact that it was often in competition with more than one language. All the Vlach languages are Latin-based, and could be considered as being Romanian dialects. The most distinct dialect (different in morphology and phonology from all other Romanian dialects) is spoken by the Megleno-Romanians.

Aromanians have a representative in the European Bureau for Lesser Spoken Languages, in Greece.

4 FOLKLORE

Many Vlachs that are now encountered through the Central and Western Balkans are the descendants of shepherds that migrated there in medieval times. As such, the folklores of all these disparate groups share pastoral influences. One of the most important folklore creations in Romania is the ballad *Miorița* (The Little Ewe). The ballad tells the story of three shepherds (one from Moldova, one from Wallachia, and one from Transylvania) that meet while attending to their flocks. The Moldovan shepherd finds from an enchanted ewe that the other two shepherds have connived to kill him and steal his flock. The shepherd accepts his fate, and tells the ewe that should he be slain, it should ask his killers to bury his body by the sheep's pen. Furthermore, the ewe is to tell the flock and his mother that he married a princess, and that the moment was marked by the falling of a star.

5 RELIGION

Many Vlachs are adherents of the Eastern Orthodox religion, usually the dominant religion in the area (e.g. Greek Orthodox). Istro-Romanians are Roman Catholic. Religious practices and customs are similar to those found among the dominant populations in the area.

A very small percentage of Vlachs are Muslims. They represent the Megleno-Romanians from Greece that have been living in Turkey since the exchange of populations in 1923.

6 MAJOR HOLIDAYS

Most Vlachs follow the major holidays of the country and region where they are located. Of significant importance are the religious holidays—especially Christmas and Easter. For a short time, at the start of the 20th century, the Aromanians were recognized as a separate nation (millet) by the Ottoman Empire. The day when the so-called Aromania Iradeo (or

Turkish Irade) was signed, 23 May 1905, is celebrated by Aromanians all over the world as their National Day. In Macedonia, it is considered an official holiday.

7 RITES OF PASSAGE

Major life events, like birth, marriage, and death, are marked and celebrated within the Christian tradition—Eastern Orthodox for most Vlachs, Roman Catholic for the Istro-Romanians. Children are taught from a young age to attend church, and they participate in the social life of the parish. Social events organized by individual, or groups of villages are often the preferred medium for young people to meet, date, and potentially marry. Marriage represents an important moment in a Vlach's life, and the union between two young people is usually done after receiving the parent's blessings. If a husband dies, the wife will wear black for a full year. Often widows wear black for the rest of their lives.

8 INTERPERSONAL RELATIONS

Since Vlachs have been for the most part migratory people, they have often been treated with resentment and distrust. In Greece, the term *Koutzovlachs* is used in a derogatory way to refer to people of a lower class. Vlachs however, are good-natured people, and in their respective countries they are nowadays respected as ardent patriots and supporters of national ideals. A traveler through Greece after the end of the Second World War describes Vlachs as being kind and "patriarchally hospitable."

9 LIVING CONDITIONS

Living conditions vary depending on where the Vlach communities are located. In Romania, most of the Aromanians live in urban centers. As such, they enjoy the benefits and challenges of post-communist cities. Outside Romania, Vlachs live for the most part in rural communities. Traditionally, Aromanians and Megleno-Romanians respected a pastoral seasonal cycle (transhumance)—tending to their sheep herds in mountain villages in the summer, and leaving for the milder climates of the plains in the winter. As more and more young Vlachs get lured by the mirage of large cities, many small mountain villages are left to be tended to by older people, or are used solely for vacation purposes.

In Greece, the largest Vlach community, and the unofficial Vlach capital, is Metsovo—a town of around 4,500 located in northern Greece, in the mountains of Pindus. It is an important tourist destination and a popular ski resort.

10 FAMILY LIFE

Vlachs are family-oriented and the patriarchal system defines the family unit. Elderly are respected, and advice is sought from them in communal matters. Village life is more tranquil and sheltered from many of the ills that city life presupposes. The social life in the village revolves around major religious holidays, and families mark major moments (such as birth, marriage, and death) with complex ceremonies. In many ways, these moments have a deeper and more profound meaning than they do in cities.

11 CLOTHING

Traditionally, the clothing of Vlach shepherds was simple and comfortable. Clothing was designed to endure long migratory walks. The trousers and the shirt were for the most part white. Thick leather belts adorned the waist, and in the winter men would wear heavy sheepskin jackets. The garb worn by women was much more intricate and elaborate. Skirts and shirts were embroidered with lively patterns, and young women would wear complexly designed headgear. Older women usually wore simpler gear, and they covered their heads with a plain black scarf.

The Vlachs living in urban centers adopt urban attire, which is usually of Western influence. Even in remote villages, traditional clothing is rarely worn anymore. Shepherds continue to fabricate clothing out of sheep's skin, but they are more likely to be encountered wearing jeans and rubber boots, rather than white trousers and leather moccasins.

12 FOOD

Being for the most part shepherds, Vlachs rarely engaged in farming. They would trade wool, cheese, and leather for agricultural produce, but they would not grow them themselves. As such, the Vlach diet is fairly basic. Cheese and meat dishes are the staple in most Vlach villages. The liquid that is left over after producing cheese (*zăr*) is used to turn a Romanian staple—*mămăligă* (cornmeal mush), into a shepherd's delicacy—*balmoş*. Metsovo (Greece), the unofficial Vlach capital, is known for its cheeses and wines.

The art of cooking in Vlach villages was passed down from generation to generation, by word of mouth and by example. Nowadays, cooking in Vlach villages borrows a lot from the culinary art in their respective area.

13 EDUCATION

Vlach schools that taught in pupils in Aromanians were established through Albania and Macedonia as early as 1860, with the help of the Aromanian diaspora in Romania. In Greece, the attempts of Vlachs to upkeep their culture were viewed with distrust and were often met with resentment and anger. Even in modern times, Greece refused to recognize Vlachs as a distinct minority.

When Aromanians were recognized as a millet of the Ottoman Empire, in 1905, they were affirmed the rights to maintain their own schools and perform liturgies in the Aromanian language. Before schools were institutionalized, education took place in churches, which also maintained local culture and identity.

Following the fall of communism, there have been attempts made by the Romanian government to support Vlach communities throughout the Balkans. Thus, in the town of Divjaka, Albania, education in Romanian and Aromanian is offered at the kindergarten, primary, and secondary level. Financial help was also offered to the only Aromanian language church—Schimbarea la faţă' of Korçë. In Macedonia, pupils can study in Aromanian at the primary level, and several educational and cultural Vlach institutions are supported by the Romanian government.

14 CULTURAL HERITAGE

With the fall of communism throughout the Balkans, Aromanians grouped together and formed cultural and political societies, sparking the beginning of a national re-awakening. In Macedonia, Aromanians are recognized as an ethnic minority and are represented in the parliament. They enjoy the right to education in their own language, as well as ethnic, cultural, and religious rights. The Romanian government offers financial support to the Macedonian Vlach community, and it conditioned the recognition of Macedonia's independence on its granting of minority rights to the Vlachs. Several cultural societies and associations are present in Macedonia. Some of these include: the Union for Aromanian Culture from Macedonia, the Aromanian League of Macedonia, the International League of Aromanians, the Aromanian Community Manachia Brothers in Bitola, the Party of the Aromanians from Macedonia, and the Democratic Union of the Aromanians from Macedonia. The Macedonian government provides generous support for Aromanian cultural enterprises, such as the publication of magazines and books. Thus it is hoped that Aromanian culture, language, and history will be preserved.

Vlachs also have contributed greatly to the culture of the countries where they lived. Some of the most prominent writers in the Balkans are of Vlach origin. Constantin Noica is one of Romania's most prominent philosophers, and his works have been distributed worldwide. George Zalokostas is an important Greek writer. Mitrush Kuteli and Lasgush Poradeci are two Albanian poets. Jovan Sterija Popovic is a well-known Serbian novelist.

15 WORK

The term Vlach (*Blachos* or *Koutzovlachs*) is often used in a derogatory way in Greece, to refer to lower class people (shepherds in particular). As a consequence, most Vlach groups don't use this word when they refer to themselves. However, apart from shepherding, Vlachs have also established themselves as industrious craftsmen and merchants. Many of them have risen to positions of wealth and rank in their respective countries. George Averoff, Apostolos Arsakis, and George Stavrou are well-known 19th century Greek benefactors of Vlach origin. Gigi Becali is one of the most prominent business-men in Romania. Sotirios Bulgaris founded the Bulgari jewelry house. The Darvari and Dumba families are famous philanthropists and Austrian Imperial bankers.

16 SPORTS

Vlachs are not particularly known to be sports-minded people, even though numerous Vlachs have risen to prominence in several sports activities. Thus, Romania's best football player of all times, Gheorghe Hagi, is an Aromanian (or *Machedon*). Gigi Becali is a well known entrepreneur in Romania, and the owner of one of the largest Romanian football clubs—FC Steaua Bucharest. Before the Romanian revolution of 1989, he used to be a shepherd. His cousins, Victor and Ioan Becali, are prominent and prosperous football impresarios.

Joshko Milenkovski is a Macedonian volleyball champion and the manager of the Macedonian Volleyball team. Dominique Moceanu (born in Tampa, Florida) is a famous US gymnast, and a Macedonian Vlach by origin.

17 ENTERTAINMENT AND RECREATION

In rural areas, entertainment and recreation find an outlet in folk dances, amateur theatrical groups, music ensembles, and social gatherings. There are a number of Vlachs that have made a name for themselves in the entertainment business. Herbert von Karajan is a world famous conductor, and a Vlach from Kozani, Greece. Apostolos Kaldaras is a well-know Greek composer. Kaliopi Bukle is a popular singer in the Republic of Macedonia. In Romania, there is a large number of gifted and prominent Aromanian actors (Toma Caragiu, Alexandru Arşinel, Ion Caramitru, Sebastian Papaiani) and film makers (Dan Piţa, Sergiu Nicolaescu).

18 FOLK ART, CRAFTS, AND HOBBIES

Traditional folk art and crafts were for Vlachs both a method of survival and a way of adorning their household. Before modern civilization reached their villages, they used to make their own household articles (e.g. plates, spoons, furnaces, tables, and chairs) and weave their own clothes and wall decorations. Wood and other materials they happened to have at hand would be used for crafting decorative objects. Very few manufactured commodities were purchased directly. Their colorful and intricate designs were also used to lavish the interiors and exteriors of their churches, cemeteries, and social gathering spots.

19 SOCIAL PROBLEMS

In an area where regional and national pride and patriotism are very strong (often leading to state fragmentations along ethnic lines), the Vlachs have been content with their position in the countries where they were located. Except for a short period during the First World War (when Romania pressed for a separate Vlach church), there have been no separatist movements pursued by the Vlach populations. A Vlach specialist considers them to be the perfect Balkan citizens, as they have never resorted to war, politics, violence, or dishonesty to preserve their culture.

²⁰ GENDER ISSUES

Gender issues among the Vlach populations are congruent with the issues faced by the general population in the countries where they are located. The Vlachs living in remote villages across the Balkans still have a traditionalist view of gender relations, and homosexuality is usually scorned.

²¹ BIBLIOGRAPHY

Capidan, Theodor. *Aromânii, dialectal aromân: Studiu lingvistic,* Bucharest: Academia Română, 1932.

Friedman, Victor A. "The Vlach Minority in Macedonia: Language, Identity, Dialectology, and Standardization." In *Selected Papers in Slavic, Balkan, and Balkan Countries,* ed. Juhani Nuoluoto et. al, Helsinki: University of Helsinki, 2001.

Hupchick, Dennis P. *The Balkans: From Constantinople to Communists,* New York: Palgrave Macmillan, 2002.

Koukoudis, Asterios I. *The Vlachs: Metropolis and Diaspora,* Athens: Zitros Publications, 2003.

Wigram, W.A. *Hellenic Travel,* London: Faber and Faber, 1947.

Winnifrith, Tom J. *The Vlachs: The History of a Balkan People,* London: Duckworth, 1987.

—M. Ionescu-Heroiu

WALLOONS

LOCATION: Belgium (southern region, called Wallonia)
POPULATION: 3.5 million
LANGUAGE: French
RELIGION: Roman Catholic; Muslim; Protestant; Jewish; Russian Orthodox; and Greek Orthodox

¹ INTRODUCTION

The Walloons, who reside in Belgium's southern provinces, comprise the country's French-speaking population. Their language and history have given them a cultural identity distinct from that of the Flemings in the northern part of the country, whose language (Flemish) is similar to Dutch. While the Flemings are culturally closer to the Netherlands and Germany, the Walloons' cultural affinity is with France in particular and, in general, other countries in which Romance languages are spoken.

The historical forces dividing the two language groups date back to the 5th century AD, when the Franks, a Germanic people, invaded the territory of present-day Belgium, routing the Romans, who had ruled the region for 500 years after wresting it from its original Celtic inhabitants in 57 BC. The Franks were able to establish a stronger presence in the northern area, in which early forms of the Dutch language subsequently developed. Frankish settlements in the south were less extensive, allowing the Roman culture and Latin-based dialects already in existence to flourish. ("Walloon," a term that did not come into use until the 19th century, is derived from "Walha," the Frankish designation for the Romanized people of the south.)

Between the 9th and 12th centuries, both the northern and southern parts of the region fell under the control of feudal lords, and numerous duchies, principalities, and towns sprang up without any unifying center of power or culture, allowing the Germanic and Latin cultures of the two regions to continue developing along separate lines. In the east, Liège became a large and powerful prince-bishopric within the Holy Roman Empire. Eventually the power of the nobles was challenged by the burghers of the cities, especially those of the north, who had began to play a vital role in European trade. There was a period of Burgundian rule in the 15th century, when French—the language of the court—first became associated with power and privilege. Beginning in the 16th century, the entire region came under the rule of a succession of foreign powers: Spain, the Austrian Habsburgs, the French under Napoleon, and, finally, the Netherlands. In spite of the Flemings' cultural and linguistic ties to Holland, they joined with the Walloons in revolting against Dutch rule, and Belgium gained its independence in 1830 as a constitutional monarchy.

Throughout the 19th century, the Walloons were the dominant group in Belgium both politically and economically, even though the Flemings accounted for a majority of the population. Independence did nothing to change the tradition of French as the language of government and culture, and the richer natural resources of the south brought the mines, mills, and factories of the Industrial Revolution to that region early, while Flanders remained a poorer, primarily agricultural area. Belgium suffered enormous losses in both world wars, but was most devastated during World War I. After World War

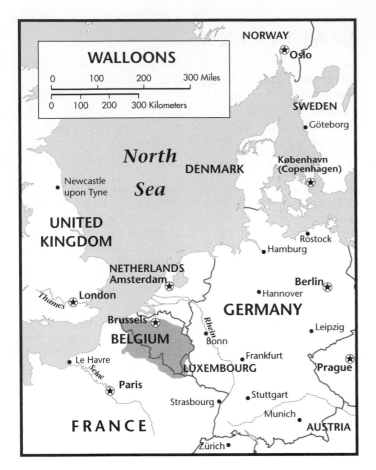

WALLOONS

II, structural and social problems had a debilitating effect on Wallonia's industries. By the 1930s Flanders had gained sufficient political and economic clout to make Flemish its official language for education, legal proceedings, and government.

In the post-World War II period, Wallonia's traditional heavy industries (notably steelmaking) have continued to decline, and its coal mines have closed. In the 1960s, the Flemings and Walloons were given increased control over their respective regions, and in 1993 Belgium's constitution was amended, making Flanders and Wallonia autonomous regions within the federal state of the Belgian Kingdom, together with the nation's bilingual capital, Brussels, and another autonomous community composed of Belgium's German-speaking population. Belgium was locked in a political stalemate beginning in June 2007 when elections failed to produce a new government. The question arose as to whether or not Belgium should cease to exist as a country, and that the territory would be split into two—Flanders and Wallonia. The crisis was temporarily resolved in March 2008 when a new government was formed, and major reforms of state were planned.

² LOCATION AND HOMELAND

The Walloons live south of an east-west line running from Aachen to a point north of Lille that divides the country's Flemish- and French-speaking regions. With an area of 17,094 km (6,600 sq mi), Wallonia covers 55% of Belgium's territory and includes the provinces of southern Brabant, Hainautl, Namur, Liège, and Luxembourg. The region's terrain rises from the

Meuse valley to the wooded hills of the Ardennes, which reach their highest elevations at 694 m (2,277 ft). Its two major rivers are the Meuse and the Escaut. Wallonia has a population of 3.5 million, or some 175 people per sq km (450 people per sq mi), making it a densely populated area. There is a growing immigrant population from southern Europe and North Africa.

³ LANGUAGE

The language of Wallonia is French, as well as various regional dialects, whose main divisions are Eastern (Liège), Central (Namur), and Western (Charleroi, La Louvière, Nivelles). There are two additional dialects called Picard and Gaumais, although all dialects in Wallonia are commonly referred to collectively as "Walloon." Dialects are spoken mainly by rural and working-class Walloons, and more often with one's family than in more formal situations, such as at work. Immigrant workers have introduced a variety of new languages into Wallonia in recent decades.

Historically, French has been the most prestigious language in Belgium since the late medieval period of Burgundian rule, when it was spoken by aristocrats at court. It remained an elite language during the periods of Spanish, Austrian, and French rule from the 16th through 18th centuries, and maintained its privileged position with the Belgian bourgeoisie even after independence in the 19th century. It was the language of government, law, the church, and education. By comparison, the Dutch-based Flemish language of northern Belgium was associated with provincialism, poverty, and a lower level of education. This language division was dramatized by the inability of French-speaking Belgian officers in World War I to communicate with their Flemish-speaking troops. Although Flemish has gained increased respectability in this century as Flanders has become more powerful economically and politically, Flemings on the whole are still more familiar with French than Walloons are with Flemish.

⁴ FOLKLORE

Traditionally, the spirits of the departed were thought to return to earth on All Saints' Day (November 1), and families still visit the cemetery to clean the tombs of their deceased relatives on that date. Walloon folklore includes many tales involving the devil, remnants of the pre-Christian Druid religion of the region. Inhabitants of some rural villages still believe in the powers of folk healers, whose methods include *toucher*, healing by touch. There is a marionette in Belgium's traditional puppet theaters called Woltje, which means "little Walloon," and others who personify particular regions or cities. Tchantchès, who is identified with the city of Liège, wears patched trousers and a floppy hat with tassels.

⁵ RELIGION

While Catholicism is the traditional religion of Wallonia, as it is throughout Belgium, the Walloons are generally less religious than the Flemings to their north, a difference that has become even more pronounced in recent years, with parish churches closing due to lack of attendance. Even the elderly who keep statues of the Virgin Mary in their windows often are not regular churchgoers. However, southern Europeans who have emigrated to the region maintain stronger religious ties than do native Walloons. Immigrants from Turkey and North Africa make up a growing Islamic community that is beginning to call for increased public recognition. Other religious minorities include Protestants, Jews, Russian Orthodox, and Greek Orthodox. Wallonia is the site of two popular pilgrimage shrines, at Beauraing and Banneaux, and Lourdes in southwestern France has traditionally drawn many pilgrims from the region.

6 MAJOR HOLIDAYS

The Walloons observe Belgium's public holidays (New Year's Day, Easter Monday, Labor Day (May 1), Independence Day (July 21), All Saints' Day (November 1), and Christmas. However, they also celebrate other dates on the Christian calendar as well as many folk holidays with origins in history and legend. Binche is notorious for its carnival festivities in the weeks before Lent. The best-known feature of the annual celebration is the dance of the Gilles, with over 1,000 people dressed in brightly colored, padded costumes throwing oranges at the spectators. Malmédy is also known for its carnival celebration, which actually continues into the Lent period, as do those in Fosses and Tilff.

7 RITES OF PASSAGE

The Walloons live in a modern, industrialized, Christian country. Although less religious than some of their fellow Belgians, most Walloon young people undergo religious rituals such as baptism and first Communion. In addition, a student's progress through the education system is marked by many families with graduation parties.

8 INTERPERSONAL RELATIONS

Walloon manners are generally formal and polite, and conversations are marked by frequent exchanges of compliments and repeated handshaking. Relatives shake hands, hug, or kiss each other on the cheek, while friends usually hug. Men and women or two female friends—but never two men—might exchange kisses on the cheek, and women can sometimes be seen walking down the street arm-in-arm.

9 LIVING CONDITIONS

The majority of Walloons are city dwellers, and most live in multistory brick row houses with large kitchens and gardens. Walloon houses, like those of other Belgians, often include (or are attached to) an area used for a family business. Walloons enjoy Belgium's high level of modern medical care by private doctors and at state-run hospitals and clinics, and the vast majority have most of their medical expenses covered by national health insurance. Located in Wallonia, the Meuse River, one of Belgium's two major waterways, is part of a network of rivers and canals whose center is the port of Antwerp, on the Scheldt River (Escaut in French), which is linked to the North Sea. Antwerp is the second largest port of Europe (after Amsterdam). Historically the connection of the Walloon city of Charleroi with Brussels and Antwerp has formed one of Belgium's major transport links.

10 FAMILY LIFE

The main type of family in Wallonia is the modern nuclear family, although it is not uncommon for an elderly grandparent to join the household. Men and women generally marry when they are in their mid- to late twenties. Wallonia's divorce rate is rising, and divorce and remarriage are considered socially acceptable.

11 CLOTHING

The Walloons, like all Belgians, wear modern Western-style clothing.

12 FOOD

While Walloon cuisine is derived from that of France, it tends to be spicier, richer, and higher in calories than modern-day French food. The most popular meats are pork and local Ardennes hams, a delicacy for which the region is famous. The main meal of the day, which is eaten at noon, might typically consist of a pork dish, potatoes, and salad with mayonnaise. Both breakfast and supper are light meals, which may include the popular regional cheese, *makèye,* served on slices of bread. Soup is a staple of the Walloon diet, as it is throughout Belgium, and it is often served as a first course for the mid-day and evening meals. Walloons drink a lot of coffee, and the common custom is to take a four o'clock coffee break called a *goûter,* often consisting of coffee and a piece of pie. Like their Flemish neighbors to the north, the Walloons like and brew beer; even the monks, for instance, in Chimay and Orval abbeys, have their own breweries. Another popular drink is straight gin, called *pèkèt.*

Local specialties in Wallonia range from venison chops and stuffed goose forestière in Luxembourg province to simple fried eggs and bacon in the area around Verviers. A favorite dish in south Belgium, adjoining the French border, is ragôut of lamb with chicory. Mussels and chips (tasty Belgian french fries) are as popular in Wallonia as they are throughout the country. In fact, when the French want to distance themselves from their Walloon neighbors across the border, they refer to them as *moules-frites* (the French term for mussels and chips).

13 EDUCATION

Education for all Belgians is compulsory from age 6 through 15, and the national literacy rate is 99%. At the secondary level, students choose between trade-oriented, business, and college-preparatory training. Wallonia has approximately 30 research centers and 300 research labs. Wallonia attracts researchers from all over the world with a high percentage of foreign researchers (15% to 20%) in Walloon universities and companies. It particularly welcomes researchers from Western and Eastern Europe.

14 CULTURAL HERITAGE

Among Belgium's early painters, the most renowned were the Flemish "Old Masters," including Van Eyck, Memling, and Rubens, although Walloons made contributions to the visual arts during all periods. In modern art, however, they came into their own with the work of surrealists René Magritte and Paul Delvaux. The best-known Walloon author is mystery writer Georges Simenon, creator of the police commissioner Maigret. There are many "French" writers who are, indeed, of Walloon origin, such as the famous poet Henri Michaux. Marguerite Yourcenar also had an international reputation; in 1980 she became the first woman elected to the Académie Française. Wallonia's most famous composer was César Franck, and the violin virtuoso Eugène Ysaye was famous for his perform-encourages the development of a diversified fabric of small and medium-sized enterprises.

¹⁶ SPORTS

Walloons share in Belgium's national passion for soccer ("football"). Thousands of fiercely partisan fans turn out for games, and many also play the sport on local or regional teams. Another favorite national pastime that the Walloons share is bicycling, either as a relaxed form of recreation or in organized races. Pigeon racing, practiced throughout Belgium, is especially popular in Wallonia.

¹⁷ ENTERTAINMENT AND RECREATION

The Walloons enjoy typical leisure-time activities such as watching television and reading. Like many Belgians, they are avid gardeners, and maintain well-tended gardens. Other typical hobbies include playing cards, stamp collecting and model trains. Popular cultural pastimes include concerts and the theater. Residents of Wallonia's towns and villages enjoy gathering with friends after hours in neighborhood cafés and discussing work, politics, sports, and other topics. The Walloons also share the general Belgian love of festivals, and their calendars are filled with celebrations of all kinds, both religious and secular.

¹⁸ FOLK ART, CRAFTS, AND HOBBIES

The talents of traditional artists can be seen in the elaborate costumes and giant figures used in festivals and processions, and also in the popular puppet and marionette theaters that have enjoyed a revival in recent years.

¹⁹ SOCIAL PROBLEMS

Wallonia was hit particularly hard by Belgium's high rate of unemployment in the 1990s, and some of its inhabitants find themselves forced to commute to jobs in Brussels or Flanders. The most lingering controversy for Walloons, as for all Belgians, has been the country's cultural, linguistic, and political division between its French- and Flemish-speaking populations. In spite of a 1993 constitution granting autonomy to both Flanders and Wallonia, separatist elements are still active on both sides. The divisiveness between the two cultural groups even threatened to divide the country in 2007 and 2008.

²⁰ GENDER ISSUES

Women make up 51.3% of Wallonia's population. As of 2008 women had a lower employment rate (48.3%) than men (63.5%), but this figure was growing, whereas the male employment rate is tending to decrease slightly. Women won the right to vote in Belgium in 1919, and restrictions on the suffrage were dropped in 1948. Abortion was only legalized in Belgium in 1990. As of 2000, women made up 24% of the lower house of parliament, and 28.8% of the upper house. Approximately 55.7% of Belgian women hold a secondary degree, 53.1% hold a bachelor's degree, and 7.6% are in senior management. The government made a concerted effort in the 1990s in involve women in politics.

Belgium decriminalized homosexuality in 1843 and legalized same-sex marriages in 2003—it was only the second country to do so worldwide. Gay and lesbian couples have the

Walloons and Flemish marched against the possible separation of Belgium in late 2007. Belgium, which had no federal government since June of 2007, was in a state of political limbo as differing factions were unable to form a coalition government. (Mark Renders/Getty Images)

ing career and also as the founder of the Queen Elisabeth of Belgium Music Competition, one of the most prestigious international music contests. The saxophone was invented by a Belgian, Adolphe Sax, who was born in Dinant in 1814.

¹⁵ WORK

Due to Wallonia's coal reserves and access to river transportation, the region underwent industrialization early. With its steel, glass, and textiles industries, it became one of Europe's leading manufacturing centers in the 19th century. However, since World War II, its coal mines have closed and its traditional heavy industries have fallen into decline. At the same time, Flanders, historically a less developed agricultural area, has caught up economically, with booming international trade through the port city of Antwerp, new industries supported by foreign aid and private investment, and a burgeoning service sector. During the 1960s, Wallonia received 50% less government aid than Flanders, with its larger work force. The Walloons were also hit harder by Belgium's high unemployment of the late 1980s and early 1990s than their neighbor to the north, where more new jobs were available. In the 21st century, Wallonia's economic future lies in high technology, the region same rights as heterosexual ones, including inheritance and adoption.

21 BIBLIOGRAPHY

Fox, Renée. *In the Belgian Château: The Spirit and Culture of a European Society in an Age of Change.* Chicago: Ivan R. Dee, 1994.

Gross, Joan. *Speaking in Other Voices: An Ethnology of Walloon Puppet Theaters.* Amsterdam: J. Benjamins, 2001.

———. "Walloons." *Encyclopedia of World Cultures (Europe).* Boston: G. K. Hall, 1992.

Hargrove, Jim. *Belgium. Enchantment of the World Series.* Chicago: Children's Press, 1988.

Hubbard, Monica M., and Beverly Baer, ed. *Cities of the World: Europe and the Middle East.* Detroit: Gale Research, 1993.

Illustrated Encyclopedia of Mankind. London: Marshall Cavendish, 1978.

Lijphart, Arend, ed. *Conflict and Coexistence in Belgium: The Dynamics of a Culturally Divided Society.* Berkeley: University of California Press, 1981.

Moss, Joyce, and George Wilson. *Peoples of the World: Western Europeans.* Detroit: Gale Research, 1993.

Pateman, Robert. *Belgium.* 2nd ed. New York: Marshall Cavendish Benchmark, 2006.

Stallaerts, Robert. *Historical Dictionary of Belgium.* 2nd ed. Lanham, MD : Scarecrow Press, 2007.

Wickman, Stephen B. *Belgium: A Country Study.* Washington, DC: U.S. Government Printing Office, 1984.

—revised by J. Hobby

WELSH

LOCATION: United Kingdom (Wales)
POPULATION: 2.97 million (2006)
LANGUAGE: English; Welsh
RELIGION: Methodist; Anglican; Presbyterian; Roman Catholic; small numbers of Jews, Muslims, Hindus, and Sikhs

1 INTRODUCTION

Occupying the western portion of the island of Great Britain, Wales is one of the four countries of the United Kingdom (the others are England, Scotland, and Northern Ireland). Its people, of Celtic origin, form a distinctive group with their own language and cultural heritage. After a Roman occupation that lasted from about AD 100 to 400, Wales was divided into tribal kingdoms which were gradually converted to the Christian religion. The southern part of Wales was colonized by Normans during the 11th century, and the last independent principality—that of Gwynedd, which had united most of North and Central Wales—was conquered by Edward I of England in 1284. Edward's oldest son was given the title Prince of Wales, and that title has been held by the oldest son of England's reigning monarch ever since. The rebellion of Owain Glyn Dwr in the 14th century briefly created a Welsh state with both a parliament in Machynlleth and recognition from the Pope, but Glyn Dwr was vanquished after a ten-year struggle. In 1536, during the reign of Henry VII of England, whose House of Tudor had Welsh ancestry and Welsh support (at least initially), Wales was officially joined with England by the Act of Union.

With the development of coal and iron mining in the 18th and 19th centuries, South Wales became heavily industrialized and many people emigrated there from the north. During the same period, the Wesleyan religious revival drew many away from the established Anglican Church, contributing to the Welsh sense of ethnic identity. In the 20th century, Wales lost much of its population—some 20% in the 1920s alone—through emigration to England and other countries, fueled by the search for better job opportunities. (During the depression of the 1930s, unemployment in some areas reached nearly 40%.) In recent decades there has been a resurgence of Welsh nationalism. The nationalist party Plaid Cymru, founded in the 1920s, had its first member elected to Parliament in 1966. That period also saw the founding of the Welsh Language Society, which has advocated the increased use and official recognition of the Welsh language and organized support for other nationalist issues.

Plans for devolution in Scotland, Wales, and Northern Ireland have long been debated in the UK, and in 1997 a referendum was held in Wales approving the introduction of the National Assembly for Wales (NAW) by a very slim margin (50.3% to 49.7%). However, support for devolution has strengthened since 1997: in 2003 more than 65% of Welsh voters supported devolution. Among those supporters there has emerged a marked preference for a more powerful form of devolution—a Parliament as in Scotland, with legislative and taxation powers—rather than the type of Assembly introduced in Wales, which has only limited legislative powers. Most Welsh think their Assembly has made no great difference on matters

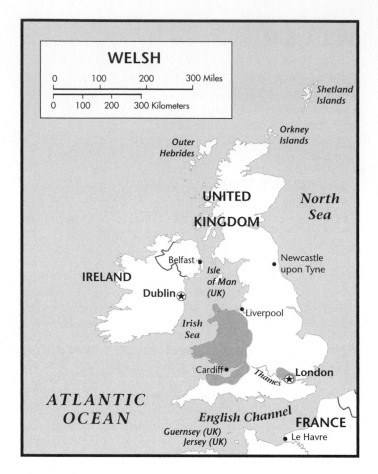

WELSH

such as health, education, and the economy. Many Welsh believe that the UK government still has too much influence on the way Wales is run, while the NAW has too little influence and should have more.

In the 21st century Wales has shown a growth in population due in large measure to inward migration from England. Birth rates have increased in recent years, and in 2005/06 Wales experienced more births than deaths for the first time in around a decade. Population projections for Wales show a growing population, but also an increase in the number of dependents per person of working age.

² LOCATION AND HOMELAND

Altogether, Wales covers an area of 20,766 sq km (8,018 sq mi), making it slightly smaller than the state of Massachusetts. It has farmland, mountains, valleys, and rivers of such scenic beauty that one-fifth of the country is classified as national parkland, yet it also has coal mining regions in which the air itself seems gray and drab.

Wales is divided into six main regions, each further divided into counties or shires. Gwynedd and Clwyd are located in the north, Powys and Dyfed in the center, and Glamorgan and Gwent in the south. The country's vegetation is mostly grasslands and forests. The rugged Cambrian mountains dominate the northern two-thirds of the country, while the terrain in the central and southern parts of the country forms plateaus and valleys. Mount Snowdon, in the northwest, is the country's highest point, at 1,085 m (3,560 ft). Of Wales's 2.97 million

people, 80% live in cities and 20% in the country. The most populous area is the south, an industrial region containing the cities of Swansea, Cardiff, and Newport.

³ LANGUAGE

Both English and Welsh are the official languages of Wales, although the use of Welsh has declined gradually over the past two centuries, while almost all Welsh people speak English. About 50% of the population spoke Welsh at the turn of the 20th century, compared with about 21% in 2001. Welsh is a Celtic language, closest to the Breton language that is spoken in a part of France. Since the 1960s there has been a movement to increase the use and recognition of Welsh, initially spearheaded by the Welsh Language Society. Welsh was recognized as an official language in 1966, and its use expanded in government forms and publications. Today the language is taught in the schools, and there are Welsh radio and television broadcasting facilities.

Welsh is known for its long words, double consonants, and scarce vowels, which often appear in unusual combinations that English speakers find quite difficult to pronounce. The Welsh language contains what is probably the longest place name in the world:
Llanfairpwllgwyngyllgogerychwyrndrobwllllantysiliogogogoch,
a town name that means "Church of St. Mary in the Hollow by the White Aspen near the Rapid Whirlpool and Church of St. Tysilio by the Red Cave." (It is usually referred to as Llanfair P.G.) In 1992 the government introduced a Welsh Language Bill, which is designed to guarantee equal status for the Welsh and English languages in Wales.

SAMPLE WORDS

llan	church
fach	small
fawr	big
blaen	head
craig	rock
cwm	valley
llyn	lake
mynydd	mountain
bach	little (one)

⁴ FOLKLORE

Welsh culture is steeped in myths and legends—even the country's national symbol, the dragon, is a mythical beast. Almost every mountain, river, and lake, as well as many farms and villages, are associated with some legend of *tylwyth teg* (fairies), magical properties or fearful beasts. The Welsh claim the legendary British hero King Arthur—who is said to be buried on the Isle of Afallon—as well as the magician Merlin and other characters who people the *Mabinogion,* the famous collection of medieval Welsh tales from which English authors from Sir Thomas Malory to Lord Tennyson took the material for their versions of the Arthurian legend. Another popular subject of Welsh legend is the prince Madog ab Owain (said to have discovered America in the 12th century). In the 16th and 18th centuries, the English actually used this legend as the basis for claims to territory in the New World.

⁵ RELIGION

The Methodism of evangelist John Wesley had a strong influence on the Welsh beginning in the 18th century, and many Welsh Christians today are Methodists (also called Nonconformists). In Wales, the Church of Wales is the leading church with about 80,900 members, followed by the Presbyterian/Reformed Churches (44,300), the Roman Catholic Church (39,500) and a few other trinitarian churches (85,600). The Welsh generally observe religious practices quite strictly, and few people work on Sundays. Wales also has small numbers of Jews, Muslims, Hindus, Sikhs and other religious minorities, concentrated mainly in the large cities of South Wales, such as Cardiff and Swansea.

⁶ MAJOR HOLIDAYS

Legal holidays in Wales include New Year's Day, St. David's Day (March 1), Good Friday, Easter Monday, a Spring Bank holiday (the last Monday in May or the first Monday in June), a Summer Bank Holiday (the last Monday in August or the first Monday in September), Christmas, and Boxing Day (December 26). St. David's Day, commemorating Wales's patron saint, is celebrated as a national holiday. Daffodils are sold everywhere, to be worn on the lapel or brought home to adorn houses throughout the country. Every January, the Festival of St Dwyhwon, the Welsh patron saint of lovers, takes place, but it is gradually being replaced by St Valentine's Day.

⁷ RITES OF PASSAGE

The Welsh live in a modern, industrialized, Christian country. Hence, many of the rites of passage that young people undergo are religious rituals, such as baptism, first Communion, confirmation, and marriage. In addition, a student's progress through the education system is marked by many families with graduation parties.

⁸ INTERPERSONAL RELATIONS

The Welsh are known for their warmth and hospitality. People are friendly with their neighbors and acquaintances always stop to chat, however briefly, when they encounter each other. Invitations to tea are readily extended and accepted.

⁹ LIVING CONDITIONS

Rural dwellers have traditionally lived in whitewashed stone cottages and farmhouses. In the past, many cottages consisted of only one or two rooms and a sleeping loft accessible by a ladder from the kitchen or an outside stairway. Another type of traditional dwelling was the longhouse, a single-story structure that housed the family at one end and livestock at the other. Today, many picturesque old cottages have been turned into vacation homes. Housing in the coalmining areas generally consists of row houses with slate roofs and stone walls and outside bathrooms, mostly built in the 19th century. Much of the older housing lacks amenities that people in the United States take for granted, such as central heating. As recently as the 1970s, it was common for people living in older housing to use coal-fired stoves for heat, with fireplaces or electric heaters used to heat rooms other than the kitchen. Many families renovate their older houses, adding rooms, porches, and modern conveniences. Semidetached houses shared by two families (similar to duplexes in the United States) are common.

Britain's comprehensive National Health Service has provided Wales with free, modern health care by physicians, surgeons, clinics, and hospitals since 1948. While there are roads linking southern Wales with London, Bristol, the West Midlands, and northwestern regions of England, many small villages in Wales itself lack an integrated transportation network, and unpaved roads are found in rural coal mining villages and agricultural areas, especially in remote mountain regions. The railroads generally run east-west, and some of the old-fashioned narrow gauge variety can still be found in more rural areas. Most major international airlines do not provide direct intercontinental service to Wales. However, Cardiff Wales Airport has regular flights to most major European cities and holiday destinations.

¹⁰ FAMILY LIFE

Family and kinship are extremely important in Wales. The Welsh dote on their children, and special occasions are spent with members of one's extended family. While the English tend to identify themselves by social class, Welsh loyalty is first and foremost to the family. When Welsh people meet, they often ask each other questions to find out if they have relatives in common. The Welsh traditionally married late and sustained lengthy courtships. In farming communities, adult sons generally remain at home working on their parents' farms until they marry, and a younger son usually inherits the farm.

Most families today have between one and three children. Welsh families spend a lot of time at home. Life in rural areas tends to be very insular, and a 32-km (20-mi) trip to a neighboring village is considered a major undertaking. On Sunday, many attend church, which is followed by Sunday dinner, the most important meal of the week. After dinner, men often meet their friends at a pub. In working class families, few women have traditionally been employed outside the home.

¹¹ CLOTHING

For ordinary casual and formal occasions, the Welsh wear typical Western style clothing. However, at festivals one can still see women wearing their traditional national costumes, consisting of checked aprons worn over long dresses, white collars similar to those of the Puritans, and tall black hats (something like witches' hats but less pointy and with a wider brim) worn over white kerchiefs. On such occasions, men may wear striped vests over white shirts and knee-length breeches with high white socks.

¹² FOOD

Traditional Welsh cuisine is unpretentious, down-to-earth farmhouse cooking using plain, everyday ingredients, such as Wales's national vegetable, the leek. Leeks are used in soups, stews, and in a popular dish known as Anglesey Eggs that also contains eggs, cheese, and potatoes. The well-known Welsh Rarebit is actually a genuine Welsh dish (although it has nothing to do with rabbit, as some mistakenly think). It consists of toast coated with a mixture of milk, eggs, cheese, and Worcestershire sauce—the original toasted cheese sandwich. Soups and stews are popular dishes, and the Welsh are known for the excellent quality of their lamb, fish, and seafood. One dish that some visitors prefer to avoid is *laverbread,* a type of seaweed, sold washed and boiled and traditionally prepared with oatmeal and bacon. The Welsh bake a variety of hearty desserts including *bara brith,* a popular bread made with raisins and currants that have been soaked in tea overnight, and Welsh gingerbread (made without ginger!). The most important meal of the week is traditionally Sunday dinner, which may include a chicken or a rolled cut of meat called a joint of beef.

13 EDUCATION

Welsh education follows the same pattern as that in England, with schooling compulsory between the ages of 5 and 16. Students take an exam at age 11, after which they attend either middle schools that prepare them for admission to college, comprehensive schools that provide a general education, or technical schools, which offer vocational training. Accredited institutions of higher learning include Cardiff University; Aberystwyth University; Bangor University; Swansea University; University of Wales, Newport; North East Wales Institute of Higher Education; University of Wales Institute, Cardiff; University of Wales, Lampeter; Swansea Institute of Higher Education; Trinity College, Carmarthen; the Royal Welsh College of Music & Drama; and the University of Glamorgan.

14 CULTURAL HERITAGE

Welsh-language literature is among the oldest continuous literary traditions in Europe, with some of its earliest masterpieces (such as "Y Gododdin" by Aneirin, and the anonymous "Canu Llywarch Her") dating from the sixth century AD. The patronage of medieval princes and later noblemen fostered the development of a unique and complex form of strict meter poetry, known as *cynghanedd.* The acknowledged master of Welsh poetry in the 16th century was Dafydd ap Gwylim, who left a great body of work. Welsh poets have gained recognition in the English-speaking world since the days of George Herbert, Thomas Vaughan, and Henry Vaughan in the 17th century. In the 20th century, W. H. Davies was known for his *Autobiography of a Super-Tramp,* Wilfred Owen for his poetry about the horrors of World War I, and R. S. Thomas for his uncompromising reflections upon Wales and the Welsh. Wales's most illustrious modern poet was Dylan Thomas, author of the beloved "A Child's Christmas in Wales," the radio play "Under Milk Wood," and many well-known poems.

The Welsh are often regarded by their neighbors in Britain and Ireland to be a very musical people, and there is a great deal of justification for this. The Welsh choral tradition includes celebrated male choirs, soloists such as Margaret Price, Geraint Evans, and Bryn Terfel, as well as pop vocalists like Tom Jones, Shirley Bassey, and Bonnie Tyler. Rock bands like the Alarm, the Manic Street Preachers, the Lostprophets, Funeral For A Friend, and Bullet For My Valentine also hail from Wales. Important cultural institutions include the Welsh Arts Council, the Welsh National Opera Company, and the National Museum of Wales. Several well-known actors are Welsh, probably the best-known being the late Richard Burton, and Sir Anthony Hopkins, who both were born in the South Welsh harbor town of Port Talbot.

15 WORK

In the century between the mid-1800s and the mid-1900s, coal mining and iron and steel production flourished in Wales. However, workers endured deprivation and harsh working conditions, and much of the wealth went to industrialists based outside the country. Other major Welsh industries included textiles and slate quarrying. The Great Depression of the 1930s left a fifth of the population unemployed by 1932, resulting in mass emigration to England. After a temporary recovery during World War II, the traditional Welsh industries declined and were replaced by light industry, plastics, chemicals, and electronics. Many people are employed in service industries including construction and power production. Tourism is also a large service industry. Dairy, cattle, and sheep farming still thrive, and the Welsh still fish in their traditional craft—called *coracles*—constructed from willow and hazel branches covered with hide. Workers in Wales's industries have a high level of unionization. Programs coordinated by the Welsh Development Agency in the late 1980s and the 1990s succeeded in attracting high levels of foreign investment in Wales. In proportion to its population, Wales gained the highest concentration of Japanese companies in Europe. The ageing of the population has affected the work force and the economy: from 1971–2006, Wales experienced a 30% increase in the number of people of retirement age. The number of people of pensionable age was expected to increase another 30% between 2006 and 2031. In 2031 (as in 2006) the UK country with the projected largest proportion of the population of pensionable age is Wales (24%).

16 SPORTS

Rugby is the most popular Welsh sport. Created at the exclusive English school whose name it bears, it was introduced to Wales about a century ago and quickly picked up by the working class as a national pastime. International matches, especially those against England, generate great national spirit and are accorded the same status as the World Series or the Super Bowl in the United States. Soccer (called football) and cricket are also widely played, and dog racing and pony racing are popular as well.

17 ENTERTAINMENT AND RECREATION

In their spare time, Welsh people enjoy movies and television. Wales has its own branch of the British Broadcasting Corporation (BBC), as well as other networks that produce high-quality programming. Many people participate in some type of music-making (choral singing is especially popular). Men commonly spend many of their leisure hours socializing in neighborhood pubs. Women's circles with weekly meetings are widespread in rural Wales, as are young farmers' clubs, and in Welsh-speaking areas the youth organization *"Urdd gobaith Cymru"* ("The Order of Hope of Wales") organizes summer camps, recreational outings, musical and dramatic productions for the under-25s, and as a message of peace to world youth. Popular outdoor activities include hunting, fishing, mountain climbing, pony trekking, golf, swimming, rock climbing, and hang gliding.

On their one-to two-week annual vacation, Welsh families enjoy traveling to seaside resort towns in various parts of the United Kingdom; Cornwall is a particularly popular destination. Travel to seaside resorts and other areas of continental Europe have also become increasingly popular in recent times, with favorite destinations being Brittany, Spain, and Greece.

18 FOLK ART, CRAFTS, AND HOBBIES

Such traditional crafts as blacksmithing, tanning, clog making, and copper-working had virtually disappeared by the

Welsh girls show their support during the U18 Six Nations Festival game between England and Wales at Sixways Stadium, Worcester, England. (John Gichigi/Getty Images)

1950s. Woodwork, metalwork and pottery remain strong, however, especially with the revived use of ancient Celtic design by many craftsmen. The old Welsh tradition of making love-spoons—intricately-carved wooden spoons bearing symbols of what a man desired of the relationship with the woman to whom he gave the spoon as a gift—also survives, although in a much-commercialized form.

The Welsh have a great tradition of choral singing that began with 18thcentury Methodist hymns which entire congregations learned by heart. The Welsh musical and poetic traditions are preserved through a series of competitive folk festivals throughout the nation that culminate in the Royal National *Eisteddfod,* an annual contest for poets and musicians attended by tens of thousands of people every August. At the end of the nine-day event, awards are presented for free and metered verse in a ceremony based on ancient Druid traditions. The festival also includes folk dancing and all types of music, from brass bands to Welsh rock groups. Competitions also take place in the fields of literature, drama, theater, and the visual arts. Many see the Eisteddfod—whose events are conducted in Welsh with instantaneous English translation—as a major force for the preservation of Welsh cultural identity. The traditions of the Eisteddfod are also shaping the way Wales presents itself to the world. The International Eisteddfod at Llangollen—a five-day festival held each July—invites competitors from all over the world to vie for prizes in traditional singing and dancing. Each year, the event attracts a huge diversity of participants, with vastly different styles such as dance troupes from India, throat singers from Tannu Tura, female choirs from Japan, instrumental soloists from Eastern Europe, and so on. Another aspect of this tradition is found in the Cardiff Singer of the Year, a competition that attracts some of the brightest young talent in the opera world, and whose prestige has launched a number of highly successful careers.

[19] SOCIAL PROBLEMS

Unemployment, especially in rural areas, accentuates concern about Wales's marginal position within the British economy. Until recently, Wales, like Scotland, had had a high level of emigration by people seeking better employment opportunities abroad. However, that trend is turning around. Some Welsh are concerned that an overemphasis on tourism promotes middleclass English interests while failing to improve the lot of the Welsh people themselves. While the movement to promote the preservation and everyday use of the Welsh language has been largely successful in gaining legal and public recognition of bilingualism and the equal status of the language in Wales, traditionalists are currently worried about the survival of rural communities in which the language thrives, and of the traditional values of the communities. Concern focuses especially upon the migration of English-speaking people from Welsh cities into the countryside, a tide which rose during the 1980s and 1990s. Furthermore, the influence exerted by the London-based mass media, whose broadcasts and circulations penetrate into rural Wales, has given reason to believe that the surreptitious adulteration of Welsh life by English influences is carried on by many means other than promoting English over Welsh. Conflicts of interest between monolingual English-speakers and bilingual Welsh-speakers are becoming important issues in many areas.

20 GENDER ISSUES

In 2006 females represented 51.3% of the population of Wales and males 48.7%. The fertility rate dropped from 2.40 births per woman in 1971 to 1.86 in 2006. In 1971, 93% of all births took place within marriage, while the figure in 2006 was 47%.

Gwenllian Morgan became Wales's first female mayor in 1910, in Brecon. Until 1918, only British males over the age of 21 were allowed to vote in elections, or to stand for election to Parliament. The leading Welsh suffragette was Margaret Haig Mackworth (née Thomas). She later became Lady Rhondda and was a successful business woman and journalist. Great Britain's Women's Freedom League was established in Swansea in 1909, and was formed as a non-violent campaigning body for women's votes. There was a large following for women's suffrage within Wales. The Cardiff branch of the National Women's Union of Suffrage Societies was the largest outside London. After years of campaigning and protesting, women over the age of 30 were granted the right to vote in 1918. In 1928 the voting age was brought into line with that for men—21.

In the 1960s and 1970s women's liberation groups in Wales campaigned for equal rights with men. Pressure from the women's movement saw the introduction of two new laws; the Equal Pay Act (1970) and the Sex Discrimination Act (1975). Welsh feminist writer Elaine Morgan's book, The Descent Of Woman, caused outrage when it was first published in 1972. Morgan questioned what she saw as the sexist angle of the theory of evolution. In the latter half of the 20th century, jobs traditionally seen as men's work (such as mining) were disappearing, while many jobs for women (especially in service industries) were being created. Nevertheless, even at the start of the 21st century full-time working women in Wales still earned on average 12% less per hour than their male counterparts.

Although homosexuality is increasingly being tolerated in Western societies, including the UK, many modern Welsh do not accept it. In 2008 a television documentary called The Only Gay in the Village looked at changing attitudes to homosexuality in Wales. It featured singer Ian "H" Watkins returning to his home area of Cwmparc to speak about his life growing up gay in the Welsh valleys, which he called "a complete nightmare." Nevertheless, there is a thriving gay community in Cardiff and other Welsh urban areas.

21 BIBLIOGRAPHY

Fuller, Barbara. *Britain. Cultures of the World*. London: Marshall Cavendish, 1994.

Illustrated Encyclopedia of Mankind. London: Marshall Cavendish, 1978.

Jenkins, Geraint H. *A Concise History of Wales*. Cambridge: Cambridge University Press, 2007.

Lloyd, Megan S. *"Speak it in Welsh": Wales and the Welsh Language in Shakespeare*. Lanham: Lexington Books, 2007.

Martin, Christopher. *A Glimpse of Heaven: Catholic Churches of England and Wales*. Swindon: English Heritage, 2007.

Moss, Joyce, and George Wilson. *Peoples of the World: Western Europeans*. Gale Research, 1993.

Sutherland, Dorothy. *Wales. Enchantment of the World Series*. Chicago: Children's Press, 1994.

Theodoratus, Robert B. "Welsh." *Encyclopedia of World Cultures (Europe)*. Boston: G. K. Hall, 1992.

Thomas, Dylan. *Child's Christmas in Wales*. New York: New Directions, 2007.

Thomas, Ruth. *South Wales*. New York: Arco Publishing, 1977.

—revised by J. Hobby

GLOSSARY

a capella: singing without musical accompaniment.

aboriginal: the first inhabitants of a country. A species of animals or plants which originated within a given area.

acupuncture: ancient practice of treating disease or relieving pain by inserting needles into pressure points on the body. The Chinese are associated with this medical treatment.

adobe: a clay from which bricks are made for use in making houses.

adult literacy: the capacity of adults to read and write.

agglutinative tongue: a language in which the suffixes and prefixes to words retain a certain independence of one another and of the stem to which they are added. Turkish is an example of an agglutinative tongue.

agrarian economy: an economy where agriculture is the dominant form of economic activity.

active volcano: a large rock mass formed by the expulsion of molten rock, or lava, which periodically erupts.

acute accent: a mark (') used to denote accentual stress of a single sound.

agglutinative tongue: a language in which the suffixes and prefixes to words retain a certain independence of one another and of the stem to which they are added. Turkish is an example of an agglutinative tongue.

agrarian economy: an economy where agriculture is the dominant form of economic activity.

agrarian society: a society where agriculture dominates the day-to-day activities of the population.

All Saints' Day: a Christian holiday on 1 November (a public holiday in many countries). Saints and martyrs who have no special festival are commemorated. In the Middle Ages, it was known as All Hallows' Day; the evening of the previous day, October 31, was called All Hallow Even, from which the secular holiday Halloween is derived.

All Souls' Day: a Christian holiday. This day, 2 November, is dedicated to prayer for the repose of the souls of the dead.

allies: groups or persons who are united in a common purpose. Typically used to describe nations that have joined together to fight a common enemy in war.

Altaic language family: a family of languages spoken by people in portions of northern and eastern Europe, and nearly the whole of northern and central Asia, together with some other regions, and divided into five branches, the Ugrian or Finno-Hungarian, Samoyed, Turkish, Mongolian, and Tungus.

altoplano: refers to the high plains of South American mountain ranges on the Pacific coast.

Amerindian: a contraction of the two words, American Indian. It describes native peoples of North, South, or Central America.

Amerindian language group: the language groups of the American Indians.

Amish: Anabaptist Protestants originally from Germany. Settled in Pennsylvania and the American Midwest.

Anabaptist: Christian sect that was founded in Switzerland during the 16th century. Rejected infant baptism as invalid.

ancestor worship: the worship of one's ancestors.

Anglican: pertaining to or connected with the Church of England.

animism: the belief that natural objects and phenomena have souls or innate spiritual powers.

anthropologist: one who studies the characteristics, customs, and development of mankind.

anti-miscegenation laws: prohibition of marriage or sexual relations between men and women of different races.

anti-Semitism: agitation, persecution, or discrimination (physical, emotional, economic, political, or otherwise) directed against the Jews.

apartheid: the past governmental policy in the Republic of South Africa of separating the races in society.

appliqué: a trimming made from one cloth and sewn onto another cloth.

aquaculture: the culture or "farming" of aquatic plants or animals.

arable land: land which can be cultivated by plowing, as distinguished from grassland, woodland, common pasture, and wasteland.

archipelago: any body of water having many islands, or the islands themselves collectively.

arctic climate: cold, frigid weather similar to that experienced at or near the North Pole.

arid: dry; without moisture; parched with heat.

aristocracy: a small minority that controls the government of a nation, typically on the basis of inherited wealth. Political power is restricted to its members. Also may referred to any privileged elite of a country.

artifacts: objects or tools that date back to an ancient period of human history.

Ash Wednesday: a Christian holiday. The first day of Lent, observed 46 days before Easter, is so called from the practice of placing ashes on the forehead of the worshipper as a sign of penitence. In the Roman Catholic Church, these ashes are obtained from burning palm branches used in the previous year's Palm Sunday observation. (Palm Sunday commemorates the entry of Jesus into Jerusalem a week before Easter Sunday, and it begins Holy Week.) On Ash Wednesday, the ashes are placed on the forehead of the communicant during Mass. The recipient is told, "Remember that you are dust, and unto dust you shall return" or "Turn away from sin and be faithful to the Gospel."

Ashura: a Muslim holiday. This fast day was instituted by Muhammad as the equivalent of the Jewish Yom Kippur but later became voluntary when Ramadan replaced it as a holiday of penance. It also commemorates Noah's leaving the ark on Mt. Ararat after the waters of the Great Flood had subsided. In Iran, the martyrdom of Husayn, grandson of Muhammad, is commemorated with passion plays on this day.

assembly: in government, a body of legislators that meets together regularly.

Assumption: a Christian holiday. This holiday, observed on 15 August in many countries, celebrates the Roman Catholic and Eastern Orthodox dogma that, following Mary's death, her body was taken into heaven and reunited with her soul.

atheist: a person who denies the existence of God, or of a supreme intelligent being.

atherosclerosis: a disease of the arteries. Characterized by blockages that prevent blood flow from the heart to the brain and other parts of the body.

atoll: a coral island, consisting of a strip or ring of coral surrounding a central lagoon. Such islands are common in the Pacific Ocean and are often very picturesque.

aurora borealis: the northern lights, consisting of bands of light across the night sky seen in northern geographical locations.

Australoid: pertains to the type of aborigines of Australia.

Austronesian language: a family of languages which includes Indonesian, Melanesian, Polynesian, and Micronesian sub-families.

B

Babushka: a head scarf worn by women.

Baltic States: the three formerly communist countries of Estonia, Latvia, and Lithuania that border on the Baltic Sea.

Bantu language group: a name applied to the south African family of tongues. The most marked peculiarity of these languages is their prevailing use of prefixes instead of suffixes in derivation and inflection. Some employ clicks and clucks as alphabetic elements.

baptism: any ceremonial bathing intended as a sign of purification, dedication, etc. Baptisms are performed by immersion of the person in water, or by sprinkling the water on the person.

Baptist: a member of a Protestant denomination which practices adult baptism by immersion.

barren land: unproductive land, partly or entirely treeless.

barter: Trade in which merchandise is exchanged directly for other merchandise or services without use of money.

bilingual: able to speak two languages. Also used to describe anything that contains or is expressed in two languages, such as directions written in both English and Spanish.

boat people: a term used to describe individuals (refugees) who attempt to flee their country by boat.

Bolshevik Revolution: pertaining to the Russian revolution of 1917. Russian communists overthrew Tsar Nicholas II and ended the feudal Russian empire.

borscht: cold beet soup, topped with sour cream.

Brahman: a member of the sacred caste among the Hindus. There are many subdivisions of the caste, often remaining in isolation from one another.

bratwurst: seasoned fresh German sausage. Made from pork or veal.

bride price: the price paid to the family of the bride by the young man who seeks to marry her.

bride wealth: the money or property or livestock a bride brings to her marriage. *See* **dowry**.

Buddhism: the religious system common in India and eastern Asia. Founded by and based upon the teachings of Gautama Buddha, Buddhism asserts that suffering is an inescapable part of life. Deliverance can only be achieved through the practice of charity, temperance, justice, honesty, and truth.

bureaucracy: a system of government which is characterized by division into bureaus of administration with their own divisional heads. Also refers to the institutional inflexibility and red tape of such a system.

bush country: a large area of land which is wild with low, bushlike vegetation.

Byzantine Empire: an empire centered in the city of Byzantium, now Istanbul in present-day Turkey.

C

Cajun: name given to Canadians who emigrated to Louisiana from Acadia, the old name for Nova Scotia. Contraction of the name Accadian.

Calvinist: a follower of the theological system of John Calvin.

Candlemas: a Christian holiday. A national holiday on 2 February in Liechtenstein, this observation is now called the Presentation of the Lord, commemorating the presentation of the infant Jesus in the Temple at Jerusalem. Before a 1969 Vatican reform, it commemorated the Purification of Mary 40 days after giving birth to a male child in accordance with a Jewish practice of the time.

capital punishment: the ultimate act of punishment for a crime; the death penalty.

capitalism: an economic system in which goods and services and the means to produce and sell them are privately owned, and prices and wages are determined by market forces.

cash crop: a crop that is grown to be sold, rather than kept for private use.

caste system: one of the artificial divisions or social classes into which the Hindus are rigidly separated according to the religious law of Brahmanism. The privileges and disabilities of a caste are passed on to each succeeding generation.

Caucasian: the "white" race of human beings, as determined by genealogy and physical features.

Caucasoid: belonging to the racial group characterized by light skin pigmentation. Commonly called the "white race," although it can refer to peoples of darker skin color.

celibate: a person who voluntarily abstains from marriage. In some religious practices, the person will often take a vow of abstention from sexual intercourse as well.

censorship: the practice of withholding certain items of news that may cast a country in an unfavorable light or give away secrets to the enemy.

census: an official counting of the inhabitants of a state or country with details of sex and age, family, occupation, possessions, etc.

Central Powers: in World War I, Germany and Austria-Hungary, and their allies, Turkey and Bulgaria.

centrally planned economy: an economic system in which all aspects are supervised and regulated by the government.

cerebrovascular: pertains to the brain and the blood vessels leading to and from the brain.

chancellery: the office of an embassy or consulate.

chaperone: an older married person, usually female, who supervises the activities of young, unmarried couples.

chattel: refers to the movable personal property of an individual or group. It cannot refer to real estate or buildings.

cholera: an acute infectious disease characterized by severe diarrhea, vomiting, and often, death.

Christianity: the religion founded by Jesus Christ.

Christmas: a Christian holiday. The annual commemoration of the nativity of Jesus is held on 25 December. A midnight Mass ushers in this joyous celebration in many Roman

Catholic churches. The custom of distributing gifts to children on Christmas Eve derives from a Dutch custom originally observed on the evening before St. Nicholas' Day (6 December). The day after Christmas—often called Boxing Day, for the boxed gifts customarily given—is a public holiday in many countries.

Church of England: the national and established church in England. The Church of England claims continuity with the branch of the Catholic Church which existed in England before the Reformation. Under Henry VIII, the spiritual supremacy and jurisdiction of the Pope were abolished, and the sovereign was declared head of the church.

chaplet: a wreath or garland of flowers placed on a woman's head.

cistern: a natural or artificial receptacle or reservoir for holding water or other fluids.

city-state: an independent state consisting of a city and its surrounding territory.

civil law: the law developed by a nation or state for the conduct of daily life of its own people.

civil rights: the privileges of all individuals to be treated as equals under the laws of their country; specifically, the rights given by certain amendments to the U.S. Constitution.

civil unrest: the feeling of uneasiness due to an unstable political climate or actions taken as a result of it.

civil war: a war between groups of citizens of the same country who have different opinions or agendas. The Civil War of the United States was the conflict between the states of the North and South from 1861 to 1865.

coca: a shrub native to South America, the leaves of which produce alkaloids which are used in the production of cocaine.

cohabitation: living together as husband and wife without being legally married.

cold war: refers to conflict over ideological differences that is carried on by words and diplomatic actions, not by military action. The term is usually used to refer to the tension that existed between the United States and the USSR from the 1950s until the breakup of the USSR in 1991.

collard greens: a hearty, leafy green vegetable. Popular part of southern American and West Indian cuisine.

collective farm: a large farm formed from many small farms and supervised by the government; usually found in communist countries.

collective farming: the system of farming on a collective where all workers share in the income of the farm.

colloquial: belonging to the language of common or familiar conversation, or ordinary, everyday speech; often especially applied to common words and phrases which are not used in formal speech.

colonial period: in the United States, the period of time when the original thirteen colonies were being formed.

colonist: any member of a colony or one who helps settle a new colony.

colony: a group of people who settle in a new area far from their original country, but still under the jurisdiction of that country. Also refers to the newly settled area itself.

commerce: the trading of goods (buying and selling), especially on a large scale, between cities, states, and countries.

commodity: any items, such as goods or services, that are bought or sold, or agricultural products that are traded or marketed.

common law: a legal system based on custom and legal precedent. The basic system of law of the United States.

common law spouse: a husband or wife in a marriage that, although not legally formalized through a religious or state-sanctioned ceremony, is legally acknowledged based on the agreement of the two people to consider themselves married.

communicable disease: referring to infectious or contagious diseases.

communion: 1. The act of partaking of the sacrament of the Eucharist; the celebration of the Lord's Supper. 2. A body of Christians who have one common faith, but not necessarily ecclesiastical union; a religious denomination. 3. Union in religious worship, or in doctrine and discipline.

communism: a form of government whose system requires common ownership of property for the use of all citizens. All profits are to be equally distributed and prices on goods and services are usually set by the state. Also, communism refers directly to the official doctrine of the former USSR.

compulsory education: the mandatory requirement for children to attend school until they have reached a certain age or grade level.

condolence: expression of sympathy.

Condomblé: American name for the Yoruba pantheon of 401 gods and goddesses.

Confucianism: the ethical system taught by the Chinese philosopher Confucius. It was enlarged upon by his contemporary Mencius so that political systems would be tested with the same ethical standards. (*See* **Taoism**)

constitution: the written laws and basic rights of citizens of a country or members of an organized group.

consumer goods: items that are bought to satisfy personal needs or wants of individuals.

Coptic Christians: members of the Coptic Church of Egypt, formerly of Ethiopia.

Corpus Christi: a Christian holiday. This holiday in honor of the Eucharist is observed on the Thursday or Sunday after Trinity Sunday, which is the Sunday after Pentecost. In the Roman Catholic and Eastern Orthodox Churches, the Eucharist is a sacrament in which the consecrated bread and wine become the body and blood of Jesus Christ, a belief stemming from New Testament accounts of the Last Supper.

corrugated steel: galvanized metal with furrows that give added strength. This metal is often used as roofing materials on houses in tropical countries because of its strength.

coup d'état: a sudden, violent overthrow of a government or its leader.

covert action: secret, concealed activities carried out without public knowledge.

cricket (sport): a game played by two teams with a ball and bat, with two wickets being defended by a batsman.

criminal law: the branch of law that deals primarily with crimes and their punishments.

crown colony: a colony established by a commonwealth over which the monarch has some control, as in colonies established by the British Commonwealth.

Crowning of Our Lady of Altagracia: a Christian holiday in honor of Mary, this day is celebrated in the Dominican Republic on 15 August with a pilgrimage to her shrine. (Altagracia Day, 21 January, is also a holiday in the Dominican Republic.)

Crusades: military expeditions by European Christian armies in the 11th, 12th, and 13th centuries to win land controlled by the Muslims in the Middle East.

cuisine: a particular style of preparing food, especially when referring to the cooking of a particular country or ethnic group.

cultivable land: land that can be prepared for the production of crops.

cursive script: a style of writing in which the letters are joined together in a flowing manner.

Cushitic language group: a group of Hamitic languages which are spoken in Ethiopia and other areas of eastern Africa.

cyclone: any atmospheric movement, general or local, in which the wind blows spirally around and in towards a center. In the northern hemisphere, the cyclonic movement is usually counter-clockwise, and in the southern hemisphere, it is clockwise.

Cyrillic alphabet: an alphabet adopted by the Slavic people and invented by Cyril and Methodius in the 9th century as an alphabet that was easier for the copyist to write. The Russian alphabet is a slight modification of it.

D

Day of Our Lady of Mercy (Las Mercedes): a Christian holiday in honor of Mary, this observance on 24 September is a holiday in the Dominican Republic.

Day of Santa Rosa of Lima: a Christian holiday. The feast day in honor of the first native-born saint of the New World, declared patron saint of South America by Pope Clement X in 1671, is 23 August, but in Peru, she is commemorated by a national holiday on 30 August.

Day of St. Peter and St. Paul: a Christian holiday. This observance, on 29 June, commemorates the martyrdom of the two apostles traditionally believed to have been executed in Rome on the same day (c. AD 67) during the persecution of Christians ordered by Emperor Nero.

deforestation: the removal of a forest ecosystem.

deity: a being with the attributes, nature, and essence of a god; a divinity.

delta: triangular-shaped deposits of soil formed at the mouths of large rivers.

democracy: a form of government in which the power lies in the hands of the people, who can govern directly, or indirectly by electing representatives.

demography: that department of anthropology which relates to vital and social statistics and their application to the comparative study of races and nations.

desegregation: the act of removing restrictions on people of a particular race that keep them separate from other groups, socially, economically, and, sometimes, physically.

détente: the official lessening of tension between countries in conflict.

developed countries: countries which have a high standard of living and a well-developed industrial base.

diacritics: as in diacritical marks, a dot, line, or other mark added or put adjacent to a letter or sign in order to give it a different sound or to indicate some particular accent, tone, stress, or emphasis. An example of diacritical marks would be those used in dictionaries to aid in pronunciation of words.

dialect: One of a number of related forms of speech regarded as descending from a common origin. The speech pattern of a locality or social class as distinguished from the generally accepted literary language.

dictatorship: a form of government in which all the power is retained by an absolute leader or tyrant. There are no rights granted to the people to elect their own representatives.

direct descendant: the offspring in an unbroken line of ancestors.

divine origin: having originated directly, or by direct descendant, from a divine being.

dogma: a principle, maxim, or tenet held as being firmly established.

domicile: a place of residence of an individual or family; a place of habitual abode.

dowry: the sum of the property or money that a bride brings to her groom at their marriage.

druid: a member of a Celtic religion practiced in ancient Britain, Ireland, and France.

Druze: a member of a religious sect of Syria, living chiefly in the mountain regions of Lebanon.

ducal: Referring to a duke or a dukedom.

dysentery: painful inflammation of the large intestine.

E

Easter: the chief Christian holiday is Easter, the annual celebration of the resurrection of Jesus Christ. Like Passover, the Jewish feast from which it is derived, the date of observation is linked to the phases of the moon. Since the Christian calendar is a solar one rather than a lunar one, the date of Easter changes from year to year. Easter is celebrated on the first Sunday after the first full moon following the spring equinox; in the Gregorian calendar, it can occur as early as 22 March or as late as 25 April. The Easter date determines the date of many other Roman Catholic holidays, such as Ash Wednesday, Ascension, and Pentecost.

Easter Monday: a Christian holiday. The day after Easter is a public holiday in many countries.

empire: a group of territories ruled by one sovereign, or supreme ruler.

Epiphany of Our Lord: a Christian holiday. Traditionally observed on 6 January but now observable on the Sunday falling between 2 January and 7 January, this feast commemorates the adoration of the Magi, who journeyed to the place of Jesus' birth. In the Orthodox churches, however, it is the feast celebrating Jesus' baptism.

episcopal: belonging to or vested in bishops or prelates; characteristic of or pertaining to a bishop or bishops.

equestrian culture: a culture that depends on horses for its livelihood. Mastery of the horse is an essential part of the culture's identity.

escarpment: a steep cliff formed from a geological fault or erosion.

ethnographic: referring to the division of anthropology which studies primitive cultures.

ethnolinguistic group: a classification of related languages based on common ethnic origin.

exodus: the departure or migration of a large body of people or animals from one country or region to another.

extinction: dying out of a species of animals or a culture of people.

F

fauna: referring to species of animals found in a specific region.

Feast of Our Lady of Angels: a Christian holiday. This feast, on 2 August, is celebrated as a national holiday in Costa Rica in honor of the Virgin Mary. Pilgrimage is made to the basilica in Cartago, which houses a black stone statue of the Virgin.

fetishism: the practice of worshipping a material object which one believes has mysterious powers residing in it or is the representation of a deity to which worship may be paid and from which supernatural aid is expected.

feudal society: In medieval times, an economic and social structure in which persons could hold land given to them by a lord (nobleman) in return for service to that lord.

Finno-Ugric language group: a subfamily of languages spoken in northeastern Europe, including Finnish, Hungarian (Ugric, Magyar), Estonian, Lapp, and others.

flora: referring to native plant life in a specific region.

folk religion: a religion with origins and traditions among the common people of a nation or region; relevant to their particular lifestyle.

folk tale: an oral story that is passed from generation to generation. Folktales are cultural records of the history and progress of different ethnic groups.

free-market economy: an economic system that relies on the market, as opposed to government planners, to set the prices for wages and products.

fundamentalist: a person who holds religious beliefs based on the complete acceptance of the words of the Bible or other holy scripture as the truth. For instance, a fundamentalist would believe the story of creation exactly as it is told in the Bible and would reject the idea of evolution.

G

gastroenteritis: inflammation of the stomach and small intestines.

geometric pattern: a design of circles, triangles, or lines on cloth.

geriatrics: the study and treatment of diseases of old age.

Germanic language group: a large branch of the Indo-European family of languages including German itself, the Scandinavian languages, Dutch, Yiddish, Modern English, Modern Scottish, Afrikaans and others. The group also includes extinct languages such as Gothic, Old High German, Old Saxon, Old English, Middle English and the like.

glottal stop: a sound formed in speech by a brief but complete closure of the glottis, the opening between the vocal cords. It is a typical sound in certain British dialects.

godparent: a male or female adult who is asked by the parents of a newborn child to assume responsibility for the care and rearing of the child in the event of the death of the parents. Godparents sometimes contribute school tuition, gifts on birthdays and holidays, as well as take an active part in the child's life.

Good Friday: a Christian holiday. The day after Holy Thursday, it is devoted to remembrance of the crucifixion of Jesus and is given to penance and prayer.

Greek Catholic: a person who is a member of an Orthodox Eastern Church.

Greek Orthodox: the official church of Greece, a self-governing branch of the Orthodox Eastern Church.

H

haiku: a form of Japanese poetry, consisting of three lines. Each line has a specific measurement of syllables.

Hanukkah: a Jewish holiday. The Festival of Lights, corresponding roughly to the winter solstice, is celebrated over an eight-day period beginning on 25 Kislev, the third month. Also known as the Feast of Dedication and Feast of the Maccabees, Hanukkah commemorates the rededication of the Temple at Jerusalem in 164 BC. According to tradition, the one ritually pure container of olive oil, sufficient to illuminate the Temple for one day, miraculously burned for eight days, until new oil could be prepared. A feature of the Hanukkah celebration is the lighting in each Jewish home of an eight-branched candelabrum, the menorah. This festival, though not a public holiday in Israel, is widely observed with the lighting of giant menorahs in public places.

harem: in a Muslim household, refers to the women (wives, concubines, and servants in ancient times) who live there and also to the area of the home they live in.

harmattan: an intensely dry, dusty wind felt along the coast of Africa between Cape Verde and Cape Lopez. It prevails at intervals during the months of December, January, and February.

Hinduism: the religion professed by a large part of the inhabitants of India. It is a development of the ancient Brahmanism, influenced by Buddhistic and other elements. Its forms are varied and numerous.

Holi: a Hindu holiday. A festival lasting 3 to 10 days, Holi closes the old year with processions and merriment. It terminates on the full moon of Phalguna, the last month, corresponding to February or March.

Holocaust: the mass slaughter of European civilians, the vast majority Jews, by the Nazis during World War II.

Holy (Maundy) Thursday: a Christian holiday. The Thursday preceding Easter commemorates the Last Supper, the betrayal of Jesus by Judas Iscariot, and the arrest and arraignment of Jesus. In Rome, the pope customarily performs a ceremony in remembrance of Jesus' washing of his apostles' feet (John 13:5–20).

Holy Roman Empire: a kingdom consisting of a loose union of German and Italian territories that existed from around the ninth century until 1806.

Holy Saturday: a Christian holiday. This day commemorates the time during which Jesus was buried and, like Good Friday, is given to solemn prayer.

homeland: a region or area set aside to be a state for a people of a particular national, cultural, or racial origin.

homogeneous: of the same kind or nature, often used in reference to a whole.

homophonic: music that has a single part with no harmonies.

Horn of Africa: the Horn of Africa comprises Djibouti, Eritrea, Ethiopia, Somalia, and Sudan.

human rights issues: any matters involving people's basic rights which are in question or thought to be abused.

humanist: a person who centers on human needs and values, and stresses dignity of the individual.

hydrology: the science of dealing with the earth's waters and their distribution above and below ground.

I

Id al-Adha: a Muslim holiday. The Great Festival, or Sacrificial Feast, celebrates the end of the special pilgrimage season, or Hajj, to Mecca and Medina, an obligation for Muslims once in their lifetime if physically and economically feasible. The slaughter of animals pays tribute to Abraham's obedience to God in offering his son to the Lord for sacrifice; a portion of the meat is supposed to be donated to the poor. The feast begins on 10 Dhu'l-Hijja and continues to 13 Dhu'l-Hijja (14 Dhu'l-Hijja in a leap year). In Malaysia and Singapore, this festival is celebrated as Hari Raya Haji; in Indonesia, Lebaran Haji; in Turkey, Kurban Bayrami.

Id al-Fitr: a Muslim holiday. The Little Festival, or Breaking-Fast-Festival, which begins just after Ramadan, on 1 Shawwal, the 10th month, is the occasion for three or four days of feasting. In Malaysia and Singapore, this festival is called Hari Raya Puasa; in Turkey, Seker Bayrami.

Iemanja: Brazilian name for Yoruba river goddess, Yemoja. Represented as a mermaid.

Immaculate Conception: a Christian holiday. This day, 8 December, celebrates the Roman Catholic dogma asserting that Mary's conception, as the future mother of God, was uniquely free from original sin. In Paraguay, it is observed as the Day of Our Lady of Caacupé.

incursion: a sudden or brief invasion or raid.

indigenous: born or originating in a particular place or country; native to a particular region or area.

indigent: person without any means of economic support.

indigo: a blue dye that is extracted from plants.

Indo-Aryan language group: the group that includes the languages of India; within a branch of the Indo-European language family.

Indo-European language family: the large family of languages that includes those of India, much of Europe, and southwestern Asia.

indulgence: a Catholic blessing given for a person's soul after death.

infant mortality: infant deaths.

infant mortality rate: the number of deaths of children less than one year old per 1,000 live births in a given year.

infanticide: the act of murdering a baby.

infidel: one who is without faith, or unbelieving; particularly, one who rejects the distinctive doctrines of a particular religion, while perhaps remaining an adherent to another religion.

inflective: refers to a language in which differences in tone and pitch give meaning to words and indicate grammatical constructions.

interferon: a drug used in the treatment of cancer in Mexico.

Inuit: an indigenous people of northwestern Canada. They are sometimes mistakenly called Eskimos.

Islam: the religious system of Mohammed, practiced by Muslims and based on a belief in Allah as the supreme being and Mohammed as his prophet. The term also refers to those nations in which it is the primary religion.

isthmus: a narrow strip of land with connecting large bodies of water on either side.

J

Jehovah's Witness: a member of a Christian sect that believes that the end of the world is near and that God should establish a theocracy on earth.

Judaism: the religious system of the Jews, based on the Old Testament as revealed to Moses and characterized by a belief in one God and adherence to the laws of scripture and rabbinic traditions.

Judeo-Christian: the dominant traditional religious makeup of the United States and other countries based on the worship of the Old and New Testaments of the Bible.

Juneteenth: an African American holiday that celebrates the freeing of slaves in America. It is thought to coincide with the surrender of the Confederacy to the Union armies.

Junkanoo: a holiday celebrated around December in the Caribbean and South America. It also has been observed in the United States in Alabama. The holiday has West African origins. Also known as John Canoe and Yancanu.

K

kale: Another hearty, green leafy vegetable that is sometimes mixed with spinach and collard greens to vary the flavor of these vegetables.

khan: a title given Genghis Khan and his successors who ruled over Turkey and Mongolia in the Middle Ages.

kielbasa: seasoned Polish sausage. Made from beef or pork.

L

lagoon: a shallow body of water connected to a larger body of water. It is sometimes separated from the larger body by reefs.

lama: a celebrated priest or ecclesiastic belonging to that variety of Buddhism known as Lamaism. The Dalai-Lama and the tesho- or bogdo-lama are regarded as supreme pontiffs.

land reforms: steps taken to create a fair distribution of farm land, especially by governmental action.

latke: potato pancake.

Leeward Islands: northern islands of the Lesser Antilles in the Caribbean that stretch from Puerto Rico southward.

leprosy: an infectious disease of the skin or nerves which can cause ulcers of the skin, loss of feeling, or loss of fingers and toes.

life expectancy: an individual's expected lifespan, calculated as an average.

lingua franca: Originally, a mixed language or jargon of Mediterranean ports, consisting of Italian mixed with Arabic, Turkish, Greek, French, and Spanish. Nowadays, the phrase is used to denote any hybrid tongue used similarly in other parts of the world; an international dialect.

linguist: a person skilled in the use of languages.

linguistic group: a group of related languages.

literacy: the ability to read and write.

lox: kosher smoked salmon.

Lutheran: of or pertaining to Martin Luther (1483–1546), the reformer, to the Evangelical Protestant Church of Germany which bears his name, or to the doctrines taught by Luther or held by the Evangelical Lutheran Church.

M

macron: a horizontal mark placed over a vowel to indicate its pronunciation as long.

maize: another name (Spanish or British) for corn or the color of ripe corn.

Malayo-Polynesian language group: also referred to as the Austronesian language group, which includes the Indonesian, Polynesian, Melanesian, and Micronesian subfamilies.

mangrove: a kind of evergreen shrub growing along tropical coasts.

marimba: a type of xylophone found in Central and South America.

massif: a central mountain-mass or the dominant part of a range of mountains. A part of a range which appears, from the position of the depression by which it is more or less isolated, to form an independent whole.

matriarchy: a society in which women are recognized as the leaders of the family or tribe.

matrifocal: a society in which women are the focus of activity or attention.

matrilineal (descent): descending from, or tracing descent through, the maternal line.

Mayan language family: the languages of the Central American Indians, further divided into two subgroups: the Maya and the Huastek.

Mecca (Mekkah): a city in Saudi Arabia; a destination of pilgrims in the Islamic world.

Mennonite: a member of the Christian denomination which originated in Friesland, Holland in the early part of the 16th century and upholds the doctrine of which Menno Simons (1492–1559) was the chief exponent.

mestizo: the offspring of a person of mixed blood; especially, a person of mixed Spanish and American Indian parentage.

metamorphosis: referring to the shamanic practice of changing from a person to an animal.

Methodist: a member of the Christian denomination founded by John Wesley (1703–1791). The name was first applied to Wesley and his companions on account of their methodical habits in study and in religious life.

millennium: any one-thousand-year period, but also refers to a real or imagined period of peace and happiness.

missionary: a person sent by ecclesiastical authority to work to spread his religious faith in a community where his church has no self-supporting organization.

Mohammed (or Muhammed or Mahomet): an Arabian prophet, known as the "Prophet of Allah" who founded the religion of Islam in 622, and wrote The Koran, the scripture of Islam. Also commonly spelled Muhammed, especially by Islamic people.

Mongol: one of an Asiatic race chiefly resident in Mongolia, a region north of China proper and south of Siberia.

Mongoloid: having physical characteristics like those of the typical Mongols (Chinese, Japanese, Turks, Eskimos, etc.).

monogamy: the practice of marrying one spouse.

monolingual: speaking one language only.

monsoon: a wind occurring in the alternation of the trade-winds in India and the north Indian Ocean. They occur between April and October when the regular northeast trade-winds are reversed and, with occasional interruptions, the wind blows at almost a steady gale from the southwest. In some areas, as in China, the change of the monsoons is followed with storms and much rain.

Moors: one of the Arab tribes that conquered Spain in the 8th century.

Mormon: an adherent of the religious body the Church of Jesus Christ of Latter-day Saints founded in 1830 by Joseph Smith.

Moslem: a follower of Mohammed (spelled Muhammed by many Islamic people), in the religion of Islam.

mosque: a Mohammedan place of worship and the ecclesiastical organization with which it is connected.

mother tongue: a tongue or language to which other languages owe their origin. One's native language.

Motown: nickname for Detroit. A contraction of Motor City Town.

mujahideen or **mujahedeen:** *see* **mujahidin.**

mujahidin: rebel fighters in Islamic countries, especially those supporting the cause of Islam.

mulatto: one who is the offspring of parents of whom one is white and the other is black.

multicultural: awareness of the effect and existence of more than one cultural viewpoint within one's value system and world view.

multilingual: having the ability to speak several languages. Also used to describe anything that contains or is expressed in several languages, such as directions written in English, Spanish, and French.

mummify: ancient method used to preserve the dead. Associated with ancient Egyptian culture.

Muslim: same as Moslem.

Muslim New Year: a Muslim holiday. Although in some countries 1 Muharram, which is the first month of the Islamic year, is observed as a holiday, in other places the new year is observed on Sha'ban, the eighth month of the year. This practice apparently stems from pagan Arab times. Shab-i-Bharat, a national holiday in Bangladesh on this day, is held by many to be the occasion when God ordains all actions in the coming year.

N

native tongue: one's natural language. The language that is indigenous to an area.

Nobel Laureate: a person awarded a prize for lifetime achievement in literature, sciences, economics, or peace. Prize founded by Swedish industrialist Alfred Nobel, inventor of dynamite.

nomad: a wanderer; member of a tribe of people who have no fixed place or abode, but move about from place to place depending on the availability of food sources.

novena: a series of prayers in honor of a saint for a specific reason.

O

obsidian: a black, shiny volcanic rock, resembling glass.

official language: the language in which the business of a country and its government is conducted.

Ottoman Empire: a Turkish empire founded by Osman I in about 1603, that variously controlled large areas of land around the Mediterranean, Black, and Caspian Seas until it was dissolved in 1918.

outback region: the rural interior region of the continent of Australia. It is sparsely populated, mainly by aboriginal peoples.

overgrazing: allowing animals to graze in an area to the point that the ground vegetation is damaged or destroyed.

P

pagan: a person who worships more than one diety. Sometimes refers to non-Christians.

pagoda: in the Far East, a sacred tower, usually pyramidal in outline, richly carved, painted, or otherwise adorned, and of several stories. They can be, but are not always, connected to a temple.

Paleoasiatic languages: languages that date back to a prehistoric or unwritten era in linguistic history.

parochial: an institution supported by a church or parish.

parody: dance or song ridiculing a serious subject in a silly manner. Usually focuses on the person or people who dominate another cultural group.

Parsi: one of the descendants of those Persians who settled in India about the end of the seventh century in order to escape Mohammedan persecution, and who still retain their ancient religion. Also Parsee.

Passover (Pesach): a Jewish holiday. Pesach, lasting seven days in Israel and eight outside it, begins on 15 Nisan, at roughly the spring equinox, and recalls the exodus of the Hebrews from Egypt and their delivery from bondage. The chief festival of Judaism, Pesach begins with a ceremonial family meal, or seder, at which special foods (including unleavened bread, or matzoh) are eaten and the Passover story (Haggadah) is read.

pastoralist: a nomadic people who move with their herds of sheep or cattle, searching for pasture and water.

patois: a dialect peculiar to a district or locality, in use especially among the peasantry or uneducated classes; hence, a rustic, provincial, or barbarous form of speech.

patriarchal system: a social system in which the head of the family or tribe is the father or oldest male. Kinship is determined and traced through the male members of the tribe.

patrilineal (descent): Descending from, or tracing descent through, the paternal line.

patrilocal: a society in which men take the larger role in activities and receive greater attention.

peccary: a pig-like animal native to North and South America and the Caribbean Islands. Noted for its musky smell, sharp tusks, and gray color.

pentatonic: music consisting of a five tone scale.

Pentecost Monday (Whitmonday): a Christian holiday. This public holiday observed in many countries occurs the day after Pentecost (derived from the ancient Greek pentekostos, "fiftieth"), or Whitsunday, which commemorates the descent of the Holy Spirit upon Jesus' apostles on the seventh Sunday after Easter and is derived from the Jewish feast of Shavuot. It was an important occasion for baptism in the early church, and the name "Whitsunday" originated from the white robes worn by the newly baptized.

Pentecostal: having to do with Pentecost, a Christian holiday celebrated the seventh Sunday after Easter, marking the day that the Holy Spirit descended upon the Apostles.

peyote: the tops of the small spineless mescal cactus. Native to the southwestern United States and northern Mexico.

phoneme: slightly different sounds in a language that are heard as the same by a native speaker.

pierogie: a Polish dumpling made from pastry dough. It contains various fillings, such as meat and potatoes.

pilgrimage: a journey to a sacred place in order to perform some religious vow or duty, or to obtain some spiritual or miraculous benefit.

polygamy: the practice of having two or more spouses at the same time.

polygyny: the practice of having two or more wives and/or mistresses.

polyphonic: combining a number of harmonic sounds. Music that has more than one sound.

polytheism: belief and worship of many gods.

post traumatic stress disorder: psychological disorder that accompanies violent or tragic experiences. Known as shell-shock during World War I.

Prayer Day: a Christian holiday. This Danish public holiday is observed on the fourth Friday after Easter.

Presbyterian: of or pertaining to ecclesiastical government by elders or by presbyteries.

Prophet Muhammed: *see* **Mohammed**.

proselytizing: inducing or persuading someone to become the adherent of some religion, doctrine, sect, or party. To convert.

Protestant: a member or an adherent of one of those Christian bodies which descended from the Reformation of the sixteenth century. Originally applied to those who opposed or protested the Roman Catholic Church.

province: an administrative territory of a country.

Purim: a Jewish holiday. This holiday, celebrated on 14 Adar (Adar Sheni in a leap year), commemorates the delivery of the Jews from potential annihilation at the hands of Haman, viceroy of Persia, as described in the Book of Esther, which is read from a scroll (megillah). The day, though not a public holiday in Israel, is widely marked by charity, exchange of edible gifts, and feasting.

R

rabbi: a Jewish religious leader; head of a congregation.

racial integration: to remove all restrictions and barriers preventing complete access to society to persons of all races.

racially homogeneous: composed of persons all of the same race.

rain forest: a tropical vegetation in the equatorial region of the world which consists of a dense growth of a wide variety of broadleaf evergreen trees and vines.

Raksha Bandhan: a Hindu holiday. During this festival, which usually falls in August, bracelets of colored thread and tinsel are tied by women to the wrists of their menfolk, thus binding the men to guard and protect them during the year. It is celebrated on the full moon of Sravana.

Ramadan: a Muslim holiday. The first day of Ramadan (the ninth month) is a public holiday in many countries, although the religious festival does not officially begin until the new moon is sighted from the Naval Observatory in Cairo, Egypt. The entire month commemorates the period in which the Prophet received divine revelation and is observed by a strict fast from sunrise to sundown. This observance is one of Islam's five main duties for believers.

Rastafarian: a member of a Jamaican cult begun in 1930 as a semi-religious, semi-political movement. Rastafarians are usually lower class men who are anti-white and advocate the return of blacks to Africa.

refugee: one who flees to a refuge, shelter or place of safety. One who in times of persecution or political commotion flees to a foreign country for safety.

respiratory: pertaining to the lungs and other breathing passages.

Roman alphabet: the alphabet of the ancient Romans from which the alphabets of most modern western European languages, including English, are derived.

Roman Catholic Church: the designation of the church of which the pope or bishop of Rome is the head, and which holds him, as the successor of St. Peter and heir of his spiritual authority, privileges, and gifts, as its supreme ruler, pastor, and teacher.

Romance language: the group of languages derived from Latin: French, Spanish, Italian, Portuguese and other related languages.

Rosh Hashanah: a Jewish holiday. The Jewish New Year is celebrated on 1 Tishri, the first month. In synagogues, the sounding of the shofar (ram's horn) heralds the new year. Rosh Hashanah begins the observance of the Ten Penitential Days, which culminate in Yom Kippur. Orthodox and Conservative Jews outside Israel celebrate 2 Tishri, the next day, as well.

runic music: music that is ancient, obscure, and mystical.

Russian Orthodox: the arm of the Orthodox Eastern Church which was the official church of czarist Russia.

S

Sacred Heart: a Christian holiday. The Friday of the week after Corpus Christi is a holiday in Colombia. The object of devotion is the divine person of Jesus, whose heart is the symbol of his love for mankind.

Samaritans: a native or an inhabitant of Samaria; specifically, one of a race settled in the cities of Samaria by the king of Assyria after the removal of the Israelites from the country.

samba: a Brazilian dance and musical tradition based on two beats to the measure.

sambo: indicates a person of visible African ancestry. Familiar form of address for an uncle from the Foulah language of West Africa.

Santer'a: Christian religion with West African origins. It merges Christian saints with Yoruban dieties.

savanna: a treeless or near treeless plain of a tropical or subtropical region dominated by drought-resistant grasses.

schistosomiasis: a tropical disease that is chronic and characterized by disorders of the liver, urinary bladder, lungs, or central nervous system.

sect: a religious denomination or group, often a dissenting one with extreme views.

self-determination: the desire of a culture to control its economic and social development.

Semitic tongue: an important family of languages distinguished by triliteral verbal roots and vowel inflections.

Seventh-day Adventist: one who believes in the second coming of Christ to establish a personal reign upon the earth. They observe the seventh day of the week as the Sabbath and believe in the existence of the spirit of prophecy among them.

shaman: holy man or woman said to have the power to heal diseases. Also thought to have magical powers.

shamanism: a religion centered on a belief in good and evil spirits that can be influenced only by shamans.

Shavuot: a Jewish holiday. This festival, on 6 Sivan, celebrates the presentation of the Ten Commandments to Moses on Mt. Sinai and the offering of the first harvest fruits at the temple in Jerusalem. The precursor of the Christian Pentecost, Shavuot takes place on the 50th day after the first day of Passover.

Shia Muslim: member of one of two great sects of Islam. Shia Muslims believe that Ali and the Imams are the rightful successors of Mohammed (also commonly spelled Muhammed). They also believe that the last recognized Imam will return as a messiah. Also known as Shiites. (*Also see* **Sunni Muslim**.)

Shiites: *see* **Shia Muslim**.

Shintoism: the system of nature- and hero-worship which forms the indigenous religion of Japan.

Shivarati (Mahashivarati): a Hindu holiday. Dedicated to the god Shiva, this holiday is observed on the 13th day of the dark half of Magha, corresponding to January or February.

Shrove Monday and Shrove Tuesday: a Christian holiday. These two days occur just prior to the beginning of Lent (a term which derives from the Middle English lente, "spring"), the Christian season of penitence that ends with Easter Sunday. These are days of Carnival, public holidays of feasting, and merriment in many lands. Shrove Tuesday is also known as Mardi Gras.

shunning: Amish practice of not interacting in any way with a person who has been cast out by the church and the community.

sierra: a chain of hills or mountains.

Sikh: a member of a politico-religious community of India, founded as a sect around 1500 and based on the principles of monotheism and human brotherhood.

Sino-Tibetan language family: the family of languages spoken in Eastern Asia, including China, Thailand, Tibet, and Burma.

slash-and-burn agriculture: a hasty and sometimes temporary way of clearing land to make it available for agriculture by cutting down trees and burning them.

slave trade: the transportation of black Africans beginning in the 1700s to other countries to be sold as slaves-people owned as property and compelled to work for their owners at no pay.

Slavic languages: a major subgroup of the Indo-European language family. It is further subdivided into West Slavic (including Polish, Czech, Slovak and Sorbian), South Slavic (including Bulgarian, Serbo-Croatian, Slovene, and Old Church Slavonic), and East Slavic (including Russian Ukrainian and Byelorussian).

Society of Friends: a religious sect founded about 1650 whose members shun military service and believe in plain dress, behavior and worship. Also referred to as the Quaker religion by those outside it.

Solemnity of Mary, Mother of God: a Christian holiday. Observed on 1 January, this celebration was, before a 1969 Vatican reform, the Feast of the Circumcision of Our Lord Jesus Christ.

sorghum: a type of tropical grass that is grown for grain, syrup, and livestock feed.

St. Agatha's Day: a Christian holiday. Celebrated on 5 February, it is the feast day of the patron saint of San Marino. St. Agatha is also the patron saint of nurses, firefighters, and jewelers.

St. Dévôte Day: a Christian holiday. Observed on 27 January in Monaco in honor of the principality's patron saint, this day celebrates her safe landing after a perilous voyage, thanks to a dove who directed her ship to the Monaco shore.

St. James's Day: a Christian holiday. Observed on 25 July, this day commemorates St. James the Greater, one of Jesus' 12 apostles. St. James is the patron saint of Spain.

St. Joseph's Day: a Christian holiday. The feast day in honor of Mary's husband is observed on 19 March as a public holiday in several countries.

St. Patrick's Day: a Christian holiday. This holiday, observed on 17 March, is celebrated in Ireland to honor its patron saint.

St. Stephen's Day: a Christian holiday. The feast day in honor of the first martyred Christian saint is 26 December, the day after Christmas. St. Stephen is the patron saint of Hungary.

steppe: a level tract of land more or less devoid of trees. It is a name given to certain parts of European and Asiatic Russia, of which the most characteristic feature is the absence of forests.

stigmatize: branding someone as a disgrace because of his or her behavior.

straits: a narrow passage of water connecting two bodies of water.

stroganoff: Russian beef stew. Sauce made from sour cream and wine.

subcontinent: a landmass of great size, but smaller than any of the continents; a large subdivision of a continent.

subsistence farming: farming that provides the minimum food goods necessary for the continuation of the farm family.

Sudanic language group: a related group of languages spoken in various areas of northern Africa, including Yoruba, Mandingo and Tshi.

Sufi: a Mohammedan mystic who believes (a) that God alone exists, and all visible and invisible beings are mere emanations from Him; (b) that, as God is the real author of all the acts of mankind, man is not a free agent, and there can be no real difference between good and evil; (c) that, as the soul existed before the body, and is confined within the latter as in a cage, death should be the chief object of desire, for only then does the soul return to the bosom of the divinity; and (d) that religions are matters of indifference, though some are more advantageous than others, and Sufism is the only true philosophy.

Sukkot: a Jewish holiday. This ancient Jewish harvest festival, which begins on 15 Tishri, recalls the period in which harvesters left their homes to dwell in the fields in sukkot, or booths—small outdoor shelters of boards, leaves, and branches—in order to facilitate gathering the crops before the seasonal rains began. In religious terms, it commemorates the 40 years of wandering in the desert by the ancient Hebrews after their exodus from Egypt. The 8th day of Sukkot (and the 22d day of Tishri) is Shmini Azeret/Simhat Torah, a joyous holiday in which the annual cycle of reading the Torah (the Five Books of Moses) is completed and begun anew. Outside of Israel, Simhat Torah and the beginning of a new reading cycle are celebrated on the next day, 23 Tishri.

sultan: a king of a Muslim state.

Sunni Muslim: Member of one of two major sects of the religion of Islam. Sunni Muslims adhere to strict orthodox traditions and believe that the four caliphs are the rightful successors to Mohammed, founder of Islam. (Mohammed is commonly spelled Muhammed, especially by Islamic people.) (*Also see* **Shia Muslim.**)

surname: a person's last name. Generally different from his or her first name.

T

taboo: a system, practice, or act whereby persons, things, places, actions, or words are placed under ban, curse, or prohibition, or set apart as sacred or privileged in some specific manner.

taiga: a coniferous forest in the far northern areas of Canada, Alaska, and Eurasia.

Taoism: the doctrine of Lao-Tzu, an ancient Chinese philosopher (about 500 BC) as laid down by him in the Tao-te-ching.

Thaipusam: a Hindu holiday. A holiday in Malaysia, Thaipusam honors Subrimaya, son of Shiva and an important deity in southern India. The three-day festival is held in the month of Magha according to when Pusam, a section of the lunar zodiac, is on the ascendant.

Tibeto-Burman language group: a subgroup of the Sino-Tibetan language family which includes Tibetan and Burmese.

Tishah b'Av: a Jewish holiday. This holiday, which takes place on 9 Av, commemorates the destruction of the First Temple by the Babylonians (Chaldeans) in 586 BC and of the Second Temple by the Romans in AD 70. It is observed by fasting.

toboggan: a kind of sled without runners or a steering mechanism.

topography: an accurate drawing representing the surface of a region on maps and charts.

toucan: a brightly colored, fruit-eating bird of tropical America with a distinctive beak.

trachoma: contagious, viral infection of the cornea. Causes scarring in the eye.

tribal society: a society based on tribal consciousness and loyalties.

tribal system: a social community in which people are organized into groups or clans descended from common ancestors and sharing customs and languages.

tsetse fly: any of the several African insects which can transmit a variety of parasitic organisms through its bite. Some of these organisms can prove fatal to both human and animal victims.

tundra: a nearly level treeless area whose climate and vegetation are more characteristically arctic due to its northern position. Although the region attains seasonal temperatures warm enough to allow a thin layer of soil on the surface to unthaw enough to support the growth of various species of plants, the subsoil is permanently frozen.

tutelary: a god or spirit who acts a guardian that watches over a person or group of people.

typhoon: a violent hurricane occurring in the China Sea or Philippine region, principally between the months of July and October.

U

unemployment rate: the overall unemployment rate is the percentage of the work force (both employed and unemployed) who claim to be unemployed. The natural unemployment rate is the lowest level at which unemployment in an economy can be maintained and still reflect a balance of the labor market and the product market.

untouchables: in 19th century India, members of the lowest caste in the caste system, a hereditary social class system.

They were considered unworthy to touch members of higher castes.

urban center: a city.

USSR: an abbreviation of Union of Soviet Socialist Republics.

V

veldt: in South Africa, an unforested or thinly forested tract of land or region, a grassland.

Vesak: this last full moon day of Visakha highlights a three-day celebration of the birth, enlightenment, and death of the Buddha. It falls in April or May.

voodoo: a belief system which is based on sorcery and other primitive rites and the power of charms and fetishes, originating in Africa.

W

wadi(s): the channel of a watercourse which is dry except in the rainy season. Also called wady.

Windward Islands: a southern group of islands stretching south to Trinidad. Part of the Lesser Antilles, but does not include Barbados.

Y

Yom Kippur: a Jewish holiday. The Day of Atonement, spent in fasting, penitence, and prayer, is the most solemn day in Judaism. It takes place on 10 Tishri.

yucca: a plant native to Mexico, Central and South America, and the southwestern United States. Can grow to the 12 feet in height.

yurt: a framework tent of stretched felt or skins. Associated with Siberia and Mongolia.

Z

Zoroastrianism: the system of religious doctrine taught by Zoroaster and his followers in the Avesta; the religion prevalent in Persia until its overthrow by the Muslims in the 7th century.

INDEX

The "v" accompanied by a numeral that precedes the colon in these index citations designates the volume number for *Worldmark Encyclopedia of Cultures and Daily Life, Second Edition*. Thus, v1 references are found in the Africa volume; v2 in Americas, v3 in Asia & Oceania, v4 in Asia and Oceania continued, and v5 in Europe. Page numbers follow the colon.